CASES AND MATERIALS ON CRIMINAL LAW

Fourth Edition

This new edition of *Cases and Materials on Criminal Law* has been thoroughly updated to provide a comprehensive selection of key materials drawn from law reports, legislation, Law Commission consultation papers and reports and Home Office publications.

Clear and highly accessible, this volume is presented in a coherent structure and provides full coverage of the topics commonly found in the criminal law syllabus. The range of thoughtfully selected materials and authoritative commentary ensures that this book provides an essential collection of materials and analysis to stimulate the reader and assist in the study of this difficult and challenging area of law.

New features include:

- revised text design with clear page layout, headings and boxed and shaded sections to aid navigation and readability
- chapter introductions to highlight the salient features under discussion
- short chapter table of contents to enable easier navigation
- "Comments and Questions" sections to encourage students to reflect on their reading
- expanded further reading to encourage students to engage further with the subject
- a Companion Website to provide regular updates to the book

This book is an invaluable reference for students on undergraduate or CPE/PG Diploma in Law criminal law courses, particularly those studying independently or on distance learning programmes.

Professor Mike Molan, BA, LLM, FHEA, Barrister, is Acting Executive Dean of the Faculty of Arts and Human Sciences at London South Bank University.

LIVERPOOL JMU LIBRARY

3 1111 01316 2118

CASES AND MATERIALS ON CRIMINAL LAW

Fourth Edition

Mike Molan

Routledge·Cavendish
Taylor & Francis Group
LONDON AND NEW YORK

First edition published 1997 by Cavendish Publishing Limited
Second edition published 2001 by Cavendish Publishing Limited
Third edition published 2005 by Cavendish Publishing Limited

Fourth edition published 2008 by Routledge-Cavendish
2 Park Square, Milton Park, Abingdon, Oxon OX14 4RN

Simultaneously published in the USA and Canada
by Routledge-Cavendish
270 Madison Ave, New York, NY 10016

Routledge-Cavendish is an imprint of the Taylor & Francis Group, an informa business

fourth edition © Molan, Mike T 2008
first edition © Taylor, Alan and Hungerford-Welch, Peter 1997
second edition © Molan, Mike T 2001
third edition © Molan, Mike T 2005

Typeset in Garamond Three and Helvetica Neue by
RefineCatch Limited, Bungay, Suffolk
Printed and bound in Great Britain by
The Cromwell Press, Trowbridge, Wiltshire

All rights reserved. No part of this book may be reprinted or
reproduced or utilised in any form or by any electronic,
mechanical, or other means, now known or hereafter
invented, including photocopying and recording, or in any
information storage or retrieval system, without permission in
writing from the publishers.

British Library Cataloguing in Publication Data
A catalogue record for this book is available from the British Library

Library of Congress Cataloging in Publication Data
A catalog record for this book has been requested

ISBN10: 0–415–42461–5 (pbk)
ISBN13: 978–0–415–42461–5 (pbk)

PREFACE

As with previous editions, this sourcebook seeks to provide a handy set of reference materials for students studying criminal law on undergraduate or CPE programmes. It does not seek to provide the more lengthy discourse one might expect from a traditional textbook, but does provide extended extracts on key topics enabling the reader to gain a better understanding of the rationale for the development of the law and the policy issues underpinning the leading cases. Coverage is therefore provided of the mainstream criminal offences through statutory and case law materials along with a comprehensive selection of key materials drawn from Law Commission consultation papers and reports, and Home Office publications.

Since the publication of the 3rd edition there have been a number of significant developments in the field of substantive criminal law and these are reflected in the structure and content of this new edition. The long awaited reform of the law relating to deception offences has now come into effect in the shape of the Fraud Act 2006 and this has had the effect of replacing all the previous deception offences with new offences under the 2006 Act. These changes are fully reflected in the text.

Recent decisions of note that are extracted and analysed include *R v Kennedy* (manslaughter based on supply of heroin); *Attorney General for Jersey v Holley* (provocation); *R v Mark* and *R v Willoughby* (elements of killing by gross negligence); *R v Barnes* (consent as a defence to sporting injuries); *Attorney General's Reference (No 3 of 2004)* (accessorial liability) and *R v Hatton* (intoxicated mistake in self-defence cases). Consideration is also given to the likely changes to the law relating to corporate manslaughter, at the time of writing contained in the Corporate Manslaughter and Corporate Homicide Bill currently before Parliament.

Two major law reform publications are extensively extracted and contextualised in this 4th edition: the Law Commission's report on Murder, Manslaughter and Infanticide (Law Com No 304) – and the Law Commission's Report on Inchoate Liability for Assisting and Encouraging Crime (Law Com 300).

I would like to extend my thanks to staff at Routledge for their support and encouragement in producing this new edition, and as always love to my 'pit lane' crew, Alison, Grace, Joy, Miles and Parker who is still a mad hound. I have endeavoured to state the law as of 1st February 2007 although some later developments have been incorporated where possible.

Professor Mike Molan
London South Bank University
May 2007

OUTLINE CONTENTS

Detailed Contents

Table of Cases

TABLE OF STATUTES

CHAPTER 1

INTRODUCTION TO CRIMINAL LAW: FRAMEWORK AND PROCEDURES

1.1 INTRODUCTION

As a source of reference materials this is not a book designed to be read from beginning to end in a linear fashion. Most readers will dip into the chapters that follow in search of material relating to a specific aspect of the substantive criminal law. The substantive criminal law does not, however, exist in a vacuum. It is hard to have an effective understanding of the doctrinal aspects of criminal law without also having a grasp of the operational context. The materials that follow in this first chapter, therefore, provide a brief overview of the sources of criminal law, the approach taken by the courts in applying criminal statutes, the procedural options open to the prosecuting authorities, and the appeals processes that give rise to many of the precedents forming the backbone of the substantive law. The materials also illustrate the impact of the Human Rights Act 1998 on the operation of domestic substantive criminal law, and the contribution of the Law Commission to the on-going programme of law reform. There are many other interesting aspects of the criminal justice system that could be considered, such as punishment, crime prevention, and theories of deviancy, but they lie beyond the scope of this text.

1.2 WHAT IS CRIMINAL LAW?

Attempts to define criminal law are generally unhelpful if they stray far beyond restating the obvious – that criminal laws are prohibitions backed up by penal sanctions imposed on the actions of individuals (and corporate bodies) by those who hold sovereignty within the state. Attempting to find some moralistic basis for criminal law proves more elusive. It is not difficult to think of immoral activities that are not criminal (arguably infidelity), and activities that are criminal that one would hesitate to denounce as immoral (e.g. failing to display a car tax disc). In any event, notions of immorality are something of a moveable feast – consider the way in which the law relating to homosexual activity between consenting adult males has changed since 1967.

How does criminal law differ from other areas of law, and how does one define the subject? In terms of purpose criminal law is properly seen as falling within the sphere of public, as opposed to private, law. Whereas the law of negligence is largely concerned with determining liability to financially compensate the victim of a tort, criminal law looks at the broader issues – should the defendant's wrongdoing be labelled as criminal; if so, what should be the degree of fault required for liability; what punishment should be imposed to ensure that others are deterred from similar wrongdoing and the public protected from the defendant? In short there are considerations that arise in criminal law that have no direct counterpart in private law. Whereas in a negligence action the victim is at the core of the case in terms of compensation, the interests of the victim in a criminal case are very much a secondary consideration. A negligence action cannot proceed unless the victim wants it to. A criminal case can proceed even with a reluctant or unwilling victim because the prosecution is in the hands of the state and its agencies. The proceedings are fulfilling a public purpose.

Criminal Law Doctrine and Theory – William Wilson (2nd ed, 2003) p 6

The major concerns of the criminal law may be expressed, therefore, as follows:

A   The support of public interests in:

1   preventing physical injury. This accounts for the crimes of murder, manslaughter, arson and other crimes of violence; also certain road traffic offences and those relating to public health and safety.

2   proscribing personal immorality deemed injurious to society's well-being. This accounts for crimes such as bigamy, incest, sado-masochism, bestiality and obscenity, drug possession and supply.

3   preventing the moral corruption of the young through crimes such as gross indecency with children and unlawful sexual intercourse.

4   maintaining the integrity of the state and the administration of justice through crimes such as treason, perjury, perverting the course of justice, tax evasion.

5   maintaining public order and security through offences such as riot, affray, breach of the peace, public drunkenness.

B   That citizens remaining free from:

(a) undesired physical interference through crimes such as rape, assault, sexual assault, false imprisonment, harassment;

(b) offence through crimes such as indecent exposure, indecency in public, solicitation;

(c) undesired interference with property through crimes such as theft, robbery, taking and driving away a road vehicle, deception.

The Definition of Crime – Glanville Williams (1955) Current Legal Problems 107

Is the effort [to define crime] worth making? The answer is that lawyers must try to clarify the notion of 'crime', because it suffuses a large part of the law. For example: there is generally no time limit for criminal proceedings, whereas civil proceedings are commenced differently, and often in different courts. A criminal prosecutor generally need not be the victim of the wrong, and a private criminal prosecutor is for many purposes not regarded as a party to the proceedings; he is certainly not 'master' of the proceedings in the sense that he can drop them at will; these rules are different in civil cases. The law of procedure may generally be waived in civil but not in criminal cases. There are many differences in the law of evidence, and several in respect of appeal . . .

. . . The common-sense approach is to consider whether there are any intrinsic differences between the acts constituting crimes and civil wrongs respectively. It is perhaps natural to suppose that since 'a crime' differs from 'a civil wrong', there must be something in a crime to make it different from a civil wrong.

As everybody knows, there is one serious hindrance to a solution of this kind. This is the overlap between crime and tort. Since the same act can be both a crime and a tort, as in murder and assault, it is impossible to divide the two branches of the law by reference to the type of act. So also it is impossible to divide them by reference to the physical consequences of the act, for if the act is the same the physical consequences must be the same.

It has occurred to some that there is a possible escape from this difficulty. Although the act, and its consequences, are the same, the act and consequences have a number of different characteristics or aspects; and it may be possible to identify some of these characteristics as criminal and some as civil. Pursuing this line of thought, two separate aspects have been seized upon as identifying crime: the aspect of moral wrong and the aspect of damage to the public . . .

The proposition that crime is a moral wrong may have this measure of truth: that the average crime is more shocking, and has graver social consequences, than the average tort. Yet crimes of strict responsibility can be committed without moral wrong, while torts and breaches of trust may be, and often are, gross moral wrongs.

Even where a forbidden act is committed intentionally, a court deciding that it is a crime is not committed to the proposition that it is a moral wrong . . .

The second intrinsic difference between crimes and civil wrongs found by some writers is in respect of the damage done. In tort there is almost invariably actual damage to some person, whereas in crime such damage is not essential, the threat being to the community as a whole . . . Again there are formidable objections. Some torts do not require damage (such as trespass and libel), while many crimes do involve private damage. Some crimes are punished as an affront to the moral feelings of the community although they cause no damage to the community as a whole. This is true of the group of crimes having in differing degrees a religious aspect: blasphemy, attempted suicide, abortion, bigamy. It is also largely true of obscenity and adult homosexuality. Even murder need not cause public damage: for example, when a mother kills her infant child. This creates no general sense of insecurity; the only material loss to society is the loss of the child, and whether that is economically a real loss or a gain depends on whether the country is under- or over-populated at the time. Evidently, the social condemnation of infant-killing rests on non-utilitarian ethics . . .

. . . We have rejected all definitions purporting to distinguish between crimes and other wrongs by reference to the sort of thing that is done or the sort of physical, economic or social consequences that follow from it. Only one possibility now remains. A crime must be defined by reference to the legal consequences of the act. We must distinguish, primarily, not between crimes and civil wrongs but between criminal and civil proceedings. A crime then becomes an act that is capable of being followed by criminal proceedings, having one of the types of outcome (punishment, etc) known to follow these proceedings . . .

As stated at the outset, there are many differences of procedure between crimes and civil wrongs. Often these differences are of no help in distinguishing between the two, because they are consequential differences – it is only when you know that the act is a crime or a civil wrong respectively that you know which procedure to select. However, some elements in procedure do assist in making the classification. When Parliament passes a statute forbidding certain conduct, it may refer in terms to certain procedural matters – such as trial on indictment, or summary conviction – which indicate that the act is to be a crime. Again, when it is disputed whether a given proceeding, such as a proceeding for a penalty, is criminal or civil, a point can be scored by showing that this proceeding has been held in the past to be governed by some procedural rule which is regarded as indicative of a criminal or civil proceeding, as the case may be . . .

Since the courts thus make use of the whole law of procedure in aid of their task of classification, an attempt to define crime in terms of one item of procedure only is mistaken. This remark applies to the test of crime adopted by Kenny, following Austin and Clark, which links crime with the ability of the Crown to remit the sanction. This test tells you whether an act is a crime only if you already know whether the sanction is remissible by the Crown. Almost always, however, the latter has to be deduced from the former, instead of vice versa. Thus Kenny defines *ignotum per ignotius*. This objection would not be open if Kenny's chosen procedural test were made available along with all the others. The procedural test does not give full assistance unless one is allowed to use the whole law of procedure.

. . . In short, a crime is an act capable of being followed by criminal proceedings having a criminal outcome, and a proceeding or its outcome is criminal if it has certain characteristics which mark it as criminal. In a marginal case the court may have to balance one feature, which may suggest that the proceeding is criminal, against another feature, which may suggest the contrary.

Walker, Crime and Criminology: A Critical Introduction (1987) pp 140–141

Objectives of the criminal law
Is it possible to discuss the proper content of the criminal law in general terms? If the contents of criminal codes are examined with a sociological eye, no fewer than fourteen different objectives can be discerned:

(a) the protection of human persons (and to some extent animals also) against intentional violence, cruelty, or unwelcome sexual approaches;

(b) the protection of people against some forms of unintended harm (for example from traffic, poisons, infections, radiation);

(c) the protection of easily persuadable classes of people (that is, the young or the weak-minded) against the abuse of their persons or property (for example by sexual intercourse or hire-purchase);

(d) the prevention of acts which, even if the participants are adult and willing, are regarded as 'unnatural' (for example incest, . . . bestiality, drug 'trips');

(e) the prevention of acts which, though not included under any of the previous headings, are performed so publicly as to shock other people (for example public nakedness, obscene language, or . . . copulation between consenting adults);

(f) the discouragement of behaviour which might provoke disorder (such as insulting words at a public meeting);

(g) the protection of property against theft, fraud, or damage;

(h) the prevention of inconvenience (for example the obstruction of roads by vehicles);

(i) the collection of revenue (for example keeping a motor car or television set without a licence);

(j) the defence of the State (for example espionage or – in some countries – political criticism);

(k) the enforcement of compulsory benevolence (for example the offence of failing to send one's children to school);

(l) the protection of social institutions, such as marriage or religious worship (for example by prohibiting bigamy or blasphemy);

(m) the prevention of unreasonable discrimination (for example against ethnic groups, religions, the female sex);

(n) the enforcement of the processes regarded as essential to these other purposes (for example offences connected with arrest, assisting offenders to escape conviction, and testimony at trials).

1.3 SOURCES OF CRIMINAL LAW

The criminal law of England and Wales is made up of a patchwork of common law and statutory offences. Offences such as theft, burglary, robbery and fraud are based on comparatively recent statutory enactments; see the Theft Acts 1968, 1978 and the Fraud Act 2006. Sexual offences are now governed by the Sexual Offences Act 2003. Other offences, whilst statute based, are somewhat venerable – see for example grievous bodily harm, wounding and actual bodily harm – all offences still governed by the Offences Against the Person Act 1861. Problems inevitably arise when trying to apply such antiquated legislation to situations that the Victorian draftsman cannot possibly have contemplated; see further Chapter 5. Perhaps surprisingly some very serious offences are not creatures of statute at all, the most notable example being murder. It would be foolish to assume that there is any particular rhyme or reason as to whether or not an offence has the common law or statute as its source. The plain fact is that legislation to create or amend criminal offences has to wait its turn in the queue for parliamentary time. Most governments in recent years have struggled to find the time to act upon proposals for fundamental reform put forward by the Law Commission; see 1.8 below. All too often parliamentary time is made available on the basis of expediency for legislation dealing with a narrow matter that happens to be exciting the general public at that particular time. Hence there has been legislation to deal with 'stalking' – see the Protection from Harassment Act 1997 (Chapter 5.6) – but no thoroughgoing reform of the Offences Against the Person Act 1861. Deception has been placed on a new statutory footing by means of the Fraud Act 2006 (see Chapter 10), but the complexities and anomalies of secondary liability at common law continue to confound juries, judges and students of criminal law (see Chapter 7).

There is a significant constitutional issue at stake here in terms of who should be creating the criminal law. In a parliamentary democracy there is a very cogent argument that new criminal offences should only be created by Parliament, and that major changes in substantive criminal law should only be sanctioned by Parliament. For judges to effect such changes is an apparent breach of the separation of powers. The reality, however, is that there are occasions where the judges feel that, given the failure of Parliament to take the initiative, they have little choice but to act.

In *Shaw v DPP* [1962] AC 220, the defendant was charged, *inter alia*, with conspiracy to corrupt public morals. The House of Lords held, by a majority, that such an offence existed, notwithstanding that there was no clear precedent to that effect. Endorsing the view of the majority that the courts could 'discover' new offences at common law if necessary, Viscount Simonds observed:

> Need I say my Lords, that I am no advocate of the right of judges to create new criminal offences . . . But . . . in the sphere of criminal law, I entertain no doubt that there remains in the courts of law a residual power to enforce the supreme and fundamental purpose of the law, to conserve not only the safety and order but also the moral welfare of the state, and that it is their duty to guard it against attacks which may be the more insidious because they are novel and unprepared for.

Against this, Lord Reid (dissenting) issued this clear warning:

> I think, or at least I hope, that it is now established that the courts cannot create new offences by individuals . . . when there is sufficient support from public opinion, Parliament does not hesitate to intervene. Where Parliament fears to tread it is not for the courts to rush in . . .

In the course of his speech in *C v DPP* [1996] AC 1, Lord Lowry reviewed the principles upon which judges ought to reflect before engaging in judicial activism. In particular he expressed the view that judges:

- should not be quick to impose their own remedies where the solution was doubtful;
- should be reluctant to act where Parliament had clearly declined to do so, or had legislated in the area without dealing with the difficulty presented by the case in hand;

- should not lightly overturn fundamental legal doctrines;
- should bear in mind that issues of social policy should be left for determination by the legislature;
- should not venture dynamic solutions unless finality was likely to result.

1.4 INTERPRETING CRIMINAL STATUTES

Where the issue is the correct interpretation of a statute, judges will often seek to substantiate their decisions by opining that they are simply giving effect to the intention of Parliament. This response masks the fact that, parliamentary sovereignty notwithstanding, judges in the higher courts have considerable discretion as to whether or not they will intervene and develop the law in new and bold directions. As Lord Reid observed in *Black-Clawson International Ltd v Papierwerke Waldhoff-Anschaffenburg* AG [1975] AC 591 (at 613):

> We often say that we are looking for the intention of Parliament, but that is not quite accurate. We are seeking the meaning of the words which Parliament used. We are seeking not what Parliament meant but the true meaning of what they said.

What principles of interpretation can be identified? In theory any ambiguity in a criminal statute should be construed in favour of the defendant, although this may have to give way to wider public policy interests if the restrictive interpretation allows a patently culpable defendant to escape liability. As Ashworth observed in 'Interpreting criminal statutes: a crisis of legality?' (1991) 107 LQR 419:

> It would not stretch the truth too far to suggest that the typical academic approach has been to emphasise liberal values and the traditional judicial approach to emphasise what they regard as social values . . . values of both kinds do and should form part of criminal law doctrine. The next step is to recognise that they will frequently conflict and that, whilst careful discussion of the principles and policies will give some indication as to how conflicts should be resolved, situations will occur in which the courts must make that choice. This makes it crucial that the policies and principles are openly discussed, rather than concealed behind high-sounding phrases about 'legislative intent', 'public policy' or 'the principle of legality'.

1.5 CLASSIFICATION OF OFFENCES

For the purposes of the powers given to police officers and citizens to effect the arrest of suspects, the Police and Criminal Evidence Act 1984 distinguishes between those offences where a power to arrest is provided without an arrest warrant having been issued (arrestable offences – see s 24), and those offences that are 'non-arrestable', that is, where a warrant would normally be required.

POLICE AND CRIMINAL EVIDENCE ACT 1984, s 24

(4)   Any person may arrest without a warrant
    (a)   anyone who is in the act of committing an arrestable offence
    (b)   anyone whom he has reasonable grounds for suspecting to be committing such an offence.
(5)   Where an arrestable offence has been committed, any person may arrest without a warrant
    (a)   anyone who is guilty of the offence
    (b)   anyone whom he has reasonable grounds for suspecting to be guilty of it.
(6)   Where a constable has reasonable grounds for suspecting that an arrestable offence has been committed, he may arrest without a warrant anyone whom he has reasonable grounds for suspecting to be guilty of the offence.
(7)   A constable may arrest without a warrant
    (a)   anyone who is about to commit an arrestable offence
    (b)   anyone whom he has reasonable grounds for suspecting to be about to commit an arrestable offence.

For these purposes an arrestable offence is one:

- in relation to which the sentence is fixed by law (for example, murder);
- in relation to which a person of 21 years of age or over (not previously convicted) may be sentenced to imprisonment for a term of five years (such as theft and robbery);
- otherwise specifically cited as coming within the scope of the s 24 powers, for example sexual assault, going equipped for stealing, s 60(8)(b) of the Criminal Justice and Public Order Act 1994 – failing to comply with requirement to remove a mask, etc.

Section 25 of the Police and Criminal Evidence Act 1984 goes on, however, to specify circumstances where a police officer can exercise a power of arrest in respect of a non-arrestable offence, notwithstanding the absence of a warrant. Under s 25 a police constable may arrest a suspect on suspicion of having committed a non-arrestable offence if satisfied that any of the general arrest conditions specified in that section are satisfied. These largely relate to circumstances that make the issuing of a summons to attend court impracticable, such as the suspect having no fixed abode, or failing to supply plausible personal details.

Criminal offences in England and Wales can also be classified by reference to the procedure used at trial. According to this taxonomy there are three types of offence:

- Indictable offences – such as rape, robbery and murder;
- Summary offences – such as insulting behaviour and common assault;
- Offences triable either way – such as theft, criminal damage (depending on the value of the property damaged), assault occasioning bodily harm contrary to s 47 of the Offences Against the Person Act 1861, and sexual assault.

Indictable offences are triable only in the Crown Court before a judge and jury. Summary offences are triable only in the magistrates' court. Offences triable either way may be tried before either court, depending on the circumstances, in particular the seriousness of the offence and the preferences expressed by the prosecution and defendant; see further s 14 of the Criminal Law Act 1977, as re-enacted by ss 17–25 of the Magistrates' Courts Act 1980.

1.6 THE DECISION TO PROSECUTE

Since the enactment of the Prosecution of Offences Act 1985 the decision to institute criminal proceedings, and the decision as to the offence to be charged has rested with the Crown Prosecution Service (CPS). The criteria borne in mind by the CPS in determining whether or not to prosecute have been published in the form of the Code for Crown Prosecutors. The current version was published in 2004.

1 INTRODUCTION

1.1 The decision to prosecute an individual is a serious step. Fair and effective prosecution is essential to the maintenance of law and order. Even in a small case a prosecution has serious implications for all involved — victims, witnesses and defendants. The Crown Prosecution Service applies the Code for Crown Prosecutors so that it can make fair and consistent decisions about prosecutions.

1.2 The Code helps the Crown Prosecution Service to play its part in making sure that justice is done. It contains information that is important to police officers and others who work in the criminal justice system and to the general public. Police officers should apply the provisions of this Code whenever they are responsible for deciding whether to charge a person with an offence.

1.3 The Code is also designed to make sure that everyone knows the principles that the Crown Prosecution Service applies when carrying out its work. By applying the same principles, everyone involved in the system is helping to treat victims, witnesses and defendants fairly, while prosecuting cases effectively.

2 GENERAL PRINCIPLES

2.1 Each case is unique and must be considered on its own facts and merits. However, there are general principles that apply to the way in which Crown Prosecutors must approach every case.

2.2 Crown Prosecutors must be fair, independent and objective. They must not let any personal views about ethnic or national origin, disability, sex, religious beliefs, political views or the sexual orientation of the suspect, victim or witness influence their decisions. They must not be affected by improper or undue pressure from any source.

2.3 It is the duty of Crown Prosecutors to make sure that the right person is prosecuted for the right offence. In doing so, Crown Prosecutors must always act in the interests of justice and not solely for the purpose of obtaining a conviction.

2.4 Crown Prosecutors should provide guidance and advice to investigators throughout the investigative and prosecuting process. This may include lines of inquiry, evidential requirements and assistance in any pre-charge procedures. Crown Prosecutors will be proactive in identifying and, where possible, rectifying evidential deficiencies and in bringing to an early conclusion those cases that cannot be strengthened by further investigation.

2.5 It is the duty of Crown Prosecutors to review, advise on and prosecute cases, ensuring that the law is properly applied, that all relevant evidence is put before the court and that obligations of disclosure are complied with, in accordance with the principles set out in this Code.

2.6 The Crown Prosecution Service is a public authority for the purposes of the Human Rights Act 1998. Crown Prosecutors must apply the principles of the European Convention on Human Rights in accordance with the Act.

3 THE DECISION TO PROSECUTE

3.1 In most cases, Crown Prosecutors are responsible for deciding whether a person should be charged with a criminal offence, and if so, what that offence should be. Crown Prosecutors make these decisions in accordance with this Code and the Director's Guidance on Charging. In those cases where the police determine the charge, which are usually more minor and routine cases, they apply the same provisions.

3.2 Crown Prosecutors make charging decisions in accordance with the Full Code Test (see section 5 below), other than in those limited circumstances where the Threshold Test applies (see section 6 below).

3.3 The Threshold Test applies where the case is one in which it is proposed to keep the suspect in custody after charge, but the evidence required to apply the Full Code Test is not yet available.

3.4 Where a Crown Prosecutor makes a charging decision in accordance with the Threshold Test, the case must be reviewed in accordance with the Full Code Test as soon as reasonably practicable, taking into account the progress of the investigation.

4 REVIEW

4.1 Each case the Crown Prosecution Service receives from the police is reviewed to make sure that it is right to proceed with a prosecution. Unless the Threshold Test applies, the Crown Prosecution Service will only start or continue with a prosecution when the case has passed both stages of the Full Code Test.

4.2 Review is a continuing process and Crown Prosecutors must take account of any change in circumstances. Wherever possible, they should talk to the police first if they are thinking about changing the charges or stopping the case. Crown Prosecutors should also tell the police if they believe that some additional evidence may strengthen the case. This gives the police the chance to provide more information that may affect the decision.

4.3 The Crown Prosecution Service and the police work closely together, but the final responsibility for the decision whether or not a charge or a case should go ahead rests with the Crown Prosecution Service.

5 THE FULL CODE TEST

5.1 The Full Code Test has two stages. The first stage is consideration of the evidence. If the case does not pass the evidential stage it must not go ahead no matter how important or serious it may be. If the case does pass the evidential stage, Crown Prosecutors must proceed to the second stage and decide if a prosecution is needed in the public interest. The evidential and public interest stages are explained below.

THE EVIDENTIAL STAGE

5.2 Crown Prosecutors must be satisfied that there is enough evidence to provide a 'realistic prospect of conviction' against each defendant on each charge. They must consider what the defence case may be, and how that is likely to affect the prosecution case.

5.3 A realistic prospect of conviction is an objective test. It means that a jury or bench of magistrates or judge hearing a case alone, properly directed in accordance with the law, is more likely than not to convict the defendant of the charge alleged. This is a separate test from the one that the criminal courts themselves must apply. A court should only convict if satisfied so that it is sure of a defendant's guilt.

5.4 When deciding whether there is enough evidence to prosecute, Crown Prosecutors must consider whether the evidence can be used and is reliable. There will be many cases in which the evidence does not give any cause for concern. But there will also be cases in which the evidence may not be as strong as it first appears. Crown Prosecutors must ask themselves the following questions:

Can the evidence be used in court?
(a) Is it likely that the evidence will be excluded by the court? There are certain legal rules which might mean that evidence which seems relevant cannot be given at a trial. For example, is it likely that the evidence will be excluded because of the way in which it was gathered? If so, is there enough other evidence for a realistic prospect of conviction?

Is the evidence reliable?
(b) Is there evidence which might support or detract from the reliability of a confession? Is the reliability affected by factors such as the defendant's age, intelligence or level of understanding?
(c) What explanation has the defendant given? Is a court likely to find it credible in the light of the evidence as a whole? Does it support an innocent explanation?
(d) If the identity of the defendant is likely to be questioned, is the evidence about this strong enough?
(e) Is the witness's background likely to weaken the prosecution case? For example, does the witness have any motive that may affect his or her attitude to the case, or a relevant previous conviction?
(f) Are there concerns over the accuracy or credibility of a witness? Are these concerns based on evidence or simply information with nothing to support it? Is there further evidence which the police should be asked to seek out which may support or detract from the account of the witness?

5.5 Crown Prosecutors should not ignore evidence because they are not sure that it can be used or is reliable. But they should look closely at it when deciding if there is a realistic prospect of conviction.

THE PUBLIC INTEREST STAGE

5.6 In 1951, Lord Shawcross, who was Attorney General, made the classic statement on public interest, which has been supported by Attorneys General ever since: 'It has never been the rule in this country — I hope it never will be — that suspected criminal offences must automatically be the subject of prosecution.' (House of Commons Debates, volume 483, column 681, 29 January 1951.)

5.7 The public interest must be considered in each case where there is enough evidence to provide a realistic prospect of conviction. Although there may be public interest factors against prosecution in a particular case, often the prosecution should go ahead and those factors should be put to the court for consideration when sentence is being passed. A prosecution will usually take place unless there are public interest factors tending against prosecution which clearly outweigh those tending in favour, or it appears more appropriate in all the circumstances of the case to divert the person from prosecution (see section 8 below).

5.8 Crown Prosecutors must balance factors for and against prosecution carefully and fairly. Public interest factors that can affect the decision to prosecute usually depend on the seriousness of the offence or the circumstances of the suspect. Some factors may increase the need to prosecute but others may suggest that another course of action would be better.

The following lists of some common public interest factors, both for and against prosecution, are not exhaustive. The factors that apply will depend on the facts in each case.

Some common public interest factors in favour of prosecution

5.9 The more serious the offence, the more likely it is that a prosecution will be needed in the public interest. A prosecution is likely to be needed if:

(a) a conviction is likely to result in a significant sentence;

(b) a conviction is likely to result in a confiscation or any other order;

(c) a weapon was used or violence was threatened during the commission of the offence;

(d) the offence was committed against a person serving the public (for example, a police or prison officer, or a nurse);

(e) the defendant was in a position of authority or trust;

(f) the evidence shows that the defendant was a ringleader or an organiser of the offence;

(g) there is evidence that the offence was premeditated;

(h) there is evidence that the offence was carried out by a group;

(i) the victim of the offence was vulnerable, has been put in considerable fear, or suffered personal attack, damage or disturbance;

(j) the offence was committed in the presence of, or in close proximity to, a child;

(k) the offence was motivated by any form of discrimination against the victim's ethnic or national origin, disability, sex, religious beliefs, political views or sexual orientation, or the suspect demonstrated hostility towards the victim based on any of those characteristics;

(l) there is a marked difference between the actual or mental ages of the defendant and the victim, or if there is any element of corruption;

(m) the defendant's previous convictions or cautions are relevant to the present offence;

(n) the defendant is alleged to have committed the offence while under an order of the court;

(o) there are grounds for believing that the offence is likely to be continued or repeated, for example, by a history of recurring conduct;

(p) the offence, although not serious in itself, is widespread in the area where it was committed; or

(q) a prosecution would have a significant positive impact on maintaining community confidence.

Some common public interest factors against prosecution

5.10 A prosecution is less likely to be needed if:

(a) the court is likely to impose a nominal penalty;

(b) the defendant has already been made the subject of a sentence and any further conviction would be unlikely to result in the imposition of an additional sentence or order, unless the nature of the particular offence requires a prosecution or the defendant withdraws consent to have an offence taken into consideration during sentencing;

(c) the offence was committed as a result of a genuine mistake or misunderstanding (these factors must be balanced against the seriousness of the offence);

(d) the loss or harm can be described as minor and was the result of a single incident, particularly if it was caused by a misjudgement;

(e) there has been a long delay between the offence taking place and the date of the trial, unless:
     the offence is serious;
     the delay has been caused in part by the defendant;
     the offence has only recently come to light; or
     the complexity of the offence has meant that there has been a long investigation;

(f) a prosecution is likely to have a bad effect on the victim's physical or mental health, always bearing in mind the seriousness of the offence;

(g) the defendant is elderly or is, or was at the time of the offence, suffering from significant mental or physical ill health, unless the offence is serious or there is real possibility that it may be repeated. The Crown Prosecution Service, where necessary, applies Home Office guidelines about how to deal with mentally disordered offenders. Crown Prosecutors must balance the desirability of diverting a defendant who is suffering from significant mental or physical ill health with the need to safeguard the general public;

(h) the defendant has put right the loss or harm that was caused (but defendants must not avoid prosecution or diversion solely because they pay compensation); or

(i) details may be made public that could harm sources of information, international relations or national security.

5.11 Deciding on the public interest is not simply a matter of adding up the number of factors on each side. Crown Prosecutors must decide how important each factor is in the circumstances of each case and go on to make an overall assessment.

The relationship between the victim and the public interest

5.12 The Crown Prosecution Service does not act for victims or the families of victims in the same way as solicitors act for their clients. Crown Prosecutors act on behalf of the public and not just in the interests of any particular individual. However, when considering the public interest, Crown Prosecutors should always take into account the consequences for the victim of whether or not to prosecute, and any views expressed by the victim or the victim's family.

5.13 It is important that a victim is told about a decision which makes a significant difference to the case in which they are involved. Crown Prosecutors should ensure that they follow any agreed procedures.

6 THE THRESHOLD TEST

6.1 The Threshold Test requires Crown Prosecutors to decide whether there is at least a reasonable suspicion that the suspect has committed an offence, and if there is, whether it is in the public interest to charge that suspect.

6.2 The Threshold Test is applied to those cases in which it would not be appropriate to release a suspect on bail after charge, but the evidence to apply the Full Code Test is not yet available.

6.3 There are statutory limits that restrict the time a suspect may remain in police custody before a decision has to be made whether to charge or release the suspect. There will be cases where the suspect in custody presents a substantial bail risk if released, but much of the evidence may not be available at the time the charging decision has to be made. Crown Prosecutors will apply the Threshold Test to such cases for a limited period.

6.4 The evidential decision in each case will require consideration of a number of factors including:

the evidence available at the time;
the likelihood and nature of further evidence being obtained;
the reasonableness for believing that evidence will become available;
the time it will take to gather that evidence and the steps being taken to do so;
the impact the expected evidence will have on the case;
the charges that the evidence will support.

6.5 The public interest means the same as under the Full Code Test, but will be based on the information available at the time of charge which will often be limited.

6.6 A decision to charge and withhold bail must be kept under review. The evidence gathered must be regularly assessed to ensure the charge is still appropriate and that continued objection to bail is justified. The Full Code Test must be applied as soon as reasonably practicable.

7 SELECTION OF CHARGES

7.1 Crown Prosecutors should select charges which:

(a) reflect the seriousness and extent of the offending;
(b) give the court adequate powers to sentence and impose appropriate post-conviction orders; and
(c) enable the case to be presented in a clear and simple way.
     This means that Crown Prosecutors may not always choose or continue with the most serious charge where there is a choice.

7.2 Crown Prosecutors should never go ahead with more charges than are necessary just to encourage a defendant to plead guilty to a few. In the same way, they should never go ahead with a more serious charge just to encourage a defendant to plead guilty to a less serious one.

7.3 Crown Prosecutors should not change the charge simply because of the decision made by the court or the defendant about where the case will be heard.

8 DIVERSION FROM PROSECUTION
ADULTS
8.1 When deciding whether a case should be prosecuted in the courts, Crown Prosecutors should consider the alternatives to prosecution. Where appropriate, the availability of suitable rehabilitative, reparative or restorative justice processes can be considered.

8.2 Alternatives to prosecution for adult suspects include a simple caution and a conditional caution.

Simple caution

8.3 A simple caution should only be given if the public interest justifies it and in accordance with Home Office guidelines. Where it is felt that such a caution is appropriate, Crown Prosecutors must inform the police so they can caution the suspect. If the caution is not administered, because the suspect refuses to accept it, a Crown Prosecutor may review the case again.

Conditional caution

8.4 A conditional caution may be appropriate where a Crown Prosecutor considers that while the public interest justifies a prosecution, the interests of the suspect, victim and community may be better served by the suspect complying with suitable conditions aimed at rehabilitation or reparation. These may include restorative processes.

8.5 Crown Prosecutors must be satisfied that there is sufficient evidence for a realistic prospect of conviction and that the public interest would justify a prosecution should the offer of a conditional caution be refused or the offender fail to comply with the agreed conditions of the caution.

8.6 In reaching their decision, Crown Prosecutors should follow the Conditional Cautions Code of Practice and any guidance on conditional cautioning issued or approved by the Director of Public Prosecutions.

8.7 Where Crown Prosecutors consider a conditional caution to be appropriate, they must inform the police, or other authority responsible for administering the conditional caution, as well as providing an indication of the appropriate conditions so that the conditional caution can be administered.

YOUTHS

8.8 Crown Prosecutors must consider the interests of a youth when deciding whether it is in the public interest to prosecute. However Crown Prosecutors should not avoid prosecuting simply because of the defendant's age. The seriousness of the offence or the youth's past behaviour is very important.

8.9 Cases involving youths are usually only referred to the Crown Prosecution Service for prosecution if the youth has already received a reprimand and final warning, unless the offence is so serious that neither of these were appropriate or the youth does not admit committing the offence. Reprimands and final warnings are intended to prevent re-offending and the fact that a further offence has occurred indicates that attempts to divert the youth from the court system have not been effective. So the public interest will usually require a prosecution in such cases, unless there are clear public interest factors against prosecution.

9 MODE OF TRIAL

9.1 The Crown Prosecution Service applies the current guidelines for magistrates who have to decide whether cases should be tried in the Crown Court when the offence gives the option and the defendant does not indicate a guilty plea. Crown Prosecutors should recommend Crown Court trial when they are satisfied that the guidelines require them to do so.

9.2 Speed must never be the only reason for asking for a case to stay in the magistrates' courts. But Crown Prosecutors should consider the effect of any likely delay if they send a case to the Crown Court, and any possible stress on victims and witnesses if the case is delayed.

10 ACCEPTING GUILTY PLEAS

10.1 Defendants may want to plead guilty to some, but not all, of the charges. Alternatively, they may want to plead guilty to a different, possibly less serious, charge because they are admitting only part of the crime. Crown Prosecutors should only accept the defendant's plea if they think the court is able to pass a sentence that matches the seriousness of the offending, particularly where there are aggravating features. Crown Prosecutors must never accept a guilty plea just because it is convenient.

10.2 In considering whether the pleas offered are acceptable, Crown Prosecutors should ensure that the interests of the victim and, where possible, any views expressed by the victim or victim's family, are taken into account when deciding whether it is in the public interest to accept the plea. However, the decision rests with the Crown Prosecutor.

10.3 It must be made clear to the court on what basis any plea is advanced and accepted. In cases where a defendant pleads guilty to the charges but on the basis of facts that are different from the prosecution case, and where this may significantly affect sentence, the court should be invited to hear evidence to determine what happened, and then sentence on that basis.

10.4 Where a defendant has previously indicated that he or she will ask the court to take an offence into consideration when sentencing, but then declines to admit that offence at court, Crown Prosecutors will consider whether a prosecution is required for that offence. Crown Prosecutors should explain to the defence advocate and the court that the prosecution of that offence may be subject to further review.

10.5 Particular care must be taken when considering pleas which would enable the defendant to avoid the imposition of a mandatory minimum sentence. When pleas are offered, Crown Prosecutors must bear in mind the fact that ancillary orders can be made with some offences but not with others.

1.7 ESTABLISHING CRIMINAL LIABILITY – THE BURDEN AND STANDARD OF PROOF

In a criminal trial the defendant is presumed to be innocent and it is for the prosecution to prove guilt. This effectively means that the prosecution has to prove each element of the offence (*actus reus* and *mens rea*). Where the burden of proof rests upon the prosecution, the standard of proof is beyond all reasonable doubt. Normally a defendant bears only an evidential burden of proof. This means that he has to raise evidence that justifies a particular defence being left to the jury – for example, evidence that he was provoked will lead to a trial judge in a murder case directing the jury as to the availability of the defence of provocation. It will then be for the prosecution to prove beyond all reasonable doubt that the defendant was not provoked. In those exceptional cases where the defendant bears the legal burden of proof, the standard of proof is balance of probabilities.

Woolmington v DPP [1935] AC 462

Lord Sankey LC:
Throughout the web of the English criminal law one golden thread is always to be seen ... that it is the duty of the prosecution to prove the prisoner's guilt ... If, at the end of and on the

whole of the case, there is a reasonable doubt, created by the evidence given by either the prosecution or the prisoner, as to whether the [elements of the offence have been made out] the prosecution has not made out the case and the prisoner is entitled to an acquittal. No matter what the charge or where the trial, the principle that the prosecution must prove the guilt of the prisoner is part of the common law of England and no attempt to whittle it down can be entertained.

1.7.1 REVERSING THE BURDEN OF PROOF

A statutory provision that seeks to place a legal burden of proof on a defendant presents difficulties in light of the fact that Art 6(2) of the European Convention on Human Rights provides that everyone charged with a criminal offence shall be presumed to be innocent until proven guilty. To survive scrutiny under the terms of the Convention any legislative provision purporting to derogate from the presumption of innocence must be a justifiable, proportionate and legitimate measure. In practical terms this means that it must infringe upon the presumption of innocence no more than is strictly necessary, must be based on clear legal authority, and must be justified by a public interest that outweighs the potential unfairness to the individual defendant. If all of these criteria are satisfied the measure in question may be held to reverse the burden of proof (although the standard of proof will still be the balance of probabilities). If the court rules that the interference with the presumption of innocence is not justified, the measure can be 'read down' so as to operate on the level of placing an evidential burden on the defendant, as opposed to a legal burden.

R v Lambert [2001] 3 All ER 577

Lambert appealed against his conviction for possession of cocaine contrary to the Misuse of Drugs Act 1971, contending that s 5(4) and s 28, which required a defendant charged with possession of a controlled drug to prove, on the balance of probabilities certain exculpatory facts, was incompatible with the presumption of innocence in Art 6(2) of the European Convention on Human Rights. The House of Lords held that to ensure compliance with Art 6(2) the provisions of the 1971 Act had to be read as imposing only an evidential burden on the defendant.

Lord Steyn:
... in a constitutional democracy limited inroads on presumption of innocence may be justified. The approach to be adopted was stated by the European Court of Human Rights in *Salabiaku v France* (1988) 13 EHRR 379, 388 (para 28) as follows:

Presumptions of fact or of law operate in every legal system. Clearly the Convention does not prohibit such presumptions in principle. It does, however, require the Contracting States to remain within certain limits in this respect as regards criminal law. Article 6(2) does not therefore regard presumptions of fact or of law provided for in the criminal law with indifference. It requires States to confine them within reasonable limits which take into account the importance of what is at stake and maintain the rights of the defence.

This test depends upon the circumstances of the individual case. It follows that a legislative interference with the presumption of innocence requires justification and must not be greater than is necessary. The principle of proportionality must be observed.

Does section 5(3) read with section 28(2) and (3) make an inroad on article 6.2? Counsel for the appellant submitted that the defence put forward by the appellant under section 28 is an ingredient of the offence under section 5(3). His argument was that knowledge of the existence and control of the contents of the container is the gravamen of the offence for which the legislature prescribed a maximum sentence of life imprisonment.The contrary argument advanced on behalf of the Director of Public Prosecutions relied on the observation of Lord Woolf CJ in the Court of Appeal [2001] 2 WLR at 221F that 'What the offence does is to make the defendant responsible for ensuring that he does not take into his possession containers which in fact contain drugs.' Taking into account that section 28 deals directly with the situation where the accused is denying moral blameworthiness and the fact that the maximum prescribed penalty is life imprisonment, I conclude that the appellant's interpretation is to be preferred. It follows that section 28 derogates from the presumption of innocence. I would, however, also reach this conclusion on broader grounds. The distinction between constituent elements of the crime and defensive issues will sometimes be unprincipled and arbitrary. After all, it is sometimes simply a matter of which drafting technique is adopted: a true constituent element can be removed from the definition of the crime and cast as a defensive issue whereas any definition of an offence can be reformulated so as to include all possible defences within it. It is necessary to concentrate not on technicalities and niceties of language but rather on matters of substance. I do not have in mind cases within the narrow exception 'limited to offences arising under enactments which prohibit the doing of an act save in specified circumstances or by persons of specified classes or with specified qualifications or with the licence or permission of specified authorities'; *R v Edwards* [1975] QB 27; *R v Hunt* [1987] AC 352; section 101 of the Magistrates' Courts Act 1980. There are other cases where the defence is so closely linked with *mens rea* and moral blameworthiness that it would derogate from the presumption to transfer the legal burden to the accused, e.g. the hypothetical case of transferring the burden of disproving provocation to an accused. In *R v Whyte* (1988) 51 DLR 4th 481 the Canadian Supreme Court rejected an argument that as a matter of principle a constitutional presumption of innocence only applies to elements of the offence and not excuses. Giving the judgment of the court Dickson CJC observed (at 493):

> The real concern is not whether the accused must disprove an element or prove an excuse, but that an accused may be convicted while a reasonable doubt exists. When that possibility exists, there is a breach of the presumption of innocence. The exact characterization of a factor as an essential element, a collateral factor, an excuse, or a defence should not affect the analysis of the presumption of innocence. It is the final effect of a provision on the verdict that is decisive. If an accused is required to prove some fact on the balance of probabilities to avoid conviction, the provision violates the presumption of innocence because it permits a conviction in spite of a reasonable doubt in the mind of the trier of fact as to the guilt of the accused.

I would adopt this reasoning. In the present case the defence under section 28 is one directly bearing on the moral blameworthiness of the accused. It is this factor alone which could justify a maximum sentence of life imprisonment. In my view there is an inroad on the presumption even if an issue under section 28 is in strict law regarded as a pure defence.

It is now necessary to consider the question of justification for the legislative interference with the presumption of innocence. I am satisfied that there is an objective justification for some interference with the burden of proof in prosecutions under section 5 of the 1971 Act. The basis for this justification is that sophisticated drug smugglers, dealers and couriers typically secrete drugs in some container, thereby enabling the person in possession of the container to say that he was unaware of the contents. Such defences are commonplace and they pose real difficulties for the police and prosecuting authorities.

That is, however, not the end of the matter. The burden is on the state to show that the legislative means adopted were not greater than necessary. Where there is objective justification for some inroad on the presumption of innocence the legislature has a choice. The first is to impose a legal burden of proof on the accused. If such a burden is created the matter in question must be taken as proved against the accused unless he satisfies the jury on a balance of probabilities to the contrary: The Eleventh Report of the CrLRC, para 138. The second is to impose an evidential burden only on the accused. If this technique is adopted the matter must be taken as proved against the accused unless there is sufficient evidence to raise an issue on the matter but, if there is sufficient evidence, then the prosecution have the burden of satisfying the jury as to the matter beyond reasonable doubt in the ordinary way: The Eleventh Report of the CrLRC, para 138. It is important to bear in mind that it is not enough for the defence merely to allege the fact in question: the court decides whether there is a real issue on the matter: The Eleventh Report of the CrLRC, para 138. A transfer of a legal burden amounts to a far more drastic interference with the presumption of innocence than the creation of an evidential burden of the accused. The former requires the accused to establish his innocence. It necessarily involves the risk that, if the jury are faithful to the judge's direction, they may convict where the accused has not discharged the legal burden resting on him but left them unsure on the point. This risk is not present if only an evidential burden is created.

The principle of proportionality requires the House to consider whether there was a pressing necessity to impose a legal rather than evidential burden on the accused. The effect of section 28 is that in a prosecution for possession of controlled drugs with intent to supply, although the prosecution must establish that prohibited drugs were in the possession of the defendant, and that he or she knew that the package contained something, the accused must prove on a balance of probabilities that he did not know that the package contained controlled drugs. If the jury is in doubt on this issue, they must convict him. This may occur when an accused adduces sufficient evidence to raise a doubt about his guilt but the jury is not convinced on a balance of probabilities that his account is true. Indeed it obliges the court to convict if the version of the accused is as likely to be true as not. This is a far reaching consequence: a guilty verdict may be returned in respect of an offence punishable by life imprisonment even though the jury may consider that it is reasonably possible that the accused had been duped. It would be unprincipled to brush aside such possibilities as unlikely to happen in practice. Moreover, as Justice has pointed out in its valuable intervention, there may be real difficulties in determining the real facts upon which the sentencer must act in such cases. In any event, the burden of showing that only a reverse legal burden can overcome the difficulties of the prosecution in drugs cases is a heavy one.

A new realism in regard to the problems faced by the prosecution in drugs cases has significantly reduced their scope. First, the relevant facts are usually peculiarly within the knowledge of the possessor of the container and that possession presumptively suggests, in the absence of exculpatory evidence, that the person in possession of it in fact knew what was in the container. This is simply a species of circumstantial evidence. It will usually be a complete answer to a no case submission. It is also a factor which a judge may squarely place before the jury. After all, it is simple common sense that possession of a package containing drugs will generally as a matter of simple common sense demand a full and adequate explanation. Secondly, the statutory provisions enabling a judge to comment on an accused's failure to mention facts when questioned or charged has strengthened the position of the prosecution: section 34 of the Criminal Justice Act 1994 . . .

[Having reviewed a number of Commonwealth authorities, his Lordship continued:]

The jurisprudence in Canada and South Africa reinforces the view that a reverse legal burden is a disproportionate means of addressing the legislative goal of easing the task of the prosecution in cases under section 5(3) of the Misuse of Drugs Act 1971.

In these circumstances I am satisfied that the transfer of the legal burden in section 28 does not satisfy the criterion of proportionality. Viewed in its place in the current legal system section 28 of the 1971 Act is a disproportionate reaction to perceived difficulties facing the prosecution in drugs cases. It would be sufficient to impose an evidential burden on the accused. It follows that section 28 is incompatible with convention rights.

[Lord Hope considered the obligations of the domestic courts under s 3(1) of the Human Rights Act 1998 to ensure, in so far at it was possible to do so, that the interpretation of domestic legislation was consistent with the demands of the European Convention on Human Rights, and continued:]

Lord Hope:
The haphazard way in which reverse burden of proof provisions have been introduced into legislation by Parliament has been identified and persuasively criticised: . . .

The lack of clarity and the inconvenience of applying a different rule to defences created by statute is obvious in the present case. Section 28(4) of the 1971 Act provides that nothing in that section shall prejudice any defence which it is open to a person when charged with an offence to which that section applies to raise apart from that section. In this case the appellant did raise such a defence. It was his defence of duress. That defence was intimately bound up with his defence under the statute, as it depended entirely upon what the jury made of his evidence. But the trial judge had to direct the jury that the onus as regards the defence of duress rested on the prosecution. The jury were not told why there was a difference as to where the onus lay. There was no need for this information to be given to them. But it would not be surprising if they found it hard to maintain a clear distinction between the two positions as to onus when they examined the evidence.

There is no doubt that it is possible, in the light of section 3(1) of the Human Rights Act 1998, to read sections 28(2) and 28(3) of the 1971 Act in such a way as to impose no more than an evidential burden on the accused. As it is a rule of construction, the exercise which section 3(1) prescribes makes it necessary to identify the words used by the legislature which would otherwise be incompatible with the Convention right and then to say how these words are to be construed according to the rule to make them compatible. But in this case there is no difficulty . . .

[Lord Hope referred to *Salabiaku v France*, as had Lord Steyn in his speech, and continued:]

Mr Owen [for the appellant] said that the court was not concerned in the Salabiaku case with a provision applicable to a person charged with a serious criminal offence which placed the burden of proof on him with respect to an essential element of it. That is true, but I do not think that this deprives it of value as a statement of principle. What it means is that, as the article 6(2) right is not absolute and unqualified, the test to be applied is whether the modification or limitation of that right pursues a legitimate aim and whether it satisfies the principle of proportionality: *Ashingdane v United Kingdom* (1985) 7 EHRR 528; see also *Brown v Stott* [2001] 2 WLR 817. It is now well settled that the principle which is to be applied requires a balance to be struck between the general interest of the community and the protection of the fundamental rights of the individual. This will not be achieved if the reverse onus provision goes beyond what is necessary to accomplish the objective of the statute.

The statutory objective is to penalise the unauthorised possession of dangerous or otherwise harmful drugs. But the statute recognises, among other things, that it would be wrong to penalise those who neither knew nor suspected nor had reason to suspect the existence of some fact alleged by the prosecution which it is necessary for the prosecution to prove if he is to be convicted of the offence charged (section 28(2)) or that the substance or product in question is a controlled drug (section 28(3)(b)(i)). That being so, it is hard to see why a person who is accused of the offence of possessing a controlled drug and who wishes to raise this defence should be deprived of the full benefit of the presumption of innocence. The systems of control and prosecution might well be in jeopardy if there were to be an initial onus on the prosecution to establish that the accused knew these things. The right to silence and the covert and unscrupulous nature of drug-related activities must be taken into account in the assessment as to whether a fair balance had been achieved. But we are not concerned here with the initial onus. As I have said in my answer to the first issue, the prosecution do not need to prove that the accused knew that the thing in his possession was a controlled drug. This is a matter which must be raised by the defence.

The choice then is between a persuasive burden, which is what the ordinary meaning of the statutory language lays down, and an evidential burden, which is the meaning which it is possible to give to the statutory language under section 3(1) of the 1998 Act. If the evidential burden were to be so slight as to make no difference – if it were to be enough, for example, for the accused merely to mention the defence without adducing any evidence – important practical considerations would suggest that in the general interest of the community the burden would have to be a persuasive one. But an evidential burden is not to be thought of as a burden which is illusory. What the accused must do is put evidence before the court which, if believed, could be taken by a reasonable jury to support his defence. That is what Professor Glanville Williams envisaged when he was giving this meaning to the words 'unless the contrary is proved': 'The Logic of "Exceptions" ' [1988] CLJ 261, 265 . . . It is what the common law requires of a defendant who wishes to invoke one of the common law defences such as provocation or duress.

The practical effect of reading section 28(2) and section 28(3) as imposing an evidential burden only on the accused and not a persuasive burden as they have been understood to impose hitherto is likely in almost every case that can be imagined to be minimal . . . The change in the nature of the burden is best understood by looking not at the accused and what he must do, but rather at the state of mind of the judge or jury when they are evaluating the evidence. That is why, in the interests of clarity and convenience as well as on grounds of principle, a fair balance will be struck by reading and giving effect to these subsections as imposing an evidential burden only on the accused.

It is worth noting in this connection that Parliament itself has recently recognised the force of the argument that as a general rule statutory provisions which require the accused to prove something as a defence to the offence with which he has been charged should be read and given effect to as if they imposed only an evidential burden on him and not a probative one. The Terrorism Act 2000 contains several provisions which say that it shall be a defence for a person charged with an offence to prove something. For example, section 57(2) provides that it shall be a defence for him to prove that his possession of an article was not for a purpose connected with the commission, preparation or instigation of an act of terrorism. But section 118(2), which applies to a number of provisions in the Act including section 57(2) which say that it is a defence for a person to prove something, provides: 'If the person adduces evidence which is sufficient to raise an issue with respect to the matter the court or jury shall assume that the defence is satisfied unless the prosecution proves beyond reasonable doubt that it is not.'

Section 53(3) of the Regulation of Investigatory Powers Act 2000 is to the same effect. It provides a defence to the offence of possession described in section 53(2). It places the onus of proving the contrary beyond a reasonable doubt on the prosecutor if sufficient evidence of that fact is adduced to raise an issue with respect to it. It is not unreasonable to think that, if Parliament were now to have an opportunity of reconsidering the words used in section 28(2) and (3) of the 1971 Act, it would be content to qualify them in precisely the same way.

I would therefore read the words 'to prove' in section 28(2) as if the words used in the subsection were 'to give sufficient evidence', and I would give the same meaning to the words 'if he proves' in section 28(3). The effect which is to be given to this meaning is that the burden of proof remains on the prosecution throughout. If sufficient evidence is adduced to raise the issue, it will be for the prosecution to show beyond reasonable doubt that the defence is not made out by the evidence.

Sheldrake v Director of Public Prosecutions [2003] 2 All ER 497

Sheldrake was charged with being in charge of a motor car in a public place whilst over the legal drink drive limit, contrary to s 5(1)(b) of the Road Traffic Act 1988. Section 5(2) of the 1988 Act, so far as material, provides that it is a defence for a person charged with an offence under subsection (1)(b) to prove that at the time he is alleged to have committed the offence the circumstances were such that there was no likelihood of his driving the vehicle whilst the proportion of alcohol in his breath, blood or urine remained likely to exceed the prescribed limit. The key issue before the House of Lords was whether s 5(2) was compliant with Art 6(2) of the European Convention on Human Rights to the extent that it placed a legal burden of proof on the defendant. Reversing the decision of the Divisional Court the House of Lords held that s 5(2) was consistent with Art 6(2) even though it did impose a legal burden of proof.

Lord Bingham:

[1] Sections 5(2) of the Road Traffic Act 1988 and 11(2) of the Terrorism Act 2000, conventionally interpreted, impose a legal or persuasive burden on a defendant in criminal proceedings to prove the matters respectively specified in those subsections if he is to be exonerated from liability on the grounds there provided. That means that he must, to be exonerated, establish those matters on the balance of probabilities. If he fails to discharge that burden he will be convicted. In this appeal by the Director of Public Prosecutions and this reference by the Attorney General these reverse burdens ('reverse' because the burden is placed on the defendant and not, as ordinarily in

criminal proceedings, on the prosecutor) are challenged as incompatible with the presumption of innocence guaranteed by Art 6(2) of the European Convention for the Protection of Human Rights and Fundamental Freedoms (1953) (Cmd 8969). Thus the first question for consideration in each case is whether the provision in question does, unjustifiably, infringe the presumption of innocence. If it does the further question arises whether the provision can and should be read down in accordance with the courts' interpretative obligation under s 3 of the Human Rights Act 1998 so as to impose an evidential and not a legal burden on the defendant. An evidential burden is not a burden of proof. It is a burden of raising, on the evidence in the case, an issue as to the matter in question fit for consideration by the tribunal of fact. If an issue is properly raised, it is for the prosecutor to prove, beyond reasonable doubt, that that ground of exoneration does not avail the defendant.

[His Lordship referred to the relevant Strasbourg case law and continued]:

[21] From this body of authority certain principles may be derived. The overriding concern is that a trial should be fair, and the presumption of innocence is a fundamental right directed to that end. The Convention does not outlaw presumptions of fact or law but requires that these should be kept within reasonable limits and should not be arbitrary. It is open to states to define the constituent elements of a criminal offence, excluding the requirement of *mens rea*. But the substance and effect of any presumption adverse to a defendant must be examined, and must be reasonable. Relevant to any judgment on reasonableness or proportionality will be the opportunity given to the defendant to rebut the presumption, maintenance of the rights of the defence, flexibility in application of the presumption, retention by the court of a power to assess the evidence, the importance of what is at stake and the difficulty which a prosecutor may face in the absence of a presumption. Security concerns do not absolve member states from their duty to observe basic standards of fairness. The justifiability of any infringement of the presumption of innocence cannot be resolved by any rule of thumb, but on examination of all the facts and circumstances of the particular provision as applied in the particular case.

[His Lordship then proceeded to explain why it was in the public interest that s 5(2) should be read as imposing a legal burden of proof on the defendant]:

[40] . . . There is an obvious risk that a person may cause death, injury or damage if he drives or attempts to drive a car when excessive consumption of alcohol has made him unfit . . . That is why such conduct has been made a criminal offence. There is also an obvious risk that if a person is in control of a car when unfit he may drive it, with the consequent risk of causing death, injury or damage already noted. That is why it has been made a criminal offence to be in charge of a car in that condition . . . But the ingredients of the offence make no reference to doing a preparatory act towards driving or forming an intention to drive. The 1872 and 1930 Acts criminalised the conduct of those who were in charge of carriages and cars respectively when drunk or unfit, but made no reference to the likelihood of driving. There could, as I understood counsel to accept, be no ground of complaint if the offence of being unfit when in charge of a motor vehicle, as laid down in 1930, had remained unaltered. As has been shown, Parliament has modified that provision in favour of the defendant. If he can show that there was no likelihood of his driving while unfit, he is deemed not to have been in charge for purposes of s 4 of the 1988 Act and has a defence under s 5(2). There appears to be no very good reason (other than history) for the adoption of these different legislative techniques, but the outcome is effectively the same. The defendant

can exonerate himself if he can show that the risk which led to the creation of the offence did not in his case exist. If he fails to establish this ground of exoneration, a possibility (but not a probability) would remain that he would not have been likely to drive. But he would fall squarely within the class of those whose conduct Parliament has, since 1930, legislated to criminalise. In *DPP v Watkins* [1989] QB 821 it was recognised, in my view rightly, that the offence does not require proof that a defendant is likely to drive: see pp 829D, 832E, 833A. This is not in my view an oppressive outcome, since a person in charge of a car when unfit to drive it may properly be expected to divest himself of the power to do so (as by giving the keys to someone else) or put it out of his power to do so (as by going well away). It may be, as was submitted in argument and suggested by Taylor LJ in *DPP v Watkins* at p 830, that the words 'in charge' have been too broadly interpreted and applied, but that is not a question which falls for decision in this appeal.

[41] It may not be very profitable to debate whether s 5(2) infringes the presumption of innocence. It may be assumed that it does. Plainly the provision is directed to a legitimate object: the prevention of death, injury and damage caused by unfit drivers. Does the provision meet the tests of acceptability identified in the Strasbourg jurisprudence? In my view, it plainly does. I do not regard the burden placed on the defendant as beyond reasonable limits or in any way arbitrary. It is not objectionable to criminalise a defendant's conduct in these circumstances without requiring a prosecutor to prove criminal intent. The defendant has a full opportunity to show that there was no likelihood of his driving, a matter so closely conditioned by his own knowledge and state of mind at the material time as to make it much more appropriate for him to prove on the balance of probabilities that he would not have been likely to drive than for the prosecutor to prove, beyond reasonable doubt, that he would. I do not think that imposition of a legal burden went beyond what was necessary. If a driver tries and fails to establish a defence under s 5(2), I would not regard the resulting conviction as unfair, as the House held that it might or would be in *R v Lambert*. I find no reason to conclude that the conviction of Mr Sheldrake was tainted by any hint of unfairness.

1.7.2 CODIFICATION AND LAW REFORM PROPOSALS – THE BURDEN AND STANDARD OF PROOF

Clause 13 of the Draft Criminal Code Bill (Law Com 177 Vol I – see 1.8 below for an overview of the Law Commission's criminal law reform project) sought to codify the law relating to burden and standard of proof in criminal trials thus:

13(1) Unless otherwise provided –
    (a) the burden of proving every element of an offence and any other fact alleged or relied on by the prosecution is on the prosecution;
    (b) where evidence is given (whether by the defendant or by the prosecution) of a defence or any other fact alleged or relied on by the defendant the burden is on the prosecution to prove that an element of the defence or such other fact did not exist.
  (2) Evidence is given of a defence or any other fact alleged or relied on by the defendant when there is such evidence as might lead a court or jury to conclude that there is a reasonable possibility that the elements of the defence or such other fact existed.

(3) The burden is on the defendant to prove any fact necessary to establish –

    (a) any plea made by him in bar to an indictment or any corresponding plea on summary trial;

    (b) the competence of any witness called by him; or

    (c) the admissibility of any evidence tendered by him.

(4) Unless otherwise provided –

    (a) where the burden of proof is on the prosecution the standard of proof required is proof beyond reasonable doubt;

    (b) where the burden of proof is on the defendant the standard of proof required is proof on the balance of probabilities, except where subsection (5) applies.

(5) Where an element of a defence is the fact that another person is guilty and liable to conviction of the offence in the same proceedings, the standard required for proof of that element is proof beyond reasonable doubt.

The commentary on these clauses observed (Law Com 177 Vol II):

6.1 Burden of proof: the general rule. Subsection (1) states the general rule in *Woolmington v DPP* . . . When the evidential burden is satisfied, the burden is on the prosecution to disprove the fact in question. The nature of the evidential burden is described in subsection (2). Unless such evidence is already before the court, the defendant must adduce evidence which might lead a court or jury to conclude that there is a reasonable possibility that the fact alleged existed.

6.2 Exceptions to the general rule. The general rule applies 'unless otherwise provided', whether expressly or by necessary implication, and subject to subsections (3) and (6). Subsection (3) provides for three cases where, under the present law, the burden of proof is, or probably is and, in our opinion, ought to be, on the defendant: to establish any fact necessary to prove (a) a plea in bar, (b) the competence of a witness called by him, (c) the admissibility of evidence tendered by him. The House of Lords in *Hunt* . . . has confirmed that section 101 of the Magistrates' Courts Act 1980 imposes the burden of proving certain defences on the defendant at a summary trial and that there is a corresponding common law rule of interpretation which achieves the same effect at a trial on indictment. Subsection (6) preserves these rules.

6.3 Standard of proof: Subsection (4) states the general rule for standard of proof – for the prosecution, proof beyond reasonable doubt and, for the defendant, proof on the balance of probabilities. The general rule applies 'unless otherwise provided', whether expressly or by necessary implication, and subject to subsection (5). This is concerned with the rare case of a special defence of the kind found in the Food Act 1984, section 100. An element of the defence is that a third person is guilty and liable to conviction in the same proceedings. The third person ought not to be convicted of the offence unless his guilt is proved beyond reasonable doubt and it is therefore necessary that that should be the standard of proof for this element of the defence.

1.8 CRIMINAL APPEALS

A defendant convicted before a magistrates' court may appeal to the Crown Court – a procedure that normally involves a complete rehearing of the case. Whatever the outcome of such proceedings, it does not normally have any value in terms of precedent, thus does not contribute to the development of the substantive criminal law. Alternatively a defendant convicted in the magistrates' court can appeal to the Divisional Court on a point of law – known as proceeding by way of case stated. This would be appropriate, for example, where the facts are not in dispute. This avenue of appeal is also available to the prosecution if a magistrates' court dismisses the case against a defendant. Rulings of the Divisional Court do create precedents binding on trial courts. Where a defendant has exercised his right to appeal from the magistrates' court to the Crown Court, he still has the option of proceeding by way of case stated in relation to a point of law, before the Divisional Court. Appeal from the Divisional Court in case stated proceedings lies directly to the House of Lords.

1.8.1 THE DEFENDANT'S OPTIONS – APPEALING AGAINST CONVICTION (FOLLOWING TRIAL ON INDICTMENT) FROM THE CROWN COURT TO THE COURT OF APPEAL

Most of the important appeal cases that give rise to developments in substantive criminal law arise where a defendant who has been convicted in the Crown Court, following trial on indictment, appeals against that conviction (as opposed to appealing against the sentence) to the Court of Appeal (Criminal Division). The statutes that govern this process are the Criminal Appeal Act 1968, and the Criminal Appeal Act 1995.

Under the 1968 Act, an accused can appeal as of right against conviction if the trial judge grants a certificate to the effect that the case is fit for appeal. In all other cases the accused will have to obtain leave to appeal from the Court of Appeal. Applications for leave are normally determined by a single judge of the Court of Appeal on the basis of written submissions. Appeal against a refusal of leave will be considered by a full court sitting of the Court of Appeal. Essentially leave should be granted if the appeal indicates that the accused has an arguable case.

Section 2(1) of the 1968 Act, as amended by the 1995 Act, provides that the Court of Appeal 'shall allow an appeal against conviction if they think that the conviction is unsafe . . . and shall dismiss such an appeal in any other case'. The use of the criterion 'unsafe' replaces the more detailed approach under the 1968 Act as originally enacted, although it is doubtful that Parliament intended to change the scope of the grounds for allowing an appeal. To this end it is instructive to note that, prior to the 1995 Act, an appeal could be allowed because of a wrong ruling on the law, material irregularity, or because (taking into account all the circumstances) the conviction was unsafe or unsatisfactory.

The extent to which a conviction can be regarded as 'safe', notwithstanding unfairness in the trial process, has had to be reconsidered following the enactment of the Human Rights Act 1998, and the decision of the European Court of Human Rights in *R v Condron* [2000] Crim LR 679. The result is that the Court of Appeal should not disengage the issue of the fairness of the trial from the issue of whether or not the conviction is safe. In essence significant violations of the right to a fair trial provided by Art 6 of the European Convention on Human Rights are, of themselves, likely to render a conviction unsafe; see further *R v Francom* (2000) *The Times*, 24 October.

In *R v Togher and Others* (2000) The Times, 21 November, Lord Woolf CJ went so far as to observe that the approach of the Court of Appeal should be in step with that of the European Court of Human Rights, with the result that the denial of a fair trial contrary to Art 6 would now inevitably lead to a finding that the resulting conviction was unsafe. Such a conclusion is a direct result of the obligation created by s 3(1) of the Human Rights Act 1998 to the effect that domestic legislation, such as the Criminal Appeal Act 1995, should be read, so far as possible, in a manner that gives effect to Convention rights. *R v Davis* (2000) *The Times*, 25 July, whilst not departing from this broad proposition, emphasises that it may still be necessary to look at the circumstances of a particular case before concluding that a violation of Art 6 has rendered a conviction unsafe – it will be a matter of fact and degree.

Even if an appeal against conviction succeeds, the accused may still face a retrial. The Court of Appeal has the discretion to order a retrial under s 7 of the 1968 Act if it appears to the court that the interests of justice so require. If there has been a total mistrial the Court of Appeal can issue a writ of *venire de novo* – setting events back to where they were before the irregularity occurred that rendered the trial a mistrial.

Some appeals against conviction will be partially successful in that the Court of Appeal can allow the appeal but substitute a conviction for a lesser-included offence – an obvious example being the quashing of a murder conviction and the substitution of a conviction for manslaughter.

1.8.2 THE DEFENDANT'S OPTIONS – CRIMINAL CASES REVIEW COMMISSION

Prior to the enactment of the Criminal Appeal Act 1995 the Home Secretary had the power to refer cases to the Court of Appeal if there was evidence to suggest that a miscarriage of justice had occurred. The significance of this discretion lay in the fact that it could be exercised notwithstanding that the time limits for lodging an appeal to the court had expired long ago. Following criticisms of the involvement of politicians in this aspect of the criminal justice process, the 1995 Act withdrew the Home Secretary's powers of referral and instead vested them in an independent body, the Criminal Cases Review Commission.

Under s 5 of the 1995 Act (amending s 23 of the Criminal Appeal Act 1968) the Court of Appeal can ask the Criminal Cases Review Commission to investigate a particular case on its behalf:

CRIMINAL APPEAL ACT 1995

5(1) After section 23 of the 1968 Act insert –

Power to order investigations. 23A(1) On an appeal against conviction the Court of Appeal may direct the Criminal Cases Review Commission to investigate and report to the Court on any matter if it appears to the Court that –

(a) the matter is relevant to the determination of the case and ought, if possible, to be resolved before the case is determined;

(b) an investigation of the matter by the Commission is likely to result in the Court being able to resolve it; and

(c) the matter cannot be resolved by the Court without an investigation by the Commission.

(4) Where the Commission have reported to the Court of Appeal on any matter which they have been directed under subsection (1) above to investigate, the Court –

(a) shall notify the appellant and the respondent that the Commission have reported; and

> (b) may make available to the appellant and the respondent the report of the Commission and any statements, opinions and reports which accompanied it.

The powers of the Commission to refer possible miscarriages of justice to the Court of Appeal of their own volition (as regards criminal proceedings in England and Wales) are provided by ss 9 (referral following trial on indictment), 11 (referral following summary trial), 13 (basis for making a referral) and 14 (further issues relating to referral) of the 1995 Act.

CRIMINAL APPEAL ACT 1995

9(1) Where a person has been convicted of an offence on indictment in England and Wales, the Commission –

(a) may at any time refer the conviction to the Court of Appeal, and (b) (whether or not they refer the conviction) may at any time refer to the Court of Appeal any sentence (not being a sentence fixed by law) imposed on, or in subsequent proceedings relating to, the conviction.

(2) A reference under subsection (1) of a person's conviction shall be treated for all purposes as an appeal by the person under section 1 of the 1968 Act against the conviction.

(3) A reference under subsection (1) of a sentence imposed on, or in subsequent proceedings relating to, a person's conviction on an indictment shall be treated for all purposes as an appeal by the person under section 9 of the 1968 Act against –

(a) the sentence, and

(b) any other sentence (not being a sentence fixed by law) imposed on, or in subsequent proceedings relating to, the conviction or any other conviction on the indictment.

(4) On a reference under subsection (1) of a person's conviction on an indictment the Commission may give notice to the Court of Appeal that any other conviction on the indictment which is specified in the notice is to be treated as referred to the Court of Appeal under subsection (1).

(5) Where a verdict of not guilty by reason of insanity has been returned in England and Wales in the case of a person, the Commission may at any time refer the verdict to the Court of Appeal; and a reference under this subsection shall be treated for all purposes as an appeal by the person under section 12 of the 1968 Act against the verdict.

(6) Where a jury in England and Wales has returned findings that a person is under a disability and that he did the act or made the omission charged against him, the Commission may at any time refer either or both of those findings to the Court of Appeal; and a reference under this subsection shall be treated for all purposes as an appeal by the person under section 15 of the 1968 Act against the finding or findings referred.

. . .

11(1) Where a person has been convicted of an offence by a magistrates' court in England and Wales, the Commission –

(a) may at any time refer the conviction to the Crown Court, and

(b) (whether or not they refer the conviction) may at any time refer to the Crown Court any sentence imposed on, or in subsequent proceedings relating to, the conviction.

(2) A reference under subsection (1) of a person's conviction shall be treated for all purposes as an appeal by the person under section 108(1) of the [1980 c 43] Magistrates' Courts Act 1980 against the conviction (whether or not he pleaded guilty).

(3) A reference under subsection (1) of a sentence imposed on, or in subsequent proceedings

relating to, a person's conviction shall be treated for all purposes as an appeal by the person under section 108(1) of the Magistrates' Courts Act 1980 against –

    (a)   the sentence, and

    (b)   any other sentence imposed on, or in subsequent proceedings relating to, the conviction or any related conviction.

(4) On a reference under subsection (1) of a person's conviction the Commission may give notice to the Crown Court that any related conviction which is specified in the notice is to be treated as referred to the Crown Court under subsection (1).

(5) For the purposes of this section convictions are related if they are convictions of the same person by the same court on the same day.

(6) On a reference under this section the Crown Court may not award any punishment more severe than that awarded by the court whose decision is referred.

(7) The Crown Court may grant bail to a person whose conviction or sentence has been referred under this section; and any time during which he is released on bail shall not count as part of any term of imprisonment or detention under his sentence.

. . .

13(1) A reference of a conviction, verdict, finding or sentence shall not be made under [ss 9 or 11] unless –

    (a)   the Commission consider that there is a real possibility that the conviction, verdict, finding or sentence would not be upheld were the reference to be made,

    (b)   the Commission so consider –

        (i)   in the case of a conviction, verdict or finding, because of an argument, or evidence, not raised in the proceedings which led to it or on any appeal or application for leave to appeal against it, or

        (ii) in the case of a sentence, because of an argument on a point of law, or information, not so raised, and

    (c)   an appeal against the conviction, verdict, finding or sentence has been determined or leave to appeal against it has been refused.

(2) Nothing in subsection (1)(b)(i) or (c) shall prevent the making of a reference if it appears to the Commission that there are exceptional circumstances which justify making it.

14(1) A reference of a conviction, verdict, finding or sentence may be made under [ss 9 or 11] either after an application has been made by or on behalf of the person to whom it relates or without an application having been so made.

(2) In considering whether to make a reference of a conviction, verdict, finding or sentence under [ss 9 or 11] the Commission shall have regard to –

    (a)   any application or representations made to the Commission by or on behalf of the person to whom it relates,

    (b)   any other representations made to the Commission in relation to it, and

    (c)   any other matters which appear to the Commission to be relevant.

(3) In considering whether to make a reference under [ss 9] the Commission may at any time refer any point on which they desire the assistance of the Court of Appeal to that Court for the Court's opinion on it; and on a reference under this subsection the Court of Appeal shall consider the point referred and furnish the Commission with the Court's opinion on the point.

(4) Where the Commission make a reference under [ss 9 or 11] the Commission shall –

    (a)   give to the court to which the reference is made a statement of the Commission's reasons for making the reference, and

> (b) send a copy of the statement to every person who appears to the Commission to be likely to be a party to any proceedings on the appeal arising from the reference.
>
> (5) Where a reference under [ss 9 or 11] is treated as an appeal against any conviction, verdict, finding or sentence, the appeal may be on any ground relating to the conviction, verdict, finding or sentence (whether or not the ground is related to any reason given by the Commission for making the reference).
>
> (6) In every case in which –
>
> (a) an application has been made to the Commission by or on behalf of any person for the reference under [ss 9 or 11] of any conviction, verdict, finding or sentence, but
>
> (b) the Commission decide not to make a reference of the conviction, verdict, finding or sentence,
>
> the Commission shall give a statement of the reasons for their decision to the person who made the application.

It may be the case that the Commission refer a case to the Court of Appeal many years after the initial conviction. In the intervening years there may have been changes in statute, common law and decisions made by the European Court of Human Rights relating to the criminal process. The way in which such factors should be dealt with by the Court of Appeal was considered in *R v Bentley* [1999] Crim LR 330, and *R v Kansal* (2001) *The Times*, June 11. Any changes in statute law between the date of the conviction and the referral, unless expressly declared to be retrospective, will be ignored. Changes in the common law, however, will be taken into account on the basis that the common law as currently stated is assumed to reflect what the law was at the time of the conviction – this may involve changes that now render a conviction unsafe. Potentially the same is true of the effect of rulings by the European Court of Human Rights. In *R v Kansal* the Court of Appeal noted that, once a case is referred to it by the Commission, it has no discretion but to hear the appeal. This, coupled with the fact that there is no time limit applicable to the convictions that can be referred by the Commission (i.e. it could refer any past conviction that meets the criteria for referral), suggests a potentially huge case load for the Court of Appeal unless the Commission clarify their policy on referral.

1.8.3 PROSECUTION APPEAL OPTIONS – APPEAL AGAINST A TRIAL JUDGE'S RULING

Whilst the prosecution cannot appeal against a jury's 'not guilty' verdict, under part 9 of the Criminal Justice Act 2003, a right of appeal does lie in respect of some rulings, made in the course of a trial, that effectively make it impossible for the prosecution case to continue. The 2003 Act, in essence, provides for an interlocutory prosecution right of appeal where there is a trial on indictment and the trial judge makes a decision that has the effect of terminating the trial (other than a decision to discharge a jury), either at a pre-trial hearing or during the trial itself. There is also a right of appeal against rulings that are so fatal to the prosecution case that the prosecution proposes to treat them as terminating. Leave to appeal must be obtained either from the judge or the Court of Appeal. The ruling against which the prosecution appeals will not take effect whilst the appeal process is in train. If the Court of Appeal subsequently confirms a terminating (or effectively terminating) ruling it must order the acquittal of the defendant. Where the prosecution appeal succeeds, the Court of Appeal may require the restoration of the Crown Court proceedings (or a fresh trial) only where this is necessary in the interests of justice.

1.8.4 PROSECUTION APPEAL OPTIONS – APPEAL ON A POINT OF LAW

If the acquittal appears to have arisen because of a misapplication of the law by the trial judge, or because of an apparent loophole in the law, the Crown can test the matter further by proceeding under s 36(1) of the Criminal Justice Act 1972. This provision allows the Attorney General to refer the relevant point of law to the Court of Appeal for a ruling. Although the outcome of the proceedings cannot affect the liability of the acquitted defendant, it does have the same status, in terms of precedent, as any other Court of Appeal decision. The nature and purpose of such a reference was considered by the House of Lords in the following case:

Attorney General's Ref (No 3 of 1994) [1997] 3 All ER 936

Lord Mustill:
The courts have always firmly resisted attempts to obtain the answer to academic questions, however useful this might appear to be. Normally, where an appeal is brought in the context of an issue between parties, the identification of questions which the court should answer can be performed by considering whether a particular answer to the question of law might affect the outcome of the dispute. The peculiarity of a reference under the Act of 1972 is that it is not a step in a dispute, so that in one sense the questions referred are invariably academic. This peculiarity might, unless limits are observed, enable the Attorney General, for the best of motives, to use an acquittal on a point of law to set in train a judicial roving commission on a particular branch of the law, with the aim of providing clear, practical and systematic solutions for problems of current interest. This is not the function of the court . . .

The option of appealing against a ruling of the Court of Appeal (Criminal Division) is open to both the prosecution and the defence. The procedure is governed by ss 33 and 34 of the Criminal Appeal Act 1968, which provide as follows:

33(1) An appeal lies to the House of Lords, at the instance of the defendant or the prosecutor, from any decision of the Court of Appeal on an appeal to that court under part I of this Act or section 9 (preparatory hearings) of the Criminal Justice Act 1987.

(2) The appeal lies only with the leave of the Court of Appeal or the House of Lords and leave shall not be granted unless it is certified by the Court of Appeal that a point of law of general public importance is involved in the decision and it appears to the Court of Appeal or the House of Lords (as the case may be) that the point is one which ought to be considered by that House.

. . .

34(1) An application to the Court of Appeal for leave to appeal to the House of Lords shall be made within the period of 14 days beginning with the date of the decision of the court and an application to the House of Lords for leave shall be made within the period of 14 days beginning with the date on which the application for leave is refused by the Court of Appeal.

1.8.5 PROSECUTION APPEAL OPTIONS – APPEAL BY THE PROSECUTION AGAINST OVER-LENIENT SENTENCES

By virtue of ss 35 and 36 of the Criminal Justice Act 1988 the prosecution may, following the conviction of the defendant in the Crown Court, appeal to the Court of Appeal (Criminal Division) in respect of the sentence passed, if it is of the view that the sentence is unduly lenient.

Section 36 of the Criminal Justice Act 1988 provides:

> (1) If it appears to the Attorney General
>   (a) that the sentencing of a person in a proceeding in the Crown Court has been unduly lenient and
>   (b) that the case is one to which this part of this Act applies,
>   he may, with the leave of the Court of Appeal, refer the case to them for them to review the sentencing of that person and on such a reference the Court of Appeal may
>   (i) quash any sentence passed on him in the proceeding and
>   (ii) in place of it pass such sentence as they think appropriate for the case and as the court
>   below had power to pass when dealing with him.
>
> . . .
>
> (6) A reference under subsection (5) above shall be made only with the leave of the Court of Appeal or the House of Lords and leave shall not be granted unless it is certified by the Court of Appeal that the point of law is of general public importance and it appears to the Court of Appeal or the House of Lords (as the case may be) that the point is one which ought to be considered by that House.

1.8.6 PROSECUTION APPEAL OPTIONS – APPLICATION TO HAVE AN ACQUITTAL QUASHED

Prior to the enactment of Part 10 of the Criminal Justice Act 2003, where a defendant was acquitted following trial on indictment, the *autre fois acquit* rule (the rule against double jeopardy) prevented the defendant being tried again for the same offence. In exceptional cases it is now possible for the prosecution to apply to the Court of Appeal for an acquittal to be quashed. This procedure requires the consent of the Director of Public Prosecutions (DPP) and only applies to a small number of serious offences such as murder, manslaughter and rape. Two criteria have to be satisfied before the Court of Appeal can order the quashing of the acquittal. First, the evidence must be new and compelling. The evidence is compelling if it is reliable, it is substantial, and in the context of the outstanding issues (ie the issues in dispute in the proceedings in which the person was acquitted), and it appears highly probative of the case against the acquitted person. Secondly, the quashing of the acquittal must be in the interests of justice. In determining whether or not this second criterion is met the court will have regard to: (a) whether existing circumstances make a fair trial unlikely (including the length of time since the offence was allegedly committed) and (b) whether the failure to adduce the evidence in earlier proceedings against the acquitted person was due to a failure by the prosecution to act with due diligence or expedition. If an acquittal is quashed the court may order a retrial as appropriate. These changes will enable the prosecution to make use of advances in technology, particularly those related to DNA evidence, whereby their examination of evidence reveals links with acquitted defendants.

R v Dunlop [2006] EWCA 1354

D was charged with murder in 1989 but acquitted following his trial. D subsequently confessed to the killing and was successfully prosecuted for perjury committed during the 1989 trial. Following the enactment of the Criminal Justice Act 2003, D was re-indicted in respect of the 1989 murder and pleaded guilty. He appealed against his conviction on a number of grounds: delay, the impossibility of his receiving a fair trial because of all the publicity surrounding his case; and the fact that it was unfair to re-indict him given that he had confessed to the murder at a time when there had been no legislative provision enabling the prosecution to proceed with a second trial for murder. The Court of Appeal dismissed the appeal, observing that issues such as delay and jury management to ensure a fair trial were routinely dealt with in other criminal trials. As to the fairness issue Phillips LCJ observed:

> In reliance on the belief that he was immune from retrial, D has provided new evidence which is not merely compelling, but overwhelming. There has been no suggestion that he is in a position to attempt to rebut this evidence. In these circumstances we suggested to Mr Owen [counsel for D] that the issue was not so much whether it was fair that he should be exposed to the jeopardy of another trial, but whether it was fair, having particular regard to the fact that he had set out to 'put the record straight' and pay the considerable penalty for perjury, that he should be exposed to further punishment for murder, the punishment in question being a mandatory life sentence. Mr Owen did not demur from this proposition.

> In considering the case for an exception to the double jeopardy rule, the Law Commission commented as follows:

>> There is, further, the spectre of public disquiet, even revulsion, when someone is acquitted of the most serious of crimes and new material (such as that person's own admission) points strongly or conclusively to guilt. Such cases may undermine public confidence in the criminal justice system as much as manifestly wrongful convictions. The erosion of that confidence, caused by the demonstrable failure of the system to deliver accurate outcomes in very serious cases, is at least as important as the failure itself.

> Those words might have been written of the present case.

> We are dealing here with the crime of murder. The Law Commission identified the unique features of this crime as providing a unique justification for an exception to the double jeopardy rule. Parliament has extended the exception further than the crime of murder, but that does not detract from the fact that the strongest justification for the exception is likely to be the case of murder.

> We have concluded that the public would rightly be outraged were the exception to the double jeopardy rule not to be applied in the present case simply on the basis that D would not have made the confessions that he did had he appreciated that they might lead to his retrial. We can see no injustice in allowing a retrial in this case. As for the sentence that D has served for perjury, that was imposed as punishment for lying under oath. It may be that the sentence reflected the consequence of the perjury, namely D's acquittal of murder, and that for this reason it should be taken into account, to some extent, when determining the minimum term to be served

should D now be convicted of that crime. That is a matter that will fall for consideration if and when a judge comes to sentence D for the offence of murder.

1.9 CODIFICATION OF THE CRIMINAL LAW

As noted above, English criminal law is drawn from a variety of common law and statutory sources. Many of the difficulties, uncertainties and absurdities encountered in an examination of English criminal law stem from the fact there has never been a systematic reappraisal of the criminal law by Parliament. Unlike other jurisdictions, there is no penal code for England and Wales. Building upon earlier work undertaken by the Criminal Law Revision Committee the Law Commission has, since 1981, been engaged in a large scale project to codify, and in certain aspects, reform the substantive criminal law of England and Wales. Volumes I and II of the Law Commission's Report (No 177) *A Criminal Code for England and Wales* attempted to lay the foundations for such a code. Subsequent Law Commission Reports have attempted to take the project further by tackling specific aspects of the substantive law such as manslaughter, nonfatal assaults and intoxication.

The recent work that has been done to date (in so far as it relates to the aspects of substantive criminal law relevant to this text) can be summarised in the table at the end of this section.

Extracts from these various reports have been included, as appropriate, in the chapters that follow. The case for codification generally was made in Volume I of Law Com 177 as follows:

Law Com 177 Vol I

1.3 English criminal law is derived from a mixture of common law and statute. Most of the general principles of liability are still to be found in the common law, though some for example, the law relating to conspiracy and attempts to commit crime have recently been defined in Acts of Parliament. The great majority of crimes are now defined by statute but there are important exceptions. Murder, manslaughter and assault are still offences at common law, though affected in various ways by statute. There is no system in the relative roles of common law and legislation. Thus, incitement to commit crime – though closely related to conspiracy and attempts – is still a common law offence. Whether an offence is defined by statute has almost always been a matter of historical accident rather than systematic organisation . . . The legislation in force extends over a very long period of time. It is true that only a very small amount of significant legislation is earlier than the midnineteenth century, but that is quite long enough for the language of the criminal law and the style of drafting to have undergone substantial changes.

1.4 There has been a steady flow of reform of the criminal law in recent years but it has been accomplished in somewhat piecemeal fashion. Some of it is derived from our own reports, where in recent years we have been pursuing a policy of putting common law offences into statutory form, and some from reports of the Criminal Law Revision Committee and committees, like the Heilbron Committee, appointed to deal with particular problems. Other reforms have resulted from the initiative of Ministers or private Members of Parliament in introducing Bills. As there is no authoritative statement of general principles of liability or of terminology to which we or these other bodies, or their draftsmen, can turn it would be surprising if there were not some inconsistencies and incongruities in the substance and language of the measures which are proposed and which become law. Some examples are pointed out below. This Report addresses the question whether it is desirable to replace the existing fluctuating mix of legislation and common law by one codifying statute . . .

Why codify the criminal law? – The aims of codification

2.1 The Code team identified the aims of codification at the present time as being to make the criminal law more accessible, comprehensible, consistent and certain. These aspirations have a number of theoretical and practical aspects which we examine in more detail below. We believe, however, that there are also fundamental constitutional arguments of principle in favour of codification which we consider first . . .

The constitutional arguments for codification

2.2 The constitutional arguments relating to codification were not stressed in the Code team's Report but were mentioned by some commentators on consultation as important arguments in favour of codifying the criminal law. These arguments were developed, in particular, by Professor ATH Smith and were conveniently summarised (as well as being endorsed) by the Society of Public Teachers of Law in their submission to us as follows:

> The virtues and advantages of a Code that [the Code team's Report] identifies (accessibility, comprehensibility, consistency and certainty) relate to essentially lawyerly concerns: what needs to be stressed is that they serve the more profound aspirations of due notice and fair warning characteristic of a system that seeks to adhere to the principle of legality. In the first place, a Code is the mechanism that will best synthesise the criminal law's conflicting aims of social protection and crime prevention with concern for legality and due process. As Professor Wechsler, principal draftsman of the Model Penal Code, has put it, a Code demonstrates that, when so much is at stake for the community and the individual, care has been taken to make law as rational and just as law can be. A Code will, secondly, provide what the mix of common law and legislation never can, one fixed starting point for ascertaining what the law is. Thirdly, because a Criminal Code makes a symbolic statement about the constitutional relationship of Parliament and the courts, it requires a judicial deference to the legislative will greater than that which the courts have often shown to isolated and sporadic pieces of legislation. Far from it being 'a possible disadvantage of codification' that it places 'limitations upon the ability of the courts to develop the law in directions which might be considered desirable', we believe that for the criminal law this is one of its greatest merits. Then, fourthly, codification will make it possible to effect many much needed and long-overdue reforms in both the General and the Special Parts of the criminal law, that have already been adumbrated in the reports of official bodies . . .

With much of this we agree. 'Due notice' or 'fair warning' – by which is meant the idea that the law should be known in advance to those accused of violating it – should clearly be regarded as a principle of major importance in our criminal justice system. While there is room for argument as to how much or how little of the content of the criminal law should be left to be developed by the common law, codification provides the opportunity for ensuring that this principle is followed over a substantial part of the criminal law. Moreover, since the criminal law is arguably the most direct expression of the relationship between a State and its citizens, it is right as a matter of constitutional principle that the relationship should be clearly stated in a criminal code the terms of which have been deliberated upon by a democratically elected legislature.

2.3 We shall return to consider some of the arguments in the passage above in more detail later, for example, the third and fourth arguments concerning codification and the role of the court and the relationship between restatement and reform. Suffice it to note here that we endorse them, subject to the considerations mentioned later. The second argument (that a code will provide a fixed starting point for ascertaining what the law is) relates to accessibility which is considered next . . .

Accessibility and comprehensibility

2.4 If the terms of the criminal law are set out in one well-drafted enactment in place of the present fluctuating mix of statute and case-law, the law must necessarily become more accessible and comprehensible to everyone concerned with the interests of criminal justice. Accessibility and comprehensibility are important values for a number of reasons.

2.5 A large and growing number of people are now involved in administering and advising upon the criminal law. One reason for this is that the volume of work in the criminal courts has hugely increased in recent years. To meet this rise, there has been a substantial increase in the numbers of Crown Court judges, recorders and assistant recorders appointed. Many of these judges are recruited from outside the ranks of specialist criminal practitioners. In the magistrates' courts, magistrates depend upon their clerks for advice on the law: in this area too the number of court clerks has risen to try to meet the increased workload. The position of the common law in criminal matters, and in particular the interface between common law and statutory provisions, undoubt-edly contributes to making the law obscure and difficult to understand for everyone concerned in the administration of justice, whether a newly-appointed assistant recorder or magistrates' clerk. Obscurity and mystification may in turn lead to inefficiency: the cost and length of trials may be increased because the law has to be extracted and clarified, and there is greater scope for appeals on misdirections on points of law. Moreover, if the law is not perceived by triers of fact to be clear and fair, there is a risk that they will return incorrect or perverse verdicts through mis-understanding or a deliberate disregard of what they are advised the law is. Finally, the criminal law is a particularly public and visible part of the law. It is important that its authority and legitim-acy should not be undermined by perceptions that it is intelligible only to experts.

2.6 Codification would help to meet all these dangers. One of its main aims would be to provide a single clear agreed text, published under the authority of Parliament. The law would immediately become more accessible; all users would have an agreed text as a common starting point and the scope for dispute about its terms and application should be reduced. The source of the general principles of criminal liability would be found in little more than fifty sections of an Act of Parlia-ment instead of many statutes, thousands of cases and the extensive commentaries on them to be found in the textbooks. While much criminal law would remain outside the Criminal Code Act, the law relating to most of the gravest crimes could be brought within it so that the reader would find it within one volume. Of course, no code or statute on a single subject can ever be truly comprehensive. The interpretive role of the judiciary will continue to be important; indeed, during the early years of legislation on a subject the judges' interpretive role is more crucial than at any time thereafter. Nor do we pretend that codification will make the law accessible to Everyman in the sense that he can pick up one volume and in it find the answer to whatever his problem is.

2.7 It is impossible to quantify the potential savings in time and costs which could be brought about by codification, but they could be substantial. The impact of presenting the criminal law in clear, modern and intelligible terms should be felt at all stages of the criminal process, from operational decisions by police officers to appeals to the higher courts. Practitioners should be assisted in advising clients and preparing for trial, trial judges should find the task of directing juries on the law easier and quicker and the length of time spent arguing points of law on appeal should be reduced.

Consistency

2.8 The Code team commented in their Report that:

> The haphazard development of the law through the cases, and a multiplicity of statutes inevitably leads to inconsistencies, not merely in terminology but also in substance. Codification must seek to remove these. If two rules actually contradict one another they cannot both be the law. The codifier cannot rationally restate both. He must restate one and abolish the other or propose some third rule to replace both. More frequently, the inconsistency is one of principle and policy rather than of mutual contradiction . . .

Inconsistency both in terminology and substance is a serious problem in English criminal law. A notable example is the use of the word 'reckless'. Recklessness is a central element of fault requirements but it has four different meanings depending on whether it is used in the context of non-fatal offences against the person, criminal damage and manslaughter, rape or driving offences. This is impossible to defend. It makes the law unnecessarily complex and less intelligible, and it results in difficulty and embarrassment in directing juries and advising magistrates. Two such offences may well be involved in the same trial when it is clearly undesirable that the law should be seen to be laying down inconsistent tests of liability without any clear policy justification. Another example concerns combinations of preliminary offences (attempt to incite, incitement to conspire, conspiracy to attempt and so on). Some combinations constitute offences known to the law, others do not. No policy can be found to support these distinctions, and the scrutiny group examining the provisions of the draft Code Bill dealing with preliminary offences agreed that in this topic the present law is an irrational mess.

2.9 This kind of inconsistency across a range of offences is not in practice remediable by use of the common law. It is most unlikely, for example, that cases will arise which raise the issue of recklessness in all the relevant offences in an appropriate form. In relation to the preliminary offences it would be impossible for the courts to reintroduce forms of liability which have been expressly abolished by statute. Codification alone, pursuing a conscious policy of the elimination of inconsistency, can deal adequately with this kind of problem. Elimination of inconsistency will also help to ensure that the offence of one accused is dealt with fairly in relation to other offences by other accused. Unjustifiable disparity of treatment can thus be avoided . . .

Certainty

2.10 In some areas of the criminal law there is substantial uncertainty as to its scope. Uncertainty can arise where the accidents of litigation and piecemeal legislation leave gaps, so that there is no law at all on a particular point. Alternatively, a statute or case may state the law obscurely, so that it is impossible to be certain as to the law to be applied to a particular problem. Uncertainty is an impediment to the proper administration of criminal justice since it may discourage the bringing of prosecutions where there is a colourable case to answer, and tend to increase the number of unmeritorious but successful submissions of 'no case to answer' if charges are brought. In either event respect for the law may be diminished. Certainty is very important to prevent unwarranted prosecutions being brought at all or prosecutions collapsing or convictions being quashed on appeal. Lack of certainty may also cause difficulties for defence lawyers advising their clients and for judges directing juries.

2.11 The common law method of resolving uncertainty by 'retrospective' declaration of the law is objectionable in principle. It may lead to the conviction of a defendant on the basis of criminal liability not known to exist in that form before he acted. Much criticism was directed at the decision of the House of Lords in *DPP v Shaw* where this was generally perceived to have happened. On the other hand, the effect of an appeal may be to narrow the law retrospectively, either by acknowledging the existence of a defence to criminal liability which was not previously recognised or by altering the definition of a criminal offence. In the . . . cases of *Moloney* . . . and *Hancock* the House of Lords restated the meaning of 'intention' as the mental element for murder [see further Chapters 3 and 4]. In doing so, the House disapproved the terms of a direction to a jury given ten years earlier in the leading case of *Hyam*. Such a change may give rise to a suggestion not only that the conviction in the earlier case was unsafe but also cast doubt on the validity of the convictions in other cases during the intervening ten-year period which had been based on the terms of the direction approved in the earlier case. Such suggestions, which are inherent in the development of the law on a case by case basis, must undermine confidence in this important branch of the law. Statutory changes, on the other hand, do not have retrospective effect. They come into force only after full Parliamentary debate with the commencement of the provisions of the statute. Earlier cases are unaffected.

Law Commission Consultation Paper	Law Commission Report	Home Office Publication
Legislating the Criminal Code: Offences Against the Person and General Principles (LCCP No 122)	Legislating the Criminal Code: Offences Against the Person and General Principles (Law Com No 218)	Violence: Reforming the Offences Against the Person Act 1861; Offences Against the Person Bill
Legislating the Criminal Code: Intoxication and Criminal Liability (LCCP No 127)	Legislating the Criminal Code: Intoxication and Criminal Liability (Law Com No 229)	Clause 19 of the Offences Against the Person Bill
Assisting and Encouraging Crime (LCCP No 131)		
Law Commission Working Paper No 50, Inchoate Offences	Criminal Law: Conspiracy to Defraud (Law Com No 228)	
Legislating the Criminal Code: Involuntary Manslaughter (LCCP No 135)	Legislating the Criminal Code: Involuntary Manslaughter (Law Com No 237)	Reforming the Law on Involuntary Manslaughter: The Government's Proposals
Criminal Law: Consent (LCCP 134)		
Criminal Law: Consent (LCCP 139)	Consent in Sex Offences: A Report to the Home Office Sex Offences Review (LC Special – 1)	Setting the Boundaries: Reforming the Law on Sex Offences
Criminal Law: Misuse of Trade Secrets (LCCP 150)		

Legislating the Criminal Code: Fraud and Deception (LCCP No 155)	Fraud (Law Com No 276)	Fraud Law Reform
Partial Defences to Murder (LCCP 173 and 173A)	Partial Defences to Murder (Law Com No 290)	
A New Homicide Act for England and Wales? (LCCP No 177)	Inchoate Liability for Assisting and Encouraging Crime (Law Com 300) Murder, Manslaughter and Infanticide (Law Com No 304)	

1.10 THE IMPACT OF THE HUMAN RIGHTS ACT 1998 ON SUBSTANTIVE CRIMINAL LAW

The conventional wisdom prevalent at the time the Human Rights Act 1998 was enacted was to the effect that it would have a very considerable impact on the criminal justice system. Since the Act came fully into force in October 2001 it has become clear that the courts are drawing a distinction between the procedural fairness aspects of the Convention, that is, those provisions that impact on criminal procedure and evidence, and those that impact on the content of the substantive law. As to the latter, there have been very few successful challenges – the doctrinal aspects of criminal law being largely a matter for signatory states provided the law in question is sufficiently clear in its ambit, is not retrospective, impinges on Convention rights only so far as is permitted under the Convention, and represents a proportionate interference with Convention rights.

Brown v Stott (Procurator Fiscal, Dunfermline) [2001] 2 All ER 97 PC

Lord Steyn:

In the first real test of the Human Rights Act 1998 it is opportune to stand back and consider what the basic aims of the convention are. One finds the explanation in the very words of the preambles of the convention. There were two principal objectives. The first was to maintain and further realise human rights and fundamental freedoms. The framers of the convention recognised that it was not only morally right to promote the observance of human rights but that it was also the best way of achieving pluralistic and just societies in which all can peaceably go about their lives. The second aim was to foster effective political democracy. This aim necessarily involves the creation of conditions of stability and order under the rule of law, not for its own sake, but as the best way to ensuring the well being of the inhabitants of the European countries. After all, democratic government has only one *raison d'etre*, namely to serve the interests of all the people. The inspirers of the convention, among whom Winston Churchill played an important role, and the framers of the convention, ably assisted by English draftsmen, realised that from time to time the fundamental right of one individual may conflict with the human right of another. Thus the principles of free speech and privacy may collide. They also realised only too well that a single-minded concentration on the pursuit of fundamental rights of individuals to the exclusion of the interests of the wider public might be subversive of the ideal of tolerant European liberal democracies. The fundamental rights of individuals are of supreme importance but those rights are not unlimited: we live in communities of individuals who also have rights. The direct lineage of this ancient idea is clear: the convention is the descendant of the Universal Declaration of Human Rights (Paris, 10 December 1948; UN TS 2 (1949); Cmd 7226) which in Art 29 expressly recognised the duties of everyone to the community and the limitation on rights in order to secure and protect respect for the rights of others. It is also noteworthy that Art 17 of the convention prohibits, among others, individuals from abusing their rights to the detriment of others. Thus, notwithstanding the danger of intolerance towards ideas, the convention system draws a line which does not accord the protection of free speech to those who propagate racial hatred against minorities: Art 10; *Jersild v Denmark* (1995) 19 EHRR 1 at 25–26 (para 31). This is to be contrasted with the categorical language of the First Amendment to the United States Constitution which provides that 'Congress shall make no law. . . abridging the freedom of speech'. The convention requires that where difficult questions arise a balance must be struck. Subject to a limited number of absolute guarantees, the scheme and structure of the convention reflects this balanced approach. It differs in material respects from other constitutional systems but as a European nation it represents our Bill of Rights. We must be guided by it. And it is a basic premise of the convention system that only an entirely neutral, impartial, and independent judiciary can carry out the primary task of securing and enforcing convention rights. This contextual scene is not only directly relevant to the issues arising on the present appeal but may be a matrix in which many challenges under the Human Rights Act should be considered.

1.10.1 ARTICLE 2 – RIGHT TO LIFE

1   Everyone's right to life shall be protected by law. No one shall be deprived of his life intentionally save in the execution of a sentence of a court following his conviction of a crime for which this penalty is provided by law.

2   Deprivation of life shall not be regarded as inflicted in contravention of this Article when it results from the use of force which is no more than absolutely necessary:

   (a)   in defence of any person from unlawful violence;

   (b)   in order to effect a lawful arrest or to prevent the escape of a person lawfully detained;

   (c)   in action lawfully taken for the purpose of quelling a riot or insurrection.

Article 2(2) provides that the right to life is not violated where death results from the use of force by the state that was no more than was absolutely necessary to prevent another suffering unlawful violence; in effecting arrest or preventing escape; in quelling a riot or insurrection. The current domestic law allows the use of lethal force by way of self-defence, including the defence of others, where it is reasonable in the circumstances. As *Andronicou v Cyprus* [1998] Crim LR 823 illustrates, there is the potential for conflict between domestic law on self-defence and the Convention. Further, *McCann v United Kingdom* (1996) 21 EHRR 97 provides that agents of the state can use lethal force under Art 2(2) where they honestly believe, with good reason, that such force is justified. This too is at odds with domestic law, which permits D to rely on an honest, albeit mistaken, belief that the use of reasonable force is justified.

1.10.2 ARTICLE 3 – PROHIBITION OF TORTURE

No one shall be subjected to torture or to inhuman or degrading treatment or punishment. In *A v UK* (1999) 27 EHRR 611, the European Court of Human Rights heard an application brought by a child who had been beaten with a stick by his stepfather. The applicant's father had been acquitted of charges of causing actual bodily harm contrary to s 47 of the Offences Against the Persons Act 1861, having relied on reasonable chastisement in the circumstances. The court concluded that there had been a violation of Art 3 on the basis that existing domestic law on the defence of lawful chastisement had failed to provide the applicant with adequate protection. Whilst the question of whether, in any given case, the treatment suffered by an applicant reached the minimum level of severity necessary to trigger the operation of Art 3 would depend on the circumstances, where the victim was a child the minimum threshold would be more easily attained. It should be noted that, whilst the court accepted that the United Kingdom could not be held responsible for the actions of a private individual, such as the applicant's stepfather, it was responsible for a system of criminal law that allowed a person inflicting serious harm upon a child to be acquitted on the grounds that the harm was justifiable chastisement. There has been no legislative response to this decision, but the courts have attempted to alleviate the shortcomings of the domestic law by offering guidelines on the availability of the defence; see *R v H (Reasonable Chastisement)* (2001) *The Times*, 18 May. Where a parent raises the defence of lawful chastisement the jury ought to be directed to consider: (i) the nature and context of the defendant's behaviour; (ii) the duration of that behaviour; (iii) the physical and mental consequences in respect of the child; (iv) the age and personal characteristics of the child; (v) the reasons given by the defendant for administering the punishment.

1.10.3 ARTICLE 5 – RIGHT TO LIBERTY AND SECURITY

1   Everyone has the right to liberty and security of person. No one shall be deprived of his liberty save in the following cases and in accordance with a procedure prescribed by law:

  (a) the lawful detention of a person after conviction by a competent court;

  (b) the lawful arrest or detention of a person for non-compliance with the lawful order of a court or in order to secure the fulfilment of any obligation prescribed by law;

  (c) the lawful arrest or detention of a person effected for the purpose of bringing him before the competent legal authority on reasonable suspicion of having committed an offence or when it is reasonably considered necessary to prevent his committing an offence or fleeing after having done so;

  (d) the detention of a minor by lawful order for the purpose of educational supervision or his lawful detention for the purpose of bringing him before the competent legal authority;

  (e) the lawful detention of persons for the prevention of the spreading of infectious diseases, of persons of unsound mind, alcoholics or drug addicts or vagrants;

  (f) the lawful arrest or detention of a person to prevent his effecting an unauthorised entry into the country or of a person against whom action is being taken with a view to deportation or extradition.

2   Everyone who is arrested shall be informed promptly, in a language which he understands, of the reasons for his arrest and of any charge against him.

3   Everyone arrested or detained in accordance with the provisions of paragraph 1(c) of this

Article shall be brought promptly before a judge or other officer authorised by law to exercise judicial power and shall be entitled to trial within a reasonable time or to release pending trial. Release may be conditioned by guarantees to appear for trial.

4 Everyone who is deprived of his liberty by arrest or detention shall be entitled to take proceedings by which the lawfulness of his detention shall be decided speedily by a court and his release ordered if the detention is not lawful.

5 Everyone who has been the victim of arrest or detention in contravention of the provisions of this Article shall have an enforceable right to compensation.

1.10.4 ARTICLE 6 – RIGHT TO A FAIR TRIAL

1 In the determination of his civil rights and obligations or of any criminal charge against him, everyone is entitled to a fair and public hearing within a reasonable time by an independent and impartial tribunal established by law. Judgment shall be pronounced publicly but the press and public may be excluded from all or part of the trial in the interest of morals, public order or national security in a democratic society, where the interests of juveniles or the protection of the private life of the parties so require, or to the extent strictly necessary in the opinion of the court in special circumstances where publicity would prejudice the interests of justice.

2 Everyone charged with a criminal offence shall be presumed innocent until proved guilty according to law.

3 Everyone charged with a criminal offence has the following minimum rights:

   (a) to be informed promptly, in a language which he understands and in detail, of the nature and cause of the accusation against him;

   (b) to have adequate time and facilities for the preparation of his defence;

   (c) to defend himself in person or through legal assistance of his own choosing or, if he has not sufficient means to pay for legal assistance, to be given it free when the interests of justice so require;

   (d) to examine or have examined witnesses against him and to obtain the attendance and examination of witnesses on his behalf under the same conditions as witnesses against him;

   (e) to have the free assistance of an interpreter if he cannot understand or speak the language used in court.

Brown v Stott (Procurator Fiscal, Dunfermline) **(above)**

Lord Steyn:

The present case is concerned with Art 6 of the convention which guarantees to every individual a fair trial in civil and criminal cases. The centrality of this principle in the convention system has repeatedly been emphasised by the European Court. But even in respect of this basic guarantee, there is a balance to be observed. First, it is well settled that the public interest may be taken into account in deciding what the right to a fair trial requires in a particular context. Thus in *Doorson v Netherlands* (1996) 22 EHRR 330 at 358 (para 70) it was held that 'principles of fair trial also require that in appropriate cases the interests of the defence are balanced against those of witnesses or victims called upon to testify'. Only one specific illustration of this balanced approach is necessary. Provided they are kept 'within reasonable limits' rebuttable presumptions of fact are permitted in criminal legislation (*Salabiaku v France* (1988) 13 EHRR 379). Secondly, once it has been determined that the guarantee of a fair trial has been breached, it is never possible to justify such breach by reference to the public interest or on any other ground. This is to be contrasted with cases where a trial has been affected by irregularities not amounting to denial of a fair trial. In such cases it is fair that a court of appeal should have the power, even when faced by the fact of irregularities in the trial procedure, to dismiss the appeal if in the view of the court of appeal the defendant's guilt is plain and beyond any doubt. However, it is a grave conclusion that a defendant has not had the substance of a fair trial. It means that the administration of justice has entirely failed. Subject to the possible exercise of a power to order a retrial where appropriate such a conviction can never be allowed to stand.

See further 1.7.2 (above) the extent to which reversing the burden of proof might violate Art 6(2).

1.10.5 ARTICLE 7 – NO PUNISHMENT WITHOUT LAW

1 No one shall be held guilty of any criminal offence on account of any act or omission which did not constitute a criminal offence under national or international law at the time when it was committed. Nor shall a heavier penalty be imposed than the one that was applicable at the time the criminal offence was committed.

2 This Article shall not prejudice the trial and punishment of any person for any act or omission which, at the time when it was committed, was criminal according to the general principles of law recognised by civilised nations.

Whilst Art 7 appears to prohibit retrospective criminal legislation, it has proved to be of rather limited scope as regards the retrospective nature of the common law. The applicant in *SW v United Kingdom* (1996) 21 EHRR 363 had been convicted of raping his wife, following the House of Lords' decision in *R v R* [1992] AC 599 to the effect that the marital exemption for rape should be abolished. He was unsuccessful in his claim that the common law operated retrospectively, in the sense that his actions, at the time they had been committed, had not constituted a criminal offence. The court ruled that Art 7 did not prohibit 'the gradual clarification of rules of criminal liability through judicial interpretation from case to case, provided that the resultant development is consistent with the essence of the offence and could be reasonably foreseen'.

'The Human Rights Act and the Substantive Criminal Law' Richard Buxton [2000] Crim LR 331

This is, however, foresight of a somewhat special sort. The accretion of exceptions to the marital rape exemption might on one view be described as an evolution [that] had reached a stage where judicial recognition of the absence of immunity had become a reasonably foresee-able development of the law; but might equally have been thought to indicate that the basic exemption, on which the complainant in *SW v United Kingdom* relied, remained intact and could only be altered by legislation. That was certainly the view of the Law Commission, which published a working paper on rape within marriage shortly before the matter came to a head in the courts, and of a number of first instance judges who, however reluctantly, had seen themselves as bound by the rule. While hesitating to appeal here to Lord Simonds' famous comparison of foresight and hindsight, if one posits an (admittedly unlikely) visit to his solicitor by Mr R to ask for advice about trying to have intercourse with his wife, it is far from clear that he would have been told with any confidence that (whatever else might be said about his conduct) he was facing a criminal conviction and a sentence of three years' imprisonment.

It would therefore seem that a 'criminal offence' under Article 7 can be an offence merely *in gremio*, provided that its appearance can be said to be foreseeable on the basis of a not very demanding standard of foresight. That adds nothing to the protection of the individual that is provided by English domestic principle, and indeed falls short of what English principle has always been thought to require.

R v Misra; R v Srivastava [2004] EWCA Crim 2375

The appellants were both senior house officers having post operative care responsibilities for the deceased, Sean Phillips. The cause of death was toxic shock syndrome, the prosecution case being that this arose from the grossly negligent way in which the appellants had overseen the deceased's care. One of the issues raised on appeal against conviction for killing by gross negligence was the extent to which the allegedly circular definition of gross negligence approved by the House of Lords in *R v Adomako* [1995] 1 AC 171 (i.e. that the negligence was 'gross' if it was so culpable as to warrant the epithet 'criminal') was inconsistent with Article 7 of the European Convention on Human Rights.

Judge LJ:

[58] We can now return to the argument based on circularity and uncertainty, and the application of Arts 6 and 7 of the ECHR. The most important passages in the speech of Lord Mackay [in R v Adomako] on the issue of circularity read:

> . . . The jury must go on to consider whether that breach of duty should be characterised as gross negligence and therefore as a crime. This will depend on the seriousness of the breach of duty committed by the defendant in all the circumstances in which the defendant was placed when it occurred. The jury will have to consider whether the extent to which the defendant's conduct departed from the proper standard of care incumbent upon him, involving as it must have done a risk of death to the patient, was such that it should be judged criminal.

> It is true that, to a certain extent, this involves an element of circularity, but in this branch of the law I do not believe that is fatal to its being correct as a test of how far conduct must depart from accepted standards to be characterised as criminal . . . The essence of the matter which is supremely a jury question is whether, having regard to the risk of death involved, the conduct of the defendant was so bad in all the circumstances as to amount in their judgment to a criminal act or omission.

[59] Mr Gledhill [counsel for Misra] suggested that this passage demonstrated that an additional specific ingredient of this offence was that the jury had to decide whether the defendant's

conduct amounted to a crime. If the jury could, or was required to, define the offence for itself, and accordingly might do so on some unaccountable or unprincipled or unexplained basis, to adopt *Bacon*, the sound given by the law would indeed be uncertain, and would then strike without warning. Mr Gledhill's argument then would be compelling.

[60] Looking at the authorities since *Bateman*, the purpose of referring to the differences between civil and criminal liability, whether in the passage in Lord Mackay's speech to which we have just referred, or in directions to the jury, is to highlight that the burden on the prosecution goes beyond proof of negligence for which compensation would be payable. Negligence of that degree could not lead to a conviction for manslaughter. The negligence must be so bad, 'gross', that if all the other ingredients of the offence are proved, then it amounts to a crime and is punishable as such.

[61] This point was addressed by Lord Atkin in Andrews at p 582, when he referred to *Williamson* (1807) 3 C&P 635: '. . . .where a man who practised as an accoucheur, owing to a mistake in his observation of the actual symptoms, inflicted on a patient terrible injuries from which she died'. To substantiate that charge – namely, manslaughter – Lord Ellenborough said, 'The prisoner must have been guilty of criminal misconduct, arising either from the grossest ignorance or the most criminal inattention.' The word 'criminal', in any attempt to define a crime, is perhaps not the most helpful: but it is plain that the Lord Chief Justice meant to indicate to the jury a high degree of negligence. So at a much later date in *Bateman* [1925] 18 Cr App R 8 a charge of manslaughter was made against a qualified medical practitioner in similar circumstances to those of Williamson's case . . . . I think with respect that the expressions used are not, indeed they were probably not intended to be, a precise definition of the crime.

[62] Accordingly, the value of references to the criminal law in this context is that they avoid the danger that the jury may equate what we may describe as 'simple' negligence, which in relation to manslaughter would not be a crime at all, with negligence which involves a criminal offence. In short, by bringing home to the jury the extent of the burden on the prosecution, they ensure that the defendant whose negligence does not fall within the ambit of the criminal law is not convicted of a crime. They do not alter the essential ingredients of this offence. A conviction cannot be returned if the negligent conduct is or may be less than gross. If, however, the defendant is found by the jury to have been grossly negligent, then, if the jury is to act in accordance with its duty, he must be convicted. This is precisely what Lord Mackay indicated when, in the passage already cited, he said, '. . .The jury must go on to consider whether that breach of duty should be charac-terised as gross negligence and therefore as a crime' (our emphasis). The decision whether the conduct was criminal is described not as 'the' test, but as 'a' test as to how far the conduct in question must depart from accepted standards to be 'characterised as criminal'. On proper analysis, therefore, the jury is not deciding whether the particular defendant ought to be convicted on some unprincipled basis. The question for the jury is not whether the defendant's negligence was gross, and whether, additionally, it was a crime, but whether his behaviour was grossly negligent and consequently criminal. This is not a question of law, but one of fact, for decision in the individual case.

[63] On examination, this represents one example, among many, of problems which juries are expected to address on a daily basis. They include equally difficult questions, such as whether a defendant has acted dishonestly, by reference to contemporary standards, or whether he has acted in reasonable self-defence, or, when charged with causing death by dangerous driving, whether the standards of his driving fell far below what should be expected of a competent and

careful driver. These examples represent the commonplace for juries. Each of these questions could be said to be vague and uncertain. If he made enquiries in advance, at most an individual would be told the principle of law which the jury would be directed to apply: he could not be advised what a jury would think of the individual case, and how it would be decided. That involves an element of uncertainty about the outcome of the decision-making process, but not unacceptable uncertainty about the offence itself.

[64] In our judgment the law is clear. The ingredients of the offence have been clearly defined, and the principles decided in the House of Lords in *Adomako*. They involve no uncertainty. The hypothetical citizen, seeking to know his position, would be advised that, assuming he owed a duty of care to the deceased which he had negligently broken, and that death resulted, he would be liable to conviction for manslaughter if, on the available evidence, the jury was satisfied that his negligence was gross. A doctor would be told that grossly negligent treatment of a patient which exposed him or her to the risk of death, and caused it, would constitute manslaughter.

[65] After Lord Williams' sustained criticism of the offence of manslaughter by gross negligence, the House of Lords in *Adomako* clarified the relevant principles and the ingredients of this offence. Although, to a limited extent, Lord Mackay accepted that there was an element of circularity in the process by which the jury would arrive at its verdict, the element of circularity which he identified did not then and does not now result in uncertainty which offends against Article 7, nor if we may say so, any principle of common law. Gross negligence manslaughter is not incompatible with the ECHR. Accordingly the appeal arising from the question certified by the trial judge must be dismissed.

[66] This conclusion in effect disposes of the Article 6 argument. It is well-understood in the European Court, and accepted, that a jury is not required to give reasons for its decision. (See, for example, *Saric v Denmark* Application 31913/96.) In the present case, by reference to the indictment in its amended form, and the summing-up of the trial judge delivered in open court, the appellants knew the case alleged against each of them, and the issues that the jury had to consider, and we, by reference to the same documents, can examine the basis on which they were convicted. The jury concluded that the conduct of each appellant in the course of performing his professional obligations to his patient was "truly exceptionally bad", and showed a high degree of indifference to an obvious and serious risk to the patient's life. Accordingly, along with the other ingredients of the offence, gross negligence too, was proved. In our judgment it is unrealistic to suggest that the basis for the jury's decision cannot readily be understood. Accordingly this contention fails.

1.10.6 ARTICLE 8 – RIGHT TO RESPECT FOR PRIVATE AND FAMILY LIFE

1 Everyone has the right to respect for his private and family life, his home and his correspondence.
2 There shall be no interference by a public authority with the exercise of this right except such as is in accordance with the law and is necessary in a democratic society in the interests of national security, public safety or the economic well-being of the country, for the prevention

> of disorder or crime, for the protection of health or morals, or for the protection of the rights and freedoms of others.

In *ADT v United Kingdom* [2000] Crim LR 1009, the applicant successfully argued that the domestic law prohibiting acts of gross indecency between men in private was incompatible with the right to privacy under Art 8. The police had raided the home of the applicant, a male homosexual. Items seized included video tape recordings of the applicant engaging in consensual group sex acts with up to four other adult men. In agreeing that the proceedings for gross indecency involved a violation of Art 8, the court noted that the activities had all taken place in the applicant's home and had not been visible to anyone other than those involved. Hence it could not agree that the interference with the applicant's privacy, resulting from the state's reliance on the gross indecency offences, was necessary in a democratic society. The applicant's activities were non-violent, raised no general public health concerns and were restricted to a small number of consenting adults.

1.10.7 ARTICLE 9 – FREEDOM OF THOUGHT, CONSCIENCE AND RELIGION

> 1 Everyone has the right to freedom of thought, conscience and religion; this right includes freedom to change his religion or belief and freedom, either alone or in community with others and in public or private, to manifest his religion or belief, in worship, teaching, practice and observance.
>
> 2 Freedom to manifest one's religion or beliefs shall be subject only to such limitations as are prescribed by law and are necessary in a democratic society in the interests of public safety, for the protection of public order, health or morals, or for the protection of the rights and freedoms of others.

1.10.8 ARTICLE 10 – FREEDOM OF EXPRESSION

> 1 Everyone has the right to freedom of expression. This right shall include freedom to hold opinions and to receive and impart information and ideas without interference by public authority and regardless of frontiers. This Article shall not prevent States from requiring the licensing of broadcasting, television or cinema enterprises.
>
> 2 The exercise of these freedoms, since it carries with it duties and responsibilities, may be subject to such formalities, conditions, restrictions or penalties as are prescribed by law and are necessary in a democratic society, in the interests of national security, territorial integrity or public safety, for the prevention of disorder or crime, for the protection of health or morals, for the protection of the reputation or rights of others, for preventing the disclosure of information received in confidence, or for maintaining the authority and impartiality of the judiciary.

1.10.9 ARTICLE 11 – FREEDOM OF ASSEMBLY AND ASSOCIATION

1   Everyone has the right to freedom of peaceful assembly and to freedom of association with others, including the right to form and to join trade unions for the protection of his interests.

2   No restrictions shall be placed on the exercise of these rights other than such as are prescribed by law and are necessary in a democratic society in the interests of national security or public safety, for the prevention of disorder or crime, for the protection of health or morals or for the protection of the rights and freedoms of others. This Article shall not prevent the imposition of lawful restrictions on the exercise of these rights by members of the armed forces, of the police or of the administration of the State.

1.10.10 WHAT IS REQUIRED OF DOMESTIC COURTS?

Section 2(1) of the Human Rights Act 1998 provides that:

A court or tribunal determining a question which has arisen in connection with a Convention right must take into account any (a) judgment, decision, declaration or advisory opinion of the European Court of Human Rights, (b) opinion of the Commission given in a report adopted under Article 31 of the Convention, (c) decision of the Commission in connection with Article 26 or 27(2) of the Convention, or (d) decision of the Committee of Ministers taken under Article 46 of the Convention . . .

When interpreting domestic legislation courts must, so far as it is possible, read and give effect to such legislation in a way that is compatible with the Convention rights; see s 3(1).

R v Lambert [2001] 3 All ER 577 HL

For the facts, see the extract above. In the course of his speech Lord Hope looked at the obligations placed upon domestic courts in criminal cases by s 3(1) of the Human Rights Act 1998.

Lord Hope:

Section 3(1) of the 1998 Act provides that, so far as it is possible to do so, primary and secondary legislation must be read and given effect in a way which is compatible with the Convention rights. I should now like to explain how, as I see it, this important and far-reaching new approach to the construction of statutes should be employed consistently with the need (a) to respect the will of the legislature so far as this remains appropriate and (b) to preserve the integrity of our statute law so far as this is possible.

The first point, as I said in paragraph 108 of my speech in *R v A* [2001] UKHL 25, is that the effect of section 3(1) is that the interpretation which it requires is to be achieved only so far as this is possible. The word 'must', which section 3(1) uses, is qualified by the phrase 'so far as it is possible to do so'. The obligation, powerful though it is, is not to be performed without regard to its limitations. Resort to it will not be possible if the legislation contains provisions, either in the words or phrases which are under scrutiny or elsewhere, which expressly contradict the meaning which the enactment would have to be given to make it compatible. The same consequence will follow if legislation contains provisions which have this effect by necessary implication. Further justification for giving this qualified meaning to section 3(1) is to be found in the words 'read and give effect.' As the side note indicates, the obligation is one which applies to the interpretation of legislation. This function belongs, as it has always done, to the judges. But it is not for them to legislate. Section 3(1) preserves the sovereignty of Parliament. It does not give power to the judges to overrule decisions which the language of the statute shows have been taken on the very point at issue by the legislator.

The second point, as I said in paragraph 110 of my speech in *R v A*, is that great care must be taken, in cases where a different meaning has to be given to the legislation from the ordinary meaning of the words used by the legislator, to identify precisely the word or phrase which, if given its ordinary meaning, would otherwise be incompatible. Just as much care must then be taken to say how the word or phrase is to be construed if it is to be made compatible. The justification for this approach to the use of section 3(1) is to be found in the nature of legislation itself. Its primary characteristic, for present purposes, is its ability to achieve certainty by the use of clear and precise language. It provides a set of rules by which, according to the ordinary meaning of the words used, the conduct of affairs may be regulated. So far as possible judges should seek to achieve the same attention to detail in their use of language to express the effect of applying section 3(1) as the parliamentary draftsman would have done if he had been amending the statute. It ought to be possible for any words that need to be substituted to be fitted into the statute as if they had been inserted there by amendment. If this cannot be done without doing such violence to the statute as to make it unintelligible or unworkable, the use of this technique will not be possible. It will then be necessary to leave it to Parliament to amend the statute and to resort instead to the making of a declaration of incompatibility.

As to the techniques that may be used, it is clear that the courts are not bound by previous authority as to what the statute means. It has been suggested that a strained or nonliteral construction may be adopted, that words may be read in by way of addition to those used by the legislator and that the words may be 'read down' to give them a narrower construction than their ordinary meaning would bear: Clayton and Tomlinson, *The Law of Human Rights*, para 4.28, p 168 (Oxford, 2000). It may be enough simply to say what the effect of the provision is without altering the ordinary meaning of the words used: see *Brown v Stott* 2000 JC 328, 355B-C, per Lord Justice General Rodger. In other cases, as in *Vasquez v The Queen* [1994] 1 WLR 1304, the words used will require to be expressed in a different language in order to explain how they are to be read in a way that is compatible. The exercise in these cases is one of translation into compatible language from language that is incompatible. In other cases, as in *R v A*, it may be necessary for words to be read in to explain the meaning that must be given to the provision if it is to be compatible. But the interpretation of a statute by reading words in to give effect to the presumed intention must always be distinguished carefully from amendment. Amendment is a legislative act. It is an exercise which must be reserved to Parliament.

Hence domestic courts are given a degree of latitude – reference to the jurisprudence of Strasbourg is mandatory – but it need only be taken into account. Legislation must be construed in a manner compatible with the Convention but only so far as is possible.

Three points are particularly worth noting:

* When applying the European Convention on Human Rights a domestic court should be

prepared to take a generous view as to whether an activity falls within the protection afforded by the Convention's Articles.

- The Convention is to be regarded as a 'living' or 'dynamic' instrument to be interpreted in the light of current conditions. More recent decisions of the European Court of Human Rights will be regarded as carrying more weight than earlier decisions.

- Where an Article of the Convention permits some state interference with the enjoyment of a right, a court assessing the extent to which that interference is compatible with the Convention should consider (i) whether the interference is provided for by law; (ii) whether it serves a legitimate purpose; (iii) whether the interference is proportionate to the end to be achieved; (iv) whether it is necessary in a democratic society; (v) whether it is discriminatory in operation; and (vi) whether the state should be allowed a margin of appreciation in its compliance with the Convention – that is, be allowed to apply the Convention to suit national standards.

1.10.11 THE 'QUALITY OF LAW' TEST

Articles 5, 6 and 7 of the European Convention on Human Rights make reference to concepts such as 'an offence', 'criminal charge' and 'criminal offence'; Arts 9–11 refer to rights being limited as 'prescribed by law'. These expressions presuppose a degree of certainty as to whether given conduct is criminal or not, and as to whether the law prescribes certain conduct or not. This in turn raises the possibility of certain aspects of domestic criminal law failing the 'quality of law' test on the basis that the scope of certain offences cannot be clearly identified – the jurisprudence of the European Convention on Human Rights requires that a 'norm' cannot be described as a law unless it can be formulated with sufficient precision so as to enable a citizen to regulate his conduct to avoid incurring liability.

For example, in *Hashman and Harrup v UK* [2000] Crim LR 185, anti-hunt protestors who were found not to have breached the peace were nevertheless ordered by the court to be bound over because they had acted *contra bono mores* (in a way that was wrong in the eyes of the majority of citizens). The European Court of Human Rights held that this was a violation of Art 10 – the expression *contra bono mores* was too vague to satisfy the 'prescribed by law' test, and could not be relied upon to justify detention under Art 5.

In *R v Hinks* [2000] 4 All ER 835 (see Chapter 9.2), Lord Hobhouse (dissenting) was concerned that the effect of the majority view in that case was to create an offence where liability hinged entirely on the issue of whether or not the accused had acted dishonestly. He was particularly concerned at the prospect of a criminal conviction based upon conduct:

> . . . which involves no inherent illegality and may only be capable of being criticised on grounds of lack of morality [that is, it is dishonest] . . . [t]his approach itself raises fundamental questions. An essential function of the criminal law is to define the boundary between what conduct is criminal and what merely immoral. Both are the subject of the disapprobation of ordinary right-thinking citizens and the distinction is liable to be arbitrary or at least strongly influenced by considerations subjective to the individual members of the tribunal. To treat otherwise lawful conduct as criminal merely because it is open to such disapprobation would be contrary to principle and open to the

> objection that it fails to achieve the objective and transparent certainty required of the criminal law by the principles basic to human rights.

See further the arguments raised in *R v Smethurst* (2001) *The Times*, 13 April, where the Court of Appeal rejected the contention that s 1 of the Protection of Children Act 1978 (offence of possession child pornography) was in conflict with Art 10 (freedom of expression). The court accepted that the concept of indecency might lack certainty, but was persuaded by the overriding public interest in protecting morality.

R v Goldstein [2004] 2 All ER 589

The Court of Appeal was asked to consider whether the common law offence of public nuisance violated the principle of legal certainty enshrined in Art 7 of the European Convention on Human Rights.

> Latham LJ:
>
> The essential principle which the offence of public nuisance is said to infringe is that a law must be formulated with sufficient precision to enable a citizen to regulate his conduct. It is similar to the concept required in Arts 8(2) and 10(2), to which we will return, that the derogation from the right protected by those articles can only be justified if it is 'in accordance with the law' (see Art 8(2)) or 'prescribed by law' (see Art 10(2)). The latter phrase was considered by the European Court of Human Rights in *Sunday Times v UK* (1979) 2 EHRR 245. It stated (at 271 (para 49)):
>
>> . . . a norm cannot be regarded as a 'law' unless it is formulated with sufficient precision to enable the citizen to regulate his conduct: he must be able – if need be with appropriate advice – to foresee, to a degree which is reasonable in all the circumstances, the consequences that a given action may entail. Those consequences need not be foreseeable with absolute certainty: experience shows this to be unattainable. Again, whilst certainty is highly desirable, it may bring in its train excessive rigidity and the law must be able to keep pace with changing circumstances. Accordingly, many laws are inevitably couched in terms which, to a greater or lesser extent, are vague and whose interpretation and application are questions of practice.
>
> In the context of Art 7, we have been referred to the decision of *X Ltd v UK* (1982) 28 DR 77 which was an application in which the European Commission of Human Rights (the Commission) considered the common law offence of blasphemous libel. The Commission stated (at 81 (para 9)):
>
>> The Commission considers that the same principles also apply to the interpretation and application of the common law. Whilst this branch of the law presents certain particularities for the very reason that it is by definition law developed by the courts, it is nevertheless subject to the rule that the law-making function of the courts must remain within reasonable limits. In particular in the area of the criminal law it is excluded, by virtue of Article 7(1) of the Convention, that any acts not previously punishable should be held by the courts to entail criminal liability, or that existing offences should be extended to cover facts which previously clearly did not constitute a criminal offence. This implies that constituent elements of an offence such as e.g. the particular form of culpability required for its completion

may not be essentially changed, at least not to the detriment of the accused, by the case law of the courts. On the other hand it is not objectionable that the existing elements of the offence are clarified and adapted to new circumstances which can reasonably be brought under the original concept of the offence.

The respondents submit that this decision is in fact helpful to them. Mr Perry submits on their behalf that the elements of the offence are perfectly clear, and their application to the present cases is merely an example of the way in which the law can be utilised to deal with new factual situations. He has referred us to *SW v UK, CR v UK* (1995) 21 EHHR 363 where the court considered and rejected complaints by two applicants who had been found guilty of raping their wives which was an undoubted extension of the concept of rape as had been previously understood. Although the Commission had declared the complaints admissible, he relies on its opinion (at 375 (para 48)), in which the Commission stated:

> It is however compatible with the requirements of Article 7(1) for the existing elements of an offence to be clarified or adapted to new circumstances or developments in society in so far as this can reasonably be brought under the original concept of the offence. The constituent elements of an offence may not however be essentially changed to the detriment of an accused and any progressive development by way of interpretation must be reasonably foreseeable to him with the assistance of appropriate legal advice if necessary.

We consider that Mr Perry's submissions are correct. If the law can be adapted to deal with new situations, it is clear that the law can be applied to new situations. The elements of the offence are sufficiently clear to enable a person, with appropriate legal advice if necessary, to regulate his behaviour. All that is required is a reasonable degree of foreseeability of the consequences which action or conduct may entail. The indictments in the present cases do no more than seek to apply the elements of the offence to the particular facts; and it is for the jury, appropriately directed, to determine whether or not the charges are made out. A citizen, appropriately advised, could foresee that the conduct identified was capable of amounting to a public nuisance. We do not accordingly consider that there has been any breach of Art 7.

We turn then to Arts 8 and 10. They essentially raise the same issue of principle and can conveniently be considered together. . . . It is submitted on behalf of the appellants that a prosecution for committing a public nuisance is capable of resulting in a breach of Arts 8(1) or 10(1), that it is not a law which is sufficiently certain to justify interference on the basis that it is either 'in accordance with the law' or 'prescribed by law' and that the interference is not 'necessary in a democratic society'.

We recognise that the offence is capable of interfering with the rights protected by Arts 8(1) and 10(1) . . . The question accordingly is whether or not the interference can be justified under Arts 8(2) and 10(2). We consider that the question of whether or not the interference was 'in accordance with the law' or 'prescribed by law' has been answered by our conclusion that there has been no breach of Art 7, and the reasons which we have given for that conclusion. The remaining question is, therefore, whether or not the offence can properly be described as 'necessary' in that it is intended to meet a pressing social need of the sort identified in each of those articles. In particular, in relation to Art 10, we accept that the right to freedom of expression includes the right to 'offend, shock or disturb' as the court stated in *Handyside v UK* (1976) 1 EHRR 737 at 754 (para 49). The jurisprudence of the Commission and the Court of Human Rights has, however, consistently pointed out that in accordance with Art 10(2) a state can legitimately impose limits to this freedom for the preservation of disorder or crime, the protection of morals and for the protection of the rights and freedoms of others. This includes the right of the public not to be outraged by the public behaviour of others.

In *S v UK* App No 17634/91 (2 September 1991, unreported), the Commission considered the common law offence of outraging public decency committed by an artist and art gallery curator who had exhibited a model with freeze-dried human foetuses as earrings. The Commission, while recognising that freedom of artistic expression fell within the ambit of Art 10, declared the application inadmissible as being manifestly ill-founded. It found that the offence of outraging public decency: (a) was prescribed by law, and (b) pursued the legitimate aim of protection of morals, and (c) was not disproportionate and could be regarded as necessary in a democratic society.

The court subsequently considered the problem in the context of the law of blasphemy. In *Wingrove v UK* (1996) 1 BHRC 509, the court held that the law of blasphemy, although imprecise, was none the less justified. The applicant had been refused a certification certificate for his video Visions of Ecstasy on the basis that it infringed the criminal law of blasphemy. The court found that the offence was prescribed by law and served the legitimate aim of protecting the rights of others. The court held (at 526–527 (para 60)) that the interference with the applicant's rights under Art 10 was not disproportionate and could be regarded as necessary in a democratic society . . . In our view, the offence of causing a public nuisance is a proper and proportionate response to the need to protect the public from acts, or omissions, which substantially interfere with the comfort and convenience of the public as being taken in the interests of public safety, for the prevention of disorder, for the protection of health and morals, and in particular the need to protect the rights of others. The level of imprecision inherent in the offence is necessary to enable it to be applied flexibly to meet new situations. We therefore reject the argument that the offence is capable of amounting to a breach of Arts 8 or 10.

FURTHER READING

Arden, M, 'Criminal law at the crossroads: the impact on human rights from the Law Commission's perspective and the need for a Code' [1999] Crim LR 439

Ashworth, A, 'Interpreting criminal statutes: a crisis of legality?' (1991) 107 LQR 419

Ashworth, A and M Blake, 'The presumption of innocence in English criminal law' [1996] Crim LR 306

Bingham, Lord CJ, 'Must we wait for ever?' [1998] Crim LR 694

Buxton, R, 'The Human Rights Act and the substantive criminal law' [2000] Crim LR 331

Dennis, I, 'The critical condition of criminal law' [1997] Current Legal Problems 213

Phillipson, G, 'The Human Rights Act, "horizontal effect" and the common law: a bang or a whimper?' (1999) 62 MLR 824

Smith, ATH, 'The Human Rights Act 1998 – (1) The Human Rights Act and the criminal lawyer: the constitutional context' [1999] Crim LR 251

Wells, C, 'Codification of the criminal law: restatement or reform?' [1986] Crim LR 314

Williams, G, 'The definition of crime' [1955] Current Legal Problems 107

CHAPTER 2

ACTUS REUS: THE EXTERNAL ELEMENTS OF AN OFFENCE

2.1 TERMINOLOGY

Criminal liability generally rests upon proof of two things – *actus reus* and *mens rea*. *Actus reus* literally means 'guilty act', but this is clearly something of a misnomer as the defendant might not bear any guilt, as in fault, for what has occurred, and, as will be seen, there are many instances where no positive act, as such, has to be established.

As Lord Diplock observed in *R v Miller* [1983] 2 AC 161 (HL):

> This expression [*actus reus*] is derived from Coke's brocard (3 Co Inst ch 1, fo 10), *actus non facit reum, nisi mens sit rea*, by converting incorrectly into an adjective the word *reus* which was there used correctly in the accusative case as a noun. As long ago as 1889 in *R v Tolson* 23 QBD 168 at 185, [1886–90] All ER Rep 26 at 36–37 Stephen J when dealing with a statutory offence, as are your Lordships in the instant case, condemned the phrase as likely to mislead, though his criticism in that case was primarily directed to the use of the expression *mens rea* . . . it is the use of the expression *actus reus* that is liable to mislead, since it suggests that some positive act on the part of the accused is needed to make him guilty of a crime and that a failure or omission to act is insufficient to give rise to criminal liability unless some express provision in the statute that creates the offence so provides . . . it would I think be conducive to clarity of analysis of the ingredients of a crime that is created by statute, as are the great majority of criminal offences today, if we were to avoid bad Latin and instead to think and speak . . . about the conduct of the accused and his state of mind at the time of that conduct, instead of speaking of *actus reus* and *mens rea*.

It is actually more sensible to think of *actus reus* as a term referring to the external elements of an offence, that is, those elements of the offence that have to be established by the prosecution, other than those that relate to the defendant's state of mind.

The type of *actus reus* that has to be established will vary according to the definition of the offence in question. Some obviously require proof of conduct on the part of the defendant, such as is the case with an offence like rape (see further Chapter 6). Other offences require proof that the defendant's actions caused a prohibited consequence. The topic of causation is dealt with in detail in the context of homicide in Chapter 4. In some cases it will be suffcient for the prosecution to establish that a particular state of affairs existed. This might be the case with an offence such as being found in the United Kingdom without having permission to remain; see R v Larsonneur considered below. Where a defendant is under a legal duty to act, his mere failure to act might give rise to the commission of an *actus reus*.

The imposition of criminal liability is based on an assumption that a defendant's acts or omissions at the time of the alleged offence were voluntary, in the sense that he was able to exercise some control over his actions or failure to act. Involuntariness can arise from a number of causes, some of which will found a defence in criminal law, some of which will not. See further intoxication (Chapter 13.1); duress and necessity (Chapter 14); insanity (Chapter 13.5) and non-insane automatism (Chapter 13.4).

2.2 A STATE OF AFFAIRS AMOUNTING TO AN *ACTUS REUS*

R v Larsonneur (1933) 24 Cr App R 74 (CA)

Lord Hewart CJ:

. . . The fact is, as the evidence shows, that the appellant is an alien. She has a French passport, which bears this statement under the date 14 March 1933, 'Leave to land granted at Folkestone this day on condition that the holder does not enter any employment, paid or unpaid, while in the United Kingdom', but on 22 March that condition was varied and one finds these words: 'The condition attached to the grant of leave to land is hereby varied so as to require departure from the United Kingdom not later than 22 March 1933'. Then follows the signature of an Under-Secretary of State. In fact, the appellant went to the Irish Free State and afterwards, in circumstances which are perfectly immaterial, so far as this appeal is concerned, came back to Holyhead. She was at Holyhead on 21 April 1933, a date after the day limited by the condition on her passport . . .

The appellant was, therefore, on 21 April 1933, in the position in which she would have been if she had been prohibited from landing by the Secretary of State and, that being so, there is no reason to interfere with the finding of the jury. She was found here and was, therefore, deemed to be in the class of persons whose landing had been prohibited by the Secretary of State, by reason of the fact that she had violated the condition on her passport. The appeal, therefore, is dismissed and the recommendation for deportation remains.

COMMENTS AND QUESTIONS

1   Given that Larsonneur was deported against her will to the United Kingdom, is there an argument as to the 'voluntariness' of her actions that brought about the *actus reus*? Lanham argues in 'Larsonneur revisited' [1976] Crim LR 276 that she was the author of her own misfortunes in going to Ireland in order to enter into an arranged marriage that would have enabled her to remain in the United Kingdom. In effect there was prior fault on her part in putting herself in a position where she risked deportation to the United Kingdom against her will.

2   In *Winzar v Chief Constable of Kent* (1983) *The Times*, 28 March (DC), the appellant was convicted of being drunk on the highway (contrary to s 12 of the Licensing Act 1872). He had been taken to a hospital; the doctors there, deciding that he was merely drunk, asked him to leave. The appellant remained in the hospital and the police were called. They placed the appellant in a police car parked in the road outside the hospital. The appellant was then charged with being drunk on the highway. It was held that the fact that his presence on the highway was not of his own volition and was momentary did not amount to a defence. The *actus reus* merely required proof of a state of affairs – drunkenness in a public place. Again an element of prior fault arises here. Winzar, of his own volition, became intoxicated and thereby put himself in a position whereby he might be found drunk and disorderly in a public place.

2.3 CODIFICATION AND LAW REFORM PROPOSALS

Clause 15 of the draft code seeks to codify the meaning to be given to the term 'act' in the following way:

A reference in this Act to an 'act' as an element of an offence refers also, where the context permits, to any result of the act, and any circumstance in which the act is done or the result occurs, that is an element of the offence, and references to a person acting or doing an act shall be construed accordingly.

As the commentary on the code observes:

> . . . Clause 15 is an interpretation clause. It does not define 'act'. It simply explains that where the Code refers to 'an act' or to a person's 'acting' or 'doing an act', the reference embraces whatever relevant results and circumstances the context permits. This clarification of the use of the word 'act' is not in fact essential; for we believe that no provision of the Code is on a fair reading truly ambiguous in its use of the term. But the clause may prove useful for the avoidance of doubt in those inexperienced in the reading of criminal statutes and as a protection against perverse reading or hopeless argument [Vol II, para 7.6].

2.4 *ACTUS REUS* MUST BE VOLUNTARY

As the quote from Lord Diplock at the beginning of this chapter indicates, *actus reus* and *mens rea* are not discrete concepts. The issue of voluntariness illustrates this. All crimes require proof of *actus reus*. Some crimes, often referred to as crimes of strict or absolute liability, require no *mens rea*. It might be thought that in relation to crimes of absolute liability no inquiry into the defendant's state of mind would be necessary. This is not the case. For an *actus* to be *reus* the prosecution must show that actions were voluntary. Voluntariness itself is a difficult concept because lack of voluntariness can arise from a number of causes. A defendant might claim that his actions were not voluntary because he acted under coercion, duress, or some other form of necessity. This does not amount to involuntariness for the purposes of the criminal law. A defendant acting under duress is aware of his actions and is controlling his actions, no matter how reluctant he may be to carry out certain acts. True involuntariness arises where D's brain is not consciously controlling his actions – such as where he is experiencing a fit of some sort. In such cases the defendant may be able to raise the complete defence of automatism, or sane automatism as it is sometimes referred to in order to distinguish it from insane automatism. The defence of automatism is considered at Chapter 13.4.

2.5 CRIMINAL LIABILITY FOR OMISSIONS

The basic principle here is that a failure to act can only give rise to the *actus reus* of an offence if the defendant was, at the time of the omission, under a legal duty to act. Legal duties can arise from statute, contract, the holding of a particular public office, or from the common law. The most obvious source of a positive legal duty to act is primary legislation. There are numerous Acts of Parliament that place individuals or companies under a legal duty to act in a particular way, whether it be the reporting of road accidents involving injury (see s 170(4) of the Road Traffic Act 1988), the duty to provide a safe working environment (see Health and Safety at Work Act 1974) or the statutory duty owed by parents and guardians towards children (see the Children and Young Persons Act 1933). See further *R v Lowe* [1973] QB 702 (CA), considered in Chapter 4.

A positive duty to act can be found in the express or implied terms of a contract of employment. An obvious example would be the contractual obligation placed upon a life-guard at a swimming pool to go to the aid of a swimmer in distress. The fact that the beneficiary of this duty is not a party to the contract is not relevant when assessing the employee's criminal liability. Similarly, the courts may be willing to identify positive legal duties arising from the fact that the defendant holds a particular office.

Common law duties are effectively residual. If the courts feel that the defendant was under a moral duty to act, and the moral duty is such that it ought to be reflected in and supported by the law, the courts will identify a common law duty to act. As the case law shows, this can arise in respect of family relationships, where one party voluntarily undertakes the care of another, or where the defendant accidentally causes harm and comes under a responsibility to act in order to mitigate the effect of the harm.

2.5.1 LIABILITY FOR FAILURE TO ACT BASED ON CONTRACT OF EMPLOYMENT

R v Pittwood (1902) 19 TLR 37 (Taunton Assizes)

The defendant was employed as a gatekeeper responsible for closing the gates of a level crossing when a train was due. On this occasion he failed to shut the gate and a hay cart crossing the line was involved in a collision with a train. A man was killed as a result. The defendant was convicted of manslaughter. As the report of the case indicates Wright J gave the judgment of the court:

> Wright J:
> . . . was clearly of opinion that in this case there was gross and criminal negligence, as the man was paid to keep the gate shut and protect the public. In his opinion there were three grounds on which the verdict could be supported: (1) There might be cases of misfeasance and cases of mere nonfeasance. Here it was quite clear there was evidence of misfeasance as the prisoner directly contributed to the accident. (2) A man might incur criminal liability from a duty arising out of contract. The learned judge quoted in support of this *R v Nicholls* (1875) 13 Cox 75; *R v Elliott* (1889) 16 Cox 710; *R v Benge* (1865) 4 F & F 594; *R v Hughes* (1857) Dears & B 248. The strongest case of all was, perhaps, *R v Instan* . . . and that case clearly governed the present charge. (3) With regard to the point that this was only an occupation road, he clearly held that it was not, as the company had assumed the liability of protecting the public whenever they crossed the road . . .

2.5.2 LIABILITY FOR OMISSION BASED ON HOLDING AN OFFICE

> ### *R v Dytham* [1979] QB 722 (CA)
>
> [Lord Widgery CJ read the following judgment of the court prepared by Shaw LJ:]
> The appellant was a police constable in Lancashire. On 17 March 1977 at about one o'clock in the morning he was on duty in uniform and was standing by a hot-dog stall in Duke Street, St Helens. A Mr Wincke was inside the stall and a Mr Sothern was by it. Some 30 yards away was the entrance to Cindy's Club. A man named Stubbs was ejected from the club by a bouncer. A fight ensued in which a number of men joined. There arose cries and screams and other indications of great violence. Mr Stubbs became the object of a murderous assault. He was beaten and kicked to death in the gutter outside the club. All this was audible and visible to the three men at the hot-dog stall. At no stage did the appellant make any move to intervene or any attempt to quell the disturbance or to stop the attack on the victim. When the hubbub had died down he adjusted his helmet and drove away. According to the other two at the hot-dog stall, he said that he was due off and was going off.
>
> His conduct was brought to the notice of the police authority. As a result he appeared on 10 October 1978 in the Crown Court at Liverpool to answer an indictment which was in these terms:
>
> > . . . the charge against you is one of misconduct of an officer of justice, in that you . . . misconducted yourself whilst acting as an officer of justice in that you being present and a witness to a criminal offence, namely a violent assault upon one . . . . Stubbs by three others

deliberately failed to carry out your duty as a police constable by wilfully omitting to take any steps to preserve the Queen's Peace or to protect the person of the said . . . Stubbs or to arrest or otherwise bring to justice [his] assailants.

On arraignment the appellant pleaded not guilty and the trial was adjourned to 7 November. On that day before the jury was empanelled counsel for the appellant took an objection to the indictment by way of demurrer. The burden of that objection was that the indictment as laid disclosed no offence known to the law. Neill J ruled against the objection and the trial proceeded. The defence on the facts was that the appellant had observed nothing more than that a man was turned out of the club. It was common ground that in that situation his duty would not have required him to take any action. The jury were directed that the crucial question for their consideration was whether the appellant had seen the attack on the victim. If he had, they could find him guilty of the offence charged in the indictment. The jury did return a verdict of guilty. Hence this appeal which is confined to the matters of law raised by the demurrer pleaded at the court of trial.

At the outset of his submissions in this court counsel for the appellant conceded two matters. The first was that a police constable is a public officer. The second was that there does exist at common law an offence of misconduct in a public office.

From that point the argument was within narrow limits though it ran deep into constitutional and jurisprudential history. The effect of it was that not every failure to discharge a duty which devolved on a person as the holder of a public office gave rise to the common law offence of misconduct in that office. As counsel for the appellant put it, nonfeasance was not enough. There must be a malfeasance or at least a misfeasance involving an element of corruption. In support of this contention a number of cases were cited from 18th and 19th century reports. It is the fact that in nearly all of them the misconduct asserted involved some corrupt taint; but this appears to have been an accident of circumstance and not a necessary incident of the offence. Misconduct in a public office is more vividly exhibited where dishonesty is revealed as part of the dereliction of duty. Indeed in some cases the conduct impugned cannot be shown to have been misconduct unless it was done with a corrupt or oblique motive . . .

In the present case it was not suggested that the appellant could not have summoned or sought assistance to help the victim or to arrest his assailants. The charge as framed left this answer open to him. Not surprisingly he did not seek to avail himself of it, for the facts spoke strongly against any such answer. The allegation made was not of mere nonfeasance but of deliberate failure and wilful neglect. This involves an element of culpability which is not restricted to corruption or dishonesty but which must be of such a degree that the misconduct impugned is calculated to injure the public interest so as to call for condemnation and punishment. Whether such a situation is revealed by the evidence is a matter that a jury has to decide. It puts no heavier burden on them than when in more familiar contexts they are called on to consider whether driving is dangerous or a publication is obscene or a place of public resort is a disorderly house . . .

The judge's ruling was correct. The appeal is dismissed.

 COMMENTS AND QUESTIONS

1   Note that Dytham was not charged with an offence that related to the injuries actually suffered by Stubbs. Is this because of the difficulties in proving causation? Could the prosecution prove that the injuries would not have been sustained had Dytham intervened?

2   What if Dytham had been off duty when the incident occurred? Do off-duty police officers have legal duties to act that do not apply to the ordinary citizen?

3   D is a consultant cardiologist flying on a plane from London to Manchester. A passenger on the flight has a heart attack and the cabin crew ask if there is a doctor on board. D does not make himself known to the crew and the passenger dies before the plane lands. Does D incur any legal liability for the death?

4   Consider further how far the law imposes a duty to act on social workers and teachers. Does the duty only extend to those children officially placed in their care? What if a teacher or social worker became aware that a neighbour was sexually abusing a child? Could failure to act result in criminal liability?

2.5.3 LIABILITY FOR OMISSION BASED ON PARENTAL RESPONSIBILITY

R v Gibbins and Proctor (1918) 13 Cr App R 134 (CA)

Proctor lived with Gibbins as his common law wife. There was evidence that Gibbins' daughter Nelly starved to death through neglect by both parents. The court considered the legal duties imposed upon both defendants.

Darling J:

. . . It has been said that there ought not to have been a finding of guilty of murder against Gibbins. The court agrees that the evidence was less against Gibbins than Proctor, Gibbins gave her money, and as far as we can see it was sufficient to provide for the wants of themselves and all the children. But he lived in the house and the child was his own, a little girl of seven, and he grossly neglected the child. He must have known what her condition was if he saw her, for she was little more than a skeleton. He is in this dilemma; if he did not see her the jury might well infer that he did not care if she died; if he did he must have known what was going on. The question is whether there was evidence that he so conducted himself as to show that he desired that grievous bodily injury should be done to the child. He cannot pretend that he showed any solicitude for her. He knew that Proctor hated her, knew that she was ill and that no doctor had been called in, and the jury may have come to the conclusion that he was so infatuated with Proctor, and so afraid of offending her, that he preferred that the child should starve to death rather than that he should be exposed to any injury or unpleasantness from Proctor. It is unnecessary to say more than that there was evidence that Gibbins did desire that grievous bodily harm should be done to the child; he did not interfere in what was being done, and he comes within the definition which I have read, and is therefore guilty of murder.

The case of Proctor is plainer. She had charge of the child. She was under no obligation to do so or to live with Gibbins, but she did so, and receiving money, as it is admitted she did, for the purpose of supplying food, her duty was to see that the child was properly fed and looked after, and to see that she had medical attention if necessary. We agree with what Lord Coleridge CJ said in *R v Instan* [1893] 1 QB 450: 'There is no case directly in point, but it would be a slur upon, and a discredit to the administration of, justice in this country if there were any doubt as to the legal principle, or as to the present case being within it. The prisoner was under a moral obligation to the deceased from which arose a legal duty towards her; that legal duty the prisoner has wilfully and deliberately left unperformed, with the consequence that there has been an acceleration of the death of the deceased owing to the non-performance of that legal duty.' Here Proctor took upon herself the moral obligation of looking after the children; she was *de facto*, though not *de jure*, the wife of Gibbins and had excluded the child's own mother. She neglected the child undoubtedly, and the evidence shows that as a result the child died. So a verdict of manslaughter at least was inevitable.

Re A (Children) (Conjoined Twins: Surgical Separation) [2000] 4 All ER 961

For the facts see Chapter 14.7 – the court was asked to rule on the legality of an operation to separate conjoined twins. The operation would enable the stronger twin (Jodie) to survive, but would inevitably result in the death of the weaker twin (Mary). Without an operation to separate, both twins would die within months. Ward LJ considered the extent to which a failure to permit medical intervention, or a refusal by the doctors to operate, might amount to a culpable omission.

Ward LJ:

I seem to be the lone voice raising the unpalatable possibility that the doctors and even – though given the horror of their predicament it is anathema to contemplate it – the parents might kill Jodie if they fail to save her life by carrying out the operation to separate her from Mary. Although I recoil at the very notion that these good people could ever be guilty of murder, I am bound to ask why the law will not hold that the doctors and the parents have come under a duty to Jodie. If the operation is in her interests the parents must consent for their duty is to act consistent with her best interests: see Lord Scarman in *Gillick* in the passages I have already set out. I know there is a huge chasm in turpitude between these stricken parents and the wretched parents in *R v Gibbins and Proctor* (1918) 13 Cr App R 134 who starved their child to death. Nevertheless I am bound to wonder whether there is strictly any difference in the application of the principle. They know they can save her. They appreciate she will die if not separated from her twin. Is there any defence to a charge of cruelty under section 1 of the Children and Young Persons Act 1933 in the light of the clarification of the law given by *R v Sheppard* [1981] AC 395 . . . Would it not be manslaughter if Jodie died through that neglect? I ask these insensitive questions not to heap blame on the parents. No prosecutor would dream of prosecuting. The sole purpose of the enquiry is to establish whether either or both parents and doctors have come under a legal duty to Jodie, as I conclude they each have, to procure and to carry out the operation which will save her life. If so then performance of their duty to Jodie is irreconcilable with the performance of their duty to Mary. Certainly it seems to me that if this court were to give permission for the operation to take place, then a legal duty would be imposed on the doctors to treat their patient in her best interests, that is, to operate upon her. Failure to do so is a breach of their duty. To omit to act when under a duty to do so may be a culpable omission . . .

The [Archbishop of Westminster, who was permitted to make written submissions] would agree. He tells us that:

> To aim at ending an innocent person's life is just as wrong when one does it by omission as when one does it by a positive act.

COMMENTS AND QUESTIONS

1   Section 5 of the Domestic Violence, Crime and Victims Act 2004 introduces a new form of liability for homicide, the offence of causing or allowing the death of a child or vulnerable adult. The offence can be committed by way of act or omission and extends to situations where D fails to intervene to protect a child or vulnerable adult who is a member of the same household; see further Chapter 4.10.

2.5.4 LIABILITY FOR OMISSION BASED ON VOLUNTARILY ASSUMING A DUTY OF CARE

R v Stone and Dobinson [1977] QB 354 (CA)

Geoffrey Lane LJ:

. . . In 1972, at 75 Broadwater, Bolton-on-Dearne in Yorkshire, there lived three people. Stone, an ex-miner now aged 67, widowed for 10 years, who is partially deaf, almost totally blind and has no appreciable sense of smell; Gwendoline Dobinson, now aged 43, who had been his housekeeper and mistress for some eight years, and Stone's son called Cyril, aged 34, who is mentally sub-normal. Stone is of low average intelligence, Dobinson is described as ineffectual and somewhat inadequate.

There was an addition to that household in 1972. Stone had a younger sister called Fanny, about 61 at the date of her death. She had been living with another sister called Rosy. For some reason, probably because Rosy could not tolerate her any longer, she had decided to leave. She came to live at No 75, where she occupied a small front room . . . She was eccentric in many ways. She was morbidly and unnecessarily anxious about putting on weight and so denied herself proper meals. She would take to her room for days. She would often stay in her room all day until the two appellants went to the public house in the evening, when she would creep down and make herself a meal.

In early spring 1975 the police called at the house. Fanny had been found wandering about in the street by herself without apparently knowing where she was. This caused the appellants to try and find Fanny's doctor. They tried to trace him through Rosy, but having walked a very consider-able distance in their search they failed. It transpired that they had walked to the wrong village. Fanny herself refused to tell them the doctor's name. She thought she would be 'put away' if she did. Nothing more was done to enlist outside professional aid.

In the light of what happened subsequently there can be no doubt that Fanny's condition over the succeeding weeks and months must have deteriorated rapidly. By July 1975 she was, it seems, unable or unwilling to leave her bed and, on 19 July, the next-door neighbour, Mrs Wilson, gallantly volunteered to help the female appellant to wash Fanny. She states:

> On 19 July Mrs Dobinson and I went to Fanny's room in order to clean her up. When I went into the room there was not a strong smell until I moved her. Her nightdress was wet and messed with her own excreta and the dress had to be cut off. I saw her back was sore; I hadn't seen anything like that before. I took the bedclothes off the bed. They were all wet through and messed. And so was the mattress. I was there for about two hours and Mrs Dobinson helped. She was raw, her back, shoulders, bottom and down below between her legs. Mrs Dobinson appeared to me to be upset because Fanny had never let her attend to her before. I advised Mrs Dobinson to go to the Social Services.

Emily West, the licensee of the local public house, the Crossed Daggers, gave evidence to the effect that during the whole of the period, from 19 July onwards, the appellants came to the public house every night at about 7.00 pm. The appellant Dobinson was worried and told Emily West that Fanny would not wash, go to the toilet or eat or drink. As a result Emily West immediately advised Dobinson to get a doctor and when told that Fanny's doctor lived at Doncaster, Emily West suggested getting a local one. It seems that some efforts were made to get a local doctor, but the neighbour who volunteered to do the telephoning (the appellants being incapable of managing the instrument themselves) was unsuccessful.

On 2 August 1975 Fanny was found by Dobinson to be dead in her bed . . . The pathologist, Dr Usher, gave evidence that the deceased was naked, emaciated, weighing five stone and five pounds, her body ingrained with dirt, lying in a pool of excrement . . . He said that the cause of death was (1) toxaemia spreading from the infected pressure areas (this could have been alleviated by keeping her clean) and (2) prolonged immobilisation.

. . . The Crown alleged that in the circumstances the appellants had undertaken the duty of caring for Fanny who was incapable of looking after herself, that they had, with gross negligence, failed in that duty, that such failure had caused her death and that they were guilty of manslaughter . . .

There is no dispute, broadly speaking, as to the matters on which the jury must be satisfied before they can convict of manslaughter in circumstances such as the present. They are: (1) that the defendant undertook the care of a person who by reason of age or infirmity was unable to care for herself; (2) that the defendant was grossly negligent in regard to his duty of care; (3) that by reason of such negligence the person died. It is submitted on behalf of the appellants that the judge's direction to the jury with regard to the first two items was incorrect.

At the close of the Crown's case submissions were made to the judge that there was no, or no sufficient, evidence that the appellants, or either of them, had chosen to undertake the care of Fanny.

That contention was advanced by counsel for the appellant before this court as his first ground of appeal. He amplified the ground somewhat by submitting that the evidence which the judge had suggested to the jury might support the assumption of a duty by the appellants did not, when examined, succeed in doing so. He suggested that the situation here was unlike any reported case. Fanny came to this house as a lodger. Largely, if not entirely due to her own eccentricity and failure to look after herself or feed herself properly, she became increasingly infirm and immobile and eventually unable to look after herself. Is it to be said, asks counsel for the appellants rhetorically, that by the mere fact of becoming infirm and helpless in these circumstances, she casts a duty on her brother and Mrs Dobinson to take steps to have her looked after or taken to hospital? The suggestion is that, heartless though it may seem, this is one of those situations where the appellants were entitled to do nothing; where no duty was cast on them to help, any more than it is cast on a man to rescue a stranger from drowning, however easy such a rescue might be.

This court rejects that proposition. Whether Fanny was a lodger or not she was a blood relation of the appellant Stone; she was occupying a room in his house; Mrs Dobinson had undertaken the duty of trying to wash her, of taking such food to her as she required. There was ample evidence that each appellant was aware of the poor condition she was in by mid-July. It was not disputed that no effort was made to summon an ambulance or the social services or the police despite the entreaties of Mrs Wilson and Mrs West. A social worker used to visit Cyril. No word was spoken to him. All these were matters which the jury were entitled to take into account when considering whether the necessary assumption of a duty to care for Fanny had been proved.

This was not a situation analogous to the drowning stranger. They did make efforts to care. They tried to get a doctor; they tried to discover the previous doctor. Mrs Dobinson helped with the washing and the provision of food. All these matters were put before the jury in terms which we find it impossible to fault. The jury were entitled to find that the duty had been assumed. They were entitled to conclude that once Fanny became helplessly infirm, as she had by 19 July, the appellants were, in the circumstances, obliged either to summon help or else to care for Fanny themselves.

2.5.5 LIABILITY FOR OMISSION BASED ON ACCIDENTALLY CREATING A DANGEROUS SITUATION

R v Miller [1983] 2 AC 161 (HL)

The appellant, a homeless man, had spent an evening drinking. He returned to the unoccupied house where he had been sleeping at night. On the evening in question he lay on a mattress and lit a cigarette. He then fell asleep with the lighted cigarette in his hand. The cigarette came into contact with the mattress and set fire to it. The appellant woke up to find the mattress on fire, but instead of extinguishing the fire he got up and went into the next room and went back to sleep. Later that night the appellant was awoken again by the emergency services called to attend a fire at the house, the fire having spread from the burning mattress. The appellant was charged on indictment with the offence of 'arson contrary to s 1(1) and (3) of the Criminal Damage Act 1971'; the particulars of offence were that he:

... on a date unknown between 13 and 16 August 1980 without lawful excuse damaged by fire a house known as No 9, Grantham Road, Sparkbrook, intending to do damage to such property or recklessly as to whether such property would be damaged ... The Court of Appeal ... certified that the following question of law of general public importance was involved:

Whether the *actus reus* of the offence of arson is present when a defendant accidentally starts a fire and thereafter, intending to destroy or damage property belonging to another or being reckless as to whether any such property would be destroyed or damaged, fails to take any steps to extinguish the fire or prevent damage to such property by that fire?

Lord Diplock:
My Lords ... the question before your Lordships in this appeal is one that is confined to the true construction of the words used in particular provisions in a particular statute, viz s 1(1) and (3) of the Criminal Damage Act 1971 ... These I now set out:

(1) A person who without lawful excuse destroys or damages any property belonging to another intending to destroy or damage any such property or being reckless as to whether any such property would be destroyed or damaged shall be guilty of an offence ...

(3) an offence committed under this section by destroying or damaging property by fire shall be charged as arson.

This definition of arson makes it a 'result-crime' . . . The crime is not complete unless and until the conduct of the accused has caused property belonging to another to be destroyed or damaged.

. . . The first question to be answered where a completed crime of arson is charged is: 'Did a physical act of the accused start the fire which spread and damaged property belonging to another (or did his act cause an existing fire, which he had not started but which would otherwise have burnt itself out harmlessly, to spread and damage property belonging to another)?' I have added the words in brackets for completeness. They do not arise in the instant case; in cases where they do, the accused, for the purposes of the analysis which follows, may be regarded as having started a fresh fire.

The first question is a pure question of causation; it is one of fact to be decided by the jury in a trial on indictment. It should be answered 'No' if, in relation to the fire during the period starting immediately before its ignition and ending with its extinction, the role of the accused was at no time more than that of a passive bystander. In such a case the subsequent questions to which I shall be turning would not arise. The conduct of the parabolical priest and Levite on the road to Jericho may have been indeed deplorable, but English law has not so far developed to the stage of treating it as criminal; and if it ever were to do so there would be difficulties in defining what should be the limits of the offence.

If, on the other hand the question, which I now confine to: 'Did a physical act of the accused start the fire which spread and damaged property belonging to another?' is answered 'Yes', as it was by the jury in the instant case, then for the purpose of the further questions the answers to which are determinative of his guilt of the offence of arson, the conduct of the accused, through-out the period from immediately before the moment of ignition to the completion of the damage to the property by the fire, is relevant; so is his state of mind throughout that period.

Since arson is a result-crime the period may be considerable, and during it the conduct of the accused that is causative of the result may consist not only of his doing physical acts which cause the fire to start or spread but also of his failing to take measures that lie within his power to counteract the danger that he has himself created. And if his conduct, active or passive, varies in the course of the period, so may his state of mind at the time of each piece of conduct. If at the time of any particular piece of conduct by the accused that is causative of the result, the state of mind that actuates his conduct falls within the description of one or other of the states of mind that are made a necessary ingredient of the offence of arson by s 1(1) of the Criminal Damage Act 1971 (ie intending to damage property belonging to another or being reckless as to whether such property would be damaged) I know of no principle of English criminal law that would prevent his being guilty of the offence created by that subsection. Likewise I see no rational ground for excluding from conduct capable of giving rise to criminal liability, conduct which consists of failing to take measures that lie within one's power to counteract a danger that one has oneself created, if at the time of such conduct one's state of mind is such as constitutes a necessary ingredient of the offence. I venture to think that the habit of lawyers to talk of *actus reus*, suggest-ive as it is of action rather than inaction, is responsible for any erroneous notion that failure to act cannot give rise to criminal liability in English law.

No one has been bold enough to suggest that if, in the instant case, the accused had been aware at the time that he dropped the cigarette that it would probably set fire to his mattress and yet had taken no steps to extinguish it he would not have been guilty of the offence of arson, since he would have damaged property of another being reckless whether any such property would be damaged.

I cannot see any good reason why, so far as liability under criminal law is concerned, it should matter at what point of time before the resultant damage is complete a person becomes aware that he has done a physical act which, whether or not he appreciated that it would at the time when he did it, does in fact create a risk that property of another will be damaged; provided that, at the moment of awareness, it lies within his power to take steps, either himself or by calling for the assistance of the fire brigade if this be necessary, to prevent or minimise the damage to the property at risk.

Let me take first the case of the person who has thrown away a lighted cigarette expecting it to go out harmlessly, but later becomes aware that, although he did not intend it to do so, it has, in the event, caused some inflammable material to smoulder and that unless the smouldering is extinguished promptly, an act that the person who dropped the cigarette could perform without danger to himself or difficulty, the inflammable material will be likely to burst into flames and damage some other person's property. The person who dropped the cigarette deliberately refrains from doing anything to extinguish the smouldering. His reason for so refraining is that he intends that the risk which his own act had originally created, though it was only subsequently that he became aware of this, should fructify in actual damage to that other person's property; and what he so intends, in fact occurs. There can be no sensible reason why he should not be guilty of arson. If he would be guilty of arson, having appreciated the risk of damage at the very moment of dropping the lighted cigarette, it would be quite irrational that he should not be guilty if he first appreciated the risk at some later point in time but when it was still possible for him to take steps to prevent or minimise the damage.

. . . My Lords, just as in the first example that I took the fact that the accused's intent to damage the property of another was not formed until, as a result of his initial act in dropping the cigarette, events had occurred which presented a risk that another person's property would be damaged, ought not under any sensible system of law to absolve him from criminal liability, so too in a case where the relevant state of mind is not intent but recklessness I see no reason in common sense and justice why, *mutatis mutandis*, a similar principle should not apply to impose criminal liability on him. If in the former case he is criminally liable because he refrains from taking steps that are open to him to try to prevent or minimise the damage caused by the risk he has himself created and he so refrains because he intends such damage to occur, so in the latter case, when, as a result of his own initial act in dropping the cigarette, events have occurred which [he realises create a risk of damage to another's property] . . . he should likewise be criminally liable if he refrains from taking steps that lie within his power to try and prevent the damage caused by the risk that he himself has created, and so refrains either because . . . he has recognised that there was some risk involved, he has nonetheless decided to take that risk.

My Lords, in the instant case the prosecution did not rely on the state of mind of the accused as being reckless during that part of his conduct that consisted of his lighting and smoking a cigarette while lying on his mattress and falling asleep without extinguishing it. So the jury were not invited to make any finding as to this. What the prosecution did rely on as being reckless was his state of mind during that part of his conduct after he awoke to find that he had set his mattress on fire and that it was smouldering, but did not then take any steps either to try to extinguish it himself or to send for the fire brigade, but simply went into the other room to resume his slumbers, leaving the fire from the already smouldering mattress to spread and to damage that part of the house in which the mattress was.

The recorder, in his lucid summing-up to the jury (they took 22 minutes only to reach their verdict), told them that the accused, having by his own act started a fire in the mattress which, when he became aware of its existence, presented an obvious risk of damaging the house, became under a duty to take some action to put it out. The Court of Appeal upheld the conviction, but its *ratio decidendi* appears to be somewhat different from that of the recorder. As I understand the judgment, in effect it treats the whole course of conduct of the accused, from the moment at which he fell asleep and dropped the cigarette onto the mattress until the time the damage to the house by fire was complete, as a continuous act of the accused, and holds that it is sufficient to constitute the statutory offence of arson if at any stage in that course of conduct the state of mind of the accused, when he fails to try to prevent or minimise the damage which will result from his initial act, although it lies within his power to do so, is that of being reckless whether property belonging to another would be damaged.

My Lords, these alternative ways of analysing the legal theory that justifies a decision which has received nothing but commendation for its accord with common sense and justice have, since the publication of the judgment of the Court of Appeal in the instant case, provoked academic controversy. Each theory has distinguished support. Professor JC Smith espouses the 'duty theory' (see [1982] Crim LR 526 at 528); Professor Glanville Williams who, after the decision of the Divisional Court in *Fagan v Metropolitan Police Comr* [1969] 1 QB 439 appears to have been attracted by the duty theory, now prefers that of the continuous act (see [1992] Crim LR 773). When applied to cases where a person has unknowingly done an act which sets in train events that, when he becomes aware of them, present an obvious risk that property belonging to another will be damaged, both theories lead to an identical result; and, since what your Lordships are concerned with is to give guidance to trial judges in their task of summing-up to juries, I would for this purpose adopt the duty theory as being the easier to explain to a jury; though I would commend the use of the word 'responsibility', rather than 'duty' which is more appropriate to civil than to criminal law since it suggests an obligation owed to another person, i.e. the person to whom the endangered property belongs, whereas a criminal statute defines combinations of conduct and state of mind which render a person liable to punishment by the state itself.

. . . where the accused is initially unaware that he has done an act that in fact sets in train events which . . . present a risk that property belonging to another would be damaged, a suitable direction to the jury would be: that the accused is guilty of the offence under s 1(1) of the Criminal Damage Act 1971 if, when he does become aware that the events in question have happened as a result of his own act, he does not try to prevent or reduce the risk of damage by his own efforts or if necessary by sending for help from the fire brigade and the reason why he does not is . . . because . . . he has . . . recognised that there was some risk involved [and] he has . . . decided not to try to prevent or reduce it.

Lord Keith of Kinkel, Lord Bridge of Harwich, Lord Brandon of Oakwood and Lord Brightman all agreed with Lord Diplock.

2.5.6 WHERE THE DEFENDANT IS ABSOLVED FROM ANY DUTY TO ACT

Airedale National Health Service Trust v Bland [1993] 1 All ER 82 (HL)

Anthony Bland was injured in the Hillsborough Stadium disaster. He suffered irreversible brain damage and was diagnosed as being in a persistent vegetative state (PVS). Expert medical evidence was to the effect that there was no hope of recovery. The Airedale NHS Trust, with the support of Bland's parents, sought a declaration that the doctors treating Bland might lawfully discontinue all life-sustaining treatment and medical treatment except that required to enable Bland to die without unnecessary distress. The Official Solicitor appealed to the House of Lords against the granting of the declaration on the basis that the withdrawal of life-support treatment would amount to murder.

> Lord Goff:
> I agree that the doctor's conduct in discontinuing life support can properly be categorised as an omission. It is true that it may be difficult to describe what the doctor actually does as an omission, for example where he takes some positive step to bring the life support to an end. But discontinuation of life support is, for present purposes, no different from not initiating life support in the first place. In each case, the doctor is simply allowing his patient to die in the sense that he is desisting from taking a step which might, in certain circumstances, prevent his patient from dying as a result of his pre-existing condition: and as a matter of general principle an omission such as this will not be unlawful unless it constitutes a breach of duty to the patient. I also agree that the doctor's conduct is to be differentiated from that of, for example, an interloper who maliciously switches off a life-support machine because, although the interloper may perform exactly the same act as the doctor who discontinues life support, his doing so constitutes interference with the life-prolonging treatment then being administered by the doctor. Accordingly, whereas the doctor, in discontinuing life support, is simply allowing his patient to die of his pre-existing condition, the interloper is actively intervening to stop the doctor from prolonging the patient's life, and such conduct cannot possibly be categorised as an omission . . . If the justification for treating a patient who lacks the capacity to consent lies in the fact that the treatment is provided in his best interests, it must follow that the treatment may, and indeed ultimately should, be discontinued where it is no longer in his best interests to provide it. The question which lies at the heart of the present case is, as I see it, whether on that principle the doctors responsible for the treatment and care of Anthony Bland can justifiably discontinue the process of artificial feeding upon which the prolongation of his life depends.
>
> It is crucial for the understanding of this question that the question itself should be correctly formulated. The question is not whether the doctor should take a course which will kill his patient, or even take a course which has the effect of accelerating his death. The question is whether the doctor should or should not continue to provide his patient with medical treatment or care which, if continued, will prolong his patient's life. The question is sometimes put in striking or emotional terms, which can be misleading. For example, in the case of a life-support system, it is sometimes asked: should a doctor be entitled to switch it off, or to pull the plug? And then it is asked: can it be in the best interests of the patient that a doctor should be able to switch the life-support system off, when this will inevitably result in the patient's death? Such an approach has rightly been criticised as misleading . . . This is because the question is not whether it is in the best interests of the patient that he should die. The question is whether it is in the best interests of the patient that his life should be prolonged by the continuance of this form of medical treatment or care.
>
> The correct formulation of the question is of particular importance in a case such as the present, where the patient is totally unconscious and where there is no hope whatsoever of any amelioration of his condition. In circumstances such as these, it may be difficult to say that it is in his best interests that the treatment should be ended. But, if the question is asked, as in my opinion it should be, whether it is in his best interests that treatment which has the effect of

artificially prolonging his life should be continued, that question can sensibly be answered to the effect that it is not in his best interests to do so.

Lord Mustill:

I turn to an argument which in my judgment is logically defensible and consistent with the existing law. In essence it turns the previous argument on its head by directing the inquiry to the interests of the patient, not in the termination of life but in the continuation of his treatment. It runs as follows. (i) The cessation of nourishment and hydration is an omission not an act. (ii) Accordingly, the cessation will not be a criminal act unless the doctors are under a present duty to continue the regime. (iii) At the time when Anthony Bland came into the care of the doctors decisions had to be made about his care which he was unable to make for himself . . . Since the possibility that he might recover still existed his best interests required that he should be supported in the hope that this would happen. These best interests justified the application of the necessary regime without his consent. (iv) All hope of recovery has now been abandoned. Thus, although the termination of his life is not in the best interests of Anthony Bland, his best interests in being kept alive have also disappeared, taking with them the justification for the non-consensual regime and the correlative duty to keep it in being. (v) Since there is no longer a duty to provide nourishment and hydration a failure to do so cannot be a criminal offence.

My Lords, I must recognise at once that this chain of reasoning makes an unpromising start by transferring the morally and intellectually dubious distinction between acts and omissions into a context where the ethical foundations of the law are already open to question. The opportunity for anomaly and excessively fine distinctions, often depending more on the way in which the problem happens to be stated than on any real distinguishing features, has been exposed by many commentators . . . All this being granted, we are still forced to take the law as we find it and try to make it work. Moreover, although in cases near the borderline the categorisation of conduct will be exceedingly hard, I believe that nearer the periphery there will be many instances which fall quite clearly into one category rather than the other . . . I therefore consider the argument to be soundly based. Now that the time has come when Anthony Bland has no further interest in being kept alive, the necessity to do so, created by his inability to make a choice, has gone; and the justification for the invasive care and treatment together with the duty to provide it have also gone. Absent a duty, the omission to perform what had previously been a duty will no longer be a breach of the criminal law.

Lord Keith, Lord Lowry and Lord Browne-Wilkinson all concurred that the appeal should be dismissed.

COMMENTS AND QUESTIONS

1   In *R v Stone and Dobinson* (above) Fanny gave Edward £1.50 per week from her pension as a contribution towards the rent. Could his liability have been based on a breach of contract?

2   Compare the position of Dobinson in this case with Proctor in *R v Gibbins and Proctor* (above). Are their roles morally indistinguishable?

3   What if Stone and Dobinson had simply refused to let Fanny into their house? Suppose she had died living 'rough'. What would their liability have been?

4   In *R v Smith* [1979] Crim LR 251 (Birmingham Crown Court) D's wife was ill but she did not want him to call a doctor. Her condition worsened and D did eventually call for medical assistance, but by this time it was too late and his wife died of puerperal fever before the doctor arrived. Medical evidence was that she could have been saved had a doctor been called earlier. D was charged with the manslaughter of his wife. The jury could not agree on the charge of manslaughter and were discharged from giving a verdict. To what extent did the court in Smith proceed on the basis that D was under no duty to summon assistance for his wife provided she was capable of making a rational decision regarding medical treatment for herself? Does this mean that the duty arises once she ceases to be capable of rational judgment? If, by that point, she has suffered irreparable harm in the sense that medical treatment will not avail her, and D fails to summon help, can it be said that his omission is the cause of her death?

5   The common law duty to limit the effect of harm accidentally caused, expounded in *R v Miller* (above), was relied upon in *DPP v Santana-Bermudez* [2003] All ER (D) 168 (Nov) to secure a conviction for actual bodily harm. The defendant was searched by a woman police constable ('WPC'). Prior to the search she specifically asked the defendant whether or not he was in possession of any needles or 'sharps' to which he answered that he was not. The WPC then put her hand into the defendant's pocket to search further and her finger was pierced by a hypodermic needle in the defendant's pocket. The Court of Appeal adopted the view that by informing the WPC that he was not in possession of any sharp items or needles, the defendant had effectively tricked her into injuring herself. The court applied *R v Miller* [1983] 1 All ER 978 on the basis that the defendant had created a dangerous situation and had then come under a duty to limit the effect of the harm caused. This he had failed to do by not telling the truth to the WPC. As an alternative basis for liability, could it be argued that the defendant's assurances that he had no sharp objects in his pocket be said to give rise to a relationship of reliance between him and the WPC?

2.5.7 CODIFICATION AND LAW REFORM PROPOSALS

The Criminal Code team's draft Code of 1985 did contain a codification of the law relating to criminal liability for omissions, but these provisions were eventually excluded from the Law Commission's draft Code Bill published in 1989. Clause 17 of the 1989 Bill does, however, make clear that results may be caused by omission. As the commentary to the Bill explains:

> The . . . Bill therefore defines homicide offences in terms of causing death rather than of killing; and other offences against the person similarly require the causing of relevant harms. It seems to us to be desirable to draft some other offences at least (most obviously, offences of damage to property) in the same way, in order to leave fully open to the courts the possibility of so construing the relevant (statutory) provisions as to impose liability for omissions. For to prefer 'cause death' to 'kill' while retaining 'destroy or damage property' might be taken to imply an intention to exclude all liability for omissions in the latter case [Vol II, para 7.13].

In its report *Legislating the Criminal Code* (Law Com 218), the Law Commission extended this approach to its proposals for a number of non-fatal offences against the person, clause 19(1) of the Bill contained in that report stating that:

> An offence to which this section applies may be committed by a person who, with the result specified for the offence, omits to do an act that he is under a duty to do at common law. Where this section applies to an offence a person may commit an offence if, with the result specified for the offence, he omits to do an act that he is under a duty to do at common law; and accordingly references to acts include references to omissions.

The issue of whether or not a duty arose would remain to be determined by the common law. The Miller principle is codified with some amendments by clause 31 of the Draft Criminal Law Bill as follows:

> Where it is an offence to be at fault in causing a result, a person who lacks the fault required when he does an act that may cause, or does cause, the result, he nevertheless commits the offence if being aware that he has done the act and that the result may occur or, as the case may be, has occurred and may continue, and with the fault required, he fails to take reasonable steps to prevent the result occurring or continuing and it does occur or continue.

The commentary on this provision indicates that D would be under a duty to take measures that lie within his power to counteract the danger he has inadvertently created – see Law Com 218, para 41.3. The Home Office draft Offences Against the Person Bill also contains a similar measure in clause 16 as regards the commission of the offences provided for in that Bill.

FURTHER READING

Ashworth, A, 'The scope of criminal liability for omission' (1989) 105 LQR 424

Buxton, R, 'The Human Rights Act and the substantive criminal law' [2000] Crim LR 331

Smart, A, 'Criminal responsibility for failing to do the impossible' (1987) 103 LQR 532

Smith, ATH, 'The Human Rights Act 1998 – (1) The Human Rights Act and the criminal lawyer: the constitutional context' [1999] Crim LR 251

Williams, G, 'What should the Code do about omissions?' (1987) 7 Legal Studies 92

Williams, G, 'Criminal omissions – the conventional view' (1991) 107 LQR 86

CHAPTER 3

MENS REA: THE MENTAL ELEMENT

CONTENTS

3.1 INTRODUCTION

The term *mens rea* (or fault element, as it is sometimes referred to) refers to the state of mind of the accused at the time of the commission of the *actus reus* of an offence. The traditional maxim is '*actus non facit reum nisi mens sit rea*': the act is not guilty unless the mind is also guilty. The only offences for which this is not a requirement are offences of 'strict liability' (as to which, see 3.8, below). This chapter examines the general principles of *mens rea*. The *mens rea* required for specific offences is dealt with as appropriate in subsequent chapters. Certain defences effectively involve a denial of *mens rea*, for example where the defendant raises issues such as insanity, diminished responsibility, intoxication or mistake. These too are dealt with in separate chapters.

3.2 *MENS REA*: INTENTION – THE BACKGROUND TO THE CURRENT LAW

For a range of offences, both statutory and common law, intention on the part of the defendant is the fault element that has to be established by the prosecution. As the following material demonstrates, defining intention has proved to be a difficult task – one that has occupied the House of Lords on at least five occasions since 1975.

In simple terms there are two types of intent. The first requires proof of purpose, that is, that it was the defendant's purpose to bring about a prohibited consequence. The second is based on evidence indicating the extent to which the defendant foresaw the prohibited consequence as resulting from his act or omission. In *DPP v Smith* [1961] AC 290 the House of Lords held that a defendant could be presumed to have foreseen the natural and probable consequences of his actions (that is, if a reasonable person would have foreseen the result then it could be presumed that the defendant had). The effect of Smith was reversed by s 8 of the Criminal Justice Act 1967 which provides:

> A court or jury, in determining whether a person has committed an offence:
>
> (a) shall not be bound in law to infer that he intended or foresaw a result of his actions by reason only of its being a natural and probable consequence of those actions; but
> (b) shall decide whether he did intend or foresee that result by reference to all the evidence, drawing such inferences from the evidence as appear proper in the circumstances.

As a result of s 8 a jury cannot conclude that the defendant must have foreseen a consequence simply because it was the natural and probable consequence of his act or omission. The fact that something is the natural and probable consequence of the defendant's act or omission is, however, evidence from which it may be inferred that the defendant intended that result to occur. One of the major difficulties facing the House of Lords in this regard has been determining the degree of foresight that could be equated with intention.

In *R v Moloney* [1985] 1 AC 905, Lord Bridge of Harwich, whilst emphasising that foresight of consequences, as an element bearing on the issue of intention, belonged not to the substantive law but to the law of evidence, expressed the view that:

> In the rare cases [of murder trials] in which it is necessary to direct a jury by reference to foresight of consequences, I do not believe it is necessary for the judge to do more than invite the jury to consider two questions. First, was death or really serious injury in a murder case (or whatever relevant consequence must be proved to have been intended in any other case) a natural consequence of the defendant's voluntary act? Second, did the defendant foresee that consequence as being a natural consequence of his act? The jury should then be told that if they answer yes to both questions it is a proper inference for them to draw that he intended that consequence . . .

The difficulty with this was the use of the phrase 'natural consequence'. At best it might leave juries uncertain; at worst it might lead juries to think that evidence that a consequence was foreseen as more likely than not was a sufficient basis for inferring intent.

The House of Lords returned to the issue in *R v Hancock and Shankland* [1986] 1 AC 455, the notorious case of the striking miners dropping a concrete block onto a motorway in order to scare off those miners continuing to work during the strike. As a result of their actions a taxi-driver taking some miners to their jobs was killed. In the course of his speech Lord Scarman observed:

In my judgment . . . the Moloney guidelines as they stand are unsafe and misleading. They require a reference to probability. They also require an explanation that the greater the probability of a consequence the more likely it is that the consequence was foreseen and that if that consequence was foreseen the greater the probability is that that consequence was also intended. But juries also require to be reminded that the decision is theirs to be reached upon a consideration of all the evidence.

Even this approach still left juries with an apparently wide discretion as regards the proper basis from which to infer whether or not a defendant who had foreseen the consequences of his actions could properly be regarded as having intended them. It fell to the Court of Appeal, in *R v Nedrick* [1986] 1 WLR 1025, to attempt a greater degree of particularisation. Lord Lane CJ offered the following:

We have endeavoured to crystallise the effect of their Lordships' speeches in *R v Moloney* and *R v Hancock* in a way which we hope may be helpful to judges who have to handle this type of case . . .

When determining whether the defendant had the necessary intent, it may therefore be helpful for a jury to ask themselves two questions:

(1) How probable was the consequence which resulted from the defendant's voluntary act?
(2) Did he foresee that consequence?

If he did not appreciate that death or serious harm was likely to result from his act, he cannot have intended to bring it about. If he did, but thought that the risk to which he was exposing the person killed was only slight, then it may be easy for the jury to conclude that he did not intend to bring about that result. On the other hand, if the jury are satisfied that at the material time the defendant recognised that death or serious harm would be virtually certain (barring some unforeseen intervention) to result from his voluntary act, then that is a fact from which they may find it easy to infer that he intended to kill or do serious bodily harm, even though he may not have had any desire to achieve that result.

Where the charge is murder and in the rare cases where the simple direction is not enough, the jury should be directed that they are not entitled to infer the necessary intention, unless they feel sure that death or serious bodily harm was a virtual certainty (barring some unforeseen intervention) as a result of the defendant's actions and that the defendant appreciated that such was the case.

Where a man realises that it is for all practical purposes inevitable that his actions will result in death or serious harm, the inference may be irresistible that he intended that result, however little he may have desired or wished it to happen. The decision is one for the jury to be reached upon a consideration of all the evidence.

3.2.1 *MENS REA* – INTENTION: THE LEADING AUTHORITY

R v Woollin [1999] 1 AC 82 (HL)

Lord Steyn:

The case in a nutshell

The appellant lost his temper and threw his three month old son on to a hard surface. His son sustained a fractured skull and died. The appellant was charged with murder. The Crown did not contend that the appellant desired to kill his son or to cause him serious injury. The issue was whether the appellant nevertheless had the intention to cause serious harm. The appellant denied that he had any such intention. Subject to one qualification, the Recorder of Leeds summed up in accordance with the guidance given by Lord Lane, CJ in *Nedrick* . . . But towards the end of his summing-up the judge directed the jury that if they were satisfied that the appellant –

> must have realised and appreciated when he threw that child that there was a substantial risk that he would cause serious injury to it, then it would be open to you to find that he intended to cause injury to the child and you should convict him of murder.

The jury found that the appellant had the necessary intention; they rejected a defence of provocation; and they convicted the appellant of murder . . .

The Court of Appeal certified the following questions as of general importance:

1   In murder, where there is no direct evidence that the purpose of a defendant was to kill or to inflict serious injury on the victim, is it necessary to direct the jury that they may only infer an intent to do serious injury, if they are satisfied:
    (a) that serious bodily harm was a virtually certain consequence of the defendant's voluntary act, and
    (b) that the defendant appreciated that fact?
2   If the answer to question 1 is 'yes,' is such a direction necessary in all cases or is it only necessary in cases where the sole evidence of the defendant's intention is to be found in his actions and their consequence to the victim?

On appeal to your Lordships' House the terrain of the debate covered the correctness in law of the direction recommended by Lord Lane CJ in *Nedrick* and, if that direction is sound, whether it should be used only in the limited category of cases envisaged by the Court of Appeal. And counsel for the appellant renewed his submission that by directing the jury in terms of substantial risk the judge illegitimately widened the mental element of murder.

The directions of the judge on the mental element

. . . it is necessary to set out the judge's relevant directions of law with a brief explanation of the context and implications. The judge reminded the jury that the Crown did not allege an intention to kill. He accordingly concentrated on intention to do really serious bodily harm. He further reminded the jury that the Crown accepted that the defendant did not want to cause the child serious injuries. The judge then directed the jury as follows: In looking at this, you should ask yourselves two questions and I am going to suggest that you write them down. First of all, how probable was the consequence which resulted from his throw, the consequence being, as you know, serious injury? How probable was the consequence of serious injury which resulted from his throw? Secondly, did he foresee that consequence in the second before or at the time of throwing? The second question is of particular importance, members of the jury, because he could not have intended serious harm could he, if he did not foresee the consequence and did not appreciate at the time that serious harm might result from his throw? If he thought, or may have thought, that in throwing the child he was exposing him to only the slight risk of being injured, then you would probably readily conclude that he did not intend to cause serious injury, because it was outside his contemplation that he would be seriously injured. But the defence say here that he never thought about the consequence at all when he threw the child. He did not give it a moment's thought. Again, if that is right, or may be right, you may readily conclude that he did not appreciate that serious harm would result. *It follows from that, if that is how you find, that you cannot infer that he intended to do Karl really serious harm unless you are sure that serious harm was a virtual certainty from what he was doing and he appreciated that that was the case.* So, members of the jury, that is how you should approach this question – and it is a vital question in the case. Are we sure that the prosecution have established that the defendant intended to cause Karl serious harm at the time that he threw him? (My emphasis added.)

The first two questions identified by the judge appear in Lord Lane's guidance in *Nedrick* . . . The [emphasised] passage is a classic direction in accordance with *Nedrick* . . . After an overnight adjournment the judge continued his summing up. He returned to the mental element which had to be established in order to find the appellant guilty of murder. On this occasion the judge did not use the *Nedrick* direction. Instead the judge directed the jury as follows:

> If you think that he had not given any thought to the consequences of what he was doing before he did it, then the Crown would have failed to prove the necessary intent, the intent to cause really serious harm, for murder and you should acquit him of murder and convict him of manslaughter. If, on the other hand, you reject that interpretation and are quite satisfied that he was aware of what he was doing and must have realised and appreciated when he threw that child that there was a substantial risk that he would cause serious injury to it, then it would be open to you to find that he intended to cause injury to the child and you should convict him of murder.

It is plain, and the Crown accepts, that a direction posing an issue as to appreciation of a 'substantial risk' of causing serious injury is wider than a direction framed in terms of appreciation of a 'virtual certainty (barring some unforeseen intervention)'. If Lord Lane correctly stated the law in *Nedrick*, the judge's direction in terms of substantial risk was wrong. But the Crown argued . . . that *Nedrick* was wrongly decided or, alternatively, that the principle as enunciated by Lord Lane does not apply to the present case.

The premises of the appeal
The first premise of any examination of the issues raised by this appeal is that it is at present settled law that a defendant may be convicted of murder if it is established (1) that he had an intent to kill or (2) that he had an intent to cause really serious bodily injury: *R v Cunningham* [1982] AC 566. In regard to (2) the intent does not correspond to the harm which resulted, ie, the causing of death. It is a species of constructive crime . . . Secondly, I approach the issues arising on this appeal on the basis that it does not follow that 'intent' necessarily has precisely the same meaning in every context in the criminal law. The focus of the present appeal is the crime of murder.

The problem facing the Court of Appeal in Nedrick
In *Hancock* Lord Scarman did not express disagreement with the test of foresight of a probability which is 'little short of overwhelming' as enunciated in *Moloney*. Lord Scarman also did not

express disagreement with the law underlying Lord Lane's model direction in Hancock which was based on a defendant having 'appreciated that what he did was highly likely to cause death or really serious bodily injury'. Lord Scarman merely said that model directions were generally undesirable. Moreover, Lord Scarman thought that where explanation is required the jury should be directed as to the relevance of probability without expressly stating the matter in terms of any particular level of probability. The manner in which trial judges were to direct juries was left unclear. Moreover, in practice juries sometimes ask probing questions which cannot easily be ignored by trial judges. For example, imagine that in a case such as *Hancock* the jury sent a note to the judge to the following effect:

> We are satisfied that the defendant, though he did not want to cause serious harm, knew that it was probable that his act would cause serious bodily harm. We are not sure whether a probability is enough for murder. Please explain.

One may alter the question by substituting 'highly probable' for 'probable'. Or one may imagine the jury asking whether a foresight of a 'substantial risk' that the defendant's act would cause serious injury was enough. What is the judge to say to the jury? *Hancock* does not rule out an answer by the judge but it certainly does not explain how such questions are to be answered. It is well known that judges were sometimes advised to deflect such questions by the statement that 'intention' is an ordinary word in the English language. That is surely an unhelpful response to what may be a sensible question. In these circumstances it is not altogether surprising that in *Nedrick* the Court of Appeal felt compelled to provide a model direction for the assistance of trial judges . . .

The direct attack on Nedrick
It is now possible to consider the Crown's direct challenge to the correctness of *Nedrick*. First, the Crown argued that *Nedrick* prevents the jury from considering all the evidence in the case relevant to intention. The argument is that this is contrary to the provisions of s 8 of the Criminal Justice Act 1967 [set out above] . . .

Paragraph (a) [of s 8] is an instruction to the judge and is not relevant to the issues on this appeal. The Crown's argument relied on paragraph (b) which is concerned with the function of the jury. It is no more than a legislative instruction that in considering their findings on intention or foresight the jury must take into account all relevant evidence . . . *Nedrick* does not prevent a jury from considering all the evidence: it merely stated what state of mind (in the absence of a purpose to kill or to cause serious harm) is sufficient for murder. I would therefore reject the Crown's first argument.

In the second place the Crown submitted that *Nedrick* is in conflict with the decision of the House in *Hancock*. Counsel argued that in order 'to bring some coherence to the process of determining intention Lord Lane specified a minimum level of foresight, namely virtual certainty'. But that is not in conflict with the decision in *Hancock* which, apart from disapproving Lord Bridge's 'natural consequence' model direction, approved *Moloney* in all other respects. And in *Moloney* Lord Bridge said that if a person foresees the probability of a consequence as little short of overwhelming, this 'will suffice to establish the necessary intent'. Nor did the House in *Hancock* rule out the framing of model directions by the Court of Appeal for the assistance of trial judges. I would therefore reject the argument that the guidance given in *Nedrick* was in conflict with the decision of the House in *Hancock*.

The Crown did not argue that as a matter of policy foresight of a virtual certainty is too narrow a test in murder. Subject to minor qualifications, the decision in *Nedrick* was widely welcomed by distinguished academic writers . . . It is also of interest that it is very similar to the threshold of being aware 'that it will occur in the ordinary course of events' in the Law Commission's draft Criminal Code . . . Moreover, over a period of twelve years since *Nedrick* the test of foresight of virtual certainty has apparently caused no practical difficulties. It is simple and clear. It is true that it may exclude a conviction of murder in the often cited terrorist example where a member of the bomb disposal team is killed. In such a case it may realistically be said that the terrorist did not foresee the killing of a member of the bomb disposal team as a virtual certainty. That may be a consequence of not framing the principle in terms of risk taking. Such cases ought to cause no substantial difficulty since immediately below murder there is available a verdict of manslaughter which may attract in the discretion of the court a life sentence. In any event, as Lord Lane eloquently argued in a debate in the House of Lords, to frame a principle for particular difficulties regarding terrorism 'would produce corresponding injustices which would be very hard to eradicate': Hansard (HL Debates), 6 November 1989, col 480. I am satisfied that the *Nedrick* test, which was squarely based on the decision of the House in *Moloney*, is pitched at the right level of foresight.

The argument that Nedrick has limited application

The Court of Appeal held that the phrase 'a virtual certainty' should be confined to cases where the evidence of intent is limited to admitted actions of the accused and the consequences of those actions. It is not obligatory where there is other evidence to consider. The Crown's alternative submission on the appeal was to the same effect. This distinction would introduce yet another complication into a branch of the criminal law where simplicity is of supreme importance. The distinction is dependent on the vagaries of the evidence in particular cases. Moreover, a jury may reject the other evidence to which the Court of Appeal refers. And in preparing his summing-up a judge could not ignore this possibility. If the Court of Appeal's view is right, it might compel a judge to pose different tests depending on what evidence the jury accepts. For my part, and with the greatest respect, I have to say that this distinction would be likely to produce great practical difficulties. But, most importantly, the distinction is not based on any principled view regarding the mental element in murder. Contrary to the view of the Court of Appeal, I would also hold that s 8(b) of the Act of 1967 does not compel such a result.

In my view the ruling of the Court of Appeal was wrong. It may be appropriate to give a direction in accordance with *Nedrick* in any case in which the defendant may not have desired the result of his act. But I accept the trial judge is best placed to decide what direction is required by the circumstances of the case.

The disposal of the present appeal

It follows that the judge should not have departed from the *Nedrick* direction. By using the phrase 'substantial risk' the judge blurred the line between intention and recklessness, and hence between murder and manslaughter. The misdirection enlarged the scope of the mental element required for murder. It was a material misdirection. At one stage it was argued that the earlier correct direction 'cured' the subsequent incorrect direction. A misdirection cannot by any means always be cured by the fact that the judge at an earlier or later stage gave a correct direction. After all, how is a jury to choose between a correct and an incorrect direction on a point of law? If a misdirection is to be corrected, it must be done in the plainest terms . . .

That is, however, not the end of the matter. For my part, I have given anxious consideration to the observation of the Court of Appeal that, if the judge had used the phrase 'a virtual certainty', the verdict would have been the same. In this case there was no suggestion of any other ill-treatment of the child. It would also be putting matters too high to say that on the evidence before the jury it was an open-and-shut case of murder rather than manslaughter. In my view the conviction of murder is unsafe. The conviction of murder must be quashed.

The status of Nedrick

In my view Lord Lane's judgment in *Nedrick* provided valuable assistance to trial judges. The model direction is by now a tried-and-tested formula. Trial judges ought to continue to use it. On matters of detail I have three observations, which can best be understood if I set out again the relevant part of Lord Lane's judgment. It was as follows:

> (A) When determining whether the defendant had the necessary intent, it may therefore be helpful for a jury to ask themselves two questions. (1) How probable was the consequence which resulted from the defendant's voluntary act? (2) Did he foresee that consequence? If he did not appreciate that death or serious harm was likely to result from his act, he cannot have intended to bring it about. If he did, but thought that the risk to which he was exposing the person killed was only slight, then it may be easy for the jury to conclude that he did not intend to bring about that result. On the other hand, if the jury are satisfied that at the material time the defendant recognised that death or serious harm would be virtually certain (barring some unforeseen intervention) to result from his voluntary act, then that is a fact from which they may find it easy to infer that he intended to kill or do serious bodily harm, even though he may not have had any desire to achieve that result. (B) Where the charge is murder and in the rare cases where the simple direction is not enough, the jury should be directed that they are not entitled to infer the necessary intention, unless they feel sure that death or serious bodily harm was a virtual certainty (barring some unforeseen intervention) as a result of the defendant's actions and that the defendant appreciated that such was the case. (C) Where a man realises that it is for all practical purposes inevitable that his actions will result in death or serious harm, the inference may be irresistible that he intended that result, however little he may have desired or wished it to happen. The decision is one for the jury to be reached upon a consideration of all the evidence. (Lettering added.)

First, I am persuaded by the speech of my noble and learned friend, Lord Hope of Craighead, that it is unlikely, if ever, to be helpful to direct the jury in terms of the two questions set out in (A). I agree that these questions may detract from the clarity of the critical direction in (B). Secondly, in their writings previously cited Glanville Williams, JC Smith and Andrew Ashworth observed that the use of the words 'to infer' in (B) may detract from the clarity of the model direction. I agree. I would substitute the words 'to find'. Thirdly, the first sentence of (C) does not form part of the model direction. But it would always be right for the judge to say, as Lord Lane put it, that the decision is for the jury upon a consideration of all the evidence in the case.

The certified questions

Given my conclusions the certified questions fall away.

R v Matthews; R v Alleyne [2003] 2 Cr App R 30

The defendants took the victim to a bridge over the River Ouse and threw him into the water. The victim could not swim and drowned as a result. The defendants were charged with murder. When directing the jury on the issue of intent, the trial judge stated:

With regard to intention to kill the prosecution will only succeed in proving . . . intent either: (i) by making you sure that this specific intention was actually in the mind/s of the defendants; or (ii) (a) by making you sure that [the deceased's death] was a virtual certainty (barring some attempt to save him), and (b) the defendant . . . had appreciated at the time that [the deceased] was thrown off the bridge that that was the case, and he then had no intentions of saving him, and knew or realised that the others did not intend to save him either.

The defendants were convicted and appealed against their convictions on the grounds that the trial judge had misdirected the jury on the issue of intent.

Rix LJ [Having referred to the trial judge's direction on intention]:
The classic form of that direction, repeated in the JSB model direction, is as follows:

> Where the charge is murder and in the rare cases where the simple direction is not enough, the jury should be directed that they are not entitled to find the necessary intention, unless they feel sure that death [or serious bodily harm] was a virtual certainty (barring some unforeseen intervention) as a result of the defendant's actions and that the defendant appreciated that such was the case.
>
> . . .

[24] We have emphasised the word find in that direction, because the original direction of Lord Lane CJ in *Nedrick* [1986] 3 All ER 2, [1986] 1 WLR 1025 contained the word 'infer'. The only change made by the House of Lords in *Woollin* [1999] AC 82, [1998] 4 All ER 103, was to substitute find for infer (see Lord Steyn at 96H of the former report and Lord Hope of Craighead at 97D of the former report).

. . .

[39] Mr Coker for the Crown on this appeal submits that in Woollin the House of Lords has finally moved away from a rule of evidence to a rule of substantive law. In this connection he drew attention to a sentence in Lord Steyn's speech at 93F where he says, immediately after setting out Lord Lane's observations in *Nedrick*, that:

> 'The effect of the critical direction is that a result foreseen as virtually certain is an intended result.'

[40] He also relies on what Professor Sir John Smith has to say in his note on *Woollin* [1998] Crim LR 890 and in Smith & Hogan, *Criminal Law*, 10th edition, at 70ff. Thus in the former, Professor Smith said this:

> A jury might still fairly ask 'We are all quite sure that D knew that it was virtually certain that his act would cause death. You tell us we are entitled to find that he intended it. Are we bound to find that? Some of us want to and some do not. How should we decide?' The implication appears to be that, even now, they are not so bound. But why not? At one point Lord Steyn says of *Nedrick* 'The effect of the critical direction is that a result foreseen as virtually certain is an intended result.' If that is right, the only question for the jury is, 'Did the defendant foresee the result as virtually certain?' If he did, he intended it. That, it is submitted is what the law should be; and it now seems that we have at last moved substantially in that direction. The *Nedrick* formula, however, even as modified ('entitled to find'), involves some ambiguity with the hint of the existence of some ineffable, undefinable notion of intent, locked in the breasts of the jurors.

[41] Moreover, in the latter treatise (at 72) Professor Smith cites Lord Lane speaking in the debate on the report of the House of Lords Select Committee on Murder (HL Paper, 78-I, 1989) as follows:

> . . . in *Nedrick* the court was obliged to phrase matters as it did because of earlier decisions in your Lordships' House by which it was bound. We had to tread very gingerly indeed in order not to tread on your Lordships' toes. As a result, *Nedrick* was not as clear as it should have been. However, I agree with the conclusions of the committee that 'intention' should be defined in the terms set out in paragraph 195 of the report on page 50. That seems to me to express clearly what in *Nedrick* we failed properly to explain.

[42] The definition referred to, as Smith & Hogan goes on to explain, is that stated in cl 18(b) of the Draft Code (itself referred to by Lord Steyn in *Woollin* [1999] AC 82, [1998] 4 All ER 103) as follows:

> A person acts 'intentionally' with respect to . . . a result when he acts either in order to bring it about or being aware that it will occur in the ordinary course of events.

[43] In our judgment, however, the law has not yet reached a definition of intent in murder in terms of appreciation of a virtual certainty. Lord Lane was speaking not of what was decided in *Nedrick* [1986] 3 All ER 2, [1986] 1 WLR 1025 (or in the other cases which preceded it) nor of what was thereafter to be decided in *Woollin* [1999] AC 82, [1998] 4 All ER 103 but of what the law in his opinion should be, as represented by the cl 18(b) definition. Similarly, although the law has progressively moved closer to what Professor Smith has been advocating (see his commentaries in the Criminal Law Review on the various cases discussed above), we do not regard Woollin as yet reaching or laying down a substantive rule of law. On the contrary, it is clear from the discussion in *Woollin* as a whole that *Nedrick* was derived from the existing law, at that time ending in *Moloney* [1985] AC 905, [1985] 1 All ER 1025 and *Hancock* [1986] 1 AC 455, [1986] 1 All ER 641, and that the critical direction in *Nedrick* was approved, subject to the change of one word.

[44] In these circumstances we think that the judge did go further than the law as it stands at present permitted him to go in redrafting the *Nedrick/Woollin* direction into a form where, as Mr Coker accepts (although we have some doubt about this), the jury were directed to find the necessary intent proved provided they were satisfied in the case of any defendant that there was appreciation of the virtual certainty of death. This is to be contrasted with the form of the approved direction which is in terms of 'not entitled to find the necessary intention, unless. . . .'

[45] Having said that, however, we think that, once what is required is an appreciation of virtual certainty of death, and not some lesser foresight of merely probable consequences, there is very little to choose between a rule of evidence and one of substantive law. It is probably this thought that led Lord Steyn to say that a result foreseen as virtually certain is an intended result. Lord Bridge had reflected the same thought when he had said, in *Moloney* at 920C of the former report, that if the defendant there had had present to his mind, when he pulled the trigger, that his gun was pointing at his stepfather's head at a distance of six feet and 'its inevitable consequence', then:

> the inference was inescapable, using words in their ordinary, everyday meaning, that he intended to kill his stepfather.

Lord Lane had also spoken in *Nedrick* of an irresistible inference.

. . .

[56] It was submitted that the judge should have directed the jury on the distinction between recklessness and the *Nedrick/Woollin* formula. However, there is no support at all in *Woollin* [1999] AC 82, [1998] 4 All ER 103, for such an additional direction. On the contrary: in *Nedrick* [1986] 3 All ER 2, [1986] 1 WLR 1025 Lord Lane had pointed up the distinction between a defendant who foresees death or serious injury but thinks that the risk is slight with the defendant who foresees death or serious injury as a virtual certainty: see the passage from Lord Lane's judgment marked as '(A)' in Lord Steyn's speech in *Woollin* [1999] AC 82, [1998] 4 All ER 103, at pp 96C/D of the former report. But Lord Steyn said that that passage should not be used, as it may detract from the clarity of the 'critical direction' (at 96G of the former report); and Lord Hope spoke to similar effect (at 97E of the former report). Under that critical direction the jury are told that they have to be sure that a defendant 'appreciated' that death or serious injury was a virtual certainty. That excludes the case of true recklessness, where the defendant does not consider consequences at all. We agree with Mr Coker's submission that a direction about recklessness was unnecessary and would have been confusing.

 COMMENTS AND QUESTIONS

1   What is the difference between inferring intention and finding intention? Is intention conceptually different from foresight?

2   What is to be made of Lord Steyn's observation that he approached the issues arising on the appeal 'on the basis that it does not follow that "intent" necessarily has precisely the same meaning in every context in the criminal law'? Does he mean that some offences require 'purpose' type intent? Or does he mean that intent might have a different meaning when used, for example, in the context of offences against the person? Is it conceivable that intent, in the context of intention to do grievous bodily harm contrary to s 18 of the Offences Against the Person Act 1861 (see further Chapter 5), would have a different meaning to that enunciated in *Woollin*? Given that intent to do grievous bodily harm will suffice for murder, this (one hopes) seems unlikely.

3   Why are the courts so reluctant to accept that the *Nedrick/Woollin* direction amounts to a definition of intent?

3.2.2 CODIFICATION AND LAW REFORM PROPOSALS

A proposed codification of intention can be found in clause 18(b) of the draft Criminal Code Bill (DCCB). The Law Commission subsequently published its proposals for reform of offences against the person (not including homicide) in *Offences Against the Person and General Principles* (Law Com 218). The draft Criminal Law Bill (DCLB) attached to that report provided for a somewhat amended definition of intention in clause 1. The most recent reform proposals are to be found in the draft Bill attached to the Home Office consultation paper *Violence: Reforming the Offences Against the Person Act 1861*, published in February 1998.

Clause 14 of the Home Office Bill proposes the following:

14(1) A person acts intentionally with respect to a result if –
   (a)   it is his purpose to cause it, or

> (b)   although it is not his purpose to cause it, he knows that it would occur in the ordinary
>   course of events if he were to succeed in his purpose of causing some other result.
>
> . . .
>
> (3)   A person intends an omission to have a result if –
>   (a)   it is his purpose that the result will occur, or
>   (b)   although it is not his purpose that the result will occur, he knows that it would occur in the
>   ordinary course of events if he were to succeed in his purpose that some other result will
>   occur.

Note that this proposed definition would only apply for the purposes of the Bill, hence it raises the prospect of intention having a different meaning in respect of other offences such as murder or criminal damage. This is clearly not a satisfactory state of affairs. If the *mens rea* for murder were to remain as 'intention to cause serious harm' it would be absurd if intent had one meaning in the context of murder, and another where the offence charged was intentionally causing serious harm under the proposed Bill.

3.3 *MENS REA* – RECKLESSNESS

A few criminal offences, such as murder, require proof of nothing less than intent. For the vast majority of criminal offences where *mens rea* has to be established, however, intention or recklessness will suffice. What meaning then is to be attributed to the term 'reckless'? On the one hand it can be seen as a fault element that justifies conviction notwithstanding that the defendant foresaw a prohibited consequence as something less than a virtually certain consequence of his act or omission – for example where the defendant foresaw that a certain harm might result. As will be seen from the extracts that follow, however, the debate in recent years has centred around the extent to which a defendant could be described as reckless notwithstanding the fact that he has not realised the risk of harm that could result from his act or omission.

Prior to the House of Lords' ruling in *Commissioner of Police of the Metropolis v Caldwell* [1982] AC 341, the accepted meaning of recklessness was that it required proof that the defendant had been aware of a more than negligible risk that a prohibited consequence would occur and had nevertheless gone on to take that risk. The decision in *Caldwell*, although effectively confined in its ambit to the offence of criminal damage under the Criminal Damage Act 1971, upset that orthodoxy by holding that, as an alternative, a defendant could be reckless if he created a risk of criminal damage that would have been obvious to the reasonable prudent adult bystander (even though not obvious to the defendant himself) and went on to take that risk. *Caldwell* recklessness was a significant departure from the subjective approach to *mens rea* in that it did not require any proof that the defendant had foreseen the risk of harm. The rule operated particularly harshly in cases involving young offenders where there was evidence that they had not possessed the intelligence to appreciate the dangerousness of their actions; see for example *Elliot v C* [1983] 1 WLR 939. What was the point of imposing liability on a defendant who would not have been aware of the 'obvious risk' even if he or she had stopped to consider the risks involved? It was never clear how the imposition of *Caldwell* recklessness was supposed to model a prospective defendant's behaviour.

3.3.1 SUBJECTIVE RECKLESSNESS

Although the Court of Appeal's decision in R v Cunningham (below) deals with an offence where the fault element was described in the relevant statute as 'maliciously', the case is the leading modern authority on the subjective nature of recklessness.

R v Cunningham [1957] 2 QB 396 (CA)

Byrne J:

The appellant was convicted at Leeds Assizes upon an indictment framed under s 23 of the Offences Against the Person Act 1861, which charged that he unlawfully and maliciously caused to be taken by Sarah Wade a certain noxious thing, namely, coal gas, so as thereby to endanger the life of the said Sarah Wade . . .

The facts were not really in dispute, and in a statement to a police officer the appellant said: 'All right, I will tell you. I was short of money, I had been off work for three days, I got eight shillings from the gas meter. I tore it off the wall and threw it away.' Although there was a stop tap within two feet of the meter the appellant did not turn off the gas, with the result that a very considerable volume of gas escaped, some of which seeped through the wall of the cellar and partially asphyxiated Mrs Wade, who was asleep in her bedroom next door, with the result that her life was endangered.

. . . The act of the appellant was clearly unlawful and therefore the real question for the jury was whether it was also malicious within the meaning of s 23 of the Offences Against the Person Act 1861 . . .

With the utmost respect to the learned judge, we think it is incorrect to say that the word 'malicious' in a statutory offence merely means wicked. We think the judge was, in effect, telling the jury that if they were satisfied that the appellant acted wickedly – and he had clearly acted wickedly in stealing the gas meter and its contents – they ought to find that he had acted maliciously in causing the gas to be taken by Mrs Wade so as thereby to endanger her life.

In our view it should have been left to the jury to decide whether, even if the appellant did not intend the injury to Mrs Wade, he foresaw that the removal of the gas meter might cause injury to someone but nevertheless removed it. We are unable to say that a reasonable jury, properly directed as to the meaning of the word 'maliciously' in the context of s 23, would without doubt have convicted.

R v G [2003] 4 All ER 765

Two boys started a fire in a refuse bin. The fire spread and caused extensive damage to some nearby shops. The boys were convicted of criminal damage on the basis that they had been reckless as to whether property would be damaged. The trial judge, following *Commissioner of Police of the Metropolis v Caldwell* [1982] AC 341, had rejected a submission that the direction to the jury regarding recklessness should reflect the fact that the defendants had been aged 11 and 12 at the time of the offence. The Court of Appeal upheld the conviction, regarding itself as bound by Caldwell and the following point of law was certified for consideration by the House of Lords:

Can a defendant properly be convicted under section 1 of the Criminal Damage Act 1971 on the basis that he was reckless as to whether property was destroyed or damaged when he gave no thought to the risk but, by reason of his age and/or personal characteristics the risk would not have been obvious to him, even if he had thought about it?

Lord Bingham:
The task confronting the House in this appeal is, first of all, one of statutory construction: what did Parliament mean when it used the word 'reckless' in section 1(1) and (2) of the 1971 Act? In so expressing the question I mean to make it as plain as I can that I am not addressing the meaning of 'reckless' in any other statutory or common law context . . .

. . . Since a statute is always speaking, the context or application of a statutory expression may change over time, but the meaning of the expression itself cannot change. So the starting point is to ascertain what Parliament meant by 'reckless' in 1971 . . . section 1 [of the 1971 Act] as enacted followed . . . the draft proposed by the Law Commission. It cannot be supposed that by 'reckless' Parliament meant anything different from the Law Commission. The Law Commission's meaning was made plain both in its Report . . . These materials . . . reveal a very plain intention to replace the old-fashioned and misleading expression 'maliciously' by the more familiar expression 'reckless' but to give the latter expression the meaning which R v Cunningham [1957] 2 QB 396 and Professor Kenny had given to the former. In treating this authority as irrelevant to the construction of 'reckless' the majority [in Caldwell] fell into understandable but clearly demonstrable error. No relevant change in the mens rea necessary for proof of the offence was intended, and in holding otherwise the majority misconstrued section 1 of the Act.

That conclusion is by no means determinative of this appeal. For the decision in R v Caldwell was made more than 20 years ago . . . Invitations to reconsider that reasoning have been rejected. The principles laid down have been applied on many occasions, by Crown Court judges and, even more frequently, by justices. In the submission of the Crown, the ruling of the House works well and causes no injustice in practice. If Parliament had wished to give effect to the intention of the Law Commission it has had many opportunities, which it has not taken, to do so. Despite its power under Practice Statement (Judicial Precedent) [1966] 1 WLR 1234 to depart from its earlier decisions, the House should be very slow to do so, not least in a context such as this.

These are formidable arguments . . . But I am persuaded by Mr Newman QC for the appellants that they should be rejected. I reach this conclusion for four reasons, taken together.

First, it is a salutary principle that conviction of serious crime should depend on proof not simply that the defendant caused (by act or omission) an injurious result to another but that his state of mind when so acting was culpable. This, after all, is the meaning of the familiar rule actus non facit reum nisi mens sit rea. The most obviously culpable state of mind is no doubt an intention to cause the injurious result, but knowing disregard of an appreciated and unacceptable risk of causing an injurious result or a deliberate closing of the mind to such risk would be readily accepted as culpable also. It is clearly blameworthy to take an obvious and significant risk of causing injury to another. But it is not clearly blameworthy to do something involving a risk of injury to another if . . . one genuinely does not perceive the risk. Such a person may fairly be accused of stupidity or lack of imagination, but neither of those failings should expose him to conviction of serious crime or the risk of punishment.

Secondly, the present case shows, more clearly than any other reported case since R v Caldwell, that the model direction formulated by Lord Diplock is capable of leading to obvious unfairness . . . it is evident that [the trial judge's direction based on the objective approach to recklessness espoused in *Caldwell*] . . . offended the jury's sense of fairness. The sense of fairness of 12 representative citizens sitting as a jury (or of a smaller group of lay justices sitting as a bench of magistrates) is the bedrock on which the administration of criminal justice in this country is built. A law which runs counter to that sense must cause concern. Here, the appellants could have been charged under section 1(1) with recklessly damaging one or both of the wheelie-bins, and they would have had little defence. As it was, jury might have inferred that boys of the appellants' age would have appreciated the risk to the building of what they did, but it seems clear that such was not their conclusion (nor, it would appear, the judge's either). On that basis the jury thought it unfair to convict them. I share their sense of unease. It is neither moral nor just to convict a defendant (least of all a child) on the strength of what someone else would have apprehended if the defendant himself had no such apprehension. Nor, the defendant having been convicted, is the problem cured by imposition of a nominal penalty.

Thirdly, I do not think the criticism of *R v Caldwell* expressed by academics, judges and practitioners should be ignored. A decision is not, of course, to be overruled or departed from simply because it meets with disfavour in the learned journals. But a decision which attracts reasoned and outspoken criticism by the leading scholars of the day, respected as authorities in the field, must command attention . . .

Fourthly, the majority's interpretation [in *Caldwell*] of 'recklessly' in section 1 of the 1971 Act was, as already shown, a misinterpretation. If it were a misinterpretation that offended no principle and gave rise to no injustice there would be strong grounds for adhering to the misinterpretation and leaving Parliament to correct it if it chose. But this misinterpretation is offensive to principle and is apt to cause injustice. That being so, the need to correct the misinterpretation is compelling.

. . . In the course of argument before the House it was suggested that the rule in *R v Caldwell* might be modified, in cases involving children, by requiring comparison not with normal reasonable adults but with normal reasonable children of the same age. This is a suggestion with some attractions but it is open to four compelling objections. First, even this modification would offend the principle that conviction should depend on proving the state of mind of the individual defendant to be culpable.

Second, if the rule were modified in relation to children on grounds of their immaturity it would be anomalous if it were not also modified in relation to the mentally handicapped on grounds of their limited understanding. Third, any modification along these lines would open the door to difficult and contentious argument concerning the qualities and characteristics to be taken into account for purposes of the comparison. Fourth, to adopt this modification would be to substitute one misinterpretation of section 1 for another. There is no warrant in the Act or in the travaux préparatoires which preceded it for such an interpretation.

A further refinement, advanced by Professor Glanville Williams in his article 'Recklessness Redefined' (1981) 40 CLJ 252, 270–271, adopted by the justices in *Elliott v C* [1983] 1 WLR 939 and commented upon by Robert Goff LJ in that case is that a defendant should only be regarded as having acted recklessly by virtue of his failure to give any thought to an obvious risk that property would be destroyed or damaged, where such risk would have been obvious to him if he had given any thought to the matter.

This refinement also has attractions, although it does not meet the objection of principle and does not represent a correct interpretation of the section. It is, in my opinion, open to the further objection of over-complicating the task of the jury (or bench of justices). It is one thing to decide whether a defendant can be believed when he says that the thought of a given risk never crossed his mind. It is another, and much more speculative, task to decide whether the risk would have been obvious to him if the thought had crossed his mind. The simpler the jury's task, the more likely is its verdict to be reliable . . . I cannot accept that restoration of the law as understood before *R v Caldwell* would lead to the acquittal of those whom public policy would require to be convicted. There is nothing to suggest that this was seen as a problem before *R v Caldwell* . . . There is no reason to doubt the common sense which tribunals of fact bring to their task. In a contested case based on intention, the defendant rarely admits intending the injurious result in question, but the tribunal of fact will readily infer such an intention, in a proper case, from all the circumstances and probabilities and evidence of what the defendant did and said at the time. Similarly with recklessness: it is not to be supposed that the tribunal of fact will accept a defendant's assertion that he never thought of a certain risk when all the circumstances and probabilities and evidence of what he did and said at the time show that he did or must have done.

. . . For the reasons I have given I would allow this appeal and quash the appellants' convictions. I would answer the certified question obliquely, basing myself on clause 18(c) of the Criminal Code Bill annexed by the Law Commission to its Report 'A Criminal Code for England and Wales Volume 1: Report and Draft Criminal Code Bill' (Law Com No 177, April 1989):

A person acts recklessly within the meaning of section 1 of the Criminal Damage Act 1971 with respect to –

(i)   a circumstance when he is aware of a risk that it exists or will exist;
(ii) a result when he is aware of a risk that it will occur;

and it is, in the circumstances known to him, unreasonable to take the risk.

Lord Steyn:
In my view the very high threshold for departing from a previous decision of the House has been satisfied in this particular case. In summary I would reduce my reasons to three propositions. First, in *Caldwell* the majority should have accepted without equivocation that before the passing of the 1971 Act foresight of consequences was an essential element in recklessness in the context of damage to property under section 51 of the Malicious Damage Act 1861. Secondly, the matrix of the immediately preceding Law Commission recommendations shows convincingly that the purpose of section 1 of the 1971 Act was to replace the out of date language of 'maliciously' causing damage by more modern language while not changing the substance of the mental element in any way. Foresight of consequences was to remain an ingredient of recklessness in regard to damage to property. Thirdly, experience has shown that by bringing within the reach of section 1(1) cases of inadvertent recklessness the decision in *Caldwell* became a source of serious potential injustice which cannot possibly be justified on policy grounds. These three propositions require some explanation.

. . . In the case before the House the two boys were 11 and 12 respectively. Their escapade of camping overnight without their parents' permission was something that many children have undertaken. But by throwing lit newspapers under a plastic wheelie bin they caused £1m of damage to a shop. It is, however, an agreed fact on this appeal that the boys thought there was no risk of the fire spreading in the way it eventually did. What happened at trial is highly significant. The jury were perplexed by the *Caldwell* directions which compelled them to treat the boys as adults and to convict them. The judge plainly thought this approach was contrary to common sense but loyally applied the law as laid down in *Caldwell*. The view of the jurors and the judge would be widely shared by reasonable people who pause to consider the matter. The only answer of the Crown is that where unjust convictions occur the judge can impose a lenient sentence. This will not do in a modern criminal justice system. Parliament certainly did not authorise such a cynical strategy.

Ignoring the special position of children in the criminal justice system is not acceptable in a modern civil society . . . The accepted meaning of recklessness involved foresight of consequences. This subjective state of mind is to be inferred 'by reference to all the evidence, drawing such inferences from the evidence as appear proper in the circumstances' . . . That is what Parliament intended by implementing the Law Commission proposals.

This interpretation of section 1 of the 1971 Act would fit in with the general tendency in modern times of our criminal law. The shift is towards adopting a subjective approach. It is generally necessary to look at the matter in the light of how it would have appeared to the defendant.

. . . The surest test of a new legal rule is not whether it satisfies a team of logicians but how it performs in the real world. With the benefit of hindsight the verdict must be that the rule laid down by the majority in *Caldwell* failed this test. It was severely criticised by academic lawyers of distinction. It did not command respect among practitioners and judges. Jurors found it difficult to understand: it also sometimes offended their sense of justice. Experience suggests that in *Caldwell* the law took a wrong turn.

That brings me to the question whether the subjective interpretation of recklessness might allow wrongdoers who ought to be convicted of serious crime to escape conviction. Experience before Caldwell did not warrant such a conclusion. In any event, as Lord Edmund-Davies explained, if a defendant closes his mind to a risk he must realise that there is a risk and, on the evidence, that will usually be decisive: 358D. One can trust the realism of trial judges, who direct juries, to guide juries to sensible verdicts and juries can in turn be relied on to apply robust common sense to the evaluation of ridiculous defences. Moreover, the endorsement by Parliament of the Law Commission proposals could not seriously have been regarded as a charter for the acquittal of wrongdoers.

In my view the case for departing from Caldwell has been shown to be irresistible.

'Caldwell Recklessness is Dead, Long Live Mens rea's Fecklessness': *Kumaralingam Amirthalingam* (2004) MLR 491

R v G's restoration of recklessness to its subjective roots may have been justified on the facts but the doctrine of *mens rea* itself needs to be restored to its normative roots of attributing blameworthiness. By emphasising blameworthiness and the community's sense of fairness but juxtaposing that with subjective *mens rea R v G* was a wrong step in the right direction . . . A modified objective test for children, where the question would be whether a reasonable person of similar age would have considered the risk to be an obvious one, was considered and rejected. The rejection of this approach is questionable given that the courts have recognised that the reasonable person may be modified in the case of professionals or experts. Lord Steyn referred to the Convention on the Rights of the Child and held that it provided a compelling argument to reject *Caldwell*, as the Convention required a child's age to be taken into account in an objective sense. The considerable experience of the tort of negligence suggests that such modifications are not only permissible but necessary.

A 'subjectivised' form of inadvertence, suggested by Glanville Williams, whereby an accused could be held reckless if the risk would have been obvious to the accused had he or she – and not the reasonable person – given any thought to the matter was also rejected. In Lord Bingham's view, juries could decide whether a defendant possessed the requisite *mens rea*, but it would be too speculative for a jury to decide whether a defendant would have considered the risk to be obvious if he or she had thought about the risk. Be that as it may the proper question in any case is not whether the defendant would have considered the risk but whether the defendant, having chosen to act in that way, should have considered the risk. This is a normative question that determines whether the *mens* was *rea* and juries are eminently capable of making such decisions.

. . . Even if one does not accept the moral blameworthiness thesis and adopts Hart's view that *mens rea* is merely about ensuring that the accused had a fair opportunity to exercise his or her physical and mental capacities to avoid infringing the law, a similar conclusion as to inadvertence is reached . . . Criminal fault is a composite of subjective and objective elements. Orthodox theory however insists on an artificial bifurcation and the inquiry into blameworthiness is hijacked by the futile exercise of labelling fault as subjective or objective. *R v C* regretfully preserves this unhelpful predilection.

. . . A subjective test is necessary to establish the existence of a relevant mental state – the '*mens*'. This ensures individual responsibility; it takes into account the accused's personal capacity so it cannot be said that the accused him or herself did not have a fair opportunity to avoid criminal liability. It is only in determining the blameworthiness of the accused's mental state – the '*rea*' – that some objectivity is necessary. This approach still honours the goal of subjectivism, as it is the accused's mental state that is at issue; unlike liability for negligence, where it is purely the accused's conduct that is at issue. Expanding negligence is not appropriate because it does not reflect the 'evil mind' that is the touchstone of criminal liability and that which distinguishes it from civil liability.

The House of Lords in *R v G* was willing to overturn an established, time tested authority in order to nurture a criminal law doctrine of fault that fairly attributes blameworthiness to the accused and accords with the community's sense of fairness and justice. On the facts, the purely subjective approach to *mens rea* was apposite, but it would be a mistake to pretend that a purely subjective doctrine is the salve to our *mens rea* woes. Lord Rodger of Earlsferry acknowledged this in his opinion where he expressed the view that Lord Diplock's broader concept of recklessness, encompassing an objective element was not undesirable in terms of legal policy; and further, held that inadvertence need not necessarily be excluded from recklessness. This observation is especially relevant to recklessness in the context of sexual offences.

. . . In a civil society there should be certain minimum duties of citizenship and every individual should have a responsibility to advert to relevant risks when actively engaging in certain conduct. Failure to live up to that can fairly be labelled culpable. This is not an objective test in the sense of ignoring the accused and asking what the reasonable person would have foreseen. The focus remains on the accused and the question is simply whether his or her mind should have been attuned to the risk.

COMMENTS AND QUESTIONS

1 Following the decision in *Caldwell* Parliament replaced the offence of causing death by reckless driving with the offence of causing death by dangerous driving; see Road Traffic Act

1991. What was the significance of the substitution of the word 'dangerous' for 'reckless'? Was it intended to make convictions easier to come by? Did the change make clear that the fault element was now totally objective?

2   Was the House of Lords correct in *R v G* to adopt an all or nothing approach to objective recklessness? Whilst few would advocate the imposition of liability on a juvenile who had not and could not have thought of the risk of harm in a given situation, is there not merit in imposing liability on a sentient adult for failing to consider a risk he would have been aware of if only he had stopped to consider it? Should thoughtlessness be elevated to a form of *mens rea*?

3   The decision in *R v Caldwell* also gave rise to what became known as the 'lacuna' argument which ran thus: if a defendant, before acting, showed that he stopped to consider a risk, and genuinely concluded that there was no risk, he should not be found to be reckless even if the risk materialised. This was because he had given thought to the risk, and thus fell outside the scope of *Caldwell* recklessness, and he did not believe he was taking a risk, hence he fell outside the scope of *Cunningham* recklessness. Following *R v G* is there any need for a lacuna argument? Is it true to say that a defendant who considers a risk but then genuinely dismisses it as remote or negligible is not reckless because he is not aware that he is taking a risk?

4   For an illustration of the effect of *R v G*, see *R v Castle* [2004] All ER (D) 289, where the appellant was charged with aggravated criminal damage being reckless as to whether life would be endangered. The Court of Appeal stressed that the objective approach to reckless-ness had been abandoned. The jury should have been directed that the defendant had acted recklessly with respect to: a circumstance if he had been aware of a risk that it had or would have existed; or that he was reckless as regards a result if he had been aware of a risk that it would occur, and it was in the circumstances known to him, unreasonable to take the risk.

5   Although Lord Bingham, in *R v G*, observed that in redefining recklessness under the Criminal Damage Act 1971 he was not referring to recklessness in any other statutory or common law context, is there any justification for recklessness having any other meaning in criminal law?

3.3.2 CODIFICATION AND LAW REFORM PROPOSALS

The definition of recklessness endorsed by the House of Lords in *R v G* is essentially that put forward in the Home Office Consultation Paper *Violence: Reforming the Offences Against the Person Act 1861*, which in turn drew upon the definition contained in the 1989 Draft Code Bill. The commentary to the DCCB is, therefore, still instructive in this regard:

8.17 'Recklessly'. Clause 18(c) provides that a person acts 'recklessly' with respect to a circum-stance when he is aware of a risk that it exists or will exist, and with respect to a result when he is aware of a risk that it will occur, it being, in either case, 'in the circumstances known to him, unreasonable to take the risk'. The use thus proposed for 'reckless' and related words is the same as that which we proposed in our Mental Element Report.

. . .

8.20 The 'subjectivist' approach to criminal liability. 'Knowledge', 'intention' and 'recklessness' (and cognate words) are terms used throughout the draft Bill with the meanings given by clause.

The modern English criminal law tradition tends to require a positive state of mind with respect to the various external elements of an offence of any seriousness; and the three key terms are the obvious terms, because of their familiarity in criminal law usage, by which to refer to some of the most common states of mind required. Although this 'subjectivist' tradition is not without its critics, we are proposing a Code that stays within the mainstream of English criminal law. But in doing so we do not exclude the possibility that Parliament may hereafter wish to create offences constructed upon a different foundation of liability. The group of House of Lords' cases led by *Caldwell* can, indeed, be interpreted as having placed some serious offences upon such a different foundation. It will, of course, be open to Parliament to pursue the line followed by those cases by rejecting or modifying the fault requirements proposed for particular offences in Part II of our draft Bill and by providing further key terms to supplement the three that we have defined.

8.21 The Code team, in their Bill, did in fact provide a term ('heedlessness') to convey the extended sense of recklessness laid down in *Caldwell*. We have not found occasion to use that expression in the definitions of offences in Part 11 of our Bill but it remains available if there should prove to be a use for it.

3.4 THE SIGNIFICANCE OF MISTAKE

Although it is common to hear mistake spoken of as a substantive defence in criminal law, in reality a defendant pleading mistake is almost always denying that he had the *mens rea* for the offence with which he has been charged. On this basis it is likely to be the case that mistake is the most commonly pleaded 'defence' in criminal law. It is possible to identify three categories of defence argument based on mistake:

(a) Where the defendant claims that he did not know that a particular activity was prohibited by law, that is, mistake of law.
(b) Where a defendant makes a mistake of fact. The key here is to distinguish between relevant and irrelevant mistakes.
  • If D burgles A's house mistaking it for P's, he has made a mistake of fact but not one that has any relevance in terms of denying the *mens rea* of the offence.
  • If D points a gun at P and pulls the trigger, wrongly believing the gun to be unloaded, with the result that P suffers injuries, D has again made a mistake of fact, but not one that necessarily denies the *mens rea* for the offence. D may not have intended to injure P, but he may still be regarded as reckless in not having checked whether or not the gun was loaded before pulling the trigger. In effect this type of mistake is a denial of foresight of consequences.
  • D fires his gun at what he believes to be a small deer. In fact it is a poacher who dies from the resultant injuries. D has made a mistake of fact, but this time it relates to an element of the offence that the prosecution has to prove – that is, on a murder charge the prosecution has to prove that D intended to kill or do grievous bodily harm to a human being. If D's mistake of fact leads him to believe he is shooting at an animal, and he therefore acts with intent to attack an animal, he lacks the *mens rea* for the offence. The mistake is evidence that D lacked the *mens rea*. As the extracts below

indicate, the debate here has centred around whether D should be judged on the facts as he believes them to be, or whether D should only be able to rely on a mistake of fact that the reasonable person would have made.

(c) D may make a mistake of fact that leads him to believe in the existence of justificatory or exculpatory circumstances. For example, he may mistakenly believe that P is consenting to what would otherwise be an assault, or D may mistakenly believe that P is about to attack him, leading D to use force on P that would be justified as self-defence if the facts were as D believed them to be; this latter aspect of mistake is considered further in Chapter 14.10.

3.4.1 MISTAKE OF FACT RELATING TO AN ELEMENT OF THE OFFENCE CHARGED

The following extracts from *DPP v Morgan* and *B v DPP* raise general issues regarding the subjectivist approach to *mens rea*, whereby the defendant is to be judged on the facts as he honestly believes them to be. Note that the offences under consideration have been significantly reformed by the Sexual Offences Act 2003, considered in Chapter 6. Under the 2003 Act, an honest belief that the complainant in a rape case was consenting will not avail the defendant, the belief in the complainant's consent must now also be reasonably held. The following extracts concern the approach to mistake of fact at common law, which remains subjective – i.e. the defendant is to be judged on the facts as he honestly believed them to be.

DPP v Morgan [1976] AC 182 (HL)

The appellant Morgan and his three co-appellants spent the evening of 15 August 1973 in one another's company. Morgan persuaded his co-defendants to return to his house in order to have sex with his wife, the complainant. He reassured them that she enjoyed being forced to have sex with strangers, and that if she offered resistance it was her way of showing that she was enjoying the sexual intercourse. The complainant was aroused from her sleep, frog-marched into another room where there was a double bed, held by each of her limbs, arms and legs apart, by the four appellants, while each of Morgan's co-appellants in turn had intercourse with her in the presence of the others. The question certified considered by the House of Lords was:

> Whether, in rape, the defendant can properly be convicted notwithstanding that he in fact believed that the woman consented if such belief was not based on reasonable grounds.

Lord Hailsham of St Marylebone:
. . . Once one has accepted, what seems to me abundantly clear, that the prohibited act in rape is non-consensual sexual intercourse, and that the guilty state of mind is an intention to commit it, it seems to me to follow as a matter of inexorable logic that there is no room either for a 'defence' of honest belief or mistake, or of a defence of honest and reasonable belief and mistake. Either the prosecution proves that the accused had the requisite intent, or it does not. In the former case it

succeeds, and in the latter it fails. Since honest belief clearly negatives intent, the reasonableness or otherwise of that belief can only be evidence for or against the view that the belief and therefore the intent was actually held, and it matters not whether, to quote Bridge J [giving the judgment of the Court of Appeal in the present case], 'the definition of a crime includes no specific element beyond the prohibited act' . . .

B v DPP [2000] 1 All ER 833

For the facts see the extract in Chapter 3.8.1.

Lord Nicholls:

Reasonable belief or honest belief
The existence of the presumption is beyond dispute, but in one respect the traditional formulation of the presumption calls for re-examination. This respect concerns the position of a defendant who acted under a mistaken view of the facts. In this regard, the presumption is expressed traditionally to the effect that an honest mistake by a defendant does not avail him unless the mistake was made on reasonable grounds. Thus, in *R v Tolson* (1889) 23 QBD 168, 181, Cave J observed:

> At common law an honest and reasonable belief in the existence of circumstances, which, if true, would make the act for which a prisoner is indicted an innocent act has always been held to be a good defence. This doctrine is embodied in the somewhat uncouth maxim 'actus non facit reum, nisi mens sit rea'. Honest and reasonable mistake stands on the same footing as absence of the reasoning faculty, as in infancy, or perversion of that faculty, as in lunacy . . . So far as I am aware it has never been suggested that these exceptions do not equally apply in the case of statutory offences unless they are excluded expressly or by necessary implication.

The other judges in that case expressed themselves to a similar effect. In *Bank of New South Wales v Piper* [1897] AC 383, 389–90, the Privy Council likewise espoused the 'reasonable belief' approach:

> . . . the absence of *mens rea* really consists in an honest and reasonable belief entertained by the accused of facts which, if true, would make the act charged against him innocent.

In *Sweet v Parsley* [1970] AC 132, 163, Lord Diplock referred to a general principle of construction of statutes creating criminal offences, in similar terms:

> . . . a general principle of construction of any enactment, which creates a criminal offence, [is] that, even where the words used to describe the prohibited conduct would not in any other context connote the necessity for any particular mental element, they are nevertheless to be read as subject to the implication that a necessary element in the offence is the absence of a belief, held honestly and upon reasonable grounds, in the existence of facts which, if true, would make the act innocent.

The 'reasonable belief' school of thought held unchallenged sway for many years. But over the last quarter of a century there have been several important cases where a defence of honest but mistaken belief was raised. In deciding these cases the courts have placed new, or renewed, emphasis on the subjective nature of the mental element in criminal offences. The courts have rejected the reasonable belief approach and preferred the honest belief approach. When *mens rea* is ousted by a mistaken belief, it is as well ousted by an unreasonable belief as by a reasonable belief. In the pithy phrase of Lawton LJ in *R v Kimber* [1983] 1 WLR 1118, 1122, it is the defendant's belief, not the grounds on which it is based, which goes to negative the intent. This approach is well encapsulated in a passage in the judgment of Lord Lane CJ in *R v Williams (Gladstone)* (1984) 78 Cr App R 276, 281:

> The reasonableness or unreasonableness of the defendant's belief is material to the question of whether the belief was held by the defendant at all. If the belief was in fact held, its unreasonableness, so far as guilt or innocence is concerned, is neither here nor there. It is irrelevant. Were it otherwise, the defendant would be convicted because he was negligent in failing to recognise that the victim was not consenting . . . and so on.

Considered as a matter of principle, the honest belief approach must be preferable. By definition the mental element in a crime is concerned with a subjective state of mind, such as intent or belief. To the extent that an overriding objective limit ('on reasonable grounds') is introduced, the subjective element is displaced. To that extent a person who lacks the necessary intent or belief may nevertheless commit the offence. When that occurs the defendant's 'fault' lies exclusively in falling short of an objective standard. His crime lies in his negligence. A statute may so provide expressly or by necessary implication. But this can have no place in a common law principle, of general application, which is concerned with the need for a mental element as an essential ingredient of a criminal offence.

The traditional formulation of the common law presumption, exemplified in Lord Diplock's famous exposition in *Sweet v Parsley*, cited above, is out of step with this recent line of authority, in so far as it envisages that a mistaken belief must be based on reasonable grounds. This seems to be a relic from the days before a defendant in a criminal case could give evidence in his own defence. It is not surprising that in those times juries judged a defendant's state of mind by the conduct to be expected of a reasonable person.

I turn to the recent authorities. The decision which heralded this development in criminal law was the decision of your Lordships' House in *Director of Public Prosecutions v Morgan* [1976] AC 182. This was a case of rape. By a bare majority the House held that where a defendant had sexual intercourse with a woman without her consent but believing she did consent, he was not guilty of rape even though he had no reasonable grounds for his belief. The intent to commit rape involves an intention to have intercourse without the woman's consent or with a reckless indifference to whether she consents or not. It would be inconsistent with this definition if an honest belief that she did consent led to an acquittal only when it was based on reasonable grounds. One of the minority, Lord Edmund-Davies, would have taken a different view had he felt free to do so. In *R v Kimber* [1983] 1 WLR 1118, a case of indecent assault, the Court of Appeal applied the approach of the majority in Morgan's case. The guilty state of mind was the intent to use personal violence to a woman without her consent. If the defendant did not so intend, he was entitled to be found not guilty. If he did not so intend because he believed she was consenting, the prosecution will have failed to prove the charge, irrespective of the grounds for the defendant's belief. The court disapproved of the suggestion made in the earlier case of *R v Phekoo* [1981] 1 WLR 1117, 1127, that this House intended to confine the views expressed in Morgan's case to cases of rape.

This reasoning was taken a step further in *R v Williams (Gladstone)* (1984) 78 Cr App R 276.

There the Court of Appeal, presided over by Lord Lane CJ, adopted the same approach in a case of assault occasioning actual bodily harm. The context was a defence that the defendant believed that the person whom he assaulted was unlawfully assaulting a third party. In *Beckford v R* [1988] AC 130 a similar issue came before the Privy Council on an appeal from Jamaica in a case involving a defence of self-defence to a charge of murder. The Privy Council applied the decisions in Morgan's case and Williams' case. Lord Griffiths said, at 144:

> If then a genuine belief, albeit without reasonable grounds, is a defence to rape because it negatives the necessary intention, so also must a genuine belief in facts which if true would justify self-defence be a defence to a crime of personal violence because the belief negatives the intent to act unlawfully.

Lord Griffiths also observed, at a practical level, that where there are no reasonable grounds to hold a belief it will surely only be in exceptional circumstances that a jury will conclude that such a belief was or might have been held. Finally in this summary, in *Blackburn v Bowering* [1994] 1 WLR 1324, the Court of Appeal, presided over by Sir Thomas Bingham MR, applied the same approach to the exercise by the court of its contempt jurisdiction in respect of an alleged assault on officers of the court while in the execution of their duty.

The Crown advanced no suggestion to your Lordships that any of these recent cases was wrongly decided. This is not surprising, because the reasoning in these cases is compelling. Thus, the traditional formulation of the common law presumption must now be modified appropriately. Otherwise the formulation would not be an accurate reflection of the current state of the criminal law regarding mistakes of fact. Lord Diplock's dictum in *Sweet v Parsley* [1970] AC 132, 163, must in future be read as though the reference to reasonable grounds were omitted.

I add one further general observation. In principle, an age-related ingredient of a statutory offence stands on no different footing from any other ingredient. If a man genuinely believes that the girl with whom he is committing a grossly indecent act is over fourteen, he is not intending to commit such an act with a girl under fourteen . . .

 COMMENTS AND QUESTIONS

1   A mistake of law will normally only amount to a defence if it is a mistake as to civil law, not criminal law. For example, it is a defence to say 'I thought that I was – as a matter of civil law – the legal owner of the property I damaged' (as in *R v Smith* [1974] QB 354, considered in Chapter 12.5.2) but it is not a defence to say 'I thought that a wild creature could not be "property" for the purposes of theft' (cf s 4(4) of the Theft Act 1968).

2   A defendant charged with theft will be able to argue that he was not dishonest if, when he appropriated the property belonging to another he did so in the honest belief that he had the right in law to take the property. Note that he does not have to provide evidence of any such right; it suffices that he believes he has the right. In this sense his mistake as to his civil law rights can provide a shield against criminal liability; see further Chapter 9.5.2.

3   A defendant who, through mental illness, is unaware that an activity is prohibited by the criminal law could be entitled to rely on the defence of insanity – see further Chapter 13.5.4.

4   Suppose D wants to fix a distinctive mascot to the front of his car and inquires at the local

police station as to whether this would be lawful. The duty officer advises him that it would be lawful. D is later stopped by the police and prosecuted because the mascot contravenes a provision in the relevant road traffic legislation. Can D plead mistake of law as a defence? Would there be any public law argument to the effect that he had a legitimate expectation that he would not be prosecuted?

5   Where a defendant makes a mistake of fact because he has, of his own volition, reduced himself to a state of intoxication, the mistake will not avail him if he is charged with a crime of basic intent – see further Chapter 13.1.3.

6   The principle that D should be judged on the facts as he honestly believes them to be should apply equally to a mistake as to the availability of a defence; see further Chapter 14.11.

3.5 CHILDREN AND PROOF OF *MENS REA*

A child under the age of 10 cannot incur criminal liability. This is established by s 50 of the Children and Young Persons Act 1933, which provides: 'It shall be conclusively presumed that no child under the age of 10 can be guilty of an offence.' Prior to 1998 it was the case that, in respect of a child between the ages of 10 and 14, *mens rea* would only be established if the defendant knew that what he had done was wrong – sometimes referred to as 'mischievous discretion'. This operated as a rebuttable presumption against a child between the ages of 10 and 14 having *mens rea*. Section 34 of the Crime and Disorder Act 1998 Act abolished the presumption as follows: 'The rebuttable presumption of criminal law that a child aged 10 or over is incapable of committing an offence is hereby abolished.'

T v United Kingdom; V v United Kingdom (1999) *The Times*, 17 December

The European Court of Human Rights was asked to rule upon whether or not the imposition of criminal liability on children as young as 10 years of age amounted to a breach of the European Convention on Human Rights.

European Court of Human Rights: Pursuant to section 50 of the Children and Young Persons Act 1933 ('the 1933 Act') as amended by section 16(1) of the Children and Young Persons Act 1963, the age of criminal responsibility in England and Wales is ten years, below which no child can be found guilty of a criminal offence. The age of ten was endorsed by the Home Affairs Select Committee (composed of Members of Parliament) in October 1993 (Juvenile Offenders, Sixth Report of the Session 1992–93, Her Majesty's Stationery Office) . . . The United Nations Standard Minimum Rules for the Administration of Juvenile Justice (the Beijing Rules) . . . were adopted by the United Nations General Assembly on 29 November 1985. These Rules are not binding in international law . . . They provide, as relevant:

4.1 In those legal systems recognising the concept of the age of criminal responsibility for juveniles, the beginning of that age shall not be fixed at too low an age level, bearing in mind the facts of emotional, mental and intellectual maturity.

Commentary: The minimum age of criminal responsibility differs widely owing to history and culture. The modern approach would be to consider whether a child can live up to the moral and psychological components of criminal responsibility; that is, whether a child, by virtue of her or his individual discernment and understanding, can be held responsible for essentially antisocial behaviour. If the age of criminal responsibility is fixed too low or if there is no lower age limit at all, the notion of criminal responsibility would become meaningless. In general, there is a close relationship between the notion of responsibility for delinquent or criminal behaviour and other social rights and responsibilities (such as marital status, civil majority, etc).

Efforts should therefore be made to agree on a reasonable lowest age limit that is applicable.

. . . The age of criminal responsibility is seven in Cyprus, Ireland, Switzerland and Liechtenstein; eight in Scotland; thirteen in France; fourteen in Germany, Austria, Italy and many Eastern European countries; fifteen in the Scandinavian countries; sixteen in Portugal, Poland and Andorra; and eighteen in Spain, Belgium and Luxembourg.

. . . The applicant alleged that the cumulative effect of the age of criminal responsibility, the accusatorial nature of the trial, the adult proceedings in a public court, the length of the trial, the jury of twelve adult strangers, the physical lay-out of the courtroom, the overwhelming presence of the media and public, the attacks by the public on the prison van which brought him to court and the disclosure of his identity, together with a number of other factors linked to his sentence gave rise to a breach of Article 3.

He submitted that, at ten years old, the age of criminal responsibility in England and Wales was low compared with almost all European countries, in the vast majority of which the minimum age of responsibility was thirteen or higher. He contended, moreover, that there was a clear developing trend in international and comparative law towards a higher age of criminal responsibility . . . He accepted that it was in principle possible for a State to attribute criminal responsibility to a child as young as ten without violating that child's rights under Article 3. However, it was then incumbent on such a State to ensure that the procedures adopted for the trial and sentencing of such young children were modified to reflect their age and vulnerability.

. . . The Government denied that the attribution of criminal responsibility to the applicant and his trial in public in an adult court breached his rights under Article 3.

With regard to the age of criminal responsibility, they submitted that the practice amongst the Contracting States was very varied, with ages ranging from seven in Cyprus, Ireland, Liechtenstein and Switzerland, to eighteen in a number of other States. There were no international principles laying down a specific age for criminal responsibility: Article 40(3) of the UN Convention required States to adopt a minimum age but imposed no specific such age. The Beijing Rules relied upon by the applicant were not binding under international law; the Preamble invited States to adopt them but left it up to States to decide whether or not to do so.

. . . The Court has considered first whether the attribution to the applicant of criminal responsibility in respect of acts committed when he was ten years old could, in itself, give rise to a violation of Article 3. In doing so, it has regard to the principle, well established in its case law that, since the Convention is a living instrument, it is legitimate when deciding whether a certain measure is acceptable under one of its provisions to take account of the standards prevailing amongst the Member States of the Council of Europe . . .

. . . In this connection, the Court observes that, at the present time there is not yet a commonly accepted minimum age for the imposition of criminal responsibility in Europe. While most of the Contracting States have adopted an age-limit which is higher than that in force in England and Wales, other States, such as Cyprus, Ireland, Liechtenstein and Switzerland, attribute criminal responsibility from a younger age. Moreover, no clear tendency can be ascertained from examination of the relevant international texts and instruments . . . Rule 4 of the Beijing Rules which, although not legally binding, might provide some indication of the existence of an international consensus, does not specify the age at which criminal responsibility should be fixed but merely invites States not to fix it too low, and Article 40(3)(a) of the UN Convention requires States Parties to establish a minimum age below which children shall be presumed not to have the capacity to infringe the criminal law, but contains no provision as to what that age should be.

The Court does not consider that there is at this stage any clear common standard amongst the member States of the Council of Europe as to the minimum age of criminal responsibility. Even if England and Wales is among the few European jurisdictions to retain a low age of criminal responsibility, the age of ten cannot be said to be so young as to differ disproportionately from the age-limit followed by other European States. The Court concludes that the attribution of criminal responsibility to the applicant does not in itself give rise to a breach of Article 3 of the Convention.

3.6 COINCIDENCE OF *ACTUS REUS* AND *MENS REA*

Establishing criminal liability normally involves the prosecution in proving that there was a coincidence of the *actus reus* and the *mens rea* for the offence in question. In the vast majority of cases the coincidence is evident from the facts. In some cases, however, the courts have had to deal with arguments based on non-coincidence and, as the following extracts indicate, they have responded by developing a somewhat elastic concept of coincidence.

Thabo Meli and Others v R [1954] 1 WLR 228 (PC)

Lord Reid:

The four appellants in this case were convicted of murder . . . The appeal which has been heard by this Board dealt with two matters: first, whether the conclusions of the learned judge on questions of fact were warranted: and, second, whether, on a point of law, the accused are entitled to have the verdict quashed.

On the first matter, there really is no ground for criticising the learned judge's treatment of the facts. It is established by evidence, which was believed and which is apparently credible, that there was a preconceived plot on the part of the four accused to bring the deceased man to a hut and there to kill him, and then fake an accident, so that the accused should escape the penalty for their act. The deceased man was brought to the hut. He was there treated to beer and was at least partially intoxicated; and he was then struck over the head in accordance with the plan of the accused. Witnesses say that while the deceased was seated and bending forward he was struck a heavy blow on the back of the head with a piece of iron like the instrument produced at the trial. But a post mortem examination showed that his skull had not been fractured and medical evidence was to the effect that a blow such as the witnesses described would have produced more severe injuries than those found at the post mortem examination. There is at least doubt whether the weapon which was produced as being like the weapon which was used could have produced the injuries that were found, but it may be that this weapon is not exactly similar to the one which was used, or it may be that the blow was a glancing blow and produced less severe injuries than those which one might expect. In any event, the man was unconscious after receiving the blow, but he was not then dead. There is no evidence that the accused then believed that he was dead, but their Lordships are prepared to assume from their subsequent conduct that they did so believe; and it is only on that assumption that any statable case can be made for this appeal. The accused took out the body, rolled it over a low krantz or cliff, and dressed up the scene to make it look like an accident. Obviously, they believed at that time that the man was dead, but it appears from the medical evidence that the injuries which he received in the hut were not sufficient to cause the death and that the final cause of his death was exposure when he was left unconscious at the foot of the krantz.

The point of law which was raised in this case can be simply stated. It is said that two acts were done: first, the attack in the hut; and, second, the placing of the body outside afterwards; and that they were separate acts. It is said that, while the first act was accompanied by *mens rea*, it was not the cause of death; but that the second act, while it was the cause of death, was not accompanied by *mens rea*; and on that ground, it is said that the accused are not guilty of murder, though they may have been guilty of culpable homicide. It is said that the *mens rea* necessary to establish murder is an intention to kill, and that there could be no intention to kill when the accused thought that the man was already dead, so their original intention to kill had ceased before they did the act which caused the man's death. It appears to their Lordships impossible to divide up what was really one series of acts in this way. There is no doubt that the accused set out to do all these acts in order to achieve their plan, and as parts of their plan; and it is much too refined a ground of judgment to say that, because they were under a misapprehension at one stage and thought that their guilty purpose had been achieved before, in fact, it was achieved, therefore they are to escape the penalties of the law. Their Lordships do not think that this is a matter which is susceptible of elaboration. There appears to be no case, either in South Africa or England, or for that matter elsewhere, which resembles the present. Their Lordships can find no difference relevant to the present case between the law of South Africa and the law of England; and they are of opinion that by both laws there can be no separation such as that for which the accused contend. Their crime is not reduced from murder to a lesser crime merely because the accused were under some misapprehension for a time during the completion of their criminal plot.

Their Lordships must, therefore, humbly advise Her Majesty that this appeal should be dismissed.

Attorney General's Ref (No 4 of 1980) [1981] 1 WLR 705 (CA)

Ackner LJ:
. . . this reference raises a single simple question, viz if an accused kills another by one or other of two or more different acts each of which, if it caused the death, is a sufficient act to establish manslaughter, is it necessary in order to found a conviction to prove which act caused the death? The answer to that question is No, it is not necessary to found a conviction to prove which act caused the death. No authority is required to justify this answer, which is clear beyond argument, as was indeed immediately conceded by counsel on behalf of the accused.

What went wrong in this case was that counsel made jury points to the judge and not submissions of law. He was in effect contending that the jury should not convict of manslaughter if the death had resulted from the 'fall', because the push which had projected the deceased over the handrail was a reflex and not a voluntary action, as a result of her digging her nails into him. If, however, the deceased was still alive when he cut her throat, since he then genuinely believed her to be dead, having discovered neither pulse nor sign of breath, but frothy blood coming from her mouth, he could not be guilty of manslaughter because he had not behaved with gross criminal negligence. What counsel and the judge unfortunately overlooked was that there was material available to the jury which would have entitled them to have convicted the accused of man-slaughter, whichever of the two sets of acts caused her death. It being common ground that the deceased was killed by an act done to her by the accused and it being conceded that the jury could not be satisfied which was the act which caused the death, they should have been directed in due course in the summing up, to ask themselves the following questions: (1) Are we satisfied beyond reasonable doubt that the deceased's 'fall' downstairs was the result of an intentional act by the accused which was unlawful and dangerous? If the answer was No, then they would acquit. It the answer was Yes, then they would need to ask themselves a second question, namely (2) Are we satisfied beyond reasonable doubt that the act of cutting the girl's throat was an act of gross criminal negligence? If the answer to that question was No, then they would acquit, but if the answer was Yes, then the verdict would be guilty of manslaughter. The jury would thus have been satisfied that, whichever act had killed the deceased, each was a sufficient act to establish the offence of manslaughter.

The fact of this case did not call for a 'series of acts direction' following the principle in *Thabo Meli v R* . . .

R v Le Brun [1992] 1 QB 61 (CA)

Lord Lane CJ:

. . . Problems of causation and remoteness of damage are never easy of solution. We have had helpful arguments from both counsel on this point, the point in the present case being, to put it in summary before coming to deal with it in more detail, that the intention of the appellant to harm his wife one way or another may have been separated by a period of time from the act which in fact caused the death, namely the fact of her falling to the ground and fracturing her skull. The second incident may have taken place without any guilty mind of the part of the appellant.

The authors of Smith and Hogan, Criminal Law, 6th edn, 1988, p 320, say:

> An intervening act by the original actor will not break the chain of causation so as to excuse him, where the intervening act is part of the same transaction, but it is otherwise if the act which causes the *actus reus* is part of a completely different transaction. For example, D, having wounded P, visits him in hospital and accidentally infects him with smallpox of which he dies.

The problem in the instant case can be expressed in a number of different ways, of which caus-ation is one. Causation on the facts as the jury in this case must have found them – I say at the best from the point of view of the appellant – is in one sense clear. Death was caused by the victim's head hitting the ground as she was being dragged away by the appellant. The only remoteness was that between the initial unlawful blow and the later moment when the skull was fractured causing death.

The question can be perhaps framed in this way. There was here an initial unlawful blow to the chin delivered by the appellant. That, again on what must have been the jury's finding, was not delivered with the intention of doing really serious harm to the wife. The guilty intent accompanying that blow was sufficient to have rendered the appellant guilty of manslaughter, but not murder, had it caused death. But it did not cause death. What caused death was the later impact when the wife's head hit the pavement. At the moment of impact the appellant's intention was to remove her, probably unconscious body to avoid detection. To that extent the impact may have been accidental. May the earlier guilty intent be joined with the later non-guilty blow which caused death to produce in the conglomerate a proper verdict of manslaughter?

[In] the present case . . . death . . . was not the result of a preconceived plan which went wrong . . . Here the death, again assuming the jury's finding to be such as it must have been, was the result of an initial unlawful blow, not intended to cause serious harm, in its turn causing the appellant to take steps possibly to evade the consequences of his unlawful act. During the taking of those steps he commits the *actus reus* but without the *mens rea* necessary for murder or manslaughter. Therefore the *mens rea* is contained in the initial unlawful assault, but the *actus reus* is the eventual dropping of the head onto the ground.

Normally the *actus reus* and *mens rea* coincide in point of time. What is the situation when they do not? Is it permissible, as the prosecution contend here, to combine them to produce a conviction for manslaughter? . . .

It seems to us that where the unlawful application of force and the eventual act causing death are parts of the same sequence of events, the same transaction, the fact that there is an appreciable interval of time between the two does not serve to exonerate the defendant from liability. That is certainly so where the appellant's subsequent actions which caused death, after the initial unlawful blow, are designed to conceal his commission of the original assault.

It would be possible to express the problem as one of causation. The original unlawful blow to the chin was a *causa sine qua non* of the later *actus reus*. It was the opening event in a series which was to culminate in death: the first link in the chain of causation, to use another metaphor. It cannot be said that the actions of the appellant in dragging the victim away with the intention of evading liability broke the chain which linked the initial blow with the death.

In short, in circumstances such as the present, which is the only concern of this court, the act which causes death, and the necessary mental state to constitute manslaughter, need not coincide in point of time . . .

Attorney General's Ref (No 3 of 1994) [1997] 3 All ER 936

The facts are set out in an extract at 3.7 below dealing with the issue of transferred malice.

Lord Mustill:
The existence of an interval of time between the doing of an act by the defendant with the necessary wrongful intent and its impact on the victim in a manner which leads to death does not in itself prevent the intent, the act and the death from together amounting to murder, so long as there is an unbroken causal connection between the act and the death.

If authority is needed for this obvious proposition it may be found in *R v Church* . . . and *R v Le Brun* . . .

Lord Hope:

As Lord Lane CJ observed in *R v Le Brun* . . . following *R v Church* . . . the act which caused the death and the mental state which is needed to constitute manslaughter need not coincide in point of time. So to this extent as least it may be said to be immaterial that the child was not alive when the defendant stabbed the mother with the intention which was needed to show that he was committing an unlawful act. It is enough that the original unlawful and dangerous act, to which the required mental state is related, and the eventual death of the victim are both part of the same sequence of events.

3.7 TRANSFERRED MALICE

Under the doctrine of transferred malice if A fires a gun at B, intending to kill him, and he misses, but succeeds in killing a bystander C, A cannot deny that he had the *mens rea* for murder. This could be explained by saying that the identity of the victim in homicide is no part of the *mens rea* (that is, the *mens rea* is intention to kill or do grievous bodily harm to a person – not a named individual). It can also, however, be expressed in terms of the 'malice' aimed at B being transferred to the actual victim, C. The same principle is applied to property offences.

R v Pembliton (1874) LR 2 CCR 119

Lord Coleridge CJ:

I am of opinion that the conviction should be quashed. The facts of the case are that there was fighting going on in the streets of Wolverhampton near the prosecutor's house, and the prisoner, after fighting for some time, separated himself from the crowd and threw a stone, which missed the person he aimed at, but struck and broke a window, doing damage to the extent of upwards of £5. The question is, whether under an indictment for unlawfully and maliciously injuring the property of the owner of the plate-glass window, these facts will support the indictment when coupled with the other facts found by the jury, that the prisoner threw the stone at the people intending to strike one or more of them, but not intending to break a window. I am of opinion that the evidence does not support the conviction. The indictment is under the 24 and 25 Vict c 97, s 51, which deals with malicious injuries to property, and the section expressly says that the act is to be unlawful and malicious. There is also the 58th section, which makes it immaterial whether the offence has been committed from malice against the owner of the property or otherwise, that is, from malice against someone not the owner of the property. In both these sections it seems to me that what is intended by the statute is a wilful doing of an intentional act. Without saying that if the case had been left to them in a different way the conviction could not have been supported, if, on these facts the jury had come to a conclusion that the prisoner was reckless of the consequence of his act, and might reasonably have expected that it would result in breaking the window, it is sufficient to say that the jury have expressly found the contrary. I do not say anything to throw doubt on the rule under the common law in cases of murder which has been referred to, but the principles laid down in such cases have no application to the statutable offence we have to consider.

R v Latimer (1886) 17 QB 359 (CCR)

The defendant aimed a blow with his belt at one person, striking him slightly. The belt also struck someone else, causing a severe wound. The court had to decide whether A could be guilty of unlawfully wounding C where A intends to strike B but strikes C instead.

Lord Coleridge CJ:

. . . It is common knowledge that a man who has an unlawful and malicious intent against another, and, in attempting to carry it out, injures a third person, is guilty of what the law deems malice against the person injured, because the offender is doing an unlawful act, and has that which the judges call general malice, and that is enough . . . [His Lordship then referred to *R v Hunt* 1 Moo CC 93 and said:] There a man intended to injure A, and said so, and, in the course of doing it, stabbed the wrong man, and had clearly malice in fact, but no intention of injuring the man who was stabbed. He intended to do an unlawful act, and in the course of doing it the consequence was that somebody was injured . . .

Lord Esher MR:

I am of the same opinion. The only case which could be cited against the well-known principle of law applicable to this case was *R v Pembliton* (1874) Law Rep 2 CC 119, but, on examination, it is found to have been decided on this ground, viz that there was no intention to injure any property at all. It was not a case of attempting to injure one man's property and injuring another's, which would have been wholly different.

Bowen LJ:

I am of the same opinion. It is quite clear that the act was done by the prisoner with malice in his mind. I use the word 'malice' in the common law sense of the term, viz a person is deemed malicious when he does an act which he knows will injure either the person or property of another. The only case that could be cited for the prisoner is *R v Pembliton* (1874) Law Rep 2 CC 119, which was founded not upon malice in general, but upon a particular form of malice, viz malicious injury to property; and the court held that though the prisoner might have been acting maliciously in the common law sense of the term, he was not malicious in the sense of the Act directed against malicious injury to property. That decision does not apply to a case under the Act where the indictment is for injury to the person. *R v Pembliton* might have been ground for an argument of some plausibility if the prisoner meant to strike at a pane of glass and had hit a person. It might have been that the malice in that case was not enough. But when, as here, an intent to injure a person is proved, that is enough.

Manisty J:

I will add only a few words, for all has been said that could be said, but the facts of this case, no doubt, raise an exceedingly important question, for the man Chapple, whom the prisoner intended to strike, and who was struck, with the belt, was standing close by the woman, and the belt bounded off and struck the prosecutrix. It seems to me that the first and second findings of the jury are quite sufficient to justify the verdict, for they find that the blow was unlawful and malicious, and that it wounded the prosecutrix. That being so, the third finding does not entitle the prisoner to acquittal. The third finding is that the striking of the prosecutrix was purely an accident, and so it was in one sense. The prisoner did not intend to strike her, but in the unlawful and malicious act of striking Chapple the prisoner did unlawfully and maliciously wound the prosecutrix, and the third finding is quite immaterial.

Attorney General's Ref (No 3 of 1994) [1997] 3 All ER 936

Lord Mustill:

My Lords . . . As will appear, the events which founder the appeal were never conclusively proved at the trial, but are assumed to have been as follows. At the time in question a young woman M was pregnant, with between 22 and 24 weeks of gestation. According to the present state of medical knowledge if her baby had been born after 22 weeks it would not have had any significant prospect of survival. Two further weeks would have increased the chance to about 10 per cent. The pregnancy was, however, proceeding normally, and the risk that it would fail to continue to full term and be followed by an uneventful birth was very small indeed. Sadly, however, the natural father B quarrelled with M and stabbed her in the face, back and abdomen with a long-bladed kitchen knife in circumstances raising a *prima facie* inference that he intended to do her grievous bodily harm. M was admitted to hospital for surgical treatment and was later discharged in an apparently satisfactory state, still carrying the baby. Unfortunately, some 17 days after the incident M went into premature labour. The baby, named S, was born alive. The birth was still grossly premature, although by that time the chance that the baby would survive had increased to 50 per cent. Thereafter S lived for 121 days, when she succumbed to broncho-pulmonary dysplasia from the effects of premature birth. After her birth it was discovered that one of the knife cuts had penetrated her lower abdomen. The wound needed surgical repair, but it is agreed that this 'made no provable contribution to her death'.

The case for the Crown at the trial of B was that the wounding of M by B had set in train the events which caused the premature birth of S and hence her failure to achieve the normal prospect of survival which she would have had if the pregnancy had proceeded to full term. In this sense, therefore, we must assume that the wounding of M, at a time when S was a barely viable foetus, was the reason why she later died when she did.

Meanwhile, B had been prosecuted for an offence of wounding the mother with intent to cause her grievous bodily harm, had pleaded guilty and had been sentenced to a term of four years' imprisonment.

After S died he was charged again, this time with the murder of S, to which he pleaded not guilty. At his trial a submission was advanced that on the evidence no criminal offence relating to S was proved. In a considered ruling the trial judge upheld that submission, as regards the offences of both murder and manslaughter. I leave aside the first submission for the defence, to the effect that causation between the wounding of the mother, the premature birth and the subsequent death of S had not been established on the evidence. This failed before the judge and has not been renewed. The gist of the ruling lay in the law, and was to the effect that both the physical and the mental elements of murder were absent. There was no relevant *actus reus*, for the foetus was not a live person; and the cause of the death was the wounding of the mother, not of S. As to *mens rea* again there was none. When B stabbed the mother he had no intent to kill or do serious harm to any live person other than the mother, or to do any harm at all to the foetus. The Crown could not make good this deficiency by reliance on the concept of 'transferred malice', for this operates only where the *mens rea* of one crime causes the *actus reus* of the same crime, albeit the result is in some respects unintended. Here, the intent to stab the mother (a live person) could not be transferred to the foetus (not a live person), an organism which could not be the victim of a crime of murder.

As to the alternative verdict of manslaughter the judge was at first exercised by the possibility that since the stabbing of M was an unlawful and dangerous act which led to the death of S a conviction could be sustained even though the act was not aimed at the ultimate victim: see *R v Mitchell* [1983] QB 741. In the end, however, he was persuaded that this approach could not be sustained where there was at the material time no victim capable of dying as a direct and immediate result.

Accordingly, the trial judge directed the jury to acquit the defendant.

Considering that this ruling should be reviewed the Attorney General referred the matter to the opinion of the Court of Appeal under s 36 of the Criminal Justice Act 1972. The point of law referred was as follows:

1.1 Subject to the proof by the prosecution of the requisite intent in either case: whether the crimes of murder or manslaughter can be committed where unlawful injury is deliberately inflicted: (i) to a child *in utero*; (ii) to a mother carrying a child *in utero* where the child is subsequently born alive, enjoys an existence independent of the mother, thereafter dies and the injuries inflicted while *in utero* either caused or made a substantial contribution to the death.

1.2 Whether the fact that the death of the child is caused solely as a consequence of injury to the mother rather than as a consequence of direct injury to the foetus can negative any liability for murder or manslaughter in the circumstances set out in question 1.1.

... In the result, the [Court of Appeal] answered the first of the referred questions in the affirmative, adding, at 598:

The requisite intent to be proved in the case of murder is an intention to kill or cause really serious bodily injury to the mother, the foetus before birth being viewed as an integral part of the mother. Such intention is appropriately modified in the case of manslaughter.

The court answered the second question in the negative, provided the jury is satisfied that causation is proved. The accused person now brings the matter before this House, and maintains that the answers given to both questions were wrong, and that the ruling of the trial judge was right ...

(a) Established rules

The able arguments of counsel were founded on a series of rules which, whatever may be said about their justice or logic, are undeniable features of the criminal law today. I will begin by stating them. Next, I shall describe two different ways in which the arguments for the Crown build on these rules, and will follow with reasons for rejecting one of these quite summarily. Closer examination is needed for the other, to see whether its historical origins are sound. Finally, an attempt will be made to see whether a principled answer can be given to the questions posed by the Attorney General. I perceive the established rules to be as follows ... [In Rule 1 Lord Mustill summarised the *mens rea* for murder.] ... 2 If the defendant does an act with the intention of causing a particular kind of harm to B, and unintentionally does that kind of harm to V, then the intent to harm B may be added to the harm actually done to V in deciding whether the defendant has committed a crime towards V.

This rule is usually referred to as the doctrine of 'transferred malice', a misleading label but one which is too firmly entrenched to be discarded. Nor would it be possible now to question the rule itself, for although the same handful of authorities are called up repeatedly in the texts they are constantly cited without disapproval ... Counsel rightly did not seek to deny the existence of the rule although, here again, it will be necessary to examine its rationale ... [Rule 3 dealt with the proposition that a foetus could not be the victim of a crime of violence; Rule 4 with coincidence of *actus reus* and *mens rea*; and Rule 5 with the proposition that violence towards a foetus that results in harm suffered by the baby once born can give rise to criminal liability.]

I prefer, so far as binding authority permits, to start afresh, and to do so by reference to the second of the arguments advanced by the Attorney General. This builds on the rules stated above by the following stages. If D struck X intending to cause her serious harm, and the blow, in fact, caused her death, that would be murder (Rule 1). If she had been nursing a baby Y which was accidentally struck by the blow and consequently died, that would also be murder (Rules 1 and 2). So, also, if an evil-doer had intended to cause harm but not death to X by giving her a poisoned substance and the substance was, in fact, passed on by X to the baby, which consumed it and died as a result (Rules 1, 2, and 3). Again, it would have been murder if the foetus had been injured *in utero* and had succumbed to the wound after being born alive (Rules 1, 2, 4 and 5). It is only a short step to make a new rule, adding together the malice towards the mother, the contemporaneous starting of a train of events, and the coming to fruition of those events in the death of the baby after being born alive.

My Lords, the attractions of this argument are plain, not least its simplicity. But for my part I find it too dependent on the piling up of old fictions, and too little on the reasons why the law takes its present shape. To look for these reasons is not, to use an expression sometimes met, 'legal archaeology' for its own sake. Except in those cases, of which the present is not one, where the rationale of the existing law is plain on its face, the common law must build for the future with materials from the past. One cannot see where a principle should go without an idea of where it has come from . . .

I turn to the second rule, of 'transferred malice'. For present purposes this is more important and more difficult. Again, one must look at its origins to see whether they provide a theme which can be applied today. Three of them are familiar. Taking Lord Coke's example of the glancing arrow we have seen how one explanation of the poacher's responsibility founded on the notion of risk. The person who committed a crime took the chance that the outcome would be worse than he expected. Amongst many sources one can find the idea in *Russell on Crime*, 4th edn (1845), p 739:

> If an action, unlawful in itself, be done deliberately, and with the intention of mischief or great bodily harm to particular individuals, or of mischief indiscriminately, fall where it may, and death ensue or beside the original intention of the party, it will be murder.

In a later edition (1855, p 759) this was exemplified by cases of particular malice to one individual falling by mistake upon another. In support are cited *R v Saunders* (1573) 2 Plowd 473 (a poisoned apple intended for the mother but given to the child) and Gore 9 Co Rep 81 (medicine poisoned by the wife to kill her husband and consumed by the apothecary to prove his innocence); also 1 Hawkins PC, c 31, 545 and 1 Hale 436. As already suggested, this doctrine does survive in some small degree today, but as the foundation of a modern doctrine of transferred malice broad enough to encompass the present case it seems to me quite unsupportable.

Secondly, there is the reversed burden of proof whereby the causing of death is *prima facie* murder, unless it falls within one of the extenuating categories recognised by the institutional writers. Again, this concept is long out of date. Nobody could seriously think of using it to make new law.

Third, there was the idea of 'general malice', of an evil disposition existing in the general and manifesting itself in the particular, uniting the aim of the offender and the result which his deeds actually produced. According to this theory, there was no need to 'transfer' the wrongful intent from the intended to the actual victim; for since the offender was (in the words of Blackstone) 'an enemy to all mankind in general', the actual victim was the direct object of the offender's enmity. Plainly, this will no longer do, for the last vestiges of the idea disappeared with the abolition of the murder/felony doctrine.

What explanation is left: for explanation there must be, since the 'transferred malice' concept is agreed on both sides to be sound law today? The sources in more recent centuries are few. Of the two most frequently cited the earlier is *R v Pembliton* . . . The ancient origins of this argument need no elaboration, and indeed the report of the argument as it developed showed that it was based on a conception of general malice. The interventions in argument are instructive. After the prosecutor had relied on the fact that the prisoner was actuated by malice, Blackburn J responded: 'But only of a particular kind, and not against the person injured.' Later, in reply to a reliance on a passage from Hale the same judge said:

> Lord Coke, 3 Inst, p 56, puts the case of a man stealing deer in a park, shooting at the deer, and by the glance of the arrow killing a boy that is hidden in a bush, and calls this murder; but can anyone say that ruling would be adopted now?

This most learned of judges continued:

> I should have told the jury that if the prisoner knew there were windows behind, and that the probable consequence of his act would be to break one of them, that would be evidence for them of malice.

The conviction was quashed. It is sufficient to quote briefly from the judgment of Blackburn J:

> We have not now to consider what would be malice aforethought to bring a given case within the common law definition of murder; here the statute says that the act must be unlawful and malicious . . . the jury might perhaps have found on this evidence that the act was malicious, because they might have found that the prisoner knew that the natural consequence of his act would be to break the glass, and although that was not his wish, yet he was reckless whether he did it or not; but the jury have not so found . . .

This decision was distinguished in *R v Latimer* . . . [see above] . . . [members of the court] . . . were able to distinguish *Pembliton* which, as Bowen LJ put the matter: 'was founded not upon malice in general but on a particular form of malice, viz, malicious injury to property . . .'

My Lords, I find it hard to base a modern law of murder on these two cases. The court in *Latimer* was, I believe, entirely justified in finding a distinction between their statutory backgrounds and one can well accept that the answers given, one for acquittal, the other for conviction, would be the same today. But the harking back to a concept of general malice, which amounts to no more than this, that a wrongful act displays a malevolence which can be attached to any adverse consequence, has long been out of date. And to speak of a particular malice which is 'transferred' simply disguises the problem by idiomatic language. The defendant's malice is directed at one objective, and when after the event the court treats it as directed at another object it is not recognising a 'transfer' but creating a new malice which never existed before. As Dr Glanville Williams pointed out (*Criminal Law*, the General Part, 2nd edn (1961), p 184) the doctrine is 'rather an arbitrary exception to general principles'. Like many of its kind this is useful enough to yield rough justice, in particular cases, and it can sensibly be retained notwithstanding its lack of any sound intellectual basis. But it is another matter to build a new rule upon it.

I pause to distinguish the case of indiscriminate malice from those already discussed, although even now it is sometimes confused with them. The terrorist who hides a bomb in an aircraft provides an example. This is not a case of 'general malice' where under the old law any wrongful act sufficed to prove the evil disposition which was taken to supply the necessary intent for homicide. Nor is it transferred malice, for there is no need of a transfer. The intention is already aimed directly at the class of potential victims of which the actual victim forms part. The intent and the *actus reus* completed by the explosion are joined from the start, even though the identity of the ultimate victim is not yet fixed. So also with the shots fired indiscriminately into a crowd. No ancient fictions are needed to make these cases of murder . . .

The fourth rule is an exception to the generally accepted principle that *actus reus* and *mens rea* must coincide. A continuous act or continuous chain of causes leading to death is treated by the law as if it happened when first initiated. The development of this into the fifth rule, which links an act and intent before birth with a death happening after a live delivery, causes a little more strain, given the incapacity of the foetus to be the object of homicide. If, however, it is possible to interpret the situation as one where the mental element is directed, not to the foetus but to the human being when and if it comes into existence, no fiction is required.

My Lords, the purpose of this enquiry has been to see whether the existing rules are based on principles sound enough to justify their extension to a case where the defendant acts without an intent to injure either the foetus or the child which it will become. In my opinion they are not. To give an affirmative answer requires a double 'transfer' of intent: first from the mother to the foetus and then from the foetus to the child as yet unborn. Then one would have to deploy the fiction (or at least the doctrine) which converts an intention to commit serious harm into the *mens rea* of murder. For me, this is too much. If one could find any logic in the rules I would follow it from one fiction to another, but whatever grounds there may once have been have long since disappeared. I am willing to follow old laws until they are overturned, but not to make a new law on a basis for which there is no principle.

Moreover, even on a narrower approach the argument breaks down. The effect of transferred malice, as I understand it, is that the intended victim and the actual victim are treated as if they were one, so that what was intended to happen to the first person (but did not happen) is added to what actually did happen to the second person (but was not intended to happen), with the result that what was intended and what happened are married to make a notionally intended and actually consummated crime. The cases are treated as if the actual victim had been the intended victim from the start. To make any sense of this process there must, as it seems to me, be some compatibility between the original intention and the actual occurrence, and this is, indeed, what one finds in the cases. There is no such compatibility here. The defendant intended to commit and did commit an immediate crime of violence to the mother. He committed no relevant violence to the foetus, which was not a person, either at the time or in the future, and intended no harm to the foetus or to the human person which it would become. If fictions are useful, as they can be, they are only damaged by straining them beyond their limits. I would not overstrain the idea of transferred malice by trying to make it fit the present case.

3.7.1 CODIFICATION AND LAW REFORM PROPOSALS

The Law Commission's Report Legislating the Criminal Code: *Offences Against the Person and General Principles* (1993) (Law Com 218) sought to codify the doctrine of transferred malice – see clause 32. A slightly amended version now appears in the draft Offences Against the Person Bill appended to the Home Office Consultation Paper, clause 17 of which provides:

17(1) This section applies in determining whether a person is guilty of an offence under this Act.

(2) A person's intention or awareness of a risk that his act will cause, a result in relation to a person capable of being the victim of the offence must be treated as an intention to cause or (as the case may be) awareness of a risk that his act cause, that result in relation to any other person affected by his act.

(3) A person's intention, or awareness of a risk, that his omission will have a result in relation to a person capable of being the victim of the offence must be treated as an intention or (as the case may be) awareness of a risk that his omission will have that result in relation to any other person affected as a result of his omission.

Given the close similarity between the Law Commission's proposed clause 32 in Law Com 218, and the provisions in the Home Office Bill, it is instructive to note the commentary on the transferred malice clause originally provided in Law Com 218.

42.1 Clause 25 of the Bill accompanying LCCP 122 restated, in the most general terms and not only in relation to offences against the person, the common law doctrine known as 'transferred intent' (subsection (1)), and provided a corresponding rule for 'transferred' defences. We received very little comment on the clause, and are satisfied, in particular, that the formulation of subsection (1) accurately represents the current law. Both subsections appear unchanged in clause 32 of the final draft Bill. Accordingly, the following explanation of the clause repeats in substance that which we gave in LCCP 122 . . .

42.3 The clause assumes that the specified result, such as serious injury, or damage to property belonging to another, is an element of a specific offence. If the actor does not cause such a result, the external elements of the offence with which he is charged are not made out. Accordingly, no question of criminal liability arises. It is only when the external elements of the offence charged have been caused by the defendant that the second question arises, of whether he acted with the fault required for that offence. This clause provides that if he acted with that fault, it can be transferred. What is required is a concurrence of fault in relation to the result specified for the offence and the occurrence of such a result, although not in relation to the same person or thing.

42.4 The equivalent clause in the Draft Code referred in terms to 'recklessness' and not, like the draft in LCCP 122 or clause 32 of the Criminal Law Bill, to 'awareness of a risk'. 'Recklessness' will have a prescribed meaning under the Bill for the purposes of offences against the person, but will continue to have its other meaning or meanings in other contexts. It is therefore necessary to avoid the term in a provision of general application. The only state of mind, other than intention, with which the subsection needs to deal is awareness of a risk. It is this aspect of recklessness that may call for 'transfer'. The provision is not needed in relation to the limb of *Caldwell* reckless-ness concerned with failure to advert to an obvious risk. In order to apply that limb to (for example) the causing of damage to the property actually affected, it is sufficient to ask: was there an obvious risk that that property (or such property) would be damaged and did the defendant fail to advert to that risk? It is irrelevant that there was a risk to other property of which the defendant should have been, but was not, aware.

42.5 Awareness of a relevant risk does not alone establish recklessness. It is necessary also that the risk be one that it was unreasonable to take in the circumstances known to the actor. If a defendant unreasonably took a known risk in relation to X, the risk-taking in relation to Y that the subsection treats as having occurred must similarly be unreasonable before reckless-ness is established in relation to Y. Conversely if, in the circumstances known to the defend-ant, it was reasonable to take the risk in relation to X that he knowingly took, the taking of the risk in relation to Y that he is treated as having knowingly taken can hardly be regarded as reckless.

42.6 Clause 32(2) enables a person who affects an uncontemplated victim to rely on a defence that would have been available to him if he had affected the person or thing he had in contempla-tion. The provision will be useful for the avoidance of doubt.

3.8 STRICT LIABILITY

There are certain offences where a defendant can be convicted notwithstanding that he did not have any *mens rea*. These offences are generally referred to as offences of strict liability. To say that these offences do not require proof of any *mens rea* may, however, be too sweeping. There are offences where no fault element at all arises – it is perhaps better to classify these as offences of absolute liability. Many so called strict liability offences do in fact require some *mens rea* in relation to some elements of the offence. The significant factor is that there may be some elements of the *actus reus* in relation to which no *mens rea* is required. When dealing with a statutory offence that is silent as to *mens rea* the task of the court lies in determining whether or not Parliament actually intended the offence to operate without proof of fault. The exercise is, largely, one of statutory interpretation. As the following extracts indicate, the factors taken into account by the courts can be summarised as follows:

(a) There is a presumption in favour of *mens rea* – that is, even if the statute is silent as to *mens rea* the courts will assume that some is required unless there is evidence to the contrary.

(b) The presumption in favour of *mens rea* can be rebutted by express wording in the statute or by necessary implication.

(c) The presumption in favour of *mens rea* is stronger where the offence is truly criminal – as opposed to merely regulatory. Factors such as the stigma attaching to a conviction and the penalty imposed will be significant here.

(d) The presumption in favour of *mens rea* may be rebutted by the subject matter of the offence, for example where the prohibition relates to a grave social danger or matter of public concern.

(e) The presumption in favour of *mens rea* is less likely to be rebutted where there is little evidence that the imposition of strict liability will help to achieve the aims and objects of the legislation.

3.8.1 THE PRESUMPTION IN FAVOUR OF *MENS REA*: READING THE STATUTE AS A WHOLE

Sweet v Parsley [1970] AC 132 (HL)

The defendant was a schoolteacher who had let premises, Fries Farm, to students. A police raid of the premises found that the students were using the premises for smoking cannabis. The defendant was convicted under s 5 of the Dangerous Drugs Act 1965, which provided as follows:

If a person:
(a) being the occupier of any premises, permits those premises to be used for the purpose of smoking cannabis or cannabis resin or of dealing in cannabis resin (whether by sale or otherwise); or,
(b) is concerned in the management of any premises used for any such purpose as aforesaid,

he shall be guilty of an offence against this Act.

The issue for the House of Lords was as to whether a defendant could incur liability under s 5 in the absence of any direct knowledge that the premises were being used for drug taking.

> Lord Morris of Borth-y-Gest:
> My Lords, it has frequently been affirmed and should unhesitatingly be recognised that it is a cardinal principle of our law that *mens rea*, an evil intention or a knowledge of the wrongfulness of the act, is in all ordinary cases an essential ingredient of guilt of a criminal offence. It follows from this that there will not be guilt of an offence created by statute unless there is *mens rea* or unless Parliament has by the statute enacted that guilt may be established in cases where there is no *mens rea*.
> . . . But as Parliament is supreme, it is open to Parliament to legislate in such a way that an offence may be created of which someone may be found guilty though *mens rea* is lacking.
> The intention of Parliament is expressed in the words of an enactment. The words must be looked at in order to see whether either expressly or by necessary implication they displace the general rule or presumption that *mens rea* is a necessary prerequisite before guilt of an offence can be found. Particular words in a statute must be considered in their setting in the statute and having regard to all the provisions of the statute and to its declared or obvious purpose . . .
> It must be considered, therefore, whether by the words of a penal statute it is either express or implied that there may be a conviction without *mens rea* or, in other words, whether what is called an absolute offence is created . . .
> The inquiry must be made, therefore, whether Parliament has used words which expressly enact or impliedly involve that an absolute offence is created. Though sometimes help in construction is derived from noting the presence or the absence of the word 'knowingly', no conclusive test can be laid down as a guide in finding the fair, reasonable and common sense meaning of language. But in considering whether Parliament has decided to displace what is a general and somewhat fundamental rule it would not be reasonable lightly to impute to Parliament an intention to create an offence in such a way that someone could be convicted of it who by all reasonable and sensible standards is without fault. . .

If someone is concerned in management there must at least be knowledge of what it is that is being managed: otherwise there could be no concern in it. If someone is concerned in the management of a building containing a number of separately let residential flats the concern in such case would be in the arrangements for the lettings and in the arrangements relating to lifts or staircases or the structure of the building as a whole. The concern would be in the management of premises used for residential purposes. In the ordinary course of things the landlord or the manager would have no right of entry into a flat and would have no concern with any normal, reasonable and lawful activity within a flat. If a tenant, who was a non-smoker, had a guest one day who smoked a pipe of tobacco in the flat, it would be a strained and unnatural use of language to describe the flat which the tenant rented as being premises used for the purpose of smoking. It would be equally strained and unnatural to describe the landlord or his agent as being concerned in the management of premises used for the purpose of smoking. If on an isolated occasion a tenant gave a showing of some cinematograph films to his friends, it would be unreasonable to describe the manager of the flats (who had no occasion to know of the film showing) as being one who was concerned in the management of premises used for the purpose of exhibiting films.

If a tenant took sugar with his tea it would be fanciful to describe the flat as premises used for the purpose of putting sugar into tea.

It seems to me, therefore that the words 'premises . . . used for the purpose of smoking cannabis' are not happily chosen if they were intended to denote premises in which at any time cannabis is smoked. In my opinion, the words 'premises . . . used for the purpose of . . .' denote a purpose which is other than quite incidental or casual or fortuitous: they denote a purpose which is or has become either a significant one or a recognised one though certainly not necessarily an only one. There is no difficulty in appreciating what is meant if it is said that premises are used for the purposes of a dance hall or a billiard hall or a bowling alley or a hairdressing saloon or a cafe. A new or additional use might, however, arise. It might happen that a house let as a private dwelling might come to be used as a brothel or for the purposes of prostitution. A room let for private occupation might come to be the resort of a number of people who wished to smoke opium so that the time would come when the room could rationally be described as a room used for the purpose of smoking opium.

The words 'concerned in the management of any premises used for the purpose of' are, in my view, to be considered together and as one phrase. Even so the phrase may be capable of two meanings. It could denote the management of premises used for a certain purpose in the sense that the management is limited to management in respect of the premises themselves. It could denote the management of premises used for a certain purpose in the sense that the management was concerned either additionally or perhaps separately with the purpose for which the premises were used. Thus, if someone is said so to be concerned in the management of premises used for the purpose of dancing, he could be someone concerned only in the management of the premises themselves, or he could be someone who additionally or possibly separately was concerned with the dancing. On either approach and with an ordinary use of words, it would seem to me that the person would be one who would have and would need to have knowledge of the use of the premises for the particular purpose . . .

For the reasons that I have indicated I consider that on a fair reading of the phrase 'concerned in the management of premises used for the purpose of' a link is denoted between management and user for a purpose. To say that someone is concerned in the management of premises used for the purpose of smoking cannabis involves, in my view, that his management is with knowledge that the premises are so used. The wording of s 5(b) contains positive indications that *mens rea* is an essential ingredient of an offence. Even if, contrary to my view, it is not affirmatively enacted that there must be *mens rea* I cannot read the wording as enacting that there need not be *mens rea*. I find it wholly impossible to say that the statute has either clearly, or by necessary implication, ruled out *mens rea* as a constituent part of guilt.

On the findings of the magistrates it follows that the appellant was not guilty. I would, therefore, allow the appeal. Accordingly, in my view, the case should be remitted to the Divisional Court with a direction to quash the conviction.

Pharmaceutical Society of Great Britain v Storkwain Ltd [1986] 1 WLR 903 (HL)

The defendants had supplied controlled drugs on production of what transpired to be a forged prescription. The House of Lords had to consider whether the relevant legislation – s 58 of the Medicines Act 1968 – could be construed so as to impose criminal liability on the defendants even though they had had no knowledge of the forgery.

Lord Goff of Chieveley:
My Lords, this appeal is concerned with a question of construction of s 58 of the Medicines Act 1968. Section 58(2)(a) of the Act provides:

(2) Subject to the following provisions of this section:
   (a) no person shall sell by retail, or supply in circumstances corresponding to retail sale, a medicinal product of a description, or falling within a class specified in an order under this section except in accordance with a prescription given by an appropriate practitioner . . .

By s 67(2) of the Act of 1968, it is provided that any person who contravenes, *inter alia*, s 58 shall be guilty of an offence. The question which has arisen for decision in the present case is whether, in accordance with the well-organised presumption, there are to be read into s 58(2)(a) words appropriate to require *mens rea*, on the principle stated in *R v Tolson* (1889) 23 QBD 168, and *Sweet v Parsley* [1970] AC 132.

. . . it is, in my opinion, clear from the Act of 1968 that Parliament must have intended that the presumption of *mens rea* should be inapplicable to s 58(2)(a). First of all, it appears from the Act of 1968 that, where Parliament wished to recognise that *mens rea* should be an ingredient of an offence created by the Act, it has expressly so provided. Thus, taking first of all offences created under provisions of Part II of the Act of 1968, express requirements of *mens rea* are to be found both in s 45(2) and in s 46(1), (2) and (3) of the Act. More particularly, in relation to offences created by Part III and Parts V and VI of the Act of 1968, s 121 makes detailed provision for a requirement of *mens rea* in respect of certain specified sections of the Act, including ss 63–65 (which are contained in Part III), but significantly not s 58, nor indeed ss 52 and 53 . . . It is very difficult to avoid the conclusion that, by omitting s 58 from those sections to which s 121 is expressly made applicable, Parliament intended that there should be no implication of a requirement of *mens rea* in s 58(2)(a). This view is fortified by subsections (4) and (5) of s 58 itself. Subsection (4)(a) provides that any order made by the appropriate ministers for the purposes of s 58 may provide that s 58(2)(a) or (b), or both, shall have effect subject to such exemptions as may be specified in the order. From this subsection alone it follows that the ministers, if they think it right, can provide for exemption where there is no *mens rea* on the part of the accused. Subsection (5) provides that any exemption conferred by an order in accordance with subsection (4)(a) may be conferred subject to such conditions or limitations as may be specified in the order. From this it follows that if the ministers, acting under subsection (4), were to confer an exemption relating to sales where the vendor lacked the requisite *mens rea* they may nevertheless circumscribe their exemption with conditions and limitations which render the exemption far narrower than the implication for which Mr Fisher (for the defendants) contends should be read into the statute itself. I find this to be very difficult to reconcile with the proposed implication.

It comes as no surprise to me, therefore, to discover that the relevant order in force at that time, the Medicines (Prescription Only) Order 1980, is drawn entirely in conformity with the construction of the statute which I favour. It is unnecessary, in the present case, to consider whether the relevant articles of the Order may be taken into account in construing s 58 of the Act of 1968; it is enough, for present purposes, that I am able to draw support from the fact that the ministers, in making the Order, plainly did not read s 58 as subject to the implication proposed by Mr Fisher. So, for example, Article 11 of the order (which is headed 'Exemption in cases involving another's default') reads as follows:

> The restrictions imposed by s 58(2)(a) (restrictions on sale and supply) shall not apply to the sale or supply of a prescription only medicine by a person who, having exercised all due diligence believes on reasonable grounds that the product sold or supplied is not a prescription only medicine, where it is due to the act or default of another person that the product is a product to which s 58(2)(a) applies.

This provision which, by including the words 'having exercised due diligence', provides for a narrower exemption than that which Mr Fisher has submitted should be read by implication into the statute, in the limited circumstances specified in the concluding words of the paragraph, is plainly inconsistent with the existence of any such implication. Likewise, Article 13(1) provides that, for the purposes of s 58(2)(a), a prescription only medicine shall not be taken to be sold or supplied in accordance with a prescription given by a practitioner unless certain specified conditions are fulfilled. Those conditions, which are very detailed, are set out in Article 13(2); and they all presuppose the existence of a valid prescription. Furthermore, Article 13(3) provides:

> The restrictions imposed by s 58(2)(a) (restrictions on sale and supply) shall not apply to a sale or supply of a prescription only medicine which is not in accordance with a prescription given by an appropriate practitioner by reason only that a condition specified in paragraph (2) is not fulfilled, where the person selling or supplying the prescription only medicine, having exercised all due diligence believes on reasonable grounds that that condition is fulfilled in relation to that sale or supply.

So here again we find a provision which creates an exemption in narrower terms than that which Mr Fisher submits is to be found, by implication, in s 58(2)(a) itself. It follows that Article 13, like Article 11, of the Order is inconsistent with the existence of any such implication.

For these reasons, which are substantially the same as those which are set out in the judgments of Farquharson and Tudor Price JJ in the Divisional Court [1985] 3 All ER 4, I am unable to accept the submissions advanced on behalf of the defendants. I gratefully adopt as my own the following passage from the judgment of Farquharson J, at 10:

It is perfectly obvious that pharmacists are in a position to put illicit drugs and perhaps other medicines on the market. Happily this rarely happens but it does from time to time. It can therefore be readily understood that Parliament would find it necessary to impose a heavier liability on those who are in such a position, and make them more strictly accountable for any breaches of the Act.

I would therefore answer the certified question in the negative, and dismiss the appeal with costs.

B v DPP [2000] 1 All ER 833

The appellant, aged 15 at the material time, sat next to a 13 year old girl who was a passenger on a bus. The appellant asked the girl several times to perform oral sex with him. She repeatedly refused. The appellant was charged with inciting a girl under 14 to commit an act of gross indecency contrary to section 1(1) of the Indecency with Children Act 1960. The appellant pleaded not guilty, relying on the fact that he honestly believed that the girl was over 14 years. The defence argued that on the admitted facts the appellant was entitled to be acquitted. The prosecution submitted that the offence was one of strict liability. The appellant was convicted and appealed. [NB liability in this area would now be governed by the Sexual Offences Act 2003, as to which see further Chapter 6.]

Lord Steyn

[considering the extent to which the offence in question could be read as one that imposed strict liability].

The correct approach

My Lords, it will be convenient to turn to the approach to be adopted to the construction of section 1(1) of the Act of 1960. While broader considerations will ultimately have to be taken into account, the essential point of departure must be the words of section 1(1). The language is general and nothing on the face of section 1(1) indicates one way or the other whether section 1(1) creates an offence of strict liability. In enacting such a provision Parliament does not write on a blank sheet. The sovereignty of Parliament is the paramount principle of our constitution. But Parliament legislates against the background of the principle of legality ... Recently, in *R v Secretary of State for the Home Department ex p Simms* [1999] 3 WLR 328 the House applied the principle to subordinate legislation: see in particular the speeches of Lord Hoffmann (at 341F–G), myself (at 340G–H) and Lord Browne-Wilkinson (at 330E). In *ex p Simms* Lord Hoffmann explained the principle as follows (at 341F–G):

But the principle of legality means that Parliament must squarely confront what it is doing and accept the political cost. Fundamental rights cannot be overridden by general or ambiguous words. This is because there is too great a risk that the full implications of their unqualified meaning may have passed unnoticed in the democratic process. In the absence of express language or necessary implication to the contrary, the courts therefore presume that even the most general words were intended to be subject to the basic rights of the individual.

This passage admirably captures, if I may say so, the rationale of the principle of legality. In successive editions of his classic work Professor Sir Rupert Cross cited as the paradigm of the principle the ' "presumption" that *mens rea* is required in the case of statutory crimes': Statutory Interpretation 3rd edn (1995), p 166. Sir Rupert explained that such presumptions are of general application and are not dependent on finding an ambiguity in the text. He said they 'not only supplement the text, they also operate at a higher level as expressions of fundamental principles governing both civil liberties and the relations between Parliament, the executive and the courts. They operate as constitutional principles which are not easily displaced by a statutory text'. In other words, in the absence of express words or a truly necessary implication, Parliament must be presumed to legislate on the assumption that the principle of legality will supplement the text. This is the theoretical framework against which section 1(1) must be interpreted. It is now necessary to examine the practical application of the principle as explained by the House in *Sweet v Parsley* . . . Lord Reid drew a distinction between 'a truly criminal act' and acts which are not truly criminal in any real sense, but are 'acts which in the public interest are prohibited under a penalty': at 149F . . . he said that in cases of truly criminal acts it is wrong to take into account 'no more than the wording of the Act and the character and seriousness of the mischief which constitutes the offence': at 150A . . .

Counsel for the Crown accepted that the approach as outlined in *Sweet v Parsley*, and in particular in the speech of Lord Reid, is an authoritative and accurate statement of the law. It is only necessary to refer one further decision. In *Lim Chin Aik v R* [1963] AC 160, at 174, the Privy Council observed that in considering how the presumption can be displaced 'it is not enough in their Lordships' opinions merely to label the statute as one dealing with a grave social evil and from that to infer that strict liability was intended'. Their Lordships no doubt had in mind that the prevalence of even a grave social evil does not necessarily throw light on the question of what technique was adopted to combat the evil, viz the creation of an offence of strict liability or an offence of which *mens rea* is an ingredient.

Concentrating still on the wording of section 1(1) of the Act of 1960, I now address directly the question whether the presumption is *prima facie* applicable. Two distinctive features of section 1(1) must be taken into account. First, the *actus reus* is widely defined. Unlike the position under sections 14 and 15 of the Act of 1956, an assault is not an ingredient of the offence under section 1(1). Any act of gross indecency with or towards a child under the age of 14, or incitement to such an act, whether committed in public or private, is within its scope. The subsection is apt to cover acts of paedophilia and all responsible citizens will welcome effective legislation in respect of such a great social evil. But it also covers any heterosexual or homosexual contact between teenagers if one of them is under 14. And the *actus reus* extends to incitement of a child under 14: words are enough. The subsection therefore extends to any verbal sexual overtures between teenagers if one of them is under 14 . . . For the law to criminalise such conduct of teenagers by offences of strict liability would be far reaching and controversial. The second factor is that section 1(1) creates an offence of a truly criminal character. It was initially punishable on indictment by a custodial term of up to two years and by subsequent amendment the maximum term has been increased to ten years' imprisonment. Moreover, as Lord Reid observed in *Sweet v Parsley* (at 146H) 'a stigma still attaches to any person convicted of a truly criminal offence, and the more serious or more disgraceful the offence the greater the stigma.' Taking into account the cumulative effect of these two factors, I am persuaded that, if one concentrates on the language of section 1(1), the presumption is *prima facie* applicable. It is, however, now necessary to examine weighty contrary arguments based on the broader context in which section 1(1) must be seen.

Since counsel for the Crown adopted as part of his argument the reasoning of the Divisional Court, and in particular the reasoning of Rougier J, it is unnecessary to summarise the judgments. Instead I propose to examine directly the major planks of the reasoning contained in the judgments of the Divisional Court and in the submissions of counsel for the Crown. But I would respectfully record my tribute to the careful and elegant judgments in the Divisional Court . . .

[Turning to the legislative policy underpinning the 1956 and 1960 Acts] Counsel for the Crown next submitted that a necessary implication negativing *mens rea* as an ingredient of the offence is to be found in the general legislative policy of the Act of 1956 to protect girls under the age of 16: see sections 5, 6, 14, 15, 26 and 28. It is undoubtedly right that there is a clear legislative policy prohibiting the sexual exploitation of girls. It is unquestionably a great social evil as Lord Hutton has so clearly explained. Whatever can be done sensibly and justly to stamp it out ought to be done.

The real question is: what does this policy tell us about the critical question whether section 1(1) is an offence of strict liability or not? It is not enough to label the statute as one dealing with a grave social evil and from that to infer that strict liability was intended . . . Moreover, upon analysis the argument is far from compelling. It infers from the premise of the legislative policy directed against the mischief a conclusion that the legislature gave clear expression to a choice of the solution of creating an offence of strict liability rather than an offence containing *mens rea* as an ingredient. The cardinal principle of construction described by Lord Reid in *Sweet v Parsley* is not to be displaced by such speculative considerations as to the chosen legislative technique. I would reject this argument.

Prince's case
Counsel for the Crown also relied on what he described as a principle of construction established in *R v Prince* (1875) LR 2 CCR 154. In *Prince* the defendant was convicted under a Victorian statute of unlawfully taking an unmarried girl under the age of 16 out of the possession of her father. The defendant *bona fide* and on reasonable grounds believed that the girl was over 16. The judge referred the question of the availability of the defence to the Court for Crown Cases Reserved. The court consisted of 16 judges. The prisoner was not represented. By a majority of 15 to 1 the court held that there was no such defence. The leading judgment was given by Blackburn J with the concurrence of nine other judges. Blackburn J relied strongly on a drafting flaw in sections 50 and 51 of the Offences Against the Person Act 1861. The two sections respectively provided for offences of sexual intercourse with a girl under ten (section 50) and above the age of ten years and under the age of twelve years (section 51). The first was a felony and the latter a misdemeanour. Blackburn J produced what Professor Sir Rupert Cross in a magisterial article described as a 'knock-out' argument: 'Centenary reflections on Prince's case' (1975) 91 LQR 540. The passage in Blackburn's J judgment reads as follows:

It seems impossible to suppose that the intention of the legislature in those two sections could have been to make the crime depend upon the knowledge of the prisoner of the girl's actual age. It would produce the monstrous result that a man who had carnal connection with a girl, in reality not quite ten years old, but whom he on reasonable grounds believed to be a little more than ten, was to escape altogether. He could not, in that view of the statute, be convicted of the felony, for he did not know her to be under ten. He could not be convicted of the misdemeanour, because she was in fact not above the age of ten. It seems to us that the intention of the legislature was to punish those who had connection with young girls, though with their consent, unless the girl was in fact old enough to give a valid consent.The man who has connection with a child, relying on her consent, does it at his peril, if she is below the statutable age. The 55th section, on which the present case arises, uses precisely the same words as those in sections 50 and 51, and must be construed in the same way.

Eventually the distinction between felonies and misdemeanours was abolished and the drafting flaw in the earlier legislation no longer exists. The principal ground of the decision of Blackburn J has disappeared. It is true that Bramwell B gave a separate judgment in which seven judges concurred. This judgment is largely based on the view that the defendant was guilty in law because if the facts had been as he supposed he would have acted immorally. For the further reasons given by Sir Rupert Cross in his article one can be confident that the reasoning of Bramwell B, if tested in a modern court, would not be upheld: see also *DPP v Morgan* [1976] AC 182, at 238, per Lord Fraser of Tullybelton; and the valuable discussion by Brooke LJ of the context of Prince's case: at 130B–32B. Significantly, Prince's case was cited in *Sweet v Parsley* but was not mentioned in any of the judgments. The view may have prevailed that it was not necessary to overrule it because its basis had gone and that the principle laid down in *Sweet v Parsley* would in future be the controlling one. In any event, I would reject the contention that there is a special rule of construction in respect of age-based sexual offences which is untouched by the presumption as explained in *Sweet v Parsley*.

Lord Nicholls:

The construction of section 1 of the Indecency with Children Act 1960
In section 1(1) of the Indecency with Children Act 1960 Parliament has not expressly negatived the need for a mental element in respect of the age element of the offence. The question, therefore, is whether, although not expressly negatived, the need for a mental element is negatived by necessary implication. 'Necessary implication' connotes an implication which is compellingly clear. Such an implication may be found in the language used, the nature of the offence, the mischief sought to be prevented and any other circumstances which may assist in determining what intention is properly to be attributed to Parliament when creating the offence.

I venture to think that, leaving aside the statutory context of section 1, there is no great difficulty in this case. The section created an entirely new criminal offence, in simple unadorned language. The offence so created is a serious offence. The more serious the offence, the greater is the weight to be attached to the presumption, because the more severe is the punishment and the graver the stigma which accompany a conviction. Under section 1 conviction originally attracted a punishment of up to two years' imprisonment. This has since been increased to a maximum of ten years' imprisonment. The notification requirements under Part I of the Sex Offenders Act 1997 now apply, no matter what the age of the offender: see Schedule 1, paragraph 1(1)(b). Further, in addition to being a serious offence, the offence is drawn broadly ('an act of gross indecency'). It can embrace conduct ranging from predatory approaches by a much older paedophile to consensual sexual experimentation between precocious teenagers of whom the offender may be the younger of the two. The conduct may be depraved by any acceptable standard, or it may be relatively innocuous behaviour in private between two young people. These factors reinforce, rather than negative, the application of the presumption in this case. The purpose of the section is, of course, to protect children. An age ingredient was therefore an essential ingredient of the offence. This factor in itself does not assist greatly. Without more, this does not lead to the conclusion that liability was intended to be strict so far as the age element is concerned, so that the offence is committed irrespective of the alleged offender's belief about the age of the 'victim' and irrespective of how the offender came to hold this belief. Nor can I attach much weight to a fear that it may be difficult sometimes for the prosecution to prove that the defendant knew the child was under fourteen or was recklessly indifferent about the child's age. A well known passage from a judgment of that great jurist, Sir Owen Dixon, in *Thomas v R* (1937) 59 CLR 279, 309, bears repetition:

> The truth appears to be that a reluctance on the part of courts has repeatedly appeared to allow a prisoner to avail himself of a defence depending simply on his own state of knowledge and belief. The reluctance is due in great measure, if not entirely, to a mistrust of the tribunal of fact – the jury. Through a feeling that, if the law allows such a defence to be submitted to the jury, prisoners may too readily escape by deposing to conditions of mind and describing sources of information, matters upon which their evidence cannot be adequately tested and contradicted, judges have been misled into a failure steadily to adhere to principle. It is not difficult to understand such tendencies, but a lack of confidence in the ability of a tribunal correctly to estimate evidence of states of mind and the like can never be sufficient ground for excluding from inquiry the most fundamental element in a rational and humane criminal code.

Similarly, it is far from clear that strict liability regarding the age ingredient of the offence would further the purpose of section 1 more effectively than would be the case if a mental element were read into this ingredient. There is no general agreement that strict liability is necessary to the enforcement of the law protecting children in sexual matters . . .

Is there here a compellingly clear implication that Parliament should be taken to have intended that the ordinary common law requirement of a mental element should be excluded in respect of the age ingredient of this new offence? Thus far, having regard especially to the breadth of the offence and the gravity of the stigma and penal consequences which a conviction brings, I see no sufficient ground for so concluding.

Indeed, the Crown's argument before your Lordships did not place much reliance on any of the matters just mentioned. The thrust of the Crown's argument lay in a different direction: the statutory context. This is understandable, because the statutory background is undoubtedly the Crown's strongest point. The Crown submitted that the law in this field has been regarded as settled for well over one hundred years, ever since the decision in *R v Prince* (1875) LR 2 CCR 154. That well known case concerned the unlawful abduction of a girl under the age of sixteen. The defendant honestly believed she was over sixteen, and he had reasonable grounds for believing this. No fewer than fifteen judges held that this provided no defence. Subsequently, in *R v Maughan* (1934) 24 Cr App R 130 the Court of Criminal Appeal (Lord Hewart CJ, Avory and Roche JJ) held that a reasonable and honest belief that a girl was over sixteen could never be a defence to a charge of indecent assault. The court held that this point had been decided in *R v Forde* (1923) 17 Cr App R 99. The court also observed that in any event the answer was to be found in Prince's case. Building on this foundation Mr Scrivener QC submitted that the Sexual Offences Act 1956 was not intended to change this established law, and that section 1 of the Indecency with Children Act 1960 was to be read with the 1956 Act. The preamble to the 1960 Act stated that its purpose was to make 'further' provision for the punishment of indecent conduct towards young people. In this field, where Parliament intended belief as to age to be a defence, this was stated expressly: see, for instance, the 'young man's defence' in section 6(3) of the 1956 Act.

This is a formidable argument, but I cannot accept it. I leave on one side Mr O'Connor QC's sustained criticisms of the reasoning in Prince's case and Maughan's case. Where the Crown's argument breaks down is that the motley collection of offences, of diverse origins, gathered into the Sexual Offences Act 1956 displays no satisfactorily clear or coherent pattern. If the interpretation of section 1 of the Act of 1960 is to be gleaned from the contents of another statute, that other statute must give compelling guidance. The Act of 1956 as a whole falls short of this standard. So do the two sections, sections 14 and 15, which were the genesis of section 1 of the Act of 1960.

Accordingly, I cannot find, either in the statutory context or otherwise, any indication of sufficient cogency to displace the application of the common law presumption. In my view the necessary mental element regarding the age ingredient in section 1 of the Act of 1960 is the absence of a genuine belief by the accused that the victim was fourteen years of age or above. The burden of proof of this rests upon the prosecution in the usual way. If Parliament considers that the position should be otherwise regarding this serious social problem, Parliament must itself confront the difficulties and express its will in clear terms. I would allow this appeal.

I add a final observation. As just mentioned, in reaching my conclusion I have left on one side the criticisms made of Prince's case and Maughan's case. Those cases concerned different offences and different statutory provisions. The correctness of the decisions in those cases does not call for decision on the present appeal. But, without expressing a view on the correctness of the actual decisions in those cases, I must observe that some of the reasoning in Prince's case is at variance with the common law presumption regarding *mens rea* as discussed above. To that extent, the reasoning must be regarded as unsound. For instance, Bramwell B (at p 174) seems to have regarded the common law presumption as ousted because the act forbidden was 'wrong in itself'. Denman J (at p 178) appears to have considered it was 'reasonably clear' that the Act of 1861 was an Act of strict liability so far as the age element was concerned. On its face this is a lesser standard than necessary implication. And in the majority judgment, Blackburn J reached his conclusion by inference from the intention Parliament must have had when enacting two other, ineptly drawn, sections of the Act. But clumsy parliamentary drafting is an insecure basis for finding a necessary implication elsewhere, even in the same statute. Prince's case, and later decisions based on it, must now be read in the light of this decision of your Lordships' House on the nature and weight of the common law presumption.

Lord Hutton:

... the Act of 1960 is an appendix to the Act of 1956, and the wording of sections 5 and 6 of the 1956 Act relating respectively to intercourse with a girl under thirteen and to intercourse with a girl under sixteen, but with the latter section providing in subsection (3) for 'the young man's defence', makes it plain that the offence under section 5 is an offence of strict liability. Therefore it is clear that in the Act of 1956 Parliament intended that there should be strict liability when a man had sexual intercourse with a girl under thirteen, and accordingly it can be argued that it is in accordance with the intention of Parliament that there should be strict liability when a person is guilty of gross indecency towards a child under fourteen. The second point is that in addition to section 6(3) there are a number of sections in the Act of 1956 which expressly provide for a defence of mistake. In the case of intercourse with a woman who is a defective section 7(2) provides a defence if the man does not know and has no reason to suspect the woman to be a defective. The same applies to the offence of procurement of a defective: see section 9(2). The same defence applies to indecent assault on a woman defective: see section 14(4). The same defence is available in respect of permitting a defective to use premises for intercourse or causing or encouraging the prostitution of a defective: see section 27(2) and section 29(2). Therefore the Crown can argue with considerable force that when Parliament intends that there should be a defence of mistake it makes express provision for this defence, so that where there is no express provision for such a defence the statute by implication intends that the defence will not be available. This point is well stated by Tucker J in his judgment at p 127H:

> I deduce from all these statutory provisions that it is the clear intention of Parliament to protect young children and to make it an offence to commit offences against children under a certain age whether or not the defendant knows of the age of the victim, and that it was intended that, save where expressly provided, a mistaken or honest belief in the victim's age should not afford a defence.

Therefore I consider that it would be reasonable to infer that it was the intention of Parliament that liability under section 1(1) of the Act of 1960 should be strict so that an honest belief as to the age of the child would not be a defence. But the test is not whether it is a reasonable implication that the statute rules out *mens rea* as a constituent part of the crime – the test is whether it is a necessary implication. Applying this test, I am of opinion that there are considerations which point to the conclusion that it is not a necessary implication. One is that the various provisions of the Act of 1956 have not been drafted to give effect to a consistent scheme but are a collection of diverse provisions derived from a variety of sources: . . . A further consideration is that in *Sweet v Parsley* Lord Reid stated at p 149D:

> It is also firmly established that the fact that other sections of the Act expressly require *mens rea*, for example because they contain the word 'knowingly', is not in itself sufficient to justify a decision that a section which is silent as to *mens rea* creates an absolute offence.

Whilst, as I have stated, I think there is force in the view expressed by Blackburn J at pp 171–72 of *R v Prince*, I am of opinion that to the extent that Prince's case can be viewed as establishing a general rule that mistake as to age does not afford a defence in age-based sexual offences, that rule cannot prevail over the presumption stated by this House in *Sweet v Parsley*.

Therefore, for the reasons which I have stated, I would allow this appeal and I would answer the first certified question in the negative. For the reasons which have been stated by my noble and learned friend Lord Steyn, and with which I agree, I would answer part (a) of the second certified question in the affirmative, and I would answer part (b) by stating that the burden of proof rests on the Crown once the defendant has raised some evidence before the jury or magistrates that he or she honestly believed the child was over fourteen.

I am conscious that the decision by this House to allow this appeal may make it more difficult to convict those who are guilty of an offence under Section 1(1) of the Act of 1960 and thus reduce the protection given to children, but I have come to the conclusion that as Parliament has failed to state by express provision or by necessary implication that *mens rea* as to age is not necessary, the legal presumption stated by Lord Reid that *mens rea* is required must be applied. If Parliament regards the decision in this case as giving rise to undesirable consequences it will be for it to change the law, and I share the regret of Brooke LJ expressed in his judgment at p 136A–H that Parliament does not take account of the expert advice which it has received over the years from the Criminal Law Revision Committee and the Law Commission, and does not address its mind, in enacting legislation creating or restating criminal offences, to the issue whether *mens rea* should be a constituent part of the offences and does not state in clear terms whether or not *mens rea* is required.

3.8.2 THE SERIOUSNESS OF THE OFFENCE: STIGMA AND PUNISHMENT VERSUS MERELY REGULATORY

Alphacell Ltd v Woodward [1972] AC 824 (HL)

The appellant company had been convicted, under the Rivers (Prevention of Pollution) Act 1951, of the offence of causing or knowingly permitting to enter a stream 'any poisonous, noxious or polluting matter' (s 2(1)(a)). The following extracts focus upon the extent to which the imposition of strict liability can be justified where the prohibition is essentially regulatory in substance, as opposed to 'truly criminal'.

Viscount Dilhorne:

. . . This Act, in my opinion, is one of those Acts to which my noble and learned friends, Lord Reid and Lord Diplock, referred in *Sweet v Parsley* [1970] AC 132, 149, 163 which, to apply the words of Wright J in *Sherras v De Rutzen* [1895] 1 QB 918, 922 deals with acts which 'are not criminal in any real sense, but are acts which in the public interest are prohibited under a penalty'.

What, then, is meant by the word 'caused' in the subsection? If a man, intending to secure a particular result, does an act which brings that about, he causes that result. If he deliberately and intentionally does certain acts of which the natural consequence is that certain results ensue, may he not also be said to have caused those results even though they may not have been intended by him? I think he can, just as he can be said to cause the result if he is negligent, without intending that result . . .

We have not here to consider what the position would be if pollution were caused by an inadvertent and unintentional act without negligence. In such case it might be said that the doer of the act had not caused the pollution although the act had caused it. Here the acts done by the appellants were intentional. They were acts calculated to lead to the river being polluted if the acts done by the appellants, the installation and operation of the pumps, were ineffective to prevent it. Where a person intentionally does certain things which produce a certain result, then it can truly be said that he has caused that result, and here in my opinion the acts done intentionally by the appellants causes the pollution . . .

Lord Salmon:

My Lords . . . The appellants contend that, even if they caused the pollution, still they should succeed since they did not cause it intentionally or knowingly or negligently. Section 2(1)(a) of the Rivers (Prevention of Pollution) Act 1951 is undoubtedly a penal section. It follows that if it is capable of two or more meanings then the meaning most favourable to the subject should be adopted. Accordingly, so the argument runs, the words 'intentionally' or 'knowingly' or 'negligently' should be read into the section immediately before the word 'causes'. I do not agree. It is of the utmost public importance that our rivers should not be polluted. The risk of pollution, particularly from the vast and increasing number of riparian industries, is very great. The offences created by the Act of 1951 seem to me to be prototypes of offences which 'are not criminal in any real sense, but are acts which in the public interest are prohibited under a penalty': *Sherras v De Rutzen* [1895] 1 QB 918, per Wright J at 922, referred to with approval by my noble and learned friends, Lord Reid and Lord Diplock, in *Sweet v Parsley* [1970] AC 132, at 149, 162. I can see no valid reason for reading the word 'intentionally', 'knowingly' or 'negligently' into s 2(1)(a) and a number of cogent reasons for not doing so. In the case of a minor pollution such as the present, when the justices find that there is no wrongful intention or negligence on the part of the defendant, a comparatively nominal fine will no doubt be imposed. This may be regarded as a not unfair hazard of carrying on a business which may cause pollution on the banks of a river. The present appellants were fined £20 and ordered to pay, in all, £24 costs. I should be surprised if the costs of pursuing this appeal to this House were incurred for the purpose of saving these appellants £44.

If this appeal succeeded and it were held to be the law that no conviction could be obtained under the Act of 1951 unless the prosecution could discharge the often impossible onus of proving that the pollution was caused intentionally or negligently, a great deal of pollution would go unpunished and undeterred to the relief of many riparian factory owners. As a result, many rivers which are now filthy would become filthier still and many rivers which are now clean would lose their cleanliness. The legislature no doubt recognised that as a matter of public policy this would be most unfortunate. Hence s 2(1)(a) which encourages riparian factory owners not only to take reasonable steps to prevent pollution but to do everything possible to ensure that they do not cause it . . .

Wings Ltd v Ellis [1985] AC 272 (HL)

A Mr Wade booked a foreign holiday with the defendant company on the strength of information contained in its travel brochure that was subsequently found to be untrue. The House of Lords had to consider whether the relevant legislation, s 14 of the Trade Descriptions Act 1968, created an offence of strict liability.

Lord Scarman:
My Lords, this appeal turns on the construction properly to be put upon a few ordinary English words in the context of s 14 of the Trade Descriptions Act 1968. Put very shortly, the basic issue between the parties is whether upon its proper construction s 14(1)(a) creates an offence of strict, or more accurately, semi-strict, liability or is one requiring the existence of full *mens rea* . . . Section 14, so far as material, is in these terms:

(1) It shall be an offence for any person in the course of any trade or business:
    (a) to make a statement which he knows to be false; or
    (b) recklessly to make a statement which is false;
as to any of the following matters, that is to say: (1) the provision in the course of any trade or business of any services, accommodation or facilities . . .

It is no exaggeration to say that the social impact of the class of business which I have described and in which the respondent company is engaged has been immense. It has brought about a dramatic change in the lifestyle of millions. People rely on the brochures issued by the companies engaged in this highly competitive business when choosing their annual holidays abroad. Some, like Mr and Mrs Wade in this case, choose to travel great distances to far-away places very different from anything which they have experienced at home upon their faith in a description which they have read in a brochure but which they cannot check.

The Trade Descriptions Act 1968 is plainly a very important safeguard for those members of the public (and they run into millions) who choose their holidays in this way. If the protection is not to be undermined, the Act must be widely known (as indeed it is), easily understood (as, having heard the arguments in this case, I fear that it may not be), and must be of general application save in situations specifically excepted by the statute itself. The Act is not based on the law of contract or tort. It operates by prohibiting false descriptions under the pain of penalties enforced through the criminal courts. But it is not a truly criminal statute. Its purpose is not the enforcement of the criminal law but the maintenance of trading standards. Trading standards, not criminal behaviour, are its concern.

Its prohibitions include false trade descriptions applied to goods (s 1); misleading indications as to the price of goods (s 11); false representations as to royal approval or awards (s 12); and false statements as to the nature of services, accommodation, or facilities provided in the course of business (s 14). It provides for certain defences to be available, two of which could have been relevant in this case. They are defences made available under ss 23 and 24, to which I shall return later. Neither section was invoked at the hearing before the justices, who consequently made no finding upon either of them. Indeed, it was argued by the respondent in your Lordships' House that neither was applicable to an offence charged under s 14.

The Act, of course, to be of any value at all in modern conditions, has to cover trades and businesses conducted on a large scale by individual proprietors, by firms, and by bodies corporate. The day-to-day business activities of large enterprises, whatever their legal structure, are necessarily conducted by their employees, and particularly by their sales staff. It follows that many of the acts prohibited by the Act will be the acts of employees done in the course of the trade or business and without the knowledge at the time of those who direct the business. It will become clear that the Act does cover such acts when one comes to consider the terms of the two statutory defences to which I have already referred. The Act also makes specific provision consistent with this view of its operation in respect of businesses carried on by bodies corporate. Section 20 provides that where an offence has been committed by a body corporate and was committed with the consent or is attributable to the neglect of a director or other officer of the company, he 'as well as the body corporate' is guilty of the offence . . .

My Lords, the subject-matter and structure of the Act make plain that the Act belongs to that class of legislation which prohibits acts which 'are not criminal in any real sense, but are acts which in the public interest are prohibited under a penalty', as Wright J put it in *Sherras v De Rutzen* [1895] 1 QB 918, 922. In construing the offence-creating sections of the Act it will, therefore, be necessary to bear in mind that it may well have been the intention of the legislature 'in order to guard against the happening of the forbidden thing, to impose a liability upon a principal even though he does not know of, and is not a party to, the forbidden act done by his servant': see per Viscount Reading CJ in *Mousell Brothers Ltd v London and North-Western Railway Co* [1917] 2 KB 836, 844.

While, however, the subject-matter of the Act is such that the presumption recognised by Lord Reid in *Sweet v Parsley* [1970] AC 132, 148G as applicable to truly criminal statutes 'that Parliament did not intend to make criminals of persons who were in no way blameworthy in what they did' is not applicable to this Act, it does not necessarily follow that merely because an offence-creating section in the Act is silent as to *mens rea* its silence must be construed as excluding *mens rea*. As Lord Reid said, at 149, in the absence of a clear indication that an offence is intended to be an absolute offence one must examine all relevant circumstances in order to establish the intention of Parliament . . . At the end of the day the question whether an offence created by statute requires *mens rea*, guilty knowledge or intention, in whole, in part, or not at all, turns on the subject-matter, the language and the structure of the Act studied as a whole, on the language of the particular statutory provision under consideration construed in the light of the legislative purpose embodied in the Act, and on 'whether strict liability in respect of all or any of the essential ingredients of the offence would promote the object of the provision': *Gammon's* case at 16 and see *Sweet v Parsley* [1970] AC 132, 163, per Lord Diplock . . .

3.8.3 PRESUMPTION IN FAVOUR OF *MENS REA* REBUTTED BY SUBJECT MATTER: THE NEED TO PROTECT SOCIETY

Gammon (Hong Kong) Ltd v AG of Hong Kong [1985] 1 AC 1 (PC)

The defendant company was charged with breaching building regulations in Hong Kong (the 'Ordinances'). The issue for the Privy Council was as to whether or not the Ordinances created offences of strict liability.

Lord Scarman:
. . . The issue in the appeal is whether the offences charged are offences of strict liability or require proof of *mens rea* as to their essential facts . . . In their Lordships' opinion, the law relevant to this appeal may be stated in the following propositions . . .: (1) there is a presumption of law that *mens rea* is required before a person can be held guilty of a criminal offence; (2) the presumption is particularly strong where the offence is 'truly criminal' in character; (3) the presumption applies to statutory offences, and can be displaced only if this is clearly or by necessary implication the effect of the statute; (4) the only situation in which the presumption can be displaced is where the statute is concerned with an issue of social concern, and public safety is such an issue; (5) even where a statute is concerned with such an issue, the presumption of *mens rea* stands unless it can also be shown that the creation of strict liability will be effective to promote the objects of the statute by encouraging greater vigilance to prevent the commission of the prohibited act.
. . . Whether, therefore, a particular provision of the statute creates an offence of full *mens rea* or of strict liability must depend upon the true meaning of the words of the particular provision construed with reference to its subject-matter and to the question whether strict liability in respect of all or any of the essential ingredients of the offence would promote the object of the provision . . .

3.8.4 WHETHER THE IMPOSITION OF STRICT LIABILITY HELPS TO ACHIEVE THE LEGISLATIVE PURPOSE

Sherras v De Rutzen [1895] 1 QB 918 (QBD)

Day J:

I am clearly of opinion that this conviction ought to be quashed. This police constable comes into the appellant's public house without his armlet, and with every appearance of being off duty. The house was in the immediate neighbourhood of the police station, and the appellant believed, and he had very natural grounds for believing, that the constable was off duty. In that belief he accordingly served him with liquor. As a matter of fact, the constable was on duty; but does that fact make the innocent act of the appellant an offence? I do not think it does. He had no intention to do a wrongful act; he acted in the *bona fide* belief that the constable was off duty. It seems to me that the contention that he committed an offence is utterly erroneous . . .

Wright J:

I am of the same opinion. There are many cases on the subject, and it is not very easy to reconcile them. There is a presumption that *mens rea*, an evil intention, or a knowledge of the wrongfulness of the act, is an essential ingredient in every offence; but that presumption is liable to be displaced either by the words of the statute creating the offence or by the subject-matter with which it deals, and both must be considered: *Nichols v Hall* Law Rep 8 CP 322. One of the most remarkable exceptions was in the case of bigamy. It was held by all the judges, on the statute 1 Jac 1, c 11, that a man was rightly convicted of bigamy who had married after an invalid Scotch divorce, which had been obtained in good faith, and the validity of which he had no reason to doubt: *Lolley's* case R & R 237. Another exception, apparently grounded on the language of a statute, is *Prince's* case Law Rep 2 CC 154, where it was held by 15 judges against one that a man was guilty of abduction of a girl under 16, although he believed, in good faith and on reasonable grounds, that she was over that age. Apart from isolated and extreme cases of this kind, the principal classes of exceptions may perhaps be reduced to three. One is a class of acts which, in the language of Lush J in *Davies v Harvey* Law Rep 9 QB 433, are not criminal in any real sense, but are acts which in the public interest are prohibited under a penalty. Several such instances are to be found in the decisions on the Revenue Statutes, e.g. *AG v Lockwood* 9 M & W 378, where the innocent possession of liquorice by a beer retailer was held an offence. So under the Adulteration Acts, *R v Woodrow* 15 M & W 404, as to innocent possession of adulterated tobacco; *Fitzpatrick v Kelly* Law Rep 8 QB 337 and *Roberts v Egerton* Law Rep 9 QB 494 as to the sale of adulterated food . . .

. . . Another class comprehends some, and perhaps all, public nuisances: *R v Stephens* Law Rep 1 QB 702 where the employer was held liable on indictment for a nuisance caused by workmen without knowledge and contrary to his orders . . . Last, there may be cases in which, although the proceeding is criminal in form, it is really only a summary mode of enforcing a civil right: see per Williams and Willes JJ in *Morden v Porter* 7 CB (NS) 641; 29 LJ (MC) 213, as to unintentional trespass in pursuit of game; *Lee v Simpson* 3 CB 871, as to unconscious dramatic piracy; and *Hargreaves v Diddams* Law Rep 10 QB 582, as to a *bona fide* belief in a legally impossible right to fish. But, except in such cases as these there must in general be guilty knowledge on the part of the defendant, or of someone whom he has put in his place to act for him, generally, or in the particular matter, in order to constitute an offence. It is plain that if guilty knowledge is not necessary, no care on the part of the publican could save him from a conviction . . . since it would be as easy for the constable to deny that he was on duty when asked, or to produce a forged permission from his superior officer, as to remove his armlet before entering the public house. I am, therefore, of opinion that this conviction ought to be quashed.

Lim Chin Aik v R [1963] AC 160 (PC)

Lord Evershed:

... What should be the proper inferences to be drawn from the language of the statute or statutory instrument under review – in this case of ss 6 and 9 of the Immigration Ordinance? More difficult, perhaps, still, what are the inferences to be drawn in a given case from the 'subject-matter with which [the statute or statutory instrument] deals'?

Where the subject-matter of the statute is the regulation for the public welfare of a particular activity – statutes regulating the sale of food and drink are to be found among the earliest examples – it can be and frequently has been inferred that the legislature intended that such activities should be carried out under conditions of strict liability. The presumption is that the statute or statutory instrument can be effectively enforced only if those in charge of the relevant activities are made responsible for seeing that they are complied with. When such a presumption is to be inferred, it displaces the ordinary presumption of *mens rea* ...

But it is not enough in their Lordships' opinion merely to label the statute as one dealing with a grave social evil and from that to infer that strict liability was intended. It is pertinent also to inquire whether putting the defendant under strict liability will assist in the enforcement of the regulations. That means that there must be something he can do, directly or indirectly, by supervision or inspection, by improvement of his business methods or by exhorting those whom he may be expected to influence or control, which will promote the observance of the regulations. Unless this is so, there is no reason in penalising him, and it cannot be inferred that the legislature imposed strict liability merely in order to find a luckless victim ...

Where it can be shown that the imposition of strict liability would result in the prosecution and conviction of a class of persons whose conduct could not in any way affect the observance of the law, their Lordships consider that, even where the statute is dealing with a grave social evil, strict liability is not likely to be intended. Their Lordships apply these general observations to the Ordinance in the present case. The subject-matter, the control of immigration, is not one in which the presumption of strict liability has generally been made. Nevertheless, if the courts of Singapore were of the view that unrestricted immigration is a social evil which it is the object of the Ordinance to control most rigorously, their Lordships would hesitate to disagree. That is a matter peculiarly within the cognisance of the local courts. But [counsel for the Crown] was unable to point to anything that the appellant could possibly have done so as to ensure that he complied with the regulations. It was not, for example, suggested that it would be practicable for him to make continuous inquiry to see whether an order had been made against him. Clearly one of the objects of the Ordinance is the expulsion of prohibited persons from Singapore, but there is nothing that a man can do about it if, before the commission of the offence, there is no practical or sensible way in which he can ascertain whether he is a prohibited person or not.

[Counsel], therefore, relied chiefly on the text of the Ordinance and their Lordships return, accordingly, to the language of the two material sections. It is to be observed that the Board is here concerned with one who is said (within the terms of s 6(3)) to have 'contravened' the subsection by 'remaining' in Singapore (after having entered) when he had been 'prohibited' from entering by an 'order' made by the Minister containing such prohibition. It seems to their Lordships that, where a man is said to have contravened an order or an order of prohibition, the common sense of the language presumes that he was aware of the order before he can be said to have contravened it. Their Lordships realise that this statement is something of an oversimplification when applied to the present case; for the 'contravention' alleged is of the unlawful act, prescribed by subsection (2) of the section, of remaining in Singapore after the date of the order of prohibition. Nonetheless it is their Lordships' view that, applying the test of ordinary sense to the language used, the notion of contravention here alleged is more consistent with the assumption that the person charged had knowledge of the order than the converse. But such a conclusion is in their Lordships' view much reinforced by the use of the word 'remains' in its context. It is to be observed that if the respondent is right a man could lawfully enter Singapore and could thereafter lawfully remain in Singapore until the moment when an order of prohibition against his entering was made; that then, instanter, his purely passive conduct in remaining – that is, the mere continuance, quite unchanged, of his previous behaviour, hitherto perfectly lawful – would become criminal. These considerations bring their Lordships clearly to the conclusion that the sense of the language here in question requires for the commission of a crime thereunder *mens rea* as a constituent of such crime; or at least that there is nothing in the language used which suffices to exclude the ordinary presumption. Their Lordships do not forget the emphasis placed by [counsel] on the fact that the word 'knowingly' or the phrases 'without reasonable cause' or 'without reasonable excuse' are found in various sections of the Ordinance (as amended) but find no place in the section now under consideration – see, for example, ss 16(4), 18(4), 19(2), 29, 31(2), 41(2) and 56(d) and (e) of the Ordinance. In their Lordships' view the absence of such a word or phrase in the relevant section is not sufficient in the present case to prevail against the conclusion which the language as a whole suggests. In the first place, it is to be noted that to have inserted such words as 'knowingly' or 'without lawful excuse' in the relevant part of s 6(3) of the Act would in any case not have been sensible. Further, in all the various instances where the word or phrase is used in the other sections of the Ordinance before-mentioned the use is with reference to the doing of some specific act or the failure to do some specific act as distinct from the mere passive continuance of behaviour theretofore perfectly lawful. Finally, their Lordships are mindful that in the *Sherras* case [1895] 1 QB 918 itself the fact that the word 'knowingly' was not found in the subsection under consideration by the court but was found in another subsection in the same section was not there regarded as sufficient to displace the ordinary rule.

Their Lordships have accordingly reached the clear conclusion, with all respect to the view taken in the courts below, that the application of the rule that *mens rea* is an essential ingredient in every offence has not in the present case been ousted by the terms or subject-matter of the Ordinance, and that the appellant's conviction and sentence cannot stand . . .

Sweet v Parsley [1970] AC 132 (HL)

The facts are given in the earlier extract at the beginning of this chapter. The following passage indicates that strict liability ought not to be imposed on those who cannot take action to prevent a prohibited circumstance arising.

Lord Morris of Borth-y-Gest:

It is said that the intention of Parliament was to impose a duty on all persons concerned in the management of any premises to exercise vigilance to prevent the smoking of cannabis. If that had been the intention of Parliament different words would have been used. It would be possible for Parliament to enact, though it would be surprising if it did, that if anyone should at any time smoke cannabis on any premises, then all those concerned in the management of those premises, whether they knew of the smoking or not, should automatically be guilty of a criminal offence. Yet this is in effect what it is now said that Parliament has enacted. The implications are astonishing. Parliament would not only be indirectly imposing a duty upon persons concerned in the management of any premises requiring them to exercise complete supervision over all persons who enter the premises to ensure that no one of them should smoke cannabis, but Parliament would be enacting that the persons concerned in the management would become guilty of an offence if, unknown to them, someone by surreptitiously smoking cannabis eluded the most elaborately devised measures of supervision. There would not be guilt by reason of anything done nor even by reasons of any carelessness, but by reason of the unknown act of some unknown person whom it had not been found possible to control. When the range of possible punishments is remembered the unlikelihood that Parliament intended to legislate in such way becomes additionally apparent.

Lord Pearce:

My Lords, the prosecution contend that any person who is concerned in the management of premises where cannabis is in fact smoked even once, is liable, though he had no knowledge and no guilty mind. This is, they argue, a practical act intended to prevent a practical evil. Only by convicting some innocents along with the guilty can sufficient pressure be put upon those who make their living by being concerned in the management of premises. Only thus can they be made alert to prevent cannabis being smoked there. And if the prosecution have to prove knowledge or *mens rea*, many prosecutions will fail and many of the guilty will escape. I find that argument wholly unacceptable.

The notion that some guilty mind is a constituent part of crime and punishment goes back far beyond our common law. And at common law *mens rea* is a necessary element in a crime. Since the Industrial Revolution the increasing complexity of life called into being new duties and crimes which took no account of intent. Those who undertake various industrial and other activities, especially where these affect the life and health of the citizen, may find themselves liable to statutory punishment regardless of knowledge or intent, both in respect of their own acts or neglect and those of their servants. But one must remember that normally *mens rea* is still an ingredient of any offence. Before the court will dispense with the necessity for *mens rea* it has to be satisfied that Parliament so intended. The mere absence of the word 'knowingly' is not enough. But the nature of the crime, the punishment, the absence of social obloquy, the particular mischief and the field of activity in which it occurs, and the wording of the particular section and its context, may show that Parliament intended that the act should be prevented by punishment regardless of intent or knowledge.

Viewing the matter of these principles, it is not possible to accept the prosecution's contention. Even granted that this were in the public health class of case, such as, for instance, are offences created to ensure that food shall be clean, it would be quite unreasonable. It is one thing to make a man absolutely responsible for all his own acts and even vicariously liable for his servants if he engages in a certain type of activity. But it is quite another matter to make him liable for persons over whom he has no control. The innocent hotel-keeper, the lady who keeps lodgings or takes paying guests, the manager of a cinema, the warden of a hostel, the matron of a hospital, the housemaster and matron of a boarding school, all these, it is conceded, are, on the prosecution's argument, liable to conviction the moment that irresponsible occupants smoke cannabis cigarettes. And for what purpose is this harsh imposition laid on their backs? No vigilance by night or day can make them safe. The most that vigilance can attain is advance knowledge of their own guilt. If a smell of cannabis comes from a sitting room, they know that they have committed the offence. Should they then go at once to the police and confess their guilt in the hope that they will not be prosecuted? They may think it easier to conceal the matter in the hope that it may never be found out. For if, though morally innocent, they are prosecuted they may lose their livelihood, since thereafter, even though not punished, they are objects of suspicion. I see no real, useful object achieved by such hardship to the innocent. And so wide a possibility of injustice to the innocent could not be justified by any benefit achieved in the determent and punishment of the guilty. If, therefore, the words creating the offence are as wide in their application as the prosecution contend, Parliament cannot have intended an offence to which absence of knowledge or *mens rea* is no defence . . .

 ## COMMENTS AND QUESTIONS

1   The corollary to the argument that there is no point in imposing strict liability upon a defendant who could not have taken action to avoid liability is that strict liability can be justified where D has a choice as to whether or not to participate in a particular trade or activity. A trader serving food to the public is regarded as having accepted the risk of liability for selling contaminated food, even where he has no knowledge of the contamination, as an occupational hazard. If he thinks such liability is unfair he should engage in a less hazardous trade. The purpose of strict liability in such cases is to ensure vigilance and to prevent the courts being flooded with 'unmeritorious' defences based on lack of knowledge. As Lord Russell CJ observed in *Parker v Alder* [1899] 1 QB 20, when referring to the imposition of strict liability on a defendant selling adulterated milk:

> Now, assuming that the respondent was entirely innocent morally, and had no means of protecting himself from the adulteration of this milk in the course of transit, has he committed an offence against the Acts? I think that he has. When the scope and object of these Acts are considered, it will appear that if he were to be relieved from responsibility a wide door would be opened for evading the beneficial provisions of this legislation . . . This is one of the class of cases in which the legislature has, in effect, determined that *mens rea* is not necessary to constitute the offence . . .

2   The 'implausible defence' issue was obviously a factor in the court's ruling in *R v Bradish* (1990) 90 Cr App R 271, where the appellant was convicted of possessing a prohibited weapon contrary to s 5(1) of the Firearms Act 1968. He had contended that he had not known that the container in his possession was a CS gas canister. Auld J observed:

> . . . the possibilities and consequences of evasion would be too great for effective control, even if the burden of proving lack of guilty knowledge were to be on the accused. The difficulty of enforcement, when presented with such a defence, would be particularly difficult where there is a prosecution for possession of a component part of a firearm or prohibited weapon, as provided for by sections 1 and 5 when read with section 57(1) of the 1968 Act. It would be easy for an accused to maintain, lyingly but with conviction, that he did not recognise the object in his possession as part of a firearm or prohibited weapon. To the argument that the innocent possessor or carrier of firearms or prohibited weapons or parts of them is at risk of unfair conviction under these provisions there has to be balanced the important public policy behind the legislation of protecting the public from the misuse of such dangerous weapons. Just as the Chicago-style gangster might plausibly maintain that he believed his violin case to contain a violin, not a sub-machine gun, so it might be difficult to meet a London lout's assertion that he did not know an unmarked plastic bottle in his possession contained ammonia rather than something to drink.

3   In *Harrow LBC v Shah* [1999] 3 All ER 302, the Divisional Court held that a defendant could be convicted of selling a lottery ticket to a person under the age of 16, even though there was no fault established on the part of the defendant retailer. Mitchell J observed that the imposition of strict liability would '. . . unquestionably encourage greater vigilance in preventing the commission of the prohibited act' and that '. . . no sort of stigma attaches to [the] offence . . .'.

3.8.5 CODIFICATION AND LAW REFORM PROPOSALS

Clause 20 of the draft Criminal Code Bill provides as follows:

20(1) Every offence requires a fault element of recklessness with or respect to each of its elements other than fault elements, unless otherwise provided.

As the commentary in Vol II explains:

> An enactment creating an offence should ordinarily specify the fault required for the offence or expressly provide that the offence is one of strict liability in respect of one or more identified elements. It is necessary, however, to have a general rule for the interpretation of any offence the definition of which does not state, in respect of one or more elements, whether fault is required or what degree of fault is required. The absence of a consistent rule of interpretation has been a regrettable source of uncertainty in English law . . . We considered a suggestion that the clause should seek to make the presumption displaceable only by express provision requiring some fault other than recklessness, or stating that no fault is required, with respect to an element of an offence. We do not think that this would be appropriate. We are mindful of the 'constitutional platitude' pointed out by Lord Ackner in *Hunt* [1987] AC 352 at 380 that the courts must give effect to what Parliament has provided not only 'expressly' but also by 'necessary implication'. If the terms of a future enactment creating an offence plainly implied an intention to displace the presumption created by clause 20(1), the courts would no doubt feel obliged to give effect to that intention even if the present clause were to require express provision for the purpose [Vol II, paras 8.25–8.28].

3.9 CORPORATE BODIES AND PROOF OF *MENS REA*

Where Parliament creates regulatory schemes, such as those that seek to prevent pollution, ensure minimum building standards, or ensure the quality of foodstuffs sold for public consumption, it often reinforces compliance by creating criminal offences that can be charged against those causing prohibited results. In many cases the parties subject to these regulations will be corporations rather than real people. The concept of *mens rea* is, of course, one that has developed in relation to the human mind, not the artificial legal identity of the corporation. In order to avoid the difficulty of establishing *mens rea* on the part of a corporation, many regulatory offences operate on the basis of strict liability – that is, liability without fault; see 3.9 above.

Where, however, a corporation is charged with an offence requiring proof of fault the question arises as to how that can be established. Which officer of the corporation is to be deemed to be the 'controlling mind' of the corporation? Is it a question of seniority? Can the *mens rea* of several managers be aggregated to provide a 'composite' *mens rea* for the corporation as a whole? The issue has particularly come to the fore in the context of corporate liability for manslaughter – a matter considered in Chapter 4.11. The following extracts concern the general principles of identifying corporate *mens rea*.

Tesco Ltd v Nattrass [1972] AC 153 (HL)

Lord Reid:

My Lords, the appellants own a large number of supermarkets in which they sell a wide variety of goods. The goods are put out for sale on shelves or stands, each article being marked with the price at which it is offered for sale. The customer selects the articles he wants, takes them to the cashier, and pays the price. From time to time the appellants, apparently by way of advertisement, sell 'flash packs' at prices lower than the normal price. In September 1969 they were selling Radiant washing powder in this way. The normal price was 3s 11d but these packs were marked and sold at 2s 11d. Posters were displayed in the shops drawing attention to this reduction in price.

These prices were displayed in the appellants' shop at Northwich on 26 September. Mr Coane, an old age pensioner, saw this and went to buy a pack. He could only find packs marked 3s 11d. He took one to the cashier who told him that there were none in stock for sale at 2s 11d. He paid 3s 11d and complained to an inspector of weights and measures. This resulted in a prosecution under the Trade Descriptions Act 1968 and the appellants were fined £25 and costs.

Section 11(2) provides:

> If any person offering to supply any goods gives, by whatever means, any indication likely to be taken as an indication that the goods are being offered at a price less than that at which they are in fact being offered he shall, subject to the provisions of this Act, be guilty of an offence.

It is not disputed that that section applies to this case. The appellants relied on s 24(1) which provides:

In any proceedings for an offence under this Act it shall, subject to subsection (2) of this section, be a defence for the person charged to prove: (a) that the commission of the offence was due to a mistake or to reliance on information supplied to him or to the act or default of another person, an accident or some other cause beyond his control; and (b) that he took all reasonable precautions and exercised all due diligence to avoid the commission of such an offence by himself or any person under his control.

The relevant facts as found by the magistrates were that on the previous evening a shop assistant, Miss Rogers, whose duty it was to put out fresh stock, found that there were no more of the specially marked packs in stock. There were a number of packs marked with the ordinary price so she put them out. She ought to have told the shop manager, Mr Clement, about this, but she failed to do so. Mr Clement was responsible for seeing that the proper packs were on sale, but he failed to see to this although he marked his daily return 'all special offers OK'. The magistrates found that if he had known about this he would either have removed the poster advertising the reduced price or given instructions that only 2s 11d was to be charged for the packs marked 3s 11d.

Section 24(2) requires notice to be given to the prosecutor if the accused is blaming another person and such notice was duly given naming Mr Clement.

In order to avoid conviction the appellants had to prove facts sufficient to satisfy both parts of s 24(1) of the Act of 1968. The magistrates held that they: '. . . had exercised all due diligence in devising a proper system for the operation of the said store and by securing so far as was reasonably practicable that it was fully implemented and thus had fulfilled the requirements of s 24(1)(b)'.

But they convicted the appellants because in their view the requirements of s 24(1)(a) had not been fulfilled: they held that Clement was not 'another person' within the meaning of that provision.

The Divisional Court held that the magistrates were wrong in holding that Clement was not 'another person'. The respondent did not challenge this finding of the Divisional Court so I need say no more about it than that I think that on this matter the Divisional Court was plainly right. But that court sustained the conviction on the ground that the magistrates had applied the wrong test in deciding that the requirements of s 24(1)(b) had been fulfilled. In effect that court held that the words 'he took all reasonable precautions . . .' do not mean what they say: 'he' does not mean the accused, it means the accused and all his servants who were acting in a managerial or supervisory capacity. I think that earlier authorities virtually compelled the Divisional Court to reach this strange construction. So the real question in this appeal is whether these earlier authorities were rightly decided.

But before examining those earlier cases I think it necessary to make some general observations.

Over a century ago courts invented the idea of an absolute offence. The accepted doctrines of the common law put them in a difficulty. There was a presumption that when Parliament makes the commission of certain acts an offence it intends that *mens rea* shall be a constituent of that offence whether or not there is any reference to the knowledge or state of mind of the accused. And it was and is held to be an invariable rule that where *mens rea* is a constituent of any offence the burden of proving *mens rea* is on the prosecution. Some day this House may have to re-examine that rule, but that is another matter. For the protection of purchasers or consumers Parliament in many cases made it an offence for a trader to do certain things. Normally those things were done on his behalf by his servants and cases arose where the doing of the forbidden thing was solely the fault of a servant, the master having done all he could to prevent it and being entirely ignorant of its having been done. The just course would have been to hold that, once the facts constituting the offence had been proved, *mens rea* would be presumed unless the accused proved that he was blameless. The courts could not, or thought they could not, take that course. But they could and did hold in many such cases on a construction of the statutory provision that Parliament must be deemed to have intended to depart from the general rule and to make the offence absolute in the sense that *mens rea* was not to be a constituent of the offence.

This has led to great difficulties. If the offence is not held to be absolute the requirement that the prosecutor must prove *mens rea* makes it impossible to enforce the enactment in very many cases. If the offence is held to be absolute that leads to the conviction of persons who are entirely blameless: an injustice which brings the law into disrepute. So Parliament has found it necessary to devise a method of avoiding this difficulty. But instead of passing a general enactment that it shall always be a defence for the accused to prove that he was no party to the offence and had done all he could to prevent it, Parliament has chosen to deal with the problem piecemeal, and has in an increasing number of cases enacted in various forms with regard to particular offences that it shall be a defence to prove various exculpatory circumstances.

In my judgment the main object of these provisions must have been to distinguish between those who are in some degree blameworthy and those who are not, and to enable the latter to escape from conviction if they can show that they were in no way to blame. I find it almost impossible to suppose that Parliament or any reasonable body of men would as a matter of policy think it right to make employers criminally liable for the acts of some of their servants but not for those of others and I find it incredible that a draftsman, aware of that intention, would fail to insert any words to express it. But in several cases the courts, for reasons which it is not easy to discover, have given a restricted meaning to such provisions. It has been held that such provisions afford a defence if the master proves that the servant at fault was the person who himself did the prohibited act, but that they afford no defence if the servant at fault was one who failed in his duty of supervision to see that his subordinates did not commit the prohibited act. Why Parliament should be thought to have intended this distinction or how as a matter of construction these provisions can reasonably be held to have that meaning is not apparent.

In some of these cases the employer charged with the offence was a limited company. But in others the employer was an individual and still it was held that he, though personally entirely blameless, could not rely on these provisions if the fault which led to the commission of the offence was the fault of a servant in failing to carry out his duty to instruct or supervise his subordinates.

Where a limited company is the employer difficult questions do arise in a wide variety of circumstances in deciding which of its officers or servants is to be identified with the company so that his guilt is the guilt of the company.

I must start by considering the nature of the personality which by a fiction the law attributes to a corporation. A living person has a mind which can have knowledge or intention or be negligent and he has hands to carry out his intentions. A corporation has none of these: it must act through living persons, though not always one or the same person. Then the person who acts is not speaking or acting for the company. He is acting as the company and his mind which directs his acts is the mind of the company. There is no question of the company being vicariously liable. He is not acting as a servant, representative, agent or delegate. He is an embodiment of the company or, one could say, he hears and speaks through the persona of the company, within his appropriate sphere, and his mind is the mind of the company. If it is a guilty mind then that guilt is the guilt of the company. It must be a question of law whether, once the facts have been ascertained, a person in doing particular things is to be regarded as the company or merely as the company's servant or agent. In that case any liability of the company can only be a statutory or vicarious liability.

In *Lennard's Carrying Co Ltd v Asiatic Petroleum Co Ltd* [1915] AC 705 the question was whether damage had occurred without the 'actual fault or privity' of the owner of a ship. The owners were a company. The fault was that of the registered managing owner who managed the ship on behalf of the owners and it was held that the company could not dissociate itself from him so far as to say that there was no actual fault or privity on the part of the company. Viscount Haldane LC said, at 713, 714:

> For if Mr Lennard was the directing mind of the company, then his action must, unless a corporation is not to be liable at all, have been an action which was the action of the company itself within the meaning of s 502 . . . It must be upon the true construction of that section in such a case as the present one that the fault or privity is the fault or privity of somebody who is not merely a servant or agent for whom the company is liable upon the footing respondeat superior, but somebody for whom the company is liable because his action is the very action of the company itself.

Reference is frequently made to the judgment of Denning LJ in *HL Bolton (Engineering) Co Ltd v T J Graham and Sons Ltd* [1957] 1 QB 159. He said, at 172:

> A company may in many ways be likened to a human body. It has a brain and nerve centre which controls what it does. It also has hands which hold the tools and act in accordance with directions from the centre. Some of the people in the company are mere servants and agents who are nothing more than hands to do the work and cannot be said to represent the mind or will. Others are directors and managers who represent the directing mind and will of the company, and control what it does. The state of mind of these managers is the state of mind of the company and is treated by the law as such.

In that case the directors of the company only met once a year, they left the management of the business to others, and it was the intention of those managers which was imputed to the company. I think that was right. There have been attempts to apply Lord Denning's words to all servants of a company whose work is brain work, or exercise some managerial discretion under the direction of superior officers of the company. I do not think that Lord Denning intended to refer to them. He only referred to those who 'represent the directing mind and will of the company, and control what it does'.

I think that it is right for this reason. Normally the board of directors, the managing director and perhaps other superior officers of a company carry out the functions of management and speak and act as the company. Their subordinates do not. They carry out orders from above and it can make no difference that they are given some measure of discretion. But the board of directors may delegate some part of their functions of management giving to their delegate full discretion to act independently of instructions from them. I see no difficulty in holding that they have thereby put such a delegate in their place so that within the scope of the delegation he can act as the company. It may not always be easy to draw the line but there are cases in which the line must be drawn. *Lennard's* case [1915] AC 705 was one of them.

In some cases the phrase alter ego has been used. I think it is misleading. When dealing with a company the word alter is I think misleading. The person who speaks and acts as the company is not alter. He is identified with the company. And when dealing with an individual no other individual can be his alter ego. The other individual can be a servant, agent, delegate or representative but I know of neither principle nor authority which warrants the confusion (in the literal or original sense) of two separate individuals . . .

[Where a statute introduces a] defence if the accused proved that 'he used all due diligence' I think that it [means] what it [says]. As a matter of construction I can see no ground for reading in 'he and all persons to whom he has delegated responsibility'. And if I look to the purpose and apparent intention of Parliament in enacting this defence I think that it was plainly intended to make a just and reasonable distinction between the employer who is wholly blameless and ought to be acquitted and the employer who was in some way at fault, leaving it to the employer to prove that he was in no way to blame.

What good purpose could be served by making an employer criminally responsible for the misdeeds of some of his servants but not for those of others? It is sometimes argued – it was argued in the present case – that making an employer criminally responsible, even when he has done all that he could to prevent an offence, affords some additional protection to the public because this will induce him to do more. But if he has done all he can how can he do more? I think that what lies behind this argument is a suspicion that magistrates too readily accept evidence that an employer has done all he can to prevent offences. But if magistrates were to accept as sufficient a paper scheme and perfunctory efforts to enforce it they would not be doing their duty – that would not be 'due diligence' on the part of the employer.

Then it is said that this would involve discrimination in favour of a large employer like the appellants against a small shopkeeper. But that is not so. Mr Clement was the 'opposite number' of the small shopkeeper and he was liable to prosecution in this case. The purpose of this Act must have been to penalise those at fault, not those who were in no way to blame.

The Divisional Court decided this case on a theory of delegation in that they were following some earlier authorities, but they gave far too wide a meaning to delegation. I have said that a board of directors can delegate part of their functions of management so as to make their delegate an embodiment of the company within the sphere of the delegation. But here the board never delegated any part of their functions. They set up a chain of command through regional and district supervisors, but they remained in control. The shop managers had to obey their general directions and also take orders from their superiors. The acts or omissions of shop managers were not acts of the company itself.

In my judgment the appellants established the statutory defence. I would therefore allow this appeal.

Lord Morris of Borth-y-Gest:

. . . My Lords, with respect I do not think that there was any feature of delegation in the present case. The company had its responsibilities in regard to taking all reasonable precautions and exercising all due diligence. The careful and effective discharge of those responsibilities required the directing mind and will of the company. A system had to be created which could rationally be said to be so designed that the commission of offences would be avoided. There was no delegation of the duty of taking precautions and exercising diligence. There was no such delegation to the manager of a particular store. He did not function as the directing mind or will of the company. His duties as the manager of one store did not involve managing the company. He was one who was being directed. He was one who was employed but he was not a delegate to whom the company passed on its responsibilities. He had certain duties which were the result of the taking by the company of all reasonable precautions and of the exercising by the company of all due diligence. He was a person under the control of the company and on the assumption that there could be proceedings against him, the company would by s 24(1)(b) be absolved if the company had taken all proper steps to avoid the commission of an offence by him. To make the company automatically liable for an offence committed by him would be to ignore the subsection. He was, so to speak, a cog in the machine which was devised: it was not left to him to devise it. Nor was he within what has been called the 'brain area' of the company. If the company had taken all reasonable precautions and exercised all due diligence to ensure that the machine could and should run effectively then some breakdown due to some action or failure on the part of 'another person' ought not to be attributed to the company or to be regarded as the action or failure of the company itself for which the company was to be criminally responsible. The defence provided by s 24(1) would otherwise be illusory . . .

Meridian Global Funds Management Asia v Securities Commission
[1995] 3 WLR 413 (PC)

Through two of its employees (Koo and Ng) the appellant company, Meridian Global Funds Management Asia, acquired a controlling interest in another company (Euro-National Corporation Ltd). In doing so the appellant company failed to comply with s 20 of the (New Zealand) Securities Amendment Act 1988, which required any person who became a substantial security holder in another company to give notice of the fact. Notwithstanding that the activities of Koo and Ng had not been authorised by the appellant company, the Court of Appeal in New Zealand held that Koo's knowledge was attributable to the appellant company under the 'directing mind and will' doctrine. The Privy Council dismissed the company's appeal.

Lord Hoffmann:
Any proposition about a company necessarily involves a reference to a set of rules. A company exists because there is a rule (usually in a statute) which says that a *persona ficta* shall be deemed to exist and to have certain of the powers, rights and duties of a natural person. But there would be little sense in deeming such a *persona ficta* to exist unless there were also rules to tell one what acts were to count as acts of the company. It is therefore a necessary part of corporate personality that there should be rules by which acts are attributed to the company. These may be called 'the rules of attribution'.

The company's primary rules of attribution will generally be found in its constitution, typically the articles of association, and will say things such as 'for the purpose of appointing members of the board, a majority vote of the shareholders shall be a decision of the company' or 'the decisions of the board in managing the company's business shall be the decisions of the company'. There are also primary rules of attribution which are not expressly stated in the articles but implied by company law, such as:

> . . . the unanimous decision of all the shareholders in a solvent company about anything which the company under its memorandum of association has power to do shall be the decision of the company: see *Multinational Gas and Petrochemical Co v Multinational Gas and Petrochemical Services Ltd* [1983] Ch 258.

These primary rules of attribution are obviously not enough to enable a company to go out into the world and do business. Not every act on behalf of the company could be expected to be the subject of a resolution of the board or a unanimous decision of the shareholders. The company therefore builds upon the primary rules of attribution by using general rules of attribution which are equally available to natural persons, namely, the principles of agency. It will appoint servants and agents whose acts, by a combination of the general principles of agency and the company's primary rules of attribution, count as the acts of the company. And having done so, it will also make itself subject to the general rules by which liability for the acts of others can be attributed to natural persons, such as estoppel or ostensible authority in contract and vicarious liability in tort.

It is worth pausing at this stage to make what may seem an obvious point. Any statement about what a company has or has not done, or can or cannot do, is necessarily a reference to the rules of attribution (primary and general) as they apply to that company. Judges sometimes say that a company 'as such' cannot do anything; it must act by servants or agents. This may seem an unexceptionable, even banal, remark. And of course the meaning is usually perfectly clear. But a reference to a company 'as such' might suggest that there is something out there called the company of which one can meaningfully say that it can or cannot do something. There is in fact no such thing as the company as such . . . only the applicable rules. To say that a company cannot do something means only that there is no one whose doing of that act would, under the applicable rules of attribution, count as an act of the company.

The company's primary rules of attribution together with the general principles of agency, vicarious liability and so forth are usually sufficient to enable one to determine its rights and obligations. In exceptional cases, however, they will not provide an answer. This will be the case when a rule of law, either expressly or by implication, excludes attribution on the basis of the general principles of agency or vicarious liability. For example, a rule may be stated in language primarily applicable to a natural person and require some act or state of mind on the part of that person 'himself', as opposed to his servants or agents. This is generally true of rules of the criminal law, which ordinarily impose liability only for the *actus reus* and *mens rea* of the defendant himself. How is such a rule to be applied to a company?

One possibility is that the court may come to the conclusion that the rule was not intended to apply to companies at all; for example, a law which created an offence for which the only penalty was community service. Another possibility is that the court might interpret the law as meaning that it could apply to a company only on the basis of its primary rules of attribution, ie, if the act giving rise to liability was specifically authorised by the resolution of the board or a unanimous agreement of the shareholders. But there will be many cases in which neither of these solutions is satisfactory; in which the court considers that the law was intended to apply to companies and that, although it excludes ordinary vicarious liability, insistence on the primary rules of attribution would in practice defeat that intention. In such a case, the court must fashion a special rule of attribution for the particular substantive rule. This is always a matter of interpretation: given that it was intended to apply to a company, how was it intended to apply? Whose act (or knowledge, or state of mind) was for this purpose intended to count as the act etc of the company? One finds the answer to this question by applying the usual canons of interpretation, taking into account the language of the rule (if it is a statute) and its content and policy.

The fact that the rule of attribution is a matter of interpretation or construction of the relevant substantive rule is shown by the contrast between two decisions of the House of Lords, *Tesco Supermarkets Ltd v Nattrass* [1972] AC 153 and in *Re Supply of Ready Mixed Concrete (No 2)* [1995] 1 AC 456 . . . [In the latter case] . . . a restrictive arrangement in breach of an undertaking by a company to the Restrictive Practices Court was made by executives of the company acting within the scope of their employment. The board knew nothing of the arrangement; it had in fact given instructions to the company's employees that they were not to make such arrangements. But the House of Lords held that for the purposes of deciding whether the company was in contempt, the act and state of mind of an employee who entered into an arrangement in the course of his employment should be attributed to the company. This attribution rule was derived from a construction of the undertaking against the background of the Restrictive Trade Practices Act 1976: such undertakings by corporations would be worth little if the company could avoid liability for what its employees had actually done on the ground that the board did not know about it. [His Lordship referred to *Tesco Supermarkets Ltd v Nattrass*, and continued]

. . . The policy of s 20 of the Securities Amendment Act 1988 is to compel, in fast-moving markets, the immediate disclosure of the identity of persons who become substantial security-holders in public issuers. Notice must be given as soon as that person knows that he has become a substantial security-holder. In the case of a corporate security-holder, what rule should be implied as to the person whose knowledge for this purpose is to count as the knowledge of the company? Surely the person who, with the authority of the company, acquired the relevant interest. Otherwise the policy of the Act would be defeated. Companies would be able to allow employees to acquire interests on their behalf which made them substantial security-holders but would not have to report them until the board or someone else in senior management got to know about it. This would put a premium on the board paying as little attention as possible to what its investment managers were doing. Their Lordships would therefore hold that upon the true construction of s 20(4)(e), the company knows that it has become a substantial security-holder when that is known to the person who had authority to do the deal. It is then obliged to give notice under s 20(3). The fact that Koo did the deal for a corrupt purpose and did not give such notice because he did not want his employers to find out cannot in their Lordships' view affect the attribution of knowledge and the consequent duty to notify.

It was therefore not necessary in this case to inquire into whether Koo could have been described in some more general sense as the 'directing mind and will' of the company. But their Lordships would wish to guard themselves against being understood to mean that whenever a servant of a company has authority to do an act on its behalf, knowledge of that act will for all purposes be attributed to the company. It is a question of construction in each case as to whether the particular rule requires that the knowledge that an act has been done, or the state of mind with which it was done, should be attributed to the company. Sometimes, as in *In re Supply of Ready Mixed Concrete (No 2)* [1995] 1 AC 456 and this case, it will be appropriate. Likewise in a case in which a company was required to make a return for revenue purposes and the statute made it an offence to make a false return with intent to deceive, the Divisional Court held that the *mens rea* of the servant authorised to discharge the duty to make the return should be attributed to the company: see *Moore v I Bresler Ltd* [1944] 2 All ER 515. On the other hand, the fact that a company's employee is authorised to drive a lorry does not in itself lead to the conclusion that if he kills someone by reckless driving, the company will be guilty of manslaughter. There is no inconsistency. Each is an example of an attribution rule for a particular purpose, tailored as it always must be to the terms and policies of the substantive rule.

Attorney General's Ref (No 2 of 1999) [2000] 3 All ER 182

The appeal arose out of a failed prosecution of a rail operating company in respect of the deaths of several passengers following a train crash involving the company's trains. For the full facts see the extract in Chapter 4.8.2 dealing with corporate manslaughter. The following extracts concern the basis upon which the courts would seek to identify the *mens rea* of a corporate body.

Rose LJ:

The court's opinion is sought in relation to two questions referred by the Attorney General under s 36 of the Criminal Justice Act 1972. [The second of these is] . . . Can a non-human defendant be convicted of the crime of manslaughter by gross negligence in the absence of evidence establishing the guilt of an identified human individual for the same crime? . . .

As to question (2), Mr Lissack [for the Attorney General] accepted that policy considerations arise. Large companies should be as susceptible to prosecution for manslaughter as one-man companies. Where the ingredients of a common law offence are identical to those of a statutory offence there is no justification for drawing a distinction as to liability between the two and the public interest requires the more emphatic denunciation of a company inherent in a conviction for manslaughter. He submitted that the ingredients of the offence of gross negligence manslaughter are the same in relation to a body corporate as to a human being, namely grossly negligent breach of a duty to a deceased causative of his death. It is, he submitted, unnecessary and inappropriate to inquire whether there is an employee in the company who is guilty of the offence of manslaughter who can properly be said to have been acting as the embodiment of the company. The criminal law of negligence follows the civil law of negligence as applied to corporations: the only difference is that, to be criminal, the negligence must be gross. Of the three theories of corporate criminal liability, namely vicarious liability, identification and personal liability, it is personal liability which should here apply. In the present case, it would have been open to the jury to convict if they were satisfied that the deaths occurred by reason of a gross breach by the defendant of its personal duty to have a safe system of train operation in place. The identification theory, attributing to the company the mind and will of senior directors and managers, was developed in order to avoid injustice: it would bring the law into disrepute if every act and state of mind of an individual employee was attributed to a company which was entirely blameless . . .

Before turning to Mr Lissack's submission in relation to personal liability it is convenient first to refer to the speech of Lord Hoffmann in *Meridian Global Funds Management Asia Ltd v Securities Commission* . . . on which Mr Lissack relied as the lynchpin of this part of his argument. It was a case in which the chief investment officer and senior portfolio manager of an investment management company, with the company's authority but unknown to the board of directors and managing director, used funds managed by the company to acquire shares, but failed to comply with a statutory obligation to give notice of the acquisition to the Securities Commission. The trial judge held that the knowledge of the officer and manager should be attributed to the company and the Court of Appeal of New Zealand upheld the decision on the basis that the officer was the directing mind and will of the company. The Privy Council dismissed an appeal. Lord Hoffmann, giving the judgment of the Privy Council, said that the company's primary rules of attribution were generally found in its constitution or implied by company law . . . But, in an exceptional case, where the application of those principles would defeat the intended application of a particular provision to companies, it was necessary to devise a special rule of attribution . . . Lord Hoffmann went on to comment that it was not necessary in that case to inquire whether the chief investment officer could be described as the 'directing mind and will' of the company. He said:

MENS REA: THE MENTAL ELEMENT

It is a question of construction in each case as to whether the particular rule requires that the knowledge that an act has been done, or the state of mind in which it was done, should be attributed to the company.

Mr Lissack's submission that personal liability on the part of the company is capable of arising in the present case was based on a number of authorities in addition to the Meridian case.

In *R v British Steel plc* [1995] 1 WLR 1356 the defendant was prosecuted, as was the present defendant, for a breach of ss 3(1) and 33(1)(a) of the 1974 Act. A worker was killed because of the collapse of a steel platform during a re-positioning operation which a competent supervisor would have recognised was inherently dangerous. The defence was that the workmen had disobeyed instructions and, even if the supervisor was at fault, the company at the level of its directing mind had taken reasonable care. An appeal against conviction was dismissed by the Court of Appeal, Criminal Division. The judgment was given by Steyn LJ who said (at 1362–63):

> . . . counsel for British Steel plc concedes that it is not easy to fit the idea of corporate criminal liability only for acts of the 'directing mind' of the company into the language of section 3(1). We would go further. If it be accepted that Parliament considered it necessary for the protection of public health and safety to impose, subject to the defence of reasonable practicability, absolute criminal liability, it would drive a juggernaut through the legislative scheme if corporate employers could avoid criminal liability where the potentially harmful event is committed by someone who is not the directing mind of the company . . . That would emasculate the legislation.

In a commentary on this decision Professor Sir John Smith QC said in relation to the 'directing mind' argument ([1995] Crim LR 655):

> Where a statutory duty to do something is imposed on a particular person (here an 'employer') and he does not do it, he commits the *actus reus* of an offence. It may be that he has failed to fulfil his duty because his employee or agent has failed to carry out his duties properly but this is not a case for vicarious liability. If the employer is held liable, it is because he, personally, has failed to do what the law requires him to do and he is personally, not vicariously liable. There is no need to find someone – in the case of a company, the 'brains' and not merely the 'hands' – for whose act the person with the duty be held liable. The duty on the company in this case was 'to ensure' – i.e. to make certain – that persons are not exposed to risk. They did not make it certain. It does not matter how; they were in breach of their statutory duty and, in the absence of any requirement for *mens rea*, that is the end of the matter.

. . . For the defendant, Mr Caplan submitted, in relation to question (2), that *R v Adomako* [1994] 3 All ER 79, [1995] 1 AC 171 was not concerned with corporate liability. It is necessarily implicit in the Law Commission's recommendation, in Law Com No 237, that Parliament should enact a new offence of corporate killing, that the doctrine of identification still continues to apply to gross negligence manslaughter since *R v Adomako. Tesco Supermarkets Ltd v Nattrass* [1971] 2 All ER 127, [1972] AC 153 is still authoritative (see *Seaboard Offshore Ltd v Secretary of State for Transport* [1994] 2 All ER 99, [1994] 1 WLR 541) and it is impossible to find a company guilty unless its alter ego is identified. None of the authorities since *Tesco Supermarkets Ltd v Nattrass* relied on by Mr Lissack supports the demise of the doctrine of identification: all are concerned with statutory construction of different substantive offences and the appropriate rule of attribution was decided having regard to the legislative intent, namely whether Parliament intended companies to be liable. There is a sound reason for a special rule of attribution in relation to statutory offences rather than common law offences, namely there is, subject to a defence of reasonable practicability, an absolute duty imposed by the statutes. The authorities on statutory offences do not bear on the common law principle in relation to manslaughter. Lord Hoffmann's speech in the *Meridian* case is a restatement not an abandonment of existing principles: see, for example, *Tesco Supermarkets Ltd v Nattrass* [1971] 2 All ER 127 at 156, [1972] AC 153 at 200 per Lord Diplock: '. . . there may be criminal statutes which on their true construction ascribe to a corporation criminal responsibility for the acts of servants and agents who would be excluded by the test that I have stated . . .' (viz those exercising the powers of the company under its articles of association). The Law Commission's proposals were made after the *Meridian* and *British Steel* cases. Identification is necessary in relation to the *actus reus*, i.e. whose acts or omissions are to be attributed to the company, and *R v Adomako*'s objective test in relation to gross negligence in no way affects this. Furthermore, the civil negligence rule of liability for the acts of servants or agents has no place in the criminal law – which is why the identification principle was developed. That principle is still the rule of attribution in criminal law whether or not *mens rea* needs to be proved.

[Having confirmed that corporate *mens rea* could only be established by means of the 'identification' doctrine, as opposed to the 'aggregation' doctrine, Rose LJ concluded:]

Finally, Mr Caplan [for the defendant] relied on the speech of Lord Lowry in *C v DPP* [1995] 2 All ER 43, [1996] AC 1 and invited this court to reject the prosecution's argument for extending corporate liability for manslaughter. Lord Lowry said, with regard to the propriety of judicial law making:

(1) if the solution is doubtful, the judges should beware of imposing their own remedy; (2) caution should prevail if Parliament has rejected opportunities of clearing up a known difficulty or has legislated while leaving the difficulty untouched; (3) disputed matters of social policy are less suitable areas for judicial intervention than purely legal problems; (4) fundamental legal doctrines should not be lightly set aside; (5) judges should not make a change unless they can achieve finality and certainty. (See [1995] 2 All ER 43 at 52, [1996] AC 1 at 28.)

Each of these considerations, submitted Mr Caplan, is pertinent in the present case.

There is, as it seems to us, no sound basis for suggesting that, by their recent decisions, the courts have started a process of moving from identification to personal liability as a basis for corporate liability for manslaughter. In *R v Adomako* the House of Lords were, as it seems to us, seeking to escape from the unnecessarily complex accretions in relation to recklessness arising from *R v Lawrence* [1981] 1 All ER 974, [1982] AC 510 and *R v Caldwell* [1981] 1 All ER 961, [1982] AC 341.

To do so, they simplified the ingredients of gross negligence manslaughter by re-stating them in line with *R v Bateman* (1925) 19 Cr App R 8, [1925] All ER Rep 45. But corporate liability was not mentioned anywhere in the submissions of counsel or their Lordships' speeches. In any event, the identification principle is in our judgment just as relevant to the *actus reus* as to mens rea. In *Tesco Supermarkets Ltd v Nattrass* [1971] 2 All ER 127 at 134, [1972] AC 153 at 173 Lord Reid said:

> ... the judge must direct the jury that if they find certain facts proved then as a matter of law they must find that the criminal act of the officer, servant or agent including his state of mind, intention, knowledge or belief is the act of the company.

In *R v HM Coroner ex p Spooner* (1989) 88 Cr App R 10 at 16 Bingham LJ said:

> For a company to be criminally liable for manslaughter ... it is required that the *mens rea* and the *actus reus* of manslaughter should be established ... against those who were to be identified as the embodiment of the company itself.

In *R v P & O European Ferries (Dover) Ltd* (1991) 93 Cr App R 72 at 84 Turner J, in his classic analysis of the relevant principles, said:

> ... where a corporation, through the controlling mind of one of its agents, does an act which fulfils the prerequisites of the crime of manslaughter, it is properly indictable for the crime of manslaughter.

In our judgment, unless an identified individual's conduct, characterisable as gross criminal negligence, can be attributed to the company the company is not, in the present state of the common law, liable for manslaughter. Civil negligence rules, e.g. as enunciated in *Wilsons and Clyde Coal Co Ltd v English* [1937] 3 All ER 628, [1938] AC 57, are not apt to confer criminal liability on a company.

None of the authorities relied on by Mr Lissack as pointing to personal liability for manslaughter by a company supports that contention. In each, the decision was dependent on the purposive construction that the particular statute imposed, subject to a defence of reasonable practicability, liability on a company for conducting its undertaking in a manner exposing employees or the public to health and safety risk. In each case there was an identified employee whose conduct was held to be that of the company. In each case it was held that the concept of directing mind and will had no application when construing the statute. But it was not suggested or implied that the concept of identification is dead or moribund in relation to common law offences. Indeed, if that were so, it might have been expected that Lord Hoffmann, in *R v Associated Octel Ltd* [1996] 4 All ER 846, [1996] 1 WLR 1543, would have referred to the ill-health of the doctrine in the light of his own speech, less than a year before, in the *Meridian* case. He made no such reference, nor was the *Meridian* case cited in *R v Associated Octel Ltd*. It therefore seems safe to conclude that Lord Hoffmann (and, similarly, the members of the Court of Appeal, Criminal Division in *R v British Steel plc* [1995] 1 WLR 1356 and in *R v Gateway Foodmarkets Ltd* [1997] 3 All ER 78) did not think that the common law principles as to the need for identification have changed. Indeed, Lord Hoffmann's speech in the Meridian case, in fashioning an additional special rule of attribution geared to the purpose of the statute, proceeded on the basis that the primary 'directing mind and will' rule still applies although it is not determinative in all cases. In other words, he was not departing from the identification theory but re-affirming its existence.

This approach is entirely consonant with the Law Commission's analysis of the present state of the law and the terms of their proposals for reform in their report (Law Com 237) published in March 1996. In this report, both the House of Lords' decision in *R v Adomako* and the Privy Council's decision in the *Meridian* case were discussed. In the light of their analysis, the Law

Commission (para 6.27 ff and para 7.5) concluded that, in the present state of the law, a corporation's liability for manslaughter is based solely on the principle of identification and they drafted a Bill to confer liability based on management failure not involving the principle of identification (see cl 4 of the draft Bill annexed to their report). If Mr Lissack's submissions are correct there is no need for such a Bill and, as Scott Baker J put it, the Law Commission have missed the point. We agree with the judge that the Law Commission have not missed the point and Mr Lissack's submissions are not correct: the identification principle remains the only basis in common law for corporate liability for gross negligence manslaughter.

We should add that, if we entertained doubt on the matter, being mindful of the observations of Lord Lowry in *C v DPP* [1995] 2 All ER 43 at 52, [1996] AC 1 at 28, we would not think it appropriate for this court to propel the law in the direction which Mr Lissack seeks. That, in our judgment, taking into account the policy considerations to which Mr Lissack referred, is a matter for Parliament, not the courts. For almost four years, the Law Commission's draft Bill has been to hand as a useful starting point for that purpose.

It follows that, in our opinion, the answer to question (2) is No.

3.9.1 CODIFICATION AND LAW REFORM PROPOSALS

The DCCB has provisions, clauses 30 and 31, that seek to codify and clarify the common law relating to the imposition of criminal liability on corporations – see also the commentary in Vol II, paras 10.1–10.25. Since then, however, the focus of reform proposals has shifted to the area of corporate liability for manslaughter. The current reform proposals are considered in Chapter 4.12.

FURTHER READING

Jackson, BS, 'Storkwain: a case study in strict liability and self-regulation' [1991] Crim LR 892

Kaveny, MC, 'Inferring Intention from Foresight' (2004) 120 LQR 81

Keating, H, 'Reckless Children?' [2007] Crim LR 546

Lanham, DJ, 'Larsonneur revisited' [1976] Crim LR 276

Leigh, L, *Strict and Vicarious Liability*, 1982, London: Sweet & Maxwell

Lynch, ACE, 'The mental element in the *actus reus*' (1982) 98 LQR 109

Norrie, A, 'After Woollin' [1999] Crim LR 532

Richardson, G, 'Strict liability for regulatory crime: the empirical research' [1987] Crim LR 295

Simester, AP and W Chan, 'Intention thus far' [1997] Crim LR 704

CHAPTER 4

HOMICIDE

4.1 INTRODUCTION

This chapter brings together material related to homicide, that is, the unlawful killing of a human being. The offences that come within the scope of homicide are:

- murder;
- voluntary manslaughter (ie where a defendant has a defence specific to murder);
- involuntary manslaughter by an unlawful act;
- killing by gross negligence (including corporate manslaughter).

All forms of homicide have a common *actus reus* – the prosecution must prove that D has caused (in fact and in law) the death of a human being. Once the *actus reus* is made out, the defendant's liability will be considered against the backdrop of the current two category structure of homicide offences – i.e. either as a murder case (where certain defences may be available) or as a manslaughter case. For murder the prosecution will have to show that the killing was caused with the necessary *mens rea* (intent). Even if the *actus reus* and *mens rea* are made out, the defendant may still be able to rely on certain partial defences that are specific to murder, such as provocation, diminished responsibility, or infanticide. These defences will, if made out, reduce D's liability to manslaughter.

If D causes the death of a human being but is not proved to have had the intention to kill there are two common law forms of manslaughter in respect of which he might be convicted:

- Unlawful act manslaughter (sometimes called constructive manslaughter); and killing by gross negligence.
- The significance of being convicted of manslaughter rather than murder, is that whilst the sentence for murder is fixed by law at life imprisonment, the sentence for manslaughter is at the discretion of the court (although it could, in theory, be life imprisonment).

In November 2006, the Law Commission published its Report entitled *Murder, Manslaughter and Infanticide* (Law Com No 304). As will be seen throughout this chapter the Report makes proposals in relation to the structure of homicide offences, the fault element in murder, the partial defences to murder, and mercy killings. Extracts are set out at appropriate points in the chapter.

In summary the Report recommends the enactment of a new Homicide Act (although no draft Bill is appended to the Report) which would have the effect of replacing the current murder/manslaughter dichotomy with a ladder of offences ranging from first degree murder, second degree murder through to manslaughter. The Report also recommends reforms to partial defences such as provocation and diminished responsibility both of which would operate so as to reduce the defendant's liability from first degree murder to second degree murder.

4.1.1 LAW COM NO 304: *PROPOSALS FOR A NEW 'LADDER' OF HOMICIDE OFFENCES*

1.34 Our consultees almost all agreed that the two-category structure of the general law of homicide is no longer fit for purpose. Consequently, we are proposing to replace the two-tier structure with a three-tier structure. Such a structure will be much better equipped to deal with the stresses and strains on the law and with the issues of appropriate labelling and sentencing. The three tiers in descending order of seriousness would be first degree murder, second degree murder and manslaughter.

1.35 Under our recommendations, first degree murder would encompass:

(1) intentional killing; or

(2) killing through an intention to do serious injury with an awareness of a serious risk of causing death.

1.36 Second degree murder would encompass:

(1) killing through an intention to do serious injury (even without an awareness of a serious risk of causing death); or

(2) killing where there was an awareness of a serious risk of causing death, coupled with an intention to cause either:

(a) some injury;

(b) a fear of injury; or

(c) a risk of injury.

1.37 Second degree murder would also be the result when a partial defence of provocation, diminished responsibility or killing pursuant to a suicide pact is successfully pleaded to first degree murder.

1.38 Manslaughter would encompass:

(1) where death was caused by a criminal act intended to cause injury, or where the offender was aware that the criminal act involved a serious risk of causing injury; or

(2) where there was gross negligence as to causing death.

. . .

1.63 We recommend that there should be a new Homicide Act for England and Wales. The new Act should replace the Homicide Act 1957. The new Act should, for the first time, provide clear and comprehensive definitions of the homicide offences and the partial defences. In addition, the new Act should extend the full defence of duress to the offences of first degree and second degree murder and attempted murder, and improve the procedure for dealing with infanticide cases.

1.64 In structuring the general homicide offences we have been guided by a key principle: the 'ladder' principle. Individual offences of homicide should exist within a graduated system or hierarchy of offences. This system or hierarchy should reflect the offence's degree of seriousness, without too much overlap between individual offences. The main reason for adopting the 'ladder' principle is as Lord Bingham has recently put it (in a slightly different context):

The interests of justice are not served if a defendant who has committed a lesser offence is either convicted of a greater offence, exposing him to greater punishment than his crime deserves, or acquitted altogether, enabling him to escape the measure of punishment which his crime deserves. The objective must be that defendants are neither over-convicted nor under-convicted . . .

(*Coutts* [2006] UKHL 39, [2006] 1 WLR 2154 at [12])

The structure of offences

1.67 We believe that the following structure would make the law of homicide more coherent and comprehensible, whilst respecting the principles just set out above:

(1) First degree murder (mandatory life penalty)

    (a) Killing intentionally.

    (b) Killing where there was an intention to do serious injury, coupled with an awareness of a serious risk of causing death.

(2) Second degree murder (discretionary life maximum penalty)

    (a) Killing where the offender intended to do serious injury.

    . . .

    (b) Killing where the offender intended to cause some injury or a fear or risk of injury, and was aware of a serious risk of causing death.

    (c) Killing in which there is a partial defence to what would otherwise be first degree murder.

(3) Manslaughter (discretionary life maximum penalty)

    (a) Killing through gross negligence as to a risk of causing death.

    (b) Killing through a criminal act:

        (i) intended to cause injury; or

        (ii) where there was an awareness that the act involved a serious risk of causing injury.

    (c) Participating in a joint criminal venture in the course of which another participant commits first or second degree murder, in circumstances where it should have been obvious that first or second degree murder might be committed by another participant.

Partial defences reducing first degree murder to second degree murder

1.68 The following partial defences would reduce first degree murder to second degree murder:

(1) provocation (gross provocation or fear of serious violence);

(2) diminished responsibility;

(3) participation in a suicide pact.

. . .

The different fault elements and the 'ladder' approach

3.4 In this Part, we consider the meanings of 'intention', 'awareness' of risk, and 'serious' risk. We set out what we believe should be the fault element of what hitherto has been known as 'unlawful and dangerous act' manslaughter. Finally, we recommend the adoption of our existing recommendations for the meaning of 'gross negligence' manslaughter's fault element.

3.5 Different fault elements serve to create a 'ladder' of crime seriousness, both in the existing law and in our recommendations. It is of vital importance to remember that any scheme that divides offences using varying fault elements will necessarily involve some degree of overlap: the most culpable cases in a lower tier may well appear worse than the least culpable cases in the next tier up. This phenomenon will occur in any sophisticated system for grading offences. This overlap does not weaken the case for having clear boundaries between offences. Neither does it necessarily mean that the boundaries have been drawn in the wrong place nor that the wrong terms have been used to mark those boundaries.

3.6 Under our recommendations, the fault elements create a 'ladder' of crime seriousness in one or both of at least two important ways. First, the less serious crimes typically have less grave fault elements. So, for example, manslaughter can be committed by gross negligence whereas murder cannot.

3.7 Secondly, the 'ladder' of crime seriousness is shaped by the nature or degree of harm or injury to which a fault element relates. Where death has been caused, a simple intention to do some injury is sufficient for a manslaughter conviction. However, if an awareness of a serious risk of causing death accompanied that intention, a conviction for second degree murder is justified. Further up the ladder, whilst an intention to do serious injury suffices to convict a killer of second degree murder, something more is required to justify a first degree murder conviction. First degree murder requires nothing short of an intention to kill or the morally equivalent intention to do serious injury in the awareness that this involves a serious risk of causing death.

3.8 This 'ladder' approach produces the following structure . . .

(1) First degree murder

    (a) An intention to kill; or

    (b) an intention to do serious injury, aware that one's conduct involves a serious risk of causing death.

(2) Second degree murder
   (a) An intention to do serious injury; or
   (b) an intention to cause:
      (i) injury;
      (ii) a fear of injury; or
      (iii) a risk of injury
   in the awareness that one's conduct involves a serious risk of causing death.
(3) Manslaughter
   (a) Manifesting gross negligence as to a risk of causing death;
   (b) doing a criminal act that the defendant intends to cause injury, or that he or she is aware involves a serious risk of causing some injury.

4.2 THE *ACTUS REUS* OF HOMICIDE – THE VICTIM MUST BE A 'LIFE IN BEING'

The prosecution must prove that the victim in a murder or manslaughter case was a 'reasonable creature' – this means a creature capable of reasoning: that is, any human being. Many of the old cases that dealt with this issue arose out of botched abortions or deliveries; hence the term 'life in being' came to mean a child that had been fully expelled from its mother's body and capable of existence independent of its mother. With the introduction of statutory offences specifically designed to protect the unborn, in particular the Infant Life (Preservation) Act 1929, the matter has given rise to less litigation. The 1929 Act provides that any person who intentionally causes the death of a child capable of being born alive commits an offence carrying with it the possibility of life imprisonment. The Act contains a rebuttable presumption in s 1(2) that a child is capable of being born alive once 28 weeks of gestation have passed. If there was doubt, therefore, as to whether a child had been killed whilst *in utero*, or after having been born, the prosecution would simply proceed on the basis of alternative counts, murder and a charge under the 1929 Act. Two cases have, however, given rise to a consideration of the issue in the modern era, and are thus worthy of consideration on this point.

Attorney General's Ref (No 3 of 1994) [1997] 3 All ER 936

For the facts see the extract from this case at Chapter 4.5. The following extract deals with the extent to which a foetus could be the victim of a homicide.

Lord Mustill:
Except under statute an embryo or foetus in utero cannot be the victim of a crime of violence. In particular, violence to the foetus which causes its death *in utero* is not a murder.

The foundation authority is the definition by Sir Edward Coke of murder . . . The proposition was developed by the same writer into examples of prenatal injuries as follows:

If a woman be quick with child, and by a potion or otherwise killeth it in her womb; or if a man beat her, whereby the child dieth in her body, and she is delivered of a dead child; this is a great misprision, and no murder . . .

> It is unnecessary to look behind this statement to the earlier authorities, for its correctness as a general principle, as distinct from its application to babies expiring in the course of delivery or very shortly thereafter, has never been controverted . . .

Lord Mustill then turned to consider the two arguments put forward by the Crown on this point.

> The decision of the Court of Appeal founded on the proposition that the foetus is part of the mother, so that an intention to cause really serious bodily injury to the mother is equivalent to the same intent directed towards the foetus. This intent could be added to the *actus reus*, constituted (as I understand it) by the creation of such a change in the environment of the foetus through the injury to the mother that the baby would be born at a time when, as events proved, it would not survive. I must dissent from this proposition for I believe it to be wholly unfounded in fact. Obviously, nobody would assert that once the mother [M] had been delivered of S [the baby], the baby and her mother were in any sense 'the same'. Not only were they physically separate, but they were each unique human beings, though no doubt with many features of resemblance. The reason for the uniqueness of S was that the development of her own special characteristics had been enabled and bounded by the collection of genes handed down not only by M but also by the natural father. This collection was different from the genes which had enabled and bounded the development of M, for these had been handed down by her own mother and natural father. S and her mother were closely related but, even apart from differing environmental influences, they were not, had not been, and in the future never would be 'the same'. There was, of course, an intimate bond between the foetus and the mother, created by the total dependence of the foetus on the protective physical environment furnished by the mother, and on the supply by the mother through the physical linkage between them of the nutriments, oxygen and other substances essential to foetal life and development. The emotional bond between the mother and her unborn child was also of a very special kind. But the relationship was one of bond, not of identity. The mother and the foetus were two distinct organisms living symbiotically, not a single organism with two aspects. The mother's leg was part of the mother; the foetus was not.
>
> The only other ground for identifying the foetus with the mother that I can envisage is a chain of reasoning on the following lines. All the case law shows that the child does not attain a sufficient human personality to be the subject of a crime of violence, and in particular of a crime of murder, until it enjoys an existence separate from its mother; hence, whilst it is in the womb it does not have a human personality; hence it must share a human personality with its mother. This seems to me an entire *non sequitur*, for it omits the possibility that the foetus does not (for the purposes of the law of homicide and violent crime) have any relevant type of personality but is an organism *sui generis* lacking at this stage the entire range of characteristics both of the mother to which it is physically linked and of the complete human being which it will later become. The argument involves one fiction too far, and I would reject it . . .
>
> *The second argument: the foetus as a separate organism . . .*
> I would, therefore, reject the reasoning which assumes that since (in the eyes of English law) the foetus does not have the attributes which make it a 'person' it must be an adjunct of the mother.

Eschewing all religious and political debate I would say that the foetus is neither. It is a unique organism. To apply to such an organism the principles of a law evolved in relation to autonomous beings is bound to mislead . . .

I turn to deal more briefly with the remaining rules. The third rule, it will be recalled, is that a foetus cannot be the victim of murder. I see no profit in an attempt to treat the medieval origins of this rule. It is sufficient to say that is established beyond doubt for the criminal law, as for the civil law (*Burton v Islington Health Authority* [1993] QB 204) that the child *en ventre sa mère* does not have a distinct human personality, whose extinguishment gives rise to any penalties or liabilities at common law.

Re A (Children) (Conjoined Twins) [2000] 4 All ER 961

The court was asked to rule on the legality of an operation to separate conjoined twins, Jodie and Mary. Mary, the weaker of the two conjoined twins, was incapable of independent existence. If the operation went ahead Jodie's life would be saved but Mary would definitely die. One of the issues was whether or not, given that she lacked the capability of sustaining her own life, Mary should be regarded as a human being for the purposes of homicide.

Brooke LJ:

Is Mary a reasonable creature?

For the reasons given by Ward LJ and Robert Walker LJ, with which I agree, I am satisfied that Mary's life is a human life that falls to be protected by the law of murder. Although she has for all practical purposes a useless brain, a useless heart and useless lungs, she is alive, and it would in my judgment be an act of murder if someone deliberately acted so as to extinguish that life unless a justification or excuse could be shown which English law is willing to recognise.

In recent editions of Archbold, including the 2000 edition, the editors have suggested that the word 'reasonable' in Coke's definition (which they wrongly ascribe to Lord Hale in para 19.1) related to the appearance rather than the mental capacity of the victim and was apt to exclude 'monstrous births'. Spurred on by this suggestion, and because the present case broke so much novel ground, we explored with counsel some of the thinking of seventeenth century English philosophers in an effort to ascertain what Coke may have meant when he used the expression 'any reasonable creature' as part of his definition. We had in mind their absorbing interest in the nature of 'strange and deformed births' and 'monstrous births' (see Thomas Hobbes, *Elements of Law*, II.10.8, and John Locke, *An Essay Concerning Human Understanding*, III.III.17, III.VI.15 and 26 and III.XI.20).

In *Attorney General's Ref (No 3 of 1994)* [1998] AC 245 Lord Mustill referred at p 254F to another statement in Coke's Institutes, not mentioned in that passage in Archbold, where after referring to prenatal injuries which lead to the delivery of a dead child, Coke writes (Co Inst Pt III, Ch 7, p 50):

'if the childe be born alive, and dieth of the potion, battery, or other cause, this is murder; for in law it is accounted a reasonable creature, in rerum natura, when it is born alive'.

In these circumstances I have no hesitation in accepting the submission by Miss Davies QC (whose assistance, as the friend of the court, was of the greatest value), which was in these terms:

In *The Sanctity of Life and the Criminal Law* (1958), Professor Glanville Williams stated at p 31:

"There is, indeed some kind of legal argument that a 'monster' is not protected even under the existing law. This argument depends upon the very old legal writers, because the matter has not been considered in any modern work or in any court judgment."

After discussing the meaning of the word 'monster' (which might originally have connoted animal paternity) he states at pp 33–34:

'Locked (Siamese) twins present a special case, though they are treated in medical works as a species of monster. Here the recent medical practice is to attempt a severance, notwithstanding the risks involved. Either the twins are successfully unlocked, or they die' [emphasis added].

It is implicit in this analysis that the author is of the view that 'Siamese' twins are capable of being murdered and the *amicus curiae* supports this view.

Advances in medical treatment of deformed neonates suggest that the criminal law's protection should be as wide as possible and a conclusion that a creature in being was not reasonable would be confined only to the most extreme cases, of which this is not an example. Whatever might have been thought of as 'monstrous' by Bracton, Coke, Blackstone, Locke and Hobbes, different considerations would clearly apply today. This proposition might be tested in this way: suppose an intruder broke into the hospital and stabbed twin M causing her death. Clearly it could not be said that his actions would be outside the ambit of the law of homicide.

Modern English statute law has mitigated the prospective burden that might otherwise fall on the parents of severely handicapped children and their families if they are willing to avail themselves of its protection at any time up to the time the child (or children) is born. Section 1(1)(d) of the Abortion Act 1967, as substituted by s 37(1) of the Human Fertilisation and Embryology Act 1990, provides:

Subject to the provisions of this section, a person shall not be guilty of an offence under the law relating to abortion when a pregnancy is terminated by a registered medical practitioner if two registered medical practitioners are of the opinion, formed in good faith . . . that there is a substantial risk that if the child were born it would suffer from such physical or mental abnormalities as to be severely handicapped.

Once a seriously handicapped child is born alive, the position changes, and it is as much entitled to the protection of the criminal law as any other human being. The governing principle is sometimes described as the universality of rights. In the Canadian case of *Perka v R* 13 DLR (4th) 1 Wilson J said at p 31 that the principle of the universality of rights demands that all individuals whose actions are subjected to legal evaluation must be considered equal in standing.

It follows that unless there is some special exception to which we can have recourse, in the eyes of the law Mary's right to life must be accorded equal status with her sister Jodie's right to life. In this context it is wholly illegitimate to introduce considerations that relate to the quality, or the potential quality, of each sister's life.

4.3 CAUSATION

Some criminal offences, such as murder and wounding, are referred to as 'result crimes' on the basis that establishing the *actus reus* involves proof that the defendant caused the prohibited result (that is, the death of the victim, or the wounding) both as a matter of fact and as a matter of law. In effect the prosecution must establish a chain of causation between the defendant's act (or in some cases omission) and the prohibited consequence. As will be seen, it may be possible for a defendant to provide evidence that the chain of causation has been broken by a *novus actus interveniens* (new intervening act), in which case liability for the completed crime cannot be established, although the defendant might still bear liability for having attempted to commit the offence; see further Chapter 8. The majority of case extracts in this chapter are drawn from cases that involve defendants charged with murder or manslaughter. This is not surprising given that homicide cases are likely to throw up interesting and novel problems of causation. It should be borne in mind, however, that the general principles of causation enunciated by the courts are of application to the vast majority of result crimes.

4.3.1 CAUSATION IN FACT

The first step in establishing a chain of causation is for the prosecution to prove that the defendant's act or omission is a cause in fact of the prohibited result. This is normally done by applying the 'but for' test. The question asked is: 'But for the defendant's act or omission would the result have occurred?' If the answer is 'no' causation in fact is established. If the answer is 'yes', it means that the result would have occurred in any event – thus the defendant's act or omission was not a cause in fact of the result.

R v White [1908–10] All ER Rep 340 (CA)

The defendant placed poison in his mother's drink. She was found dead on the sofa a little later. The expert evidence revealed that she had died from some external cause such as fright or heart failure before the poison could take effect. The defendant was convicted of attempted murder and appealed unsuccessfully against his conviction.

Bray J:

[The defendant] . . . therefore, perfectly well knew the deadly character of this poison, and supposed that a very small quantity would produce an instant effect. Upon consideration of all the evidence, including the denial of the prisoner that he had put anything into the wine glass at all, we are of opinion that there was sufficient evidence to warrant the jury also in coming to the conclusion that the appellant put the cyanide in the glass with intent to murder his mother.

The next point made was that, if he put it there with that intent, there was no attempt at murder; that the jury must have acted upon a suggestion of the learned judge in his summing-up that this was one, the first or some later, of a series of doses which he intended to administer and so cause her death by slow poisoning, and if they did act on that suggestion there was no attempt at murder, because the act of which he was guilty – the putting of poison in the wine glass – was a completed act and could not be and was not intended by the appellant to have the effect of killing her at once. It could not kill unless it were followed by other acts which he might never have done. There seems no doubt that the learned judge in effect did tell the jury that, if this was a case of slow poisoning, the appellant would be guilty of the attempt to murder. We are of opinion that this direction was right, and that the completion or attempted completion of one of a series of acts intended by a man to result in killing is an attempt to murder even though this completed act would not, unless followed by the other acts, result in killing. It might be the beginning of the attempt, but would none the less be an attempt. While saying this, we must say also that we do not think it likely the jury acted on this suggestion, because there was nothing to show that the administration of small doses of cyanide of potassium, would have a cumulative effect; we think it much more likely, having regard to the statement made by the prisoner to the witness Carden, that the appellant supposed he had put sufficient poison in the glass to kill her. This, of course, would be an attempt to murder . . .

4.3.2 CAUSATION IN LAW: BASIC PRINCIPLES

Assuming causation in fact can be established, attention shifts to whether or not the defendant can be said to have caused the death as a matter of law. This is a question of fact that will be determined by the jury in the light of the trial judge's directions as to the relevant law. In the vast majority of cases no specific direction is required – it will be obvious that the defendant caused the death and no issue arises as to any intervening cause. A simple direction in terms of whether or not the defendant's act was an operating and substantial cause of death will suffice – see further *R v Smith* [1959] 2 QB 35, extracted below. Where there is some intervening cause of death the issue for the jury will be to decide whether the death was nevertheless a reasonably foreseeable consequence of the defendant's act. Only if the intervening cause amounts to a 'novus actus', that is, something that breaks the chain of causation, will the prosecution have failed to establish causation in law.

R v Smith [1959] 2 QB 35 (CA)

The appellant, a private soldier in the King's Regiment, took part in a fight between a company of his regiment and a company of the Gloucestershire Regiment, who were sharing barracks in Germany, on the night of 13 April 1958. Three men of the Gloucesters received stab wounds. One of them subsequently died. One of the issues before the Court of Appeal was the extent to which the inadequacies of the treatment received by the deceased might be regarded as the cause of death, as opposed to the stab wounds inflicted by the defendant.

Lord Parker CJ:
. . . The second ground concerns a question of causation . . . It seems to the court that if at the time of death the original wound is still an operating cause and a substantial cause, then the death can properly be said to be the result of the wound, albeit, that some other cause of death is also

operating. Only if it can be said that the original wounding is merely the setting in which another cause operates can it be said that the death does not result from the wound. Putting it in another way, only if the second cause is so overwhelming as to make the original wound merely part of the history can it be said that the death does not flow from the wound . . . In the present case it is true that the judge-advocate did not in his summing-up go into the refinements of causation. Indeed, in the opinion of this court he was probably wise to refrain from doing so. He did leave the broad question to the court whether they were satisfied that the wound had caused the death in the sense that the death flowed from the wound, albeit that the treatment he received was in the light of after-knowledge a bad thing. In the opinion of this court that was on the facts of the case a perfectly adequate summing-up on causation; I say 'on the facts of the case' because, in the opinion of the court, they can only lead to one conclusion: a man is stabbed in the back, his lung is pierced and haemorrhage results; two hours later he dies of haemorrhage from that wound; in the interval there is no time for a careful examination, and the treatment given turns out in the light of subsequent knowledge to have been inappropriate and, indeed, harmful. In those circumstances no reasonable jury or court could, properly directed, in our view possibly come to any other conclusion than that the death resulted from the original wound. Accordingly, the court dismisses this appeal.

R v Warburton and another [2006] EWCA Crim 627, confirms that a simple direction in terms of whether or not the acts for which D was responsible significantly contributed to P's death will suffice.

4.3.3 *NOVUS ACTUS INTERVENIENS* – CAN THE CHAIN OF CAUSATION BE BROKEN BY THE ACTIONS OF THE VICTIM IN REFUSING MEDICAL TREATMENT?

R v Blaue [1975] 1 WLR 1411 (CA)

Lawton LJ:

. . . The victim was a young girl aged 18. She was a Jehovah's Witness. She professed the tenets of that sect and lived her life by them. During the late afternoon of 3 May 1974 the appellant came into her house and asked her for sexual intercourse. She refused. He then attacked her with a knife inflicting four serious wounds. One pierced her lung. The appellant ran away. The girl staggered out into the road. She collapsed outside a neighbour's house. An ambulance took her to hospital, where she arrived at about 7.30 pm. Soon afterwards she was admitted to the intensive care ward. At about 8.30 pm she was examined by the surgical registrar who quickly decided that serious injury had been caused which would require surgery. As she had lost a lot of blood, before there could be an operation there would have to be a blood transfusion. As soon as the girl appreciated that the surgeon was thinking of organising a blood transfusion for her, she said that she should not be given one and that she would not have one. To have one, she said, would be contrary to her religious beliefs as a Jehovah's Witness. She was told that if she did not have a blood transfusion she would die. She said that she did not care if she did die. She was asked to acknowledge in writing that she had refused to have a blood transfusion under any circumstances. She did so. The Crown admitted at the trial that had she had a blood transfusion when advised to have one she would not have died. She did so at 12.45 am the next day. The evidence called by the Crown proved that at all relevant times she was conscious and decided as she did deliberately, and knowing what the consequences of her decision would be. In his final speech to the jury, counsel for the Crown accepted that the girl's refusal to have a blood transfusion was a cause of her death. The prosecution did not challenge the defence evidence that the appellant was suffering from diminished responsibility.

Towards the end of the trial and before the summing-up started counsel on both sides made submissions as to how the case should be put to the jury. Counsel then appearing for the appellant invited the judge to direct the jury to acquit the appellant generally on the count of murder. His argument was that the girl's refusal to have a blood transfusion had broken the chain of causation between the stabbing and her death. As an alternative he submitted that the jury should be left to decide whether the chain of causation had been broken. Counsel for the Crown submitted that the judge should direct the jury to convict, because no facts were in issue and when the law was applied to the facts there was only one possible verdict, i.e. manslaughter by reason of diminished responsibility . . .

The physical cause of death in this case was bleeding into the pleural cavity arising from the penetration of the lung. This had not been brought about by any decision made by the deceased girl but by the stab wound.

Counsel for the appellant tried to overcome this line of reasoning by submitting that the jury should have been directed that if they thought the girl's decision not to have a blood transfusion was an unreasonable one, then the chain of causation would have been broken. At once the question arises – reasonable by whose standards? Those of Jehovah's Witnesses? Humanists? Roman Catholics? Protestants of Anglo-Saxon descent? The man on the Clapham omnibus? But he might well be an admirer of Eleazar who suffered death rather than eat the flesh of swine (see 2 Maccabees, Chapter 6 vv 18–31) or of Sir Thomas More who, unlike nearly all his contemporaries, was unwilling to accept Henry VIII as Head of the Church of England. Those brought up in the Hebraic and Christian traditions would probably be reluctant to accept that these martyrs caused their own deaths.

As was pointed out to counsel for the appellant in the course of argument, two cases, each raising the same issue of reasonableness because of religious beliefs, could produce different verdicts depending on where the cases were tried. A jury drawn from Preston, sometimes said to be the most Catholic town in England, might have different views about martyrdom to one drawn from the inner suburbs of London . . . It has been the policy of the law that those who use violence on other people must take their victims as they find them. This in our judgment means the whole man, not just the physical man. It does not lie in the mouth of the assailant to say that his victim's religious beliefs which inhibited her from accepting certain kinds of treatment were unreasonable. The question for decision is what caused her death. The answer is the stab wound. The fact that the victim refused to stop this end coming about did not break the causal connection between the act and death.

. . . The issue of the cause of death in a trial for either murder or manslaughter is one of fact for the jury to decide. But if, as in this case, there is no conflict of evidence and all the jury has to do is to apply the law to the admitted facts, the judge is entitled to tell the jury what the result of that application will be. In this case the judge would have been entitled to have told the jury that the appellant's stab wound was an operative cause of the death. The appeal fails.

See further *R v Holland* (1841) 2 Mood & R 351.

4.3.4 *NOVUS ACTUS INTERVENIENS* – CAN THE CHAIN OF CAUSATION BE BROKEN BY THE VICTIM'S SELF-ADMINISTRATION OF DRUGS?

Cases involving the supply of controlled drugs by D to P, where P consumes what transpires to be a lethal quantity of the drugs of his own volition, have presented difficulties for the courts. The issue of causation in law is plain – had D not supplied the drugs to P the death would not have occurred. As regards causation in law, the operating and substantial cause of death is the self-administration of the drugs by P. As Waller LJ observed when dealing with such a scenario in *R v Dalby* [1982] 1 All ER 916: 'In this case the supply of drugs would itself have caused no harm unless the deceased had subsequently used the drugs in a form and quantity which was dangerous.' Similarly in *R v Dias* [2002] Crim LR 490, Keene LJ observed:

> . . . [the] supply of heroin was undoubtedly unlawful, but the difficulty about relying on it as a basis for manslaughter would have been one of causation. [The deceased] was an adult and able to decide for himself whether or not to inject the heroin. His own action in injecting himself might well have been seen as an intervening act between the supply of the drug by the appellant and the death of [the deceased]. The chain of causation was probably broken by that intervening act . . . We accept that there may be situations where a jury could find manslaughter in cases such as this, so long as they were satisfied so as to be sure that the chain of causation was not broken . . . The recipient does not have to inject the drug which he is encouraged and assisted to take. He has a choice. It may be that in some circumstances the causative chain will still remain. That is a matter for the jury to decide . . . It may seem to some that there is morally not a great deal between this situation where A hands B a syringe containing a drug such as heroin, with death resulting, and that where A injects B with his consent with the contents of the syringe. But the vital difference (and this is why causation cannot be assumed) is that the former situation involves an act of B's taken voluntarily and leading to his death.

R v Finlay [2003] EWCA Crim 3868

D prepared a syringe containing a heroin mixture that the victim, Jasmine Grosvenor, used to inject herself. The dosage proved fatal. D appealed, unsuccessfully, on the basis that the victim's voluntary act had broken the chain of causation.

> Buxton LJ:
> The test is one of causation. In this case, could it be said that the act of the deceased in taking up the syringe and using it on herself, which are to be assumed to be the facts, prevented Mr Finlay's previous acts being causative of the injection . . . In . . . *Environment Agency v Empress Car Company* [1999] 2 AC 22, [1998] 1 All ER 481 . . . Lord Hoffmann said that the prosecution need not prove that the Defendant did something which was the immediate cause of the death. When the prosecution had identified an act done by the Defendant, the court had to decide, particularly when a necessary condition of the event complained of was the act of a third party, whether that

act should be regarded as a matter of ordinary occurrence which would not negative the effect of the Defendant's act; or something extraordinary, on the other hand which would leave open a finding that the Defendant did not cause the criminal act or event. That, said Lord Hoffmann, with the agreement of the rest of the House of Lords, was a question of fact and degree to which, in the case before him, the justices had to apply their common sense, as in a jury trial the jury has to apply its common sense. That was exactly the way in which the judge directed himself in his observations on the application that count 2 should be removed from the jury.

And that is exactly how he directed the jury when he came to sum up. At p 14F he said this:

> Whether or not the Defendant caused heroin to be administered to or taken by the deceased is a question of fact and degree which you have to decide, and you should decide it by applying your common sense and knowledge of the world to the facts that you find to be proved by the evidence. The prosecution do not have to show that what the defendant did or said was a sole cause of the injection of heroin into the deceased. Where the Defendant has produced the situation in which there is the possibility for heroin to be administered to or taken by Jasmine Grosvenor, but the actual injection of heroin involves an act on part of another – in this case Jasmine herself – then if the injection of heroin is to be regarded in your view as a normal fact of life, in the situation proved by the evidence, then the act of the other person will not prevent the Defendant's deeds or words being a cause, or one of the causes, of that injection. On the other hand, if in the situation proved by the evidence, injection is to be regarded as an extraordinary event, then it would be open to you to conclude that the defendant did not cause heroin to be administered to or taken by the deceased.

. . . Mr Gibson-Lee [for the appellant] really advances two reasons why the judge should not have taken that view . . . The first is that on the assumption that it was the deceased who injected herself, that act of itself breaks the chain of causation between whatever it was that the accused did and the actual event of injection . . . We have to say that that approach is not correct. It seeks to make the existence of what used to be called a *novus actus interveniens*, and can now more simply be regarded as an act of another person, as something that as a matter of law breaks the chain of causation. It was that view or assumption that was rejected by the House of Lords in the Empress Car case. Intervening acts are only a factor to be taken into account by the jury in looking at all the circumstances, as the judge told them to do.

Secondly, Mr Gibson-Lee says that in any event the facts of this case were such that it simply was not open to the jury to conclude that Mr Finlay had caused the injection. He had done no more than form part of the background, or provide the opportunity of which the deceased availed herself: in other words, that the case was so extreme or so clear that it was not appropriate for the jury to look at it as a case of causation at all. The judge did not take that view, nor do we. The unhappy circumstances of this case, and in particular the unhappy circumstances of this lady's life and condition, in our view indicate that it was certainly open to a jury to conclude in Empress Car terms that in those circumstances, and we emphasise that, it was what Lord Hoffmann described as an 'ordinary' occurrence for the purpose of the law of causation that she should have taken advantage of whatever it was that Mr Finlay did towards her or with her. It is not necessary for that conclusion to decide, as Mr Gibson-Lee suggested it was, that she was incapable of knowing what she was doing or had ceased entirely to be a rational being. All that is necessary, in our judgment, is that the circumstances should be such that it could properly be said to fall within the ambit of possible and ordinary events that she will take the opportunity given her. We quite accept that, on facts different from these, there might be more difficulty in coming to that conclusion.

R v Kennedy [2005] EWCA Crim 685

D prepared a dose of heroin for P and gave P a syringe ready for self injection. P injected himself and shortly after experienced breathing difficulties brought on by the effect of the heroin. Following P's death D was convicted of manslaughter. D's original appeal against conviction was dismissed – see [1999] Crim LR 65. In the light of subsequent decisions, however, D's case was referred back to the Court of Appeal by the Criminal Cases Review Commission under s 9 of the Criminal Appeal Act 1995. The key argument before the Court of Appeal on the referral back was as to whether a free, deliberate and informed act by P in deciding to inject himself with the heroin would break the chain of causation between the supply of the heroin by D and the death of P.

Lord Woolf CJ (dismissing the appeal):
. . . before turning to [*R v Finlay* [2003] EWCA Crim 3868] . . . it is important to point out where the authorities that we have already cited take us;

i) That a person who kills himself is not committing a crime.

ii) Contrary to part of the judgment of Waller LJ (Junior) on the first appeal, even though a person may encourage another to take his own life, he is not an accessory to manslaughter on this ground alone as there is no principal of whom he is the accessory.

iii) If, however, the role played by the defendant, in concert with the deceased, amounts to administering or causing the drug to be administered, then that person will have committed an offence under s 23 of the 1861 Act and he will be guilty of an unlawful act. The fact that the deceased may die does not affect that situation. Furthermore, if the defendant participates in an offence involving the administration of the drug, there could be no question of difficulties in relation to causation.

iv) On the first appeal, Waller LJ (Junior) was right when he regarded 'the critical question to which the jury must direct its mind, where (as in the instance case) there is an act causative of death performed by, in this case the deceased himself, is whether the appellant can be said to be jointly responsible for the carrying out of that act' (emphasis added).

v) The critical comments in relation to the judgment on the first appeal are directed to other parts of Waller LJ's judgment, when he indicates that it would be sufficient if the appellant was an accessory. Waller LJ, for example, stated 'if the appellant assisted in and wilfully encouraged that unlawful conduct [i.e. the self-injection] he would himself be acting unlawfully' (emphasis added). If the encouragement is isolated from the assisting, then there would be a basis for the criticism.

. . .

40. In *Finlay*, Buxton LJ was suggesting that the approach the House of Lords appropriately applied in the Empress case to a statute dealing with pollution could be applied equally here to the issues of causation where the statutory context is very different. It is, however, to be noted

that the question of causation can arise on a charge of manslaughter when s 23 of the 1861 Act is not relied upon, and in two different circumstances when s 23 is relied upon. It can arise on the general question of whether the defendant's unlawful action caused the deceased's death. It can also arise on the question of whether the defendant caused to be administered 'any poison or other destructive or noxious thing contrary to s 23'. These are distinct situations.

41. In his summing-up in *Finlay*, the trial judge referred to the need for the prosecution, in relation to the s 23 offence, to prove that the defendant caused the heroin to be administered to, or to be taken by, the deceased. In that context he referred to the Empress case. As we understand the position, it was to this context that Buxton LJ was addressing himself when he referred with approval to the approach of the judge to establishing causation in accordance with Lord Hoffmann's speech in the Empress case. In that context, this appears to us to be, with respect, an unnecessary sophistication. All the jury had to decide as to causation was whether Finlay's actions were as a matter of fact causative of the deceased taking the action to administer the drug. If it was, his conduct contravened s 23 and was unlawful. Otherwise it was not.

42. It has to be remembered that when considering whether the defendant's act has caused death, what amounts to causation in a case of this nature is not dependent upon a particular statutory context. Accordingly if a defendant is acting in concert with the deceased, what the deceased does in concert with the defendant will not break the chain of causation, even though the general principles as to causation have to be applied. This was recognised by Lord Steyn when he qualified the general position when saying in *R v Latif & Others* [1996] 2 Cr App R 92 at p 104:

> The free, deliberate and informed intervention of a second person, who intends to exploit the situation created by the first, *but is not acting in concert with him* is held to relieve the first actor of criminal responsibility. (Emphasis added)

43. If Kennedy either caused the deceased to administer the drug or was acting jointly with the deceased in administering the drug, Kennedy would be acting in concert with the deceased and there would be no breach in the chain of causation.

44. The exception made for the person 'acting in concert' is of considerable importance. The fact that a person who takes his own life does not commit an unlawful act by so doing, does not mean that a person who helps him to commit that act, if that helping act is contrary to s 23, does not commit an unlawful act. On the contrary, the helper does commit an unlawful act and could be charged under s 23 and convicted. He could also be convicted of manslaughter if the person he was helping dies in consequence. The requirement of an unlawful act is fulfilled. There should, in the appropriate case, be no difficulty in establishing foreseeability of risk. Nor should there be difficulty in establishing causation because the participants were acting in concert.

. . .

Conclusions

51. In view of the conclusions that we have come to as a result of our examination of the authorities, it appears to us that it was open to the jury to convict the appellant of manslaughter. To convict, the jury had to be satisfied that, when the heroin was handed to the deceased 'for immediate injection', he and the deceased were both engaged in the one activity of administering the heroin. These were not necessarily to be regarded as two separate activities; and the question that remains is whether the jury were satisfied that this was the situation. If the jury were satisfied

of this then the appellant was responsible for taking the action in concert with the deceased to enable the deceased to inject himself with the syringe of heroin which had been made ready for his immediate use.

52. In our view, the jury would have been entitled to find (and indeed it is an appropriate finding) that in these circumstances the appellant and the deceased were jointly engaged in administering the heroin. This was the conclusion of this Court on the first appeal, as we understand Waller LJ's judgment, and we do not feel it necessary to take a different view, though we do accept that the issue could have been left by the trial judge to the jury in more clear terms than it was.

53. The point in this case is that the appellant and the deceased were carrying out a 'combined operation' for which they were jointly responsible. Their actions were similar to what happens frequently when carrying out lawful injections: one nurse may carry out certain preparatory actions (including preparing the syringe) and hand it to a colleague who inserts the needle and administers the injection, after which the other nurse may apply a plaster. In such a situation, both nurses can be regarded as administering the drug. They are working as a team. Both their actions are necessary. They are interlinked but separate parts in the overall process of administering the drug. In these circumstances, as Waller LJ stated on the first appeal, they 'can be said to be jointly responsible for carrying out that act'.

54. Whether the necessary linkage existed between the actions of the appellant and the deceased was very much a matter for the jury to determine. The question then arises as to whether the trial judge in the summing-up expressed the issue in sufficiently clear terms for the jury? As to this, we share similar reservations to those expressed by Waller LJ in his judgment on the first appeal. There was no need for the jury to find the encouragement that Waller LJ thought was necessary. However, the jury did have to find that the appellant and the deceased were acting in concert in administering the heroin.

55. In addition, there is the fact that Mr Montrose, who represented the appellant at the trial, was not allowed to address the jury on the question of causation. However, here we have less reservations than the court on the first appeal, since if the deceased and the appellant were acting in concert in administering the heroin, it seems to us inevitable that the unlawful act, contrary to s 23 of the 1861 Act, was causative of the deceased's death.

4.3.5 *NOVUS ACTUS INTERVENIENS* – CAN THE CHAIN OF CAUSATION BE BROKEN BY THE ACTIONS OF THE VICTIM IN SEEKING TO ESCAPE FROM THE DEFENDANT?

R v Roberts (1971) 56 Cr App R 95 (CA)

P left a party at about 3 am, having agreed to travel with D in his car to another party. After travelling some distance D made indecent advances towards P and she jumped out of the car. She suffered some concussion and grazing and was detained in hospital for three days. The defendant was charged with assault occasioning actual bodily harm. One of the issues before the court was whether or not P had broken the chain of causation by jumping from the moving car.

Stephenson LJ:

... [The jury] had to consider: was the appellant guilty of occasioning [the victim] actual bodily harm? Of course, for that to be established, it had to be established that he was responsible in law and in fact for her injuries caused by leaving in a hurry the moving car ... This court thinks that that correctly states the law ...

... The test is: Was it [the action of the victim which resulted in actual bodily harm] the natural result of what the alleged assailant said and did, in the sense that it was something that could reasonably have been foreseen as the consequence of what he was saying or doing? As it was put in one of the old cases, it had got to be shown to be his act, and if of course the victim does something so 'daft', in the words of the appellant in this case, or so unexpected, not that this particular assailant did not actually foresee it but that no reasonable man could be expected to foresee it, then it is only in a very remote and unreal sense a consequence of his assault, it is really occasioned by a voluntary act on the part of the victim which could not reasonably be foreseen and which breaks the chain of causation between the assault and harm or injury.

R v Williams and Another [1992] 1 WLR 380 (CA)

The deceased, John Shephard, had been hitch-hiking to a free festival at Glastonbury. He was picked up in a car driven by Williams. Davis and the co-accused Bobat were passengers in that car. After travelling approximately five miles, the deceased jumped from the car, and died from head injuries caused by falling onto the road. The evidence was that the car had been travelling at approximately 30 mph at the time of this incident. The prosecution case was that the deceased had tried to escape from the defendants who were intent on robbing him. One of the issues for the Court of Appeal was the extent to which the deceased had, by his actions, broken the chain of causation in law between the defendants' acts and his death.

Stuart-Smith LJ:

... [I]n some cases, and in our judgment this is one of them, it is necessary to give the jury a direction on causation, and explain the test by which the voluntary act of the deceased may be said to be caused by the accused's act and not a *novus actus interveniens*, breaking the chain of causation between the threat of violence and the death. There must be some proportionality between the gravity of the threat and the action of the deceased in seeking to escape from it ... But the nature of the threat is of importance in considering both the foreseeability of harm to the victim from the threat and the question whether the deceased's conduct was proportionate to the threat, that is to say that it was within the ambit of reasonableness and not so daft as to make it his one voluntary act which amounted to a *novus actus interveniens* and consequently broke the chain of causation. It should of course be borne in mind that a victim may in the agony of the moment do the wrong thing.

In this case there was an almost total lack of evidence as to the nature of the threat. The prosecution invited the jury to infer the gravity of the threat from the action of the deceased. The judge put it this way:

... what he was frightened of was robbery, that this was going to be taken from him by force, and the measure of the force can be taken from his reaction to it. The prosecution suggest that if he is prepared to get out of a moving car, then it was a very serious threat involving him in the risk of, as he saw it, serious injury.

In our judgment that was a wholly impermissible argument and was simply a case of the prosecution pulling itself up by its own bootstraps.

Moreover in a case of robbery the threat of force is made to persuade the victim to hand over money: if the money is handed over actual violence may not eventuate. The jury should consider two questions: first, whether it was reasonably foreseeable that some harm, albeit not serious harm, was likely to result from the threat itself; and, second, whether the deceased's reaction in jumping from the moving car was within the range of responses which might be expected from a victim placed in the situation which he was. The jury should bear in mind any particular characteristic of the victim and the fact that in the agony of the moment he may act without thought and deliberation . . .

COMMENTS AND QUESTIONS

1   The ability of the victim to assess the degree of risk or danger inherent in his chosen course of action may be impaired by disability or the effect of drugs. How does this sit with the test for reasonable foreseeability? In *R v Corbett* [1996] Crim LR 594 (CA), the victim was a mentally handicapped man of 26 who suffered from time to time with mental illness and had problems with high alcohol consumption. On the day of his death he had been drinking all day. At about 9.30 pm the appellant had an argument with the victim and started to hit and head-butt him. The victim ran away and fell into the gutter where he was struck by a passing car and killed. The Court of Appeal upheld the conviction, thereby rejecting submission to the effect that the actions of the deceased could amount to a *novus actus interveniens*. The decision suggests strongly that the *R v Blaue* principle, to the effect that the defendant must take his victim as he finds him or her, is of overriding application.

2   *R v Majoram* [2000] Crim LR 372 confirms that the issue of causation is to be assessed objectively. There is no need to prove that the defendant had any foresight of the harmful consequences in order to establish causation. For these purposes the reasonable person does not share any of the defendant's personal attributes. In the course of his judgment Roch LJ cited with approval the passage from R v Roberts (above) to the effect that the chain of causation would be broken if P did something so unexpected it might be described as 'daft'.

3   The doctrine that the defendant should take his victim as he finds him or her, as expressed in Blaue, would suggest that even a 'daft' action by the victim should not break the chain of causation. To what extent can this apparent contradiction be resolved by arguing that: (i) Blaue is to be preferred because it is the later case; (ii) the 'take your victim as you find him or her' doctrine is part of the ratio of Blaue; (iii) Blaue is preferable as a matter of public policy (i.e. the defendant should not be absolved because of the unforeseen 'peculiarities' of the victim).

4   Whether or not P's suicide would amount to a *novus actus interveniens* has been a matter of conjecture. On the one hand it could fall within the 'Blaue' principle, on the other the suicide could be seen as a 'daft' escape by P. In *R v Dhaliwal* [2006] EWCA CRIM 1139 (an appeal under s 58 of the Criminal Justice Act 2003), the court noted (per curiam) that, subject to evidence and argument on the issue of causation, in cases where D inflicted unlawful

violence on an P, (P being an individual with a fragile and vulnerable personality), and where D's violence was proved to be a material cause of death, D could be convicted of manslaughter even where P had taken his own life as a result of the violence. The violence does not have to involve physical contact for these purposes but could extend to cases of psychiatric harm inflicted by D, for example through bullying, harassment or torture.

4.3.6 *NOVUS ACTUS INTERVENIENS* – CAN THE CHAIN OF CAUSATION BE BROKEN BY THE ACTIONS OF A THIRD PARTY?

R v Pagett (1983) 76 Cr App R 279 (CA)

In the early hours of one morning on the first floor of a block of flats where he lived, the appellant, who was armed with a shotgun and cartridges, shot at police officers who were attempting to arrest him for various serious offences. The appellant had with him a 16 year old girl who was pregnant by him, and against her will used her body to shield him from any retaliation by the officers. The officers in fact returned the appellant's fire and as a result the girl was killed. The appellant was charged, *inter alia*, with her murder.

Robert Goff LJ:

. . . [I]t was pressed upon us by Lord Gifford [counsel for the appellant] that there either was, or should be, a comparable rule of English law, whereby, as a matter of policy, no man should be convicted of homicide (or, we imagine, any crime of violence to another person) unless he himself, or another person acting in concert with him, fired the shot (or, we imagine, struck the blow) which was the immediate cause of the victim's death (or injury).

No English authority was cited to us in support of any such proposition, and we know of none. So far as we are aware, there is no such rule in English law; and, in the absence of any doctrine of constructive malice, we can see no basis in principle for any such rule in English law. Lord Gifford urged upon us that, in a case where the accused did not, for example, fire the shot which was the immediate cause of the victim's death, he will inevitably have committed some lesser crime, and that it would be sufficient that he should be convicted of that lesser crime. So, on the facts of the present case, it would be enough that the appellant was convicted of the crime of attempted murder of the two police officers, DS Sartain and DC Richards. We see no force in this submission. In point of fact, it is not difficult to imagine circumstances in which it would manifestly be inadequate for the accused merely to be convicted of a lesser offence; for example, a man besieged by armed terrorists in a house might attempt to make his escape by forcing some other person to act as a shield, knowing full well that that person would in all probability be shot, and possibly killed, in consequence. For that man merely to be convicted of an assault would, if the person he used as a shield were to be shot and killed, surely be inadequate in all the circumstances; we can see no reason why he should not be convicted at least of manslaughter. But in any event there is, so far as we can discern, no basis of legal principle for Lord Gifford's submission. We are therefore unable to accept it.

In our judgment, the question whether an accused person can be held guilty of homicide, either murder or manslaughter, of a victim the immediate cause of whose death is the act of another person must be determined on the ordinary principles of causation, uninhibited by any such rule of policy as that for which Lord Gifford has contended. We therefore reject the second ground of appeal.

We turn to the first ground of appeal, which is that the learned judge erred in directing the jury that it was for him to decide as a matter of law whether by his unlawful and deliberate acts the appellant caused or was a cause of Gail Kinchen's death . . .

We have no intention of embarking in this judgment on a dissertation of the nature of causation, or indeed of considering any matters other than those which are germane to the decision of the issues now before us. Problems of causation have troubled philosophers and lawyers throughout the ages; and it would be rash in the extreme for us to trespass beyond the boundaries of our immediate problem. Our comments should therefore be understood to be confined not merely to the criminal law, but to cases of homicide (and possibly also other crimes of violence to the person); and it must be emphasised that the problem of causation in the present case is specifically concerned with the intervention of another person (here one of the police officers) whose act was the immediate cause of the death of the victim, Gail Kinchen.

In cases of homicide, it is rarely necessary to give the jury any direction on causation as such. Of course, a necessary ingredient of the crimes of murder and manslaughter is that the accused has by his act caused the victim's death. But how the victim came by his death is usually not in dispute. What is in dispute is more likely to be some other matter: for example, the identity of the person who committed the act which indisputably caused the victim's death; or whether the accused had the necessary intent; or whether the accused acted in self-defence, or was provoked. Even where it is necessary to direct the jury's minds to the question of causation, it is usually enough to direct them simply that in law the accused's act need not be the sole cause, or even the main cause, of the victim's death, it being enough that his act contributed significantly to that result. It is right to observe in passing, however, that even this simple direction is a direction of law relating to causation, on the basis of which the jury are bound to act in concluding whether the prosecution has established, as a matter of fact, that the accused's act did in this sense cause the victim's death. Occasionally, however, a specific issue of causation may arise. One such case is where, although an act of the accused constitutes a causa sine qua non of (or necessary condition for) the death of the victim, nevertheless the intervention of a third person may be regarded as the sole cause of the victim's death, thereby relieving the accused of criminal responsibility. Such intervention, if it has such an effect, has often been described by lawyers as a *novus actus interveniens*. We are aware that this time-honoured Latin term has been the subject of criticism. We are also aware that attempts have been made to translate it into English; though no simple translation has proved satisfactory, really because the Latin term has become a term of art which conveys to lawyers the crucial feature that there has not merely been an intervening act of another person, but that act was so independent of the act of the accused that it should be regarded in law as the cause of the victim's death, to the exclusion of the act of the accused. At the risk of scholarly criticism, we shall for the purposes of this judgment continue to use the Latin term.

Now the whole subject of causation in the law has been the subject of a well-known and most distinguished treatise by Professors Hart and Honore, Causation in the Law. Passages from this book were cited to the learned judge, and were plainly relied upon by him . . . the learned authors consider the circumstances in which the intervention of a third person, not acting in concert with the accused, may have the effect of relieving the accused of criminal responsibility. The criterion which they suggest should be applied in such circumstances is whether the intervention is voluntary, i.e. whether it is 'free, deliberate and informed'. We resist the temptation of expressing the judicial opinion whether we find ourselves in complete agreement with that definition; though we certainly consider it to be broadly correct and supported by authority. Among the examples which the authors give of non-voluntary conduct, which is not effective to relieve the accused of responsibility, are two which are germane to the present case, viz a reasonable act performed for the purpose of self-preservation, and an act done in performance of a legal duty.

There can, we consider, be no doubt that a reasonable act performed for the purpose of self-preservation, being of course itself an act caused by the accused's own act, does not operate as a *novus actus interveniens*. If authority is needed for this almost self-evident proposition, it is to be found in such cases as *Pitts* (1842) C & M 284, and *Curley* (1909) 2 Cr App R 96. In both these cases, the act performed for the purpose of self-preservation consisted of an act by the victim in attempting to escape from the violence of the accused, which in fact resulted in the victim's death. In each case it was held as a matter of law that, if the victim acted in a reasonable attempt to escape the violence of the accused, the death of the victim was caused by the act of the accused. No one form of self-preservation is self-defence; for present purposes, we can see no distinction in principle between an attempt to escape the consequences of the accused's act, and a response which takes the form of self-defence. Furthermore, in our judgment, if a reasonable act of self-defence against the act of the accused causes the death of a third party, we can see no reason in principle why the act of self-defence, being an involuntary act caused by the act of the accused, should relieve the accused from final responsibility for the death of the third party. Of course, it does not necessarily follow that the accused will be guilty of the murder, or even of the manslaughter, of the third party; though in the majority of cases he is likely to be guilty at least of manslaughter. Whether he is guilty of murder or manslaughter will depend upon the question whether all the ingredients of the relevant offence have been proved; in particular, on a charge of murder, it will be necessary that the accused had the necessary intent . . .

No English authority was cited to us, nor we think to the learned judge, in support of the proposition that an act done in the execution of a legal duty, again of course being an act itself caused by the act of the accused, does not operate as a *novus actus interveniens* . . . Even so, we agree with the learned judge that the proposition is sound law, because as a matter of principle such an act cannot be regarded as a voluntary act independent of the wrongful act of the accused. A parallel may be drawn with the so-called 'rescue' cases in the law of negligence, where a wrongdoer may be held liable in negligence to a third party who suffers injury in going to the rescue of a person who has been put in danger by the defendant's negligent act . . . in cases where there is an issue whether the act of the victim or of a third party constituted a *novus actus interveniens*, breaking the causal connection between the act of the accused and the death of the victim, it would be appropriate for the judge to direct the jury, of course in the most simple terms, in accordance with the legal principles which they have to apply. It would then fall to the jury to decide the relevant factual issues which, identified with reference to those legal principles, will lead to the conclusion whether or not the prosecution have established the guilt of the accused of the crime of which he is charged . . .

COMMENTS AND QUESTIONS

1   To what extent do you think the police might have been grossly negligent in returning fire in the circumstances described in *Pagett*? If gross negligence on the part of a police

officer had been established, would this have constituted a *novus actus interveniens*? See the consideration of gross negligence on the part of doctors in *R v Cheshire*, considered below.

2   See further *R v Watson* [1989] 1 WLR 684, considered below at 4.7.3. Suppose D burgles P's house, and there is evidence that P dies of a heart attack several hours later, the attack being brought on by P's exertions in making his property safe. Do P's actions amount to a *novus actus interveniens*. Alternatively, what if the medical evidence indicates that the heart attack was brought on by the stress of dealing with the police inquiries following the burglary? Can the interventions of the police officers be seen as a *novus actus interveniens*?

3   In *R v Shohid and another* [2003] All ER (D) 216, the Court of Appeal upheld a conviction for manslaughter in a case where D had forced P onto a railway line and P was killed by a train, having been prevented from getting off the line by others. Emphasising that it was not necessary for the prosecution to show that D's actions were the sole or major cause of death, the court held that there had been no *novus actus interveniens*. Neither was there any requirement that D should have foreseen that others might prevent the victim from escaping from the path of the approaching train.

4.3.7 *NOVUS ACTUS INTERVENIENS* – CAN THE CHAIN OF CAUSATION BE BROKEN BY MEDICAL TREATMENT?

R v Jordan (1956) 40 Cr App R 152 (CA)

Jordan stabbed a man named Beaumont. Beaumont was hospitalised as a result and received treatment for his injuries. There was evidence that, at a time when the wound was healing, doctors treating the victim administered an antibiotic, terramycin, a drug to which Beaumont was intolerant. Expert evidence suggested that this treatment had been 'palpably wrong'. The issue for the Court of Appeal was whether or not the medical treatment could properly be regarded as a *novus actus interveniens*.

Hallett J:

. . . We are disposed to accept it as the law that death resulting from any normal treatment employed to deal with a felonious injury may be regarded as caused by the felonious injury, but we do not think it necessary to examine the cases in detail or to formulate for the assistance of those who have to deal with such matters in the future the correct test which ought to be laid down with regard to what is necessary to be proved in order to establish causal connection between the death and the felonious injury. It is sufficient to point out here that this was not normal treatment. Not only one feature, but two separate and independent features, of treatment were, in the opinion of the doctors, palpably wrong and these produced the symptoms discovered at the post mortem examination which were the direct and immediate cause of death, namely the pneumonia resulting from the condition of oedema which was found.

The question then is whether it can be said that, if that evidence had been before the jury, it ought not to have, and in all probability would not have, affected their decision. We recognise that the learned judge, if this matter had been before him, would have had to direct the jury correctly on how far such supervening matters could be regarded as interrupting the chain of causation; but we felt that in the end it would have been a question of fact for the jury depending on what evidence they accepted as correct and the view they took on that evidence. We feel no uncertainty at all that, whatever direction had been given to the jury and however correct it had been, the jury would have felt precluded from saying that they were satisfied that death was caused by the stab wound.

For these reasons we come to the conclusion that the appeal must be allowed and the conviction set aside.

R v Smith [1959] 2 QB 35 (CA)

For the facts see 4.3.2 above. The following extract concerns the extent to which poor medical treatment might have amounted to a *novus actus interveniens*.

Lord Parker CJ:
. . . The second ground concerns a question of causation. The deceased man in fact received two bayonet wounds, one in the arm and one in the back. The one in the back, unknown to anybody, had pierced the lung and caused haemorrhage. There followed a series of unfortunate occurrences. A fellow member of his company tried to carry him to the medical reception station. On the way he tripped over a wire and dropped the deceased man. He picked him up again, went a little farther, and fell apparently a second time, causing the deceased man to be dropped onto the ground. Thereafter he did not try a third time but went for help, and ultimately the deceased man was brought into the reception station. There, the medical officer, Captain Millward, and his orderly were trying to cope with a number of other cases, two serious stabbings and some minor injuries, and it is clear that they did not appreciate the seriousness of the deceased man's condition or exactly what had happened. A transfusion of saline solution was attempted and failed. When his breathing seemed impaired he was given oxygen and artificial respiration was applied, and in fact he died after he had been in the station about an hour, which was about two hours after the original stabbing. It is now known that having regard to the injuries which the man had in fact suffered, his lung being pierced, the treatment that he was given was thoroughly bad and might well have affected his chances of recovery. There was evidence that there is a tendency for a wound of this sort to heal and for the haemorrhage to stop. No doubt his being dropped on the ground and having artificial respiration applied would halt or at any rate impede the chances of healing. Further, there were no facilities whatsoever for blood transfusion, which would have been the best possible treatment. There was evidence that if he had received immediate and different treatment, he might not have died. Indeed, had facilities for blood transfusion been available and been administered, Dr Camps, who gave evidence for the defence, said that his chances of recovery were as high as 75% . . . Mr Bowen placed great reliance on a case decided in this court of *R v Jordan* (1956) 40 Cr App R 152 . . . The court is satisfied that Jordan's case was a very particular case depending upon its exact facts. It incidentally arose in this court on the grant of an application to call further evidence, and leave having been obtained, two well-known medical experts gave evidence that in their opinion death had not been caused by the stabbing but by the introduction of terramycin after the deceased had shown that he was intolerant to it, and by the

intravenous introduction of abnormal quantities of liquid. It also appears that at the time when that was done the stab wound which had penetrated the intestine in two places had mainly healed. In those circumstances the court felt bound to quash the conviction because they could not say that a reasonable jury properly directed would not have been able on that to say that there had been a break in the chain of causation; the court could only uphold the conviction in that case if they were satisfied that no reasonable jury could have come to that conclusion.

R v Malcherek; R v Steel [1981] 1 WLR 690 (CA)

In these conjoined appeals both appellants had attacked women causing their victims serious injuries. In both cases the victims were placed on life support machines. In both cases doctors treating the victims decided to switch off the machines on the basis that there was no prospect of recovery. The appellants contended that the actions of the doctors in each case should have been regarded as a *novus actus interveniens* breaking the chain of causation in law between the attacks and the deaths.

Lord Lane CJ:
. . . This is not the occasion for any decision as to what constitutes death. Modern techniques have undoubtedly resulted in the blurring of many of the conventional and traditional concepts of death. A person's heart can now be removed altogether without death supervening; machines can keep the blood circulating through the vessels of the body until a new heart can be implanted in the patient, and even though a person is no longer able to breathe spontaneously a ventilating machine can, so to speak, do his breathing for him, as is demonstrated in the two cases before us. There is, it seems, a body of opinion in the medical profession that there is only one true test of death and that is the irreversible death of the brain stem, which controls the basic functions of the body such as breathing. When that occurs it is said the body has died, even though by mechanical means the lungs are being caused to operate and some circulation of blood is taking place.

We have had placed before us, and have been asked to admit, evidence that in each of these two cases the medical men concerned did not comply with all the suggested criteria for establishing such brain death. Indeed, further evidence has been suggested and placed before us that those criteria or tests are not in themselves stringent enough. However, in each of these two cases there is no doubt that whatever test is applied the victim died; that is to say, applying the traditional test, all body functions, breathing and heartbeat and brain function came to an end, at the latest, soon after the ventilator was disconnected. The question posed for answer to this court is simply whether the judge in each case was right in withdrawing from the jury the question of causation. Was he right to rule that there was no evidence on which the jury could come to the conclusion that the assailant did not cause the death of the victim?

The way in which the submissions are put by counsel for Malcherek on the one hand and by counsel for Steel on the other is as follows: the doctors, by switching off the ventilator and the life support machine, were the cause of death or, to put it more accurately, there was evidence which the jury should have been allowed to consider that the doctors, and not the assailant, in each case may have been the cause of death.

In each case it is clear that the initial assault was the cause of the grave head injuries in the one case and of the massive abdominal haemorrhage in the other. In each case the initial assault was the reason for the medical treatment being necessary. In each case the medical treatment given was normal and conventional. At some stage the doctors must decide if and when treatment has become otiose. This decision was reached, in each of the two cases here, in circumstances which have already been set out in some detail. It is no part of the task of this court to inquire whether the criteria, the Royal Medical College confirmatory tests, are a satisfactory code of practice. It is no part of the task of this court to decide whether the doctors were, in either of these two cases, justified in omitting one or more of the so called 'confirmatory tests'. The doctors are not on trial; *Steel* and *Malcherek* respectively were.

There are two comparatively recent cases which are relevant to the consideration of this problem. The first is *R v Jordan* (1956) 40 Cr App R 152 . . .

In the view of this court, if a choice has to be made between the decision in R v Jordan and that in *R v Smith*, which we do not believe it does (*R v Jordan* being a very exceptional case), then the decision in *R v Smith* is to be preferred . . .

There is no evidence in the present case here that at the time of conventional death, after the life support machinery was disconnected, the original wound or injury was other than a continuing, operating and indeed substantial cause of the death of the victim, although it need hardly be added that it need not be substantial to render the assailant guilty.There may be occasions, although they will be rare, when the original injury has ceased to operate as a cause at all, but in the ordinary case if the treatment is given *bona fide* by competent and careful medical practitioners, then evidence will not be admissible to show that the treatment would not have been administered in the same way by other medical practitioners. In other words, the fact that the victim has died, despite or because of medical treatment for the initial injury given by careful and skilled medical practitioners, will not exonerate the original assailant from responsibility for the death. It follows that so far as the ground of appeal in each of these cases relates to the direction given on causation, that ground fails. It also follows that the evidence which it is sought to adduce now, although we are prepared to assume that it is both credible and was not available properly at the trial (and a reasonable explanation for not calling it at the trial has been given), if received could, under no circumstances, afford any ground for allowing the appeal.

The reason is this. Nothing which any of the two or three medical men whose statements are before us could say would alter the fact that in each case the assailant's actions continued to be an operating cause of the death. Nothing the doctors could say would provide any ground for a jury coming to the conclusion that the assailant in either case might not have caused the death. The furthest to which their proposed evidence goes, as already stated, is to suggest, first, that the criteria or the confirmatory tests are not sufficiently stringent and, second, that in the present case they were in certain respects inadequately fulfilled or carried out. It is no part of this court's function in the present circumstances to pronounce on this matter, nor was it a function of either of the juries at these trials. Where a medical practitioner adopting methods which are generally accepted comes *bona fide* and conscientiously to the conclusion that the patient is for practical purposes dead, and that such vital functions as exist (for example, circulation) are being maintained solely by mechanical means, and therefore discontinues treatment, that does not prevent the person who inflicted the initial injury from being responsible for the victim's death. Putting it in another way, the discontinuance of treatment in those circumstances does not break the chain of causation between the initial injury and the death.

Although it is unnecessary to go further than that for the purpose of deciding the present point, we wish to add this thought. Whatever the strict logic of the matter may be, it is perhaps somewhat bizarre to suggest, as counsel have impliedly done, that where a doctor tries his conscientious best to save the life of a patient brought to hospital *in extremis*, skilfully using sophisticated methods, drugs and machinery to do so, but fails in his attempt and therefore discontinues treatment, he can be said to have caused the death of the patient.

R v Cheshire [1991] 1 WLR 844 (CA)

D shot P following an argument in a fish and chip shop in Greenwich. P was hospitalised as a result and, having undergone surgery, was placed in an intensive care unit. P died whilst in hospital, the post mortem suggesting that his windpipe had become obstructed due to narrowing near the site of a tracheotomy scar. The deceased's windpipe had become so narrowed that even a small amount of mucus could block it and cause asphyxiation. D contended that at the time of death the original wound was no longer life-threatening and that death had resulted from negligent medical care. The Court of Appeal dismissed his appeal.

Beldam J:

Whatever may be the differences of policy between the approach of the civil and the criminal law to the question of causation, there are we think reasons for a critical approach when importing the language of the one to the other.

Since the apportionment of responsibility for damage has become commonplace in the civil law, judges have sought to distinguish the blameworthiness of conduct from its causative effect. Epithets suggestive of degrees of blameworthiness may be of little help in deciding how potent the conduct was in causing the result. A momentary lapse of concentration may lead to more serious consequences than a more glaring neglect of duty. In the criminal law the jury considering the factual question, did the accused's act cause the deceased's death, will we think derive little assistance from figures of speech more appropriate for conveying degrees of fault or blame in questions of apportionment. Unless authority suggests otherwise, we think such figures of speech are to be avoided in giving guidance to a jury on the question of causation. Whilst medical treatment unsuccessfully given to prevent the death of a victim with the care and skill of a competent medical practitioner will not amount to an intervening cause, it does not follow that treatment which falls below that standard of care and skill will amount to such a cause. As Professors Hart and Honoré comment, treatment which falls short of the standard expected of the competent medical practitioner is unfortunately only too frequent in human experience for it to be considered abnormal in the sense of extraordinary. Acts or omissions of a doctor treating the victim for injuries he has received at the hands of an accused may conceivably be so extraordinary as to be capable of being regarded as acts independent of the conduct of the accused but it is most unlikely that they will be . . .

. . . when the victim of a criminal attack is treated for wounds or injuries by doctors or other medical staff attempting to repair the harm done, it will only be in the most extraordinary and unusual case that such treatment can be said to be so independent of the acts of the accused that it could be regarded in law as the cause of the victim's death to the exclusion of the accused's acts.

Where the law requires proof of the relationship between an act and its consequences as an element of responsibility, a simple and sufficient explanation of the basis of such relationship has proved notoriously elusive.

In a case in which the jury have to consider whether negligence in the treatment of injuries inflicted by the accused was the cause of death we think it is sufficient for the judge to tell the jury that they must be satisfied that the Crown have proved that the acts of the accused caused the death of the deceased adding that the accused's acts need not be the sole cause or even the main cause of death it being sufficient that his acts contributed significantly to that result. Even though negligence in the treatment of the victim was the immediate cause of his death, the jury should not regard it as excluding the responsibility of the accused unless the negligent treatment was so independent of his acts, and in itself so potent in causing death, that they regard the contribution made by his acts as insignificant.

It is not the function of the jury to evaluate competing causes or to choose which is dominant provided they are satisfied that the accused's acts can fairly be said to have made a significant contribution to the victim's death. We think the word 'significant' conveys the necessary substance of a contribution made to the death which is more than negligible . . . Accordingly, we dismiss the appeal.

R v Mellor [1996] 2 Cr App R 245

P was attacked and later died of his injuries in hospital. The immediate cause of death was broncho-pneumonia brought on directly by the injuries inflicted by the appellant. There was evidence that if P had been administered sufficient oxygen in time, the broncho-pneumonia would not have been fatal. The appellant, therefore, contended that the medical treatment, being negligent, could be regarded as an independent cause of death.

Schiemann LJ:
. . . In homicide cases where the victim of the alleged crime does not die immediately, supervening events will occur which are likely to have some causative effect leading to the victim's death; for example, a delay in the arrival of the ambulance, a delay in resuscitation, the victim's individual response to medical or surgical treatment, and the quality of medical, surgical and nursing care. Sometimes such an event may be the result of negligence or mistake or bad luck. It is a question of fact and degree in each case for the jury to decide, having regard to the gravity of the supervening event, however caused, whether the injuries inflicted by the defendant were a significant cause of death.

The onus on the Crown is to make the jury sure that the injuries inflicted by the defendant were a significant cause of death. However, the Crown has no onus of establishing that any supervening event was not a significant cause of death or that there was no medical negligence in the deceased's treatment.

If the issue of medical negligence is raised, the jury must have regard to the evidence adduced on the issue. If they conclude that there was or may have been medical negligence, they must have regard to that conclusion when answering the all-important question: 'Has the Crown proved that the injuries inflicted by the defendant were a significant cause of death?' In appropriate cases the jury can be told that there may be a number of significant causes leading to a victim's death. So as long as the Crown proves that the injuries inflicted by the defendant were at least a significant, if not the only, cause of death that will be sufficient to prove the nexus between injury and death . . .

His Lordship referred to *R v Cheshire* (above) and *R v Pagett* (above) and continued:

In our judgment, Beldam LJ (in Cheshire) was not intending to put any gloss on Goff LJ's suggested direction in *Pagett*, which was not a medical negligence case, but relating it to a medical negligence case. He made it clear at the end of the passage which we have cited that the question for the jury was whether they were satisfied that the accused's acts significantly contributed to the victim's death. That was the question for the jury in the present case.

What the Crown had to prove in the present case was that the injuries inflicted by the appellant significantly contributed to Mr Sims's death. There was no onus whatever on the Crown to negative medical negligence. Equally, there was no onus on the appellant to establish medical negligence. However, if negligence was established it was a factor to be taken into account by the jury in deciding whether the Crown had established that, notwithstanding this negligence, the injuries inflicted by the appellant had significantly contributed to Mr Sims's death. In the event of a jury being sure that medical negligence has been negatived by the Crown as a significant contributory cause of death, the medical negligence factor would be out of the equation.

In our judgment, it is undesirable in most cases for juries to be asked to embark upon the question of whether medical negligence as a significant contributory cause of death has been negatived because it diverts the jury from the relevant question, namely has the accused's act contributed significantly to the victim's death? . . .

An appropriate, but we do not suggest the only appropriate, form of words on the particular facts of this case would have been:

> You must acquit the defendant of murder unless the Crown has made you sure that the injuries that he inflicted contributed significantly to Mr Sims's death. Provided you are sure of that, it matters not whether incompetence or mistake in treatment at the hospital may have also contributed significantly to the death.

In our judgment, if the medical/causation issue had been put in this way there could only have been one answer. The evidence was overwhelming that having regard to the extent and nature of the injuries inflicted upon the 71 year old Mr Sims those injuries significantly contributed to his death less than two days later . . .

4.3.8 CAUSATION – CODIFICATION AND LAW REFORM PROPOSALS

Clause 17 of the draft Code Bill seeks to restate the common law position regarding causation. It provides:

17(1) Subject to subsections (2) and (3), a person causes a result which is an element of an offence when:
(a) he does an act which makes a more than negligible contribution to its occurrence; or
(b) he omits to do an act which might prevent its occurrence and which he is under a duty to do according to the law relating to the offence.

Regarding *novus actus interveniens*, clause 17(2) states:

A person does not cause a result where, after he does such an act or makes such an omission, an act or event occurs:

(a) which is the immediate and sufficient cause of the result;

>   (b)   which he did not foresee; and
>   (c)   which could not in the circumstances reasonably have been foreseen.

The commentary on the draft code Bill observes:

> [Clause 17(2)] appears to restate satisfactorily for criminal law the principles which determine whether intervening acts or events are sufficient to break the chain of causation . . . According to this provision a person will still be liable if his intended victim suffers injury in trying to escape from the threatened attack unless the victim has done something so improbable that it can properly be said not to have been reasonably foreseeable. Equally, liability for homicide will be unaffected if the victim refuses medical treatment for a wound caused by the defendant. Even if the refusal could be said to be unforeseeable, it is not sufficient in itself to cause the victim's death – in such a case, to use the language of the cases, the original wound is still the 'operating and substantial cause' of death [Vol II, para 7.17].

Note that the Law Commission's Report (Law Com No 304): *Murder, Manslaughter And Infanticide* does not deal with issues relating to causation in homicide.

4.4 THE GAP IN TIME BETWEEN THE DEFENDANT'S ACT AND THE VICTIM'S DEATH

It used to be the case that, for a person to be convicted of murder or manslaughter, the death of the victim had to occur within a year and a day of the act or omission which caused the death. Section 1 of the Law Reform (Year and a Day Rule) Act 1996, however, abolishes this rule. Section 2 of the Act provides instead:

> **Section 2 of the Law Reform (Year and a Day) Act 1996**
> (1)   Proceedings to which this section applies may only be instituted by or with the consent of the Attorney General.
> (2)   This section applies to proceedings against a person for a fatal offence if:
>   (a)   the injury alleged to have caused the death was sustained more than three years before the death occurred; or
>   (b)   the person has previously been convicted of an offence committed in circumstances alleged to be connected with the death.
> (3)   In subsection (2) 'fatal offence' means:
>   (a)   murder, manslaughter, infanticide or any other offence of which one of the elements is causing a person's death; or
>   (b)   the offence of aiding, abetting, counselling or procuring a person's suicide.

An example of the operation of s 2(2)(b) would be where a person is convicted of causing grievous bodily harm and, after the conviction, the victim dies; in such a case, the consent of the Attorney General must be obtained before the person is prosecuted for murder (even if three years have not elapsed since the date of the assault).

Murder and manslaughter are both result crimes, in the sense that the defendant must be proved to have caused the death of the victim in fact and in law.

4.5 THE *MENS REA* FOR MURDER

For a defendant to be convicted of murder he must have caused the death of a human being and must be shown to have acted with the requisite *mens rea* – an intention to kill a human being, or an intention to cause a human being grievous bodily harm. The nature of intention, particularly in the context of murder, was considered in Chapter 3: see in particular *R v Woollin* [1999] 1 AC 82. The term 'malice aforethought' is often used to denote the *mens rea* required for murder – see the classic definition of murder set out in Coke's Institutes (3 Co Inst 47): 'Murder is when a [person] . . . unlawfully killeth . . . any reasonable creature in rerum natura under the Queen's peace, with malice aforethought . . . so as the party wounded or hurt, etc dies of the wound or hurt' – but it is submitted that, in the modern context, this phrase is likely to mislead. The defendant charged with murder does not need to have displayed any 'malice' towards his victim – it may, for example, be a mercy killing. Further, there is no need for the prosecution to prove that the killing was in any way premeditated or planned. All in all, notwithstanding that Parliament used the phrase in the Homicide Act 1957 (see below) the phrase is best avoided.

> **Homicide Act 1957**
>
> [Section 1] Where a person kills another in the course or furtherance of some other offence, the killing shall not amount to murder unless done with the same malice aforethought (express or implied) as is required for the killing to amount to murder when not done in the course or furtherance of another offence.

The effect of s 1 of the 1957 Act is to abolish the doctrine of constructive malice, whereby a defendant who killed in the course of committing a felony was deemed to have the *mens rea* for murder. Hence, prior to the Act coming into effect, a defendant who killed in the course of committing a robbery would have faced a murder charge – the *mens rea* for murder being 'constructed' from the *mens rea* for robbery. Following the enactment of s 1 the *mens rea* for murder must be established in its own right. The effect of the provision has been undermined to a degree, however, by the decision in *R v Vickers* [1957] 2 QB, where the Court of Appeal confirmed that, notwithstanding s 1, an intention to do grievous bodily harm would suffice for the *mens rea* for murder. The extracts that follow provide a critique of this restatement of the law. It is suffice to note here that it amounts to a partial re-introduction of constructive malice. A defendant who kills in the course of intentionally committing grievous bodily harm is deemed to have the *mens rea* for murder.

4.5.1 CRITICISMS OF THE CURRENT *MENS REA* FOR MURDER

Attorney General's Ref (No 3 of 1994) [1997] 3 All ER 936

Lord Mustill:

My Lords, murder is widely thought to be the gravest of crimes. One could expect a developed system to embody a law of murder clear enough to yield an unequivocal result on a given set of facts, a result which conforms with apparent justice and has a sound intellectual base. This is not so in England, where the law of homicide is permeated by anomaly, fiction, misnomer and obsolete reasoning. One conspicuous anomaly is the rule which identifies the 'malice aforethought' (a doubly misleading expression) required for the crime of murder not only with a conscious intention to kill but also with an intention to cause grievous bodily harm. It is, therefore, possible to commit a murder not only without wishing the death of the victim but without the least thought that this might be the result of the assault. Many would doubt the justice of this rule, which is not the popular conception of murder and (as I shall suggest) no longer rests on any intellectual foundation. The law of Scotland does very well without it, and England could perhaps do the same. It would, however, be fruitless to debate this here, since the rule has been established beyond doubt by *R v Cunningham* [1982] AC 566. This rule, which I will call the 'grievous harm' rule, is the starting point of the present appeal . . .

. . . My Lords, since the original concepts are no longer available to explain why an intent to cause grievous bodily harm will found a conviction for murder the reason must be sought elsewhere: for reason, in regard to such a grave crime, there must surely be. The obvious recourse is to ascribe this doctrine to the last vestiges of the murder/felony rule, and to see in it a strong example of that rule, for unlike the more extravagant early manifestations it offers at least some resemblance in nature and degree between the intended act and its unintended consequences. It would follow, therefore, that when the murder/felony rule was expressly abolished by section 1 of the Homicide Act 1957 the only surviving justification for the 'grievous harm' rule fell away, with nothing left. This proposition was indeed advanced soon after the 1957 Act in *R v Vickers* [1957] 2 QB 664, where it was dismissed out-of-hand. The same concept was developed in *Hyam v DPP* [1975] AC 55, where after close analysis it was adopted by Lord Diplock, and in a concurring speech by Lord Kilbrandon. The majority in the House did not agree. The question was raised again in *R v Cunningham* [1982] AC 566, and this time a decisive answer was given. The 'grievous harm' rule had survived the abolition of the murder/felony principle. The speeches show that it did so because a solid and long-lasting line of authority had decreed that this was the law, and the House saw no need to change a rule which answered practical needs.

My Lords, in a system based on binding precedent there could be no ground for doubting a long course of existing law, and certainly none which could now permit this House even to contemplate such a fundamental change as to abolish the grievous harm rule: and counsel rightly hinted at no such idea. But when asked to strike out into new territory it is, I think, right to recognise that the grievous harm rule is an outcropping of old law from which the surrounding strata of rationalisations have weathered away. It survives but exemplifies no principle which can be applied to a new situation.

R v Powell and Daniels; R v English [1999] AC 1

For the facts, see Chapter 7.9.1.

Lord Steyn:

In English law a defendant may be convicted of murder who is in no ordinary sense a murderer. It is sufficient if it is established that the defendant had an intent to cause really serious bodily injury. This rule turns murder into a constructive crime. The fault element does not correspond to the conduct leading to the charge, i.e. the causing of death. A person is liable to conviction for a more serious crime than he foresaw or contemplated . . . This is a point of considerable importance. The Home Office records show that in the last three years for which statistics are available mandatory life sentences for murder were imposed in 192 cases in 1994; in 214 cases in 1995; and in 257 cases in 1996. Lord Windlesham, writing with great Home Office experience, has said that a minority of defendants convicted of murder have been convicted on the basis that they had an intent to kill: *Responses to Crime*, Vol 3 (1996), at 342, n 29.That assessment does not surprise me. What is the justification for this position? There is an argument that, given the unpredictability whether a serious injury will result in death, an offender who intended to cause serious bodily injury cannot complain of a conviction of murder in the event of a death. But this argument is outweighed by the practical consideration that immediately below murder there is the crime of manslaughter for which the court may impose a discretionary life sentence or a very long period of imprisonment. Accepting the need for a mandatory life sentence for murder, the problem is one of classification.The present definition of the mental element of murder results in defendants being classified as murderers who are not in truth murderers. It happens both in cases where only one offender is involved and in cases resulting from joint criminal enterprises. It results in the imposition of mandatory life sentences when neither justice nor the needs of society require the classification of the case as murder and the imposition of a mandatory life sentence . . . In my view the problem ought to be addressed. There is available a precise and sensible solution, namely, that a killing should be classified as murder if there is an intention to kill or an intention to cause really serious bodily harm coupled with awareness of the risk of death: 14th Report of the Law Revision Committee (1980), para 31, adopted in the Criminal Code for England and Wales (Law Com 177, 1986), clause 54(1). This solution was supported by the House of Lords Select Committee on Murder and Life Imprisonment, HL Paper 78–1, 1989, para 68.

4.5.2 MURDER – REFORM PROPOSALS

The Law Commission's Report (Law Com No 304) Murder: *Manslaughter And Infanticide* reflects the criticisms of the fault element in murder expressed in the foregoing extracts, highlighting the over- and under-inclusive nature of the current definition.

2.4 To bring greater order, fairness and clarity to the law of homicide, the scope of and distinctions between individual homicide offences must be made clearer and more intelligible, as well as being morally more defensible. Achieving this goal has not proved possible within a two-tier structure of general homicide offences. As we have seen, the constraining effect of the two-tier structure gives rise to a definition of murder that leaves it in one respect too broad and in another respect too narrow.

2.5 The definition is too broad in so far as it encompasses killings committed through an intention to do harm the jury judges to be serious, even if the defendant (D) had no intention to endanger life and did not imagine that his or her acts might lead to the victim's (V) death.

2.6 The definition is too narrow in that it excludes cases where D, without intending to kill or to cause serious injury, nonetheless realised that his or her conduct posed a serious risk of causing death and went ahead regardless.

2.7 The over- and under-inclusiveness of murder's current definition inevitably has the undesirable consequence of making it unduly difficult to devise a fair sentencing structure for both murder and manslaughter. We believe that the introduction of a further tier into the general law of homicide will do a great deal to resolve this problem.

Rationale for first degree murder
How our recommendation would be an improvement on the existing law

2.63 The fault element we are recommending for first degree murder improves on murder's existing fault element in several ways.

2.64 First, as further recommendations which we set out below [para 2.70] make clear, our recommendation for what should constitute first degree murder forms part of the creation of a proper 'ladder' of homicide offences, in order of seriousness, which the present law fails to provide. The recommendation would do this by eliminating the legal anomalies identified in Part 1 which result in the definition of murder being in some respects too narrow and in some respects too broad.

2.65 Secondly, implementation of the recommendation for what should constitute first degree murder would bring the law somewhat closer to what Parliament (mistakenly, as it turned out) thought the law was when it decided against providing a comprehensive definition of the fault element for murder in the Homicide Act 1957.

2.66 Thirdly, under our recommendations, if the jury found that one or other of the fault elements for first degree murder ((1) or (2) in paragraph 2.50) was present and convicted of murder, the judge would no longer have to go on to decide for sentencing purposes which one of those fault elements the jury had found proven. This seemingly technical but important point needs addressing in more detail.

2.67 Under the present law, Parliament has acknowledged that there is potentially a large gap in point of culpability within murder, namely between an intention to kill and an intention to do serious harm (where there was no awareness of a risk of death). In consequence, Parliament now requires a judge to decide which of these intentions D acted on and to take that into account when determining the length of the initial period in custody of the mandatory life sentence. In one way, that is a commendable attempt to see that justice is done. It is, however, open to the objection that it requires the judge to trespass on what should be a question for the jury: the question of D's intent (whether there was an intention to kill or only an intention to do serious harm).

2.68 Under our recommendations, there would no longer be such a large gap in the degree of culpability involved, as between the alternative fault elements in first degree murder ((1) and (2) in paragraph 2.50 above). This is because a conviction for murder would require a finding that there was at least an intention to do serious injury in the awareness that there was a serious risk of causing death. The two alternative fault elements for first degree murder should be regarded as morally equivalent. Consequently, there would be no need for the judge, when sentencing, to determine which fault element it was that D acted on in killing.

2.69 We recommend that first degree murder should encompass:

(1) intentional killings, and

(2) killings with the intent to cause serious injury where the killer was aware that his or her conduct involved a serious risk of causing death.

2.70 We recommend that second degree murder should encompass:

(1) killings intended to cause serious injury; or

(2) killings intended to cause injury or fear or risk of injury where the killer was aware that his or her conduct involved a serious risk of causing death; or

(3) killings intended to kill or to cause serious injury where the killer was aware that his or her conduct involved a serious risk of causing death but successfully pleads provocation, diminished responsibility or that he or she killed pursuant to a suicide pact.

2.71 We also recommend that second degree murder should attract a maximum sentence of life imprisonment, with guidelines issued on appropriate periods in custody for different kinds of killing falling within second degree murder. . . .

2.72 Second degree murder would be a new offence, constituting a second or middle tier in the structure of general homicide offences. As an offence, second degree murder would perform three functions.

2.73 First, it would capture some cases that, to date, have been treated as plain murder, namely cases in which someone killed when intending to do an injury that the jury regards as serious but which D had no idea might cause death. This could be referred to as the new offence's 'mitigating' role.

2.74 Secondly, the new offence would capture some cases that, to date, have been treated as only manslaughter, namely cases in which someone has killed intending to cause harm or fear or risk of harm and was aware of a serious risk of causing death. This could be referred to as the new offence's 'aggravating' role.

2.75 Second degree murder would perform a third function. It would capture those who success-fully raise a partial defence and who are currently convicted of manslaughter. This could be referred to as the new offence's 'labelling' role. Why killing through an intention to do serious injury (but without awareness that there was a risk of causing death) should be treated as second degree murder.

2.94 We are recommending that second degree murder should attract a discretionary maximum life sentence. This means that, where appropriate, judges can take account of the kind and degree of injury actually intended in determining the sentence that they pass. That is not possible, at present, because the life sentence is mandatory when the jury has brought in a verdict of murder on the basis that there was an intention to do harm they (the jury) regard as serious. The discretion the judge would have, in sentencing in cases of second degree murder, means that it is not necessary to complicate the law further by seeking to fix a definition of 'serious' injury.

2.95 In the CP we provisionally proposed that within second degree murder, alongside killing through the intention to do serious injury, there should be killing by 'reckless indifference'.

2.96 Under the present law, killing through reckless conduct, however culpable, can be treated as nothing more serious than manslaughter. In Part 1 we said that we believe that this constitutes a significant anomaly or weakness within the law. Some reckless killers ought to be convicted of second degree murder and not simply of manslaughter.

2.97 Under our recommendations, if someone foresaw death as virtually certain to occur if he or she acted as intended, and death did thereby occur, he or she could be convicted of first degree murder. Under the current law, if someone sees the causing of death as a serious risk from their conduct (even if it is not considered to be virtually certain to result), they can only be convicted of manslaughter. However, in certain circumstances it ought to be possible to convict them of the middle tier offence, second degree murder and not merely of manslaughter.

2.98 The example of the bomber who gives an inadequate warning is a case that ought to fall within the ambit of the middle tier offence. Some other examples (based on real cases) which at present commonly fall within manslaughter but ought to be candidates for treatment as second degree murder are:

(1) D sets fire to V's house at night, knowing that V is asleep inside. His intention is to give the occupants a severe fright. V is killed trying to escape.

(2) D burgles the house of an elderly man, tying him up securely and leaving him, although she appreciates that the house is isolated and that the man has few visitors. V, unable to escape his bonds or summon help, dies.

(3) D injects V with an illegal drug that D realises may contain impurities dangerous to life. V goes into a coma, and consequently dies.

(4) D intentionally accelerates his car towards a police officer standing in the road at a road-block. His intention is to frighten the officer by swerving the car out of the way only at the last possible second D's attempt to swerve out of the way is unsuccessful and the officer is killed.

ADVANTAGES OF THE NEW FORMULA

2.108 We believe that the recommended formula will make the place of second degree murder within the overall structure, or 'ladder', of offences much clearer than 'reckless indifference' would do. We also believe that the recommended formula will keep faith with the viewpoint of those who endorsed the inclusion of reckless indifference within second degree murder. We anticipate that the recommended formula will produce results at variance with the reckless indifference formula only in very rare or unusual kinds of case. In such cases, the offender can expect to receive a long prison sentence for manslaughter.

2.109 As important as what the recommended formula includes is what it excludes. It will not be sufficient for conviction of second degree murder simply that the killer was aware that his or her conduct involved a serious risk of causing death (recklessness as to causing death). If the killer was aware that his or her conduct involved a risk of death, he or she stands to be convicted only of manslaughter. To be convicted of second degree murder, in addition to showing that the offender had this awareness, it must also be shown that the killer intended to cause injury or fear or risk of injury.

2.110 We regard this extra element as of great importance in preventing a large and uncertain overlap developing between second degree murder and gross negligence manslaughter. Many of those currently convicted of gross negligence manslaughter will, in fact, have been aware that their conduct posed a risk of causing death. They will, however, have foolishly acted in the belief that the chance of the harm materialising was remote. That would be true, for example, of an electrician who is mistakenly confident that he or she can cut corners on health and safety's 'bureaucratic requirements' (as he or she sees them) without posing undue risks to customers. We do not believe that such an offender should necessarily be guilty of second degree murder if he or she kills. The electrician will almost certainly be guilty of, and can be punished severely for, manslaughter, if the cost-cutting measures lead to someone's death. That will usually be punishment enough.

2.111 The extra element ensures that those who kill through simple carelessness or disregard, but without anything that could (speaking very loosely) be called a hostile or aggressive act directed at someone, should be guilty only of manslaughter. The degree of their carelessness or disregard can be reflected in the sentence received upon conviction for manslaughter. In the electrician example just given, the electrician does not intend to cause injury or fear or risk of injury. So, in spite of his or her awareness of the possibly fatal consequences of corner-cutting, he or she should not be convicted of second degree murder if death results.

The report then looked at the proposed *mens rea* for first degree murder in more detail. As outlines above, the report recommends that first degree murder should encompass situations where D intentionally kills or where D kills intending to do serious injury whilst aware that his actions create a serious risk of causing death.

Reforming the mental element in murder
The serious harm rule
1.17 Under the current law, D is liable for murder not only if he or she kills intentionally but also if he or she kills while intentionally inflicting harm which the jury considers to have been serious. In our view, the result is that the offence of murder is too wide. Even someone who reasonably believed that no one would be killed by their conduct and that the harm they were intentionally inflicting was not serious, can find themselves placed in the same offence category as the contract or serial killer. Here is an example:

> D intentionally punches V in the face. The punch breaks V's nose and causes V to fall to the ground. In falling, V hits his or her head on the curb causing a massive and fatal brain haemorrhage.

It is sometimes argued that manslaughter by recklessness and by gross negligence form one single category of manslaughter with two alternative fault requirements. We will be recommending that any reform of the law should adopt this approach . . .

1.18 This would be murder if the jury decided that the harm that D intended the punch to cause (the broken nose) can be described as 'serious'. Whilst it is clear that a person who kills in these circumstances should be guilty of a serious homicide offence, it is equally clear to the great majority of our consultees that the offence should not be the top tier or highest category offence.

1.19 . . . Parliament, when it passed the Homicide Act 1957, never intended a killing to amount to murder – at that time a capital offence – unless (amongst other things) the defendant ("D") realised that his or her conduct might cause death. The widening of the law of murder beyond such cases came about through an unexpected judicial development of the law immediately following the enactment of the 1957 legislation. . . .

1.20 The inclusion of all intent-to-do-serious-harm cases within murder distorts the sentencing process for murder. The fact that an offender only intended to do serious harm, rather than kill, is currently regarded as a mitigating factor that justifies the setting of a shorter initial custodial period as part of the mandatory life sentence. On the face of it, this seems perfectly reasonable. However, there is a strong case for saying that when an offence carries a mandatory sentence, there should be no scope for finding mitigation in the way in which the basic or essential fault elements come to be fulfilled.

1.21 We have been informed by research, carried out by Professor Barry Mitchell, into public opinion about murder. This shows that the public assumes that murder involves an intention to kill or its moral equivalent, namely a total disregard for human life. The latter may not be evident in a case where someone has intentionally inflicted harm the jury regards as serious, as when D intentionally breaks someone's nose. Indeed, some members of the public regarded deaths caused by intentionally inflicted harm that was not inherently life-threatening as being in some sense 'accidental'.

1.22 Having said that, we do not recommend that killing through an intention to do serious injury should simply be regarded as manslaughter. Manslaughter is an inadequate label for a killing committed with that degree of culpability. In any event, to expand the law of manslaughter still further would be wrong because manslaughter is already an over-broad offence.

1.23 We will be recommending that the intent-to-do-serious-injury cases should be divided into two. Cases where D not only intended to do serious injury but also was aware that his or her conduct posed a serious risk of death should continue to fall within the highest category or top tier offence. This is warranted by the kind of total disregard for human life that such Ds show. They are morally equivalent to cases of intentional killing. Cases where D intended to do serious injury but was unaware of a serious risk of killing should fall (along with some instances of reckless killing) into a new middle tier homicide offence.

Reckless manslaughter

1.24 The scope of murder is both too broad and too narrow. Where the scope of murder is too narrow, the scope of manslaughter is correspondingly too broad. In particular, the law is too generous to some who kill by 'reckless' conduct, that is those who do not intend to cause serious harm but do realise that their conduct involves an unjustified risk of causing death. The law is too generous in treating all those who realise that their conduct poses a risk of causing death but press on regardless as guilty only of manslaughter. Again, the problems have arisen from the way that periodic judicial development of the law in individual cases, albeit well-intentioned, has changed the boundaries of homicide offences.

1.25 . . . When the Homicide Act 1957 was passed, it was still accepted by both Parliament and by the courts that the archaic language of 'malice aforethought' governed the fault element in murder. But malice aforethought has never been a term with very clear boundaries and differences soon emerged between the courts and Parliament over how it should be understood . . .

1.26 At that time, the courts treated malice aforethought as covering cases in which the offender: either (a) intended to kill; or (b) intended to cause serious harm; or (c) had knowledge that the act which causes death will probably cause the death of or grievous bodily harm to some person. However, during the passage of the Homicide Act 1957, Parliament was led to believe that (b) was not a species of malice aforethought and that malice aforethought could not be established without D being proven to have at least been aware that the harm done was life-threatening. This was the basis upon which the Homicide Act 1957 was passed. Parliament's belief was founded on the Lord Chief Justice's evidence to the Royal Commission on Capital Punishment, whose report led to the passing of the Homicide Act 1957.

1.27 Defined either way, however, malice aforethought provided sufficient coverage to ensure that the worst kinds of reckless killer could be convicted of murder. Here is an example:

D, intending to cause fear and disruption, plants a bomb. D gives a warning which D believes might be sufficient to permit the timely evacuation of the area but probably would not be. In the ensuing explosion, someone is killed.

1.28 At the time of the enactment of the Homicide Act 1957, such a person would have been regarded by both Parliament and the courts as acting with 'malice aforethought' and would be guilty of murder . . .

1.29 Immediately after the passing of the Homicide Act 1957, however, the Court of Appeal indicated that only an intention to kill or to cause serious harm – ((a) and (b) in paragraph 1.26 above) – would suffice as proof of 'malice aforethought'. In 1975, there was what can be interpreted as an attempt by the House of Lords to reconcile this new view with the older and broader understanding of malice aforethought, that is, as including exposing others to a probable risk of serious harm or death. It was held that a jury could find that D intended to kill or to cause serious harm if he or she foresaw one or other of these results was a highly probable result of his or her conduct. However, developments did not stop there.

1.30 In 1985, the use of the label 'malice aforethought' to describe the fault element for murder was overtly criticised by the House of Lords, even though it is at the heart of section 1 of the Homicide Act 1957. Further, the House of Lords made it clear beyond doubt that intention should not be construed as to automatically include the mere foresight of probable consequences. That development led to a series of further cases on the exact width of the law. What has emerged is that murder no longer includes killing by reckless risk-taking, as such, however heinous the killing. Such killings, although they can be encompassed by the woolly language of 'malice aforethought', are not intentional. Consequently, from 1985 onwards, the hypothetical bomber described in paragraph 1.27 above could no longer be guilty of murder because he or she did not intend to kill or to cause serious injury. He or she could only be guilty of (reckless) manslaughter.

. . .

INTENTION

3.9 One or more of the fault elements for first degree murder, second degree murder and manslaughter use the term 'intention'. The courts have often struggled with the meaning of this key term. However, the law has now reached a reasonably stable state. The question is whether a definition is needed that significantly alters the common law understanding of intention. We have concluded that there is no such need but that the existing law governing the meaning of intention should be codified.

. . .

3.12 At common law, someone must be taken to have intended something if they acted in order to bring it about. In that respect, 'intention' is partly defined by the common law. However, in unusual cases, typically murder cases, that definition has proven to be too narrow. It excludes from murder those cases that should be murder given D's especially high level of culpability.

3.13 Accordingly, the following rule has been developed at common law. The jury may – but not must – find that the defendant (D) intended the result if D thought it would be a certain consequence (barring some extraordinary intervention) of his or her actions, whether he or she desired it or not. Take the following examples:

> D is in the process of stealing V's car. V leaps onto the car bonnet to deter D from driving off. D accelerates to 100 miles per hour and continues at that speed. Eventually V's grip loosens and V falls off the car. The fall kills V. D claims he did not intend to kill V or to cause V serious injury but was simply determined to escape come what may.

Given that we are not engaged in a drafting exercise, we will not distinguish in what follows between the phrases 'foresight of virtual certainty', 'foresight of certainty (barring some extraordinary intervention)' and 'foresight that X will/would happen'.

> D is jogging along a narrow path that follows a cliff edge. V is walking slowly ahead of him. D wantonly barges V over the cliff rather than slowing down and asking V to step aside so that D can pass. V is killed by the fall. D says that his intention was to keep running at the same speed at all costs, and he was not concerned with whether V lived or died.

3.14 In both these examples, the jury should be directed that they may find that D intended to kill V or to cause V serious injury, if they are sure that D realised that V was certain (barring an extraordinary intervention) to die or suffer serious injury, if D did what he or she was set upon doing. We would expect the jury to find a intention to kill or cause serious harm in both cases.

. . .

3.19 Someone should be taken to 'intend' a result if they act in order to bring it about. That is the basic definition of intention . . .

3.20 Very occasionally, there will be cases where the judge believes that justice may not be done unless an expanded understanding of intention is given (two examples were given in paragraph 3.13 above). In such cases, the judge should direct the jury that they may find intention to kill if D thought that his or her action would certainly (barring an extraordinary intervention) kill, even if the death was undesired.

3.21 We acknowledge that this approach gives the jury an element of discretion in deciding whether, in cases such as those within the examples in paragraph 3.13 above, a verdict of (first degree) murder can and should be returned. The result in such cases will not be wholly determined by legal rules governing the meaning of intention. We believe that it is sometimes necessary and desirable that juries should have that element of discretion if the alternative is a more complex set of legal rules that they must apply. It is the price of avoiding complexity. Complexity must be kept to a minimum if the new structure of homicide offences is to be acceptable to Parliament, the public and the legal profession.

3.22 Some academics have suggested that it would be simpler to abandon the pretence, as they see it, that it is true 'intention' that is found by the jury when it exercises this discretion. They claim it would be simpler and more honest to say that someone can be found guilty of first degree murder either if they intend to kill (or to cause serious injury aware of a serious risk of causing death) or if they know or believe that death or serious injury (aware of a serious risk of death) will occur. On this view, intention, knowledge and belief, are alternate forms of fault element . . .

3.23 Naturally, we recognise that there are differences between intention, knowledge and belief. The law would certainly be little worse off for taking an alternative approach in which these mental states are carefully separated. However, we do not believe that this approach would be a substantial improvement, at least in the context of homicide. There is, for example, no evidence that the existing law gives rise to any confusion in the jury room. If the law confused juries we would expect juries to be consistently sending notes to judges asking for further explanation. We have not received reports that this has occurred.

3.24 In some areas of the law it may be necessary to distinguish between intention and knowledge or belief that something will happen. This may be necessary where criminal liability depends upon which of these alternate fault elements is established. It is not clear that the distinction between these fault elements does or should serve this purpose in homicide cases.

3.25 For example, the distinction between intentionally and knowingly killing would matter if the defences of necessity or duress of circumstances were available to those who knowingly killed (that is, where death was foreseen as certain to occur) but not in cases where someone acted in order to kill. If duress and necessity became defences to first degree murder, we do not believe that this approach would attract the courts. There can be cases of intentional killing that these defences should cover. Conversely, there can be cases where death was foreseen as certain to occur in which the defence should be denied. In many instances, D's exact state of mind would simply affect the jury's assessment of whether the reasonable person might have done as D did. So, distinguishing formally between these states of mind would increase, rather than reduce, the complexities involved in deciding whether these defences should apply in first degree murder cases.

3.26 Giving the jury the power to find intention when they find that D foresaw the result as virtually certain widens the fault element in the law of homicide. However, it does this whilst avoiding the much greater uncertainty involved in the use of evaluative terms such as 'recklessness' or 'extreme indifference'. That the law expands the fault element through letting the jury decide when intention should be found, rather than through requiring the jury to apply yet further legal rules governing inference-drawing, can thus be regarded as a strength and not a weakness.

3.27 We recommend that the existing law governing the meaning of intention is codified as follows:

(1) A person should be taken to intend a result if he or she acts in order to bring it about.
(2) In cases where the judge believes that justice may not be done unless an expanded understanding of intention is given, the jury should be directed as follows: an intention to bring about a result may be found if it is shown that the defendant thought that the result was a virtually certain consequence of his or her action.

'AWARENESS' OF RISK

3.28 In Part 2, we recommended that a person should be guilty of first degree murder if he or she killed intending to do serious injury and was aware that his or her conduct involved a serious risk of death. We also recommended that a person should be guilty of second degree murder if he or she intended to cause some injury or a risk or a fear of serious injury and was aware that his or her conduct involved a serious risk of death.

3.29 We do not believe that the use of the terms 'aware' and 'awareness' will give rise to practical difficulties. However, to avoid doubt, we stress that awareness involves conscious advertence to the risk. In particular, someone should not be said to have been aware of a risk at the time of the alleged offence, unless it was brought to mind at the relevant time. Merely having knowledge of the risk stored in one's memory ought not to suffice. Take the following example:

D is told that V is a haemophiliac, whose life is endangered by any serious flesh wound. Some months later, D has a violent argument with V, picks up a knife and stabs V once in the leg. V bleeds to death in spite of being taken promptly to hospital.

3.30 In this example, it may well be that the prosecution can show (a) that D intended to do serious injury (the stab to the leg) and (b) that D was aware that V consequently faced a serious risk of bleeding to death because of his haemophilia. If so, under our recommendations, D would be guilty of first degree murder.

3.31 However, it should not be enough for the prosecution to simply show that D had been told of V's condition in the past. The prosecution should have to show that D was aware of V's condition and the resulting risk of death at the time of the stabbing. It is a matter for the jury whether, on the particular facts, D consciously adverted to, or thought of, the risk when stabbing V. In that regard, however, as Lord Bingham (*R v G* [2003] UKHL 50, [2004] 1 AC 1034 at [39]) has observed:

. . . it is not to be supposed that the tribunal of fact will accept a defendant's assertion that he never thought of a certain risk when all the circumstances and probabilities and evidence of what he did and said at the time show that he did or must have done.

3.32 A final point. Both first and second degree murder should be regarded as crimes of 'specific intent'. This means that if D did not kill with the requisite fault element, he or she must be acquitted of murder although he or she may still be guilty of manslaughter. In particular, D should be entitled to rely on any evidence tending to show that he or she did not have the intent or awareness in question, including evidence of intoxication.

. . .

'SERIOUS' RISK
3.36 By 'serious' risk, we mean a risk that ought to be taken seriously. We do not mean a risk that by definition is 'likely to', or 'probably will' result in harm done. Probability may come into the question of whether a risk is 'serious' but it is not determinative of the question. It is merely one factor determining whether the risk ought to be taken seriously. The Australian High Court has succinctly and clearly expressed what we mean by serious risk in Boughey [(1986) 161 CLR 10] with the following formulation [at p 15] : 'a substantial or real chance, as distinct from a mere possibility'.

4.6 VOLUNTARY MANSLAUGHTER

There are four defences that are uniquely available to a defendant who is charged with murder. They are:

- diminished responsibility;
- provocation;

- infanticide;
- suicide pact.

All four operate as partial defences in the sense that, if they are made out, the defendant's liability is reduced from murder to manslaughter, thus avoiding the consequences of the mandatory life sentence for murder. Diminished responsibility and provocation are by far the more important of the four and are considered in more detail in the extracts that follow.

4.6.1 INFANTICIDE

The current defence of infanticide was introduced by the Infanticide Act 1938, s 1 of which provides:

> 1(1) Where a woman by any wilful act or omission causes the death of her child being a child under the age of 12 months, but at the time of the act or omission the balance of her mind was disturbed by reason of her not having fully recovered from the effect of giving birth to the child or by reason of the effect of lactation consequent upon the birth of the child, then, notwithstanding that the circumstances were such that but for this Act the offence would have amounted to murder, she shall be guilty of [an offence], to wit of infanticide, and may for such offence be dealt with and punished as if she had been guilty of the offence of manslaughter of the child.

The provision creates an offence of infanticide, but also makes clear that it operates as a defence to murder – typically the mother who kills her baby whilst suffering from post-natal depression. The provision is rarely invoked – in the region of five convictions a year are based on infanticide. This perhaps also reflects a reluctance to prosecute at all in such cases. One difficulty that has been identified however, (as the following extract indicates) relates to those women who kill as a result of post-natal depression, but who refuse to acknowledge their condition – and hence do not provide the prosecution with the basis for this alternative to murder.

R v Kai-Whitewind [2005] EWCA Crim 1092

The defendant gave birth to a baby boy but had difficulty bonding with him. She told her health visitor that she was suffering from depression but was not taking her medication because she was breastfeeding. The defendant also admitted that, for a fleeting moment, she had felt like killing the child. A few weeks later the child died whilst in the sole care of the defendant. Post-mortem examinations of the child revealed, *inter alia*, new and old blood in the lungs, consistent with two distinct episodes of upper airway obstruction. At her trial the defendant did not give evidence (although the defence maintained that death had arisen from natural causes) and she was convicted of murder. The defendant appealed unsuccessfully to the Court of Appeal. Given that there was evidence that the defendant had intentionally caused the death of the child, and given her refusal to raise the defences of infanticide or diminished responsibility, the Court of Appeal had no option but to uphold the conviction. In the course of delivering the judgment of the court Judge LJ made the following observations on the need for reform of the defence of infanticide:

135. . . . Infanticide remains both as a defence to murder, available to the mother who causes the death of her infant before it reaches twelve months, but simultaneously, as an offence in its own right where the mother has killed the baby, and it is nevertheless accepted that the balance of her mind was disturbed.

136. For many years now there has been some considerable discussion about infanticide, its definition, and indeed whether it should continue to be an offence, or alternatively, a defence to murder. Thus the *Report of the Committee on Mentally Abnormal Offenders* (Cmnd 6244 Chairman: Right Hon. Lord Butler of Saffron Walden (1975)) believed that assuming, contrary to its own 'decided preference' the mandatory life sentence for murder were retained, diminished responsibility should be re-worded so as to apply where the defendant was 'suffering from a form of mental disorder . . . such as to be an extenuating circumstance . . .'. Infanticide would then cease to be of any practical value.

137. The Report pointed out at paragraph 19.23 that 'the medical principles on which the Infanticide Act is based may no longer be relevant. The theory behind the Act was that childbirth produced an hormonal disorder which caused mental illness. But. . . . the operative factors in child-killing are often the stress of having to care for the infant, who may be unwanted or difficult, and personality problems . . .'. In the next paragraph the Committee quoted at length from 'perhaps the most impressive evidence' received on the subject from the Governor and staff of Holloway Prison. 'The disturbance of the "balance of mind" that the Act requires can rarely be said to arise directly from incomplete recovery from the effects of childbirth, and even less so from the effects of lactation . . . A combination of environmental stress and personality disorder . . . are the usual aetiological factors . . . and the relationship to "incomplete recovery from the effects of childbirth or lactation" specified in the Infanticide Act is often somewhat remote.'

138. In its *Fourteenth Report on Offences Against the Person*, Cmnd 7844 (1980), the Criminal Law Revision Committee suggested that infanticide should be retained, but recommended that it should be extended to cases where the balance of the mother's mind was disturbed by "environmental or other stresses". Clause 64(1) of the Draft Criminal Code Bill provided that a mother is guilty of infanticide:

> . . . if her act is done when the child is under the age of 12 months and the balance of her mind is disturbed by reason of the effect of giving birth or of circumstances consequent upon the birth.

The *Report of the Select Committee of the House of Lords on Murder and Life Imprisonment* (HL Paper 78) (1989) did not recommend that there should be a change in the law, but suggested that it should be 'further considered'.

139. The issues raised in these cases are delicate and sensitive. In October 2004 the Home Office announced a comprehensive review of the law of murder. The recently published Law Commission, Ninth Programme of Law Reform, anticipates that it will be involved in and contribute to this review. The public interest requires that the problems arising from and connected to the offence of infanticide should be included in any review. We shall highlight two particular areas of concern. The first is whether, as a matter of substantive law, infanticide

should extend to circumstances subsequent to the birth, but connected with it, such as the stresses imposed on a mother by the absence of natural bonding with her baby: in short, whether the current definition of infanticide reflects modern thinking. The second problem arises when the mother who has in fact killed her infant is unable to admit it. This may be because she is too unwell to do so, or too emotionally disturbed by what she has in fact done, or too deeply troubled by the consequences of an admission of guilt on her ability to care for any surviving children. When this happens, it is sometimes difficult to produce psychiatric evidence relating to the balance of the mother's mind. Yet, of itself, it does not automatically follow from denial that the balance of her mind was not disturbed: in some cases it may indeed help to confirm that it was.

140. The law relating to infanticide is unsatisfactory and outdated. The appeal in this sad case demonstrates the need for a thorough re-examination.

4.6.1.1 Reforming infanticide

The Law Commission's Report (Law Com No 304) *Murder, Manslaughter And Infanticide* considered the need for changes to the offence/defence of infanticide and made these proposals.

1.47 A particular anomaly is that D is entitled to have evidence that he or she was provoked to lose self-control put before the jury no matter how unlikely it is that the defence will succeed. Thus, if D claims that he was provoked to lose his self-control by V's failure to cook his steak medium rare as ordered, the defence has to be put to the jury even though it has no merit and ought to be rejected. By way of contrast, if instead of being provoked, D's killing was a fear-driven over-reaction to a threat of future serious violence, he or she has no defence to murder at all, however well founded the fear. The courts have declined to create or extend a partial defence to cover such cases. Accordingly, reform of this area now depends upon legislative action by Parliament.

1.48 In 2004 we recommended reform of the partial defence of provocation. We set out how we thought the defence should be reformed to create greater certainty and to correct the lop-sided character of the law. During the current consultation, consultees have again broadly agreed that the defence should be reformed along the lines we are recommending . . .

1.51 Where the offence of infanticide is concerned, the problem is not so much the definition but, rather, the procedure for ensuring that evidence of a mother's mental disturbance at the time of the killing is heard at trial. A mother may be 'in denial' about having killed her infant. She may, therefore, be unwilling to submit to a psychiatric examination if the point of this examination seems to her to be to find out why she did it. This is because she cannot accept that she did do it. In such circumstances, she is unlikely to have another defence and is, therefore, likely to be convicted of murder. This is not in the public interest. However, this is not an easy problem to solve. We recommend the adoption of a post-trial procedure designed to do justice in these cases . . .

Missing defences
1.52 Whereas there has recently been controversy over whether provocation should continue to be a partial defence to murder, other strong claims for mitigation of the offence of murder have

failed to gain legal recognition. Judges have decided that they would prefer Parliament to decide whether there should be new partial defences to murder but Parliament has not had the time to consider the matter.

. . .

8.23 Based on the responses to our consultation and recent research, we recommend that the offence/defence of infanticide be retained without amendment (subject to 'murder' being replaced with 'first degree murder or second degree murder').

. . .

8.46 We provisionally proposed that:

in circumstances where infanticide is not raised as an issue at trial and the defendant (biological mother of a child aged 12 months or less) is convicted by the jury of murder [first degree murder or second degree murder], the trial judge should have the power to order a medical examination of the defendant with a view to establishing whether or not there is evidence that at the time of the killing the requisite elements of a charge of infanticide were present. If such evidence is produced and the defendant wishes to appeal, the judge should be able to refer the application to the Court of Appeal and to postpone sentence pending the determination of the application.

4.6.2 SUICIDE PACT

Section 4(1) of the Homicide Act 1957 introduced the defence of suicide pact. It provides:

4(1) It shall be manslaughter, and shall not be murder, for a person acting in pursuance of a suicide pact between him and another to kill the other or be a party to the other being killed by a third person.

For these purposes a suicide pact is defined by s 4(3) as: '. . . a common agreement between two or more persons having for its object the death of all of them, whether or not each is to take his own life, but nothing done by a person who enters into a suicide pact shall be treated as done by him in pursuance of the pact unless it is done while he has the settled intention of dying in pursuance of the pact'.

Note that in its Report (Law Com No 304) *Murder, Manslaughter And Infanticide* the Law Commission concluded that any reform of the suicide pact defence should be considered in the context of a wider review of 'mercy' killings.

4.6.3 DIMINISHED RESPONSIBILITY

Diminished responsibility was introduced as a partial defence to murder by the Homicide Act 1957.

Section 2 of the Homicide Act 1957 provides:

(1) Where a person kills or is party to the killing of another, he shall not be convicted of murder if he was suffering from such abnormality of mind (whether arising from a condition of arrested or retarded development of mind or any inherent causes or induced by disease or injury) as substantially impaired his mental responsibility for his acts or omissions in doing or being a party to the killing.

(2) On a charge of murder, it shall be for the defence to prove that the person charged is by virtue of this section not liable to be convicted of murder.

(3) A person who but for this section would be liable, whether as principal or as accessory, to be convicted of murder shall be liable instead to be convicted of manslaughter.

(4) The fact that one party to a killing is by virtue of this section not liable to be convicted of murder shall not affect the question whether the killing amounted to murder in the case of any other party to it.

4.6.3.1 'Abnormality of the mind'

R v Byrne [1960] 2 QB 396 (CA)

Lord Parker CJ:

The appellant was convicted of murder . . . The victim was a young woman whom he strangled in the YWCA hostel, and after her death he committed horrifying mutilations upon her dead body. The facts as to the killing were not disputed, and were admitted in a long statement made by the accused. The only defence was that in killing his victim the accused was suffering from diminished responsibility as defined by s 2 of the Homicide Act 1957, and was accordingly, guilty not of murder but of manslaughter.

Three medical witnesses were called by the defence, the senior medical officer at Birmingham Prison and two specialists in psychological medicine. Their uncontradicted evidence was that the accused was a sexual psychopath, that he suffered from abnormality of mind, as indeed was abundantly clear from the other evidence in the case, and that such abnormality of mind arose from a condition of arrested or retarded development of mind or inherent causes. The nature of the abnormality of mind of a sexual psychopath, according to the medical evidence, is that he suffers from violent perverted sexual desires which he finds it difficult or impossible to control. Save when under the influence of his perverted sexual desires he may be normal. All three doctors were of opinion that the killing was done under the influence of his perverted sexual desires, and although all three were of opinion that he was not insane in the technical sense of insanity laid down in the M'Naghten Rules it was their view that his sexual psychopathy could properly be described as partial insanity . . .

[Lord Parker CJ referred to the provisions of s 2 of the 1957 Act and continued:] 'Abnormality of mind', which has to be contrasted with the time-honoured expression in the M'Naghten Rules 'defect of reason', means a state of mind so different from that of ordinary human beings that the reasonable man would term it abnormal. It appears to us to be wide enough to cover the mind's activities in all its aspects, not only the perception of physical acts and matters, and the ability to form a rational judgment as to whether an act is right or wrong, but also the ability to exercise will-power to control physical acts in accordance with that rational judgment. The expression 'mental responsibility for his acts' points to a consideration of the extent to which the accused's mind is answerable for his physical acts which must include a consideration of the extent of his ability to exercise willpower to control his physical acts.

Whether the accused was at the time of the killing suffering from any 'abnormality of mind' in the broad sense which we have indicated above is a question for the jury. On this question medical evidence is no doubt of importance, but the jury are entitled to take into consideration all the evidence, including the acts or statements of the accused and his demeanour. They are not bound to accept the medical evidence if there is other material before them which, in their good judgment, conflicts with it and outweighs it.

The aetiology of the abnormality of mind (namely whether it arose from a condition of arrested or retarded development of mind or any inherent causes, or was induced by disease or injury) does, however, seem to be a matter to be determined on expert evidence.

Assuming that the jury are satisfied on the balance of probabilities that the accused was suffering from 'abnormality of mind' from one of the causes specified in parentheses in the subsection, the crucial question nevertheless arises: was the abnormality such as substantially impaired his mental responsibility for his acts in doing or being a party to the killing? This is a question of degree and essentially one for the jury. Medical evidence is, of course, relevant, but the question involves a decision not merely as to whether there was some impairment of the mental responsibility of the accused for his acts but whether such impairment can properly be called 'substantial', a matter upon which juries may quite legitimately differ from doctors.

Furthermore, in a case where the abnormality of mind is one which affects the accused's self-control the step between 'he did not resist his impulse' and 'he could not resist his impulse' is, as the evidence in this case shows, one which is incapable of scientific proof. *A fortiori* there is no scientific measurement of the degree of difficulty which an abnormal person finds in controlling his impulses. These problems which in the present state of medical knowledge are scientifically insoluble, the jury can only approach in a broad, common sense way. This court has repeatedly approved directions to the jury which have followed directions given in Scots cases where the doctrine of diminished responsibility forms part of the common law. We need not repeat them. They are quoted in *R v Spriggs* [1958] 1 QB 270. They indicate that such abnormality as 'substantially impairs his mental responsibility' involves a mental state which in popular language (not that of the M'Naghten Rules) a jury would regard as amounting to partial insanity or being on the borderline of insanity . . .

. . . Inability to exercise willpower to control physical acts, provided that it is due to abnormality of mind from one of the causes specified in parentheses in the subsection is, in our view, sufficient to entitle the accused to the benefit of the section; difficulty in controlling his physical acts depending on the degree of difficulty, may be. It is for the jury to decide on the whole of the evidence whether such inability or difficulty has, not as a matter of scientific certainty but on the balance of probabilities, been established, and in the case of difficulty whether the difficulty is so great as to amount in their view to a substantial impairment of the accused's mental responsibility for his acts. The direction in the present case thus withdrew from the jury the essential determination of fact which it was their province to decide . . .

R v Sanders (1991) 93 Cr App R 245

The appellant was charged with the murder of his wife. He sought, unsuccessfully, to rely on the defence of diminished responsibility, supported by expert evidence. The Crown conceded that the appellant suffered from an abnormality of the mind, but contested the point as to whether or not it affected his responsibility for his actions. On appeal the appellant raised the point that the trial judge had failed to direct the jury expressly on the fact that the expert testimony had been unanimous in finding that the requirements of s 2(1) of the Homicide Act 1957 were satisfied. The appeal was dismissed.

Watkins LJ:
We were referred to the following authorities. *Matheson* (1958) 42 Cr App R 145; [1958] 2 All ER 87, was a five judge court and it was held that where on a charge of murder a defence of diminished responsibility is relied on, and the medical evidence that diminished responsibility exists is uncontradicted and the jury return a verdict of guilty of murder, if there are facts entitling the jury to reject or differ from the opinions of the medical men the Court of Criminal Appeal will not interfere with the verdict unless it can be said that the verdict would amount to a miscarriage of justice. There may be cases where evidence of the conduct of the accused before, at the time of and after the killing may be a relevant consideration for the jury in determining this issue. Where, however, there is unchallenged medical evidence of abnormality of mind and consequent substantial impairments of mental responsibility and no facts or circumstances appear which can displace or throw doubt on that evidence a verdict of guilty of murder is one which cannot be supported having regard to the evidence within the meaning of s 4(1) of the Criminal Appeal Act 1907. In the course of the judgment of the court, which was given by Lord Goddard CJ, he said at p 151 and p 89 respectively:

> Here it is said there was evidence of premeditation and undoubtedly there was, but an abnormal mind is as capable of forming an intention and desire to kill as one that is normal; it is just what an abnormal mind might do. A desire to kill is quite common in cases of insanity . . . Where a defence of diminished responsibility is raised, a plea of guilty to manslaughter on this ground should not be accepted; the issue must be left to the jury, as in the case of a defence of insanity.

It was complained in the perfected grounds in this case if not in the course of submissions to us that the judge had made no reference to premeditation being not necessarily inconsistent with diminished responsibility. That complaint was, we think, quite unjustified for the judge said of it in the green bundle at p 4C:

> Even if the killing was premeditated, the doctors say that does not exclude or discount diminished responsibility as a defence, or in any way alter their opinions. Although Dr Holland accepted that if the killing was in fact premeditated that would mean that the defendant had not told him the truth. It is for you to assess that evidence and say what you make of it.

The next case which we were referred to was *Bailey* in 1961; reported in (1978) 66 Cr App R 31 [as a note, following *Walton v R*, below]. In that case a 17 year old youth was convicted of murder and sentenced to be detained at Her Majesty's pleasure. The Lord Chief Justice in giving the judgment of the court said at p 32:

This court has said on many occasions that of course juries are not bound by what the medical witness say, but at the same time they must act on evidence, and if there is nothing before them, no facts and no circumstances shown before them which throw doubt on the medical evidence, then that is all they are left with, and the jury, in those circumstances, must accept it. That was the effect of the decision of this court, sitting as a court of five judges, in the case of *Matheson* and as we understand it, nothing that this court said in the case of *Byrne* (1960) 44 Cr App R 246 throws any doubt upon what was said in Matheson's case.

In *Walton v R* (1978) 66 Cr App R 25; [1978] AC 788, a Privy Council case, in the course of giving the opinion of the Board, Lord Keith of Kinkel stated at p 30 and p 793:

These cases make clear that upon an issue of diminished responsibility the jury are entitled and indeed bound to consider not only the medical evidence but the evidence upon the whole facts and circumstances of the case. These include the nature of the killing, the conduct of the accused before, at the time of and after it and any history of mental abnormality. It being recognised that the jury on occasion may properly refuse to accept medical evidence, it follows that they must be entitled to consider the quality and weight of that evidence. As was pointed out by Lord Parker CJ in *Byrne* (1960) 44 Cr App R 246, 254 what the jury are essentially seeking to ascertain is whether at the time of the killing the accused was suffering from a state of mind bordering on but not amounting to insanity. That task is to be approached in a broad common sense way.

Finally, we were asked to look at *Kiszko* (1979) 68 Cr App R 62. In that case Bridge LJ, giving the judgment of the court, stated at p 69:

The most recent pronouncement on this subject, in a judgment of the Privy Council in the case of *Walton v R* (1978) 66 Cr App R 25 seems to us still to encapsulate the law entirely accurately and not to require any modification in the light of the provisions of s 2(1)(a) of the Criminal Appeal Act 1968. After referring to earlier authorities, the judgment delivered by Lord Keith of Kinkel is in these terms at p 30. . . .

He then sets out the passage which I have already read. From these cases, in our opinion, two clear principles emerge where the issue is diminished responsibility. The first is that if there are no other circumstances to consider, unequivocal, uncontradicted medical evidence favourable to a defendant should be accepted by a jury and they should be so directed. The second is that where there are other circumstances to be considered the medical evidence, though it be unequivocal and uncontradicted, must be assessed in the light of the other circumstances.

 COMMENTS AND QUESTIONS

1   According to Edmund Davies J in *R v Lloyd* [1967] 1 QB 175, whether or not a defendant's responsibility for his actions has been substantially impaired, as opposed to moderately, is a question of fact for the jury. As he put it: '. . . Substantial does not mean total, that is to say, the mental responsibility need not be totally impaired, so to speak, destroyed altogether. At the other end of the scale substantial does not mean trivial or minimal. It is something in between and Parliament has left it to . . . juries to say on the evidence, was the mental responsibility impaired, and, if so, was it substantially impaired?'

2   The courts have tended to take a liberal view as to what can give rise to diminished responsi-
     bility. In *R v Reynolds* [1988] Crim LR 679, it was, in effect, accepted that premenstrual
     syndrome and post-natal depression could be causes. In *R v Hobson* (1997) *The Times*,
     25 June, the Court of Appeal held that 'battered woman syndrome', having been included in
     the British classification of mental diseases recognised by the psychiatric profession, could
     form the basis of a plea of diminished responsibility.

3   Diminished responsibility will only be available as a defence where death has actually
     occurred, hence it is not available to a defendant charged with attempted murder; see *R v
     Campbell* [1997] Crim LR 495.

4   The fact that s 2(2) of the 1957 Act places the legal burden of proof on the defendant seeking
     to raise the defence of diminished responsibility has survived scrutiny under the Human
     Rights Act 1998. In *R v Lambert* [2001] 1 All ER 1014, the Court of Appeal confirmed that the
     sub-section did not require the defendant to prove any matter that could be said to be an
     element of the offence of murder. Placing the burden of proof on defendants as regards
     defences was not contrary to Art 6 of the European Convention on Human Rights.

4.6.3.2 Diminished responsibility and intoxication

R v Tandy [1989] 1 WLR 350 (CA)

The appellant was an alcoholic. She normally drank Cinzano. On one occasion, however, she
consumed 90% of a bottle of vodka (which contains more alcohol than Cinzano). Later that
day, she strangled her 11 year old daughter.

Watkins LJ:

. . . So in this case it was for the appellant to show:

(1) that she was suffering from an abnormality of mind at the time of the act of
     strangulation;

(2) that that abnormality of mind was induced by disease, namely the disease of alcohol-
     ism; and

(3) that the abnormality of mind induced by the disease of alcoholism was such as sub-
     stantially impaired her mental responsibility for her act of strangling her daughter.

The principles involved in seeking answers to these questions are, in our view, as follows. The
appellant would not establish the second element of the defence unless the evidence showed
that the abnormality of mind at the time of the killing was due to the fact that she was a chronic
alcoholic. If the alcoholism had reached the level at which her brain had been injured by the
repeated insult from intoxicants so that there was gross impairment of her judgment and emotional responses, then the defence of diminished responsibility was available to her, provided that
she satisfied the jury that the third element of the defence existed. Further, if the appellant were
able to establish that the alcoholism had reached the level where although the brain had not been
damaged to the extent just stated, the appellant's drinking had become involuntary, that is to say
she was no longer able to resist the impulse to drink then the defence of diminished responsibility
would be available to her, subject to her establishing the first and third elements, because if her

drinking was involuntary, then her abnormality of mind at the time of the act of strangulation was induced by her condition of alcoholism.

On the other hand, if the appellant had simply not resisted an impulse to drink and it was the drink taken on the [day of the killing] which brought about the impairment of judgment and emotional response, then the defence of diminished responsibility was not available to the appellant.

. . . The appellant had chosen to drink vodka on the Wednesday rather than her customary drink of Cinzano. Her evidence was that she might not have had a drink at all on the Tuesday. She certainly did not tell the jury that she must have taken drink on the Tuesday or Wednesday because she could not help herself. She had been able to stop drinking at 6.30 pm on the Wednesday evening although her supply of vodka was not exhausted. Thus her own evidence indicated that she was able to exercise some control even after she had taken the first drink, contrary to the view of the doctors. There was the evidence of Dr Lawson that the appellant would have had the ability on that Wednesday to abstain from taking the first drink of the day . . .

The three matters on which the appellant relies in the perfected grounds of appeal for saying that there was a misdirection can be dealt with shortly. As to the first, in our judgment the judge was correct in telling the jury that if the taking of the first drink was not involuntary, then the whole of the drinking on the Wednesday was not involuntary. Further, as we have pointed out, the appellant's own evidence indicated that she still had control over her drinking on that Wednesday after she had taken the first drink.

As to the second, the jury were told correctly that the abnormality of mind with which they were concerned was the abnormality of mind at the time of the act of strangulation and as a matter of fact by that time on that Wednesday the appellant had drunk 90% of the bottle of vodka.

On the third point, we conclude that for a craving for drinks or drugs in itself to produce an abnormality of mind within the meaning of s 2(1) of the Act of 1957, the craving must be such as to render the accused's use of drink or drugs involuntary . . .

R v Gittens [1984] 1 QB 698 (CA)

The essential issue in this case was whether the abnormality of mind from which the appellant suffered when he killed his wife and stepdaughter was caused by the alcohol and drugs which he had taken prior to the killing or whether it was due to inherent causes coupled with the drink and drugs.

Lord Lane CJ:

. . . Where alcohol or drugs are factors to be considered by the jury, the best approach is that adopted by the judge and approved by this court in R v Fenton (1975) 61 Cr App R 261. The jury should be directed to disregard what, in their view, the effect of the alcohol or drugs upon the defendant was, since abnormality of mind induced by alcohol or drugs is not (generally speaking) due to inherent causes and is not therefore within the section. Then the jury should consider whether the combined effect of the other matters which do fall within the section amounted to such abnormality of mind as substantially impaired the defendant's mental responsibility within the meaning of 'substantial' set out in R v Lloyd [1967] 1 QB 175.

R v Sanderson (1994) 98 Cr App R 325

The appellant was convicted of killing a woman – a Miss Glasgow. On appeal the court had to consider the proper approach to be taken where there was evidence to suggest that diminished responsibility might be caused by inherent factors, upbringing, and drug abuse.

Roch LJ:

In this case there could not have been any real issue that the appellant, at the time he killed Miss Glasgow, was suffering from an abnormality of mind. He had no reason to want her death apart from his deluded beliefs for weeks. The way in which he inflicted death upon her and his subsequent behaviour all indicated that at the time his judgment and control over his emotions were not those of a normal mind. The first issue which arose on the medical evidence was the nature of that abnormality of mind: was it a paranoid psychosis, that is to say a serious disorder of the mind in which the appellant was suffering from fixed delusions centring around some perverted idea which had some important bearing on his actions, or was he suffering from simple paranoia?

The second issue which arose out of the medical evidence was the cause of the abnormality of mind. Was the abnormality of mind due to inherent causes, the appellant's childhood and upbringing, possibly exacerbated by drug addiction, or simply a side effect or consequence of his drug-taking? It is now well established by authority that for abnormality of the mind to come within the subsection it must be caused by one of the matters listed in the subsection; that is to say it must arise from a condition of arrested or retarded development of mind – of which there is no suggestion in this case – or from inherent causes or be induced by disease or injury.

Dr Bowden's evidence was that the appellant did not have the mental illness of paranoid psychosis and that as far as he was aware medical science showed that the taking of heroin and cocaine could not injure the structures of the brain. Consequently, his evidence was to the effect that the appellant did not and had not had any injury or disease which could have induced the paranoia. Further, his evidence denied that the paranoia arose from inherent cause; it arose simply because the appellant used cocaine. There was no evidence that his use of cocaine was involuntary.

In those circumstances, in our judgment the Common Serjeant was quite correct to direct the jury that if they accepted the evidence of Dr Bowden and rejected that of Dr Coid the defence of diminished responsibility had to fail. In our judgment the jury could not have found that the appellant was suffering from an abnormality of mind within section 2(1) on the evidence of Dr Bowden. Consequently, the first ground of appeal fails.

The court considers that there is substance in the second and third submissions made by the appellant's counsel, and that for the reasons which we shall give shortly, the jury's verdict in this case is unsafe and unsatisfactory.

Cases of diminished responsibility can become difficult and confusing for a jury, and it is important that the judge in directing the jury should tailor his directions to suit the facts of the particular case. We think it will rarely be helpful to the jury to read to them section 2(1) in its entirety. Further, we consider that Annex F would have been of greater assistance had the words in brackets been confined to 'arising from any inherent cause or induced by disease', there being no evidence of arrested or retarded development or of injury.

The judge in his directions to the jury at p 9G, which we have already cited, then summarising the defendant's medical evidence and comparing it with the Crown's medical evidence, referred to the abnormality of mind arising from any inherent cause or disease on three occasions. In his final direction to the jury on diminished responsibility at the end of the summing up, the judge again referred to those two potential causes when he said:

> Has the defendant proved that he was suffering from an abnormality of mind through inherent cause or induced by disease, that is to say a paranoid psychosis which is a mental illness, whether exacerbated by drugs or not?

Again the jury were being directed to consider whether the abnormality of mind arose either from inherent cause or was induced by disease. Further, that direction was so worded that the jury could understand the disease to be the mental illness of paranoid psychosis.

However, earlier in the summing up, the judge summarised Dr Coid's opinion in this way:

> Dr Coid's opinion was this: 'The defendant was at the time of the killing and is now suffering from paranoid psychosis, a mental illness, forming incorrect and abnormal beliefs about other people. This was there already, irrespective of drug abuse. Although paranoid psychosis can be exacerbated by the use of cocaine over the years and much worse, nonetheless, quite apart from the drugs, paranoid psychosis, the mental illness, was there and that amounted to an abnormality of mind,' which is, when you call it inherent or resulting from disease.

We take it the last part should read: 'which it is, whether you call it inherent or resulting from disease'.

Thus the jury were being told Dr Coid was saying that the abnormality of mind was paranoid psychosis. In our opinion it was those apparently contradictory directions which must have given rise to the jury's questions. Although their questions are not free from ambiguity the jury were probably asking:

1 What is meant by induced by disease or injury, that is to say what does induced mean?
2 Is paranoid psychosis a disease or injury which can induce an abnormality of mind?

The judge interpreted the second question as being: 'Can a paranoid psychosis be induced by disease or injury?' and told the jury that he did not know; that 'nobody speaks of paranoid psychosis arising from disease of injury'. That was simply not correct.

The judge had summarised the appellant's doctor's evidence at p 9H:

> It is said for the defence through Dr Coid that there was an underlying paranoid psychosis or mental illness which amounted to an abnormality of mind within the Act. It arose from an inherent cause or disease of long-standing.

Again, at p 23E in summarising Dr Coid's evidence the judge told the jury that Dr Coid was saying that paranoid psychosis amounted to an abnormality of mind which it was whether one said it arose from inherent cause or was induced by disease.

The judge should have sought clarification of the jury's questions, and then, if the real difficulty was whether the mental illness or paranoid psychosis was a disease within the meaning of the subsection, he should have directed them that the medical evidence they had was that this abnormality of mind was the mental illness of paranoid psychosis, if Dr Coid was right, and if Dr Coid was correct as to the aetiology of that mental illness, then it came within the words: 'arising from any inherent cause' and was therefore within the subsection. In our judgment the answers that the judge gave failed to answer the questions which we believe the jury were asking, and would, in any event have confused them rather than have helped them.

Mr Worsley for the Crown submits that the central issue was left to the jury. The judge finally left to the jury the substantive defence which the appellant was raising. The jury were being told, correctly, that if they accepted Dr Coid's evidence, then the defence, subject to their view on the second question set out in Annex F, would succeed, whereas if they preferred Dr Bowden's evidence, the defence failed. Thus, submits Mr Worsley, even if the questions had been clarified and direct answers given, the jury's verdict would have been the same. He invites us to apply the proviso.

To that submission, Mr Jones replied that the questions themselves showed that the jury were inclined to accept that there was a paranoid psychosis, i.e. Dr Coid's evidence, rather than Dr Bowden's simple paranoia resulting from the taking of cocaine. The jury's concern was whether the paranoid psychosis came within the subsection. The jury should have been directed that the paranoid psychosis described by Dr Coid could, as a matter of law, come within the subsection. Had that direction been given, the probable verdict would have been one of manslaughter.

We agree with that submission by Mr Jones . . . For those reasons we allow this appeal, quash the conviction of murder and substitute the conviction of manslaughter.

R v Dietschmann [2003] 1 All ER 897

The defendant attacked and killed the victim, Nicholas Davies by punching him and kicking him on the head. There was evidence that the defendant had been heavily intoxicated at the time of the attack, and that he had also been suffering from a mental abnormality known as adjustment disorder, a condition triggered by the grief felt by the defendant following the death of a close relative. The jury rejected the defendant's defence of diminished responsibility and he was convicted of murder. Following an unsuccessful appeal to the Court of Appeal the following question was certified as raising a point of law of general importance:

(1) Does a defendant seeking to prove a defence of diminished responsibility under s 2(1) of the 1957 Act in a case where he had taken drink prior to killing the victim, have to show that if he had not taken drink (a) he would have killed as he in fact did; and (b) he would have been under diminished responsibility when he did so?

(2) If not, what direction ought to be given to a jury as to the approach to be taken to self-induced intoxication which was present at the material time in conjunction with an abnormality of mind which falls within s 2(1) of the 1957 Act?

Lord Hutton:

. . . In a case where the defendant suffered from an abnormality of mind of the nature described in s 2(1) and had also taken alcohol before the killing and where (as the Court of Appeal held in this case) there was no evidence capable of establishing alcohol dependence syndrome as being an abnormality of mind within the subsection, the meaning to be given to the subsection would appear on first consideration to be reasonably clear. I would read the subsection to mean that if the defendant satisfies the jury that, notwithstanding the alcohol he had consumed and its effect on him, his abnormality of mind substantially impaired his mental responsibility for his acts in doing the killing, the jury should find him not guilty of murder but (under sub-s 3) guilty of manslaughter. I take this view because I think that in referring to substantial impairment of mental responsibility the subsection does not require the abnormality of mind to be the sole cause of the defendant's acts in doing the killing. In my opinion, even if the defendant would not have killed if he had not taken drink, the causative effect of the drink does not necessarily prevent an abnormality of mind suffered by the defendant from substantially impairing his mental responsibility for his fatal acts.

. . . [a number of] . . . points clearly emerge from the judgment of the Court of Appeal in *R v Gittens*. (i) Where a defendant suffers from an abnormality of mind arising from arrested or retarded development of mind or inherent causes or induced by disease or injury and has also taken drink before the killing, the abnormality of mind and the effect of the drink may each play a part in impairing the defendant's mental responsibility for the killing. (ii) Therefore the task for the jury is to decide whether, despite the disinhibiting effect of the drink on the defendant's mind, the abnormality of mind arising from a cause specified in sub-s 2(1) nevertheless substantially impaired his mental responsibility for his fatal acts. (iii) Accordingly it is not correct for the judge to direct the jury that unless they are satisfied that if the defendant had not taken drink he would have killed, the defence of diminished responsibility must fail. Such a direction is incorrect because it fails to recognise that the abnormality of mind arising from a cause specified in the subsection and the effect of the drink may each play a part in impairing the defendant's mental responsibility for the killing.

. . . When, in *R v Gittens*, the Court of Appeal stated that the jury should be directed 'to disregard what, in their view, the effect of the alcohol or drugs on the defendant was' the court were referring to the effect of the alcohol on his abnormality of mind and were making it clear that in deciding whether the defendant was suffering from an abnormality of mind within the meaning of the section and had impairment of mental responsibility arising from that abnormality, the alcohol was to be left out of account. This is clear because after the words I have set out the court continued 'since abnormality of mind induced by alcohol or drugs is not, generally speaking, due to inherent causes and is not therefore within the section'. In other words (as is stated in an article by Mr GR Sullivan on 'Intoxicants and Diminished Responsibility' [1994] Crim LR 156 at 160) the defendant's drinking is to be left out of account in so far as it exacerbated his abnormality of mind. But, of course, alcohol can have a disinhibiting effect and can lead to violence on the part of a person who does not suffer from an abnormality of mind within the meaning of s 2(1), and the jury can take this into account in deciding whether the defendant's underlying mental abnormality did substantially impair his mental responsibility for the fatal acts, notwithstanding the drink he had taken.

This point is well put in Simester and Sullivan *Criminal Law: Theory and Doctrine* (2000) pp 580, 581:

> . . . the taking of intoxicants should not disentitle D from successfully pleading diminished responsibility if the abnormality of mind caused by factors internal to [him] is sufficient, of itself, substantially to impair [his] responsibility . . . The drink does not supervene over his underlying subnormality. That underlying condition remains, and so does the question whether that condition substantially impaired his responsibility for the killing.

. . . Therefore I would answer the first part of the certified question in the negative. As regards the second part of the question, without attempting to lay down a precise form of words as the judge's directions are bound to depend to some extent on the facts of the case before him, I consider that the jury should be directed along the following lines:

Assuming that the defence have established that the defendant was suffering from mental abnormality as described in s 2, the important question is: did that abnormality substantially impair his mental responsibility for his acts in doing the killing? You know that before he carried out the killing the defendant had had a lot to drink. Drink cannot be taken into account as something which contributed to his mental abnormality and to any impairment of mental responsibility arising from that abnormality. But you may take the view that both the defendant's mental abnormality and drink played a part in impairing his mental responsibility for the killing and that he might not have killed if he had not taken drink. If you take that view, then the question for you to decide is this: has the defendant satisfied you that, despite the drink, his mental abnormality substantially impaired his mental responsibility for his fatal acts, or has he failed to satisfy you of that? If he has satisfied you of that, you will find him not guilty of murder but you may find him guilty of manslaughter. If he has not satisfied you of that, the defence of diminished responsibility is not available to him.

4.6.3.3 Diminished responsibility – law reform proposals

The Law Commission's Report (Law Com No 304) *Murder, Manslaughter And Infanticide* supports the retention of the partial defence of diminished responsibility but with refinements that would enable it to address issues of emotional immaturity more effectively, and a format that would provide the flexibility to accommodate future changes in diagnostic practice.

THE DEFINITION OF DIMINISHED RESPONSIBILITY

5.109 There has been consistent criticism of the way in which diminished responsibility was defined in the 1957 Homicide Act . . . There are two principal problems.

5.110 First, the definition says nothing about what is involved in a 'substantial impairment [of] mental responsibility'. The implication is that the effects of an abnormality of mind must significantly reduce the offender's culpability. The Act neither makes this clear, nor says in what way the effects of an abnormality of mind can reduce culpability for an intentional killing, such that a manslaughter verdict is the right result.

5.111 Secondly, the definition has not been drafted with the needs and practices of medical experts in mind, even though their evidence is crucial to the legal viability of any claim of diminished responsibility. 'Abnormality of mind' is not a psychiatric term, so its meaning has had to be developed by the courts from case to case. Further, diagnostic practice in diminished responsibility cases has long since developed beyond identification of the narrow range of permissible 'causes' of an abnormality of mind stipulated in the bracketed part of the definition. In any event, the stipulated permissible causes have never had an agreed psychiatric meaning. The outmoded stipulation of permissible causes has become as much a hindrance as a help. As Dr Madelyn Hicks put it to us:

[A]ttempting to specify the cause of mental disorders . . . is irrelevant [and] misleading, and in fact there are almost always multiple causes stemming from the interaction between genetic vulnerability and life events. [The CP, para 6.40. Dr Hicks is a Consultant Psych-iatrist and Honorary Lecturer, Institute of Psychiatry, King's College London.]

5.112 To address these problems, in our CP83 we provisionally proposed a new definition of diminished responsibility, developed from a definition adopted in the state of New South Wales in 1997. That definition received very broad support when we first proposed a version of it in 2004. Once again, it has had the support of a majority of consultees, but we have also had some helpful suggestions for improvement. In response to comments and analysis that we have received, we recommend adoption of the following definition:

(a) a person who would otherwise be guilty of first degree murder is guilty of second degree murder if, at the time he or she played his or her part in the killing, his or her capacity to:
(i) understand the nature of his or her conduct; or
(ii) form a rational judgement; or
(iii) control him or herself,
was substantially impaired by an abnormality of mental functioning arising from a recognised medical condition, developmental immaturity in a defendant under the age of eighteen, or a combination of both; and
(b) the abnormality, the developmental immaturity, or the combination of both provides an explanation for the defendant's conduct in carrying out or taking part in the killing.

5.113 It is envisaged that this definition would improve the present law in the following ways.

5.114 First, the law will no longer be constrained by a fixed and out-of-date set of causes from which an abnormality of mental functioning ('mental functioning' is a term preferred by psychi-atrists to 'mind') must stem. The issue will be whether the abnormality was brought about by a 'recognised medical condition'

. . .

5.116 In law it is sufficient that a condition is 'more than trivial'. What matters is that it has the effect of substantially impairing D's capacities. It follows that, alongside the familiar psychotic disorders that fall within the scope of the provisions, neurotic disorders, for example, may also do so. An example of the latter would be a post traumatic stress disorder suffered by a woman due to violent abuse suffered over many years.

5.117 Secondly, we believe the provisions make clearer the relationship between the role of the expert and the role of the jury. It is for the experts to offer an opinion on:

(1) whether D was suffering from an abnormality of mental functioning stemming from a recog-nised medical condition; and
(2) whether and in what way the abnormality had an impact on D's capacities, as these are explained in the new provisions.

5.118 It is then for the jury to say whether, in the light of that (and all the other relevant) evidence they regard the relevant capacities of D to have been 'substantially impaired'.

. . .

5.121 Thirdly, the new provisions seek to make clear what impact on capacity the effects of an abnormality of mental functioning must have, if the abnormality is to be the basis for a successful plea of diminished responsibility. It might be helpful to illustrate this by example, although it is not our case that on the actual facts given below the defence should necessarily succeed.

(1) Substantially impaired capacity to 'understand the nature of his or her conduct':

    (a) a boy aged 10 who has been left to play very violent video games for hours on end for much of his life, loses his temper and kills another child when the child attempts to take a game from him. When interviewed, he shows no real understanding that, when a person is killed they cannot simply be later revived, as happens in the games he has been continually playing.

(2) Substantially impaired capacity to 'form a rational judgement':

    (a) a woman suffering from post traumatic stress disorder, consequent upon violent abuse suffered at her husband's hands, comes to believe that only burning her husband to death will rid the world of his sins;

    (b) a mentally sub-normal boy believes that he must follow his older brother's instructions, even when they involve taking take part in a killing. He says, 'I wouldn't dream of disobeying my brother and he would never tell me to do something if it was really wrong';

    (c) a depressed man who has been caring for many years for a terminally ill spouse, kills her, at her request. He says that he had found it progressively more difficult to stop her repeated requests dominating his thoughts to the exclusion of all else, so that 'I felt I would never think straight again until I had given her what she wanted.'

(3) Substantially impaired capacity to 'control him or herself':

    (a) a man says that sometimes the devil takes control of him and implants in him a desire to kill, a desire that must be acted on before the devil will go away.

5.122 Fourthly, it has never been entirely clear whether, under the existing law, the abnormality of mind must, in some sense, 'cause' D to kill. The law simply states that the abnormality of mind must substantially impair D's mental responsibility for his acts in doing or being a party to the killing.

. . .

5.124 The final choice of particular words is a matter for those drafting the legislation. However, we have framed the issue in these terms: the abnormality of mind, or developmental immaturity, or both, must be shown to be 'an explanation' for D's conduct. This ensures that there is an appropriate connection (that is, one that grounds a case for mitigation of the offence) between the abnormality of mental functioning or developmental immaturity and the killing. It leaves open the possibility, however, that other causes or explanations (like provocation) may be admitted to have been at work, without prejudicing the case for mitigation.

DEVELOPMENTAL IMMATURITY

5.125 We recommend that:

    It should be possible to bring in a verdict of diminished responsibility on the grounds of the developmental immaturity of an offender who was under 18 at the time he or she played his or her part in the killing.

. . .

5.128 A very important aspect of this recommendation is that evidence of developmental immaturity can be combined with evidence of an abnormality of mental functioning, to make a case for a verdict of second degree murder. As we explained in the CP, experts may find it impossible to distinguish between the impact on D's mental functioning of developmental immaturity, and the impact on that functioning of a mental abnormality. To force experts – as the law currently does – to assess the impact of the latter, whilst disregarding the effect of the former, is wholly unrealistic and unfair.

. . .

5.130 It is important to recognise the nature and limits of what we are suggesting. In England and Wales, criminal liability for murder can be imposed on an offender if he or she was at least 10 years of age at the time of the offence. We are not suggesting that imposing liability for murder on a child of this age is always unfair or inappropriate. Some 10-year-old killers may be sufficiently advanced in their judgment and understanding that such a conviction would be fair.

5.131 What we are suggesting is that it is unrealistic and unfair to assume that all children aged 10 or over who kill must have had the kind of developed sense of judgement, control and understanding that makes a first degree murder conviction the right result (provided the fault element was satisfied). Instead, our recommendation is that it should be for the jury to decide in the individual case whether D had such a sense of judgement, control, or understanding. Moreover, it will be for D to prove that his or her capacity for judgement, control and understanding was substantially impaired by developmental immaturity.

5.132 D may wish to prove substantial impairment by developmental immaturity through appeal either to biological factors, or to social and environmental influences, or to a combination of both. For example, D may wish to give evidence that his or her power of control over his or her actions was substantially impaired by a biological factor such as poor frontal lobe development . . .

5.133 As this final sentence implies, however, in an individual case involving a child under 14 years of age, it would be open to the prosecution to seek to rebut evidence of poor frontal lobe development by arguing that this particular D had matured to a sufficient degree to be fairly convicted of first degree murder. The jury should be trusted to reject implausible claims, as they are with other defences based on expert evidence.

4.6.4 PROVOCATION

Provocation has a long history as a common law defence to murder. As Lord Hoffmann observed in *R v Smith (Morgan)* [2000] 4 All ER 289:

. . . although the doctrine has much earlier roots, it emerged in recognisably modern form in the late 17th and early 18th centuries. It comes from a world of Restoration gallantry in which gentlemen habitually carried lethal weapons, acted in accordance with a code of honour which required insult to be personally avenged by instant angry retaliation and in which the mandatory penalty for premeditated murder was death. To show anger 'in hot blood' for a proper reason by an appropriate response was not merely permissible but the badge of a man of honour. The human frailty to which the defence of provocation made allowance was the possibility that the man of honour might overreact and kill when a lesser retaliation would have been appropriate. Provided that he did not grossly overreact in the extent or manner of his retaliation, the offence would be manslaughter and execution avoided.

The modern basis for the defence is to be found in *R v Duffy* [1949] 1 All ER 932 (Note), where Lord Goddard CJ quoted with approval the direction given to the jury by the trial judge Devlin J: 'Provocation is some act, or series of acts, done by the dead man to the accused which would cause in any reasonable person, and actually causes in the accused, a sudden and temporary loss of self-control, rendering the accused so subject to passion as to make him or her for the moment not master of his mind . . .'. Parliament subsequently enacted s 3 of the Homicide Act 1957, but this simply clarifies certain aspects of the defence. It does not place it on a statutory basis.

Section 3 of the Homicide Act 1957 provides:

> Where on a charge of murder there is evidence on which a jury can find that the person charged was provoked (whether by things done or by things said or by both together) to lose his self-control, the question whether the provocation was enough to make a reasonable man do as he did shall be left to be determined by the jury; and in determining that question the jury shall take into account everything both done and said according to the effect which, in their opinion, it would have on a reasonable man.

That there should be a defence of provocation at all has been questioned – not least because it may be seen as offering an excuse to abusive or excessively jealous and possessive men who kill their partners when relationships deteriorate. The development of the defence since 1957 has revealed a tension between those who believe that it should demand a degree of self-control from the defendant such as could be expected of the reasonable person, and those who believe that the defence should be couched in terms that reflect the characteristics of the defendant touching upon his ability to deal with the provocation that he encountered. This debate between what might loosely be termed the objectivist and subjectivist camps was referred to by Lord Hoffmann in *R v Smith (Morgan)*, where he observed that:

> . . . it is impossible to read even a selection of the extensive modern literature on provocation without coming to the conclusion that the concept has serious logical and moral flaws. But your Lordships must take the law as it stands. Whatever your decision in this case, the result is not likely to be wholly satisfactory. The doctrine of provocation has always been described as a concession to human frailty and the law illustrates Kant's dictum that, from the crooked timber of humanity, nothing completely straight can be made.

4.6.4.1 Determining whether or not the defence of provocation has been raised

It is for the defendant to provide some evidence of provocation for the jury to act upon, but once this evidential burden is discharged, the legal burden rests upon the prosecution to prove, beyond all reasonable doubt, that the defendant was not acting under provocation at the time of the killing.

R v Stewart [1995] 4 All ER 999 (CA)

Stuart-Smith LJ:

. . . It is now well established that even if the defence do not raise the issue of provocation, and even if they would prefer not to because it is inconsistent with and will detract from the primary defence, the judge must leave the issue for the jury to decide if there is evidence which suggests that the accused may have been provoked; and this is so even if the evidence of provocation is slight or tenuous in the sense that the measure of the provocative acts or words is slight: see *R v Rossiter* [1994] 2 All ER 752 and *R v Cambridge* [1994] 2 All ER 760, [1994] 1 WLR 971 . . .

In our judgment, where the judge must, as a matter of law, leave the issue of provocation to the jury, he should indicate to them, unless it is obvious, what evidence might support the conclusion that the appellant lost his self-control . . .

R v Acott [1997] 1 All ER 706 (HL)

Lord Steyn:

. . . The Court of Appeal (Criminal Division) certified that there was a point of law of general public importance involved in the decision to dismiss the appeal, namely: In a prosecution for murder, before the judge is obliged to leave the issue of provocation to the jury, must there be some evidence, either direct or inferential, as to what was either done or said to provoke the alleged loss of self-control? . . .

. . . Strictly, the certified question need not be answered in order to dispose of the appeal. But it seems possible to summarise the legal position in terms which might be helpful. Section 3 is only applicable 'if there is evidence . . . that the person charged was provoked (whether by things done or things said or by both together) to lose his self-control'. A loss of self-control caused by fear, panic, sheer bad temper or circumstances (eg a slow down of traffic due to snow) would not be enough. There must be some evidence tending to show that the killing might have been an uncontrolled reaction to provoking conduct rather than an act of revenge. Moreover, although there is no longer a rule of proportionality as between provocation and retaliation, the concept of proportionality is nevertheless still an important factual element in the objective inquiry. It necessarily requires of the jury an assessment of the seriousness of the provocation. It follows that there can only be an issue of provocation to be considered by the jury if the judge considers that there is some evidence of a specific act or words of provocation resulting in a loss of self-control. It does not matter from what source that evidence emerges or whether it is relied on at trial by the defendant or not. If there is such evidence, the judge must leave the issue to the jury. If there is no such evidence, but merely the speculative possibility that there had been an act of provocation, it is wrong for the judge to direct the jury to consider provocation. In such a case there is simply no triable issue of provocation . . .

Counsel for the appellant invited your Lordships to go further and state what would be sufficient evidence of provocation to justify a trial judge in leaving the issue of provocation for the jury to consider. The invitation was attractively put. But it must be rejected. What is sufficient in this particular context is not a question of law. Where the line is to be drawn depends on a judgment involving logic and common sense, the assessment of matters of degree and an intense focus on the circumstances of a particular case. It is unwise to generalise on such matters: it is a subject best left to the good sense of trial judges. For the same reason it is not useful to compare the facts of decided cases on provocation with one another.

For my part the certified question can be answered in the general way in which I have indicated. But the reasoning in this judgment is subject to the overriding principle that the legal burden rests on the Crown to disprove provocation on a charge of murder to the required standard of proof. In *Lee Chun-Chuen v R* [1963] AC 220 at 229 Lord Devlin summed up the legal position as follows:

> It is not of course for the defence to make out a *prima facie* case of provocation. It is for the prosecution to prove that the killing was unprovoked. All that the defence need do is to point to material which could induce a reasonable doubt.

That remains the position.

I would dismiss the appeal.

4.6.4.2 The 'subjective' stage: was there 'cooling time' between the provocation and the killing?

R v Ibrams and Gregory (1981) 74 Cr App R 154

Ibrams was sharing a flat with his fiancée, Laura Adronik. An ex-boyfriend of Laura's, John Monk, was released from borstal and regularly visited the flat to bully and terrorise Ibrams and Adronik. On some occasions Gregory was also at the flat. On Sunday 7 October 1979 the police were contacted twice but did nothing. As it seemed that the police were not going to protect them, Ibrams, Adronik and Gregory felt that they had to protect themselves. On Wednesday 10 October they met together and drew up a plan for dealing with Monk. In essence, the plan was that they would get Monk drunk and he would be encouraged to go to bed with Adronik. Ibrams and Gregory would then enter the flat and attack Monk whilst he was in bed. This plan was carried out on Friday 12 October. The injuries inflicted by Ibrams and Gregory were so serious that Monk died of his injuries.

The trial judge, McNeill J, held that there was no evidence of provocation for the jury to consider. The Court of Appeal upheld this decision on the basis that the final incident of provocation had taken place several days before the attack on the deceased and that the attack had been planned in advance; accordingly, there was no evidence of the sudden and temporary loss of self-control necessary to establish provocation.

Lawton LJ:
. . . [His Lordship referred to the speech of Lord Diplock in *DPP v Camplin* [1978] AC 705 where Lord Diplock sets out the history of the law relating to provocation.] That history shows that, in the past at any rate, provocation and loss of self-control tended to be regarded by the courts as taking place with a very short interval of time between the provocation and the loss of self-control . . . In our judgment, Lord Diplock clearly thought that the loss of self-control must occur at or about the time of the act of provocation . . .

His Lordship then cited with approval part of the direction of Devlin J in *R v Duffy* [1949] 1 All ER 932:

> Indeed, circumstances which induce a desire for revenge are inconsistent with provocation, since the conscious formulation of a desire for revenge means that a person has had time to think, to reflect, and that would negative a sudden temporary loss of self-control, which is of the essence of provocation . . .
>
> . . . [The appellants] were masters of their minds when carrying [their plan] out, because they worked out the details with considerable skill; and in pursuing the plan as they did on the Friday night they were still masters of their own minds. They were doing what they had planned to do . . . It follows . . . that McNeill J was right in ruling that there was no evidence of loss of self-control . . .

R v Ahluwalia [1992] 4 All ER 889 (CA)

The appellant, an Asian woman, entered into an arranged marriage with the deceased. She had to endure several years of violence and abuse. Her husband regularly assaulted her; he had threatened to kill her; he taunted her with the fact that he was having an affair with another woman. During the evening of 8 May 1989 her husband threatened to beat her up and threatened to burn her face with an iron. That night, the appellant poured some petrol, which she had previously purchased, into a bucket (to make it easier to throw); she lit a candle on the gas cooker and carried the bucket and the candle upstairs, taking an oven glove for self-protection, and a stick. She went into her husband's bedroom, threw in some petrol, lit the stick with the candle and threw it into the room. Her husband suffered severe burns from which he died a few days later.

> Lord Taylor CJ:
>
> . . . Section 3 of the Homicide Act 1957 did not provide a general or fresh definition of provocation which remains a common law not a statutory defence. The changes effected by the 1957 Act are conveniently summarised in Smith and Hogan, Criminal Law, 6th edn, 1988:
>
> (1) It made it clear that 'things said' alone may be sufficient provocation, if the jury should be of the opinion that they would have provoked a reasonable man . . .
> (2) It took away the power of the judge to withdraw the defence from the jury on the ground that there was no evidence on which the jury could find that a reasonable man would have been provoked to do as the defendant did . . .
> (3) It took away the power of the judge to dictate to the jury what were the characteristics of the reasonable man . . .
>
> The phrase 'sudden and temporary loss of self-control' encapsulates an essential ingredient of the defence of provocation in a clear and readily understandable phrase. It serves to underline that the defence is concerned with the actions of an individual who is not, at the moment when he or she acts violently, master of his or her own mind . . .
>
> . . . [I]t is open to the judge, when deciding whether there is any evidence of provocation to be left to the jury and open to the jury when considering such evidence, to take account of the

interval between the provocative conduct and the reaction of the defendant to it. Time for reflection may show that after the provocative conduct made its impact on the mind of the defendant, he or she kept or regained self-control. The passage of time following the provocation may also show that the subsequent attack was planned or based on motives such as revenge or punishment, inconsistent with the loss of self-control and therefore with the defence of provocation. In some cases, such an interval may wholly undermine the defence of provocation; that, however, depends entirely on the facts of the individual case and is not a principle of law.

[Counsel for the appellant] referred to the phrase 'cooling-off period' which has sometimes been applied to an interval of time between the provocation relied upon and the fatal act. He suggests that although in many cases such an interval may indeed be a time for cooling and regaining self-control so as to forfeit the protection of the defence, in others the time lapse has an opposite effect. He submits, relying on expert evidence not before the trial judge, that women who have been subjected frequently over a period to violent treatment may react to the final act or words by what he calls a 'slow-burn' reaction rather than by an immediate loss of self-control.

We accept that the subjective element in the defence of provocation would not as a matter of law be negatived simply because of the delayed reaction in such cases, provided that there was at the time of the killing a 'sudden and temporary loss of self-control' caused by the alleged provocation. However, the longer the delay and the stronger the evidence of deliberation on the part of the defendant, the more likely it will be that the prosecution will negative provocation . . .

R v Baillie [1995] 2 Cr App R 31

The appellant's sons were threatened by a drug dealer called Robert McCubbin. On hearing of this the appellant, who had been drinking, set off in a rage to attack McCubbin. Having retrieved a sawn-off shotgun from the attic of his house, and having armed himself with a cut-throat razor, the appellant drove to McCubbin's house (stopping en route to fill up with petrol). The appellant confronted McCubbin at his house, attacking him with the razor. McCubbin fled out of the back of the house, and the appellant pursued him, firing the shotgun twice after him. McCubbin died as a result. The appellant invited the Court of Appeal to consider the trial judge's refusal to leave the defence of provocation before the jury on the ground that there had been a gap in time between the provocation and the killing.

Henry LJ:
Lady Mallalieu [counsel for the appellant] points to the scheme of section 3 [of the Homicide Act 1957], under which the jury is the sole arbiter of the make-up of the reasonable man, and what would or would not have provoked him. She accepts, as she must, that on the wording of the section, provocation only comes into the picture where there is evidence fit for consideration by the jury that the defendant was, or might have been, suffering from a sudden and temporary loss of self-control at the time he did the fatal act. Here the judge ruled that there was no such evidence, and the question is whether she was right to do so.

The question is necessarily one of a value judgment, a matter of degree. The judge clearly expressed the view that in her judgment (our emphasis) this was not a case of provocation because any sudden or temporary loss of self-control must have ceased by the time of the fatal act. She so expresses it in the terms of her judgment: 'I am not persuaded . . .', 'in my judgment . . .', 'that seems to me to be . . .'

It seems to us that that approach is too austere an approach for the purposes of section 3. Having regard to the clear intention of Parliament to move the test of provocation from the judge's province to that of the jury (while reserving to the judge a screening process), the provisions of that section must be construed paying proper and sensible regard to human frailty in answering the essential jury question.

. . . We are dealing with threats to sons in their middle to late teens. We are dealing with threats by one who is supplying them with narcotics which may lead to the ruin of their lives quite independently of whether the actual physical threats are carried out or not. We are dealing with a father who, though no stranger to drink, behaved on this evening in a way apparently quite inconsistent with anything that he had done before. We are dealing with a case in which (depending on your view of the petrol stop) there was arguably no 'natural break' between the conversation with his son which caused him to go up to the attic to find the shotgun hidden there, and the shooting itself. Now, there are many and obvious difficulties in such a defence succeeding, but Lady Mallalieu has referred us to cases where the matter has been left to juries (and the defence has succeeded) even though there are the same qualities of the desire for revenge, as great a lapse of time, as much planning and as many of the features as point against a sudden and temporary loss of control. In our judgment, this is a matter which should have been left to the jury as being fit for their consideration. We say this while recognising that there are formidable, perhaps insuperable, obstacles in the jury arriving at a verdict of manslaughter because of provocation.

 ## COMMENTS AND QUESTIONS

1   Anything can be provocation – even the crying of a baby; see *R v Doughty* (1986) 83 Cr App R 319. The issue is whether the defendant's response to the provocation was reasonable. The more trivial the provocation, however, the less likely the jury are to believe that D actually was provoked at the time of the killing.

2   The defence of provocation is available to both the principal offender who is charged with murder, and an accomplice; see *R v Marks* [1998] Crim LR 676, although it seems likely that there would be considerable evidential difficulties in actually making out the defence.

3   If a jury is invited to consider only the incident that provokes the defendant and sparks the killing, its verdict might be based on too narrow a basis. Often words or deeds are provoking because they are the culmination of some long running dispute between the parties, or reflect the stage in an abusive relationship where the defendant could no longer cope. The Court of Appeal, as the following extracts indicate, has accepted that in such cases a jury ought to be directed to look at the relationship between the parties in context; see *R v Humphreys* [1995] 4 All ER 889.

4   A defendant may rely on the defence of provocation even if he or she has been partly responsible for bringing that provocation about. In *R v Johnson* [1989] 1 WLR 740, Watkins LJ observed: '. . . we find it impossible to accept that the mere fact that a defendant caused a reaction in others, which in turn led him to lose his self-control, should result in the issue of

provocation being kept outside a jury's consideration. Section 3 [of the Homicide Act 1957] clearly provides that the question is whether things done or said or both provoked the defendant to lose his self-control.

4.6.4.3 The objective stage: what degree of self-control is to be expected from the defendant?

Assuming there is evidence of provocation to put before a jury, and assuming that there are no issues related to 'cooling time', how is the objective part of the test for provocation to be applied? As the extracts from *DPP v Camplin* (below) indicate – to apply a reasonable adult test without qualification to a juvenile defendant would result in unfairness, if not absurdity – hence the reasonable person may be imbued with the age of the accused. But what other characteristics are relevant? Gender? Ethnicity? Disability? It was also recognised by the House of Lords in *DPP v Camplin* that some characteristics of the accused would have to be taken into account to explain why the provocation produced such a violent reaction on the part of the accused – for example if D were impotent and he was taunted about this. It was assumed, however, that such characteristics would have no bearing on the measure used to assess whether or not the accused had displayed the degree of self-control to be expected of the reasonable person.

DPP v Camplin [1978] AC 705 (HL)

Camplin, who was 15 years of age at the time, killed a man named Khan by splitting his skull with a chapati pan. Khan had raped Camplin and then taunted Camplin about the incident. Camplin relied upon the defence of provocation but was convicted of murder. The point of law of general public importance involved in the case has been certified as being:

> Whether on the prosecution for murder of a boy of 15, where the issue of provocation arises, the jury should be directed to consider the question under s 3 of the Homicide Act 1957 whether the provocation was enough to make a reasonable man do as he did by reference to a 'reasonable adult' or by reference to a 'reasonable boy of 15'.

Lord Diplock:
... [F]or the purposes of the law of provocation the 'reasonable man' has never been confined to the adult male. It means an ordinary person of either sex, not exceptionally excitable or pugnacious, but possessed of such powers of self-control as everyone is entitled to expect that his fellow citizens will exercise in society as it is today ... [N]ow that the law has been changed so as to permit of words being treated as provocation even though unaccompanied by any other acts, the gravity of verbal provocation may well depend upon the particular characteristics or circumstances of the person to whom a taunt or insult is addressed. To taunt a person because of his race, his physical infirmities or some shameful incident in his past may well be considered by the jury to be more offensive to the person addressed, however equable his temperament, if the facts on which the taunt is founded are true than it would be if they were not ...

In my opinion a proper direction to a jury on the question left to their exclusive determination by s 3 of the Act of 1957 would be on the following lines. The judge should state what the question is using the very terms of the section. He should then explain to them that the reasonable man referred to in the question is a person having the power of self-control to be expected of an ordinary person of the sex and age of the accused, but in other respects sharing such of the accused's characteristics as they think would affect the gravity of the provocation to him; and that the question is not merely whether such a person would in like circumstances be provoked to lose his self-control but also whether he would react to the provocation as the accused did . . .

Lord Simon of Glaisdale:
. . . In my judgment the reference to 'a reasonable man' at the end of [s 3 of the Homicide Act 1957] means 'a man of ordinary self-control'. If this is so the meaning satisfies what I have ventured to suggest as the reason for importing into this branch of the law the concept of the reasonable man – namely to avoid the injustice of a man being entitled to rely on his exceptional excitability or pugnacity or ill-temper or on his drunkenness . . .

I think that the standard of self-control which the law requires before provocation is held to reduce murder to manslaughter is still that of the reasonable person (hence his invocation in s 3); but that, in determining whether a person of reasonable self-control would lose it in the circumstances, the entire factual situation, which includes the characteristics of the accused, must be considered . . .

4.6.4.4 The *Camplin* approach doubted

The decision in *DPP v Camplin* gave rise to a succession of cases in which the Court of Appeal adopted the view that *personal* characteristics other than *just* age and gender could be attributed to the reasonable person for the purposes of assessing whether or not the defendant had displayed the expected degree of self-control. Hence in *R v Dryden* [1995] 4 All ER 987, the court accepted that the defendant's obsession with his property and his eccentric character should have been left to the jury for consideration as part of the objective test. Similarly in *R v Newell* (1980) 71 Cr App R 331, *R v Raven* [1982] Crim LR 51 (22-year-old with a mental age of 9 judged by the standard of a reasonable 22-year-old with a mental age of 9), and *R v Ahluwalia* [1992] 4 All ER 889.

The Privy Council in *Luc Thiet Thuan v R* [1997] AC 131, expressed the contrary view, holding that the actual characteristics of the accused were relevant only to the gravity of the provocation. Only age and sex were to be attributed to the reasonable person for the purpose of expressing the standard of self-control to be expected. The House of Lords in *R v Smith (Morgan)* [2000] 4 All ER 289 endorsed the Court of Appeal's thinking on this issue, effectively abandoning the *Camplin* approach in favour of a test that asked juries to consider (assuming there was evidence of provocation) whether the defendant had exercised (what was for him) reasonable self-control. In assessing the extent to which the defendant had acted reasonably the jury would be entitled to take into account all relevant characteristics of the defendant. In Morgan Smith's case, for example, this included evidence that he suffered from depression. Whilst the change in the law represented by Morgan Smith was welcomed in some quarters on the basis that it was not fair to expect a defendant to display more self-control than could be reasonably expected of him, uncertainties arose concerning those characteristics that were relevant for the purposes of the Morgan Smith approach and those that were not. For example, in *R v Weller*

[2004] 1 Cr App R 1, the Court of Appeal suggested it would be wrong to tell a jury to ignore characteristics such as male possessiveness and jealousy. In *R v Rowland* [2003] EWCA Crim 3636, Potter LJ (reviewing the effect of these decisions) went so far as to conclude:

> ... it seems clear that, in the context of the law of provocation, the reasonable man is now to be regarded as an archetype best left lurking in the statutory undergrowth, lest his emergence should lead the jury down a false trail of reasoning en route to their verdict. That is not to say that reference to the reasonable man is proscribed; that could scarcely be so in the light of the wording of the statute. However, since the invocation of the reasonable man was traditionally employed by judges in summing-up in connection with characteristics with which he would not normally be expected to be endowed, his utility is diminished once it is clear that the application of the objective test is to be regarded exclusively as a matter for the jury ...

4.6.4.5 *Camplin* restored

As will be seen from the extracts that follow, the issue of how a jury should be directed on the objective stage of the test for provocation has been revisited by the Privy Council in *AG v Holley* with the effect that the *DPP v Camplin* approach has effectively been resurrected – the defendant's characteristics can be taken into account to explain the gravity of the provocation, but in assessing whether or not he exercised reasonable self-control, only age and gender are to be taken into account.

Attorney General for Jersey v Holley (Jersey) [2005] UKPC 23

Holley was a chronic alcoholic convicted of murdering his longstanding girl friend with an axe while under the influence of alcohol. On appeal the Court of Appeal of Jersey set aside the conviction of murder and substituted a conviction for manslaughter, on the ground that the Deputy Bailiff had misdirected the jury on the issue of provocation. The Attorney General for Jersey appealed to the Privy Council. The issue for the Privy Council was whether the law relating to provocation as stated by the House of Lords in *R v Morgan Smith* was to be preferred to the more objective approach suggested in *DPP v Camplin*. The majority judgment delivered by Lord Nicholls of Birkenhead, held that *R v Morgan Smith* was not to be followed.

> Per Lord Nicholls of Birkenhead:
>
> 8. ... In the leading case of *R v Camplin* [1978] AC 705, 717, Lord Diplock gave a much quoted explanation of the meaning of the phrase 'reasonable man' for the purposes of the law of provocation:
>
> > It means an ordinary person of either sex, not exceptionally excitable or pugnacious, but possessed of such powers of self-control as everyone is entitled to expect that his fellow citizens will exercise in society as it is today.

Lord Simon of Glaisdale said the same, at page 726. The reference to 'a reasonable man' at the end of section 3, he said, means 'a man of ordinary self-control'. Similarly in *R v Morhall* [1996] AC 90, 98, Lord Goff of Chieveley commented that, despite the express words of the statute, to speak of the degree of self-control attributable to the ordinary person is 'certainly less likely to mislead' than to do so with reference to the reasonable person.

9. An external standard of this character, whether expressed in terms of reasonableness or a reasonable man or an ordinary person, has long been an essential element of the defence . . .

10. Before 1957 loss of self-control had to be brought about by things done. Words would not suffice to constitute provocation. Section 3 extended the scope of the defence by providing that in future loss of self-control could be provoked either by things done or by things said or by both together. This extension had an effect on what evidence was relevant, and therefore admissible, on the issue of the gravity of the provocation, that is, the first element in the objective ingredient. As explained by Lord Diplock in the case of Camplin, at page 717, when words alone could not amount to provocation the gravity of provocation depended primarily on degrees of violence. Once words could amount to provocation, the gravity of provocation could depend upon 'the particular characteristics or circumstances of the person to whom a taunt or insult is addressed'. Lord Diplock expressed his view, at page 718, on what would be a proper direction to a jury on the question left to their determination by section 3:

> He should . . . explain to them that the reasonable man referred to in the question is a person having the power of self-control to be expected of an ordinary person of the sex and age of the accused, but in other respects sharing such of the accused's character-istics as they think would affect the gravity of the provocation to him; and that the question is not merely whether such a person would in like circumstances be provoked to lose his self-control but also whether he would react to the provocation as the accused did . . .

11. Hence if a homosexual man is taunted for his homosexuality it is for the jury to consider whether a homosexual man having ordinary powers of self-control might, in comparable circum-stances, be provoked to lose his self-control and react to the provocation as the defendant did. Authority for this proposition, if needed, is the 'glue-sniffer' case of *R v Morhall* [1996] AC 90. There the deceased nagged the defendant about his addiction to glue-sniffing. The problem before the House of Lords was whether this addiction should have been taken into account at the defendant's trial as affecting the gravity of the provocation: see page 97D. Lord Goff of Chieveley, with whose speech all members of the House agreed, said it should. The thrust of his reasoning was that, for this purpose, 'the entire factual situation' was to be taken into account. This includes matters not falling strictly within the description 'characteristics'. It also includes matters which are discreditable to the defendant. Lord Goff said, at page 99:

> suppose that a man who has been in prison for a sexual offence, for example rape, has after his release been taunted by another man with reference to that offence. It is difficult to see why, on ordinary principles, his characteristic or history as an offender of that kind should not be taken into account as going to the gravity of the provocation.

12. Of course, assessing the conduct of a glue-sniffing defendant against the standard of a glue-sniffing man having ordinary powers of self-control may mean the defendant is assessed against a standard of self-control he cannot attain. He may be exceptionally excitable or

pugnacious. But this is so with every defendant who seeks to rely upon provocation as a defence. The objective standard of self-control is the standard set by the common law and, since 1957, by the statutory reference to a 'reasonable man'. It is of general application. Inherent in the use of this prescribed standard as a uniform standard applicable to all defendants is the possibility that an individual defendant may be temperamentally unable to achieve this standard.

13. Taking into account the age and sex of a defendant, as mentioned in *Camplin*, is not an exception to this uniform approach. The powers of self-control possessed by ordinary people vary according to their age and, more doubtfully, their sex. These features are to be contrasted with abnormalities, that is, features not found in a person having ordinary powers of self-control. The former are relevant when identifying and applying the objective standard of self-control, the latter are not.

14. That Lord Diplock intended to draw this distinction in *Camplin* is plain from the terms of his suggested direction to a jury, quoted above. The statutory reasonable man has the power of self-control to be expected of an ordinary person of like sex and age. In other respects, that is, in respects other than power of self-control, the reasonable man shares such of the defendant's characteristics as the jury think would affect the gravity of the provocation to the defendant. This direction, approved by the other members of the House, was clearly intended to be a model direction, of general application in cases of provocation.

Persons of diminished responsibility

15. Before proceeding further it is important to pause and note that when adopting the 'reasonable man' standard in section 3 of the Homicide Act 1957 Parliament recognised that, standing alone, this provision might work harshly on defendants suffering from mental abnormality. Accordingly, cheek by jowl with section 3 Parliament introduced into English law the partial defence of diminished responsibility. In short, under section 2 a person is not to be convicted of murder if he shows he was suffering from such abnormality of mind, whether arising from a condition of arrested or retarded development of mind or any inherent causes or induced by disease or injury, as 'substantially impaired' his mental responsibility for his acts and omissions in killing or being a party to the killing. In such a case the defendant is liable to be convicted of manslaughter. The burden of proof rests on the defendant who seeks to rely on this defence.

16. This provision, which is reproduced in article 3 of the Jersey law, is apt to embrace some cases where it is inappropriate to apply to the defendant the standard of self-control of an ordinary person. Section 3, with its objective standard, is to be read with this in mind. The statutory provision regarding diminished responsibility in section 2 represents the legislature's view on how cases of mental abnormality are to be accommodated in the law of homicide. *R v Raven* [1982] Crim LR 51 appears to be an instance of a case where this defence would have been relevant. There a 22-year-old defendant had a mental age of 9 years. Similarly in *R v Ahluwalia* [1992] 4 All ER 889, where a defence of provocation failed, the Court of Appeal ordered a retrial on the issue of diminished responsibility. Section 2 should not be distorted to accommodate the types of case for which section 3 was specifically enacted.

The two views

17. Against this background their Lordships turn to consider the point where the substantial difference in judicial views has emerged. Exceptional excitability or pugnacity is one thing. But

what if the defendant is suffering from serious mental abnormality, as in the *Morgan Smith* case where the defendant suffered from severe clinical depression? Is he, for the purposes of the defence of provocation, to be judged by the standard of a person having ordinary powers of self-control?

18. The view of the minority in the case of Morgan Smith is that he is. The standard is a constant, objective standard in all cases. The jury should assess the gravity of the provocation to the defendant. In that respect, as when considering the subjective ingredient of provocation (did the defendant lose his self-control?), the jury must take the defendant as they find him, 'warts and all', as Lord Millett observed. But having assessed the gravity of the provocation to the defendant, the standard of self-control by which his conduct is to be evaluated for the purpose of the defence of provocation is the external standard of a person having and exercising ordinary powers of self-control. That is the standard the jury should apply when considering whether or not the provocation should be regarded as sufficient to bring about the defendant's response to it: see Lord Millett, at page 211.

19. This view accords with the approach applied by their Lordships' Board in *Luc Thiet Thuan v The Queen* [1997] AC 131, an appeal from Hong Kong. On a trial for murder the defendant relied on the defences of diminished responsibility and provocation. Medical evidence showed the defendant suffered from brain damage and was prone to respond to minor provocation by losing his self-control and acting explosively. The trial judge directed the jury that this medical evidence was not relevant on the defence of provocation. The jury rejected both defences. The correctness of the judge's direction on provocation was the issue on the appeal. The Board, Lord Steyn dissenting, upheld the judge's direction. Lord Goff of Chieveley noted that mental infirmity of the defendant, if itself the subject of taunts by the deceased, may be taken into account as going to the gravity of the provocation. He continued, at page 146:

> But this is a far cry from the defendant's submission that the mental infirmity of a defendant impairing his power of self-control should as such be attributed to the reasonable man for the purposes of the objective test.

20. The majority view expressed in *Morgan Smith* rejects this approach. According to this view, the standard of self-control required by the common law and by the statute is not the constant standard of a person having and exercising ordinary self-control. The required standard is more flexible. The jury should apply the standard of control to be expected of the particular individual. The jury must ask themselves whether the defendant 'exercised the degree of self-control *to be expected of someone in his situation*' (emphasis added): see Lord Slynn of Hadley, at page 155. Lord Hoffmann expressed the view, at page 163, that the effect of the change in the law made by section 3 of the Homicide Act was that in future the jury 'were to determine not merely whether the behaviour of the accused complied with some legal standard but could determine for themselves what the standard in the particular case should be'. Lord Hoffmann continued, at page 173:

> The law expects people to exercise control over their emotions. A tendency to violent rages or childish tantrums is a defect in character rather than an excuse. The jury must think that the circumstances were such as to make the loss of self-control sufficiently excusable to reduce the gravity of the offence from murder to manslaughter. This is entirely a question for the jury. In deciding what should count as a sufficient excuse, they have to apply what they consider to be appropriate standards of behaviour; on the one hand

making allowance for human nature and the power of the emotions but, on the other hand, not allowing someone to rely upon his own violent disposition.

21. Lord Clyde, at page 179, expressed the expected standard of self-control in these terms:

the standard of reasonableness in this context should refer to a person exercising the ordinary power of self-control over his passions *which someone in his position is able to exercise* and is expected by society to exercise. By position I mean to include all the characteristics which the particular individual possesses and which may in the circumstances bear on his power of control other than those influences which have been self-induced (emphasis added).

22. This majority view, if their Lordships may respectfully say so, is one model which could be adopted in framing a law relating to provocation. But their Lordships consider there is one compelling, overriding reason why this view cannot be regarded as an accurate statement of English law. It is this. The law of homicide is a highly sensitive and highly controversial area of the criminal law. In 1957 Parliament altered the common law relating to provocation and declared what the law on this subject should thenceforth be. In these circumstances it is not open to judges now to change ('develop') the common law and thereby depart from the law as declared by Parliament. However much the contrary is asserted, the majority view does represent a departure from the law as declared in section 3 of the Homicide Act 1957. It involves a significant relaxation of the uniform, objective standard adopted by Parliament. Under the statute the sufficiency of the provocation ('whether the provocation was enough to make a reasonable man do as [the defendant] did') is to be judged by one standard, not a standard which varies from defendant to defendant. Whether the provocative act or words and the defendant's response met the 'ordinary person' standard prescribed by the statute is the question the jury must consider, not the altogether looser question of whether, having regard to all the circumstances, the jury consider the loss of self-control was sufficiently excusable. The statute does not leave each jury free to set whatever standard they consider appropriate in the circumstances by which to judge whether the defendant's conduct is 'excusable'.

23. On this short ground their Lordships, respectfully but firmly, consider the majority view expressed in the Morgan Smith case is erroneous.

Points arising

24. Their Lordships mention some ancillary points. The first is relevant to the facts in the present case. It concerns application of the principles discussed above in circumstances where the defendant acted under the influence of alcohol or drugs and, therefore, at a time when his level of self-control may have been reduced. If the defendant was taunted on account of his intoxication, that may be a relevant matter for the jury to take into account when assessing the gravity of the taunt to the defendant. But the defendant's intoxicated state is not a matter to be taken into account by the jury when considering whether the defendant exercised ordinary self-control. The position is the same, so far as provocation is concerned, if the defendant's addiction to alcohol has reached the stage that he is suffering from the disease of alcoholism.

25. The second point their Lordships wish to mention concerns the three examples given by Lord Steyn in his dissenting opinion in *Luc Thiet Thuan v The Queen* [1997] AC 131, 149. Lord Steyn instanced cases of women who are more prone to lose their self-control because they are suffering from postnatal depression, or 'battered woman syndrome', or a personality disorder. Lord

Steyn suggested that, on the majority view of the law expressed in that case, in those three instances the judge would have to direct the jury that on the defence of provocation the evidence of the woman's condition was admissible on the 'first and subjective inquiry' but not on the 'second and objective inquiry'. Their Lordships respectfully differ. This is not wholly correct. As explained above, the evidence of the woman's condition may be relevant on two issues: whether she lost her self-control, and the gravity of the provocation for her. The jury will then decide whether in their opinion, having regard to the actual provocation and their view of its gravity for the defendant, a woman of her age having ordinary power of self-control might have done what the defendant did. More importantly, in each of these three cases the defendant will in principle have available to her the defence of diminished responsibility. The potential availability of this defence in these cases underlines the importance of not viewing the defence of provocation in isolation from the defence of diminished responsibility. These two defences must be read together to obtain an overall, balanced view of the law in this field.

26. Next, in recent years much play has been made of the 'mental gymnastics' required of jurors in having regard to a defendant's 'characteristics' for one purpose of the law of provocation but not another. Their Lordships consider that any difficulties in this regard have been exaggerated. The question is largely one of presentation. It will be noted that their Lordships have eschewed use of the expression 'characteristics', accompanied as that expression now is with much confusing baggage. The better approach is summarised by Lord Hobhouse of Woodborough in the *Morgan Smith* case at page 205C-H.

27. The final point is this. In expressing their conclusion above their Lordships are not to be taken as accepting that the present state of the law is satisfactory. It is not. The widely held view is that the law relating to provocation is flawed to an extent beyond reform by the courts: see the Law Commission Report *Partial Defences to Murder* (Law Com No 290) (2004 Cm 6301), para 2.10. Their Lordships share this view. But the law on provocation cannot be reformulated in isolation from a review of the law of homicide as a whole. In October 2004 the Home Secretary announced the government's intention to review the law of murder. Given the importance of this area of the criminal law it is imperative that a review, of all aspects of the law of murder, should be undertaken as soon as possible.

Note that Lords Bingham, Hoffmann and Carswell delivered dissenting judgments

 COMMENTS AND QUESTIONS

1   *AG for Jersey v Holley* was followed by the Court of Appeal in *R v Mohammed* [2005] EWCA 1880, and *R v James: R v Karimi* [2006] EWCA 14. In the latter case Lord Phillips acknowledged that normally the Court of Appeal would have regarded itself as bound by a decision of the House of Lords (i.e. *R v Morgan Smith*) rather than the Privy Council (i.e. *AG for Jersey v Holley*). Looked at pragmatically, bearing in mind that the majority in *Holley* had represented half of the Appellate Committee of the House of Lords, it was likely that any appeal to the House of Lords would result in the approach in *Holley* being endorsed. The Court of Appeal refused permission to appeal to the House of Lords, but certified that points of law of general public importance were involved in the decision, namely (i) whether an opinion of the Judicial Board of the Privy Council could take precedence over an existing opinion of the Judicial

Committee of the House of Lords, and if so, in what circumstances; and (ii) whether the majority opinion in *Holley* was to be preferred to the majority decision in *Morgan Smith*. See further *R v Grigson* [2006] All ER (D) 99.

4.6.4.6 Reforming the defence of provocation

The Law Commission's Report (Law Com No 304) *Murder, Manslaughter And Infanticide* described the partial defence of provocation as a 'confusing mixture of judge-made law and legislative provision' plagued by uncertainties regarding its scope that the courts appeared to be unable to resolve. Against this backdrop the Report proposes a return to the '*Camplin*' approach to provocation, but with refinements relating to the role of the judge in leaving the defence to the jury, the availability of the defence where the provocation is incited by the defendant, and the extension of the defence to situations where the defendant overreacts to a fear of serious violence. If put into effect, these reforms would recreate a clear distinction between the defences of provocation and diminished responsibility, as originally intended by Parliament in enacting the Homicide Act 1957.

THE SUBSTANCE OF THE DEFENCE

5.11 In our review of the defence of provocation in 2004, we concluded that the circumstances in which it should in future be available ought to be changed [see *Partial Defences to Murder* (2004) Law Com No 290] . . . Our conclusions were reached after widespread and detailed consultation. We see no compelling reason to depart from them in substance, although we will indicate below where our conclusions remain controversial and, therefore, where there is an issue that could profitably be taken further in the next stage of the review. We are recommending that the defence be reformed as follows:

(1) Unlawful homicide that would otherwise be first degree murder should instead be second degree murder if:

   (a) the defendant acted in response to:

   (i) gross provocation (meaning words or conduct or a combination of words and conduct) which caused the defendant to have a justifiable sense of being seriously wronged; or

   (ii) fear of serious violence towards the defendant or another; or

   (iii) a combination of both (i) and (ii); and

   (b) a person of the defendant's age and of ordinary temperament, i.e. ordinary tolerance and self-restraint, in the circumstances of the defendant might have reacted in the same or in a similar way.

(2) In deciding whether a person of the defendant's age and of ordinary temperament, i.e. ordinary tolerance and self-restraint, in the circumstances of the defendant might have reacted in the same or in a similar way, the court should take into account the defendant's age and all the circumstances of the defendant other than matters whose only relevance to the defendant's conduct is that they bear simply on his or her general capacity for self-control.

(3) The partial defence should not apply where:

   (a) the provocation was incited by the defendant for the purpose of providing an excuse to use violence; or

   (b) the defendant acted in considered desire for revenge.

(4) A person should not be treated as having acted in considered desire for revenge if he or she acted in fear of serious violence, merely because he or she was also angry towards the deceased for the conduct which engendered that fear.

(5) A judge should not be required to leave the defence to the jury unless there is evidence on which a reasonable jury, properly directed, could conclude that it might apply.

. . .

The unnecessary and undesirable loss of self-control requirement

5.17 For 250 years or more, the law took the uncomplicated view that the defence of provocation could be pleaded whenever D was provoked into a towering rage or temper and killed before the rage or temper subsided. In the nineteenth century, this subjective requirement was turned into a requirement that D 'lost self-control' at the time of the killing. Judges have since struggled to interpret and apply this notion as a description of the necessary state of mind. It remains unclear to what extent a delay between the provocation and the loss of self-control will undermine a provocation plea.

5.18 In addition, the requirement of a loss of self-control has been widely criticised as privileging men's typical reactions to provocation over women's typical reactions. Women's reactions to provocation are less likely to involve a 'loss of self-control', as such, and more likely to be comprised of a combination of anger, fear, frustration and a sense of desperation. This can make it difficult or impossible for women to satisfy the loss of self-control requirement, even where they otherwise deserve at least a partial defence.

5.19 This is why in our previous report and in the CP, we took the view that a positive requirement of loss of self-control was unnecessary and undesirable. Our current recommendations have not sought to resurrect it.

. . .

Uncertainty over the 'reasonable person' requirement

5.33 At present a provocation plea cannot succeed unless the jury decide that a reasonable person might have responded to the provocation in question by doing as D did, namely losing self-control and killing. We set out above, in paragraph 5.11, 1(b) and 2, our recommendation for the way in which this 'reasonable person requirement' should be understood. We believe the law needs clarification on this point for the following reasons.

5.34 In a series of cases in recent years, the Court of Appeal, the House of Lords, and the Privy Council, have disagreed over how broadly or narrowly to construe the reasonable person requirement. The result has been uncertainty over its scope and nature, although in no case has the justification for having the restriction in some form been doubted. In the Privy Council case of *Attorney-General for Jersey v Holley* [1995] UKPC 23, [2005] 2 AC 580, departing from an approach to the reasonable person requirement adopted by the House of Lords only four years previously, [*Smith (Morgan)* [2001] AC 146] Lord Nicholls said:

> In expressing their conclusion . . . their Lordships are not to be taken as accepting that the present state of the law is satisfactory. It is not. The widely held view is that the law relating to provocation is flawed to an extent beyond reform by the courts . . . Their Lordships share this view. But the law on provocation cannot be reformulated in isolation from a review of the law of homicide as a whole [[2005] 2 AC 580, 594 to 595].

5.35 Disagreement in the courts has focused on the extent to which D's own characteristics, or other factors, can, or must, be taken into account in judging how the reasonable person might have responded to the provocation.

5.36 One key question in making that judgment is 'how gravely provocative really was the provocation'? It is obvious that D's own characteristics must be relevant to this question. To give a simple example, D's own height would be relevant in assessing the gravity of the provocation constituted by an accusation that he or she was 'a midget'. The courts have not encountered significant difficulties in recent years in deciding how such characteristics or factors affecting the gravity of provocation should be dealt with in law. The jury is obliged to take such characteristics into account.

5.37 More controversial has been the question whether the jury should be required, or permitted, to take into account individual characteristics of D (or other factors) liable to affect the level of self-control that he or she can be expected to show in the face of any provocation. It may be, for example, that a drunken D, an immature D or a mentally deficient D, is unable to exercise the same level of self-control, in the face of provocation generally, as a sober adult with normal mental capacities. The courts have disagreed over whether the jury should be required or permitted to take such factors into account.

5.38 We will not retrace the history of the courts' attempts to introduce clarity to the law on this question. In our view, the function of the reasonable person requirement is to test D's own reaction against the standards of someone of his or her age possessed of an ordinary temperament: someone who is neither intolerant nor lacking in a reasonable measure of self-restraint when facing provocation. Unless the jury concludes that D's reaction might have been that of such a person, the defence ought to fail, even if D only killed as a result of a provoked and momentary loss of temper.

5.39 We are reluctant to speculate on how the courts would interpret the provisions in 1(b) and (2) in paragraph 5.11 above. Still less would we wish to insist that they interpret them in a given way. None the less, the following examples may provide some guidance on the kinds of distinctions we think that it would be helpful to draw.

5.40 Our provisions impose a duty on the judge to instruct the jury to ignore factors that affect D's general capacity to exercise self-control. Alcoholism, for example, or another mental deficiency or disorder that is liable to affect temper and tolerance are obvious examples. A person who has killed because his or her capacity for self-control was reduced by such a characteristic must look to the defence of diminished responsibility for a partial defence, because such characteristics constitute an abnormality of mental functioning, unlike, for example, D's age.

5.41 Abnormal states of mind, such as intoxication or irritability, should also be left out, as should other factors that affect a general capacity to exercise adequate self-control, like a claim that D is 'more jealous or obsessive than most'. This approach to the general capacity to exercise adequate self-control will produce some hard cases. Examples might be ones in which, at the time of the provoked killing, D's general capacity for self-control was temporarily impaired by the effect of taking prescribed medicine, by having suffered a stroke, by involuntary intoxication, by an allergic reaction of some kind or by a bang on the head.

5.42 In such cases, the individual might well be accurately described in general terms as someone with adequate powers of self-restraint. It is just that their reaction could (albeit for good reason) not be expected to be the reaction of such a person in the particular circumstances. We believe that if their reaction was not one that might have been the reaction of a person exercising ordinary powers of self-restraint in the particular circumstances, that very fact means the provocation defence must fail. The fact that the individual in question could, putting on one side their reaction in the circumstances, be described as someone with adequate powers of self-restraint is quite irrelevant to the provocation plea. They must instead look to diminished responsibility for a defence. As Professor Gardner expresses the point:

> [T]he question, for excusatory purposes, is obviously not whether the person claiming the excuse lived up to expectations in the predictive sense of being true to form . . . The question is whether that person lived up to expectations in a *normative* sense . . . In the face of . . . taunts, did this person exhibit as much self-restraint as we have a right to demand of someone in her situation? The character standards which are relevant to these and other excuses are not the standards of our own characters, nor even the standards of most people's characters, but rather the standards to which our characters should, minimally, conform . . . those standards cannot be capped according to the capacities (be they past, present or even future) of the person to whom the excuse is supposed to apply. For, such incapacity, far from militating against unfitness [for playing the role of someone with adequate powers of self-control], is a mode of unfitness in its own right. [John Gardner, 'The Gist of Excuses' (1998) 1 Buffalo Criminal Law Review 575, 579 to 587 (Gardner's emphasis).]

5.43 By way of contrast, a low IQ could be taken into account as part of the circumstances of D (see 1(b) in paragraph 5.11 above) if it meant, for example, that D misinterpreted a provocation, thinking it to be more grave than a person of higher intelligence might have done. To give a different example, the fact that D was dumb and thus unable to respond verbally, is a factor that might legitimately be taken into account when considering D's reaction to a particular provocation given on a particular occasion. In each example, the characteristic is not being used as evidence that the D lacked a general capacity to exercise adequate self-control.

5.44 By way of contrast, some of the evidence given by a psychiatrist in Roberts would not be relevant to the provocation plea, under our recommendations. This was evidence that 'irrational violence was to be expected from some immature prelingually deaf persons when emotionally disturbed'. This is evidence relevant to a plea of diminished responsibility, rather than to a plea of provocation, because it is evidence of an impaired general capacity for self-control.

5.45 In many instances, the circumstances liable quite properly to influence the jury in D's favour will bear on how 'gross' the provocation was, or on how justifiable it was for D to feel seriously wronged (see 1(a)(i) in paragraph 5.11 above). An example is the cumulative effect of repeated provocations given, quite possibly over many years, in circumstances where it may also have been impossible for D to escape the provocation's effects. There is usually no theoretical difficulty about taking such background factors into account because they do not necessarily suggest that D is someone with a reduced general capacity to exercise self-control. A classic example would be the intimidated spouse who has been subject to abuse, the cumulative effect of which has become intolerable over the years.

5.46 This area of law will always remain difficult. As we indicated in the CP, however, a trial judge is under a duty to explain to the jury the full context in which a provoked killing has taken place, and the form of his or her direction ought to be discussed in advance with prosecution and defence advocates. These safeguards should go some way towards minimising the chance of misdirections, and hence appeals.

A NEW BASIS FOR THE DEFENCE: FEAR OF SERIOUS VIOLENCE

5.48 In 1(a)(ii) we recommend that:

> the partial defence of provocation should be expanded to encompass cases in which the defendant overreacted to a fear of serious violence.

5.49 Historically, the common law treated as provocation (sufficient to reduce murder to manslaughter) an overreaction to illegal conduct, such as violence towards or (threatened) false imprisonment of the accused. This line of cases lost its authority when the 'loss of self-control' and 'reasonable person' requirements became established. As we have said, the provocation defence is currently available only when there is evidence that D was provoked to lose his or her self-control. The defence is concerned with angry, spur-of-the-moment reactions to provocation. It is not concerned with reactions prompted by fear, unaccompanied by a loss of self-control, even if the fear in question was that the victim would have inflicted serious violence on D if the victim had not been killed.

. . .

5.50 . . . Here are two examples where the law is currently deficient:

> Example 1: D and V live together, but their relationship is a violent one. V frequently hits D when he (V) comes home drunk. One night, when V comes home drunk and threatens to beat D yet again, she goes to the kitchen, fetches a knife, and stabs V in the chest while he is off his guard. V dies.

> Example 2: D is an armed police officer called to a house where a neighbour has said there is a man (V) with what looked like a gun. When the officer enters the house, V appears to have something in his hand. D demands that V show him what is in his hand but V does not respond. D shoots V and V dies. It turns out that V had a small metal bar in his hand. V may not have heard what D said because he (V) suffered from deafness.

5.51 In both examples, assuming he or she cannot plead diminished responsibility, D has only two effective choices under the existing law if he or she admits having acted with the fault element for murder. D can plead self-defence, a justificatory plea that, if successful, will end in complete acquittal. Alternatively, D can seek a manslaughter verdict by pleading provocation.

5.52 To succeed in a plea of self-defence, D must make a case that what he or she did was within the bounds of reasonableness, as a means of averting a threat posed by V. In both examples it is possible, given the circumstances, that a jury will accept this. It is also quite possible, however, that the prosecution will persuade the jury in each case that acting with intent to kill or do serious harm was not within the bounds of reasonableness as a response to the threat posed by V.

5.53 Under the present law, if D's killing of V is regarded as an overreaction in self-defence, he or she must be convicted of murder unless he or she can succeed in a plea of provocation (with the result that the offence is reduced to manslaughter). In example 1, D would be required to frame the partial defence in terms of the provocation constituted by V's threat, in the context of V's history of violence. In example 2, the provocation would have to be framed in terms of V's failure to respond to D's request, coupled with the fact that V is holding what D believes to be a gun. In both examples, that is an artificial way to analyse the basis for a partial defence. Further, D will in both examples have to show that the provocation caused him or her to lose self-control at the time of the killing. It is not enough that D was frightened, but still in control of himself or herself.

5.54 In some circumstances, cases on facts such as those in Examples 1 and 2 should end in a first degree murder verdict. In our view, however, a rational approach to reaching the right verdict is currently hampered by arbitrariness and unfairness in the way that the provocation defence is structured. In particular, D should not be prejudiced because he or she overreacted in fear or panic, instead of over-reacting due to an angry loss of self-control.

5.55 Consequently, we are recommending that the provocation defence should be available where D killed in response to a fear of serious violence. D will be allowed to say that the effect of the fear of the threat, or of the fear of the threat coupled with the impact of the gross provocation received, was such that, in the circumstances, someone of D's age and of an ordinary temperament might have reacted in the same or in a similar way. The frequently close relationship between anger and fear in someone's reaction makes us confident that it is right to link these elements together in a single partial defence of provocation.

4.7 INVOLUNTARY MANSLAUGHTER: UNLAWFUL ACT MANSLAUGHTER

Where a defendant is proved to have caused death but is not shown to have had the intention to kill or to cause grievous bodily harm, the jury will have to consider whether or not he can be convicted of involuntary manslaughter. At common law involuntary manslaughter charges will normally be formed on one of two bases:

- Unlawful act, or constructive, manslaughter;
- Killing by gross negligence.

The elements of killing by gross negligence are considered at 4.8, below. In order to prove unlawful act manslaughter, the prosecution will have to establish that D committed:

- A positive act – an omission will not suffice;
- Which was also a criminal act – a tortuous act will not suffice;
- Which was also dangerous;
- That D had the necessary *mens rea* for the unlawful act.

4.7.1 THE NEED FOR A POSITIVE CRIMINAL ACT

R v Lowe [1973] QB 702 (CA)

Phillimore LJ:

Robert Lowe appeals against his conviction at Nottingham Crown Court on 25 July 1972 . . . [H]e was convicted on count 2 of the indictment of cruelty to a child by wilfully neglecting it so as to cause unnecessary suffering or injury to health contrary to the provisions of s 1(1) of the Children and Young Persons Act 1933. He was also convicted on count 1 of manslaughter of the child on the grounds that his cruelty alleged under count 2 caused its death . . .

The trial judge . . . directed the jury that if they found the appellant guilty of the second count they must, as a matter of law, find him guilty of the first, namely of manslaughter. Having found him guilty of the second count they also found him guilty of the first and made it clear that they did so solely as a result of the direction by the trial judge; in other words, they did not find the appellant guilty of reckless conduct resulting in the child's death.

. . . This court feels that there is something inherently unattractive in a theory of constructive manslaughter. It seems strange that an omission which is wilful solely in the sense that it is not inadvertent, the consequences of which are not in fact foreseen by the person who is neglectful should, if death results, automatically give rise to an indeterminate sentence instead of the maximum of two years which would otherwise be the limit imposed.

We think there is a clear distinction between an act of omission and an act of commission likely to cause harm. Whatever may be the position in regard to the latter it does not follow that the same is true of the former. In other words if I strike a child in a manner likely to cause harm it is right that if the child dies I may be charged with manslaughter. If, however, I omit to do something with the result that it suffers injury to health which results in its death, we think that a charge of manslaughter should not be an inevitable consequence, even if the omission is deliberate.

4.7.2 THE POSITIVE ACT MUST BE A CRIME

R v Dias [2002] Crim LR 490

Dias prepared a syringe containing a heroin solution. Escott, the deceased, injected himself with the solution and died shortly afterwards from the resulting overdose. Following Dias' conviction for unlawful act manslaughter, he appealed on the ground that, as the self-injection by the deceased had not been an unlawful act, Dias had not committed an unlawful act in encouraging the deceased to inject himself. The trial judge granted a certificate in the following terms: 'Was I correct as a matter of law to direct the jury that it is unlawful for a man to inject heroin into himself?'

Keene LJ:
Although there were several possible bases relied on by the Crown for the manslaughter charge, the possibilities were narrowed down by the time the matter was left to the jury . . . The Crown had . . . relied on s 23 of the Offences against the Person Act 1861 which insofar as material provides:

Whosoever shall unlawfully and maliciously administer to, or cause to be administered to or taken by any other person any poison, or other destructive or noxious thing, so as thereby to endanger the life of such person . . . shall be guilty of an offence . . .

The argument was that if the appellant's actions came within the terms of that section then they were unlawful and would support a verdict of unlawful and dangerous act manslaughter . . . The direction actually given to the jury was in the following terms:

... manslaughter, is proved in this particular case if the prosecution satisfy you so that you are sure that the defendant assisted and deliberately encouraged Mr Escott to take the heroin.

... That formulation is appropriate where someone is charged with aiding and abetting an offence. It would render him liable as the secondary party in circumstances where he does not cause the *actus reus* because the voluntary act of another intervenes.

... The jury were told that there was no dispute that the heroin in the syringe was a cause of death. The direction given by the judge, which we have just quoted, was the result of a ruling made by him after extensive legal argument. He ruled that following the decision in *R v Kennedy* [1999] Crim LR 65, the self-injection by Escott of the heroin was itself an unlawful act. It followed that aiding and abetting such an offence would make the appellant criminally liable as a secondary party for that unlawful act which in turn had caused the death of Escott.

It will be observed that it was not contended that the manslaughter charge could properly be based merely on the supply of the heroin to Escott ... We return to the question whether the judge was correct to rule that the self-injection by Escott with heroin was an unlawful act. In this context 'unlawful' means that the act has to be a criminal offence: see *Franklin* (1883) 15 Cox CC 163, and *Lamb* [1967] 2 QB 981 ... On behalf of the appellant Mr Rumfitt QC relies on the decision of this court in *R v Cato* [1976] 1 All ER 260, (1976) 62 Cr App Rep 41. That was a case where the appellant Cato had injected the deceased with morphine with his consent, but bringing about his death. The court upheld the conviction for manslaughter by an unlawful and dangerous act because there was an offence committed by the appellant under s 23 of the 1861 Act, namely administering a noxious thing. That was a case where the appellant had injected the deceased, not one of self-injection by the deceased. Mr Rumfitt relies on a passage at p 47 of the latter report where the court in its judgment given by Lord Widgery CJ said this:

> Of course, on the first approach to manslaughter in this case it was necessary for the prosecution to prove that Farmer had been killed in the course of an unlawful act. Strangely enough, or it may seem strange to most of us, although the possession or supply of heroin is an offence, it is not an offence to take it ...

That, it is submitted, is clearly right. The possession or the supply of heroin is made an offence under the Misuse of Drugs Act 1971, but nowhere does that statute make it an offence to inject oneself with drugs.

It is sought on behalf of the appellant to distinguish the case of *Kennedy* [1999] Crim LR 65 relied upon by the trial judge. The facts of that case were very similar to those of the present appeal. Kennedy had heated heroin and water in a teaspoon, put some of it into a syringe and handed the syringe to the deceased in return for money. The deceased immediately injected it into his own arm. He died as a result. In upholding the conviction for manslaughter, the court relied upon another passage in *Cato* [1976] 1 All ER 260, (1976) 62 Cr App Rep 41, where it had been said at p 47 of the latter report that, quite apart from the appellant's act being unlawful under s 23:

> We think that there would have been an unlawful act here and we think the unlawful act would be described as injecting the deceased Farmer with a mixture of heroin and water which at the time of the injection and for the purposes of the injection the accused had unlawfully taken into his possession.

In *Kennedy* [1999] Crim LR 65 Waller LJ, giving the judgment of the court, said at p 6 of the transcript:

. . . the injection of the heroin into himself by Bosque [the victim] was itself an unlawful act, and if the appellant assisted in and wilfully encouraged that unlawful conduct, he would himself be acting unlawfully.

It is contended by Mr Rumfitt that the court in *Kennedy* [1999] Crim LR 65 misinterpreted *Cato* [1976] 1 All ER 260, (1976) 62 Cr App Rep 41. It is said that the injection was unlawful in *Cato* because administering a drug to another would be contrary to s 23. There is, emphasised Mr Rumfitt, no offence of injecting heroin into oneself; consequently, aiding and abetting the self-administration of heroin is not unlawful. So far as s 23 is concerned, and its reference to 'administering a noxious substance or causing such a matter to be taken', it is emphasised that the judge did not leave any issue to the jury on the basis of s 23. It is argued that it cannot be said that the actions of the appellant caused the heroin to be taken by Escott because there was here an intervening act of Mr Escott. The trial judge seems to have accepted that. That is why he did not leave to the jury the issue of whether the acts on the part of the appellant had caused Escott's death. Mr Rumfitt submits that there is a line to be drawn, and it is to be drawn where the voluntary act of the deceased intervenes.

For the prosecution Mr Coker QC contends that there is no conflict between *Cato* [1976] 1 All ER 260, (1976) 62 Cr App Rep 41 and *Kennedy* and that the latter was rightly decided. However, he does not seek to argue that self-injection with heroin is of itself an unlawful act. In his words the prosecution 'is not happy' with the judge's conclusion to that effect. Nonetheless, it is submitted that the conviction can be upheld, albeit on a somewhat different basis. It is argued that all the ingredients of manslaughter were present in the case with which we are dealing; that the unlawful act was the supply of the heroin; and that that was a dangerous act because of the likelihood that Escott would take it to his ill-effect.

. . . It is argued that, if the unlawful act is the supply and the handing of the mixture in a syringe to the victim, one can find manslaughter properly based on the facts of the case such as the present. In *Kennedy* [1999] Crim LR 65 the jury had found that there was an unlawful supply of drugs and that that, plus the encouragement given by Kennedy, caused the death of the victim. That was a dangerous act because the encouragement carried with it the risk of harm. In the present case it is suggested that the jury's findings that the appellant's acts assisted and encouraged Escott must be sufficient to show causation.

We begin with the authorities which have been cited to us. The earliest in time, *Cato* [1976] 1 All ER 260, (1976) 62 Cr App Rep 41, undoubtedly arrived at the right result since to inject someone with heroin and water would normally be an offence under s 23 of the 1861 Act. That was the basis of the decision, and both the passages relied on (one by each side) from p 47 of the report were strictly *obiter*. The case was in any event concerned with the injection by one person of another with heroin and water, not with self-injection. The statement that injecting the deceased with that mixture was an unlawful act, irrespective of s 23, is not explained at any length. It may be that it was based on the fact that the appellant was thereby supplying heroin to the deceased . . .

In *Dalby* [1982] 1 All ER 916 . . . the appellant had supplied the deceased with a class A drug (Diconal) in tablet form and both had then injected themselves intravenously. It was not contended that the act of self-injection was unlawful. The supply of the tablets clearly was, and the case turned on the issue of causation. But the end result was that the conviction for manslaughter was quashed.

The facts of *Kennedy* [1999] Crim LR 65 have already been set out earlier in this judgment. However, it is not easy to see on what basis the court concluded that the act of self-injection was unlawful because there is no real elaboration of this point. It is not surprising that the Crown in this present appeal finds it difficult to uphold that particular sentence in the report . . . If Kennedy is rightly decided on this aspect, then it would seem that *Dalby* [1982] 1 All ER 916, (1982) 74 Cr App Rep 348 should have had a different result since on the facts there seems to have been a comparable degree of assistance and encouragement by the appellant in the latter case to that which took place in Kennedy. There is no offence under the Misuse of Drugs Act 1971, or other statute, or at common law, of injecting oneself with a prohibited drug.

There is the offence of possession of such a drug, and that offence was committed by Escott, the deceased. We have considered, therefore, whether that renders the act of injection unlawful for these purposes, but we find it difficult to see that it can do so. The causative act (the act causing death) was essentially the injection of the heroin rather than the possession of it. Self-injection undoubtedly requires unlawful possession in a case such as this, but it is not in itself a separate offence. No one could be charged with injecting himself with heroin, only with the possession of it. The deceased was in possession of the heroin before he injected it and also after he had injected it. Such possession amounted to an offence, but the act of injecting was not itself part of the offence. It was merely made possible by the unlawful possession of the heroin.

It seems therefore to this court that the dictum of Lord Widgery CJ in *Cato* . . . namely that it is not an offence to take heroin, was soundly based. To inject another person with heroin, as in *Cato*, is likely to be unlawful, not merely because of s 23 but also because it would amount to a supply of a prohibited drug. But that is not this case.

There is a further problem about the basis of the present conviction, given the direction by the trial judge. The case was not left to the jury on the footing that the appellant might have caused the death of Escott, and that is perhaps understandable since the act of self-injection was seen by the judge as a voluntary act of an adult not labouring under any mistake as to what he was doing. The judge seems to have taken the view that the chain of causation would have been broken by Escott's own action. It follows from that that the appellant could only have been guilty of manslaughter as a secondary party and not as a principal. But in that case who is the principal guilty of manslaughter? As there is no offence of self-manslaughter, it is difficult to see how the appellant could be guilty of that offence as a secondary party because of his encouragement or assistance to Escott over the injection of the drug . . . this conviction cannot be regarded as safe and it follows that it will be quashed. This appeal is allowed.

 COMMENTS AND QUESTIONS

1   In *R v Rogers* [2003] 1 WLR 1374, the Court of Appeal held that applying a tourniquet to the deceased's arm so that the deceased could raise a vein amounted to an unlawful act on the part of the appellant, thus justifying his conviction for unlawful act manslaughter where the deceased died from a self-injected overdose of heroin. Rose LJ expressed the view that it was artificial and unreal to separate the application of the tourniquet from the injection; thus by applying the tourniquet, the appellant had played a part in the mechanics of the injection that caused death. How can *R v Rogers* be reconciled with *R v Dias*? Does the application of the tourniquet amount to 'administration' of the heroin by the defendant? Assisting self-administration cannot be an unlawful act, as the self-administration itself is not unlawful.

2   Following the decision in *R v Dalby* [1982] 1 WLR 621, in particular the *obiter* statement from

Waller LJ, to the effect that '. . ., where the charge of manslaughter is based on an unlawful and dangerous act, it must be an act directed at the victim and likely to cause immediate injury, however slight . . .', there was some support for the notion that the unlawful act in constructive manslaughter had to be an offence against the person – how else could the unlawful act be directed at the victim? Choosing to rationalise the decision in *R v Dalby* as one where the chain of causation was broken by the voluntary consumption of drugs by the victim, the Court of Appeal in *R v Goodfellow* (1986) 83 Cr App R 23 made clear that there was no requirement in law that the unlawful act should be directed at the victim. In that case it was held that criminal damage would suffice as the basis of an unlawful act manslaughter charge.

3   There is no need for the prosecution to prove that the person at whom the defendant's unlawful act is aimed must also be the person whose death is caused. As Staughton J observed in *R v Mitchell* [1983] QB 741: 'We can see no reason of policy for holding that an act calculated to harm A cannot be manslaughter if it in fact kills B. The criminality of the doer of the act is precisely the same whether it is A or B who dies. A person who throws a stone at A is just as guilty if, instead of hitting and killing A, it hits and kills B.'

4.7.3 THE CRIMINAL ACT MUST BE DANGEROUS

R v Dawson, Nolan and Walmsley (1985) 81 Cr App R 150 (CA)

The three appellants attempted to rob a petrol filling station but fled when the attendant pressed an alarm button. The attendant, who suffered from a heart condition, collapsed and died shortly afterwards. The appellants were convicted of manslaughter. At their trial, medical experts were of the opinion that the attempted robbery was responsible for the attendant's death; but they could not rule out the possibility of a heart attack having occurred before the attempted robbery.

Watkins LJ:
. . . It has, in our experience, been generally understood that the harm referred to in the second element of the offence of manslaughter, namely the unlawful act, must be one that all sober and reasonable people would realise was likely to cause some, albeit not serious, harm, means physical harm . . .
. . . [T]here seems to us to be no sensible reason why shock produced by fright should not come within the definition of harm in this context . . . Shock can produce devastating and lasting effects, for instance upon the nervous system. That is surely harm, i.e. injury to the person. Why not harm in this context?
. . . We shall assume without deciding the point, although we incline to favour the proposition, that harm in the context of manslaughter includes injury to the person through the operation of shock emanating from fright . . .
. . . In our judgment, a proper direction would have been that the requisite harm is caused if the unlawful act so shocks the victim as to cause him physical injury.
. . . [The] test [of knowledge] can only be undertaken upon the basis of the knowledge gained by a sober and reasonable man as though he were present at the scene of and watched the

unlawful act being performed and who knows that, as in the present case, an unloaded replica gun was in use, but that the victim may have thought it was a loaded gun in working order. In other words, he has the same knowledge as the man attempting to rob and no more. It was never suggested that any of these appellants knew that their victim had a bad heart. They knew nothing about him . . .

R v Watson [1989] 1 WLR 684 (CA)

Lord Lane CJ:

. . . The facts of the case, in so far as they are relevant, were as follows. Late at night on 11 December 1986 two men, one of whom was the appellant, broke into the home of a man called Harold Moyler. Mr Moyler was 87 years old and suffered from a serious condition of the heart. He lived alone. The two men first threw a brick through the window and, having made entry to the house, confronted Mr Moyler as he woke up, abused him verbally and then made off without stealing anything.

Mr Moyler died an hour and a half later as the result of a heart attack. The case for the Crown was that the heart attack was a direct consequence of the unlawful actions of the appellant and his colleague . . .

It was accepted that the judge correctly defined the offence of manslaughter as it applied to the circumstances as follows:

> Manslaughter is the offence committed when one person causes the death of another by an act which is unlawful and which is also dangerous, dangerous in the sense that it is an act which all sober and reasonable people would inevitably realise must subject the victim to the risk of some harm resulting whether the defendant realised that or not.

The first point taken on behalf of the appellant is this. When one is deciding whether the sober and reasonable person (the bystander) would realise the risk of some harm resulting to the victim, how much knowledge of the circumstances does one attribute to the bystander? The appellant contends that the unlawful act here was the burglary as charged in the indictment.

The charge was laid under s 9(1)(a) of the Theft Act 1968, the allegation being that the appellant had entered the building as a trespasser with intent to commit theft. Since that offence is committed at the first moment of entry, the bystander's knowledge is confined to that of the defendant at that moment. In the instant case there was no evidence that the appellant, at the moment of entry, knew the age or physical condition of Mr Moyler or even that he lived there alone.

The judge clearly took the view that the jury were entitled to ascribe to the bystander the knowledge which the appellant gained during the whole of his stay in the house and so directed them. Was this a misdirection? In our judgment it was not. The unlawful act in the present circumstances comprised the whole of the burglarious intrusion and did not come to an end upon the appellant's foot crossing the threshold or window sill. That being so, the appellant (and therefore the bystander) during the course of the unlawful act must have become aware of Mr Moyler's frailty and approximate age, and the judge's directions were accordingly correct . . .

COMMENTS AND QUESTIONS

1   What if the burglary in *R v Watson* had taken place in complete darkness – the appellant not being able to see the occupant? How if at all would the direction to the jury on dangerousness have to be altered to reflect this?

2   In *R v Ball* [1989] Crim LR 730, the defendant's conviction for unlawful act manslaughter was upheld where he had fired a gun at the victim believing the cartridges to be blanks. The appellant had admitted mixing up live and blank rounds. The unlawful act was clear, but as to the issue of dangerousness the appellant contended that a reasonable person could also have made the same mistake regarding whether or not he was loading a live or blank cartridge into the gun. The Court of Appeal refused to impute this error to the reasonable sober bystander. The question of whether the act was dangerous was to be judged not by the appellant's appreciation but by that of the sober reasonable man, and it was impossible to impute into his appreciation the mistaken belief that what he was doing was not dangerous because he thought he had a blank cartridge in the chamber. Is this consistent with the notion in *R v Dawson* that the reasonable person sees what the defendant sees and knows what the defendant knows – nothing more nor less?

4.7.4 THE *MENS REA* FOR UNLAWFUL ACT MANSLAUGHTER

Identifying the *mens rea* for unlawful act manslaughter has been hampered by the rather opaque explanations delivered by appeal courts asked to rule upon this issue. There is common consent that the offence requires *mens rea* (although see *R v Andrews*, considered below). What is less clear is exactly what that *mens rea* is.

R v Lamb [1967] 2 QB 981 (CA)

Sachs LJ:

. . . The defendant, Terence Walter Lamb, aged 25, had become possessed of a Smith & Wesson revolver. It was a revolver in the literal old-fashioned sense, having a five-chambered cylinder which rotated clockwise each time the trigger was pulled. The defendant, in jest, with no intention to do any harm, pointed the revolver at the deceased, his best friend, when it had two bullets in the chambers, but neither bullet was in the chamber opposite the barrel. His friend was similarly treating the incident as a joke. The defendant then pulled the trigger and thus killed his friend, still having no intention to fire the revolver. The reason why the pulling of the trigger produced that fatal result was that its pulling rotated the cylinder and so placed a bullet opposite the barrel so that it was struck by the striking pin or hammer.

The defendant's defence was that, as neither bullet was opposite the barrel, he thought they were in such chambers that the striking pin could not hit them; that he was unaware that the pulling of the trigger would bring one bullet into the firing position opposite the barrel; and that the killing was thus an accident. There was not only no dispute that that was what he in fact thought, but the mistake he made was one which three experts agreed was natural for somebody who was not aware of the way the revolver mechanism worked . . .

The defence of accident was, however, in effect withdrawn from the jury by the trial judge . . . [who] made no mention of the word 'accident' in his summing-up nor of the evidence of the experts save that he at one stage directed the jury that their evidence was not relevant . . .

Dealing with manslaughter in the sense of an unlawful act resulting in death his Lordship said:

> . . . The trial judge took the view that the pointing of the revolver and the pulling of the trigger was something which could of itself be unlawful even if there was no attempt to alarm or intent to injure . . .
>
> [Counsel for the Crown] however, had at all times put forward the correct view that for the act to be unlawful it must constitute at least what he then termed 'a technical assault'. In this court moreover he rightly conceded that there was no evidence to go to the jury of any assault of any kind. Nor did he feel able to submit that the acts of the defendant were on any other ground unlawful in the criminal sense of that word. Indeed no such submission could in law be made: if, for instance, the pulling of the trigger had had no effect because the striking mechanism or the ammunition had been defective no offence would have been committed by the defendant.
>
> Another way of putting it is that *mens rea*, being now an essential ingredient in manslaughter (compare *Andrews v DPP* [1937] AC 576 and *R v Church* [1966] 1 QB 59), that could not in the present case be established in relation to the first ground except by proving that element of intent without which there can be no assault.
>
> It is perhaps as well to mention that when using the phrase 'unlawful in the criminal sense of that word' the court has in mind that it is long settled that it is not in point to consider whether an act is unlawful merely from the angle of civil liabilities . . .' [Therefore] the verdict cannot stand . . .

DPP v Newbury and Jones [1977] AC 500 (HL)

Lord Salmon:

My Lords, on 11 October 1974, the train travelling from Pontypridd to Cardiff was approaching a bridge which crossed the railway line. The guard was sitting next to the driver of the train in the front cab. The driver noticed the heads of three boys above the parapet of the bridge. He saw one of the boys push something off the parapet towards the oncoming train. This proved to be part of a paving stone which some workmen had left on the parapet. It came through the glass window of the cab in which the driver and the guard were sitting, struck the guard and killed him. There was ample evidence that just as the train was about to reach the bridge the two appellants, who were each about 15 years of age, were jointly concerned in pushing over the parapet the piece of paving stone which killed the guard. They were jointly charged with manslaughter . . . The point of law certified to be of general public importance is 'can a defendant be properly convicted of manslaughter, when his mind is not affected by drink or drugs, if he did not foresee that his act might cause harm to another?'

The learned trial judge did not direct the jury that they should acquit the appellants unless they were satisfied beyond a reasonable doubt that the appellants had foreseen that they might cause harm to someone by pushing the piece of paving stone off the parapet into the path of the approaching train. In my view the learned trial judge was quite right not to give such a direction to the jury . . . In *R v Larkin* (1942) 29 Cr App R 18, Humphreys J said at 23:

Where the act which a person is engaged in performing is unlawful, then if at the same time it is a dangerous act, that is, an act which is likely to injure another person, and quite inadvertently the doer of the act causes the death of that other person by that act, then he is guilty of manslaughter.

... [T]hat is an admirably clear statement of the law which has been applied many times. It makes it plain (a) that an accused is guilty of manslaughter if it is proved that he intentionally did an act which was unlawful and dangerous and that that act inadvertently caused death and (b) that it is unnecessary to prove that the accused knew that the act was unlawful or dangerous. This is one of the reasons why cases of manslaughter vary so infinitely in their gravity. They may amount to little more than pure inadvertence and sometimes to little less than murder ...

... In judging whether the act was dangerous the test is not did the accused recognise that it was dangerous but would all sober and reasonable people recognise its danger ...

Lord Edmund Davies delivered a concurring speech.

Attorney General's Reference (No 3 of 1994) [1997] 3 All ER 936

Lord Hope

... the accused must be proved to have intended to do what he did, it is not necessary to prove that he knew that his act was unlawful or dangerous. So it must follow that it is unnecessary to prove that he knew that his act was likely to injure the person who died as a result of it. All that need be proved is that he intentionally did what he did ... As Lord Salmon put it in *DPP v Newbury* ... manslaughter is one of those crimes in which only what is called a basic intention need be proved – that is, an intention to do the act which constitutes the crime.

 COMMENTS AND QUESTIONS

1   Do these authorities specify the *mens rea* for unlawful act manslaughter? Does the defendant have to have the actual *mens rea* required for the unlawful act (ie in R v Watson – burglary; in *R v Dawson* – attempted robbery), or is it sufficient, as Lord Hope indicates in *Attorney General's Reference (No 3 of 1994)* [1997] 3 All ER 936 (above), that the defendant '... intended to do what he did ...'?

2   What if the dangerous criminal act is one of strict liability? *R v Andrews* [2003] Crim LR 477 suggests that the *mens rea* requirement for unlawful act manslaughter follows the contours of the underlying offence. In that case the prosecution based its case on the fact that the defendant had committed an offence contrary to s 58(2)(b) of the Medicines Act 1968, in supplying insulin that had been lawfully prescribed for another person. D injected P who died as a result of the injection. The offence under the 1968 Act did not require proof of *mens rea*. In order to reflect the gravity of the offence of manslaughter, should the prosecution have been required to base its case on s 23 or s 24 of the Offences Against the Person Act 1861 (considered at Chapter 5.4)?

4.8 INVOLUNTARY MANSLAUGHTER: KILLING BY GROSS NEGLIGENCE

Whereas unlawful act manslaughter requires proof of a positive act, many instances of killing by gross negligence are characterised by the defendant's failure to discharge the duty of care owed to the deceased – in contrast to unlawful act manslaughter, liability for killing by gross negligence can be based on a failure to act. The essence of this form of manslaughter is that the defendant was engaged in an activity that was, *per se*, lawful. His criminality lies in the fact that he has carried out this activity so negligently – death being the result – that he deserves to incur not only tortuous liability, but also the stigmatisation and punishment that accompanies a conviction for manslaughter. A common factor in killing by gross negligence cases is the existence of the duty of care owed by the defendant to the deceased. Hence many of the early cases involved the death of patients through poor medical treatment. In *R v Bateman* [1925] 94 LJKB 791, where D operated on a woman who died, the Court of Appeal allowed an appeal against a conviction for killing by gross negligence because the trial judge had failed to distinguish between the degree of negligence required for civil liability and that required for manslaughter. Lord Hewart CJ indicated the rationale for this form of manslaughter when he observed that a defendant could only be convicted of the offence if the prosecution could show negligence so gross in that it went beyond a mere matter of compensation between subjects – i.e. was so serious, it could not be left to the civil law to resolve the issue of fault. The purpose of the prosecution, at least in part, was to publicly label the defendant's actions as criminal.

What are the elements of killing by gross negligence?

- Act or omission by D;
- D owed P a duty of care;
- D's breach of duty caused P's death in fact and in law;
- D breached that duty of care in circumstances amounting to gross negligence.

4.8.1 WHEN WILL A DUTY OF CARE ARISE?

R v Wacker [2002] Crim LR 839

Fifty-eight Chinese illegal immigrants died whilst being smuggled from Holland to the United Kingdom concealed in the back of the appellant's lorry. The immigrants had been loaded into a specially adapted partition, hidden from view by a consignment of tomatoes. The container was refrigerated and the deaths resulted from a lack of ventilation. The appellant was convicted, *inter alia*, of 58 offences of gross negligence manslaughter. Part of the appellant's argument had been that the doctrine of *ex turpi causa non oritur actio* applied (i.e. that the law of negligence did not recognise the relationship between those involved in a criminal enterprise as giving rise to a duty of care owed by one participant to another). On this basis he contended that he had not owed the immigrants any duty of care, as they too must have been involved in an illegal enterprise.

Kay LJ:

There are occasions when it is helpful when considering questions of law for the court to take a step back and to look at an issue of law that arises without first turning to, and becoming embroiled in, the technicalities of the law. This is such a case. We venture to suggest that all right minded people would be astonished if the propositions being advanced on behalf of the appellant correctly represented the law of the land. The concept that one person could be responsible for the death of another in circumstances such as these without the criminal law being able to hold him to account for that death even if he had shown not the slightest regard for the welfare and life of the other is one that would be unacceptable in civilised society. Taking this perspective of the case causes one immediately to question whether the whole approach adopted by both counsel and the judge in the court below can be correct, and we must, therefore, examine this matter.

The first question that it is pertinent to ask is why it is that the civil law has introduced the concept of *ex turpi causa*. The answer is clear from the authorities . . . as a matter of public policy the courts will not 'promote or countenance a nefarious object or bargain which it is bound to condemn'.

In other situations, it is clear that the criminal law adopts a different approach to the civil law in this regard. A person who sold a harmless substance to another pretending that it was an unlawful dangerous drug could not be the subject of a successful civil claim by the purchasers for the return of the purchase price. However the criminal law would, arising out of the same transaction, hold that he was guilty of the offence of obtaining property by deception [since replaced by sections 2 to 4 of the Fraud Act 2006]. Many other similar examples readily come to mind.

Why is then, therefore, this distinction between the approach of the civil law and the criminal law? The answer is that the very same public policy that causes the civil courts to refuse the claim points in a quite different direction in considering a criminal offence. The criminal law has as its function the protection of citizens and gives effect to the state's duty to try those who have deprived citizens of their rights of life, limb or property. It may very well step in at the precise moment when civil courts withdraw because of this very different function. The withdrawal of a civil remedy has nothing to do with whether as a matter of public policy the criminal law applies. The criminal law should not be disapplied just because the civil law is disapplied. It has its own public policy aim which may require a different approach to the involvement of the law.

Further the criminal law will not hesitate to act to prevent serious injury or death even when the persons subjected to such injury or death may have consented to or willingly accepted the risk of actual injury or death. By way of illustration, the criminal law makes the assisting another to commit suicide a criminal offence and denies a defence of consent where significant injury is deliberately caused to another in a sexual context (*Brown* [1994] 1 AC 212). The state in such circumstances has an overriding duty to act to prevent such consequences.

Thus looked at as a matter of pure public policy, we can see no justification for concluding that the criminal law should decline to hold a person as criminally responsible for the death of another simply because the two were engaged in some joint unlawful activity at the time or, indeed, because there may have been an element of acceptance of a degree of risk by the victim in order to further the joint unlawful enterprise. Public policy, in our judgment, manifestly points in totally the opposite direction.

The next question that we are bound to ask ourselves is whether in any way we are required by authority to take a different view. The foundation for the contention that *ex turpi causa* is as much a part of the law of manslaughter as it is a part of the law of negligence is the passage from the speech of Lord Mackay in *Adomako* . . . In particular it is Lord Mackay's reference to 'the ordinary principles to negligence'.

37 *Adomako* was a case where an anaesthetist had negligently brought about the death of a patient. It, therefore, involved no element of unlawful activity on the part of either the anaesthetist or the victim. We have no doubt that issues raised in the case we are considering would never have crossed the minds of those deciding that case in the House of Lords. Insofar as Lord Mackay referred to 'ordinary principles of the laws of negligence' we do not accept for one moment that he was intending to decide that the rules relating to *ex turpi causa* were part of those ordinary principles. He was doing no more than holding that in an 'ordinary' case of negligence, the question whether there was a duty of care was to be judged by the same legal criteria as governed whether there was a duty of care in the law of negligence. That was the only issue relevant to that case and to give the passage the more extensive meaning accepted in the court below was in our judgment wrong.

38 The next question which is posed is whether it is right to say in this case that no duty of care can arise because it is impossible or inappropriate to determine the extent of that duty. We do not accept this proposition. If, at the moment when the vent was shut, one of the Chinese had said 'you will make sure that we have enough air to survive', the appellant would have had no difficulty understanding the proposition and clearly by continuing with the unlawful enterprise in the way that he did, he would have been shouldering the duty to take care for their safety in this regard. The question was such an obvious one that it did not need to be posed and we have no difficulty in concluding that in these circumstances the appellant did voluntarily assume the duty of care for the Chinese in this regard. He was aware that no one's actions other than his own could realistically prevent the Chinese from suffocating to death and if he failed to act reasonably in fulfilling this duty to an extent that could be characterised as criminal, he was guilty of manslaughter if death resulted.

39 One further issue merits consideration, namely is it any answer to a charge of manslaughter for a defendant to say 'we were jointly engaged in a criminal enterprise and weighing the risk of injury or death against our joint desire to achieve our unlawful objective, we collectively thought that it was a risk worth taking'. In our judgment it is not. The duty to take care cannot, as a matter of public policy, be permitted to be affected by countervailing demands of the criminal enterprise. Thus, in this case, the fact that keeping the vent shut increased the chances of the Chinese succeeding in entering the United Kingdom without detection was not a factor to be taken into account in deciding whether the appellant had acted reasonably or not . . .

COMMENTS AND QUESTIONS

1   The court in *R v Wacker* rejected a challenge on the point of jurisdiction. The duty of care may have arisen in Holland but it continued as the lorry came within the jurisdiction of the British courts – arguably on a British registered vessel.

2   Does the illegal supplier of controlled drugs owe a duty of care to his client? In *R v Khan* [1998] Crim LR 830, the Court of Appeal declined to rule on whether a drug pusher owed a duty of care to a 15-year-old prostitute, to whom he had supplied a quantity of heroin. The girl

consumed twice the amount that might be consumed by an experienced user of heroin and fell into a coma whilst on the appellant's premises. The appellant then left P alone, and she died shortly afterwards. Could it be said that the appellant had created a reliance relationship given the girl's age and the fact that she was on the appellant's property with his permission? Presumably the extent of the duty of care will depend upon the expertise and autonomy of the victim, as well as the extent of any reliance placed upon the defendant by the deceased.

3 Does the supplier of an unlicensed firearm owe a duty of care to the recipient who turns it on himself and commits suicide?

4 In *R v Singh* [1999] Crim LR 582, the Court of Appeal more readily identified a duty of care where the appellants, a landlord and a gas fitter, had their convictions for killing by gross negligence upheld, following the death of one of the landlord's tenants from carbon monoxide poisoning.

5 In *Lewin v CPS* [2002] EWHC 1049, the court considered whether there ought to have been a prosecution for killing by gross negligence where D left P asleep in a car overnight and P, remaining asleep once in the car during the following day, died from the effects of the heat. Kennedy LJ observed:

> [A duty of care] . . . could only persist in a way which would be relevant to the offence of manslaughter if a reasonable person would have foreseen that by leaving the deceased in the vehicle parked in that position [the deceased] was being exposed to the risk not merely of injury or even of serious injury but of death . . . there was, as it seems to me, no realistic possibility of demonstrating beyond reasonable doubt that a reasonable person in the position of [the appellant] would have foreseen the risk of death.

6 If objective recklessness is no longer a basis for criminal liability – see *R v G* [2003] – can the objective approach to liability for killing by gross negligence be justified? See further *R v Mark* [2004] All ER (D) 35.

7 In *R v Willoughby* [2004] All ER (D) 79 the appellant had set fire to his business premises in order to solve his financial problems. He had spread petrol inside the premises causing a fire and an explosion that caused the death of the victim who had been assisting the appellant. The Court of Appeal rejected the argument that the appellant had owed the victim a duty of care simply because he had been the owner of the premises. The duty arose because the appellant had enlisted the victim's help in carrying out the acts amounting to arson.

4.8.2 WHEN WILL THE NEGLIGENCE ACCOMPANYING A BREACH OF DUTY BE CHARACTERISED AS 'GROSS'?

In *R v Stone and Dobinson* [1977] QB 354 (considered in Chapter 2.5.4), Geoffrey Lane LJ described gross negligence as a form of recklessness. He observed: 'What the Crown has to prove is a breach of that duty in such circumstances that the jury feel convinced that the defendant's conduct can properly be described as reckless. That is to say a reckless disregard of danger to the health and welfare of the infirm person. Mere inadvertence is not enough.

The defendant must be proved to have been indifferent to an obvious risk of injury to health, or actually to have foreseen the risk but to have determined nevertheless to run it.' This raised questions as to whether killing by gross negligence was really a species of reckless manslaughter, and if it was, a further question arose as to what type of recklessness was involved – subjective or objective. Answering these questions was not made any easier by the terminology deployed by Geoffrey Lane LJ – what did he mean by the distinction between inadvertence and indifference?

As more recent authorities (extracted below) illustrate, that debate has become somewhat redundant. Gross negligence is really a fault term that describes the way in which the defendant conducted himself. It can be established without any direct evidence as to the defendant's state of mind, although any such evidence may be considered by the jury in determining whether or not the negligence was gross.

R v Adomako [1994] 3 WLR 288

The defendant was a *locum tenens* anaesthetist employed at a hospital. He was assisting during an operation on a patient for a detached retina. During the operation the tube from the patient's ventilator became detached. By the time D became aware that something had gone wrong the damage caused to the patient had become irreversible and he died. D was convicted of manslaughter following a direction from the trial judge, in terms of gross negligence as the basis for liability rather than recklessness. The Court of Appeal certified that a point of law of general public importance was involved in the decision to dismiss the appeal, namely:

In cases of manslaughter by criminal negligence not involving driving but involving a breach of duty is it a sufficient direction to the jury to adopt the gross negligence test set out by the Court of Appeal in the present case following *R v Bateman* (1925) 19 Cr App R 8 and *Andrews v DPP* [1937] AC 576 . . .?

Lord Mackay of Clashfern LC:

. . . [having referred to *R v Bateman* 19 Cr App R 8, continued] To support an indictment for manslaughter the prosecution must prove the matters necessary to establish civil liability (except pecuniary loss), and, in addition, must satisfy the jury that the negligence or incompetence of the accused went beyond a mere matter of compensation and showed such disregard for the life and safety of others as to amount to a crime against the state and conduct deserving punishment.

Next I turn to *Andrews v DPP* [1973] AC 576 which was a case of manslaughter through dangerous driving of a motor car. In a speech with which all the other members of this House who sat agreed, Lord Atkin said at 581–82:

. . . of all crimes manslaughter appears to afford most difficulties of definition, for it concerns homicide in so many and so varying conditions. From the early days when any homicide involved penalty the law has gradually evolved 'through successive differentiations and integrations' until it recognises murder on the one hand, based mainly, though not exclusively, on an intention to kill, and manslaughter on the other hand, based mainly, though not exclusively, on the absence of intention to kill but with the presence of an

element of 'unlawfulness' which is the elusive factor. In the present case it is only necessary to consider manslaughter from the point of view of an unintentional killing caused by
negligence, that is, the omission of a duty to take care . . .

Lord Atkin then referred to the judgment of Lord Hewart CJ [in *R v Bateman*] from which I have
already quoted and went on at 583:

Here again I think with respect that the expressions used are not, indeed they were probably not intended to be, a precise definition of the crime. I do not myself find the connotations of *mens rea* helpful in distinguishing between degrees of negligence, nor do the ideas
of crime and punishment in themselves carry a jury much further in deciding whether in a
particular case the degree of negligence shown is a crime and deserves punishment. But
the substance of the judgment is most valuable, and in my opinion is correct. In practice it
has generally been adopted by judges in charging juries in all cases of manslaughter by
negligence, whether in driving vehicles or otherwise. The principle to be observed is that
cases of manslaughter in driving motor cars are but instances of a general rule applicable
to all charges of homicide by negligence. Simple lack of care such as will constitute civil
liability is not enough: for purposes of the criminal law there are degrees of negligence: and
a very high degree of negligence is required to be proved before the felony is established.
Probably of all the epithets that can be applied 'reckless' most nearly covers the case. It is
difficult to visualise a case of death caused by reckless driving in the connotation of that
term in ordinary speech which would not justify a conviction for manslaughter: but it is
probably not all-embracing, for 'reckless' suggests an indifference to risk whereas the
accused may have appreciated the risk and intended to avoid it and yet shown such a high
degree of negligence in the means adopted to avoid the risk as would justify a conviction. If
the principle of *Bateman's* case 19 Cr App R 8 is observed it will appear that the law of
manslaughter has not changed by the introduction of motor vehicles on the road. Death
caused by their negligent driving, though unhappily much more frequent, is to be treated
in law as death caused by any other form of negligence: and juries should be directed
accordingly.

In my opinion the law as stated in these two authorities is satisfactory as providing a proper basis
for describing the crime of involuntary manslaughter. Since the decision in *Andrews* was a decision of your Lordships' House, it remains the most authoritative statement of the present law
which I have been able to find . . . On this basis in my opinion the ordinary principles of the law of
negligence apply to ascertain whether or not the defendant has been in breach of a duty of care
towards the victim who has died. If such breach of duty is established the next question is
whether that breach of duty caused the death of the victim. If so, the jury must go on to consider
whether that breach of duty should be characterised as gross negligence and therefore as a
crime. This will depend on the seriousness of the breach of duty committed by the defendant in all
the circumstances in which the defendant was placed when it occurred. The jury will have to
consider whether the extent to which the defendant's conduct departed from the proper standard
of care incumbent upon him, involving as it must have done a risk of death to the patient, was
such that it should be judged criminal.

It is true that to a certain extent this involves an element of circularity, but in this branch of the
law I do not believe that is fatal to its being correct as a test of how far conduct must depart from
accepted standards to be characterised as criminal. This is necessarily a question of degree and

an attempt to specify that degree more closely is I think likely to achieve only a spurious precision. The essence of the matter which is supremely a jury question is whether having regard to the risk of death involved, the conduct of the defendant was so bad in all the circumstances as to amount in their judgment to a criminal act or omission . . .

Attorney General's Reference (No 2 of 1999) [2000] 3 All ER 182

The prosecution arose from a collision which occurred in September 1997, between a high speed train (HST) from Swansea to London Paddington, operated by the defendant company, and a freight train crossing from the down relief line to Southall Yard. Seven passengers died. There was evidence that the various safety warning devices installed to assist the driver had been switched off with the result that the train went through several signals set at red.

The company operating the HST was charged with killing by gross negligence.

Rose LJ:

As a result of *R v Adomako*, Mr Lissack [for the Attorney-General] submitted, gross negligence manslaughter can be proved without the need to inquire into the state of the defendant's mind. This proposition is supported by a passage in *Smith and Hogan's Criminal Law* (7th edn, 1992) pp 90, 91, which culminates in contrasting crimes requiring *mens rea* with crimes of negligence. The *Adomako* test was derived from *R v Bateman* (1925) 19 Cr App R 8, [1925] All ER Rep 45, which was an objective test (see *Criminal Law: Involuntary Manslaughter* (Law Com 135, para 3.32)).

For the defendant Mr Caplan QC, in relation to question (1), submitted that there is a difference between whether *mens rea* must be proved and whether it may be relevant. He accepted that it need not be proved for gross negligence. But, he said, it may be relevant because the *Adomako* test requires the jury, when deciding if the breach is criminal, to consider it in all the circumstances. Furthermore, in *R v Adomako* [1994] 3 All ER 79 at 87, [1995] 1 AC 171 at 187 Lord Mackay LC went on to say that it was perfectly appropriate to use the word 'reckless' in cases of involuntary manslaughter, in its ordinary connotation as in *R v Stone, R v Dobinson* [1977] 2 All ER 341, [1977] QB 354. In *R v Stone, R v Dobinson* Lord Lane CJ said that, where a defendant had undertaken a duty of care for the health and welfare of an infirm person the prosecution had to prove:

> a reckless disregard of danger to the health and welfare of the infirm person. Mere inadvertence is not enough. The defendant must be proved to have been indifferent to an obvious risk of injury to health, or actually to have foreseen the risk but to have determined nevertheless to run it.

On this question, we accept the submissions of both Mr Lissack and Mr Caplan . . . Although there may be cases where the defendant's state of mind is relevant to the jury's consideration when assessing the grossness and criminality of his conduct, evidence of his state of mind is not a prerequisite to a conviction for manslaughter by gross negligence. The *Adomako* test is objective, but a defendant who is reckless as defined in *R v Stone, R v Dobinson* may well be the more readily found to be grossly negligent to a criminal degree.

R v Misra; R v Srivastava [2004] EWCA Crim 2375

The facts are set out at Chapter 2.9.5. The following extracts concern the court's evaluation of the *mens rea* requirement in the offence of killing by gross negligence.

Judge LJ:

[53] Adomako further explained that with involuntary manslaughter, notwithstanding Seymour, recklessness as explained in the Lawrence/Caldwell sense had no application. The use of the word 'reckless' by the trial judge, as part of his exposition of the concept of gross negligence in an appropriate case, was permissible. In the single speech agreed by the other members of the House, as we have already indicated, Lord Mackay approved *Stone and West London Coroner, ex parte Grey* as examples of an acceptable use of the word 'reckless' in its ordinary connotation. In *Stone*, Geoffrey Lane LJ described examples of 'recklessness', and reflected the observations of Lord Atkin in *Andrews* that reckless 'was an appropriate epithet for the very high degree of negligence required before the defendant could be convicted of manslaughter by gross negligence'. Although the word 'reckless' might be deployed in summing-up to the jury, its use simply reflected one way of describing the ingredients of the offence. At the end of his speech Lord Mackay's language was quite unequivocal:

> While therefore I have perhaps said in my view it is perfectly open to a trial judge to use the word 'reckless' if it appears appropriate in the circumstances of a particular case, as indicating the extent to which the defendant's conduct must deviate from that of a proper standard of care, I do not think it right to require that this should be done, and certainly not right that it should incorporate the full detail required in *Lawrence*.

[54] The point of law certified for the decision of the House of Lords was answered:

> In cases of manslaughter by criminal negligence involving a breach of duty, it is a sufficient direction to the jury to adopt the gross negligence tests set out by the Court of Appeal in the present case, following *R v Bateman* 19 Cr App R 8, and *Andrews v Director of Public Prosecutions* [1937] AC 576, and that it is not necessary to refer to the definition of recklessness in *R v Lawrence* [1982] AC 510, although it is perfectly open to the trial judge to use the word 'reckless' in its ordinary meaning as part of his exposition of the law if he deems it appropriate in the circumstances of the particular case.

The result of the appeal was that the continuing existence of the offence of manslaughter by gross negligence was confirmed. The attempt to replace manslaughter by gross negligence with manslaughter by recklessness was rejected.

[55] It is convenient now to address the argument that the decision in *R v G and Another* should lead us to reassess whether gross negligence manslaughter should now be replaced by and confined to reckless manslaughter. As we have shown, precisely this argument by Lord Williams of Mostyn was rejected in *Adomako*. We also note, first, that Parliament has not given effect to possible reforms on this topic discussed by the Law Commission and, second, notwithstanding that *Adomako* was cited in argument in *R v G and Another*, it was not subjected to any reservations or criticisms. Indeed in his speech Lord Bingham of Cornhill emphasised that in *R v G* he was not addressing the meaning of 'reckless' in any other statutory or common law context than s 1(1) and (2) of the Criminal Damage Act 1971. In these circumstances, although we gave leave to

Mr Gledhill [counsel for Misra] to amend his grounds of appeal to enable him to deploy the argument, we reject it.

[56] We can now reflect on Mr Gledhill's associated contention that if recklessness is not a necessary ingredient of this offence, the decision in *Attorney General's Reference (No. 2 of 1999)* [2000] QB 796, [2000] 3 All ER 182 led to the unacceptable conclusion that manslaughter by gross negligence did not require proof of any specific state of mind, and that the defendant's state of mind was irrelevant. In our judgment the submission is based on a narrow reading of the decision that a defendant may properly be convicted of gross negligence manslaughter in the absence of evidence as to his state of mind. However when it is available, such evidence is not irrelevant to the issue of gross negligence. It will often be a critical factor in the decision (see *R (on the application of Rowley) v DPP* [2003] EWHC 693). In *Adomako* itself, Lord Mackay directed attention to 'all' of the circumstances in which the defendant was placed: he did not adopt, or endorse, or attempt to redefine the list of states of mind to which Lord Taylor CJ referred in *Prentice*, which was not in any event 'exhaustive' of possible relevant states of mind. It is therefore clear that the defendant is not to be convicted without fair consideration of all the relevant circumstances in which his breach of duty occurred. In each case, of course, the circumstances are fact-specific.

[57] Mr Gledhill nevertheless contended that even so, the problem of *mens rea* remains. This, he argued was a necessary, but absent ingredient of the offence. We have reflected, of course, that if the defendant intends death or really serious harm, and acts in such a way to cause either, and death results, he would be guilty of murder. If he intends limited injury, and causes death, he would be guilty of manslaughter in any event. We are here concerned with the defendant who does not intend injury, but who in all the contemporaneous circumstances is grossly negligent. As a matter of strict language, '*mens rea*' is concerned with an individual defendant's state of mind. Speaking generally, negligence is concerned with his failure to behave in accordance with the standards required of the reasonable man. Looked at in this way, the two concepts are distinct. However the term '*mens rea*' is also used to describe the ingredient of fault or culpability required before criminal liability for the defendant's actions may be established. In *Sweet v Parsley* [1970] AC 132, [1969] 1 All ER 347, Lord Reid explained that there were occasions when gross negligence provided the 'necessary mental element' for a serious crime. Manslaughter by gross negligence is not an absolute offence. The requirement for gross negligence provides the necessary element of culpability.

COMMENTS AND QUESTIONS

1   Lord Mackay in *R v Adomako* (above) conceded that the definition of gross negligence was necessarily somewhat circular in nature (ie the negligence is gross if it is criminal and vice versa). As to whether this offends the requirement of legal certainty required by Art 7 of the European Convention on Human Rights see further Chapter 1.10.5.

2   Causing death by dangerous driving, contrary to s 1 of the Road Traffic Act 1988 carries the possibility of 14 years' imprisonment and can be committed without direct evidence of the defendant's state of mind – all that is required is proof that the driving was dangerous and that it caused the death. Whether or not driving is dangerous can be determined objectively. The Road Safety Act 2006 introduced the offence of causing death by careless or inconsiderate driving. This offence is similarly based on an objective fault element (albeit a lower fault

element than dangerousness) and this lower level of culpability is reflected in the lower maxium sentence of five years' imprisonment. Is it appropriate that a defendant might face a 5-year sentence for the consequences of an 'inconsiderate' act? Should not cases of human error be more appropriately dealt with in the civil courts?

4.9 CAUSING OR ALLOWING THE DEATH OF A CHILD OR VULNERABLE ADULT

Section 5 of the Domestic Violence, Crime and Victims Act 2004 introduces a new form of liability for homicide, causing or allowing the death of a child or vulnerable adult. Liability can arise in a number of ways. The most straightforward is where the child or vulnerable adult ('V'):

- was a member of the same household as D;
- had frequent contact with D at that time when there was a significant risk of serious physical harm being caused to V by the unlawful act of D; and
- D was the person whose act caused V's death.

Alternatively D can incur liability where the child or vulnerable adult ('V'):

- dies as a result of the unlawful act of a person ('X') who was a member of the same household as V, and had frequent contact with V; and
- D was also a member of the same household as V, and had frequent contact with V; and
- at that time there was a significant risk of serious physical harm being caused to V by the unlawful act of X; and
- D was, or ought to have been, aware that there was a significant risk of serious physical harm being caused to V by the unlawful act of X; and
- D failed to take such steps as he could reasonably have been expected to take to protect V from the risk; and
- the act of X causing V's death occurred in circumstances of the kind that D foresaw or ought to have foreseen.

Note that for the purposes of this offence, a child is a person under the age of 16. A vulnerable adult is defined as '. . . a person aged 16 or over whose ability to protect himself from violence, abuse or neglect is significantly impaired through physical or mental disability or illness, through old age or otherwise'; see s 5(6). Where D is not the mother or father of V no liability can arise unless D was over the age of 16 at the time of the act that caused V's death. The expression 'member of the same household' is inevitably somewhat vague. Section 5(4) seeks to clarify this somewhat by providing that: '. . . a person is to be regarded as a "member" of a particular household, even if he does not live in that household, if he visits it so often and for such periods of time that it is reasonable to regard him as a member of it.'

Although the offence is expressed in terms of acts causing death, s 5(6) makes it clear that for these purposes 'act' includes a course of conduct and also includes omission.

For the purposes of s 5 an 'unlawful' act is one that constitutes an offence. Where the unlawful act is one committed by X (see above), an 'unlawful' act is one that constitutes an offence or one that would constitute an offence but for being the act of a person under the age of ten, or a person entitled to rely on a defence of insanity.

The offence carries a maximum penalty of 14 years' imprisonment following conviction on indictment.

The aim of this new offence is to close a loophole in existing law whereby parents or carers can escape liability if the prosecution cannot establish which member of the household was responsible for the death. As s 5(2) makes clear, D can be convicted where he himself caused the death through his act or omission, or where he allowed the death to be caused by another under the terms of s 5(1)(d). The prosecution does not have to specify which mode of liability is being alleged.

4.10 CODIFICATION AND LAW REFORM PROPOSALS

As noted above (see 4.1.2 Law Com No 304: *Proposals for a new 'ladder' of homicide offences*) the Law Commission's Report (Law Com No 304) *Murder, Manslaughter And Infanticide* proposes a ladder of offences based around first degree and second degree murder, with a third category of unlawful killing comprising manslaughter – defined as:

- killing another person through the commission of a criminal act intended by the defendant to cause injury ('criminal act manslaughter'), or
- killing another person through the commission of a criminal act that the defendant was aware involved a serious risk of causing some injury ('criminal act manslaughter'), or
- killing another person through gross negligence ('gross negligence manslaughter').

As Law Com No 304 explained:

> 2.164 Our recommendation with regard to gross negligence manslaughter reflects the current legal position. Our recommendation with regard to criminal act manslaughter is almost identical to the proposal put forward by the Government for replacing 'unlawful and dangerous act' manslaughter . . .
>
> 2.165 As we have already indicated, not all reckless killings will fall into the category of second degree murder. Will they be covered by the concept of gross negligence, within manslaughter? We believe that they will. If someone realises that there is a risk of causing death, but unjustifiably carries on with his or her conduct, that can be regarded as a kind of 'gross' negligence. It can be regarded as a failure to take account of the interests of potential victims so highly culpable that it should amount to a homicide offence against the person killed. There is, in consequence, no need for the addition of 'reckless killing' to killing by gross negligence in the lower tier of homicide, manslaughter.
>
> . . .

3.46 The organisation Justice suggested to us that, in the absence of an intention to injure, manslaughter should require an awareness of a risk of serious injury. We can see considerable force behind this suggestion as a way of limiting the scope of the offence.

3.47 However, we are not recommending that manslaughter, in the absence of an intention to injure, should require the awareness of a risk of serious injury. This is because we believe that such a limitation would introduce excessive complexity into the law. The jury would have to be told that whilst a criminal act that causes death and which was intended by D to do some injury is manslaughter, if the criminal act was one that D was only aware might cause some injury, D could only be convicted of manslaughter if he or she was aware that it might cause serious injury.

3.48 Such a definition would encourage forensic disputes about whether an assault (say, a punch) causing death was actually intended to cause injury or was only a criminal act that D thought might cause some injury (but not serious injury). If the former, D would be guilty of manslaughter, but if the latter, D would only be guilty of an assault. We do not believe liability for manslaughter should turn on such fine distinctions. D's lack of awareness that serious harm or death might occur can be taken into account in sentencing. So we, along with almost all of our consultees, support the wider formulation endorsed by the Home Office in 2000.

3.49 However, while we are not attracted to liability for criminal act manslaughter being dependent on awareness of a risk of serious injury, we do believe that liability should be dependent on the risk of injury being a serious risk.

. . .

3.51 In the context of the current review of homicide it was necessary to reconsider at least some of the elements of gross negligence manslaughter. We took as our template the Home Office's own proposals in 2000 for reform. Our recommendation for gross negligence manslaughter reflects the essence of those proposals. However, there are two significant changes.

The first change – structure
3.52 Under our recommendations, some forms of 'reckless' killing would constitute second degree murder and not merely manslaughter. A 'reckless' killing involves an unjustified killing where the killer was aware that there was a risk of killing but nonetheless went on to engage in the risky conduct. Under our recommendations, explained in Part 2, if D is reckless, in the sense that he or she realises that there is a serious risk that his or her conduct may kill, he or she can be guilty of second degree murder but only if, additionally, he or she intended by his her conduct to cause some injury or a fear or risk of injury.

3.53 Under our recommendations, not all cases of 'reckless' killing will fall into second degree murder. These will be killings where there is an awareness of a risk that conduct may cause death but the extra element is missing: there is no intention to cause injury or a fear or risk of injury. Almost all of our consultees were in favour of treating 'reckless' killing (without any further aggravating factor) as manslaughter. We believe that such cases should be treated as falling within gross negligence manslaughter. In other words, there should cease to be a separate category of 'reckless manslaughter'. The Crown Prosecution Service and Professor Taylor expressly said that they would favour this course.

3.54 We believe that there would be little point in continuing with a category of 'reckless manslaughter' when the worst cases of recklessness (those in which there was also an intention to cause injury or a fear or risk of injury) are accounted for within second degree murder. Under our recommendations, 'reckless manslaughter' would become a very narrow category, in many cases all but indistinguishable from gross negligence manslaughter. The Crown Prosecution Service thought that the law would become too complicated if reckless manslaughter were retained as a separate category. We agree.

3.55 In many cases treated as ones of gross negligence manslaughter, D would be hard-pressed to deny that he or she was in broad terms perfectly well aware of the risk of his or her conduct killing someone. In other words, in many cases it would be hard for D (if pushed) to deny that he or she was reckless as well as grossly negligent, unless he or she had, in his or her own mind, positively ruled out the possibility that death might be caused. An example is Lidar, where D drove off knowing that the victim was hanging from the car window with his body half in the car. In such a case, D would be hard-pressed to deny being both grossly negligence and reckless.

3.56 Recent case law has reinforced our belief that reckless manslaughter can be subsumed within gross negligence manslaughter. For example, the Court of Appeal has said that D's state of mind can be 'relevant to the jury's consideration when assessing the grossness and criminality of his conduct'. This cuts both ways. On the one hand, the fact that D was aware of a risk but pressed on regardless strengthens the case for saying that his or her conduct was grossly negligent (in the sense of showing a blatant disregard for the safety of others). On the other hand, the fact that D genuinely (albeit stupidly) thought that there was little or no risk weakens, without wholly undermining, the case for saying that his or her conduct showed such disregard or was grossly negligent.

3.57 The term 'reckless' has an unhappy history in the context of homicide. Although the House of Lords brought some welcome clarity to the definition of that term in another context, we now believe that the law of homicide is better off without it.

The second change – fault
3.58 The second change relates to gross negligence manslaughter's fault element. We recommend that the prosecution be required to show that there was gross negligence as to the risk of causing death (not merely as to causing serious injury). That change in effect means our recommendations restate, rather than extend, the common law. We do not believe that this recommendation will prove controversial in any significant way. This change was supported by the vast majority of consultees.

3.59 Gross negligence manslaughter can be committed even when D was unaware that his or her conduct might cause death, or even injury. This is because negligence, however gross, does not necessarily involve any actual realisation that one is posing a risk of harm: it is a question of how glaringly obvious the risk would have been to a reasonable person. If liability for an offence as serious as manslaughter is to be justified in the absence of an awareness that one is posing a risk, D's negligence must relate to the risk of bringing about the very harm he or she has caused: the risk of causing death. Otherwise, the crime of manslaughter becomes unduly wide and a misleading label for what the offender has done.

3.60 We recommend the adoption of the definition of causing death by gross negligence given in our earlier report on manslaughter:

(1) a person by his or her conduct causes the death of another;

(2) a risk that his or her conduct will cause death . . . would be obvious to a reasonable person in his or her position;

(3) he or she is capable of appreciating that risk at the material time; and

(4) . . . his or her conduct falls far below what can reasonably be expected of him or her in the circumstances. . . .

4.11 CORPORATE MANSLAUGHTER

In principle corporate bodies can incur criminal liability just as any natural person can. In practice there are two key limitations. The first is that certain offences require the positive action of a human being – such as rape. The second is that most serious offences require proof of *mens rea*. Hence, whilst securing the conviction of a corporate body for a strict liability offence is often quite straightforward, establishing the fault required for an offence such as manslaughter can be problematic. As the law currently stands a company can be charged with killing by gross negligence, but this requires proof that a 'directing mind' of the company (such as a managing director, or other board member) also has the required degree of fault. This is sometimes referred to as the 'identification principle'. The difficulty with this approach is that various senior employees may have a degree of fault but no one senior employee may have sufficient fault to warrant a prosecution. The courts have been reluctant to aggregate the fault of various employees and attribute this to a corporate body. The problems created by this common law approach are illustrated in the following extract concerning the failure of the prosecution arising out of sinking of the 'Herald of Free Enterprise' at Zeebrugge.

R v P & O European Ferries (Dover) Ltd (1990) 93 Cr App R 72 (Central Criminal Court)

In 1987 the ferry 'Herald of Free Enterprise' capsized whilst leaving Zeebrugge harbour. The evidence suggested that the sinking was caused by the ship leaving port with the bow doors still open. The owners and operators of the ferry, P & O European Ferries (Dover) Ltd, were charged with manslaughter in respect of the passengers and crew that died as a result of the capsizing. The prosecution was unsuccessful, but the court did consider the extent to which an indictment would lie against a corporation for the offence of manslaughter.

Turner J:

. . . The main thrust of the argument for the company in support of the submission that the four counts of manslaughter in this indictment should be quashed was not merely that English law does not recognise the offence of corporate manslaughter but that, as a matter of positive English law, manslaughter can only be committed when one natural person kills another natural person. Hence it was no accident that there is no record of any corporation or non-natural person having been successfully prosecuted for manslaughter in any English court. It was, however, accepted that there is no conceptual difficulty in attributing a criminal state of mind to a corporation. The broad argument advanced on behalf of the prosecution was that, there being no all-embracing statutory definition of murder or manslaughter there is, in principle, no reason why a corporation, or other non-natural person, cannot be found guilty of most offences in the criminal calendar. The exceptions to such a broad proposition could be found either in the form of punishment, which would be inappropriate for a corporation, or in the very person nature of individual crimes or categories of crime such as offences under the Sexual Offences Act, bigamy and, arguably, perjury. It was further argued that the definitions of homicide to be found in the works of such as Coke, Hale, Blackstone and Stephen, and which were strongly relied upon by the company, were not intended to be exclusive, but reflected the historical fact that, at the dates when these definitions originated, the concept of criminal liability of a corporation, just as their very existence, was not within the contemplation of the courts or the writers of the legal treatises referred to. Before the days when corporate crime was in contemplation, it can be a matter of no surprise to find that the definition of homicide did not include the possibility of a corporation committing such a crime . . .

Since the 19th century there has been a huge increase in the numbers and activities of corporations whether nationalised, municipal or commercial, which enter the private lives of all or most of 'men and subjects' in a diversity of ways. A clear case can be made for imputing to such corporations social duties including the duty not to offend all relevant parts of the criminal law. By tracing the history of the cases decided by the English courts over the period of the last 150 years, it can be seen how, first tentatively and finally confidently, the courts have been able to ascribe to corporations a 'mind' which is generally one of the essential ingredients of common law and statutory offences. Indeed, it can be seen that in many Acts of Parliament the same concept has been embraced. The parliamentary approach is, perhaps, exemplified by s 18 of the Theft Act 1968 which provides for directors and managers of a limited company to be rendered liable to conviction if an offence under ss 15, 16 or 17 of the Act are proved to have been committed – and I quote – 'with the consent, connivance of any director, manager, secretary . . . purporting to act in such capacity, then such director, manager or secretary shall be guilty of the offence'. Once a state of mind could be effectively attributed to a corporation, all that remained was to determine the means by which that state of mind could be ascertained and imputed to a non-natural person. That done, the obstacle to the acceptance of general criminal liability of a corporation was overcome. *Cessante ratione legis, cessat ipsa lex.* As some of the decisions in other common law countries indicate, there is nothing essentially incongruous in the notion that a corporation should be guilty of an offence of unlawful killing. I find unpersuasive the argument of the company that the old definitions of homicide positively exclude the liability of a non-natural person to conviction of an offence of manslaughter. Any crime, in order to be justiciable must have been committed by or through the agency of a human being. Consequently, the inclusion in the definition of the expression 'human being' as the author of the killing was either tautologous or, as I think more probable, intended to differentiate those cases of death in which a human being played no direct part and which would have led to forfeiture of the inanimate, or if animate non-human, object which caused the death (deodand) from those in which the cause of death was initiated by human activity albeit the instrument of death was inanimate or if animate non-human. I am confident that the expression 'human being' in the definition of homicide was not intended to have the effect of words of limitation as might have been the case had it been found in some Act of Parliament or legal deed. It is not for me to attempt to set the limits of corporate liability for criminal offences in English law. Examples of other crimes which may or may not be committed by corporations will, no doubt, be decided on a case by case basis in conformity with the manner in which the common law has adapted itself in the past. Suffice it that where a corporation, through the controlling mind of one of its agents, does an act which fulfils the prerequisites of the crime of manslaughter, it is properly indictable for the crime of manslaughter . . .

4.12 REFORM OF CORPORATE MANSLAUGHTER

The current proposals for the reform of the law relating to corporate manslaughter can be traced back to the Law Commission's 1996 Report: *Legislating the Criminal Code: Involuntary Manslaughter* (Law Com 237). This in turn led to the Home Office publication: *Reforming the Law on Involuntary Manslaughter: The Government's Proposals*, which was published in May 2000.

The Home Office paper commented on the need for reform of the law in these terms:

The need for reform

3.1.5 There have been a number of disasters in recent years which have evoked demands for the use of the law of manslaughter and failures to successfully prosecute have led to an apparent perception among the public that the law dealing with corporate manslaughter is inadequate. This perception has been heightened because the disasters have been followed by inquiries which have found corporate bodies at fault and meriting very serious criticism and in some instances there have been successful prosecutions for offences under the Health and Safety at Work etc Act 1974, as amended ('the 1974 Act'). These disasters have included:

- The Herald of Free Enterprise disaster on 6 March 1987 where the jury at the inquest returned verdicts of unlawful killing in 187 cases and the DPP launched prosecutions against 7 individuals and the company. The case failed because the various acts of negligence could not be aggregated and attributed to any individual who was a directing mind.
- The King's Cross fire on 18 November 1987 which claimed 31 lives. London Underground were criticised for not guarding against the unpredictability of the fire and because no one person was charged with overall responsibility.
- The Clapham rail crash on 12 December 1988 which caused 35 deaths. British Rail were criticised for allowing working practices which were 'positively dangerous' and it was said that the errors went much wider and higher in the organisation than merely to be the responsibility of those who were working that day.
- The Southall rail crash on 19 September 1997 which resulted in 7 deaths and 151 injuries. In July 1999 Great Western Trains (GWT) pleaded guilty to contravening Section 3(1) of the 1974 Act in that they failed to ensure that the public were not exposed to risks to their health and safety. They received a record fine for a health and safety offence of £1.5 million for what Mr Justice Scott Baker described as 'a serious fault of senior management'. The judge had earlier ruled that a charge of manslaughter could not succeed because of the need to identify some person whose gross negligence was that of GWT itself.

3.1.6 It is not only the law's apparent inability to hold accountable companies responsible for large scale disasters which led the Law Commission to propose that the law be reformed. The result of the operation of the identification doctrine has meant that there have been only a few prosecutions of a corporation for manslaughter in the history of English law and only three successful prosecutions . . . all of these were small companies.

A draft Corporate Manslaughter Bill (Cm 6497) was published in March 2005, and following further scrutiny by the Home Affairs and Work and Pensions Committees in the House of Commons, a Corporate Manslaughter and Corporate Homicide Bill was introduced in the House of Commons in 2006.

The Bill creates an offence of corporate manslaughter (corporate homicide in Scotland), that would be committed where an organisation (as a result of the way it manages or organises its activities) causes a person's death, and in circumstances amounting to a gross breach of a relevant duty of care owed by the organisation to the deceased. The offence would apply to any corporate body (other than a corporation sole), government departments as specified in the Bill and police forces.

There are a number of hurdles for the prosecution to clear in order to secure a conviction under these proposals:

An organisation would only be guilty of an offence if the way in which its activities are managed or organised by its senior management is a substantial element in the breach of duty of care causing death. Senior managers for this purpose are either those who play a significant role in making decisions about how the whole or a substantial part of the organisation's activities are to be managed or organised, or those responsible for the actual managing or organising of the whole or a substantial part of those activities.

The duty of care must be one that is relevant, i.e. it is one that is owed to its employees or to other persons working for the organisation or performing services for it; owed as occupier of premises; owed in connection with the supply by the organisation of goods or services, the carrying on by the organisation of any construction or maintenance operations, the carrying on by the organisation of any other activity on a commercial basis, or the use or keeping by the organisation of any plant, vehicle or other thing.

Clause 3 of the Bill excludes liability for any breach of duty of care arising in connection with public policy decisions, exclusively public functions and statutory inspections. Similarly clause 4 excludes liability in respect of operational aspects of military activities. Clause 6 further limits the scope of liability for emergency services and NHS bodies responding to emergency circumstances.

Assuming a relevant duty of care exists, the breach of the duty of care must be 'gross' – i.e. conduct that falls far below what can reasonably be expected of the organisation in the circumstances. Clause 8 provides that in determining the extent of the breach of duty the jury should '. . . consider whether the evidence shows that the organisation failed to comply with any health and safety legislation that relates to the alleged breach, and if so—a) how serious that failure was; (b) how much of a risk of death it posed'. A jury will also be entitled to consider the '. . . extent to which the evidence shows that there were attitudes, policies, systems or accepted practices within the organisation that were likely to have encouraged any such . . . [breach of duty]'.

What is immediately evident is that these proposals shift the emphasis of the prosecution from the search for a controlling mind of the company displaying the requisite degree of fault to an examination of objective factors such as the way in which the company was organised. If a company was convicted of corporate manslaughter under clause 1 of the Bill the court would have the power to issue a remedial order under clause 9 to remedy the breach of duty that caused the death and to order the organisation to deal with any deficiencies in its health and safety procedures. Although clause 16 provides a bar to any individual liability for aiding, abetting counselling or procuring the offence of corporate manslaughter, nothing in the Bill would prevent criminal proceedings being brought against individual directors of a company for killing by gross negligence contrary to common law if the evidence warranted such a charge.

FURTHER READING

Benyon, H, 'Causation, omissions and complicity' [1987] Crim LR 539

Chalmers, J, 'Merging Provocation and Diminished Responsibility: Some Reasons for Scepticism' [2004] Crim LR 198

Gardner, J and T Macklem, 'No Provocation Without Responsibility: A Reply to Mackay and Mitchell' [2004] Crim LR 213

Hart, HLA and AM Honore, *Causation in the Law*, 2nd edn, 1985, Oxford: OUP

Herring, J and E Palser, 'The Duty of Care in Gross Negligence Manslaughter' [2007] Crim LR 24

Holton, R and S Shute, 'Self-control in the modern provocation defence' (2007) 27 Oxford JLS 1

Horder, J and L McGowan, 'Manslaughter by Causing Another's Suicide' [2006] Crim LR 1035

Mackay, RD, 'The abnormality of the mind factor in diminished responsibility' [1999] Crim LR 117

Mackay, RD and BJ Mitchell, 'Provoking Diminished Responsibility: Two Pleas Merging into One?' [2003] Crim LR 745

Mackay, RD and BJ Mitchell, 'Replacing Provocation: More on a Combined Plea' [2004] Crim LR 219

Norrie, A, 'A critique of criminal causation' (1991) 54 MLR 685

Ormerod, D and R Fortson, 'Drug Suppliers as Manslaughterers (Again)' [2005] Crim LR 819

Phippen, L and D Radlett, 'Drugs and Manslaughter', 155 NLJ 1054

Power, H, 'Provocation and Culture' [2006] Crim LR 871

Simester, AP, 'Murder, *mens rea* and the House of Lords – again' (1999) 115 LQR 17

Stannard, JE, 'Medical treatment and the chain of causation' (1993) JCL 88

Sullivan, W, 'Corporate killing – some Government proposals' [2001] Crim LR 31

Williams, G, 'Finis for *novus actus*?' (1989) 48 CLJ 391

CHAPTER 5

NON-FATAL OFFENCES AGAINST THE PERSON

<table>
<tr><td colspan="3" align="center">**CONTENTS**</td></tr>
<tr><td>5.1</td><td>Introduction</td><td>252</td></tr>
<tr><td>5.2</td><td>Section 18 Offences Against the Person Act 1861 – wounding or grievous bodily harm with intent</td><td>253</td></tr>
<tr><td>5.3</td><td>Section 20 Offences Against the Person Act 1861 – malicious wounding or grievous bodily harm</td><td>257</td></tr>
<tr><td>5.4</td><td>Section 47 Offences Against the Person Act 1861 – assault occasioning actual bodily harm</td><td>264</td></tr>
<tr><td>5.5</td><td>Poisoning</td><td>275</td></tr>
<tr><td>5.6</td><td>Common assault and battery</td><td>279</td></tr>
<tr><td>5.7</td><td>'Stalking'</td><td>283</td></tr>
<tr><td>5.8</td><td>Racially motivated assaults and harassment</td><td>284</td></tr>
<tr><td>5.9</td><td>Codification and law reform proposals</td><td>287</td></tr>
<tr><td>5.10</td><td>Consent to physical harm as a defence</td><td>293</td></tr>
</table>

5.1 INTRODUCTION

The material selected for this chapter aims to cover the mainstream non-fatal offences against the person, as well as the related issue of consent to harm. Sexual offences are considered in Chapter 6. The law relating to non-fatal offences against the person is to be found in a hotchpotch of common law and statutory provisions. It is an area crying out for reform and rationalisation. Despite the existence of workable proposals for codification, there is little sign of any government having the desire to take the political initiative.

The major offences are:

- s 18 Offences Against the Person Act 1861 – wounding or grievous bodily harm with intent;
- s 20 Offences Against the Person Act 1861 – malicious wounding or grievous bodily harm;
- s 47 Offences Against the Person Act 1861 – assault occasioning actual bodily harm;

- common assault; and
- common battery.

In addition there are offences of poisoning, harassment, and racially aggravated forms of assault. The prosecution may also seek to rely on public order offences such as affray and riot – see ss 1 to 5 of the Public Order Act 1985 as amended.

5.2 SECTION 18 OFFENCES AGAINST THE PERSON ACT 1861 – WOUNDING OR GRIEVOUS BODILY HARM WITH INTENT

Whosoever shall unlawfully and maliciously by any means whatsoever wound or cause any grievous bodily harm to any person . . . with intent . . . to do some . . . grievous bodily harm to any person, or with intent to resist or prevent the lawful apprehension or detainer of any person, shall be guilty of [an offence], and being convicted thereof shall be liable . . . to [imprisonment] for life . . .

5.2.1 WHAT CONSTITUTES A WOUND?

C (A Minor) v Eisenhower (sub nom JJC v Eisenhower) [1983] 3 WLR 537

The defendant, a juvenile, had been charged (together with another juvenile) with unlawful and malicious wounding contrary to s 20 of the Offences Against the Person Act 1861. The only point at issue was whether the victim's injuries constituted a 'wound'.

Robert Goff LJ:

. . . The offence arose in the following circumstances. These two boys were both 15 at the relevant time. The defendant's co-accused, in company with the defendant, purchased an air pistol and some pellets from a shop. A few days later, on 21 January 1982, they were walking together along Flexmere Road, Tottenham, when they became aware of a young man called Martin Cook, together with another young man and two girls, on the opposite side of the road. As the defendant and his co-accused walked along, the co-accused aimed the air pistol in the direction of those four young people. He fired once. A little later he fired again. Martin Cook was hit in the area of the left eye by a pellet from the air pistol.

The justices in the case found that the injuries sustained by Martin Cook amounted to a bruise just below the left eyebrow and that fluid filling the front part of his left eye for a time afterwards abnormally contained red blood cells . . .

The question stated by the justices is as follows:

The question for the opinion of the High Court is whether in the light of the facts as we found them and the law applied to those facts we were right to find the [defendant] guilty of the offence with which he had been charged.

. . . In *R v M'Loughlin* (1838) 8 Car & P 635, it was held by Coleridge J, other judges being present, that it must be the whole skin that is broken. He, of course, was referring to the fact that the human skin has two layers, an outer layer called the epidermis or the cuticle, and an underlayer which is sometimes called the dermis or the true skin. In that case there was evidence of an abrasion of the skin, with blood issuing from it. It was made plain to the jury by Coleridge J that:

> if it is necessary to constitute a wound, that the skin should be broken, it must be the whole skin, and it is not sufficient to show a separation of the cuticle only.

It was therefore not enough that there had been an abrasion affecting only the cuticle. There had to be a break in the continuity of the whole skin.

His Lordship then referred to two more old cases: see *R v Shadbolt* (1833) 5 Car & P 504 and *R v Waltham* (1849) 3 Cox CC 442; his Lordship went on:

These cases show that there can be a break in the continuity of the skin sufficient to constitute a wound if the skin which was broken is the skin of an internal cavity of the body, being a cavity from the outer surface of the body where the skin of the cavity is continuous with the outer skin of the body. So, for example, in *Shadbolt* it was held that it was sufficient if there had been a break in the skin of the internal surface of the lips inside the mouth. In *Waltham*, which is possibly the most extreme of the cases cited to us, it was held by Cresswell J that there would be a wounding if there had been a rupture of the lining membrane of the urethra causing a small flow of blood into the urine, because that membrane was of precisely the same character as that which lined the cheek and the internal skin of the lip.

So we can see a picture emerging. There must be a break in the continuity of the skin. It must be a break in the continuity of the whole skin, but the skin may include not merely the outer skin of the body but the skin of an internal cavity of the body where the skin of the cavity is continuous with the outer skin of the body . . .

In my judgment, having regard to the cases there is a continuous stream of authority – to which I myself can find no exception at all – which does establish that a wound is, as I have stated, a break in the continuity of the whole skin . . . This has become such a well-established meaning of the word 'wound' that in my judgment it would be very wrong for this court to depart from it.

We now turn to the case stated for our consideration by the justices. The justices concluded that there was a wound because, although they described the injury as a bruise just below the left eyebrow with fluid filling the front part of his left eye for a time afterwards which abnormally contained red blood cells, they thought that the abnormal presence of red blood cells in the fluid in Martin Cook's left eye indicated at least the rupturing of a blood vessel or vessels internally; and this they thought was sufficient to constitute a wound for the purposes of s 20 of the Offences Against the Person Act 1861.

In my judgment, that conclusion was not in accordance with the law. It is not enough that there has been a rupturing of a blood vessel or vessels internally for there to be a wound under the statute because it is impossible for a court to conclude from that evidence alone whether or not there has been any break in the continuity of the whole skin. There may have simply been internal bleeding of some kind or another, the cause of which is not established. Furthermore, even if there had been a break in some internal skin, there may not have been a break in the whole skin. In these circumstances, the evidence is not enough, in my judgment, to establish a wound within the statute. In my judgment, the justices erred in their conclusion on the evidence before them.

The question posed for the opinion of this court is whether, in the light of the facts found by the justices and the law applied to those facts, they were right to find the defendant guilty of the offence with which he had been charged, viz, the unlawful and malicious wounding of Martin Cook contrary to s 20 of the Offences Against the Person Act 1861. I would answer that question in the negative.

5.2.2 WHAT CONSTITUTES GRIEVOUS BODILY HARM?

The word 'grievous' is not defined in the 1861 Act, but in modern times the courts have adopted the view that it is sufficient to direct the jury in terms of 'serious' or 'really serious' harm; see *Director of Public Prosecutions v Smith* [1961] AC 290. For a more recent illustration consider *R v Doyle* [2004] EWCA Crim 2714, where the defendant's conviction under s 18 was upheld after he had, *inter alia*, bitten the victim in the genital area through his trousers. The Court of Appeal confirmed that it was perfectly adequate on the facts for the judge to leave the issue with the jury on the basis that grievous bodily harm had been caused if they viewed it as serious harm.

5.2.3 INTENT

The offence under s 18 of the 1861 Act requires proof of an intention to do some grievous bodily harm. It is submitted that, given that intention to do grievous bodily harm is sufficient *mens rea* for murder, intention in this context ought to have the same meaning as that attributed to it in *R v Woollin* [1998] 4 All ER 103; see Chapter 3.2.1.

5.2.4 CROWN PROSECUTION CHARGING STANDARDS

In 1994 the Crown Prosecution Service published the Charging Standards used to guide prosecutors as to the appropriate charge to proceed with in cases of non-sexual, non-fatal assault. The general principles regarding charging practice provide that prosecutors should select charge(s) that 'accurately reflect the extent of the defendant's alleged involvement and responsibility, thereby allowing the courts the discretion to sentence appropriately'. In particular, the guidelines provide that:

- the choice of charges should ensure the clear and simple presentation of the case, particularly where there is more than one defendant;
- it is wrong to encourage a defendant to plead guilty to a few charges by selecting more charges than are necessary;
- it is wrong to select a more serious charge which is not supported by the evidence in order to encourage a plea of guilty to a lesser allegation.

5.2.4.1 Crown prosecution charging standards: wounding/causing grievous bodily harm with intent, contrary to s 18 of the Act

9.4 The distinction between charges under section 18 and section 20 is one of intent.

9.5 The gravity of the injury resulting is not the determining factor although it may provide some evidence of intent.

9.6 When charging an offence involving grievous bodily harm, consideration should be given to the fact that a section 20 offence requires the infliction of harm, whereas a section 18 offence requires the causing of harm. This is especially significant when considering alternative verdicts (see paragraph 11 below).

9.7 Factors which may indicate the specific intent include:

- a repeated or planned attack;
- deliberate selection of a weapon or adaptation of an article to cause injury, such as breaking a glass before an attack;
- making prior threats;
- using an offensive weapon against, or kicking, the victim's head.

9.8 The evidence of intent required is different if the offence alleged is a wounding or the causing of grievous bodily harm with intent to resist or prevent the lawful apprehension or detainer of any person. This part of section 18 is of assistance in more serious assaults upon police officers, where the evidence of an intention to prevent arrest is clear, but the evidence of an intent to cause grievous bodily harm is in doubt.

9.9 It is not bad for duplicity to indict for wounding with intent to cause grievous bodily harm or to resist lawful apprehension in one count, although it is best practice to include the allegations in separate counts. This will enable a jury to consider the different intents and the court to sentence on a clear basis of the jury's finding.

5.2.4.2 Crown prosecution charging standards: s 18 or attempted murder?

10.3 Unlike murder, which requires an intention to kill or cause grievous bodily harm, attempted murder requires evidence of an intention to kill alone. This makes it a difficult allegation to sustain and careful consideration must be given to whether the more appropriate charge is under section 18.

10.4 The Courts will pay particular attention to counts of attempted murder and justifiably will be highly critical of any such count unless there is clear evidence of an intention to kill.

10.5 It should be borne in mind that the actions of the defendant must be more than preparatory and although words and threats may provide *prima facie* evidence of an intention to kill, there may be doubt as to whether they were uttered seriously or were mere bravado.

10.6 Evidence of the following factors may assist in proving the intention to kill:

- calculated planning;

- selection and use of a deadly weapon;
- threats (subject to paragraph 10.5) above;
- severity or duration of attack;
- relevant admissions in interview.

5.3 SECTION 20 OFFENCES AGAINST THE PERSON ACT 1861 – MALICIOUS WOUNDING OR GRIEVOUS BODILY HARM

Section 20: inflicting bodily injury, with or without weapon

Whosoever shall unlawfully and maliciously wound or inflict any grievous bodily harm upon any other person, either with or without any weapon or instrument, shall be guilty of [an offence], and being convicted thereof shall be liable . . . to [imprisonment for not more than five years] . . .

For the meaning of 'wounding' and 'grievous bodily harm', see 5.2.1 and 5.2.2 above.

5.3.1 INFLICTING

R v Mandair [1994] 2 WLR 700 (HL)

Lord Mackay of Clashfern LC:
The indictment contained a single count alleging causing grievous bodily harm with intent, contrary to s 18 of the Offences Against the Person Act 1861. The particulars of offence were that the defendant on 31 January 1991 unlawfully caused grievous bodily harm to Amarjit Mandair with intent to do her grievous bodily harm.

The recorder, applying s 6(3) of the Criminal Law Act 1967, left open to the jury the option of returning a lesser verdict under s 20 of the Offences Against the Person Act 1861. After sundry procedure the jury returned a verdict of not guilty on the charge against the defendant of causing grievous bodily harm with intent contrary to s 18 and a verdict of guilty on the alternative charge against the defendant of causing grievous bodily harm contrary to s 20 . . .

In my view 'cause' in s 18 is certainly sufficiently wide to embrace any method by which grievous bodily harm could be inflicted under s 20 and since causing grievous bodily harm in s 18 is an alternative to wounding I regard it as clear that the word 'cause' in s 18 is wide enough to include any action that could amount to inflicting grievous bodily harm under s 20 where the word 'inflict' appears as an alternative to 'wound'. For this reason, in my view, following the reasoning of this House in R v Wilson (Clarence) [1984] AC 242 an alternative verdict under s 20 was open on the terms of this indictment . . .

Lord Templeman:
My Lords, the criminal law is already overburdened with technicalities. In my opinion: (1) an allegation of causing grievous bodily harm includes an allegation of inflicting grievous bodily

harm. (2) A jury may convict of an offence under s 20 of the Offences Against the Person Act 1861 as an alternative to a charge of convicting of an offence under s 18 of that Act. (3) The Court of Appeal may substitute a conviction under s 20 for a conviction under s 18 . . .

I agree, therefore, with the order proposed by my noble and learned friend, Lord Mackay of Clashfern LC.

R v Ireland; R v Burstow [1997] 4 All ER 225

In *R v Burstow* the Court of Appeal certified the following point as of general importance, namely:

Whether an offence of inflicting grievous bodily harm under section 20 of the Offences against the Person Act 1861 can be committed where no physical violence is applied directly or indirectly to the body of the victim.

Lord Steyn outlined the facts giving rise to the appeal in *R v Burstow* as follows:

In *R v Burstow* the appellant was indicted on one count of unlawfully and maliciously inflicting grievous bodily harm, contrary to section 20 of the Act of 1861 . . . Burstow had a social relationship with a woman. She broke it off. He could not accept her decision. He proceeded to harass her in various ways over a lengthy period. His conduct led to several convictions and periods of imprisonment. During an eight-month period in 1995 covered by the indictment he continued his campaign of harassment. He made some silent telephone calls to her. He also made abusive calls to her. He distributed offensive cards in the street where she lived. He was frequently, and unnecessarily, at her home and place of work. He surreptitiously took photographs of the victim and her family. He sent her a note which was intended to be menacing, and was so understood. The victim was badly affected by this campaign of harassment. It preyed on her mind. She was fearful of personal violence. A consultant psychiatrist stated that she was suffering from a severe depressive illness. In the Crown Court counsel asked for a ruling whether an offence of unlawfully and maliciously inflicting grievous bodily harm contrary to section 20 may be committed where no physical violence has been applied directly or indirectly to the body of the victim. The judge answered this question in the affirmative. Burstow thereupon changed his plea to guilty. The judge sentenced him to three years' imprisonment. Burstow applied for leave to appeal against conviction. The Court of Appeal heard full oral argument on the application, and granted the application for leave to appeal but dismissed the appeal.

He continued:

The decision in *Chan-Fook* opened up the possibility of applying sections 18, 20 and 47 in new circumstances. The appeal of *Burstow* lies in respect of his conviction under section 20. It was conceded that in principle the wording of section 18, and in particular the words 'cause any grievous bodily harm to any person' do not preclude a prosecution in cases where the *actus reus* is the causing of psychiatric injury. But counsel laid stress on the difference between 'causing' grievous bodily harm in section 18 and 'inflicting' grievous bodily harm in section 20. Counsel argued that the difference in wording reveals a difference in legislative intent: inflict is a narrower concept than cause. This argument loses sight of the genesis of sections 18 and 20. In his commentary on the Act of 1861 Greaves, the draftsman, explained the position: *The Criminal Law Consolidation and Amendment Acts*, 2nd edn (1862). He said (at pp 3–4):

> If any question should arise in which any comparison may be instituted between different sections of any one or several of these Acts, it must be carefully borne in mind in what manner these Acts were framed. None of them was re-written; on the contrary, each contains enactments taken from different Acts passed at different times and with different views, and frequently varying from each other in phraseology, and ... these enactments, for the most part, stand in these Acts with little or no variation in their phraseology, and, consequently, their differences in that respect will be found generally to remain in these Acts. It follows, therefore, from hence, that any argument as to a difference in the intention of the legislature, which may be drawn from a difference in the terms of one clause from those in another, will be entitled to no weight in the construction of such clauses; for that argument can only apply with force where an Act is framed from beginning to end with one and the same view, and with the intention of making it thoroughly consistent throughout.

The difference in language is therefore not a significant factor.

Counsel for Burstow then advanced a sustained argument that an assault is an ingredient of an offence under section 20. He referred your Lordships to cases which in my judgment simply do not yield what he sought to extract from them. In any event, the tour of the cases revealed conflicting dicta, no authority binding on the House of Lords, and no settled practice holding expressly that assault was an ingredient of section 20. And, needless to say, none of the cases focused on the infliction of psychiatric injury. In these circumstances I do not propose to embark on a general review of the cases cited: compare the review in Smith and Hogan, *Criminal Law*, 8th edn (1996), pp 440–41. Instead I turn to the words of the section.

Counsel's argument can only prevail if one may supplement the section by reading it as providing 'inflict by assault any grievous bodily harm'. Such an implication is, however, not necessary. On the contrary, section 20, like section 18, works perfectly satisfactorily without such an implication. I would reject this part of counsel's argument. But counsel had a stronger argument when he submitted that it is inherent in the word 'inflict' that there must be a direct or indirect application of force to the body. Counsel cited the speech of Lord Roskill in *R v Wilson (Clarence)* [1984] AC 242, 259E–260H, in which Lord Roskill quoted with approval from the judgment of the full court of the Supreme Court of Victoria in *R v Salisbury* [1976] VR 452. There are passages that give assistance to counsel's argument. But Lord Roskill expressly stated (at p 260H) that he was 'content to accept, as did the [court in Salisbury] that there can be the infliction of grievous bodily harm contrary to section 20 without an assault being committed'. In the result the effect of the decisions in *Wilson* and *Salisbury* is neutral in respect of the issue as to the meaning of 'inflict'. Moreover, in *Burstow* [1997] 1 Cr App R 144, 149, the Lord Chief Justice pointed out that in *R v Mandair* [1995] 1 AC 208, 215, Lord Mackay of Clashfern LC observed with the agreement of the majority of the House of Lords: 'In my opinion ... the word "cause" is wider or at least not narrower than the word "inflict".' Like the Lord Chief Justice I regard this observation as making clear that in the context of the Act of 1861 there is no radical divergence between the meaning of the two words.

That leaves the troublesome authority of the decision Court for Crown Cases Reserved in *R v Clarence* (1888) 22 QBD 23. At a time when the defendant knew that he was suffering from a venereal disease, and his wife was ignorant of his condition, he had sexual intercourse with her.

He communicated the disease to her. The defendant was charged and convicted of inflicting grievous bodily harm under section 20. There was an appeal. By a majority of nine to four the court quashed the conviction. The case was complicated by an issue of consent. But it must be accepted that in a case where there was direct physical contact the majority ruled that the requirement of infliction was not satisfied. This decision has never been overruled. It assists counsel's argument. But it seems to me that what detracts from the weight to be given to the *dicta* in *Clarence* is that none of the judges in that case had before them the possibility of the inflicting, or causing, of psychiatric injury. The criminal law has moved on in the light of a developing understanding of the link between the body and psychiatric injury. In my judgment *Clarence* no longer assists.

The problem is one of construction. The question is whether as a matter of current usage the contextual interpretation of 'inflict' can embrace the idea of one person inflicting psychiatric injury on another. One can without straining the language in any way answer that question in the affirmative. I am not saying that the words cause and inflict are exactly synonymous. They are not. What I am saying is that in the context of the Act of 1861 one can nowadays quite naturally speak of inflicting psychiatric injury. Moreover, there is internal contextual support in the statute for this view. It would be absurd to differentiate between sections 18 and 20 in the way argued on behalf of *Burstow*. As the Lord Chief Justice observed in *Burstow* [1997] 1 Cr App R 144, 149F, this should be a very practical area of the law. The interpretation and approach should so far as possible be adopted which treats the ladder of offences as a coherent body of law. Once the decision in *Chan-Fook* [1994] 1 WLR 689 is accepted the realistic possibility is opened up of prosecuting under section 20 in cases of the type which I described in the introduction to this judgment.

For the reasons I have given I would answer the certified question in Burstow in the affirmative.

Lord Hope:

. . . The question is whether there is any difference in meaning, in this context, between the word 'cause' and the word 'inflict'. The fact that the word 'caused' is used in section 18, whereas the word used in section 20 is 'inflict', might be taken at first sight to indicate that there is a difference. But for all practical purposes there is, in my opinion, no difference between these two words. In *R v Mandair* [1995] 1 AC 208, 215B Lord Mackay of Clashfern LC, said that the word 'cause' is wider or at least not narrower than the word 'inflict'. I respectfully agree with that observation. But I would add that there is this difference, that the word 'inflict' implies that the consequence of the act is something which the victim is likely to find unpleasant or harmful. The relationship between cause and effect, when the word 'cause' is used, is neutral. It may embrace pleasure as well as pain. The relationship when the word 'inflict' is used is more precise, because it invariably implies detriment to the victim of some kind.

In the context of a criminal act therefore the words 'cause' and 'inflict' may be taken to be interchangeable. As the Supreme Court of Victoria held in *Salisbury* [1976] VR 452, it is not a necessary ingredient of the word 'inflict' that whatever causes the harm must be applied directly to the victim. It may be applied indirectly, so long as the result is that the harm is caused by what has been done. In my opinion it is entirely consistent with the ordinary use of the word 'inflict' in the English language to say that the appellant's actions 'inflicted' the psychiatric harm from which the victim has admittedly suffered in this case. The issues which remain are issues of fact and, as the appellant pled guilty to the offence, I would dismiss his appeal.

5.3.2 MALICIOUSLY

R v Mowatt [1968] 1 QB 421 (CA)

Mowatt attacked another man in the street in a dispute over a £5 note. The attack left the victim almost unconscious. Mowatt was arrested and convicted under s 20 of the 1861 Act. He appealed contending that the trial judge had not directed the jury adequately as regards the meaning of the word malicious.

Diplock LJ:

. . . The learned judge in summing-up explained to the jury the meaning of 'unlawfully' . . . but nowhere in the summing-up did the judge mention the word 'maliciously' or give the jury any directions as to its meaning . . .

. . . In s 18 the word 'maliciously' adds nothing. The intent expressly required by that section is more specific than such element of foresight of consequences as is implicit in the word 'maliciously' and in directing a jury about an offence under this section the word 'maliciously' is best ignored. In the offence under s 20, and in the alternative verdict which may be given on a charge under s 18 – for neither of which is any specific intent required – the word 'maliciously' does import on the part of the person who unlawfully inflicts the wound or other grievous bodily harm an awareness that his act may have the consequence of causing some physical harm to some other person . . . It is quite unnecessary that the accused should have foreseen that his unlawful act might cause physical harm of the gravity described in the section i.e. a wound or serious physical injury. It is enough that he should have foreseen that some physical harm to some person, albeit of a minor character, might result . . .

. . . There may, of course, be cases where the accused's awareness of the possible consequences of his act is genuinely in issue. *R v Cunningham* [1957] 2 QB 396 is a good example. But where the evidence for the prosecution, if accepted, shows that the physical act of the accused which caused the injury to another person was a direct assault which any ordinary person would be bound to realise was likely to cause some physical harm to the other person (as, for instance, an assault with a weapon or the boot or violence with the hands) and the defence put forward on behalf of the accused is not that the assault was accidental or that he did not realise that it might cause some physical harm to the victim, but is some other defence such as that he did not do the alleged act or that he did it in self-defence, it is unnecessary to deal specifically in the summing-up with what is meant by the word 'maliciously' in the section. It can only confuse the jury to invite them in the summing-up to consider an improbability not previously put forward and to which no evidence has been directed, to wit, that the accused did not realise what any ordinary person would have realised was a likely consequence of his act, and to tell the jury that the onus lies, not on the accused to establish, but on the prosecution to negative, that improbability, and to go on to talk about presumptions. To a jury who are not jurisprudents that sounds like jargon. In the absence of any evidence that the accused did not realise that it was a possible consequence of his act that some physical harm might be caused to the victim, the prosecution satisfy the relevant onus by proving the commission by the accused of an act which any ordinary person would realise was likely to have that consequence. There is no issue here to which the jury need direct their minds and there is no need to give to them any specific directions about it . . . In the view of this court, this was clearly a case where in relation to the lesser offence of which the appellant was convicted it was quite unnecessary for the learned judge to give the jury any instructions on the meaning of the word 'maliciously' . . .

R v Savage; R v Parmenter [1992] 1 AC 699 (HL)

One of the certified questions asked the House of Lords to consider whether, in order to establish an offence under s 20 of the 1861 Act, the prosecution had to prove that the defendant actually foresaw that his act would cause harm, or whether it was sufficient to prove that he ought to have foreseen the harm.

[Lord Ackner (with whom Lord Keith of Kinkel, Lord Brandon of Oakbrook, Lord Jauncey of Tullichettle and Lord Lowry agreed):]

[Having determined that *R v Caldwell* [1982] AC 341 was of no application in relation to s 20 his Lordship concluded:] . . . in order to establish an offence under s 20 the prosecution must prove either that the defendant intended or that he actually foresaw that his act would cause harm . . .

. . . In order to establish an offence under s 20 is it sufficient to prove that the defendant intended or foresaw the risk of some physical harm or must he intend or foresee either wounding or grievous bodily harm?

. . . My Lords, I am satisfied that the decision in *R v Mowatt* [1968] 1 QB 421 was correct and that it is quite unnecessary that the accused should either have intended or have foreseen that his unlawful act might cause physical harm of the gravity described in s 20, i.e. a wound or serious physical injury. It is enough that he should have foreseen that some physical harm to some person, albeit of a minor character, might result.

In the result I would dismiss the appeal in Savage's case but allow the appeal in Parmenter's case, but only to the extent of substituting, in accordance with the provisions of s 3(2) of the Criminal Appeal Act 1968, verdicts of guilty of assault occasioning actual bodily harm contrary to s 47 of the 1861 Act for the four s 20 offences of which he was convicted.

See further *Director of Public Prosecutions v W and another* [2006] All ER (D) 76 (Jan) confirming that foresight of the risk of some physical harm will suffice, and *R v Brady* [2006] EWCA Crim 2413.

5.3.3 CROWN PROSECUTION CHARGING STANDARDS: UNLAWFUL WOUNDING/ INFLICTING GRIEVOUS BODILY HARM, CONTRARY TO S 20 OF THE ACT

8.4 The definition of wounding may encompass injuries which are relatively minor in nature, for example a small cut or laceration. An assault resulting in such minor injuries should more appropriately be charged contrary to section 47. An offence contrary to section 20 should be reserved for those wounds considered to be serious (thus equating the offence with the infliction of grievous, or serious, bodily harm under the other part of the section).

8.5 Grievous bodily harm means serious bodily harm. Examples of this are:

- injury resulting in permanent disability or permanent loss of sensory function;
- injury which results in more than minor permanent, visible disfigurement;
- broken or displaced limbs or bones, including fractured skull; compound fractures, broken cheek bone, jaw, ribs, etc;
- injuries which cause substantial loss of blood, usually necessitating a transfusion;
- injuries resulting in lengthy treatment or incapacity. (When psychiatric injury is alleged appropriate expert evidence is essential to prove the injury.)

8.6 In accordance with the recommendation in *R v McCready* [1978] 1 WLR 1376, if there is any reliable evidence that a sufficiently serious wound has been inflicted, then the charge under section 20 should be of unlawful wounding, rather than of inflicting grievous bodily harm.

Where both a wound and grievous bodily harm have been inflicted, discretion should be used in choosing which part of section 20 more appropriately reflects the true nature of the offence.

8.7 The prosecution must prove under section 20 that either the defendant intended, or actually foresaw, that the act would cause some harm. It is not necessary to prove that the defendant either intended or foresaw that the unlawful act might cause physical harm of the gravity described in section 20. It is enough that the defendant foresaw that some physical harm to some person, albeit of a minor character, might result: *R v Savage, R v Parmenter* (supra).

5.3.3.1 Crown prosecution charging standards: Alternative verdicts where s 18 or s 20 are charged

11.1 In certain circumstances, it is possible for a jury to find the accused not guilty of the offence charged, but guilty of some other alternative offence. The general provisions are contained in section 6(3), Criminal Law Act 1967, and are supplemented by other provisions which relate to specific offences.

11.2 For offences against the person, the following alternatives may be found by a jury:

(a) causing grievous bodily harm with intent, contrary to section 18 of the Act;
- attempting to cause grievous bodily harm with intent;
- inflicting grievous bodily harm, contrary to section 20 of the Act;
- unlawful wounding, contrary to section 20 of the Act.

(b) wounding with intent, contrary to section 18 of the Act;
- attempting wounding with intent;
- unlawful wounding, contrary to section 20 of the Act;
- assault occasioning actual bodily harm, contrary to section 47 of the Act.

(c) inflicting grievous bodily harm, contrary to section 20 of the Act;
- assault occasioning actual bodily harm, contrary to section 47 of the Act.

(d) unlawful wounding, contrary to section 20 of the Act;
- assault occasioning actual bodily harm, contrary to section 47 of the Act.

11.3 It is essential, however, that the charge which most suits the circumstances of the case is always preferred. It will never be appropriate to charge a more serious offence in order to obtain a conviction (whether by plea or verdict) to a lesser offence.

11.4 There is authority to support the proposition that a jury may convict of wounding, contrary to section 20 of the Act, as an alternative to a count of causing grievous bodily harm with intent, contrary to section 18 of the Act: *R v Wilson, R v Jenkins & Jenkins* (1984) 77 Cr App R 319, HL, *R v Mandair* [1994] 2 WLR 1376, HL.

11.5 Notwithstanding that authority, prosecutors should nevertheless include a separate count on the indictment alleging wounding, contrary to section 20, where there is a realistic likelihood that the jury will convict the defendant of the lesser offence.

11.6 Common assault is not available as an alternative to any offence contrary to sections 18, 20 or 47 of the Act. A specific count alleging common assault must be included on the indictment pursuant to the provisions of section 40, Criminal Justice Act 1988.

 COMMENTS AND QUESTIONS

1   Proof that D acted maliciously will require evidence that he foresaw some physical harm – foresight that the victim would merely be shocked or frightened will not suffice; see *R v Sullivan* [1981] Crim LR 46.

2   Confirmation that the infliction of grievous bodily harm can occur without an assault (ie even with the victim's apparent consent) is provided by *R v Dica* [2004] 3 All ER 593 – see further Chapter 5.10.3.

5.4 SECTION 47 OFFENCES AGAINST THE PERSON ACT 1861 – ASSAULT OCCASIONING ACTUAL BODILY HARM

Section 47 of the Offences Against the Person Act 1861 provides:

Whosoever shall be convicted upon an indictment of any assault occasioning actual bodily harm shall be liable . . . to [imprisonment for five years].

For these purposes assault bears either its narrow meaning, that is, D causing P to apprehend immediate physical violence, or it can be used in its broad sense to encompass battery.

5.4.1 WHAT IS AN ASSAULT?

In its narrow sense common assault is committed where D causes P to apprehend immediate physical violence. No physical contact is necessary. A battery is any unlawful touching of P by D. Hence, technically, no assault is committed where D hits P from the rear, although the term 'assault' is still used in its general sense of assault and battery; see *R v Lynsey* [1995] 2 All ER 654

Fagan v Metropolitan Police Commissioner [1969] 1 QB 439

On 31 August 1967 the appellant was reversing a motor car in Fortunegate Road, London NW10, when Police Constable David Morris directed him to drive the car forwards to the kerbside and, standing in front of the car, pointed out a suitable place in which to park. At first the appellant stopped the car too far from the kerb for the officer's liking. Morris asked him to park closer and indicated a precise spot. The appellant drove forward towards him and stopped the car with the offside wheel on Morris's left foot. 'Get off, you are on my foot,' said the officer. 'Fuck you, you can wait,' said the appellant. The engine of the car stopped running. Morris repeated several times 'Get off my foot'. The appellant said reluctantly, 'OK, man, OK' and then slowly turned on the ignition of the vehicle and reversed it off the officer's foot. The appellant had either turned the ignition off to stop the engine or turned it off after the engine had stopped running.

The justices at quarter sessions on those facts were left in doubt as to whether the mounting of the wheel on to the officer's foot was deliberate or accidental. They were satisfied, however, beyond all reasonable doubt that the appellant 'knowingly, provocatively and unnecessarily allowed the wheel to remain on the foot after the officer said, "Get off, you are on my foot"'. They found that on those facts an assault was proved.

James J:

... The sole question is whether the prosecution proved facts which in law amounted to an assault.

[Counsel for the appellant] . . . contends that on the finding of the justices the initial mounting of the wheel could not be an assault and that the act of the wheel mounting the foot came to an end without there being any *mens rea*. It is argued that thereafter there was no act on the part of the appellant which could constitute an *actus reus* but only the omission or failure to remove the wheel as soon as he was asked. That failure, it is said, could not in law be an assault, nor could it in law provide the necessary *mens rea* to convert the original act of mounting the foot into an assault.

[Counsel for the Crown] argues that the first mounting of the foot was an *actus reus* which act continued until the moment of time at which the wheel was removed. During that continuing act, it is said, the appellant formed the necessary intention to constitute the element of *mens rea* and once that element was added to the continuing act, an assault took place . . .

In our judgment, the question arising, which has been argued on general principles, falls to be decided on the facts of the particular case. An assault is any act which intentionally – or possibly recklessly – causes another person to apprehend immediate and unlawful personal violence. Although 'assault' is an independent crime and is to be treated as such, for practical purposes today 'assault' is generally synonymous with the term 'battery', and is a term used to mean the actual intended use of unlawful force to another person without his consent. On the facts of the present case, the 'assault' alleged involved a 'battery'. Where an assault involved a battery, it matters not, in our judgment, whether the battery is inflicted directly by the body of the offender or through the medium of some weapon or instrument controlled by the action of the offender. An assault may be committed by the laying of a hand on another, and the action does not cease to be an assault if it is a stick held in the hand and not the hand itself which is laid on the person of the victim. So, for our part, we see no difference in principle between the action of stepping onto a person's toe and maintaining that position and the action of driving a car onto a person's foot and sitting in the car while its position on the foot is maintained.

To constitute this offence, some intentional act must have been performed; a mere omission to act cannot amount to an assault. Without going into the question whether words alone can constitute an assault, it is clear that the words spoken by the appellant could not alone amount to an assault; they can only shed light on the appellant's action. For our part, we think that the crucial question is whether, in this case, the act of the appellant can be said to be complete and spent at the moment of time when the car wheel came to rest on the foot, or whether his act is to be regarded as a continuing act operating until the wheel was removed. In our judgment, a distinction is to be drawn between acts which are complete, though results may continue to flow, and those acts which are continuing. Once the act is complete, it cannot thereafter be said to be a threat to inflict unlawful force on the victim. If the act, as distinct from the results thereof, is a continuing act, there is a continuing threat to inflict unlawful force. If the assault involves a battery and that battery continues, there is a continuing act of assault. For an assault to be committed, both the elements of *actus reus* and *mens rea* must be present at the same time. The *actus reus* is the action causing the effect on the victim's mind: see the observations of Parke B, in *R v St George* (1840) 9 C & P 483. The *mens rea* is the intention to cause that effect. It is not necessary that *mens rea* should be present at the inception of the *actus reus*; it can be superimposed on an existing act. On the other hand, the subsequent inception of *mens rea* cannot convert an act which has been completed without *mens rea* into an assault.

In our judgment, the Willesden magistrates and quarter sessions were right in law. On the facts found, the action of the appellant may have been initially unintentional, but the time came when, knowing that the wheel was on the officer's foot, the appellant (1) remained seated in the car so that his body through the medium of the car was in contact with the officer, (2) switched off the ignition of the car, (3) maintained the wheel of the car on the foot, and (4) used words indicating the intention of keeping the wheel in that position. For our part, we cannot regard such conduct as mere omission or inactivity.

There was an act constituting a battery which at its inception was not criminal because there was no element of intention, but which became criminal from the moment the intention was formed to produce the apprehension which was flowing from the continuing act. The fallacy of the appellant's argument is that it seeks to equate the facts of this case with such a case where a motorist has accidentally run over a person and, that action having been completed, fails to assist the victim with the intent that the victim should suffer . . .

Lord Parker CJ expressed agreement with **James J**; Lord Bridge delivered a dissenting judgment.

5.4.2 THE IMPORTANCE OF THE VICTIM'S PERCEPTIONS

Smith v Chief Superintendent, Woking Police Station (1983) 76 Cr App R 234 (DC)

Kerr LJ:

. . . In view of the question of law I must also refer shortly to the evidence on the basis of which the justices convicted. The incident happened at about 11 pm, when Miss Mooney was in her room wearing a pink, knee-length nightie. There was a bay window and a side window. The curtains were drawn but they left a gap. She saw the defendant peering in and stated that he was right up against the window. She said: 'I instantly recognised him. I was very scared, very shocked. He was there about three or four seconds. I walked backwards and could no longer see him. I turned and he was at the other window, again right against the glass. I just stood and stared at him, didn't know what to do. He was just standing there, didn't seem he was going to go away. I jumped across the bed towards the window and screamed. I was terrified, absolutely terrified. He must have seen me look at him. He moved away when I went across the bed. I looked at him for about 20 seconds at the side window. I called the police.'

Then she says that she was scared and after the incident she was very jumpy and shocked. The defendant, having first denied the incident, later admitted it and agreed that he would be scared stiff in the situation in which Miss Mooney found herself . . .

It is . . . common ground that the definition of an assault . . . [is] 'any act which intentionally – or recklessly – causes another to apprehend immediate and unlawful violence' . . . [T]here must be, on the part of the defendant, a hostile intent calculated to cause apprehension in the mind of the victim.

In the present case, on the findings which I have summarised, there was quite clearly an intention to cause fear, an intention to frighten, and that intention produced the intended effect as the result of what the defendant did, in that it did frighten and indeed terrify Miss Mooney to the extent that she screamed. It is not a case where she was merely startled or surprised or ashamed to be seen in her nightclothes; she was terrified as the result of what the defendant deliberately did, knowing and either intending or being reckless as to whether it would cause that fear in her . . .

When one is in a state of terror one is very often unable to analyse precisely what one is frightened of as likely to happen next. When I say that, I am speaking of a situation such as the present, where the person who causes one to be terrified is immediately adjacent, albeit on the other side of the window . . .

In the present case the defendant intended to frighten Miss Mooney and Miss Mooney was frightened. As it seems to me, there is no need for a finding that what she was frightened of, which she probably could not analyse at that moment, was some innominate terror of some potential violence. It was clearly a situation where the basis of the fear which was instilled in her was that she did not know what the defendant was going to do next, but that, whatever he might be going to do next, and sufficiently immediately for the purposes of the offence, was something of a violent nature. In effect, as it seems to me, it was wholly open to the justices to infer that her state of mind was not only that of terror, which they did find, but terror of some immediate violence . . .

5.4.3 WORDS AS AN ASSAULT

R v Ireland; R v Burstow [1997] 4 All ER 225

In Ireland's case the certified question of law of general public importance was whether the making of a series of silent telephone calls could amount in law to an assault.

Lord Steyn outlined the facts giving rise to the appeal in *R v Ireland* as follows:

... the appellant was convicted on his plea of guilty of three offences of assault occasioning actual bodily harm, contrary to section 47 of the Act of 1861 ... The case against Ireland was that during a period of three months in 1994 covered by the indictment he harassed three women by making repeated telephone calls to them during which he remained silent. Sometimes, he resorted to heavy breathing. The calls were mostly made at night. The case against him, which was accepted by the judge and the Court of Appeal, was that he caused his victim to suffer psychiatric illness [see extracts below relating to whether or not such harm could constitute actual bodily harm]. *Ireland* had a substantial record of making offensive telephone calls to women. The judge sentenced him to a total of three years' imprisonment.

Lord Steyn then considered whether or not there could be an assault by words alone or by silence.

It is now necessary to consider whether the making of silent telephone calls causing psychiatric injury is capable of constituting an assault under section 47. The Court of Appeal, as constituted in the *Ireland* case, answered that question in the affirmative. There has been substantial academic criticism of the conclusion and reasoning in Ireland: see Archbold News, Issue 6, 12 July 1996; *Archbold's Criminal Pleading, Evidence & Practice* (1995), Supplement No 4 (1996), pp 345–47; Smith and Hogan, *Criminal Law*, 8th edn, 413; 'Assault by telephone' by Jonathan Herring [1997] CLJ 11; 'Assault' [1997] Crim LR 434, 435–36. Counsel's arguments, broadly speaking, challenged the decision in *Ireland* on very similar lines. Having carefully considered the literature and counsel's arguments, I have come to the conclusion that the appeal ought to be dismissed.

The starting point must be that an assault is an ingredient of the offence under section 47. It is necessary to consider the two forms which an assault may take. The first is battery, which involves the unlawful application of force by the defendant upon the victim. Usually, section 47 is used to prosecute in cases of this kind. The second form of assault is an act causing the victim to apprehend an imminent application of force upon her: see *Fagan v Metropolitan Police Commissioner* [1969] 1 QB 439, 444D–E.

One point can be disposed of, quite briefly. The Court of Appeal was not asked to consider whether silent telephone calls resulting in psychiatric injury is capable of constituting a battery. But encouraged by some academic comment it was raised before your Lordships' House. Counsel for Ireland was most economical in his argument on the point. I will try to match his economy of words. In my view it is not feasible to enlarge the generally accepted legal meaning of what is a battery to include the circumstances of a silent caller who causes psychiatric injury.

It is to assault in the form of an act causing the victim to fear an immediate application of force to her that I must turn. Counsel argued that as a matter of law an assault can never be committed by words alone and therefore it cannot be committed by silence. The premise depends on the slenderest authority, namely, an observation by Holroyd J to a jury that 'no words or singing are equivalent to an assault': *Meade's and Belt's Case* (1823) 1 Lew CC 184. The proposition that a gesture may amount to an assault, but that words can never suffice, is unrealistic and indefensible. A thing said is also a thing done. There is no reason why something said should be incapable of causing an apprehension of immediate personal violence, e.g. a man accosting a woman in a dark alley saying 'Come with me or I will stab you.' I would, therefore, reject the proposition that an assault can never be committed by words.

That brings me to the critical question whether a silent caller may be guilty of an assault. The answer to this question seems to me to be 'Yes, depending on the facts.' It involves questions of fact within the province of the jury. After all, there is no reason why a telephone caller who says to a woman in a menacing way 'I will be at your door in a minute or two' may not be guilty of an assault if he causes his victim to apprehend immediate personal violence. Take now the case of the silent caller. He intends by his silence to cause fear and he is so understood. The victim is assailed by uncertainty about his intentions. Fear may dominate her emotions, and it may be the fear that the caller's arrival at her door may be imminent. She may fear the possibility of immediate personal violence. As a matter of law the caller may be guilty of an assault: whether he is or not will depend on the circumstance and in particular on the impact of the caller's potentially menacing call or calls on the victim. Such a prosecution case under section 47 may be fit to leave to the jury. And a trial judge may, depending on the circumstances, put a common sense consideration before jury, namely what, if not the possibility of imminent personal violence, was the victim terrified about? I conclude that an assault may be committed in the particular factual circumstances which I have envisaged. For this reason I reject the submission that as a matter of law a silent telephone caller cannot ever be guilty of an offence under section 47. In these circumstances no useful purpose would be served by answering the vague certified question in *Ireland*.

Having concluded that the legal arguments advanced on behalf of *Ireland* on section 47 must fail, I nevertheless accept that the concept of an assault involving immediate personal violence as an ingredient of the section 47 offence is a considerable complicating factor in bringing prosecutions under it in respect of silent telephone callers and stalkers. That the least serious of the ladder of offences is difficult to apply in such cases is unfortunate. At the hearing of the appeal of *Ireland* attention was drawn to the Bill which is annexed to the Law Commission Report, Legislating the Criminal Code: Offences Against the Person and General Principles, Consultation Paper (Law Com 218, Cmnd 2370, 1993). Clause 4 of that Bill is intended to replace section 47. Clause 4 provides that 'A person is guilty of an offence if he intentionally or recklessly causes injury to another.' This simple and readily comprehensible provision would eliminate the problems inherent in section 47. In expressing this view I do not, however, wish to comment on the appropriateness of the definition of 'injury' in clause 18 of the Bill, and in particular the provision that 'injury' means 'impairment of a person's mental health'.

Lord Hope:
There is no clear guidance on this point either in the statute or in the authorities. On the one hand in *Meade's and Belt's* Case (1823) 1 Lew CC 184 Holroyd J said that no words or singing can amount to an assault. On the other hand in *R v Wilson* [1955] 1 WLR 493, 494 Lord Goddard CJ said that the appellant's words, 'Get out knives' would itself be an assault. The word 'assault' as used in section 47 of the Act of 1861 is not defined anywhere in that Act. The legislation appears to have been framed on the basis that the words which it used were words which everyone would understand without further explanation. In this regard the fact that the statute was enacted in the middle of the last century is of no significance. The public interest, for whose benefit it was enacted, would not be served by construing the words in a narrow or technical way. The words used are ordinary English words, which can be given their ordinary meaning in the usage of the present day. They can take account of changing circumstances both as regards medical knowledge and the means by which one person can cause bodily harm to another.

The fact is that the means by which a person of evil disposition may intentionally or recklessly cause another to apprehend immediate and unlawful violence will vary according to the circum-stances. Just as it is not true to say that every blow which is struck is an assault – some blows, which would otherwise amount to battery, may be struck by accident or in jest or may otherwise be entirely justified – so also it is not true to say that mere words or gestures can never constitute an assault. It all depends on the circumstances. If the words or gestures are accompanied in their turn by gestures or by words which threaten immediate and unlawful violence, that will be sufficient for an assault. The words or gestures must be seen in their whole context.

In this case the means which the appellant used to communicate with his victims was the telephone. While he remained silent, there can be no doubt that he was intentionally communicating with them as directly as if he was present with them in the same room. But whereas for him merely to remain silent with them in the same room, where they could see him and assess his demeanour, would have been unlikely to give rise to any feelings of apprehension on their part, his silence when using the telephone in calls made to them repeatedly was an act of an entirely different character. He was using his silence as a means of conveying a message to his victims. This was that he knew who and where they were, and that his purpose in making contact with them was as malicious as it was deliberate. In my opinion silent telephone calls of this nature are just as capable as words or gestures, said or made in the presence of the victim, of causing an apprehension of immediate and unlawful violence.

5.4.4 WHAT IS ACTUAL BODILY HARM?

In the absence of any statutory definition in the 1861 Act the courts have had to develop an open-textured working definition of actual bodily harm for the purposes of s 47. In *R v Donovan* [1934] 2 KB 498, Swift J referred to 'hurt or injury calculated to interfere with the health or comfort of the [victim]'. Similarly in *R v Miller* [1954] 2 QB 282, where Lynskey J endorsed this approach and added:

There was a time when shock was not regarded as bodily hurt, but the day has gone by when that could be said. It seems to me now that if a person is caused hurt or injury resulting, not in any physical injury, but in an injury to her state of mind for the time being, that is within the definition of actual bodily harm, and on that point I would leave the case to the jury. In *Director of Public Prosecutions v Smith* [2006] All ER (D) 69 (Jan) it was held that cutting another's hair without their consent could amount to actual bodily harm provided it was not so trivial as to be without significance. Actual bodily harm was not limited to harm to the skin, flesh and bones; it applied to all parts of the body, even it if technically constituted dead tissue.

R v Ireland; R v Burstow [1997] 4 All ER 225

One of the issues common to both *R v Ireland* and *R v Burstow* was the extent to which any psychiatric illness caused by the activities of the appellants could amount to actual bodily harm (Ireland) or grievous bodily harm (*Burstow*).

Lord Steyn:
It will now be convenient to consider the question which is common to the two appeals, namely, whether psychiatric illness is capable of amounting to bodily harm in terms of sections 18, 20 and 47 of the Act of 1861. The answer must be the same for the three sections.

The only abiding thing about the processes of the human mind, and the causes of its disorders and disturbances, is that there will never be a complete explanation. Psychiatry is and will always remain an imperfectly understood branch of medical science. This idea is explained by Vallar's psychiatrist in Iris Murdoch's The Message to the Planet:

> Our knowledge of the soul, if I may use that unclinical but essential word, encounters certain seemingly impassable limits, set there perhaps by the gods, if I may refer to them, in order to preserve their privacy, and beyond which it may be not only futile but lethal to attempt to pass and though it is our duty to seek for knowledge, it is also incumbent on us to realise when it is denied us, and not to prefer a fake solution to no solution at all.

But there has been progress since 1861. And courts of law can only act on the best scientific understanding of the day. Some elementary distinctions can be made. The appeals under consideration do not involve structural injuries to the brain such as might require the intervention of a neurologist. One is also not considering either psychotic illness or personality disorders. The victims in the two appeals suffered from no such conditions. As a result of the behaviour of the appellants they did not develop psychotic or psychoneurotic conditions. The case was that they developed mental disturbances of a lesser order, namely neurotic disorders. For present purposes the relevant forms of neurosis are anxiety disorders and depressive disorders. Neuroses must be distinguished from simple states of fear, or problems in coping with every day life. Where the line is to be drawn must be a matter of psychiatric judgment. But for present purposes it is important to note that modern psychiatry treats neuroses as recognisable psychiatric illnesses: see *Liability for Psychiatric Injury*, Law Commission Consultation Paper 137 (1995) Part III (The Medical Background); Mullany and Hanford, *Tort Liability for Psychiatric Damages* (1993), discussion on 'The medical perspective,' at pp 24–42, and in particular at 30, fn 88. Moreover, it is essential to bear in mind that neurotic illnesses affect the central nervous system of the body, because emotions such as fear and anxiety are brain functions.

The civil law has for a long time taken account of the fact that there is no rigid distinction between body and mind. In *Bourhill v Young* [1943] AC 92, 103 Lord Macmillan said:

> The crude view that the law should take cognisance only of physical injury resulting from actual impact has been discarded, and it is now well recognised that an action will lie for injury by shock sustained through the medium of the eye or the ear without direct physical contact. The distinction between mental shock and bodily injury was never a scientific one . . .

This idea underlies the subsequent decisions of the House of Lords regarding post-traumatic stress disorder in *McLoughlin v O'Brian* [1983] 1 AC 410, 418, per Lord Wilberforce; and *Page v Smith* [1996] AC 155, 181A–D, per Lord Browne-Wilkinson. So far as such cases are concerned with the precise boundaries of tort liability they are not relevant. But so far as those decisions are based on the principle that the claimant must be able to prove that he suffered a recognis-able psychiatric illness or condition they are by analogy relevant. The decisions of the House of Lords on post-traumatic stress disorder hold that where the line is to be drawn is a matter for expert psychiatric evidence. By analogy those decisions suggest a possible principled approach to the question whether psychiatric injury may amount to bodily harm in terms of the Act of 1861.

The criminal law has been slow to follow this path. But in *R v Chan-Fook* [1994] 1 WLR 689 the Court of Appeal squarely addressed the question whether psychiatric injury may amount to bodily harm under section 47 of the Act of 1861. The issue arose in a case where the defendant had aggressively questioned and locked in a suspected thief. There was a dispute as to whether the defendant had physically assaulted the victim. But the prosecution also alleged that even if the victim had suffered no physical injury, he had been reduced to a mental state which amounted to actual bodily harm under section 47. No psychiatric evidence was given. The judge directed the jury that an assault which caused an hysterical and nervous condition was an assault occasioning actual bodily harm. The defendant was convicted. Upon appeal the conviction was quashed on the ground of misdirections in the summing-up and the absence of psychiatric evidence to support the prosecution's alternative case. The interest of the decision lies in the reasoning on psychiatric injury in the context of section 47. In a detailed and careful judgment given on behalf of the court Hobhouse LJ said (at p 695G–H):

> The first question on the present appeal is whether the inclusion of the word 'bodily' in the phrase 'actual bodily harm' limits harm to the skin, flesh and bones of the victim . . . The body of the victim includes all parts of his body, including his organs, his nervous system and his brain. Bodily injury therefore may include injury to any of those parts of his body responsible for his mental and other faculties.

In concluding that 'actual bodily harm' is capable of including psychiatric injury Hobhouse LJ emphasised (at p 696C) that

> it does not include mere emotions such as fear or distress nor panic nor does it include, as such, states of mind that are not themselves evidence of some identifiable clinical condition.

He observed that in the absence of psychiatric evidence a question whether or not an assault occasioned psychiatric injury should not be left to the jury.

The Court of Appeal, as differently constituted in *Ireland* and *Burstow*, was bound by the decision in *Chan-Fook*. The House is not so bound. Counsel for the appellants in both appeals submitted that bodily harm in Victorian legislation cannot include psychiatric injury. For this reason they argued that *Chan-Fook* was wrongly decided. They relied on the following observation of Lord Bingham of Cornhill CJ in *Burstow* [1997] 1 Cr App R 144, 148:

> Were the question free from authority, we should entertain some doubt whether the Victorian draftsman of the 1861 Act intended to embrace psychiatric injury within the expressions 'grievous bodily harm' and 'actual bodily harm'.

Nevertheless, the Lord Chief Justice observed that it is now accepted that in the relevant context the distinction between physical and mental injury is by no means clear-cut. He welcomed the ruling in *Chan-Fook* at p 149B. I respectfully agree. But I would go further and point out that, although out of considerations of piety we frequently refer to the actual intention of the draftsman, the correct approach is simply to consider whether the words of the Act of 1861 considered in the light of contemporary knowledge cover a recognisable psychiatric injury . . .

The proposition that the Victorian legislator when enacting sections 18, 20 and 47 of the Act 1861, would not have had in mind psychiatric illness is no doubt correct. Psychiatry was in its infancy in 1861. But the subjective intention of the draftsman is immaterial. The only relevant enquiry is as to the sense of the words in the context in which they are used. Moreover the Act of 1861 is a statute of the 'always speaking' type: the statute must be interpreted in the light of the best current scientific appreciation of the link between the body and psychiatric injury.

For these reasons I would, therefore, reject the challenge to the correctness of *Chan-Fook* [1994] 1 WLR 689. In my view the ruling in that case was based on principled and cogent reasoning and it marked a sound and essential clarification of the law. I would hold that 'bodily harm' in sections 18, 20 and 47 must be interpreted so as to include recognisable psychiatric illness.

5.4.5 THE ASSAULT MUST CAUSE THE ACTUAL BODILY HARM

R v Roberts (1971) 56 Cr App R 95 (CA)

The appellant made indecent advances towards, and indecent suggestions to, the complainant, a young woman who was a passenger in his car. The prosecution case was that the complainant jumped out of the appellant's car whilst it was moving in order to escape from his advances. Her resulting injuries caused her to be taken to hospital, where she was treated for some concussion and for some grazing, and was detained for three days. The defendant was convicted of assault occasioning actual bodily harm. He appealed on the ground that the complainant's jumping from his moving car was a *novus actus interveniens*, breaking the chain of causation between his actions and her injuries.

Stephenson LJ:
... [The jury] had to consider: was the appellant guilty of occasioning [the victim] actual bodily harm? Of course, for that to be established, it had to be established that he was responsible in law and in fact for her injuries caused by leaving in a hurry the moving car . . .

We have been . . . referred to . . . *Beech* (1912) 7 Cr App R 197, which was a case of a woman jumping out of a window and injuring herself . . . In that case the Court of Criminal Appeal (at p 200) approved the direction given by the trial judge in these terms: 'Will you say whether the conduct of the prisoner amounted to a threat of causing injury to this young woman, was the act of jumping the natural consequence of the conduct of the prisoner, and was the grievous bodily harm the result of the conduct of the prisoner?' That, said the court, was a proper direction as far as the law went, and they were satisfied that there was evidence before the jury of the prisoner causing actual bodily harm to the woman. 'No-one could say,' said Darling J when giving the judgment of the court, 'that if she jumped from the window it was not a natural consequence of the prisoner's conduct. It was a very likely thing for a woman to do as the result of the threats of a man who was conducting himself as this man indisputably was.'

This court thinks that that correctly states the law . . .

. . . The test is: Was it [the action of the victim which resulted in actual bodily harm] the natural result of what the alleged assailant said and did, in the sense that it was something that could reasonably have been foreseen as the consequence of what he was saying or doing? As it was put in one of the old cases, it had got to be shown to be his act, and if of course the victim does something so 'daft', in the words of the appellant in this case, or so unexpected, not that this particular assailant did not actually foresee it but that no reasonable man could be expected to foresee it, then it is only in a very remote and unreal sense a consequence of his assault, it is really occasioned by a voluntary act on the part of the victim which could not reasonably be foreseen and which breaks the chain of causation between the assault and harm or injury.

5.4.6 THE *MENS REA* FOR S 47

R v Venna [1976] QB 421 (CA)

The appellant lashed out at a police constable who was attempting to arrest him. The appellant caused the constable to suffer a fractured hand, and was convicted under s 47. He appealed on the basis that he did not know or suspect that there was a police officer in the way or that his foot might strike a police officer's hand.

> James LJ:
> . . . In our view the element of *mens rea* in the offence of battery is satisfied by proof that the defendant intentionally or recklessly applied force to the person of another. If it were otherwise, the strange consequence would be that an offence of unlawful wounding contrary to s 20 of the Offences Against the Person Act 1861 could be established by proof that the defendant wounded the victim either intentionally or recklessly, but if the victim's skin was not broken and the offence was therefore laid as an assault occasioning actual bodily harm contrary to s 47 of the 1861 Act, it would be necessary to prove that the physical force was intentionally applied.

R v Savage; R v Parmenter [1992] 1 AC 699 (HL)

In *R v Savage*, the defendant had intended to throw the contents of a beer glass at the victim, a Ms Beal. Because the glass was wet it slipped from her hand and cut Ms Beal's wrist. In *R v Parmenter* the defendant had been convicted under s 20 of the 1861 Act after harming his infant son. Both appeals raised the issue of whether or not a defendant charged under s 47 had to be shown to have intended (or to have been reckless as to whether the victim would suffer) actual bodily harm.

> Lord Ackner (with whom Lord Keith of Kinkel, Lord Brandon of Oakbrook, Lord Jauncey of Tullichettle and Lord Lowry agreed):
> Can a verdict of assault occasioning actual bodily harm be returned upon proof of an assault together with proof of the fact that actual bodily harm was occasioned by the assault, or must the prosecution also prove that the defendant intended to cause some actual bodily harm or was reckless as to whether such harm would be caused?
> Your Lordships are concerned with the mental element of a particular kind of assault, an assault 'occasioning actual bodily harm'. It is common ground that the mental element of assault is an intention to cause the victim to apprehend immediate and unlawful violence or recklessness whether such apprehension be caused: see *R v Venna* [1976] QB 421. It is of course common ground that Mrs Savage committed an assault upon Miss Beal when she threw the contents of her glass of beer over her. It is also common ground that however the glass came to be broken and Miss Beal's wrist thereby cut, it was, on the finding of the jury, Mrs Savage's handling of the glass which caused Miss Beal 'actual bodily harm'. Was the offence thus established or is there a further mental state that has to be established in relation to the bodily harm element of the offence? Clearly the section, by its terms, expressly imposes no such requirement. Does it do so

by necessary implication? It neither uses the word 'intentionally' nor the word 'maliciously'. The words 'occasioning actual bodily harm' are descriptive of the word 'assault', by reference to a particular kind of consequence . . .

. . . [O]nce the assault was established, the only remaining question was whether the victim's conduct was the natural consequence of that assault. The word 'occasioning' raised solely a question of causation, an objective question which does not involve enquiring into the accused's state of mind . . .

. . . The decision in *R v Roberts* 56 Cr App R 95 was correct. The verdict of assault occasioning actual bodily harm may be returned upon proof of an assault together with proof of the fact that actual bodily harm was occasioned by the assault. The prosecution are not obliged to prove that the defendant intended to cause some actual bodily harm or was reckless as to whether such harm would be caused . . .

5.4.7 CROWN PROSECUTION CHARGING STANDARDS: ASSAULT OCCASIONING ACTUAL BODILY HARM, CONTRARY TO S 47 OF THE ACT

7.3 As is made clear in paragraph 4.6 above, the only factor in law which distinguishes a charge under section 39 from a charge under section 47 is the degree of injury. By way of example, the following injuries should normally be prosecuted under section 47:

- loss or breaking of a tooth or teeth;
- temporary loss of sensory functions (which may include loss of consciousness);
- extensive or multiple bruising;
- displaced broken nose;
- minor fractures;
- minor, but not merely superficial, cuts of a sort probably requiring medical treatment (eg stitches);
- psychiatric injury which is more than fear, distress or panic. (Such injury will be proved by appropriate expert evidence.)

 COMMENTS AND QUESTIONS

1   The House of Lords' decision in *R v Savage; R v Parmenter* [1992] 1 AC 699 (above) makes it clear that a verdict of guilty of assault occasioning actual bodily harm is a permissible alternative verdict on a count alleging unlawful wounding contrary to s 20 of the 1861 Act; see further s 6(3) of the Criminal Law Act 1967.

5.5 POISONING

Sections 23 and 24 of the Offences Against the Person Act 1861 provide:

23 Whosoever shall unlawfully and maliciously administer to or cause to be administered to or taken by any other person any poison or other destructive or noxious thing, so as thereby to endanger the life of such person, or so as thereby to inflict upon such person any grievous bodily harm, shall be guilty of felony, and being convicted thereof shall be liable to be kept in penal servitude for any term not exceeding ten years.

24 Whosoever shall unlawfully and maliciously administer to or cause to be administered to or taken by any other person any poison or other destructive or noxious thing, with intent to injure, aggrieve, or annoy such person, shall be guilty of a misdemeanour, and being convicted thereof shall be liable to be kept in penal servitude.

5.5.1 ADMINISTERING

R v Gillard (1988) 87 Cr App R 189 (CA (Crim Div))

The court considered whether spraying CS gas constituted an 'administration' of a substance for the purposes of s 24 of the 1861 Act.

McNeill J:

Mr Boyd put his argument in this court in this way. He relied on the use in section 24 of the word 'administered' in conjunction with the word 'taken' as indicating Parliament's intention in this section to make criminal only acts which by physical contact obliged the victim to ingest the noxious thing. Where there was no physical contact and so no battery the act could nevertheless be charged and should be charged as an assault: to spray CS gas into someone's face is, he said, an assault in law.

The *Shorter Oxford English Dictionary* includes among definitions of 'administer', 'to apply, as medicine, etc. Hence to dispense, give (anything beneficial; also (jocular) a rebuke, a blow, etc)'.

The court does not find the dictionary definitions helpful: too many and too diverse alternatives are offered.

. . . A well established canon of construction is that if the words of a section are capable on their own of bearing a clear and ascertainable meaning there is no scope for reference over to other sections of the same statute; such recourse may only be had in the event of ambiguity or uncertainty or if that meaning is apparently inconsistent with the general intention of the statute. This is not the case here.

Where, in the view of this court, the learned recorder was in error was in holding that 'administering' and 'taking' were to be treated effectively as synonymous or as conjunctive words in the section; on the contrary, the repeated use of the word 'or' makes it clear that they are disjunctive. The word 'takes' postulates some 'ingestion' by the victim; 'administer' must have some other meaning and there is no difficulty in including in that meaning such conduct as spraying the victim with noxious fluid or vapour, whether from a device such as a gas canister or, for example, hosing down with effluent. There is no necessity when the word 'administer' is used to postulate any form of entry into the victim's body, whether through any orifice or by absorption; a court dealing with such a case should not have to determine questions of pathology such as, for example, the manner in which skin irritation results from exposure to CS gas or the manner in which the eye waters when exposed to irritant. The word 'ingest' should be reserved to its natural meaning of intake into the digestive system and not permitted to obscure the statutory words.

In the view of this court, the proper construction of 'administer' in section 24 includes conduct which not being the application of direct force to the victim nevertheless brings the noxious thing into contact with his body.

While such conduct might in law amount to an assault, this court considers that so to charge it would tend to mislead a jury.

The court has been assisted by the note by Professor JC Smith in the report of *Dones* [1987] Crim LR 682. The learned recorder, as the note submits, was correct in treating the question as one of construction and as a matter of law, following *R v Maginnis* (1987) 85 Cr App R 127.

In this respect, Judge Butler was in error in following as he presumably did the approach of the House of Lords in *Brutus v Cozens* (1972) 56 Cr App R 799, [1973] AC 854 which, in relation to the word 'insulting' regarded the meaning of that word as a matter of fact for the jury. This court regards the word 'administer' as one to be construed as was the word 'supply' in *R v Maginnis*. However, the trial judge's error – and an understandable error – was, if anything, to the advantage of the defendant, as he then was, and can in no way be regarded as a material irregularity.

As Mr Recorder Walsh correctly said: 'It is for the court to interpret and construe the word here, as having a particular meaning, and for the court to direct the jury as to what it means.' In concluding as follows: 'I am satisfied that the word "administer" does not apply to a situation such as this,' that is squirting ammonia from a plastic lemon – he was in error.

Accordingly, this appeal is dismissed.

5.5.2 NOXIOUS SUBSTANCE

R v Cato [1976] 1 WLR 110 (CA)

The appellant injected the deceased, a friend of the appellant's named Farmer, with a fatal dosage of heroin. The injection had been at Farmer's request. The following extract concerns the extent to which the heroin solution constituted a noxious substance for the purposes of s 23 of the 1861 Act.

Lord Widgery CJ:

... What is a noxious thing, and in particular is heroin a noxious thing? The authorities show that an article is not to be described as noxious for present purposes merely because it has a potentiality for harm if taken in an overdose.

There are many articles of value in common use which may be harmful in overdose, and it is clear on the authorities when looking at them that one cannot describe an article as noxious merely because it has that aptitude. On the other hand, if an article is liable to injure in common use, not when an overdose in the sense of an accidental excess is used but is liable to cause injury in common use, should it then not be regarded as a noxious thing for present purposes?

When one has regard to the potentiality of heroin in the circumstances which we read about and hear about in our courts today we have no hesitation in saying that heroin is a noxious thing and we do not think that arguments are open to an accused person in a case such as the present, whereby he may say: 'Well the deceased was experienced in taking heroin: his tolerance was high,' and generally to indicate that the heroin was unlikely to do any particular harm in a particular circumstance. We think there can be no doubt, and it should be said clearly, that heroin is a noxious thing for the purposes of s 23.

. . . We think in this case where the act was entirely a direct one that the requirement of malice is satisfied if the syringe was deliberately inserted into the body of Farmer, as it undoubtedly was, and if Cato at a time when he so inserted the syringe knew that the syringe contained a noxious substance. That is enough, we think, in this type of direct injury case to satisfy the requirement of maliciousness.

5.5.3 *MENS REA* FOR THE 'POISONING' OFFENCES

For both sections 23 and 24, the defendant's administration of the noxious substance must be 'malicious' – as to which see *R v Cunningham* [1957] 2 QB 396. For s 24 an ulterior intent, namely to 'injure, aggrieve or annoy', must be established. The meaning of this was considered by the House of Lords in *R v Hill* (extracted below).

R v Hill (1986) 83 Cr App R 386

The respondent gave some young boys tablets (tenuate dospan, used as an aid in slimming cures). He hoped that the tablets might affect the boys so as to make them less inhibited and more amenable to indulging in homosexual activities with him. The respondent was convicted under s 24 and appealed contending that he had not had the required ulterior intent. The Court of Appeal certified a question of law of general public importance in the following form:

Whether the offence of administering a noxious thing with intent to injure contrary to section 24 of the Offences Against the Person Act 1861 is capable of being committed when a noxious thing is administered to a person without lawful excuse with the intention only of keeping that person awake.

Lord Griffiths [having referred to the trial judge's summing-up on intent and the Court of Appeal's criticism of it]:

In this passage from the summing-up the judge is explaining to the jury the meaning of injury in the section and relating it to the circumstances of this case. He is rightly directing the jury that injury includes causing harm to the body and pointing out to them that they would be entitled to conclude that to give drugs to children with the intention of interfering with their metabolism so that they would stay awake for an unnatural period could amount to causing injury in the sense of harm.

I am quite unable to read this passage in the summing-up as a direction that an intention to keep a child awake by itself say for some benevolent purpose such as enjoying the fireworks, or to greet his father on a late return from work could amount to an intent to injure and I am sure it would not have been so understood by the jury.

Furthermore, far from other passages in the summing-up being to the same effect, as the Court of Appeal supposed, the whole tenor of the summing-up was that the jury must be sure that the respondent intended to cause harm to the health of the boys . . .

> The summing-up read as a whole, as a summing-up should always be read, made it clear beyond peradventure that the jury should only convict if they were sure that the respondent intended to injure the boys in the sense of causing them physical harm by the administration of the drugs. This was a correct direction. The respondent did, in fact, cause some physical harm and there was overwhelming evidence that this was his intention. I would accordingly allow this appeal and restore the convictions.
>
> My Lords, on the view I take of the summing-up this question does not call for an answer. It is, in any event, a question which it is not sensible to attempt to answer without knowing the factual background against which it is asked. If the noxious thing is administered for a purely benevolent purpose such as keeping a pilot of an aircraft awake the answer will almost certainly be no, but if administered for a malevolent purpose such as a prolonged interrogation the answer will almost certainly be yes. I would, my Lords, therefore decline to answer the certified question.
>
> Your Lordships declined to give leave to the respondent to argue that the conviction should be quashed on the ground that the judge failed to direct the jury on the issue of consent. This issue was never raised by the defence at the trial and if it had been it would have had no prospect of success. In the circumstances, the judge was under no duty to refer to it in the summing up.

Lord Mackay, Lord Ackner, Lord Bridge and Lord Brandon agreed that the appeal should be allowed for the reasons given.

R v Gantz [2004] All ER (D) 69 (Oct), confirms that where D surreptitiously puts an ecstasy tablet in P's drink in order to make her more susceptible to his advances a trial judge can direct the jury that D intends to 'injure' – the stimulating effect of the judge sufficing for these purposes.

5.6 COMMON ASSAULT AND BATTERY

The offences of common assault (intentionally or recklessly causing another to apprehend immediate physical violence) and battery (intentionally or recklessly causing physical contact with another) are only triable on a summary basis, and thus carry a maximum penalty of six months' imprisonment. Although they are offences at common law, charges of common assault and common battery will be brought under s 39 of the Criminal Justice Act 1988.

5.6.1 COMMON LAW OR STATUTORY OFFENCES?

DPP v Taylor; DPP v Little [1992] 1 QB 645 (DC)

The basic issue in both cases was the effect of s 39 on the offences of common assault and battery. In *Taylor*, an information had been laid by the DPP. It was argued that it could only be laid by the victim, and that s 39 did not affect the common law in this respect. In *Little*, the question was simply whether an information alleging assault and battery was bad for duplicity. In each case, the magistrates dismissed the information. The DPP's appeal in *Taylor* was allowed, but was dismissed in *Little*.

Mann LJ:

Assault and battery are treated in the statute [Criminal Justice Act 1988] as separate offences. They have always been separate offences. Thus in *R v Mansfield Justices ex p Sharkey* [1985] QB 613, 627, Lord Lane CJ said:

> An assault is any act by which the defendant intentionally, or recklessly, causes the victim to apprehend immediate unlawful violence. There is no need for it to proceed to physical contact. If it does, it is an assault and a battery. Assault is a crime independent of battery and it is important to remember that fact.

The resolution of the debate as to whether the offences are statutory offences cannot in my view be achieved without an examination of some history. Assault and battery were born at the common law. Prosecutions for battery are rare but prosecutions for assault are frequent. The term 'assault' has by usage come to have a meaning in practice which would not commend itself to the philologist (as to whom see Robert Goff LJ, *Collins v Wilcock* [1984] 1 WLR 1172, 1177A). In *Fagan v Metropolitan Police Commissioner* [1969] 1 QB 439 James J (with whom Lord Parker CJ entirely agreed) said, at p 444:

> Although 'assault' is an independent crime and is to be treated as such, for practical purposes today 'assault' is generally synonymous with the term 'battery', and is a term used to mean the actual intended use of unlawful force to another person without his consent.

More recently in *R v Williams (Gladstone)* (1984) 78 Cr App R 276 Lord Lane CJ said, at p 279:

> 'Assault' in the context of this case, that is to say using the word as a convenient abbreviation for assault and battery, is an act by which the defendant, intentionally or recklessly, applies unlawful force to the complainant.

The usage has also been employed by Parliament. The Offences Against the Person Act 1861 contains a group of sections (sections 36 to 47) under the heading 'Assaults'. [In] Section 47 . . . can be seen Parliament's employment of 'assault' as including the use of force for without force it would only be in a most unusual case that an assault could occasion actual bodily harm. Such a case would be that of a person who is put in such fear of force being about to be used against him, that he jumps from a high window with injurious consequences. It is now far too late to even contemplate that the familiar offence of 'actual bodily harm' is confined to unusual cases of that nature. The phrase 'common assault' must be, and in practice has long been, construed in a consistent and similar sense. The adjective 'common' serves only to differentiate from particular assaults for which specific provision is or was made, elsewhere . . . in [the 1861 Act] . . .

My conclusion upon the question of whether the offences of common assault and battery are statutory offences is that they are and have been such since 1861 and accordingly that they should now be charged as being 'contrary to section 39 of the Criminal Justice Act 1988'.

I turn to the question of how a charge of common assault should be formulated so as to avoid duplicity where the case is one of actual as well as apprehended unlawful force. The form which is hallowed by long use is 'did assault and beat' the victim: *Stone's Justices' Manual 1991*, vol 3, p 5595, paras 9–90. Mr Godfrey, who appeared for the defendant, Stephen Little, described this form as 'lazy "conventional" language'. A proper language, said Mr Godfrey, would be 'assault by beating' where force had been used and 'assault by threatening' where it had not.

Although duplicity is a matter of form it is a fundamental matter of form. If an information is duplicitous the prosecutor must elect on which offence he wishes to proceed and if he does not do so the information must be dismissed. In my judgment the unusual allegation of 'assault and batter' in the information against Stephen Little was duplicitous. I cannot accept the submission of Mr Collins for the DPP that 'and batter' is to be taken as no more than 'and beat' expressed in archaic language. I think that in 1990 an informant who uses 'batter' must be taken as referring to the offence of battery rather than as employing archaic language. The word 'assault' must therefore, by virtue of the contrast with 'batter', be taken as used in its pure sense of putting in fear of force. The result is an assertion of two offences. I think the justices were right in their conclusion that the information was duplicitous.

The phrase 'assault and beat' by reference to which many thousands of people must have been convicted without objection is not directly before us. The phrase is free of the vice of a contrast with 'batter', and the event to which the charge relates is a single occasion, albeit apprehension and receipt of force may be separable by a small unit of time. I think that now may be too late to regard the formulation as objectionable. However, undeniably a more accurate form would avoid a conjunction and use a preposition. Thus 'assault by beating' would be immune from argument. Mr Collins accepted that it would be, and I think that in the future prosecutors should avoid conjunctive forms.

The [Criminal Justice] Act of 1988 repealed section 42 of the Act of 1861 . . . and the effect of section 39 is that all common assaults and batteries are now triable summarily . . .

5.6.2 CROWN PROSECUTION CHARGING STANDARDS: COMMON ASSAULT – CONTRARY TO S 39 OF THE CRIMINAL JUSTICE ACT 1988

4.5 Where there is a battery the defendant should be charged with 'assault by beating': *DPP v Little* [1992] 1 All ER 299.

4.6 The only factor which distinguishes common assault from assault occasioning actual bodily harm, contrary to section 47 of the Offences Against the Person Act 1861, is the degree of injury which results. Normally, aggravating factors which may be relevant to sentence and to mode of trial decisions are irrelevant when deciding whether the degree of injury justifies a charge under section 47.

4.7 Where battery results in injury, a choice of charge is available. The Code for Crown Prosecutors recognises that there will be factors which may properly lead to a decision not to prefer or continue with the gravest possible charge. Thus, although any injury can be classified as actual bodily harm, the appropriate charge will be contrary to section 39 where injuries amount to no more than the following:

- grazes;
- scratches;
- abrasions;
- minor bruising;
- swellings;
- reddening of the skin;
- superficial cuts;
- a 'black eye'.

4.8 You should always consider the injuries first and in most cases the degree of injury will determine whether the appropriate charge is section 39 or section 47. There will be borderline cases, such as where an undisplaced broken nose has resulted. When the injuries amount to no more than those described at paragraph 4.7 above, any decision to charge an offence contrary to section 47 would only be justified in the most exceptional circumstances, or where the maximum available sentence in the magistrates' court would be inadequate.

4.9 As common assault is not an alternative verdict to more serious offences of assault, a jury may only convict of common assault if the count has been preferred in the circumstances set out in section 40 Criminal Justice Act 1988 (see paragraph 11.6 [set out] below).

4.10 Where a charge contrary to section 47 has been preferred, the acceptance of a plea of guilty to an added count for common assault will rarely be justified in the absence of a significant change in circumstances that could not have been foreseen at the time of review.

COMMENTS AND QUESTIONS

1   Although the vast majority of battery cases will involve D using force directly on P, this need not be the case. In *Haystead v DPP* [2000] 2 Cr App R 339, D was convicted under s 39 of the Criminal Justice Act 1988, where he frightened a woman into dropping her baby on the floor. The court certified the following point of law under s 1(2) of the Administration of Justice Act 1960: 'Whether the *actus reus* of the offence of battery requires that there be direct physical contact between the defendant and the complainant?' Leave to appeal to the House of Lords was refused. The same reasoning as regards indirect battery would apply if D set dogs on P to frighten him; see *R v Dume* (1987) *The Times*, 16 October.

2   By virtue of s 10 of the Domestic Violence, Crime and Victims Act 2004, common assault is made an arrestable offence for the purposes of the Police and Criminal Evidence Act 1984.

3   Section 38 of the Offences Against the Person Act 1861 creates the following offence: 'Whosoever . . . shall assault any person with intent to resist or prevent the lawful apprehension or detainer of himself or of any other person for any offence, shall be guilty of [an offence], and being convicted thereof shall be liable . . . to be imprisoned for any term not exceeding two years . . .'. For this offence to be made out, the arrest must be a lawful one. Where the arrest is carried out by a member of the public (not a police officer), this means that an arrestable offence must have been committed; see *R v Self* [1992] 1 WLR 657 and *R v Lee* [2000] Crim LR 991. Section 38 may be used for assaults on persons such as store detectives, who may be trying to apprehend or detain an offender.

4   When a police officer is assaulted, a charge under section 89(1) of the Police Act 1996 is often more appropriate. Unlike section 89(1), a charge under section 38 is triable on indictment and may therefore be coupled with other offences to be tried on indictment. Section 89 states:

> (1) Any person who assaults a constable in the execution of his duty, or a person assisting a constable in the execution of his duty, shall be guilty of an offence and liable on summary conviction to imprisonment for a term not exceeding six months or to a fine not exceeding [£5,000] or to both.

> (2) Any person who resists or wilfully obstructs a constable in the execution of his duty, or a person assisting a constable in the execution of his duty, shall be guilty of an offence and liable on summary conviction to imprisonment for a term not exceeding one month or to a fine not exceeding [£1,000] or to both.

The provisions of the Police Act 1996 consolidate provisions in the Police Act 1964. The elements of the offence under s 89(1) are: (a) an assault; (b) on a police officer; (c) who is acting in the execution of his duty. It does not matter that the defendant did not realise that the person he assaulted was a police officer, although this would be good mitigation and would result in a lesser punishment for the assault. The elements of the offence under s 89(2) are: (a) obstruction; (b) of a police officer; (c) who is acting in the execution of his duty. For the meaning of 'assault', see above.

5.7 'STALKING'

Parliament's response to the problem posed by what is popularly referred to as 'stalking' took the form of the Protection from Harassment Act 1997.

The Protection from Harassment Act 1997 was introduced in response to concerns about the inability of the existing civil and criminal law to deal adequately with the problem of stalking. The conduct prohibited is detailed in s 1 in the following terms:

> 1(1) A person must not pursue a course of conduct –
> (a) which amounts to harassment of another, and
> (b) which he knows or ought to know amounts to harassment of the other.
> 1(2) For the purposes of this section, the person whose course of conduct is in question ought to know that it amounts to harassment of another if a reasonable person in possession of the same information would think the course of conduct amounted to harassment of the other.
> 1(3) Subsection (1) does not apply to a course of conduct if the person who pursued it shows –
> (a) that it was pursued for the purpose of preventing or detecting crime,
> (b) that it was pursued under any enactment or rule of law or to comply with any condition or requirement imposed by any person under any enactment, or
> (c) that in the particular circumstances the pursuit of the course of conduct was reasonable.

Under s 2(1) it is a summary offence to pursue a course of conduct which amounts to a breach of the prohibition laid down in s 1. More serious harassment is made an offence (triable either way) under s 4 which provides:

> 4(1) A person whose course of conduct causes another to fear, on at least two occasions, that violence will be used against him is guilty of an offence if he knows or ought to know that his course of conduct will cause the other so to fear on each of those occasions.

4(2) For the purposes of this section, the person whose course of conduct is in question ought to know that it will cause another to fear that violence will be used against him on any occasion if a reasonable person in possession of the same information would think the course of conduct would cause the other so to fear on that occasion.

4(3) It is a defence for a person charged with an offence under this section to show that –

(a) his course of conduct was pursued for the purpose of preventing or detecting crime,

(b) his course of conduct was pursued under any enactment or rule of law or to comply with any condition or requirement imposed by any person under any enactment, or

(c) the pursuit of his course of conduct was reasonable for the protection of himself or another or for the protection of his or another's property.

 COMMENTS AND QUESTIONS

1   The objective nature of the test laid down in s 1(2) is emphasised in *R v Colohan* (2001) *The Times*, 14 June, where it was held that D's schizophrenia could not be taken into account in determining whether he ought to have known that his course of conduct would have amounted to harassment of another. Hughes J observed that to take into account the mental illness of the accused in applying the objective test laid down by 1(2) would undermine the very purpose of the 1997 Act, given that it was aimed at the activities of persons who might be expected to suffer from some form of mental illness.

2   Facts giving rise to a charge under the 1997 Act may also provide the basis for an assault charge. Much will depend on whether D's activities can be said to amount to a course of conduct as that phrase is understood under the 1997 Act; compare *R v Hills* [2001] Crim LR 318 and *Pratt v DPP* (2001) *The Times*, 22 August.

3   The Criminal Justice and Police Act 2001 introduces additional police powers to give directions to stop the harassment of a person in his home (s 42), and amends the 1997 Act by introducing measures to deal with collective harassment.

5.8   RACIALLY MOTIVATED ASSAULTS AND HARASSMENT

As part of a response to racially motivated violence the courts were given increased sentencing powers in respect of offences of violence and harassment with a proven racial element under the Crime and Disorder Act 1998. Section 39 of the Anti-Terrorism, Crime and Security Act 2001 amended the nature of the aggravating factor further to include religious aggravation – the extracts from the 1998 Act set out below are as amended by the 2001 Act.

28 Meaning of 'racially or religiously aggravated'

(1) An offence is racially or religiously aggravated for the purposes of sections 29 to 32 below if

(a) at the time of committing the offence, or immediately before or after doing so, the offender demonstrates towards the victim of the offence hostility based on the victim's membership (or presumed membership) of a racial or religious group; or

(b)   the offence is motivated (wholly or partly) by hostility towards members of a racial or religious group based on their membership of that group.

(2)   In subsection (1)(a) above

'membership', in relation to a racial or religious group, includes association with members of that group, 'presumed' means presumed by the offender.

(3)   It is immaterial for the purposes of paragraph (a) or (b) of subsection (1) above whether or not the offender's hostility is also based, to any extent, on any other factor not mentioned in that paragraph.

(4)   In this section 'racial group' means a group of persons defined by reference to race, colour, nationality (including citizenship) or ethnic or national origins.

(5)   In this section 'religious group' means a group of persons defined by reference to religious belief or lack of religious belief.

29 Racially or religiously aggravated assaults

(1)   A person is guilty of an offence under this section if he commits

(a)   an offence under section 20 of the Offences Against the Person Act 1861 (malicious wounding or grievous bodily harm);

(b)   an offence under section 47 of that Act (actual bodily harm); or

(c)   common assault,

which is racially or religiously aggravated for the purposes of this section.

(2)   A person guilty of an offence falling within subsection (1)(a) or (b) above shall be liable

(a)   on summary conviction, to imprisonment for a term not exceeding six months or to a fine not exceeding the statutory maximum, or to both;

(b)   on conviction on indictment, to imprisonment for a term not exceeding seven years or to a fine, or to both.

(3)   A person guilty of an offence falling within subsection (1)(c) above shall be liable

(a)   on summary conviction, to imprisonment for a term not exceeding six months or to a fine not exceeding the statutory maximum, or to both;

(b)   on conviction on indictment, to imprisonment for a term not exceeding two years or to a fine, or to both.

. . .

32 Racially or religiously aggravated harassment etc

(1)   A person is guilty of an offence under this section if he commits

(a)   an offence under section 2 of the Protection from Harassment Act 1997 (offence of harassment); or

(b)   an offence under section 4 of that Act (putting people in fear of violence),

which is racially or religiously aggravated for the purposes of this section.

(2)   In section 24(2) of the 1984 Act (arrestable offences), after paragraph (o) there shall be inserted

'(p) an offence falling within section 32(1)(a) of the Crime and Disorder Act 1998 (racially or religiously aggravated harassment)'.

(3)   A person guilty of an offence falling within subsection (1)(a) above shall be liable

(a)   on summary conviction, to imprisonment for a term not exceeding six months or to a fine not exceeding the statutory maximum, or to both;

(b)   on conviction on indictment, to imprisonment for a term not exceeding two years or to a fine, or to both.

(4)   A person guilty of an offence falling within subsection (1)(b) above shall be liable

(a) on summary conviction, to imprisonment for a term not exceeding six months or to a fine not exceeding the statutory maximum, or to both;

(b) on conviction on indictment, to imprisonment for a term not exceeding seven years or to a fine, or to both.

(5) If, on the trial on indictment of a person charged with an offence falling within subsection (1)(a) above, the jury find him not guilty of the offence charged, they may find him guilty of the basic offence mentioned in that provision.

(6) If, on the trial on indictment of a person charged with an offence falling within subsection (1)(b) above, the jury find him not guilty of the offence charged, they may find him guilty of an offence falling within subsection (1)(a) above.

The courts have avoided a narrowly legalistic approach to the scope of the offences under ss 28 to 23 of the 1998 Act. In *Attorney General's Reference (No 4 of 2004)* [2005] EWCA Crim 889, D had assaulted a doctor whilst referring to him as an 'immigrant doctor'. The trial judge had ruled that the use of this phrase could not necessarily turn the assault into one that was racially aggravated on the basis that the term 'immigrant' was too wide to constitute an ethnic or national group. Allowing the prosecution's appeal, the Court of Appeal held that a person who was an immigrant to the United Kingdom, and who was, therefore, non-British could, as such, be a member of a racial group within s 28(4) of the 1998 Act. The issue of whether D had used the term 'immigrant doctor' to highlight that the victim was not British, or whether it was evidence of her hostility to him within the terms of s 28(1)(a) of the 1998 (i.e. a reference to his race and/or his colour and/or his nationality and/or his ethnic or national origins) involved the determination of a question of fact that should have been left to the jury.

R v Rogers [2005] EWCA Crim 2863

D became involved in an altercation with a group of Spanish women during the course of which he referred to them as 'bloody foreigners', and told them to 'go back to your own country'. He was convicted of using racially aggravated abusive or insulting words or behaviour with the intent to cause fear or provoke violence, contrary to s 31(1)(a) of the 1998 Act and appealed unsuccessfully against his conviction.

Lord Phillips CJ:

13. . . . two separate issues can arise in relation to section 28 of the 1998 Act. For an offence to be aggravated under that section the defendant must first form the view that the victim is a member of a racial group, within the definition in section 28(4). He must then say something which demonstrates hostility towards the victim based on membership of that group. The words used may or may not expressly identify the racial group to which the defendant believes the victim belongs.

. . .

19. . . . [the facts giving rise to the current appeal] suggest that the only relevant characteristic that the appellant identified in relation to the victims of his assault was that they were foreign. There is no evidence that there was anything in their appearance that indicated a relevant racial characteristic. The defendant simply heard them speaking a foreign language, or with a foreign accent. If 'foreigners' constitute a racial group within the definition in section 28(4), there was plainly a case to go to the jury that he had demonstrated hostility towards his victims because they were foreigners . . .

20. . . . Hostility demonstrated to foreigners because they are foreign can be just as objectionable as hostility based on a more limited racial characteristic. All who are black form a racial group, defined by reference to colour, within section 28(4), as do all who are white. This demonstrates the width of the concept of racial group in this context. It is no great extension of the concept to embrace within a single racial group all who are foreign.

. . .

24. The very width of the meaning of racial group for the purposes of section 28(4) gives rise to a danger that charges of aggravated offences may be brought where vulgar abuse has included racial epithets that did not, when all the relevant circumstances are considered, indicate hostility to the race in question. Section 28 is designed to address racist behaviour and prosecutors should not bring charges based on its provisions unless satisfied that the facts truly suggest that the offence charged was aggravated by racism.

5.9 CODIFICATION AND LAW REFORM PROPOSALS

In 1998 the Home Office published its consultation document *Violence: Reforming the Offences Against the Person Act 1861*. The paper was based upon the Law Commission's Report *Legislating the Criminal Code: Offences Against the Person and General Principles*.

The key provisions of the draft Bill accompanying the Home Office paper were as follows:

Injury and assault

1(1) A person is guilty of an offence if he intentionally causes serious injury to another.

(2) A person is guilty of an offence if he omits to do an act which he has a duty to do at common law, the omission results in serious injury to another, and he intends the omission to have that result.

(3) An offence under this section is committed notwithstanding that the injury occurs outside England and Wales if the act causing injury is done in England and Wales or the omission resulting in injury is made there.

(4) A person guilty of an offence under this section is liable on conviction on indictment to imprisonment for life.

2(1) A person is guilty of an offence if he recklessly causes serious injury to another.

(2) An offence under this section is committed notwithstanding that the injury occurs outside England and Wales if the act causing injury is done in England and Wales.

(3) A person guilty of an offence under this section is liable –

    (a) on conviction on indictment, to imprisonment for a term not exceeding 7 years;

    (b) on summary conviction, to imprisonment for a term not exceeding 6 months or a fine not exceeding the statutory maximum or both.

3(1) A person is guilty of an offence if he intentionally or recklessly causes injury to another.

(2) An offence under this section is committed notwithstanding that the injury occurs outside England and Wales if the act causing injury is done in England and Wales.

(3) A person guilty of an offence under this section is liable –

    (a) on conviction on indictment, to imprisonment for a term not exceeding 5 years;

    (b) on summary conviction, to imprisonment for a term not exceeding 6 months or a fine not exceeding the statutory maximum or both.

4(1) A person is guilty of an offence if –

    (a) he intentionally or recklessly applies force to or causes an impact on the body of another, or

    (b) he intentionally or recklessly causes the other to believe that any such force or impact is imminent.

(2) No such offence is committed if the force or impact, not being intended or likely to cause injury, is in the circumstances such as is generally acceptable in the ordinary conduct of daily life and the defendant does not know or believe that it is in fact unacceptable to the other person.

(3) A person guilty of an offence under this section is liable on summary conviction to imprisonment for a term not exceeding 6 months or a fine not exceeding level 5 on the standard scale or both.

5(1) A person is guilty of an offence if he assaults –

    (a) a constable acting in the execution of his duty, or

    (b) a person assisting a constable acting in the execution of his duty.

(2) For the purposes of this section a person assaults if he commits the offence under section 4.

(3) A reference in this section to a constable acting in the execution of his duty includes a reference to a constable who is a member of a police force maintained in Scotland or Northern Ireland when he is executing a warrant, or otherwise acting in England and Wales, by virtue of an enactment conferring powers on him in England and Wales.

(4) For the purposes of subsection (3) each of the following is a police force –

    (a) a police force within the meaning given by section 50 of the Police (Scotland) Act 1967;

    (b) the Royal Ulster Constabulary and the Royal Ulster Constabulary Reserve.

(5) A person guilty of an offence under this section is liable on summary conviction to imprisonment for a term not exceeding 6 months or a fine not exceeding level 5 on the standard scale or both.

6(1) A person is guilty of an offence under this section if he causes serious injury to another intending to resist, prevent or terminate the lawful arrest or detention of himself or a third person.

(2) The question whether the defendant believes the arrest or detention is lawful must be determined according to the circumstances as he believes them to be.

(3) A person guilty of an offence under this section is liable on conviction on indictment to imprisonment for life.

7(1) A person is guilty of an offence if he assaults another intending to resist, prevent or terminate the lawful arrest or detention of himself or a third person.

(2) The question whether the defendant believes the arrest or detention is lawful must be determined according to the circumstances as he believes them to be.

(3) For the purposes of this section a person assaults if he commits the offence under section 4.

(4) A person guilty of an offence under this section is liable –

    (a) on conviction on indictment, to imprisonment for a term not exceeding 2 years;

    (b) on summary conviction, to imprisonment for a term not exceeding 6 months or a fine not exceeding the statutory maximum or both.

    . . .

Other offences

10(1) A person is guilty of an offence if he makes to another a threat to cause the death of, or serious injury to, that other or a third person, intending that other to believe that it will be carried out.

(2) A person guilty of an offence under this section is liable –

    (a) on conviction on indictment, to imprisonment for a term not exceeding 10 years;

    (b) on summary conviction, to imprisonment for a term not exceeding 6 months or a fine not exceeding the statutory maximum or both.

11(1) A person is guilty of an offence if –

    (a) he administers a substance to another or causes it to be taken by him and (in either case) he does so intentionally or recklessly,

    (b) he knows the substance is capable of causing injury to the other, and

    (c) it is unreasonable to administer the substance or cause it to be taken having regard to the circumstances as he knows or believes them to be.

(2) A person guilty of an offence under this section is liable –

    (a) on conviction on indictment, to imprisonment for a term not exceeding 5 years;

    (b) on summary conviction, to imprisonment for a term not exceeding 6 months or a fine not exceeding the statutory maximum or both. . . .

12(1) A person is guilty of an offence if he intentionally inflicts severe pain or suffering on another and he does the act –

    (a) in the performance or purported performance of his official duties as a public official, or

    (b) at the instigation or with the consent or acquiescence of a public official who is performing or purporting to perform his official duties.

(2) A person is guilty of an offence if –

    (a) he omits to do an act which he has a duty to do at common law,

    (b) he makes the omission as mentioned in subsection (1)(a) or (b),

    (c) the omission results in the infliction of severe pain or suffering on another, and

    (d) he intends the omission to have that result.

(3) The following are immaterial –

    (a) the nationality of the persons concerned;

    (b) whether anything occurs in the United Kingdom or elsewhere;

    (c) whether the pain or suffering is physical or mental.

(4) References in this section to an official include references to a person acting in an official capacity.

(5) Proceedings for an offence under this section may be instituted only by or with the consent of the Attorney General.

(6) A person guilty of an offence under this section is liable on conviction on indictment to imprisonment for life.

For clause 14 dealing with proposed fault terms, see Chapter 3.

. . .

15(1) In this Act 'injury' means –
    (a) physical injury, or
    (b) mental injury.
(2) Physical injury does not include anything caused by disease but (subject to that) it includes pain, unconsciousness and any other impairment of a person's physical condition.
(3) Mental injury does not include anything caused by disease but (subject to that) it includes any impairment of a person's mental health.
(4) In its application to section 1 this section applies without the exceptions relating to things caused by disease.

The commentary to the Home Office proposals observed as follows:

3.5 The Government's proposals on the offence of assault go rather further than those of the Law Commission. The Commission proposed to replace common assault and battery with a new offence of assault that would combine the two existing offences. In doing this the Commission were concerned to clarify the meaning of assault and to remove the need for separate offences of assault. However, although the Commission considered the effect of their proposals on a number of different assault offences, they did not undertake a comprehensive survey of all other statutory offences of assault. The Government is concerned to ensure that the courts are able to apply a single definition of assault in all those many offences which use the concept of assault, wherever they occur. In considering this issue, we identified over 70 different uses of assault in law. It is vital that in considering cases involving any of these offences, judges, lawyers and juries know exactly what is meant by the term assault.

3.6 The Government is therefore proposing to apply the definition of assault in this Bill to all assault offences . . . This proposal builds on the initial premise of the Law Commission but goes much further than their recommendation. Schedule 1 to the draft Bill sets out the precise impact of these changes on each piece of legislation. The list is long and detailed; at this stage the Government is only proposing to align meanings. This paper does not address the separate question of whether all these offences of assault are now necessary.

. . .

3.7 The Government shares the Law Commission's view that in general, the proposed new general offences offer protection for everyone, and that in principle special protection in law for particular classes or individuals should not normally be necessary. There are however some exceptions to this general principle. Some sections of society may require or deserve the additional protection of a specific provision in law. The Government has included in the Crime and Disorder Bill, now before Parliament, new aggravated offences for racially motivated violence which are based on existing offences of violence against the person in the Offences Against the Person Act 1861. Using these well-established and familiar offences will allow the courts to build on the existing law in dealing with those who commit these offences. The Government recognises that any subsequent implementation of its proposals to reform the Offences Against the Person Act 1861 will also have to amend the way in which these aggravated offences are formulated. The intention would be to re-state these offences following the model of the new offences against the person in the draft Bill. The Government recognises that it is unusual for Parliament to be asked to consider the same offences in quick succession in this way; however any such re-enactment would be a consolidation exercise to ensure that the law remained consistent.

3.8 The Law Commission recognised that the police and those carrying out a lawful arrest, had a legitimate and well-justified case for special recognition in the law, as they do at present. The Government agrees with this view. The Government is proposing to retain a number of particular offences relating to the police. The Law Commission had proposed to retain the offence of assaulting a police officer; the Government proposes to retain this offence and the offences of assault in resisting arrest. Clauses 5 to 7 therefore set out specific offences against the police. We recognise that Clause 6 does not fully mirror exactly the same approach of motivation and intent adopted by the Law Commission to the substantive offences in Clauses 1 to 4 of this Bill, in that it does not require intent or recklessness to be proved. These offences are intended to replicate the present provisions relating to assaults on the police or in resisting arrest, so preserving the current legal position. The Government does not wish to reduce the protection given to the police in this law reform. The offences in Clauses 5 to 7 are derived partly from the 1861 Act, but also reflect recent statutory changes.

. . .

3.9 A number of updated offences, mainly replacing offences currently contained in the 1861 Offences Against the Person Act, appear in Clauses 8 to 13. Those relating to dangerous substances (Clauses 8 and 9) are a reworking of the 1861 provisions to reflect the new substantive offences against the person, and to provide comprehensive protection against particular kinds of dangerous activity. The Law Commission had recommended that these provisions should be reviewed, and we have taken this opportunity to do so. Clause 8 is little changed in essence from the earlier provision; Clause 9 has been amended to mirror the provisions of Clause 8 where injury, rather than serious injury is caused, reflecting the structure of the first three clauses of the draft Bill. These changes are fully in accord with the principles of the Law Commission's report.

3.10 The Government accepts the Law Commission's reasoning that the existing offence of making threats to kill should be extended to threats to cause serious injury and also to threats made to a second person to harm a third person. This extended offence fills a gap in the equivalent 1861 Act offence, by creating a specific offence of threatening a third party. It is set out in Clause 10. The new offence of administering a substance capable of causing injury (Clause 11) was proposed by the Law Commission to replace the old poisoning offences. It has been revised slightly to remove any possibility that it could apply to *bona fide* medical treatment. Clause 12 re-states the law on torture (presently set out in section 134 of the Criminal Justice Act 1988). Clause 13 sets out an updated version of the 1861 Act offences of causing danger on railways. These reflect and build on the Law Commission's work but are set out in the body of the Bill rather than in a Schedule as the Commission had proposed.

. . .

3.12 Clause 15 defines the meaning of injury in the Bill. This clarifies the meaning of the new offences in clauses 1 to 4. There is however no definition of what is a serious injury. The Government, like the Law Commission, is content for the courts to decide what is appropriate in individual cases. The definition of injury does however raise a number of important questions. It is sufficiently wide to encompass psychological and psychiatric harm as well as physical harm. The definition will also allow the transmission of disease to be included in the Clause 1 offence of intentionally causing serious injury.

3.13 In seeking to reform an archaic and outdated law, the Government has to consider what the present law includes, how the courts have interpreted it, and how any replacement law should replicate or alter the present law. That is the context in which the question of whether the intentional transmission of disease ought to fall within the criminal law is being considered. In LC 218 the Law Commission were unequivocal that the Offences Against the Person Act 1861 could be used to prosecute the transmission of disease, and recommended that the proposed new offences should enable the intentional or reckless transmission of disease to be prosecuted in appropriate cases. The Government has not accepted this recommendation in full.

3.14 There are few decided cases on this point, so the position in the criminal law is not entirely clear. The most commonly cited case, that of Clarence (1888), seems to indicate that the 1861 Act could not be successfully used to prosecute the reckless transmission of disease. However it is now accepted that the judgment related to one specific offence and to the issue of consent, and that in principle it may well be possible to prosecute individuals for transmitting illness and disease at least when they do so intentionally. Although this has not been tested in the courts in recent years, in *Ireland* and *Burstow* the House of Lords held that the 1861 Act could be used to prosecute the infliction of psychiatric injury. In reforming the law, the issue of whether and if so how, the transmission of disease should fall within the criminal law needs the most careful consideration.

3.15 The Government recognises that this is a very sensitive issue. The criminal law deals with behaviour that is wrong in intent and in deed. The Law Commission's original proposal, which included illness and disease in the definition of injury, would have resulted in the intentional or reckless transmission of disease being open to prosecution. They argued that the width of their proposal would be balanced by the fact that prosecution would only be appropriate in the most serious cases. The Government has considered their views very carefully, but is not persuaded that it would be right or appropriate to make the range of normal everyday activities during which illness could be transmitted, potentially criminal.

We think it would be wrong to criminalise the reckless transmission of normally minor illnesses such as measles or mumps, even though they could have potentially serious consequences for those vulnerable to infection.

3.16 An issue of this importance has ramifications beyond the criminal law, into the wider considerations of social and public health policy. The Government is particularly concerned that the law should not seem to discriminate against those who are HIV positive, have AIDS or viral hepatitis or who carry any kind of disease. Nor do we want to discourage people from coming forward for diagnostic tests and treatment, in the interests of their own health and that of others, because of an unfounded fear of criminal prosecution.

3.17 The Government therefore considered whether it should exclude all transmission of disease from the criminal law, and concluded that that too would not be appropriate. The existing law extends into this area, even though it has not been used. There is a strong case for arguing that society should have criminal sanctions available for use to deal with evil acts. It is hard to argue that the law should not be able to deal with the person who gives a disease causing serious illness to others with intent to do them such harm. That is clearly a form of violence against the person. Such a gap in the law would be difficult to justify.

3.18 The Government therefore proposes that the criminal law should apply only to those whom it can be proved beyond reasonable doubt had deliberately transmitted a disease intending to cause a serious illness. This aims to strike a sensible balance between allowing very serious intentional acts to be punished whilst not rendering individuals liable for prosecution for unintentional or reckless acts, or for the transmission of minor disease. The Government believes that this is close to the effect of the present law, and that it is right in principle to continue to allow the law to be used in those rare grave cases where prosecution would be justified. This proposal will clarify the present law which, because it is largely untested is unclear; by doing so the effect of the law will be confined to the most serious and culpable behaviour.

3.19 It is important to emphasise that this proposal does not reflect a significant change in the law. Prosecutions for the transmission of disease are very rare for very good reasons. Any criminal charge has to be supported by evidence and proved to a court beyond reasonable doubt. It is very difficult to prove both the causal linkage of the transmission and also to prove that it was done intentionally. To do so beyond reasonable doubt is even more difficult. The Government does not expect that the proposed offence will be used very often, but considers that it is important that it should exist to provide a safeguard against the worst behaviour.

3.20 Clause 15 provides for the intentional transmission of serious injury or disease to be included for the purposes of Clause 1 (intentional serious injury), but not for any other purpose. This means that only those who transmit diseases with intent to cause serious injury, will be criminally liable . . .

5.10 CONSENT TO PHYSICAL HARM AS A DEFENCE

Allowing the consent of the victim to operate as a defence in criminal law raises some interesting issues of legal policy. At the core of the debate is the conflict between the need, on the one hand, to maintain the rule of law, and on the other, the need to allow an appropriate degree of individual autonomy. This debate often takes place around the issue of euthanasia – whether the law should sanction the deliberate taking of life where the victim gives full, free and informed consent. In criminal law consent can often operate to negate liability in respect of crimes against property, for example criminal damage; see further Chapter 12. In theft a defendant may not be dishonest where he genuinely believes that the owner would have consented to his appropriation of property; see further Chapter 9.5.3. In sexual relations between adults consent may operate to render activities lawful; see further Chapter 6.3.1. It is in respect of the deliberate infliction of physical harm that the law has encountered difficulties in determining where the line should be drawn to mark the limits of personal autonomy. The matter is complicated further by questions as to what constitutes informed consent, and whether the law does and should distinguish between consent to inevitable physical harm and consent to the risk of harm. In very broad terms the current position might be summarised thus:

	Activity with low social utility	Activity with high social utility
Harm amounts to actual bodily harm or worse	Consent not a defence	Consent may be a defence
Harm does not amount to actual bodily harm	Consent may be a defence	Consent may be a defence

5.10.1 IDENTIFYING THE LIMITS OF CONSENT

R v Donovan [1934] 2 KB 498 (CA)

Swift J:

It was established by the evidence, and was not in dispute, that on 8 March last, in the evening, the appellant induced Norah Eileen Harrison, a girl 17 years of age, to go with him to a garage at Morden, and there he beat her with a cane in circumstances of indecency. The defence was that it lay upon the prosecution to prove absence of consent, and that in fact the girl had consented to everything that was done by the appellant. It is not necessary to narrate the facts in detail. It appeared that the appellant was addicted to a form of sexual perversion, and there was no doubt that during a series of telephone conversations he had made suggestions to the prosecutrix which, if they were taken seriously, meant that he intended or desired to beat her. According to the evidence of the appellant, and of a young woman who said that she had overheard some of the telephone conversations, there was talk between the appellant and the prosecutrix which left no doubt that she had expressed her willingness to submit herself to the kind of conduct to which he was addicted . . .

. . . We have no doubt that the facts proved in the present case were such that the jury might reasonably have found consent; it is, indeed, difficult to reconcile some of the admitted facts with absence of consent. It was therefore of importance (if consent was in issue) that there should be no possibility of doubt in the minds of the jury upon the question whether it was for the Crown to negative consent, or for the defence to prove it. A second observation which may fairly be made is that consent, being a state of mind, is to be proved or negatived only after a full and careful review of the behaviour of the person who is alleged to have consented. Unless a jury is satisfied beyond reasonable doubt that the conduct of the person has been such that, viewed as a whole, it shows that she did not consent, then the prisoner is entitled to be acquitted . . .

. . . If an act is unlawful in the sense of being in itself a criminal act, it is plain that it cannot be rendered lawful because the person to whose detriment it is done consents to it. No person can license another to commit a crime. So far as the criminal law is concerned, therefore, where the act charged is in itself unlawful, it can never be necessary to prove absence of consent on the part of the person wronged in order to obtain the conviction of the wrongdoer. There are, however, many acts in themselves harmless and lawful which become unlawful only if they are done without the consent of the person affected. What is, in one case, an innocent act of familiarity or affection, may, in another, be an assault, for no other reason than that, in the one case there is consent, and in the other consent is absent. As a general rule, although it is a rule to which there are well-established exceptions, it is an unlawful act to beat another person with such a degree of violence that the infliction of bodily harm is a probable consequence, and when such an act is proved, consent is immaterial.

. . . Always supposing, therefore, that the blows which he struck were likely or intended to do bodily harm, we are of opinion that [the appellant] was doing an unlawful act, no evidence having been given of facts which would bring the case within any of the exceptions to the general rule. In our view, on the evidence given at the trial, the jury should have been directed that, if they were satisfied that the blows struck by the prisoner were likely or intended to do bodily harm to the prosecutrix, they ought to convict him, and that it was only if they were not so satisfied, that it became necessary to consider the further question whether the prosecution had negatived consent . . .

Attorney General's Ref (No 6 of 1980) [1981] QB 715 (CA)

Lord Lane CJ:

. . . The point of law on which the court is asked to give its opinion is as follows:

> Where two persons fight (otherwise than in the course of sport) in a public place can it be a defence for one of those persons to a charge of assault arising out of the fight that the other consented to fight?

The facts out of which the reference arises are these. The respondent, aged 18, and a youth aged 17, met in a public street and argued together. The respondent and the youth decided to settle the argument there and then by a fight. Before the fight the respondent removed his watch and handed it to a bystander for safe keeping and the youth removed his jacket. The respondent and the youth exchanged blows with their fists and the youth sustained a bleeding nose and bruises to his face caused by blows from the respondent . . .

We think that it can be taken as a starting point that it is an essential element of an assault that the act is done contrary to the will and without the consent of the victim; and it is doubtless for this reason that the burden lies on the prosecution to negative consent. Ordinarily, then, if the victim consents, the assailant is not guilty.

But the cases show that the courts will make an exception to this principle where the public interest requires: see *R v Coney* (1882) 8 QBD 534 ('the prize fight case') . . .

The answer to this question, in our judgment, is that it is not in the public interest that people should try to cause, or should cause, each other actual bodily harm for no good reason. Minor struggles are another matter. So, in our judgment, it is immaterial whether the act occurs in private or in public; it is an assault if actual bodily harm is intended and/or caused. This means that most fights will be unlawful regardless of consent.

Nothing which we have said is intended to cast doubt on the accepted legality of properly conducted games and sports, lawful chastisement or correction, reasonable surgical interference, dangerous exhibitions, etc. These apparent exceptions can be justified as involving the exercise of a legal right, in the case of chastisement or correction, or as needed in the public interest, in the other cases.

Our answer to the point of law is 'No', but not, as the reference implies, because the fight occurred in a public place, but because, wherever it occurred, the participants would have been guilty of assault, subject to self-defence, if, as we understand was the case, they intended to and/or did cause actual bodily harm . . .

R v Brown and Others [1994] 1 AC 212 (HL)

Lord Templeman:

My Lords, the appellants were convicted of assaults occasioning actual bodily harm contrary to s 47 of the Offences Against the Person Act 1861. Three of the appellants were also convicted of wounding contrary to s 20 of the 1861 Act. The incidents which led to each conviction occurred in the course of consensual sadomasochistic homosexual encounters. The Court of Appeal upheld the convictions and certified the following point of law of general public importance:

> Where A wounds or assaults B occasioning him actual bodily harm in the course of a sadomasochistic encounter, does the prosecution have to prove lack of consent on the part of B before they can establish A's guilt under s 20 or s 47 of the Offences Against the Person Act 1861?

. . . In the present case each appellant pleaded guilty to an offence under [s 47 of the 1861 Act] when the trial judge ruled that consent of the victim was no defence.

His Lordship then quoted s 20 of the 1861 Act and continued:

. . . Three of the appellants pleaded guilty to charges under s 20 when the trial judge ruled that the consent of the victim afforded no defence.

In the present case each of the appellants intentionally inflicted violence upon another (to whom I shall refer as 'the victim') with the consent of the victim and thereby occasioned actual bodily harm or in some cases wounding or grievous bodily harm. Each appellant was therefore guilty of an offence under s 47 or s 20 of the Act of 1861 unless the consent of the victim was effective to prevent the commission of the offence or effective to constitute a defence to the charge.

In some circumstances violence is not punishable under the criminal law. When no actual bodily harm is caused, the consent of the person affected precludes him from complaining. There can be no conviction for the summary offence of common assault if the victim has consented to the assault. Even when violence is intentionally inflicted and results in actual bodily harm, wounding or serious bodily harm the accused is entitled to be acquitted if the injury was a foreseeable incident of a lawful activity in which the person injured was participating. Surgery involves intentional violence resulting in actual or sometimes serious bodily harm but surgery is a lawful activity. Other activities carried on with consent by or on behalf of the injured person have been accepted as lawful notwithstanding that they involve actual bodily harm or may cause serious bodily harm. Ritual circumcision, tattooing, ear-piercing and violent sports including boxing are lawful activities . . .

My Lords, the authorities dealing with the intentional infliction of bodily harm do not establish that consent is a defence to a charge under the Act of 1861. They establish that the courts have accepted that consent is a defence to the infliction of bodily harm in the course of some lawful activities. The question is whether the defence should be extended to the infliction of bodily harm in the course of sadomasochistic encounters . . .

[His Lordship set out some of the dangers inherent in the activities in which the defendants had participated and went on:]

In principle there is a difference between violence which is incidental and violence which is inflicted for the indulgence of cruelty. The violence of sadomasochistic encounters involves the indulgence of cruelty by sadists and the degradation of victims. Such violence is injurious to the participants and unpredictably dangerous. I am not prepared to invent a defence of consent for sadomasochistic encounters which breed and glorify cruelty and result in offences under ss 47 and 20 of the Act of 1861.

... Society is entitled and bound to protect itself against a cult of violence. Pleasure derived from the infliction of pain is an evil thing. Cruelty is uncivilised. I would answer the certified question in the negative and dismiss the appeals of the appellants against conviction.

Lord Jauncey of Tullichettle:

... It was accepted by all the appellants that a line had to be drawn somewhere between those injuries to which a person could consent to infliction upon himself and those which were so serious that consent was immaterial ...

... In my view the line properly falls to be drawn between assault at common law and the offence of assault occasioning actual bodily harm created by s 47 of the Offences Against the Person Act 1861, with the result that consent of the victim is no answer to anyone charged with the latter offence or with a contravention of s 20 unless the circumstances fall within one of the well-known exceptions such as organised sporting contests and games, parental chastisement or reasonable surgery. There is nothing in ss 20 and 47 of the Act of 1861 to suggest that consent is either an essential ingredient of the offences or a defence thereto. If consent is to be an answer to a charge under s 47 but not to one under s 20, considerable practical problems would arise ... These problems would not arise if consent is an answer only to common assault. I would therefore dispose of these appeals on the basis that the infliction of actual or more serious bodily harm is an unlawful activity to which consent is no answer ...

... Without going into details of all the rather curious activities in which the appellants engaged it would appear to be good luck rather than good judgment which has prevented serious injury from occurring. Wounds can easily become septic if not properly treated, the free flow of blood from a person who is HIV positive or who has Aids can infect another and an inflicter who is carried away by sexual excitement or by drink or drugs could very easily inflict pain and injury beyond the level to which the receiver had consented ...

... If it is to be decided that such activities as the nailing by A of B's foreskin or scrotum to a board or the insertion of hot wax into C's urethra followed by the burning of his penis with a candle or the incising of D's scrotum with a scalpel to the effusion of blood are injurious neither to B, C and D nor to the public interest then it is for Parliament with its accumulated wisdom and sources of information to declare them to be lawful.

... There was argument as to whether lack of consent was a necessary ingredient of the offence of assault or whether consent, where available [ie in the case of common assault], was merely a defence ... If it were necessary, which it is not in this appeal, to decide which argument was correct, I would hold that consent could be a defence to assault but that lack of consent was not a necessary ingredient in assault.

Lord Lowry:

My Lords, I have had the advantage of reading in draft the speeches of your Lordships. I agree with the reasoning and conclusions of my noble and learned friends, Lord Templeman and Lord Jauncey of Tullichettle, and I, too, would answer the certified question in the negative and dismiss the appeals.

In stating my own further reasons for this view I shall address myself exclusively to the cases in which, as has been informally agreed, one person has acted upon another in private, occasioning him actual bodily harm but nothing worse . . .

. . . Everyone agrees that consent remains a complete defence to a charge of common assault and nearly everyone agrees that consent of the victim is not a defence to a charge of inflicting really serious personal injury (or 'grievous bodily harm'). The disagreement concerns offences which occasion actual bodily harm: the appellants contend that the consent of the victim is a defence to one charged with such an offence, while the respondent submits that consent is not a defence. I agree with the respondent's contention for reasons which I now explain . . .

I suggest that the following points should be noted . . .

- Wounding is associated in ss 18 and 20 with the infliction of grievous bodily harm and is naturally thought of as a serious offence, but it may involve anything from a minor breaking or puncture of the skin to a near fatal injury. Thus wounding may simply occasion actual bodily harm or it may inflict grievous bodily harm. If the victim's consent is a defence to occasioning actual bodily harm, then, so far as concerns the proof of guilt, the line is drawn, as my noble and learned friend Lord Jauncey of Tullichettle puts it . . . 'somewhere down the middle of s 20', which I would regard as a most unlikely solution.
- According to the appellants' case, if an accused person charged with wounding relies on consent as a defence, the jury will have to find whether anything more than actual bodily harm was occasioned, something which is not contemplated by s 20.
- The distinction between common assault and all other attacks on the person is that common assault does not necessarily involve significant bodily injury. It is much easier to draw the line between no significant injury and some injury than to differentiate between degrees of injury. It is also more logical, because for one person to inflict any injury on another without good reason is an evil in itself (*malum in se*) and contrary to public policy.
- That consent is a defence to a charge of common assault is a common law doctrine which the Act of 1861 has done nothing to change.

. . . If, as I, too, consider, the question of consent is immaterial, there are *prima facie* offences against s 20 and 47 and the next question is whether there is good reason to add sado-masochistic acts to the list of exceptions contemplated in the Attorney General's Reference. In my opinion, the answer to that question is 'No'.

In adopting this conclusion I follow closely my noble and learned friends, Lord Templeman and Lord Jauncey. What the appellants are obliged to propose is that the deliberate and painful infliction of physical injury should be exempted from the operation of statutory provisions the object of which is to prevent or punish that very thing, the reason for the proposed exemption being that both those who will inflict and those who will suffer the injury wish to satisfy a perverted and depraved sexual desire. Sadomasochistic homosexual activity cannot be regarded as conducive to the enhancement or enjoyment of family life or conducive to the welfare of society. A relaxation of the prohibitions in ss 20 and 47 can only encourage the practice of homosexual sadomasochism, with the physical cruelty that it must involve (which can scarcely be regarded as a 'manly diversion'), by withdrawing the legal penalty and giving the activity a judicial *imprimatur*. As well as all this, one cannot overlook the physical danger to those who may indulge in sadomasochism. In this connection, and also generally, it is idle for the appellants to claim that they are educated exponents of 'civilised cruelty'. A proposed general exemption is to be tested by considering the likely general effect. This must include the probability that some sado-masochistic activity, under the powerful influence of the sexual instinct, will get out of hand and result in serious physical damage to the participants and that some activity will involve a danger of infection such as these particular exponents do not contemplate for themselves . . .

Lord Mustill and Lord Slynn of Hadley delivered dissenting speeches.

5.10.2 EXCEPTIONS TO THE ACTUAL BODILY HARM LIMIT: TATTOOING, HORSEPLAY AND SPORT

R v Wilson [1996] 3 WLR 125 (CA)

The appellant was charged with assault occasioning actual bodily harm contrary to s 47 of the Offences Against the Person Act 1861. The appellant's wife was examined by her doctor and he noticed that she had marks on both her buttocks. The marks had been caused by the appellant branding his initials on his wife's buttocks at her request. The trial judge, following *R v Brown*, ruled that there was no defence of consent available to the appellant. The appellant was convicted and conditionally discharged for a period of 12 months. The issue for the Court of Appeal was whether or not the trial judge's decision to reject the defence of consent had been correct.

Russell LJ:

In the court below, and before us, reference was predictably made to *R v Donovan* [1934] 2 KB 498, a decision of the Court of Criminal Appeal, and to *R v Brown (Anthony)* [1994] 1 AC 212, a decision of the House of Lords. They are the two authorities to which the trial judge referred in the observations we have cited . . .

We are abundantly satisfied that there is no factual comparison to be made between the instant case and the facts of either *R v Donovan* [1934] 2 KB 498 or *R v Brown* 1 AC 212: Mrs Wilson not only consented to that which the appellant did, she instigated it. There was no aggressive intent on the part of the appellant. On the contrary, far from wishing to cause injury to his wife, the appellant's desire was to assist her in what she regarded as the acquisition of a desirable piece of personal adornment, perhaps in this day and age no less understandable than the piercing of nostrils or even tongues for the purposes of inserting decorative jewellery.

In our judgment *R v Brown* is not authority for the proposition that consent is no defence to a charge under s 47 of the Act of 1861, in all circumstances where actual bodily harm is deliberately inflicted. It is to be observed that the question certified for their Lordships in *R v Brown* related only to a 'sadomasochistic encounter'. However, their Lordships recognised in the course of their speeches, that it is necessary that there must be exceptions to what is no more than a general proposition. The speeches of Lord Templeman at 231, Lord Jauncey of Tullichettle at 245, and the dissenting speech of Lord Slynn of Hadley at 277, all refer to tattooing as being an activity which, if carried out with the consent of an adult, does not involve an offence under s 47, albeit that actual bodily harm is deliberately inflicted.

For our part, we cannot detect any logical difference between what the appellant did and what he might have done in the way of tattooing. The latter activity apparently requires no state authorisation, and the appellant was as free to engage in it as anyone else. We do not think that we are entitled to assume that the method adopted by the appellant and his wife was any more dangerous or painful than tattooing. There was simply no evidence to assist the court on this aspect of the matter.

Does public policy or the public interest demand that the appellant's activity should be visited by the sanctions of the criminal law? The majority in *R v Brown* clearly took the view that such considerations were relevant. If that is so, then we are firmly of the opinion that it is not in the public interest that activities such as the appellant's in this appeal should amount to criminal behaviour. Consensual activity between husband and wife, in the privacy of the matrimonial home, is not, in our judgment, normally a proper matter for criminal investigation, let alone criminal prosecution. Accordingly we take the view that the judge failed to have full regard to the facts of this case and misdirected himself in saying that *R v Donovan* [1934] 2 KB 498 and *R v Brown* [1994] 1 AC 212 constrained him to rule that consent was no defence.

In this field, in our judgment, the law should develop upon a case-by-case basis rather than upon general propositions to which, in the changing times in which we live, exceptions may arise from time to time not expressly covered by authority.

We shall allow the appeal and quash the conviction . . .

R v Aitken and Others [1992] 1 WLR 1066 (Courts-Martial Court of Appeal)

The appellants were RAF officers who, during the course of a drunken bout of horseplay, had set fire to the fire-resistant suit worn by a colleague, Flying Officer Gibson. They were convicted of offences under s 20 of the 1861 Act. On appeal the Courts-Martial Appeal Court allowed the appeals on the basis that the judge advocate's direction had not dealt satisfactorily with the issue of consent.

Cazalet J:

The appellants submit that the nature of the horseplay and pranks in which Gibson had been involved that evening before the incident when he sustained his injuries were such that he must be taken to have given his consent to being involved in the sort of boisterous activities which had been taking place throughout much of the evening. The appellants pray in aid the fact that Gibson had been present throughout and had taken part in the various spirited events in the officers' mess at the earlier stage. He had also accompanied the others to Bell's married quarters after the bar had closed when there had been various further jokes and undisciplined pranks, including the two incidents of setting fire to the trousers of Huskisson and Thomas. He then elected to return with the others to the officers' mess where there had been further drinking before the incident in question.

It was submitted that viewed overall in the context of a celebratory evening in the mess such as this, it was clearly arguable that the rough and undisciplined horseplay which the three appellants had perpetrated on Gibson was not *per se* unlawful. In seeking to restrain him from leaving the room, grappling him to the ground and then, as he was getting up, trying to carry out the same type of burning incident as had happened earlier in the evening the appellants were acting in a manner consistent with what had been going on during much of the time. The fact that Gibson struggled, albeit weakly through drink, to avoid the attentions of the three during the incident in question should not, it was submitted on the appellants' behalf, be taken in isolation. The totality of the circumstances, his knowledge of the course which celebration evenings such as the one in question was likely to take and his continued presence with the others demonstrated an acceptance by him that horseplay of the nature perpetrated upon him might well take place.

It was submitted that the judge advocate had not fully or properly directed the court in regard to this and that, in particular, he had failed to give any direction to the effect that since the Crown accepted that none of the appellants intended to inflict any harm on Gibson, the fact that a much larger quantity of white spirit had been poured on to his clothing than had been the case with Thomas could be viewed as an accident, and thus not unlawful. Additionally, submitted the appellants, given that it was open to the court to find that the horseplay with Gibson was not of itself unlawful, it was incumbent upon the judge advocate, following the decision in *R v Jones* (Terence), 83 Cr App R 375 to give further directions, first that such conduct, if not unlawful, would only have become unlawful if Gibson had not consented to it, and second that even if Gibson had not consented, the court must consider whether in the circumstances any of the appellants genuinely believed, whether reasonably or not, that Gibson had so consented.

Mr Hucker [for the prosecution] conceded that the judge advocate had not given the court either of these two latter directions. He contended that such were not necessary on the unchallenged facts of the case. He submitted that the incident involving Gibson must have been unlawful. The sequence of the incidents of setting fire to the clothing of others had, he submitted, escalated to a serious degree. From a mild flame with brandy more dangerous flames had sprung up with the use of white spirit on Thomas's trouser leg. He referred to Aitken's written statement which had recounted how the heat from the flames had woken Thomas, who had then had difficulty in putting out the flames with Bell being required to help smother them. That, he contended, demonstrated a dangerous build-up of this particular conduct, such that the incident with Gibson, once again involving the white spirit and a burning, clearly raised a risk of serious injury to Gibson. This, he maintained, took the activity outside the realm of rough and undisciplined horseplay such that this incident was plainly unlawful from the outset and accordingly the question of consent did not arise.

However although it must, on the evidence, have been open to the court to find that the incident involving Gibson was *per se* unlawful, we do not consider, for the reasons submitted to us by Mr Butterfield, that this was so plain that the judge advocate was absolved from a direction that it was in the circumstances open to the court to find that the activities of the appellants were not *per se* unlawful. In this event the judge advocate should then have directed the court as to the necessity of considering whether Gibson gave his consent as a willing participant to the activities in question, or whether the appellants may have believed this, whether reasonably or not.

In the circumstances we consider that the judge advocate in what was, on any view, a difficult and complex case on the law, failed properly to direct the court on these two important matters as to consent.

R v Barnes [2004] EWCA Crim 3246

The appellant tackled P, an opposing team member, during an amateur football match with the result that P sustained serious leg injuries. The appellant was charged under s 20 of the 1861 Act, the prosecution alleging that the injury had been the result of a crushing tackle, which had been late, unnecessary, and reckless. The appellant contended that the challenge had been legitimate in that it was what might be expected during the course of a competitive fixture. Following a direction from the trial judge that the jury could only return a guilty verdict if the prosecution had proved that what had occurred had not been by way of 'legitimate sport', the appellant was convicted under s 20 and appealed successfully to the Court of Appeal.

Lord Woolf CJ:

11. The advantage of identifying that the defence [of consent] is based upon public policy is that it renders it unnecessary to find a separate jurisprudential basis for application of the defence in the various different factual contexts in which an offence could be committed. For example, it explains why boxing, despite the fact that participants intend to hurt each other, is ordinarily considered a lawful sport, whereas prize-fighting is not. It also means that changing public attitudes can affect the activities which are classified as unlawful, as the judgment in [R v Dica [2004] 3 All ER 593, considered below at 5.10.3] demonstrates. However, so far as contact sports are concerned, the recognition that public policy is the foundation of the defence should not detract from the value of recognising that public policy limits the defence to situations where there has been implicit consent to what occurred.

12. The fact that the participants in, for example, a football match, implicitly consent to take part in a game, assists in identifying the limits of the defence. If what occurs goes beyond what a player can reasonably be regarded as having accepted by taking part in the sport, this indicates that the conduct will not be covered by the defence. What is implicitly accepted in one sport will not necessarily be covered by the defence in another sport . . .

13. The general position as to contact sports was helpfully considered by the Law Commission in *Consent and offences against the person*: Law Commission Consultation Paper No. 134.

The Commission indicated its approval of the approach adopted by the Criminal Injuries Compensation Board which we would also approve. This is that "in a sport in which bodily contact is a commonplace part of the game, the players consent to such contact even if, through unfortunate accident, injury, perhaps of a serious nature, may result. However, such players do not consent to being deliberately punched or kicked and such actions constitute an assault for which the Board would award compensation". (10.12)

14. Subject to what we have to say hereafter we would in general accept the view of the Commission that:

the present broad rules for sports and games appear to be :
(i)   the intentional infliction of injury enjoys no immunity;
(ii) a decision as to whether the reckless infliction of injury is criminal is likely to be strongly influenced by whether the injury occurred during actual play, or in a moment of temper or over-excitement when play has ceased, or "off the ball";
(iii) although there is little authority on the point, principle demands that even during play injury that results from risk-taking by a player that is unreasonable, in the light of the conduct necessary to play the game properly, should also be criminal. (10.18)

15. On the other hand, the fact that the play is within the rules and practice of the game and does not go beyond it, will be a firm indication that what has happened is not criminal. In making a judgment as to whether conduct is criminal or not, it has to be borne in mind that, in highly competitive sports, conduct outside the rules can be expected to occur in the heat of the moment, and even if the conduct justifies not only being penalised but also a warning or even a

sending off, it still may not reach the threshold level required for it to be criminal. That level is an objective one and does not depend upon the views of individual players. The type of the sport, the level at which it is played, the nature of the act, the degree of force used, the extent of the risk of injury, the state of mind of the defendant are all likely to be relevant in determining whether the defendant's actions go beyond the threshold.

16. Whether conduct reaches the required threshold to be criminal will therefore depend on all the circumstances. However, there will be cases that fall within a 'grey area', and then the tribunal of fact will have to make its own determination as to which side of the line the case falls. In a situation such as we have on this appeal, to determine this type of question the jury would need to ask themselves among other questions whether the contact was so obviously late and/or violent that it could not be regarded as an instinctive reaction, error or misjudgement in the heat of the game.

17. In the case of offences against the person contrary to Sections 18 and 20 of the 1861 Act, it is a requirement of the offence that the conduct itself should be unlawful. Where the offending act is alleged to fall within the implicit consent derived from the victim's participation in the sport (so that a defence to the alleged offence exists), the defendant can be said not to be guilty of the offence because his conduct was not unlawful as required by the 1861 Act. In the case of an offence contrary to Section 20, the 1861 Act also requires that the conduct be inflicted 'maliciously'. In that context, 'maliciously' means either intending to cause some bodily harm (however slight) or causing the harm recklessly. (See *R v Cunningham* [1957] 2 QB 396.) 'Recklessly' in this context means no more than that the defendant foresaw the risk that some bodily harm (however slight) might result from what he was going to do and yet, ignoring that risk, the defendant went on to commit the offending act. (See *DPP v Parmenter* [1992] 1 AC 699.) In a sport like football, anyone going to tackle another player in possession of the ball can be expected to have the necessary malicious intent according to this approach, and in the great majority of criminal cases, the existence of a malicious intent is not likely to be in issue. This being so, in many situations, as Lord Diplock pointed out in *R v Mowatt*, [1968] 1 Q.B. 421 (at pages 426E to 427F) it will only confuse the jury to make unnecessary reference to the word 'maliciously' and invite them to consider the improbability that the defendant did not foresee the risk. However, this is a subject which it will be prudent for the trial judge to discuss with counsel before he starts his summing-up.

[Having considered the facts giving rise to the appeal and the trial judge's direction to the jury, his Lordship continued]:

28. We appreciate the difficulty that the judge had summing-up this case because of the state of the authorities. The concept of 'legitimate sport' in itself is not unhelpful. However, it required an explanation of how the jury should identify what is and what is not 'legitimate' in the context of the relevant sport. The case called out for the jury to be given help as to the approach they should adopt in determining what is or is not 'legitimate sport'. The judge should have given the jury a direction to determine for themselves what actually happened at the critical time when the injury was inflicted. Broadly speaking, were they satisfied that the case for the prosecution was correct? They should have been told that if they were not, and they thought that the appellant's description of what occurred might be correct, then that was in all probability the end of the case. It should have been pointed out to the jury that even if the offending contact was a foul, it was still

necessary for them to determine whether it could be anticipated in a normal game of football or was it something quite outside what could be expected to occur in the course of a football game. The summing-up should also have made it clear that even if a tackle results in a player being sent off, it may still not reach the necessary threshold to constitute criminal conduct.

29. The jury were not given any examples of conduct which could be regarded as 'legitimate sport' and those which were not 'legitimate sport' for the purposes of determining whether they were criminal. The jury did not need copies of the rules, but they did need to be told why it was important to determine where the ball was at the time the tackle took place. They should have been told the importance of the distinction between the appellant going for the ball, albeit late, and his 'going for' the victim.

30. Having carefully considered the summing-up as a whole, we can well understand why the jury felt they needed further assistance after they retired. The further direction they received, did not give them that assistance. Without it, it is difficult to determine what they thought they had to decide in order to find the appellant guilty. This being the position, we are forced to come to the conclusion that the summing-up was inadequate, and that as a result the conviction is unsafe. Accordingly the appeal will be allowed and the orders made set aside.

 ## COMMENTS AND QUESTIONS

1   What is the social utility in tattooing and body piercing that justifies any public policy exception to the limits of valid consent to harm?

2   Are the facts that the victim in *R v Wilson* instigated the actions of the defendant, and that the events occurred within a husband and wife relationship, of any significance in distinguishing the case from *R v Brown* as regards the effect of the victim's consent to harm?

3   Why is consent recognised as a defence to harm caused in the course of rough horseplay, but not when caused during sadomasochistic sexual activity?

4   The Female Genital Mutilation Act 2003 makes it an offence to carry out female circumcision, unless the activity falls within the medical exceptions as defined by the Act. The performance of such operations in the belief that they are required as a matter of custom or ritual is expressly stated by s 1(5) of the Act to be immaterial for the purposes of providing any justification for the activity. The offence under the 2003 Act carries with it the possibility of 14 years' imprisonment.

5   Lord Lane CJ in *Attorney General's Ref (No 6 of 1980)* (above), and Lord Jauncey in *R v Brown* (above), both refer to the lawful chastisement of children as falling within the exceptions where the infliction of harm amounting to actual bodily harm or worse is permitted by law. Is lawful chastisement really a situation where the victim consents? Any such exception must now operate within the confines of the European Convention on Human Rights, in particular the right not to be subjected to inhuman and degrading treatment; see further Art 3. In *R v H* [2002] 1 Cr App R 59, the Court of Appeal held that a jury should be directed to have regard to whether the chastisement in question was reasonable and moderate. Relevant factors would include the nature, context and duration of the defendant's behaviour; the physical and mental consequences for the child, bearing in mind his age and personal characteristics; and the justification given by the defendant for the beating.

6   In *R v Barnes* (above) Lord Woolf CJ indicated that the discretion to prosecute should be
     used sparingly in respect of injury caused during legitimate sporting activity because most
     serious incidents would come within the jurisdiction of the sports governing body, and further
     because the injured party would normally be able to pursue a civil action for compensation.
     This is broadly in line with the view that criminal liability ought to be imposed where the harm
     done goes beyond being simply a private matter between parties

7   Does a participant in a legitimate contact sport consent to harm or the risk of harm? Clearly
     there is consent to contact *per se*, but the extent to which there is submission to inevitable
     physical harm must vary with the sport and the level at which it is played. By convention a
     'friendly' football match would not be played in such a competitive spirit as a cup final. On the
     other hand, it is hard to see the attraction of boxing for those who view it as a sport, if it
     merely involves participants consenting to the risk of harm. In such sports the participants
     arguably consent to the risk of death; see further 5.10.3 below.

8   Lord Woolf CJ in *R v Barnes* refers to the *actus reus* of offences under s 18 and s 20 not being
     made out where P impliedly consents to the (risk of) harm on the basis that if there is consent
     D cannot be said to be acting unlawfully. Viewed this way consent, when raised, is not so
     much a true defence, but a denial of one of the elements of the offence charged – as such it is
     for the prosecution to prove beyond all reasonable doubt that P was not impliedly consenting
     to the harm done, or the risk of the harm being caused.

5.10.3 CONSENTING TO THE RISK OF HARM

The above authorities indicate that, subject to certain exceptions recognised at common law, a
victim cannot validly consent to the deliberate (i.e. inevitable) infliction of actual bodily harm
or worse. The courts have begun to clarify, however, the distinction between consenting to
harm and consenting to the risk of harm. Participation in a dangerous exhibition, for example
volunteering to stand in front of the knife thrower's target at a circus, involves consenting to
a risk of harm, but there would presumably be no volunteers if it involved consenting to
inevitable harm. Should the knife thrower make an error and stab his volunteer he may be
liable to a civil action for negligence, but may well be able to invoke consent as a bar to any
criminal prosecution.

R v Dica [2004] 3 All ER 593

The appellant was diagnosed as HIV+ in 1995 and informed as to his condition. Subsequently
he had unprotected sexual intercourse with a number of women who subsequently became
HIV+. The prosecution accepted that in each case the women had consented to sexual intercourse, hence there was no basis for a rape charge (at least under the pre-Sexual Offences Act
2003 offence). The women, however, gave evidence to the effect that they would not have
consented to the unprotected sexual intercourse had they been aware of the risk of becoming
HIV+. The appellant was charged with maliciously inflicting grievous bodily harm, contrary
to s 20 of the Offences Against the Person Act 1861. The trial judge took the view that, even
if the women had consented to the risk of becoming HIV+ through sexual connection with
the appellant their consent would not have been relevant, thus no direction was given to the
jury on the issue of consent.

The appellant was convicted and appealed contending that the trial judge's ruling on consent was in error. The appeal was allowed and a retrial ordered. The appellant had sought to rely on *R v Clarence* [1886–90] All ER Rep 133, to the effect that consent to the sexual intercourse meant that there could be no assault upon which to base liability for the s 20 offence. The court rejected this contention, holding that *R v Clarence* was not to be followed. It was a decision based on the outmoded notion that a wife was assumed to consent to sexual intercourse with her husband, and on the now discredited argument that the infliction of harm contrary to s 20 necessarily required proof of an assault. As Judge J observed:

> . . . the reasoning which led the majority in *Clarence* to decide that the conviction under s 20 should be quashed has no continuing application. If that case were decided today, the conviction under s 20 would be upheld. Clarence knew, but his wife did not know, and he knew that she did not know that he was suffering from gonorrhoea. Nevertheless he had sexual intercourse with her, not intending deliberately to infect her, but reckless whether she might become infected, and thus suffer grievous bodily harm.

As to the issue of consent, it was clear that if the women had not been aware of the appellant's condition they had not consented, and thus the appellant would have had no consent defence to a s 20 charge. Conversely if, as the appellant contended, the women had been aware that he was HIV+, the issue arose as to whether any such consent would be effective in law.

> Judge LJ:
> As a general rule, unless the activity is lawful, the consent of the victim to the deliberate infliction of serious bodily injury on him or her does not provide the perpetrator with any defence. Different categories of activity are regarded as lawful. Thus no-one doubts that necessary major surgery with the patient's consent, even if likely to result in severe disability (eg an amputation) would be lawful. However the categories of activity regarded as lawful are not closed, and equally, they are not immutable. Thus, prize fighting and street fighting by consenting participants are unlawful: although some would have it banned, boxing for sport is not. Coming closer to this case, in *Bravery v Bravery* [1954] 3 All ER 59 at 68, [1954] 1 WLR 1169 at 1180, Denning LJ condemned in the strongest terms, and as criminal, the conduct of a young husband who, with the consent of his wife, underwent a sterilisation operation, not so as to avoid the risk of transmitting a hereditary disease, or something similar, but to enable him to 'have the pleasure of sexual intercourse without shouldering the responsibilities attaching to it'. He thought that such an operation, for that reason, was plainly 'injurious to the public interest'. This approach sounds dated, as indeed it is. Denning LJ's colleagues expressly and unequivocally dissociated themselves from it. However, judges from earlier generations, reflecting their own contemporary society, might have agreed with him. We have sufficiently illustrated the impermanence of public policy in the context of establishing which activities involving violence may or may not be lawful.
> The present policy of the law is that, whether or not the violent activity takes place in private, and even if the victim agrees to it, serious violence is not lawful merely because it enables the perpetrator (or the victim) to achieve sexual gratification. Judge Philpot [at first instance] was impressed with the conclusions to be drawn from the well-known decision in *R v Brown* . . . Sadomasochistic

activity of an extreme, indeed horrific kind, which caused grievous bodily harm, was held to be unlawful, notwithstanding that those who suffered the cruelty positively welcomed it . . .

The same policy can be seen in operation in *R v Donovan* [1934] 2 KB 498, [1934] All ER Rep 207, where the violence was less extreme and the consent of the victim, although real, was far removed from the enthusiastic co-operation of the victims in *R v Brown*.

R v Boyea (1992) 156 JP 505 represents another example of the application of the principle in *R v Donovan*. If she consented to injury by allowing the defendant to put his hand into her vagina and twist it, causing, among other injuries, internal and external injuries to her vagina and bruising on her pubis, the woman's consent (if any) would have been irrelevant. Recognising that social attitudes to sexual matters had changed over the years, a contemporaneous approach to these matters was appropriate. However, 'the extent of the violence inflicted . . . went far beyond the risk of minor injury to which, if she did consent, her consent would have been a defence' ((1992) 156 JP 505 at 513). On close analysis, however, this case was decided on the basis that the victim did not in fact consent.

In *R v Emmett* (unreported, 18 June 1999), as part of their consensual sexual activity, the woman agreed to allow her partner to cover her head with a plastic bag, tying it tightly at the neck. On a different occasion, she agreed that he could pour fuel from a lighter onto her breasts and set fire to the fuel. On the first occasion, she was at risk of death, and lost consciousness. On the second, she suffered burns, which became infected. This court did not directly answer the question posed by the trial judge in his certificate, but concluded that *R v Brown* demonstrated that the woman's consent to these events did not provide a defence for her partner.

These authorities demonstrate that violent conduct involving the deliberate and intentional infliction of bodily harm is and remains unlawful notwithstanding that its purpose is the sexual gratification of one or both participants. Notwithstanding their sexual overtones, these cases were concerned with violent crime, and the sexual overtones did not alter the fact that both parties were consenting to the deliberate infliction of serious harm or bodily injury on one participant by the other. To date, as a matter of public policy, it has not been thought appropriate for such violent conduct to be excused merely because there is a private consensual sexual element to it. The same public policy reason would prohibit the deliberate spreading of disease, including sexual disease.

In our judgment the impact of the authorities dealing with sexual gratification can too readily be misunderstood. It does not follow from them, and they do not suggest, that consensual acts of sexual intercourse are unlawful merely because there may be a known risk to the health of one or other participant. These participants are not intent on spreading or becoming infected with disease through sexual intercourse. They are not indulging in serious violence for the purposes of sexual gratification. They are simply prepared, knowingly, to run the risk – not the certainty – of infection, as well as all the other risks inherent in and possible consequences of sexual intercourse, such as, and despite the most careful precautions, an unintended pregnancy. At one extreme there is casual sex between complete strangers, sometimes protected, sometimes not, when the attendant risks are known to be higher, and at the other, there is sexual intercourse between couples in a long-term and loving, and trusting relationship, which may from time to time also carry risks.

The first of these categories is self-explanatory and needs no amplification. By way of illustration we shall provide two examples of cases which would fall within the second.

In the first, one of a couple suffers from HIV. It may be the man: it may be the woman. The circumstances in which HIV was contracted are irrelevant. They could result from a contaminated blood transfusion, or an earlier relationship with a previous sexual partner, who unknown to the sufferer with whom we are concerned, was himself or herself infected with HIV. The parties are Roman Catholics. They are conscientiously unable to use artificial contraception. They both know of the risk that the healthy partner may become infected with HIV. Our second example is that of a young couple, desperate for a family, who are advised that if the wife were to become pregnant and give birth, her long-term health, indeed her life itself, would be at risk. Together the couple decide to run that risk, and she becomes pregnant. She may be advised that the foetus should be aborted, on the grounds of her health, yet, nevertheless, decides to bring her baby to term. If she does, and suffers ill health, is the male partner to be criminally liable for having sexual intercourse with her, notwithstanding that he knew of the risk to her health? If he is liable to be prosecuted, was she not a party to whatever crime was committed? And should the law interfere with the Roman Catholic couple, and require them, at the peril of criminal sanctions, to choose between bringing their sexual relationship to an end or violating their consciences by using contraception?

These, and similar risks, have always been taken by adults consenting to sexual intercourse. Different situations, no less potentially fraught, have to be addressed by them. Modern society has not thought to criminalise those who have willingly accepted the risks, and we know of no cases where one or other of the consenting adults has been prosecuted, let alone convicted, for the consequences of doing so.

The problems of criminalising the consensual taking of risks like these include the sheer impracticability of enforcement and the haphazard nature of its impact. The process would undermine the general understanding of the community that sexual relationships are pre-eminently private and essentially personal to the individuals involved in them. And if adults were to be liable to prosecution for the consequences of taking known risks with their health, it would seem odd that this should be confined to risks taken in the context of sexual intercourse, while they are nevertheless permitted to take the risks inherent in so many other aspects of everyday life, including, again for example, the mother or father of a child suffering a serious contagious illness, who holds the child's hand, and comforts or kisses him or her goodnight.

In our judgment, interference of this kind with personal autonomy, and its level and extent, may only be made by Parliament.

This, and similar questions, have already been canvassed in a number of different papers. These include the efforts made by the Law Commission to modernise the 1861 Act altogether, and replace it with up-to-date legislation. In relation to sexually transmitted disease, much of the discussion initially focused on the decision in *R v Clarence*, and its perceived consequences, which as we have now concluded is entirely bereft of any authority in relation to s 20 of the 1861 Act. In its report *Criminal Law, Legislating the Criminal code, Offences against the Person and General Principles* (1993) (Law Com no 218), the Law Commission expressed the view that intentional or reckless transmission of disease should be capable of constituting an offence against the person (paras 15.15–15.17). A second publication, *Criminal Law, Consent in the Criminal Law* (1995) (Law Commission Consultation Paper No 139) made a provisional proposal that precluded a defence of consent for the proposed offence of recklessly causing seriously disabling injury (para 4.46–4.51). In 1998, in response to the activities of the Law Commission, the Home Office issued a consultation paper entitled *Reforming the Offences Against the Person Act 1861*. In this paper, the Home Office indicated that the government had not accepted the recommendation that there should be offences to enable the intentional or reckless transmission of disease to be prosecuted. It pointed out that the issue had ramifications going beyond the criminal law into wider considerations of social and public health policy. It stated (para 3.16) that the government 'is particularly concerned that the law should not seem to discriminate against those who are HIV positive, have AIDS or viral hepatitis or who carry any kind of disease'. It then went on to say that there is a strong case for arguing that society should have criminal sanctions available for use to deal with evil acts, and that it was hard to argue that the law should not be able to deal with the person who gives the disease causing serious illness to others with intent to do them such harm. It then proposed that the criminal law should apply only to those whom it can be proved beyond reasonable doubt had deliberately transmitted a disease, intending to cause serious injury. It added (para 3.18):

> This aims to strike a sensible balance between allowing very serious intentional acts to be punished while not rendering individuals liable for prosecution of unintentional or reckless acts or for the transmission of minor disease.

On this approach it would seem that the policy at that stage would have been to criminalise conduct of the nature we are considering when it fell within s 18 of the 1861 Act, but not when it falls within s 20. In the Law Commission's report in 2000, *Consent in Sex Offences*, no view was expressed on this topic, but it was assumed that any forthcoming legislation would not impose criminal liability for recklessly communicating HIV or other disease.

We have taken note of the various points made by the interested organisations. These include the complexity of bedroom and sex negotiations, and the lack of realism if the law were to expect people to be paragons of sexual behaviour at such a time, or to set about informing each other in advance of the risks or to counsel the use of condoms. It is also suggested that there are significant negative consequences of disclosure of HIV, and that the imposition of criminal liability could have an adverse impact on public health because those who ought to take advice, might be discouraged from doing so. If the criminal law was to become involved at all, this should be confined to cases where the offender deliberately inflicted others with a serious disease.

In addition to this material our attention has been drawn to the decisions in *R v Mwai* [1995] 3 NZLR 149, [1995] 4 LRC 719, a decision of the Court of Appeal in New Zealand, and *R v Cuerrier* [1998] 2 SCR 371, [1999] 2 LRC 29, in the Supreme Court of Canada. Both cases arose out of legislative provisions different to our own. Nevertheless, if we may say so, the judgments were illuminating, not least in the context of the views expressed in *R v Cuerrier*, which were inconsistent with some of the arguments put to us by the interested organisations. We also notice Professor Spencer's illuminating conclusion on the question of recklessness:

> To infect an unsuspecting person with a grave disease you know you have, or may have, by behaviour that you know involves a risk of transmission, and that you know you could easily modify to reduce or eliminate the risk, is to harm another in a way that is both needless and callous. For that reason, criminal liability is justified unless there are strong countervailing reasons. In my view there are not. (See NLJ, 26 March 2004, p 471.)

Although we have considered these judgments, and the remaining material to which our attention was drawn, in this court we are concerned only to decide what the law is now, and in this jurisdiction. Having done so, it is for Parliament if it sees fit, to amend the law as we find it to be.

In Judge Philpot's second ruling, he accepted the Crown's argument that the possible consent of the victims was irrelevant. That position, as we have already explained, was not maintained by the Crown before us. For the reasons we have now given, the ruling was wrong in law.

5.10.4 THE NEED FOR INFORMED CONSENT

Once the courts accept the distinction between consenting to inevitable harm and consenting to the risk of harm, an issue inevitably arises as to P's understanding of the risks involved in the activity being undertaken by D. To go back to the example used at 5.10.3 (above), an audience member might assume, when volunteering to stand in front of the knife thrower's target, that the knife thrower is experienced and a competent professional. Suppose the knife thrower has a history of mistakes resulting in serious injuries to volunteers? Must he make this plain when asking for a volunteer? Is P's consent to the risk of harm vitiated without such a disclosure? Consider the extent to which the following extract provides guidance on this issue.

R v Konzani [2005] EWCA Crim 706

D was informed that he was HIV positive and proceeded to have unprotected sexual intercourse with a number of women, each of whom, as a result of contact with D, contracted the HIV virus. The women gave evidence to the effect that D had not informed them of his HIV status prior to the sexual intercourse and that they consented to the risk of catching the HIV virus from D. At his trial D contended that the women had consented to unprotected sexual intercourse and had thus consented to the risk of contracting the HIV virus. The trial judge directed the jury that only informed and willing consent to the risk of contracting HIV could provide D with a defence. D was convicted under s 20 of the 1861 Act and appealed unsuccessfully.

Judge LJ:

34. Referring to HIV, the [trial] judge . . . [in directing the jury] returned to the clear and important distinction between 'running a risk on one hand and consenting to run that risk on the other', pointing out that the prosecution had to establish that the complainant 'did not willingly consent to the risk of suffering the infection in the sense of her having consciously thought about it at the time and decided to run it' . . .

35. In short, the judge explained that before the consent of the complainant could provide the appellant with a defence, it was required to be an informed and willing consent to the risk of contracting HIV.

36. Mr Timothy Roberts QC [for Konzani] submitted first, that the judge wrongly declined to leave to the jury the issue whether the appellant may have had an honest, even if unreasonable, belief that the complainant was consenting to the risk of contracting the HIV virus, and second, that he misdirected the jury on the issue of consent as it applied to the present case. Notwithstanding the express and uncontradicted evidence of the complainants, he submitted that as a matter of inference the appellant may have had an honest, even if unreasonable, belief that the complainant was consenting, simply because she had sexual intercourse with him in the circumstances in which she did, and so accepted all possible consequent risks . . .

38. To examine Mr Roberts' submissions, and his criticisms of the directions to the jury, we must turn to *R v Dica* [2004] EWCA Crim 1103, where the issue of consent was addressed (a) in the context of the long-standing decision in *R v Clarence* (1888) 22 QBD 23 that the consent of a wife to sexual intercourse carried with it consent to the risks inherent in sexual intercourse, including the risk of sexually transmitted disease, and (b) the trial judge's ruling that the consent of the complainants to sexual intercourse with an individual who was known to them to be suffering from the HIV virus could provide no defence.

39. In *R v Barnes* [2004] EWCA Crim. 3246, Lord Woolf CJ summarised the effect of the decision in *Dica* in this way. An HIV positive male defendant who infected a sexual partner with the HIV virus would be guilty of an offence 'contrary to s 20 of the 1861 Act if, being aware of his condition, he had sexual intercourse . . . without disclosing his condition'. On the other hand, he would have a defence if he had made the partner aware of his condition, who 'with that knowledge consented to sexual intercourse with him because [she was] still prepared to accept the risks involved'.

40. *R v Dica* represented what Lord Mustill in *R v Brown* described as a 'new challenge', and confirmed that in specific circumstances the ambit of the criminal law extended to consensual sexual intercourse between adults which involved a risk of the most extreme kind to the physical health of one participant. In the context of direct physical injury, he pointed out that cases involving the '. . . consensual infliction of violence are special. They have been in the past, and will continue to be in the future, the subject of special treatment by the law'. In his subsequent detailed examination of the 'situations in which the recipient consents or is deemed to consent to the infliction of violence upon him', activity of the kind currently under consideration did not remotely fall within any of the ten categories which he was able to identify. *Brown* itself emphatically established the clear principle that the consent of the injured person does not form a kind of all-purpose species of defence to an offence of violence contrary to s 20 of the 1861 Act.

41. We are concerned with the risk of and the actual transmission of a potentially fatal disease through or in the course of consensual sexual relations which did not in themselves involve unlawful violence of the kind prohibited in *R v Brown*. The prosecution did not seek to prove that the disease was deliberately transmitted, with the intention required by s 18 of the 1861 Act. The allegation was that the appellant behaved recklessly on the basis that knowing that he was suffering from the HIV virus, and its consequences, and knowing the risks of its transmission to a sexual partner, he concealed his condition from the complainants, leaving them ignorant of it. When sexual intercourse occurred these complainants were ignorant of his condition. So although they consented to sexual intercourse, they did not consent to the transmission of the HIV virus. *Dica* analysed two different sets of assumed facts arising from the issue of the complainants' consent, by distinguishing between the legal consequences if, as they alleged, the truth of his condition was concealed from his sexual partners by Dica, and the case that he would have developed at trial if he had not been prevented from doing so by the judge's ruling, that far from concealing his condition from the complainants, he expressly informed them of it, and they, knowing of his condition because he had told them of it, consented to unprotected sexual intercourse with him. There is a critical distinction between taking a risk of the various, potentially adverse and possibly problematic consequences of sexual intercourse, and giving an informed consent to the risk of infection with a fatal disease. For the complainant's consent to the risks of contracting the HIV virus to provide a defence, it is at least implicit from the reasoning in *R v Dica*, and the observations of Lord Woolf CJ in *R v Barnes* confirm, that her consent must be an informed consent. If that proposition is in doubt, we take this opportunity to emphasise it. We must therefore examine its implications for this appeal.

42. The recognition in *R v Dica* of informed consent as a defence was based on but limited by potentially conflicting public policy considerations. In the public interest, so far as possible, the spread of catastrophic illness must be avoided or prevented. On the other hand, the public interest also requires that the principle of personal autonomy in the context of adult non-violent sexual relationships should be maintained. If an individual who knows that he is suffering from the HIV virus conceals this stark fact from his sexual partner, the principle of her personal autonomy is

not enhanced if he is exculpated when he recklessly transmits the HIV virus to her through consensual sexual intercourse. On any view, the concealment of this fact from her almost inevitably means that she is deceived. Her consent is not properly informed, and she cannot give an informed consent to something of which she is ignorant. Equally, her personal autonomy is not normally protected by allowing a defendant who knows that he is suffering from the HIV virus which he deliberately conceals, to assert an honest belief in his partner's informed consent to the risk of the transmission of the HIV virus. Silence in these circumstances is incongruous with honesty, or with a genuine belief that there is an informed consent. Accordingly, in such circumstances the issue either of informed consent, or honest belief in it will only rarely arise: in reality, in most cases, the contention would be wholly artificial.

43. This is not unduly burdensome. The defendant is not to be convicted of this offence unless it is proved that he was reckless. If so, the necessary *mens rea* will be established. Recklessness is a question of fact, to be proved by the prosecution. Equally the defendant is not to be convicted if there was, or may have been an informed consent by his sexual partner to the risk that he would transfer the HIV virus to her. In many cases, as in *Dica* itself, provided recklessness is established, the critical factual area of dispute will address what, if anything, was said between the two individuals involved, one of whom knows, and the other of whom does not know, that one of them is suffering the HIV virus. In the final analysis, the question of consent, like the issue of recklessness is fact-specific.

44. In deference to Mr Roberts' submission, we accept that there may be circumstances in which it would be open to the jury to infer that, notwithstanding that the defendant was reckless and concealed his condition from the complainant, she may nevertheless have given an informed consent to the risk of contracting the HIV virus. By way of example, an individual with HIV may develop a sexual relationship with someone who knew him while he was in hospital, receiving treatment for the condition. If so, her informed consent, if it were indeed informed, would remain a defence, to be disproved by the prosecution, even if the defendant had not personally informed her of his condition. Even if she did not in fact consent, this example would illustrate the basis for an argument that he honestly believed in her informed consent. Alternatively, he may honestly believe that his new sexual partner was told of his condition by someone known to them both. Cases like these, not too remote to be fanciful, may arise. If they do, no doubt they will be explored with the complainant in cross-examination. Her answers may demonstrate an informed consent. Nothing remotely like that was suggested here. In a different case, perhaps supported by the defendant's own evidence, material like this may provide a basis for suggesting that he honestly believed that she was giving an informed consent. He may provide an account of the incident, or the affair, which leads the jury to conclude that even if she did not give an informed consent, he may honestly have believed that she did. Acknowledging these possibilities in different cases does not, we believe, conflict with the public policy considerations identified in *R v Dica*. That said, they did not arise in the present case.

45. Why not? In essence because the jury found that the complainants did not give a willing or informed consent to the risks of contracting the HIV virus from the appellant. We recognise that where consent does provide a defence to an offence against the person, it is generally speaking correct that the defendant's honest belief in the alleged victim's consent would also provide a defence. However for this purpose, the defendant's honest belief must be concomitant with the consent which provides a defence. Unless the consent would provide a defence, an honest belief in it would not assist the defendant. This follows logically from *R v Brown*. For it to do so here, what was required was some evidence of an honest belief that the complainants, or any one of

them, were consenting to the risk that they might be infected with the HIV virus by him. There is not the slightest evidence, direct or indirect, from which a jury could begin to infer that the appellant honestly believed that any complainant consented to that specific risk. As there was no such evidence, the judge's ruling about 'honest belief' was correct. In fact, the honest truth was that the appellant deceived them.

46. In our judgment, the judge's directions to the jury sufficiently explained the proper implications to the case of the consensual participation by each of the complainants to sexual intercourse with the appellant. The jury concluded, in the case of each complainant, that she did not willingly or consciously consent to the risk of suffering the HIV virus. Accordingly the appeal against conviction will be dismissed.

 ## COMMENTS AND QUESTIONS

1   In *R v Richardson* [1998] 3 WLR 1292, D had provided dental treatment despite having been suspended from practice by the General Dental Council and was convicted under s 47 of the 1861 Act on the basis that her patients had not consented to the treatment. Her appeal to the Court of Appeal was allowed, *inter alia*, on the basis that informed consent had no place in criminal law.

Otton J observed:

> It was suggested in argument that we might be assisted by the civil law of consent, where such expressions as 'real' or 'informed' consent prevail. In this regard the criminal and the civil law do not run along the same track. The concept of informed consent has no place in the criminal law. It would also be a mistake, in our view, to introduce the concept of a duty to communicate information to a patient about the risk of an activity before consent to an act can be treated as valid. The gravamen of the defendant's conduct in the instant case was that the complainants consented to treatment from her although their consent had been procured by her failure to inform them that she was no longer qualified to practise. This was clearly reprehensible and may well found the basis of a civil claim for damages. But we are quite satisfied that it is not a basis for finding criminal liability in the field of offences against the person.

Although *R v Richardson* was not cited in *R v Konzani* it is submitted that the approach in *Konzani* is to be preferred.

2.   What if the appellant in *R v Richardson* had been suffering from AIDS but had not informed anyone? Would the apparent consent of her patients have been vitiated by her deception?

3.   Compare *R v Richardson* (above) with *R v Tabassum* [2000] Crim LR 686. The appellant was convicted of indecent assault [now sexual assault] having persuaded women to allow him to touch their breasts on the basis that he was carrying out research into breast cancer. The women gave evidence that they had only consented because they thought the appellant had either medical qualifications or relevant training. He had neither. The court held that there was

no valid consent on the basis that the women had consented to a *bona fide* medical examination, not an indecent assault. Rose LJ observed:

> In *Richardson*, the case proceeded solely by reference to the point on identity . . . the prosecution in that case did not at trial or on appeal rely on the nature or quality of the act . . . In the present case the motive and intent of the defendant were irrelevant . . . [t]he nature and quality of the defendant's acts in touching the breasts of women to whom, in sexual terms he was a stranger, was unlawful and an indecent assault unless the complainants consented to that touching . . . On the evidence . . . consent was given . . . [on the basis that] the touching was for a medical purpose. As this was not so, there was no true consent. They were consenting to touching for medical purposes not to indecent behaviour, that is, there was consent to the nature of the act but not its quality.

Is the distinction here between nature and quality of the act sustainable? Surely there was consent to the nature of the act – the appellant touching the women's breasts. If so, how can a mere mistake as to the nature of the act be sufficient to render consent void? What if the appellant had been properly qualified, and conducting a perfectly proper medical examination that he nevertheless found sexually arousing? Assuming the patient would not have consented had she known this, is her consent void?

4. In *R v Cort* [2004] QB 388, the defendant's conviction for kidnapping was upheld where he had persuaded women to accept lifts in his car after falsely telling them that the bus they had been waiting for would not arrive. The Court of Appeal held that where kidnapping was effected by fraud, consent would never be a defence, as the victim would never consent to being taken away by fraud. Where, as in this case, there was no fraud as to the giving of the lift or the defendant's intention to take his passengers safely to their desired destinations, can it be said that the deception really vitiates the consent, in the sense of rendering it void? The women consented to lifts in his car and that is precisely what he provided.

5.10.5 D'S BELIEF IN P'S CONSENT

Suppose the appellant in *R v Dica* had claimed that he honestly (but mistakenly) believed his sexual partners had known about his being HIV+, and that he had therefore honestly believed them to have been consenting to the risk of harm? On the basis that D should be judged on the facts as he honestly believed them to be (provided of course this claimed belief is not disproved beyond all reasonable doubt by the prosecution) D should be acquitted, as the following extract from *R v Kimber* suggests.

R v Kimber [1983] 1 WLR 1118 (CA)

The appellant was convicted of indecently assaulting a woman. He contended that he should have been acquitted as he honestly believed that the woman was consenting. (Note that the offence of indecent assault considered here has since been repealed with the offence of sexual assault under s 3 of the Sexual Offences Act 2003 – see further Chapter 6.)

Lawton LJ:

. . . can a defendant charged with indecent assault on a woman raise the defence that he believed she had consented to what he did? . . . Second, if he could, did the jury have to consider merely whether his belief was honestly held or, if it was, did they have to go on to consider whether it was based on reasonable grounds? Another way of putting these points is to ask whether the principles upon which the House of Lords decided *R v Morgan* [1976] AC 182 should be applied to a charge of indecent assault on a woman.

The victim was a female patient in a mental hospital. Her mental disorder had been diagnosed as schizophrenia . . . Although she was not a defective within the meaning of ss 7 and 45 of the Sexual Offences Act 1956 . . . she was suffering from a severe degree of mental disorder . . . [T]he appellant admitted trying to have sexual intercourse with [the victim] but said he had not succeeded . . . and that he had interfered with her in a way which clearly amounted to an indecent assault if it had been done without her consent . . .

[In evidence, the appellant had said that he thought the victim was 'unstable' but he 'thought she was giving consent to have sexual intercourse'; he also said that he 'was not really interested in [her] feelings at all'.]

. . . At the close of the prosecution's case the [trial judge] ruled that the sole issue for the jury was whether [the victim] had given her real and genuine consent . . . He said:

It is no defence that the defendant thought or believed [the victim] was consenting. The question is: was she consenting? It does not matter what he thought or believed. Before this court it was accepted by counsel for the prosecution . . . that this direction was wrong. The [trial judge] had not had his attention drawn to *R v Tolson* (1889) 23 QBD 168. Before us [counsel for the prosecution] submitted that the jury should have been directed that the appellant had a defence if he had believed that [the victim] was consenting and he had had reasonable grounds for thinking so. On the facts the appellant could not have had any such grounds . . . We agree that on the evidence the appellant had no reasonable grounds for thinking that [the victim] was consenting and no jury other than a perverse one could have thought he had.

[Counsel for the appellant] argued, relying on the decision in *R v Morgan* [1976] AC 182, that the sole issue was whether the appellant had honestly believed that [the victim] was consenting. Unless the jury was sure that he had not so believed, he was entitled to be acquitted. The grounds for his belief were irrelevant save in so far as they might have assisted the jury to decide whether he did believe what he said he did . . .

The offence of indecent assault is . . . statutory: see s 14 of the Sexual Offences Act 1956. The prosecution had to prove that the appellant made an indecent assault on [the victim]. As there are no words in the section to indicate that Parliament intended to exclude *mens rea* as an element in this offence, it follows that the prosecution had to prove that the appellant intended to commit it. This could not be done without first proving that the appellant intended to assault [the victim]. In this context assault clearly includes battery. An assault is an act by which the defendant intentionally or recklessly causes the complainant to apprehend, or to sustain, unlawful personal violence: see *R v Venna* [1976] QB 421 at 428–29. In this case the appellant by his own admissions did intentionally lay his hands on [the victim]. That would not, however, have been enough to prove the charge. There had to be evidence that the appellant had intended to do what he did unlawfully. When there is a charge of indecent assault on a woman, the unlawfulness [of the assault] can be proved, as was sought to be done in *R v Donovan* [1934] 2 KB 498, by evidence that the defendant intended to cause bodily harm. In most cases, however, the prosecution tries to prove that the complainant did not consent to what was being done. The burden of proving lack of consent rests on the prosecution: see *R v May* [1912] 3 KB 572 at 575 per Lord Alverstone CJ.

The consequence is that the prosecution has to prove that the defendant intended to lay hands on his victim without her consent. If he did not intend to do this, he is entitled to be found not guilty; and if he did not so intend because he believed she was consenting, the prosecution will have failed to prove the charge. It is the defendant's belief, not the grounds on which it was based, which goes to negative the intent.

In analysing the issue in this way we have followed what was said by the majority in *R v Morgan* [1976] AC 182: see Lord Hailsham of St Marylebone at 214F–H and Lord Fraser of Tullybelton at 237E–G. If, as we adjudge, the prohibited act in indecent assault is the use of personal violence to a woman without her consent, then the guilty state of mind is the intent to do it without her consent. Then, as in rape at common law, the inexorable logic, to which Lord Hailsham referred in *R v Morgan*, takes over and there is no room either for a 'defence' of honest belief or mistake, or of a 'defence' of honest and reasonable belief or mistake: see [1976] AC 182 at 214F–H.

His Lordship then went on to criticise the decisions of the Divisional Court in *Albert v Lavin* [1982] AC 546 and *R v Phekoo* [1981] 1 WLR 1117.

His Lordship concluded:

In our judgment the [trial judge] should have directed the jury that the Crown had to make them sure that the appellant never had believed that [the victim] was consenting. [However, despite the judge's failure to so direct the jury] a reasonable jury would inevitably have decided that he had no honest belief that [the victim] was consenting. His own evidence showed that his attitude to her was one of indifference to her feelings and wishes. This state of mind is aptly described in the colloquial expression, 'couldn't care less'. In law this is recklessness. Had the jury been directed on recklessness we are sure they would have found that [the appellant] had acted recklessly. That would have been enough to support a conviction of the offence charged . . .

5.10.6 CODIFICATION AND LAW REFORM PROPOSALS

The Law Commission has addressed the issue of consent to harm in two Consultation Papers: LCCP 134, and more recently *Consent in the Criminal Law* (LCCP 139). What follows is an extract from Part XVI of LCCP 139, summarising the provisional proposals of the Law Commission, and indicating those areas where responses were requested. References in parentheses are to the main body of LCCP 139.

In this second, extended Consultation Paper we have raised a large number of issues, and have made provisional proposals on many of them. We summarise here our provisional proposals and the other issues on which we are seeking respondents' views . . .

The need for the same principles to be adopted in relation to consent in other criminal offences in which consent is an issue
1 We provisionally propose that the proposals contained in paragraphs 12–30 below should apply not only to offences against the person and sexual offences but also to every other criminal

offence in which the consent of a person other than the defendant is or may be a defence to criminal liability.

[Paragraphs 1.24 – 1.27]

Intentional causing of seriously disabling injury

2p We provisionally propose that the intentional causing of seriously disabling injury (as defined at paragraph 7 below) to another person should continue to be criminal, even if the person injured consents to such injury or to the risk of such injury.

[Paragraphs 4.3–4.6 and 4.47]

Reckless causing of seriously disabling injury

3 We provisionally propose that –

(1) the reckless causing of seriously disabling injury (as defined at paragraph 7 below) should continue to be criminal, even if the injured person consents to such injury or to the risk of such injury; but

(2) a person causing seriously disabling injury to another person should not be regarded as having caused it recklessly unless –

  (a) he or she was, at the time of the act or omission causing it, aware of a risk that such injury would result, and

  (b) it was at that time contrary to the best interests of the other person, having regard to the circumstances known to the person causing the injury (including, if known to him or her, the fact that the other person consented to such injury or to the risk of it), to take that risk.

[Paragraphs 4.7–4.28 and 4.48]

Secondary liability for consenting to seriously disabling injury

4 We provisionally propose that, where a person causes seriously disabling injury to another person who consented to injury or to the risk of injury of the type caused, and the person causing the injury is guilty of an offence under the proposals in Paragraphs 2 and 3 above, the ordinary principles of secondary liability should apply for the purpose of determining whether the person injured is a party to that offence.

[Paragraphs 1.20–1.23]

Intentional causing of other injuries

5 We provisionally propose that the intentional causing of any injury to another person other than seriously disabling injury as defined at paragraph 7 below (whether or not amounting to 'grievous bodily harm' within the meaning of the Offences Against the Person Act 1861 or to 'serious injury' within the meaning of the Criminal Law Bill) should not be criminal if, at the time of the act or omission causing the injury, the other person consented to injury of the type caused.

[Paragraphs 4.29 and 4.49]

Reckless causing of other injuries

6 We provisionally propose that the reckless causing of any injury to another person other than seriously disabling injury as defined at paragraph 7 below (whether or not amounting to 'grievous bodily harm' within the meaning of the Offences Against the Person Act 1861 or to 'serious injury' within the meaning of the Criminal Law Bill) should not be criminal if, at the time of the act or omission causing the injury, the other person consented to injury of the type caused, to the risk of such injury or to the act or omission causing the injury.

[Paragraphs 4.29 and 4.50]

Definition of seriously disabling injury

7 We provisionally propose that for the purpose of paragraphs 2–6 above 'seriously disabling injury' should be taken to refer to an injury or injuries which –

(1) cause serious distress, and

(2) involve the loss of a bodily member or organ or permanent bodily injury or permanent functional impairment, or serious or permanent disfigurement, or severe and prolonged pain, or serious impairment of mental health, or prolonged unconsciousness; and, in determining whether an effect is permanent, no account should be taken of the fact that it may be remediable by surgery.

[Paragraphs 4.29–4.40 and 4.51]

Meaning of consent

8 We provisionally propose that for the purposes of the above proposals –

(1) 'consent' should mean a valid subsisting consent to an injury or to the risk of an injury of the type caused, and consent may be express or implied;

(2) a person should be regarded as consenting to an injury of the type caused if he or she consents to an act or omission which he or she knows or believes to be intended to cause injury to him or her of the type caused; and

(3) a person should be regarded as consenting to the risk of an injury of the type caused if he or she consents to an act or omission which he or she knows or believes to involve a risk of injury to him or her of the type caused.

[Paragraphs 4.3–4.28 and 4.52]

. . .

Persons without capacity

12 We provisionally propose that for the purposes of any offence to which consent is or may be a defence, a valid consent may not be given by a person without capacity.

[Paragraphs 5.19–5.21]

Definition of persons without capacity

13 We provisionally propose that a person should be regarded as being without capacity if when he or she gives what is alleged to be his or her consent –

(1) he or she is under the age of 18 and is unable by reason of age or immaturity to make a decision for himself or herself on the matter in question;

(2) he or she is unable by reason of mental disability to make a decision for himself or herself on the matter in question; or

(3) he or she is unable to communicate his or her decision on that matter because he or she is unconscious or for any other reason.

[Paragraphs 5.19–5.21]

Capacity and minors

14 We provisionally propose that –

(1) in relation to those matters in which a person under the age of 18 may give a valid consent under our proposals, such a person should be regarded as unable to make a decision by reason of age or immaturity if at the time the decision needs to be made he or she does not have sufficient understanding and intelligence to understand the information relevant to the decision, including information about the reasonably foreseeable consequences of deciding one way or another or of failing to make the decision; and

(2) in determining whether a person under the age of 18 has sufficient understanding and intelligence for the above purposes, a court should take into account his or her age and maturity as well as the seriousness and implications of the matter to which the decision relates.

[Paragraphs 5.1–5.11 and 5.21–5.22]

. . .

Exception for recognised sport

40 We provisionally propose that a person should not be guilty of an offence of causing injury if he or she caused the relevant injury in the course of playing or practising a recognised sport in accordance with its rules.

[Paragraphs 12.1–12.63 and 12.68]

41 We wish to receive views on the precise formulation of the rule we suggest, since we do not wish a player to lose its protection, for example, merely because he or she happened to be offside on the football field.

[Paragraphs 12.1–12.63 and 12.69]

42 We provisionally propose that in the context of these proposals:

(1) the expression 'recognised sport' should mean all such sports, martial arts activities and other activities of a recreational nature as may be set out from time to time in a list to be kept and published by the UK Sports Council in accordance with a scheme approved by the appropriate minister for the recognition of sports, and the rules of a recognised sport should mean the rules of that sport as approved in accordance with the provisions of such a scheme;

(2) when carrying out its duties in relation to the recognition of any such activity the UK Sports Council should consult such organisations as appear to it to have expert knowledge in relation to that activity.

[Paragraphs 13.1–13.19]

43 We would welcome views not only in relation to the desirability of the recognition scheme we propose, but also on any points of detail we ought to bear in mind when formulating our final recommendations.

[Paragraph 13.20]

Dangerous exhibitions

44 We ask whether it would be appropriate, in relation to any particular type of dangerous exhibition, to set an age limit below which a consent to a risk of injury would not be valid.

[Paragraphs 12.64–12.67]

Fighting and horseplay

45 We provisionally propose that:

(1) the intentional or reckless causing of all types of injury in the course of fighting, otherwise than in the course of a recognised sport, should continue to be criminal, even if the person injured consented to injury or to the risk of injury of the type caused; but

(2) an exception to this rule should continue to be available where any injury, other than seriously disabling injury, is caused in the course of undisciplined consensual horseplay.

[Paragraphs 14.1–14.20]

46 We wish to receive views as to possible definitions of 'fighting' and 'undisciplined horseplay' that would achieve an acceptable degree of clarity and certainty.

[Paragraph 14.21]

Mistaken belief in consent: offences against the person

9 We ask –

(1) whether it should in itself be a defence to an offence of causing injury to another person that –

    (a) at the time of the act or omission causing the injury, the defendant believed that the other person consented to injury or to the risk of injury of the type caused, or to that act or omission, and

    (b) he or she would have had a defence under our proposals in paragraphs 5 and 6 above if the facts had been as he or she then believed them to be; or

(2) whether such a belief should be a defence only if, in addition, either

    (a) it would not have been obvious to a reasonable person in his or her position that the other person did not so consent, or

    (b) he or she was not capable of appreciating that that person did not so consent.

[Paragraphs 7.1–7.28 and 7.31]

. . .

Burden of proof on the issue of consent or mistaken belief in consent in relation to offences against the person

11 If the proposals in paragraphs 5 and 6 above were accepted, we ask –

(1) whether it should be for the defence to prove, on the balance of probabilities,

    (a) that the person injured consented to injury of the type caused, or (in the case of injury recklessly caused) to the risk of such injury or to the act or omission causing the injury, or

    (b) that the defendant believed that that person so consented (and, if such in paragraph 9(2) is satisfied, that one of those conditions is satisfied); a belief were to be a defence only where one of the conditions set out or

(2) whether it should be for the prosecution to prove) beyond reasonable doubt,

    (a) that that person did not consent, and

    (b) that the defendant did not so believe (or, if such a belief were to be a defence only where one of the conditions set out in Paragraph 9(2) is satisfied, that neither of those conditions is satisfied).

[Paragraphs 4.41–4.45, 4.53 and 7.33]

Types of deception that may nullify consent

19 We provisionally propose that a person should not be treated as having given a valid consent, for the purposes of any offence of doing an act without such consent, if he or she gives such consent because he or she has been deceived as to –

(1) the nature of the act; or

(2) the identity of the other person or persons involved in the act.

[Paragraphs 6.11–6.18 and 6.79]

Other types of fraudulent misrepresentation that may nullify consent

20 We ask

(1) whether a fraudulent misrepresentation that a person has been found to be free from HIV and/or other sexually transmitted diseases should form an exception to the general rule that

fraud should nullify consent only where it goes to the nature of the act or the identity of the other person or persons involved in the act;

(2) if so, in what terms this new class of misrepresentation should be formulated; and

(3) whether there are any other specific types of misrepresentation that also call for extraordinary treatment.

[Paragraphs 6.19 and 6.80]

An offence of procuring consent by deception

21 We provisionally propose that a person should be guilty of an offence, punishable on conviction on indictment with five years' imprisonment, if he or she does any act which, if done without the consent of another, would be an offence so punishable, and he or she has procured that other's consent by deception.

[Paragraphs 6.18 and 6.81]

A definition of 'deception'

22 We provisionally propose that for the purposes of this offence 'deception' should mean any deception (whether deliberate or reckless) by words or conduct as to fact or as to law, including a deception as to the present intentions of the person using the deception or any other person.

[Paragraphs 6.7 and 6.82]

Inducing another person to perform an act on oneself by deception

23 We ask –

(1) whether it should be a specific offence for a person to induce a man by deception to have sexual intercourse (vaginal or anal) with him or her;

(2) if so, whether the offence should be confined to deceptions as to a particular kind of circumstance, and if so what; and

(3) whether it should include inducing another person by deception to perform any acts other than sexual intercourse, and if so what.

[Paragraph 6.20–6.21 and 6.83]

The duty to communicate information

24 We ask whether there are any particular circumstances in which the criminal law should impose an express duty to communicate information upon a person who wishes to rely on a consent to the causation of injury or to the risk of injury caused by him or her.

[Paragraphs 6.22–6.23 and 6.84]

Self-induced mistake

25 We provisionally propose that a person should not be treated as having given a valid consent to an act if he or she gives consent because of a mistake as to –

(1) the nature of the act,

(2) the identity of the other person or persons involved in the act, or

(3) any other circumstance such that, had the consent been obtained by a deception as to that circumstance, it would not have been treated as valid, if the defendant knows that such a mistake has been made or is aware that such a mistake may have been made.

[Paragraphs 6.24–6.27 and 6.85]

Non-disclosure

26 We invite views on –

(1) how the law should deal with the obtaining of consent by the non-disclosure of material facts;

(2) whether (if it is thought that any such non-disclosure should be criminal) the law should act out, in respect of each class of offence, the facts that must be disclosed;

(3) if so, what those facts should be in each case; and

(4) whether it should be a specific offence for one person to induce another, by non-disclosure of such a fact, to perform an act (and if so what kinds of act) upon him or her.

[Paragraphs 6.29–6.33 and 6.86]

FURTHER READING

Bronitt, S, 'Spreading disease and the criminal law' [1994] Crim LR 21

Gardner, J, 'Rationality and the rule of law in offences against the person' [1994] CLJ 502

Gardner, S, 'Stalking' (1998) 114 LQR 33

Gunn, M and DC Omerod, 'The legality of boxing' [1995] 15 Legal Studies 181

Horder, J, 'Reconsidering psychic assault' [1998] Crim LR 392

Omerod, DC, 'The Second Law Commission Consultation Paper on Consent: consent – a second bash' [1996] Crim LR 694

Roberts, P, 'Consent to injury: how far can you go?' (1997) 113 LQR 27

Roberts, P, 'The philosophical foundations of consent in the criminal law' (1997) 17 OJLS 389

Shute, S, 'The Second Law Commission Consultation Paper on Consent: something old, something new, something borrowed: three aspects of the project' [1996] Crim LR 684

Smith, JC, 'Offences against the person: the Home Office Consultation Paper' [1998] Crim LR 317

Spencer, JR, 'Liability for Reckless Infection' [2004] NLJ 384 and 448

Stone, R, 'It's bad to talk: assault by telephone' (1997) 113 LQR 407

Wells, C, 'Stalking: the criminal response' [1997] Crim LR 463

Withey, C, 'Biological GBH: Overruling Clarence?' [2003] NLJ 1698

CHAPTER 6

SEXUAL OFFENCES

6.1 INTRODUCTION

The term 'sexual offences' covers a very wide range of activities from key offences such as rape and sexual assault, through to exhibitionism, voyeurism, bestiality, offences related to prostitution and offences against minors and those lacking the ability to consent to sexual activity. In a sense some of these offences can be seen as aggravated forms of assault, for example the offence of 'sexual assault' (prior to 2003, known as indecent assault). The prohibited activities are regarded as meriting specific prohibition as sexual offences, partly to provide the appropriate label to the defendant's behaviour, partly to provide for enhanced powers of sentencing, and partly to reflect the stigma attached to sexual offences. There may also be repercussions for the defendant in terms of being placed on the sex offenders' register.

The law governing this area has been thoroughly reviewed in recent years. In July 2000 the Home Office published its Consultation Paper *Setting the Boundaries: Reforming the Law on Sex Offences*. The terms of reference for the reform were to review the sex offences in the common and statute law of England and Wales, and make recommendations that would:

- provide coherent and clear sex offences which protect individuals, especially children and the more vulnerable, from abuse and exploitation;
- enable abusers to be appropriately punished; and

- be fair and non-discriminatory in accordance with the European Convention on Human Rights ('ECHR') and Human Rights Act.

Regarding the need for a review of the law in this area the Summary Report observed:

[The current law] . . . is a patchwork quilt of provisions ancient and modern that works because people make it do so, not because there is a coherence and structure. Some is quite new – the definition of rape for example was last changed in 1994. But much is old, dating from nineteenth century laws that codified the common law of the time, and reflected the social attitudes and roles of men and women of the time. With the advent of a new century and the incorporation of the European Convention on Human Rights into our law, the time was right to take a fresh look at the law to see that it meets the need of the country today [para 02].

The Summary Report set out in more details the scope, style and purpose of the review:

0.6 The law on sex offences is the part of the criminal law which deals with the most private and intimate part of life – sexual relationships – when they are non-consensual, inappropriate or wrong. As such it embodies society's view of what is right and wrong in sexual relations. Our guiding principle was that this judgment on what is right and wrong should be based on an assessment of the harm done to the individual (and through the individual to society as a whole). In considering what was harmful we took account of the views of victims/survivors and of academic research. The victims of sexual violence and coercion are mainly women. They must be offered protection and redress and the law must ensure that male victims/survivors are protected too. The law must make special provision for those who are too young or otherwise not able to look after themselves, and offer greater protection to children and vulnerable people within the looser structures of modern families. In order to deliver effective protection to all, the law needs to be framed on the basis that offenders and victims can be of either sex. We have recommended offences that are gender-neutral in their application, unless there was good reason to do otherwise.

0.7 Our other key guiding principle was that the criminal law should not intrude unnecessarily into the private life of adults. Applying the principle of harm means that most consensual activity between adults in private should be their own affair, and not that of the criminal law. But the criminal law has a vital role to play where sexual activity is not consensual, or where society decides that children and other very vulnerable people require protection and should not be able to consent. It is quite proper to argue in such situations that an adult's right to exercise sexual autonomy in their private life is not absolute, and society may properly apply standards through the criminal law which are intended to protect the family as an institution as well as individuals from abuse. In addition to this, the ECHR ensures that the state must uphold its responsibility to provide a remedy in law so that a complainant can seek justice.

0.8 We also thought it was vital that the law was clear and well understood, particularly in this field of sexual behaviour where there is much debate about the ground-rules. There is no Highway Code for sexual relations to give a clear indication of what society expects or will tolerate. The law should ensure respect for an individual's own decisions about withholding sexual activity and protect every person from sexual coercion and violence.

In November 2002 the Government published the White Paper, *Protecting the Public: strengthening protection against sex offenders and reforming the law on sexual offences* (Cm 5668), which set the Government's intentions for reforming the law on sexual offences and for strengthening measures to protect the public from sexual offending. The outcome of this review process was a very far reaching reform of all aspects of the statutory regulation of sexual conduct – the Sexual Offences Act 2003.

The offences of rape and indecent assault, as enacted in the Sexual Offences Act 1956, are replaced under the 2003 Act by four new offences:

Section 1: Rape;

Section 2: Assault by penetration;

Section 3: Sexual assault; and

Section 4: Causing a person to engage in sexual activity without consent.

These provisions need to be considered in the context of the statutory framework developed in the 2003 Act to determine the issue of whether or not the complainant was consenting; see ss 74–76. Each is considered in turn below.

6.2 RAPE – THE NEED FOR REFORM

Prior to the enactment of the Sexual Offences Act 2003, the offence of rape was provided for by the Sexual Offences Act 1956 s 1 as amended by s 142 of the Criminal Justice and Public Order Act 1994. A man was guilty of rape if he had sexual intercourse with a person (whether vaginal or anal) who at the time of the intercourse did not consent to it; and at the time he knew that the person did not consent to the intercourse or was reckless as to whether that person consented to it.

The offence was limited in scope. It did not cover vaginal or anal penetration with objects other than a penis, did not cover penile penetration of the mouth, and did not protect transsexuals.

Determining whether or not a complainant had in fact consented to sexual intercourse in cases where there was no clear evidence of the complainant being physically overpowered depended very much on the view of the facts taken by the jury. The standard guidance in such cases was based on the Court of Appeal's decision in *R v Olugboja* [1982] QB 320, where Dunn LJ observed that:

> Although 'consent' is [a] common word it covers a wide range of states of mind in the context of intercourse between a man and a woman, ranging from actual desire on the one hand to reluctant acquiescence on the other. We do not think that the issue of consent should be left to a jury without some further direction. What this should be will depend on the circumstances of each case. The jury will have been reminded of the burden and standard of proof required to establish each ingredient including lack of consent, of the offence. They should be directed that consent, or the absence of it, is to be given its ordinary meaning and if need be, by way of example, that there is a difference between consent and submission; every consent involves a submission,

> but it by no means follows that a mere submission involves consent ... [I]n the ... type of case where intercourse takes place after threats not involving violence or the fear of it ... we think that ... a jury will have to be ... directed to concentrate on the state of mind of the victim immediately before the act of sexual intercourse, having regard to ... their combined good sense, experience and knowledge of human nature and modern behaviour to all the relevant facts of that case.

Giving so much discretion to the jury, as this type of direction inevitably did, increased the likelihood of inconsistent verdicts, and raised the possibility that a jury might be reluctant to return a guilty verdict in trials (such as those involving so called 'date rape, or 'acquaintance rape') where the facts did not resemble popular conceptions of rape (violent attack by a stranger).

Even where the *actus reus* was established (ie the absence of consent) the prosecution still faced the problem of proving *mens rea*, that is, that the defendant knew the complainant was not consenting or was at least reckless as to whether the complainant was consenting. In *R v Morgan* [1975] 2 All ER 347, the House of Lords held that a defendant who genuinely, albeit mistakenly, believed that the complainant was consenting could not be guilty of rape. As Lord Hailsham observed:

> ... the mental element is and always has been the intention to commit that act [of sexual intercourse] or the equivalent intention of having intercourse willy-nilly not caring whether the victim consents or no. A failure to prove this involves an acquittal because the intent, an essential ingredient, is lacking ... in particular it matters not that the intention is lacking only because of a belief not based on reasonable grounds. ...

The Home Office Consultation Paper *Setting the Boundaries: Reforming the Law on Sex Offences* observed:

> 2.8.1 The first issue we thought about was the criminal behaviour that should be included in the crime of rape. We considered the various sexual violations that are perpetrated on men and women by other men and women, and the impact of differing kinds of sexual assaults on the victim in order to assess the relative seriousness of the different kinds of behaviour. We also wondered how the public might understand the law. We looked at what solutions other countries had adopted and sought information on how effective they had been. (The latter was particularly difficult as the letter of the law is only one of many variables in the way the criminal justice process operates.)
>
> 2.8.2 We decided that the essence of rape was the sexual penetration of a person by another person without consent. However, penetration comes in many forms. Men put their penis into the vagina, anus and mouth. Other parts of the body (notably fingers and tongues) are inserted into the genitalia and the anus. Objects are inserted into the vagina and anus of victims. Both men and

women may perform such penetration. These are all extremely serious violations of victims which can leave them physically and psychologically damaged for many years. We did consider whether there was evidence that a woman could force a man to penetrate her against his will but, although we found a little anecdotal evidence, we did not discover sufficient to convince us that this was the equivalent of rape. (However we do recognise the existence of such coercive behaviour and think it should be subject to the criminal law. We make separate recommendations about offences of compelling sexual penetration in para 2.20 following.)

2.8.3 Having decided that all coerced sexual penetration was very serious, the question was how the law should best deal with it. There seemed to be two potential approaches – that of defining any sexual penetration as rape, and that of treating penile penetration separately from other forms of penetration.

2.8.4 We were uneasy about extending the definition of rape to include all forms of sexual penetration. We felt rape was clearly understood by the public as an offence that was committed by men on women and on men. We felt that the offence of penile penetration was of a particularly personal kind, it carried risks of pregnancy and disease transmission and should properly be treated separately from other penetrative assaults. We therefore set aside our presumption of gender-neutrality as regards the perpetrator for offences for the crime of rape and propose that it be limited to penile penetration. We also recognised the concerns of transsexuals that the law could except them from the protection of the criminal justice system. If modem surgical techniques could provide sexual organs, the law should be clear enough to show that penetration of or by such organs would be contained within the scope of the offence. The law must give protection from all sexual violence. Whether or not sexual organs are surgically created, the law should apply. Accordingly we thought to put it beyond doubt that the law should apply to surgically constructed organs – whether vaginal or penile.

Note that the Consultation Paper rejected the idea that the law should be reformed so as to recognise degrees of rape:

2.8.6 An issue that was raised in Home Office research, and by a few respondents, was whether there should be any gradation or degrees of rape. The argument put is that there are 'serious' rapes (those which involve violence, by strangers etc) and less serious rapes – the 'date rape' or 'he just went a bit too far' type of rape. Some people argued that such a gradation with lower sentences for 'lesser' crimes would encourage juries to convict more readily. Without research into juries' thinking, we do not have any firm evidence to support this view.

. . .

2.8.7. A more serious question is whether there are genuinely lesser rapes. Victim/survivor organisations told us that although all victim/survivors were deeply affected by rape, there was often greater victimisation in rapes that were seen as lesser than the traditional model of stranger rape. A woman or man attacked in the street is a chance victim – it is truly appalling, but no blame attaches to the victim. To be raped by someone you know and trust, whom you may let into your house, or when you visit theirs, is not such a matter of chance. The victim has made decisions to put their trust in the other person. There may or may not be overt physical violence but those victims face additional issues of betrayal of trust and being seen as, or feeling, guilty for being in that situation. Some research indicates that the level of violence in partner/ex-partner rape is second only to stranger rape. We were told by those who counsel victim/survivors that those raped by friends or family often find it much harder to recover and may take longer to do so. In addition to these powerful arguments, it is hard to see how degrees of rape could be defined – when does a stranger become an acquaintance or a friend? The crime of rape is so serious that it needs to be considered in its totality rather than being constrained by any relationship between the parties.

. . .

2.8 If we are to consider a rape as being not just an offence of violence, but a violation of the integrity of another person, then there is neither justification nor robust grounds for grading rape into lesser or more serious offences. The impact on victims is no less, and indeed there are arguments that it can be more serious and long-lasting. Rape is a very serious crime but sentences can, and should, reflect the seriousness of each individual case within an overall maximum. Gradation of the seriousness of a particular offence is best reflected in the sentence finally imposed rather than creating separate offences.

The Government White Paper, *Protecting the Public: strengthening protection against sex offenders and reforming the law on sexual offences* (Cm 5668), outlined the need for reform thus:

39 Sexual activity without the consent of one of the parties involved is a non-consensual offence. This is the case whether the offender intends to engage in sexual activity with another person in the full knowledge that he or she does not consent, or when he could not care less whether consent was given or not. These non-consensual offences are acts of sexual violation and often involve force. Such crimes can cause long-lasting physical and psychological damage to the victim(s). Our new set of non-consensual offences creates a more coherent structure for criminalising such acts and addresses a number of problems in existing law. It increases the protection offered by the law and sets penalties for these offences that reflect the seriousness of the abuse involved. It will still be for the prosecution to prove that the victim did not consent.

40 Rape is one of the most serious and abhorrent crimes a person can commit. It is a crime that generates fear and alarm in the community and from which everyone needs to be protected. To maximise the protection offered by the criminal law the definition of rape will be widened to include penile penetration of the vagina, anus or mouth and will cover surgically reconstructed male and female genitalia (for example when a person has undergone an operation to change sex). Rape will continue to attract a maximum penalty of life imprisonment.

41 Date rape has recently received much attention in the media and there have been calls for the creation of a separate offence of date rape. Our view is that rape is rape, and cannot be divided in this way into more and less serious offences. It can be just as traumatic to be raped by someone you know and trust who has chosen you as his victim, as by a stranger who sexually assaults the first man or woman who passes by. It is up to the courts to take all the particular circumstances of a case into account before determining the appropriate penalty. One of the principles underlying our new offences is that they should not be gender-specific. However, the offence of rape is

clearly understood to be non-consensual penile penetration perpetrated by a man, on a woman or a man. The anatomical differences between men and women must sensibly direct that the offence of rape should remain an offence that can only be physically performed by a man (although women can be guilty as accessories to the crime), it will therefore not apply to circumstances where a woman compels a man to penetrate her without his consent. However, this form of sexual offending will be caught within the scope of a new offence of causing another person to perform an indecent act without consent, which will, in relation to sexual penetration, carry a maximum penalty of life.

42 Drug-assisted rape has received plenty of press coverage in recent years and is a real cause for concern. Existing law includes an offence of administering drugs in order for a man to have unlawful sexual intercourse with a woman and carries a maximum penalty of 2 years. We intend to retain this offence, amended so that it covers the administering of drugs or other substances with intent to stupefy a victim in order that they can be subjected to an indecent act without their consent, and to increase the maximum penalty to 10 years' imprisonment. This offence can apply both where the substance has been administered to sexually exploit a person even though the sexual activity does not for whatever reason take place and where the purpose is for the victim to be subjected to sexual activity with someone other then the person who administers the drugs.

6.3 THE REFORMED OFFENCE OF RAPE

Section 1 of the Sexual Offences Act 2003 states:

(1)   1 A person (A) commits an offence if –
  (a)   he intentionally penetrates the vagina, anus or mouth of another person (B) with his penis,
  (b)   B does not consent to the penetration, and
  (c)   A does not reasonably believe that B consents.
(2)   Whether a belief is reasonable is to be determined having regard to all the circumstances, including any steps A has taken to ascertain whether B consents.
(3)   Sections 75 and 76 apply to an offence under this section.

Section 79(2) provides that penetration, for these purposes, is a continuing act from entry to withdrawal. Note that the offences extend to penile penetration of the mouth (ie forced oral sex), and by virtue of s 79(3), references to a part of the body now include references to a part surgically constructed (in particular, through gender reassignment surgery). The offence of rape continues to carry a maximum penalty of life imprisonment.

6.3.1 PROVING THE COMPLAINANT DID NOT CONSENT

The Government White Paper, *Protecting the Public: strengthening protection against sex offenders and reforming the law on sexual offences* (Cm 5668), summarised the need for a fresh approach to the issue of consent in sexual offences:

28 The issue of whether the complainant consented or not is central to establishing whether a sex offence actually took place. It is vital that the law is as clear as possible about what consent means in order to prevent miscarriages of justice that result in an innocent party being convicted or the guilty walking free. Juries must decide that they are sure, beyond reasonable doubt, whether the complainant was consenting or not. This is an important and often difficult role.

29 Human beings have devised a complex set of messages to convey agreement or lack of it. Agreement or lack of agreement is not necessarily verbal, but both parties should understand it. Each must respect the right of the other to demonstrate or say 'no' and mean it. We do not of course wish to formalise such understanding into an unnecessary or semi-contractual agreement; it is not the role of Government or the law to prescribe how consent should be sought and given. It is, however, the role of the law to make it unambiguously clear that intimate sexual acts should only take place with the agreement of both parties.

30 The current law on the issue of consent is set out in case law, and is complex. There is little general guidance in case law as to the meaning of consent, except that it has been held that consent is different from submission. We intend to make statutory provision on this issue that is clear and unambiguous. In line with current law, where a person is deceived as to the nature of sexual activity or where his or her consent is induced by impersonation of someone else, that person will be deemed not to consent to it.

31 In order to protect victims of all ages we will be including in statute the following list of circumstances in which it should be presumed that consent was most unlikely to have been present, i.e. where the victim:

- was subject to force or the fear of force;
- was subject to threats or fear of serious harm or serious detriment to themselves or another person;
- was abducted or unlawfully detained;
- was unconscious;
- was unable to communicate his or her decision by reason of physical disability; or
- had agreement given for them by a third party.

32 It would be for the prosecution to prove, beyond a reasonable doubt, that sexual activity took place in one of the circumstances on the list. If so, it would then be for a defendant to show, on the balance of probabilities, that in the particular circumstances in question the victim did indeed give their consent. The intention is to strike the right balance between protecting victims and ensuring fairness under the law for defendants by helping juries with the fundamental questions of whether the victim was able to, and did in fact give his or her consent on the occasion in question. Including such a list in statute will also send a clear signal to the public about the circumstances in which sexual activity is likely to be wrong and will help encourage genuine victims to bring cases to court.

33 We will also be modifying the test of mistaken belief in relation to non-consensual offences. The current defence of an 'honest' belief in consent means that no crime is committed when a person is forced against their will to have sexual intercourse with a person who can convince the court that they 'honestly' interpreted their protestations or actions as consent to sex, however unreasonable such a belief might be. We believe the difficulty in proving that some defendants did not truly have an 'honest' belief in consent contributes in some part to the low rate of convictions

for rape. This in turn leads many victims, who feel that the system will not give them justice, not to report incidents or press for them to be brought to trial.

34 We will therefore alter the test to include one of reasonableness under the law. This will make it clear that, where the prosecution can prove that there is reasonable room for uncertainty about whether someone was consenting and that the defendant did not take reasonable action in the circumstances to ensure that the other person was willing to take part in the sexual acts, he will commit an offence. 'Reasonable' will be judged by reference to what an objective third party would think in the circumstances. The jury would however have to take into account the actions of both parties, the circumstances in which they have placed themselves and the level of responsibility exercised by both. The jury would also expect, where relevant, to take account of the circumstances in which the accusation or revelation is delivered (including any media involvement) and the time that has elapsed.

The 2003 Act creates a staged approach to establishing whether or not the complainant (P) consented to D's actions. Regard must first be had to those situations, outlined under s76, where P is conclusively presumed not to have consented. If these are not made out, regard is had, under s 75, to those situations where P is presumed not to have consented – the presumption being rebuttable depending on the evidence provided by D.

Under s 76, the situations where P is conclusively presumed not to have consented to the sexual activity of D arise where D intentionally deceived P as to the nature or purpose of the relevant act; or D intentionally induced P to consent to the relevant act by impersonating someone known personally to P.

Under s 75 of the 2003 Act, where D intentionally penetrates the vagina, anus or mouth of P and any one of the following circumstances existed, namely:

(i)   any person was, at the time of the relevant act or immediately before it began, using violence against P or causing P to fear that immediate violence would be used against him; or

(ii)   any person was, at the time of the relevant act or immediately before it began, causing P to fear that violence was being used, or that immediate violence would be used, against another person; or

(iii)   P was, and D was not, unlawfully detained at the time of the relevant act; or

(iv)   P was asleep or otherwise unconscious at the time of the relevant act; or

(v)   because of P's physical disability, P would not have been able at the time of the relevant act to communicate to D whether P consented; or

(vi)   any person had administered to or caused to be taken by P, without P's consent, a substance which, having regard to when it was administered or taken, was capable of causing or enabling the complainant to be stupefied or overpowered at the time of the relevant act,

and D knew that any one of these circumstances existed, the jury can presume that P did not consent to the relevant act, unless sufficient evidence is adduced to raise an issue as to whether P consented.

Where there is no factual basis for recourse to ss 76 and 75 (i.e. no basis for concluding that P did not consent or presuming that P did not consent), the jury will have to be directed in accordance with s 74 of the 2003 Act, which provides that: '. . . a person consents if he agrees by choice, and has the freedom and capacity to make that choice'. Setting aside issues of age – children being protected by specific offences – capacity to consent will essentially be a matter of evidence as to the mental health of the complainant, or the effect of any intoxicating substances on P's rationality.

Note that in *R v B* (Court of Appeal, Criminal Division) 16 October 2006, where D had been convicted of rape, the prosecution had been permitted to adduce evidence that D knew he was HIV positive at the time of the sexual intercourse and he admitted that he had not informed the complainant of his HIV status. The defence case was that the sexual intercourse had been consensual. The trial judge had held that the fact that D had not informed the complainant of his HIV status was a matter which the jury were entitled to take into account when deciding whether the complainant had consented.

The appeal was allowed, the court ruling that the fact that a defendant's failure to disclose his HIV status was not, in law, a matter which could, in any way, be relevant to the issue of consent to sexual activity within the meaning of s 74 of the 2003 Act. The only deceptions explicitly declared by the 2003 Act as vitiating consent are deceptions as to the nature and quality of the sexual act. Whether or not criminal liability should arise from a failure to disclose a sexually transmittable disease was a matter requiring debate not in a court of law but as a matter of public and social policy.

The Sexual Offences Act 2003 (1) Rape, Sexual Assaults and the Problems of Consent
[2004] Crim LR 328

Jennifer Temkin and Andrew Ashworth

Some criticisms of the new scheme

By introducing a three-track approach to matters of consent and belief in consent – irrebuttable presumptions, rebuttable presumptions, and a general definition of consent – the Act raises a number of questions. Are the three categories intended to reflect some kind of moral hierarchy, so that the most serious cases of non-consent give rise to irrebuttable presumptions and the next most serious to rebuttable presumptions, with the remainder falling within the general definition? Or is the organising principle one of clarity and certainty, so that it is the clearest cases (not necessarily the worst) that give rise to irrebuttable presumptions and the next clearest to rebuttable presumptions, with the remainder falling within the general definition? Or is it a mixture of the two, with an added element of common law history? One would have thought that consideration ought to be given to marking out the worst cases of non-consent by means of irrebuttable presumptions, but that appears not to have happened. Various criticisms may be advanced.

(i) Are the types of fraud that give rise to the conclusive presumptions in s 76(2) the worst cases of non-consent?

A preliminary question here is whether the types of fraud singled out by s 76(2) are necessarily the worst types of deception, compared with deception as to intentions, powers and other matters . . . A more pressing question, however, is whether obtaining compliance by fraud or deception is worse than other ways of avoiding true consent, such as using threats or violence, administering drugs, or taking advantage of a sleeping or unconscious person. Obtaining compliance by using violence or threats of immediate violence seems no less heinous than doing so by deception, and yet the Act creates a conclusive presumption in the latter case and only a rebuttable presumption in the former.

There is also a case to be made for a conclusive presumption in the situation set out in s 75(2)(f), where it is proved beyond doubt that C had a substance administered to her without her consent which was capable of stupefying or overpowering her at the time of the relevant act and D knew this. Of course D must have, as he does under this provision, the opportunity to argue that the presumption does not apply because the substance administered was incapable of causing C to be stupefied or overpowered. But if the stupefying effect is established, it is questionable whether D should be able to argue that C nevertheless consented to the subsequent sexual act and that the drug or alcohol did not in fact prevent her from consenting. Can freedom and capacity to make a choice really exist in any meaningful sense in this situation? The present terms of s 75(2)(f) leave it open to the defence to enter into an impossible area of speculation about the precise effect of the substance on C, a matter which can only confuse the jury and cannot satisfactorily be resolved.

Is there any good reason why it should be the case that, if D deceives C by means of impersonation or as to the nature of the act, non-consent is conclusively proved under s 76, but if D has sex with C when C is asleep or unconscious this supports only a rebuttable presumption? The common law drew no such distinction between these situations. The Home Office Minister, Beverley Hughes, asserted that 'one of the principles behind the proposal [in respect of the presumptions] is that we should take steps to clarify existing case law and incorporate it into statute'. However, it has always been the law that consent must be present at the time of the sexual act. This means that consent is necessarily regarded as absent once it is proved beyond doubt that C was asleep or unconscious at the time sexual intercourse took place. If absence of consent is not conclusively presumed in these situations, as it was at common law, then the law is being taken backwards rather than forwards. This new departure reflects the more far reaching and entirely unfortunate proposal of the Law Commission that consent should be defined as a subsisting, free and genuine agreement, which would have invited the defence to argue that a consent given previously had not been withdrawn.

Those who are uncomfortable with the full implications of sexual autonomy may not share the view that a conclusive presumption of absence of consent should apply where D has sex with C who is asleep at the time. The provisions of the Act on consent apply not only to rape and assault by penetration but also to touching which falls within sexual assault or causing sexual activity. A conclusive presumption of absence of consent and absence of reasonable belief in consent, if applied to all situations where C was asleep at the time, would render D liable for sexual assault if he sexually touched his partner C while C was asleep even though D was in the habit of doing so and C had not objected to this in the past. Even though complaints are unlikely to be made in such cases, this may be regarded as casting the law's net too wide. However, there was another solution, recommended by the Report: that the list of non-consent situations should apply only to rape and assault by penetration, with other cases being left to the general definition of consent. Whilst the interests of consistency and coherence argue in favour of the list of rebuttable presumptions applying to all four offences, it might have been preferable to follow the common law in cases where C was asleep at the time and to enact an irrebuttable presumption of absence of consent applying only to penetrative acts.

(ii) Should the list of circumstances in s 75 be more extensive and non-exhaustive?
In Canada and the Australian jurisdictions which have a statutory list of non-consent situations, the list is non-exhaustive. The exhaustive list in s 75 leaves no scope for further situations to be added through the common law. Only Parliament will be able to make additions to the list. The Report, on

the other hand, considered that the list simply reflected obvious situations where consent was likely to be absent, including those already recognised at common law. It was just a starting point from which 'the courts will continue to develop the common law as they consider cases where different circumstances apply'. The Minister's justification for the list was that there was 'real value in making a statement in the legislation about circumstances in which sexual activity is not acceptable'. Elsewhere the Government has claimed that 'it will provide juries with a clear framework within which to make fair and just decisions. It should also serve as a clear statement to the public more widely'. If those are among its primary purposes, the brevity of the list might be thought to be troubling, as might its potential to undermine the definition of consent in s 74. For example, it omits threats other than of immediate violence, no matter how serious such threats might be. In both the Report and Protecting the Public the list included threats or fear of serious harm or serious detriment to the complainant or to others. The Government rejected amendments that would have added other serious threats to the list, arguing that terms such as serious harm and serious detriment were too imprecise and would give rise to too much uncertainty. This gesture towards the principle of maximum certainty is laudable but unconvincing. The definition of consent itself positively sprouts uncertainties. Moreover, by restricting the fear of violence in the presumption to fear of immediate violence, the Act imposes a limitation which is not present in existing law and not required in defences such as duress and self-defence.

During the passage of the Bill through Parliament, one presumption was added to the list in s 75 (administering a stupefying substance) but another disappeared entirely. In the Report and in Protecting the Public, cases where the complainant's willingness to engage in sexual activity with the defendant was indicated only by a third party were included in the list of circumstances. The Report expressed the matter cogently as follows: 'Free agreement is an issue between sexual partners and cannot be given by others, whether husbands, partners or those in authority over the complainant.' In Canada the law provides that 'no consent is obtained where the agreement is expressed by the words or conduct of a person other than the complainant'. The Government was so persuaded by the force of these arguments that the original Bill provided that, where absence of consent was proved, belief in consent based only on evidence of anything said or done by a third party should lead to a conclusive presumption of absence of reasonable belief in consent. However, this provision was opposed on two main grounds. Some argued that it tipped the scales too far against defendants, in cases where it was simply one person's word against another's: the cogency of this argument depends on whether people have been put on notice that they should never accept a third party's word in matters of sexual autonomy. The other objection was that people with a learning disability or mental disorder could not be expected to know that they were being deceived: insofar as this has substance it is an argument against almost all objective tests in the criminal law, and might best be dealt with by way of exception or defence. In the end these two objections led the Government to abandon the presumption, not only as a conclusive presumption but also as a rebuttable presumption. Cases of this kind now fall to be dealt with on general principles.

The Report further recommended that the list should include the situation where C was 'too affected by alcohol or drugs to give free agreement'. This proposal was not adopted in Protecting the Public and s 75(2)(f) is considerably narrower, since it relates only to situations where C's intoxication is patently blameless. Whilst contributory negligence has no place in the criminal law, it is apparent that such ideas had an influence on the Government's thinking. Those who take alcohol or drugs voluntarily are placed in a different moral category from those who have had alcohol or drugs 'administered' to them by the defendant. Thus, the list of presumptions, which the Government has invested with great moral symbolism, is there to protect those who can be constructed as the 'innocent' victims of sexual assault.The many women who get raped when they are drunk and whose inebriation is more or less voluntary will have to take their chances in the legal process without the benefit of evidential presumptions. Where the intoxicant had the effect of rendering C unconscious, the presumption under s 75(2)(d) will apply.

The Sexual Offences Act 2003: Intoxicated Consent and Drug Assisted Rape Revisited
[2004] Crim LR 789
E Finch and VE Munro

. . . the position under the Sexual Offences Act 1956 was subjected to considerable criticism for its failure to provide adequate guidance in terms of how to delineate between consent and non-consent. In marked contrast to the non-prescriptive stance adopted in the previous statute, the Sexual Offences Act 2003 attempts to impose a determinate framework for guiding jury decision making on the presence or absence of consent. Under s 74 of the 2003 Act, the meaning of consent is explained: 'a person consents if he agrees by choice, and had the freedom and capacity to make that choice.' The incorporation of this definition has the potential to offer more than semantic clarification. In requiring that a person must have the freedom and capacity to make the relevant choice, this provision directs attention to the context in which consent is given or refused. In turn, this promotes a less one-dimensional understanding that acknowledges the reality that the outcome of the consent binary cannot be radically divorced from the circum-stances under which the relevant choice is made.This suggests a positive protection of the idea and value of sexual autonomy which, if interpreted broadly, could permit a more complex analysis of the power dynamics and cultural pressures that operate to constrain a person's freedom and capacity to make sexual choices. While such a development could have significant ramifications for understanding of the consent threshold, it remains to be seen whether this possibility will be embraced with the necessary enthusiasm and innovation by the legal community.

. . . It is clear that there are complexities inherent in [the situation where D administers intoxi-cants to P so as to stupefy or overpower P in order that D should have sexual intercourse with P] . . . that stem largely from the effects of the intoxicants involved but also from the failure of the law to tackle the distinction between the use of intoxicants to procure intercourse and the use of intoxicants to procure consent. An approach which involves an interpretation of stupefaction as involving virtual unconsciousness excludes many commonplace abuses of intoxicants for sexual purposes from the scope of the section, whilst an approach that involves lowering the threshold for what counts as stupefaction requires direct engagement with the different levels of intoxica-tion short of unconsciousness and the extent to which they permit a residual capacity for decision making.

Since these questions are not adequately addressed in the context of what it means to 'stupefy' a victim, it might be hoped that the inclusion within s 75(2)(f) of the alternative requirement that the substance be capable of 'overpowering' the victim might provide fertile ground. Certainly, the specific inclusion of the alternative does indicate a recognition of the fact that a drug may be administered to a victim which, whilst not rendering her insentient or unconscious at the time of intercourse, will negatively impact on her ability to refuse consent. Unfortunately, however, the legislation provides no further guidance as to the meaning of 'overpowering'. In a context in which the concept of overpowering in sexual offences to date has implied the use of force, this lack of definition would seem to suggest that a substance will only be one which overpowers the victim if it is capable of rendering her physical resistance impossible. Once again, it is most unlikely that this notion of overpowering, narrowly defined, will offer redress to many of those victims who have ingested intoxicants, including Rohypnol, which do not necessarily lead to this kind of insentience or ineptitude.

Thus, there is a considerable need for further clarification as to what is envisaged by the requirement that the intoxicant must be one capable of stupefying or overpowering the victim. To the extent that resolution of this question requires consideration of whether there is a stage of intoxication short of unconsciousness at which a victim is incapable of giving meaningful consent, it is apparent that the provisions under s 75(2)(f) do not resolve the fundamental debate at the core of legal responses to intoxicated consent under the Sexual Offences Act 1956. In addition, there is one final problem with this aspect of the s 75(2)(f) presumption that ought to be discussed, namely the extent to which it is necessary to establish a causal link between the administration of the intoxicant and the stupefaction or susceptibility of the victim to being overpowered. Given that it is common practice for date-rape drugs to be administered in alcohol, it may be difficult to ascertain the extent to which the victim's condition is the inevitable result of her voluntary consumption of alcohol or the result of the administration of the intoxicant. This problem will be exacerbated in situations in which the victim's alcoholic drink has been spiked with additional alcohol. Moreover, the calculation of the impact of any amount of alcohol on a particular person is rather an imprecise science at the best of times, given the individualistic reaction to alcohol that exists as between different people. If this is to be further muddied by the difficulty of ascertaining how much alcohol the victim consumed on a voluntary basis and how much can be attributed to a non-consensual administration, it is easy to envisage that it would be almost impossible to assess the relative contribution of the two to the state that the victim was in at the time of intercourse. Given the commonplace occurrence of the misuse of alcohol in socio-sexual situations, this seemingly insoluble dilemma is likely to fall for resolution by the courts at some stage in the future.

Convicting Rapists and Protecting Victims – Justice for Victims of Rape A Consultation Paper (2006) Office for Criminal Justice Reform

Consent is at the heart of most cases of rape. This is not simply saying 'yes' or 'no' but doing so through choice, and with the freedom and capacity to make that choice. We are seeking views on whether we need to define that capacity in law to assist the courts and juries in cases where drink or drugs may have impacted upon the complainant's ability to choose . . . In July 2000 the Government published *Setting the boundaries: reforming the law on sex offences*. It was a detailed account of the consultation exercise and made a number of recommendations. The subsequent Command Paper *Protecting the public: strengthening protection against sex offenders and reforming the law on sexual offences* put forward proposals to strengthen the law on sex offenders and to modernise penalties and the law on sex offending to increase public confidence and better protect the public. Those proposals were articulated in the Sexual Offences Act 2003.

Recommendation 6 of *Setting the boundaries* was that the law should include a non-exhaustive list of examples of where consent was not present including where a person was 'too affected by alcohol . . . to give free agreement'.

However, in the 2002 White Paper, *Protecting the Public*, the Home Secretary, when stating the Government's intention to create a set of evidential presumptions, indicated that these would not cover voluntary intoxication leading to incapacity falling short of sleep or a lack of consciousness:

> I have rejected the suggestion that someone who is inebriated could claim they were unable to give consent – as opposed to someone who is unconscious for whatever reason, including because of alcohol – on the ground that we do not want mischievous accusations.

The Sexual Offences Act 2003 sought to create greater legal protection for victims by clarifying the law on consent . . . Section 74 of the Act defines consent by stating that 'a person consents if he agrees by choice, and has the freedom and capacity to make that choice'. It also provides, at section 75, a list of circumstances in which it is presumed a complainant did not consent.These include: where the victim was asleep or unconscious, or could not communicate consent because of a physical disability; and where the victim had been given a substance without their consent that was capable of causing them to be overpowered at the time the alleged rape took place.This includes the scenario when a victim's drink is spiked.

These circumstances do not include, however, where the victim was voluntarily intoxicated. Nor does the Act define what is meant by 'capacity'.

So, taken in conjunction with the evidential presumptions about consent provided for by s 75, in a case where a complainant was rendered unconscious by drink, then it could be presumed that she had not consented. However, where the complainant was severely intoxicated but remained conscious, the presumption would not arise and it would be for the jury to consider whether or not the complainant had consented to sexual activity or not and central to that argument would be whether or not the complainant had the capacity to give her consent.

Capacity however is not defined in the Sexual Offences Act 2003. In *Sexual Offences: Law and Practice* (3rd edn, 2004,Thomson Sweet and Maxwell) the authors Rook and Ward suggest that, in the absence of such a definition, the courts may look for assistance to the common law, although they acknowledge that there were at common law no clear principles governing whether a person had capacity to consent to sexual acts. They conclude: 'Adapting the common law on capacity to the definition of consent in s 74, a complainant will not have had the capacity to agree by choice where their understanding and knowledge were so limited that they were not in a position to decide whether or not to agree' (Rook and Ward, *Sexual Offences: Law and Practice*, 1.81–1.94).

R v Dougal [2005] Swansea Crown Court

The case of *R v Dougal* concerned an allegation of rape by a female student at Aberystwyth University. In that case, the judge directed the jury to enter a 'not guilty' verdict when the prosecution informed the judge that it did not propose to proceed further because it was unable to prove that the complainant had not given consent because of her level of intoxication.

What was not addressed at the trial was whether or not the victim had the capacity to consent to sexual activity given her level of intoxication. It could be argued that these were matters that could quite properly have been put before a jury and the matter left for them to decide whether or not the complainant's level of drunkenness had meant that she was not capable of consenting to sexual activity. However, the case has also raised questions about the possible need for 'capacity' to be defined in statute.

The case of *R v Dougal* has undoubtedly raised concerns amongst some about the effectiveness of the Sexual Offences Act 2003 and caused them to question whether or not the Act offers adequate protection to persons at times of particular vulnerability. The absence of a clear definition has, they argue, led to a lack of clarity the result of which has been that not all cases that should have gone to the jury have done so.

Others have argued to the contrary, saying that *R v Dougal* has not brought into question the effectiveness of the legislation but merely raised questions about the prosecution of such cases. They contend that in such a case the question about whether or not the level of alcohol consumed by the complainant had left her incapable of consenting could quite rightly be put to the jury. Moreover, seeking to change the law in this area would do little to address underlying weaknesses in the criminal justice system relating to the manner in which such cases are handled.

Does the law need to be changed?

Where the victim is so drunk that she becomes unconscious or where the accused 'spikes' the victim's drinks the law on consent is clear. But where the victim has voluntarily taken drink or drugs, the issues become more difficult. Inevitably, if a person continues to drink heavily throughout an evening, they will reach a point at which they become so intoxicated that they will lose the capacity to give meaningful consent to sexual activity. What is difficult to establish is when is that point reached? There are many levels to intoxication and different people will be able to consume varying amounts of alcohol and suffer different effects.

It is also the case that alcohol is a disinhibitor and can make individuals do things that they would not choose to do when they are sober. There is a distinction to be drawn therefore between intoxication that results in a lack of capacity to consent; and intoxication that alters a person's choices but does not deprive him or her of the capacity to consent. Regretting an act the following day does not mean that you did not engage in it willingly, if foolishly, at the time.

Given the evident complexities in this area, the question that needs to be asked is: does the existing legislation need to be changed or is it sufficiently robust as it stands to prosecute these particularly challenging rape cases?

The offence of rape at section 1 of the Sexual Offences Act 2003 has 3 central elements which the prosecution must prove beyond reasonable doubt: the intentional penetration of the vagina, anus or mouth of a person by the penis of another; that the victim did not consent to the penetration; and that the perpetrator did not reasonably believe the victim had consented. In many cases, it is not doubted or disputed that penetration occurred and therefore the key to the case is the issue of consent. And this is where the difficulties lie because consent is not simply about demonstrating that the complainant said 'yes' or 'no'. Rather, it is about the complainant having the capacity to make that decision and that choice, a capacity for which alcohol (or drugs or other things) may have deprived her. Moreover where the complainant is publicly intoxicated it may well be the case that there are witnesses to that incapacity as well as to the fact that the perpetrator could not have reasonably believed that she was able to consent by choice, freely and ably.

A statutory definition of capacity?

As mentioned previously, Rook and Ward in their book *Sexual Offences: Law and Practice* have suggested a definition of the central elements of capacity based on understanding and knowledge, with further reference to the limits placed upon them by, amongst other things, alcohol. While the issues about whether and to what degree an individual's understanding and knowledge, and therefore capacity, were limited through drink undoubtedly raise some difficult questions for courts and juries to contemplate, the question on which views are sought, is whether the inclusion of such a definition would serve to reinforce the importance of capacity as a key consideration and provide a clearer reference point to aid juries in determining this issue.

Evidential presumptions

As also discussed previously, s 75 of the Act provides a list of circumstances where, if it is proved that they existed, it is presumed that the complainant did not consent. These include unconsciousness and the complainant being asleep. There is clearly a link here with alcohol, as - many intoxicated persons will reach a point when the effect of the drink is such that they will pass into unconsciousness. But this is often a drawn-out process, involving a gradual passage through mild drunkenness to intoxication to passing out. In many cases, a person's ability to function properly and to have the capacity to consent to certain acts will be severely impaired at the point that an individual drifts into unconsciousness or sleep.

Given this complex picture, would the creation of a further evidential presumption based upon extreme drunkenness be helpful in ensuring that, in general, it is the jury that decides whether or not the complainant had the capacity to give consent?

We have given careful consideration to this question. Creating an evidential presumption would raise many difficult questions, especially as alcohol affects people differently. This is also a matter about which other concerns have already been expressed such as those of the Home Secretary quoted at the beginning of this chapter. The existing presumptions all relate to circumstances where the complainant is not able to freely consent due to factors outside of his or her control. That would not apply to self-induced intoxication.

Moreover, there is little evidence that the existing evidential presumptions have enjoyed great usage. The presumptions apply unless the defendant raises "sufficient evidence" to raise an issue as to whether the victim consented. Where the defendant does raise such evidence, the judge will direct the jury that the presumption does not apply and the jury should consider the issue of consent in the normal way. In practice, it is not particularly onerous for defendants to enter the witness box and give 'sufficient evidence' to disengage the presumption. Therefore, we believe that the arguments for creating an additional evidential presumption are not strong and the better course would be to proceed by legislating to provide for a clearer definition of capacity.

 COMMENTS AND QUESTIONS

1   Questions arise as to why deception and impersonation cases lead to a conclusive presumption against consent but cases where P is asleep or has been drugged do not. Surely the latter are more serious and more conclusive?

2   Issues of choice and freedom to consent under s 74 may yet prove troublesome. Suppose a cashier is spotted by a security guard stealing from a cash register. He offers to ignore the incident if she has sex with him. If she agrees to have sexual intercourse has she consented as that term is understood within the context of s 74?

3   In *R v Linekar* [1995] 3 All ER 69, D agreed to pay P, a prostitute, £25 for sex. After sexual intercourse had taken place D, in breach of the agreement he had made with P, made off without paying. Would this activity fall within the revised definition of rape? Has D deceived P as to the nature of the sexual act (thus creating a conclusive presumption that P did not consent) – that is, he purported that it would be sex that was paid for, when this was never his intention.

4   See *R v B* (above). Why is D's silence as to his having a sexually transmittable disease not a deception as to the 'quality' of the act if the evidence is that P would not have consented to the sexual intercourse if he or she had been aware of D's condition? Why is a conviction for grievous bodily harm in such situations possible, but not a conviction for a sexual offence? See further *R v Dica* [2004] 3 All ER 593, considered in Chapter 5.10.3.

5   Where P's consent to intercourse is predicated on D's compliance with a precondition and D fails to meet that precondition, could the subsequent intercourse be regarded as having occurred without P's consent? The matter was addressed, albeit *obiter*, in *A-G's Ref (No 28 of 1996)* [1997] 2 Cr App R (S) 206. The appellant had been convicted of a number of rapes of women working as prostitutes. The common factor was that the prostitutes had agreed to have sexual intercourse with the appellant on the basis that he would be wearing a condom. In each case the appellant had removed the condom immediately before penetration. Lord Bingham CJ observed:

> . . . prostitutes are as much entitled to the protection of the law as anyone else: they are entitled to insist that they are not willing to permit sexual intercourse unless their sexual partner is protected. It is undoubtedly rape for any defendant to insist upon sexual intercourse without protection when the woman does not consent, and even more so if he imposes his sexual demands by force. [Prostitutes] . . . are in particular need of the law's protection because they are vulnerable to infection. . .

Deception as to wearing a condom would appear to be caught under the conclusive presumption provisions of s 75 – unprotected sexual intercourse arguably being an act of a different nature to protected sexual intercourse. If however, D makes no pretence of wearing a condom and simply ignores P's precondition the matter falls to be considered under s 74. It would be odd if behaviour that was clearly regarded as falling within the old offence of rape was regarded as falling outside the reformed offence.

6.3.2 *MENS REA* FOR RAPE

As noted above, the *mens rea* for rape is (in addition to an intent to commit the prohibited acts) the absence of any reasonable belief in the consent of the complainant. Under s 1(2) whether or not a belief is reasonable is to be determined having regard to all the circumstances, including any steps the defendant took to ascertain whether or not the complainant was consenting (on the scope of 'circumstances' see *Attorney General's Reference (No 79 of 2006) R v Whitta* [2006] EWCA Crim 2626 (below)).

Under s 1 of the 2003 Act, the prosecution must prove that D intended to engage in penile penetration of P's vagina/mouth/anus, and that D had no reasonable belief that P was consenting. Under s 76 of the Act, D is conclusively presumed not to have believed that P consented if he intentionally deceived P as to the nature or purpose of the relevant act; or D intentionally induced P to consent to the relevant act by impersonating someone known personally to P. If these circumstances are found to exist, therefore, no direct evidence of D's state of mind is required to secure a conviction.

If the circumstances referred to in s 76 are not made out, the jury will still be entitled to presume that D did not reasonably believe that P consented if any one of the situations referred to in s 75 is established by the prosecution, and that D knew that any one of these circumstances existed. The situations are that:

(i)   any person was, at the time of the relevant act or immediately before it began, using violence against P or causing P to fear that immediate violence would be used against him; or

(ii)   any person was, at the time of the relevant act or immediately before it began, causing P to fear that violence was being used, or that immediate violence would be used, against another person; or

(iii)   P was, and D was not, unlawfully detained at the time of the relevant act; or

(iv)   P was asleep or otherwise unconscious at the time of the relevant act; or

(v)   because of P's physical disability, P would not have been able at the time of the relevant act to communicate to D whether P consented;

(vi)   any person had administered to or caused to be taken by P, without P's consent, a substance which, having regard to when it was administered or taken, was capable of causing or enabling the complainant to be stupefied or overpowered at the time of the relevant act.

Where there is no factual basis for recourse to ss 76 and 75 in order to make presumptions, conclusive or otherwise, about D's state of mind, the prosecution, in proving that D had no reasonable belief as to P's consent, can ask the jury to consider all the circumstances, including any steps D took to ascertain whether P was consenting. The aim of these provisions is clearly to replace the subjective approach to the *mens rea* of rape established in *DPP v Morgan*, with a more objective approach where the onus lies on the man to ascertain consent before engaging in sexual activity. Note that a degree of subjectivity could be introduced where the jury is directed to have regard to the circumstances, as these could include the mental capacity of the defendant.

Attorney General's Reference (No 79 of 2006) R v Whitta [2006] EWCA Crim 2626

D had attended a party at C's house at the invitation of C's son. During the party D met S, a young woman with whom he became friends. Having spent the night out with friends C returned home and joined in with the party for a short period of time before retiring to bed. S also stayed the night in C's house. When the party broke up D was shown a bedroom in which he was invited to stay for the night. Once in his bedroom D decided to visit the bedroom of S, believing she would be amenable to sexual intercourse with him. D entered what he believed to be S's room. In fact if was C's bedroom. D approached C, who was asleep, and penetrated her vagina with his finger. C woke and told D to desist. D, realising his error, apologised and left. C subsequently reported the incident to the police and D was charged with rape contrary to s 1 of the Sexual offences Act 2003, and assault by penetration contrary to s 2 of the Sexual

Offences Act 2003. At the subsequent trial D's argument was that he had reasonably believed C was consenting because he had mistakenly believed C to be S. HHJ Fingret ruled that the evidence put forward by D did not amount to a defence. In his view the requirement that the jury consider the reasonableness of a defendant's belief in the victim's consent 'having regard to all the circumstances' was limited to whatever had taken place between the defendant and the named complainant in the indictment. In his view the jury could not be directed to consider the defendant's state of mind in relation to any third party. Consequently D pleaded guilty to the s 2 charge and the prosecution offered no evidence on the s 1 rape charge. D was sentenced to a supervision order for three years and the Attorney General sought leave to refer the sentence to the Court of Appeal pursuant to s 36 of the Criminal Justice Act 1988 as being unduly lenient. The Court of Appeal refused to increase the sentence.

Hooper LJ:

7. If the ruling [by HHJ Fingret] is right it will apply equally to offences under sections 1 and 3 of the SOA ['Sexual Offences Act 2003'] . . .

10. This reference is not concerned with either the correctness of the judge's ruling, or the correctness of the conviction which resulted from it. However, it is fair to say that, at the outset of the hearing, the court expressed the view that it had doubts about the ruling of the judge . . .

11. Some analysis of the ruling and the consequences flowing from it is necessary, however, in order to understand on what factual matrix the offender fell to be sentenced.

12. The effect of the SOA 2003, in particular the provisions of sections 1(1)(c), 2(1)(d) and 3(1)(d), is to make the offences of rape, assault by penetration and sexual assault crimes that can be committed negligently. Miss Whitehouse (for the Attorney-General) sought to support the judge's ruling by saying that the judge had decided that the offender's belief was not reasonable. She submitted that the offender had not taken the necessary care to ascertain who was in the bed and that he had committed the offence of sexual penetration 'by omission'.

13. We disagree with this analysis of the ruling. The effect of the judge's ruling is that it is not a defence to a charge under sections 1 or 2 of the SOA if the defendant has made a mistake, however reasonable, as to the identity of the person to whom the sexual activity is directed. In his ruling the judge did not decide that the offender's belief was not reasonable or that he had omitted to take the necessary care. He decided that the offender's belief was irrelevant because he did not believe that C consented.

14. If the ruling is right, then the three offences are offences of strict responsibility as far as, and only as far as, the identity of the complainant is concerned. This being so, the judge must determine the level of the defendant's culpability, if any, in order to determine the appropriate sentence.

15. We note in passing that a possible alternative way of dealing with this very rare set of circumstances would be to hold that the offence is committed if a reasonable (and therefore sober) person would have realised that the person being penetrated or sexually touched was not the person whom the defendant thought he was consensually penetrating or touching.

6.3.3 THE BACKGROUND TO REFORMING THE *MENS REA* FOR RAPE

The Home Office Consultation Paper, Setting the Boundaries: Reforming the Law on Sex Offence, reviewed the arguments for and against a subjective approach to *mens rea* in the offence of rape; in particular the effect of the decision in *DPP v Morgan*, whereby a defendant who honestly, but mistakenly, believed a complainant to have been consenting was held not to be guilty of rape:

2.13 Honest belief in consent

2.13.1 The question of honest, albeit mistaken, belief in consent, is used as a defence in court, and rouses strong passions in those responding to the review, and amongst the members of the review. About a third of the representations we received on rape argued that the decision in *Morgan* ... should be reversed to an honest and reasonable belief. The seminar on rape also unanimously concluded that *Morgan* needed to be changed. The External Reference Group [ERG] of the review, which advised the Steering Group, endorsed the view that the *Morgan* judgment should be set aside and a requirement of reasonableness be reintroduced into the law.

2.13.2 This issue is often discussed in theoretical terms: for instance, in terms of rape, the extent to which criminality depends on the state of mind of the accused, and whether or not he should be found guilty of a crime that he did not intend to commit. The law at present does not require the reasonableness of a defendant's belief to be tested (although other tests are possible) so making it possible for a defendant to claim he held a completely irrational but honest belief in the consent of the woman: if this is upheld, he must be acquitted. In terms of subjectivist legal principle this is right. In terms of social policy, it makes some very large assumptions. By allowing the belief of the accused to be paramount, the law risks saying to a victim/survivor who feels violated and betrayed that they were not really the victim of crime, and that what they thought, said or did was immaterial. It is seen to validate male assumptions that they can assume consent without asking. It is an issue that utterly divides opinion, and divided those of us undertaking the review.

2.13.3 Internationally the issue divides common law jurisdictions. No US state has ever extended the subjective bias towards the defendant as far as *Morgan*, and the honest belief of the defendant is subject to a test of reasonableness. Some have limited its use even further, California for example, limits its use to situations where the complainant's behaviour was 'equivocal'. In Australia the common law states (ACT, Victoria, NSW and South Australia) uphold the subjective test set out in *Morgan*. Indeed Victoria and South Australia adopted the subjective approach before *Morgan*. Those states which adopted their Criminal Codes in the 1920s (Tasmania, Queensland, W Australia) have retained the pre-*Morgan* position of an objective test of reasonableness on the defendant's honest belief. The Model Criminal Code proposals argue for retaining honest belief. New Zealand has reversed *Morgan*. They have developed what they call a 'subjective and objective test' – the defendant could hold a subjective honest belief but that belief is subject to an objective test of reasonableness.

2.13.4 In the UK, the Law Commission reviewed the *mens rea* for rape in detail in their Consultation Paper No 139 (Consent in the Criminal Law: Chapter 7) and their view was that the *Morgan* rule should be qualified by an objective test, and they sought views on that. They said: 'we think it would be remarkable if the *Morgan* rule did not sometimes have the effect of encouraging a jury to accept a bogus defence.' In their policy paper to the review, the Law Commission now recommend that honest belief should be preserved but that judges should direct the jury to the effect that in judging whether honest belief is genuine they should have regard as to whether he sought to ascertain consent, and that if his belief in consent arose from self-induced intoxication, it is not a defence.

2.13.5 The review spent many careful hours discussing this issue. We looked at the present subjectivist view and were all agreed that it could not be retained in its current form. We then looked at a variety of solutions to try to ensure that the defendant is not compromised but the victim is ensured justice. The first thing we established was that in practice, the defence of honest albeit mistaken belief in consent is usually run in tandem with consent. We could not find evidence of it being critical in a trial. The Sexual Offences (Amendment) Act 1976 requires the jury to have regard to the 'presence or absence of reasonable grounds for such a belief . . . in considering whether he so believed'. We noted research by the Law Commission in Victoria to try to determine whether it was more difficult to convict if the belief was run as a defence. In a study of 53 prosecutions, the defendant's belief was relevant in 23% of cases. 6% used mistaken belief as a primary defence, 17% as part of a defence. Of the 12 cases, 6 were convicted (50%). It is impossible to tell whether putting an objective test onto the reasonableness of that belief would have made a difference in the remaining 6 cases.

2.13.6 The arguments given for the full subjective test are:

- The law should punish people not just for what they did but for what they intended to do. This underlies most modern law, and underpins for example the distinction between intentional killing being charged as murder whilst a death that results from poor driving, although deeply tragic, is not regarded as so blameworthy because there was no specific intent, and in terms of the law is a less serious offence.
- A test of reasonableness is applying external standards. Should a person be found guilty of a very serious crime because they did not apply the same personal standards of reasonableness as those who determined the accused's guilt or innocence? Is it right to apply external standards when the accused did not think they were doing wrong, for whatever cultural or other factors? What if they did not have the capacity to realise there was no consent?
- How should a reasonableness test be applied? Does it have to be reasonable for a person of the same class, culture or level of intelligence? If so does this not risk accentuating and perpetuating stereotypes about behaviour?
- The nature of the belief and its reasonableness or lack of it are issues to be tested by evidence on the facts of the case. The testing of the nature of the belief by the prosecution is an essential part of the case.

2.13.7 The arguments against the subjective test are:

- It implicitly authorises the assumption of consent, regardless of the views of the victim, or whatever they say or do.
- It encourages people to adhere to myths about sexual behaviour and in particular that all women like to be overborne by a dominant male, and that 'no' really means 'yes'. It undermines the fundamental concept of sexual autonomy.
- The mistaken belief arises in a situation where it is easy to seek consent and the cost to the victim of the forced penetration is very high. It is not unfair to any person to make them take care that their partner is consenting and be at risk of a prosecution if they do not do so.
- There is no justice in a situation whereby a woman (or a man) who has been raped in fact (because she or he did not consent) sees an assailant go free because of a belief system that

society as a whole would find unreasonable – for example that he saw some or all women (or women of certain types) as sexual objects.

- It is easy to raise the defence but hard to disprove it.
- The Youth Justice and Criminal Evidence Act 1999 limits the use of a complainant's sexual history in court. One of the exceptional cases where it may be introduced is when the defence of honest belief in consent is raised and sexual history is relevant to that belief. The concern is that this provision will significantly increase the use of the honest belief defence because that would open the door to introducing the element of previous sexual history as part of the defence, allowing cross-examination of the complainant on this issue.

2.13.8 In balancing these arguments, there was a disagreement between the External Reference Group who unanimously wanted the law restoring to its pre-*Morgan* state of requiring any honest belief in consent to be subject to a test of reasonableness, and the Steering Group. The Steering Group did not take the ERG's advice on this issue but identified an effective way of fettering an inappropriate use of honest belief, without re-introducing the external test of reasonableness that the courts had rejected.

2.13.9 The Steering Group aimed to ensure that their proposals gave proper weight to the victim's need for justice while maintaining the golden thread of the presumption of innocence of the defendant and ensuring that he was convicted for what he intended to do. It was essential that the law should be acceptable to the public, and to give victims and the wider public confidence that the law offers protection. We thought this confidence was lacking at present. The review is recommending changes to the law to define the meaning of consent as free agreement, and setting out when consent is not present. The Steering Group thought that these changes would create a rather different dynamic in rape cases where it would be more difficult to run a spurious defence of honest belief. The best way forward was to limit the use of the defence of honest belief in a way that fitted with our broader proposals, emphasised the importance of free agreement and made it much harder to run a dishonest defence.

2.13.10 The Steering Group was very attracted to the Canadian solution to this very difficult problem. In Canada the law retains an honest but mistaken belief defence but fetters when it can be used in a way that ties in with the definition of consent. The intention was to introduce an 'air of reality' into the use of a defence that relies on establishing what was happening in the defendant's mind at the time of the offence. The Canadian Criminal Code states:

273.2 It is not a defence . . . where
(a) the accused's belief arose from the accused's
    (i)   self-induced intoxication
    (ii)   reckless or wilful blindness; or
(b) the accused did not take reasonable steps, in the circumstances known to him at the time, to ascertain that the complainant was consenting.

2.13.11 This provides several useful concepts with which to moderate the dishonest or inappropriate use of the defence of honest belief. The requirement on the accused to have considered the issue of consent in order to provide a defence of honest belief is particularly important. The accused cannot invoke the defence unless they proved that they took all reasonable steps, in the circumstances known to them at the time, to ascertain whether the complainant was consenting. This undermines the belief that a defendant can make large assumptions about the attitude of the complainant and should mean, for example, in situations where a defendant thinks that all women fight, or say no when they mean yes, they had not sought free agreement at the time.

2.13.12 Self-induced intoxication because of drink or drugs does not reduce the criminal liability of a defendant, and this is set out in the Majewski Rules. A defendant is liable for his actions if he has voluntarily become drunk or high – because that was a matter of his own choice. He must be responsible for any consequences that flow from his actions when drunk or high. As drink and drugs are often an element in cases of rape, and we are concerned that the law should be clear, then it seems to be important to set out the principle in this context.

. . .

2.13.14 A further important point to ensure is that in retaining an honest belief in consent defence, in future any belief in consent will have to be a belief in free agreement – our definition of consent. The use of the qualifying conditions for the use of any belief in free agreement (ie that it was based on self-intoxication, arose from recklessness and that they did not take reasonable steps to ascertain free agreement) would create some sensible safeguards, while enabling the use of a defence when it is genuinely relevant. Accordingly we recommend that the defence of honest belief should be expressed in terms of free agreement, and be subject to limitations as to its use. This does not impose an external and objective requirement of reasonableness on the defendant, as our External Reference Group wanted, but it does reinterpret the doctrine of honest belief as set out by the House of Lords in the *Morgan* judgment, and provides new conditions for its use. The External Reference Group fully support this proposal, but would like to see it linked to a separate requirement that any belief in consent should be reasonable.

In relation to indecent assault the review recommended the introduction of a new offence of sexual assault '. . . to cover sexual touching (defined as behaviour that a reasonable bystander would consider to be sexual) that is done without the consent of the victim'.

The Sexual Offences Act 2003 (1) Rape, Sexual Assaults and the Problems of Consent
[2004] Crim LR 328

Jennifer Temkin and Andrew Ashworth

The absence of reasonable belief in consent

. . . under the new Act the *mens rea* of rape and the accompanying sexual assault offences has radically changed. The requirement of knowledge or reckless knowledge of the absence of consent, supported by the 'couldn't care less' test, has been replaced by the need to prove that 'A does not reasonably believe that B consents' (s I(l)(c)). Should this be seen as an improvement in the law? To answer this, we need to consider several other questions.

Why was the *Morgan* approach thought unsatisfactory? This landmark decision was widely applauded by subjectivists for its general effects on the criminal law, since it emphasised that people ought to be judged on the facts as they believed them to be, and not on facts to which they had not given thought. If an offence requires proof of intention or recklessness in respect of a consequence or circumstance, then it is a matter of 'inexorable logic' that a mistaken belief in that respect should negative liability. Whatever the justifications for this as a general approach in the criminal law, it seemed to many that those justifications were outweighed in the case of sexual offences, where the two parties are necessarily in close proximity and where intercourse without consent would be a fundamental violation of the victim. Surely, out of respect for the autonomy and sexual choice of B, A should take the opportunity to be clear that B does consent. In most situations this is an easy thing to do, and there is a strong reason for doing it. This is not to suggest strict liability as to the absence of consent: it is to suggest a requirement that A acted as a reasonable person should have done in the situation in respect of ascertaining consent.

Why was the Bill changed during its parliamentary progress? The Government departed from Setting the Boundaries by opting for a reasonableness standard rather than the 'couldn't care less' test, but the clause as originally drafted was unduly complex. Moreover, its formulation turned on whether the defendant had acted as a reasonable person would, and this was attacked on the ground that a defendant with, for example, a learning disability would be judged by standards he could not attain. The Bill was then amended, so that s 1(2) now states:

> Whether a belief is reasonable is to be determined having regard to all the circumstances, including any steps A has taken to ascertain whether B consents.

This wording discards the 'reasonable person' in favour of a general test of what is reasonable in the circumstances. The Home Affairs Committee applauded the change as avoiding the 'potential injustice' of a test that would operate regardless of individual characteristics: 'by focusing on the individual defendant's belief, the new test will allow the jury to look at characteristics – such as learning disability or mental disorder – and take them into account'. A different approach would have been to retain the reasonable person standard but to add a defence for those mentally incapable of attaining it. The difficulty with s 1(2) is that it could empty the reasonableness test of most of its content, and justify the kind of direction laid down in the self-defence case of *United States v King* 34 F302, 309 (CCEDKY 1888):

> In determining whether it is founded on reasonable grounds, the jury are not to conceive of some ideally reasonable person, but they are to put themselves in the position of the assailed person, with his physical and mental equipment surrounded with the circumstances and exposed to the influences with which he was surrounded and to which he was exposed at the time.

Has Parliament replaced the 'couldn't care less' test with one that is more demanding on the prosecution and more favourable to the defence? Much depends on how the phrase 'all the circumstances' comes to be interpreted. The Government's view was that 'it is for the jury to decide whether any of the attributes of the defendant are relevant to their deliberations, subject to directions from the judge where necessary'. Beverley Hughes expressed the matter slightly differently, stating that it would be for the judge 'to decide whether it is necessary to introduce consideration of a defendant's characteristics and which characteristics are relevant . . . The judge or jury can take into account all or any characteristics and circumstances that they wish to, and it is best that we leave that decision to the judge and jury for each case.' By what standards is it to be decided which characteristics are 'relevant'? Much will depend on the Specimen Directions and the approach of the Court of Appeal. But, as L'Heureux-Dube J famously stated in *Seaboyer* (1991) 83 DLR (4th) 193 at 228, 'The content of any relevancy decision will be filled by the particular judge's experience, common sense and /or logic . . . This area of the law has been particularly prone to the utilisation of stereotype in the determination of relevance.'

In Protecting the Public the Government expressed its concern that the *Morgan* test 'leads many victims who feel that the system will not give them justice, not to report incidents or press for them to be brought to trial'. Accordingly, it decided to alter the test 'to include one of reasonableness under the law'. But the present formulation is unlikely to provide the incentive to report or pursue the case that the Government is seeking. The broad reference to 'all the circumstances' is an invitation to the jury to scrutinise the complainant's behaviour to determine whether there was anything about it which could have induced a reasonable belief in consent. In this respect the Act contains no real challenge to society's norms and stereotypes about either the relationship between men and women or other sexual situations, and leaves open the possibility that those stereotypes will determine assessments of reasonableness. Is B's sexual history to be taken to be a relevant part of the circumstances? In answer to a question raised in Committee, the Minister agreed that the section 'should focus the court's attention on what is happening at the time of the offence' and 'should make the previous sexual history of the complainant far less relevant'. But this does not seem to reflect the natural meaning of the words 'all the circumstances', which contain no limitation to circumstances existing at the time of the event in question. Further, it is true that s 1(2) requires consideration of 'any steps A has taken to ascertain whether B consents', however, if A enquires about consent; B says no, but A concludes that B's 'no' is tantamount to 'yes', is his culturally engendered belief to be regarded as reasonable or not? In deciding what it is 'relevant' to consider, what is to prevent the influence of stereotypes about B's dress, B's frequenting of a particular place, an invitation to have a drink, and so forth?

It therefore seems possible that the new element of absence of reasonable belief in consent, which forms part of the four major offences in the Act, may not impose greater duties on defendants than does the present law. Of course, the prosecution may take advantage of the various presumptions in ss 76 (conclusive) and 75 (rebuttable) . . . but there will be many cases that fall outside that list of circumstances. The Act requires the prosecution to establish beyond reasonable doubt that A did not reasonably believe that B consented. Was the Government right to abandon its proposal for placing the onus of proof on the defence, once the basis for one of the rebuttable presumptions has been established?

6.4 'QUASI-RAPE' – ASSAULT BY PENETRATION

Section 2 Sexual Offences Act 2003 provides:

(1) A person (A) commits an offence if –
  (a) he intentionally penetrates the vagina or anus of another person (B) with a part of his body or anything else,
  (b) the penetration is sexual,
  (c) B does not consent to the penetration, and
  (d) A does not reasonably believe that B consents.
(2) Whether a belief is reasonable is to be determined having regard to all the circumstances, including any steps A has taken to ascertain whether B consents.
(3) Sections 75 and 76 apply to an offence under this section.

The offence carries the possibility of life imprisonment and can be committed by a man or a woman. Where the defendant is male the offence could be committed by means of penile penetration, but such cases are already dealt with under s 1. The mischief s 2 is aimed at involves penetration with fingers, or objects such as sticks, bottles, vibrators etc. The offence is limited to penetration of the vagina or anus – otherwise nonconsensual 'French kissing' would carry the possibility of life imprisonment. Note that the offence does not require proof of an assault.

The penetration must be 'sexual', which is further defined by s 78 of the 2003 Act in these terms:

> . . . penetration, touching or any other activity is sexual if a reasonable person would consider that –
>
> (a) whatever its circumstances or any person's purpose in relation to it, it is because of its nature sexual, or
> (b) because of its nature it may be sexual and because of its circumstances or the purpose of any person in relation to it (or both) it is sexual.

This is essentially an objective test to be approached in two stages. First the act may be such that, regardless of the circumstances or the purpose of D, the reasonable person would regard it as sexual. If the act is not regarded as sexual on that basis, the second approach would be to ask whether the act is of a nature that could be regarded as sexual if regard is had to the circumstances and the purpose of D. The intention of these provisions is that an act that, *per se*, could not reasonably be regarded as sexual should not fall within the ambit of the s 2 offence simply because of a secret sexual gratification derived by D. For an endorsement and application of this two-stage test see further *R v H* [2005] All ER (D) 16 (Feb), considered below.

The penetration referred to in s 2 must be an act to which P does not consent. The way in which the absence of consent is established follows the same process as that outlined above in relation to rape – the conclusive assumption, the rebuttable assumption, and the general direction to the jury.

In relation to the *mens rea* for the s 2 offence, D's penetration must be intentional, and the prosecution must prove that D had no reasonable belief that P was consenting; see further *Attorney General's Reference (No 79 of 2006) R v Whitta* [2006] EWCA Crim 2626 at 6.2.2 (above). Again the provisions regarding conclusive presumptions about the absence of any reasonable belief in consent, and the rebuttable presumptions about D's reasonable belief in P's consent follow the pattern established under ss 76, 75 and 74 in relation to rape.

6.5 SEXUAL ASSAULT

The 2003 Act introduces a new offence of sexual assault in place of the two indecent assault offences provided by the Sexual Offences Act 1956, ss 14 and 15. Three issues in particular proved problematic under the 1956 Act. First, the statute referred to assault, when in fact the vast majority of offences actually involved battery. Secondly, the concept of indecency was uncertain. In *R v Court* [1989] AC 28, the House of Lords adopted the approach that indecency involved a contravention of standards of decent behaviour in regard 'to sexual modesty or privacy', but debate continued over whether D's state of mind could be taken into account in determining whether an activity should rightly be regarded as indecent. Thirdly, the issue of consent remained at least partly unresolved in those situations where D exercised a deception in order to carry out an indecent assault; see further *R v Tabassum* [2000] 2 Cr App R 328.

The new offence of sexual assault is set out in s 3 of the Sexual Offences Act 2003, which provides:

(1) A person (A) commits an offence if –
    (a) he intentionally touches another person (B),
    (b) the touching is sexual,
    (c) B does not consent to the touching, and
    (d) A does not reasonably believe that B consents.
(2) Whether a belief is reasonable is to be determined having regard to all the circumstances, including any steps A has taken to ascertain whether B consents.
(3) Sections 75 and 76 apply to an offence under this section.

Section 79(8) of the 2003 Act provides that 'touching' includes touching: (a) with any part of the body; (b) with anything else; (c) through anything, and in particular includes touching amounting to penetration.

In *R v H* [2005] All ER (D) 16 (Feb), D had approached P, asked her 'Do you fancy a shag?', and then grabbed her tracksuit bottoms in the area of her right hand pocket. D was convicted under s.3 of the Sexual Offences Act 2003 despite the defence submission of no case to answer, based on the assertion that touching P's tracksuit bottoms had not amounted to 'touching' within s 79(8) of the 2003 Act. The Court of Appeal upheld the conviction, holding that touching of that clothing being worn by P constituted 'touching' for the purposes of the offence contrary to s 3 of the Act.

The touching must be sexual, as to which see s 2 (see 6.3 above). *R v Kumar* [2006] EWCA CRIM 1946, although dealing with a case of indecent assault under the 1956 Act is instructive on this issue (the defendant would have been charged with sexual assault if the 2003 Act had been in force at the time of his offence). D was a doctor who carried out a breast cancer examination on a patient. An examination was clinically necessary, but what D did went far beyond the bounds of acceptable practice. Upholding the conviction the Court of Appeal appeared to endorse the trial judge's direction to the jury to the effect that an assault was indecent (i.e. sexual for the purposes of the 2003 Act) if they were satisfied that D had intended to obtain sexual gratification. Four possibilities were identified.

(i) D's sole intention had been to gain sexual gratification (D guilty);
(ii) D's sole intention had been to gain clinical information (not guilty);
(iii) D had a dual intention, namely, legitimate breast examination as cover with intention to gain sexual gratification from the outset (D guilty);
(iv) D had, in the course of a legitimate medical examination, gained sexual gratification (D not guilty).

Situations (i) and (iii) would come within s 78(b) of the 2003 Act given the admissibility of evidence as to D's purpose.

The issue of consent is dealt with as explained above in relation to the offence of rape.

To establish the *mens rea*, the prosecution must prove that D's touching of P was intentional and that D had no reasonable belief that P was consenting – see further *Attorney General's Reference (No 79 of 2006) R v Whitta* [2006] EWCA Crim 2626 at 6.2.2 (above).

Provisions for establishing whether or not D had any reasonable belief in P's consent are as outlined above in relation to the offence of rape.

6.6 CAUSING A PERSON TO ENGAGE IN SEXUAL ACTIVITY WITHOUT CONSENT

Section 4 of the 2003 Act creates a new offence of causing a person to engage in sexual activity without consent. Section 4(1) provides that:

(1) A person (A) commits an offence if –
    (a) he intentionally causes another person (B) to engage in an activity,
    (b) the activity is sexual,
    (c) B does not consent to engaging in the activity, and
    (d) A does not reasonably believe that B consents.
(2) Whether a belief is reasonable is to be determined having regard to all the circumstances, including any steps A has taken to ascertain whether B consents.
(3) Sections 75 and 76 apply to an offence under this section.

Where the 'activity' caused involves

(a) penetration of B's anus or vagina,
(b) penetration of B's mouth with a person's penis,
(c) penetration of a person's anus or vagina with a part of B's body or by B with anything else, or
(d) penetration of a person's mouth with B's penis . . .

the defendant will be liable, on conviction on indictment, to imprisonment for life. Otherwise the offence is punishable by six months' imprisonment following summary conviction. The offence is wide enough to cover pimping, female 'rape' of a man, forcing a victim to undress under threats or forcing a victim to masturbate; see for example *R v Sargeant* (1997) 161 JP 127. As the Government White Paper, *Protecting the Public: strengthening protection against sex offenders and reforming the law on sexual offences* (Cm 5668), observed:

46 We intend to close a gap in existing legislation which does not expressly provide for the prosecution of someone who forces another person to perform sexual or indecent acts, either on themselves or the offender, or to engage in sexual activity with another person, against their will.

> Where compulsion is used, this is itself very frightening in addition to the highly distressing nature of the sexual behaviour itself. Forcing someone else to carry out a sexual act on themselves or with another person can leave those who are compelled feeling guilty and ashamed, although they had no choice but to engage in the activity. The offence of causing another person to perform an indecent act without consent makes it clear that the guilt lies with the person who causes the act to happen rather then the immediate victims. This offence will also provide an equivalent to the charge of rape where, for example, a woman compels a man to have sexual intercourse with her. It will have a maximum penalty of life imprisonment where sexual penetration is involved; non-penetrative acts will carry a maximum penalty of 10 years' imprisonment.

As with the offences under ss 2 and 3 the activity must be sexual, and must be one to which P does not consent. The issue of consent is dealt with as explained above in relation to the offence of rape.

In terms of *mens rea*, D must be proved to have intentionally caused the activity whilst having no reasonable belief that P was consenting. Provisions for establishing whether or not D had any reasonable belief in P's consent are as outlined above in relation to the offence of rape.

6.7 OFFENCES AGAINST CHILDREN UNDER THE AGE OF 13

Amongst the key aims of the Sexual Offences Act 2003 was the desire to enhance the protection offered to young children in the area of sexual offences and to simplify the task of the prosecution in establishing the elements of liability. To this end, ss 8 to 11 of the 2003 Act introduce four new offences that can only be committed where the victim is a child under the age of 13. These offences effectively mirror the structure of the four offences introduced under ss 1 to 4, but it will be noted that, as a child under 13 cannot give any effective consent to sexual activity, the provisions in ss 1 to 4 regarding consent are excluded. The offence of rape of a child under the age of 13 (s 8) is a strict liability offence, hence provisions relating to the defendant's intention and belief are also excluded in respect of that offence. The offence of causing a child under 13 to engage in sexual activity contrary to s 8 differs from the 'adult' version of the offence under s 4 only in that liability is extended to a defendant who incites such activity. Liability can therefore arise under s 8 even if the sexual activity never takes place. Whilst these offences are necessary to ensure the protection of children from adult sexual predators, they do, in theory, create the prospect of young adolescents engaged in sexual experimentation with each other being sentenced to life imprisonment (see s 6). It is assumed that sensible prosecution guidelines will be developed so as not to permit inappropriate prosecutions to reach the courts.

Section 5 Rape of a child under 13

(1) A person commits an offence if –

    (a) he intentionally penetrates the vagina, anus or mouth of another person with his penis, and

    (b) the other person is under 13.

(2)   A person guilty of an offence under this section is liable, on conviction on indictment, to imprisonment for life.

Section 6 Assault of a child under 13 by penetration

(1)   A person commits an offence if –
   (a)   he intentionally penetrates the vagina or anus of another person with a part of his body or anything else,
   (b)   the penetration is sexual, and
   (c)   the other person is under 13.
(2)   A person guilty of an offence under this section is liable, on conviction on indictment, to imprisonment for life.

Section 7 Sexual assault of a child under 13

(1)   A person commits an offence if –
   (a)   he intentionally touches another person,
   (b)   the touching is sexual, and
   (c)   the other person is under 13.
(2)   A person guilty of an offence under this section is liable –
   (a)   on summary conviction, to imprisonment for a term not exceeding 6 months or a fine not exceeding the statutory maximum or both;
   (b)   on conviction on indictment, to imprisonment for a term not exceeding 14 years.

Section 8 Causing or inciting a child under 13 to engage in sexual activity

(1)   A person commits an offence if –
   (a)   he intentionally causes or incites another person (B) to engage in an activity,
   (b)   the activity is sexual, and
   (c)   B is under 13.
(2)   A person guilty of an offence under this section, if the activity caused or incited involved –
   (a)   penetration of B's anus or vagina,
   (b)   penetration of B's mouth with a person's penis,
   (c)   penetration of a person's anus or vagina with a part of B's body or by B with anything else, or
   (d)   penetration of a person's mouth with B's penis, is liable, on conviction on indictment, to imprisonment for life.
(3)   Unless subsection (2) applies, a person guilty of an offence under this section is liable –
   (a)   on summary conviction, to imprisonment for a term not exceeding 6 months or to a fine not exceeding the statutory maximum or both;
   (b)   on conviction on indictment, to imprisonment for a term not exceeding 14 years.

6.8 PROTECTION OF CHILDREN BETWEEN 13 AND 16

Sections 9 to 13 of the Sexual Offences Act 2003 provide a further raft of offences designed to protect children under the age of 16. Clearly there will be a degree of overlap with the offences created by ss 5 to 8, considered above, but the assumption is that where the victim is under the age of 13 it is the offences under ss 5 to 8 that will be invoked, where it is felt that this is appropriate in terms of labelling the criminal activity involved, and where it is necessary to do so in order to provide the court with appropriate sentencing powers in the event of a conviction.

The four areas of activity criminalised by ss 9 to 12 of the 2003 Act are:

- sexual activity with a child;
- causing or inciting a child to engage in sexual activity;
- engaging in sexual activity in the presence of a child;
- causing a child to watch a sexual act.

In each case (subject to s 13 considered below) the offence can only be committed where the defendant is aged 18 or over at the time of the offence and the complainant is under the age of 16. The consent of the complainant is irrelevant. Where the complainant is between the ages of 13 and 16 the prosecution must prove that D had no reasonable belief that the complainant was over the age of 16. There is no longer any offence of unlawful sexual intercourse as was provided by s 6 of the Sexual Offences Act 1956. The options open to the prosecution now are:

- charge D with rape of a child under the age of 13;
- charge D with rape contrary to s 1; or
- charge D with sexual activity with a child if the complainant consented but was under the age of 16 – the provisions of s 9(2) applying to provide for trial on indictment (see below).

Section 9 Sexual activity with a child

(1) A person aged 18 or over (A) commits an offence if –

    (a) he intentionally touches another person (B),

    (b) the touching is sexual, and

    (c) either –

        (i)   B is under 16 and A does not reasonably believe that B is 16 or over, or

        (ii) B is under 13.

(2) A person guilty of an offence under this section, if the touching involved –

    (a) penetration of B's anus or vagina with a part of A's body or anything else,

    (b) penetration of B's mouth with A's penis,

    (c) penetration of A's anus or vagina with a part of B's body, or

    (d) penetration of A's mouth with B's penis,

    is liable, on conviction on indictment, to imprisonment for a term not exceeding 14 years.

(3) Unless subsection (2) applies, a person guilty of an offence under this section is liable –

    (a) on summary conviction, to imprisonment for a term not exceeding 6 months or to a fine not exceeding the statutory maximum or both;

    (b) on conviction on indictment, to imprisonment for a term not exceeding 14 years.

Section 10 Causing or inciting a child to engage in sexual activity

(1) A person aged 18 or over (A) commits an offence if –

    (a) he intentionally causes or incites another person (B) to engage in an activity,

    (b) the activity is sexual, and

    (c) either –

(i)   B is under 16 and A does not reasonably believe that B is 16 or over, or

(ii) B is under 13.

(2) A person guilty of an offence under this section, if the activity caused or incited involved –

(a) penetration of B's anus or vagina,

(b) penetration of B's mouth with a person's penis,

(c) penetration of a person's anus or vagina with a part of B's body or by B with anything else, or

(d) penetration of a person's mouth with B's penis,

is liable, on conviction on indictment, to imprisonment for a term not exceeding 14 years.

(3) Unless subsection (2) applies, a person guilty of an offence under this section is liable –

(a) on summary conviction, to imprisonment for a term not exceeding 6 months or to a fine not exceeding the statutory maximum or both;

(b) on conviction on indictment, to imprisonment for a term not exceeding 14 years.

Section 11 Engaging in sexual activity in the presence of a child

(1) A person aged 18 or over (A) commits an offence if –

(a) he intentionally engages in an activity,

(b) the activity is sexual,

(c) for the purpose of obtaining sexual gratification, he engages in it –

(i)   when another person (B) is present or is in a place from which A can be observed, and

(ii) knowing or believing that B is aware, or intending that B should be aware, that he is engaging in it, and

(d) either –

(i)   B is under 16 and A does not reasonably believe that B is 16 or over, or

(iii) B is under 13.

(2) A person guilty of an offence under this section is liable –

(a) on summary conviction, to imprisonment for a term not exceeding 6 months or a fine not exceeding the statutory maximum or both;

(b) on conviction on indictment, to imprisonment for a term not exceeding 10 years.

Section 12 Causing a child to watch a sexual act

(1) A person aged 18 or over (A) commits an offence if –

(a) for the purpose of obtaining sexual gratification, he intentionally causes another person (B) to watch a third person engaging in an activity, or to look at an image of any person engaging in an activity,

(b) the activity is sexual, and

(c) either –

(i)   B is under 16 and A does not reasonably believe that B is 16 or over, or

(ii) B is under 13.

(2) A person guilty of an offence under this section is liable –

(a) on summary conviction, to imprisonment for a term not exceeding 6 months or a fine not exceeding the statutory maximum or both;

(b) on conviction on indictment, to imprisonment for a term not exceeding 10 years.

Note that, as confirmed in *R v Abdullahi* [2006] All ER (D) 334 (Jul), it was not the intention of Parliament that liability under s 12 should be limited to situations where the display of the relevant material or act was contemporaneous or simultaneous to D's sexual gratification. Neither is the nature of the sexual gratification obtained defined under s 12.

Section 13 of the Sexual Offences Act 2003 provides that where D is aged between 10 and 17, he or she can incur liability for the offences created by ss 9 to 12, but in the event of a successful prosecution the sentencing powers are more limited. It states:

Section 13 Child sex offences committed by children or young persons

(1) A person under 18 commits an offence if he does anything which would be an offence under any of sections 9 to 12 if he were aged 18.

(2) A person guilty of an offence under this section is liable –

    (a) on summary conviction, to imprisonment for a term not exceeding 6 months or a fine not exceeding the statutory maximum or both;

    (b) on conviction on indictment, to imprisonment for a term not exceeding 5 years.

The mischief that the provisions under ss 9 to 12 are aimed at is clearly the sexual exploitation of young persons by predatory adults. The difficulty, however, is that s 13 will bring within the scope of the criminal law much of the consensual sexual activity that can take place between adolescents in an affectionate non-exploitative relationship, for example, so called 'heavy petting' between two 14-year-olds. As is the case with the offences under ss 5 to 8, unless clear and sensible prosecution policies are promulgated and adhered to, much harm could be caused by the inappropriate use of these provisions.

Sections 16 to 19 of the 2003 Act restate the offences set out in ss 9 to 12 in the context of abuse of a position of trust, thereby re-enacting the provisions of the Sexual Offences (Amendment) Act 2000 in terms that reflect the new framework of sexual offences designed to protect children. As with the previous law relating to abuse of a position of trust, children up to the age of 18 are protected by these provisions.

Summary of the main provisions of the Sexual Offences Act 2003

Rape	*P is under the age of 13*	*P is aged between 13 and 15*	*P is aged 16 or over*
D is under the age of 10	No liability	No liability	No liability
D is aged between 10 and 17	D charged under s 5	D could be charged under s 1 or under s 9 by virtue of s 13	D charged under s 1
D is aged 18 or over	D charged under s 5	D charged under s 1 although s 9 would be an alternative	D charged under s 1

Assault by penetration	P is under the age of 13	P is aged between 13 and 15	P is aged 16 or over
D is under the age of 10	No liability	No liability	No liability
D is aged between 10 and 17	D charged under s 6	D could be charged under s 2 or under s 9 by virtue of s 13	D charged under s 2
D is aged 18 or over	D charged under s 6	D charged under s 2 although s 9 would be an alternative	D charged under s 2
Sexual assault	P is under the age of 13	P is aged between 13 and 15	P is aged 16 or over
D is under the age of 10	No liability	No liability	No liability
D is aged between 10 and 17	D charged under s 7	D could be charged under s 3 or under s 9 by virtue of s 13	D charged under s 3
D is aged 18 or over	D charged under s 7	D charged under s 3 although s 9 would be an alternative	D charged under s 3
Causing a person to engage in a sexual activity without consent	P is under the age of 13	P is aged between 13 and 15	P is aged 16 or over
D is under the age of 10	No liability	No liability	No liability
D is aged between 10 and 17	D charged under s 8	D could be charged under s 4 or under s 10 by virtue of s 13	D charged under s 4
D is aged 18 or over	D charged under s 8	D charged under s 10 although s 4 would be an alternative	D charged under s 4

FURTHER READING

Gardner, S, 'Appreciating Olugboja' [1996] 16 Legal Studies 275

Gross, H, 'Rape, Moralism and Human rights' [2007] Crim LR 220

Herring, J, 'Mistaken Sex' [2005] Crim LR 511

Herring, J, 'Human Rights and Rape: a Reply to Hyman Gross' [2007] Crim LR 228

Lacey, N, 'Beset by boundaries: the Home Office Review of Sex Offences' [2001] Crim LR 3

ACCESSORIAL LIABILITY

7.1 INTRODUCTION

A criminal offence that involves the activities of more than one defendant can present particular difficulties in terms of ascribing fault to those who play some part. At common law, three possibilities exist:

(a)   two or more defendants act together to commit a crime – as where D1 and D2 rob their victim, D1 punching the victim and D2 grabbing her bag. In this case both D1 and D2 are committing robbery – they would normally be regarded as co-principals. In such cases issues of accessorial liability should not arise (even though they may technically have been helping each other to commit the crime) as they can each be shown to have committed the completed offence as principals in their own right.

(b)   D1 carries out the robbery using a gun supplied by D2. In this case D1 is clearly the principal offender. D2 is not even at the scene of the crime. D2 may incur liability, however, on the basis of the part he played in providing the weapon. The type of liability D2 incurs here is sometimes referred to as secondary liability.

(c) D1 robs the victim whilst D2 acts as a lookout. Here D2 is at the scene of the crime and the law tends to view such cases as a particular type of secondary liability sometimes called joint venture. Typically D2 will be regarded as having aided and abetted the robbery. In many cases it will not matter whether D2 is a secondary party or is involved in a joint venture, but as will be seen below, the courts have developed some complex rules governing the liability of those engaged in joint ventures where the principal offender has gone beyond the agreed or understood scope of the joint venture.

The terminology used in this area of law can be confusing. The principal is the defendant who commits the completed crime (although note above there can be co-principals). The generic term for those who help in some way before or at the time of the commission of the offence by the principal offender is accomplices. Section 8 of the Accessories and Abettors Act 1861 provides that there are actually four ways in which a defendant can be an accomplice – they are:

- aiding;
- abetting;
- counselling;
  and
- procuring.

These four modes should not be regarded as mutually exclusive. Aiding and abetting typically occurs at the scene of the crime, whilst counselling and procuring tends to occur prior to the commission of the offence. Section 8 of the 1861 Act stipulates that an accomplice is liable to be tried, indicted and punished in the same way as a principle offender. Section 44(1) of the Magistrates' Courts Act 1980 makes similar provision for summary offences (i.e. offences triable only in a magistrates' court).

The law in this area is generally regarded as being overly complex and in need of urgent and radical reform. The most significant defect in the existing law of accessorial liability is that the accomplice's liability is derivative – i.e. it depends on the liability of the principal offender. In the example (b) above – if D1 decides, having obtained the gun from D2 – not to commit the robbery, D2 cannot incur any accessorial liability as no crime is carried out by D1. This is problematic because D2 has done all he ever intended to do in the furtherance of the offence and is as morally culpable as he would be if the offences had been carried out by D1. There are inchoate offences that the prosecution could consider in respect of D2, such as incitement and conspiracy (see Chapter 8), but these offence are not always appropriate. Hence the Law Commission (*Inchoate Liability for Assisting and Encouraging Crime* (2006) Law Com 300) has proposed the abolition of incitement and the creation of a new offence of assisting crime – these matters are considered further in Chapter 8. For the moment the Law Commission is recommending the retention of secondary liability, subject to reforms to be set out in a report to be published in the future. In its report on *Murder Manslaughter and Infanticide* (2006) (Law Com 304) the Commission did make a number of recommendations for reform of the law relating to complicity in murder, and these are set out below at 7.9.4.

7.2 MODES OF PARTICIPATION: COUNSELLING

Counselling is a broad term that encompasses encouragement, advice and instructions given before the commission of the offence. Although the term suggests a consensual arrangement between the parties it extends to cover those situations where A orders B to commit an offence and B acts under duress in so doing.

R v Calhaem [1985] 1 QB 808 (CA)

Parker LJ:

The prosecution case was that the applicant had counselled or procured the commission of the offence by one Zajac, a private detective, on 23 February 1983. On 5 September 1983 Zajac pleaded guilty to the murder and was duly sentenced therefore. The prosecution case against the applicant was that she had hired Zajac to commit the murder in order to get rid of the victim, who had for some time had an affair with the applicant's solicitor, Mr Pigot, with whom she was infatuated; that she had made a down-payment to Zajac of some £5,000 at a meeting on 28 January 1983 and that he had thereafter committed the murder.

The principal witness for the prosecution was Zajac. He testified to the hiring, the receipt of the money, and the murder itself. He said that on the day of the murder he went to Mrs Rendell's house, having first ensured that her husband was out, taking with him a hammer, a knife, and a shotgun loaded with cartridges from which he had removed the shot, the gun being in a gift-wrapped parcel. He had, he said, no intention of killing Mrs Rendell, having decided in the preceding days not to do so. He had on arrival at the house rung the bell, and when Mrs Rendell came to the door he had asked her to sign for the gift-wrapped parcel. She went to get a pen, and when she returned and found him in the hall she screamed. He had intended to do no more than act out a charade, so that both Mrs Rendell and the applicant would think that an attempt had been made to murder her. However, when Mrs Rendell screamed, he said, he had gone berserk, hit her several times with the hammer and killed her. Thereafter, it appears, he had stabbed her in the neck with his knife.

The first point taken by Mr Carman on the applicant's behalf was that the judge had seriously misdirected the jury on the law as to the ingredients of the offence of counselling . . . Put in summary form, the submission which was made was that (a) the Crown were bound by Zajac's evidence as to his state of mind before and at the time of the murder; (b) both procuring and counselling require a substantial causal connection between the acts of the secondary offender and the commission of the offence; and (c) on Zajac's evidence there was no causal connection, or at any rate no substantial causal connection.

So far as presently material, at the end of [this] submission . . . the judge ruled as follows:

> In my judgment, therefore, the appropriate direction in this case is to this effect. 'To counsel' means to incite, solicit, instruct or authorise. The Crown have to prove that the defendant counselled Zajac in this sense to kill Mrs Rendell and that in fact Mrs Rendell was killed by Zajac in circumstances that amounted to murder, and that such killing was within the scope of that instruction or authorisation.

. . . The direction given by the judge was, Mr Carman submits, wrong in law. He should have directed the jury that, in the case of counselling as in the case of procuring, the counselling must be a substantial cause . . .

Such authority as there is does not, in our view, take the matter much further; although assistance as to the general approach is to be gained from *AG's Ref (No 1 of 1975)* [1975] QB 773 at 778 . . .

We must . . . approach the question raised on the basis that we should give to the word 'counsel' its ordinary meaning, which is, as the judge said, 'advise', 'solicit', or something of that sort. There is no implication in the word itself that there should be any causal connection between the counselling and the offence. It is true that, unlike the offence of incitement at common law, the actual offence must have been committed, and committed by the person counselled. To this extent there must clearly be, first, contact between the parties, and, second, a connection between the counselling and the murder. Equally, the act done must, we think, be done within the scope of the authority or advice, and not, for example, accidentally when the mind of the final murderer did not go with his actions. For example, if the principal offender happened to be involved in a football riot in the course of which he laid about him with a weapon of some sort and killed someone who, unknown to him, was the person whom he had been counselled to kill, he would not, in our view, have been acting within the scope of his authority; he would have been acting entirely outside it, albeit what he had done was what he had been counselled to do . . .

The natural meaning of the word does not imply the commission of the offence. So long as there is counselling – and there was ample evidence in this case of that fact – so long as the principal offence is committed by the one counselled, and so long as the one counselled is acting within the scope of his authority, and not in the accidental way or some such similar way as I have suggested with regard to an incident in a football riot, we are of the view that the offence is made out . . .

7.3 MODES OF PARTICIPATION: PROCURING

Procuring is the least obvious of the four modes of participation and arises where the accomplice causes the offence to be committed by the principal offender. There is no need for there to be any agreement between accomplice and principal in order for procuring to be established.

Attorney General's Ref (No 1 of 1975) [1975] QB 773 (CA)

The Court of Appeal was asked to rule upon whether or not A who placed alcohol in the drink of B, a car driver, could be convicted of procuring the offence of driving with excess alcohol contrary to s 6(1) of the Road Traffic Act 1972, if B was subsequently found to have committed this offence having consumed the alcohol placed in his drink by A.

Lord Widgery CJ:
This case comes before the court on a reference from the Attorney General, under s 36 of the Criminal Justice Act 1972, and by his reference he asks the following question:

Whether an accused, who surreptitiously laced a friend's drinks with double measures of spirits when he knew that his friend would shortly be driving his car home, and in consequence his friend drove with an excess quantity of alcohol in his body and was convicted of the offence under s 6(1) of the Road Traffic Act 1972, is entitled to a ruling of no case to answer on being later charged as an aider and abettor, counsellor and procurer, on the ground that there was no shared intention between the two, that the accused did not by accompanying him or otherwise positively encourage the friend to drive, or on any other ground.

... The present question has no doubt arisen because in recent years there have been a number of instances, where men charged with driving their motor cars with an excess quantity of alcohol in the blood have sought to excuse their conduct by saying that their drinks were 'laced', as the jargon has it; that is to say, some strong spirit was put into an otherwise innocuous drink and as a result the driver consumed more alcohol than he had either intended to consume or had the desire to consume. The relevance of all that is not that it entitles the driver to an acquittal because such driving is an absolute offence, but that it can be relied on as a special reason for not disqualifying the driver from driving. Hence, no doubt, the importance which has been attached in recent months to the possibility of this argument being raised in a normal charge of driving with excess alcohol.

The question requires us to say whether on the facts posed there is a case to answer and, needless to say, in the trial from which this reference is derived the judge was of the opinion that there was no case to answer and so ruled. We have to say in effect whether he is right.

The language in the section which determines whether a 'secondary party', as he is sometimes called, is guilty of a criminal offence committed by another embraces the four words 'aid, abet, counsel or procure'. The origin of those words is to be found in s 8 of the Accessories and Abettors Act 1861 . . .

Thus, in the past, when the distinction was still drawn between felony and misdemeanour, it was sufficient to make a person guilty of a misdemeanour if he aided, abetted, counselled or procured the offence of another. When the difference between felonies and misdemeanours was abolished in 1967, s 1 of the Criminal Law Act 1967 in effect provided that the same test should apply to make a secondary party guilty either of treason or felony.

Of course it is the fact that in the great majority of instances where a secondary party is sought to be convicted of an offence there has been a contact between the principal offender and the secondary party. Aiding and abetting almost inevitably involves a situation in which the secondary party and the main offender are together at some stage discussing the plans which they may be making in respect of the alleged offence, and are in contact so that each knows what is passing through the mind of the other.

In the same way it seems to us that a person, who counsels the commission of a crime by another, almost inevitably comes to a moment when he is in contact with that other, when he is discussing the offence with that other and when, to use the words of the statute, he counsels the other to commit the offence.

The fact that so often the relationship between the secondary party and the principal will be such that there is a meeting of minds between them caused the trial judge in the case from which this reference is derived to think that this was really an essential feature of proving or establishing the guilt of the secondary party and, as we understand his judgment, he took the view that in the absence of some sort of meeting of minds, some sort of mental link between the secondary party and the principal, there could be no aiding, abetting or counselling of the offence within the meaning of the section.

So far as aiding, abetting and counselling are concerned we would go a long way with that conclusion. It may very well be, as I said a moment ago, difficult to think of a case of aiding, abetting or counselling when the parties have not met and have not discussed in some respects the terms of the offence which they have in mind. But we do not see why a similar principle should apply to procuring. We approach s 8 of the Act of 1861 on the basis that the words should be given their ordinary meaning, if possible. We approach the section on the basis also that if four words are employed here, 'aid, abet, counsel or procure', the probability is that there is a difference between each of those four words and the other three, because, if there were no such difference, then Parliament would be wasting time in using four words where two or three would do. Thus, in deciding whether that which is assumed to be done under our reference was a criminal offence, we approach the section on the footing that each word must be given its ordinary meaning.

To procure means to produce by endeavour. You procure a thing by setting out to see that it happens and taking the appropriate steps to produce that happening. We think that there are plenty of instances in which a person may be said to procure the commission of a crime by another even though there is no sort of conspiracy between the two, even though there is no attempt at agreement or discussion as to the form which the offence should take. In our judgment the offence described in this reference is such a case.

If one looks back at the facts of the reference: the accused surreptitiously laced his friend's drink. This is an important element and, although we are not going to decide today anything other than the problem posed to us, it may well be that, in similar cases where the lacing of the drink or the introduction of the extra alcohol is known to the driver, quite different considerations may apply. We say that because, where the driver has no knowledge of what is happening, in most instances he would have no means of preventing the offence from being committed. If the driver is unaware of what has happened, he will not be taking precautions. He will get into his car seat, switch on the ignition and drive home and, consequently, the conception of another procuring the commission of the offence by the driver is very much stronger where the driver is innocent of all knowledge of what is happening, as in the present case where the lacing of the drink was surreptitious.

The second thing which is important in the facts set out in our reference is that, following and in consequence of the introduction of the extra alcohol, the friend drove with an excess quantity of alcohol in his blood. Causation here is important. You cannot procure an offence unless there is a causal link between what you do and the commission of the offence, and here we are told that in consequence of the addition of this alcohol the driver, when he drove home, drove with an excess quantity of alcohol in his body.

Giving the words their ordinary meaning in English, and asking oneself whether in those circumstances the offence has been procured, we are in no doubt that the answer is that it has. It has been procured because, unknown to the driver and without his collaboration, he has been put in a position in which in fact he has committed an offence which he never would have committed otherwise. We think that there was a case to answer and that the trial judge should have directed the jury that an offence is committed if it is shown beyond reasonable doubt that the defendant knew that his friend was going to drive, and also knew that the ordinary and natural result of the additional alcohol added to the friend's drink would be to bring him above the recognised limit of 80 milligrams per 100 millilitres of blood.

It was suggested to us that, if we held that there may be a procuring on the facts of the present case, it would be but a short step to a similar finding for the generous host, with somewhat bibulous friends, when at the end of the day his friends leave him to go to their own homes in circumstances in which they are not fit to drive and in circumstances in which an offence . . . is committed. The suggestion has been made that the host may in those circumstances be guilty with his guests on the basis that he has either aided, abetted, counselled or procured the offence.

The first point to notice in regard to the generous host is that that is not a case in which the alcohol is being put surreptitiously into the glass of the driver. That is a case in which the driver knows perfectly well how much he has to drink and where to a large extent it is perfectly right and proper to leave him to make his own decision.

Furthermore, we would say that, if such a case arises, the basis on which the case will be put against the host is, we think, bound to be on the footing that he has supplied the tool with which the offence is committed. This, of course is a reference back to such cases as those where oxyacetylene equipment was bought by a man knowing it was to be used by another for a criminal offence: see *R v Bainbridge* [1960] 1 QB 129. There is ample and clear authority as to the extent to which supplying the tools for the commission of an offence may amount to aiding and abetting for present purposes.

Accordingly, so far as the generous host type of case is concerned we are not concerned at the possibility that difficulties will be created, as long as it is borne in mind that in those circumstances the matter must be approached in accordance with well-known authority governing the provision of the tools for the commission of an offence, and never forgetting that the introduction of the alcohol is not there surreptitious, and that consequently the case for saying that the offence was procured by the supplier of the alcohol is very much more difficult.

Our decision on the reference is that the question posed by the Attorney General should be answered in the negative.

7.4 AIDING AND ABETTING

Aiding implies assistance given before or at the scene of the offence. Abetting involves encouraging the commission of the offence, typically at the scene of the crime, as encouragement prior to the commission of the offence could be charged as counselling.

Wilcox v Jeffery [1951] 1 All ER 464 (KBD)

Lord Goddard CJ:

This is a case stated by the metropolitan magistrate at Bow Street Magistrates' Court before whom the appellant, Herbert William Wilcox, the proprietor of a periodical called 'Jazz Illustrated', was charged on an information that 'on 11 December 1949, he did unlawfully aid and abet one Coleman Hawkins in contravening Art 1(4) of the Aliens Order, 1920, by failing to comply with a condition attached to a grant of leave to land, to wit, that the said Coleman Hawkins should take no employment paid or unpaid while in the United Kingdom, contrary to Art 18(2) of the Aliens Order, 1920'. Under the Aliens Order, Art 1(1), it is provided that:

> . . . an alien coming . . . by sea to a place in the United Kingdom: (a) shall not land in the United Kingdom without the leave of an immigration officer . . .

It is provided by Art 1(4) that:

> An immigration officer, in accordance with general or special directions of the Secretary of State, may, by general order or notice or otherwise, attach such conditions as he may think fit to the grant of leave to land, and the Secretary of State may at any time vary such conditions in such manner as he thinks fit, and the alien shall comply with the conditions so attached or varied . . .

If the alien fails to comply, he is to be in the same position as if he has landed without permission, i.e. he commits an offence.

The case is concerned with the visit of a celebrated professor of the saxophone, a gentleman by the name of Hawkins who was a citizen of the United States. He came here at the invitation of two gentlemen of the name of Curtis and Hughes, connected with a jazz club which enlivens the neighbourhood of Willesden. They, apparently, had applied for permission for Mr Hawkins to land and it was refused, but, nevertheless, this professor of the saxophone arrived with four French musicians. When they came to the airport, among the people who were there to greet them was the appellant. He had not arranged their visit, but he knew they were coming and he was there to report the arrival of these important musicians for his magazine. So, evidently, he was regarding the visit of Mr Hawkins as a matter which would be of interest to himself and the magazine which he was editing and selling for profit. Messrs Curtis and Hughes arranged a concert at the Princes Theatre, London. The appellant attended that concert as a spectator. He paid for his ticket. Mr Hawkins went on the stage and delighted the audience by playing the saxophone. The appellant did not get up and protest in the name of the musicians of England that Mr Hawkins ought not to be here competing with them and taking the bread out of their mouths or the wind out of their instruments. It is not found that he actually applauded, but he was there having paid to go in, and, no doubt, enjoying the performance, and then lo and behold, out comes his magazine with a most laudatory description, fully illustrated, of this concert. On those facts the magistrate has found that he aided and abetted.

Reliance is placed by the prosecution on *R v Coney* (1882) 8 QBD 534 which dealt with a prize-fight. This case relates to a jazz band concert, but the particular nature of the entertainment provided, whether by fighting with bare fists or playing on saxophones, does not seem to me to make any difference to the question which we have to decide. The fact is that a man is charged with aiding and abetting an illegal act, and I can find no authority for saying that it matters what that illegal act is, provided that the aider and abettor knows the facts sufficiently well to know that they would constitute an offence in the principal. In *R v Coney* the prize-fight took place in the neighbourhood of Ascot, and four or five men were convicted of aiding and abetting the fight. The conviction was quashed on the ground that the chairman had not given a correct direction to the jury when he told them that, as the prisoners were physically present at the fight, they must be held to have aided and abetted. That direction, the court held, was wrong, it being too wide. The matter was very concisely put by Cave J, whose judgment was fully concurred in by that great master of the criminal law, Stephen J. Cave J said (8 QBD 534 at 540):

> Where presence may be entirely accidental, it is not even evidence of aiding and abetting. Where presence is *prima facie* not accidental it is evidence, but no more than evidence, for the jury.

There was not accidental presence in this case. The appellant paid to go to the concert and he went there because he wanted to report it. He must, therefore, be held to have been present, taking part, concurring, or encouraging, whichever word you like to use for expressing this conception. It was an illegal act on the part of Hawkins to play the saxophone or any other instrument at this concert. The appellant clearly knew that it was an unlawful act for him to play. He had gone there to hear him, and his presence and his payment to go there was an encouragement. He went there to make use of the performance, because he went there, as the magistrate finds and was justified in finding, to get 'copy' for his newspaper. It might have been entirely different, as I say, if he had gone there and protested, saying: 'The Musicians' Union do not like you foreigners coming here and playing and you ought to get off the stage.' If he had booed, it might have been some evidence that he was not aiding and abetting. If he had gone as a member of a claque to try to drown the noise of the saxophone, he might very likely be found not guilty of aiding and abetting. In this case it seems clear that he was there, not only to approve and encourage what was done, but to take advantage of it by getting 'copy' for his paper. In those circumstances there was evidence on which the magistrates could find that the appellant aided and abetted, and for these reasons I am of opinion that the appeal fails.

7.5 PRESENCE AT THE SCENE OF THE CRIME AND FAILING TO PREVENT THE COMMISSION OF OFFENCES

Normally, mere presence at the scene of a crime will not, of itself, result in a person being convicted as an accomplice to the offence in question. As the following extracts indicate, however, if presence at the scene of the crime encourages its commission, and the defendant is aware of this, it may be possible to impose accessorial liability. Similarly where a defendant is in a position of authority and has the right to prevent an activity taking place that he realises involves the commission of a criminal offence, his failure to intervene could lead to his being convicted as an accomplice to the offence.

R v Coney and Others (1882) 8 QBD 534

Cave J:

. . . The evidence was that on 16 June last, at the close of Ascot races, Burke and Mitchell had engaged in a fight near the road from Ascot to Maidenhead; that a ring was formed with posts and ropes; that a large number of persons were present looking on, some of whom were undoubtedly encouraging the fight; that the men fought for some time; and that the three prisoners were seen in the crowd, but were not seen to do anything, and there was no evidence how they got there or how long they stayed there.

The chairman of quarter sessions directed the jury in the words of *Russell on Crimes*, Vol 1, p 818:

There is no doubt that prize-fights are illegal, indeed just as much so as that persons should go out to fight with deadly weapons, and it is not at all material which party strikes the first blow, and all persons who go to a prize-fight to see the combatants strike each other, and who are present when they do so are, in point of law, guilty of an assault.

And the chairman added, in the words of Littledale J, in *R v Murphy* 6 C & P 103: 'If they were not casually passing by, but stayed at the place, they encouraged it by their presence, although they did not say or do anything.'

. . . Now it is a general rule in the case of principals in the second degree that there must be participation in the act, and that, although a man is present whilst a felony is being committed, if he takes no part in it, and does not act in concert with those who commit it, he will not be a principal in the second degree merely because he does not endeavour to prevent the felony, or apprehend the felon . . .

. . . Where presence may be entirely accidental, it is not even evidence of aiding and abetting. Where presence is *prima facie* not accidental it is evidence, but no more than evidence, for the jury . . .

This summing-up unfortunately appears to me capable of being understood in two different ways. It may mean either that mere presence unexplained is evidence of encouragement, and so of guilt, or that mere presence unexplained is conclusive proof of encouragement, and so of guilt. If the former is the correct meaning, I concur in the law so laid down, if the latter, I am unable to do so. It appears to me that the passage tending to convey the latter view is that which was read by the chairman in this case to the jury, and I cannot help thinking that the chairman believed himself, and meant to direct the jury, and at any rate I feel satisfied that the jury understood him to mean, that mere presence unexplained was conclusive proof of encouragement, and so of guilt; and it is on this ground I hold that this conviction ought not to stand.

Lopes J:

. . . I understand the ruling of the chairman to amount to this, that mere presence at a prize-fight, unexplained, is conclusive proof of aiding and abetting, even if there be no evidence that the person or persons so present encouraged, or intended to encourage the fight by his or their presence. I cannot hold, as a proposition of law, that the mere looking on is *ipso facto* a participation in or encouragement of a prize-fight. I think there must be more than that to justify a conviction for an assault. If, for instance, it was proved that a person went to a prize-fight, knowing it was to take place, and remained there for some time looking on, I think that would be evidence from which a jury might infer that such person encouraged, and intended to encourage, the fight by his presence. In the present case, the three prisoners were merely seen in the crowd, were not seen to do anything, and there was no evidence why or how they came there, or how long they stayed.

Applying the direction of the chairman to this state of facts, I think it was wrong.

Hawkins J:

. . . In summing-up the case the chairman directed the jury that all persons who went to a prize-fight to see the combatants strike each other, and who were present when they did so, were, in point of law, guilty of an assault, for 'if they were not casually passing by, but stayed at the place, they encouraged it by their presence, although they did not do or say anything'. The jury, on that direction, found the defendants guilty, but they also found expressly that they were not aiding or abetting. The whole question, therefore, for us to determine, as a matter of law, is not whether voluntary presence at a prize-fight is evidence of an aiding and abetting, but whether inactive presence at a prize-fight as a voluntary spectator thereof, amounts of itself to such encouragement of it as to render a man amenable to the criminal law as an aider and abettor in that breach of the peace . . .

In my opinion, to constitute an aider and abettor some active steps must be taken by word, or action, with the intent to instigate the principal, or principals. Encouragement does not of necessity amount to aiding and abetting, it may be intentional or unintentional, a man may unwittingly encourage another in fact by his presence, by misinterpreted words, or gestures, or by his silence, on non-interference, or he may encourage intentionally by expressions, gestures, or actions intended to signify approval. In the latter case he aids and abets, in the former he does not. It is no criminal offence to stand by, a mere passive spectator of a crime, even of a murder. Non-interference to prevent a crime is not itself a crime. But the fact that a person was voluntarily and purposely present witnessing the commission of a crime, and offered no opposition to it, though he might reasonably be expected to prevent and had the power so to do, or at least to express his dissent, might under some circumstances, afford cogent evidence upon which a jury would be justified in finding that he wilfully encouraged and so aided and abetted. But it would be purely a question for the jury whether he did so or not. So if any number of persons arrange that a criminal offence shall take place, and it takes place accordingly, the mere presence of any of those who so arranged it would afford abundant evidence for the consideration of a jury of an aiding and abetting . . .

Huddleston B:

. . . The mere staying at the place where a fight is going on is not necessarily encouragement; the detective sent to report what is taking place and to bring the offenders to justice cannot be said to be encouraging what is going on; a person casually passing, but who stays to see what happens and interferes to prevent, or retires in disgust, or is hemmed in so that he cannot retire, cannot be said to be encouraging . . . The finding of the jury was in fact one of not guilty. They bow with respect to the chairman's direction in point of law, but by adding that the prisoners were not aiding and abetting, I conclude that they intend to convey that by no act of theirs were they countenancing or encouraging the fight, a conclusion fully supported by the evidence in the case.

Manisty J:

. . . It is said that if the ruling of the chairman is not upheld a great impetus will be given to prize-fighting. I do not share in that apprehension. It is well-settled law that every person who by his presence or otherwise encourages a fight, be it a prize or an ordinary fight, is guilty of a criminal offence, that is to say, of an assault or manslaughter, as the case may be, but it is for the jury in each particular case to say as a matter of fact whether the accused did by his presence or otherwise encourage the combatants to fight. To hold the contrary would, in my opinion, be erroneous in point of law, and very injurious in its consequences.

Suppose that the fight in question had resulted in the death of one of the combatants, then, if the direction given to the jury was right, every person who was in the crowd was in point of law guilty of manslaughter, though he neither spoke nor did anything, and notwithstanding that in the opinion of the jury he neither aided nor abetted the combatants. I cannot believe such is the law of England . . .

R v Clarkson and Others [1971] 1 WLR 1402 (Courts-Martial Appeal Court)

The appellants, Clarkson and Carroll, were present whilst a young woman was raped by some soldiers in a barracks. There was no evidence that either appellant had committed any positive act to assist in the rape. The appeal court approached the case on the assumption that the presence of the appellants in the room where the offence was taking place was not accidental, and that they entered the room when the crime was committed because of what they had heard, which indicated that a woman was being raped, and they remained there.

Megaw LJ:

... *R v Coney* (1882) 8 QBD 534 decided that non-accidental presence at the scene of the crime is not conclusive of aiding and abetting. The jury has to be told by the judge, or as in this case the court-martial has to be told by the judge-advocate, in clear terms what it is that has to be proved before they can convict of aiding and abetting; what it is of which the jury or the court martial, as the case may be, must be sure as matters of inference before they can convict of aiding and abetting in such a case where the evidence adduced by the prosecution is limited to non-accidental presence. [Having referred to the judgment of Hawkins J in *R v Coney* his Lordship continued:]

It is not enough, then, that the presence of the accused has, in fact, given encouragement. It must be proved that the accused intended to give encouragement; that he wilfully encouraged. In a case such as the present, more than in many other cases where aiding and abetting is alleged, it was essential that that element should be stressed; for there was here at least the possibility that a drunken man with his self-discipline loosened by drink, being aware that a woman was being raped, might be attracted to the scene and might stay on the scene in the capacity of what is known as a voyeur; and, while his presence and the presence of others might in fact encourage the rapers or discourage the victim, he himself, enjoying the scene or at least standing by assenting, might not intend that his presence should offer encouragement to rapers and would-be rapers or discouragement to the victim; he might not realise that he was giving encouragement; so that, while encouragement there might be, it would not be a case in which, to use the words of Hawkins J, the accused person 'wilfully encouraged'.

A further point is emphasised in passages in the judgment of the Court of Criminal Appeal in *R v Allan* [1965] 1 QB 130 at 135, 138. That was a case concerned with participation in an affray. Edmund Davies J, giving the judgment of the court, said:

In effect, it amounts to this: that the learned judge thereby directed the jury that they were duty bound to convict an accused who was proved to have been present and witnessing an affray if it was also proved that he nursed an intention to join in if help were needed by the side which he favoured, and this notwithstanding that he did nothing by words or deeds to evince his intention and outwardly played the role of purely passive spectator. It was said that, if that direction be right, where A and B behave themselves to all outward appearances in an exactly similar manner, but it be proved that A had the intention to participate if needs be, whereas B had no such intention, then A must be convicted of being a principal in the second degree to the affray, whereas B should be acquitted. To do that, it is objected, would be to convict A on his thoughts, even though they found no reflection in his actions.

The other passage in the judgment is this:

> In our judgment, before a jury can properly convict an accused person of being a principal in the second degree to an affray, they must be convinced by the evidence that, at the very least, he by some means or other encouraged the participants. To hold otherwise would be, in effect, as counsel for the appellants rightly expressed it, to convict a man on his thoughts, unaccompanied by any physical act other than the fact of his mere presence.

From that it follows that mere intention is not in itself enough. There must be an intention to encourage; and there must also be encouragement in fact, in cases such as the present case.

So we come to what was said by the judge-advocate . . .

The judge-advocate draws the analogy which is commonly drawn where direction is given of two persons jointly indicted, for example, of committing burglary. One actually enters the house and the other stands outside to keep watch. That analogy, in the view of this court, is misleading in relation to what was involved in the present case, for it presupposes a prior meeting of minds between the persons concerned as to the crime to be committed. The man who stands outside and does not go in is guilty of burglary; but it cannot in such a case properly be said that he has taken no active step in the commission of the offence. He has gone to the place where he is, and he has conducted himself as he does, as a part of the joint plan which, in its totality, is intended to procure commission of the crime.

In the view of this court the echo of that false analogy unfortunately continued throughout when the judge-advocate came to sum up the matter to the court-martial . . .

R v JF Alford Transport Ltd; R v Alford; R v Payne [1997] 2 Cr App R 326

The appellant company's managing director and transport manager were convicted of aiding and abetting offences under the Transport Act 1968. The court found that they had been aware that drivers employed by the company had been making false entries on tachograph records contrary to s 99(5) of the 1968 Act, and had not intervened to prevent the practice. Their appeals against conviction were allowed, on the basis that there was insufficient evidence of *mens rea* to be accomplices. Kennedy LJ, however, considered the extent to which failure to act could amount to giving positive encouragement:

Kennedy LJ:

. . . if the prosecution could show that the individual defendants, or either of them, knew that the drivers were illegally falsifying tachograph records, and if it could be shown that the individual defendants took no steps to prevent misconduct it was open to the jury in the absence of any alternative explanation, to infer that the individual defendant whom they happened to be considering, and thus the company, was positively encouraging what was going on . . . [Counsel for the appellant] submitted that in [previous cases, such as *Tuck v Robson* and *Du Cros v Lambourne* [1907] 1 KB 40] it was critical that the aider and abettor was present at the time of the commission of the principal offence. In our judgment nothing turned on actual presence. What mattered was knowledge of the principal offence, the ability to control the action of the offender, and the deliberate decision to refrain from doing so . . . in the context of the present case it would have to be proved that the defendant under consideration intended to do the acts which he knew to be capable of assisting or encouraging the commission of the crime, but he need not have intended that the crime be committed . . . [T]hus if the management's reason for turning a blind eye was to keep the drivers happy rather than to encourage the production of false tachograph records, that would afford no defence.

COMMENTS AND QUESTIONS

1   For aiding and abetting by omission where D is under a duty to act, see further *Rubie v Faulkner* [1940] 1 KB 571, where the defendant was supervising the driving of a learner driver and failed to prevent the driver from performing a dangerous overtaking manoeuvre that resulted in the driver being convicted of driving without due care and attention. Lord Hewart CJ held that for the appellant to refrain from doing anything when he could see that an unlawful act was about to be done (it being his duty to prevent an unlawful act if he could), was for him to aid and abet.

2   Similarly in *Tuck v Robson* [1970] 1 WLR 741, the appellant was convicted of aiding and abetting the consumption of alcohol after hours, where he failed to prevent customers from drinking after the permitted 'drinking up' time had expired. Lord Parker CJ observed that the magistrate was entitled to draw the inference that there was '. . . passive assistance in the sense of presence with no steps being taken to enforce his right either to eject the customers or at any rate to revoke their licence to be on the premises. In my judgment the magistrate was entitled to draw that inference, and accordingly I would dismiss this appeal'.

3   Where a statute creates an offence aimed at protecting a class of people, a member of that class cannot be an accessory to such an offence, even if the offence is committed with his or her assistance, encouragement or consent. In *R v Tyrrell* [1894] 1 QB 710, the court had to consider whether it was an offence for 'a girl between the ages of 13 and 16 to aid and abet a male person in the commission of the misdemeanour of having unlawful carnal connection with her, or to solicit and incite a male person to commit that misdemeanour'. Lord Coleridge CJ observed: '[the relevant provision] was passed for the purpose of protecting women and girls against themselves . . . it is impossible to say that the Act, which is absolutely silent about aiding or abetting, or soliciting or inciting, can have intended that the girls for whose protection it was passed should be punishable under it for the offences committed upon themselves.' Mathew J agreed, observing: '. . . I do not see how it would be possible to obtain convictions under the statute if the contention for the Crown were adopted, because nearly every section which deals with offences in respect of women and girls would create an offence in the woman or girl. Such a result cannot have been intended by the legislature. There is no trace in the statute of any intention to treat the woman or girl as criminal.'

4   See further s 5 of the Domestic Violence, Crime and Victims Act 2004, which introduces liability for causing or allowing the death of a child or vulnerable adult. Under s 5(d)(i)–(iii), D can incur liability by failing to intervene to prevent harm being caused to a child or vulnerable adult. See further Chapter 4.9.

7.6 HOW CAN AN ACCOMPLICE WITHDRAW FROM PARTICIPATION IN THE COMMISSION OF AN OFFENCE?

As the following extracts indicate, a party who has a change of mind and wishes to withdraw from a joint enterprise must communicate to the other parties his intention to withdraw from the enterprise and must do so in sufficient time before the commission of the offence:

R v Becerra and Cooper (1975) 62 Cr App R 212 (CA)

Becerra, Cooper and a third man agreed to burgle a house divided into flats. Cooper was armed with a knife and Becerra knew this. During the burglary Cooper became involved in a fight with one of the occupants of the house, a Mr Lewis, and used the knife to stab Mr Lewis to death. Becerra, hearing the altercation between Cooper and Lewis, fled through an open window. At the subsequent trial Becerra maintained that he was not an accomplice to the killing of Lewis as he had, by making his escape, withdrawn from the criminal enterprise.

Roskill LJ:

. . . It is necessary, before dealing with that argument in more detail, to say a word or two about the relevant law. It is a curious fact, considering the number of times in which this point arises where two or more people are charged with criminal offences, particularly murder or manslaughter, how relatively little authority there is in this country upon the point. But the principle is undoubtedly of long standing.

Perhaps it is best first stated in *Saunders and Archer* (1577) 2 Plowd 473 (in the 18th year of the first Queen Elizabeth) at 476, in a note by Plowden, thus:

> . . . for if I command one to Kill JS and before the Fact done I go to him and tell him that I have repented, and expressly charge him not to kill JS and he afterwards kills him, there I shall not be Accessory to this Murder, because I have countermanded my first Command, which in all Reason shall discharge me, for the malicious Mind of the Accessory ought to continue to do ill until the Time of the Act done, or else he shall not be charged; but if he had killed JS before the Time of my Discharge or Countermand given, I should have been Accessory to the Death, notwithstanding my private Repentance.

The next case to which I may usefully refer is some 250 years later, but over 150 years ago: *Edmeads and Others* (1828) 3 C & P 390, where there is a ruling of Vaughan B at a trial at Berkshire Assizes, upon an indictment charging Edmeads and others with unlawfully shooting at gamekeepers. At the end of his ruling the learned Baron said on the question of common intent at 392:

> that is rather a question for the jury; but still, on this evidence, it is quite clear what the common purpose was. They all draw up in lines, and point their guns at the gamekeepers, and they are all giving their countenance and assistance to the one of them who actually fires the gun. If it could be shown that either of them separated himself from the rest, and showed distinctly that he would have no hand in what they were doing, the objection would have much weight in it.

I can go forward over 100 years. Mr Owen (to whose juniors we are indebted for their research into the relevant Canadian and United States cases) referred us to several Canadian cases, to only one of which is it necessary to refer in detail, a decision of the Court of Appeal of British Columbia in *Whitehouse* (alias *Savage*) (1941) 1 WWR 112. I need not read the headnote. The Court of Appeal held that the trial judge concerned in that case, which was one of murder, had been guilty of misdirection in his direction to the jury on this question of 'withdrawal'. The matter is, if I may most respectfully say so, so well put in the leading judgment of Sloan JA, that I read the whole of the passage at pp 115 and 116:

> Can it be said on the facts of this case that a mere change of mental intention and a quitting of the scene of the crime just immediately prior to the striking of the fatal blow will absolve those who participate in the commission of the crime by overt acts up to that moment from all the consequences of its accomplishment by the one who strikes in ignorance of his companions' change of heart? I think not. After a crime has been committed and before a prior abandonment of the common enterprise may be found by a jury there must be, in my view, in the absence of exceptional circumstances, something more than a mere mental change of intention and physical change of place by those associates who wish to dissociate themselves from the consequences attendant upon their willing assistance up to the moment of the actual commission of that crime. I would not attempt to define too closely what must be done in criminal matters involving participation in a common unlawful purpose to break the chain of causation and responsibility. That must depend upon the circumstances of each case but it seems to me that one essential element ought to be established in a case of this kind: Where practicable and reasonable there must be timely communication of the intention to abandon the common purpose from those who wish to dissociate themselves from the contemplated crime to those who desire to continue in it. What is 'timely communication' must be determined by the facts of each case but where practicable and reasonable it ought to be such communication, verbal or otherwise, that will serve unequivocal notice upon the other party to the common unlawful cause that if he proceeds upon it he does so without the further aid and assistance of those who withdraw. The unlawful purpose of him who continues alone is then his own and not one in common with those who are no longer parties to it nor liable to its full and final consequences.

The learned judge then went on to cite a passage from *Hale's Pleas of the Crown* 618 and the passage from Saunders and Archer to which I have already referred.

In the view of each member of this court, that passage, if we may respectfully say so, could not be improved upon and we venture to adopt it in its entirety as a correct statement of the law which is to be applied in this case.

The last case, an English one, is *Croft* [1944] 1 KB 295, a well-known case of a suicide pact where, under the old law, the survivor of a suicide pact was charged with and convicted of murder. It was sought to argue that he had withdrawn from the pact in time to avoid liability (as the law then was) for conviction for murder.

The Court of Criminal Appeal, comprising Lawrence J (as he then was), Lewis and Wrottesley JJ dismissed the appeal and upheld the direction given by Humphreys J to the jury at the trial. Towards the end of the judgment Lawrence J said at pp 297 and 298:

> . . . counsel for the appellant complains – although I do not understand that the point had ever been taken in the court below – that the summing-up does not contain any reference

to the possibility of the agreement to commit suicide having been determined or counter-manded. It is true that the learned judge does not deal expressly with that matter except in a passage where he says: 'Even if you accept his statement in the witness box that the vital and second shot was fired when he had gone through that window, he would still be guilty of murder if she was then committing suicide as the result of an agreement which they had mutually arrived at that that should be the fate of both of them, and it is no answer for him that he altered his mind after she was dead and did not commit suicide himself.' . . . The authorities, such as they are, show in our opinion, that where a person has acted as an accessory before the fact, in order that he should not be held guilty as an accessory before the fact, he must give express and actual countermand or revocation of the advising, counselling, procuring, or abetting which he had given before.

It seems to us that those authorities make plain what the law is which has to be applied in the present case.

We therefore turn back to consider the direction which the learned judge gave in the present case to the jury and what was the suggested evidence that Becerra had withdrawn from the common agreement. The suggested evidence is the use by Becerra of the words 'Come on, let's go', coupled, as I said a few moments ago, with his act in going out through the window. The evidence, as the judge pointed out, was that Cooper never heard that nor did the third man. But let it be supposed that that was said and the jury took the view that it was said.

On the facts of this case, in the circumstances then prevailing, the knife having already been used and being contemplated for further use when it was handed over by Becerra to Cooper for the purpose of avoiding (if necessary) by violent means the hazards of identification, if Becerra wanted to withdraw at that stage, he would have to 'countermand', to use the word that is used in some of the cases or 'repent' to use another word so used, in some manner vastly different and vastly more effective than merely to say 'Come on, let's go' and go out through the window.

It is not necessary, on this application, to decide whether the point of time had arrived at which the only way in which he could effectively withdraw, so as to free himself from joint responsibility for any act Cooper thereafter did in furtherance of the common design, would be physically to intervene so as to stop Cooper attacking Lewis, as the judge suggested, by interposing his own body between them or somehow getting in between them or whether some other action might suffice. That does not arise for decision here. Nor is it necessary to decide whether or not the learned judge was right or wrong, on the facts of this case, in that passage which appears at the bottom of p 206, which Mr Owen criticised: 'and at least take all reasonable steps to prevent the commission of the crime which he had agreed the others should commit'. It is enough for the purposes of deciding this application to say that under the law of this country as it stands, and on the facts (taking them at their highest in favour of Becerra), that which was urged as amounting to withdrawal from the common design was not capable of amounting to such withdrawal. Accordingly Becerra remains responsible, in the eyes of the law, for everything that Cooper did and continued to do after Becerra's disappearance through the window as much as if he had done them himself.

Cooper being unquestionably guilty of murder, Becerra is equally guilty of murder. Mr Owen's careful argument must therefore be rejected and the application by Becerra for leave to appeal against conviction fails . . .

R v Whitefield (1983) 79 Cr App R 36 (CA)

Dunn LJ:

. . . The facts of the burglary were as follows. Between 4 pm on 3 November and 11 pm on 5 November 1982, a quantity of goods were taken from a flat in London SE16 when the occupier was away. On his return the latter reported the matter to the police. On 23 November the police interviewed the appellant after two other persons (Anthony Gallagher and Helen Coffey) had been arrested and charged with the burglary. Contemporaneous notes of the interviews were made and signed by the appellant. The appellant stated at the interview that he never took part in the burglary, but admitted telling Gallagher one evening that the flat that was next to his own was unoccupied. He also admitted that he had agreed to break into the flat with Gallagher by way of his own flat and balcony. They discussed how the property should be disposed of and the proceeds divided. Subsequently the appellant decided that he would not take part, and so informed Gallagher before the burglary took place. However, he knew that the burglary was to take place on a particular night. He heard it being committed, but did nothing to prevent it. He denied having spoken to Gallagher since the burglary. He had received none of the property or proceeds from its disposal . . .

The law upon withdrawal is stated in *Becerra and Cooper . . . and Grundy* [1977] Crim LR 543. So far as material to the facts of this case, the law may be shortly stated as follows. If a person has counselled another to commit a crime, he may escape liability by withdrawal before the crime is committed, but it is not sufficient that he should merely repent or change his mind. If his participation is confined to advice or encouragement, he must at least communicate his change of mind to the other, and the communication must be such as 'will serve unequivocal notice upon the other party to the common unlawful cause that if he proceeds upon it he does so without the aid and assistance of those who withdraw'. (See the Canadian case of *Whitehouse* [1941] 1 WWR 112, 116 per Sloan JA, approved in *Becerra and Cooper and Grundy*.)

In this case there was, if the jury accepted it, evidence in the answers given by the appellant to the police that he had served unequivocal notice on Gallagher that if he proceeded with the burglary he would do so without the aid or assistance of the appellant. In his ruling the judge stated that such notice was not enough, and that in failing to communicate with the police or take any other steps to prevent the burglary he remained 'liable in law for what happened, for everything that was done that night'. In the judgment of this court, in making that statement the judge fell into an error of law. The direct result of it was that the appellant changed his plea to one of guilty. A change of plea founded upon an error of law by the judge cannot stand, and the conviction must be quashed and the appeal allowed . . .

R v Rook [1993] 1 WLR 1005 (CA)

Lloyd LJ:

. . . The case concerns a so-called contract killing. Afsar was a taxi driver in Nottingham. He wished to be rid of his wife, Shaheen. On Tuesday 19 December 1989 he met the appellant, Armstrong, and a man called Barker, when they hired his taxi. During the journey there was some conversation. Afsar asked whether the appellant wanted to earn some money. A friend of his, said Afsar, wanted to have a woman beaten up. As the conversation continued, it became clear that the 'friend' wanted the woman murdered. There was some discussion between the appellant, Afsar and Armstrong about money. The appellant named a price of £20,000. The price agreed was £15,000 cash, and £5,000 worth of jewellery which the woman would be wearing. Afsar said it was to be a murder on credit. In the event he paid no more than £50.

Barker said he wanted nothing to do with it; so the following day, Wednesday 20 December 1989, the appellant recruited Leivers. He said to Leivers: 'Look Mark, it's murder.' Leivers replied: 'Yea, it's all right. I'll be there.' It was arranged that Afsar would pick up the other three at about 4.30 pm. They drove to Colwick Park, by the side of the lake. There was some discussion between all four as to how the murder should be committed. Afsar said that when they were ready he would bring the woman in his car. It was agreed that the murder would take place the following day.

On the evening of Wednesday 20 December there was a further discussion between the appellant, Armstrong and Leivers about the method of killing. They decided to use a knife and a piece of wood. Armstrong said that he wanted some money 'up front'. The appellant said that they would need money in order to buy new clothes after the murder.

On Thursday 21 December 1989 Afsar drove Armstrong and Leivers to Colwick Park, and dropped them as arranged. The appellant could not be found. Afsar went back to collect Shaheen. When he returned, Armstrong and Leivers dragged her from the car and killed her most brutally. Her body was found in the lake the next day.

The appellant was interviewed and made certain admissions. He also gave evidence at the trial. His defence was that he never intended the woman to be killed. He hoped to get some money from Afsar 'up front', and then disappear. At first he 'tagged along' to see how serious the others were. He was not sure whether they would go through with it or not. Then he tried to stall them, because he never intended to go through with it himself. Finally, on the Thursday, he deliberately absented himself. He said he thought that, if he were not there, Armstrong and Leivers would not go ahead without him . . .

. . . Mr Maxwell QC [for the appellant] submits that where a person has given assistance, for example by providing a gun, in circumstances which would render him liable as a secondary party if he does not withdraw, then in order to escape liability he must 'neutralise' his assistance. He must, so it was said, break the chain of causation between his act of assistance, and the subsequent crime, by recovering the gun, or by warning the victim to stay away, or by going to the police. Mr Hockman submits, on the other hand, that the Crown must prove that the defendant continued ready to help until the moment the crime is committed; and if there is doubt as to the defendant's state of mind on the day in question, or his willingness to provide further help if required, then the jury must acquit.

As between these two extreme views, we have no hesitation in rejecting the latter. In R v Croft [1944] KB 295 the surviving party of a suicide pact was held to be guilty of murder. Lawrence J, giving the judgment of the court, said ([1944] KB 295 at 298):

The authorities, however, such as they are, show, in our opinion, that the appellant, to escape being held guilty as an accessory before the fact must establish that he expressly countermanded or revoked the advising, counselling, procuring or abetting which he had previously given.

In R v Whitehouse [1941] 1 WWR 112 at 114 Sloan JA said:

Can it be said on the facts of this case that a mere change of mental intention and a quitting of the scene of the crime just immediately prior to the striking of the fatal blow will absolve those who participate in the commission of the crime by overt acts up to that moment from all the consequences of its accomplishment by the one who strikes in ignorance of his companions' change of heart? I think not. After a crime has been committed and before a prior abandonment of the common enterprise may be found by a jury there must be, in my view, in the absence of exceptional circumstances, something more than a mere mental change of intention and physical change of place by those associates who wish to dissociate themselves from the consequences attendant upon their willing assistance up to the moment of the actual commission of that crime. I would not attempt to define too closely what must be done in criminal matters involving participation in a common unlawful purpose to break the chain of causation and responsibility. That must depend upon the circumstances of each case but it seems to me that one essential element ought to be established in a case of this kind: Where practicable and reasonable there must be timely communication of the intention to abandon the common purpose from those who wish to dissociate themselves from the contemplated crime to those who desire to continue in it. What is 'timely communication' must be determined by the facts of each case but where practicable and reasonable it ought to be such communication, verbal or otherwise, that will serve unequivocal notice upon the other party to the common unlawful cause that if he proceeds upon it he does so without the further aid and assistance of those who withdraw. The unlawful purpose of him who continues alone is then his own and not one in common with those who are no longer parties to it nor liable to its full and final consequences.

. . .

In the present case the appellant never told the others that he was not going ahead with the crime. His absence on the day could not possibly amount to 'unequivocal communication' of his withdrawal. In his evidence-in-chief, in a passage already quoted, he said that he made it quite clear to himself that he did not want to be there on the day. But he did not make it clear to the others. So the minimum necessary for withdrawal from the crime was not established on the facts. In these circumstances, as in *R v Becerra*, it is unnecessary for us to consider whether communication of his withdrawal would have been enough, or whether he would have had to take steps to 'neutralise' the assistance he had already given.

Mr Maxwell rightly drew our attention to a sentence in the judgment of Sloan JA, already quoted, where he refers to the service of notice on the other party that if he proceeds he does so without further aid from those who withdraw. This may suggest that aid already afforded need not be neutralised. We agree with Mr Maxwell that this attaches too much importance to a single word. But that is as far as we are prepared to go in this case. We are not prepared, as at present advised, to give our approval to his proposition in its extreme form. In *Criminal Law: The General Part*, 2nd edn, 1961, para 127, Glanville Williams quotes a graphic phrase from an American authority (*Eldredge v US* (1932) 62 F 2d 449, per McDermott J):

> A declared intent to withdraw from a conspiracy to dynamite a building is not enough, if the fuse has been set; he must step on the fuse.

It may be that this goes too far. It may be that it is enough that he should have done his best to step on the fuse. Since this is as much a question of policy as a question of law, and since it does not arise on the facts of the present case, we say no more about it . . .

R v O'Flaherty; R v Ryan; R v Toussaint [2004] EWCA Crim 526

The three appellants were involved in disturbances outside a nightclub in Luton involving an attack on a victim named Hall. This attack took place in Flowers Way. In the first disturbance O'Flaherty was armed with a baseball bat, Ryan with a broken bottle, and Toussaint with a claw hammer. Shortly afterwards Hall was pursued by another group of men, all three armed with weapons. This group attacked Hall in Park Street West. O'Flaherty went to Park Street West, still holding the cricket bat, and was seen to advance to within a few feet of the prone body of Hall, and then move away. The expert medical evidence concluded that the cause of Hall's death had been multiple stab wounds. The appellants were convicted of murder and appealed contending that the judge should have made it clear to the jury that, irrespective of whether there was one incident or two, they had to determine which injuries had brought about Hall's death, where those injuries had taken place, and whether a particular defendant had played a part in causing those injuries. The prosecution's argument was that once a defendant became a party to a joint enterprise, unless the event causing the fatal injury or injuries was separate from the event into which the individual had joined, it was irrelevant that at some stage the individual defendant had taken no further part in the action. The Court of Appeal dismissed O'Flaherty's appeal, but allowed the appeals of *Ryan* and *Toussaint*. The following extract deals with the issue of withdrawal from a joint enterprise.

Mantell LJ:

58. While, as we suggest later in this judgment, a strict view of what will in fact constitute withdrawal can properly be taken, the preclusion of withdrawal in any circumstances cannot in our view be correct, either in principle or as a matter of policy. A person who unequivocally withdraws from the joint enterprise before the moment of the actual commission of the crime by the principal, here murder, should not be liable for that crime, although his acts before withdrawing may render him liable for other offences. That this is so is seen from an earlier case involving an appellant called Grundy. In *R v Grundy* [1977] Crim L Rev 543 this Court recognised that a person can withdraw until the acts of the principal offender reach the stage of an attempt. The line was probably crossed in *R v Perman* [1996] 1 Cr App R 24, 34, decided on another ground. In *R v Perman* this Court doubted that it is possible for a party who becomes a party to a joint enterprise to withdraw once the criminal activity falling within that joint enterprise has commenced. This is, however, not inconsistent with *R v Grundy* [1977] Crim LR 543 because in *R v Perman* the criminal activity within the joint enterprise was a robbery and the robbery had commenced before the defendant left the shop where the robbery was taking place.

59. The 1989 decision in *R v Grundy* (1989) 89 Cr App Rep 333, relied on in the Crown's submissions to the judge, is, moreover, clearly distinguishable from the present case. First, in that case no issue of disengagement or withdrawal arose. G joined in an attack that others had started and did so after the infliction of the broken nose, the only injury he and possibly the trial judge considered could amount to grievous bodily harm. The facts in this case also suggest that care should be taken in applying it to a case of murder such as the present case. Here the Crown accepts that if a particular defendant joined an incident after the infliction of the fatal injury that defendant is not guilty of murder. But, substituting 'serious injury' for 'fatal injury', that is exactly

what the appellant in *Grundy* argued had occurred in his case. The difference may lie in the fact that in grievous bodily harm it is the totality of the injuries which determines whether they are really serious; whereas an injury is or is not causative of death. More fundamentally, in Grundy's case, this Court did not accept that the broken nose was the only injury that amounted to grievous bodily harm: (1989) 89 Cr App Rep 333, at p 339.The Court stated that there was ample evidence of the infliction of grievous bodily harm in the part of the attack in which G as well as his co-defendants participated.

60. We have noted that for there to be withdrawal, mere repentance does not suffice. To disengage from an incident a person must do enough to demonstrate that he or she is withdrawing from the joint enterprise.This is ultimately a question of fact and degree for the jury. Account will be taken of *inter alia* the nature of the assistance and encouragement already given and how imminent the infliction of the fatal injury or injuries is, as well as the nature of the action said to constitute withdrawal. In cases of assistance it has sometimes been suggested that, for there to be an effective withdrawal, reasonable steps must have been taken to prevent the crime. It is clear, however, this is not necessary. In *R v Whitehouse* (1941) 4 WWR 112, a decision of the Court of Appeal of British Columbia approved by this Court on several occasions (see *R v Becerra and Cooper* (1975) 62 Cr App R 212; *R v Grundy* [1977] Cr L Rev 543; *R v Whitefeld* (1983) 79 Cr App Rep 36) Soan JA stated (at p 115) that after a crime has been committed:

> . . . [I]n the absence of exceptional circumstances, something more than a mere mental change of intention and physical change of location by those associated who wish to disassociate themselves from the consequences attendant upon their willing assistance up to the moment of the actual commission of that crime. I would not attempt to define too closely what must be done in criminal matters involving participation in a common unlawful purpose to break the chain of causation and responsibility. That must depend upon the circumstances of each case but it seems to me that one essential element ought to be established in a case of this kind: Where practicable and reasonable there must be timely communication of the intention to abandon the common purpose from those who wish to dissociate themselves from the contemplated crime to those who desire to continue in it. What is 'timely communication' must be determined by the facts of each case but where practicable and reasonable it ought to be such communication, verbal or otherwise, that will serve unequivocal notice upon the other party to the common unlawful cause that if he proceeds upon it he does so without the further aid and assistance of those who withdraw.

61. There is no reference to a requirement that reasonable steps must have been taken to prevent the crime. The old decision of *R v Hyde* Hale 1 Pleas of the Crown 537 (1672) and *R v Grundy* [19771 Cr L Rev 543 are also illustrations of the recognition that this is not necessary. Furthermore, the decision in *R v Mitchell and King* (1998) 163 JP 75, so far as we can see, an authority not brought to the attention of the judge, shows that in a case of spontaneous violence in principle it is possible to withdraw by ceasing to fight, throwing down one's weapons and walking away. In that case one of Mitchell's defences was that he had withdrawn before the fatal injuries had been inflicted. It was stated by the Court (p 81) that in those circumstances the jury had to be directed (a) that they must be satisfied that the fatal injuries were sustained whilst the joint enterprise was continuing and that the defendant was still acting within that joint enterprise, and (b) that they must be satisfied that the acts which caused the death were within the scope of the joint enterprise.

62. In *R v Mitchell and King* this Court also considered Soan JA's statement in *R v Whitefeld* that 'where practicable and reasonable there must be timely communication of the intention to abandon the common purpose'. It held that while communication of withdrawal is a necessary condition for disassociation from pre-planned violence it is not necessary when the violence is spontaneous.

63. For these reasons a defendant who effectively disengages or withdraws before the fatal injury is or injuries are inflicted is not guilty of murder because he was not party to and did not partici-pate in any unlawful violence which caused the fatal injury or injuries. We consider that the question whether or not the violence formed one evolving incident or was two separate and discreet incidents is only relevant in helping to decide whether a particular defendant disengaged before the fatal injury or injuries were caused or joined in after they had been caused. Another way of looking at the matter is that suggested in *R v Perman*, i.e. that the issue of disengagement or withdrawal may be no more than a consideration of the scope of the joint enterprise. In the absence of such disengagement or withdrawal, however, it is sufficient for there to be a conviction for murder for the prosecution to prove that a defendant participated in unlawful violence which caused injury or injuries which formed a significant cause of death provided that the cause or causes of death cumulatively assessed arose out of a single evolving incident and that the defendant had the necessary intention or foresight.

64. Accordingly, we consider, as this Court did in *R v Mitchell and King* (1998) 163 JP 75 that the jury should have been directed that they must be satisfied (a) that the fatal injuries were sustained when the joint enterprise was continuing and that the defendant was still acting within that joint enterprise, and (b) that the acts which caused the death were within the scope of the joint enterprise . . .

 COMMENTS AND QUESTIONS

1   In *R v Mitchell* [1999] Crim LR 496, the Court of Appeal held that a distinction was to be drawn between pre-planned and spontaneous violence, in the sense that where violence was pre-planned, communication of withdrawal from the planned violence was necessary for that withdrawal to be effective. Where the violence was spontaneous, communication of the intention to withdraw was not necessarily required. Is this distinction justifiable?

2   Simply moving a few feet away from a victim, having already stabbed him with a knife, and shouting 'I'm not doing it' is not sufficient to amount to a withdrawal from participation in the victim's death; see *R v Baker* [1994] Crim LR 444. The words were quite capable of mean-ing no more than 'I will not myself strike any more blows'. They were not an unequivocal indication that he did not intend to take any further part in any further assault on the victim.

7.7 THE *MENS REA* OF ACCOMPLICES

As *Johnson v Youden and Others* (extracted below) indicates, an accomplice cannot be convicted without some evidence that he knew of the facts that constituted the offence. The difficulty, however, has been in determining just how precise the accomplice's *mens rea* must be. Where there is evidence that he was certain as to what the principal offender intended to do, liability is easy to establish. As can be imagined, however, many of those who are questioned about the role they might have had to play in the commission of an offence by another may be rather vague as to what they thought this other person might do. Hence the courts have had to develop a slightly different approach to *mens rea* where the liability of accomplices is concerned. Instead of concepts such as foresight, the courts have preferred expressions such as 'contemplation'. The problem remains, however. How likely must the commission of the offence by the principal offender have seemed to the accomplice to justify a court in concluding that the accomplice had sufficient *mens rea* to be convicted as such?

7.7.1 NO ACCESSORIAL LIABILITY WITHOUT *MENS REA*

Johnson v Youden and Others [1950] 1 KB 544 (DC)

One Dolbear, a builder, built a house under the authority of a licence granted under a Defence Regulation subject to a condition limiting the price for which the house might be sold to £1,025. The builder induced a purchaser to agree to pay for the house £250 in excess of the price permitted. That £250 was paid to the builder in advance. He then instructed a firm of solicitors, in which the three defendants were partners, to act for him in the sale. He concealed from the defendants the fact that he had received the additional £250, and the first two defendants did not know of it at any material time.

On 6 April 1949, however, the purchaser's solicitors wrote a letter to the third defendant stating that they had not proceeded to completion because the builder was in breach of s 7 of the Building Materials and Housing Act 1945. The third defendant sought an explanation from the builder, who said that he had placed the £250 in question in a separate deposit account, and that it was to be spent on payment for work, as and when he would be able lawfully to execute it in the future, on the house on the purchaser's behalf. The third defendant accepted that explanation, and, having read the Act of 1945, formed the opinion that the payment of £250 was lawful and called on the purchaser to complete.

The builder was charged on information with offering to sell the house for a greater price than that permitted, contrary to s 7(1) of the Building Materials and Housing Act 1945; and informations were preferred against the three defendants charging them with aiding and abetting him in the commission of that offence.

On 5 July 1949, the builder was convicted, but the justices dismissed the three informations against the other defendants as they were of the opinion that *mens rea* was a constituent of the offence of aiding and abetting an offence under s 7(1) of the Act of 1945. They found that the third defendant honestly believed the explanation given to him by the builder regarding the £250. The prosecutor appealed.

Lord Goddard CJ:
Before a person can be convicted of aiding and abetting the commission of an offence he must at least know the essential matters which constitute that offence. He need not actually know that an offence has been committed, because he may not know that the facts constitute an offence and

ignorance of the law is not a defence. If a person knows all the facts and is assisting another person to do certain things, and it turns out that the doing of those things constitutes an offence, the person who is assisting is guilty of aiding and abetting that offence, because to allow him to say, 'I knew of all those facts but I did not know that an offence was committed', would be allowing him to set up ignorance of the law as a defence.

The reason why, in our opinion, the justices were right in dismissing the informations against the first two defendants is that they found, and found on good grounds, that they did not know of the matters which in fact constituted the offence; and, as they did not know of those matters, it follows that they cannot be guilty of aiding and abetting the commission of the offence.

With regard to their partner, the third defendant, a different state of affairs arises. His client, the builder, told him a story which, even if it were true, was on the face of it obviously a colourable evasion of the Act. The builder told him that he had received another £250, that he had placed the sum in a separate deposit account, 'and that it was to be spent on payment for work as and when he, the builder, would be lawfully able to execute it in the future on the house on behalf of the said purchaser'. It seems impossible to imagine that anyone could believe such a story. Who has ever heard of a purchaser putting money into the hands of the builder when he bought a house from him because he might want some work done thereafter? Surely, if the builder did not think that the purchaser could pay for the work, he would say: 'Will you pay something on account?' A story of that kind, on the face of it, is a mere colourable evasion of the Act.

It is more than likely, I think, that, in reading the Act, the third defendant did not read as carefully as he might have done s 7(5). If he had read that subsection carefully, I cannot believe that he – or indeed any solicitor, or even a layman – would not have understood that the arrangement which the builder said that he had made was just the kind of thing that subsection prohibited.

How could anybody say that the story which the builder told the third defendant was not a story with regard to a transaction with which the sale was associated? If that subsection had been read by the third defendant and appreciated by him, he would have seen at once that the extra £250 which the builder was obtaining was an unlawful payment; but unfortunately he did not realise it, and either misread the Act or did not read it carefully; and the next day he called on the purchaser to complete. Therefore he was clearly aiding and abetting the builder in the offence which the latter was committing.

The result is that, as far as the first two defendants are concerned, the appeal fails and must be dismissed; but as far as the third defendant is concerned, the case must go back to the justices with an intimation that an offence has been committed, and that he must be convicted.

National Coal Board v Gamble [1959] 1 QB 11 (QBD)

On 3 October 1957, an employee of a firm of hauliers took his lorry to a National Coal Board colliery, where it was filled with coal from a hopper and was then taken to a weighbridge, where the weighbridge operator (Haslam, an employee of the NCB) weighed the lorry and its load and told the driver (Mallender) that the load was nearly four tons overweight. The driver, saying that he would risk taking the overload, took the weighbridge ticket from the weighbridge operator and left the colliery. He was subsequently stopped by the police. His employers were later convicted of contravening the Motor Vehicles (Construction and Use) Regulations 1955. The hauliers were collecting the coal for carriage to a power station, to whom the NCB were bound by contract to supply a bulk quantity of coal. The NCB were charged with aiding and abetting the hauliers in the commission of an offence. The weighbridge operator knew that an offence would be committed if the lorry was driven with an overweight load. Property in the coal did not pass to the purchaser until the ticket was given by the weighbridge operator.

> Devlin J:
> A person who supplies the instrument for a crime or anything essential to its commission aids in the commission of it; and if he does so knowingly and with intent to aid, he abets it as well and is therefore guilty of aiding and abetting. I use the word 'supplies' to comprehend giving, lending, selling, or any other transfer of the right of property . . . In the transfer of property there must be either a physical delivery or a positive act of assent to a taking. But a man who hands over to another his own property on demand, although he may physically be performing a positive act, in law is only refraining from detinue. Thus in law the former act is one of assistance voluntarily given and the latter is only a failure to prevent the commission of the crime by means of a forcible detention, which would not even be justified except in the case of felony. Another way of putting the point is to say that aiding and abetting is a crime that requires proof of *mens rea*, that is to say, of intention to aid as well as of knowledge of the circumstances, and that proof of the intent involves proof of a positive act of assistance voluntarily done . . .
> . . . No doubt evidence of an interest in the crime or of an express purpose to assist it will greatly strengthen the case for the prosecution. But an indifference to the result of the crime does not of itself negative abetting. If one man deliberately sells to another a gun to be used for murdering a third, he may be indifferent about whether the third man lives or dies and interested only in the cash profit to be made out of the sale, but he can be still an aider and abettor. To hold otherwise would be to negative the rule that *mens rea* is a matter of intent only and does not depend on desire or motive . . .
> . . . For the reasons I have given I think that the law cannot be so stated and that the appeal should be dismissed.

7.8 ESTABLISHING THE *MENS REA* OF ACCOMPLICES

R v Bainbridge [1960] 1 QB 129 (CA)

On the night of 30 October 1958 the Stoke Newington branch of the Midland Bank was broken into by cutting the bars of a window, the doors of the strong room and of a safe inside the strong room. This was done by a means of oxygen cutting equipment. The cutting equipment was left behind and it was later discovered that it had been bought by the appellant some six weeks earlier. The appellant was convicted of being an accessory before the fact to the burglary.

Lord Parker CJ:

The case against him [the appellant] was that he had bought this cutting equipment on behalf of one or more of the thieves with the full knowledge that it was going to be used, if not against the Stoke Newington branch of the Midland Bank, at any rate for the purposes of breaking and entering premises.

The appellant's case, as given in his evidence, was this:

> True, I had bought this equipment from two different firms. I had gone there with a man called Shakeshaft to buy it for him. As a result of a conversation which I had with him I was suspicious that he wanted it for something illegal, I thought it was for breaking up stolen goods which Shakeshaft had received, and as a result in those purchases I gave false names and addresses, but I had no knowledge that the equipment was going to be used for any such purpose as it was used.

The complaint here is that Judge Aarvold, who tried the case, gave the jury a wrong direction in regard to what it was necessary for them to be satisfied of in order to hold the appellant guilty of being an accessory before the fact. The passages in question are these. He said:

> To prove that, the prosecution have to prove these matters: first of all they have to prove the felony itself was committed. Of that there is no doubt. That is not contested. Second, they have to prove the defendant, this man Bainbridge, knew that a felony of that kind was intended and was going to be committed, and with that knowledge he did something to help the felons commit the crime. The knowledge that is required to be proved in the mind of this man Bainbridge is not the knowledge of the precise crime. In other words, it need not be proved he knew the Midland Bank, Stoke Newington branch, was going to be broken and entered and money stolen from that particular bank, but he must know the type of crime that was in fact committed. In this case it is a breaking and entering of premises and the stealing of property from those premises. It must be proved he knew that sort of crime was intended and was going to be committed. It is not enough to show that he either suspected or knew that some crime was going to be committed, some crime which might have been a breaking and entering or might have been disposing of stolen property or anything of that kind. That is not enough. It must be proved he knew the type of crime which was in fact committed was intended . . .

Mr Simpson, who has argued this case very well, contends that that direction is wrong. As he puts it, in order that a man should be convicted of being accessory before the fact, it must be shown that at the time he bought the equipment in a case such as this he knew that a particular crime was going to be committed, and by a particular crime Mr Simpson means that the premises in this case which were going to be broken into were known to the appellant and contemplated by him, and not only the premises in question but the date when the breaking was going to occur; in other words, that he must know that on a particular date the Stoke Newington branch of the Midland Bank is intended to be broken into.

The court fully appreciates that it is not enough that it should be shown that a man knows that some illegal venture is intended. To take this case, it would not be enough if he knew – he says he only suspected – that the equipment was going to be used to dispose of stolen property. That would not be enough. Equally, this court is quite satisfied that it is unnecessary that knowledge of the particular crime which was in fact committed should be shown to his knowledge to have been intended, and by 'particular crime' I am using the words in the same way in which Mr Simpson used them, namely on a particular date and particular premises.

It is not altogether easy to lay down a precise form of words which will cover every case that can be contemplated but, having considered the cases and the law this court is quite clear that the direction of Judge Aarvold in this case cannot be criticised . . .

Judge Aarvold in this case, in the passage to which I have referred, makes it clear that there must be not merely suspicion but knowledge that a crime of the type in question was intended, and that the equipment was bought with that in view. In his reference to the felony of the type intended it was, as he stated, the felony of breaking and entering premises and the stealing of property from those premises. The court can see nothing wrong in that direction . . .

R v Bryce [2004] EWCA Crim 1231

B was convicted of aiding and abetting, counselling and procuring X to murder the deceased, Patrick Moore. X had been convicted of the murder of Patrick Moore having shot him in the head at close range as he slept in his bed. The case against B was that he had transported X to a caravan near to Moore's home so that X could wait for an opportunity to carry out the killing, and had supplied the gun used by X to shoot Moore. B claimed that he had simply given X a lift on the night in question and had not seen any weapons.

The trial judge directed the jury that they could convict if B had: (a) done an act which in fact assisted X; (b) deliberately done what was alleged against him knowing it to be capable of assisting X to commit the offence; (c) done the acts alleged knowing or contemplating as a real (not a fanciful) possibility that X, with the help he was supplying, either would or might kill the victim deliberately and unlawfully, intending to do so, or at least would or might intentionally do the victim some really serious injury.

Following conviction as an accomplice to murder, B appealed on the grounds that his actions had been too remote from the killing to amount to aiding and abetting the murder; were performed at a time when the principal offender (X) had not yet formed the intent to commit any criminal offence; and that the trial judge had misdirected the jury in relation to the mental element required to constitute the offence of aiding and abetting murder.

Potter LJ:

. . . it is necessary to preserve the distinction between the perpetrator and secondary parties because the mental element or *mens rea* for the secondary party is not necessarily the same as for the perpetrator. This stems from the fact that the *actus reus* of being an accessory involves two concepts: (a) an act (or possibly an omission) which aids, abets, counsels or procures (b) the commission by the perpetrator of the principal offence.

. . . As to (a) it is necessary to show firstly that the act which constitutes the aiding, abetting etc was done intentionally in the sense of deliberately and not accidentally and secondly that the accused knew it to be an act capable of assisting or encouraging the crime. In this case, as in most cases, the first requirement will not be in issue. The act of taking X to the caravan with the gun was obviously done deliberately. However, on the defence which the appellant sought to advance through his counsel, the second requirement was implicitly in issue in that Mr Foy wished to submit to the jury that the appellant's actions were intended to impede rather than assist.

As to (b), it is now well established that it is not necessary to prove that the secondary party at the time of the act of aiding, abetting etc intended the crime to be committed.

. . . Thus, if it is proved that the defendant intended to do the acts of assistance or encouragement, it is no defence that he hoped that events might intervene to prevent the crime taking place. So, where the defendant drove the perpetrator to a place where he knew that the perpetrator intended to murder a policeman, his intentional driving of the car to that place amounted to an aiding and abetting of the offence despite his unwillingness that the killing should take place . . .

. . . We turn to Rook . . . Rook is, in our view, authority for the proposition that it is not necessary to show that the secondary party intended the commission of the principal offence and that it is sufficient if the secondary party at the time of his actions relied on as lending assistance or encouragement contemplates the commission of the offence, that is knows that it will be committed or realises that it is a real possibility that it will be committed.

The issue in the present case is whether, in addition to proving that the act of assistance relied on was deliberate and that the secondary party contemplated the commission of the offence, the prosecution must prove an intention to assist. It was the defendant's case through his counsel that his intention was not to assist, but to hinder, the plan which was apparently in existence between Black [the drug dealer who wanted X to carry out the killing] and X.

. . . We are of the view that, outside the Powell and English situation (violence beyond the level anticipated in the course of a joint criminal enterprise), where a defendant, D, is charged as the secondary party to an offence committed by P in reliance on acts which have assisted steps taken by P in the preliminary stages of a crime later committed by P in the absence of D, it is necessary for the Crown to prove intentional assistance by D in the sense of an intention to assist (and not to hinder or obstruct) P in acts which D knows are steps taken by P towards the commission of the offence. Without such intention the *mens rea* will be absent whether as a matter of direct intent on the part of D or by way of an intent sufficient for D to be liable on the basis of 'common purpose' or 'joint enterprise'. Thus, the prosecution must prove:

(a) an act done by D which in fact assisted the later commission of the offence,
(b) that D did the act deliberately realising that it was capable of assisting the offence,
(c) that D at the time of doing the act contemplated the commission of the offence by A i.e. he foresaw it as a 'real or substantial risk' or 'real possibility', and
(d) that D when doing the act intended to assist A in what he was doing.

The court went on to hold that an accomplice could incur liability even though, at the time of the assistance given, the principal offender had not fully made up his mind to commit the offence.

Potter LJ:

. . . in relation to secondary liability in respect of acts committed by an accused in anticipation of a crime, because of the uncertainty which may exist as to the precise intentions of the eventual perpetrator (whose identity may be unknown to the accessory at the time he renders his assistance) all that is necessary in the secondary party is foresight of the real possibility that an offence will be committed by the person to whom the accessory's acts of assistance are directed. In those circumstances, whereas it will be usual in the case of assistance given directly to the perpetrator prior to the commission of the crime, that both have at the time the *mens rea* appropriate to their role, it is by no means essential. The point would be more immediately obvious if the position had been one where the appellant . . . had himself directly counselled X to commit the murder and X had at first refused but had thereafter changed his mind and carried out the murder according to the appellant's advice or instructions. It cannot be thought that in such a case the appellant should properly avoid liability.

7.8.1 THE 'BLANK CHEQUE' PROBLEM

The emphasis in *R v Bainbridge* and similar cases on the need for the prosecution to prove that an accomplice at least contemplated the type of crime committed by the principal, raises the prospect of the accomplice attempting to avoid liability by claiming to have had a wide range of crimes in contemplation, sometimes referred to as the 'blank cheque' argument. Not surprisingly, the courts have not been sympathetic to such claims.

DPP for Northern Ireland v Maxwell [1978] 1 WLR 1350 (HL)

The appellant drove members of a terrorist gang to the Crosskeys Inn where they carried out a bombing. He was charged with aiding and abetting various offences relating to the use of explosives. The appellant contended that he did not know what offence the gang members were planning to commit – i.e. it could have been any one of a range of terrorist activities. The House of Lords dismissed his appeal against the conviction.

Lord Fraser of Tullybelton:
The possible extent of his guilt was limited to the range of crimes any of which he must have known were to be expected that night. Doing acts with explosives and possessing explosives were within that range and when they turned out to be crimes committed on that night he was therefore guilty of them. If another member of the gang had committed some crime that the appellant had no reason to expect, such as perhaps throwing poison gas into the inn, the appellant would not have been guilty of using poison gas.

Lord Scarman:
My Lords, I also would dismiss this appeal. The question it raises is as to the degree of knowledge required by law for the attachment of criminal responsibility to one who assists another (or others) to commit or attempt crime . . . [the appellant] . . . may have in contemplation only one offence, or several; and the several which he contemplates he may see as alternatives. An accessory who leaves it to his principal to choose is liable, provided always the choice is made from the range of offences from which the accessory contemplates the choice will be made. Although the court's formulation of the principle goes further than the earlier cases, it is a sound development of the law and in no way inconsistent with them. I accept it as good judgemade law in a field where there is no statute to offer guidance.

On the facts as found by the trial (there was no jury because of the Northern Ireland (Emergency Provisions) Act 1973), the appellant knew he was guiding a party of men to the Crosskeys Inn on a UVF military-style 'job', i.e. an attack by bomb, incendiary or bullet on persons or property. He did not know the particular type of offence intended, but he must have appreciated that it was very likely that those whom he was assisting intended a bomb attack on the inn.

If the appellant contemplated, as he clearly did, a bomb attack as likely, he must also have contemplated the possibility that the men in the car, which he was leading to the inn, had an explosive substance with them. Though he did not know whether they had it with them or not, he must have believed it very likely that they did. In the particular circumstances of this case, the inference that the two offences of possessing the explosive and using it with intent to cause injury or damage were within the appellant's contemplation is fully justified on the evidence. The appellant was rightly convicted, and I would dismiss his appeal.

7.8.2 PUBLIC POLICY EXCEPTIONS

Gillick v West Norfolk and Wisbech Area Health Authority and Department of Health and Social Security [1986] 1 AC 112 (HL)

Victoria Gillick sought a declaration as to the legality of a DHSS circular advising doctors that girls below the age of 16 could be prescribed the contraceptive pill without parental consent. One of the arguments before the House of Lords was as to whether a doctor following the advice in the circular, knowing that a girl under the age of 16 was intending to have sexual intercourse if the prescription was given to her, would be guilty of aiding and abetting unlawful sexual intercourse.

Lord Scarman:

. . . Clearly a doctor who gives a girl contraceptive advice or treatment not because in his clinical judgment the treatment is medically indicated for the maintenance of restoration of her health but with the intention of facilitating her having unlawful sexual intercourse may well be guilty of a criminal offence. It would depend . . . upon the doctor's intention – a conclusion hardly to be wondered at in the field of criminal law. The department's guidance avoids the trap of declaring that the decision to prescribe the treatment is wholly a matter of the doctor's discretion. He may prescribe only if she has the capacity to consent or if exceptional circumstances exist which justify him in exercising his clinical judgment without parental consent. The adjective 'clinical' emphasises that it must be a medical judgment based upon what he honestly believes to be necessary for the physical, mental, and emotional health of his patient. The *bona fide* exercise by a doctor of his clinical judgment must be a complete negation of the guilty mind which is an essential ingredient of the criminal offence of aiding and abetting the commission of unlawful sexual intercourse.

The public policy point fails for the same reason. It cannot be said that there is anything necessarily contrary to public policy in medical contraceptive treatment if it be medically indi-cated as in the interest of the patient's health, for the provision of such treatment is recognised as legitimate by Parliament: s 5 of the National Health Service Act 1977. If it should be prescribed for a girl under 16 the fact that it may eliminate a health risk in the event of the girl having unlawful sexual intercourse is an irrelevance unless the doctor intends to encourage her to have that intercourse. If the prescription is the *bona fide* exercise of his clinical judgment as to what is best for his patient's health, he has nothing to fear from the criminal law or from any public policy based on the criminality of a man having sexual intercourse with her.

It can be said by way of criticism of this view of the law that it will result in uncertainty and leave the law in the hands of the doctors. The uncertainty is the price which has to be paid to keep the law in line with social experience, which is that many girls are fully able to make sensible decisions about many matters before they reach the age of 16. I accept that great responsibilities will lie on the medical profession. It is, however, a learned and highly trained profession regulated by statute and governed by a strict ethical code which is vigorously enforced. Abuse of the power to prescribe contraceptive treatment for girls under the age of 16 would render a doctor liable to severe professional penalty. The truth may well be that the rights of parents and children in this sensitive area are better protected by the professional standards of the medical profession than by a *priori* legal lines of division between capacity and lack of capacity to consent since any such general dividing line is sure to produce in some cases injustice, hardship, and injury to health . . .

 COMMENTS AND QUESTIONS

1. In *R v Lomas* (1913) 9 Cr App R 220, a burglary was committed by a man named King, who had used for the purpose a housebreaking implement known as a jemmy. He was convicted as a principal. On the day on which the burglary was committed the jemmy had been in the possession of the appellant who had originally received it from King. At King's request the appellant had returned it to him. The appellant was convicted of being an accessory before the fact (the terminology then used), but his conviction was quashed on appeal on the basis that he could not aid and abet by returning King's property to him as the appellant had been under a legal duty to deliver up the item. Compare this with the situation where A sells such an implement to P knowing that P intends to use it to commit a burglary. In that case A will be an accomplice as he has no duty to sell the item to P (see further *National Coal Board v Gamble* [1959] 1 QB 11).

7.9 WHERE THE PRINCIPAL COMMITS ACTS OUTSIDE THE CONTEMPLATION OF THE ACCOMPLICE

It is a not uncommon feature of criminal cases involving accessorial liability that, once those involved are apprehended, the accomplice attempts to argue that the acts carried out by the principal offender were not part of any plan or understanding between them. The point is a crucial one. If the principal offender was acting in his own right, and not in furtherance of a common scheme, the accomplice should be relieved of liability – in simple terms he ceases to be an accomplice.

Dealing with these arguments involves untangling a number of issues:

(a) Were the actions of the principal offender beyond the scope of the express or implied understanding between the parties? If not, the accomplice has no basis for contending that he is not liable at least as a secondary party.

(b) If the principal's actions did exceed the common design did the principal deliberately go beyond what was planned, or was the result an accidental consequence of the principal's actions?

For example – suppose A and P agree to rob P, A acting as a look out. They agree that no weapons will be used.

(i) P carries out the robbery as planned but uses a knife to force P to hand over his money. P will be guilty of robbery as a principal offender – A will be an accomplice. The use of the knife was a departure from the plan by P but the crime committed was still robbery as contemplated by A.

(ii) P carries out the robbery, but in the course of doing so deliberately stabs P with a knife causing grievous bodily harm. P will be guilty of robbery and grievous bodily harm. A will only be an accomplice to the robbery.

(iii) P carries out the robbery as planned, during the course of which V dies of shock – there being no physical contact between P and V. P will be guilty of manslaughter. A will be an accomplice to manslaughter, even though that result was not planned. It came about as an accidental consequence of the agreed course of conduct being carried out; see *R v Betts and Ridley* (1930) 22 Cr App R 148; and *R v Baldessare* (1930) 22 Cr App R 70.

The above is a somewhat simplistic analysis. In real life the facts may contain many shades and nuances of difference. An obvious example is where P does not use a weapon during the robbery but does punch V hard in the face, causing grievous bodily harm. Is this a departure from the plan? Much will depend upon the evidence of A and P as to what was agreed and what A contemplated P doing.

7.9.1 JOINT ENTERPRISE – *MENS REA* FOR ACCOMPLICES TO MURDER

What *mens rea* is required where a defendant is charged with being an accomplice to murder? One might expect the fault element to be that required on the part of the principal offender – namely intention to kill or to do grievous bodily harm. As will be seen below, however, to require the same level of foresight on the part of an accomplice to murder as is required on the part of the principal offender, would be overly burdensome on the prosecution. The accomplice could in many cases plausibly argue that he did not know exactly what the principal offender was going to do. For this reason the courts have embraced the notion of 'contemplation' as descriptive of the fault element required of accomplices in these cases. The requirement is merely that the accomplice foresaw that the principal might kill or do grievous bodily harm with intent to kill, or intent to do grievous bodily harm.

R v Powell and Daniels; R v English [1999] AC 1

Powell and Daniels, along with a third man, went to purchase drugs from a drug dealer. The drug dealer was shot dead when he came to the door. The case for the Crown was that, on the basis that the third man had fired the gun, the two appellants were guilty of murder because they knew that the third man was armed with a gun and realised that he might use it to kill or cause really serious injury to the drug dealer. The issue for the House of Lords was whether this constituted sufficient *mens rea* for murder on the part of an accomplice to a joint enterprise, the certified question being put thus:

Is it sufficient to found a conviction for murder for a secondary party to a killing to have realised that the primary party might kill with intent to do so or must the secondary party have held such intention himself.

Lord Hutton:

. . . My Lords, the . . . question gives rise, in my opinion, to two issues. The first issue is whether there is a principle established in the authorities that where there is a joint enterprise to commit a crime, foresight or contemplation by one party to the enterprise that another party to the enterprise may in the course of it commit another crime, is sufficient to impose criminal liability for that crime if committed by the other party even if the first party did not intend that criminal act to be carried out. (I shall consider in a later part of this judgment whether the foresight is of a possibility or of a probability.) The second issue is whether, if there be such an established principle, it can stand as good law in the light of the decisions of this House that foresight is not sufficient to constitute the *mens rea* for murder in the case of the person who actually causes the death and that guilt only arises if that person intends to kill or cause really serious injury.

My Lords, I consider that there is a strong line of authority that where two parties embark on a joint enterprise to commit a crime, and one party foresees that in the course of the enterprise the other party may carry out, with the requisite *mens rea*, an act constituting another crime, the former is liable for that crime if committed by the latter in the course of the enterprise. This was decided by the Court of Appeal, constituted by five judges, in *R v Smith (Wesley)* [1963] 1 WLR 1200 . . .

However it is clear from a number of decisions, in addition to the judgment of the Court of Appeal in *R v Smith* [1963] 1 WLR 1200, that as stated by the High Court of Australia in *McAuliffe v R* (1995) 69 ALJR 621, 624 (in a judgment to which I will refer later in more detail),'The scope of the common purpose is to be determined by what was contemplated by the parties sharing that purpose.' Therefore when two parties embark on a joint criminal enterprise one party will be liable for an act which he contemplates may be carried out by the other party in the course of the enterprise even if he has not tacitly agreed to that act.

The principle stated in *R v Smith* was applied by the Privy Council in *Chan Wing-Siu v R* [1985] AC 168 in the judgment delivered by Sir Robin Cooke who stated, at p 175G:

The case must depend rather on the wider principle whereby a secondary party is criminally liable for acts by the primary offender of a type which the former foresees but does not necessarily intend. That there is such a principle is not in doubt. It turns on contemplation or, putting the same idea in other words, authorisation, which may be express or is more usually implied. It meets the case of a crime foreseen as a possible incident of the common unlawful enterprise. The criminal culpability lies in participating in the venture with that foresight.

The principle stated by Sir Robin Cooke in *Chan Wing-Siu's* case was followed and applied in the judgment of the Court of Appeal in *R v Hyde* [1991] 1 QB 134, where Lord Lane CJ took account of Professor Smith's comment in *R v Wakeley* that there is a distinction between tacit agreement and foresight and made it clear that the latter is the proper test . . .

There is therefore a strong line of authority that participation in a joint criminal enterprise with foresight or contemplation of an act as a possible incident of that enterprise is sufficient to impose criminal liability for that act carried out by another participant in the enterprise . . . The second issue which arises on these appeals is whether the line of authority exemplified by *R v Smith* and *Chan Wing-Siu* is good law in the light of the decisions of this House in *R v Moloney* [1985] AC 905 and *R v Hancock* [1986] AC 455 . . .

In reliance upon *R v Moloney* and *R v Hancock* Mr Feinberg, on behalf of the appellants Powell and Daniels, submitted to this House, as he submitted to the Court of Appeal, that as a matter of principle there is an anomaly in requiring proof against a secondary party of a lesser *mens rea* than needs to be proved against the principal who commits the *actus reus* of murder. If foreseeability of risk is insufficient to found the *mens rea* of murder for a principal then the same test of liability should apply in the case of a secondary party to the joint enterprise. Mr Feinberg further submitted that it is wrong for the present distinction in mental culpability to operate to the disadvantage of a party who does not commit the *actus reus* and that there is a manifest anomaly where there is one test for a principal and a lesser test for a secondary party.

My Lords, I recognise that as a matter of logic there is force in the argument advanced on behalf of the appellants, and that on one view it is anomalous that if foreseeability of death or really serious harm is not sufficient to constitute *mens rea* for murder in the party who actually carries out the killing, it is sufficient to constitute *mens rea* in a secondary party. But the rules of the common law are not based solely on logic but relate to practical concerns and, in relation to crimes committed in the course of joint enterprises, to the need to give effective protection to the public against criminals operating in gangs. As Lord Salmon stated in *R v Majewski* [1977] AC 443, 482E, in rejecting criticism based on strict logic of a rule of the common law, 'this is the view that has been adopted by the common law of England, which is founded on common sense and experience rather than strict logic'.

In my opinion there are practical considerations of weight and importance related to considerations of public policy which justify the principle stated in *Chan Wing-Siu* and which prevail over considerations of strict logic. One consideration is that referred to by Lord Lane CJ in *R v Hyde* [1991] 1 QB 134, 139C, where he cited with approval the observation of Professor Smith in his comment on *R v Wakeley*:

> If B realises (without agreeing to such conduct being used) that A may kill or intentionally inflict serious injury, but nevertheless continues to participate with A in the venture, that will amount to a sufficient mental element for B to be guilty of murder if A, with the requisite intent, kills in the course of the venture. As Professor Smith points out, B has in those circumstances lent himself to the enterprise and by so doing he has given assistance and encouragement to A in carrying out an enterprise which B realises may involve murder.

A further consideration is that, unlike the principal party who carries out the killing with a deadly weapon, the secondary party will not be placed in the situation in which he suddenly has to decide whether to shoot or stab the third person with intent to kill or cause really serious harm. There is, in my opinion, an argument of considerable force that the secondary party who takes part in a criminal enterprise (for example, the robbery of a bank) with foresight that a deadly weapon may be used, should not escape liability for murder because he, unlike the principal party, is not suddenly confronted by the security officer so that he has to decide whether to use the gun or knife or have the enterprise thwarted and face arrest. This point has been referred to in cases where the question has been discussed whether in order for criminal liability to attach the secondary party must foresee an act as more likely than not or whether it suffices if the secondary party foresees the act only as a possibility.

. . . Therefore for the reasons which I have given I would answer the certified question of law in the appeals of Powell and Daniels . . . by stating that (subject to the observations which I make in relation to the second certified question in the case of English) it is sufficient to found a conviction for murder for a secondary party to have realised that in the course of the joint enterprise the primary party might kill with intent to do so or with intent to cause grievous bodily harm. Accordingly I would dismiss the appeals of Powell and Daniels.

Lord Steyn:

My Lords, . . . the established principle is that a secondary party to a criminal enterprise may be criminally liable for a greater criminal offence committed by the primary offender of a type which the former foresaw but did not necessarily intend. The criminal culpability lies in participating in the criminal enterprise with that foresight. Foresight and intention are not synonymous terms. But foresight is a necessary and sufficient ground of the liability of accessories. That is how the law has been stated in two carefully reasoned decisions of the Privy Council: see *Chan Wing-Sui v R* [1985] AC 168 and *Hui Chi-Ming v R* [1992] 1 AC 34. In a valuable article Professor Sir John Smith has recently concluded that there is no doubt that this represents English law: 'Criminal liability of accessories: law and law reform' (1997) 113 LQR 453, 455. And Lord Hutton has demonstrated in his comprehensive review of the case law that the law is as stated in the two Privy Council decisions. That does not mean that the established principle cannot be re-examined and, if found to be flawed, re-formulated. But the existing law and practice forms the starting point.

Counsel for the appellants argued that the secondary party to a criminal enterprise should only be guilty of a murder committed by the primary offender if the secondary party has the full *mens rea* sufficient for murder, i.e. an intent to kill or to cause grievous bodily harm. Their arguments fell into three parts, namely (1) that there is a disharmony between two streams of authority; (2) that the accessory principle involves a form of constructive criminal liability; and (3) that it is anomalous that a lesser form of culpability is sufficient for a secondary party than for the primary offender. The first part of the argument centred on the scope of decisions of the House of Lords in *R v Moloney* [1985] AC 905 and *R v Hancock* [1986] AC 455. Those decisions distinguish between foresight and intention and require in the case of murder proof of intention to kill or cause serious bodily injury. But those decisions were intended to apply to a primary offender only. The liability of accessories was not in issue. Plainly the House did not intend in those decisions to examine or pronounce on the accessory principle. The resort to authority must therefore fail.

That brings me to the second argument. If the application of the accessory principle results in a form of constructive liability that would be contrary to principle and it would be a defect in our criminal law. But subject to a qualification about the definition of the *mens rea* required for murder to which I will turn later, I would reject the argument that the accessory principle as such imposes a form of constructive liability. The accessory principle requires proof of a subjective state of mind on the party of a participant in a criminal enterprise, viz foresight that the primary offender might commit a different and more serious offence. Professor Sir John Smith, 'Criminal liability of accessories: law and law reform' (1997) 113 LQR 464, explained how the principle applies in the case of murder:

Nevertheless, as the critics point out it is enough that the accessory is reckless, whereas, in the case of the principal, intention must be proved. Recklessness . . . [however] death be caused is a sufficient *mens rea* for a principal offender in manslaughter, but not murder. The accessory to murder, however, must be proved to have been reckless, not merely whether death might be caused, but whether murder might be committed: he must have been aware, not merely that death or grievous bodily harm might be caused, but that it might be caused intentionally, by a person whom he was assisting or encouraging to commit a crime. Recklessness whether murder be committed is different from, and more serious than, recklessness whether death be caused by an accident. The foresight of the secondary party must be directed to a real possibility of the commission by the primary offender in the course of the criminal enterprise of the greater offence. The liability is imposed because the secondary party is assisting in and encouraging a criminal enterprise which he is aware might result in the commission of a greater offence. The liability of an accessory is predicated on his culpability in respect of the greater offence as defined in law. It is undoubtedly a lesser form of *mens rea*. But it is unrealistic to say that the accessory principle as such imposes constructive criminal liability.

At first glance there is substance in the third argument that it is anomalous that a lesser form of culpability is required in the case of a secondary party, viz foresight of the possible commission of the greater offence, whereas in the case of the primary offender the law insists on proof of the specific intention which is an ingredient of the offence. This general argument leads, in the present case, to the particular argument that it is anomalous that the secondary party can be guilty of murder if he foresees the possibility of such a crime being committed while the primary can only be guilty if he has an intent to kill or cause really serious injury. Recklessness may suffice in the case of the secondary party but it does not in the case of the primary offender. The answer to this supposed anomaly, and other similar cases across the spectrum of criminal law, is to be found in practical and policy considerations. If the law required proof of the specific intention on the part of a secondary party, the utility of the accessory principle would be gravely undermined. It is just that a secondary party who foresees that the primary offender might kill with the intent sufficient for murder, and assists and encourages the primary offender in the criminal enterprise on this basis, should be guilty of murder. He ought to be criminally liable for harm which he foresaw and which in fact resulted from the crime he assisted and encouraged. But it would in practice almost invariably be impossible for a jury to say that the secondary party wanted death to be caused or that he regarded it as virtually certain. In the real world proof of an intention sufficient for murder would be well nigh impossible in the vast majority of joint enterprise cases. Moreover, the proposed change in the law must be put in context. The criminal justice system exists to control crime. A prime function of that system must be to deal justly but effectively with those who join with others in criminal enterprises. Experience has shown that joint criminal enterprises only too readily escalate into the commission of greater offences. In order to deal with this important social problem the accessory principle is needed and cannot be abolished or relaxed. For these reasons I would reject the arguments advanced in favour of the revision of the accessory principle.

7.9.2 WHERE THE PRINCIPAL DELIBERATELY EXCEEDS THE SCOPE OF THE JOINT ENTERPRISE BY USING A MORE DANGEROUS WEAPON

As noted at 7.9 above, an accomplice will not normally be a party to the actions of the principal offender that involve the principal in deliberately departing from the common design. This raises particular problems in homicide cases. If A foresees that P might kill V with intent to kill in the course of an agreed attack, does it matter how P chooses to kill V? If the agreement was that P should strangle V to death with his hands, and P uses a rope to strangle V that can hardly avail A as an argument that P has deliberately departed from the plan. Logically, therefore, A would have no argument on those facts if P had used a knife to kill V, or indeed shot him dead. The agreed outcome has been achieved. The same logic cannot be applied, however, where A foresees P causing V grievous bodily harm and further foresees that by doing so P might kill V or might cause V grievous bodily harm. Admittedly such foresight should suffice to make A an accomplice to murder, but the courts have been willing to recognise that it is possible for A to foresee grievous bodily harm that is not necessarily life threatening. If P proceeds to cause grievous bodily harm in a more dangerous way than that contemplated by A, and P in fact kills V, A may well escape liability.

R v Powell and Daniels; R v English [1999] AC 1

The appeal in *R v English* was conjoined with that in *R v Powell and Daniels* as they both raised important issues regarding liability for participation in a joint enterprise. In *R v English* the appellant and another young man, Weddle, took part in an attack on a police officer, Sergeant Forth. In the course of the attack Weddle used a knife with which he stabbed Sergeant Forth to death. The Crown accepted that it was a reasonable possibility that English had no knowledge that Weddle was carrying a knife.

Weddle and English were convicted of murder and their appeals were rejected by the Court of Appeal. English appealed to the House of Lords, on the basis of two certified questions:

(i) Is it sufficient to found a conviction for murder for a secondary party to a killing to have realised that the primary party might kill with intent to do so or with intent to cause grievous bodily harm or must the secondary party have held such an intention himself? Note that this matter was addressed in the appeal of *R v Powell* and *Daniels*, considered above.

(ii) Is it sufficient for murder that the secondary party intends or foresees that the primary party would or may act with intent to cause grievous bodily harm, if the lethal act carried out by the primary party is fundamentally different from the acts foreseen or intended by the secondary party?

The second certified question in the appeal of English arose because of the last sentence in the following passage in the trial judge's summing-up to the jury: If he had the knife and English knew that Weddle had the knife, what would have been – must have been – in the mind of English, bearing in mind whatever condition you find that he was in as a result of drink? So you have to ask that question. If he did not know of the knife then you have to consider whether nevertheless he knew that there was a substantial risk that Weddle might cause some really serious injury with the wooden post which was used in the manner which you find it to have been used.

Lord Hutton: In *R v Anderson; R v Morris* [1966] 2 QB 110 the primary party (Anderson) killed the victim with a knife. The defence of the secondary party (Morris) was that even though he may have taken part in a joint attack with Anderson to beat up the victim, he did not know that Anderson was armed with a knife. In his summing-up the trial judge told the jury that they could convict Morris of manslaughter even though he had no idea that Anderson had armed himself with a knife. The Court of Appeal held that this was a misdirection in respect of Morris and quashed his conviction for manslaughter.

In delivering the judgment of the Court of Appeal Lord Parker CJ accepted, at p 118, the principle formulated by Mr Geoffrey Lane QC (as he then was) on behalf of Morris:

> ... where two persons embark on a joint enterprise, each is liable for the acts done in pursuance of that joint enterprise, that that includes liability for unusual consequences if they arise from the execution of the agreed joint enterprise but (and this is the crux of the matter) that, if one of the adventurers goes beyond what had been tacitly agreed as part of the common enterprise, his co-adventurer is not liable for the consequences of that unauthorised act. Finally, he says it is for the jury in every case to decide whether what was done was part of the joint enterprise, or went beyond it and was in fact an act unauthorised by that joint enterprise.

As a matter of strict analysis there is, as Professor JC Smith pointed out in his commentary on *R v Wakely* [1990] Crim LR 119, 120, a distinction between a party to a common enterprise contemplating that in the course of the enterprise another party may use a gun or knife and a party tacitly agreeing that in the course of the enterprise another party may use such a weapon. In many cases the distinction will in practice be of little importance because as Lord Lane CJ observed in *R v Wakely*, at p 120, with reference to the use of a pick axe handle in a burglary, 'Foreseeability that the pick axe handle might be used as a weapon of violence was practically indistinguishable from tacit agreement that the weapon should be used for that purpose.' Nevertheless it is possible that a case might arise where a party knows that another party to the common enterprise is carrying a deadly weapon and contemplates that he may use it in the course of the enterprise, but, whilst making it clear to the other party that he is opposed to the weapon being used, nevertheless continues with the plan. In such a case it would be unrealistic to say that, if used, the weapon would be used with his tacit agreement.

> ... In *R v Hyde* [1991] 1 QB 134, as already set out, Lord Lane stated, at p 139C:
> If B realises (without agreeing to such conduct being used) that A may kill or intentionally inflict serious injury, but nevertheless continues to participate with A in the venture, that will amount to a sufficient mental element for B to be guilty of murder if A, with the requisite intent, kills in the course of the venture.

However, in *Hyde* the attack on the victim took place without weapons and the Crown case was that the fatal blow to the victim's head was a heavy kick. The problem raised by the second certified question is that, if a jury is directed in the terms stated in *Hyde*, without any qualification (as was the jury in English), there will be liability for murder on the part of the secondary party if he foresees the possibility that the other party in the criminal venture will cause really serious harm by kicking or striking a blow with a wooden post, but the other party suddenly produces a knife or a gun, which the secondary party did not know he was carrying, and kills the victim with it.

Mr Sallon, for the appellant, advanced to your Lordships' House the submission (which does not appear to have been advanced in the Court of Appeal) that in a case such as the present one where the primary party kills with a deadly weapon, which the secondary party did not know that he had and therefore did not foresee his use of it, the secondary party should not be guilty of murder. He submitted that to be guilty under the principle stated in *Chan Wing-Siu* the secondary party must foresee an act of the type which the principal party committed, and that in the present case the use of a knife was fundamentally different to the use of a wooden post.

My Lords, I consider that this submission is correct. It finds strong support in the passage of the judgment of Lord Parker in *R v Anderson; R v Morris* [1966] 2 QB 110, 120B which I have set out earlier, but which it is convenient to set out again in this portion of the judgment:

> It seems to this court that to say that adventurers are guilty of manslaughter when one of them has departed completely from the concerted action of the common design and has suddenly formed an intent to kill and has used a weapon and acted in a way which no party to that common design could suspect is something which would revolt the conscience of people today.

The judgment in *Chan Wing-Siu's* case [1985] AC 168 also supports the argument advanced on behalf of the appellant because Sir Robin Cooke stated, at p 175F: The case must depend rather on the wider principle whereby a secondary party is criminally liable for *acts by the primary offender of a type* which the former foresees but does not necessarily intend. [emphasis added]

There is also strong support for the appellant's submission in the decision of Carswell J (as he then was), sitting without a jury in the Crown Court in Northern Ireland, in *R v Gamble* [1989] NI 268. In that case the four accused were all members of a terrorist organisation, the Ulster Volunteer Force, who had a grievance against a man named Patton. The four accused entered upon a joint venture to inflict punishment upon him, two of them, Douglas and McKee, contemplating that Patton would be subjected to a severe beating or to 'kneecapping' (firing a bullet into his kneecap). In the course of the attack upon him Patton was brutally murdered by the other two accused. His throat was cut with a knife with great force which rapidly caused his death. In addition he was shot with four bullets, and two of the bullet wounds would have been fatal had his death not been caused by the cutting of his throat. Douglas and McKee had not foreseen killing with a knife or firing of bullets into a vital part of the body. It was argued, however, on behalf of the prosecution that the joint enterprise of committing grievous bodily harm, combined with the rule that an intent to cause such harm grounded a conviction for murder in respect of a resulting death, was sufficient to make the two accused liable for murder notwithstanding that they had not foreseen the actions which actually caused death. After citing the relevant authorities Carswell J rejected this argument and stated, at p 283F:

> When an assailant 'kneecaps' his victim, i.e. discharges a weapon into one of his limbs, most commonly into the knee joint, there must always be the risk that it will go wrong and that an artery may be severed or the limb may be so damaged that gangrene sets in, both potentially fatal complications. It has to be said, however, that such cases must be very rare among victims of what is an abhorrent and disturbingly frequent crime. Persons who

take a part in inflicting injuries of this nature no doubt do not generally expect that they will endanger life, and I should be willing to believe that in most cases they believe that they are engaged in a lesser offence than murder. The infliction of grievous bodily harm came within the contemplation of Douglas and McKee, and they might therefore be regarded as having placed themselves within the ambit of life-threatening conduct. It may further be said that they must be taken to have had within their contemplation the possibility that life might be put at risk. The issue is whether it follows as a consequence that they cannot be heard to say that the murder was a different crime from the attack which they contemplated, and so cannot escape liability for the murder on the ground that it was outside the common design. To accept this type of reasoning would be to fix an accessory with consequences of his acts which he did not foresee and did not desire or intend. The modern development of the criminal law has been away from such an approach and towards a greater emphasis on subjective tests of criminal guilt, as Sir Robin Cooke pointed out in *Chan Wing-Sui*. Although the rule remains well entrenched that an intention to inflict grievous bodily harm qualifies as the *mens rea* of murder, it is not in my opinion necessary to apply it in such a way as to fix an accessory with liability for a consequence which he did not intend and which stems from an act which he did not have within his contemplation. I do not think that the state of the law compels me to reach such a conclusion, and it would not in my judgment accord with the public sense of what is just and fitting.

In my opinion this decision was correct in that a secondary party who foresees grievous bodily harm caused by kneecapping with a gun should not be guilty of murder where, in an action unforeseen by the secondary party, another party to the criminal enterprise kills the victim by cutting his throat with a knife. The issue (which is one of fact after the tribunal of fact has directed itself, or has been directed, in accordance with the statement of Lord Parker in *R v Anderson; R v Morris* [1966] 2 QB 110, 120B) whether a secondary party who foresees the use of a gun to kneecap, and death is then caused by the deliberate firing of the gun into the head or body of the victim, is guilty of murder is more debatable although, with respect, I agree with the decision of Carswell J on the facts of that case.

Accordingly, in the appeal of English, I consider that the direction of the learned trial judge was defective (although this does not constitute a criticism of the judge, who charged the jury in conformity with the principle stated in *Hyde*) because in accordance with the principle stated by Lord Parker in *R v Anderson*, at p 120B, he did not qualify his direction on foresight of really serious injury by stating that if the jury considered that the use of the knife by Weddle was the use of a weapon and an action on Weddle's part which English did not foresee as a possibility, then English should not be convicted of murder. As the unforeseen use of the knife would take the killing outside the scope of the joint venture the jury should also have been directed, as the Court of Appeal held in *R v Anderson*, that English should not be found guilty of manslaughter.

On the evidence the jury could have found that English did not know that Weddle had a knife. Therefore the judge's direction made the conviction of English unsafe and in my opinion his appeal should be allowed and the conviction for murder quashed.

English was guilty of a very serious attack on Sergeant Forth, striking him a number of violent blows with a wooden post at the same time as Weddle attacked him with a wooden post. Therefore English was fully deserving of punishment for that attack, but it is unnecessary for your Lordships to give any further consideration to this point as English has already served a number of years in detention pursuant to the sentence of the trial judge.

I have already stated that the issue raised by the second certified question in the appeal of English is to be resolved by the application of the principle stated by Lord Parker in *R v Anderson*, at p 120B. Having so stated and having regard to the differing circumstances in which the issue may arise I think it undesirable to seek to formulate a more precise answer to the question in case such an answer might appear to prescribe too rigid a formula for use by trial judges. However I would wish to make this observation: if the weapon used by the primary party is different to, but as dangerous as, the weapon which the secondary party contemplated he might use, the secondary party should not escape liability for murder because of the difference in the weapon, for example, if he foresaw that the primary party might use a gun to kill and the latter used a knife to kill, or vice versa.

In conclusion I would wish to refer to a number of other points which arise from the submissions in these appeals. The first issue is what is the degree of foresight required to impose liability under the principle stated in *Chan Wing-Siu* [1985] AC 168. On this issue I am in respectful agreement with the judgment of the Privy Council in that case that the secondary party is subject to criminal liability if he contemplated the act causing the death as a possible incident of the joint venture, unless the risk was so remote that the jury take the view that the secondary party genuinely dismissed it as altogether negligible.

Secondly, as the Privy Council also stated in *Chan Wing-Siu*, in directing the jury the trial judge need not adopt a set of fixed formulae, and the form of the words used should be that best suited to the facts of the individual case. In this judgment I have cited two passages from the judgment of Lord Parker in *R v Anderson; R v Morris* [1966] 2 QB 110. One passage commences at p 118F, the second passage commences at p 120B. Trial judges have frequently based their directions to the jury in respect of the liability of a secondary party for an action carried out in a joint venture on the first passage. There is clearly no error in doing so. However in many cases there would be no difference in result between applying the test stated in that passage and the test of foresight, and if there would be a difference the test of foresight is the proper one to apply. I consider that the test of foresight is a simpler and more practicable test for a jury to apply than the test of whether the act causing the death goes beyond what had been tacitly agreed as part of the joint enterprise.

Therefore, in cases where an issue arises as to whether an action was within the scope of the joint venture, I would suggest that it might be preferable for a trial judge in charging a jury to base his direction on the test of foresight rather than on the test set out in the first passage in *R v Anderson; R v Morris*. But in a case where, although the secondary party may have foreseen grievous bodily harm, he may not have foreseen the use of the weapon employed by the primary party or the manner in which the primary party acted, the trial judge should qualify the test of foresight stated in *R v Hyde* [1991] 1 QB 134 in the manner stated by Lord Parker in the second passage in *Anderson v Morris*.

As I have already observed in referring to the decision in *R v Gamble* [1989] NI 268, in applying the second passage in *R v Anderson* there will be cases giving rise to a fine distinction as to whether or not the unforeseen use of a particular weapon or the manner in which a particular weapon is used will take a killing outside the scope of the joint venture, but this issue will be one of fact for the common sense of the jury to decide.

R v Rahman and Others [2007] EWCA Crim 342

The defendants were involved in an attack on the victim Tyrone Clark. During the attack Clark was stabbed to death by a member of the group. The defendants were convicted as accomplices to the murder on the basis of their being involved in a joint enterprise. One of the issues arising during the course of these unsuccessful appeals against conviction was the extent to which an accomplice who foresaw that a principal offender might cause grievous bodily harm, and in the course of so doing might kill the victim, could escape liability where the principal caused death by using a fundamentally different weapon.

Hooper LJ:

20. . . . As we see below the second certified question in Powell and English was concerned with a defendant who intends or foresees that the primary party would or may act with intent to cause grievous bodily harm. That defendant has the 'advantage' of the 'fundamentally different' rule. Nothing in Powell and English suggests that a defendant who realised that one of the attackers might kill with intent to kill can enjoy the benefit of the rule. The liability of such a person is not 'parasitic', to use the words in Smith and Hogan, pages 192–193. He realises that the crime of murder may be committed . . .

21. It might be thought that a defendant who foresees that P might kill with intent to cause really serious bodily harm would also be guilty of murder even though P's act was fundamentally different. The second certified question does not specifically deal with a foresight of this kind. It deals with the defendant who foresees or realises that P would or may act with intent to cause grievous bodily harm. However, Lord Hutton in Powell and English (at page 29) approves of the passage in *Gamble* [1989] NI 268, at 283–284. The kneecappers, it could be said, 'must be taken to have had within their contemplation the possibility that life might be put at risk'. Given the nature of kneecapping, this must be right. Nonetheless, so it seems, they will not be guilty of murder if P's act was fundamentally different. Mr Smith [counsel for the Crown] did not dissent from the proposition that this category of defendants may take advantage of the 'fundamentally different' rule. (Cf *Attorney General's Reference No 3 of 2004* [2005] EWCA Crim 1882, paragraph 29.)

. . .

68. Before leaving this ground; we think it helpful to set out, albeit with trepidation, a more concise route to verdict in a case of this kind, avoiding the directions which were too favourable to the defendants. We assume an attack by a group of armed people on a person (V) who is killed during the attack. It is the prosecution's case that the defendants were parties to that murder. The prosecution accept that none of the defendants on trial can be shown to have caused the death of V and there is no dispute that a distinct member of the group whom we shall call P caused the death. The prosecution's case is that all of the defendants participated in the attack intending (at the least) that really serious harm would be caused to V.

69. In order to convict D of murder the jury must first be sure that P unlawfully caused the death of V intending to kill him or cause him really serious bodily harm and secondly be sure that D played some part in the attack on V. The route to verdict could then be:

1. Are you sure that D intended that one of the attackers would kill V intending to kill him or that D realised that one of the attackers might kill V with intent to kill him? If yes, guilty of murder. If no, go to 2.

2. Are you sure that either:
   a) D realised that one of the attackers might kill V with intent to cause him really serious bodily harm; or
   b) D intended that serious really bodily harm would be caused to V; or
   c) D realised that one of the attackers might cause serious bodily harm to V intending to cause him such harm?
   If no, not guilty of murder. If yes, go to question 3.

3. What was P's act which caused the death of V? (e.g. stabbing, shooting, kicking, beating). Go to question 4.

4. Did D realise that one of the attackers might do this act? If yes, guilty of murder. If no, go to question 5.

5. What act or acts are you sure D realised that one of the attackers might do to cause V really serious harm? Go to question 6.

6. Are you sure that this act or these acts (which D realised one of the attackers might do) is/are not of a fundamentally different nature to P's act which caused the death of V? If yes, guilty of murder. If no, not guilty of murder.

70. Mr Smith submitted that the expression 'fundamentally different' would normally need no further clarification, albeit that the judge would summarise the competing arguments as the judge did in the present case. We agree.

 ## COMMENTS AND QUESTIONS

1 Uncertainty remains as regards the extent to which the principal's use of a weapon other than that contemplated by the accomplice results in the principal exceeding the scope of the common design. In *R v Uddin* [1998] 2 All ER 744, the appellant was involved in a group attack on S who was stabbed to death. The principal offender was convicted of murder, and the appellant was convicted of murder as an accomplice.

Beldam LJ observed (at p 751):

> In deciding whether the actions [of the principal are of an entirely different type to those contemplated by the accomplice] the use by [the principal] of a weapon is a significant factor. If the character of the weapon, e.g. its propensity to cause death is different from any weapon used or contemplated by the others and if it is used with specific intent to kill, the others are not responsible for the death unless it is proved that they knew or foresaw the likelihood of the use of such a weapon.

In practice it will be for the jury to determine whether the weapon used by the principal is sufficiently different from that contemplated by the accomplice for there to be a departure from the joint enterprise, but it can be imagined how difficulties might arise where, for example, the agreement is to hit the victim with bare fists and the principal kicks him whilst wearing steel-capped boots. Are the boots a fundamentally different type of weapon?

2   P may use the weapon contemplated by A, and with intent contemplated by A, but in a way that causes more life threatening injuries than those contemplated by A. For example, A and P agree that P will attack V with a baseball bat and cause grievous bodily harm by breaking P's arms. In the event P attacks V with the baseball bat, intending to cause V grievous bodily harm, by striking V on the head. V dies from his injuries. P may be convicted of murder, and A (in theory) could be convicted as an accomplice, given his *mens rea*. Can it not be argued, however, in the light of *Gamble* (see above) that by choosing to attack V and causing more life-threatening GBH, P deliberately departed from the common design? See further *R v Bamborough* [1996] Crim LR 744, where the Court of Appeal proceeded on the basis that it would be sufficient, in order to substantiate A's conviction for murder as an accomplice, that he had contemplated grievous bodily harm as a possible incident of the common design, the court not being overly concerned at how A might have foreseen the grievous bodily harm being caused by P.

3   The Court of Appeal rejected the argument, advanced in *R v Concannon* [2002] Crim LR 213, to the effect that ruling in *R v Powell and Daniels* (above), resulting in a significant disparity between the *mens rea* to be established as regards a defendant charged with murder as a principal offender and one charged with murder as an accomplice in cases of joint enterprise, was incompatible with the European Convention of Human Rights (Art 6). Predictably, the court confirmed that Art 6 was concerned with procedural fairness, not the fairness of the substantive law of signatory states.

4   One important exception to the rule that if A foresees P killing V it matters not how P chooses to do it arises where the identity of the victim is an element of the joint enterprise. If A and P agree that P will shoot V dead as he comes out of his house and, on seeing V's wife X come out of V's house P deliberately shoots her dead, A should escape liability as an accomplice to murder even though he foresaw death as something that might happen. By deliberately choosing a different victim P has gone beyond the scope of the joint enterprise. If the evidence was that P had accidentally shot and killed X, A would be an accomplice to manslaughter; see *R v Saunders and Archer* (1573) 2 Plowd 473. A supplied S with poison, concealed in a roasted apple, so that S could kill his wife. S gave the apple to his wife who, instead of eating it herself, gave it to their young daughter, who consumed the apple and died. S was present throughout this chain of events. It was held that by deliberately allowing his daughter to die, rather than his wife, S had exceeded the scope of the common design between S and A. See also *R v Leahy* [1985] Crim LR 99, for a more modern application of this doctrine.

7.9.3 RESIDUAL LIABILITY FOR MANSLAUGHTER WHERE THE PRINCIPAL IS CONVICTED OF MURDER

Thus far we have seen that if A foresees P causing the death of V with the *mens rea* for murder as something that might occur in the course of the joint enterprise he can be an accomplice to murder. Similarly if A contemplates P causing V grievous bodily harm with intent and V dies from those injuries.

Where P murders V but A contemplates neither death nor grievous bodily harm, but merely that P might cause some harm to V falling short of grievous bodily harm, A cannot be an accomplice to murder. A can, however, be an accomplice to manslaughter, on the basis that he foresaw P committing a dangerous and unlawful act that caused V's death.

Provided P's act is one contemplated by A as part of the joint enterprise establishing the liability of A as an accomplice to manslaughter should be unproblematic. As the following extracts show, where A contends that the actions of P were as contemplated but P acted with more *mens rea* than contemplated (and thus A should be acquitted because P has exceeded the common design) the courts have had more difficulty.

R v Stewart and Schofield [1995] 3 All ER 159 (CA)

Two young women – Rothwell and Stewart – visited a shop and noticed the shopkeeper, a Mr Dada, removing money from the cash register and placing it in his pocket. Shortly afterwards Rothwell and Stewart met up with two men, Schofield and Lambert, and they agreed to return to the shop in order to rob Mr Dada. Lambert, Schofield and Stewart took out of the car a scaffolding bar and a knife. Lambert put on a balaclava and a long coat. Whilst Schofield kept watch outside, Lambert and Stewart went into the shop, Lambert armed with the bar and Stewart armed with the knife. Mr Dada was viciously beaten and later died from his injuries. Schofield had admitted knowledge of the weapons with which Lambert and Stewart were armed. Both said that they had not contemplated that Mr Dada would be more than threatened, and that they did not know at that time that Lambert was a person who was deeply motivated by racial hatred or would be liable to use such excessive violence. They contended that Lambert's attack went far beyond anything that they contemplated and was motivated not by the needs of the robbery but by vicious racial hatred. The appellants were convicted as accomplices to manslaughter and appealed.

Hobhouse LJ:
The allegation that a defendant took part in the execution of a crime as a joint enterprise is not the same as an allegation that he aided, abetted, counselled or procured the commission of that crime. A person who is a mere aider or abettor etc is truly a secondary party to the commission of whatever crime it is that the principal has committed although he may be charged as a principal. If the principal has committed the crime of murder, the liability of the secondary party can only be a liability for aiding and abetting murder. In contrast, where the allegation is joint enterprise, the allegation is that one defendant participated in the criminal act of another. This is a different principle. It renders each of the parties to a joint enterprise criminally liable for the acts done in the course of carrying out that joint enterprise. Where the criminal liability of any given defendant depends upon the further proof that he had a certain state of mind, that state of mind must be proved against that defendant. Even though several defendants may, as a result of having engaged in a joint enterprise, be each criminally responsible for the criminal act of one of those defendants done in the course of carrying out the joint enterprise, their individual criminal responsibility will, in such a case, depend upon what individual state of mind or intention has been proved against them. Thus, each may be a party to the unlawful act which caused the victim's death. But one may have had the intent either to kill him or to cause him serious harm and be guilty of murder, whereas another may not have had that intent and may be guilty only of manslaughter.

Mens rea
An allegation that a defendant was part of a criminal joint enterprise with others includes an allegation that he was aware of the character of the joint enterprise in which he was joining and

foresaw that the relevant criminal acts were liable to be involved. Thus, the allegation of joint enterprise involves an allegation concerning the state of the defendant's mind at the time of his participation in the joint enterprise. Normally the fact that the defendant had the state of mind sufficient to prove his guilt of the offence charged is proved by proof that he was a party to the joint enterprise in the course of which the criminal acts were committed. But joint enterprises vary. They may have a purpose, say the infliction of grievous bodily harm, which corresponds to the specific intent for a particular crime, say murder or an offence contrary to s 18 of the Offences Against the Person Act 1861, in which case participation in the joint enterprise will prove the relevant *mens rea*. But in other cases the purpose of the joint enterprise may have been more limited and the relevant criminal liability may only have arisen from some undesired consequence. Provided that the joint enterprise is proved in relation to the relevant acts, then it is not an answer that consequences of those acts were unusual or unexpected. Even if unusual or unexpected consequences arose from the execution of the plan, each participant is responsible for those consequences. In such cases the liability of an individual defendant may depend upon whether his intention at the time the act was done included an intention that the consequences should follow. A defendant who had that intention may have a more serious criminal liability than one who did not. This is because the *mens rea* for the more serious offence can be proved against the one but not against the other.

Archbold

The analysis which we have shortly summarised is that followed by the editors of Archbold and by way of summary we are content to adopt what they say:

> A person who is a party to a joint enterprise, the pursuance of which results in the causing of another's death may be criminally liable for that death either on the basis that he is guilty of murder or on the basis that he is guilty of manslaughter. It is fundamental to a conviction of either offence that the accused must have been a party to the act which caused death. The application of the law concerning joint enterprise in cases of homicide in practice raises two problems, (1) whether in the circumstances the accused was party to the act which caused death; (2) if he was, whether his state of mind was such as to make him guilty of murder or of manslaughter.

[Hobhouse LJ considered the authorities and continued:]

The authorities do not support the appellants' submission. There is no suggestion that *R v Reid* was wrongly decided nor that there is an inconsistency between what Lawton LJ there said and what was said in *R v Anderson and Morris* by Lord Parker CJ. The distinction between the various cases is that, as one would expect, in different factual situations there may be different verdicts open to a jury. The latest case, *Hui Chi-Ming v R*, confirms again that it is possible that a person may be a party to a joint enterprise which leads to death and be guilty of manslaughter although the actual killer may be guilty of murder.

Conclusion

The directions given by Morland J in the present case disclose no error of law. The verdicts of manslaughter were properly open to the jury and were correctly left to them. It is possible to identify a number of confusions in the appellants' arguments and, it appears, in the academic comment. Cases of joint enterprise, properly so termed, should not be confused with cases of counselling or procuring. It may often be the case that the proof of a defendant's *mens rea* is sufficiently proved by proof of this participation in the joint enterprise; the cases cited emphasise this. But it does not follow that this will, or must, always be the case. It is possible that a defendant, whilst being a participant in a joint enterprise and responsible for the unintended consequences of acts done in the course of carrying out that joint enterprise, may lack a specific intent possessed by another participant. In any given case the issue may arise what was the scope of the joint enterprise; depending upon what answer is given to that question, a further question may arise where a crime of specific intent is charged, what was the state of mind of the defendant. The *mens rea* of the defendant may be proved by either method, by proof of participation in a joint enterprise having the requisite character, or, where the joint enterprise proved does not have that character, by proof of a specific intent. Where proof of participation in the joint enterprise during the course of which the relevant act was done is considered to prove only the *mens rea* appropriate to a lesser offence, only the lesser crime will have been proved against that defendant, although the act in question may have involved the commission of a more serious crime by another against whom a specific intent can be proved.

The question whether the relevant act was committed in the course of carrying out the joint enterprise in which the defendant was a participant is a question of fact not law. If the act was not so committed then the joint enterprise ceases to provide a basis for a finding of guilt against such a defendant. He ceases to be responsible for the act. This is the fundamental point illustrated by *R v Anderson and Morris* and *R v Lovesey, R v Peterson*. But it does not follow that a variation in the intent of some of the participants at the time the critical act is done precludes the act from having been done in the course of carrying out the joint enterprise, as is illustrated by *R v Betty* and *R v Reid*.

The appeals against conviction must accordingly be dismissed.

R v Perman [1996] 1 Cr App R 24 (CA)

The appellant knew that the principal offender was armed with a gun but denied any knowledge that it was loaded. The principal offender shot dead a customer in a shop during a robbery. On appeal the court had to consider whether the appellant could be an accomplice to manslaughter.

Roch LJ:

... The Crown's case against the appellant was that there was a joint enterprise between the appellant and his co-defendant to rob this newsagent's, that the appellant had known that his co-defendant had a gun and would use it to threaten and intimidate those in the shop and that in the shop the appellant had played an active, albeit minor, part in the robbery. The unlawful use of the gun had been part of and within the scope of the joint enterprise. Consequently the appellant was guilty of manslaughter, although in the circumstances of the case the Crown did not seek conviction of the appellant on the charge of murder. The appellant's case, as we have already observed, was simply that there was no such joint enterprise and that he had not taken any part at all in the robbery . . .

In the present case, if the appellant did not know that the gun was loaded, and believed that it was unloaded, the scope of the joint enterprise in which he joined was the robbery of those in the shop by the putting of such persons as were in the shop in fear by the use of an unloaded and therefore innocuous gun. The appellant's knowledge that the gun was loaded was crucial to the Crown's case, because if it were proved that he knew the gun was loaded then he was party to a joint enterprise in which those in the shop were to be threatened with a lethal weapon, that is to say were to be subjected to the obvious risk of that weapon being fired in the excitement and tensions of the occasion. That would make him guilty of manslaughter, as is demonstrated by the case of *Reid*.

A joint enterprise to cause fright or hysteria through threats being made with an unloaded and innocuous gun was not sufficient to found a conviction of manslaughter in the circumstances of this case. It was, of course, sufficient to found convictions in respect of the counts of robbery and possession of an offensive weapon with intent. Nevertheless, the judge directed that the defence to the manslaughter count was the same as the defence to the counts of robbery and possession of the offensive weapon with intent. Here again the implication was that even if the appellant did not know the gun was loaded, and believed it to be unloaded, he would be not guilty of murder but he would be guilty of all the other charges he faced, including manslaughter. The true distinction between the appellant being guilty of murder and the appellant being guilty of manslaughter in the circumstances of this case was not the appellant's knowledge that the gun was loaded but the appellant's knowledge that the co-defendant was likely to use the loaded gun to kill or cause grievous bodily harm on the one hand, or was simply going to use the loaded gun to frighten on the other. We conclude that there was here a material misdirection in respect of count 4 . . .

R v Gilmour [2000] 2 Cr App R 407

G appealed successfully against his conviction as an accomplice to murder. He had driven members of a terrorist organisation to a house on the basis that it was to be firebombed. Three young boys living in the house were killed in the ensuing fire. The Court of Appeal of Northern Ireland held that as G had not foreseen the risk that anyone would suffer death or grievous bodily harm, he could not be an accomplice to murder. A conviction for manslaughter could be substituted, however, as G had contemplated the unlawful acts, that is, the petrol bombing, that had caused the deaths.

Carswell LCJ:

. . . The issue then is whether [Gilmour] can be found guilty of manslaughter on the first three counts, on the basis that if the principals had thrown the petrol bomb into the house without the intention of killing or inflicting grievous bodily harm on any person they would have properly been convicted of that offence. It was argued on behalf of the appellant that if he did not share the intention of the principals he should not be found guilty of either murder or manslaughter, in the same way as if the principals go outside the contemplated acts involved in the joint enterprise the accessory cannot be convicted of either offence: see . . . *R v Powell and English* . . .

The issue is discussed in *Blackstone's Criminal Practice* . . . in which the example is posed where the principal and accessory agree that the principal will post an incendiary device to the victim, the accessory contemplating only superficial injuries but the principal foreseeing and hoping that the injuries will be serious or fatal. The principal will be guilty of murder and the accessory will not. The editors conclude that the accessory should in such a case be convicted of manslaughter, because the act done by the principal is precisely what was envisaged.

In our opinion this is the correct principle to apply in the present case. The appellant foresaw that the principals would carry out the act of throwing a petrol bomb into the house, but did not realise that in so doing they intended to kill or do grievous bodily harm to the occupants. To establish that a person charged as an accessory to a crime of specific intent is guilty as an accessory, it is necessary to prove that he realised the principal's intention . . . The line of authority represented by such cases as *Anderson and Morris* [19661 2 QB 110, approved in *R v Powell and English*, deals with situations where the principal departs from the contemplated joint enterprise and perpetrates a more serious act of a different kind unforeseen by the accessory. In such cases it is established that the accessory is not liable at all for such unforeseen acts. It does not follow that the same result should follow where the principal carries out the very act contemplated by the accessory, though the latter does not realise that the principal intends a more serious consequence from the act.

We do not consider that we are obliged by authority to hold that the accessory in such a case must be acquitted of manslaughter as well as murder. The cases in which an accessory has been found not guilty both of murder and manslaughter all concern a departure by the principal from the *actus reus* contemplated by the accessory, not a difference between the parties in respect of the *mens rea* of each. In such cases the view has prevailed that it would be wrong to hold the accessory liable when the principal committed an act which the accessory did not contemplate or authorise. We do not, however, see any convincing policy reason why a person acting as an accessory to a principal who carries out the very deed contemplated by both should not be guilty of the degree of offence appropriate to the intent with which he so acted. It is of course conceivable, as is suggested in Blackstone . . . that in some cases the nature of the principal's *mens rea* may change the nature of the act committed by him and take it outside the type of act contemplated by the accessory, but it does not seem to us that the existence of such a possibility affects the validity of the basic principle which we have propounded. A verdict of guilty of manslaughter on this basis was upheld by the Court of Appeal in Stewart and Schofield (above) . . . Even if there may be ground for criticism of some of the propositions enunciated in the court's judgment, the principle accepted as its basis is in our view sustainable.

Attorney General's Reference (No 3 of 2004) [2005] EWCA Crim 1882

H had hired K and C to terrorise R by threatening R with a loaded gun, discharging it in the vicinity of R if necessary. K and C visited R and killed him by firing the gun at R from point blank range. K and C were convicted of murder and H was convicted of manslaughter. H subsequently appealed successfully against his conviction, the Court of Appeal ordering a retrial. A pre-trial hearing was convened at the start of the second trial to determine whether, even if the Crown could prove the facts it set out to prove, the jury would in law be entitled to conclude that H was guilty of manslaughter. It was agreed that the judge would have to decide the issue on the basis of the following assumed facts: (i) that H had sent K and C to apply pressure on R through terror; (ii) that H had known that K and C would have with them a loaded firearm; (iii) that H had known that, in order to maximise the pressure on R, the firearm might be deliberately discharged near R; and (iv) that H had not intended physically to injure or kill R and had not foreseen the possibility of physical injury or death. On these assumed facts, the trial judge ruled that H's liability as an accomplice to manslaughter could not been made out. The Crown offered no evidence against H and a verdict of not guilty was entered. The Attorney General, under s 36 of the Criminal Justice Act 1972, referred the following point of law for consideration by the Court of Appeal: 'Where a secondary party to a joint enterprise contemplates that the carrying out of the joint enterprise will involve the commission of an act intended to frighten the victim (for example by the discharge of a firearm) and the principal carries out the act with an intention to kill or cause serious bodily harm thus causing the death of the victim, does the variation in the intent of the participants at the time the act is done preclude the act from being part of the joint enterprise or may a jury nevertheless convict the secondary party of manslaughter?' Although the Court of Appeal noted that a complete answer could not be given to the question, partly because of its complexity, and partly because of the rather unusual nature of the assumed facts in this case, the trial judge's decision on there not being a basis for liability as an accomplice to manslaughter had been correct.

Hooper LJ:

18. There is no dispute that, on the assumed facts, H could have been convicted of manslaughter if the deliberate discharge of the firearm by K or C had accidentally caused R's death or if the firearm had accidentally been discharged and caused R's death. Both H and the principals would be guilty of manslaughter by an unlawful act if the jury found that 'all sober and reasonable people would inevitably realise [that such an act] must subject the victim to, at least, the risk of some harm resulting therefrom, albeit not serious harm' (*Church* [1966] 1 QB 59, at 70) . . .

19. What caused the death of R was the deliberate discharge by K of the firearm aimed at R. However, the judge had to assume that H had not foreseen the possibility of physical injury or death, let alone the deliberate causing of death. H had contemplated the deliberate discharge of the firearm (on the assumed facts) but not at R. The question in this case is whether the fact that H had not foreseen the possibility of physical injury or death means that he is not guilty of manslaughter even though he could have been guilty of manslaughter (the other ingredients being satisfied) if the gun had been deliberately discharged and had accidentally killed R or had accidentally been discharged with the same fatal result.

20. The Attorney General submits that H is guilty of manslaughter because if the primary party had carried out his plan and R had been shot accidentally, H would have been guilty of manslaughter. The fact that the primary party went further and murdered R should not affect H's criminal responsibility for manslaughter.

21. Mr Perry [for the Attorney-General] relies on public policy to support his argument. If H would have been guilty of manslaughter if death had been caused accidentally by the primary party carrying out the plan to frighten R, then it would be quite wrong if the fact that the primary party went outside the scope of the plan prevented his conviction for manslaughter. What distinguishes

what was planned to happen and what did happen is only the decision by K to shoot R rather than frighten R by discharging the gun. Instead of discharging the gun with the intent to frighten, K discharged the gun with intent to kill (or cause grievous bodily harm).

22. Courts have recognised the apparent anomaly in acquitting a party of manslaughter when the primary party goes beyond the scope of the joint enterprise and kills. As Carswell J said in *Gamble* [1989] N.I. 268, at 284, the anomaly is on its face difficult to accept . . .

23. It is sometimes suggested that the rule enables a defendant in these circumstances to escape criminal liability altogether. It does not. Mr Perry accepted that if the trial indictment had contained a count or counts to reflect the criminality of the plan to frighten with a gun, H could have duly been convicted and received substantial punishment. Not only, so Mr Perry submits, would it be difficult for the prosecution to anticipate what counts are needed, but the additional count or counts would overload the indictment. We find this an unconvincing argument. To convict a person of manslaughter simply because of the supposed difficulty of drafting appropriate alternative counts (or because of the failure to do so at the first trial) seems wrong to us. Prosecutors were warned of the danger of not including alternative offences in *Greatrex and Bates* [1999] 1 C App R 126.

24. Whether the rule is a good rule or a bad rule, there is no doubt, and Mr Perry accepts this, that if the primary party goes outside the scope of the joint enterprise (whatever that may mean) then the secondary party is not guilty of murder or manslaughter. He would not be guilty of manslaughter even though he would be guilty of manslaughter (the other ingredients being satisfied) if the plan had been carried out as envisaged and death had accidentally been caused. There is no dispute about that and could not be on the law as it stands, confirmed as it was in Powell and English.

25. Thus if the killing is within the scope of joint enterprise, the secondary party is guilty of murder, if he has the necessary *mens rea* for a secondary party (foresight of possibility), or manslaughter if he has the necessary very reduced *mens rea* for manslaughter – provided, of course, the other ingredients of the relevant offence are established.

26. In this case, if the killing of R was inside the scope of the joint enterprise, then the jury could properly have convicted H of manslaughter on the assumed facts in the particular circumstances set out in paragraph 18 above.

27. There is no dispute that the same joint enterprise principles to a secondary party whether he is present or absent from the scene (see e.g. *Rook* [1997] Cr App R 327). The same issues arise in the case of H and C, although the answers may well be different.

28. This case is concerned with the test for deciding whether an act is or is not within the scope of a joint enterprise. Other phrases are also used to describe 'joint enterprise', such as common design and joint venture, but we shall use the phrase 'joint enterprise'.

29. It is clear after Powell and English that if the secondary party realised that in the course of the joint enterprise the primary party might kill with intent to do so or with intent to cause grievous bodily harm, then the secondary party is guilty of murder. The killing, with the necessary intent, having been foreseen as a possibility by the secondary party, will be or will, as Mr Cox [counsel for H] accepted, almost certainly be within the scope of the joint enterprise. On the assumed facts, H did not have that foresight.

30. It would also follow that if the secondary party realised that in the course of the joint enterprise the primary party might kill in circumstances which in law amounted to manslaughter, then the secondary party is guilty of manslaughter. The killing, having been foreseen as a possibility by the secondary party, will be (or almost certainly will be) within the scope of the joint enterprise. On the assumed facts H did not have that foresight.

31. The first question referred to this Court by the Attorney General asks whether the secondary party is guilty of manslaughter if he contemplates the commission of an unlawful act to frighten and the principal carries out that act with the necessary intention for murder. Would the killing be within the scope of the joint enterprise?

32. Mr Perry concedes (rightly in our view) that the test for whether what the primary party did is within or outside the scope of the joint enterprise requires the application of a subjective test. Did the secondary party foresee the possibility that the primary party would do what he did? It is preferable to define the scope of the joint enterprise in this way rather than by using such language as 'Did the act go beyond what had tacitly been agreed?' or 'Did he depart from the concerted action of the common design?'. That is established by Powell and English (see e.g. 31C–D). Nor is a test fashioned on the law of causation probably very helpful. Earlier cases which talk of 'must have anticipated' may also now be ignored.

33. The issue in this case is what does the secondary party have to have foreseen as a possibility? There is no dispute between Mr Perry and Mr Cox that it is an act and in the case of English, as in this case, it is the act which caused the death. Lord Hutton in Powell and English said:

> The first issue is what is the degree of foresight required to impose liability under the principle stated in *Chan Wing-Siu* [1985] AC 168. On this issue I am in respectful agreement with the judgment of the Privy Council in that case that the secondary party is subject to criminal liability if he contemplated *the act causing the death* as a possible incident of the joint venture, unless the risk was so remote that the jury take the view that the secondary party genuinely dismissed it as altogether negligible. [Emphasis added]

34. Mr Perry says: the act which caused the death in the instant case was the deliberate discharge of a loaded gun. If H foresaw that as a possibility (and H did on the assumed facts), he could be convicted of manslaughter, the deliberate discharge of the gun being within the scope of the joint enterprise. Given that the risk of manslaughter was within the scope of the joint enterprise to frighten by discharging a loaded gun, the fact, in this case, that the primary party went further and deliberately shot R with the loaded gun does not and cannot take the act of the primary party outside the scope of the joint enterprise.

35. Mr Cox says: the act which caused the death was the deliberate discharge of a loaded gun deliberately pointed at R. Anything less than the foresight of the possibility of the deliberate discharge of the gun at R takes the killing outside the scope of the joint enterprise and H is not guilty of manslaughter.

36. We note in passing that, if the defendant had that foresight then, as a matter of fact, he is likely to be convicted of murder. A jury is likely to conclude that the defendant realised that in the course of the joint enterprise the primary party might kill with intent to do so or with intent to cause grievous bodily harm. However a conviction is not inevitable as the case of *Gamble* shows.

37. The problem of defining the test to determine whether the act of the primary party was, or was not, within the scope of the joint enterprise is further complicated by the fact that manslaughter and murder both require the defendant to have unlawfully caused the death of someone and that the difference between the two offences lies only in the mental element. Murder requires intent to kill or cause grievous bodily harm (for the primary party) whereas manslaughter requires only the *mens rea* of the unlawful act which caused the death. There is the added complication that the offence of manslaughter requires no foresight even of injury. Mr Perry argues that the only difference between what H had in mind and what happened was that K had the necessary *mens rea* for murder. That he submits, relying on authority, is insufficient to take the deliberate shooting at K outside the scope of the joint enterprise. . . .

39. The question (it is agreed) being 'What was the act which caused the death?', we take the view, untrammelled by any authority, that the answer to that question is the answer given by Mr Cox and not that given by Mr Perry. If a person was asked what caused R's death, he would answer, we think, K shot him and he might add at point blank range. If he did give Mr Perry's answer (he deliberately discharged the loaded gun), the questioner would then say 'At him?', to which the answer would be 'Yes'.

40. In *Powell and English*, Lord Hutton said:

> . . . there will be cases giving rise to a fine distinction as to whether or not the unforeseen use of a particular weapon or the manner in which a particular weapon is used will take a killing outside the scope of the joint venture, but this issue will be one of fact for the common sense of the jury to decide.

41. Mr Cox stresses the words 'the manner in which a particular weapon is used'. On the assumed facts, H knew that the gun would be discharged to frighten, K's use of it to shoot R takes it outside the scope of the joint venture. Applying Lord Hutton's words to this case, it seems to us that Mr Cox must be right.

42. Nor do we think that Mr Perry's public policy arguments are as strong as he contends. If A and B agree that B will unlawfully give V a light punch and, unforeseen as a possibility by A, B 'goes mad' and, by punching kills V intending to kill V or cause him grievous bodily harm, why should A be guilty of manslaughter simply because if V had fallen to the ground as a result of the slap, A would have been guilty of manslaughter?

43. The public policy argument may seem to have more force in this case because of the assumed facts. But the assumed facts have a measure of unreality about them. If H had been charged with murder and, on the assumption that the jury were sure of the assumed facts, then a jury might have had little difficulty in concluding that H realised that the primary party might kill in circumstances amounting to manslaughter. The jury might well find that unlawfully discharging a loaded gun near R carried with it that risk and that H was aware of that risk. However, in this case, the assumed facts precluded such a finding because, on the assumed facts, H had not foreseen the possibility of physical injury or death to V. The peculiar 'facts' of this case should not be used in support of Mr Perry's public policy argument. Nor does the public policy argument find support in Powell and English.

. . .

54. In the instant case Sir Stephen Mitchell ruled that the act done by K was of a fundamentally different character from any act contemplated by H. We agree.

COMMENTS AND QUESTIONS

1   A and P agree that P will attack V with an iron bar whilst A acts as a look-out. They agree that P will only wound V. P attacks V intending to cause grievous bodily harm and V dies from his injuries. P is convicted of murder. On the basis of *R v Stewart and Schofield* (above) A will be an accomplice to manslaughter. Why is it that P's decision to use the iron bar with more deadly intent than that agreed between A and P is not a deliberate departure from the scope of the joint enterprise? Is it right to anchor the concept of the scope of the joint enterprise to the principal's actions and not the intent with which he carries them out? See further *R v Robert Roberts, Stephens and Day* [2001] EWCA Crim 1594 where Laws LJ gave the following example:

> Suppose that the participants in a joint enterprise all propose or foresee the same kind of violence being inflicted on their victim, let it be punching with the possibility of kicking to follow. On that they are at one. But two of them harbour a subjective intention to inflict very serious injury by means of such violence. The third harbours only, or foresees or intends only, that some harm might be done. One of those actuated by intent to do grievous bodily harm punches or kicks the victim just as all three foresaw. The victim falls and suffers a subdural haemorrhage and dies. The principal is guilty of murder as he had the *mens rea* required. So also is the accessory who, like him, intended or contemplated the infliction of the serious injury. What of the third adventurer? Mr Fitzgerald submits he must escape altogether because he did not foresee a murderous state of mind would be harboured by his fellows. Yet if his fellows had entertained only an intention to do some harm and otherwise the facts were the same all three would be guilty of manslaughter. It does not seem to us that that can be right. In such a case there was a joint enterprise at least to inflict some harm, and that is not negated by the larger intentions of the other two adventurers. In our judgment in such a case there is no reason why the participants should not be convicted and sentenced appropriately as their several states of mind dictate . . .

See further *R v D* [2005] EWCA 1981.

7.9.4 LAW REFORM PROPOSALS

In Law Com 300, *Inchoate Liability for Assisting and Encouraging Crime*, the Law Commission set out its recommendations for reforming the law relating to defendants who play some preparatory role towards the commission of an offence where the principal offender, for whatever reason, does not commit the completed offence. The details of these reforms are considered at Chapter 8.2.4.

The Law Commission has moved from its previous position, to the effect that secondary liability should be abolished, to a position that it should be retained but reformed. The recommendations for reform are likely to be published in 2007. In Law Com 300, however, the Commission outlined the drivers for the reforms:

1.21 In relation to secondary liability, there is a major issue on which we would like to have the benefit of informed views before we make a final decision. The issue is the correct approach to be adopted (as a matter of policy) to the drafting of new statutory offences to replace the existing common law on secondary liability, particularly against the background of our continuing commitment to codification of the criminal law. The choice for us is, in essence, between two competing approaches.

1.22 The first approach would be to cast the inculpatory provisions imposing secondary liability in quite detailed terms, catering for a variety of circumstances. Adopting this approach would require broad defences to ensure that the Bill did not impose secondary liability where it would be unreasonable to do so. The other approach would be a draft Bill that imposes secondary liability in a more open-textured form, leaving greater scope for judicial development of the principles of liability laid down in the Bill. The provisions imposing secondary liability would, on this approach, be supplemented by a limited number of specific defences and exemptions.

1.23 The issue of the correct approach to the drafting of the Bill as respects secondary liability has greatly exercised us and, indeed, continues to do so. The same issue does not, in our view, arise in relation to the specific new statutory inchoate offences to prohibit the encouragement or assistance of crime. It is for this reason that we feel able to proceed with this report and the draft Bill that accompanies it, before publishing our proposals for reforming the law of secondary liability. In addition, we believe that inchoate liability for encouraging or assisting crime is a matter that merits urgent attention.

Despite its preference for deferring a review of secondary liability as a whole, In Law Com 304 – *Murder, Manslaughter and Infanticide*, the Commission opted to review the law relating accessorial liability for murder. Reflecting the proposals for the reform of the homicide offences contained in the main body of the report, the Commission recommended that (using D for accomplice and P for principal offender):

4.47 . . . D should be liable to be convicted of P's offence of first or second degree murder (as the case may be) if:

(1)   D intended to assist or encourage P to commit the relevant offence; or
(2)   D was engaged in a joint criminal venture with P, and realised that P, or another party to the joint venture, might commit the relevant offence.

4.48 . . . D should be liable for manslaughter if the following conditions are met:

(1)   D and P were parties to a joint venture to commit an offence;
(2)   P committed the offence of first degree murder or second degree murder in relation to the fulfilment of that venture;
(3)   D intended or foresaw that (non-serious) harm or the fear of harm might be caused by a party to the venture; and
(4)   a reasonable person in D's position, with D's knowledge of the relevant facts, would have foreseen an obvious risk of death or serious injury being caused by a party to the venture.

The Report provides the background to these conclusions:

Complicity in murder committed by another person

1.39 A serious problem has arisen in murder cases with regard to what lawyers call the doctrine of 'complicity', that is, involving oneself in a criminal enterprise with another who commits murder. A typical example might be where A, B and C see V (a supporter of a rival football team), walking home alone. They set upon V punching and kicking him. When V falls over, B produces a knife and stabs V through the heart. A and C say that (i) although they knew that B sometimes carried a knife, they did not know he would use it on this occasion, and (ii) they did not have murder in mind when attacking V.

1.40 In this example, B is likely to be found guilty of murder as a principal offender. The question is: are A and C involved in the killing in some way that is sufficiently culpable to warrant being guilty of a homicide offence? The law currently answers this question by telling the jury to ask itself whether there was a 'fundamental difference' between what A and C thought might happen and what B did. If the jury thinks that there was such a fundamental difference, then A and C are guilty of no homicide offence at all. A and C will be guilty of assaulting V, but assault is obviously a much lesser offence than murder or manslaughter.

1.41 We believe that this represents a gap in the law. It should be possible to convict A and C of a homicide offence. This gap appears especially significant when people in A and C's position knew from the start of the joint criminal venture that the person who eventually commits the murder was armed. In such circumstances, the mere fact that they did not foresee that the armed participant would actually commit murder should not absolve A and C from all responsibility for the homicide.

1.42 In the CP, we put forward a proposal for filling this gap. It was that A and C should be guilty of manslaughter if:

(1) they were engaged in a joint criminal venture with B; and
(2) it should have been obvious to them that B might commit first or second degree murder in the course of that joint criminal venture.

This would mean that A and C could not escape responsibility for the homicide simply by denying that they knew B might commit murder if this should have been obvious to them. This is especially likely to be the case when they knew that the eventual killer was already armed. The vast majority of consultees supported the proposal . . .

1.43 Moreover, we will also recommend that if A, B and C are engaged in a joint criminal enterprise and A and C do realise that B might commit murder in the fulfilment of the joint venture, or intend that B does so, then A and C should be guilty of murder along with B. The crucial difference is A and C's awareness of what B may or will do. This awareness makes it justifiable to convict A and C of murder, not just manslaughter . . .

PART 4 COMPLICITY IN MURDER – OUR RECOMMENDATIONS
D'S LIABILITY FOR FIRST DEGREE MURDER
4.9 Our view is that the concept of 'joint venture' should be defined broadly to cover criminal ventures following on from a conspiracy or an informal 'tacit agreement' involving two or more individuals; but it should also extend to the type of situation where D encouraged or assisted P to commit a crime (such as an offence of violence outside a public house) and they acted with a common purpose notwithstanding the absence of any prior agreement between them. . . .

4.11 We expected the third basis for determining D's liability to be the most controversial aspect of our proposals on complicity, given that D would be guilty of first degree murder on the 'mere' basis that D foresaw that another party to the joint venture might commit it. However, this third basis, reflecting the position at common law, was strongly supported by most of our consultees who addressed the issue. Our view continues to be that this foundation for liability is fully justifiable, on the following basis:

(1) We are recommending a narrower fault requirement for the offence of first degree murder than currently applies to murder, albeit broader than the definition we originally proposed in the CP. The prosecution would have to prove beyond reasonable doubt, first, that both D and P were parties to a joint criminal venture and, secondly, that D foresaw that P or another party might act with the intention to kill (or with the intention to cause serious injury allied with awareness of a serious risk of death). What justifies D's liability for first degree murder is not simply that D was aware that P might act with extreme violence in the course of their joint venture, but that P might do so with one of these intentions.

(2) D carries additional fault on account of being involved in a joint venture with P to commit a crime. Individuals who perform criminal acts in groups have been shown to be more disposed to act violently than those who act alone, and this can be taken to be common knowledge.

(3) A test of foresight of a realistic possibility is an acceptable basis for joint venture liability, given the increased culpability that comes with being involved in a criminal venture; but it is in any event the only practicable test for criminal proceedings in England and Wales. In particular, D should not be able to avoid liability for first degree murder on the mere basis of a mistaken understanding of the degree of likelihood involved, and the prosecution should not be expected to prove (beyond reasonable doubt) the actual degree of likelihood D contemplated.

4.12 Nevertheless, we accept that some consultees regard this test of foresight as unduly harsh, given that a perpetrator can be liable for first degree murder under our proposals only if he or she intended to kill or intended to cause serious injury with awareness of a serious risk of death . . .

D'S LIABILITY FOR SECOND DEGREE MURDER

4.31 Some of our consultees wondered what the position would be under our proposals in relation to second degree murder. The answer, of course, is that the general principles of our proposed doctrine of secondary liability would apply in this context too.

4.32 Suppose D assists or encourages P, or agrees with P, to attack V with a view to causing V serious harm, but not death; or suppose that D and P agree to commit burglary and D foresees that P might intentionally attack a householder (V) with the intention to cause serious harm, but not death. Then, if P committed second degree murder against V by virtue of P's having the intention to cause serious harm and causing V's death, D too would be liable for second degree murder.

4.33 A similar position obtains with respect to our recommended alternative fault element for second degree murder (see Part 2). Under our recommendations D would be liable for second degree murder if P killed V with the intention to cause harm or fear or risk of harm, in the belief that his or her conduct involved a serious risk of causing death, if D acted with the same state of mind or D believed that P might act with that state of mind during the course of the burglary.

> 4.34 D is also guilty of second degree murder if he or she assists or encourages P, or agrees with P, to inflict serious harm on V, but P goes on to commit first degree murder in consequence. In committing first degree murder P also necessarily commits second degree murder and D possessed the fault element for the latter offence. The discretionary life sentence, which would apply to second degree murder, will ensure that justice is done in these types of case, in terms of the appropriate penalty D should suffer bearing in mind what he or she intended or contemplated.

7.10 THE RELATIONSHIP BETWEEN THE LIABILITY OF THE PRINCIPAL AND THE ACCOMPLICE

As noted above, the common law approach to accessorial liability is derivative, in the sense that the liability of the accomplice is derived from that of the principal offender. If there are difficulties in establishing the liability of the principal offender there may be consequences for accessorial liability.

A number of possibilities exist:

- Principal offender acquitted because no *actus reus* is proved against him;
- Principal offender acquitted because he lacks *mens rea*;
- Principal offender charged with or convicted of a less serious offence than the accomplice because he has less *mens rea* than the accomplice;
- Principal offender has a partial offence not available to the accomplice that reduces his liability;
- Principal offender has a complete defence not available to the accomplice.

Only the first of these possibilities presents an insurmountable problem for the prosecution. Whatever the principal's *mens rea*, for accessorial liability there has to be an *actus reus* to which the accomplice is a party.

7.10.1 NO *ACTUS REUS* ON THE PART OF THE PRINCIPAL OFFENDER

> ### *Thornton v Mitchell* [1940] 1 All ER 339 (KBD)
>
> Lord Hewart LCJ:
> In my opinion, it is quite clear that this appeal must be allowed. Informations were preferred by the respondent, a superintendent of police, against a certain motor driver, one Hollinrake, for driving a motor vehicle – that is to say, an omnibus – without due care and attention, contrary to s 12(1) of the Road Traffic Act 1930, and also against the same driver for driving a motor vehicle – that is to say, a motor omnibus – without reasonable consideration for other persons using the road. At the same time, the bus conductor was charged as an aider and abettor. The information alleged that Hollinrake did unlawfully drive the motor vehicle without due care and attention, and that the

present appellant, who was a bus conductor, unlawfully did aid, abet counsel and procure Hollinrake to do and commit that offence. There was a further charge against the bus conductor under the second information, whereby the driver was charged with driving 'without reasonable consideration for other persons using the road'. In the result, the justices dismissed the two charges against the driver, but convicted the appellant of unlawfully aiding, abetting counselling and procuring the driver to do and commit the offence of driving without due care and attention, contrary to s 12(1). They say in para 8:

> We, being of opinion that the conductor [had been very negligent], held that he was guilty of aiding and abetting, counselling and procuring the said Hollinrake to drive without due care and attention, and accordingly we inflicted a fine.

In my opinion, this case is *a fortiori* upon *Morris v Tolman* [1923] 1 KB 166, to which our attention has been directed. I will read one sentence from the judgment of Avory J at 171:

> . . . in order to convict, it would be necessary to show that the respondent was aiding the principal, but a person cannot aid another in doing something which that other has not done.

That, I think is the very thing which these justices have decided that this bus conductor did. In one breath they say that the principal did nothing which he should not have done, and in the next breath they hold that the bus conductor aided and abetted the driver in doing something which had not been done or in not doing something which he ought to have done. I really think that, with all respect to the ingenuity of counsel for the respondent, the case is too plain for argument, and this appeal must be allowed and the conviction quashed.

R v Loukes [1996] 1 Cr App R 444 (CA)

Auld LJ:

. . . Mr Loukes and his brother, Ian Loukes, were partners in a haulage contractors. Mr Loukes's role in the business was to oversee the maintenance and servicing by the firm's mechanics of its fleet of vehicles. Ian Loukes drove some of the vehicles and had other responsibilities, but none of them included the servicing of vehicles. Ronnie Kennedy was one of the firm's drivers.

On 10 July 1993 Mr Kennedy was driving an ERF tipper truck of the firm along the northbound carriageway of the M1. Part of the prop shaft broke free and flew across the crash barrier into the path of a vehicle travelling in the southbound carriageway, killing its driver. The police examined the vehicle, and as a result Mr Kennedy was charged with causing death by dangerous driving, and Mr Loukes and his brother were charged with aiding, abetting, counselling or procuring that offence.

At the trial the prosecution case against Mr Loukes was that he caused the truck to be driven by Mr Kennedy when he, Mr Loukes, knew or ought to have known that it was in a dangerous state. PC Logan, an accident investigation officer, gave evidence about the truck's transmission system of which the prop shaft was a part. He said that the system had several pre-accident defects which, together, had caused lateral movements in the sliding joints of the system, which in turn had caused the prop shaft to become loose and fly off . . .

As to the mechanics of the prop shaft breaking free, PC Logan's opinion was that the nut had become loose and had eventually become detached from the flange, allowing the flange to move partly away from the shaft, hence the worn splines and grooves on the shaft. He said that he would have expected that last damage to have occurred about four hours before the castellated nut worked its way completely free of the flange, allowing the prop shaft to break away. He added that during that period of loosening of the nut there would have been additional noise and vibration detectable to the driver. His conclusion in summary was that an examination of the underside of the vehicle before the accident would have revealed the defects in the flange, and that it would have been obvious there was a danger of that part of the prop shaft breaking free and causing an accident . . .

At the close of the prosecution case the judge upheld submissions of no case to answer on behalf of Ian Loukes and Ronnie Kennedy, but rejected a similar submission on behalf of Mr Loukes.

Mr Loukes did not give evidence or call any witnesses. His defence, as presented by his counsel to the jury, was that, although the truck had been in a dangerous state, there was no evidence that the defects alleged to have been dangerous and to have caused the accident, did cause it, and, in any event, no evidence that he had known of its dangerous state.

The first ground of appeal is that the judge, having directed the jury to acquit Mr Kennedy of the principal offence, misdirected the jury by directing them that Mr Loukes could be found guilty of the secondary offence. His case, in reliance on the well-known authority of *Thornton v Mitchell* [1940] 1 All ER 339, is that the judge directed the acquittal of Mr Kennedy because there was no evidence that he had committed the *actus reus* of the offence, and that, therefore, he, Mr Loukes, could not be convicted of procuring it. He accepts, in reliance on *Millward* [1994] Crim LR 527, that if the judge properly directed the acquittal of Mr Kennedy only for want of evidence of *mens rea*, he, Mr Loukes, could be convicted of the secondary offence.

The principle upon which the court proceeded in *Millward* was that the procurer of another to commit the *actus reus* of an offence may be convicted of procuring it even if that other is not guilty of it for want of *mens rea*. The critical question here is 'What is the *actus reus* of the new offence of causing death by dangerous driving?'

Mr Loukes was charged with aiding, abetting, counselling or procuring Mr Kennedy to cause death by dangerous driving, contrary to ss 1 and 2A(2) of the Road Traffic Act 1988, as amended on 1 July 1992 by the Road Traffic Act 1991. The effect of that amendment was to substitute the offence of causing death by dangerous driving for that of causing death by reckless driving. The material provisions of ss 1 and 2A of the 1988 Act read:

1 A person who causes the death of another by driving a mechanically propelled vehicle dangerously on a road or other public place is guilty of an offence.

2A(1) For the purposes of s 1 . . . above a person is to be regarded as driving dangerously if (and, subject to subsection (2) below, only if):

 (a) the way he drives falls far below what would be expected of a competent and careful driver, and

 (b) it would be obvious to a competent and careful driver that driving in that way would be dangerous.

(2) A person is also to be regarded as driving dangerously for the purposes of s 1 . . . if it would be obvious to a competent and careful driver that driving the vehicle in its current state would be dangerous.

(3) . . . in determining . . . what would be . . . obvious to . . . a competent and careful driver

in a particular case, regard shall be had not only to the circumstances of which he could be expected to be aware but also to any circumstances shown to have been within the knowledge of the accused.

By reference to ss 1 and 2A(2), the principal offence charged, giving rise to the secondary charge against Mr Loukes, was that Mr Kennedy caused death by driving the vehicle when it would have been obvious to a competent and careful driver that to do so in its then state would be dangerous . . .

It is implicit in the judge's ruling on the submission on behalf of Mr Loukes that he did not regard the *actus reus* as including any element of constructive knowledge of a notional competent and careful driver. In his definition of the *actus reus* he was clearly influenced by the decision of this court in Millward, a case concerning the procuring of the former offence of causing death by reckless driving, the recklessness relating to a defect in the vehicle and not to the manner of driving. The court there held that the *actus reus* of the principal offence lay in the taking of the vehicle on the road in a defective condition so as to cause death. It held that a procurer could be found guilty even though the driver was not, and that the *mens rea* of the procurer lay in the causing of that *actus reus* knowing of the vehicle's defective condition, whether or not it was or should have been known to the driver. The decision has been expressly approved by another division of this court in *Wheelhouse* [1994] Crim LR 756. As Professor Sir John Smith observed in a commentary in [1994] Crim LR 528–30, it:

. . . breaks new ground, being the first case to decide that procuring the *actus reus* of an offence is itself that offence . . .

The drafting of the new provisions is tortuous, but their intent is plain, namely that a driver is guilty of an offence if, measured by an objective standard, his driving is dangerous. The standard might be said to be one of constructive blameworthiness, namely a constructive knowledge of danger – what should have been obvious to him because it would have been obvious to a competent and careful driver who also knew what he did. This is close to the first, alternative part of the Lawrence test of recklessness applicable to the former offence of reckless driving, namely driving in a way so as to create an obvious risk of danger without having given any thought to it . . .

The purpose of the 1991 amendment was to resolve that uncertainty by introducing a wholly objective test and thus an absolute offence. In our view, it has achieved that. *Mens rea* plays no part in the principal offence. Proof of guilt depends on an objective standard of driving, namely what would have been obvious to a competent and careful driver. The accused driver's state of mind is relevant only if and to the extent that it attributes additional knowledge to the notional competent and careful driver. See the commentary to *Woodward* [1995] Crim LR 487; and the commentary to *Skelton* [1995] Crim LR 635. It should be noted too that the threshold of proof is high. It must be shown that the defect was 'obvious' to a 'competent and careful driver'. It is not enough to show in the case of such a driver that, say, if he had examined the vehicle by going underneath it, he would have seen the defect. See *Strong* [1995] Crim LR 428.

The effect of the judge's ruling in withdrawing from the jury the case against Mr Kennedy was that there was no dangerous driving here because, not only was there no evidence that he knew of the dangerous condition, but also – the critical test – no evidence that it would have been obvious to a competent and careful driver. It follows that the effect, though not the form, of the judge's ruling was that there was no evidence of the commission of the *actus reus* of the offence.

Where does that conclusion leave the conviction of Mr Loukes as an alleged procurer of a non-existent offence? We do not consider Millward to be of help in the new statutory context. It was essential to the decision in that case that there was evidence of the commission of the *actus reus*. Scott Baker J, giving the judgment of the court, said:

> ... the *actus reus* ... was the taking of the vehicle in the defective condition on the road so as to cause the death.

For reasons we have given, the *actus reus* of the new offence of dangerous driving is broader, its criterion being the objective one of obviousness to a competent and careful driver, whether or not supplemented by any particular knowledge of the accused driver. In the offence of reckless driving, there was scope for consideration of *mens rea*, however faint on the first alternative in the Lawrence test, and it was certainly an element of the second alternative. Here there is no room for it.

Accordingly, we are of the view that the Millward principle does not enable conviction of an alleged procurer of causing death by dangerous driving where the dangerous driving as defined in s 2A(2) has not been established. In our view, this case is governed by *Thornton v Mitchell*. A man cannot be convicted of procuring an offence where the *actus reus* is not established. That is enough to dispose of the appeal in Mr Loukes's favour ...

... [F]or the reasons that we have given, we allow the appeal on the first ground, that Mr Loukes could not procure an offence, the *actus reus* of which – all of the offence in this case – has not been committed. The case of *Millward* [1994] Crim LR 527 was decided after the change in the law, and the problem that the court had to consider there does not appear to have been considered in the Road Traffic Review Report (the North Report), Department of Transport and Home Office 1988, the Government White Paper, The Road User and the Law, February 1989 (Cmd 576) or in the passage of the Bill which became the 1991 Act through Parliament. If we are correct in our interpretation of the new provisions, a person who, knowing of the dangerous state of a vehicle, procures another, innocent of that dangerous state, to drive it, and where there is no evidence that that state would have been obvious to a competent and careful driver, will escape conviction. In our view, that injustice can only be cured by legislation ...

7.10.2 PRINCIPAL OFFENDER LACKS *MENS REA* OR HAS LESS *MENS REA* THAN THE ACCOMPLICE

R v Cogan and Leak [1976] 1 QB 217 (CA)

Lawton LJ:

... The indictment in the statement of offence charged Cogan with rape and Leak as 'being aider and abettor to the same offence'. The particulars of offence against Cogan were in common form. As against Leak they were as follows: 'at the same time and place did aid and abet counsel and procure John Rodney Cogan to commit the said offence'.

The victim of the conduct which the prosecution submitted was rape by both defendants was Leak's wife, a slightly built young woman in her early 20s. They had been married in 1969. There had been many quarrels and some violence. On 9 July 1974, Leak came home in the evening under the influence of alcohol. He asked his wife for money. She refused to give him any. Shortly afterwards he attacked her. He knocked her down and while she was on the floor he kicked her many times. She sustained numerous bruises on her back and hip. At his trial he pleaded guilty to this assault.

The next day Leak came home at about 6 pm with Cogan. Both had been drinking. Leak told his wife that Cogan wanted to have sexual intercourse with her and that he, Leak, was going to see she did. She was frightened of him and what he might do, as well she might have been. He made her go upstairs where he took her clothes off and lowered her on to a bed. Cogan then came into the room. Leak asked him twice whether he wanted sexual intercourse with her. On both occasions he said that he did not. Leak then had sexual intercourse with her in the presence of Cogan. When he had finished, Leak again asked Cogan if he wanted sexual intercourse with his wife. This time Cogan said he did. He asked Leak to leave the room but he refused to do so. Cogan then had sexual intercourse with Mrs Leak. Her husband watched. While all this was going on for most of the time, if not all, Mrs Leak was sobbing. She did not struggle when Cogan was on top of her but she did try to turn away from him. When he had finished, he left the room. Leak then had intercourse with her again and behaved in a revolting fashion to her. When he had finished he joined Cogan and the pair of them left the house to renew their drinking. Mrs Leak dressed. She went to a neighbour's house and then to the police. The two defendants were arrested about three-quarters of an hour later. Both made oral and written statements. Leak did not give evidence.

Leak's statement amounted to a confession that he had procured Cogan to have sexual intercourse with his wife. He admitted that while Cogan was having sexual intercourse with her she was 'sobbing on and off not all the time'. There was ample evidence from the terms of his statement that she had not consented to Cogan having intercourse with her. The whole tenor of this statement was that he had procured Cogan to do what he did in order to punish her for past misconduct. He intended that she should be raped and that Cogan's body should provide the physical means to an end.

Cogan, in his written statement, admitted that he had had sexual intercourse with Mrs Leak at Leak's suggestion and that while he was on top of her she had been upset and had cried. At the trial Cogan gave evidence that he thought Mrs Leak had consented. The basis of his belief was what he had heard from her husband about her. The drink he had had seems to have been a reason, if not the only one, for mistaking her sobs and distress for consent . . .

Cogan's appeal against conviction was based on the ground that the decision of the House of Lords in *R v Morgan* [1976] AC 182 applied. It did. There is nothing more to be said. It was for this reason that we allowed the appeal and quashed his conviction.

Leak's appeal against conviction was based on the proposition that he could not be found guilty of aiding and abetting Cogan to rape his wife if Cogan was acquitted of that offence as he was deemed in law to have been when his conviction was quashed: see s 2(3) of the Criminal Appeal Act 1968 . . .

. . . [H]ere one fact is clear – the wife had been raped. Cogan had had sexual intercourse with her without her consent. The fact that Cogan was innocent of rape because he believed that she was consenting does not affect the position that she was raped.

Her ravishment had come about because Leak had wanted it to happen and had taken action to see that it did by persuading Cogan to use his body as the instrument for the necessary physical act. In the language of the law the act of sexual intercourse without the wife's consent was the *actus reus*: it had been procured by Leak who had the appropriate *mens rea*, namely his intention that Cogan should have sexual intercourse with her without her consent. In our judgment it is irrelevant that the man whom Leak had procured to do the physical act himself did not intend to have sexual intercourse with the wife without her consent. Leak was using him as a means to procure a criminal purpose.

Before 1861 a case such as this, pleaded as it was in the indictment, might have presented a court with problems arising from the old distinctions between principals and accessories in felony. Most of the old law was swept away by s 8 of the Accessories and Abettors Act 1861 and what remained by s 1 of the Criminal Law Act 1967. The modern law allowed Leak to be tried and punished as a principal offender. In our judgment he could have been indicted as a principal offender . . .

Had Leak been indicted as a principal offender, the case against him would have been clear beyond argument. Should he be allowed to go free because he was charged with 'being aider and abettor to the same offence'? If we are right in our opinion that the wife had been raped (and no one outside a court of law would say that she had not been), then the particulars of offence accurately stated what Leak had done, namely he had procured Cogan to commit the offence. This would suffice to uphold the conviction. We would prefer, however, to uphold it on a wider basis. In our judgment convictions should not be upset because of mere technicalities of pleading in an indictment. Leak knew what the case against him was and the facts in support of that case were proved. But for the fact that the jury thought that Cogan in his intoxicated condition might have mistaken the wife's sobs and distress for expressions of her consent, no question of any kind would have arisen about the form of pleading. By his written statement Leak virtually admitted what he had done. As Judge Chapman said in *R v Humphreys* [1965] 3 All ER 689, 692:

> It would be anomalous if a person who admitted to a substantial part in the perpetration of a misdemeanour as aider and abettor could not be convicted on his own admission merely because the person alleged to have been aided and abetted was not or could not be convicted.

In the circumstances of this case it would be more than anomalous: it would be an affront to justice and to the common sense of ordinary folk . . .

7.10.3 PRINCIPAL OFFENDER HAS A DEFENCE NOT AVAILABLE TO THE ACCOMPLICE

R v Bourne [1939] 1 KB 687 (CA)

Lord Goddard CJ:

The appellant was indicted before Hallett J at the last assizes for Worcestershire and convicted of aiding and abetting his wife to commit the offence commonly called bestiality. The circumstances were such that nobody can approach this case without feeling the utmost repulsion, and indeed the learned judge thought it right, and I think he was quite right, to have a special report on the sanity of the appellant before he tried him. Without going into more of the revolting facts of this case than one can help, the appellant, who is only 28 years of age, his wife being a year or two younger, compelled her on two occasions to submit to the insertion of the male organ of a dog which he had excited into her vagina. That such a man should be allowed to be at large is almost intolerable and dreadful. Though he denied the offence when he went into the witness box, he had admitted it to the police. He had gone to the police to inquire where his wife and children were. The police meantime had been informed of what had been going on, I suppose on complaint by the wife, and they told him what had been suggested and he made a full confession to them, saying he admitted he had been a brute to his wife . . .

The case against the appellant was that he was a principal in the second degree to the crime of buggery which was committed by his wife, because if a woman has connection with a dog, or allows a dog to have connection with her, that is the full offence of buggery. She may be able to show that she was forced to commit the offence. I will assume that the plea of duress could have been set up by her on the evidence, and in fact we have allowed Mr Green to argue this case on the footing that the wife would have been entitled to be acquitted on the ground of duress. The learned judge left no question to the jury on duress, but the jury have found that she did not consent . . . I am willing to assume for the purpose of this case, and I think my brethren are too, that if this woman had been charged herself with committing the offence, she could have set up the plea of duress, not as showing that no offence had been committed, but as showing that she had no *mens rea* because her will was overborne by threats of imprisonment or violence so that she would be excused from punishment. But the offence of buggery whether with man or beast does not depend upon consent; it depends on the act, and if an act of buggery is committed, the felony is committed.

A point is raised here that the appellant was charged with being not merely an accessory before the fact but with being an aider and abettor. So he was, because the charge is: 'you being present aided and abetted, counselled and procured . . .'

In the opinion of the court, there is no doubt that the appellant was properly indicted for being a principal in the second degree to the commission of the crime of buggery. That is all that it is necessary to show. The evidence was, and the jury by their verdict have shown they accepted it, that he caused his wife to have connection with a dog, and if he caused his wife to have connection with a dog he is guilty, whether you call him an aider and abettor or an accessory, as a principal in the second degree. For that reason, this appeal fails and is dismissed.

R v Howe and Others [1987] 1 AC 417 (HL)

For the facts see Chapter 14.

Lord Mackay of Clashfern:
. . . In dismissing the appeals the court certified [*inter alia*, the following point of law] of general public importance . . . namely: . . .

(2) Can the one who incites or procures by duress another to kill or to be a party to a killing be convicted of murder if that other is acquitted by reason of duress? . . .

. . . Clarkson's appeal is concerned with the second question in respect of which he contends that if Burke was acquitted by reason of duress he could not be convicted of murder as one who had incited or procured by duress Burke to kill or to be a party to a killing . . .

Question 2

I turn now to the second certified question. In the view that I take on question one the second does not properly arise. However, I am of opinion that the Court of Appeal reached the correct conclusion upon it as a matter of principle.

Giving the judgment of the Court of Appeal Lord Lane CJ said [1986] QB 626 at 641–42:

> The judge based himself on a decision of this court in *R v Richards* [1974] QB 776. The facts in that case were that Mrs Richards paid two men to inflict injuries on her husband which she intended should 'put him in hospital for a month'. The two men wounded the husband but not seriously. They were acquitted of wounding with intent but convicted of unlawful wounding. Mrs Richards herself was convicted of wounding with intent, the jury plainly, and not surprisingly, believing that she had the necessary intent, though the two men had not. She appealed against her conviction on the ground that she could not properly be convicted as accessory before the fact to a crime more serious than that committed by the principals in the first degree. The appeal was allowed and the conviction for unlawful wounding was substituted. The court followed a passage from Hawkins' Pleas of the Crown,Vol 2 c 29, para 15: 'I take it to be an uncontroverted rule that [the offence of the accessory can never rise higher than that of the principal]; it seeming incongruous and absurd that he who is punished only as a partaker of the guilt of another, should be adjudged guilty of a higher crime than the other'.

James LJ delivering the judgment in *R v Richards* [1974] QB 776 said at 780:

> If there is only one offence committed, and that is the offence of unlawful wounding, then the person who has requested that offence to be committed, or advised that that offence be committed, cannot be guilty of a graver offence than that in fact which was committed.

The decision in *R v Richards* has been the subject of some criticism. Counsel before us posed the situation where A hands a gun to D informing him that it is loaded with blank ammunition only and telling him to go and scare X by discharging it. The ammunition is in fact live, as A knows, and X is killed. D is convicted only of manslaughter, as he might be on those facts. It would seem absurd that A should thereby escape conviction for murder. We take the view that *R v Richards* was incorrectly decided, but it seems to us that it cannot properly be distinguished from the instant case.

I consider that the reasoning of Lord Lane CJ is entirely correct and I would affirm his view that where a person has been killed and that result is the result intended by another participant, the mere fact that the actual killer may be convicted only of the reduced charge of manslaughter for some reason special to himself does not, in my opinion in any way, result in a compulsory reduction for the other participant . . .

FURTHER READING

Clarkson, CMV, 'Complicity, Powell and manslaughter' [1998] Crim LR 556

Duff, RA, 'Can I help you? Accessorial liability and the intention to assist' (1990) 10 Legal Studies 165

Lanham, DJ, 'Accomplices and withdrawal' (1981) 97 LQR 575

Padfeld, N, 'Assisting and encouraging crime' [1994] 58 JCL 297

Simester, AP, 'The Mental Element in Complicity' (2006) 122 LQR 578

Smith, JC, 'Criminal liability of accessories: law and law reform' (1997) 113 LQR 453

Smith, KJM, 'The Law Commission Consultation Paper on Complicity: A Blueprint for Rationalisation' [1994] Crim LR 239

Spencer, JN, 'Trying to help another person commit a crime', in P Smith (ed), *Criminal Law: Essays in Honour of JC Smith*, 1987, London: Butterworths

Sullivan, GR, 'Fault elements and joint enterprise' [1994] Crim LR 252

Williams, G, 'Letting offences happen' [1990] Crim LR 780

CHAPTER 8

INCHOATE OFFENCES

CONTENTS		

8.1 INTRODUCTION

The three forms of liability for inchoate offences in English criminal law are incitement, conspiracy and attempt. In each case liability can be imposed on the defendant even though the completed offence is not committed (inchoate simply means incomplete).

There are broadly two justifications for such offences. The first can be encapsulated in the notion that prevention is better than cure. To intervene and arrest whilst a bombing campaign is being discussed, agreed or arranged, is far better than to deal with its aftermath. The second is based on the argument that by suggesting, agreeing to commit, or trying to commit a crime a defendant has demonstrated his willingness that the crime should be committed. Therein lies the culpability that justifies punishment. In that sense it matters not whether the completed crime is ever committed. There is a further practical matter that should not be overlooked. Even where there is evidence that a completed offence has been committed, it may be easier for the prosecution to secure a conviction for incitement, conspiracy or attempt to commit the crime. The prosecution is at liberty to take this course of action, provided the indictment does not allege an inchoate and completed form of the same offence.

8.2 INCITEMENT

To incite another to commit a criminal offence is itself an offence at common law. The offence requires proof that:

(a) The inciter communicated his incitement to an incitee.
(b) The act incited would be an offence if carried out by the incitee.
(c) The incitee was aware of the facts that would make the conduct incited an offence.
(d) The inciter intended to communicate the incitement.
(e) The inciter intended the incitement to be acted upon.

In addition to the common law offence Parliament has, from time to time, created statutory offences of incitement where the conduct incited would not, of itself, involve the commission of a criminal offence. Examples include incitement to racial hatred, and incitement to disaffection amongst troops.

8.2.1 WHAT CONSTITUTES INCITEMENT?

As Lord Denning observed in *Race Relations Board v Applin* [1973] QB 815, at 825G: '[It was] suggested that to "incite" means to urge or spur on by advice, encouragement, and persuasion, and not otherwise. I do not think the word is so limited, at any rate in this context. A person may "incite" another to do an act by threatening or by pressure, as well as persuasion.' In *R v Smith* [2004] All ER (D) 79 the Court of Appeal confirmed that incitement also encompassed situations where the inciter stimulated a desire on the part of the incitee to commit an offence.

Normally D will be seeking to incite a particular incitee, but an incitement can be unilateral, for example where it forms part of an advertisement or broadcast; see *R v Most* (1881) 7 QBD 244.

Invicta Plastics Ltd and Another v Clare [1976] RTR 251 (DC)

A company, Invicta Plastics Ltd, were manufacturers of a device called 'Radatec', which was advertised as enabling drivers to detect speed traps set by the police. The company faced four offences of incitement to use unlicensed apparatus for wireless telegraphy, contrary to s 1(1) of the Wireless Telegraphy Act 1949. That section, as amended, provides, *inter alia*:

No person shall . . . use any apparatus for wireless telegraphy except under the authority of a licence in that behalf granted by the Secretary of State . . . and any person who . . . uses any apparatus for wireless telegraphy except under and in accordance with such a licence shall be guilty of an offence . . .

Park J:
The first question which the justices had to decide was whether a person who used the Radatec in his motor car without a licence from the Secretary of State would be using apparatus for wireless telegraphy contrary to s 1 of the Act of 1949. On the evidence before them they decided that such a person would be committing such an offence. There is no submission to this court that the justices were wrong in coming to that conclusion. So, on the first summons, which concerned the company, the question was whether the company by the advertisement in the magazine incited its readers to commit an offence under the Act . . .

It is submitted on behalf of the company that, before the offence of incitement could be committed by means of the advertisement, there had to be in it an incitement to use the device which was advertised; that, if not, any matter in the advertisement would not constitute incitement, as it would not be sufficiently proximate to the offence alleged to have been incited; and that, as the advertisement merely encouraged readers to find out more about the device, it did not amount to incitement in fact or in law.

I think that it is necessary to look at the advertisement as a whole. Approaching it in this way, I have come to the conclusion that the company did incite a breach of the Act by means of the advertisement. I think, therefore, that justices were right to convict the company of this offence.

It is conceded that on the other summons against the company the case is much stronger because it depends upon the view taken by the justices of the pamphlet. [Counsel for the defendants], in the course of his argument, conceded that this pamphlet would amount to incitement except for two sentences, which I have read, which he submits amount to 'disclaimers'. Those two sentences are those where the pamphlet states that the majority of X band transmissions are not intended for public use and, therefore, their deliberate reception is illegal unless licensed by the Post Office, and where it states that it is illegal to employ Radatec specifically for the reception of, for instance, police radar transmissions.

Again, looking at the pamphlet as a whole, as the justices did, it is plain that from the words used readers were being persuaded and incited to use the Radatec device. In my view, therefore, the justices were also right to convict the company on that charge . . .

8.2.2 THE INCITEE MUST KNOW OF THE FACTS THAT CONSTITUTE THE OFFENCE

R v Curr [1968] 2 QB 944 (CA)

Fenton Atkinson J:

. . . The facts shortly were these, that he was in fact a trafficker in family allowance books. His method was to approach some married woman who had a large family of children and lend her money on the security of her family allowance book. A woman would borrow from him, let us say, £6 and would sign three of the vouchers in her family allowance book to the value of, let us say, £9, and hand over the book to him as security. He then had a team of women agents whom he sent out to cash the vouchers, and he would pocket the proceeds in repayment of the loans and thereafter return the books. He admitted quite freely in evidence that he had done, as he put it, 40 to 80 books a week, and he said, in February 1966, he had between three and five women agents assisting him in this matter, and when he was arrested he had about 80 family allowance books in his possession. He agreed quite frankly that he knew he was not legally entitled to receive these payments, and that it could be risky; in dealing with the husband of one of the women concerned he said: 'When you're doing business like this, you should keep your big mouth shut.' So it is quite plain that the dealings of this man were highly objectionable, and the assistant recorder who tried the case clearly had very strong views about it; on two occasions in his summing-up he spoke of preying on these women with large families, and he finished up his direction to the jury with words to this effect: 'If you are getting interest at 800% per annum it is not bad, is it? That is what the prosecution say here, that the whole system was corrupt', and the language there used was no whit too strong.

But the very nature of the case being bound to arouse strong prejudice in the mind of any right-thinking juror, for that reason it was all the more important to put the law on each count clearly to the jury, and to make sure that the defence was clearly put before them . . .

... [The defendant was charged] that on a day unknown [he] unlawfully 'solicited a woman unknown to obtain on his behalf from HM's Postmaster General the sum of £2 18s on account of an allowance knowing that it was not properly receivable by her' ...

[The relevant legislation, the Family Allowances Act 1945, contained a section headed] 'Penalty for obtaining or receiving payment wrongfully' [which provided:]

> If any person: ... (b) obtains or receives any such sum as on account of an allowance, either as in that person's own right or as on behalf of another, knowing that it was not properly payable, or not properly receivable by him or her; that person shall be liable on summary conviction to imprisonment for a term not exceeding three months or to a fine not exceeding £50 or to both such imprisonment and such fine.

[Defence counsel's] argument was that if the woman agent in fact has no guilty knowledge, knowing perhaps nothing of the assignment, or supposing that the defendant was merely collecting for the use and benefit of the woman concerned, then she would be an innocent agent, and by using her services in that way the defendant would be committing the summary offence himself, but would not be inciting her to receive money knowing that it was not receivable by her. He contends that it was essential to prove, to support this charge, that the woman agent in question in this transaction affecting a Mrs Currie knew that the allowances were not properly receivable by her. [Prosecuting counsel's] answer to that submission was that the woman agent must be presumed to know the law, and if she knew the law, she must have known, he contends, that the allowance was not receivable by her ...

The argument is that in no other circumstances may an agent lawfully collect for the use and benefit of the book holder, and [counsel for the prosecution] was ready to contend, for example, that if a mother with, say, eight children to look after at home asks a neighbour to go and collect her allowance for her, and the neighbour does so, the neighbour would be committing an offence under the 1945 Act, and the mother would be guilty of the offence of soliciting. We are by no means satisfied that any agent who collects with the full authority of the book holder and for her use and benefit would commit an offence under that subsection. There appears to be no express prohibition, certainly we were referred to no express prohibition, in the Family Allowance Act 1945, or any orders making such collection unlawful. On the evidence, the Post Office in practice appears to allow this to be done in certain cases; in our view there can be situations, or may be situations, in which an agent, however well she may know the statute and regulations, could properly suppose that her action in receiving an allowance of this kind was lawful.

In our view the prosecution argument here gives no effect to the word 'knowing' in the 1945 Act, and in our view the defendant could only be guilty if the woman solicited, that is, the woman agent sent to collect the allowance, knew that the action she was asked to carry out amounted to an offence. As has already been said, the defendant himself clearly knew that his conduct in the matter was illegal and contrary to the 1945 Act, but it was essential in our view for the jury to consider the knowledge, if any, of the woman agent. The assistant recorder dealt with this count by referring to soliciting as follows: 'Solicited means encouraged or incited another person to go and draw that money which should have been paid, you may think, to Mrs Currie.' He later dealt with ignorance of the law being no excuse. He went on to deal with statutory offences, under the Family Allowances Act 1945, telling the jury in effect that, apart from the case of sickness, nobody else could legally receive these allowances, and then went on to consider the position of the defendant, asking the rhetorical question whether he could be heard to say with his knowledge of this matter and his trafficking in these books that it was not known to be wrong to employ an agent to go and collect the family allowance. But the assistant recorder never followed that with the question of the knowledge of the woman agents, and in the whole of the summing-up dealing with this matter he proceeded on the assumption that either guilty knowledge in the woman agent was irrelevant, or, alternatively, that any woman agent must be taken to have known that she was committing an offence under the Act.

If the matter had been left on a proper direction for the jury's consideration, they might well have thought that the woman agents, other than Mrs Nicholson, whom they acquitted, must have known very well that they were doing something wrong; some of them were apparently collecting as many as 10 of these weekly payments. But the matter was never left to them for their consideration, and here again, so it seems to this court, there was a vital matter where the defence was not left to the jury at all and there was no sufficient direction; it would be quite impossible to say that on a proper direction the jury must have convicted on this count . . .

 ## COMMENTS AND QUESTIONS

1   In *Curr*, did the court treat the knowledge of the incitees as part of the *actus reus* that had to be established, or is the court saying that the inciter must know that the incitee will be acting with the necessary *mens rea*? Consider further *DPP v Armstrong* [2000] Crim LR 379, where A incited J (where J, unknown to A, was an undercover police officer) to supply child pornography. A was acquitted on the basis that there could be no liability for incitement unless J had parity of *mens rea* – on the facts J had no intention of supplying the pictures. Allowing the prosecutor's appeal the Divisional Court held that strict parity of *mens rea* was not required in incitement cases. J knew of the facts that would constitute the offence even though he had no intention of supplying the material requested. Had J done what was requested by A, J would have been committing an offence.

2   The fact that the incitee may be willing to commit an offence even without the incitement committed by the incitee is irrelevant. Hence if A asks B, a drugs dealer, to supply drugs, the request is the incitement. The fact that B was in any event a supplier does not provide A with a defence; see *R v Goldman* [2001] Crim LR 822.

3   Can D1 be guilty of incitement where he requests that D2 commit an offence, for example the supply of child pornography, by means of visiting D2's website and eliciting an automated response to his order? *R (on the application of O) v Coventry Magistrates Court* [2004] Crim LR 948 suggests that he can, but the ruling is problematic as it rests on the argument that D1 will have incited the programmer who designed the website to commit the offence of supplying child pornography. In reality the task of building the site would have occurred before the *actus reus* of incitement by D1.

4   The *mens rea* of common law incitement comprises an intention on the part of the inciter to communicate with the incitee. Further it requires evidence that the inciter intended or believed that the incitee would commit the *actus reus* of the offence incited with the requisite *mens rea*.

5   *R v C* [2005] EWCA Crim 2817, confirms that no offence is committed where D encourages P to commit an offence that P is legally incapable of committing (in this case the offence of buggery by a boy under the age of 14, there being at the time an irrebuttable presumption

that a boy under 14 could not commit the offence). As far as sexual offences with children are concerned, this loophole has now been closed by the enactment of s 11 of the Sexual Offences Act 2003 – see Chapter 6.8, but that change does not apply to cases of incitement to commit buggery before the presumption was abrogated in relation to acts committed after 20 September 1993; see also *R v Whitehouse* [1995] 1 Cr App R 420.

8.2.3 INCITEMENT AND IMPOSSIBILITY

How should the criminal law deal with a defendant who suggests the commission of an offence which, unknown to him at the time he makes the suggestion, cannot be carried out? As will be seen (at 8.3.5 and 8.4.4) in relation to both statutory conspiracy and attempt Parliament has intervened to ensure that impossibility is no bar to the imposition of liability in respect of those two forms of liability for inchoate offences. Incitement, however, is largely a common law offence, and the courts have opted to apply the common law rules on impossibility (derived from as laid down in *DPP v Nock* [1978] AC 979, considered below) to incitement – the result being an inconsistency of approach across the three forms of liability for inchoate offences that is difficult to justify in terms of legal logic.

R v Fitzmaurice [1983] QB 1083 (CA)

Neill J:

On 22 July 1981, Robert Fitzmaurice was convicted at the Central Criminal Court of unlawfully inciting three men, Terence Bonham, James Brown and Steven Brown to commit robbery by robbing a woman at Bow . . .

The facts of the case were unusual. They have been set out in a convenient form in an agreed statement of facts as follows:

(1) On 28 September 1978, Bonham, James Brown and Steven Brown were arrested in Bow in a green van. Bonham was the driver and the Browns were each armed with an imitation firearm. All had sleeve masks and there was a pickaxe handle in the van.

(2) Bonham and the others believed that they were there to carry out a wages snatch from a woman walking from her place of work to the bank. A security van was due to visit the National Westminster Bank in Bow Road at that time, and police officers had received information from the appellant's father that a robbery on the security van had been planned. All three were subsequently charged with conspiracy to rob a person on the basis of their account that they were there to rob a woman of money on her way to the bank and not the security van. At their trial they pleaded guilty to the conspiracy count and were sentenced to imprisonment.

(3) Subsequent investigations revealed that the three men were victims of a trick by the appellant's father, and had been set up to carry out a robbery by him so that he and his accomplice Skipp could collect the reward money for informing the police of an intended raid on the security van. That information was false and the invention of the appellant's father.

(4) The appellant's father asked the appellant if he could find someone to carry out a robbery. The appellant approached Bonham and informed him of the proposed robbery, describing it as a 'wages snatch'. The appellant brought Bonham to an address where the appellant's

father outlined the plan. The plan was to snatch wages from a woman carrying money from a factory to a bank in Bow, east London. The appellant offered to participate, but was excluded. Bonham agreed to the plan. Later Bonham, who had recruited the two Browns, visited Bow with the appellant's father, but not the appellant. They saw a woman, in fact Skipp's girlfriend, walking from the factory to the bank. She was carrying a bag. The following week the appellant's father took Bonham and the two Browns to Bow again and pointed out where the getaway car would be left. On the day appointed, Bonham and the others met at the appellant's house. Imitation guns and masks were distributed. Bonham and the others left the premises and were subsequently arrested. The appellant believed throughout that the robbery plan was genuine and agreed to accept £200 and a television for his part.

(5)   On 5 June 1981 Bonham had his conviction for conspiracy set aside by the Court of Appeal on the grounds that the crime which he had conspired to commit was impossible of fulfilment. O'Connor LJ said:

> However morally culpable, the truth is that these three men had been fraudulently induced to agree to commit a crime which could not be committed in the strict sense; they were themselves the victims of a different conspiracy to which they were not parties.

In support of the appellant's appeal to this court, [counsel for the appellant] put forward two submissions: (a) that the trial judge had misdirected the jury as to the meaning of 'incitement'; and (b) that the appellant could not be guilty of inciting other men to commit a crime which in fact could not be committed.

On his first submission, [counsel for the appellant] drew our attention to a passage in the summing-up where the judge said:

> The word 'incitement' is a word which is used in widely differing circumstances. A person can incite another to envy or hatred. A person can also be incited to loyalty and patriotism. Here, the charge is that the accused incited Mr Bonham to commit a crime. Now, the original approach by the defendant to Mr Bonham is not denied. There is no dispute about the fact that the defendant approached Mr Bonham, and it was an approach to him to commit a crime. There is no question about that. The defendant does not deny that Mr Bonham was an old friend of his, and that he knew at the time that he was out of work and needed money. You may conclude that an approach to Mr Bonham in those circumstances by the defendant, whether it was a suggestion, a proposal or a request, was an approach that embodied naturally the promise of reward, that if he engaged in the enterprise he would get money. That prospect, you may think, was the most persuasive factor in the approach. If you take that view, then clearly you may think that there was incitement to commit the crime, in the broad sense I have indicated.

[Counsel for the appellant] criticised this passage on the basis that it provided an unsatisfactory and inadequate definition of incitement because the judge did not sufficiently instruct the jury as to the necessity of proof that the appellant had persuaded or encouraged the commission of the robbery. He submitted that there was a clear distinction between the mere procurement of a crime and incitement. Procuration, he said, did not necessarily involve any persuasion or counselling of a third party by the defendant to commit the crime. Similarly, said [counsel], a person may be liable as an accessory before the fact, for example, by providing the tools for a crime, but, in the absence of any proof of persuasion to commit the crime, he will not be guilty of incitement . . .

We have considered this submission in the context of the present case. In our judgment the judge gave a perfectly adequate definition to deal with the facts which the jury had to consider. We are satisfied that in some cases a person who is deputed to collect men together to take part in a crime may well not be guilty of incitement. For example, his role may be limited to informing certain named individuals that the planner of the enterprise would like to see them. But in the present case the judge could point to the fact that Bonham was out of work and needed money. The suggestion, proposal or request was accompanied by an implied promise of reward. Indeed, by using the words 'That proposal, you may think, was the most persuasive factor in the approach', the judge rightly focused the attention of the jury on the element of persuasion which it was necessary for the prosecution to prove. We therefore see no reason to fault the judge's summing-up in this respect.

[Counsel's] second submission, however, is at first sight more formidable. Incitement is one of the three inchoate offences, incitement, conspiracy and attempt. [Counsel] argued that there was no logical basis for treating the three offences differently when considering their application in circumstances where the complete offence would be impossible to commit, and that therefore the court should apply the principles laid down by the House of Lords in the case of attempts in *R v Smith (Roger)* [1975] AC 476 and in the case of conspiracy in *DPP v Nock* [1978] AC 979 . . .

In our view . . . the right approach in a case of incitement is the same as that which was underlined by Lord Scarman in *DPP v Nock* [1978] AC 979 when he considered the offence of conspiracy. In every case it is necessary to analyse the evidence with care to decide the precise offence which the defendant is alleged to have incited. Lord Scarman said, at 995:

> The indictment makes plain that the Crown is alleging in this case a conspiracy to commit a crime: and no one has suggested that the particulars fail to disclose an offence known to the law. But the appellants submit, and it is not disputed by the Crown, that the agreement as proved was narrower in scope than the conspiracy charged. When the case was before the Court of Appeal, counsel on both sides agreed that the evidence went to prove that the appellants agreed together to obtain cocaine by separating it from the other substance or substances contained in a powder which they had obtained from one of their co-defendants, a Mr Mitchell. They believed that the powder was a mixture of cocaine and lignocaine, and that they would be able to produce cocaine from it. In fact the powder was lignocaine hydrochloride, an anaesthetic used in dentistry, which contains no cocaine at all. It is impossible to produce, by separation or otherwise, cocaine from lignocaine . . . The trial judge in his direction to the jury, and the Court of Appeal in their judgment dismissing the two appeals, treated this impossibility as an irrelevance. In their view the agreement was what mattered: and there was plain evidence of an agreement to produce cocaine, even though unknown to the two conspirators it could not be done. Neither the trial judge nor the Court of Appeal thought it necessary to carry their analysis of the agreement further. The trial judge described it simply as an agreement to produce cocaine. The Court of Appeal thought it enough that the prosecution had proved 'an agreement to do an act which was forbidden by s 4 of the Misuse of Drugs Act 1971'. Both descriptions are accurate, as far as they go. But neither contains any reference to the limited nature of the agreement proved; it was an agreement upon a specific course of conduct with the object of producing cocaine, and limited to that course of conduct. Since it could not result in the production of cocaine, the two appellants by pursuing it could not commit the statutory offence of producing a controlled drug.

In our view these words suggest the correct approach at common law to any inchoate offence. It is necessary in every case to decide on the evidence what was the course of conduct which was (as the case may be) incited or agreed or attempted. In some cases the evidence may establish that the persuasion by the inciter was in quite general terms whereas the subsequent agreement of the conspirators was directed to a specific crime and a specific target. In such cases where the committal of the specific offence is shown to be impossible it may be quite logical for the inciter to be convicted even though the alleged conspirators (if not caught by s 5 of the Criminal Attempts Act 1981) may be acquitted. On the other hand, if B and C agree to kill D and A, standing beside B and C, though not intending to take any active part whatever in the crime, encourages them to do so, we can see no satisfactory reason, if it turns out later that D was already dead, why A should be convicted of incitement to murder whereas B and C at common law would be entitled to an acquittal on a charge of conspiracy. The crucial question is to establish on the evidence the course of conduct which the alleged inciter was encouraging.

We return to the facts of the instant case. [Counsel for the appellant] submitted that the 'crime' which Bonham and the two Browns were being encouraged to commit was a mere charade. The appellant's father was not planning a real robbery at all and therefore the appellant could not be found guilty of inciting the three men to commit it. In our judgment, however, the answer to [counsel's] argument is to be found in the facts which the prosecution proved against the appellant. As was made clear by [counsel for the Crown], the case against the appellant was based on the steps he took to recruit Bonham. At that stage the appellant believed that there was to be a wages snatch and he was encouraging Bonham to take part in it. As [counsel] put it, 'The appellant thought he was recruiting for a robbery not for a charade.' It is to be remembered that the particulars of offence in the indictment included the words 'by robbing a woman at Bow'. By no stretch of the imagination was that an impossible offence to carry out and it was that offence which the appellant was inciting Bonham to commit.

For these reasons, therefore we are satisfied that the appellant was rightly convicted. The appeal is dismissed.

 ## COMMENTS AND QUESTIONS

1   In *R v Pickford* [1995] 1 Cr App R 420, the appellant contested his conviction for inciting his son to have sexual intercourse with his (the appellant's) wife, on the basis that, at the time of the alleged offence, the appellant's son would have been under the age of 14, and thus presumed at common law to have been incapable of having sexual intercourse (a presumption since abolished by statute). The essence of the appeal was that the appellant had been charged with inciting a non-existent crime. Dismissing the appeal, the court noted that the common law presumption of incapacity existed to protect young boys in respect of crimes committed by them, not to protect adults committing offences against them. As Laws J observed: 'The reasons for the presumption, however they may have been articulated in the old cases, cannot begin to justify its application in a case where the boy is not the perpetrator of the offence, but its victim. Accordingly, the appellant in the present case would rightly have been found guilty of inciting the mother to have intercourse with her son, even if it were plain beyond argument that he was under 14 at the time . . .'

2   In *DPP v Armstrong* (above), A had contended that the offence he had incited was impossible to carry out as the incitee (unknown to A at the relevant time) was an undercover police officer who would never have supplied the pornography requested by A. This argument was

rejected by the Divisional Court on the basis that the incitee could have had access to and supplied the material if he had wanted to. J could have supplied the material had he so wished.

3   As part of the Government's response to concerns over 'sexual tourism' – principally the sexual exploitation of children in countries overseas facilitated by individuals in the United Kingdom – Parliament enacted the Sexual Offences (Conspiracy and Incitement) Act 1996. Section 2 of the Act applies where:

> 2(1) . . .
>   (a) any act done by a person in England and Wales would amount to the offence of incitement to commit a listed sexual offence but for the fact that what he had in view would not be an offence triable in England and Wales,
>   (b) the whole or part of what he had in view was intended to take place in a country or territory outside the United Kingdom, and
>   (c) what he had in view would involve the commission of an offence under the law in force in that country or territory.
>
> The term 'listed sexual offence' is defined in the Schedule to the Sexual Offences (Conspiracy and Incitement) Act 1996, as amended by the Sexual Offences Act 2003 – the offences covered are under any of sections 1 to 12, 14 and 15 to 26 of the Sexual Offences Act 2003.

If these conditions are satisfied, what the defendant had in view is to be treated as that listed sexual offence for the purpose of any charge of incitement brought in respect of that act, and any such charge is accordingly triable in England and Wales (s 2(2)). Under s 2(3) any act of incitement by means of a message (however communicated) is to be treated as done in England and Wales if the message is sent or received in England and Wales.

4   The scope of the domestic courts' jurisdiction over incitement to commit offences abroad was further extended by the coming into force of provisions of the Criminal Justice Act 1993, on 1 June 1999. Under the 1993 Act, courts in England and Wales have jurisdiction over what are referred to as 'Group B' offences – this includes incitement to commit a range of offences abroad involving dishonest and fraudulent conduct – provided the conduct incited would amount to an offence triable by the courts in England and Wales, were the conduct incited to be carried out within the jurisdiction.

8.2.4 CODIFICATION AND LAW REFORM PROPOSALS – INCITEMENT

The Law Commission's Consultation Paper *Assisting and Encouraging Crime* (LCCP No 131) outlined some radical reforms in relation to incitement – essentially the abolition of the offence and its replacement with a new offence of 'encouraging crime'. In the subsequent report, *Inchoate Liability for Encouraging and Assisting Crime* (Law Com No 300), the Commission has refined its proposals, in the light of consultations, and is proposing:

The abolition of common law incitement

The introduction of a new inchoate offence of assisting in crime

Reforming secondary liability but retaining the common law doctrine of joint venture (to be the subject of a later report).

Addressing the shortcomings of the current common law offence of incitement, Law Com No 300 observes;

1.5 In contrast to acts of assistance, if D encourages P to commit an offence which P does not go on to commit, D will be guilty of incitement provided he or she satisfies the fault element of the offence. However, the offence of incitement has a number of unsatisfactory features:

(1) there is uncertainty as to whether it must be D's purpose that P should commit the offence that D is inciting;

(2) the fault element of the offence has been distorted by decisions of the Court of Appeal. These decisions have focused, wrongly, on the state of mind of P rather than on D's state of mind;

(3) there is uncertainty as to whether and, if so, to what extent it is a defence to act in order to prevent the commission of an offence or to prevent or limit the occurrence of harm;

(4) there is uncertainty as to the circumstances in which D is liable for inciting P to do an act which, if done by P, would not involve P committing an offence, for example because P is under the age of criminal responsibility or lacks a guilty mind;

(5) the rules governing D's liability in cases where D incites P to commit an inchoate offence have resulted in absurd distinctions;

(6) D may have a defence if the offence that he or she incites is impossible to commit whereas impossibility is not a defence to other inchoate offences, apart from common law conspiracies.

The offence of incitement is therefore in need of clarification and reform.

. . .

1.25 We are recommending that there should be two new inchoate offences:

(1) encouraging or assisting the commission of an offence ('the principal offence') intending to encourage or assist its commission ('the clause 1 offence');

(2) encouraging or assisting the commission of an offence ('the principal offence') believing that it will be committed ('the clause 2(1) offence').

Each offence targets very culpable conduct. In order to be convicted of the clause 1 offence, D must not only deliberately seek to encourage or assist P but also do so with the intention that P should commit the principal offence or be encouraged or assisted to commit it. In order to be convicted of the clause 2(1) offence, D must not only deliberately do something capable of encouraging or assisting P but also do so believing that it will encourage or assist P to commit the principal offence and that P will commit the principal offence:

Example 1F
D knows that P wishes to murder V. D, who hates V, provides P with information regarding the whereabouts of V. D's intention is that P should murder V. Meanwhile, Z alerts V to the fact that P intends to kill him. As a result, V goes abroad and P abandons the plan to murder V.

D has committed the clause 1 offence, namely encouraging or assisting murder intending to encourage or assist its commission.

Example 1G
D is a key holder at the office where he works. In return for payment, D makes a copy of the key and gives it to P believing that P will use the key to commit a burglary at the premises. However, D hopes that P will change his mind. P is arrested in connection with another matter before he can even attempt to commit the burglary. P informs the police of what D has done.

In this example, D has committed the clause 2(1) offence because, although not intending that P should commit burglary, D believed that P would commit the offence and that, by giving P a copy of the keys, he would help P to do so.

1.26 The two offences would replace the existing common law offence of incitement and fill the existing gap whereby at common law a person incurs no criminal liability for assisting the commission of an offence unless and until the offence is committed or attempted. Each offence may be committed whether or not the principal offence is committed.

Liability for encouraging or assisting more than one principal offence
1.27 Sometimes D may do an act that is capable of encouraging or assisting the commission of more than one principal offence:

Example 1H
In return for payment, D drives P to the house of V. D is not sure whether P will commit burglary, arson or murder. However, D believes that P will commit at least one of those three offences. D drops P near the premises and drives off. P's intention is to commit all three offences but, suspecting that he is being watched, P decides to abandon the project.

D's state of mind is such that, although he or she believes that at least one of three offences will be committed, in relation to each of the three offences the belief is no more than that the offence might be committed.

1.28 We are recommending that if D's act is capable of encouraging or assisting the commission of one or more of a number of different principal offences and:

(1) D believes that at least one of them will be committed;
(2) D has no belief as to which particular offence will be committed; and
(3) D believes that his or her act will encourage or assist the commission of at least one of those offences,

D may be prosecuted and convicted of encouraging or assisting the commission of any offence that he or she believed might be committed ('the clause 2(2) offence'). However, the prosecution will only be able to prosecute D for one of the offences that he or she believed might be committed.

The penalty for each offence
1.29 Subject to one exception, we are recommending that the maximum penalty on conviction of either the clause 1 offence or a clause 2 offence should be the same as if D had been convicted of the principal offence. The exception is where the principal offence is murder. We are recommending that for encouraging or assisting murder, D should be liable to a maximum sentence of life imprisonment rather than the mandatory life sentence.

Defences and exemptions

1.30 We are recommending that it should be a defence to both the clause 1 and a clause 2 offence if D proves on a balance of probabilities that he or she acted in order to prevent the commission of an offence or the occurrence of harm and that it was reasonable to act as D did:

> *Example 1J*
>
> D is the manager of a public house. P enters the premises with a view to carrying out an assault on a customer, V, because of an unpaid debt. D encourages P instead to take V's briefcase. Before P can take the case, another customer overpowers him.
>
> D has encouraged P to commit theft. However, it might be thought that D ought to be able to say that he or she acted in order to prevent the commission of a more serious offence and that it was reasonable in all the circumstances to encourage P to commit theft. The harm that D was seeking to prevent was greater than any harm resulting from the theft.

1.31 We are also recommending that it should be a defence to a clause 2 offence, but not the clause 1 offence, if D proves on the balance of probabilities that he or she acted reasonably in all the circumstances:

> *Example 1K*
>
> D works as a typist for P. P tells D to type a statement addressed to the solicitors acting for P's wife. D knows that the statement is for the purpose of divorce and ancillary financial relief proceedings that are currently before the county court. In typing the statement, D realises that it contains deliberately misleading information about P's assets.
>
> By typing the letter, D is assisting P to commit an offence. However, it ought to be possible for D to say that he or she acted reasonably because he or she was following her employer's instructions.

1.32 Acting reasonably in all the circumstances would not be a defence to the clause 1 offence. If D intends his or her encouragement or assistance to lead to the commission of an offence, it ought not to be possible for D to have a defence by claiming that what he or she did was within the bounds of reasonableness.

1.33 Our scheme also preserves and refines the common law Tyrrell exemption. In Tyrrell P, an adult, had unlawful sexual intercourse with D, a child aged between 13 and 16. It was alleged that D had encouraged P to commit the offence. It was held that D could not be convicted of committing the offence as an accessory or of inciting the offence because the offence has been enacted for the purpose of protecting a category of persons and D fell within the category.

1.34 We are recommending that it should be a defence to the clause 1 offence and a clause 2 offence if:

(1) the principal offence is one that exists for the protection of a particular category of person;

(2) D falls within that category; and

(3) D is the victim of the principal offence or would have been had the principal offence been committed.

Regarding the 'defence' of impossibility, the Report concluded:

6.61 We believe that impossibility should not be a defence to the new offences that we are recommending. D's state of mind and, therefore his or her culpability, is unaffected by the unknown impossibility of the principal offence being committed. Further, if D can be liable notwithstanding that, contrary to D's belief, P never intends to commit the principal offence, it would be illogical if D was able to plead that it would have been impossible to commit the principal offence.

6.62 We do not believe that it is necessary for the Bill to include a clause expressly addressing the issue. In Part 5, we explained that D's liability is in relation to an abstract and not a particular principal offence. In order to be convicted of the new offences, D must do an act that is capable of encouraging or assisting the doing of a criminal act. 'Criminal act' refers to no more than the conduct element of the principal offence. If D gives P a weapon, D has done an act capable of assisting the doing of the criminal act of a number of different offences against the person. D's liability will turn on whether he or she intended or expected that P would use the weapon to attack another human being and, if so, with what consequences.

6.63 Accordingly, if D, in return for payment, provides P with a weapon believing that P will use it to attack V1 (intending to kill V1), D is guilty of assisting murder irrespective of whether P uses the weapon to attack anyone. Were P to attack and murder V2, instead of V1, D would be equally guilty of encouraging or assisting murder. If P attacked V2 because V1 was already dead at the time that D provided the weapon, D would still be guilty of encouraging or assisting murder. It may have been impossible for V1 to be murdered but, nonetheless, D had done an act capable of encouraging or assisting the conduct element of murder, namely an attack on any human being.

8.3 STATUTORY CONSPIRACY

The offence of conspiracy essentially involves an agreement between two or more persons that a criminal offence will be committed. As with other inchoate offences the criminality lies in the conspirators' willingness that the agreement should be carried out – this culpability exists regardless of whether or not the agreement is in fact acted upon. Until the enactment of the Criminal Law Act 1977 conspiracy was a common law offence. Although s 5(1) of the Criminal Law Act 1977 states that it has the effect of abolishing common law conspiracy, s 5(2) provides that this '. . . does not affect the offence of conspiracy at common law so far as it relates to conspiracy to defraud'. Subsection (3) goes on to preserve common law conspiracy to corrupt public morals or outrage public decency – see 8.3.4 (below). The vast majority of conspiracies are charged as offences under the 1977 Act – it is best to think of common law conspiracy to defraud as providing a residual form of liability for conspiracies falling outside the 1977 Act.

CRIMINAL LAW ACT 1977

1(1) Subject to the following provisions of this part of this Act, if a person agrees with any other person or persons that a course of conduct shall be pursued which, if the agreement is carried out in accordance with their intentions, either:

(a) will necessarily amount to or involve the commission of any offence or offences by one or more of the parties to the agreement; or

(b) would do so but for the existence of facts which render the commission of the offence or any of the offences impossible,

he shall be guilty of conspiracy to commit the offence or offences in question.

1(2) Where liability for any offence may be incurred without knowledge on the part of the person committing it of any particular fact or circumstance necessary for the commission of the offence, a person shall nevertheless not be guilty of conspiracy to commit that offence by virtue of subsection (1) above unless he and at least one other party to the agreement intend or know that the fact or circumstance shall or will exist at the time when the conduct constituting the offence is to take place.

8.3.1 THE *ACTUS REUS* OF STATUTORY CONSPIRACY

The *actus reus* of conspiracy is the agreement to commit the offence: *R v Gill* (1993) 97 Cr App R 215 (CA). This agreement is usually proved by evidence of acts carried out to fulfil the agreement: see *R v Cooper* (extracted below). Nevertheless, because it is the agreement itself which amounts to the conspiracy, it does not matter if the acts actually carried out differ from those agreed: see *R v Bolton* (1992) 94 Cr App R 74.

R v Cooper and Compton [1947] 2 All ER 701 (CA)

Humphreys J:

These two appellants were tried at the Central Criminal Court on an indictment which contained nine counts. The first count was a charge of conspiracy to steal. The second, third, fourth and fifth counts alleged that in four separate cases the appellants had been guilty of robbing four separate persons, that is, forcing them to give their money or goods as the result of threats and owing to fear. The next four counts charged that in those same cases they had stolen the money of those four persons, simple larceny.

The main ground of this appeal is put well in the grounds of appeal. The jury found a verdict of guilty on the first count. They found a verdict of not guilty on each and all of the remaining counts, and it is argued in support of the appeals that in those circumstances a verdict of not guilty on the substantive counts 2 and 9 leaves the first count unsupported by sufficient, or any, evidence . . .

. . . The jury . . . returned the verdict of guilty on the first count and not guilty on each of the others . . .

. . . All we can say is that the jury has said in terms: 'We are not satisfied with the case for the prosecution on counts 2–9. We are satisfied with the case for the prosecution on count 1.'

Is it possible that this court can uphold that verdict as being reasonable? In a great many cases there is no doubt that a verdict of guilty of conspiracy, but not guilty of the particular acts charged, is a perfectly proper and reasonable one. In such cases it would be wrong not to insert in the indictment a charge of conspiracy. Criminal lawyers know it often happens that, while a general conspiracy to do such a thing as to steal is likely to be inferred by the jury from the evidence, it may be that the evidence of the particular acts constituting the larcenies charged in the indictment are supported by rather nebulous evidence. That is a case where the jury may say, and very likely will say, not guilty of larceny but guilty of being concerned with others to commit larceny . . .

In the present case it appears to us that there was no necessity from any point of view for the insertion of any charge of conspiracy. A verdict of guilty could only be supported if the jury believed the general story, and the general story was told by four different persons, each of whom, if he was believed, proved conclusively a charge of stealing . . .

R v Bolton (1992) 94 Cr App R 74 (CA)

The defendant was charged with conspiracy to procure the execution of valuable securities by deception. The appeal concerned the question whether it mattered that the defendant expected a cheque but in fact money was transferred by electronic means.

Woolf LJ:

. . . [His Lordship referred to *R v Siracusa* (1990) 90 Cr App R 340, *R v Anderson* [1986] AC 27 and *R v Reed* [1982] Crim LR 819.] In the latter case Donaldson LJ said:

> . . . A and B agree to drive from London to Edinburgh in a time which can be achieved without exceeding the speed limits, but only if the traffic which they encounter is exceptionally light. Their agreement will not necessarily involve the commission of any offence, even if it is carried out in accordance with their intentions, and they do arrive . . . within the agreed time. Accordingly the agreement does not constitute the offence of statutory conspiracy.

[Woolf LJ went on to say:] there can be a distinction between the manner in which the conspirators intend to achieve their objective and how that objective is in fact achieved. Taking the example given by Donaldson LJ in the case of *Reed*, if A and B agree and intend to drive from London to Edinburgh in excess of the speed limit because they expect heavy traffic, the fact that it proves unnecessary for them to do so because the traffic is light does not avoid them being guilty of conspiracy. Their agreement was to do something which necessarily would involve the commission of an offence, namely exceeding the speed limit and they embarked on the commission of that offence. So in this case, if Roger Bolton and his co-conspirators agree dishonestly etc to procure the building societies to make a mortgage advance by executing a valuable security and this was what they set out to achieve, it would not mean the conspirators were not guilty of conspiracy, if contrary to what they intended, the building societies happened always to use a method of advancing the mortgage moneys which did not involve the use of a valuable security. In the case of conspiracy as opposed to the substantive offence, it is what is agreed to be done and not what was in fact done which is all important . . .

 COMMENTS AND QUESTIONS

1   Certain persons cannot be guilty of conspiracy – notably the intended victim of the conspiracy and children under the age of 10. Similarly, a person cannot be guilty of conspiracy if the only other parties to the conspiracy are his spouse; a child under the age of 10; or the intended victim; see further s 2 of the 1977 Act.

2   In *Practice Note* [1977] 2 All ER 540, Lord Widgery CJ at the sitting of the court announced the following practice direction made after consultation with the judges of the Queen's Bench Division:

(1) In any case where an indictment contains substantive counts and a related conspiracy count, the judge should require the prosecution to justify the joinder, or, failing justification, to elect whether to proceed on the substantive or on the conspiracy counts.

(2) A joinder is justified for this purpose if the judge considers that the interests of justice demands it.

3   Where D1 and D2 are charged with conspiracy, the acquittal of D1 does not necessarily mean that D2 must be acquitted as well. Under s 5 of the Criminal Law Act 1977, the court will have regard to whether or not, in all the circumstances of the case, the conviction of D2 is inconsistent with the acquittal of D1.

8.3.2 THE *MENS REA* OF STATUTORY CONSPIRACY

In one sense the *mens rea* of statutory conspiracy can be easily stated: D must intend to enter into an agreement with another person, and in doing so must intend that a course of conduct is followed that will result in the commission of an offence.

R v Saik [2006] UKHL 18

Lord Nicholls:

4. . . . under [s 1(1) of the Criminal Law Act 1977] the mental element of the offence, apart from the mental element involved in making an agreement, comprises the intention to pursue a course of conduct which will necessarily involve commission of the crime in question by one or more of the conspirators. The conspirators must intend to do the act prohibited by the substantive offence. The conspirators' state of mind must also satisfy the mental ingredients of the substantive offence. If one of the ingredients of the substantive offence is that the act is done with a specific intent, the conspirators must intend to do the prohibited act and must intend to do the prohibited act with the prescribed intent. A conspiracy to wound with intent to do grievous bodily harm contrary to section 18 of the Offences of the Person Act 1861 requires proof of an intention to wound with the intent of doing grievous bodily harm. The position is the same if the prescribed state of mind regarding the consequence of the prohibited act is recklessness. Damaging property, being reckless as to whether life is endangered thereby, is a criminal offence: Criminal Damage Act 1971, section 1(2). Conspiracy to commit this offence requires proof of an intention to damage property, and to do so recklessly indifferent to whether this would endanger life.

5. An intention to do a prohibited act is within the scope of section 1(1) even if the intention is expressed to be conditional on the happening, or non-happening, of some particular event. The question always is whether the agreed course of conduct, if carried out in accordance with the parties' intentions, would necessarily involve an offence. A conspiracy to rob a bank tomorrow if the coast is clear when the conspirators reach the bank is not, by reason of this qualification, any less a conspiracy to rob. In the nature of things, every agreement to do something in the future is hedged about with conditions, implicit if not explicit. In theory if not in practice, the condition

could be so far-fetched that it would cast doubt on the genuiness of a conspirator's expressed intention to do an unlawful act. If I agree to commit an offence should I succeed in climbing Mount Everest without the use of oxygen, plainly I have no intention to commit the offence at all. Fanciful cases apart, the conditional nature of the agreement is insufficient to take the conspiracy outside section 1(1).

Difficulties have arisen in conspiracy cases where there is some doubt as to the extent to which the defendant actually intended that the agreement be carried out, particularly where he himself intends to play no part in the execution of the agreement. Whilst Lord Bridge in *Anderson* (below) thought a conspirator would have to intend to play some part in carrying out the agreement, the Court of Appeal in *Siracusa* (below) quickly clarified this by explaining that the only *mens rea* required was an intention to agree that other parties to the conspiracy should carry out the agreed course of conduct.

R v Anderson [1986] AC 27 (HL)

The appellant agreed that he would purchase and supply diamond wire, a cutting agent capable of cutting through metal bars, to be smuggled into the prison by either Assou or Mohammed Andaloussi. The plan was that either Assou or Mohammed Andaloussi would pass the cutting wire on to an inmate in the prison, Ahmed Andaloussi in order that he should use the wire to escape from his cell. The appellant was to be paid £20,000 for his part in the escape scheme. The appellant actually received from Assou a payment of £2,000 on account of the agreed fee of £20,000. Shortly after this the appellant was injured in a road accident and thereafter took no further step in pursuance of the escape plan. The appellant was convicted of conspiring to effect the escape of a prisoner, and appealed on the basis that he had only agreed to supply the wire. He had been indifferent as to whether the escape plan would actually work, and therefore did not have the *mens rea* for conspiracy. His appeal was dismissed by the Court of Appeal, and the following questions were certified for consideration by the House of Lords:

(1) Is a person who 'agrees' with two or more others, who themselves intend to pursue a course of conduct which will necessarily involve the commission of an offence, and who has a secret intention himself to participate in part only of that course of conduct, guilty himself of conspiracy to commit that offence under s 1(1) of the Criminal Law Act 1977?
(2) If not, is he liable to be indicted as a principal offender under s 8 of the Accessories and Abettors Act 1861? . . .

Lord Bridge of Harwich:
. . . The Criminal Law Act of 1977, subject to exceptions not presently material, abolished the offence of conspiracy at common law. It follows that the elements of the new statutory offence of conspiracy must be ascertained purely by interpretation of the language of s 1(1) of the Act of 1977. For purposes of analysis it is perhaps convenient to isolate the three clauses each of which must be taken as indicating an essential ingredient of the offence as follows:

(1) 'if a person agrees with any other person or persons that a course of conduct shall be pursued'

(2) 'which will necessarily amount to or involve the commission of any offence or offences by one or more of the parties to the agreement'

(3) 'if the agreement is carried out in accordance with their intentions'.

Clause (1) presents, as it seems to me, no difficulty. It means exactly what it says and what it says is crystal clear. To be convicted, the party charged must have agreed with one or more others that 'a course of conduct shall be pursued'. What is important is to resist the temptation to introduce into this simple concept ideas derived from the civil law of contract. Any number of persons may agree that a course of conduct shall be pursued without undertaking any contractual liability. The agreed course of conduct may be a simple or an elaborate one and may involve the participation of two or any larger number of persons who may have agreed to play a variety of roles in the course of conduct agreed.

Again, clause (2) could hardly use simpler language. Here what is important to note is that it is not necessary that more than one of the participants in the agreed course of conduct shall commit a substantive offence. It is, of course, necessary that any party to the agreement shall have assented to play his part in the agreed course of conduct, however innocent in itself, knowing that the part to be played by one or more of the others will amount to or involve the commission of an offence.

It is only clause (3) which presents any possible ambiguity. The heart of the submission for the appellant is that in order to be convicted of conspiracy to commit a given offence the language of clause (3) requires that the party charged should not only have agreed that a course of conduct shall be pursued which will necessarily amount to or involve the commission of that offence by himself or one or more other parties to the agreement, but must also be proved himself to have intended that that offence should be committed. Thus, it is submitted here that the appellant's case that he never intended that Andaloussi should be enabled to escape from prison raised an issue to be left to the jury, who should have been directed to convict him only if satisfied that he did so intend. I do not find it altogether easy to understand why the draftsman of this provision chose to use the phrase 'in accordance with their intentions'. But I suspect the answer may be that this seemed a desirable alternative to the phrase 'in accordance with its terms', or any similar expression, because it is a matter of common experience in the criminal courts that the 'terms' of a criminal conspiracy are hardly ever susceptible of proof. The evidence from which a jury may infer a criminal conspiracy is almost invariably to be found in the conduct of the parties. This was so at common law and remains so under the statute. If the evidence in a given case justifies the inference of an agreement that a course of conduct should be pursued, it is a not inappropriate formulation of the test of the criminality of the inferred agreement to ask whether the further inference can be drawn that a crime would necessarily have been committed if the agreed course of conduct had been pursued in accordance with the several intentions of the parties. Whether that is an accurate analysis or not, I am clearly driven by consideration of the diversity of roles which parties may agree to play in criminal conspiracies to reject any construction of the statutory language which would require the prosecution to prove an intention on the part of each conspirator that the criminal offence or offences which will necessarily be committed by one or more of the conspirators if the agreed course of conduct is fully carried out should in fact be committed. A simple example will illustrate the absurdity to which this construction would lead. The proprietor of a car hire firm agrees for a substantial payment to make available a hire car to a gang for use in a robbery and to make false entries in his books relating to the hiring to which he can point if the number of the car is traced back to him in connection with the robbery. Being fully aware of the circumstances of the robbery in which the car is proposed to be used he is plainly a party to the conspiracy to rob. Making his car available for use in the robbery is as much part of the relevant agreed course of conduct as the robbery itself. Yet, once he has been paid, it will be a matter of complete indifference to him whether the robbery is in fact committed or not. In these days of highly organised crime the most serious statutory conspiracies will frequently involve an elaborate and complex agreed course of conduct in which many will consent to play necessary but subordinate roles, not involving them in any direct participation in the commission of the offence or offences at the centre of the conspiracy. Parliament cannot have intended that such parties should escape conviction of conspiracy on the basis that it cannot be proved against them that they intended that the relevant offence or offences should be committed.

There remains the important question whether a person who has agreed that a course of conduct will be pursued which, if pursued as agreed, will necessarily amount to or involve the commission of an offence, is guilty of statutory conspiracy irrespective of his intention, and, if not, what is the *mens rea* of the offence? I have no hesitation in answering the first part of the question in the negative. There may be many situations in which perfectly respectable citizens, more particularly those concerned with law enforcement, may enter into agreements that a course of conduct shall be pursued which will involve commission of a crime without the least intention of playing any part in furtherance of the ostensibly agreed criminal objective, but rather with the purpose of exposing and frustrating the criminal purpose of the other parties to the agreement. To say this is in no way to encourage schemes by which police act, directly or through the agency of informers, as *agents provocateurs* for the purpose of entrapment. That is conduct of which the courts have always strongly disapproved. But it may sometimes happen, as most of us with experience in criminal trials well know, that a criminal enterprise is well advanced in the course of preparation when it comes to the notice either of the police or of some honest citizen in such circumstances that the only prospect of exposing and frustrating the criminals is that some innocent person should play the part of an intending collaborator in the course of criminal conduct proposed to be pursued. The *mens rea* implicit in the offence of statutory conspiracy must clearly be such as to recognise the innocence of such a person, notwithstanding that he will, in literal terms, be obliged to agree that a course of conduct be pursued involving the commission of an offence.

I have said already, but I repeat to emphasise its importance, that an essential ingredient in the crime of conspiring to commit a specific offence or offences under s 1(1) of the Act of 1977 is that the accused should agree that a course of conduct be pursued which he knows must involve the commission by one or more of the parties to the agreement of that offence or those offences. But, beyond the mere fact of agreement, the necessary *mens rea* of the crime is, in my opinion, established if, and only if, it is shown that the accused, when he entered into the agreement, intended to play some part in the agreed course of conduct in furtherance of the criminal purpose which the agreed course of conduct was intended to achieve. Nothing less will suffice; nothing more is required.

Applying this test to the facts which, for the purposes of the appeal, we must assume, the appellant, in agreeing that a course of conduct be pursued that would, if successful, necessarily involve the offence of effecting Andaloussi's escape from lawful custody, clearly intended, by providing diamond wire to be smuggled into the prison, to play a part in the agreed course of conduct in furtherance of that criminal objective. Neither the fact that he intended to play no further part in attempting to effect the escape, nor that he believed the escape to be impossible, would, if the jury had supposed they might be true, have afforded him any defence.

In the result, I would answer the first part of the certified question in the affirmative and dismiss the appeal. Your Lordships did not find it necessary to hear argument directed to the second part of the certified question and it must, therefore, be left unanswered.

R v Siracusa (1990) 90 Cr App R 340 (CA)

O'Connor LJ:

. . . The case arises out of the operations of an organisation of smugglers engaged in moving massive quantities of heroin from Thailand and cannabis from Kashmir to Canada via England. The scheme was simple. The drugs were to be housed in secret compartments in selected items of locally produced furniture, which would be included in substantial shipments of furniture. The object of passing the consignments through England was to support the manifests to be presented to the Canadian customs declaring the country of origin of the goods as England.

On 13 December 1984 a consignment of 52 packing cases of furniture from India consigned to Elongate Ltd arrived at Felixstowe. Customs officers found in some articles of furniture cannabis with a street value of £0.5 million in England and £3 million in Canada. They repacked and waited and watched. The consignment was cleared by shipping agents and delivered to a warehouse, Unit 5, Batsworth Road, Mitcham. The customs moved in on 18 December 1984, seized the consignment and arrested Siracusa and a man named Gaultieri. Unit 5 is a spacious warehouse. There was nothing in it except the 52 cases of furniture and a fork-lift truck. The work in hand was the painting out of the Indian shipping marks with black paint.

On 28 May 1985, a consignment of 84 packing cases of furniture from Thailand consigned to Ital Provisions Ltd arrived at Southampton. Customs officers found in some articles of furniture heroin with a street value of £15 million in England and £75 million in Canada. They repacked some of the heroin and waited and watched. The consignment was not delivered in this country, but trans-shipped and left for Canada on 8 June 1985.

After delivery in Canada on 21 June 1985, enforcement officers moved in, seized the consignment and arrested three men. It was found that they had gone unerringly to the cases containing the pieces in which heroin was concealed. In England, Monteleone, Luciani and Di Carlo were arrested on 21 June 1985 . . .

The appellants contend that . . . the prosecution had to prove against each defendant that he knew that the Kashmir operation involved cannabis and that the Thailand operation involved heroin . . .

His Lordship referred to the speech of Lord Bridge in *R v Anderson* [1986] AC 27 and commented:

. . . We think it obvious that Lord Bridge cannot have been intending that the organiser of a crime who recruited others to carry it out would not himself be guilty of conspiracy unless it could be proved that he intended to play some active part himself thereafter . . .

The present case is a classic example of such a conspiracy. It is the hallmark of such crimes that the organisers try to remain in the background and more often than not are not apprehended. Second, the origins of all conspiracies are concealed and it is usually quite impossible to establish when or where the initial agreement was made, or when or where other conspirators were recruited. The very existence of the agreement can only be inferred from overt acts. Participation in a conspiracy is infinitely variable: it can be active or passive. If the majority shareholder and director of a company consents to the company being used for drug smuggling carried out in the company's name by a fellow director and minority shareholder, he is guilty of conspiracy.

Consent, that is the agreement or adherence to the agreement, can be inferred if it is proved that he knew what was going on and the intention to participate in the furtherance of the criminal purpose is also established by his failure to stop the unlawful activity. Lord Bridge's dictum does not require anything more.

His Lordship then referred to the *dictum* of Lord Bridge that:

. . . an essential ingredient in the crime of conspiring to commit a specific offence or offences under s 1(1) of the Act of 1977 is that the accused should agree that a course of conduct be pursued which he knows must involve the commission by one or more of the parties to the agreement of that offence or those offences.

And O'Connor LJ went to observe that:

Lord Bridge plainly does not mean that the prosecution have to prove that persons who agree to import prohibited drugs into this country know that the offence which will be committed will be in contravention of s 170(2) of the Customs and Excise Management Act. He is not to be taken as saying that the prosecution must prove that the accused knew the name of the crime. We are satisfied that Lord Bridge was doing no more than applying the words of s 1 of the Criminal Law Act 1977, namely that when the accused agreed to the course of conduct, he knew that it involved the commission of an offence.

The *mens rea* sufficient to support the commission of a substantive offence will not necessarily be sufficient to support a charge of conspiracy to commit that offence. An intent to cause grievous bodily harm is sufficient to support the charge of murder, but is not sufficient to support a charge of conspiracy to murder or of attempt to murder.

We have come to the conclusion that if the prosecution charge a conspiracy to contravene s 170(2) of the Customs and Excise Management Act by the importation of heroin, then the prosecution must prove that the agreed course of conduct was the importation of heroin. This is because the essence of the crime of conspiracy is the agreement and in simple terms, you do not prove an agreement to import heroin by proving an agreement to import cannabis.

We are confident that in coming to this conclusion, we are not making the enforcement of the anti-drug laws more difficult. If the facts suggest that the agreement was to import prohibited drugs of more than one class that can be appropriately laid because s 1(1) of the Criminal Law Act expressly provides for the agreed course of conduct to involve the commission of more than one offence . . .

Yip Chiu-Cheung v R [1994] 3 WLR 514 (PC)

Lord Griffiths:
. . . The prosecution case was based primarily on the evidence of Philip Needham who was an undercover drug enforcement officer of the United States of America and named in the indictment

as a co-conspirator. The other conspirator, referred to in the indictment as a person unknown, was introduced to Needham by the defendant under the name of Hom.

In outline Needham's evidence was that he had a series of meetings in Thailand with the defendant, at one of which Hom also took part, at which it was arranged that Needham would act as a courier to carry five kilos of heroin from Hong Kong to Australia, travelling by air.

The arrangement was that Needham would fly to Hong Kong on 22 October 1989 under the name of Larsen, where he would be met by the defendant. He would then stay at the Nathan Hotel in Kowloon for a few days and then fly on to Australia with five kilos of heroin supplied by the defendant. For this service he would be paid US $16,000. In fact Needham did not fly to Hong Kong on 22 October because the flight was delayed and he missed the rescheduled flight. Needham said he had no way of contacting the defendant in Hong Kong and had been advised by the Hong Kong authorities that the Nathan Hotel would be a dangerous place for him to stay. Needham therefore proceeded no further with the plan, and did not go to Hong Kong.

The defendant was arrested in Hong Kong on 15 November, a piece of paper with the name Larsen was found in the defendant's possession and it was admitted that he had come to the airport to meet Needham's flight on 22 October.

Needham said that throughout his dealings with the defendant and Hom he kept the authorities in Hong Kong and Australia informed of the plans and they agreed that he would not be prevented from carrying the heroin out of Hong Kong and into Australia. It was obviously the intention to try to identify and arrest both the suppliers and the distributors of the drug . . .

On the principal ground of appeal it was submitted that the trial judge and the Court of Appeal were wrong to hold that Needham, the undercover agent, could be a conspirator because he lacked the necessary *mens rea* or guilty mind required for the offence of conspiracy. It was urged upon their Lordships that no moral guilt attached to the undercover agent who was at all times acting courageously and with the best of motives in attempting to infiltrate and bring to justice a gang of criminal drug dealers. In these circumstances it was argued that it would be wrong to treat the agent as having any criminal intent, and reliance was placed upon a passage in the speech of Lord Bridge of Harwich in *R v Anderson* [1986] AC 27, 38–39; but in that case Lord Bridge was dealing with a different situation from that which exists in the present case. There may be many cases in which undercover police officers or other law enforcement agents pretend to join a conspiracy in order to gain information about the plans of the criminals, with no intention of taking any part in the planned crime but rather with the intention of providing information that will frustrate it. It was to this situation that Lord Bridge was referring in *R v Anderson*. The crime of conspiracy requires an agreement between two or more persons to commit an unlawful act with the intention of carrying it out. It is the intention to carry out the crime that constitutes the necessary *mens rea* for the offence. As Lord Bridge pointed out, an undercover agent who has no intention of committing the crime lacks the necessary *mens rea* to be a conspirator.

The facts of the present case are quite different. Nobody can doubt that Needham was acting courageously and with the best of motives; he was trying to break a drug ring. But equally there can be no doubt that the method he chose and in which the police in Hong Kong acquiesced involved the commission of the criminal offence of trafficking in drugs by exporting heroin from Hong Kong without a licence. Needham intended to commit that offence by carrying the heroin through the customs and onto the aeroplane bound for Australia.

Neither the police, nor customs, nor any other members of the executive have any power to alter the terms of the ordinance forbidding the export of heroin, and the fact that they may turn a blind eye when the heroin is exported does not prevent it from being a criminal offence . . .

Naturally, Needham never expected to be prosecuted if he carried out the plan as intended. But the fact that in such circumstances the authorities would not prosecute the undercover agent does not mean that he did not commit the crime albeit as part of a wider scheme to combat drug dealing.

The judge correctly directed the jury that they should regard Needham as a conspirator if they found that he intended to export the heroin . . .

8.3.3 CONSPIRACY TO COMMIT STRICT OR ABSOLUTE LIABILITY OFFENCES

Section 1(2) of the Criminal Law Act 1977 provides:

Where liability for any offence may be incurred without knowledge on the part of the person committing it of any particular fact or circumstance necessary for the commission of the offence, a person shall nevertheless not be guilty of conspiracy to commit that offence by virtue of sub-section (1) above unless he and at least one other party to the agreement intend or know that the fact or circumstance shall or will exist at the time when the conduct constituting the offence is to take place.

This provision not only requires proof of *mens rea* even where D is charged with conspiring to commit a strict or absolute liability offence, it also means that less onerous forms of *mens rea* required for completed crimes, such as 'suspicion' or 'recklessness' will not suffice if conspiracy is charged. The defendant must know of the facts that will constitute the offence, or intend that they will exist at the time of the offence.

R v Saik [2006] UKHL 18

The defendant was convicted of conspiring to convert the proceeds of drug trafficking and/or criminal conduct contrary to s 1(1) of the Criminal Law Act 1977. The substantive offence, created by s 93C(2) of the Criminal Justice Act 1988 provided that: 'A person is guilty of an offence if, knowing or having reasonable grounds to suspect that any property is, or in whole or in part directly or indirectly represents, another person's proceeds of criminal conduct, he—(a) conceals or disguises that property; or (b) converts or transfers that property or removes it from the jurisdiction, for the purpose of assisting any person to avoid prosecution for an offence to which this Part of this Act applies or the making or enforcement in his case of a confiscation order.'

The defendant contended that he could not be guilty of conspiring to commit the offence contrary to s 93 of the 1988 Act as it required proof that he knew or had reasonable grounds to suspect that the property in question represented the proceeds of crime. In support of his contention he cited s 1(2) of the Criminal Law Act 1977, which provides that: 'Where liability for any offence may be incurred without knowledge on the part of the person committing it of any particular fact or circumstance necessary for the commission of the offence, a person shall nevertheless not be guilty of conspiracy to commit that offence by virtue of subsection (1) above unless he and at least one other party to the agreement intend or know that that fact or circumstance shall or will exist at the time when the conduct constituting the offence is to take place.'

The issue for the House of Lords was, therefore, whether or not the prosecution had to prove that the defendant had known the property in question represented the proceeds of crime.

Lord Nicholls:

6. Section 1(2) qualifies the scope of the offence created by section 1(1). This subsection is more difficult. Its essential purpose is to ensure that strict liability and recklessness have no place in the offence of conspiracy . . .

7. Under this subsection conspiracy involves a third mental element: intention or knowledge that a fact or circumstances necessary for the commission of the substantive offence will exist. Take the offence of handling stolen goods. One of its ingredients is that the goods must have been stolen. That is a fact necessary for the commission of the offence. Section 1(2) requires that the conspirator must intend or know that this fact will exist when the conduct constituting the offence takes place.

8. It follows from this requirement of intention or knowledge that proof of the mental element needed for the commission of a substantive offence will not always suffice on a charge of conspiracy to commit that offence. In respect of a material fact or circumstance conspiracy has its own mental element. In conspiracy this mental element is set as high as 'intend or know'. This subsumes any lesser mental element, such as suspicion, required by the substantive offence in respect of a material fact or circumstances. In this respect the mental element of conspiracy is distinct from and supersedes the mental element in the substantive offence. When this is so, the lesser mental element in the substantive offence becomes otiose on a charge of conspiracy. It is an immaterial averment. To include it in the particulars of the offence of conspiracy is potentially confusing and should be avoided.

9. The phrase 'fact or circumstance necessary for the commission of the offence' is opaque. Difficulties have sometimes arisen in its application. The key seems to lie in the distinction apparent in the subsection between 'intend or know' on the one hand and any particular 'fact or circumstance necessary for the commission of the offence' on the other hand. The latter is directed at an element of the actus reus of the offence. A mental element of the offence is not itself a 'fact or circumstance' for the purposes of the subsection.

10. This contrast can be illustrated by the offence of entering into an arrangement whereby the retention by another person (A) of A's proceeds of crime is facilitated, knowing or suspecting A has been engaged in crime: section 93A of the Criminal Justice Act 1988, now repealed. The requirement that the defendant must know or suspect A's criminal history is an element of the offence, but it is a mental element. The need for the defendant to have this state of mind is not a fact or circumstance within section 1(2). Another ingredient of the offence is that the property involved must be the proceeds of crime. That is a fact necessary for the commission of the offence and section 1(2) applies to that fact . . .

11. The genesis of this feature of the legislation lies in the ingredients of the common law offence of conspiracy as enunciated by your Lordships' House in *R v Churchill* [1967] 2 AC 224. There the

defendant was charged with the common law offence of conspiracy to commit a statutory offence. The statutory offence was an offence of strict liability. The House held that the conspirator was not guilty of the offence of conspiracy if on the facts known to him the act he agreed to do was lawful.

12. This principle was accepted by the Law Commission in its subsequent report on *Conspiracy and Criminal Law Reform* (Law Com No 76) . . . This report led to the enactment of the Criminal Law Act 1977.

13. The rationale underlying this approach is that conspiracy imposes criminal liability on the basis of a person's intention. This is a different harm from the commission of the substantive offence. So it is right that the intention which is being criminalised in the offence of conspiracy should itself be blameworthy. This should be so, irrespective of the provisions of the substantive offence in that regard.

14. Against that background I turn to some issues concerning the scope and effect of section 1(2). The starting point is to note that this relieving provision is not confined to substantive offences attracting strict liability. The subsection does not so provide. Nor would such an interpretation of the subsection make sense. It would make no sense for section 1(2) to apply, and require proof of intention or knowledge, where liability for the substantive offence is absolute but not where the substantive offence has built into it a mental ingredient less than knowledge, such as suspicion.

15. So much is clear. A more difficult question arises where an ingredient of the substantive offence is that the defendant must know of a material fact or circumstance. On its face section 1(2) does not apply in this case. The opening words of section 1(2), on their face, limit the scope of the subsection to cases where a person may commit an offence without knowledge of a material fact or circumstance.

16. Plainly Parliament did not intend that a person would be liable for conspiracy where he lacks the knowledge required to commit the substantive offence. That could not be right. Parliament could not have intended such an absurd result. Rather, the assumption underlying section 1(2) is that, where knowledge of a material fact is an ingredient of a substantive offence, knowledge of that fact is also an ingredient of the crime of conspiring to commit the substantive offence.

17. There are two ways this result might be achieved. One is simply to treat section 1(2) as inapplicable in this type of case. This would mean that the knowledge requirement in the substantive offence would survive as a requirement which must also be satisfied in respect of a conspiracy. In the same way as a conspirator must intend to do the prohibited act with any specific intent required by the substantive offence, so he must intend to do the prohibited act having the knowledge required by the substantive offence. Accordingly, on this analysis, where knowledge of a fact is an ingredient of the substantive offence, section 1(2) is not needed.

18. The other route is to adopt the interpretation of section 1(2) suggested by Sir John Smith. The suggestion is that section 1(2) applies in such a case despite the opening words of the subsection. Section 1(2) is to be read as applicable even 'where liability for an offence may be incurred without knowledge [etc]'. It is difficult to see what other function the word 'nevertheless' has in the subsection. This may seem a slender peg on which to hang a conclusion of any substance, but it is enough: see 'Some Answers' [1978] Crim LR 210.

19. The first route accords more easily with the language of section 1(2), but I prefer the second route for the following reason. A conspiracy is looking to the future. It is an agreement about future conduct. When the agreement is made the 'particular fact or circumstance necessary for the commission' of the substantive offence may not have happened. So the conspirator cannot be said to know of that fact or circumstance at that time. Nor, if the happening of the fact or circumstance is beyond his control, can it be said that the conspirator will know of that fact or circumstance.

20. Section 1(2) expressly caters for this situation. The conspirator must 'intend or know' that this fact or circumstance 'shall or will exist' when the conspiracy is carried into effect. Although not the happiest choice of language, 'intend' is descriptive of a state of mind which is looking to the future. This is to be contrasted with the language of substantive offences. Generally, references to 'knowingly' or the like in substantive offences are references to a past state of affairs. No doubt this language could be moulded appropriately where the offence charged is conspiracy. But the more direct and satisfactory route is to regard section 1(2) as performing in relation to a conspiracy the function which words such as 'knowingly' perform in relation to the substantive offence. That approach accords better with what must be taken to have been the parliamentary intention on how the phrase 'intend or know' in section 1(2) would operate in this type of case. Thus on a charge of conspiracy to handle stolen property where the property has not been identified when the agreement is made, the prosecution must prove that the conspirator intended that the property which was the subject of the conspiracy would be stolen property.

21. In my view, therefore, the preferable interpretation of section 1(2) is that the subsection applies to all offences. It applies whenever an ingredient of an offence is the existence of a particular fact or circumstance. The subsection applies to that ingredient.

8.3.4 CONSPIRACY TO COMMIT A CRIME ABROAD

The courts in England and Wales have always had jurisdiction at common law to try a defendant for conspiracy to commit murder, regardless of whether or not the murder was planned to occur with the jurisdiction. This was recognised by Parliament in enacting s 1 (4) of the Criminal Law Act 1977 which provides:

In this part of this Act 'offence' means an offence triable in England and Wales, except that it includes murder notwithstanding that the murder in question would not be so triable if committed in accordance with the intentions of the parties to the agreement.

This should now be read subject to the provisions of the Criminal Justice (Terrorism and Conspiracy) Act 1998, the provisions of which repeal those aspects of the Sexual Offences (Conspiracy and Incitement) Act 1996, and the Criminal Justice Act 1993, in so far as those enactments dealt with the extra-territorial jurisdiction of the domestic courts in respect of conspiracy.

CRIMINAL JUSTICE (TERRORISM AND CONSPIRACY) ACT 1998

5(1) The following section shall be inserted after section 1 of the Criminal Law Act 1977 (conspiracy) –

Conspiracy to commit offences outside the United Kingdom

(1A)—(1) Where each of the following conditions is satisfied in the case of an agreement, this Part of this Act has effect in relation to the agreement as it has effect in relation to an agreement falling within section 1(1) above.

(2) The first condition is that the pursuit of the agreed course of conduct would at some stage involve – (a) an act by one or more of the parties, or (b) the happening of some other event, intended to take place in a country or territory outside the United Kingdom.

(3) The second condition is that that act or other event constitutes an offence under the law in force in that country or territory.

(4) The third condition is that the agreement would fall within section 1(1) above as an agreement relating to the commission of an offence but for the fact that the offence would not be an offence triable in England and Wales if committed in accordance with the parties' intentions.

(5) The fourth condition is that –

(a) a party to the agreement, or a party's agent, did anything in England and Wales in relation to the agreement before its formation, or

(b) a party to the agreement became a party in England and Wales (by joining it either in person or through an agent), or

(c) a party to the agreement, or a party's agent, did or omitted anything in England and Wales in pursuance of the agreement.

(6) In the application of this Part of this Act to an agreement in the case of which each of the above conditions is satisfied, a reference to an offence is to be read as a reference to what would be the offence in question but for the fact that it is not an offence triable in England and Wales.

(7) Conduct punishable under the law in force in any country or territory is an offence under that law for the purposes of this section, however it is described in that law.

(8) Subject to subsection (9) below, the second condition is to be taken to be satisfied unless, not later than rules of court may provide, the defence serve on the prosecution a notice –

(a) stating that, on the facts as alleged with respect to the agreed course of conduct, the condition is not in their opinion satisfied,

(b) showing their grounds for that opinion, and

(c) requiring the prosecution to show that it is satisfied.

(9) The court may permit the defence to require the prosecution to show that the second condition is satisfied without the prior service of a notice under subsection (8) above.

(10) In the Crown Court the question whether the second condition is satisfied shall be decided by the judge alone, and shall be treated as a question of law for the purposes of –

(a) section 9(3) of the Criminal Justice Act 1987 (preparatory hearing in fraud cases), and

(b) section 31(3) of the Criminal Procedure and Investigations Act 1996 (preparatory hearing in other cases).

(11) Any act done by means of a message (however communicated) is to be treated for the purposes of the fourth condition as done in England and Wales if the message is sent or received in England and Wales.

(12) In any proceedings in respect of an offence triable by virtue of this section, it is immaterial to guilt whether or not the accused was a British citizen at the time of any act or other event proof of which is required for conviction of the offence.

(13) References in any enactment, instrument or document (except those in this Part of this Act) to an offence of conspiracy to commit an offence include an offence triable in England and Wales as such a conspiracy by virtue of this section (without prejudice to subsection (6) above).

(14) Nothing in this section –

(a) applies to an agreement entered into before the day on which the Criminal Justice (Terrorism and Conspiracy) Act 1998 was passed, or

(b) imposes criminal liability on any person acting on behalf of, or holding office under, the Crown.

(2) At the end of section 4 of that Act (restrictions on the institution of proceedings) there shall be added –

(5) Subject to subsection (6) below, no proceedings for an offence triable by virtue of section 1A above may be instituted except by or with the consent of the Attorney General.

(6) The Secretary of State may by order provide that subsection (5) above shall not apply, or shall not apply to any case of a description specified in the order.

(7) An order under subsection (6) above –

(a) shall be made by statutory instrument, and

(b) shall not be made unless a draft has been laid before, and approved by resolution of, each House of Parliament.

8.3.5 COMMON LAW CONSPIRACY TO DEFRAUD

There are two types of conspiracy to defraud. One involves agreeing dishonestly to deprive a person of something to which he is entitled or to which he might be entitled; no actual deception need be proved. See *Scott v Metropolitan Police Commissioner* [1975] AC 819 and *R v Hollinshead* [1985] AC 975. The other form, which does require proof of deception, consists of dishonestly deceiving a person into acting contrary to his public duty. See, for example, *Welham v DPP* [1961] AC 103 and *R v Moses* [1991] Crim LR 617. As noted above, the prosecution should regard conspiracy to defraud as a residual form of liability. If the defendants have agreed on a course of conduct that will involve the commission of a substantive offence, statutory conspiracy should be charged. Where, however, the agreement is to engage in a dishonest course of conduct that will cause loss to another, but which may not actually amount to a substantive offence, common law conspiracy may provide the basis for a prosecution.

Scott v Metropolitan Police Commissioner [1975] AC 818 (HL)

Viscount Dilhorne:

. . . The Court of Appeal certified that a point of law of general public importance was involved in the decision to dismiss the appeal against conviction on count 1, namely:

Whether, on a charge of conspiracy to defraud, the Crown must establish an agreement to deprive the owners of their property by deception; or whether it is sufficient to prove an agreement to prejudice the rights of another or others without lawful justification and in circumstances of dishonesty . . .

In this case it is not necessary to decide that a conspiracy to defraud may exist even though its object was not to secure a financial advantage by inflicting an economic loss on the person at whom the conspiracy was directed. But for myself I see no reason why what was said by Lord Radcliffe in relation to forgery should not equally apply in relation to conspiracy to defraud.

In this case the accused bribed servants of the cinema owners to secure possession of films in order to copy them and in order to enable them to let the copies out on hire. By so doing Mr Blom-Cooper conceded they inflicted more than nominal damage to the goodwill of the owners of the copyright and distribution rights of the films. By so doing they secured for themselves profits which but for their actions might have been secured by those owners just as in *R v Button* 3 Cox CC 229 the defendants obtained profits which might have been secured by their employer. In the circumstances it is, I think, clear that they inflicted pecuniary loss on those owners . . .

Reverting to the questions certified by the Court of Appeal, the answer to the first question is in my opinion in the negative. I am not very happy about the way in which the second question is phrased although the word 'prejudice' has been not infrequently used in this connection. If by 'prejudice' is meant 'injure', then I think the answer to that question is yes, for in my opinion it is clearly the law that an agreement by two or more by dishonesty to deprive a person of something which is his or to which he is or would be or might be entitled and an agreement by two or more by dishonesty to injure some proprietary right of his, suffices to constitute the offence of conspiracy to defraud.

In my opinion this appeal should be dismissed.

Lord Diplock:
My Lords, I have had the advantage of reading the speech of my noble and learned friend, Viscount Dilhorne. I agree with it. The authorities he cites and others cited in the speeches in this House in the contemporaneous appeal in *R v Withers* [1975] AC 751, in my view, established the following propositions: . . .

(2) Where the intended victim of a 'conspiracy to defraud' is a private individual the purpose of the conspirators must be to cause the victim economic loss by depriving him of some property or right, corporeal or incorporeal, to which he is or would or might become entitled. The intended means by which the purpose is to be achieved must be dishonest. They need not involve fraudulent misrepresentation such as is needed to constitute the civil tort of deceit. Dishonesty of any kind is enough.

(3) Where the intended victim of a 'conspiracy to defraud' is a person performing public duties as distinct from a private individual it is sufficient if the purpose is to cause him to act contrary to his public duty, and the intended means of achieving this purpose are dishonest. The purpose need not involve causing economic loss to anyone.

In the instant case the intended victims of the conspiracy to defraud were private individuals. The facts bring it squarely within proposition 2 above. The dishonest means to be employed were clandestine bribery.

I would dismiss the appeal.

> **R v Hollinshead [1985] 1 AC 975 (HL)**
>
> Lord Roskill:
>
> . . . The Court of Appeal (Criminal Division) certified two points of law as of general public importance:
>
> 1 If parties agree (a) to manufacture devices whose only use is fraudulently to alter electricity meters and (b) to sell those devices to a person who intends merely to re-sell them and not himself to use them, does that agreement constitute a common law conspiracy to defraud?
>
> 2 Alternatively, is such an agreement properly charged as a statutory conspiracy to aid, abet, counsel or procure persons unknown to commit offences under s 2 of the Theft Act 1978? [see now ss 2 to 4 of the Fraud Act 2006]. . . .

His Lordship quoted from the speech of Lord Bridge of Harwich in *R v Ayres* [1984] AC 447 and continued:

> I therefore turn to consider whether it was necessary for the prosecution in order to secure a conviction on count 2 to aver and prove a dishonest agreement actually to use the black boxes so as to defraud the intended victims, various electricity boards . . .
>
> The real question . . . is whether in order to secure conviction on count 2 it was necessary to aver and prove a dishonest agreement by the respondents actually to use the black boxes, the submission being that it was not enough to show only an intention that such a dishonest use should follow their dishonest manufacture and sale . . .

His Lordship referred to a number of authorities including *Attorney General's Ref (No 1 of 1982)* [1983] QB 751, concerning a dishonest agreement to produce, label and distribute bottles of whiskey so as to represent them as containing whiskey of a well-known brand which in fact they did not contain, and said:

> In my view the respondents were liable to be convicted of conspiracy to defraud because they agreed to manufacture and sell and thus put into circulation dishonest devices, the sole purpose of which was to cause loss just as the former defendants in the case just referred to would, apart from the jurisdictional problem, have been liable to be convicted to defraud because they agreed dishonestly to produce, label and distribute bottles of whiskey, the sole purpose of the sale of which was to defraud potential purchasers of those bottles . . .
>
> In the result I would allow the appeals, answer certified question 1 'Yes' and certified question 2 'No'. I would restore the convictions of the respondents on count 2 . . .

Welham v DPP [1961] AC 103 (HL)

Lord Radcliffe:

. . . Now, I think that there are one or two things that can be said with confidence about the meaning of this word 'defraud'. It requires a person as its object: that is, defrauding involves doing something to someone. Although in the nature of things it is almost invariably associated with the obtaining of an advantage for the person who commits the fraud, it is the effect upon the person who is the object of the fraud that ultimately determines its meaning. This is nonetheless true because since the middle of the last century the law has not required an indictment to specify the person intended to be defrauded or to prove intent to defraud a particular person.

Second, popular speech does not give, and I do not think ever has given, any sure guide as to the limits of what is meant by 'to defraud'. It may mean to cheat someone. It may mean to practise a fraud on someone. It may mean to deprive someone by deceit of something which is regarded as belonging to him or, though not belonging to him, as due to him or his right. It passes easily into metaphor, as does so much of the English natural speech. Murray's *New English Dictionary* instances such usages as defrauding a man of his due praise or his hopes. Rudyard Kipling in the First World War wrote of our 'angry and defrauded young'. There is nothing in any of this that suggests that to defraud is in ordinary speech confined to the idea of depriving a man by deceit of some economic advantage or inflicting upon him some economic loss.

Has the law ever so confined it? In my opinion there is no warrant for saying that it has . . .

Of course, as I have said, in 99 cases out of 100 the intent to deceive one person to his prejudice merely connotes the deceiver's intention of obtaining an advantage for himself by inflicting a corresponding loss upon the person deceived. In all such cases the economic explanation is sufficient. But in that special line of cases where the person deceived is a public authority or a person holding a public office, deceit may secure an advantage for the deceiver without causing anything that can fairly be called either a pecuniary or an economic injury to the person deceived. If there could be no intent to defraud in the eyes of the law without an intent to inflict a pecuniary or economic injury, such cases as these could not have been punished as forgeries at common law, in which an intent to defraud is an essential element of the offence, yet I am satisfied that they were regularly so treated . . .

Lord Denning:

. . . If a drug addict forges a doctor's prescription so as to enable him to get drugs from a chemist, he has, I should have thought, an intent to defraud, even though he intends to pay the chemist the full price and no one is a penny the worse off . . .

. . . It has long been ruled that it is no answer to a charge of forgery to say that there was no intent to defraud any particular person, because a general intent to defraud is sufficient to constitute the crime. So also it is no answer to say that there was no intent to defraud the recipient, if there was intent to defraud somebody else: see *R v Taylor* (1779) 1 Leach 214 . . .

R v Landy [1981] 1 WLR 355 (CA)

Lawton LJ:

. . . What the prosecution had to prove was a conspiracy to defraud which is an agreement dishonestly to do something which will or may cause loss or prejudice to another. The offence is one of dishonesty. This is the all-important ingredient which must be stressed by the judge in his directions to the jury and must not be minimised in any way. There is always a danger that a jury may think that proof of an irregularity followed by loss is proof of dishonesty. The dishonesty to be proved must be in the minds and intentions of the defendants. It is to their states of mind that the jury must direct their attention. What the reasonable man or the jurors themselves would have believed or intended in the circumstances in which the defendants found themselves is not what the jury have to decide; but what a reasonable man or they themselves would have believed or intended in similar circumstances may help them to decide what in fact individual defendants believed or intended. An assertion by a defendant that throughout a transaction he acted honestly does not have to be accepted but has to be weighed like any other piece of evidence. If that was the defendant's state of mind, or may have been, he is entitled to be acquitted. But if the jury, applying their own notions of what is honest and what is not, conclude that he could not have believed that he was acting honestly, then the element of dishonesty will have been established. What a jury must not do is to say to themselves: 'If we had been in his place we would have known we were acting dishonestly so he must have known he was.' What they can say is: 'We are sure he was acting dishonestly because we can see no reason why a man of his intelligence and experience would not have appreciated, as right-minded people would have done, that what he was doing was dishonest.' In our judgment this is the way *R v Feely* [1973] QB 530 should be applied in cases where the issue of dishonesty arises. It is also the way in which the jury should have been directed in this case but, unfortunately, they were not . . .

Wai Yu-Tsang v R [1992] 1 AC 269 (PC)

Lord Goff of Chieveley:
. . . [*Welham v DPP* [1961] AC 103] establishes that the expression 'intent to defraud' is not to be given a narrow meaning, involving an intention to cause economic loss to another. In broad terms, it means simply an intention to practise a fraud on another, or an intention to act to the prejudice of another man's right . . .

His Lordship then referred to *R v Scott* [1975] AC 819 and to the speech of Lord Diplock and said:

With the greatest respect to Lord Diplock, their Lordships consider this categorisation to be too narrow. In their opinion, in agreement with the approach of Lord Radcliffe in *Welham v DPP* [1961] AC 103, the cases concerned with persons performing public duties are not to be regarded as a special category in the manner described by Lord Diplock, but rather as exemplifying the general principle that conspiracies to defraud are not restricted to cases of intention to cause the victim economic loss . . .
. . . In *R v Allsop* 64 Cr App R 29 what the defendant agreed to do was to present the company with false particulars, in reliance upon which, as he knew, the company would decide whether to enter into hire-purchase transactions. It is then necessary to consider whether that could constitute a conspiracy to defraud, notwithstanding that the defendant's underlying purpose or motive

was not to damage any economic interest of the company but to ensure that the transaction went through so that he would earn his commission. Their Lordships can see no reason why such an agreement should not be a conspiracy to defraud the company, substantially for the reasons given by the Court of Appeal. The defendant was, for his own purposes, dishonestly supplying the company with false information which persuaded it to accept risks which it would or might not have accepted if it had known the true facts. Their Lordships cannot see why this was not an agreement to practise a fraud on the company because . . . it was a dishonest agreement to employ a deceit which imperilled the economic interests of the company . . .

. . . Their Lordships are . . . reluctant to allow this part of the law to become enmeshed in a distinction, sometimes artificially drawn, between intention and recklessness. The question whether particular facts reveal a conspiracy to defraud depends upon what the conspirators have dishonestly agreed to do, and in particular whether they have agreed to practise a fraud on somebody. For this purpose it is enough for example that, as in *R v Allsop* and in the present case, the conspirators have dishonestly agreed to bring about a state of affairs which they realise will or may deceive the victim into so acting, or failing to act, that he will suffer economic loss or his economic interests will be put at risk. It is however important in such a case, as the Court of Appeal stressed in *R v Allsop*, to distinguish a conspirator's intention (or immediate purpose) dishonestly to bring about such a state of affairs from his motive (or underlying purpose). The latter may be benign to the extent that he does not wish the victim or potential victim to suffer harm; but the mere fact that it is benign will not of itself prevent the agreement from constituting a conspiracy to defraud. Of course, if the conspirators were not acting dishonestly, there will have been no conspiracy to defraud; and in any event their benign purpose (if it be such) is a matter which, if they prove to be guilty, can be taken into account at the stage of sentence . . .

COMMENTS AND QUESTIONS

1   Common law conspiracy to defraud may be a useful tool in the armoury of the prosecution, but is it appropriate to exploit an offence that essentially comprises an allegation that the defendants agreed to engage in a course of conduct which (albeit it was dishonest), if completed, would not result in the commission of a substantive offence? See criticisms below at 8.3.6

2   For evidence of the offences of common law conspiracy to corrupt public morals, and conspiracy to outrage public decency, see further *Shaw v DPP* [1962] AC 220 and *Knuller v DPP* [1973] AC 435. These offences have been interpreted very restrictively. In essence, 'corrupting public morals' involves undermining the very fabric of society; 'outraging public decency' means going considerably further than shocking reasonable people.

3   In cases where there is an overlap between statutory conspiracy and conspiracy to defraud, the prosecution can make a choice as to which form of conspiracy should be charged. As s 12 of the Criminal Justice Act 1987 provides, the fact that a statutory conspiracy could be charged (ie an agreement to commit a criminal offence) does not preclude a charge of conspiracy to defraud being brought.

8.3.6 CODIFICATION AND LAW REFORM PROPOSALS

The Law Commission, in its Report *Criminal Law: Conspiracy to Defraud* (Law Com 228, 1994), concluded:

> We believe that for practical reasons conspiracy to defraud performs a useful role in the present law of dishonesty, and we have concluded that it should remain intact pending our comprehensive review of the law. We have resolved that it would be inappropriate, at a time when we are about to re-examine the whole scheme of dishonesty offences, to make piecemeal recommendations for reform of other aspects of the law of dishonesty . . . [para 1.20].

The Report went on, however, to consider some of the more significant criticisms of the offence of conspiracy to defraud, notably:

- that it should not be a criminal offence to agree to a course of conduct which, if carried out, would not involve the commission of a criminal offence, notwithstanding that dishonesty would be involved.
- that the offence was potentially too wide (over-inclusive).
- that the parameters of the offence were vague and uncertain. Having reviewed the subject of fraud offences in depth, the Commission went on to recommend, in its report *Fraud* (Law Com 276), that the offence of conspiracy to defraud at common law ought to be abolished.

Following consultations on the proposals in Law Com 276 however, the government (in its response paper Fraud Law Reform (2005)) opted to retain, at least for the time being, an offence of conspiracy to defraud at common law, for the reasons set out in the extracts below:

> *Fraud law reform – Government response to consultations*
>
> 39. The repeal of Common Law Conspiracy to Defraud was the only proposal to which there was widespread opposition. It is normally fundamental to a codification exercise such as this, that the common law should be repealed in favour of the new statute. A large minority of respondents agreed with the Law Commission that it was illogical that what was legal for one person should be criminal for many, and that the offence is unfairly uncertain, and so wide it has the potential to catch behaviour that should not be criminal. They took the view that the new statutory offences, together with the possibility of charging statutory conspiracy to commit these new offences, and bearing in mind other possible charges – such as the new offence of cheating at gambling that is in the current Gambling Bill – cover all the behaviour that in practice should be covered by the criminal law.
>
> 40. However the repeal was opposed by the majority of consultees. The main argument was that, at least until we have experience of how the new offences operate in practice, it would be rash to repeal conspiracy to defraud as it provides flexibility in dealing with a wide variety of frauds. They argued that it was not clear that the new offences could successfully replace it in every case, especially bearing in mind developing technology and possible new types of fraud.

41. It was argued that conspiracy to defraud was well defined [e.g. *Welham v DPP* (extracted above)]and is not tied to economic gain or loss, but only requires that the conduct prejudices another person's rights. That makes it particularly useful in intellectual property cases and in cases where no economic loss has been suffered. An example of the latter was *Terry* [1984] AC 374 where the defendants made use of vehicle excise licences in a fraudulent manner. It is also useful in dealing with cases where the fraudulent nature of a transaction only becomes apparent in the context of several other transactions.

42. Some respondents referred to limitations on statutory conspiracy (under the Criminal Law Act 1977) – in particular that the parties to it must intend that the substantive offence will be perpetrated by one or more of the conspirators. This is not required for conspiracy to defraud. In *Hollinshead* [1985] 1 All ER 850 for example the defendants conspired to market devices for use by third parties to avoid paying for electricity used. The Court of Appeal held that this did not amount to a conspiracy to commit offences under section 2 of the 1978 Act, as the defendants themselves were not practising the fraud on the electricity companies, but it did constitute conspiracy to defraud. One respondent said that this situation often arose in cases involving intellectual property: for example a group of people conspire to manufacture counterfeit goods but do not themselves commit any deception in selling them on to another person, who makes the actual public sale.

43. In their 2002 report, the Law Commission suggested that this issue is more appropriately dealt with in the context of their work on assisting and encouraging crime rather than in the Fraud Bill. This work is not yet complete, though it should be published early in 2005.

44. A compromise position was proposed, under which repeal would be enacted but not implemented until after a transitional period during which experience may show it is no longer being used, having been successfully replaced in practice by the new offences. We are not attracted by this approach, which is somewhat untidy and unlikely to work in the absence of a solution to the *Hollinshead* type of case.

45. Bearing in mind in particular the Hollinshead type of case, we decided to accept the view of the majority and retain common law conspiracy to defraud for the present. However it remains our long-term aim to repeal this common law crime and we will review the position in the context of the Law Commission's forthcoming report and any action to implement it. This should also allow any final decision to be made in the light of some experience of the Fraud Bill in operation.

8.3.7 IMPOSSIBILITY AS A DEFENCE TO CONSPIRACY

As far as statutory conspiracy is concerned, there is no longer any defence based on impossibility, save where the allegation is that the defendants agreed to commit an offence unknown to law. The removal of any impossibility based defence was effected by the Criminal Attempts Act 1981, which amended the 1977 Act by providing that: '. . . if a person agrees with any other person or persons that a course of conduct shall be pursued which, if the agreement is carried out in accordance with their intentions . . . will necessarily amount to or involve the commission of any offence or offences by one or more of the parties to the agreement, or *would do so but for the existence of facts which render the commission of the offence or any of the offences impossible*, he is guilty of conspiracy to commit the offence or offences in question.' (emphasis added)

Hence, provided the defendant believes, at the time of the agreement, that the course of conduct agreed upon will result in the commission of an offence, he can be convicted of conspiracy. For common law conspiracy, the defence of impossibility remains as detailed below in *DPP v Nock*.

DPP v Nock [1978] AC 979 (HL)

Lord Scarman:

. . . Five persons, including the two appellants, David Michael Nock and Kevin Charles Alsford, appeared at the Snaresbrook Crown Court on 5 January 1977, to answer an indictment charging them with a number of drug offences. Nock and Alsford were convicted upon several counts but your Lordships' House is concerned only with their conviction upon the first count in the indictment. It charged them (and others) with conspiracy to contravene s 4 of the Misuse of Drugs Act 1971. The section provides by subsection (1) that subject to regulations (which are of no present relevance) it shall not be lawful for a person to produce a controlled drug and by subsection (2) that it is an offence to produce a controlled drug in contravention of subsection (1). The particulars of offence, after being amended, were as follows:

Kevin Charles Alsford, David Michael Nock [and three other named defendants] on divers days before 23 September 1975, conspired together and with other persons unknown to produce a controlled drug of Class A, namely cocaine.

The indictment makes plain that the Crown is alleging in this case a conspiracy to commit a crime: and no one has suggested that the particulars fail to disclose an offence known to the law. But the appellants submit, and it is not disputed by the Crown that the agreement as proved was narrower in scope than the conspiracy charged. When the case was before the Court of Appeal, counsel on both sides agreed that the evidence went to prove that the appellants agreed together to obtain cocaine by separating it from the other substance or substances contained in a powder which they had obtained from one of their co-defendants, a Mr Mitchell. They believed that the powder was a mixture of cocaine and lignocaine, and that they would be able to produce cocaine from it. In fact the powder was lignocaine hydrochloride, an anaesthetic used in dentistry, which contains no cocaine at all. It is impossible to produce, by separation or otherwise, cocaine from lignocaine. The agreement between the appellants was correctly summarised by the Court of Appeal, when certifying the point of law, as an agreement 'to pursue a course of action which could never in fact have produced cocaine'.

The appellants made a number of attempts – all of them, of course, unsuccessful – to extract cocaine from their powder. It was not until after they had been arrested and the powder seized by the police and sent for analysis that they learnt to their surprise that there was no way in which cocaine could be produced from it.

The trial judge in his direction to the jury, the Court of Appeal in their judgment dismissing the two appeals, treated this impossibility as an irrelevance. In their view the agreement was what mattered: and there was plain evidence of an agreement to produce cocaine, even though unknown to the two conspirators it could not be done. Neither the trial judge nor the Court of Appeal thought it necessary to carry their analysis of the agreement further. The trial judge described it simply as an agreement to produce cocaine. The Court of Appeal thought it enough that the prosecution had proved 'an agreement to do an act which was forbidden by s 4 of the Misuse of Drugs Act 1971'. Both descriptions are accurate, as far as they go. But neither contains any reference to the limited nature of the agreement proved: it was an agreement upon a specific course of conduct with the object of producing cocaine, and limited to that course of conduct. Since it could not result in the production of cocaine, the two appellants by pursuing it could not commit the statutory offence of producing a controlled drug. The appellants, who did get a chemist to take on the impossible job of extracting cocaine from the powder, may perhaps be treated as having completed their agreed course of conduct: if so, they completed it without committing the statutory offence. Perhaps, however, it would be more accurate to treat them as having desisted before they had completed all that they had agreed to do: but it makes no difference because, had they completed all that they had agreed to do, no cocaine would have been produced.

If, therefore, their agreement, limited as it was to a specific course of conduct which could not result in the commission of the statutory offence, constituted (as the Court of Appeal held) a criminal conspiracy, the strange consequence ensues, that by agreeing upon a course of conduct which was not criminal (or unlawful) the appellants were guilty of conspiring to commit a crime.

Upon these facts the appellants submit that the evidence reveals no 'conspiracy at large', by which they mean an agreement in general terms to produce cocaine if and when they could find a suitable raw material, but only the limited agreement, to which I have referred. Counsel for the appellants concedes that, if two or more persons decide to go into business as cocaine producers, or, to take another example, as assassins for hire (eg 'Murder Incorporated'), the mere fact that in the course of performing their agreement they attempt to produce cocaine from a raw material which could not possibly yield it or (in the second example), stab a corpse, believing it to be the body of a living man, would not avail them as a defence: for the performance of their general agreement would not be rendered impossible by such transient frustrations. But performance of the limited agreement proved in this case could not in any circumstances have involved the commission of the offence created by the statute.

The answer sought to be made by the Crown (and accepted by the Court of Appeal) is that the offence of conspiracy is committed when an agreement to commit, or to try to commit, a crime is reached, whether or not anything is, or can be, done to perform it. It is wrong, upon their view, to treat conspiracy as a 'preliminary' or 'inchoate' crime: for its criminality depends in no way upon its being a step towards the commission of the substantive offence (or, at common law, the unlawful act). Upon this view of the law the scope of agreement is irrelevant: all that is needed to constitute the crime is the intention to commit the substantive offence and the agreement to try to do so.

. . . In *Board of Trade v Owen* [1957] AC 602, 623–25 Lord Tucker, quoting with approval some observations from RS Wright J's little classic, *The Law of Criminal Conspiracies and Agreements* (1873) and some passages from Sir William Holdsworth's (somewhat larger) work, *The History of English Law*, accepted that the historical basis of the crime of conspiring to commit a crime (the case with which we are now concerned) was that it developed as an 'auxiliary' (RS Wright's word) to the law which creates the crime agreed to be committed. Lord Tucker accepted Holdsworth's comment (at 625) that 'it was inevitable therefore, as Stephen has said, that conspiracy should come to be regarded as a form of attempt to commit a wrong'. Lord Tucker concluded his survey with these words at 626:

> Accepting the above as the historical basis of the crime of conspiracy, it seems to me that the whole object of making such agreements punishable is to prevent the commission of the substantive offence before it has even reached the stage of an attempt . . .

Lord Tucker, in whose opinion the other noble and learned Lords sitting with him concurred, by stressing the 'auxiliary' nature of the crime of conspiracy and by explaining its justification as being to prevent the commission of substantive offences, has placed the crime firmly in the same class and category as attempts to commit a crime. Both are criminal because they are steps towards the commission of a substantive offence. The distinction between the two is that, whereas a 'proximate' act is that which constitutes the crime of attempt, agreement is the necessary ingredient in conspiracy. The importance of the distinction is that agreement may, and usually will, occur well before the first step which can be said to be an attempt. The law of conspiracy thus makes possible an earlier intervention by the law to prevent the commission of the substantive offence. But the distinction has no relevance in determining whether the impossibility of committing the substantive offence should be a defence. Indeed upon the view of the law authoritatively explained and accepted in *Owen's* case [1957] AC 602, logic and justice would seem to require that the question as to the effect of the impossibility of the substantive offence should be answered in the same way, whether the crime charged be conspiracy or attempt . . .

The Crown's argument, as developed before your Lordships, rests, in my judgment, upon a misconception of the nature of the agreement proved. This is a case not of an agreement to commit a crime capable of being committed in the way agreed upon, but frustrated by a supervening event making its completion impossible, which was the Crown's submission, but of an agreement upon a course of conduct which could not in any circumstances result in the statutory offence alleged, i.e. the offence of producing the controlled drug, cocaine . . .

8.4 ATTEMPT

Until 1981 the offence of attempt was governed by the common law. With the enactment of the Criminal Attempts Act 1981 it was placed on a statutory footing. Unlike the position with incitement and conspiracy, there is no surviving form of common law attempt.

Section 1 of the Criminal Attempts Act 1981

(1) If, with intent to commit an offence to which this section applies, a person does an act which is more than merely preparatory to the commission of the offence, he is guilty of attempting to commit the offence.

(2) A person may be guilty of attempting to commit an offence to which this section applies even though the facts are such that the commission of the offence is impossible.

(3) In any case where:

    (a) apart from this subsection a person's intention would not be regarded as having amounted to an intent to commit an offence; but

    (b) if the facts of the case had been as he believed them to be, his intention would be so regarded, then for the purposes of subsection (1) above, he shall be regarded as having an intent to commit that offence.

8.4.1 *ACTUS REUS*: AN ACT WHICH IS MORE THAN MERELY PREPARATORY

Various tests of what constituted an attempt existed prior to the Criminal Attempts Act 1981: for example, whether the defendant had gone past the point of no return ('crossing the Rubicon'), and the 'uninterrupted series of acts' test set out in *Davey v Lee* [1968] 1 QB 366. However, pre-1981 case law is only persuasive; the correct approach is to give the words of the statute their ordinary and natural meaning. Was the act alleged 'more than merely preparatory to the commission of the offence'? See, for example, *R v Gullefer* [1990] 1 WLR 1063; *R v Jones* [1990] 1 WLR 1057; *Attorney General's Ref (No 1 of 1992)* [1993] 1 WLR 274.

Section 4(3) of the Criminal Attempts Act 1981 provides:

> Where, in proceedings against a person for an offence under s 1 above, there is evidence sufficient in law to support a finding that he did an act falling within subsection (1) of that section, the question whether or not his act fell within that subsection is a question of fact.

The effect is that if there is a *prima facie* case that the defendant did an act which was more than merely preparatory, the jury must be left to decide whether the act was indeed more than merely preparatory.

R v Gullefer [1990] 1 WLR 1063 (Note)

Lord Lane CJ:

On 26 February 1986 before the Crown Court at Snaresbrook the appellant was convicted of attempted theft and sentenced to six months' imprisonment.

The judge certified that the case was fit for appeal on the ground that:

> ... a submission was made that the action alleged as constituting the attempt (as to which there was no dispute, because his action was filmed on video tape, which the jury and I saw) could not amount to an attempt to steal, even if the jury were satisfied that what the defendant did was done with the object of dishonestly receiving a sum of money equivalent to his stake from a bookmaker ...

The facts were as follows. On 5 March 1985 the appellant attended the Greyhound Racing Stadium at Romford. During the last race, as the dogs rounded the final bend, he climbed the fence on to the track in front of the dogs, waving his arms and attempting to distract them. His efforts were only marginally successful, and the stewards decided that it was unnecessary to declare 'no race'. Had they made such a declaration, by the rules the bookmakers would have been obliged to repay the amount of his stake to any punter, but would not have been liable to pay any winnings to those punters who would have been successful if the race had been valid.

When interviewed by the police the appellant said the reasons for his behaviour were partly that a year earlier he had lost a large bet at the stadium by reason of one of the stadium's staff leaning over the rails and distracting the dog on which he had gambled. He also admitted that he had attempted to stop the race because the dog on which he had staked £18 was losing. He hoped that by his actions the dogs would be distracted, that the stewards would declare 'no race' and that he would therefore recover his stake from the bookmaker . . .

His Lordship quoted ss 1(1) and 4(3) of the Criminal Attempts Act and continued:

Thus the judge's task is to decide whether there is evidence upon which a jury could reasonably come to the conclusion that the appellant had gone beyond the realm of mere preparation and had embarked upon the actual commission of the offence. If not, he must withdraw the case from the jury. If there is such evidence, it is then for the jury to decide whether the defendant did in fact go beyond mere preparation . . .

The first task of the court is to apply the words of the Act of 1981 to the facts of the case. Was the appellant still in the stage of preparation to commit the substantive offence, or was there a basis of fact which would entitle the jury to say that he had embarked on the theft itself? Might it properly be said that when he jumped on to the track he was trying to steal £18 from the bookmaker?

Our view is that it could not properly be said that at that stage he was in the process of committing theft. What he was doing was jumping onto the track in an effort to distract the dogs, which in its turn, he hoped, would have the effect of forcing the stewards to declare 'no race', which would in its turn give him the opportunity to go back to the bookmaker and demand the £18 he had staked. In our view there was insufficient evidence for it to be said that he had, when he jumped on to the track, gone beyond mere preparation.

So far at least as the present case is concerned, we do not think that it is necessary to examine the authorities which preceded the Act of 1981, save to say that the sections we have already quoted in this judgment seem to be a blend of various decisions, some of which were not easy to reconcile with others . . .

It seems to us that the words of the Act of 1981 seek to steer a midway course. They do not provide, as they might have done, that the *R v Eagleton* test is to be followed, or that, as Lord Diplock suggested, the defendant must have reached a point from which it was impossible for him to retreat before the *actus reus* of an attempt is proved. On the other hand the words give perhaps as clear a guidance as is possible in the circumstances on the point of time at which Stephen's 'series of acts' begin. It begins when the merely preparatory acts come to an end and the defendant embarks upon the crime proper. When that is, will depend of course upon the facts in any particular case . . .

R v Jones (Kenneth Henry) [1990] 1 WLR 1057 (CA)

Taylor LJ:
read the following judgment of the court. This case raises a point of law as to the true construction of s 1 of the Criminal Attempts Act 1981 . . .

The appellant, a married man, started an affair with a woman named Lynn Gresley in 1985. She lived with him in Australia during 1986. In September 1987, back in England, she began a relationship with the victim, Michael Foreman. She continued, however, to see the appellant to whom she was still very attached. In November 1987 she decided to break off the relationship with the appellant, but he continued to write to her, begging her to come back to him.

On 12 January 1988 the appellant applied for a shotgun certificate, and three days later bought two guns in company with two companions. He bought two more guns a few days later on his own. On 23 January he shortened the barrel of one of them and test fired it twice the following day.

The appellant told a colleague at work that he would be away on Tuesday 26 January. On 24 January he phoned Lynn Gresley in a distraught state. The next day he apologised, but she again refused his invitation to resume their relationship. The appellant then told his wife he had packed a bag as he was going to Spain to do some work on their chalet. On 26 January he left home dressed normally for work, saying he would telephone his wife as to whether he was leaving for Spain that evening.

That same morning, the victim, Michael Foreman, took his daughter to school by car as usual. After the child left the car, the appellant appeared, opened the door and jumped into the rear seat. He was wearing overalls, a crash helmet with the visor down, and was carrying a bag. He and the victim had never previously met. He introduced himself, said he wanted to sort things out and asked the victim to drive on. When they stopped on a grass verge, the appellant handed over a letter he had received from Lynn. Whilst the victim read it, the appellant took the sawn-off shotgun from the bag. It was loaded. He pointed it at the victim at range of some 10 to 12 inches. He said, 'You are not going to like this', or similar words. The victim grabbed the end of the gun and pushed it sideways and upwards. There was a struggle during which the victim managed to throw the gun out of the window. As he tried to get out, he felt a cord over his head pulling him back. He managed to break free and run away, taking the gun with him.

From a nearby garage he telephoned the police.

Meanwhile, the appellant drove off in the victim's car. He was arrested jogging away from it carrying his holdall. He said he had done nothing and only wanted to kill himself. His bag contained a hatchet, some cartridges and a length of cord. He also had a sharp kitchen knife which he threw away. In the appellant's car parked near the school was £1,500 sterling together with a quantity of French and Spanish money. The evidence showed that the safety catch of the shotgun had been in the on position. The victim was unclear as to whether the appellant's finger was ever on the trigger. When interviewed, the appellant declined to make any comment.

At the end of the prosecution case, after the above facts had been given in evidence, a submission was made to the judge that the charge of attempted murder should be withdrawn from the jury. It was argued that since the appellant would have had to perform at least three more acts before the full offence could have been completed, i.e. remove the safety catch, put his finger on the trigger and pull it, the evidence was insufficient to support the charge. There was a discussion as to the proper construction of s 1(1) of the Criminal Attempts Act 1981. After hearing full argument, the judge ruled against the submission and allowed the case to proceed on count 1. Thereafter, the appellant gave evidence. In the result, the jury convicted him unanimously of attempted murder. It follows that they found he intended to kill the victim.

The sole ground of appeal is that the judge erred in law in his construction of s 1(1) and ought to have withdrawn the case.

His Lordship then quoted s 1(1) and s 4(3) of the Criminal Attempts Act 1981.

[Counsel for the appellant] says that for about a century, two different tests as to the *actus reus* of attempt have been inconsistently applied by the courts. In *R v Eagleton* (1855) Dears CC 515, the defendant was charged with attempting to obtain money from the guardians of a parish by falsely pretending to the relieving officer that he had delivered loaves of bread of proper weight to the poor when in fact the loaves were underweight. In the course of giving the judgment of the court, Parke B said at 538:

> Acts remotely leading towards the commission of the offence are not to be considered as attempts to commit it, but acts immediately connected with it are; and if, in this case, after the credit with the relieving officer for the fraudulent overcharge, any further step on the part of the defendant had been necessary to obtain payment, as the making out a further account or producing the vouchers to the board, we should have thought that the obtaining credit in account with the relieving officer would not have been sufficiently proximate to the obtaining the money. But, on the statement in this case, no other act on the part of the defendant would have been required. It was the last act, depending on himself towards the payment of the money, and therefore it ought to be considered as an attempt.

Accordingly, the test deriving from *R v Eagleton* was said to be the 'last act' test. It was adopted in a number of cases, e.g. *R v Robinson* [1915] 2 KB 342. In *DPP v Stonehouse* [1978] AC 55, 68, Lord Diplock referred to *R v Eagleton* as the *locus classicus*, adopted some of the words of Parke B and summarised them in the graphic phrase: 'In other words, the offender must have crossed the Rubicon and burnt his boats.'

The other test referred to by [counsel for the appellant] derives from Stephen's *Digest of the Criminal Law*, 9th edn, 1950, Chapter 4, art 29 where it was stated, at pp 24–25:

> An attempt to commit a crime is an act done with intent to commit that crime, and forming part of a series of acts, which would constitute its actual commission if it were not interrupted.

Lord Edmund-Davies noted in *Stonehouse's* case at 86, that Stephen's definition has been repeatedly cited with approval. He referred to its adoption in *Hope v Brown* [1954] 1 WLR 250, 253, and *Davey v Lee* [1968] 1 QB 366. It was also applied in *R v Linneker* [1906] 2 KB 99 where *Eagleton's* case was not cited.

In some cases, including three since the Act of 1981, both tests have been considered, and the court has found it unnecessary to decide between them, holding that the result in those cases would have been the same, whichever applied: see *R v Ilyas* (1984) 78 Cr App R 17; *R v Widdowson* (1986) 82 Cr App R 314 and *R v Boyle* (1986) 84 Cr App R 270 . . .

. . . The Act of 1981 is a codifying statute. It amends and sets out completely the law relating to attempts and conspiracies. In those circumstances the correct approach is to look first at the natural meaning of the statutory words, not to turn back to earlier case law and seek to fit some previous test to the words of the section . . .

[His Lordship then quoted with approval from the judgment of Lord Lane CJ in *R v Gullefer* (Note) [1990] 1 WLR 1063.]

... We do not accept [the appellant's] contention that s 1(1) of the Act of 1981 in effect embodies the 'last act' test derived from *R v Eagleton*. Had Parliament intended to adopt that test, a quite different form of words could and would have been used.

It is of interest to note that the Act of 1981 followed a report from the Law Commission on *Attempt, and Impossibility in Relation to Attempt Conspiracy and Incitement* (1980) Law Com No 102. At paragraph 2.47 the report states:

> The definition of sufficient proximity must be wide enough to cover two varieties of cases; first, those in which a person has taken all steps towards the commission of a crime which he believes to be necessary as far as he is concerned for that crime to result, such as firing a gun at another and missing. Normally such cases cause no difficulty. Second, however, the definition must cover those instances where a person has to take some further step to complete the crime, assuming that there is evidence of the necessary mental element on his part to commit it; for example, when the defendant has raised the gun to take aim at another but has not yet squeezed the trigger. We have reached the conclusion that, in regard to these cases, it is undesirable to recommend anything more complex than a rationalisation of the present law.

In paragraph 2.48 the report states:

> The literal meaning of 'proximate' is 'nearest, next before or after (in place, order, time, connection of thought, causation, etc)'. Thus, were this term part of a statutory description of the *actus reus* of attempt, it would clearly be capable of being interpreted to exclude all but the 'final act'; this would not be in accordance with the policy outlined above.

Clearly, the draftsman of s 1(1) must be taken to have been aware of the two lines of earlier authority and of the Law Commission's report. The words 'an act which is more than merely preparatory to the commission of the offence' would be inapt if they were intended to mean 'the last act which lay in his power towards the commission of the offence'.

Looking at the plain natural meaning of s 1(1) in the way indicated by the Lord Chief Justice [in *R v Gullefer*], the question for the judge in the present case was whether there was evidence from which a reasonable jury, properly directed, could conclude that the appellant had done acts which were more than merely preparatory. Clearly his actions in obtaining the gun, in shortening it, in loading it, in putting on his disguise, and in going to the school could only be regarded as preparatory acts. But, in our judgment, once he had got into the car, taken out the loaded gun and pointed it at the victim with the intention of killing him, there was sufficient evidence for the consideration of the jury on the charge of attempted murder. It was a matter for them to decide whether they were sure those acts were more than merely preparatory. In our judgment, therefore, the judge was right to allow the case to go to the jury, and the appeal against conviction must be dismissed.

R v Geddes (1996) 160 JP 697 (CA)

Lord Bingham of Cornhill CJ:

The background to the case may be shortly summarised. On 20 July 1994 the appellant went into the boys' lavatory block at Dorothy Stringer School, Brighton. He had no connection with the school and had no right to be there. At about midday a teacher saw him in the boys' lavatory and spoke to him. He had a rucksack with him. A woman police officer, who, by chance, was on the premises, saw him and shouted at him, but he left. In a cubicle in the lavatory block there was a cider can which had belonged to the appellant. In the course of leaving the school the appellant discarded his rucksack which was found in some bushes. Its contents included several articles: a large kitchen knife, some lengths of rope and a roll of masking tape. The appellant was arrested three days later. The teacher and some pupils from the school identified him.

The prosecution alleged that the presence of the cider can showed that the appellant had been inside a cubicle in the lavatory block. They further alleged that the contents of the rucksack could be used to catch and restrain a boy who entered the lavatory. The rope could have been used to tie the boy; the knife to frighten him; and the tape to cover his mouth to prevent him screaming.

The defence resisted the charge on the basis that the prosecution case was based on specula-tion. It was contested that the cider can showed that the appellant had been hiding in the cubicle, since he could well have entered the cubicle for normal purposes and left the cider can there. Alternatively, since the partitions of the lavatory did not extend from the floor to the ceiling, the can could have rolled or been thrown into the position where it was ultimately found. It was argued that there were other explanations for the contents of the rucksack . . .

. . . The cases show that the line of demarcation between acts which are merely preparatory and acts which may amount to an attempt is not always clear or easy to recognise. There is no rule of thumb test. There must always be an exercise of judgment based on the particular facts of the case. It is, we think, an accurate paraphrase of the statutory test and not an illegitimate gloss upon it to ask whether the available evidence, if accepted, could show that a defendant has done an act which shows that he has actually tried to commit the offence in question, or whether he has only got ready or put himself in a position or equipped himself to do so.

In the present case . . . there is not much room for doubt about the appellant's intention. Furthermore, the evidence is clearly capable of showing that he made preparations, that he equipped himself, that he got ready, that he put himself in a position to commit the offence charged. We question whether the cider can in the cubicle is of central importance, but would accept that in the absence of any explanation it could lead to the inference that the appellant had been in the cubicle. But was the evidence sufficient in law to support a finding that the appellant had actually tried or attempted to commit the offence of imprisoning someone? Had he moved from the realm of intention, preparation and planning into the area of execution or implementa-tion? . . . Here it is true that the appellant had entered the school; but he had never had any contact or communication with any pupil; he had never confronted any pupil at the school in any way . . . [The] contents of the rucksack, which gave a clear indication as to what the appellant may have had in mind, but do not throw light on whether he had begun to carry out the commission of the offence [and so must be treated as irrelevant]. On the facts of this case we feel bound to conclude that the evidence was not sufficient in law to support a finding that the appellant did an act which was more than merely preparatory to wrongfully imprisoning a person unknown. In those circumstances we conclude that the appeal must be allowed and the conviction quashed.

8.4.2 JURISDICTIONAL ISSUES

Section 1(4) of the Criminal Attempts Act 1981 provides that s 1 applies to '. . . any offence which, if it were completed, would be triable in England and Wales as an indictable offence . . .'. One effect of this is that an attempt can comprise acts outside the jurisdiction that would have lead to the commission of the completed offence within the jurisdiction; see *DPP v Stonehouse* [1978] AC 55. Jurisdiction over attempts with a foreign element has been widened further by the provisions of the Criminal Justice Act 1993, which provides that courts in England and Wales have jurisdiction to deal with attempts to commit 'Class A' offences (defined in the 1993 Act as offences of dishonesty and fraud) provided certain conditions are met. It achieves this by inserting a s 1A after s 1 in the Criminal Attempts Act 1981:

Section 1A: Extended jurisdiction in relation to certain attempts

(1) If this section applies to an act, what the person doing the act had in view shall be treated as an offence to which section 1(1) above applies.

(2) This section applies to an act if –
   (a) it is done in England and Wales, and
   (b) it would fall within section 1(1) above as more than merely preparatory to the commission of a Group A offence but for the fact that that offence, if completed, would not be an offence triable in England and Wales.

(3) In this section 'Group A offence' has the same meaning as in Part 1 of the Criminal Justice Act 1993.

(4) Subsection (1) above is subject to the provisions of section 6 of the Act of 1993 (relevance of external law).

(5) Where a person does any act to which this section applies, the offence which he commits shall for all purposes be treated as the offence of attempting to commit the relevant Group A offence.

The commentary in *Blackstone's Criminal Practice*, 11th edn, at A6.38 observes:

The [Criminal Justice Act 1993] inserts a new s 1A in the Criminal Attempts Act 1981, supposedly to cover cases where the accused in England and Wales attempts to commit abroad something that would be a Group A offence, but for the fact that it is not triable under English law. This provision is fundamentally at odds with itself. If a Group A offence is instigated by conduct within England and Wales, that offence will inevitably be triable under English law. Section 1A is merely a trap for unwary prosecutors, who may be tempted to use it instead of s 1.

8.4.3 *MENS REA*: WITH INTENT TO COMMIT THE COMPLETE OFFENCE

The *mens rea* for an attempt is the intention to commit the complete offence; recklessness as to whether or not the prohibited consequence will occur is not enough: *R v Pearman* (1984) 80 Cr App R 259. Recklessness as to circumstances may still suffice, however; see *R v Khan* (below). It follows that the *mens rea* for an attempt is normally the same as the *mens rea* for the completed offence: *R v Millard* [1987] Crim LR 393; *R v Khan* [1990] 1 WLR 813; *AG's Ref (No 3 of 1992)* [1994] 1 WLR 409.

R v Pearman (1984) 80 Cr App R 259 (CA)

The appellant was charged with attempting to cause grievous bodily harm. He had driven his car at a police officer. His defence was that he did not intend to harm the police officer and did not foresee that his actions could cause serious injury to anybody.

Stuart-Smith J:

... This court, in the case of *Mohan* [1976] QB 1 dealt with the question of the mental element in an attempt before passing to that Act. It is not necessary to deal with the facts of the case. James LJ gave the judgment of the court. After reviewing the speeches of the House of Lords in *Hyam v DPP*, he said at p 11:

> In our judgment, evidence of knowledge of likely consequences, or from which knowledge of likely consequences can be inferred, is evidence by which intent may be established but it is not in relation to the offence of attempt to be equated with intent. If the jury find such knowledge established, they may, and using common sense, they probably will find intent proved, but it is not the case that they must do so. An attempt to commit crime is itself an offence. Often it is a grave offence. Often it is as morally culpable as the completed offence which is attempted but not in fact committed. Nevertheless it falls within the class of conduct which is preparatory to the commission of the crime and is one step removed from the offence which is attempted. The court must not strain to bring within the offence of attempt conduct which does not fall within the well-established bounds of the offence. On the contrary, the court must safeguard against extension of those bounds save by the authority of Parliament. The bounds are presently set requiring proof of specific intent, a decision to bring about, in so far as it lies within the accused's power, the commission of the offence which it is alleged the accused attempted to commit, no matter whether the accused desired that consequence of his act or not.

The last few words of that sentence, 'no matter whether the accused desired that consequence of his act or not', has given rise to debate amongst textbook writers as to what is meant by it, but it is clear from that passage that if the law is, as stated by James LJ in *Mohan* (above), still the same, that foresight of the consequences might be something from which the jury can infer intent, it is not to be equated with intent. We see no reason why the passing of the 1981 Act should have altered the law as to what is meant by the word 'intent'. The purpose of the Act was to deal with other matters rather than the content of the word 'intent'. We can see no reason why the judgment of the court in that case should not still be binding upon this court. It was, to some extent, based on the earlier decision of this court in *Whybrow* (1951) 35 Cr App R 141, where it was held that in the case of attempted murder although the *mens rea* for the completed offence of murder must be intent to kill or to cause really serious bodily harm, that was not sufficient in a case of attempted murder and it was necessary to prove the intent to kill.

As Parker LJ said in the course of argument, it would be an illogical conclusion and one offensive to common sense and offensive to any notion of an attempt if a man, who was in fact trying his best to avoid something coming about, could be guilty of an attempted offence simply because he foresaw that his actions might so involve him in committing it. It is offensive to common sense to suppose that simply because he could foresee it, he would be intending the offence to come about.

The words of James LJ which he used at the end of that passage, namely 'no matter whether the accused desired that consequence of his act or not', are probably designed to deal with a case where the accused has, as a primary purpose, some other object, for example, a man who plants a bomb in an aeroplane which he knows is going to take off, it being his primary intention that he should claim the insurance on the aeroplane when the freight goes down into the sea. The jury would not be put off from saying that he intended to murder the crew simply by saying that he did not want or desire to kill the crew, but that was something that he inevitably intended to do. Similarly, for example, a man who is cornered by the police when he is in a car may have the primary purpose of simply escaping from that situation. If he drives straight at the police officers at high speed, a jury is likely to conclude that he intended to injure a police officer and maybe cause him serious grievous bodily harm.

In the ordinary way, it would seem to this court to be sufficient for the judge to have told the jury that the Crown has to prove intent to cause grievous bodily harm on the part of the accused man . . .

R v Khan [1990] 1 WLR 813 (CA)

Russell LJ:

. . . These appeals raise the short but important point of whether the offence of attempted rape is committed when the defendant is reckless as to the woman's consent to sexual intercourse. The appellants submit that no such offence is known to the law . . .

In our judgment an acceptable analysis of the offence of rape [N.B. the appellant was charged with rape under the Sexual Offences Act 1956, the Sexual Offences Act 2003 introduced a different definition of the offence, see further Chapter 6] is as follows: (1) the intention of the offender is to have sexual intercourse with a woman; (2) the offence is committed if, but only if, the circumstances are that: (a) the woman does not consent; and (b) the defendant knows that she is not consenting or is reckless as to whether she consents.

Precisely the same analysis can be made of the offence of attempted rape: (1) the intention of the offender is to have sexual intercourse with a woman; (2) the offence is committed if, but only if, the circumstances are that: (a) the woman does not consent; *and* (b) the defendant knows that she is not consenting or is reckless as to whether she consents.

The only difference between the two offences is that in rape sexual intercourse takes place whereas in attempted rape it does not, although there has to be some act which is more than preparatory to sexual intercourse. Considered in that way, the intent of the defendant is precisely the same in rape and in attempted rape and the *mens rea* is identical, namely an intention to have intercourse plus a knowledge of or recklessness as to the woman's absence of consent. No question of attempting to achieve a reckless state of mind arises; the attempt relates to the physical activity; the mental state of the defendent is the same. A man does not recklessly have sexual intercourse, nor does he recklessly attempt it. Recklessness in rape and attempted rape arises not in relation to the physical act of the accused but only in his state of mind when engaged in the activity of having or attempting to have sexual intercourse.

If this is the true analysis, as we believe it is, the attempt does not require any different intention on the part of the accused from that for the full offence of rape. We believe this to be a desirable result which in the instant case did not require the jury to be burdened with different directions as to the accused's state of mind, dependent on whether the individual achieved or failed to achieve sexual intercourse.

We recognise, of course, that our reasoning cannot apply to all offences and all attempts. Where, for example, as in causing death by reckless driving or reckless arson, no state of mind other than recklessness is involved in the offence, there can be no attempt to commit it.

In our judgment, however, the words 'with intent to commit an offence' to be found in s 1 of the 1981 Act mean, when applied to rape, 'with intent to have sexual intercourse with a woman in circumstances where she does not consent and the defendant knows or could not care less about her absence of consent'. The only 'intent', giving that word its natural and ordinary meaning, of the rapist is to have sexual intercourse. He commits the offence because of the circumstances in which he manifests that intent – i.e. when the woman is not consenting and he either knows it or could not care less about the absence of consent . . .

Petition: The Appeal Committee of the House of Lords (Lord Keith of Kinkel, Lord Brandon of Oakbrook and Lord Lowry) dismissed petitions by Khan, Dhokia and Faiz for leave to appeal.

Attorney General's Ref (No 3 of 1992) [1994] 1 WLR 409 (CA)

Schiemann J:

The court has heard a reference made under s 36(1) of the Criminal Justice Act 1972. The point of law which has been referred to us was formulated as follows:

> Whether on a charge of attempted arson in the aggravated form contemplated by s 1(2) of the Criminal Damage Act 1971, in addition to establishing a specific intent to cause damage by fire, it is sufficient to prove that the defendant was reckless as to whether life would thereby be endangered.

The acquittals which have given rise to this reference had the following background according to the prosecution evidence. Following previous attacks upon their property the complainants maintained a night-time watch over their premises from a motor car (a Ford Granada). In the early hours of the morning the respondents came upon the scene in a vehicle. Inside this car, a Sierra, was a milk crate containing a number of petrol bombs, matches, a petrol can and some rags. As the Sierra approached the complainants, four inside their car and two persons on the pavement talking to them, a lighted petrol bomb was thrown towards them from the Sierra. The prosecution's case was that it was thrown at the Granada and its occupants. The petrol bomb in fact passed over the top of the Granada and smashed against the garden wall of a house a pavement's width away from the car. The Sierra accelerated away but crashed, and the respondents were arrested . . .

So far as attempting to commit the . . . offence [under s 1(1) of the Criminal Damage Act 1971] is concerned, in order to convict on such a charge it must be proved that the defendant: (a) did an act which was more than merely preparatory to the commission of the offence; and (b) did an act intending to damage any property belonging to another.

One way of analysing the situation is to say that a defendant, in order to be guilty of an attempt, must be in one of the states of mind required for the commission of the full offence, and did his best, as far as he could, to supply what was missing from the completion of the offence. It is the policy of the law that such people should be punished notwithstanding that in fact the intentions of such a defendant have not been fulfilled.

If the facts are that, although the defendant had one of the appropriate states of mind required for the complete offence, but the physical element required for the commission of the complete offence is missing, the defendant is not to be convicted unless it can be shown that he intended to supply the physical element. This was the state of affairs in *R v Millard and Vernon* [1987] Crim LR 393, of which we have seen the transcript. There the defendants were convicted of attempting to damage property. The particulars of the offence were that they 'attempted to damage a wooden wall at the . . . stadium . . . intending to damage the . . . wall or being reckless as to whether the . . . wall was damaged'. The trial judge directed the jury that recklessness was sufficient. Mustill LJ, delivering the judgment of the Court of Appeal, stated:

> The result which would have been achieved if the offence had been taken to fruition was damage to the stand . . . the prosecution had to show . . . that it was this state of affairs which each appellant had decided, so far as in him lay, to bring about.

In consequence, mere recklessness was not sufficient and the convictions were quashed.

We turn finally to the attempt to commit the aggravated offence [under s 1(2) of the Criminal Damage Act 1971]. In the present case, what was missing to prevent a conviction for the completed offence was damage to the property referred to in the opening lines of s 1(2) of the Act of 1981, what in the example of a crane, which we gave earlier in this judgment, we referred to as 'the first-named property'. Such damage is essential for the completed offence. If a defendant does not intend to cause such damage he cannot intend to commit the completed offence. At worst he is reckless as to whether the offence is committed. The law of attempt is concerned with those who are intending to commit crimes. If that intent cannot be shown, then there can be no conviction.

However, the crime here consisted of doing certain acts in a certain state of mind in circumstances where the first-named property and the second-named property were the same, in short where the danger to life arose from the damage to the property which the defendant intended to damage. The substantive crime is committed if the defendant damaged property in a state of mind where he was reckless as to whether the life of another would thereby be endangered. We see no reason why there should not be a conviction for attempt if the prosecution can show that he, in that state of mind, intended to damage the property by throwing a bomb at it. One analysis of this situation is to say that although the defendant was in an appropriate state of mind to render him guilty of the completed offence the prosecution had not proved the physical element of the completed offence, and therefore he is not guilty of the completed offence. If, on a charge of attempting to commit the offence, the prosecution can show not only the state of mind required for the completed offence but also that the defendant intended to supply the missing physical element of the completed offence, that suffices for a conviction. That cannot be done merely by the prosecution showing him to be reckless. The defendant must intend to damage property, but there is no need for a graver mental state than is required for the full offence . . .

. . . What was missing in the present case was damage to the first-named property, without which the offence was not complete. The mental state of the defendant in each case contained everything which was required to render him guilty of the full offence. In order to succeed in a prosecution for attempt, it must be shown that the defendant intended to achieve that which was missing from the full offence. Unless that is shown, the prosecution have not proved that the defendant intended to commit the offence. Thus in *R v Khan (Mohammed Iqbal)* [1990] 1 WLR 813 the prosecution had to show an intention to have sexual intercourse, and the remaining state of mind required for the offence of rape. In the present case, the prosecution had to show an intention to damage the first-named property, and the remaining state of mind required for the offence of aggravated arson . . .

We answer [the question posed by the reference] in the affirmative.

We add that, in circumstances where the first-named property is not the same as the second-named property, in addition to establishing a specific intent to cause damage by fire to the first-named property, it is sufficient to prove that the defendant was reckless as to whether any

> second-named property was damaged and reckless as to whether the life of another would be
> endangered by the damage to the second-named property.

8.4.4 IMPOSSIBILITY

There are at least three forms of impossibility that a defendant, when charged with attempt, may think will provide him with an answer to the charge. The first is impossibility of means; the second impossibility in fact; and the third, impossibility in law.

Impossibility of means has never been a defence as such. The fact that D does not use enough dynamite to blow open the doors of a safe, or that his arms are not long enough to reach the property he wants to steal, is irrelevant provided he has taken steps more than merely preparatory to the commission of the completed offence, with the necessary *mens rea*. Impossibility of fact, as for example where D fires a gun at P intending to kill him, only to discover that P had died an hour before, has presented some difficulties in the past, but is clearly now prevented from operating as any bar to liability for attempt, as *R v Shivpuri* (extracted below) indicates. Impossibility of law, where for example D handles goods that have (unknown to D), as a matter of law, ceased to be stolen, was for a time regarded as a bar to liability by the House of Lords (see *Haughton v Smith* [1973] 3 All ER 1109). The Criminal Attempts Act 1981, by virtue of s 1(2) and (3), makes clear that this decision has now been swept away, leaving the defendant with no argument based on impossibility.

In effect the only 'impossibility' argument that could now avail a defendant charged with attempt is where he takes steps more than merely preparatory to committing what he wrongly believes to be an offence, for example an attempt to import the complete works of Shakespeare into the UK. Although he believes he is committing a crime, he cannot be charged with attempt as the offence only relates to offences known to law. The House of Lords was first asked to rule upon the effect of the Criminal Attempts Act 1981 in *Anderton v Ryan* [1985] AC 560. Mrs Ryan admitted purchasing a video recorder that she believed to have been stolen. The video recorder was not recovered and the prosecution was unable to prove that it actually had been stolen goods at the time Mrs Ryan bought it. In consequence she was charged with attempting to handle stolen goods, the essence of the offence being her belief that the goods were stolen. The prosecution sought to rely on the wording of s 1 of the 1981 Act, in particular s 1(3) insofar as it provided that:

> In any case where: (a) apart from this subsection a person's intention would not be regarded as
> having amounted to an intent to commit an offence; but (b) if the facts of the case had been as he
> believed them to be, his intention would be so regarded, then for the purposes of [the offence of
> attempt] he shall be regarded as having an intent to commit that offence.

The House of Lords, whilst fully aware of what Parliament's intention had been in enacting s 1(3), held that Mrs Ryan could not be guilty of attempting to handle stolen goods. Notwithstanding her abundant *mens rea*, the prosecution had failed to establish an element of the *actus reus*, i.e. that the video recorder was stolen property. Her belief that it was stolen could not make good that omission. The House of Lords rejected the notion of liability based on the defendant's *mens rea* alone. This decision left the 1981 Act in disarray as far as its purpose in reforming the law on attempt and impossibility was concerned. Less than a year later, however, in a stunning judicial *volte-face*, the House of Lords conceded that the approach in *Anderton v Ryan* was erroneous. The reasons for this change of view, and the House of Lords' acceptance of the efficacy of the 1981 Act in removing any defence of impossibility in respect of a charge of attempting to commit an offence, are set out in the extracts from *R v Shivpuri* (below).

R v Shivpuri [1987] 1 AC 1 (HL)

The appellant visited India and, whilst there, was approached by a man named Desai, who offered to pay him £1,000 if, on his return to England, he would receive a suitcase which a courier would deliver to him containing packages of drugs that the appellant was then to distribute according to instructions he would receive. The suitcase was duly delivered to him in Cambridge. Acting on instructions, the appellant went to Southall Station to deliver a package of drugs to a third party. Outside the station he and the man he had met by appointment were arrested. A package containing a powdered substance was found in the appellant's shoulder bag. At the appellant's flat in Cambridge, he produced to customs officers the suitcase from which the lining had been ripped out and the remaining packages of the same powdered substance. The appellant made a full confession of having played his part as recipient and distributor of illegally imported drugs. The appellant believed the drugs to be either heroin or cannabis. In due course the powdered substance in the several packages was scientifically analysed and found not to be a controlled drug but snuff or some similar harmless vegetable matter. The appellant was convicted of being knowingly concerned in dealing with (count 1) and in harbouring (count 2) a Class A controlled drug, namely diamorphine, with intent to evade the prohibition of importation imposed by s 3(1) of the Misuse of Drugs Act 1971, contrary to s 170(1)(b) of the Customs and Excise Management Act 1979.

The Court of Appeal dismissed his appeal against conviction but certified a point of law of general public importance and granted leave to appeal to the House of Lords. The certified question asked:

> Does a person commit an offence under s 1 of the Criminal Attempts Act 1981 where, if the facts were as that person believed them to be, the full offence would have been committed by him, but where on the true facts of the offence which that person set out to commit was in law impossible, e.g. because the substance imported and believed to be heroin was not heroin but a harmless substance?

Lord Bridge of Harwich:

The . . . Criminal Attempts Act 1981. That Act marked an important new departure since, by s 6, it abolished the offence of attempt at common law and substituted a new statutory code governing attempts to commit criminal offences. It was considered by your Lordships' House last year in *Anderton v Ryan* [1985] AC 560 after the decision in the Court of Appeal which is the subject of the present appeal. That might seem an appropriate starting point from which to examine the issues arising in this appeal. But your Lordships have been invited to exercise the power under the *Practice Statement (Judicial Precedent)* [1966] 1 WLR 1234 to depart from the reasoning in that decision if it proves necessary to do so in order to affirm the convictions appealed against in the instant case. I was not only a party to the decision in *Anderton v Ryan*, I was also the author of one of the two opinions approved by the majority which must be taken to express the House's *ratio*. That seems to me to afford a sound reason why, on being invited to re-examine the language of the statute in its application to the facts of this appeal, I should initially seek to put out of mind what I said in *Anderton v Ryan*. Accordingly I propose to approach the issue in the first place as an exercise in statutory construction, applying the language of the Act to the facts of the case, as if the matter were *res integra*. If this leads me to the conclusion that the appellant was not guilty of any attempt to commit a relevant offence, that will be the end of the matter. But if this initial exercise inclines me to reach a contrary conclusion, it will then be necessary to consider whether the precedent set by *Anderton v Ryan* bars that conclusion or whether it can be surmounted either on the ground that the earlier decision is distinguishable or that it would be appropriate to depart from it under the *Practice Statement*.

His Lordship set out s 1 of the Criminal Attempts Act 1981 and continued:

Applying this language to the facts of the case, the first question to be asked is whether the appellant intended to commit the offences of being knowingly concerned in dealing with and harbouring drugs of Class A or Class B with intent to evade the prohibition on their importation. Translated into more homely language the question may be rephrased, without in any way altering its legal significance, in the following terms: did the appellant intend to receive and store (harbour) and in due course pass on to third parties (deal with) packages of heroin or cannabis which he knew had been smuggled into England from India? The answer is plainly yes, he did. Next, did he in relation to each offence, do an act which was more than merely preparatory to the commission of the offence? The act relied on in relation to harbouring was the receipt and retention of the packages found in the lining of the suitcase. The act relied on in relation to dealing was the meeting at Southall Station with the intended recipient of one of the packages. In each case the act was clearly more than preparatory to the commission of the intended offence; it was not and could not be more than merely preparatory to the commission of the actual offence, because the facts were such that the commission of the actual offence was impossible. Here then is the nub of the matter. Does the 'act which is more than merely preparatory to the commission of the offence' in s 1(1) of the Act of 1981 (the *actus reus* of the statutory offence of attempt) require any more than an act which is more than merely preparatory to the commission of the offence which the defendant intended to commit? Section 1(2) must surely indicate a negative answer; if it were otherwise, whenever the facts were such that the commission of the actual offence was impossible, it would be impossible to prove an act more than merely preparatory to the commission of that offence and subsections (1) and (2) would contradict each other.

This very simple, perhaps oversimple, analysis leads me to the provisional conclusion that the appellant was rightly convicted of the two offences of attempt with which he was charged. But can this conclusion stand with *Anderton v Ryan*? The appellant in that case was charged with an attempt to handle stolen goods. She bought a video recorder believing it to be stolen. On the facts as they were to be assumed it was not stolen. By a majority the House decided that she was entitled to be acquitted. I have re-examined the case with care. If I could extract from the speech of Lord Roskill or from my own speech a clear and coherent principle distinguishing those cases of attempting the impossible which amount to offences under the statute from those which do not, I should have to consider carefully on which side of the line the instant case fell. But I have to confess that I can find no such principle.

Running through Lord Roskill's speech and my own in *Anderton v Ryan* [1985] AC 560 is the concept of 'objectively innocent' acts which, in my speech certainly, are contrasted with 'guilty acts'. A few citations will make this clear. Lord Roskill said at 580:

> My Lords, it has been strenuously and ably argued for the respondent that these provisions involve that a defendant is liable to conviction for an attempt even where his actions are innocent but he erroneously believes facts which, if true, would make those actions criminal, and further, that he is liable to such conviction whether or not in the event his intended course of action is completed.

He proceeded to reject the argument. At p 582 I referred to the appellant's purchase of the video recorder and said: 'Objectively considered, therefore, her purchase of the recorder was a perfectly proper commercial transaction'. A further passage from my speech proceeded, at pp 582–83:

> The question may be stated in abstract terms as follows. Does s 1 of the Act of 1981 create a new offence of attempt where a person embarks on and completes a course of conduct which is objectively innocent, solely on the ground that the person mistakenly believes facts which, if true, would make that course of conduct a complete crime? If the question must be answered affirmatively it requires convictions in a number of surprising cases: the classic case, put by Bramwell B in *R v Collins* (1864) 9 Cox CC 497, of the man who takes away his own umbrella from a stand, believing it not to be his own and with intent to steal it; the case of the man who has consensual intercourse with a girl over 16 believing her to be under that age; the case of the art dealer who sells a picture which he represents to be and which is in fact a genuine Picasso, but which the dealer mistakenly believes to be a fake. The common feature of all these cases, including that under appeal, is that the mind alone is guilty, the act is innocent.

I then contrasted the case of the man who attempts to pick the empty pocket, saying:

> Putting the hand in the pocket is the guilty act, the intent to steal is the guilty mind, the offence is appropriately dealt with as an attempt, and the impossibility of committing the full offence for want of anything in the pocket to steal is declared by [subsection (2)] to be no obstacle to conviction.

If we fell into error, it is clear that our concern was to avoid convictions in situations which most people, as a matter of common sense, would not regard as involving criminality. In this connection it is to be regretted that we did not take due note of paragraph 2.97 of the Law Commission's report *Criminal Law: Attempt, and Impossibility in Relation to Attempt, Conspiracy and Incitement* (1980) Law Com 102 which preceded the enactment of the Act of 1981, which reads:

> If it is right in principle that an attempt should be chargeable even though the crime which it is sought to commit could not possibly be committed, we do not think that we should be deterred by the consideration that such a change in our law would also cover some

extreme and exceptional cases in which a prosecution would be theoretically possible. An example would be where a person is offered goods at such a low price that he believes that they are stolen, when in fact they are not; if he actually purchases them, upon the principles which we have discussed he would be liable for an attempt to handle stolen goods. Another case which has been much debated is that raised in argument by Bramwell B in *R v Collins* (1864) 9 Cox CC 497. If A takes his own umbrella, mistaking it for one belonging to B and intending to steal B's umbrella, is he guilty of attempted theft? Again, on the principles which we have discussed he would in theory be guilty, but in neither case would it be realistic to suppose that a complaint would be made or that a prosecution would ensue.

The prosecution in *Anderton v Ryan* itself falsified the Commission's prognosis in one of the 'extreme and exceptional cases'. It nevertheless probably holds good for other such cases, particularly that of the young man having sexual intercourse with a girl over 16, mistakenly believing her to be under that age, by which both Lord Roskill and I were much troubled.

However that may be, the distinction between acts which are 'objectively innocent' and those which are not is an essential element in the reasoning in *Anderton v Ryan* and the decision, unless it can be supported on some other ground, must stand or fall by the validity of this distinction. I am satisfied on further consideration that the concept of 'objective innocence' is incapable of sensible application in relation to the law of criminal attempts. The reason for this is that any attempt to commit an offence which involves 'an act which is more than merely preparatory to the commission of the offence' but for any reason fails, so that in the event no offence is committed, must *ex hypothesi*, from the point of view of the criminal law, be 'objectively innocent'. What turns what would otherwise, from the point of view of the criminal law, be an innocent act into a crime is the intent of the actor to commit an offence. I say 'from the point of view of the criminal law' because the law of tort must surely here be quite irrelevant. A puts his hand into B's pocket. Whether or not there is anything in the pocket capable of being stolen, if A intends to steal, his act is a criminal attempt; if he does not so intend, his act is innocent. A plunges a knife into a bolster in a bed. To avoid the complication of an offence of criminal damage, assume it to be A's bolster. If A believes the bolster to be his enemy B and intends to kill him, his act is an attempt to murder B; if he knows the bolster is only a bolster, his act is innocent. These considerations lead me to the conclusion that the distinction sought to be drawn in *Anderton v Ryan* between innocent and guilty acts considered 'objectively' and independently of the state of mind of the actor cannot be sensibly maintained.

Another conceivable ground of distinction which was to some extent canvassed in argument, both in *Anderton v Ryan* and in the instant case, though no trace of it appears in the speeches in *Anderton v Ryan*, is a distinction which would make guilt or innocence of the crime of attempt in a case of mistaken belief dependent on what, for want of a better phrase, I will call the defendant's dominant intention. According to the theory necessary to sustain this distinction, the appellant's dominant intention in *Anderton v Ryan* was to buy a cheap video recorder, her belief that it was stolen was merely incidental. Likewise in the hypothetical case of attempted unlawful sexual intercourse, the young man's dominant intention was to have intercourse with the particular girl; his mistaken belief that she was under 16 was merely incidental. By contrast, in the instant case the appellant's dominant intention was to receive and distribute illegally imported heroin or cannabis.

Whilst I see the superficial attraction of this suggested ground of distinction, I also see formidable practical difficulties in its application. By what test is a jury to be told that a defendant's dominant intention is to be recognised and distinguished from his incidental but mistaken belief? But there is perhaps a more formidable theoretical difficulty. If this ground of distinction is relied on to support the acquittal of the appellant in *Anderton v Ryan*, it can only do so on the basis that her mistaken belief that the video recorder was stolen played no significant part in her decision to buy it and therefore she may be acquitted of the intent to handle stolen goods. But this line of reasoning runs into head-on collision with s 1(3) of the Act of 1981. The theory produces a situation where, apart from the subsection, her intention would not be regarded as having amounted to any intent to commit an offence. Section 1(3)(b) then requires one to ask whether, if the video recorder had in fact been stolen, her intention would have been regarded as an intent to handle stolen goods. The answer must clearly be yes, it would. If she had bought the video recorder knowing it to be stolen, when in fact it was, it would have availed her nothing to say that her dominant intention was to buy a video recorder because it was cheap and that her knowledge that it was stolen was merely incidental. This seems to me fatal to the dominant intention theory.

I am thus led to the conclusion that there is no valid ground on which *Anderton v Ryan* can be distinguished. I have made clear my own conviction, which as a party to the decision (and craving the indulgence of my noble and learned friends who agreed in it) I am the readier to express, that the decision was wrong. What then is to be done? If the case is indistinguishable, the application of the strict doctrine of precedent would require that the present appeal be allowed. Is it permissible to depart from precedent under the *Practice Statement (Judicial Precedent)* [1966] 1 WLR 1234 notwithstanding the especial need for certainty in the criminal law? The following considerations lead me to answer that question affirmatively. First, I am undeterred by the consideration that the decision in *Anderton v Ryan* was so recent. The *Practice Statement* is an effective abandonment of our pretention to infallibility. If a serious error embodied in a decision of this House has distorted the law, the sooner it is corrected the better. Second, I cannot see how, in the very nature of the case, anyone could have acted in reliance on the law as propounded in *Anderton v Ryan* in the belief that he was acting innocently and now find that, after all, he is to be held to have committed a criminal offence. Third, to hold the House bound to follow *Anderton v Ryan* because it cannot be distinguished and to allow the appeal in this case would, it seems to me, be tantamount to a declaration that the Act of 1981 left the law of criminal attempts unchanged following the decision in *R v Smith* [1975] AC 476. Finally, if, contrary to my present view, there is a valid ground on which it would be proper to distinguish cases similar to that considered in *Anderton v Ryan*, my present opinion on that point would not foreclose the option of making such a distinction in some future case.

I cannot conclude this opinion without disclosing that I have had the advantage, since the conclusion of the argument in this appeal, of reading an article by Professor Glanville Williams entitled 'The Lords and impossible attempts, or *quis custodiet ipsos custodes*?' [1986] CLJ 33. The language in which he criticises the decision in *Anderton v Ryan* is not conspicuous for its moderation, but it would be foolish, on that account, not to recognise the force of the criticism and churlish not to acknowledge the assistance I have derived from it.

I would answer the certified question in the affirmative and dismiss the appeal.

8.5 DOUBLY INCHOATE OFFENCES – INCITING INCITEMENT

There are a number of combinations of inchoate offences that can give rise to what is sometimes referred to as doubly inchoate liability. There is, at present, a lack of coherency regarding which inchoate offences can be combined and which cannot. The table below summarises the position and also shows the relationship between inchoate offences and accessorial liability. The extract from *R v Sirat* sets out the rationale for this form of liability as regards inciting incitement.

	Incite	Conspire	Attempt	Aid, abet, counsel and procure
Incite to . . .	Yes; see *R v Sirat* (1986) 83 Cr App Rep 41	No – expressly abolished; see s 5(7) Criminal Law Act 1977	Theoretically possible but unlikely	No
Conspire to . . .	Still a possibility	Never charged	Theoretically possible but unlikely	Doubtful; Smith and Hogan suggest that this falls outside the 1977 Act
	Incite	*Conspire*	*Attempt*	*Aid, abet, counsel and procure*
Attempt to . . .	Yes – see *R v Ransford* (1874) 13 Cox CC 9; *R v Rowley* (1992) 94 Cr App R 95	No – expressly abolished; see s 5(7) Criminal Law Act 1977	Never charged	No – expressly excluded by s 1(4)(b) Criminal Attempts Act 1981
Aid, abet, counsel or procure to . . .	Possible	Possible – see criticisms of *R v Siracusa* (above)	Yes – see *R v Dunnington* (1984)	No such form of liability

---

R v Sirat (1986) 83 Cr App R 41 (CA)

Parker LJ:

. . . The charges on the indictment were as follows:

Count 1: soliciting to murder contrary to s 4 of the Offences Against the Person Act 1861.

Particulars of offence: Mohammed Sirat between the 15th and 21st days of August 1984 solicited encouraged persuaded or endeavoured to persuade Mohammed Bashir to murder Raquia Begum by the act of Mohammed Bashir and/or by the acts of another or others.

Count 2: incitement to cause grievous bodily harm.

Particulars of offence: Mohammed Sirat between the 15th and 21st days of August 1984 unlawfully incited Mohammed Bashir to cause grievous bodily harm to Raquia Begum by the acts of Mohammed Bashir and/or by the acts of another or others.

The facts may be shortly stated. Between Thursday 16 August 1984, and Monday 20 August, both dates inclusive, the appellant had four meetings with Mr Bashir, the last of which was recorded by the police, to whom Mr Bashir had reported after the first two had taken place. It is unnecessary to set out the details of the conversations. It is sufficient to say that they plainly showed that the appellant desired the death of his wife or, if not that, her serious injury, and that he was urging Bashir to (1) either kill or injure her himself, or (2) pay a man who was in fact non-existent to do so, or (3) procure the result, whether by doing the deed himself or by paying someone else, not necessarily the non-existent man, to do so.

At the close of the prosecution case it was submitted on behalf of the appellant that (1) there was no such offence in law as inciting a person to counsel or abet a third person to commit an offence, and (2) there was not sufficient evidence to go to the jury that the appellant had incited Bashir himself to murder or cause grievous bodily harm to the appellant's wife. The judge rightly rejected the second of those two submissions and no complaint is made as to that.

We are now only indirectly concerned with the ruling on the first submission; for what now matters is not the ruling itself but the subsequent direction to the jury which was based on it. Of this complaint is made. In the only ground of appeal which was pursued it is contended that the learned judge erred in law 'in directing the jury that if the defendant urged the witness Bashir to incite a third man to cause grievous bodily harm to the defendant's wife the defendant was guilty of the offence charged in count 2 of the indictment and in rejecting a submission by defence counsel that there was no such offence in law as inciting a person to counsel or abet a third person to commit an offence'.

There is no doubt that at common law incitement to commit a crime is an offence. This being so, it follows logically that if A incites B to incite C to commit a crime, e.g. to wound D, A is guilty of incitement to commit a crime, namely incitement. This however is subject to the qualification that if C is non-existent, being either dead or fictional, A would not be guilty, because he would be inciting the commission of an impossible crime. B cannot incite C, because C does not exist. On the basis of *Fitzmaurice* [1983] QB 1083, the judge rightly so directed the jury. Hence, since the jury convicted on count 2, it follows that they must have concluded that the appellant had not urged Bashir to get the fictional man and no other to do the deed.

With regard to the remaining possibilities, the essence of the learned judge's directions appears from the following passages in his summing up:

If a man wants a murder to be committed and he tries to persuade somebody else to commit it or he tries to persuade that second person to get a third person to commit it, then the first man is guilty of the crime of incitement . . . incitement to murder.

If you are sure that in reality the effect of what he was saying to Bashir was this, 'I want you to get her seriously injured, do it yourself or get the white man from Leeds to do it', then what Sirat was proposing was a possibility because the white man from Leeds was only one way in which he was making his proposal. Another, on the basis that I am putting it to you, was that Bashir might do it himself and that was obviously possible, so in that event he would be guilty of count 2 and, equally, if the effect of what he was saying was this, 'I want you to get her seriously injured, get the white man from Leeds to do it if you like, get somebody else to do it if you like, so long as you get somebody', if that is the effect of what he was saying, then once again the serious injury which he wanted brought about would be a possibility and he would then be guilty of count 2.

Similarly with count 2, you have to be sure before you can convict him that he desired his wife to be seriously injured and that he tried to persuade Bashir to bring about her serious injury in a way which was, in fact, possible.

In principle there is nothing wrong with these directions, but complication is introduced by the provisions of the Criminal Law Act 1977. Section 1 of that Act created the statutory offence of conspiracy and s 5(1), subject to exceptions which do not matter, abolished the offence of conspiracy at common law. Section 5(7) then provided: 'Incitement and attempt to commit the offence of conspiracy (whether the conspiracy incited or attempted would be an offence at common law or under s 1 above or any other enactment) shall cease to be offences.' If, therefore, A incites B to agree with C that C will wound D, A's incitement of B is by statute not an offence.

There is, in our view, no doubt that one possible view of the evidence was that the appellant was inciting Bashir to agree, with either the non-existent man or anyone else who would do it at the right price, that such person should cause grievous bodily harm to the appellant's wife. It is therefore clearly possible that the jury may have convicted him of something which by statute is no longer an offence. Moreover, as was accepted by the prosecution, they may have convicted him of an offence with which he was not charged, namely incitement to incite to cause grievous bodily harm, whereas the prosecution charged incitement to cause grievous bodily harm.

This being so, we allowed the appeal on two grounds: (a) that the appellant may have been convicted of an offence of which he was not charged, and (b) that he may have been convicted of an offence which does not exist.

Lest there be any doubt, we do not intend to indicate that the common law offence of inciting to incite no longer exists. Where however the facts are that the accused's incitement of B is actually to enter into an agreement with C for the commission of a crime, it would in our judgment be impossible to hold that the accused can be guilty of incitement, on the ground that B must of necessity propose the crime to C on the way to making the agreement. Whether other forms of incitement to incite survive will fall for decision when the question arises. It may appear to be absurd that, where a person is inciting actual agreement to be made for the commission of a crime, he should be guilty of no offence, but that where he does not seek actual agreement but mere encouragement he should be guilty. This however is not necessarily absurd, for there may well be circumstances where there is no question of an agreement being sought but where the particular form of incitement is more effective than any attempt to secure agreement.

FURTHER READING

Dennis, I, 'The rationale of criminal conspiracy' (1977) 93 LQR 39

Duff, RA, 'The circumstances of an attempt' [1991] CLJ 100

Hogan, B, 'The Criminal Attempts Act and attempting the impossible' [1984] Crim LR 584

Ormerod, D, 'Making Sense of Mens Rea in Statutory Conspiracies' (2006) 59 CLP 185

Stannard, JE, 'Making up for the missing element: a sideways look at attempts' (1987) 7 Legal Studies 194

Smith, KJM, 'Proximity in attempt: Lord Lane's "midway course" ' [1991] Crim LR 576

CHAPTER 9

THEFT

9.1 INTRODUCTION

The offence of theft is created by s 1 of the Theft Act 1968, which sets out the following definition:

Section 1 of the Theft Act 1968: basic definition of theft

(1) A person is guilty of theft if he dishonestly appropriates property belonging to another with the intention of permanently depriving the other of it; and 'thief' and 'steal' shall be construed accordingly.

. . .

(3) The five following sections of this Act shall have effect as regards the interpretation and operation of this section (and, except as otherwise provided by this Act, shall apply only for purposes of this section).

Section 7 of the Theft Act 1968: punishment

A person guilty of theft shall on conviction on indictment be liable to imprisonment for a term not exceeding [seven years].

There are thus five elements to the offence;

- Property

- Appropriation
- Belonging to another
- Dishonesty
- Intention to permanently deprive

9.2 PROPERTY: THE STATUTORY DEFINITION

Property is defined very widely in s 4 of the Theft Act 1968. It should be noted that the statutory definition excludes land but includes 'things in action'. A 'thing (or 'chose') in action' describes 'all personal rights of property which can only be claimed or enforced by [taking legal] action, and not by taking physical possession' (*Torkington v Magee* [1902] 2 KB 427 at 430, *per* Channell J). A good example of a 'thing in action' is a debt. The term therefore includes bank and building society accounts (if my bank account is in credit, then the bank owes me a debt equivalent to the amount of my credit balance). A cheque is a piece of paper and therefore amounts to 'property', and this is so whether or not the account on which the cheque is drawn is in credit.

Electricity cannot be stolen (*Low v Blease* [1975] Crim LR 513), but there is the specific offence of abstracting electricity under s 13 of the Theft Act 1968 (see below).

9.2.1 SECTION 4 OF THE THEFT ACT 1968: 'PROPERTY'

(1) 'Property' includes money and all other property, real or personal, including things in action and other intangible property.

(2) A person cannot steal land, or things forming part of land and severed from it by him or by his directions, except in the following cases, that is to say:

    (a) when he is a trustee or personal representative, or is authorised by power of attorney, or as liquidator of a company, or otherwise, to sell or dispose of land belonging to another, and he appropriates the land or anything forming part of it by dealing with it in breach of the confidence reposed in him; or

    (b) when he is not in possession of the land and appropriates anything forming part of the land by severing it or causing it to be severed, or after it has been severed; or

    (c) when, being in possession of the land under a tenancy, he appropriates the whole or part of any fixture or structure let to be used with the land.

    For purposes of this subsection 'land' does not include incorporeal hereditaments; 'tenancy' means a tenancy for years or any less period and includes an agreement for such a tenancy, but a person who after the end of a tenancy remains in possession as statutory tenant or otherwise is to be treated as having possession under the tenancy, and 'let' shall be construed accordingly.

(3) A person who picks mushrooms growing wild on any land, or who picks flowers, fruit or foliage from a plant growing wild on any land, does not (although not in possession of the land) steal what he picks, unless he does it for reward or for sale or other commercial purpose.

> For purposes of this subsection 'mushroom' includes any fungus, and 'plant' includes any shrub or tree.
>
> (4) Wild creatures, tamed or untamed, shall be regarded as property; but a person cannot steal a wild creature not tamed nor ordinarily kept in captivity, or the carcase of any such creature, unless either it has been reduced into possession by or on behalf of another person and possession of it has not since been lost or abandoned, or another person is in course of reducing it into possession.

9.2.2 STEALING INTANGIBLE PROPERTY

R v Kohn (1979) 69 Cr App R 395

The court considered whether the balance of an account in credit, or the right to withdraw funds under an agreed overdraft, could amount to intangible property under s 4 of the Theft Act 1968.

Geoffrey Lane LJ:

We now turn to the counts which cover the situation when the account was overdrawn, but the amount of the cheque was within the agreed limits of the overdraft. So far as this aspect of the matter is concerned, Mr Tyrrell [counsel for the appellant] submits that the grant of facilities for an overdraft does not create a debt. He submits that all it does is to give a right of action in the event of a breach.

. . . the meaning of the word 'debt' is perhaps not quite so simple . . .

One turns to *Director of Public Prosecutions v Turner* (1973) 57 Cr App R 932; [1974] AC 357. This was a case involving consideration of section 16(2) of the Theft Act, obtaining a pecuniary advantage by deception [an offence now replaced by ss 2 to 4 of the Fraud Act 2006]. It is a passage in the speech of Lord Reid which does cast some light on this abstruse problem. He said:

> I turn then to paragraph (a). The first question is what is meant by the word 'debt'. I get no assistance from its being linked with the word 'charge' because during the argument no one was able to suggest any case to which 'charge' could apply in this context. Debt normally has one or other of two meanings: it can mean an obligation to pay money or it can mean a sum of money owed. It cannot have the latter meaning here. The paragraph deals with cases where a debt is 'reduced', 'evaded' or 'deferred'. No doubt you can reduce a sum of money, but to speak of a sum of money being evaded or deferred is nonsense. It is an elementary principle of construction that a word must be given the same meaning in different parts of the same provision. The same word used in different sections or subsections of the same Act may in some cases have different meanings. But in this paragraph the word 'debt' is only used once and it would, I think, be totally wrong to allow it to mean one thing when considering whether a debt has been reduced and something different when considering whether a debt has been evaded or deferred.

If the account is in credit, as we have seen, there is an obligation to honour the cheque. If the account is within the agreed limits of the overdraft facilities, there is an obligation to meet the cheque. In either case it is an obligation which can only be enforced by action. For purposes of this case it seems to us that that sufficiently constitutes a debt within the meaning of the word as explained by Lord Reid. It is a right of property which can properly be described as a thing in action and therefore potentially a subject of theft under the provisions of the 1968 Act . . . Miss Goddard on behalf of the Crown has drawn our attention to a number of useful passages to some of which, it is right, we should make reference. The first of these authorities is *William Rouse v The Bradford Banking Co Ltd* [1894] AC 586, where at pp 595 and 596 Lord Herschell LC said:

> It is not necessary to consider what the rights of the bank were with regard to their debtors when they had agreed to an overdraft. The transaction is of course of the commonest. It may be that an overdraft does not prevent the bank who have agreed to give it from at any time giving notice that it is no longer to continue, and that they must be paid their money. This I think at least it does; if they have agreed to give an overdraft they cannot refuse to honour cheques or drafts, within the limit of that overdraft, which have been drawn and put in circulation before any notice to the person to whom they have agreed to give the over-draft that the limit is to be withdrawn. That effect I think it has in point of law; whether it has more than that in point of law it is unnecessary to consider.

. . . It seems to us, in the light of those authorities and in the light of the wording of the Theft Act 1968, that in this situation, when the order to a bank is within the agreed limits of the overdraft, a thing in action certainly exists and accordingly the judge was right in rejecting the submission. The appeal so far as those particular counts are concerned must fail.

That leads us to the third situation, which affects only count 7, that being, it will be remembered, the count which dealt with the cheque presented to the bank at a time when the account was over the agreed overdraft limit which had been imposed by the bank.

The situation here is that there is no relationship of debtor and creditor, even notionally. The bank has no duty to the customer to meet the cheque. It can simply mark the cheque 'Refer to drawer'. It can decline to honour the cheque. The reasons for that are obvious. If then a bank declines to honour a cheque, there is no right of action in the customer. If they do as a matter of grace – that is all it can be – honour the cheque then that is a course which does not retro-spectively create any personal right of property in the customer and does not create any duty retrospectively in the bank. It seems, therefore, on that bald statement of principle, that this count which alleges a theft of a thing in action when the account was over the agreed limit must be quashed, unless some external reason can be found for saving it.

The only way in which Miss Goddard on behalf of the Crown seeks to support the conviction on this count is this. It is only fair to her to say that with characteristic fairness she dealt with this very delicately and her arguments were somewhat faintly put forward. She suggests that it is possible to say that there may be a moment between the bank's decision to honour a cheque and the actual moment when the cheque is honoured, when an obligation upon the bank of a corresponding right in the customer may be said to exist. It seems to us that this is first of all something which would be almost impossible in any particular case to prove, even if it were possible to bring all the necessary witnesses from the particular branch before the court, which would be very unlikely; but a much more serious objection is that, such an argument would be too artificial when one is dealing with what after all is a serious criminal offence which may well, as it did in this case, involve a loss of liberty. Furthermore, it would be impossible for the learned judge to explain to a jury so that a jury can understand precisely what this highly artificial concept really meant.

R v Navvabi [1986] 1 WLR 1311 (CA)

The appellant opened a number of bank accounts and was supplied with cheque books and cheque guarantee cards. Knowing the accounts were not in funds, and not having secured an agreed overdraft facility, the appellant drew a number of cheques in favour of casinos, supported by his cheque guarantee card. One of the issues considered by the Court of Appeal was whether or not the appellant had appropriated any identifiable property.

Lord Lane CJ:

Before the trial judge and again in this court counsel for the appellant submitted that no identifiable property was appropriated, because the contractual obligation imposed on the bank was referable not to any asset which it had at the time the cheque was drawn and delivered to the casino, but to those funds which it had at the time of presentation by the casino. It was further submitted that, if there was identifiable property, its appropriation took place when the bank honoured the cheque and the funds were transferred to the casino by the bank, and not at the time the cheque was drawn and delivered to the casino. Furthermore it was contended that theft in such a way was so academic a concept that only an academically-minded person understanding such niceties would be able to form the necessary intention permanently to deprive the owner. Counsel for the appellant conceded, though this court doubts the correctness of that concession, that if the prosecution case had been presented on the basis that the appropriation took place at the time the funds were transferred by the bank to the casino, the conviction would be unimpeachable . . .

[Regarding the assertion based on in *R v Kohn* to the effect that theft does not occur until the transaction involving the cheque has gone through to completion] . . . It suggests (and has been taken by Professor Griew in his article 'Stealing and obtaining bank credits' [1986] Crim LR 356 . . . to mean that theft occurs at the time when the bank transfers the funds. But Professor Smith has argued . . . that the delivery of the cheque to the payee is 'an assumption of the rights of an owner' and therefore the appropriation. There may, however, as Professor Griew points out, be practical difficulties with this approach, for the state of the account may be much more difficult to ascertain when the cheque is delivered to the payee than when it is presented to the bank. Such difficulties, however, do not arise, or call for resolution, in the present case . . .

. . . [The] use of the cheque card and delivery of the cheque did no more than give the casino a contractual right as against the bank to be paid a specified sum from the bank's funds on presentation of the guaranteed cheque. That was not in itself an assumption of the rights of the bank to that part of the bank's funds to which the sum specified in the cheque corresponded: there was therefore no appropriation by the drawer either on delivery of the cheque to the casino or when the funds were ultimately transferred to the casino.

9.2.3 WHAT CANNOT BE STOLEN?

9.2.3.1 Information

***Oxford v Moss* (1978) 68 Cr App R 183 (DC)**

Smith J:

... On 5 May 1976, an information was preferred by the prosecutor against the defendant alleging that the defendant stole certain intangible property, namely confidential information being examination questions for a civil engineering examination to be held in the month of June 1976 at Liverpool University, the information being the property of the Senate of the University, and the allegation being that the respondent intended permanently to deprive the said Senate of the said property.

The facts can be stated very shortly indeed. They were agreed facts. They are set out in the case and they are as follows. In May 1976 the defendant was a student at Liverpool University. He was studying engineering. Somehow (and this court is not concerned precisely how) he was able to acquire the proof of an examination paper for an examination in civil engineering to be held in the University during the following month, that is to say June 1976. Without doubt the proof, that is to say the piece of paper, was the property of the University. It was an agreed fact, as set out in the case, that the respondent at no time intended to steal what is described as 'any tangible element' belonging to the paper; that is to say it is conceded that he never intended to steal the paper itself.

In truth and in fact, and in all common sense, what he was about was this. He was borrowing a piece of paper hoping to be able to return it and not be detected in order that he should acquire advance knowledge of the questions to be set in the examination and thereby, I suppose, he would be enabled to have an unfair advantage as against other students who did not possess the knowledge that he did.

By any standards, it was conduct which is to be condemned, and to the layman it would readily be described as cheating. The question raised is whether it is conduct which falls within the scope of the criminal law ...

... The question for this court, shortly put, is whether confidential information can amount to property within the meaning of the Theft Act 1968 ...

The question for this court is whether confidential information of this sort falls within that definition contained in s 4(1) ...

In my judgment, it is clear that the answer to that question must be no. Accordingly, I would dismiss the appeal.

9.2.3.2 Human corpse

***R v Kelly* [1999] 2 WLR 384**

Rose LJ:

On 3rd April 1998 at Southwark Crown Court, these appellants were convicted of one offence of theft. Kelly was sentenced to 9 months' imprisonment, and Lindsay to 6 months' imprisonment suspended for 2 years. They appeal against conviction by certificate of the trial judge, His Honour Judge Rivlin QC, in the following terms:

Whether the trial Judge was correct in ruling as a matter of law that there is an exception to the traditional common law rule that 'there is no property in a corpse', namely, that once a human body or body part has undergone a process of skill by a person authorised to perform it, with the object of preserving for the purpose of medical or scientific examination or for the benefit of medical science, it becomes something quite different from an interred corpse. It thereby acquires a usefulness or value. It is capable of becoming property in the usual way, and can be stolen.

The facts were these. Between 1992 and 1994, the appellant, Kelly, who is an artist, had privileged access to the premises of the Royal College of Surgeons in order to draw anatomical specimens held on display and used for training surgeons. The appellant, Lindsay, was employed by the college during that period as a junior technician. Between 1993 and 1994, Kelly, who was then in his late thirties, asked Lindsay, who was under 21, to remove a number of human body parts from the college. Some 35 to 40 such parts, including three human heads, part of a brain, six arms or parts of an arm, ten legs or feet, and part of three human torsos were removed and taken to Kelly's home. He made casts of the parts, some of which were exhibited in an art gallery. Neither appellant intended to return the body parts, many of which Kelly buried in a field in the grounds of his family home. Part of a leg was kept in the attic of his home. The remaining parts were recovered from the basement of a flat occupied by one of Kelly's friends.

The crucial issue for the jury, when the matter was left for their consideration, was whether the appellants had acted dishonestly or whether, at the time they took the body parts, they acted in the honest belief that they had the right to do so. It was accepted, for the purposes of the hearing, that all the specimens in question antedated in age the Anatomy Act of 1984 which had come into force in early 1988. All the specimens taken had been preserved or fixed by college staff or other medical agencies. All were subject to a regular scheme of inspection, preservation, and maintenance and most of them had been the subject of further work, by prosecution, whereby they had been expertly dissected so as to reveal, in highlighted form, the inner workings of the body.

There was evidence that the appellants would not have been permitted to remove body parts from the building under any circumstances. Permission could only be given by a licensed teacher of anatomy for the disposal of the specimens. It was elicited in cross-examination that some of the specimens at the college were no longer in use because of their poor condition due to age, and that other parts had, on occasions, left the college for the purposes of burial or cremation. There was evidence that the preparation of the specimens by prosecution, to which we have referred, would have involved many hours, sometimes weeks, of skilled work. There was also evidence that the type of dissection indicated that the work was that of a previous generation of anatomists, thereby throwing some light on the age of the parts. There was evidence that parts kept in the demonstration room would be up to 20 years old, but those in the basement store would be much older. It was not possible to say whether the specimens taken by the appellants had come from the demonstration room or the basement. There was evidence from the current inspector of anatomy to the effect that the college had full authority to be in possession of these specimens. In cross-examination, he said it was his understanding that the 1832 Anatomy Act did not apply. There was similar evidence from the inspector of anatomy at the time the parts were taken, between 1991 and 1995.

There was a good deal of material placed before the jury, in the form of a jury bundle, which is before this court, containing letters written by various people, in 1944, on the basis of which arguments were advanced as to the belief as to whether or not the possession of the Royal

College of Surgeons was lawfully well-founded. We have to say that, for our part, we find no relevance whatever in those documents to any issue which was before the jury.

Kelly was interviewed on a number of occasions by the police. He said he understood the body parts were old, but that they were extremely valuable to the college. He thought that after 4 years the college required a certificate to retain the parts, which they did not have, and he considered that he was intercepting the parts which were 'on their way to the grave'. Nobody, he agreed, had given him permission to remove the items. He said at first that he had buried all of them but subsequently he gave the address of a friend, to which earlier we referred, where some of the parts were stored. When he was charged with theft and dishonest handling he said he did not intend to commit either such offence.

The appellant, Lindsay, in interview, referred to the age of the anatomical specimens and to the unusual access given to Kelly to the demonstration rooms and basement store. He said that his understanding of the law was that the college was only allowed to keep specimens for a period of 3 years, after which they had to be buried. He said that Kelly had asked him to remove the items, so that castings could be made in the way which we have described and he, Lindsay, agreed to that on condition that Kelly buried the parts afterwards. Lindsay said he took the items from the anatomy store or the storage tanks which were usually in the demonstration rooms. He removed the identification labels which he threw in a bin. Kelly had paid him £400 for his services but, he said, his main interest was in having the pieces buried.

A submission was made to the learned judge on behalf of the defence at the close of the prosecution. The first part of that submission was that parts of bodies were not in law capable of being property, and therefore could not be stolen. The judge ruled, in favour of the Crown, that the specimens were property, because of an exception to the common law rule, in the terms of the certificate which he has given for the purposes of the appeal to this court, the basis of that exception being a decision of the High Court of Australia in *R v Doodeward and Spence* (1908) 6 CLR 406.

. . . On behalf of the appellant, Lindsay, in submissions adopted by counsel on behalf of Kelly, Mr Thornton QC submits, as we have indicated, that the jury's verdict was unsafe, first, because the body parts were not property and therefore could not be stolen, secondly, because they did not belong to the Royal College of Surgeons because they were not lawfully in their possession, and thirdly, because the judge's direction that the college was in lawful possession was a preju-dicial misdirection of the jury.

In support of those submissions, Mr Thornton advanced eight propositions. First, that the common law rule applies to corpses to be buried but not yet buried. Such, he submits, are not property. Secondly there has been, until this case, no prosecution for theft of a body or body parts, although there do exist in other Acts, in particular the Anatomy Act of 1832, certain statutory offences, in relation to corpses and parts of corpses, which are – it is perhaps worth noting in passing – susceptible to a maximum sentence of imprisonment of 3 months. Thirdly, the common law rule extends to parts of bodies as well as to the entire corpse. Fourthly, the body parts in the present case were not property, they were intended by their donors for burial, and the resolution of that matter, clearly one of fact, was one which could only be favourable to the defence. Fifthly, there is no exception to the general common law rule.

For this part of his submission, it was pertinent for him to take the court, as he did, to *Doodeward and Spence*, to which we have already referred. The first of the two majority judg-ments in that Australian case was given by Griffith CJ at p 413 of the report. He said this:

It is idle to contend in these days that the possession of a mummy, or of a prepared skeleton, or of a skull, or other parts of a human body, is necessarily unlawful; if it is, the many valuable collections of anatomical and pathological specimens or preparations formed and maintained by scientific bodies, were formed and are maintained in violation of the law.

In my opinion there is no law forbidding the mere possession of a human body, whether born alive or dead, for purposes other than immediate burial. *A fortiori* such possession is not unlawful if the body possesses attributes of such a nature that its preservation may afford valuable or interesting information or instruction.

Towards the foot of p 414:

. . . a human body, or a portion of a human body, is capable by law of becoming the subject of property. It is not necessary to give an exhaustive enumeration of the circumstances under which such a right may be acquired, but I entertain no doubt that, when a person has by the lawful exercise of work or skill so dealt with a human body or part of a human body in his lawful possession that it has acquired some attributes differentiating it from a mere corpse awaiting burial, he acquires a right to retain possession of it, at least as against any person not entitled to have it delivered to him for the purpose of burial, but subject, of course, to any positive law which forbids its retention under the particular circumstances.

Barton J at p 417 said this:

I have read the judgment of the Chief Justice, and I entirely agree with the reasons it embodies, which I hold it unnecessary to amplify.

Higgins J gave a dissenting judgment at p 417. He referred at p 422, to the transformation of a corpse into a mummy, by the skill of an embalmer turning it into something different. He went on at p 423 to say that such traffic as there is in skulls and bones is clandestine. If they come from dissecting rooms, they come in violation of the law. He went on to say that no dead body could be used for dissection except under very stringent conditions and when the dissection was over the body must be decently interred. He said this, which is much relied upon by the appellants in this court:

. . . I rather think that sundry contraventions of the strict law as to dead bodies are winked at in the interests of medical science, and also for the practical reasons that no one can identify the bones or parts, and that no one is interested in putting the law in motion.

At the conclusion of judgment, at p 424, he said this:

A right to keep possession of a human corpse seems to me to be just the thing which the British law, and, therefore, the New South Wales law, declines to recognise.

Mr Thornton draws attention to the fact that that authority, which related to a two-headed stillborn fetus preserved as a curio, arose from a claim in detinue and he relies, as we have said, on the dissenting judgment of Higgins J. The facts of that case, he says, are plainly distinguishable from the present, because the nature of the object there in dispute rendered it something wholly different from a corpse or part of a corpse.

He submitted that there cannot be property for the purposes of the Theft Act, unless there is a permanent right to possession vested in the person from whom the property is taken. He submitted that the decision of the English Court of Appeal in *Dobson v North Tyneside Health Authority* [1996] 4 All ER 474, does not lend succour to the *Doodeward* exception. He submitted that no amount of skill expended on a body part can affect its ownership; at the highest, it might affect possessory rights.

. . . Mr Campbell-Tiech, on behalf of the prosecution, advanced before this court a submission which was not made to the learned trial judge, namely, that a corpse and parts of a corpse are property within section 4 of the Theft Act; a thing is either property or not. The status of the holder of the thing is irrelevant to determination of whether it is property or not, as is equally irrelevant the intention of the holder of the thing. Section 4 deals with property. Section 5 deals with rights over property. There is no overlap between the two sections. The common law in relation to corpses and parts of corpses deals with rights over things, and that is the province of section 5, not section 4. The common law doctrine as to who has the right to possession or control is irrelevant to whether a thing is property. Parts of a corpse have all the properties of a thing; the common law relates to rights not things. In the Theft Act, Parliament did not declare that a corpse was not property and could not be stolen. As a matter of statutory construction, a corpse or part of a corpse is within the definition of property in section 4.

We have sought summarily to rehearse Mr Campbell-Tiech's argument lest this matter proceed further. But, as we indicated to him and other counsel in the case, bearing in mind that the submission was not made before the learned trial judge, bearing in mind the way in which the matter proceeded before him and bearing in mind the terms of his certificate to this court, Mr Campbell-Tiech's submission is not one which we shall regard as being in any way determinative of this appeal. We merely comment that the draftsmen of the Theft Act must presumably have been well aware of the state of the common law for the last 150 years or more, and they do not appear to have made any exception in the Theft Act by reference to it.

We return to the first question, that is to say whether or not a corpse or part of a corpse is property. We accept that, however questionable the historical origins of the principle, it has now been the common law for 150 years at least that neither a corpse, nor parts of a corpse, are in themselves and without more capable of being property protected by rights (see, for example, Earl J, in *R v Sharp* (1857) Dears & Bell 160, at p 163, where he said:

> Our law recognises no property in a corpse, and the protection of the grave at common law as contradistinguished from ecclesiastic protection to consecrated ground depends on this form of indictment.

He was there referring to an indictment which charged not theft of a corpse but removal of a corpse from a grave.

If that principle is now to be changed, in our view, it must be by Parliament, because it has been express or implicit in all the subsequent authorities and writings to which we have been referred that a corpse or part of it cannot be stolen.

To address the point as it was addressed before the trial judge and to which his certificate relates, in our judgment, parts of a corpse are capable of being property within section 4 of the Theft Act, if they have acquired different attributes by virtue of the application of skill, such as dissection or preservation techniques, for exhibition or teaching purposes: see *Doodeward and Spence*, in the judgment of Griffith CJ to which we have already referred and *Dobson v North Tyneside Health Authority* where, at p 479, this proposition is not dissented from and appears, in the judgment of this court, to have been accepted by Peter Gibson LJ; otherwise, his analysis of the facts of *Dobson*, which appears at that page in the judgment, would have been, as it seems to us, otiose. Accordingly the trial judge was correct to rule as he did.

Furthermore, the common law does not stand still. It may be that if, on some future occasion, the question arises, the courts will hold that human body parts are capable of being property for the purposes of section 4, even without the acquisition of different attributes, if they have a use or significance beyond their mere existence. This may be so if, for example, they are intended for use in an organ transplant operation, for the extraction of DNA or, for that matter, as an exhibit in a trial. It is to be noted that in *Dobson*, there was no legal or other requirement for the brain, which was then the subject of litigation, to be preserved . . .

9.2.3.3 Dishonestly abstracting electricity

In order to avoid technical arguments as to whether there can be an intention to permanently deprive the owner of electricity, the Theft Act 1968 makes special provision for the dishonest use of electricity. Section 13 provides:

> 13(1) A person who dishonestly uses without due authority, or dishonestly causes to be wasted or diverted, any electricity shall on conviction on indictment be liable to imprisonment for a term not exceeding five years.

The offence is normally committed by those who tamper with metering equipment either by reconnecting the supply without authority, or interfering with the operation of the meter so that it does not fully record the amount of electricity consumed; see *Collins v DPP* (1987) *The Times*, 20 October. A defendant would still incur liability, however, if he were to move into an empty house as a squatter and make use of an existing supply simply by plugging in electrical equipment; see *R v McCreadie and Tume* (1992) 96 Cr App R 143.

> **Boggeln v Williams [1978] 1 WLR 873 (DC)**
>
> Lloyd J:
>
> . . . The question for the opinion of the court is whether a person can be convicted of dishonestly abstracting electricity contrary to s 13 of the Theft Act 1968, if he intends to pay for the electricity when payment is due, and that intention is based on a genuine belief that he will be able to do so . . .
>
> The facts are these. On 27 October 1976, a representative of the East Midlands Electricity Board had disconnected the defendant's supply of electricity after due warning had been given by reason of the defendant's failure to pay an outstanding amount of £39.65. The defendant thereupon spoke to one of the board's employees and informed him that he was intending to reconnect the supply himself. Shortly thereafter he broke the seal on the board's main fuse box and reconnected the supply by means of a piece of wire which he inserted in place of the main fuse which the board's employees had removed. The way in which he carried out the

re-connection meant that the electricity which he used would continue to be recorded on the meter in the usual way.

There is then this important finding of fact in paragraph 2(5) of the case [stated by the justices]:

> As a result of the said conversation the [defendant] did not believe that the Board consented to reconnection by him. The [defendant] nevertheless did believe that, by giving notice of his intention and by ensuring that consumption was duly recorded through the meter, he was not acting dishonestly in reconnecting.

. . . There is then another important finding of fact in paragraph 2(8) [of the case stated by the justices]:

> At the time when the [defendant] reconnected the supply, the [defendant] believed, as he asserted, that he would be in a position to pay for the electricity consumed thereafter at the date when payment was due. We were satisfied that this belief was a genuine one and we were not satisfied that it was unreasonable.

There is no specific finding anywhere in the case as to the defendant's intention to pay for the electricity, but it is common ground in this case that that can be inferred. Finally, in paragraph 5 of the case it is stated:

> We were of the opinion that the defendant did believe that, when payment became due, he would be able to pay for the electricity consumed; that this belief was not proved to be unreasonable; and that the defendant's state of mind at the relevant time (ie when reconnecting the supply) was not dishonest.

The question for the opinion of the court is as follows:

> Is an intention to pay for electricity knowingly used without the authority of the Electricity Board capable of affording a defence to a charge under s 13 of the Theft Act 1968, if that intention is based on a genuine belief that the user will be able to pay at the due time for payment?

. . . The fact that the defendant did not believe at the time he reconnected his supply that he had the consent of the board does not of itself make the defendant's conduct dishonest in law. It is a question of fact in each case for the tribunal of fact whether the necessary dishonesty is proved or not . . .

O'Connor J and Lord Widgery CJ delivered concurring judgments.

9.2.4 STEALING OF PART CAN BE STEALING OF WHOLE

Pilgram v Rice-Smith [1977] 2 All ER 659 (DC)

Lord Widgery CJ:
. . . At the Crown Court the following facts were found. The first respondent was an assistant employed by International Stores, the victims of the alleged theft. She worked in their shop at East

Dereham. The second respondent was known to, and I think one can fairly say a friend of, the first respondent.

On the day in question the second respondent went to the counter where the first respondent was serving, and at that time corned beef was 18p a quarter and bacon was 72p a pound. The first respondent, who (it will be remembered) was behind the counter and an employee of the shop, served the second respondent with a quantity of corned beef which appeared to be well over a quarter and marked the price as 20p on the wrapping. She then weighed just over a pound of bacon and marked the price as 38p on the wrapping. Both articles were handed to the second respondent.

The second respondent then went around the store and bought some further articles. At the check-out she paid for all the articles in the total sum of £1.04. This included the 20p for the corned beef and the 38p for the bacon. The appellant alleged that the second respondent should have paid 83p more than that in respect of an undercharge on the bacon and the corned beef.

As the second respondent was leaving the store she was spoken to by the store detective and the usual investigation followed . . .

In the result I analyse the case in this way. It seems to me clear that we must treat the two respondents as having been in league with one another from the outset. It is proper to treat the parcel of bacon and corned beef as a single parcel for this purpose. The fraud was inspired from the very beginning and therefore it operated from before the time when the goods were handed over to the purchaser, and accordingly the transaction of sale, or the purported transaction of sale, was a nullity from the start. It was a nullity from the start because from the start the lady behind the counter had no authority on the part of her employer to sell these goods at under value. She just did not have that authority. Consequently no contract of sale was entered into at all. That opens the door immediately for a conviction of theft in respect of the whole of the goods, and it is well established that it matters not in a case such as this that you have charged only the theft of part and proved the whole. You can nevertheless obtain a conviction in respect of what has been charged . . .

9.2.5 CODIFICATION AND LAW REFORM PROPOSALS

In its Consultation Paper *Legislating the Criminal Code: Misuse of Trade Secrets* (LCCP 150), the Law Commission provisionally proposed that information, in the form of trade secrets, should come within the protection of the criminal law. The summary of the Paper explained the rationale for this position:

At present trade secrets cannot be stolen as they do not constitute 'property' for the purpose of the Theft Act 1968. The law has been strongly criticised because 'it is not too much to say that we live in a country where the theft of the boardroom table is punished far more severely than the theft of the boardroom secrets'.

Other jurisdictions have extended the protection of the criminal law to the misuse of confidential business information: for example, the majority of the American states and a number of European countries, including France and Germany, provide criminal sanctions against the misuse of trade secrets.

The Consultation Paper itself sets out the position under the existing criminal law in more detail:

> 1.4 At present the criminal law gives no specific protection to trade secrets. In particular, trade secrets cannot, in law, be stolen: they do not constitute 'property' for the purpose of the Theft Act 1968 . . . In the leading case, *Oxford v Moss*, an undergraduate obtained the proof of an examination paper before the examination. After reading the proof he returned it, retaining the information for his own use. He was held not guilty of stealing the information.
>
> 1.5 The principle is strikingly illustrated by *Absolom*, which followed *Oxford v Moss*. The defendant, a geologist, obtained and then tried to sell to a rival company details of a leading oil company's exploration for oil off the Irish coast. The information, which was contained in a 'graphalog' (a record of geological data and an indication of the prospects of finding oil), was unique, since the company was the only oil company exploring the area. The company had invested £13 million in drilling operations, and the information could have been sold for between £50,000 and £100,000. Although the judge stated that the defendant had acted in 'utmost bad faith', he directed the jury to acquit him of theft, on the ground that the information in the graphalog was not capable of founding such a charge.
>
> 1.6 A further difficulty with applying the law of theft to the misappropriation of a trade secret arises from the requirement that the defendant must intend permanently to deprive the owner of the property. 'It is difficult to see how there is any question of deprivation where someone has, in breach of confidence, forced the original holder to share, but not forget, his secret.'
>
> 1.7 Normally the information amounting to a trade secret will be recorded on a physical medium such as paper, microfiche or a computer disk. In that case, the physical medium is property, and a dishonest taking of it can therefore be charged as theft. But a charge of stealing an object worth a few pence would scarcely represent the gravamen of the defendant's conduct. And even this charge is unavailable if the information is absorbed without the taking of the medium on which it is recorded, or if (as in *Oxford v Moss*) there is no intention permanently to deprive the secrets owner of the medium (as distinct from the secret).
>
> 1.8 There are, however, a number of existing offences of infringing rights in intellectual property; and there are other offences which are not primarily concerned with intellectual property but which might be committed in the course of acquiring, using or disclosing another's trade secret.
>
> . . .
>
> 1.21 Where two or more people dishonestly use or disclose another's trade secret, they may be guilty of the common law offence of conspiracy to defraud. The element of fraud is so widely defined that, on such facts, it may be readily established. The main reason why conspiracy to defraud is not a complete solution under the existing law is the requirement of conspiracy: it is probably illegal for two people to agree to 'steal' a trade secret, but not for one person to do it alone.
>
> . . .

1.23 Although trade secret misuse is not an offence in itself, the way in which a secret is obtained may incidentally trigger liability for a more general offence. Where secret information is obtained by deception, for example, on the understanding that it has been or will be paid for, there may be an obtaining of services by deception, contrary to section 1 of the Theft Act 1978 [see now s 11 of the Fraud Act 2006]. Obtaining information by bribery or corruption may be an offence under the Prevention of Corruption Acts 1889 to 1916. Again, industrial espionage may involve the commission of the offence of intercepting post or of telephone tapping. But there is no offence if an employee simply discloses or uses the secret in breach of confidence, or an outsider obtains it in a manner not specifically prohibited.

1.24 It thus appears that the protection afforded to trade secrets by the existing criminal law is limited. There may be no offence if an individual, acting alone, dishonestly uses or discloses secret information (not protected by copyright or a registered trademark, and not amounting to personal data protected by the Data Protection Act 1984) without authority, provided that that individual

(1) obtains the information with the consent of its owner (albeit in confidence) for example where an employee is given the information for the purposes of his or her work or

(2) though not authorised to have the information at all, obtains it without resorting to deception, corruption, unauthorised access to a computer, intercepting post, telephone tapping or any other prohibited means. A simple example would be the industrial spy who gains access to premises without forcing entry (which would involve an offence of criminal damage) and inspects the contents of an unlocked filing cabinet.

The summary of the Consultation Paper's proposals continues:

Should there be criminal sanctions for trade secret misuse?
We provisionally conclude there should be criminal sanctions because:

- There is no distinction between the harm caused by theft and by the misuse of trade secrets. In both cases, the property of another is being used for the benefit of the wrongdoer, and the owner is likely to suffer damage.
- The imposition of legal sanctions is necessary in order to protect investment and research. Vast sums of money are spent on producing certain types of trade secret such as manufacturing formulae and other technical data and it seems strange that the criminal law does not provide a sanction.
- It is inconsistent for the law to provide criminal sanctions for the infringement of copyright and registered trademarks, but not for misuse of trade secrets.
- Civil remedies alone are insufficient to discourage trade secret misuse, as many wrongdoers are unable to satisfy any judgment against them. At present the law has no effective sanctions against the person who dishonestly misuses trade secrets and has no assets.
- The criminalisation of trade secret misuse would help to preserve standards in business life.

What trade secrets are covered?
We provisionally propose that the definition of a 'trade secret' should include a requirement that its owner had indicated – expressly or impliedly – a wish to keep it secret. We invite views on

whether the definition of trade secrets should make a reference to the use of the information in a trade or business and, if so, whether the definition should extend to information used in a profession or in non-commercial research.

It is our provisional view that an element of the definition of a trade secret should be that the information is not generally known; but we believe that the prosecution should not have to prove that the information was not generally known unless there is some evidence to suggest that it was.

What wrong-doings in connection with trade secrets should be covered?

We provisionally conclude that the new offence should be committed by any person who uses or discloses a trade secret belonging to another without that other's consent. By 'belonging to another' we mean the person who is entitled to the benefit of the trade secret. Our provisional view is that consent to the use or disclosure of a trade secret should not negative liability for the offence if it was obtained by deception.

We provisionally propose that it should be an element of the new offence that the defendant:

- knows that the information in question is a trade secret belonging to another, and
- is aware that the other does not (or may not) consent to the use or disclosure; but it should not be an offence if the person who uses or discloses the trade secret does so in the belief that every person to whom the secret belongs would consent to the use or disclosure if he or she knew of it and the circumstances of it.

Defences

We are concerned that there should be a public interest defence, and therefore provisionally propose that the new offence should not apply to: the use or disclosure to an appropriate person of information for the purpose of the prevention, detection or exposure of a crime, fraud or breach of statutory duty, whether committed or contemplated, conduct which is in the nature of a fraud on the general public, or matters constituting a present or future threat to the health or welfare of the community, or any use or disclosure of information which under the law of confidence would be justified on grounds of public interest.

We also provisionally propose that the new offence should not apply to: any disclosure of information by a person who under any form of legislation is obliged or permitted to make it, disclosure of information pursuant to a court order, or otherwise in the course of civil or criminal legal proceedings, or the lawful exercise of an official function with regard to national security or the prevention, investigation or prosecution of crime.

Should there be criminal liability for the dishonest acquisition of a trade secret?

We invite views on whether the law should be extended to cover the acquisition of a trade secret; and, if so, whether this should be achieved by creating an offence of acquiring a trade secret with the intention of using or disclosing it, or an offence of acquiring a trade secret by wrongful methods, or an offence defined in some other way (and, if so, what)?

9.3 APPROPRIATION

Section 3 of the Theft Act 1968: 'appropriates'

(1) Any assumption by a person of the rights of an owner amounts to an appropriation, and this includes, where he has come by the property (innocently or not) without stealing it, any later assumption of a right to it by keeping or dealing with it as owner.

(2) Where property or a right or interest in property is or purports to be transferred for value to a person acting in good faith, no later assumption by him of rights which he believed himself to be acquiring shall, by reason of any defect in the transferor's title, amount to theft of the property.

Note that s 1(2) of the 1968 Act provides that: 'It is immaterial whether the appropriation is made with a view to gain, or is made for the thief's own benefit.'

Section 3(1) makes no reference to whether or not the absence of consent on the part of the owner is a matter that has to be established by the prosecution. It might seem logical to assume that where the owner genuinely consents to property being appropriated there can be no theft; where the owner is tricked into consenting, the appropriate charge would be one of fraud by false pretences contrary to s 2 of the Fraud Act 2006 [formerly obtaining property by deception contrary to s 15 of the Theft Act 1968]. Where the owner does not consent the appropriate charge would be theft. As a number of House of Lords decisions such as *R v Lawrence, R v Gomez,* and *R v Hinks* (all extracted below) reveal, however, s 3(1) creates no onus on the prosecution to prove the absence of consent. *Any* assumption of *any* right of the owner will suffice. The objection to this broad approach to appropriation, as will be seen from the extracts below, is that it blurred the distinction between theft (in the sense of theft being the unauthorised taking of property) and deception (where D obtains possession by tricking P into handing over the property). To some extent the debate is now academic given that the Fraud Act 2006 has swept away the deception offences, including obtaining property by deception contrary to s 15 of the 1968 Act, replacing them with a range of inchoate offences, including the use of false pretences with the intention of gaining property. The authorities extracted below are still relevant, however, to the debate over the nature of appropriation – is it an act that can be committed with the owner's consent or does it have to be something that is unauthorised?

Lawrence v Metropolitan Police Commissioner [1972] AC 626 (HL)

Mr Occhi, an Italian who spoke little English, arrived at Victoria Station on his first visit to England. He approached the appellant, a taxi driver, and showed him a piece of paper on which an address in Ladbroke Grove was written. The appellant said that it was very far and very expensive. Mr Occhi got into the taxi, took a £1 note out of his wallet and gave it to the appellant who then, the wallet being still open, took a further £6 out of it. The appellant then drove Mr Occhi to Ladbroke Grove. The correct lawful fare for the journey was in the region of 50p in current coinage. The appellant was charged with and convicted of the theft of the £6. The appellant contended that he could not be guilty of theft as there had been no appropriation, Mr Occhi having consented to his taking the money from the wallet.

Viscount Dilhorne:

I see no ground for concluding that the omission of the words 'without the consent of the owner' [from s 1(1) of the Theft Act 1968] was inadvertent and not deliberate, and to read the subsection as if they were included is, in my opinion, wholly unwarranted. Parliament by the omission of these words has relieved the prosecution of the burden of establishing that the taking was without the owner's consent. That is no longer an ingredient of the offence . . .

. . . That there was appropriation in this case is clear. Section 3(1) states that any assumption by a person of the rights of an owner amounts to an appropriation. Here there was clearly such an assumption. That an appropriation was dishonest may be proved in a number of ways. In this case it was not contended that the appellant had not acted dishonestly. Section 2(1) provides, *inter alia*, that a person's appropriation of property belonging to another is not to be regarded as dishonest if he appropriates the property in the belief that he would have the other's consent if the other knew of the appropriation and the circumstances of it. *A fortiori*, a person is not to be regarded as acting dishonestly if he appropriates another's property believing that with full knowledge of the circumstances that other person has in fact agreed to the appropriation. The appellant, if he believed that Mr Occhi, knowing that £7 was far in excess of the legal fare, had nevertheless agreed to pay him that sum, could not be said to have acted dishonestly in taking it.

. . . Belief or the absence of belief that the owner had with such knowledge consented to the appropriation is relevant to the issue of dishonesty, not to the question whether or not there has been an appropriation. That may occur even though the owner has permitted or consented to the property being taken. So proof that Mr Occhi had consented to the appropriation of £6 from his wallet without agreeing to paying a sum in excess of the legal fare does not suffice to show that there was not dishonesty in this case. There was ample evidence that there was.

I now turn to the third element, 'property belonging to another' . . . [T]he money in the wallet which [the appellant] appropriated belonged to another, to Mr Occhi.

There was no dispute about the appellant's intention being permanently to deprive Mr Occhi of the money.

The four elements of the offence of theft as defined in the Theft Act 1968 were thus clearly established and, in my view, the Court of Appeal was right to dismiss the appeal.

Having done so, they granted a certificate that a point of law of general public importance was involved . . .

The first question posed in the certificate was:

Whether s 1(1) of the Theft Act 1968 is to be construed as though it contained the words 'without having the consent of the owner' or words to that effect.

In my opinion, the answer is clearly No.

The second question was:

Whether the provisions of s 15(1) [the offence of obtaining property by deception, now replaced by ss 2 to 4 of the Fraud Act 2006] and of s 1(1) of the Theft Act 1968, are mutually exclusive in the sense that if the facts proved would justify a conviction under s 15(1) there cannot lawfully be a conviction under s 1(1) on those facts.

Again, in my opinion, the answer is No. There is nothing in the Act to suggest that they should be regarded as mutually exclusive and it is by no means uncommon for conduct on the part of an accused to render him liable to conviction for more than one offence. Not infrequently there is some overlapping of offences. In some cases the facts may justify a charge under s 1(1) and also a charge under s 15(1). On the other hand, there are cases which only come within s 1(1) and some which are only within s 15(1). If in this case the appellant had been charged under s 15(1), he would, I expect, have contended that there was no deception, that he had simply appropriated the money and that he ought to have been charged under s 1(1). In my view, he was rightly charged under that section . . .

Lord Pearson, Lord Diplock, Lord Cross, and Lord Donovan also agreed that the appeal should be dismissed.

Dobson v General Accident Fire and Life Assurance Corp plc [1990] 1 QB 274 (CA)

This was a civil case involving a claim under a home insurance policy, which included cover for loss by theft. The plaintiff had advertised an expensive watch for sale. He was visited in his house by a purchaser who bought the watch, providing the plaintiff with a cheque that subsequently proved to be worthless. The plaintiff contended that his loss was covered by his household insurance policy as he had been the victim of a theft. The insurance company refused to pay out on the basis that there had been no theft as the plaintiff had consented to the purchaser taking the watch. The issue for the Court of Appeal (Civil Division), therefore, was whether theft could occur even where the owner consented to the taking of the property. The court held that the plaintiff had been the victim of a theft.

Parker LJ:
. . . The issue for determination on the appeal is whether the circumstances constituted a theft of the watch and ring by the rogue.
. . . On the basis of *Lawrence v Commissioner of Police for the Metropolis* [1972] AC 626, the facts of the present case appear to establish that the rogue assumed all the rights of an owner when he took or received the watch and ring from the plaintiff. That he did so dishonestly and with the intention of permanently depriving the plaintiff of them are matters beyond doubt. It was however submitted that the third element was not satisfied because, at the time of appropriation, if there was one, the watch and ring were not property belonging to another. The property had, it was submitted, already passed to the rogue at the time the articles were delivered to him.
. . . Having regard to the terms of the contract, the conduct of the parties and the circum-stances of the case, I have no doubt that the property was not intended to pass in this case on contract but only in exchange for a valid building society cheque, but even if it may be regarded as intended to pass in exchange for a false, but believed genuine, building society cheque it will not in my view avail the insurers . . .
It was further submitted on the part of the insurers that, notwithstanding the emphatic statement of the House of Lords that absence of consent on the part of the owner was not an ingredient of the offence and was not relevant to the question whether there had been an appropriation, the later decision of the House in *R v Morris* [1984] AC 320 at 332, that appropriation 'involves not an act expressly or impliedly authorised by the owner but an act by way of adverse interference with

or usurpation of those rights', must lead in the present case to the conclusion that there had been no theft.

The difficulties caused by the apparent conflict between the decision in *Lawrence's* case and *R v Morris* have provided, not surprisingly, a basis for much discussion by textbook writers and contributors of articles to law journals. It is, however, clear that their Lordships in *R v Morris* did not regard anything said in that case as conflicting with *Lawrence's* case for it was specifically referred to in Lord Roskill's speech, with which the other members of the Appellate Committee all agreed, without disapproval or qualification. The only comment made was that, in *Lawrence's* case, the House did not have to consider the precise meaning of 'appropriation' in s 3(1) (see [1984] AC 320 at 331). With respect, I find this comment hard to follow in the light of the first of the questions asked in *Lawrence's* case and the answer to it . . . the fact that it was specifically argued that 'appropriates' is meant in a pejorative, rather than a neutral, sense in that the appropriation is against the will of the owner (see [1972] AC 626 at 631), and finally that dishonesty was common ground. I would have supposed that the question in *Lawrence's* case was whether appropriation necessarily involved an absence of consent . . .

. . . the insurers' contention that there was no theft is based on consent and the fact that there was a clear s 15(1) offence, both of which are negatived as answers to appropriation by *Lawrence's* case, and the fact that the contract of sale between the plaintiff and the rogue was voidable only and not void, which is not relevant according to *R v Morris*.

If, then, the insurers are deprived of their arguments to defeat the only element of the offence of theft which was in doubt once the 'belonging to another' argument has been rejected, they cannot in my judgment succeed on the basis of Lord Roskill's statement in *R v Morris* that there must be an act by way of adverse interference with or usurpation of the owner's rights. If consent and the existence of a voidable contract under which property passes are irrelevant, there was in my judgment a plain interference with or usurpation of the plaintiff's rights.

I am fully conscious of the fact that in so concluding I may be said not to be applying *R v Morris*. This may be so, but in the light of the difficulties inherent in the decision, the very clear decision in *Lawrence's* case and the equally clear statement in *R v Morris* that the question whether a contract is void or only voidable is irrelevant, I have been unable to reach any other conclusion. I would therefore dismiss the appeal.

Bingham LJ:

. . . It . . . appears that A commits theft if he dishonestly assumes any of the rights of an owner over B's property intending to deprive B of that property permanently.

This simple analysis may be applied to the everyday example of a customer selecting goods from a supermarket shelf and putting them in the wire basket or trolley provided. The goods on the shelves belong to the supermarket. They continue to belong to the supermarket until paid for by a customer: see *Lacis v Cashmarts* [1969] 2 QB 400. The customer assumes some of the rights of an owner when he takes them into his (or her) possession and exercises control over them by putting them in a basket or trolley. The customer, not intending to return the goods to the supermarket, intends to deprive the supermarket of the goods permanently. In the ordinary case the customer will honestly intend to pay the market price for the goods at the cash desk, so no offence of theft will be committed. But a customer who dishonestly intends not to pay the marked price will be guilty of theft, at the time of dishonest appropriation. On this analysis it is irrelevant that the supermarket displays the goods for sale and invites, perhaps even tempts, customers to put them in their baskets or trolleys. The acid test is whether when doing so the customer acts honestly or dishonestly. (I need not discuss the case where a customer initially appropriates goods honestly intending to pay and later forms a dishonest intention to keep the goods without paying) . . .

I do not find it easy to reconcile [the] ruling of Viscount Dilhorne [in *Lawrence's* case, that appropriation may occur even though the owner has permitted or consented to the property being taken], which was as I understand central to the answer which the House of Lords gave to the certified question, with the reasoning of the House in *R v Morris*. Since, however, the House in *R v Morris* considered that there had plainly been an appropriation in *Lawrence's* case, this must (I think) have been because the Italian student, although he had permitted or allowed his money to be taken, had not in truth consented to the taxi driver taking anything in excess of the correct fare. This is not a wholly satisfactory reconciliation, since it might be said that a super-market consents to customers taking goods from its shelves only when they honestly intend to pay and not otherwise. On the facts of the present case, however, it can be said, by analogy with *Lawrence's* case, that although the plaintiff permitted and allowed his property to be taken by the rogue, he had not in truth consented to the rogue becoming owner without giving a valid draft drawn by the building society for the price. On this basis I conclude that the plaintiff is able to show an appropriation sufficient to satisfy s 1(1) of the 1968 Act when the rogue accepted delivery of the articles.

On the facts here the plaintiff has no difficulty in showing dishonesty and an intention perman-ently to deprive on the part of the rogue. It is, however, argued for the insurers that when the rogue appropriated the ring and the watch they were not property belonging to another because owner-ship of the goods had already, before delivery, passed to the rogue under the contract of sale.

The courts have been enjoined so far as possible to eschew difficult questions of contract law relating to title to goods: see *R v Morris* [1984] AC 320 at 334. But whether, in the ordinary case to which s 5 of the 1968 Act does not apply, goods are to be regarded as belonging to another is a question to which the criminal law offers no answer and which can only be answered by reference to civil law principles. Applying these principles, I would without much doubt impute an intention to the plaintiff and the rogue that property in the watch and the ring should pass to the rogue on delivery of the goods to him and not before. That would also, as I think, be the moment of appropriation. If, therefore, it were necessary for the plaintiff to show that the goods still belonged to him at the moment of appropriation I would doubt whether he could do so, appropriation and transfer of title being simultaneous. Happily for the plaintiff, the point was raised in *Lawrence v Commissioner of Police for the Metropolis* [1972] AC 626 at 632 and decided in his favour . . .

. . . Just as it is enough to satisfy s 15 that the goods belong to the victim up to the time of obtaining, so it is enough for the plaintiff that the watch and ring belonged to him up to the time of appropriation . . .

R v Gomez [1993] AC 442 (HL)

Gomez was employed as assistant manager at a shop trading by retail in electrical goods. He was asked by an acquaintance called Ballay to supply goods from the shop and to accept payment by two stolen building society cheques, one for £7,950 and the other for £9,250, which were undated and bore no payee's name. Gomez agreed, and prepared a list of goods to the value of £7,950 which he submitted to the manager, Mr Gilberd, saying that it repre-sented a genuine order by one Johal and asking him to authorise the supply of the goods in return for a building society cheque in that sum. Mr Gilberd instructed Gomez to confirm with the bank that the cheque was acceptable, and Gomez later told him that he had done so and that such a cheque was 'as good as cash'. Mr Gilberd agreed to the transaction, Gomez paid the cheque into the bank, and a few days later Ballay took possession of the goods, Gomez helping him to load them into his vehicle. Shortly afterwards a further consignment of goods to the value of £9,250 was ordered and supplied in similar fashion (apart from one item valued at £1,002.99 which was not delivered), against the second stolen building society cheque. Mr Gilberd agreed to this transaction without further inquiry. Later the two cheques were returned by the bank marked 'Orders not to pay. Stolen cheque'. Gomez was convicted of theft and appealed, contending that there could be no theft where the owner had been deceived into consenting to the property being taken. The Court of Appeal certified that a point of law of general public importance was involved, namely:

> When theft is alleged and that which is alleged to be stolen passes to the defendant with the consent of the owner, but that consent has been obtained by a false representation, has (a) an appropriation within the meaning of s 1(1) of the Theft Act 1968 taken place, or (b) must such a passing of property necessarily involve an element of adverse [interference] with or usurpation of some right of the owner?

Lord Keith of Kinkel:

My Lords, this appeal raises the question whether two decisions of your Lordships' House upon the proper construction of certain provisions of the Theft Act 1968 are capable of being reconciled with each other, and, if so, in what manner. The two decisions are *R v Lawrence (Alan)* [1972] AC 626 and *R v Morris (David)* [1984] AC 320 . . .

. . . It will be seen that Viscount Dilhorne's speech [in *Lawrence's* case] contains two clear pronouncements, first that it is no longer an ingredient of the offence of theft that the taking should be without the owner's consent and second, that an appropriation may occur even though the owner has permitted or consented to the property being taken . . .

In my opinion Lord Roskill [in *R v Morris*] was undoubtedly right when he said . . . that the assumption by the defendant of any of the rights of an owner could amount to an appropriation within the meaning of s 3(1), and that the removal of an article from the shelf and the changing of the price label on it constituted the assumption of one of the rights of the owner and hence an appropriation within the meaning of the subsection. But there are observations in the passage which, with the greatest possible respect to Lord Roskill, I must regard as unnecessary for the decision of the case and as being incorrect. In the first place, it seems to me that the switching of price labels on the article is in itself an assumption of one of the rights of the owner, whether or not it is accompanied by some other act such as removing the article from the shelf and placing it in a basket or trolley. No one but the owner has the right to remove a price label from an article or to place a price label upon it. If anyone else does so, he does an act, as Lord Roskill puts it, by way of adverse interference with or usurpation of that right. This is no less so in the case of the practical joker figured by Lord Roskill than in the case of one who makes the switch with dishonest intent. The practical joker, of course, is not guilty of theft because he has not acted dishonestly and does not intend to deprive the owner permanently of the article. So the label switching in itself constitutes an appropriation and so to have held would have been sufficient for the dismissal of both appeals. On the facts of the two cases it was unnecessary to decide whether, as argued by [counsel for the prosecution], the mere taking of the article from the shelf and putting it in a trolley or other receptacle amounted to the assumption of one of the rights of the owner, and hence an appropriation. There was much to be said in favour of the view that it did, in respect that doing so gave the shopper control of the article and the capacity to exclude any other shopper from taking it. However, Lord Roskill expressed the opinion that it did not, on the ground that the concept of appropriation in the context of s 3(1):

> involves not an act expressly or impliedly authorised by the owner but an act by way of adverse interference with or usurpation of those rights.

While it is correct to say that appropriation for purposes of s 3(1) includes the latter sort of act, it does not necessarily follow that no other act can amount to an appropriation and in particular that no act expressly or impliedly authorised by the owner can in any circumstances do so. Indeed, *R v Lawrence* [1972] AC 626 is a clear decision to the contrary since it laid down unequivocally that an act may be an appropriation notwithstanding that it is done with the consent of the owner. It does not appear to me that any sensible distinction can be made in this context between consent and authorisation.

In the civil case of *Dobson v General Accident and Life Assurance Corporation plc* [1990] 1 QB 274 a Court of Appeal consisting of Parker and Bingham LJJ considered the apparent conflict between *R v Lawrence* and *R v Morris* and applied the former decision.

His Lordship then quoted extensively from the judgment of Parker LJ and from the judgment of Bingham LJ in *Dobson* and continued:

> It was argued for the defendant in the present appeal that *Dobson v General Accident Fire and Life Assurance Corporation plc* [1990] 1 QB 274 was wrongly decided. I disagree, and on the contrary find myself in full agreement with those parts of the judgment of Parker LJ to which I have referred. As regards the attempted reconciliation by Bingham LJ of the reasoning in *R v Morris* . . . with the ruling in *R v Lawrence*, it appears to me that the suggested basis of reconciliation, which is essentially speculative, is unsound. The actual decision in *Morris* was correct, but it was erroneous, in addition to being unnecessary for the decision, to indicate that an act expressly or impliedly authorised by the owner could never amount to an appropriation. There is no material distinction between the facts in *Dobson* and those in the present case. In each case the owner of the goods was induced by fraud to part with them to the rogue. *Lawrence* makes it clear that consent to or authorisation by the owner of the taking by the rogue is irrelevant. The taking amounted to an appropriation within the meaning of s 1(1) of the Act of 1968. *Lawrence* also makes it clear that it is no less irrelevant that what happened may also have constituted the offence of obtaining property by deception under s 15(1) of the 1968 Act.
>
> . . . The decision in *Lawrence* was a clear decision of this House upon the construction of the word 'appropriates' in s 1(1) of the 1968 Act, which had stood for 12 years when doubt was thrown upon it by *obiter dicta* in *Morris*. *Lawrence* must be regarded as authoritative and correct, and there is no question of it now being right to depart from it . . .
>
> There were cited to your Lordships a number of cases involving the abstraction of moneys from a limited company by a person who was in a position to give the consent of the company to the abstraction. It is sufficient to say that I agree with what my noble and learned friend, Lord

Browne-Wilkinson, has to say about these cases in the speech to be delivered by him and that in my opinion a person who thus procures the company's consent dishonestly and with the intention of permanently depriving the company of the money is guilty of theft contrary to s 1(1) of the Act 1968.

My Lords, for the reasons which I have given I would answer branch (a) of the certified question in the affirmative and branch (b) in the negative, and allow the appeal.

Lord Browne-Wilkinson:

My Lords, I have read the speech of my noble and learned friend, Lord Keith of Kinkel, with which I agree . . .

The fact that Parliament used that composite phrase 'dishonest appropriation' in my judgment casts light on what is meant by the word 'appropriation'. The views expressed (*obiter*) by this House in *R v Morris* [1984] AC 320 that 'appropriation' involves an act by way of adverse interference with or usurpation of the rights of the owner treats the word appropriation as being tantamount to 'misappropriation'. The concept of adverse interference with or usurpation of rights introduces into the word appropriation the mental state of both the owner and the accused. So far as concerns the mental state of the owner (did he consent?), the 1968 Act expressly refers to such consent when it is a material factor: see ss 2(1)(b), 11(1), 12(1) and 13. So far as concerns the mental state of the accused, the composite phrase in s 1(1) itself indicates that the requirement is dishonesty.

For myself, therefore, I regard the word 'appropriation' in isolation as being an objective description of the act done irrespective of the mental state of either the owner or the accused. It is impossible to reconcile the decision in *Lawrence* (that the question of consent is irrelevant in considering whether there has been an appropriation) with the views expressed in *Morris*, which latter views in my judgment were incorrect.

It is suggested that this conclusion renders s 15 of the Act of 1968 otiose since a person who, by deception, persuades the owner to consent to part with his property will necessarily be guilty of theft within s 1. This may be so though I venture to doubt it. Take for example a man who obtains land by deception. Save as otherwise expressly provided the definitions in ss 4 and 5 of the 1968 Act apply only for the purposes of interpreting s 1 of that Act: see s 1(3). Section 34(1) applies ss 4(1) and 5(1) generally for the purposes of the 1968 Act. Accordingly the other subsections of s 4 and s 5 do not apply to s 15. Suppose that a fraudster has persuaded a victim to part with his house: the fraudster is not guilty of theft of the land since s 4(2) provides that you cannot steal land. The charge could only be laid under s 15 which contains no provisions excluding land from the definition of property. Therefore, although there is a substantial overlap between s 1 and s 15, s 15 is not otiose.

Lords Slynn and Jauncey concurred.

Lord Lowry (dissenting):

In my opinion, any attempt to reconcile the statement of principle in *Lawrence* and *Morris* is a complete waste of time . . . [I]t is clear that, whether they succeeded or not, both the Criminal Law Revision Committee and the draftsman must have intended to give the word one meaning, which would be the same in the Act as in the committee's report. To simplify the law, where possible, is a worthy objective but, my Lords, I maintain that the law, as envisaged in the report, is simple enough: there is no problem (and there would have been none in *Lawrence, Morris* and the present case) if one prosecutes under section 15 all offenders involving obtaining by deception and prosecutes theft in general under section 1. In that way some thefts will come under section 15, but no false pretences will come under section 1.

R v Hinks [2000] 4 All ER 835

The appellant, a 38-year-old woman, befriended a 53-year-old man, John Dolphin. He was a man of limited intelligence; his IQ was in the range between 70 to 80 (the average being 90 to 110). Expert evidence suggested that Mr Dolphin was a naïve and trusting person having no idea of the value of his assets or the ability to calculate their value. Despite this there was evidence that Mr Dolphin was capable of making a valid gift and understood the concept of ownership. In the period April to November 1996 Mr Dolphin withdrew sums totalling around £60,000 from his building society account, and that these sums were deposited in the appellant's account. During the summer of that year Mr Dolphin made withdrawals of the maximum permissible sum of £300 almost every day. Towards the end of this period Mr Dolphin had lost most of his savings and moneys inherited from his father. In 1997 the appellant was charged with six counts of theft, five counts covering moneys withdrawn and one count of a television set transferred by Mr Dolphin to the appellant. At her trial the appellant made a submission that in law there was no case to answer. The submission was based on the contention that the moneys were a gift from Mr Dolphin, and that the title in the moneys had passed to the appellant, and that there could therefore be no theft. The trial judge's direction to the jury on the issue of appropriation was as follows:

> The second ingredient is appropriates, dishonestly appropriates. You must be sure on any count that the property referred to in that count passed from Mr Dolphin to Miss Hinks so that she acquired it and treated it as her own to deal with. That can include, obviously, members of the jury, a straightforward taking or transfer of the property concerned. It can also include acquiring it by way of gift, either for herself or on behalf of her young son.

The appellant was convicted and appealed unsuccessfully to the Court of Appeal. The certified question before the House was as follows:

> Whether the acquisition of an indefeasible title to property is capable of amounting to an appropriation of property belonging to another for the purposes of section 1(1) of the Theft Act 1968. In other words, the question is whether a person can 'appropriate' property belonging to another where the other person makes him an indefeasible gift of property, retaining no proprietary interest or any right to resume or recover any proprietary interest in the property.

Lord Steyn:
My Lords ... [s]ince the enactment of the Theft Act 1968 the House of Lords has on three occasions considered the meaning of the word 'appropriates' in section 1(1) of the Act, namely in

R v Lawrence [1972] AC 626; in *R v Morris* [1984] AC 320; and in *R v Gomez* [1993] AC 442. The law as explained in *Lawrence* and *Gomez*, and applied by the Court of Appeal in the present case (*R v Hinks* [2000] 2 Cr App R 1) has attracted strong criticism from distinguished academic lawyers: see for example, JC Smith [1993] Crim LR 304 and [1998] Crim LR 904; Edward Griew, *The Theft Acts*, 7th edn, 1995, 41–59; ATH Smith, 'Gifts and the law of theft' [1999] CLJ 10. These views have however been challenged by equally distinguished academic writers: Glazebrook [1993] CLJ 191–94; Gardner, 'Property and theft' [1998] Crim LR. The academic criticism of *Gomez* provided in substantial measure the springboard for the present appeal . . . the question [raised by the current appeal] is whether a person can 'appropriate' property belonging to another where the other person makes him an indefeasible gift of property, retaining no proprietary interest or any right to resume or recover any proprietary interest in the property. Before the enactment of the Theft Act 1968 English law required a taking and carrying away of the property as the *actus reus* of the offence. In 1968 Parliament chose to broaden the reach of the law of theft by requiring merely an appropriation. The relevant sections of the Act of 1968 are as follows . . .

His Lordship set out ss 1, 2, and 3 of the 1968 Act and continued:

. . . My Lords, counsel for the appellant has not expressly asked the House to depart from the previous decisions of the House. He did, however, submit with the aid of the writings of Sir John Smith that the conviction of a donee for receiving a perfectly valid gift is a completely new departure. Relying on the academic criticism of the earlier decisions of the House counsel submitted that their reach should not be extended. Counsel cited as evidence of the true intention of the draftsman a passage from a note by Sir John Smith on the decision in *Hinks*: [1998] Crim LR 904. The passage reads as follows (904–05):

In a memorandum dated January 15, 1964 the distinguished draftsman of the Theft Act (Mr JS Fiennes, as he then was) wrote to members of the Larceny Sub-Committee of the Criminal Law Revision Committee: I trust the Sub-Committee will not agree with Dr [Glanville] Williams when he says . . . that a person appropriates for himself property of which another person is the owner every time he gratefully accepts a gift or buys an apple. If this is what the words mean, then the whole language of the clause ought to be changed, because one really cannot have a definition of stealing which relies on the word 'dishonestly' to prevent it covering every acquisition of property.

Sir John Smith returned to this point in 'The sad fate of the Theft Act 1968', an essay in *The Search for Principle, Essay in Honour of Lord Goff of Chieveley*, ed by W Swadling and G Jones, pp 97, 100–01. While this anecdote is an interesting bit of legal history, it is not relevant to the question before the House. Given counsel's use of it, as well as aspects of Sir John Smith's writing on the point in question, which have played such a large role in the present case, it is necessary to state quite firmly how the issue of interpretation should be approached. In *Black-Clawson International Ltd v Papierwerke Waldhoff-Anschaffenburg AG* [1975] AC 591, 613 Lord Reid observed:

We often say that we are looking for the intention of Parliament, but that is not quite accurate. We are seeking the meaning of the words which Parliament used. We are seeking not what Parliament meant but the true meaning of what they said.

This does not rule out or diminish relevant contextual material. But it is the critical point of departure of statutory interpretation. It also sets logical limits to what may be called in aid of statutory interpretation. Thus the published Eighth Report of the Criminal Law Revision Committee on *Theft and Related Offences* (Cmnd 2977, 1966), and in particular para 35, may arguably be relevant as part of the background against which Parliament enacted the Bill which became the Act of 1968. How far it in fact takes one is a matter considered in *Gomez* [1993] AC 442. Relevant publicly available contextual materials are readily admitted in aid of the construction of statutes. On the other hand, to delve into the intentions of individual members of the Committee, and their communications, would be to rely on material which cannot conceivably be relevant. If statutory interpretation is to be a rational and coherent process a line has to be drawn somewhere. And what Mr Fiennes wrote to the Larceny Sub-Committee was demonstrably on the wrong side of the line.

The starting point must be the words of the statute as interpreted by the House in its previous decisions. The first case in the trilogy is *R v Lawrence* . . . Lord Dilhorne expressly [stated] that belief that the passenger gave informed consent (ie knowing that he was paying in excess of the fare) 'is relevant to the issue of dishonesty, not to the question whether or not there has been an appropriation': . . . the appeal was dismissed. The *ratio decidendi* of *Lawrence*, namely that in a prosecution for theft it is unnecessary to prove that the taking was without the owner's consent, goes to the heart of the certified question in the present case.

The second decision of the House was *Morris* . . . The third decision of the House was in *Gomez* . . . the House was expressly invited to hold that 'there is no appropriation where the entire proprietary interest passes' . . . That submission was rejected. The leading judgment in *Gomez* was therefore in terms which unambiguously rule out the submission that section 3(1) does not apply to a case of a gift duly carried out because in such a case the entire proprietary interest will have passed.

. . . In other words it is immaterial whether the act was done with the owner's consent or authority. It is true of course that the certified question in *Gomez* referred to the situation where consent had been obtained by fraud. But the majority judgments do not differentiate between cases of consent induced by fraud and consent given in any other circumstances. The *ratio* involves a proposition of general application. *Gomez* therefore gives effect to section 3(1) of the Act by treating 'appropriation' as a neutral word comprehending 'any assumption by a person of the rights of an owner'. If the law is as held in *Gomez*, it destroys the argument advanced on the present appeal, namely that an indefeasible gift of property cannot amount to an appropriation.

Counsel for the appellant submitted in the first place that the law as expounded in *Gomez* and *Lawrence* must be qualified to say that there can be no appropriation unless the other party (the owner) retains some proprietary interest, or the right to resume or recover some proprietary interest, in the property. Alternatively, counsel argued that 'appropriates' should be interpreted as if the word 'unlawfully' preceded it. Counsel said that the effect of the decisions in *Lawrence* and *Gomez* is to reduce the *actus reus* of theft to 'vanishing point'.

. . . He argued that the result is to bring the criminal law 'into conflict' with the civil law. Moreover, he argued that the decisions in *Lawrence* and *Gomez* may produce absurd and grotesque results. He argued that the mental requirements of dishonesty and intention of permanently depriving the owner of property are insufficient to filter out some cases of conduct which should not sensibly be regarded as theft. He did not suggest that the appellant's dishonest and repellent conduct came within such a category. Instead he deployed four examples for this purpose, namely the following:

(1) S makes a handsome gift to D because he believes that D has obtained a First. D has not and knows that S is acting under that misapprehension. He makes the gift. There is here a motivational mistake which, it is submitted, does not avoid the transaction. (Glanville Williams, *Textbook*, 1st edn, at p 788.)

(2) P sees D's painting and, thinking he is getting a bargain, offers D £100,000 for it. D realises that P thinks the painting is a Constable, but knows that it was painted by his sister and is worth no more than £100. He accepts P's offer. D has made an enforceable contract and is entitled to recover and retain the purchase price. (Smith and Hogan, *Criminal Law*, 9th edn, pp 507–08.)

(3) A buys a roadside garage business from B, abutting on a public thoroughfare; unknown to A but known to B, it has already been decided to construct a bypass road which will divert substantially the whole of the traffic from passing A's garage. There is an enforceable contract and A is entitled to recover and retain the purchase price. The same would be true if B knew that A was unaware of the intended plan to construct a bypass road. (Compare Lord Atkin in *Bell v Lever Brothers* [1932] AC 161, 224.)

(4) An employee agrees to retire before the end of his contract of employment, receiving a sum of money by way of compensation from his employer. Unknown to the employer, the employee has committed serious breaches of contract which would have enabled the employer to dismiss him without compensation. Assuming that the employee's failure to reveal his defaults does not affect the validity of the contract, so that the employee is entitled to sue for the promised compensation, is the employee liable to be arrested for the theft the moment he receives the money? (Glanville Williams: 'Theft and voidable title' [1981] Crim LR 666, 672.)

My Lords, at first glance these are rather telling examples. They may conceivably have justified a more restricted meaning of section 3(1) than prevailed in *Lawrence* . . . and *Gomez* . . . The House ruled otherwise and I am quite unpersuaded that the House overlooked the consequences of its decision. On the facts set out in the examples a jury could possibly find that the acceptance of the transfer took place in the belief that the transferee had the right in law to deprive the other of it within the meaning of section 2(1)(a) of the Act. Moreover, in such cases a prosecution is hardly likely and if mounted, is likely to founder on the basis that the jury will not be persuaded that there was dishonesty in the required sense. And one must retain a sense of perspective. At the extremity of the application of legal rules there are sometimes results which may seem strange. A matter of judgment is then involved. The rule may have to be recast. Sir John Smith has eloquently argued that the rule in question ought to be recast. I am unpersuaded. If the law is restated by adopting a narrower definition of appropriation, the outcome is likely to place beyond the reach of the criminal law dishonest persons who should be found guilty of theft. The suggested revisions would unwarrantably restrict the scope of the law of theft and complicate the fair and effective prosecution of theft. In my view the law as settled in *Lawrence* and *Gomez* does not demand the suggested revision. Those decisions can be applied by judges and juries in a way which, absent human error, does not result in injustice.

Counsel for the appellant further pointed out that the law as stated in *Lawrence* and *Gomez* creates a tension between the civil and the criminal law. In other words, conduct which is not wrongful in a civil law sense may constitute the crime of theft. Undoubtedly, this is so. The question whether the civil claim to title by a convicted thief, who committed no civil wrong, may be defeated by the principle that nobody may benefit from his own civil or criminal wrong does not arise for decision. Nevertheless there is a more general point, namely that the interaction between criminal law and civil law can cause problems . . . The purposes of the civil law and the criminal law are somewhat different. In theory the two systems should be in perfect harmony. In a practical world there will sometimes be some disharmony between the two systems. In any event, it would be wrong to assume on *a priori* grounds that the criminal law rather than the civil law is defective. Given the jury's conclusions, one is entitled to observe that the appellant's conduct should constitute theft, the only available charge. The tension between the civil and the criminal law is therefore not in my view a factor which justifies a departure from the law as stated in *Lawrence* and *Gomez*. Moreover, these decisions of the House have a marked beneficial consequence. While in some contexts of the law of theft a judge cannot avoid explaining civil law concepts to a jury (eg in respect of section 2(1)(a)), the decisions of the House of Lords eliminate the need for such explanations in respect of appropriation. That is a great advantage in an overly complex corner of the law.

My Lords, if it had been demonstrated that in practice *Lawrence* and *Gomez* were calculated to produce injustice that would have been a compelling reason to revisit the merits of the holdings in those decisions. That is however, not the case. In practice the mental requirements of theft are an adequate protection against injustice. In these circumstances I would not be willing to depart from the clear decisions of the House in *Lawrence* and *Gomez*. This brings me back to counsel's principal submission, namely that a person does not appropriate property unless the other (the owner) retains, beyond the instant of the alleged theft, some proprietary interest or the right to resume or recover some proprietary interest. This submission is directly contrary to the holdings in *Lawrence* and *Gomez*. It must be rejected. The alternative submission is that the word 'appropriates' should be interpreted as if the word 'unlawfully' preceded it so that only an act which is unlawful under the general law can be an appropriation. This submission is an invitation to interpolate a word in the carefully crafted language of the Act of 1968. It runs counter to the decisions in *Lawrence* and *Gomez* and must also be rejected. It follows that the certified question must be answered in the affirmative.

In his judgment my noble and learned friend Lord Hutton concluded that the trial judge's summing-up on dishonesty was materially defective in particular respects which he lists and that the appeal should be allowed on this ground. In reluctant disagreement with Lord Hutton I take a different view. The House is clearly not confined to the certified question. I agree that in the interests of justice one must look at the matter in the round. It is, however, relevant to bear in mind the context in which the points arise. First, the trial judge was not invited to give such special directions. Secondly, these points were not contained in the written grounds of appeal before the Court of Appeal. Thirdly, the points of criticism were not contained in the Statement of Facts and Issues or in the printed cases. Fourthly, the House has not seen transcripts of evidence. The relevance of this factor is that the House is inadequately informed as to the way in which the defence case was deployed before the judge and jury. And a summing-up must always be tailored to the particular circumstances of each case.

My Lords, for my part the position would have been different if I had any lurking doubt about the guilt of the appellant on the charges for which she was convicted. In the light of a fair and balanced summing-up and a very strong prosecution case, the jury accepted the prosecution case and rejected the appellant's account as untruthful. They found that she had acted dishonestly by systematically raiding the savings in a building society account of a vulnerable person who trusted her. Even if one assumes that the judge ought to have directed more fully on dishonesty I am satisfied that the convictions are entirely safe. In these circumstances it is not necessary and indeed undesirable for the House to pronounce upon what directions should be given on dishonesty in cases akin to the present. My Lords I would dismiss the appeal to the House.

Lord Slynn and Lord Jauncey also agreed, for the reasons given by Lord Steyn that the appeal should be dismissed.

Lord Hutton (dissenting):

[Having considered the provisions of sections 1, 2 and 3 of the Theft Act 1968] . . . I therefore turn to consider dishonesty where the defendant contends, as in this case, that she received the money or property as a gift. My Lords, it appears contrary to common sense that a person who receives money or property as a gift could be said to act dishonestly, no matter how much ordinary and decent people would think it morally reprehensible for that person to accept the gift. Section 2(1)(b) of the Act recognises this common sense view by providing:

(1) A person's appropriation of property belonging to another is not to be regarded as dishonest . . . (b) if he appropriates the property in the belief that he would have the other's consent if the other knew of the appropriation and the circumstances of it;

It follows, *a fortiori*, that a person's appropriation of property belonging to another should not be regarded as dishonest if the other person actually gives the property to him. Thus in *R v Lawrence* [1972] AC 626, 632C Viscount Dilhorne said:

Section 2(1) provides, *inter alia*, that a person's appropriation of property belonging to another is not to be regarded as dishonest if he appropriates the property in the belief that he would have the other's consent if the other knew of the appropriation and the circumstances of it. *A fortiori*, a person is not to be regarded as acting dishonestly if he appropriates another's property believing that with full knowledge of the circumstances that other person has in fact agreed to the appropriation. The appellant, if he believed that Mr Occhi, knowing that £7 was far in excess of the legal fare, had nevertheless agreed to pay him that sum, could not be said to have acted dishonestly in taking it. When Megaw LJ said that if there was true consent, the essential element of dishonesty was not established, I understand him to have meant this. Belief or the absence of belief that the owner had with such knowledge consented to the appropriation is relevant to the issue of dishonesty, not to the question whether or not there has been an appropriation.

Therefore I consider that in *R v Mazo* [1997] 2 Cr App R 518 after referring to a sentence in the above passage of the speech of Viscount Dilhorne, Pill LJ was right to say at p 521C: 'It is implicit in that statement that if in all the circumstances there is held to be a valid gift there can be no theft'. The reason why there is no theft is because there is no dishonesty.

But the simple proposition that a person who receives property as a gift is not to be regarded as dishonest becomes more difficult to apply where the prosecution alleges that the gift was void or voidable by reason of circumstances known to the defendant. This situation was discussed by Megaw LJ in *Lawrence* [1971] 1 QB 373, 377C:

Of course, where there is true consent by the owner of property to the appropriation of it by another, a charge of theft under section 1(1) must fail. This is not, however, because the words 'without consent' have to be implied in the new definition of theft. It is simply because, if there is such true consent, the essential element of dishonesty is not established. If, however, the apparent consent is brought about by dishonesty, there is nothing in the words of section 1(1), or by reason of any implication that can properly be read into those words, to make such apparent consent relevant as providing a defence. The prosecution have to prove the four elements already mentioned, and no more. No inference to the contrary is to be drawn from the words of section 2(1)(b), already quoted. That reference does no more than show that the essential element of dishonesty does not exist if the defendant when he appropriates the property believes that the owner would consent if he knew the circumstances. 'The circumstances' are, of course, all the relevant circumstances. 'The belief' is an honest belief. That paragraph does not give rise to the inference that an appropriation of property is not theft when there is a 'consent' – if it can be rightly so described – which is founded upon the dishonesty of the defendant.

There was no difficulty in applying that concept in the case of *Lawrence* itself because, as Viscount Dilhorne observed at p 632C and E, it was not contended that the defendant had not acted dishonestly, and there was ample evidence of dishonesty. . . . I think that in a case where the prosecution contends that the gift was invalid because of the mental incapacity of the donor it is necessary for the jury to consider that matter. I further consider that the judge must make it clear to the jury that they cannot convict unless they are satisfied (1) that the donor did not have the mental capacity to make a gift and (2) that the donee knew of this incapacity.

. . . My Lords, in the present state of the law relating to theft when the defendant claims that he or she received the money or property as a gift, a Crown Court judge faces a difficult task in summing-up to a jury. In this case the judge gave a fair and careful summary of the evidence. In the passage which I have set out he rightly told the jury that the mere fact that they disapproved of what the defendant did, or thought that it was morally reprehensible, did not necessarily mean that it was dishonest. It is also clear that the third and fourth paragraphs in the passage of the summing-up which I have set out above were based on the guidance given by the Court of Appeal in *R v Ghosh* [1982] 1 QB 1053.

But in my opinion in a case where the defendant contends that he or she received a gift, a direction based only on *Ghosh* is inadequate because it fails to make clear to the jury that if there was a valid gift there cannot be dishonesty, and in the present case there is the danger that, if the gift was not void for want of mental capacity, the jury might nevertheless convict on the basis that ordinary and decent people would think it dishonest for a younger woman to accept very large sums of money which constituted his entire savings from a naïve man of low intelligence, and that the woman would have realised this.

. . . Therefore I consider that in this case: (1) It was necessary for the judge to make clear to the jury that if there was a valid gift the defendant could not be found to be dishonest no matter how much they thought her conduct morally reprehensible. (2) If the Crown were making the case that the gifts were invalid because Mr Dolphin was mentally incapable of making a gift, it was necessary for the judge to give the jury a specific direction as to what degree of mental weakness would, in the light of the value of the gifts and the other circumstances of the case, make the donor incapable of making a valid gift. (3) The jury should have been directed that if they were satisfied that Mr Dolphin was mentally incapable of making a gift, they should not convict unless they were satisfied that what the defendant did was dishonest by the standards of ordinary decent people and that the defendant must have realised this. (4) If the Crown were making the case that the gift was invalid because of undue influence or coercion exercised by the defendant, it was necessary for the judge to give the jury a specific direction as to what would constitute undue influence or coercion. (5) The jury should have been directed that if they were satisfied that the gifts were invalid by reason of undue influence or coercion, they should not convict unless they were satisfied that what the defendant did was dishonest by the standards of ordinary decent people and that the defendant must have realised this.

The conduct of the defendant was deplorable and it may be that if the issues had been more clearly defined a jury would have been entitled to convict, but in my opinion the summing-up was defective in the ways which I have described and the convictions should not stand. I consider, with respect, that the Court of Appeal erred in the present case because . . . it rejected the appellant's submission as to dishonesty by referring to the separate issue of appropriation.

Accordingly, for the reasons which I have stated, I would allow the appeal and quash the convictions.

Lord Hobhouse (dissenting):

My Lords . . . Another point which has arisen from the general intention of the Act and its drafting is the assumption that all questions arising in connection with the law of theft should now be capable of answer without involving any concept or rule derived from the civil law or using any technical legal terminology. Whilst there can be no doubt about the general intention of the Act, to proceed from such a general intention to that assumption is simplistic and erroneous. It is, of course, part of the duty and function of the judge at the criminal trial to separate the questions of law from the questions of fact and only direct the jury on matters of law so far as the issues in the case make it necessary for them to know the law in order to decide the issues of fact and determine the defendant's guilt or innocence; but, when there are relevant questions of law, they must be recognised and the jury directed accordingly.

The truth is that theft is a crime which relates to civil property and, inevitably, property concepts from the civil law have to be used and questions answered by reference to that law . . . Section 1(1) uses the expression 'belonging to another'. Thus, in some criminal cases, it may be necessary to determine whether the relevant property belonged to the alleged victim or to the defendant.

. . . The discussion in the present case has been marked by a failure to consider the law of gift. Perhaps most remarkable is the statement of the Court of Appeal that 'a gift may be clear evidence of appropriation'. The making of a gift is the act of the donor. It involves the donor in forming the intention to give and then acting on that intention by doing whatever it is necessary for him to do to transfer the relevant property to the donee. Where the gift is the gift of a chattel, the act required to complete the gift will normally be either delivery to the donee or to a person who is to hold the chattel as the bailee of the donee; money can be transferred by having it credited to the donee's bank account – and so on. Unless the gift was conditional, in which case the condition must be satisfied before the gift can take effect, the making of the gift is complete once the donor has carried out this step. The gift has become the property of the donee. It is not necessary for the donee to know of the gift. The donee, on becoming aware of the gift, has the right to refuse (or reject) the gift in which case it revests in the donor with resolutive effect . . .

What consequences does this have for the law of theft? Once the donor has done his part in transferring the property to the defendant, the property, subject to the special situations identified in the subsections of s 5, ceases to be 'property belonging to another'. However wide a meaning one were to give to 'appropriates', there cannot be a theft. For it to be possible for there to be a theft there will have to be something more, like an absence of a capacity to give or a mistake satisfying s 5(4). Similarly, where the donee himself performs the act necessary to transfer the property to himself, as he would if he himself took the chattel out of the possession of the donor or, himself, gave the instructions to the donor's bank, s 5(1) would apply and mean that that constituent of the crime of theft would at that time have been satisfied.

If one treats the 'acceptance' of the gift as an appropriation, and this was the approach of the judge and is implicit in the judgment of the Court of Appeal (despite their choice of words), there are immediate difficulties with s 2(1)(a). The defendant did have the right to deprive the donor of the property. The donor did consent to the appropriation; indeed, he intended it. There are also difficulties with s 6 as she was not acting regardless of the donor's rights; the donor has already surrendered his rights. The only way that these conclusions can be displaced is by showing that the gift was not valid. There are even difficulties with s 3 itself. The donee is not 'assuming the rights of an owner': she has them already.

. . . The considerations which I have discussed now at some length all lead to the conclusion that sections 1 to 6 of the Theft Act should be read as a cohesive whole and that to attempt to isolate and compartmentalise each element only leads to contradictions. This vice is particularly clear where alleged gifts are involved. In such a situation greater care in the analysis is required under sections 2, 3 and 5 and it will normally be necessary to direct the jury in fuller terms and not merely ask them if they think that the defendant fell below the standards of an ordinary and decent person and realised that such persons would so regard his conduct.

. . . My Lords, the relevant law is contained in sections 1 to 6 of the Act. They should be construed as a whole and applied in a manner which presents a consistent scheme both internally and with the remainder of the Act. The phrase 'dishonestly appropriates' should be construed as a composite phrase. It does not include acts done in relation to the relevant property which are done in accordance with the actual wishes or actual authority of the person to whom the property belongs. This is because such acts do not involve any assumption of the rights of that person within s 3(1) or because, by necessary implication from s 2(1), they are not to be regarded as dishonest appropriations of property belonging to another.

Actual authority, wishes, consent (or similar words) mean, both as a matter of language and on the authority of the three House of Lords cases, authorisation not obtained by fraud or mis-representation. The definition of theft therefore embraces cases where the property has come to the defendant by the mistake of the person to whom it belongs and there would be an obligation to restore it – s 5(4) – or property in which the other still has an equitable proprietary interest – s 5(1). This would also embrace property obtained by undue influence or other cases coming within the classes of invalid transfer recognised in *Re Beaney*.

In cases of alleged gift, the criteria to be applied are the same. But additional care may need to be taken to see that the transaction is properly explained to the jury. It is unlikely that a charge of theft will be brought where there is not clear evidence of at least some conduct of the defendant which includes an element of fraud or overt dishonesty or some undue influence or knowledge of the deficient capacity of the alleged donor. This was the basis upon which the prosecution of the appellant was originally brought in the present case. On this basis there is no difficulty in explain-ing to the jury the relevant parts of s 5 and s 2(1) and the effect of the phrase 'assumption of the rights of an owner'. Where the basis is less specific and the possibility is that there may have been a valid gift of the relevant article or money to the defendant, the analysis of the prosecution case will break down under sections 2 and 5 as well as s 3 and it will not suffice simply to invite the jury to convict on the basis of their disapprobation of the defendant's conduct and their attribution to him of the knowledge that he must have known that they and other ordinary and decent persons would think it dishonest. Theft is a crime of dishonesty but dishonesty is not the only element in the commission of the crime. I would answer the certified question in the negative. But, in any event, I would allow the appeal and quash the conviction because the summing-up failed to direct the jury adequately upon the other essential elements of theft, not just appropriation.

R v Briggs [2004] 1 Cr App R 34

The appellant had a great aunt and uncle (the 'Reids') who wished to sell their home (Ascot Drive) and purchase a house ('Welwynd Lodge') closer to the appellant's. The sale of Ascot Drive was handled by a firm called Bentons, for whom the appellant had worked in the past. A firm called Metcalfs handled the sale of Welwynd Lodge for the vendors. In October 1997, the appellant wrote to Bentons enclosing a letter of authority, written by the appellant but signed by the Reids, instructing Bentons to send the proceeds of the sale of Ascot Drive (£49,950) to Metcalfs by telegraphic transfer. In November 1997, after the sale of 4 Ascot Drive was completed, these instructions were carried out, and title in Ascot Drive was transferred to and registered in the name of the appellant and her father, Mr West. The prosecution alleged that this transfer of title had been against the wishes of the Reids, and the appellant was convicted of theft of the £49,950. On appeal the main issue was whether or not there had been an appropriation of that money by the appellant.

Judge LJ:

The central issue [is] . . . whether there was an 'appropriation', which is a necessary ingredient for the offence of theft. Mr Barry for the prosecution contends as he did at the trial that the credit balance was appropriated by the appellant when she caused Bentons to transfer the sale proceeds to Metcalfs for her own purposes. Those purposes were to pay the purchase price of Welwynd Lodge, which, against the wishes of the Reids was then transferred into the name of the appellant and her father. Miss Felix on behalf of the appellant submits that such a payment cannot amount to an 'appropriation', as it was made in accordance with and as a result of the Reids' instructions.

. . . The trial judge dealt with the issue of appropriation in his summing-up on count 1 by saying:

I direct you that there may be an appropriation of the credit balance in count 1 notwithstanding that it was transferred with the Reids' consent, if that consent was induced by fraud. The prosecution say that this is such a case in that the entire transaction was fraudulent – in other words, the prosecution say that the [appellant], throughout, intended to use the proceeds from the Reids' Felixstowe property to purchase Welwynd Lodge and put the latter in her name and her father's without Mrs Reid's knowledge or consent and knowing Mrs Reid would not consent if she had known. It is for you to decide whether the Reids' consent was induced by fraud. If you are sure it was, then there can be an appropriation notwithstanding the Reids' consent to the transfer.

Miss Felix submits that this direction, which accords with the trial judge's reason for rejecting an earlier application there was no case to answer, was wrong because a party does not appropriate an item if by fraud he or she induces the owner to part with that item. In support of this, she relies on the statement of Hutchison LJ giving the judgment of this court in *Naviede* [1997] Crim L R 662, where he explained that:

> We are not satisfied that a misrepresentation which persuades the account holder to direct payment out of his account is an assumption of the rights of the account holder as owner, such as to amount to an appropriation of his rights within section 3(1) of the 1968 Act.

A similar approach has been suggested by the late Professor Sir John Smith in his cogent and persuasive commentary on *Naviede* [1997] Crim L R 665 where he explained that:

> In Archbold News (Issue 9, November 14, 1996) I considered the question and, referring to my commentary in *Caresana* [1996] Crim L R 667, doubted whether it could be theft 'because the diminution in V's thing in action is effected by V or by V's agents and it is not easy to discern the necessary act of appropriation. The opinion of the court [in *Naviede* quoted in paragraph 8 above] seems to be exactly the same . . .
>
> I distinguished the case where D induces V to make a telegraphic transfer from that where D dishonestly presents a cheque drawn on V's account causing it to be debited. This, it is submitted, does amount to an appropriation of the thing in action belonging to V . . . In the telegraphic case it is true that D procures the whole course of events resulting in V's account being debited; but the telegraphic transfer is initiated by V and his voluntary intervening acts break the chain of causation. It is the same as if V is induced by deception to take money out of his safe to pay to D. D does not at that moment 'appropriate' it – V is not acting as his agent. D commits theft only if and when the money is put into his hands.

In response, Mr Barry contends that there was an appropriation in this case as is illustrated by the decision of this court in *Hilton* [1997] 2 Cr App R 445, which was a case in which a defendant on a theft charge, who was one of the designated signatories to a bank account had caused monies to be transferred out of that account to other accounts. This Court held that the instructions of the defendant had caused the bank to make the transfers and therefore the defendant had appropriated the charity's credit balance by assuming the charity's right to the balance.

In that case, we consider that there was a clear act of appropriation because, in the words of the late Professor Sir John Smith in the case note on *Naviede* to which we have already referred:

> There, [the defendant] had direct control of a bank account belonging to a charity. He caused payments to be made from that account to settle his personal debts. That was a completely straightforward case of theft of a chose in action belonging to another.

We also agree with his further comment that that is a totally different case from the situation in cases such as *Naviede*, which 'were all concerned with [the defendant] by deception induces [the victim] to initiate a transaction whereby [the victim's] bank account is debited and that of the [defendant] is credited' ([1997] Crim L R at 666). In other words, we consider that where a victim causes a payment to be made in reliance on deceptive conduct by the defendant, there is no 'appropriation' by the defendant.

We are fortified in coming to that view by [a number of] . . . factors . . . no case has been cited to us where it has been held that an 'appropriation' occurs where the relevant act is committed by the victim albeit as a result of deception . . . we have already referred to the explanation of the word 'appropriation' in section 3(1) of the Theft Act 1968 and it is a word which connotes a physical act rather than a more remote action triggering the payment which gives rise to the charge. The Oxford English Dictionary defines 'appropriation' as 'to take possession for one's own, to take to oneself'. It is not easy to see why an act of deceiving an owner to do something would fall within the meaning of 'appropriation'.

Indeed, we consider that in this case the appropriate charge might have been for an offence of deception. Our conclusion is that the conviction on count I must be quashed as there was no appropriation by the appellant of £49,950.

9.3.1 HOW MANY TIMES CAN D APPROPRIATE THE SAME PROPERTY?

Where a 'thief' does several acts in respect of a particular item, are the acts of appropriation a continuing process that is complete only when the final act has been done, or can an item be appropriated on more than one occasion? On what basis should the prosecution point to the exact moment when the goods are stolen? In most cases this will not matter (since the jury or magistrates will only have to consider whether the goods were stolen by the defendant on a particular date: the exact time of the appropriation does not matter). However, uncertainty over when the theft is complete creates a particular problem with the regard to the offence of handling stolen goods, since this offence cannot be committed until the goods have been 'stolen'. In *R v Atakpu* [1994] QB 69 the Court of Appeal gave some guidance on when the appropriation takes place.

R v Atakpu and Abrahams [1994] QB 69 (CA)

The appellants operated a scheme whereby they hired expensive motor cars abroad, drove them into the United Kingdom, made changes to the vehicles, and sold them on to unsuspecting purchasers. The issues for the Court of Appeal were: (1) whether the theft committed abroad continued within the jurisdiction so that it could be established by the retention of the car after the hire period had expired, or by altering the cars, or by some other fresh appropriation; (2) whether cars stolen abroad could be stolen again, and again and again, within the jurisdiction each time an appropriation of them is made.

Ward J:

. . . [I]t would seem that: (1) theft can occur in an instant by a single appropriation but it can also involve a course of dealing with property lasting longer and involving several appropriations before the transaction is complete; (2) theft is a finite act – it has a beginning and it has an end; (3) at what point the transaction is complete is a matter for the jury to decide upon the facts of each case; (4) though there may be several appropriations in the course of a single theft or several appropriations of different goods each constituting a separate theft . . . no case suggests that there can be successive thefts of the same property (assuming of course that possession is constant and not lost or abandoned, later to be assumed again).

Can these conclusions stand in the light of *R v Gomez* [1993] AC 442? Whilst we see the logic of the argument that if there are several appropriations each one can constitute a separate theft, we flinch from reaching that conclusion.

His Lordship then approved the following passage by Professor Glanville Williams in [1978] Crim LR 69:

A man steals a watch, and two weeks later sells it. In common sense and ordinary language he is not guilty of a second theft when he sells it. Otherwise it would be possible, in theory, to convict a thief of theft of a silver teapot every time he uses it to make tea.

His Lordship then quoted s 3(1) of the Theft Act 1968, above and continued:

If, therefore, he has come by the property by stealing it then his later dealing with the property is by implication not included among the assumptions of the rights of an owner which amount to an appropriation within the meaning of s 3(1). We reject the speculation that he would not have come by the property by stealing it if an indictment for the theft would not lie because the theft occurred abroad. There is no reason to restrict the plain ordinary words of s 3(1) in such a narrow legalistic way. We note that one is guilty of handling stolen property under s 24 and the provisions of the Act apply whether the stealing occurred in England or Wales or elsewhere. 'Stealing' must have the same meaning in s 3(1) as it has in s 24. In our judgment, if goods have once been stolen, even if stolen abroad, they cannot be stolen again by the same thief exercising the same or other rights of ownership over the property.

We find it more difficult to answer the first question we posed as to whether or not theft is a continuous offence. On a strict reading of *R v Gomez* [1993] AC 442 any dishonest assumption of the rights of the owner made with the necessary intention constitutes theft, and that leaves little room for a continuous course of action.

We would not wish that to be the law. Such restriction and rigidity may lead to technical anomalies and injustice. We would prefer to leave it for the common sense of the jury to decide that the appropriation can continue for so long as the thief can sensibly be regarded as in the act of stealing or, in more understandable words, so long as he is 'on the job' ... Since the matter is not strictly necessary for our decision we ... will leave it open for further argument. It is not necessary for us to decide because no jury properly directed could reasonably arrive at a conclusion that the theft of these motor cars was still continuing days after the appellants had first taken them. If the jury had been asked when and where these motor cars were stolen they could only have answered that they were stolen in Frankfurt or Brussels. The theft was complete abroad and the thieves could not steal again in England. For these reasons the appeal must be allowed ...

COMMENTS AND QUESTIONS

1   If the appellant, in *R v Hinks*, acquired property under a valid *inter vivos* transfer, how could she have been appropriating property that still belonged to another? What was this appropriation? When did it occur?

9.4 PROPERTY BELONGING TO ANOTHER

The expression 'belonging to another' is given an extended definition by s 5(1) of the 1968 Act, and the deeming provisions of s 5(3) and s 5(4). The term 'belonging' is not to be regarded as synonymous with 'owned'. Hence property can belong to another because they have it in their possession or control – even where, as a matter of civil law, legal ownership is vested in the defendant; see *R v Turner (No 2)*, below.

Section 5(1) provides:

> Property shall be regarded as belonging to any person having possession or control of it, or having in it any proprietary right or interest (not being an equitable interest arising only from an agreement to transfer or grant an interest).

9.4.1 POSSESSION AND CONTROL

R v Turner (No 2) [1971] 1 WLR 901 (CA)

Lord Parker CJ:

. . . The defendant was at the material time living in Seymour Road, East Ham, with a Miss Nelson and their children. Three miles away a man called Arthur Edwin Brown ran a garage in Carlyle Road, Manor Park. There is no doubt that at some time prior to 7 March 1969, the defendant took a Sceptre car of which he was the registered owner to Mr Brown's garage for repairs. It was Mr Brown's case that he did those repairs, that as he was short of space he left the car in Carlyle Road some 10 to 20 yards from the garage. The ignition key had been handed to him by the defendant, and this he retained on the keyboard in his office. According to Mr Brown, on 7 March 1969, the defendant called at the garage and asked if the car was ready. On being told that it was except that it might require to be tuned, the defendant said that he would return on the next day, Saturday 8 March, and would pay Mr Brown for the repairs and pick up the car. A few hours later, however, Mr Brown found that the Sceptre car had gone; moreover whoever had taken it had a key, because the key that Mr Brown had was still on the keyboard. He reported the matter to the police.

Apparently night after night thereafter until 16 March Mr Brown, according to him, went round the neighbouring streets to see if he could find the car, and sure enough on Sunday 16 March, he found it parked in a street near the defendant's flat. It was, moreover, his evidence that he did not know the defendant's full name or his address and only knew of him as Frank.

What Mr Brown then did was to take the car back to his garage, to take out the engine and then tow it back less the engine to the place from which he had taken it. Meanwhile, the police made enquiries of the defendant and there is no doubt in the light of what happened afterwards that he, the defendant, told lie after lie to the police. He said that Mr Brown had never had his Sceptre car at all, that the car had never been to the garage, and that the only work that Mr Brown had done was to a Zephyr car on an earlier occasion. However, a time came when he abandoned those denials and agreed that he had taken the car to the garage, and that he had taken it away and had never paid for it. In saying that, however, he emphasised that he had taken it away with the consent of Mr Brown. It was on those short facts that the jury . . . found the defendant guilty of the theft of his own car . . .

His Lordship quoted s 5(1) of the Theft Act 1968 and went on:

The sole question was whether Mr Brown had possession or control. This court is quite satisfied that there is no ground whatever for qualifying the words 'possession or control' in any way. It is sufficient if it is found that the person from whom the property is taken, or to use the words of the Act, appropriated, was at the time in fact in possession or control . . . The only question was whether Mr Brown was in fact in possession or control . . .

His Lordship then turned to the question of dishonesty and said:

The whole test of dishonesty is the mental element of belief. No doubt, although the defendant may for certain purposes be presumed to know the law, he would not at the time have the vaguest idea whether he did have in law a right to take the car back again, and accordingly when one looks at his mental state, one looks at it in the light of what he believed. The jury were properly told that if he believed that he had a right, albeit there was none, he would nevertheless fall to be acquitted . . .

R v Woodman [1974] 2 All ER 955

Lord Widgery CJ:
. . . The facts of the case were these. On 20 March 1973 the appellant and his son, and another man called Davey who was acquitted, took a van to some premises at Wick near Bristol and loaded onto the van one ton six cwt of scrap metal, which they proceeded to drive away.

The premises from which they took this scrap metal were a disused factory belonging to English China Clays, and the indictment alleged that the scrap metal in question was the property of English China Clays. Whether that was entirely true or not depends on the view one takes of the events immediately preceding this taking of scrap metal, because what had happened, according to the prosecution evidence, was that the business run by English China Clays at this point had been run-down. In August 1970 the business had ceased. There was at that time a great deal of miscellaneous scrap metal on the site, and English China Clays, wishing to dispose of this, sold the scrap metal to the Bird Group of companies, who thereupon had the right and title to enter on the site and remove the scrap metal which they had bought. They or their sub-contractor went onto the site. They took out the bulk of the scrap metal left there by English China Clays, but a certain quantity of scrap was too inaccessible to be removed to be attractive to the Bird Group of companies so that it was left on the site and so it seems to have remained for perhaps a couple of years until the appellant and his son came to take it away, as I have already recounted.

Also in the history of the matter, and important in it, is the fact that when the site had been cleared by the Bird Group of companies a barbed wire fence was erected around it obviously to exclude trespassers. The site was still in the ownership of the English China Clays and their occupation, and the barbed wire fence was no doubt erected by them. Within the barbed wire fence were these remnants of scrap which the Bird Group had not taken away.

English China Clays took further steps to protect their property because a number of notices giving such information as 'Private Property. Keep Out' and 'Trespassers will be prosecuted' were exhibited around the perimeter of the site. A Mr Brooksbank, who was an employee of English China Clays, gave evidence that he had visited the site about half a dozen times over a period of two or three years, and indeed he had visited it once as recently as between January and March 1973. He did not notice that any scrap metal had been left behind, and it is perfectly clear that there is no reason to suppose that English China Clays or their representatives appreciated that there was any scrap remaining on the site after the Bird Group had done their work . . .

His Lordship referred to the provisions of s 5(1) of the 1968 Act and continued:

. . . The recorder took the view that the contract of sale between English China Clays and the Bird Group had divested English China Clays of any proprietary right to any scrap on the site. It is unnecessary to express a firm view on that point, but the court are not disposed to disagree with the conclusion that the proprietary interest in the scrap had passed.

The recorder also took the view on the relevant facts that it was not possible to say that English China Clays were in possession of the residue of the scrap. It is not quite clear why he took that view. It may have been because he took the view that difficulties arose by reason of the fact that English China Clays had no knowledge of the existence of this particular scrap at any particular time. But the recorder did take the view that so far as control was concerned there was a case to go to the jury on whether or not this scrap was in the control of English China Clays, because if it was, then it was to be regarded as their property for the purposes of a larceny charge even if they were not entitled to any proprietary interest . . .

We have formed the view without difficulty that the recorder was perfectly entitled to do what he did, that there was ample evidence that English China Clays were in control of the site and had taken considerable steps to exclude trespassers as demonstrating the fact that they were in control of the site, and we think that in ordinary and straightforward cases if it is once established that a particular person is in control of a site such as this, then *prima facie* he is in control of articles which are on the site . . .

So far as this case is concerned, arising as it does under the Theft Act 1968, we are content to say that there was evidence of English China Clays being in control of the site and *prima facie* in control of articles on the site as well. The fact that it could not be shown that they were conscious of the existence of this or any particular scrap iron does not destroy the general principle that control of a site by excluding others from it is *prima facie* control of articles on the site as well . . .

9.4.2 THEFT FROM A THIEF

R v Kelly [1999] 2 WLR 384

For the facts see above. The following extracts relate to the issue of whether 'possession and control' for the purposes of s 5 has to be lawful.

Rose LJ:

The further submission was made that the specimens were not in the lawful possession of the college at the time they were taken, and therefore could not have been stolen. It was, however, accepted that the college was physically in possession of the specimens, but the submission was made at that time that that possession was governed by the provisions of the Anatomy Act 1832 and, in consequence, the college's possession was unlawful because the specimens had been retained beyond the period of 2 years, referred to in that Act by way of amendment, before burial. The learned judge rejected that submission on the basis that possession and control in the accepted terms of those words for the purposes of the Theft Act, was not in issue. He found that there was certainly no evidence before the court to support the suggestion that the college's possession and control was unlawful. To those submissions, which have been repeated in this court, we shall in a moment return in a little more detail . . .

[Mr Thornton, for the second appellant, made a sixth submission to the effect that] . . . the body parts in question did not belong to anybody. He further submitted, in his seventh submission, that the Royal College of Surgeons, albeit in control and factual possession, were not in lawful possession because of the expiry of the 2-year period under the 1832 Anatomy Act, and he drew attention to certain sections in that Act.

He drew the court's attention to the case of *R v Turner (No 2)* . . .

. . . Mr Thornton submits that that case has not only been criticised by Professor Sir John Smith QC in an article to which he drew our attention, but it is to be understood as limited to the facts of the particular case and should not be regarded as any authority, for present purposes, as to the construction of section 5(1) of the Theft Act.

. . . So far as the question of possession by the Royal College of Surgeons is concerned, in our judgment the learned judge was correct to rule that the college had possession, sufficiently for the purposes of and within section 5(1) of the Theft Act 1968. We are unable to accept that possession, for the purposes of that section, is in any way dependent on the period of possession, i.e. whether it is for a limited time, or an indefinite time. In our judgment, the evidence, so far as it was material, before the jury, was to the effect that factually, the parts were in the custody of the Royal College of Surgeons. They were, as it seems to us, in their control and possession within the meaning of section 5(1).

That conclusion is, as it seems to us, reinforced by the judgment of the Court of Appeal in *Turner (No 2)*. We do not accept that the passage in Lord Parker's judgment which we have read is to be regarded as limited to the facts of that particular case. In expressing the view that no other word such as 'lawful' was to be read into section 5(1), by reference to possession, that court was construing section 5 entirely consonantly with the construction which we now place upon it for the purposes of this appeal.

There remains the submission as to the judge's direction that the college was in lawful possession of the parts. It is implicit in what we have already said that the lawfulness of the possession was not a matter for necessary enquiry in the trial. There was, as we have said, evidence before the jury as to the fact of possession of these parts, coming from the inspectors of anatomy. Their views as to the law, as we have already indicated, seem to us to be a matter of no relevance or materiality in relation to any issue which the jury had to determine. It follows that it was not necessary for the judge to direct the jury that the college was in lawful possession rather than merely in possession. The question which arises is whether that direction was of a nature to undermine and prejudice the defence of the appellants. We, in the light of the other passages in the summing-up in relation to dishonesty which we have already cited, are wholly unpersuaded that that is a tenable view.

It follows that for none of the reasons ably advanced before this court, can the convictions of either of these appellants be regarded as unsafe. Accordingly, the appeals against conviction are dismissed.

9.4.3 SECTION 5(3) OF THE THEFT ACT 1968: OBLIGATION TO DEAL WITH PROPERTY

Under s 5(3) of the Theft Act 1968, where a person receives property from another and is under an obligation to deal with that property in a particular way, the property is to be regarded as belonging to that other person. The obligation to deal with property in a particular way must be a *legal* obligation (ie one which is enforceable by civil proceedings): see *R v Gilks* [1972] 1 WLR 1341 (a case decided under s 5(4) of the Theft Act 1968).

Section 5(3) provides:

Where a person receives property from or on account of another, and is under an obligation to the other to retain and deal with that property or its proceeds in a particular way, the property or proceeds shall be regarded (as against him) as belonging to the other.

R v Hall (1972) 56 Cr App R 547

The appellant was in business as a travel agent. He received a payment from a customer by way of a deposit on some airline tickets. The funds were not used by the appellant to secure the tickets and, in due course, the customer failed to receive his tickets. The Court of Appeal was asked to consider whether or not the funds paid over by the customer could be construed as being property belonging to another by virtue of s 5(3).

Edmund-Davies LJ:
[at the instigation of counsel for the appellant referred to a passage in the Eighth Report of the Criminal Law Revision Committee (Cmnd 2977), at p 127] . . .

Subsection (3) provides for the special case where property is transferred to a person to retain and deal with for a particular purpose and he misapplies it or its proceeds. An example would be the treasurer of a holiday fund. The person in question is in law the owner of the property; but the subsection treats the property, as against him, as belonging to the persons to whom he owes the duty to retain and deal with the property as agreed. He will therefore be guilty of stealing from them if he misapplies the property or its proceeds.

Mr Jolly [counsel for the appellant] . . . submits that the position of a treasurer of a solitary fund is quite different from that of a person like the appellant, who was in general (and genuine) business as a travel agent, and to whom people pay money in order to achieve a certain object – in the present cases, to obtain charter flights to America. It is true, he concedes, that thereby the travel agent undertakes a contractual obligation in relation to arranging flights and at the proper time paying the airline and any other expenses . . . But what Mr Jolly resists is that in such circumstances the travel agent 'is under an obligation' to the client 'to retain and deal with . . . in a particular way' sums paid to him in such circumstances.

What cannot of itself be decisive of the matter is the fact that the appellant paid the money into the firm's general trading account. As Widgery J (as he then was) said in *Yule* (1963) 47 Cr App R 229, at p 234; [1964] 1 QB 5, at p 10, decided under section 20(1)(iv) of the Larceny Act 1916: 'The fact that a particular sum is paid into a particular banking account . . . does not affect the right of persons interested in that sum or any duty of the solicitor either towards his client or towards third parties with regard to disposal of that sum.' Nevertheless, when a client goes to a firm carrying on the business of travel agents and pays them money, he expects that in return he will, in due course, receive the tickets and other documents necessary for him to accomplish the trip for which he is paying, and the firm are 'under an obligation' to perform their part to fulfil his expectation and are liable to pay him damages if they do not. But, in our judgment, what was not here established was that these clients expected them to 'retain and deal with that property or its proceeds in a particular way', and that an 'obligation' to do so was undertaken by the appellant.

We must make clear, however, that each case turns on its own facts. Cases could, we suppose, conceivably arise where by some special arrangement (preferably evidenced by documents), the client could impose upon the travel agent an 'obligation' falling within section 5(3). But no such special arrangement was made in any of the seven cases here being considered . . . It follows from this that, despite what on any view must be condemned as scandalous conduct by the appellant, in our judgment, upon this ground alone this appeal must be allowed and the convictions quashed.

But as, to the best of our knowledge, this is one of the earliest cases involving section 5(3), we venture to add some observations:

. . .

(b) Where the case turns, wholly or in part, on section 5(3) a careful exposition of the subsection is called for . . . it was nowhere quoted or even paraphrased by the learned Commissioner in his summing-up. Instead he unfortunately ignored it and proceeded upon the assumption that, as the accused acknowledged the purpose for which clients had paid him money, *ipso facto* there arose an 'obligation . . . to retain and deal with' it for that purpose. He therefore told the jury: 'The sole issue to be determined in each count is this: Has it been proved that the money was stolen in the sense I have described, dishonestly appropriated by him for purposes other than the purpose for which the monies were handed over? Bear in mind that this is not a civil claim to recover money that has been lost.' We have to say respectfully that this will not do . . .

(c) Whether in a particular case the Crown has succeeded in establishing an 'obligation' of the kind coming within section 5(3) . . . may be a difficult question . . . to illustrate what we have in mind, mixed questions of law and fact may call for consideration. For example, if the transaction between the parties is wholly in writing, is it for the judge to direct the jury that, as a matter of law, the defendant had thereby undertaken an 'obligation' within section 5(3)? On the other hand, if it is wholly (or partly) oral, it would appear that it is for the judge to direct them that, if they find certain facts proved, it would be open to them to find that an 'obligation' within section 5(3) had been undertaken – but presumably not that they must so find, for so to direct them would be to invade their territory. In effect, however, the learned Commissioner unhappily did something closely resembling that in the present case by his above-quoted direction that the only issue for their consideration was whether the accused was proved to have been actuated by dishonesty.

R v Wain [1995] 2 Cr App R 660 (CA)

The appellant took part in raising money for a 'telethon' organised for charity by Yorkshire Television. He raised £2,833.25, which he paid into a separate bank account. When asked by Yorkshire Television for the money he made a number of excuses. Eventually the company gave him permission to pay the money into his own bank account. The appellant then handed the company a cheque drawn on that account. The cheque was not met. Meanwhile, the appellant withdrew cash from that account.

At trial, it was submitted on the appellant's behalf that, under s 5(3) of the Theft Act 1968, the debt owed to the charity could not be said to be the proceeds of the money which he had been paid, because the proceeds were the things purchased with the money. This submission was rejected by the trial judge and the appellant was convicted. His appeal to the Court of Appeal was dismissed.

McCowan LJ:
. . . [I]t seems to us that by virtue of s 5(3), the appellant was plainly under an obligation to retain, if not the actual notes and coins, at least their proceeds, that is to say the money credited in the bank account which he opened for the trust with the actual property. When he took the money credited to that account and moved it over to his own bank account, it was still the proceeds of the notes and coins donated which he proceeded to use for his own purposes, thereby appropriating them . . .

We would add this. Whether a person in the position of the appellant is a trustee is to be judged on an objective basis. It is an obligation imposed on him by law. It is not essential that he should have realised that he was a trustee, but of course the question remains as to whether he was acting honestly or dishonestly in using the money for his own purposes. That is a matter of fact for the jury.

9.4.4 SECTION 5(4) OF THE THEFT ACT 1968: OBLIGATION TO RESTORE PROPERTY

Under s 5(4) of the Theft Act 1968, where A receives money from B as the result of a mistake on B's part, and A is under a legal obligation to return some or all of that money to B, the money which should be returned to B is regarded as property belonging to B for the purposes of theft.

Section 5(4) provides:

> Where a person gets property by another's mistake, and is under an obligation to make restoration (in whole or in part) of the property or its proceeds or of the value thereof, then to the extent of that obligation the property or proceeds shall be regarded (as against him) as belonging to the person entitled to restoration, and an intention not to make restoration shall be regarded accordingly as an intention to deprive that person of the property or proceeds.

R v Gilks [1972] 1 WLR 1341 (CA)

Cairns LJ:

. . . The facts were as follows. On 27 March 1971 the appellant went into Ladbrokes' betting shop at North Cheam and placed some bets on certain horses: one of his bets was on a horse called 'Fighting Scot'. 'Fighting Scot' did not get anywhere in the race which was in fact won by a horse called 'Fighting Taffy'. Because of a mistake on the part of the relief manager in the betting shop, the appellant was paid out as if he had backed the successful horse with the result that he was overpaid to the extent of £106.63. He was paid £117.25 when the amount he had won (on other races) was only £10.62. At the very moment when he was being paid the appellant knew that a mistake had been made and that he was not entitled to the money, but he kept it. He refused to consider repaying it, his attitude being that it was Ladbrokes' hard lines . . .

The trial judge held that it was unnecessary for the prosecution to rely on s 5(4) [of the Theft Act 1968] because the property in the £106.63 never passed to the appellant. In the view of this court that ruling was right. The subsection introduced a new principle into the law of theft but long before it was enacted it was held in *R v Middleton* (1873) LR 2 CCR 38 that where a person was paid by mistake . . . a sum in excess of that properly payable, the person who accepted the overpayment with knowledge of the excess was guilty of theft . . .

The gap in the law which s 5(4) was designed to fill was . . . that which is illustrated by the case of *Moynes v Cooper* [1956] 1 QB 439. There a workman received a pay packet containing £7 more than was due to him but did not become aware of the overpayment until he opened the envelope some time later. He then kept the £7. This was held not to be theft because there was no *animus furandi* at the moment of taking . . .

An alternative ground on which the [trial judge] held that the money should be regarded as belonging to Ladbrokes was that 'obligation' in s 5(4) meant an obligation whether a legal one or not. In the opinion of this court that was an incorrect ruling. In a criminal statute, where a person's criminal liability is made dependent on his having an obligation, it would be quite wrong to construe that word so as to cover a moral or social obligation as distinct from a legal one . . .

The appeal against conviction was dismissed.

Attorney General's Ref (No 1 of 1983) [1985] QB 182 (CA)

Lord Lane CJ:

. . . The respondent is a woman police officer and she received her pay from the Receiver of the Metropolitan Police. Owing to an error in the Receiver's department she was credited (in a way which will have to be described in more detail in a moment) with the sum of £74.74 for wages and overtime in respect of a day when she was not at work at all. That amount, together with other sums which were properly due to her, was paid into her bank by direct debit by the Receiver's bank. She knew nothing of the error until later, though it was not proved precisely when. There was some evidence before the jury that she had decided to say nothing about this unsolicited windfall which had come her way, and had decided to take no action about it after she discovered the error. No demand for payment of the sum was made by the Receiver of the Metropolitan Police or anyone else . . .

The question comes up to this court on the Attorney General's reference in the following form:

> Whether a person who receives overpayment of a debt due to him or her by way of a credit to his or her bank account through the 'direct debit' system operated by the banks and who knowing of that overpayment intentionally fails to repay the amount of the overpayment 'may be' [which is an amendment which counsel for the Attorney General has asked us to make to the reference] guilty of theft of the credit to the amount of the overpayment . . .

[W]hat the respondent . . . got was simply the debt due to her from her own bank. That is so unless her account was overdrawn or overdrawn beyond any overdraft limit, in which case she did not even get that right to money. That point is made in a decision of this court in *R v Kohn* (1979) 69 Cr App R 395 . . .

The property in the present case was the debt owed by the bank to the respondent [his Lordship then quoted the definition of property in s 4(1) of the Theft Act, which includes 'things in action', and continued:] The debt here was a thing in action, therefore the property was capable of being stolen.

It will be apparent that, at first blush, that debt did not belong to anyone except the respondent herself. She was the only person who had the right to go to her bank and demand the handing over of that £74.74 . . .

His Lordship then referred to s 5(4) of the Theft Act 1968.

In order to determine the effect of that subsection on this case one has to take it piece by piece to see what the result is read against the circumstances of this particular prosecution. First of all: did the respondent get property? The word 'get' is about as wide a word as could possibly have been adopted by the draftsman of the Act. The answer is Yes; the respondent in this case did get her chose in action, that is her right to sue the bank for the debt which they owed her, money which they held in their hands to which she was entitled by virtue of the contract between bank and customer.

Second: did she get it by another's mistake? The answer to that is plainly Yes, the Receiver of the Metropolitan Police made the mistake of thinking she was entitled to £74.74 when she was not entitled to that at all.

Was she under an obligation to make restoration of either the property or its proceeds or its value? We take each of those in turn. Was she under an obligation to make restoration of the 'property', the chose in action? The answer to that is No, it was something which could not be restored in the ordinary meaning of the word. Was she under an obligation to make restoration of its proceeds? The answer to that is No, there were no proceeds of the chose in action to restore. Was she under an obligation to make restoration of the value thereof, the value of the chose in action? The answer to that seems to us to be Yes.

I should say here, in parentheses, that a question was raised during the argument this morning whether 'restoration' is the same as 'making restitution'. We think that, on the wording of s 5(4) as a whole, the answer to that question is Yes. One therefore turns to see whether, under the general principles of restitution, the respondent was obliged to restore or pay for the benefit which she received. Generally speaking the respondent, in these circumstances, is obliged to pay for a benefit received when the benefit has been given under a mistake as to a material fact on the part of the giver. The mistake must be as to a fundamental or essential fact and the payment must have been due to that fundamental or essential fact. The mistake here was that this police officer had been working on a day when she had been at home and not working at all . . .

In the present case, applying that principle to the facts of this case, the value of the chose in action (the property) was £74.74 and there was a legal obligation on the respondent to restore that value to the receiver when she found that the mistake had been made. One continues to examine the contents of s 5(4). It follows from what has already been said that the extent of that obligation, the chose in action, has to be regarded as belonging to the person entitled to restoration, that is the Receiver of the Metropolitan Police.

As a result of the provisions of s 5(4) the debt of £74.74 due from the respondent's bank to the respondent notionally belonged to the Receiver of the Metropolitan Police, therefore the prosecution, up to this point, have succeeded in proving (remarkable though it may seem) that the 'property' in this case belonged to another within the meaning of s 1 in the 1968 Act from the moment when the respondent became aware that this mistake had been made and that her account had been credited with the £74.74 and she consequently became obliged to restore the value. Furthermore, by the final words of s 5(4), once the prosecution succeed in proving that the respondent intended not to make restoration, that is notionally to be regarded as an intention to deprive the receiver of that property which notionally belongs to him . . .

 COMMENTS AND QUESTIONS

1   Whether an 'obligation' arises for the purposes of s 5(3) or 5(4) is to be determined by the civil law, and the trial judge should direct the jury accordingly; see *R v Breaks and Huggan* [1998] Crim LR 349.

2   Under s 5(2), property subject to a trust is regarded as belonging to any person having a right to enforce the trust, for example, beneficiaries. In cases involving misappropriation of charitable funds the person with the right to enforce the trust is the Attorney General; see further *R v Dyke and Munroe* [2002] Crim LR 153.

3   Where P disposes of his property with *animus revocandi* (an intention to relinquish ownership) it ceases to be property belonging to another for the purposes of theft, and hence cannot be stolen. Where, by contrast, P simply loses or mislays his property, it remains

property belonging to another for the purposes of theft; see further *R v Rostron* [2003] All ER (D) 269 (D guilty of theft of golf balls from golf course).

4   Resort to s 5(4) may not always be necessary where property is given to D as a result of P's error. In *R v Williams* [1980] Crim LR 589, the appellant exchanged obsolete foreign currency (knowing it to be obsolete) for sterling at a bureau de change in a department store. The Court of Appeal, dismissing his appeal against conviction for theft, held that there had been a 'fundamental mistake' operating on the mind of the cashier handing over the money, hence the transaction was void *ab initio*. As such, no property in the money could pass to the appellant, and he appropriated it when he put it in his pocket. The money could be regarded as property belonging to another simply by virtue of s 5(1).

5   Since consent does not prevent an appropriation from taking place, a company director cannot say that he can give consent on behalf of the company for the appropriation of the company's property. It also follows from the fact that a limited liability company is a separate legal entity from its directors and shareholders, that a director or shareholder takes property 'belonging to another' if he takes property belonging to the company (cf *Attorney General's Ref (No 2 of 1982)* [1984] QB 624, approved in *R v Gomez*).

6   *R v Bonner* [1970] 1 WLR 838 makes clear that, as regards theft of property owned by a partnership, provided the other elements of theft are made out, one partner can commit theft of partnership property just in the same way that one individual can commit the theft of the property of another individual with whom he has no connection nor relationship.

9.5 DISHONESTY

Given the extended definition of appropriation resulting from the decisions of the House of Lords in *Lawrence, Gomez* and *Hinks* (considered above) and the wide ambit of the term 'belonging to another', there will be few situations in which D deals with P's property where the elements of appropriating property belonging to another cannot be made out by the prosecution. This means that in most theft cases, liability will hinge on the issue of *mens rea*, specifically whether or not the defendant was dishonest. The scheme adopted by the Theft Act 1968 is to provide a negative statutory definition of dishonesty – essentially three situations where the defendant is not regarded as having been dishonest. If a defendant cannot bring himself within one of the three, he may yet escape liability if, following a direction on the common law definition of dishonesty, the jury conclude that he was not dishonest.

9.5.1 THE NEGATIVE STATUTORY DEFINITION OF DISHONESTY

Section 2 of the Theft Act 1968 provides:
(1) A person's appropriation of property belonging to another is not to be regarded as dishonest:
   (a) if he appropriates the property in the belief that he has in law the right to deprive the other of it, on behalf of himself or of a third person; or
   (b) if he appropriates the property in the belief that he would have the other's consent if the other knew of the appropriation and the circumstances of it; or

> (c) (except where the property came to him as trustee or personal representative) if he appropriates the property in the belief that the person to whom the property belongs cannot be discovered by taking reasonable steps.

Where a defendant is charged with theft, or an offence which requires proof of theft (such as robbery, or some burglaries), regard should first be had to the terms of s 2(1)(a)–(c) in order to determine whether or not D is dishonest. Only if D appears to fall outside these provisions should consideration be given to the approach to dishonesty at common law exemplified in *R v Ghosh* (below).

9.5.2 DISHONESTY UNDER S 2 – CLAIM OF RIGHT

Under s 2(1)(a) the defendant will not be dishonest if he honestly believes he has the right in law to deprive the other party of the property. *R v Holden* [1991] Crim LR 478 makes clear that reasonable belief is not the relevant test; however, the reasonableness of the belief might be relevant to the question of whether the defendant could have had an honest belief that he was entitled to take the tyres. It follows, as the test is subjective, that the defendant does not have to have had any actual legal right. To this extent his mistake of civil law provides him with a basis for his defence.

9.5.3 DISHONESTY UNDER S 2 – BELIEF IN THE OWNER'S CONSENT

> **Attorney General's Ref (No 2 of 1982) [1984] QB 624 (CA)**
>
> Kerr LJ:
> On this reference by the Attorney General under s 36 of the Criminal Justice Act 1972, the court is asked to give its opinion on the following point of law:
>
> > Whether a man in total control of a limited liability company (by reason of his shareholding and directorship) is capable of stealing the property of the company; and whether two men in total control of a limited liability company (by reason of their shareholdings and director-ships) are (while acting in concert) capable of jointly stealing the property of the company . . .
>
> The counts of theft were specimen counts alleging the appropriation by the defendants for their own private purposes of funds of various companies of which they were the sole shareholders and directors. The total amounts involved ran into millions. Some of the counts related to X alone, some to Y alone, and in some of them they were charged jointly. However, it is common ground that, in relation to all of them, each acted with the consent of the other: indeed, all the alleged thefts appear to have been carried out by means of cheques drawn on various accounts of the companies concerned and signed in each case by X and Y jointly. There is no question of X or Y having been the victim of the dishonesty of the other . . .
>
> It was submitted that since the defendants were the sole owners of the company and, through their shareholding, the sole owners of all its property, they could not, in effect, be charged with

stealing from themselves. In particular, it was submitted that there was no issue to go to the jury on the ingredient of 'dishonesty'. The defendants were the sole will and directing mind of the company. The company was therefore bound to consent to all to which they themselves consented . . . Further, the defendants relied on the wide 'objects' clauses of the memorandum of association of the various companies concerned and submitted that the defendants' acts were covered by these and were accordingly *intra vires* . . .

. . . The basic fallacy in the submission on behalf of the defendants is the contention that, in effect, in a situation such as the present a jury is bound to be directed that, when all the members and directors of a company act in concert in appropriating the property of their company, they cannot, as a matter of law, be held to have acted dishonestly; or that, on such facts, any reasonable jury is bound to reach this conclusion. We entirely disagree with both these propositions . . .

. . . In our view there is no substance whatever in the submission that s 2(1)(b) would preclude a jury from concluding, as a matter of law, that the defendants had acted dishonestly in these cases. Nor can we accept for one moment that any jury would be bound to conclude, on the facts alleged that dishonesty had not been established.

. . . [I]t does not by any means follow that the members and directors of a company which is wholly owned by them cannot properly be charged with theft of the company's property, or that the defendants cannot rely on s 2 of the 1968 Act in answer to such a charge. Their appropriate defence in such cases is provided by s 2(1)(a) of the Act, the belief of a defendant, which must of course be an honest belief, 'that he has in law the right to deprive [the company] of [the property]'.

In effect, the defendants' answer to the charges in the present case, assuming that the prosecution establishes the facts alleged, would have been: 'We honestly believed that we were entitled to do what we did. They were our companies, and we honestly believed that we were entitled to draw all the cheques and expend all the moneys which are now charged as acts of theft.' This is the defence provided by s 2(1)(a). To obtain a conviction, the prosecution would have had to establish the contrary to the satisfaction of the jury . . .

. . . In our view the *vires* of the company may be of evidential relevance to, but not determinative of, the crucial issue as to the defendants' honesty or dishonesty. Of course, in asserting an honest belief in his right to act as he did, a defendant may wish to refer to the objects for which the company was constituted, and to the terms of its memorandum, to assist him in his defence that he had acted honestly . . .

The converse equally applies to the case for the prosecution. Thus, although the prosecutor may seek to prove by reference to the company's memorandum that on its true construction the acts charged were *ultra vires*, the prosecution will not thereby inevitably establish that the defendant had acted dishonestly. The defendant would of course be perfectly entitled to assert that in all the circumstances, and especially because he at all times believed his acts to be *intra vires*, he had not acted dishonestly. Whether or not the defendant had acted *ultra vires* is a matter which the jury would then be entitled to take into account, giving it such weight as they thought proper in deciding the ultimate question, namely: has the prosecution proved that the defendant had acted dishonestly?

9.5.4 DISHONESTY UNDER S 2 – BELIEF THAT THE OWNER CANNOT BE FOUND BY TAKING REASONABLE STEPS

Section 2(1)(c) covers appropriation of property which the defendant honestly believes to be lost or abandoned property. Again, the reasonableness of the belief rests on whether that belief was genuinely held.

R v Small (1988) 86 Cr App R 170 (CA)

The appellant was charged with theft of a car; having admitted to the police that he had stolen it, his defence at trial was that he believed the car to have been abandoned.

> Henry J:
>
> . . . The appellant when he was called gave evidence that he lived in a road adjacent to Links Road and that he had seen the car [in Links Road] every day for about two weeks, during which time it had not moved. He said it was parked at an angle on a corner, the doors were unlocked and the keys were in the ignition. According to him the car was in a somewhat forlorn state. The tyre was flat, as was the battery. The petrol tank was empty and the windscreen wipers did not work. He thought it was 'dumped', he said . . .
>
> The appellant told the court how he got petrol, bump started the car and drove it round the corner. There it remained for a few days, when he and his co-accused decided to go for a drive with Williams driving. He said that it had not occurred to him until the police flashed their lights that the car was stolen, but it did occur to him then. He then panicked and ran away.
>
> In cross-examination he said that he thought the car had been dumped, abandoned by the true owner. He accepted that he did not have the right to take it. He said he intended to leave it with the keys in it after he had driven it. He said he had initially told the police that he had stolen the car because he had not in fact paid for it. He said that he did not know that the fact that the car was being dumped might offer him a defence at the time when he admitted to the police that he had stolen it.

Counsel for the appellant contended (1) that one cannot steal abandoned property, and (2) that an honest belief that property was abandoned is a defence.

> In considering whether a belief is honest or not, it seems to us that a belief can, in certain circumstances, be honest or genuinely held, even though it is not reasonably held. The relevance of reasonableness is this. It is certainly relevant as to whether the belief was in fact held, because the fact that such a belief would be objectively viewed as unreasonable is a factor – and a strong factor – for the jury to take into account first in considering whether that belief was held, and second, if held, in considering whether it was honestly held . . .

9.5.5 DISHONESTY AT COMMON LAW

In theft cases, resort to the common law definition of dishonesty should be the last resort, not the first. Most defendants charged with theft who are found to be not guilty because they were not dishonest will have been excluded from liability by virtue of s 2(1)(a)–(c) of the 1968 Act. The problem with attempting a general definition of dishonesty lies in striking the right balance between objectivity – the standards to be expected of individuals – and subjectivity – what the defendant thought of what he was doing. As will be seen, *R v Ghosh* does not actually provide a common law definition; more a direction to assist the jury in determining the right balance between the competing demands of objectivity and subjectivity.

R v Ghosh [1982] QB 1053 (CA)

Lord Lane CJ:

. . . At all material times the appellant was a surgeon acting as a *locum tenens* consultant at a hospital. The charges alleged that he had falsely represented that he had himself carried out a surgical operation to terminate pregnancy or that money was due to himself or an anaesthetist for such an operation, when in fact the operation had been carried out by someone else, and/or under the National Health Service provisions.

His defence was that there was no deception; that the sums paid to him were due for consultation fees which were legitimately payable under the regulations, or else were the balance of fees properly payable; in other words that there was nothing dishonest about his behaviour on any of the counts . . .

. . . *R v Feely* [1973] QB 530 . . . is often treated as having laid down an objective test of dishonesty for the purpose of s 1 of the Theft Act 1968. But what it actually decided was: (1) that it is for the jury to determine whether the defendant acted dishonestly and not for the judge; (2) that the word 'dishonestly' can only relate to the defendant's own state of mind; and (3) that it is unnecessary and undesirable for judges to define what is meant by 'dishonestly' . . .

. . . Is 'dishonestly' in s 1 of the Theft Act 1968 intended to characterise a course of conduct? Or is it intended to describe a state of mind? If the former, then we can well understand that it could be established independently of the knowledge or belief of the accused. But if, as we think, it is the latter, then the knowledge and belief of the accused are at the root of the problem.

Take for example a man who comes from a country where public transport is free. On his first day here he travels on a bus. He gets off without paying. He never had any intention of paying. His mind is clearly honest; but his conduct, judged objectively by what he has done, is dishonest. It seems to us that in using the word 'dishonestly' in the Theft Act 1968, Parliament cannot have intended to catch dishonest conduct in that sense, that is to say conduct to which no moral obloquy could possibly attach. This is sufficiently established by the partial definition in s 2 of the Theft Act 1968 itself. All the matters covered by s 2(1) relate to the belief of the accused. Section 2(2) relates to his willingness to pay. A man's belief and his willingness to pay are things which can only be established subjectively. It is difficult to see how a partially subjective definition can be made to work in harness with the test which in all other respects is wholly objective.

If we are right that dishonesty is something in the mind of the accused . . . then if the mind of the accused is honest, it cannot be deemed dishonest merely because members of the jury would have regarded it as dishonest to embark on that course of conduct. So we would reject the simple uncomplicated approach that the test is purely objective, however attractive from the practical point of view that solution may be.

There remains the objection that to adopt a subjective test is to abandon all standards but that of the accused himself, and to bring about a state of affairs in which 'Robin Hood would be no robber' . . . This objection misunderstands the nature of the subjective test. It is no defence for a man to say 'I knew that what I was doing is generally regarded as dishonest; but I do not regard it as dishonest myself. Therefore I am not guilty'. What he is, however, entitled to say is, 'I did not know that anybody would regard what I was doing as dishonest'. He may not be believed; just as he may not be believed if he sets up 'a claim of right' under s 2(1) of the Theft Act 1968, or asserts that he believed in the truth of a misrepresentation under s 15 of the 1968 Act. But if he is believed, or raises a real doubt about the matter, the jury cannot be sure that he was dishonest.

In determining whether the prosecution has proved that the defendant was acting dishonestly, a jury must first of all decide whether according to the ordinary standards of reasonable and honest people what was done was dishonest. If it was not dishonest by those standards, that is the end of the matter and the prosecution fails.

If it was dishonest by those standards, then the jury must consider whether the defendant himself must have realised that what he was doing was by those standards dishonest. In most cases, where the actions are obviously dishonest by ordinary standards, there will be no doubt about it. It will be obvious that the defendant himself knew that he was acting dishonestly. It is dishonest for a defendant to act in a way which he knows ordinary people consider to be dishonest, even if he asserts or genuinely believes that he is morally justified in acting as he did. For example, Robin Hood or those ardent anti-vivisectionists who remove animals from vivisection laboratories are acting dishonestly, even though they may consider themselves to be morally justified in doing what they do, because they know that ordinary people would consider these actions to be dishonest . . .

 COMMENTS AND QUESTIONS

1   If D can appropriate property even though P consents to the actions constituting the appropriation, why should D's belief that P consents to the appropriation provide a basis for denying dishonesty?

2   Section 2(2) of the 1968 Act provides that: 'A person's appropriation of property belonging to another may be dishonest notwithstanding that he is willing to pay for the property.' Hence, even if D takes P's property and leaves money far in excess of the market value of the property, a jury will not be precluded from concluding that D acted dishonestly.

3   How should a jury be directed in accordance with *R v Ghosh*, where the defendant contends that he gave no thought to what ordinary decent people would have thought of his actions, or contends that he considered this but was unable to come to a view?

4   In its Consultation Paper *Legislating the Criminal Code: Fraud and Deception* (LCCP 155), the Law Commission identified theft as being one of a number of offences where: '. . . the conduct elements of the offence are very broadly defined, such that they include a wide range of beneficial or innocuous activities. Dishonesty is the one factor which renders the conduct criminal. In such offences, dishonesty "does all the work" . . . Theft . . . [is an offence] . . . in

which dishonesty operates as a positive element . . .' For details of the Law Commission review of dishonesty, in particular its role in relation to offences of dishonesty, see its Report *Fraud* (Law Com No 276), considered at Chapter 10.8

9.6 INTENTION TO PERMANENTLY DEPRIVE

The second element of the *mens rea* of theft is provided by proof that the defendant intended to permanently deprive the other party of the property. The main purpose of this element of the *mens rea* is to ensure that the courts make the necessary distinction between borrowing and theft, although as will be seen, the section does not actually define intention to permanently deprive. What it does is to provide a number of specific instances where a defendant who does not actually have any intention to permanently deprive can nevertheless be deemed to have such an intention because of the way in which he has dealt with the property. Section 6 provides:

> (1) A person appropriating property belonging to another without meaning the other permanently to lose the thing itself is nevertheless to be regarded as having the intention of permanently depriving the other of it if his intention is to treat the thing as his own to dispose of regardless of the other's rights; and a borrowing or lending of it may amount to so treating it if, but only if, the borrowing or lending is for a period and in circumstances making it equivalent to an outright taking or disposal.
>
> (2) Without prejudice to the generality of subsection (1) above, where a person, having possession or control (lawfully or not) of property belonging to another, parts with the property under a condition as to its return which he may not be able to perform, this (if done for purposes of his own and without the other's authority) amounts to treating the property as his own to dispose of regardless of the other's rights.

9.6.1 WHERE THE DEFENDANT TREATS THE THING AS HIS OWN TO DISPOSE OF REGARDLESS OF THE OTHER'S RIGHTS

R v Marshall; R v Coombes; R v Eren [1998] 2 Cr App R 282

As part of an operation by London Underground Limited at Victoria Station the appellants were observed and videoed obtaining used travel tickets from passengers leaving the underground and selling them at a reduced rate to persons intending to travel. The tickets, which had been issued by London Underground Limited, remained valid in the sense that their usefulness had not been exhausted. Thereby London Underground Limited was deprived of revenue which it might have expected to receive from those persons who had bought the tickets. Each of the appellants pleaded guilty to theft of the tickets following the trial judge's ruling on the elements of the offence, and appealed.

Mantell LJ:

This appeal could have implications for all ticket touts and even for the ordinary motorist who passes on the benefit of an unexpired parking ticket . . . A number of submissions were made to the learned Judge. The first was that the travel tickets were not the property of London Underground Limited within the meaning of section 1 of the Theft Act 1968. The Judge rejected the submission ruling that although the tickets had passed into the possession and control of the customers, London Underground retained a proprietary right or interest in the tickets which were to be regarded therefore as the property of London Underground pursuant to section 5(1) of the Act. As a secondary reason for rejecting the submission he referred to the express term on the reverse of each ticket to the effect that it remained throughout the property of LRT, of which London Underground Limited is a part.

A second submission was made that in the circumstances there had been no appropriation so as to bring the case within the basic definition of theft. In rejecting the submission the judge referred to section 3(1) [set out above] . . . and to the decision of the House of Lords in *R v Morris* . . . in which it was held that it was not necessary to demonstrate an assumption by the accused of all the owner's rights, simply to show the assumption of some of the rights of the owner of the goods in question. The learned Judge considered that the use of the ticket to the detriment of London Underground was inconsistent with London Underground's rights and consequently that the actions of the appellants amounted to an appropriation in law.

Thirdly and lastly it was submitted that on the agreed facts there was no evidence of an intention to permanently deprive. That submission also was rejected, the learned Judge taking the view that the provisions of section 6(1) of the Theft Act covered the position. It will be necessary to refer to the terms of the subsection later in this judgment.

. . . As indicated, although a number of submissions were made to the learned Judge and subsequently reproduced in the grounds of appeal, only one such has been pursued before this court. It is set out in the skeleton argument of Mr Taylor of counsel who appears for the appellants Marshall and Coombes. It was adopted by Mr Simpson on behalf of Eren.

> It is submitted by the appellants that in the circumstances although there was an assumption of the rights of the owner contrary to section 3 of the Theft Act 1968 which amounted to an appropriation there was nevertheless no intention on their part to deprive London Underground Limited of the said ticket. They intended either to return them directly to London Underground Limited or to do so through the third party buyer without resale to London Underground Limited and without any loss in the virtue of the ticket when returned.

The argument proceeds,

> The ticket forms are pieces of paper printed over with information about the ticket. When returned to London Underground Limited they had no more and no less value than when they were originally purchased. The return to London Underground, notwithstanding these intervening transactions involved no loss of virtue to London Underground Limited's property.

It was submitted section 6(1) of the Theft Act 1968 did not apply as that was only to be resorted to where there was a resale of the property to the original owner. It was further submitted that the issuing of a travel ticket was analogous to the drawing of a cheque and that as both were choses in action the reasoning in *R v Preddy* [1996] 3 WLR 255 was equally applicable.

It will be seen that the submission made on what is accepted to be the single issue in the appeal depends in part upon the misapprehension that the ticket forms would necessarily find their way back into the possession of London Underground. That was the factual basis upon which the learned Judge ruled. As mentioned, we are content to deal with this appeal on a similar basis.

On this point the Judge ruled as follows:

> I am satisfied that the essence of section 6 of the Theft Act 1968 is whether there was an intention to treat the tickets as their own regardless of the owner's rights. Mr Taylor has drawn my attention in particular to the cases of *Duru* (1972) 58 CAR 151 and *Preddy and Others* . . . and referred me to the commentary by Professor Smith to the case of *R v Mitchell* . . . I note that all these cases involved cheques and for my part I am not prepared to extend to the underground what the High Court have found in relation to cheques.

For the reasons which follow we consider that the judge was right.

His Lordship recited the provisions of s 6(1) of the Theft Act 1968, and continued:

> . . . On its face the subsection would seem apt to cover the facts of the present case. The ticket belongs to London Underground. It has been appropriated by an appellant. It is the exclusive right of London Underground to sell tickets. By acquiring and re-selling the ticket the appellant has an intention to treat the ticket as his own to dispose of regardless of London Underground's right. However Mr Taylor and Mr Simpson have reminded us of what was said by Lord Lane, Lord Chief Justice in the case of *R v Lloyd* . . .
>
> > Bearing in mind the observation of Edmund Davis LJ in *Warner* (1970) 55 Cr App R 93, we would try to interpret the section in such a way as to ensure that nothing is construed as an intention permanently to deprive which would not prior to the 1968 Act have been so construed. Thus the first part of section 6(1) seems to us to be aimed at the sort of case where a defendant takes things and then offers them back to the owner for the owner to buy if he wishes. If the taker intends to return them to the owner only upon such payment, then, on the wording of section 6(1) that is deemed to amount to the necessary intention permanently to deprive . . .
>
> It is submitted, therefore, that the subsection is to be construed narrowly and confined to the sort of case of which Lord Lane gave an example and of which the present is not one. However, this court had to consider a similar situation in the case of *R v Fernandez* [1996] 1 Cr App R 175 where at p 188 Lord Justice Auld giving the judgment of the court said this:
>
> > In our view section 6(1), which is expressed in general terms, is not limited in its application to the illustrations given by Lord Lane CJ in *Lloyd*. Nor in saying that in most cases it would be unnecessary to refer to the provision, did Lord Lane suggest it should be so limited. The critical notion, stated expressly in the first limb and incorporated by reference in the second is, whether a defendant intended to 'treat the thing as his own to dispose of regardless of the other's rights'. The second limb of subsection (1) and also subsection (2) are merely specific illustrations of the application of that notion. We consider that section 6 may apply to a person in possession or control of another's property who, dishonestly and for his own purpose, deals with that property in such a manner that he knows he is risking its loss.

In our judgment and following *Fernandez* the subsection is not to be given the restricted interpretation for which the appellants contend.

The principal submission put forward on behalf of the appellants is that the issuing of the ticket is analogous to the drawing of a cheque in that in each instance a chose in action is created which in the first case belongs to the customer and in the second to the payee. So by parity of reasoning with that advanced by Lord Goff in *Preddy* . . . the property acquired belonged to the customer and not London Underground and there can have been no intention on the part of the appellant to deprive London Underground of the ticket which would in due course be returned to the possession of London Underground. Attractive though the submission appears at first blush we do not think that it can possibly be correct.

. . . On the issuing of an underground ticket a contract is created between London Underground and the purchaser. Under that contract each party has rights and obligations. Theoretically those rights are enforceable by action. Therefore it is arguable, we suppose, that by the transaction each party has acquired a chose in action. On the side of the purchaser it is represented by a right to use the ticket to the extent which it allows travel on the underground system. On the side of London Underground it encompasses the right to insist that the ticket is used by no one other than the purchaser. It is that right which is disregarded when the ticket is acquired by the appellant and sold on. But here the charges were in relation to the tickets and travel cards themselves and a ticket form or travel card and, dare we say, a cheque form is not a chose in action. The fact that the ticket form or travel card may find its way back into the possession of London Underground, albeit with its usefulness or 'virtue' exhausted, is nothing to the point. Section 6(1) prevails for the reasons we have given.

The appellants by their pleas having acknowledged that they were acting dishonestly it seems to us that there is no reason to consider the convictions unsafe and these appeals must be dismissed.

9.6.2 WHERE THE DEFENDANT BORROWS OR LENDS THE PROPERTY FOR A PERIOD AND IN CIRCUMSTANCES MAKING IT EQUIVALENT TO AN OUTRIGHT TAKING OR DISPOSAL

This aspect of s 6(1) effectively brings certain instances of borrowing within the scope of theft. It will be a question of fact for the jury to determine whether or not the borrowing should be treated as amounting to an outright taking, but relevant factors will be the perishable nature of the property, the duration of the borrowing, and the transient nature of the rights represented by the tangible property. Thus to borrow P's ice cream whilst it melts and then to return it to P could be theft. The same could be true where D borrows P's ticket to a concert, returning it to P the day after the performance. The borrowing has the effect of removing the value from the tangible property – just the mischief that this limb of s 6(1) is aimed at.

R v Lloyd, Bhuee and Ali [1985] QB 829 (CA)

The appellant was employed as chief projectionist at the Odeon Cinema at Barking. The other two appellants, Ali and Bhuee, were employed by a man called Mustafa. The case against the appellants was that over a period of months Lloyd had been clandestinely removing feature films which were due to be shown at the Odeon Cinema at Barking and lending them to his co-defendants, who had equipment that enabled them to copy the films onto a master video tape, and, as a result, produce pirated versions of the film. The films were only out of the cinema for a few hours, and were always back in time for their projection to take place at the advertised times to those people who attended the cinema to see them. The appellants were caught redhanded in the process of copying a film called *The Missionary* onto the master tape. Following the appellants' convictions for theft, the trial judge issued a certificate (that the case was fit for appeal) by posing the following question:

Whether the offence of conspiracy to steal is committed when persons dishonestly agree to take a film from a cinema without authority intending it should be returned within a few hours but knowing that many hundreds of copies will be subsequently made and that the value of the film so returned will thereby be substantially reduced?

Lord Lane CJ:

. . . [His Lordship quoted s 6(1) of the Theft Act 1968 and said that it] is abstruse. But it must mean, if nothing else, that there are circumstances in which a defendant may be deemed to have the intention permanently to deprive, even though he may intend the owner eventually to get back the object which has been taken . . .

. . . The first part of s 6(1) seems to us to be aimed at the sort of case where a defendant takes things and then offers them back to the owner for the owner to buy if he wishes. If the taker intends to return them to the owner only on such payment, then, on the wording of s 6(1), that is deemed to amount to the necessary intention permanently to deprive: see, for instance, *R v Hall* (1848) 1 Den 381, where the defendant took fat from a candlemaker and then offered it for sale to the owner. His conviction for larceny was affirmed. There are other cases of similar intent: for instance, 'I have taken your valuable painting. You can have it back on payment to me of £X,000. If you are not prepared to make that payment, then you are not going to get your painting back.'

It seems to us that in this case we are concerned with the second part of s 6(1), namely the words after the semicolon:

and a borrowing or lending of it may amount to so treating it if, but only if, the borrowing or lending is for a period and in circumstances making it equivalent to an outright taking or disposal.

These films, it could be said, were borrowed by Lloyd from his employers in order to enable him and the others to carry out their 'piracy' exercise.

Borrowing is *ex hypothesi* not something which is done with an intention permanently to deprive. This half of the subsection, we believe, is intended to make it clear that a mere borrowing is never enough to constitute the necessary guilty mind unless the intention is to return the 'thing' in such a changed state that it can truly be said that all its goodness or virtue has gone: for example *R v Beecham* (1851) 5 Cox CC 181, where the defendant stole railway tickets intending that they should be returned to the railway company in the usual way only after the journeys had been completed. He was convicted of larceny. The judge in the present case gave another example, namely the taking of a torch battery with the intention of returning it only when its power is exhausted.

That being the case, we turn to inquire whether the feature films in this case can fall within that category. Our view is that they cannot. The goodness, the virtue, the practical value of the films to the owners has not gone out of the article. The film could still be projected to paying audiences, and, had everything gone according to the conspirators' plans, would have been projected in the ordinary way to audiences at the Odeon Cinema, Barking, who would have paid for their seats. Our view is that those particular films which were the subject of this alleged conspiracy had not themselves diminished in value at all. What had happened was that the borrowed film had been used or was going to be used to perpetrate a copyright swindle on the owners whereby their commercial interests were grossly and adversely affected in the way that we have endeavoured to describe at the outset of this judgment. The borrowing, it seems to us, was not for a period, or in such circumstances, as made it equivalent to an outright taking or disposal. There was still virtue in the film.

9.6.3 INTENTION TO PERMANENTLY DEPRIVE: CONDITIONAL INTENT

R v Easom [1971] 2 QB 315 (CA)

Edmund Davies LJ:

. . . This is an appeal by the appellant against his conviction . . . on an indictment charging him with theft, the particulars of the charge being that, on 27 December 1969, he 'stole one handbag, one purse, one notebook, a quantity of tissues, a quantity of cosmetics and one pen, the property of Joyce Crooks'.

The circumstances giving rise to the charge may be shortly stated. On the evening of 27 December 1969, Woman Police Sergeant Crooks and other plain-clothes officers went to the Metropole Cinema in Victoria. Sergeant Crooks sat in an aisle seat and put her handbag (containing the articles enumerated in the charge) alongside her on the floor. It was attached to her right wrist by a piece of black cotton. Police Constable Hensman sat next to her on the inside seat. When the house lights came on during an interval, it was seen that the appellant was occupying the aisle seat in the row immediately behind Sergeant Crooks and that the seat next to him was vacant. Within a few minutes of the lights being put out, Sergeant Crooks felt the cotton attached to her wrist tighten. She thereupon gave Police Constable Hensman a pre-arranged signal. The cotton was again pulled, this time so strongly that she broke it off. Moments later the officers could hear the rustle of tissues and the sound of her handbag being closed. Very shortly afterwards the appellant left his seat and went to the lavatory. The officers then turned round and found Sergeant Crook's handbag on the floor behind her seat and in front of that which the appellant had vacated. Its contents were intact. When the appellant emerged from the lavatory and seated himself in another part of the cinema, he was approached by the police officers. When the offence of theft was put to him, he denied it . . .

. . . In every case of theft the appropriation must be accompanied by the intention of permanently depriving the owner of his property. What may be loosely described as a 'conditional' appropriation will not do. If the appropriator has it in mind merely to deprive the owner of such of his property as, on examination, proves worth taking and then, finding that the booty is valueless to the appropriator, leaves it ready to hand to be repossessed by the owner, the appropriator has not stolen. If a dishonest postal sorter picks up a pile of letters, intending to steal any which are registered, but, on finding that none of them are, replaces them, he has stolen nothing, and this is so notwithstanding the provisions of s 6(1) of the Theft Act 1968 . . .

But does it follow from all this that the appellant . . . has to go scot-free? Can he not, as counsel for the Crown originally submitted, be convicted at least of attempted theft?

. . . [M]uch depends on the manner in which the charge is framed. Thus, 'if you indict a man for stealing your watch, you cannot convict him of attempting to steal your umbrella' (*per* Cockburn CJ in *R v M'Pherson* (1857) Dears & B 197, 200) – unless, of course, the court of trial has duly exercised the wide powers of amendment conferred by s 5 of the Indictments Act 1915 . . . No amendment was sought or effected in the present case, which accordingly has to be considered in relation to the articles enumerated in the theft charge and nothing else. Furthermore, it is implicit in the concept of an attempt that the person acting intends to do the act attempted, so that the *mens rea* of an attempt is essentially that of the complete crime . . . That being so, there could be no valid conviction of the appellant of attempted theft on the present indictment unless it were established that he was animated by the same intention permanently to deprive Sergeant Crooks of the goods enumerated in the particulars of the charge as would be necessary to establish the full offence. We hope that we have already made sufficiently clear why we consider that, in the light of the evidence and of the direction given, it is impossible to uphold the verdict on the basis that such intention was established in this case. For these reasons, we are compelled to allow the appeal and quash the conviction.

 ## COMMENTS AND QUESTIONS

1   Suppose D takes £100 in notes and coins from his employer's cash register on a Friday night, intending to place £100 in the cash register on the following Monday morning. A jury may infer dishonesty from the fact that D knows he has no legal right to take the money, knows his employer does not consent, and the fact that he does not leave a note indicating that he has removed the funds. In relation to intention to permanently deprive, D may seek to argue that his intention to put £100 in the cash register on the Monday negates this element of *mens rea*. *R v Velumyl* [1989] Crim LR 299, however, indicates that D would have the requisite intention of permanently depriving his employer of the money because he had no intention to return the objects which he had taken. His intention would have been to return objects of equivalent value – a matter relevant to dishonesty, not s 6(1).

2   Has the enactment of the Criminal Attempts Act 1981, in particular s 1(2) and (3) dealing with the removal of impossibility as a bar to liability for attempt (see further Chapter 8.3.4) provided an alternative way of dealing with the problem of conditional intent? Could Easom now be charged with attempting to steal property unknown from persons unknown?

3   Suppose D takes a piece of jewellery from P without P's knowledge, inn order to have it valued. D intends to keep the jewellery if the valuation shows it to be worth more than £1,000. At the time he takes the jewellery does D commit theft? Alternatively, does he commit attempted theft when he takes the jewellery?

9.7 MAKING OFF WITHOUT PAYMENT

The offence of making off without payment was created by s 3 of the Theft Act 1968 in order to close a loophole in the law arising where, for example, D entered a restaurant, ordered a meal, consumed the meal, and then decided to leave without paying. A charge of theft would not have been possible because D would have been honest when eating the food. A deception charge under the pre-Fraud Act 2006 law would also have failed because there would have been no deception prior to D's obtaining of the food, and no subsequent deception as to non-payment. Similarly where D drove onto a petrol station forecourt, filled his petrol tank, decided not to pay and drove off; see *Edwards v Ddin* [1976] 1 WLR 942. Hence the need for s 3 of the Theft Act 1978, to cover cases where D claims that he formed the intention not to pay for the goods or services *after* he had obtained them. It should be noted that such conduct might now be caught by s 2 of the Fraud Act where D changes his mind about payment and falsely represents himself as someone who intends to pay – see further Chapter 10.2.2. Where there are no false representations by D, however, s 3 of the 1978 Act will have to be relied upon.

Section 3 of the Theft Act 1978 provides as follows:

> (1) Subject to subsection (3) below, a person who, knowing that payment on the spot for any goods supplied or service done is required or expected from him, dishonestly makes off without having paid as required or expected and with intent to avoid payment of the amount due shall be guilty of an offence.

The elements of the offence created by s 3 of the Theft Act 1978 are that the defendant:

> (1) knowing that payment on the spot (for goods already supplied or services already done) is required or expected . . .
> (2) dishonestly . . .
> (3) makes off without having paid . . .
> (4) with intent to avoid payment of the amount due.

9.7.1 PAYMENT ON THE SPOT

This term is partially defined by s 3(2), which provides that:

> For purposes of this section 'payment on the spot' includes payment at the time of collecting goods on which work has been done or in respect of which service has been provided.

The phrase therefore means little more than 'immediate payment' – see further *R v Aziz* [1993] Crim LR 708.

Under s 3(3) there can be no liability where the supply of the goods or the doing of the service is contrary to law, or where the service done is such that payment is not legally enforceable; hence failing to pay a prostitute after sexual intercourse has taken place would not be an offence under s 3 (although it could be an offence under s 1 of the Theft Act 1978). In *Troughton v The Metropolitan Police* [1987] Crim LR 138, a taxi driver agreed to take the appellant to his home somewhere in Highbury. The appellant, having had a great deal to drink, had not told the driver his address. The driver had to stop to obtain directions from the appellant at some point. There was an argument, the appellant accusing the driver of making an unnecessary diversion. The taxi driver, being unable to get an address from the appellant, drove to the nearest police station to see if someone else could help. The court held that the basis for allowing this appeal was that the journey had not been completed and the consequence of that was a breach of contract by the taxi driver. Instead of resolving the argument about further instructions during the journey the driver broke away from the route which would have taken the appellant home and in order to go to the police station. The driver, being in breach of contract, was not lawfully able to demand the fare at any time thereafter. For that reason, among others, the appellant was never in a situation in which he was bound to pay or even tender the money for the journey, and thus it could not be contended that he made off without payment.

9.7.2 MAKING OFF

In most cases, no further explanation of the words 'making off' is necessary. They simply mean that the customer leaves without paying. However, the offence can be committed where the supplier of the goods or services allows the customer to leave as the result of some false representation (although a charge of fraud contrary to s 2 of the Fraud Act 2006 may be more appropriate). Handing over a worthless cheque and then making off could, in principle, be an offence under s 3. However, a charge under s 2 of the 2006 Act would again be more appropriate. 'Making off' normally entails leaving the premises. Thus, if the customer starts to leave but is prevented from doing so, he is guilty only of an attempt to make off. In *R v McDavitt* [1981] Crim LR 843 (Croydon Crown Court), the defendant had a meal with three friends in a restaurant. At the end of the meal his friends left the restaurant and the defendant remained at the table where they had all been sitting. The bill was brought and an argument ensued between the defendant and the owner of the restaurant which ended with the defendant refusing to pay any of the bill. He went towards the door whereupon someone standing by the door advised him not to leave as the police were being called. The defendant then went to the toilet in the restaurant where he remained until the police arrived. The jury was directed that 'makes off' referred to making off from the spot where payment was required or expected. What was the spot depended on the circumstances of each case. In this case the spot was the restaurant.

The jury were directed that it was not open to them to find the defendant guilty of the offence on the indictment but that it was open to them to find him guilty of an attempt to commit the offence.

R v Brooks and Brooks (1982) 76 Cr App R 66 (CA)

The appellants, father and daughter, along with a person named Smith, had a meal together one evening in the upstairs room of a restaurant. At 10.30pm the daughter was seen leaving the premises in haste. The manager went upstairs and saw the two men were not there but found Smith downstairs waiting outside the men's lavatory.

Nearby was a door inside the premises which led into the yard. Smith made no comment when asked about the unpaid bill but, after entering the lavatory, later made off through the outer door. The manager chased after him and asked him to come back. While they were re-entering the restaurant, the father came out of it. All three then went back inside. All the father could offer for payment for the bill of £8.52 was a cheque for £130 in his favour, which later turned out to be valueless. Smith said in the father's hearing that the payment was not due from him, Smith. When the daughter was later interviewed by the police she maintained that Smith had met them earlier that night for the first time and had generously offered to treat her and her father to a meal. Both father and daughter were charged with making off without payment contrary to s 3(1) of the Theft Act 1978.

Kilner Brown J:

. . . In our opinion, the words 'dishonestly makes off' are words easily understandable by any jury which, in the majority of cases, require no elaboration in a summing up. The jury should be told to apply the words in their ordinary natural meaning and to relate them to the facts of the case. We agree with the decision in *R v McDavitt* [1981] Crim LR 843 that 'making off' involves a departure from the spot where payment is required . . .

On the facts of this case, it was not necessary to elaborate on the necessity to establish that there was a departure from the spot. The evidence of this was there. Both went outside the premises. However, in a case where the accused is stopped before passing the spot where payment is required, a jury should be directed that that may constitute an attempt to commit the offence, rather than the substantive offence, provided that the other ingredients are established . . .

In the case of the appellant Julie Brooks, there is a further and different consideration . . .

. . . [T]he jury were never told that upon the evidence that she left earlier and in haste and her defence that she went to the restaurant at the other man's invitation believing that he would pay, they would have to draw the inference that at the time she left she intended dishonestly to evade payment, before she could be convicted. If the jury had been alerted to this necessity, it is quite possible that they may not have been satisfied of her guilt . . .

9.7.3 INTENT TO AVOID PAYMENT

In addition to proving that D made off dishonestly (dishonesty here being based on the *R v Ghosh* direction; see 9.4.5), the prosecution must also prove that the defendant intended to make permanent default; in other words, never to pay for the goods or services supplied. If the defendant is merely trying to postpone payment, then an offence under s 3 is not committed.

R v Allen [1985] AC 1029 (HL)

Lord Hailsham of St Marylebone LC:

. . . Count 2 of the indictment, which resulted in the conviction appealed from, read as follows:

Statement of Offence: Making off without payment, contrary to s 3 of the Theft Act 1978.

Particulars of Offence: Christopher Allen, on a day between 8 and 11 February 1983, knowing that payment on the spot for goods supplied and services done was required or expected from him, dishonestly made off without having paid as required or expected and with intent to avoid payment of the £1,286.94 due.

The facts, which are not disputed . . . were as follows. The respondent, Christopher Allen, booked a room at a hotel for 10 nights from 15 January 1983. He stayed on thereafter and finally left on 11 February 1983 without paying his bill in the sum of £1,286.94. He telephoned two days later to explain that he was in financial difficulties because of some business transactions and arranged to return to the hotel on 18 February 1983 to remove his belongings and leave his Australian passport as security for the debt. He was arrested on his return and said that he genuinely hoped to be able to pay the bill and denied he was acting dishonestly. On 3 March 1983, he was still unable to pay the bill and provided an explanation to the police of his financial difficulties. The respondent's defence was that he had acted honestly and had genuinely expected to pay the bill from the proceeds of various business ventures . . .

The judgment of the Court of Appeal, with which I agree, was delivered by Boreham J. He said [1985] 1 WLR 50, 57:

To secure a conviction under s 3 of the 1978 Act the following must be proved:
(1) that the defendant in fact made off without making payment on the spot;
(2) the following mental elements:
    (a) knowledge that payment on the spot was required or expected of him; and
    (b) dishonesty; and
    (c) intent to avoid payment [that is, 'of the amount due'].

I agree with this analysis. To this the judge adds the following comment:

If (c) means, or is taken to include, no more than an intention to delay or defer payment of the amount due it is difficult to see what it adds to the other elements. Anyone who knows that payment on the spot is expected or required of him and who then dishonestly makes off without paying as required or expected must have at least the intention to delay or defer payment. It follows, therefore, that the conjoined phrase 'and with intent to avoid payment of the amount due' adds a further ingredient – an intention to do more than delay or defer – an intention to evade payment altogether.

My own view, for what it is worth, is that the section thus analysed is capable only of this meaning . . . Even on the assumption that, in the context, the word 'avoid' without the addition of the word 'permanently' is capable of either meaning, which Boreham J was inclined to concede, I find myself convinced by his final paragraph, which reads:

Finally, we can see no reason why, if the intention of Parliament was to provide, in effect, that an intention to delay or defer payment might suffice, Parliament should not have said so in explicit terms. This might have been achieved by the insertion of the word 'such' before 'payment' in the phrase in question. It would have been achieved by a grammatical reconstruction of the material part of s 3(1) thus, 'dishonestly makes off without having paid and with intent to avoid payment of the amount due as required or expected'. To accede to the Crown's submission would be to read the section as if it were constructed in that way. That we cannot do. Had it been intended to relate the intention to avoid 'payment' to 'payment as required or expected' it would have been easy to say so. The section does not say so. At the very least it contains an equivocation which should be resolved in favour of the appellant.

There is really no escape from this argument . . .

Lord Scarman, Lord Diplock, Lord Bridge of Harwich and Lord Brightman all agreed with Lord Hailsham LC.

 COMMENTS AND QUESTIONS

1   No liability arises under s 3 of the 1978 Act if D, by a false representation, persuades P to allow him to leave without paying so that he can return and repay the debt at a later date. Notwithstanding D's deception, P no longer expects payment 'on the spot'; see *R v Vincent* [2001] Crim LR 488. D should, instead, be charged under s 2 of the Fraud Act 2006 – fraud by a false representation, provided the prosecution can prove that D was dishonest at the time of the false representation.

2   Suppose D persuades P, the proprietor of a hotel, to allow him to leave without paying the bill in full (or at all), and D does, at the time of his departure, genuinely intend to return to pay the bill. D is not dishonest and does not commit a deception; hence there can be no liability for any offence under s 2 of the Fraud Act 2006. What if D, on arriving home, resolves not to return to settle the bill? Is this simply a debtor and creditor relationship to be governed by the civil law?

3   Payment by means of a stolen credit card would clearly not be payment as required and expected under s 3. What if D pays by cheque drawn on his own account, supported by a cheque guarantee card, that D has no authority to draw as he has exceeded his overdraft limit?

9.8 TAKING A MOTOR VEHICLE OR OTHER CONVEYANCE WITHOUT AUTHORITY

The Theft Act 1968 creates a specific offence of taking a vehicle without the owner's consent because, in many such cases, a charge of theft would fail due to the inability of the prosecution to establish that the defendant had any intention to permanently deprive the owner of the car. The difficulty arises from the fact that abandoned cars are easily reunited with their owners through the licence plate details held at Driver Vehicle Licensing Centre. Only where the car is modified in some way as to disguise its origins would a charge of theft be more appropriate. Where D sells P's car purporting to be the owner, D can obviously be charged with theft (or attempted theft) or fraud contrary to s 2 of the Fraud Act 2006. Section 12(4) of the 1968 Act provides further that if on the trial of an indictment for theft the jury are not satisfied that D committed theft, but it is proved that he committed the offence of taking a motor vehicle or other conveyance without authority contrary to s 12(1), the jury may find D guilty of taking a motor vehicle or other conveyance without authority.

The elements of the offence under s 12 of the Theft Act 1968 are that the defendant:

(a) takes
(b) a conveyance (as defined in s 12(7)(a))
(c) for his own or another's use
(d) without the owner's consent or
(a) knowing that the conveyance has been taken without the owner's consent
(b) drives it or allows himself to be carried in it.

Section 12 provides:

(1) Subject to subsections (5) and (6) below, a person shall be guilty of an offence if, without having the consent of the owner or other lawful authority, he takes any conveyance for his own or another's use or, knowing that any conveyance has been taken without such authority, drives it or allows himself to be carried in or on it.

. . .

(5) Subsection (1) above shall not apply in relation to pedal cycles; but, subject to subsection (6) below, a person who, without having the consent of the owner or other lawful authority, takes a pedal cycle for his own or another's use, or rides a pedal cycle knowing it to have been taken without such authority, shall on summary conviction be liable to a fine not exceeding [level 3 on the standard scale].

(6) A person does not commit an offence under this section by anything done in the belief that he has lawful authority to do it or that he would have the owner's consent if the owner knew of his doing it and the circumstances of it.

(7) For purposes of this section:

(a) 'conveyance' means any conveyance constructed or adapted for the carriage of a person or persons whether by land, water or air, except that it does not include a conveyance constructed or adapted for use only under the control of a person not carried in or on it, and 'drive' shall be construed accordingly; and

(b) 'owner', in relation to a conveyance which is the subject of a hiring agreement or hire-purchase agreement, means the person in possession of the conveyance under that agreement.

9.8.1 'TAKING'

The word 'taking' requires that the conveyance must be moved, albeit by a small distance. Merely starting the vehicle's engine is not enough (although it may amount to an attempt to commit the full offence).

R v Bogacki and Others [1973] QB 832 (CA)

Roskill LJ:

These three young men, the defendants, Bogacki, Tillwach and Cox, were charged ... with attempting, and I venture to underline the word 'attempting', to take a motor vehicle without authority ...

... The evidence for the Crown was to a large extent undisputed. At about 3.45 am on New Year's Day 1972, these three young men, who had been having a lot to drink at a New Year's Eve party, went to Ponders End bus garage. There they tried to change a 50p piece in order to purchase cigarettes from a machine. They were refused change and told to go away. As they went they boarded a single decker bus which was standing on the forecourt of the garage. One of them turned the engine over with the starter as if to start it. It was common ground that after three or four minutes they left the garage quite openly. They walked to the police station where they were given change for the 50p piece which they had been refused at the bus station. Very shortly thereafter they were arrested. According to the police evidence, Cox first of all denied he had ever boarded the bus. Tillwach made a written statement in which he admitted that he had been on the bus and he alleged that Bogacki had sat in the driving seat and tried to start the engine.

There was no doubt, and [counsel] for the defendants has not sought to contend otherwise, that one of those three young men acting in concert with the others got on board that bus and attempted to start the engine. The bus never moved. Indeed the weight of the evidence was that the engine never started and this court deals with the appeal on that assumption ...

... The word 'take' is an ordinary simple English word ...

... [T]he court accepts [the defendants'] submission that there is still built in, if I may use the phrase, to the word 'takes' in the subsection the concept of movement and that before a man can be convicted of the completed offence under s 12(1) it must be shown that he took the vehicle, that is to say that there was an unauthorised taking possession or control of the vehicle by him adverse to the rights of the true owner or person otherwise entitled to such possession or control, coupled with some movement, however small ... of that vehicle following such unauthorised taking.

Here, had the judge given the jury a correct direction, there was abundant evidence to justify convictions for attempting to take the bus because what was done must on the verdict of the jury clearly be taken to have been an act to which all these men were joint parties, preparatory to putting the bus into motion after an unauthorised taking of possession or control ...

9.8.2 '... FOR HIS OWN OR ANOTHER'S USE ...'

'Use' means use as a conveyance; the defendant's motive is immaterial (*R v Bow* (1976) 64 Cr App R 54). As Bridge LJ observed, once '... a conveyance is taken and moved in a way which necessarily involves its use as a conveyance, the taker cannot be heard to say that the taking was not for that use. If he has in fact taken the conveyance and used it as such ...'.

R v Marchant and McCallister (1984) 80 Cr App R 361 (CA)

Two police officers gave evidence to the effect that they saw the two appellants pushing a car. They said that they saw the two appellants succeeding in moving the car, by pushing it, although moving it only a very short distance, about two or three feet.

The two appellants gave evidence to the effect that they did not know who the car belonged to. They said that they were moving it because it was badly parked and sticking out from the kerb. McCallister, however, also said that he was looking out for a car like that, and that he thought it was abandoned; and Marchant also gave evidence to the effect that McCallister was looking for a car of this kind.

Robert Goff LJ:

. . . [Section 12 of the Theft Act 1968] simply provides that the offence is committed if a person takes a conveyance for his own use, without prior consent or lawful authority. So, to be guilty of the offence, the accused must have both taken the vehicle, i.e. have taken control of it and caused it to be moved, and he must have done so for his own or another's use. The latter requirement has been said to mean 'for his own use or another's as a conveyance': see *R v Bow* (1976) 64 Cr App R 54 at 57, *per* Bridge LJ. Even so, as we see it, if a person takes a vehicle for that use, i.e. to use it as a conveyance, without the consent of the owner or lawful authority, he commits the offence . . . Suppose a man finds a car in the street. He needs a car for a day's expedition. He forms the intent to take the car for that use, though intending to return it later to that place where he found it. He knows he cannot start it then, so he pushes it round the corner to his home with the intention of getting it going for use on his expedition. The police catch up with him and find the car parked in his yard. Has that person committed the offence of taking a conveyance for his own use, without having the necessary consent or authority? In our judgment, he has. He has certainly taken it because he has moved it a certain distance. In my judgment his purpose for taking it is plain. It was for use as a conveyance. So in those circumstances, the offence has been committed.

Director of Public Prosecution v Spriggs [1994] RTR 1 (DC)

Tudor Evans J:

. . . The car had originally been taken from the car park of a company which owned the car during the course of the afternoon or early evening on 23 November 1990. It was taken without the consent of the owner or other lawful authority. The prosecution did not suggest that the defendant took the vehicle from the car park or that he was in any way involved in the original taking.

The case for the prosecution was that, much later on the day of the original taking, he was seen by police officers at the wheel of the car, that it was being driven very slowly in convoy with another vehicle which drove off at the approach of the police car, and that, when the police car stopped the car, the defendant tried to run away and both he and Mr Staff were arrested. The evidence showed that there were obvious signs of damage to the door and the ignition of the car and the defendant was found with a bent screwdriver in his possession.

The account given by him at interview was that Mr Staff had been giving him a lift home in another vehicle when they came across the car in question which they saw had been left blocking the road with the engine running. The defendant's account was that, whilst he accepted that he should never have got into the car and whilst he accepted that he had driven it for about 200 yards, he was simply moving the car preparatory to notifying the police of what he had found. He accepted that he realised that the car had been stolen when he got into it . . .

The question for the opinion of the court is whether a person, not being the person who is responsible for the original and unlawful taking of a vehicle from the place where its lawful owner last left it, is capable in law of committing the offence of taking a conveyance without authority contrary to s 12(1) of the Theft Act 1968 by reason only of a later and separate taking of the same vehicle from some other place . . .

. . . This is a case in which the car was taken and then possession of it was abandoned, as is quite plain on the facts as found. There was then a fresh assumption of possession and taking within the language of the subsection.

In those circumstances, where a vehicle is abandoned, it seems to me that it must inevitably follow that, if there is a subsequent taking which falls within the language of the first part of s 12(1), then the offence is committed. It cannot be that offences under this subsection are limited only to facts where there has been one taking either by a single person or by his acting jointly with another.

Accordingly, I would answer the question which I have already identified with the answer 'Yes' and I would remit the matter to the Crown Court with a direction to convict. It follows that the appeal must be allowed.

9.8.3 '. . . WITHOUT THE OWNER'S CONSENT . . .'

Where the owner is deceived into allowing the defendant to take the conveyance, that consent is not vitiated by the fraud and so no offence is committed under s 12.

Whittaker and Another v Campbell [1984] QB 318 (DC)

The defendants hired a vehicle to collect a consignment of coal. Neither held a full driving licence. The defendants came into possession of a full driving licence belonging to one Derek Dunn. The defendants decided to use the licence to hire a van to remove the coal. One of the defendants, Wilson Coglan Whittaker, represented himself as being Derek Dunn and signed the name 'D Dunn' on the hire agreement form. The defendants repeated this deception in order to hire a van from the hire company on a number of occasions. Mr Robson, the hire company's director, gave evidence that on the occasion of each hire, he was deceived by the defendants into believing that the defendant Wilson Coglan Whittaker was Derek Dunn and that he was the holder of a full driving licence, and had he known that that was not the case the defendant Wilson Coglan Whittaker would not have been allowed to hire any of his (Robson's) vehicles or drive any of his vehicles. The defendants were convicted of an offence under s 12.

Robert Goff LJ:

. . . There being no general principle that fraud vitiates consent, we see the problem simply as this: can a person be said to have taken a conveyance for his own or another's use 'without

consent of the owner or other lawful authority' within those words as used in s 12(1) of
Act 1968, if he induces the owner to part with possession of the conveyance by a
it misrepresentation of the kind employed by the defendants in the present case? . . .

umstances such as those of the present case, the criminality (if any) of the act would
app__ to rest rather in the fact of the deception, inducing the person to part with the possession
of his vehicle, rather than in the fact (if it be the case) that the fraud has the effect of inducing a
mistake as to, for example, 'identity' rather than 'attributes' of the deceiver. It would be very
strange if fraudulent conduct of this kind has only to be punished if it happened to induce a
fundamental mistake; and it would be even more strange if such fraudulent conduct has only to
be punished where the chattel in question happened to be a vehicle. If such fraudulent conduct is
to be the subject of prosecution, the crime should surely be classified as one of obtaining by
deception [see now s 2 Fraud Act 2006], rather than an offence under s 12(1) of the Act of 1968,
which appears to us to be directed to the prohibition and punishment of a different form of
activity . . .

9.8.4 BELIEF IN CONSENT OF OWNER (S 12(6))

No offence is committed if, at the time of the taking (and it must be at the time of the taking
(*R v Ambler* [1979] RTR 217)), the accused genuinely believed that the owner had consented
(or would have consented) to the taking. It is for the prosecution to prove the absence of such a
belief, but before the prosecution have to do so the defence must make out a *prima facie* case
that he held this belief.

R v Gannon (1988) 87 Cr App R 254 (CA)

Kenneth Jones J:
. . . The onus was of course on the prosecution to prove the absence of the belief [that the
defendant had lawful authority to take the car] – *R v MacPherson* [1973] RTR 157. But before that
stage was reached, it was of course for the appellant to raise the issue. That means that he was
required to call evidence or at least be able to point to some evidence which tended to show that
he did hold the belief referred to in s 12(6) . . .

9.8.5 ALLOWING HIMSELF TO BE CARRIED

Again, there must have been some movement of the conveyance and it must be proved that
the accused knew that the conveyance had been taken without the owner's consent (*R v Diggin*
(1980) 72 Cr App R 204).

9.8.6 SECTION 12A OF THE THEFT ACT 1968: AGGRAVATED
VEHICLE-TAKING

This aggravated form of the s 12 offence was introduced specifically to deal with the problem
of high performance cars being taken by 'joyriders' in order to perform stunts or engage in
dangerous racing activities.

For an offence under s 12A to be committed, it must be proved that:

(a) an offence under s 12(1) of the Theft Act 1968 has been committed;

(b) the conveyance must be a 'mechanically propelled vehicle';

(c) one of the following has also occurred:

    (i) the vehicle was driven dangerously;

    (ii) as a result of the driving of the vehicle, injury has been caused to someone;

    (iii) as a result of the driving of the vehicle, property other than the vehicle has been damaged; or

    (iv) the vehicle has been damaged.

Section 12A provides:

(1) Subject to subsection (3) below, a person is guilty of aggravated taking of a vehicle if:

    (a) he commits an offence under s 12(1) above (in this section referred to as a 'basic offence') in relation to a mechanically propelled vehicle; and

    (b) it is proved that, at any time after the vehicle was unlawfully taken (whether by him or another) and before it was recovered, the vehicle was driven, or injury or damage was caused, in one or more of the circumstances set out in paragraphs (a) to (d) of subsection (2) below.

(2) The circumstances referred to in subsection (1)(b) above are:

    (a) that the vehicle was driven dangerously on a road or other public place;

    (b) that, owing to the driving of the vehicle, an accident occurred by which injury was caused to any person;

    (c) that, owing to the driving of the vehicle, an accident occurred by which damage was caused to any property, other than the vehicle;

    (d) that damage was caused to the vehicle.

(3) A person is not guilty of an offence under this section if he proves that, as regards any such proven driving, injury or damage as is referred to in subsection (1)(b) above, either:

    (a) the driving, accident or damage referred to in subsection (2) above occurred before he committed the basic offence; or

    (b) he was neither in nor on nor in the immediate vicinity of the vehicle when that driving, accident or damage occurred.

(4) A person guilty of an offence under this section shall be liable on conviction on indictment to imprisonment for a term not exceeding two years or, if it is proved that, in circumstances falling within subsection (2)(b) above, the accident caused the death of the person concerned, five years.

(5) If a person who is charged with an offence under this section is found not guilty of that offence but it is proved that he committed a basic offence, he may be convicted of the basic offence.

(6) If by virtue of subsection (5) above a person is convicted of a basic offence before the Crown Court, that court shall have the same powers and duties as a magistrates' court would have had on convicting him of such an offence.

(7) For the purposes of this section a vehicle is driven dangerously if:
  (a) it is driven in a way which falls far below what would be expected of a competent and careful driver; and
  (b) it would be obvious to a competent and careful driver that driving the vehicle in that way would be dangerous.

(8) For the purposes of this section a vehicle is recovered when it is restored to its owner or to other lawful possession or custody; and in this subsection 'owner' has the same meaning as in s 12 above.

9.8.7 AGGRAVATING CIRCUMSTANCES FOR S 12A

R v Marsh (1996) 160 JP 721 (DC)

Laws J:

. . . [The appellant had taken a motor car without the consent of the owner.] During the journey, the [passenger] noticed a figure towards the right of the car and it seemed as if it was about to cross towards the footpath on the left. The car continued down. The figure began to run over towards the left-hand side footpath and, unfortunately, it transpired that it was a lady who was running across the road. She was knocked to the ground. The appellant . . . stopped to help her. She was not, it seems, seriously injured . . .

It is right that we should note that the [passenger] was to state that throughout the journey the appellant drove at around the 30 mph mark and that, had the pedestrian remained to the right of the car, there would have been no accident. There was, therefore, no evidence of fault in the manner in which the car was driven; certainly, the Crown relied on none . . .

His Lordship quoted from s 12A(1), (2) of the Theft Act 1968 and went on:

The assertion made in the Crown Court by the defendant was that no liability could attach to him under s 12A(2)(b) unless it were proved that the accident in question had been occasioned by culpable driving on his part . . .

. . . [I]t is unhelpful, in our judgment, to gloss the statute by referring to the manner or mode of driving: the words are plain and simple. In our view, the question for the court on their proper construction is, was the driving of the vehicle a cause of an accident? Any other approach would require the court to read in words which are not there.

The learned recorder, in our view, was right to hold that the policy of this statute is to impose heavier sanctions on those who take vehicles unlawfully and then cause an accident, whether or not the accident involves any fault in the driving.

Dealing with the statutory words more distinctly, it is to be noted that there is a clear contrast between the words of s 12A(2)(a) that 'the vehicle was driven dangerously on a road' and those in (b) and (c), where the phrase is only 'owing to the driving of the vehicle'. Of course (d), the subparagraph contemplating that damage is caused to the vehicle, has nothing to say about fault at all . . .

... Applying ordinary canons of statutory construction, it is impossible to say that the words of s 12A(2)(b) import a requirement of fault in the driving of the vehicle. No word suggesting fault appears in the statutory language. It seems to us that the ordinary meaning of the words used is simply to point to a requirement that there be a causal connection between the moving of the vehicle on the road and an accident which follows . . .

FURTHER READING

Cooper, S and MJ Allen, 'Appropriation after *Gomez*' [1993] J Crim Law 186

Gardner, S, 'Appropriation in theft: the last word?' (1993) 109 LQR 194

Gardner, S, 'Property and theft' [1998] Crim LR 35

Griew, E, 'Dishonesty: the objections to *Feely* and *Ghosh*' [1985] Crim LR 341

Halpin, A, 'The test for dishonesty' [1996] Crim LR 283

Hickey, R, 'Stealing Abandoned Goods: Possessory Title in Proceedings for Theft' (2006) 26 Legal Studies 584

Puttick, K and M Molan, 'Benefits and the criminal law: "fraud" and the new parameters of welfare crime' (2007) 7 Welfare Benefits 10

Smith, JC, 'Stealing tickets' [1998] Crim LR 723

THE FRAUD ACT 2006

10.1 INTRODUCTION

The Fraud Act 2006 came into force in Janaury 2007. The Act has the effect of completely replacing the deception-based offences previously found in the Theft Acts 1968 and 1978, and the Theft (Amendment) Act 1996.

To summarise, the deception offences under the Theft Acts 1968 and 1978 were:

- s 15 Theft Act 1968 – obtaining property by deception;
- s 15(A) & (B) Theft Act 1968 – obtaining a money transfer by deception (introduced by the Theft (Amendment) Act 1996);
- s 16 Theft Act 1968 – obtaining a pecuniary advantage by deception;
- s 1 Theft Act 1978 – obtaining services by deception;
- s 2 Theft Act 1978 – evasion of a liability by deception.

In 2002 the Law Commission published its Report on the operation of fraud offences (Law Com 276). This Report broadly recommended that the various deception-based offences should be replaced with a general offence of fraud that could be committed in a variety of ways. The Report was followed by a Home Office Consultation Paper *(Fraud Law Reform-Consultations on proposals for legislation)* in 2004. The Home Office subsequently published its response to the consultation exercise and the Fraud Bill was introduced into the House of Lords in 2005. The Fraud Act 2006 eventually received the Royal Assent on 8th November 2006.

The changes in the law can be summarised thus:

Theft Act offences	Replacement provision under the Fraud Act 2006
s 15 Theft Act 1968	Fraud by one of the following means:
s 15(A) and (B) Theft Act 1968	s 2 Fraud Act 2006 – fraud by false representation;
s 16 Theft Act 1968	s 3 Fraud Act 2006 – fraud by failing to disclose information;
s 2 Theft Act 1978	s 4 Fraud Act 2006 – fraud by abuse of position;
s 1 Theft Act 1978	s 11 Fraud Act 2006 – obtaining services by deception.

10.2 WHY WAS IT NECESSARY TO REPLACE DECEPTION OFFENCES WITH FRAUD OFFENCES?

Annexe B to the Home Office response to consultations on the proposals for the reform of the law relating to fraud provides a useful summary of why reform was deemed to be necessary.

Annex B – Problems With The Existing Law Of Fraud

1. The main problems with the existing law of fraud are detailed below in an analysis that draws on that made by the Law Commission in Part III of their 2002 report.

Range of separate offences

2. Problems have arisen because the existing statutory offences in the Theft Acts are too specific and overlapping. These offences include:

(1) theft, defined as the dishonest appropriation of property belonging to another with the intention of permanently depriving the other of it; and

(2) eight offences of deception, committed by a person who dishonestly and by deception
- obtains property belonging to another
- obtains a money transfer
- obtains services
- secures the remission of an existing liability to make a payment
- induces a creditor to wait for payment or to forgo payment with intent to permanently default on the debt
- obtains an exemption from or abatement of liability to make a payment
- obtains a pecuniary advantage
- procures the execution of a valuable security.

3. This multitude of different, over-particularised deception offences leads to a position where a defendant could face the wrong charge, or too many charges. For example, in *Duru* [1974] 1 WLR 2 the deception resulted in a bank making out a cheque in the defendant's favour. He was charged with obtaining property by deception, when the correct charge was procuring the execution of a valuable security. Where the "belt and braces" approach is taken to charging, the indictments may become overly complex and result in excessively lengthy trials.

4. Having a range of particularised offences also makes it very difficult to charge a defendant with an attempted offence when the deception does not result in money being paid over to him. Where a defendant unsuccessfully makes a false representation to obtain money from another person but is indifferent as to how the money is to be paid (by cash, money transfer or cheque for example), it is unclear which offence under the Theft Act 1968 he has attempted – section 15, section 15A or section 20.

5. The range of specific fraud offences, defined with reference to different types of consequence, also leaves the law vulnerable to technical assaults. This was evidenced in *Preddy* [1996] AC 815 where the defendants made false representations when applying for mortgages and were charged with obtaining property by deception. The House of Lords held that the credit balances in the defendants' accounts were choses in action which had never belonged to the lender but were entirely new property. Consequently, there was no appropriation of property 'belonging to another'. Although section 15A of the 1968 Act was enacted to deal with this particular loophole, other similarly technical problems have arisen and may continue to arise as a result of the specificity of the deception offences. The changing nature of technology is almost certain to continue to outgrow the context-specific offences in the Theft Acts. For example there is a lack in clarity in the law as to whether or not the *Preddy* problem arises in the financial markets, such as with Eurobonds or any system where title to securities or shares is held in a pool by a broker or a clearing system and not by individuals. While this lack of clarity can be overcome by the ability to charge conspiracy to defraud that charge is not universally available as it depends on there being more than one person involved.

6. That is why fraud needs to be dealt with in a more general offence that targets the nature of fraudulent behaviour, rather than particular instances of such behaviour in a set of defined circumstances. The *Preddy* difficulty also suggests that fraud should cover situations where there is loss to a victim, whether or not the defendant or anyone else obtains (or appropriates) what the victim has lost.

Cases where there is no deception
7. Many of the Theft Act offences require deception. To say that a defendant has deceived another implies that the other person believed in the truth of the defendant's false representation. As a result of this there is a loophole in the current law in that no offence can be charged for providing false information to a machine in order to gain services, as it is impossible to 'deceive' anything but a human mind. Therefore it is not an offence for example to buy insurance online by providing false credit card details.

8. Second, sometimes a person will act on a defendant's false representation without considering whether or not it is true (or indeed caring). This argument has arisen in relation to credit cards, debit cards and cheque guarantee cards which the defendant was using without authority (either because it was stolen or the transaction exceeded his credit limit). In these circumstances, the merchant will be paid for the goods or services he provides by the card issuer in

any event. The House of Lords has held in *Charles* [1997] AC177 and *Lambie* [1982] AC 449 that the cardholder does commit the offence of obtaining goods or services 'by deception' in such cases. It held that an implied representation is made by the defendant in handing over the card that he has authority to use it; and even if the merchant did not address his mind to whether the cardholder had such authority, it can be assumed that he would not have accepted the card if he had known it was tendered without authority and this is sufficient to make out 'deception'. This reasoning is widely thought to be artificial, and can lead to acquittals if, for example, the merchant gave differing evidence to that presupposed by this reasoning in cross-examination.

9. The problem arises because the concept of deception focuses on the operative effect of the representation on the victim's mind. In various cases where a person would have acted in the way they did regardless of the false representation (for example where a bank manager signs whatever is put in front of him), an inference therefore has to be posited that the false statement was the operative inducement. This is unsatisfactory.

10. It has been suggested that there are examples where persons within an organisation can make dishonest gains through use of normal business procedures without committing any obvious deception. An example is where excessive and unauthorised advances were made to the directors of a bank which lead to its liquidation, to the detriment of its depositors and investors. A further example is where unit trust managers issued personal instructions to brokers to acquire shares in order to sell them on to the fund at a higher price.

Services
11. There is a further gap in respect of services provided where the provider does not expect to be paid, but does expect a future financial gain either for himself or another. This gap was exposed in the case of *Halai* [1983] Crim LR 624, where the defendant had opened a building society account with a bad cheque but was acquitted of the section 1 offence because the building society did not charge for the opening of an account. The building society did however expect to receive a future financial benefit from the opening of the account.

Intention to permanently deprive
12. The offence of obtaining property by deception does not cover victims who are temporarily deprived of their property. However, such deprivation can often be damaging. A person may replace the property, at their own cost, in the period before it is returned or the item may have lost its value by the time it is returned. In the case of *Scott* [1975] AC 819, the defendant temporarily obtained copies of films from projectionists in order to make pirate copies. This could have been charged as theft were it not for the requirement of the intention to permanently deprive.

13. It is also odd that where money is concerned in a case of obtaining property by deception, even if the defendant intends to repay the victim, he is very unlikely to be returning the same banknotes he took and so intention to permanently deprive is made out. (Of course, the intention to repay would go to the issue of dishonesty, so would be relevant but the situation is still odd.)

Abuse of position of trust
14. In *Tarling* (1978) 70 Cr App R 77, the House of Lords held that the company directors' failure to disclose a secret profit made in breach of fiduciary duty, even if dishonest, did not amount to conspiracy to defraud. However, in *Adams*, [1995] 1 WLR 52, the Privy Council held that a

company director had been rightly convicted for conspiracy to defraud by dishonestly making a secret profit. The distinction seems to be that in *Adams* the defendant not only failed to disclose the transactions constituting the abuse of position, but also took positive steps to conceal them. This leaves a gap in cases where the defendant abuses his position but takes no steps to conceal it (perhaps because there is no need to). Where the benefit is obtained by an abuse of trust and the victim remains in ignorance of the loss until after the event, the benefit is not obtained by deception so no statutory offence is available, and conspiracy to defraud is only available where the defendant is acting in agreement with others and they took steps to deliberately conceal their actions.

15. In the Attorney General's Reference No. 1 of 1985 it was held that there could be no theft of a secret profit made by an employee at his employer's expense because it was not property belonging to another. If the employee had taken specific steps to conceal his side-line from his employers and if he had conspired with another, conspiracy to defraud would have been available.

Deception which causes a loss and a gain which do not correspond
16. This can occur where there is fraudulent business practice. An example would be where a person starts a false rumour as a result of which his business rival's profits suffer. Although the defendant is motivated by a desire to make money at the victim's expense, the loss and gain will not relate to the same property and will not even be of corresponding value. A more sophisticated example is the Guinness fraud where Guinness plc and Argyll Group plc were competing to take over Distillers Company plc. Both made offers partly based on their own share price and the Guinness directors entered into a fraudulent share support scheme to make their offer appear more valuable. The victims included Argyll, Distillers, their shareholders, those who bought Guinness shares at falsely inflated prices, and other indirect losers for example other companies who would have received more investment without the false enthusiasm for Guinness shares. The existing deception offences could not reflect the way the gains and losses were caused. Conspiracy to defraud could have done (but could not be charged at that time for technical reasons that no longer apply).

Deception which only prejudices another's financial interests
17. The case of *Wai Yu-Tsang* [1992] 1 AC 269 involved an agreement to conceal a bank's losses or liabilities from its shareholders, creditors and depositors. This put their economic interests at substantial risk even though it was not done for the defendants' gain or to cause loss. Putting economic interests at risk without causing actual loss is not sufficient for a deception offence. It is covered by conspiracy to defraud, provided more than one person is involved. *Scott* (1975) 2 AER 162 defined conspiracy to defraud as 'an agreement by two or more by dishonesty to deprive a person of something which is his, or to which he is or might be entitled and an agreement by two or more, by dishonesty, to injure some proprietary right of his'.

10.3 SECTION 2 OF THE FRAUD ACT 2006 – FRAUD BY FALSE REPRESENTATION

Section 2 of the Fraud Act 2006 provides that:

> (1) A person is in breach of this section if he–
>   (a) dishonestly makes a false representation, and
>   (b) intends, by making the representation–
>   (i) to make a gain for himself or another, or
>   (ii) to cause loss to another or to expose another to a risk of loss.

The striking difference between the offence under s 2 and those that it effectively replaces (obtaining property by deception and obtaining a pecuniary advantage by deception under the Theft Act 1968), is that D can incur liability without actually obtaining any tangible or intangible benefit. It is sufficient that the representation is made with the necessary intent, akin to the making of a demand with menaces in the offence of blackmail (see further Chapter 11.2).

For example in *R v Jackson* [1983] Crim LR 617, D used a stolen credit card as the means of paying for petrol at a petrol station. He was convicted under s 2(1)(a) of the Theft Act 1978 on the basis that he had, by deception, secured the remission of his liability to pay for the pertrol. This was always a somewhat dubious basis for liability as it depended on proof that D had wiped out his liability to pay for the petrol on the basis of his use of a stolen credit card. Under the Fraud Act 2006 the use of the card would be the false pretences, and the intention to cause another loss would, presumably, be satisfied by evidence that the credit card company would bear the cost of the fraud. Similarly in *R v Holt and Another* [1981] 1 WLR 1000 (another s 2 Theft Act 1978 offence), where the defendants induced a waiter to forgo payment for a meal by dishonestly telling him that they had already paid one of his colleagues. Under s 2 of the Fraud Act 2006, the statement would be the false pretences and the intention to cause loss to another would be made out by evidence that the plan was to leave without paying the restaurant for the meal.

10.3.1 SECTION 2 OF THE FRAUD ACT 2006 – ELEMENTS OF THE OFFENCE – *ACTUS REUS*

* Representation
* Made by D
* Representation is false

Under s 2(3) a 'representation' means any representation as to fact or law, including a representation as to the state of mind of the person making the representation, or any other person. The representation may be express or implied. There is no need to prove that the representation is operative (i.e. that the victim believes D's representations).

Under s 2(5) a representation may be regarded as made if it (or anything implying it) is submitted in any form to any system or device designed to receive, convey or respond to communications (with or without human intervention). This provision has the effect of extending fraud offences to human interaction with machines and computers. Deception offences under the Theft Acts 1968 and 1978 required proof that the deception had operated on a human mind; see *Davies* v *Flackett* (1972) 116 Sol Jo 526.

By virtue of s 2(2) a representation is false if it is untrue or misleading, and the person making it knows that it is, or might be, untrue or misleading.

The definition of representation is similar to the s 15(4) Theft Act 1968 definition of deception. The s 2 offence under the 2006 Act is broad enough to encompass activity such as that in *DPP* v *Ray* [1974] AC 370, where D ate a meal at a restaurant and then decided to leave without paying. In order to make good his escape he waited until the waiters were otherwise engaged. The House of Lords held that by sitting at the table at the end of the meal appearing to be a diner who was going to pay for his meal, D had exercised a deception that had induced the waiters to give him the opportunity to run out without paying. It is submitted that this type of implied representation could come within the scope of false pretences under s 2 of the Fraud Act 2006 – the intention to cause loss to another is self-evident.

More problematic may be the distinction between fact and opinion. If D provides a quotation for work to be carried out that is substantially above the market rate is he making a false representation? In one sense he is honestly indicating how much he wants to charge. Looked at another way, however, it could be argued that he is representing the charge as typical of the market rate. Where there is a relationship of trust between the parties the evidence to support the latter conclusion will be more powerful, especially if P has always relied upon D to be fair in this respect.

R v Silverman (1988) 86 Cr App R 213

Over a period of 15 years D, who worked for a firm of plumbers, had carried out jobs for the two sisters who lived together. They had come to rely on D and trusted his advice as to work that needed doing. D advised the sisters that their house needed a new boiler and rewiring. The evidence was that the work was required, but the price demanded by D was well in excess of market rates. D was convicted of obtaining services by deception contrary to s 15(1) of the Theft Act 1968 and appealed successfully because the judge had failed to deal adequately with the defence case when summing-up to the jury. One of the issues dealt with by the Court of Appeal, however, was whether or not there was evidence of a deception.

> Watkins LJ:
> It seems to us that the complainants [i.e. the sisters], far from being worldly wise, were unquestionably gullible . . . they relied implicitly upon the word of the appellant about their requirements in their maisonette. In such circumstances of mutual trust, one party depending upon the other for fair and reasonable conduct, the criminal law may apply if one party takes dishonest advantage of the other by representing as a fair charge that which he but not the other knows is dishonestly excessive . . .
>
> . . . There was material for a finding that there had been a false representation although it is true that the appellant had said nothing at the time he made his representations to encourage the

sisters to accept the quotations. He applied no pressure upon them, and apart from mentioning the actual prices to be charged was silent as to the other matters that may have arisen for question in their minds . . . the situation had been built up over a long period of time. It was a situation of mutual trust and the appellant's silence on any matter other than the sums charged were, we think, as eloquent as if he had said: 'What is more, I can say to you that we are going to get no more than a modest profit out of this' . . .

Home Office Consultation Paper *Fraud Law Reform (2004)*

13. False representation (or fraudulent misrepresentation) is a well-established concept in law. It consists of the assertion of a proposition which is wrong or misleading. The person making this assertion must know that it is wrong or misleading, or be aware that it might be. This proposition can be clearly stated, implied in written or spoken word, or in non-verbal conduct. The proposition may be one of fact or law. It may be as to the current intentions or other state of mind of the defendant or any other person.

14. There are distinct similarities between fraud by false representation and deception. Both involve behaviour that is carried out dishonestly and causes a financial loss, and obviously constitute one of the ways that fraud can be committed. However, in certain examples of this offence, false representation is a more appropriate description than deception.

15. The . . . concept of deception [under the Theft Acts] implies that the victim believes the truth of the assertion made by the defendant. However in cases where a false representation is made to a shop assistant (for example by using a credit card or debit card without authorisation), it is not always the case that the person accepting the payment needs to believe the truth of the representation. By using the [credit] card [without authority], the defendant is falsely representing that he has the authority to use the card for that transaction. But the shop assistant who accepts the card for payment is not necessarily interested in whether the defendant has authority to use it – he may only be concerned that the payment is cleared. Therefore we cannot say that he has actually been deceived if the defendant has no authority. False representation would be a more accurate way to describe this form of conduct: the customer who offers the card is implying that he has the authority to use it.

Note that there is nothing in s 2 of the Fraud Act 2006 to suggest that the false pretences must be exercised upon the person to whom D intends to cause loss. In this respect the operation of s 2 follows s 15 of the Theft Act 1968; see *Metropolitan Police Commissioner v Charles* [1977] AC 177.

10.3.2 SECTION 2 OF THE FRAUD ACT 2006 – ELEMENTS OF THE OFFENCE – *MENS REA* – DISHONESTY

- Dishonesty
- Intention to make a gain for himself or another, or to cause loss to another or to expose another to a risk of loss
- Knowledge that a representation is or might be untrue or misleading

In making the false representation it must be proved that D acted dishonestly. There is no definition of dishonesty under the Fraud Act 2006, hence it should be assumed that the common law approach exemplified in *R v Ghosh* [1982] QB 1053 (extracted in Chapter 9.5.5) still applies.

The jury will be asked to consider whether D's actions were dishonest according to the standards of ordinary decent people. If they are found to be dishonest on that basis, the jury will then have to consider whether or not D realised that ordinary decent people would have regarded his actions as dishonest.

10.3.3 SECTION 2 OF THE FRAUD ACT 2006 – ELEMENTS OF THE OFFENCE – *MENS REA* – INTENTION TO MAKE A GAIN ETC

The requirement that the prosecution must prove that D dishonestly made the false representation with a view to gain for himself or another, or with intent to cause loss to another or to expose another to a risk of loss, is similar to the requirement in the offence of blackmail (Theft Act 1968 s 21 and s 34(2)(a) – see Chapter 11.2), that D must be shown to have made a menacing demand with a view to gain or causing loss to another.

For the purposes of the Fraud Act 2006, the terms 'gain' and 'loss' are further defined by s 5, which provides:

> 5 'Gain' and 'loss'
>
> (1) The references to gain and loss in sections 2 to 4 are to be read in accordance with this section.
> (2) 'Gain' and 'loss'–
>   (a) extend only to gain or loss in money or other property;
>   (b) include any such gain or loss whether temporary or permanent;
>   and 'property' means any property whether real or personal (including things in action and other intangible property).
> (3) 'Gain' includes a gain by keeping what one has, as well as a gain by getting what one does not have.
> (4) 'Loss' includes a loss by not getting what one might get, as well as a loss by parting with what one has.

Note that an intention to expose another person to the risk of loss would bring within the scope of the s 2 offence activities such as D making unauthorised use of his own cheque book and cheque guarantee card, or credit card, provided there is evidence that he did not know how the expenditure was to be financed and that he was dishonest; see as examples under the Theft Act 1968, *MPC v Charles* [1977] AC 177, and *R v Lambie* [1981] Crim LR 712.

Government Response to Consultations on Fraud Law Reform (2005)

30. Most respondents agreed that the definitions of 'gain', 'loss' and 'property' should be aligned with those used in the law of theft and accepted that the current definitions were tried and tested and had not given rise to problems . . .

31. Several respondents suggested that the definition of property should be expanded to include confidential financial data. We do not think any such change is appropriate or necessary, as simply by accessing confidential information, the offender will usually 'intend to make a gain' – albeit an economic gain from wrongful exploitation of the material, rather than a gain of the material itself. As long as that is his intention he is caught by the new offence. If he does not have that intention then fraud is arguably not the appropriate concept anyway. The Bill covers cases where, for example, an employee makes a gain by obtaining information by fraudulent means – for example, by abusing his position of trust. The new offence of being equipped to commit fraud also helps in this context: it will ensure that the possession of confidential financial information with the intent of committing fraud is a crime. In our view that strikes at the mischief, in a more practical way.

32. It was suggested that, as in the Theft Act, the term 'property' should be defined as including intangible property. We agree. That will ensure that intangible things that can be property – notably intellectual property – are covered. However, an essential problem will remain in that it is unusual for intellectual property to be 'gained' or 'lost' when someone misuses it. Normally the mischief lies in unauthorised duplication or use. But if a person abuses his position or makes a false representation in order to interfere (in some way) with intellectual property, or to access confidential information, a person will usually be aiming at an economic gain and so will be caught by the general fraud offence anyway.

10.3.4 SECTION 2 OF THE FRAUD ACT 2006 – ELEMENTS OF THE OFFENCE – *MENS REA* – KNOWLEDGE THAT A REPRESENTATION IS OR MIGHT BE UNTRUE OR MISLEADING

Proving beyond all reasonable doubt that D knew his representation to be untrue or misleading will, in many cases, present an insurmountable obstacle to the prosecution – hence the alternative here that it is sufficient to prove that D knew the representation might be untrue. This is akin to establishing liability on proof of recklessness, but as the following extract indicates, it was decided not to expressly include that as the fault element.

Home Office Consultation Paper *Fraud Law Reform* (2004)

16. For a representation to be false, the Law Commission propose that the defendant should know that the representation is untrue or misleading or be 'aware that it might be'. While this phrase may be unusual in criminal law, we believe that it fits the policy need: it can be difficult to prove that a fraudster knows in advance that his claims for any particular scheme (e.g. a 'High Yield Investment') are untrue, whilst it should be possible to show that he was 'aware that' his prospectus 'might' be untrue, by – for example – providing evidence of previous failures.

17. An alternative approach is provided by section 15(4) of the Theft Act 1968, which provides that a deception must be 'deliberate or reckless'. Recklessness is a concept well recognised and accepted in criminal law. (Clearly this would be so-called *Cunningham* recklessness, where the defendant must foresee a risk and unreasonably go on to take that risk.) However, the addition of a 'recklessness' criterion might prove troublesome. The Law Commission argued in their report that it was preferable to avoid the use of 'reckless' as it is 'somewhat problematic', in view of the different meanings it can have.

Government Reponse to Consultations on Fraud Law Reform (2005)

14. The main controversy concerned the proposal that this offence will be committed not only when the defendant knows that his representation is false or misleading, but when he is 'aware that it might be'. The phrase is precedented, for example in section 6 of the Public Order Act 1986, where one of the conditions for several offences (e.g. riot and violent disorder) is that the person is 'aware that his conduct may be' harmful in one way or another (e.g. violent). However some respondents thought the phrase is too vague and potentially too wide.

. . .

16. We therefore concentrated on the suggestions for replacement which were based on a subjective test. There were 2 main proposals:

- *Cunningham* recklessness
- 'Knowing' (that it might be)

Several respondents were specifically opposed to the use of 'reckless' in view of the problems this term has posed in the past. Those who favoured it said it is well precedented (e.g. in section 15 of the Theft Act 1968) and argued that its meaning is now clearer, following the House of Lords decision in *R v G* . . . However many law enforcers think that an offender could make a false representation without being 'reckless' at any point. In practice subjective (*Cunningham*) reck-lessness is akin to awareness, but it was pointed out to us that there is a difference in that the former includes not only awareness of the risk, but the additional test that it was unreasonable of the offender to take the risk in all the circumstances known to him. It is therefore a slightly tighter and more complex test.

17. 'Knowing' was proposed as the most straightforward alternative to 'aware'. 'Know' is one of the dictionary meanings of 'aware' and vice versa. There is therefore little if any difference between the two, but 'know' is better precedented and less likely to give rise to technical argu-ments. We therefore decided to replace 'is aware that it might be' with 'knows that it might be'. The essential point is that an offence should be committed not only where the offender knows that he is making a representation that is false or misleading, but where he knows that it might be false or misleading.

18. There was a view from a few respondents that it would be going too far to provide that an offence is committed when the defendant knows his representation 'might be' misleading. An example was given of a seller of a Renoir painting which turns out to be incorrectly attributed. It was argued that, given the inevitable uncertainties in such areas, the seller would only be able to protect himself from a fraud charge if he had said 'I honestly believe this to be a Renoir' rather

than 'This is a painting by Renoir'. We do not agree as the 'dishonesty' requirement will assist in drawing the line in marginal cases. But if the consequence were that sellers became more cautious in their statements this does not seem an undesirable result.

19. The question of the meaning of 'misleading' was raised. It was suggested that it means less than wholly true and capable of an interpretation to the detriment of the victim. We would agree with that.

20. Cases of negligent misrepresentation were also raised: one example was where a person hires a car for a fixed period but fails to return it at the end of that time. It was argued that although this may be technically an offence, prosecutors are likely to advise at present that this is a matter for the parties to resolve in the civil courts. We think that the Bill does not change this practical position.

10.4 SECTION 3 OF THE FRAUD ACT 2006 – FRAUD BY FAILING TO DISCLOSE INFORMATION

Section 3 of the Fraud Act 2006 creates the offence of fraud by failing to disclose information. Under s 3 a person is in breach of this section if he:

(a) dishonestly fails to disclose to another person information which he is under a legal duty to disclose, and
(b) intends, by failing to disclose the information–
    (i) to make a gain for himself or another, or
    (ii) to cause loss to another or to expose another to a risk of loss.

Hence the elements of the offence are:

Actus reus
- Failure to disclose (to another person)
- Information (not defined for the purposes of s 3)
- Existence of a legal duty to disclose

Mens rea
- Intention to make a gain or cause a loss – see 10.3.3 (above)
- Dishonesty – see 10.3.2 (above)

10.4.1 SECTION 3 OF THE FRAUD ACT 2006 – ELEMENTS OF THE OFFENCE – *ACTUS REUS* – DUTY TO DISCLOSE

Under s 3 no liability can arise unless D is under a legal obligation to disclose the information in question. It was originally envisaged that the offence would extend to situations where

D was in a relationship of trust with P and a reasonable person would have expected D to have disclosed the information to P, but these provisions were subsequently dropped following consultation. The main objection was that criminal liability should not be based on the somewhat uncertain concept of trust and reliance between parties, but it was also noted that an offence based on the existence of a moral duty to disclose could conflict with the doctrine of *caveat emptor*. The purchaser of a second-hand car should be expected to make his own investigations into the soundness of the vehicle, rather than relying on the vendor to disclose all. Regarding the need for an offence of fraud by omission, the Home Office Consultation Paper *Fraud Law Reform (2004)* observed:

> 18. Fraudulent conduct can arise as a result of positive steps being taken to create a false impression. However, a false impression can also be created by the failure to challenge or dispute such an impression arising naturally, or through failure to reveal information. Non-disclosure can constitute deception, particularly where there is a legal duty to disclose.
>
> 19. In their 1999 Consultation Paper, the Law Commission suggested that omission should not be enough to constitute deception. It was argued against this that, from the victim's point of view, a failure to reveal facts could have the same essential effect as deception by conduct. The Law Commission accordingly redefined their position to state that the concept of fraud should be wide enough to include cases of dishonest non-disclosure and we agree with this view.

Further, in its Report on Fraud, the Law Commission observed that:

> 7.28 .. Such a [legal] duty may derive from statute (such as the provisions governing company prospectuses), from the fact that the transaction in question is one of the utmost good faith (such as a contract of insurance), from the express or implied terms of a contract, from the custom of a particular trade or market, or from the existence of a fiduciary relationship between the parties (such as that of agent and principal).
>
> 7.29 For this purpose there is a legal duty to disclose information not only if the defendant's failure to disclose it gives the victim a cause of action for damages, but also if the law gives the victim a right to set aside any change in his or her legal position to which he or she may consent as a result of the non-disclosure. For example, a person in a fiduciary position has a duty to disclose material information when entering into a contract with his or her beneficiary, in the sense that a failure to make such disclosure will entitle the beneficiary to rescind the contract and to reclaim any property transferred under it.

A potential query remains in respect of the s 3 offence as to whether or not any contractual duty will suffice in order to satisfy the requirement of 'legal duty'. Consider *R v Rai* [2000] 1 Cr App R 242. D was convicted of obtaining services by deception contrary to s 1(1) of the Theft Act 1978. He had applied successfully to Birmingham City Council for a grant towards providing a downstairs bathroom at his room for the use of his elderly and infirm mother. Two days after the grant was awarded D's mother died, but he failed to inform the council and the building work was duly carried out. The Court of Appeal, upholding the conviction, held that there was conduct capable of amounting to deception (D's continuing implied representation that the work was required for his mother) but the question remains, was he under an (implied) duty stemming from the agreement with the council to inform them that the work was no longer required.

In *R v Firth* (1990) 91 Cr App R 217, by contrast, D was under a contractual duty to inform the NHS if he had private patients being treated in an NHS hospital and his failure to do so was relied upon as the basis of his deception. Such a case could now be prosecuted under s 3 of the Fraud Act 2006.

10.5 SECTION 4 OF THE FRAUD ACT 2006 – FRAUD BY ABUSE OF POSITION

Section 4 of the Fraud Act 2006 introduces an offence based on D's abuse of a position of trust or privilege in circumstances where he was expected to safeguard the financial interests of another party. Liability could arise, for example, where an estate agent dishonestly induces a client to sell a property at an undervalue, or where D, an employee, enters into a contract on behalf of his employer to buy goods at an inflated price from X with a view to receiving some financial inducement from X.

The elements of the offence are:

Actus reus
- D occupies a position of trust
- D is expected to safeguard, or not to act against, the financial interests of another person
- D abuses his position of trust

Mens rea
- D's abuse of position is dishonest
- D abuses the position of trust with an intent to make a gain for himself or another, or to cause loss to another or to expose another to a risk of loss

Section 4 provides:

(1) A person is in breach of this section if he –
    (a) occupies a position in which he is expected to safeguard, or not to act against, the financial interests of another person,
    (b) dishonestly abuses that position, and
    (c) intends, by means of the abuse of that position –
        (i)   to make a gain for himself or another, or
        (ii) to cause loss to another or to expose another to a risk of loss.
(2) A person may be regarded as having abused his position even though his conduct consisted of an omission rather than an act.

On the need for this offence, note the following from the Home Office Consultation Paper *Fraud Law Reform (2004)*:

> 23. Some types of behaviour amount to fraud as they are essentially an abuse of an existing position of trust. The necessary situation for an offence of this type to take place is where the victim has put the perpetrator into a privileged position where he would be expected to safeguard the victim's interests (for example he has been given access to the victim's premises, equipment, records or customers). The defendant does not need to induce the victim to any further action (either by misrepresentation or non-disclosure) because his co-operation has already been secured.
>
> 24. The type of relationships that may give rise to this situation are those between employer and employee, trustee and beneficiary, director and company, professional person and client, agent and principal, and between 2 partners. This type of offence is also possible within family relationships or the context of voluntary work. In almost all cases the relationship will involve fiduciary duties, however these duties are not essential to the commission of the offence. The judge will be able to rule, or give directions to the jury, as to whether an appropriate relationship existed between victim and defendant.
>
> 25. An example of this type of fraudulent conduct is where a bar manager uses the premises of the establishment where he works to sell barrels of his own beer, rather than the beer belonging to the landlord. Abuse of position can also be committed by omission. An example given by the Law Commission is that of an employee who fails to take up the opportunity of a crucial contract, in order that an associate of his can take it up instead (to the detriment of the employer).

Note that as originally proposed by the Law Commission the offence would have required proof that there was an element of secrecy involved, i.e. that P was unaware of what D was doing, but this element was dropped following consultation.

Reviewing responses generally to the proposals for this offence, the Government Reponse to Consultations on Fraud Law Reform (2005) observed:

> 26. There was general support for [what is now s 4 Fraud Act 2006] . . . which recognised that this type of behaviour is not well addressed by the existing law, as there may be cases where no deception is involved, or is at least difficult to prove. Examples were given of frauds by local and central government officials, internal banking frauds, the financial abuse of the elderly and Probate fraud, some of which was committed via Enduring Powers of Attorney. (It is however worth noting that in most cases where public officials are concerned the common law crime of misconduct in a public office should be available.)
>
> 27. A minority opposed [the introduction of the offence] on the grounds that it was too wide, with insufficient definition of crucial points – notably the relationships covered and the meaning of 'abuse' – and that it would bring to the police many complaints which are currently dealt with under civil law, for example by suing for beach of contract or by dismissal for gross misconduct. One respondent said they were strongly opposed to criminalising people simply as a result of the

breakdown of everyday commercial and fiduciary relationships. We think however that while 'simple' breakdown of relationships could lead to allegations of 'abuse' of position, the offence will only be committed if the defendant is dishonest and seeks to make a gain or cause a loss. That is something more than a breakdown of relationships.

28. There was wide support for 'secrecy' as an ingredient of the offence – secrecy is a 'hallmark' of fraud, as one of our respondents put it. It was accepted that an open abuse is no less reprehensible than a secret abuse, but while an open abuse might be rightly subject to sanction, the argument was that it should not fall under the criminal law of fraud. A secrecy requirement helps separate fraud from other offences (e.g. blackmail) and matters better dealt with under civil law. However some were concerned that, while secrecy would almost invariably be part of the offending behaviour in practice, it was difficult to define and represented an unnecessary complication, which could lead to technical arguments in court. There could be arguments about whether there had been an intention to disclose in the future, and about whether the employer knew what was going on, if a surveillance operation was in place. It was argued that the mischief lay in the dishonest abuse and that the value-laden concepts of 'dishonesty' and 'abuse' were sufficient in themselves to set the parameters for the offence.

29. We accept these arguments and in the light of this concern we decided to delete the secrecy requirement proposed by the Law Commission.

10.6 SECTION 11 OF THE FRAUD ACT 2006 – DISHONESTLY OBTAINING SERVICES

Section 11 of the Fraud Act 2006 creates an offence of dishonestly obtaining services. The offence replaces s 1 of the Theft Act 1978 (dishonestly, by deception, obtaining services). The fact that the s 11 offence does not require proof of an operative deception means that it can be relied upon by the prosecution in situations where the previous Theft Act 1978 offence would have been inappropriate – for example where D acts dishonestly in relation to a machine in order to obtain a service (under the previous law deception could only operate on a human mind). The offence can also operate in situations where there is simply no deception – such as where D (unseen) enters a cinema via an open fire-exit door and is able to view a film without paying the admission charge. The s 11 offence carries a maximum penalty of 5 years' imprisonment following conviction on indictment.

10.6.1 SECTION 11 OF THE FRAUD ACT 2006 – DISHONESTLY OBTAINING SERVICES – ELEMENTS OF THE OFFENCE

The elements of the s 11 offence are:

Actus reus
- Services made available on the basis that payment has been, is being, or will be made for or in respect of them
- An 'act' by D

- The obtaining of services by D
- D has not paid for the services or does not pay in full

The offence cannot be committed by omission alone – a positive act is required. Unlike the fraud offences introduced under ss 2 to 4, s 11 is not inchoate – D can only incur liability if he actually obtains the service (although a charge of attempting to obtain services would be available). It is presumed that D's dishonest act must cause the obtaining of the service.

Mens rea
- D's obtaining of the service is dishonest
- D knows that the services were, or might have been, provided on the basis that payment had been or would be made for them
- D intends not to pay for the services or not to pay in full

Section 11 of the Fraud Act 2006 provides:

> (1) A person is guilty of an offence under this section if he obtains services for himself or another –
>   (a) by a dishonest act, and
>   (b) in breach of subsection (2).
> (2) A person obtains services in breach of this subsection if –
>   (a) they are made available on the basis that payment has been, is being or will be made for or in respect of them,
>   (b) he obtains them without any payment having been made for or in respect of them or without payment having been made in full, and
>   (c) when he obtains them, he knows –
>   (i) that they are being made available on the basis described in paragraph (a), or
>   (ii) that they might be,
>   but intends that payment will not be made, or will not be made in full.

- D hands over a worthless cheque to the provider of the service, claiming thereby to be paying in advance, and then receives the service;
- D, by lying to P, persuades P (the provider of the service) to agree to a lesser payment than would otherwise have been the case (for example by claiming to be entitled to a discount).

As was the case under s 1 of the Theft Act 1968, no liability arises if D persuades P to provide the service for free, even if D is acting dishonestly in doing so, as the service will not thereafter be provided on the basis that it has been or will be paid for (for example if D pretends to have no money and thereby persuades a taxi driver to provide transportation for no charge). Such behaviour should, however, fall foul of s 2 of the Fraud Act 2006 as it involves a false pretence that is intended to cause loss to another.

10.6.2 THE NATURE OF 'SERVICES' FOR THE PURPOSES OF S 11

Responding to consultation on the proposed s 11 offence the Government Reponse to Consultations on Fraud Law Reform (2005) observed:

> 36. Examples of services which respondents thought should be covered include the opening of a bank account, the setting up of a company, downloading software or music from the internet. We believe these are all covered within the normal meaning of the term 'services'.
>
> 37. An example mentioned by the Law Commission that is not covered by the new offence is where parents, who have every intention of paying all relevant fees, lie about a child's religious upbringing in order to obtain a place at a fee-paying school. This case is in principle covered by [what was] the existing offence in section 1 of the [Theft Act 1978] . . ., as it is not necessary under that provision to show that the defendant intended to avoid payment. One respondent thought that this type of case should be covered by the criminal law as there is loss to the school in that they have accepted a pupil they would not otherwise have taken and a loss to another family whose child has not obtained a place. We, however, agree with the Law Commission that this type of gain and loss should not be a matter for the criminal law of fraud and that the new offence should apply only where there is an intention not to pay.
>
> 38. A few respondents believed that the requirement that the defendant only be 'aware that the services might be chargeable' was too low and that it would assist unscrupulous service providers (of whom they say there is an increasing number, on the net). However, the majority felt the overall dishonesty requirement provides sufficient protection for the innocent client.

Given that the definition of services under s 11 as '. . . made available on the basis that payment has been, is being or will be made for or in respect of them . . .' is so similar to the wording of the offence it replaces – s 1(2) Theft Act 1978 '. . . provided on the understanding that the [service] has been or will be paid for . . .', the Theft Act 1978 case law on this point should still be persuasive.

R v Sofroniou [2004] 1 Cr App R 35

The appellant provided false information about his identity in order to open a number of bank accounts and credit card accounts. He was convicted of a number of offences of obtaining services by deception contrary to s 1(1) of the Theft Act 1978, and appealed on the ground that there was insufficient evidence to sustain the necessary understanding or agreement that the benefit would be paid for – hence he contended that there had not been the provision of a service as that term was used in the context of s 1(1) of the 1978 Act.

> May LJ:
> It is to be supposed that obtaining services is to be contrasted with obtaining property. In ordinary use, 'services' has a wide range of meaning. Inducing someone to confer a benefit is also capable of wide application. . . . Section 1(3) of the 1978 Act now provides that inducing a bank or building

> society to make a loan, or to cause or permit a loan to be made, constitutes the obtaining of services within the section. It also provides that an understanding that any payment, by way of interest or otherwise, will be or has been made in respect of the loan is sufficient for the purposes of sub-section (2) . . . We do not see any substantial difference, in the context of obtaining services by deception, between the dishonest use of a credit card and the dishonest operation of a bank account.

Referring to the enactment of s 1(3) of the Theft Act 1978, which provides that inducing a bank or building society to make a loan, or to cause or permit a loan to be made, constitutes the obtaining of services, his Lordship continued:

> . . . Parliament was persuaded that dishonestly inducing a bank or building society to make a loan, on the understanding that interest or other payment would be made in respect of it, should constitute obtaining services within the section. In our judgment, there should no longer be any doubt but that dishonestly inducing a bank or building society to provide banking or credit card services is also within the section, provided the requirement as to payment is also satisfied. We consider that [counsel for the appellant] is right to accept that inducing a bank or building society to open an account constitutes obtaining services; and that inducing a bank or other organisation to issue a credit card constitutes obtaining services. We also consider that the dishonest operation of a bank or building society account over a period and a dishonest use of a credit card over a period constitutes obtaining services within the section. We . . . [see] . . . no proper distinction between the opening of a bank account and its subsequent operation. What the bank provides in each instance is the benefit of their participation in the banking system which can in our judgment properly be described as a service or services. We do not need to decide for the purposes of the present appeal whether dishonestly inducing a bank to negotiate a single cheque or the dishonest use of a credit card on a single occasion would constitute obtaining services within the section.

As regards the meaning of the phrase 'on the understanding it has been or will be paid for', he continued:

> The ambit of the necessary understanding as to payment is problematic . . . The section is not intended to encompass obtaining gratuitous services by deception. Banks and building societies are commercial organisations. They are not in business to provide gratuitous services and it may be assumed that, if a customer opens and operates an account, he will pay for the services so provided by some means. Banks habitually make charges for running their customers' accounts.
> They charge interest on overdrawn accounts. They often pay no interest on accounts which are in credit; or, if they do, the rate of interest is less than they themselves obtain on the same money in the market. Credit card providers sometimes make charges for operating the account, whether there is prompt repayment in full or not. American Express did this for count 3 of the present indictment. Credit card operators also charge interest, if the account is not paid in full after a stipulated short period. Even if a particular customer pays his credit card balance in full within the

stipulated period, the card provider may still be taken to make a charge to the supplier of goods purchased by means of the card, so that the amount which the customer pays for the goods is greater than it would be if the credit card service were not provided . . . Section 1(2) refers to an understanding, not an agreement. This is, we think, intended to cover situations where nothing explicitly is said about payment, but where there is a common understanding that the services will not be provided gratuitously. I can induce someone to mow my lawn on the understanding that he will do so for nothing: or the understanding may be that he will be paid. If, in the latter instance, I induce him to mow my lawn dishonestly by deception, as for instance by representing that I am able to pay him when I am not, I commit an offence within the section. This would be so even if there is no explicit articulation of the understanding as to payment . . .

. . . We accept that in a subjective sense the understanding may not in truth be mutual. The section is concerned with dishonest deception and the deception may well relate to the deceiver's intention and ability to pay. A dishonest person may well not have a subjective intention or understanding that he will pay. But we do consider that the section envisages a putative objective mutual understanding as to payment on the assumption that the inducement was not dishonest. We consider that an understanding which is mutual in this sense is the natural meaning of the use of the word 'understanding' in its context. We also consider that payment has to be an identifiable payment or payments made or to be made by or on behalf of the person obtaining the services. We recognise that there are some indications in favour of a looser construction. The words in sub-section (2) 'has been or will be paid for' do not by themselves positively require that the payment has to be by or on behalf of the person obtaining the services. The words 'any payment' and 'by way of interest or otherwise' in sub-section (3) are wide. But we consider that the general sense of the section is that the payment is to be made by or on behalf of the person obtaining the services. And we consider that the words in sub-section (3) 'on the understanding that any payment . . . will be or has been made in respect of the loan' positively connote payment by the borrower in respect of the loan. Just as we consider that the introduction of sub-section (3) clarified the ambit of 'services' beyond the specific instance of a loan; so we consider that the introduction of the sub-section clarified the meaning 'has been or will be paid for'.

. . . This construction means that, in our judgment, an understanding as to payment under the section will not be satisfied unless there is an agreement or sufficient understanding that an identifiable payment or payments have been or will be made by or on behalf of the person receiving the services to the person providing them. Although it is a common understanding that banks often make charges on accounts which are in credit and charge interest on accounts which are overdrawn, this is not invariably so. Likewise, although it is common for credit card providers to make charges and to charge interest on debit balances which are not promptly paid, it is not to be assumed that every credit card provider makes a charge irrespective of when the balance is repaid; and many people are careful to pay off their balances promptly and thus avoid interest charges. It may therefore be possible to have the benefit of a credit card without ever making any identifiable direct payment to the credit card provider.

In *R v Shortland* [1996] 1 Cr App Rep 116, the appellant opened two bank accounts under an assumed name. There was no direct evidence of any understanding that the provision of banking services had been or would be paid for. The trial judge rejected a submission of no case to answer saying that it would be an affront to commonsense to think that banking services would be provided free of charge. He ruled that the jury could infer from the opening of the bank accounts that the benefit conferred would be paid for, and he directed them accordingly. This court allowed the appellant's appeal, holding that the matter should have been withdrawn from the jury. The inference which the jury were invited to draw was not something that they could conclude with any safety or satisfaction. Mr Causer points out that the Crown did not resist the appeal and that the decision was before the amendment introducing sub-section (3) to section 1 of the 1978 Act. As to the latter, we have explained our view that sub-section (3) clarifies the requirement as to payment in the way we have indicated. Professor Smith's commentary on *Shortland* states that what was missing in that case was any evidence as to the terms of the contract made when the appellant opened the account. These terms would probably have shown that the service was to be paid for but it was not possible to infer with the necessary degree of certainty that this was so from the mere fact of the opening of the account.

It might be possible to submit, from the brevity of the report and the fact that the Crown did not resist the appeal, that we are not strictly bound by the decision in *Shortland*. We consider on balance that we are bound by that decision, but in any event it accords with our view as to the construction of the section as amended. We do not consider that inferred indirect commercial advantages to a bank, building society or credit card provider are capable of providing the necessary ingredient as to payment. These will include the difference between interest paid by a bank to an account holder and interest earned by the bank on the same money; or a charge by the credit card provider to the seller of goods bought by means of a credit card. Nor can it be safely inferred from the mere opening of a bank account or the mere obtaining of a credit card that there will be charges. But the facts of the present appeal well illustrate circumstances in which a jury could surely infer the necessary understanding as to payment. The appellant was comprehensively dishonest. He intentionally used the bank accounts in counts 1 and 2 so that they became overdrawn. For count 1 he obtained a substantial loan. The services he obtained were not just the use of bank accounts, but of bank accounts which he dishonestly intended to overdraw. It was open to the jury to infer that the banks would charge interest on accounts overdrawn in this way. Although in different circumstances an inference that interest would be charged might not safely be drawn, it did not require direct evidence that banks invariably charge interest on substantial unauthorised overdrafts to draw such an inference in the present case. Such an inference would be a sufficient putative objective mutual understanding as to payment for the purposes of the offence charged in each of these counts. For counts 4 and 5, where the appellant was charged with attempting to open a bank account and with obtaining the shop card, it was open to the jury to infer from the evidence as a whole that the appellant's intention in each instance was to overdraw the accounts so that interest would be charged. Here again the inference was capable of supporting the necessary understanding as to payment.

10.7 OTHER OFFENCES UNDER THE FRAUD ACT 2006

The Fraud Act 2006 introduces a range of fraud-related offences to augment the key provisions under ss 2, 3, 4 and 11.

Under s 6 it is an offence for D to have in his possession or under his control any article for use in the course of or in connection with any fraud. A consequence of this offence being introduced is that the offence of 'going equipped' contrary to s 25 of the Theft Act 1968 (see Chapter 11.6) is amended so that instead of relating to going equipped to commit a theft, cheat or burglary, references to 'cheat' are removed.

Section 6 of the 2006 Act provides:

'(1) A person is guilty of an offence if he has in his possession or under his control any article for use in the course of or in connection with any fraud.' The offence under s 6 carries the possibility of 5 years' imprisonment following conviction on indictment.

Examples of activities that will be covered by this offence are provided by *R v Rashid* [1977] 1 WLR 298 and *R v Doukas* [1978] 1 WLR 372. In *R v Rashid*, D was convicted of having with him articles for use in the course of or in connection with cheat [contrary to s 25(1) of the Theft Act 1968, a 'cheat' for these purposes being a deception]. D was a steward on a British Rail train. He was arrested on his way into work and found to be in possession of two loaves of sliced bread and one bag of tomatoes. The prosecution case was that D intended to use these article to make his own sandwiches and pass them off to train customers as British rail food, pocketing the proceeds of sale. On appeal it was held that the conviction under s 25 should be quashed as there was insufficient evidence that the prospective purchasers of the sandwiches would have refused to buy them from D had they been aware of their true provenance (i.e. insufficient evidence that the deception would have been operative). It is submitted that on these facts Rashid would be guilty under s 6 of the 2006 Act – he had articles in his possession, and he intended to use them in what would now be a s 2 fraud. Offering the food to passengers as British Rail food when it in fact was his own would be the false representation. The intention to take payment would be the intent to make a gain for himself, and the dishonesty is fairly self-evident. Similarly with *R v Doukas* [1978] 1 WLR 372, where D took his own wine into a hotel where he worked as a wine waiter, intending to sell his wine as if it were the hotel wine, again pocketing the proceeds of sale. Whether the false representation would have been effective, or not, is irrelevant to a charge under s 2.

Section 7 of the 2006 Act creates the offence of making or supplying articles for use in frauds. A person is guilty of an offence under s 7 if he makes, adapts, supplies or offers to supply any article knowing that it is designed or adapted for use in the course of or in connection with fraud, or intending it to be used to commit, or assist in the commission of, fraud.

10.8 SHOULD DISHONESTY HAVE BEEN RETAINED AS AN ELEMENT OF THE FRAUD ACT 2006 OFFENCES?

In Part V of its Report on the operation of fraud offences (Law Com 276), the Law Commission reviewed the role of dishonesty in criminal law and the arguments for and against the introduction of a general offence of dishonesty.

Is it possible to define dishonesty?

5.2 Legal definitions of 'moral' elements, such as dishonesty, seem to be elusive . . .

5.4 Likewise, when fact-finders are asked to consider whether the defendant's conduct was or was not dishonest, the law does not provide them with a definition of the word. The fact-finders draw the line, so that dishonesty means what they understand it to mean . . . this lack of definition has been criticised, but we are unaware of any proposed definitions which the law could adopt.

5.5 It may be that moral elements such as dishonesty can only be defined with reference to the fact-finders' judgement. Richard Tur argues that 'what may constitute a just excuse is so context-dependent that exhaustive definition must necessarily limit the range of circumstances which might excuse'. Therefore, if an exhaustive definition of 'just excuse' or 'dishonesty' were incorporated into the law, there would inevitably be examples of behaviour which were legally dishonest, but which the fact-finders would characterise as morally blameless.

The Ghosh approach

5.6 When dishonesty is a live issue, although the fact-finders are not given a definition, they are required to consider it in a structured way . . .

5.7 While [the *Ghosh*] . . . approach provides structure, and prevents defendants from running 'Robin Hood' defences, where the defendant acknowledges that his or her conduct would be regarded as dishonest by reasonable, honest people, it still involves the jury drawing the line between what is and what is not dishonest. It is not, however, merely what the jury regards as the appropriate moral standard, by reference to their view of the ordinary standards of reasonable and honest people, which counts. In addition, the jury is required to find that the defendant recognised that his or her conduct was outside the norms of what society regards as honest.

5.8 Some academic critics argue that this approach must lead to inconsistency, such that the same set of facts could produce an acquittal in one court and a conviction in another. On the other hand, we are not aware of any research or evidence to show that verdicts are in fact significantly inconsistent when dishonesty is a live issue in a case.

5.9 There is some evidence that people's moral standards are surprisingly flexible. A MORI poll for the Sunday Times in October 1985 found that only 35% of those questioned thought it morally wrong to accept payment in cash in order to evade liability for tax. On the other hand, it does not follow that the other 65%, if sitting on a jury in a case of tax evasion where dishonesty was in issue, would necessarily have acquitted. Indeed, the proportion of those questioned who thought that such conduct was morally acceptable to *most* people was only 37%. This may suggest that people do not generally assume that their own moral standards are the norm. Indeed it indicates that a majority of respondents thought that their own moral standards fell below those of most others.

5.10 It seems, therefore, that the first stage of the *Ghosh* test may not necessarily result in the jury simply applying their own standards of honesty. It may, indeed, be quite natural for fact-finders to form a view of what reasonable, honest people would consider dishonest, as distinct from their decision reflecting their own personal moral view. This approach still leaves room for inconsistent verdicts, because fact-finders might have different views on what reasonable, honest people would categorise as dishonest. Nonetheless, there must be less inconsistency than if fact-finders were expressly required to apply their own moral standards.

5.11 The second limb imposes an important brake on what might, despite its express terms, tend to be a subjective approach to the first-limb decision. First it prevents naive or innocent defendants from being found to be dishonest when the jury is not satisfied that they must have recognised that their behaviour fell outside the norms of reasonable, honest people. On the other hand it operates as a brake on the jury acquitting by virtue of the 'Robin Hood' defence.

What purpose does dishonesty serve as a defining element?

5.12 Some critics of the *Ghosh* approach have questioned whether dishonesty is a useful concept at all. Before answering this question, it is important to note a distinction between two ways that dishonesty can form part of the definition of an offence. In some crimes, such as conspiracy to defraud, the other elements of the offence are not *prima facie* unlawful, so dishonesty renders criminal otherwise lawful conduct. However, in deception offences the other elements of the offence, if proved, would normally be unlawful in themselves. If someone has practised a deception in order to gain a benefit their conduct is *prima facie* wrongful. Therefore dishonesty can be raised to rebut the inference that conduct was in fact wrongful. For ease of explanation, we will refer to the former type of crime as having a *positive* requirement of dishonesty, and the latter as having a *negative* requirement. It should be remembered, however, that even where dishonesty is a negative requirement, so that the issue is likely to be raised by the defence to rebut the Crown's case, the burden of proof remains with the Crown. Whenever dishonesty is in issue, the Crown must prove that the defendant was dishonest.

5.13 In Consultation Paper No 155, we provisionally concluded first, that it is wrong in principle to use dishonesty as a positive element; and second, that, for offences which require proof of deception, dishonesty could be more usefully replaced by specific defences. We stand by the first of these provisional proposals, and expand on that recommendation in Part V. However, we no longer propose to dispose of dishonesty as a negative requirement in fraud offences. This change in view was prompted by the consultation process, and the overall change in our approach.

5.14 Some of the respondents to the Consultation Paper, such as the Magistrates' Association, felt that the requirement of *Ghosh* dishonesty was unproblematic. This was because they appeared to take the view that there are shared community values in relation to such concepts as dishonesty. Others felt that the combined wisdom of the members of the jury meant that the potential for inconsistency between different juries should not be overstated.

5.15 Other respondents took the view that juries from different areas of the country may have substantially different views on dishonesty, depending on the prevailing financial circumstances and political views of those living in the area. However, we would question whether it is at all sensible to project an apparent divergence, on the macro level, in economic circumstances and political preference between different areas of the country onto the likelihood of a divergence in views where the focus is a decision of 12 individuals who have been asked the specific question whether reasonable, honest people would consider certain behaviour to be dishonest. Even if there is the potential for a divergence of views on such a question, we are unaware of any evidence of it.

5.16 While in principle we are against a crime of fraud which would be based on *Ghosh* dishonesty as a positive element (see paragraphs 5.20 to 5.22 below), we accept that in cases where the defendant's conduct is *prima facie* fraudulent, there is a need to ensure that those who most people would consider morally blameless are not found guilty. We have also concluded that it would not be possible to define dishonesty exhaustively while still achieving this result.

5.18 The fact that *Ghosh* dishonesty leaves open a possibility of variance between cases with essentially similar facts is, in our judgment, a theoretical risk. Many years after its adoption, the

Ghosh test remains, in practice, unproblematic. We also recognise the fact that the concept of dishonesty is now required in a very large number of criminal cases, so to reject it at this stage would have a far-reaching effect on the criminal justice system.

5.19 We have therefore concluded that dishonesty should be a negative element in any crime of fraud, so that where other elements of the crime can be proved, a lack of dishonesty will nonetheless be a defence. However, for reasons which we set out below, we do not consider it right that dishonesty should be the key, positive element in a fraud offence. It should be a *necessary* element of the offence, but it should not be *sufficient*.

FURTHER READING

Omerod, D, 'The Fraud Act 2006—Criminalising Lying?' [2007] Crim LR 193
Yeo, N, 'Bulls-Eyes' (2007) 157 NLJ 212

CHAPTER 11

ROBBERY, BLACKMAIL, BURGLARY AND GOING EQUIPPED

11.1 INTRODUCTION: ROBBERY

Robbery is essentially an aggravated form of theft, the aggravating factors being the use of force or the threatened use of force. Proof of the completed offence requires proof of all five elements of theft, as to which see Chapter 9.1 to 9.5. The offence of robbery is created by s 8 of the Theft Act 1968, which provides:

> (1) A person is guilty of robbery if he steals, and immediately before or at the time of doing so, and in order to do so, he uses force on any person or puts or seeks to put any person in fear of being then and there subjected to force.
> (2) A person guilty of robbery, or of an assault with intent to rob, shall on conviction on indictment be liable to imprisonment for life.

The offence of robbery, which (unlike other Theft Act offences such as burglary and theft) is triable only in the Crown Court, comprises the following elements:

(1) force or the threatened use of force,
(2) before or at the time of stealing,
(3) in order to steal, and
(4) theft (that is, the offence created by s 1 of the Theft Act 1968 as defined in ss 2–7 of the Act). The offence carries the possibility of life imprisonment.

11.1.1 THE USE OF FORCE OR THREATENED FORCE

Corcoran v Anderton (1980) 71 Cr App R 104 (DC)

Watkins J:

. . . At 7.55 pm on 22 February 1979, Mrs Hall was in Conran Street in Manchester. She was carrying a handbag. Two youths came along, one the defendant, Christopher Corcoran, and another his co-accused Peter Partington. They had agreed beforehand to steal Mrs Hall's handbag. They began to carry out their purpose. Partington struck her in the back, took hold of and tugged at her handbag causing her to release it. Corcoran was present and participated. Mrs Hall understandably screamed when this attack was made upon her and fell. At that these two youths ran away. So Mrs Hall managed to recover her handbag. At no time, say the justices, did Partington have sole control of the handbag. They were finally of the opinion . . . that the appropriation of the bag was complete when Partington pulled at it so causing Mrs Hall to release it . . .

They were asked to state a case. They did and asked this court this question: 'Could the tugging at the handbag, accompanied by force, amount to robbery, notwithstanding the fact that the co-accused did not have sole control of the bag at any time?'

. . . Robbery, as the Theft Act 1968 provides by s 8(1), is committed if a person steals and immediately before or at the time of doing so and in order to do so force is used on any person.

. . . [The] circumstances [found by the justices] involve the use of force upon the person of Mrs Hall so that she lost her grip upon her handbag accompanied by the intention in the minds of both the appellant and his companion to steal, that is to say to take the handbag, by force if necessary, away from Mrs Hall and permanently deprive her of that handbag or its contents . . .

. . . [C]onfining myself to the facts as found by the justices in the instant case, I think that an 'appropriation' takes place when an accused snatches a woman's handbag completely from her grasp, so that she no longer has physical control of it because it has fallen to the ground. What has been involved in such activity as that, bearing in mind the dishonest state of mind of the accused, is an assumption of the rights of the owner, a taking of the property of another . . . In my judgment there cannot possibly be, save for the instance where a handbag is carried away from the scene of it, a clearer instance of robbery than that which these justices found was committed.

Turning to the actual question posed to this court, 'Could the tugging at the handbag, accompanied by force, amount to robbery, notwithstanding the fact that the co-accused did not have sole control of the bag at any time?' In my opinion, which may be contrary to some notions of what constitutes a sufficient appropriation to satisfy the definition of that word in s 3(1) of the Theft Act the forcible tugging of the handbag of itself could in the circumstances be a sufficient exercise of control by the accused person so as to amount to an assumption by him of the rights of the owner, and therefore an appropriation of the property . . .

Eveleigh LJ:

I agree. Each, that is to say the lady and the defendant, was trying to exclude the other from exclusive claim to the bag. The lady was treating the bag as hers, as indeed it was, and resisting any efforts of his to deprive her of it. He, on the other hand, was treating the bag as his and seeking to overcome her efforts to retain it. He was thereby exercising the rights which belonged to the owner. She too was doing so. She was doing it lawfully, he was doing it unlawfully. He was, in my view, appropriating that bag . . .

11.1.2 FORCE

The use of force will normally be by means of direct force applied to the victim's person, but it can be indirect, as evidenced by *R v Clouden* [1987] Crim LR 56, where D was found guilty of robbery where the force used was to snatch a shopping bag out of the victim's hands.

R v Dawson and James (1978) 68 Cr App R 170 (CA)

The point at issue was whether 'jostling' amounted to the use of force.

> Lawton LJ:
> [Force] is a word in ordinary use. It is a word which juries understand. The learned judge left it to the jury to say whether jostling a man in the way which the victim described to such an extent that he had difficulty in keeping his balance could be said to be the use of force.
> . . . It was a matter for the jury. They were to use their common sense and knowledge of the word. We cannot say that their decision as to whether force was used was wrong. They were entitled to the view that force was used.
> Other points were discussed in the case as to whether the force had been used for the purpose of distracting the victim's attention or whether it was for the purpose of overcoming resistance. Those sorts of refinements may have been relevant under the old law, but so far as the new law is concerned the sole question is whether the accused used force on any person in order to steal. That issue in this case was left to the jury. They found in favour of the Crown.

We cannot say that this verdict was either unsafe or unsatisfactory. Accordingly the appeal is dismissed.

11.1.3 THEFT

Since theft is an essential ingredient of robbery, it follows that if the defendant is not guilty of theft he cannot be guilty of robbery (so, in *R v Robinson* [1977] Crim LR 173 it was held that since the defendant had not acted dishonestly he could not be guilty of theft and so could not be guilty of robbery).

However, the prosecution must also prove that force was used immediately before, or at the same time as, the appropriation of the property. There must be a causal link between the theft and the use or threat of force (so a direction to the jury that they can convict of robbery even if they find that the violence is unconnected with the theft is wrong in law: see *R v Shendley* [1970] Crim LR 49). It is clear that the courts take a robust attitude to the question of appropriation in the context of robbery, so as to allow the jury to take a commonsense approach to the question whether or not there was a robbery.

R v Hale (1978) 68 Cr App R 415 (CA)

Eveleigh LJ:

. . . The prosecution alleged that the appellant and one McGuire went to the house of a Mrs Carrett. When she answered the door they rushed in. Each was wearing a stocking mask. The appellant put his hand over Mrs Carrett's mouth to stop her screaming and McGuire went upstairs to search. The appellant subsequently released his hold on Mrs Carrett and she went to the settee. He undid her dressing gown and touched her. He also exposed himself. McGuire then came downstairs with a jewellery box and asked where the rest was. The telephone rang. It was a next-door neighbour who had heard Mrs Carrett scream and wanted to know if everything was all right. Under threat from the appellant she replied everything was all right. All three then went upstairs and Mrs Carrett was asked where her money was. The appellant and McGuire then used the toilet and on their return said that they would tie her up and she was not to telephone the police. They tied her ankles and hands and put socks in her mouth. They went out of the front door warning her not to telephone, saying that they would come back and do something to her little boy if she phoned the police within five minutes . . .

Section 8 of the Theft Act 1968 begins: 'A person is guilty of robbery if he steals . . .' He steals when he acts in accordance with the basic definition of theft in s 1 of the Theft Act; that is to say when he dishonestly appropriates property belonging to another with the intention of permanently depriving the other of it. It thus becomes necessary to consider what is 'appropriation' or, according to s 3, 'any assumption by a person of the rights of an owner'. An assumption of the rights of an owner describes the conduct of a person towards a particular article. It is conduct which usurps the rights of the owner. To say that the conduct is over and done with as soon as he lays hands upon the property, or when he manifests an intention to deal with it as his, is contrary to common sense and to the natural meaning of words. A thief who steals a motor car first opens the door. Is it to be said that the act of starting up the motor is no more a part of the theft?

In the present case there can be little doubt that if the appellant had been interrupted after the seizure of the jewellery box the jury would have been entitled to find that the appellant and his accomplice were assuming the rights of an owner at the time when the jewellery box was seized. However, the act of appropriation does not suddenly cease. It is a continuous act and it is a matter for the jury to decide whether or not the act of appropriation has finished. Moreover, it is quite clear that the intention to deprive the owner permanently, which accompanies the assumption of the owner's rights was a continuing one at all material times. This court therefore rejects the contention that the theft had ceased by the time the lady was tied up. As a matter of common sense the appellant was in the course of committing theft; he was stealing.

There remains the question whether there was robbery. Quite clearly the jury were at liberty to find the appellant guilty of robbery relying upon the force used when he put his hand over Mrs Carrett's mouth to restrain her from calling for help. We also think that they were entitled to rely upon the act of tying her up provided they were satisfied (and it is difficult to see how they could not be satisfied) that the force so used was to enable them to steal. If they were still engaged in the act of stealing the force was clearly used to enable them to continue to assume the rights of the owner and permanently to deprive Mrs Carrett of her box, which is what they began to do when they first seized it . . .

11.2 BLACKMAIL

The offence of blackmail requires proof that D made a:

* demand;
* with menaces;
* with a view to gain or causing loss to another;
* and the demand was unwarranted.

Section 21 of the Theft Act 1968 provides:

(1) A person is guilty of blackmail if, with a view to gain for himself or another or with intent to cause loss to another, he makes any unwarranted demand with menaces; and for this purpose a demand with menaces is unwarranted unless the person making it does so in the belief:
 (a) that he has reasonable grounds for making the demand; and
 (b) that the use of the menaces is a proper means of reinforcing the demand.
(2) The nature of the act or omission demanded is immaterial, and it is also immaterial whether the menaces relate to action to be taken by the person making the demand.
(3) A person guilty of blackmail shall on conviction on indictment be liable to imprisonment for a term not exceeding 14 years.

It should be noted that the offence does not require proof of dishonesty – this element is replaced by the need to show that the demand was unwarranted. Further, there is no need for the prosecution to prove that D did actually gain from the blackmail. The offence is made out provided the demand is made.

11.2.1 DEMAND WITH MENACES

In most instances of blackmail the demand will be express and can easily be established. In cases where it is explicit, an objective approach is adopted – would a reasonable person realise that a demand was being made; see *R v Collister and Warhurst* (1955) 39 Cr App Rep 100. As to whether the demand is accompanied by menaces *R v Lawrence and Pomroy* (1971) 57 Cr App R 64 provides that (*per* Cairns LJ) the word menaces is an ordinary English word which any jury can be expected to understand. Hence in most cases no specific direction will need to be given.

R v Clear [1968] 1 QB 670 (CA)

Sellers LJ:

. . . Words or conduct which would not intimidate or influence anyone to respond to the demand would not be menaces . . . but threats and conduct of such a nature and extent that the mind of an ordinary person of normal stability and courage might be influenced or made apprehensive so as to accede unwillingly to the demand would be sufficient for a jury's consideration . . . [The victim must be] deprived of 'that element of free, voluntary action which alone constitutes consent' in the words used by Wilde B in *R v Walton and Ogden* (1863) Le & Ca 288.

There may be special circumstances unknown to an accused which would make the threats innocuous and unavailing for the accused's demand, but such circumstances would have no bearing on the accused's state of mind and on his intention. If an accused knew that what he threatened would have no effect on the victim it might be different . . .

R v Garwood [1987] 1 WLR 319 (CA)

The appellant was convicted of blackmail, having obtained money from the victim by 'menaces'. The jury found that the victim was rather timid and that other people may not have found the appellant's behaviour menacing.

Lord Lane CJ:

. . . In our judgment it is only rarely that a judge will need to enter on a definition of the word 'menaces'. It is an ordinary word of which the meaning will be clear to any jury . . .

It seems to us that there are two possible occasions on which a further direction on the meaning of the word menaces may be required. The first is where the threats might have affected the mind of an ordinary person of normal stability but did not affect the person actually addressed. In such circumstances that would amount to a sufficient menace: see *R v Clear* [1968] 1 QB 670.

The second situation is where the threats in fact affected the mind of the victim, although they would not have affected the mind of a person of normal stability. In that case, in our judgment, the existence of menaces is proved providing that the accused man was aware of the likely effect of his action upon the victim.

If the recorder had told the jury that [the victim's] undue timidity did not prevent them from finding 'menaces' proved, provided that the appellant realised the effect his actions were having on [the victim], all would have been well . . .

11.2.2 UNWARRANTED DEMAND

It will only be in very rare cases that 'menaces [will be] a proper means of reinforcing the demand' so that the demand becomes a warranted one under s 21(1). It would not be enough that one is demanding back property to which one is entitled, since the making of menaces is not a proper means of achieving that objective: see *R v Lawrence* (1971) 57 Cr App R 64 (above); *R v Harvey* (1980) 72 Cr App R 139.

R v Harvey (1980) 72 Cr App R 139 (CA)

The appellants agreed with one Scott that they would pay him £20,000 to procure a large quantity of cannabis. Scott failed to supply the cannabis. The appellants kidnapped Scott, along with his wife and small child, and they subjected Scott to threats of what would happen to the wife and child if he did not give them their money back.

Bingham J:

. . . [T]wo points emerge with clarity: (1) [s 21(1) of the Theft Act 1968] is concerned with the belief of the individual defendant in the particular case . . . It matters not what the reasonable man, or any man other than the defendant, would believe save in so far as that may throw light on what the defendant in fact believed. Thus the factual question of the defendant's belief should be left to the jury . . . (2) In order to exonerate a defendant from liability his belief must be that the use of the menaces is a 'proper' means of reinforcing the demand. 'Proper' . . . is . . . plainly a word of wide meaning, certainly wider than (for example) 'lawful'. But the greater includes the less and no act which was not believed to be lawful could be believed to be proper within the meaning of the subsection. Thus no assistance is given to any defendant, even a fanatic or a deranged idealist, who knows or suspects that his threat, or the act threatened, is criminal, but believes it to be justified by his end or his peculiar circumstances. The test is not what he regards as justified, but what he believes to be proper. And where, as here, the threats were to do acts which any sane man knows to be against the laws of every civilised country, no jury would hesitate long before dismissing the contention that the defendant genuinely believed the threats to be a proper means of reinforcing even a legitimate demand.

. . . [T]he jury should have been directed that the demand with menaces was not to be regarded as unwarranted unless the Crown satisfied them in respect of each defendant that the defendant did not make the demand with menaces in the genuine belief both: (a) that he had had reasonable grounds for making the demand; and (b) that the use of the menaces was in the circumstances a proper (meaning for present purposes a lawful, and not a criminal) means of reinforcing the demand . . .

11.2.3 '. . . WITH A VIEW TO GAIN . . . OR WITH INTENT TO CAUSE LOSS TO ANOTHER . . .'

R v Bevans (1988) 87 Cr App R 64

The appellant appealed against his conviction for blackmail. He had forced a doctor, at gunpoint, to provide him with a painkilling injection of morphine. The appellant contended, unsuccessfully, that as his motive had been pain relief he had not made his menacing demand with a view to gain.

Jones J:

Mr Griffiths [counsel for the appellant] argued before the learned judge, and has repeated his argument before this court, that the demand for an injection of morphine was not made with a view to gain for the appellant. He argues that those words, 'with a view to gain for himself', involve the court in a consideration of the motive which lay behind the appellant's demand. It is said that that motive was unquestionably the relief from the pain which he was suffering at the time. Therefore what he had in mind was the gain of relief from pain, not for a gain in money or other property . . . Mr Griffiths argues that in no sense of the word was there here an economic interest involved. There was not in the appellant's mind either an economic gain by him or an economic loss inflicted upon the doctor.

It may be that the difficulty has arisen in this case by importing into the Act words which are not there . . . the word 'motive' is not used anywhere in the Act. The words used are, 'with a view to gain or with an intent to cause loss'. As I have said, it may well be misleading to try to import those words into the Act, and then try to understand what meaning they should bear.

In the judgment of this court the matter can be resolved quite simply and straightforwardly by reference to the Act itself. What had to be established was that the demand was made with a view to gain for the appellant; expanding those words by reference to section 34(2), that meant with a view to the appellant getting what he had not, and to getting something which consisted of money or other property.

It seems difficult, if not impossible, to argue that the liquid which constituted the substance which was to be injected into the appellant's body was not property. It clearly was. There has been no dispute but that if an ampoule containing the liquid had been handed over to the appellant instead of being transferred to a syringe and injected into his body, he would have got property in that sense. This court can see no difference between the liquid being contained in the syringe before it is passed into his body and the liquid being contained in an ampoule. There can be no question but that that morphine was property.

Again the next question would be – did the appellant have in view the getting of that morphine (that admittedly being something which, before making the demand, he had not)? Again there seems to be only one possible answer: yes. It is nothing to the point that his ultimate motive was the relief of pain through the effect which that morphine would have upon his bodily processes.

It was pointed out in the course of argument that someone may very well demand a bottle of whisky. His ultimate motive may simply be to get drunk, that is to drink it all himself and to get drunk. That does not detract in any way from the proposition that in fact he would be demanding property in the form of the bottle of whisky and in particular the bottle's contents.

By analogy exactly the same argument must apply here. This demand, which was a demand for an injection of morphine, involved two things: first of all it involved the passing of a drug to him, and secondly it involved the service by the doctor of actually carrying out the injection. The fact that he was gaining the service does not in any way mean that he was not gaining the property which consisted of the morphine. There is no suggestion anywhere in the Act that the gain must be exclusively directed to one particular object.

 ## COMMENTS AND QUESTIONS

1   Consider the case of the highwayman holding up the stagecoach shouting 'Your money or your life!' Assuming the passengers are put in fear he appears to be guilty of at least attempted robbery, but is he not also guilty of blackmail?

2   Where D holds a knife to the throat of P's baby X, and tells X to hand over her purse or X will be stabbed, D is clearly guilty of blackmail, but is he guilty of robbery?

3   D blackmails P and demands payment of £1,000 in notes. If P actually pays D, is D guilty of theft of that money?

11.3 BURGLARY

Section 9 of the Theft Act 1968 creates the offence of burglary, which can be committed in a number of ways. Simply entering a building as a trespasser with intent to commit criminal damage, theft or grievous bodily harm will suffice for the offence created by s 9(1)(a). None of these offences need be carried out. The criminality lies in D's intent at the time of entry. Under s 9(1)(b) D must have entered as a trespasser and have actually committed theft or grievous bodily harm, or at least attempted to commit either of those two offences. Note that the offence of burglary based on D's entry as a trespasser with intent to rape has been abolished and replaced with a new offence under s 68 of the Sexual Offences Act 2003; see 11.4 below.

Section 9 of the Theft Act 1968

(1) A person is guilty of burglary if:

    (a) he enters any building or part of a building as a trespasser and with intent to commit any such offence as is mentioned in subsection (2) below; or

    (b) having entered any building or part of a building as a trespasser he steals or attempts to steal anything in the building or that part of it or inflicts or attempts to inflict on any person therein any grievous bodily harm.

(2) The offences referred to in subsection (1)(a) above are offences of stealing anything in the building or part of a building in question, of inflicting on any person therein any grievous bodily harm [references to 'raping any person therein' repealed by the Sexual Offences Act 2003; see 11.4 below], and of doing unlawful damage to the building or anything therein.

(3) A person guilty of burglary shall on conviction on indictment be liable to imprisonment for a term not exceeding:

    (a) where the offence was committed in respect of a building or part of a building which is a dwelling, 14 years;

    (b) in any other case, 10 years.

(4) References in subsections (1) and (2) above to a building, and the reference in subsection (3) above to a building which is a dwelling, shall apply also to an inhabited vehicle or vessel, and shall apply to any such vehicle or vessel at times when the person having a habitation in it is not there as well as at times when he is.

11.3.1 '... BUILDING OR PART OF A BUILDING...'

To be a building, a structure must have a degree of permanence. So, a freezer trailer (which could be hooked up to a lorry and transported at any time) was held not to be a building (*Norfolk Constabulary v Seekings* [1986] Crim LR 167); but a freezer which was 25 feet long, weighed three tons, was connected to the electricity supply and had been in place for at least two years, was held to be a building (*B v Leathley* [1979] Crim LR 314). The test is that laid down by Byles J in *Stevens v Gourley* (1859) CBNS 99 at 112, that the structure must be 'of considerable size and intended to be permanent or at least to endure for a considerable period'. That entry into part of a building may amount to burglary means that a person may become a burglar (if the other elements of the offence are satisfied) by going from a part in which he is lawful visitor to a part in which he is not: see *R v Walkington* (extracted below).

R v Walkington [1979] 1 WLR 1169 (CA)

The defendant was seen to enter the three-sided enclosure where a cash register was sited on the sales floor of a department store. The area inside that partition was reserved for the staff. The defendant, having no permission to enter the partitioned area, moved into that area and pulled the drawer of the cash register open. Having looked into the drawer the defendant slammed it to and started making his way out of the shop, when he was stopped by the store detective. The defendant was convicted of burglary contrary to s 9(1)(a).

Geoffrey Lane LJ:

...What the prosecution had to prove here was that the defendant had entered a part of a building as a trespasser with intent to steal anything in that part of the building...

His Lordship then cited with approval two passages, one from Professor Griew's book, *The Theft Acts 1968 and 1978*, and the other from Professor Smith's book, *The Law of Theft*. Those passages read as follows:

A licence to enter a building may extend to part of the building only. If so, the licensee will trespass if he enters some other part not within the scope of the licence. To do so with intent to commit in that other part one of the specified offences, or to do so and then to commit or attempt to commit one of those offences therein, will be burglary. [Professor Griew]

...A customer in a shop who goes behind the counter and takes money from the till during a short absence of the shopkeeper would be guilty of burglary even though he entered the shop with the shopkeeper's permission. The permission did not extend to his going behind the counter. [Professor Smith]

...Here, it seems to us, there was a physical demarcation. Whether it was sufficient to amount to an area from which the public was plainly excluded was a matter for the jury. It seems to us that there was ample evidence on which they could come to the conclusion (a) that the management had impliedly prohibited customers entering that area and (b) that this particular defendant knew of that prohibition...

11.3.2 ENTRY AS A TRESPASSER

R v Collins [1973] QB 100 (CA)

Edmund Davies LJ:

This is about as extraordinary a case as my brethren and I have ever heard either on the bench or while at the bar. Stephen William George Collins was convicted ... of burglary with intent to commit rape ...

. . . At about 2 o'clock in the early morning of Saturday 24 July 1971, a young lady of 18 went to bed at her mother's home in Colchester. She had spent the evening with her boyfriend. She had taken a certain amount of drink, and it may be that this fact affords some explanation of her inability to answer satisfactorily certain crucial questions put to her at the trial.

She has the habit of sleeping without wearing night apparel in a bed which is very near the lattice-type window of her room. At one stage in her evidence she seemed to be saying that the bed was close up against the window which, in accordance with her practice, was wide open. In the photographs which we have before us, however, there appears to be a gap of some sort between the two, but the bed was clearly quite near the window.

At about 3.30 or 4.00 am she awoke and she then saw in the moonlight a vague form crouched in the open window. She was unable to remember, and this is important, whether the form was on the outside of the window sill or on that part of the sill which was inside the room, and for reasons which will later become clear, that seemingly narrow point is of crucial importance.

The young lady then realised several things: first of all that the form in the window was that of a male; second that he was a naked male, and third that he was a naked male with an erect penis. She also saw in the moonlight that his hair was blond. She thereupon leapt to the conclusion that her boyfriend, with whom for some time she had been on terms of regular and frequent sexual intimacy, was paying her an ardent nocturnal visit. She promptly sat up in bed, and the man descended from the sill and joined her in bed and they had full sexual intercourse. But there was something about him which made her think that things were not as they usually were between her and her boyfriend. The length of his hair, his voice as they had exchanged what was described as 'love talk', and other features led her to the conclusion that somehow there was something different. So she turned on the bedside light, saw that her companion was not her boyfriend and slapped the face of the intruder, who was none other than the defendant. He said to her, 'Give me a good time tonight', and got hold of her arm, but she bit him and told him to go. She then went into the bathroom and he promptly vanished.

The complainant said that she would not have agreed to intercourse if she had known that the person entering her room was not her boyfriend. But there was no suggestion of any force having been used on her, and the intercourse which took place was undoubtedly effected with no resistance on her part.

The defendant was seen by the police at about 11.30 am later that same morning. According to the police, the conversation which took place then elicited these points: He was very lustful the previous night. He had taken a lot of drink, and we may here note that drink (which to him is a very real problem) had brought this young man into trouble several times before, but never for an offence of this kind. He went on to say that he knew the complainant because he had worked around her house. On this occasion, desiring sexual intercourse – and according to the police evidence he added that he was determined to have a girl, by force if necessary, although that part of the police evidence he challenged – he went on to say that he walked around the house, saw a light in an upstairs bedroom, and he knew that this was the girl's bedroom. He found a step ladder, leaned it against the wall and climbed up and looked into the bedroom. What he could see inside through the wide-open window was a girl who was naked and asleep. So he descended the ladder and stripped off all his clothes with the exception of his socks, because apparently he took the view that if the girl's mother entered the bedroom it would be easier to effect a rapid escape if he had his socks on than if he was in his bare feet. That is a matter about which we are not called on to express any view, and would in any event find ourselves unable to express one.

Having undressed, he then climbed the ladder and pulled himself up on to the window sill. His version of the matter is that he was pulling himself in when she awoke. She then got up and knelt on the bed, she put her arms around his neck and body, and she seemed to pull him into the bed.

He went on:

I was rather dazed because I didn't think she would want to know me. We kissed and cuddled for about 10 or 15 minutes and then I had it away with her but found it hard because I had had so much to drink.

The police officer said to the defendant:

It appears that it was your intention to have intercourse with this girl by force if necessary, and that it was only pure coincidence that this girl was under the impression that you were her boyfriend and apparently that is why she consented to allowing you to have sexual intercourse with her.

It was alleged that he then said, 'Yes, I feel awful about this. It is the worst day of my life, but I know it could have been worse.'

Thereupon the officer said to him – and the defendant challenges this: 'What do you mean, you know it could have been worse?', to which he is alleged to have replied:

Well, my trouble is drink and I got very frustrated. As I've told you, I only wanted to have it away with a girl and I'm only glad I haven't really hurt her.

Then he made a statement under caution, in the course of which he said:

When I stripped off and got up the ladder I made my mind up that I was going to try and have it away with this girl. I feel terrible about this now, but I had too much to drink. I am sorry for what I have done.

In the course of his testimony, the defendant said that he would not have gone into the room if the girl had not knelt on the bed and beckoned him into the room. He said that if she had objected immediately to his being there or to his having sexual intercourse he would not have persisted. While he was keen on having sexual intercourse that night, it was only if he could find someone who was willing. He strongly denied having told the police that he would, if necessary, have pushed over some girl for the purpose of having intercourse . . .

Now, one feature of the case which remained at the conclusion of the evidence in great obscurity is where exactly Collins was at the moment when, according to him, the girl manifested that she was welcoming him. Was he kneeling on the sill outside the window or was he already inside the room, having climbed through the window frame, and kneeling on the inner sill? It was a crucial matter, for there were certainly three ingredients that it was incumbent on the Crown to establish. Under s 9 of the Theft Act 1968, which renders a person guilty of burglary if he enters any building or part of a building as a trespasser and with the intention of committing rape, the entry of the accused into the building must first be proved. Well, there is no doubt about that, for it is common ground that he did enter this girl's bedroom. Second, it must be proved that he entered as a trespasser. We will develop that point a little later. Third, it must be proved that he entered as a trespasser with intent at the time of entry to commit rape therein . . .

Having concluded that a defendant must be shown to have known he was trespassing, or at least to have been reckless as to whether he was, in order to be convicted of burglary, Edmund Davies LJ continued:

... Having so held, the pivotal point of this appeal is whether the Crown established that this defendant at the moment that he entered the bedroom knew perfectly well that he was not welcome there or, being reckless whether he was welcome or not, was nevertheless determined to enter.

That in turn involves consideration as to where he was at the time that the complainant indicated that she was welcoming him into her bedroom. If, to take an example that was put in the course of argument, her bed had not been near the window but was on the other side of the bedroom, and he (being determined to have her sexually even against her will) climbed through the window and crossed the bedroom to reach her bed, then the offence charged would have been established. But in this case, as we have related, the layout of the room was different, and it became a point of nicety which had to be conclusively established by the Crown as to where he was when the girl made welcoming signs, as she unquestionably at some stage did ...

... [W]hat the accused had said was, 'She knelt on the bed, she put her arms around me and then I went in.' If the jury thought he might be truthful in that assertion, they would need to consider whether or not, although entirely surprised by such a reception being accorded to him, this young man might not have been entitled reasonably to regard her action as amounting to an invitation to him to enter. If she in fact appeared to be welcoming him, the Crown do not suggest that he should have realised or even suspected that she was so behaving because, despite the moonlight, she thought he was someone else. Unless the jury were entirely satisfied that the defendant made an effective and substantial entry into the bedroom without the complainant doing or saying anything to cause him to believe that she was consenting to his entering it, he ought not to be convicted of the offence charged. The point is a narrow one, as narrow maybe as the window sill which is crucial to this case. But this is a criminal charge of gravity and, even though one may suspect that his intention was to commit the offence charged, unless the facts show with clarity that he in fact committed it he ought not to remain convicted.

Some question arose whether or not the defendant can be regarded as a trespasser *ab initio*. But we are entirely in agreement with the view ... that the common law doctrine of trespass *ab initio* has no application to burglary under the Theft Act 1968. One further matter that was canvassed ought perhaps to be mentioned. The point was raised that, the complainant not being the tenant or occupier of the dwelling house and her mother being apparently in occupation, this girl herself could not in any event have extended an effective invitation to enter, so that even if she had expressly and with full knowledge of all material facts invited the defendant in, he would nevertheless be a trespasser. Whatever the position in the law of tort, to regard such a proposition as acceptable in the criminal law would be unthinkable.

We have to say that this appeal must be allowed on the basis that the jury were never invited to consider the vital question whether this young man did enter the premises as a trespasser, that is to say knowing perfectly well that he had no invitation to enter or reckless of whether or not his entry was with permission ...

R v Ryan (1996) 160 JP 610 (CA)

Hirst LJ:

. . . The facts of the burglary are as follows. At about 2.30 am on Sunday 13 November 1994 the appellant was found stuck in a downstairs window by the elderly occupier. The window was 1 ft high and 2 ft 6 ins across. The appellant had his head and right arm inside the window and was trapped by the window itself on his neck. The rest of his body remained outside the window. On being accosted by the householder, the appellant said: 'Have you any Fairy Liquid? I'm stuck in the window.' The occupier demanded to know what he was doing there, to which he replied: 'I'm getting my baseball hat. My mate's put my baseball hat through the window.' The police were called and recovered a knife and a baseball hat from the ground outside the window in which the appellant was stuck. These two items significantly were the same knife and hat which formed the subject matter of the handling charge to which the appellant pleaded guilty. Eventually, the fire brigade had to be summoned to extricate the appellant from the window.

He was interviewed at 2.25 pm on the same day at Swindon police station and maintained his scarcely credible story that the baseball cap had been dropped through the open window by another person. He repeated the same line of defence in his evidence at the trial, which not surprisingly was disbelieved by the jury.

The appeal against conviction raises one point and one point only, namely whether as a matter of law his action was capable of constituting an entry . . .

His Lordship quoted from s 9(1) of the Theft Act 1968 and went on:

The question is, was this capable of constituting an entry? That point was conclusively decided in *R v Brown* . . . The judgment of the court was given by Watkins LJ. In that case also there was a partial entry through a window. The very same point was taken as in the present case, namely:

> Counsel for the appellant contends there can be no offence committed under the provisions of s 9(1) unless the person accused of the burglary is found upon the facts to have been at the relevant time wholly within the building.

That proposition was rejected by the court and Watkins LJ made it crystal clear in his judgment that a person can enter in the circumstances where only part of his body is actually within the premises.

[Counsel for the appellant] sought to distinguish *Brown's* case from the present case on the footing that in the former the appellant was capable of stealing property within the building, whereas in the present case, since the appellant was stuck firm by his neck in the window, he was incapable. That is a totally irrelevant distinction which in no way affects the principle laid down in *Brown* which is binding on us. There, the partial entry was capable of constituting entry. So here also this partial presence of the appellant within the building, albeit stuck in the window, was capable of constituting entry and it was therefore a matter for the jury to decide, as the learned recorder admirably directed them. The appeal against conviction will therefore be dismissed . . .

11.3.3 *MENS REA* FOR TRESPASS

R v Collins [1973] QB 100 (CA)

Edmund Davies LJ:

. . . We hold that, for the purposes of s 9 of the Theft Act 1968, a person entering a building is not guilty of trespass if he enters without knowledge that he is trespassing or at least without acting recklessly as to whether or not he is unlawfully entering . . .

. . . In the judgment of this court there cannot be a conviction for entering premises 'as a trespasser' within the meaning of s 9 of the Theft Act 1968 unless the person entering does so knowing that he is a trespasser and nevertheless deliberately enters, or, at the very least, is reckless as to whether or not he is entering the premises of another without the other party's consent.

Having so held, the pivotal point of this appeal is whether the Crown established that this defendant at the moment that he entered the bedroom knew perfectly well that he was not welcome there or, being reckless whether he was welcome or not, was nevertheless determined to enter.

R v Jones; *R v Smith* [1976] 1 WLR 672 (CA)

The appellants were charged with burglary, contrary to s 9(1)(b) of the Theft Act 1968. The prosecution case was that they had entered the house of Smith's father and stolen two television sets. Smith's father had reported the theft to the police at the time, but at the trial of Smith and Jones he gave evidence to the effect that he had given Smith unreserved permission to enter the house, stating that his son, Christopher Smith, 'would not be a trespasser in the house at any time'.

James LJ:

Mr Rose [counsel for the appellants] argues that a person who had a general permission to enter premises of another person cannot be a trespasser. His submission is as short and as simple as that. Related to this case he says that a son to whom a father has given permission generally to enter the father's house cannot be a trespasser if he enters it even though he had decided in his mind before making the entry to commit a criminal offence of theft against the father once he had got into the house and had entered the house solely for the purpose of committing that theft. It is a bold submission. Mr Rose frankly accepts that there has been no decision of the court since this statute was passed which governs particularly this point. He has reminded us of the decision in *Byrne v Kinematograph Renters Society Ltd* [1958] 2 All ER 579 . . . In that case persons had entered a cinema by producing tickets not for the purpose of seeing the show, but for an ulterior purpose. It was held in the action, which sought to show that they entered as trespassers pursuant to a conspiracy to trespass, that in fact they were not trespassers. The important words in the judgment of Harman J at p 593D are 'They did nothing that they were not invited to do . . .' That provides a distinction between that case and what we consider the position to be in this case . . . We were also referred to *Collins* (1972) 56 Cr App R 554; [1973] QB 100 and in particular to the long passage of Edmund Davies LJ, as he then was, commencing at pp 559 and 104 of the respective reports where the learned Lord Justice commenced the consideration of what is involved by the words '. . . the entry must be "as a trespasser" '. . . . In our view the passage there referred to is consonant with the passage in the well-known case of *Hillen and Pettigrew v ICI (Alkali) Ltd* [1936] AC 65 where, in the speech of Lord Atkin these words appear at p 69: 'My Lords, in my opinion this duty to an invitee only extends so long and so far as the invitee is making what can reasonably be contemplated as an ordinary and reasonable use of the premises by the invitee for the purpose for which he has been invited. He is not invited to use any part of the premises for purposes which he knows are wrongfully dangerous and constitute an improper use.' As Scrutton LJ has pointedly said [in *The Calgarth* [1926] P 93 at p 110] 'When you invite a person into your house to use the staircase you do not invite him to slide down the banisters.' That case of course was a civil case in which it was sought to make the defendant liable for a tort.

The decision in *Collins* . . . added to the concept of trespass as a civil wrong only the mental element of *mens rea*, which is essential to the criminal offence. Taking the law as expressed in *Hillen and Pettigrew v ICI Ltd* . . . and in the case of *Collins* . . . it is our view that a person is a trespasser for the purpose of section 9(1)(b) . . . if he enters premises of another knowing that he is entering in excess of the permission that has been given to him, or being reckless as to whether he is entering in excess of the permission that has been given to him to enter, providing the facts are known to the accused which enable him to realise that he is acting in excess of the permission given or that he is acting recklessly as to whether he exceeds that permission, then that is sufficient for the jury to decide that he is in fact a trespasser.

In this particular case it was a matter for the jury to consider whether, on all the facts, it was shown by the prosecution that the appellants entered with the knowledge that entry was being effected against the consent or in excess of the consent that had been given by Mr Smith senior to his son Christopher. The jury were, by their verdict, satisfied of that. It was a novel argument that we heard, interesting but one without, in our view, any foundation.

11.3.4 THE ULTERIOR INTENT REQUIRED UNDER S 9(1)(A)

R v Walkington [1979] 1 WLR 1169 (CA)

See above for the facts of this case.

Geoffrey Lane LJ:

. . . [His Lordship turned to the second issue in the appeal, namely that there was no evidence that there was anything capable of being stolen.] In this case there is no doubt that the defendant was not on the evidence in two minds as to whether to steal or not. He was intending to steal when he went to that till and it would be totally unreal to ask oneself, or for the jury to ask themselves, the question, what sort of intent did he have? Was it a conditional intention to steal if there was money in the till or a conditional intention to steal only if what he found there was worth stealing? In this case it was a cash till and what plainly he was intending to steal was the contents of the till, which was cash. The mere fact that the till happened to be empty does not destroy his undoubted intention at the moment when he crossed the boundary between the legitimate part of the store and the illegitimate part of the store . . .

. . . It seems to this court that in the end one simply has to go back to the words of the Act itself which we have already cited, and if the jury are satisfied, so as to feel sure, that the defendant has entered any building or part of a building as a trespasser, and are satisfied that at the moment of entering he intended to steal anything in the building or that part of it, the fact that there was nothing in the building worth his while to steal seems to us to be immaterial. He nevertheless had the intent to steal. As we see it, to hold otherwise would be to make a nonsense of this part of the Act and cannot have been the intention of the legislature at the time when the Theft Act 1968 was passed. Nearly every prospective burglar could no doubt truthfully say that he only intended to steal if he found something in the building worth stealing.

Attorney General's Refs (Nos 1 and 2 of 1979) [1980] QB 180 (CA)

Roskill LJ:

. . . The question referred in *Reference No 1* is:

Whether a man who has entered a house as a trespasser with the intention of stealing money therein is entitled to be acquitted of an offence against s 9(1)(a) of the Theft Act 1968 on the grounds that his intention to steal is conditional upon his finding money in the house.

The answer of this court to this question is 'No'.

In the second reference the question is:

Whether a man who is attempting to enter a house as a trespasser with the intention of stealing anything of value which he may find therein is entitled to be acquitted of the offence of attempted burglary on the ground that at the time of the attempt his said intention was insufficient to amount to 'the intention of stealing anything' necessary for conviction under s 9 of the Theft Act 1968.

The answer of this court to this question is also 'No'.

His Lordship then referred to *R v Husseyn* (1977) 67 Cr App R 131 and continued:

The indictment in *R v Husseyn* – the Registrar has supplied the court with copies – was as follows:

Statement of Offence: Attempted Theft.
Particulars of Offence: Ulus Husseyn and Andrew Demetriou on or about the 27th day of February 1976 in Greater London, attempted to steal a quantity of sub-aqua equipment belonging to David Johnson.

Here therefore the relevant count was of attempted theft and not of theft but the charge related to a specific object. Therefore it was essential, in order to establish guilt on this charge of attempted theft, that the accused's intention had been to steal, not the contents of the parked van in question, but the specific object named in the count, namely the sub-aqua equipment. Lord Scarman's judgment must be understood against the background of that fundamental fact . . .

[Lord Scarman in *R v Husseyn* said:]

> . . . it cannot be said that one who has it in mind to steal only if what he finds is worth stealing has a present intention to steal.
>
> We were asked to say that either that sentence was wrong or that it was *obiter*. We are not prepared to do either. If we may say so with the utmost deference to any statement of law by Lord Scarman, if this sentence be open to criticism, it is because in the context it is a little elliptical. If one rewrites that sentence, so that it reads: 'It must be wrong, for it cannot be said that one who has it in mind to steal only if what he finds is worth stealing has a present intention to steal *the specific item charged*' (our emphasis added), then the difficulties disappear, because, as already stated, what was charged was attempted theft of a specific object . . .
>
> I come back to what Lord Scarman himself said in *Director of Public Prosecutions v Nock* [1978] AC 979 . . .
>
> > An intention to steal can exist even though, unknown to the accused, there is nothing to steal: but, if a man be in two minds whether to steal or not, the intention required by the statute is not proved.

11.3.5 SECTION 9(1)(b) OF THE THEFT ACT 1968: THEFT AND APPROPRIATION

For there to have been a burglary there must have been a theft, and therefore there must have been an appropriation.

R v Gregory (1981) 77 Cr App R 41 (CA)

The appellant was charged with burglary of a dwelling house. He gave evidence at his trial that a man called Tony, knowing that the appellant was a general dealer, had told him that his (Tony's) parents had died and that he was clearing out their bungalow. It was agreed that the appellant should visit the bungalow to see if there was anything he wished to purchase. The appellant and Tony went to a bungalow in Broadstairs and the appellant took some jewellery. He said that he did not realise that Tony had told him a pack of lies.

> Watkins LJ:
> . . . [His Lordship referred to the judgment of Eveleigh LJ in *R v Hale* (1978) 68 Cr App R 415 at 418 and continued:] Nor do we think that in a given criminal enterprise involving theft there can necessarily be only one 'appropriation' within s 3(1) of the Theft Act 1968. It seems to us that the question of whether, when and by whom there has been an appropriation of property has always to be determined by the jury having regard to the circumstances of the case. The length of time involved, the manner in which it came about and the number of people who can properly be said to have taken part in an appropriation will vary according to those circumstances. In a case of burglary of a dwelling-house and before any property is removed from it, it may consist of a continuing process and involve either a single appropriation by one or more persons or a number of appropriations of the property in the house by several persons at different times during the same incident. If this were not a correct exposition of the law of appropriation, startling and disturbing consequences could arise out of the presence of two or more trespassers in a dwelling-house.

Thus a person who may have more the appearance of a handler than the thief can nevertheless still be convicted of theft, and thus of burglary, if the jury are satisfied that with the requisite dishonest intent he appropriated, or took part in the appropriation, of another person's goods.

COMMENTS AND QUESTIONS

1   For D to have entered a building for the purposes of burglary it is not necessary that his entire body should be within the building. In *R v Brown* [1985] Crim LR 212, the appellant was caught standing on the pavement leaning in through a broken shop window to take goods on display. It was held that this satisfied the requirements of a 'substantial and effective' entry for the purposes of the offence.

2   In *R v Collins* (above) the Court of Appeal rejected the notion that only the complainant's parents could give others permission to enter the family home, yet in *R v Jones and Smith* the court ignored the father's evidence that his own son would never be a trespasser in his house. Are these approaches reconcilable?

11.4 TRESPASS WITH INTENT TO COMMIT A SEXUAL OFFENCE

In July 2000 the Home Office published its review of sexual offences, *Setting the Boundaries: Reforming the Law on Sex Offences*. The review examined the case for reforming the aspect of s 9(1)(a) that created liability for burglary based on D's entry as a trespasser with intent to rape:

2.16 Burglary with intent to rape

2.16.1 The Theft Act 1969 contains an aggravated burglary offence of burglary with intent to rape in s 9. This is an important element in the law on rape as it covers the situation where someone may break into a house (or office or other private place) 'with the intent of having sexual intercourse with the person within, if possible with consent but if not then by committing rape'. The rape does not have to take place for the offence to be committed. Even if no rape occurs, the trauma of being seriously threatened with rape by an intruder in your own bedroom or workplace, where you think you are safe, is profound . . .

2.16.2 We considered whether this offence should be left as an aggravated burglary, or whether it was a sex offence. We concluded that the essence of the crime was the sexual intent rather than the burglary, and that hence it should be regarded as a sex offence. We thought that there was a risk that being tucked away in the Theft Act, it was an offence that could be overlooked. We also noted that it did not carry a requirement to register under the Sex Offenders Act at present.

The existing offence of burglary with intent to rape would need to be redefined to take account of our proposals to reform the law of serious sex offences. In order to differentiate our new offence, we thought that the word trespass was preferable to burglary – and covers the same elements of unwanted intrusion. We also thought that as the intent to commit a sex offence was central to the

> offence, the redefinition should apply to trespass with intent to commit a serious sex offence – rape, sexual assault by penetration, sexual assault or adult sexual abuse of a child – and that it should be codified with other sex offences.

The response to this was the enactment of a new offence of trespass with intent to commit a sexual offence. Section 63 of the Sexual Offences Act 2003 provides:

> (1) A person commits an offence if –
>   (a) he is a trespasser on any premises,
>   (b) he intends to commit a relevant sexual offence on the premises, and
>   (c) he knows that, or is reckless as to whether, he is a trespasser.
> (2) In this section –
>   • 'premises' includes a structure or part of a structure;
>   • 'relevant sexual offence' has the same meaning as in section 62;
>   • 'structure' includes a tent, vehicle or vessel or other temporary or movable structure.

Hence, by virtue of s 63, it is now an offence for D to intend to commit a 'relevant sexual offence' (ie any offence under Part 1 of the 2003 Act, including an offence of aiding, abetting, counselling or procuring such an offence), whilst he is on any premises where he is a trespasser. D must either know or be reckless as to whether he is trespassing. The offence is triable summarily or on indictment and has a maximum penalty of 10 years.

11.5 AGGRAVATED BURGLARY

The gravity of burglary by a defendant armed with a weapon is denoted by the provision of a specific offence of aggravated burglary in s 10 of the Theft Act 1968. Section 10 provides:

> (1) A person is guilty of aggravated burglary if he commits any burglary and at the time has with him any firearm or imitation firearm, any weapon of offence, or any explosive; and for this purpose:
>   (a) 'firearm' includes an airgun or air pistol, and 'imitation firearm' means anything which has the appearance of being a firearm, whether capable of being discharged or not; and
>   (b) 'weapon of offence' means any article made or adapted for use for causing injury to or incapacitating a person, or intended by the person having it with him for such use; and
>   (c) 'explosive' means any article manufactured for the purpose of producing a practical effect by explosion, or intended by the person having it with him for that purpose.
> (2) A person guilty of aggravated burglary shall on conviction on indictment be liable to imprisonment for life.

11.5.1 WEAPON OF OFFENCE

If the weapon is not 'made or adapted for causing injury to or incapacitating a person', the defendant must intend to use the weapon for such a purpose during the particular burglary with which he is charged.

R v Stones [1989] 1 WLR 156 (CA)

The appellant was charged with aggravated burglary, contrary to s 10(1) of the Theft Act 1968.

> Glidewell LJ:
> . . . The primary facts, which were not in dispute at all, were these. The appellant admitted that he had taken part in a burglary of a dwelling house in Bedlington in the early hours of 29 June 1987. A police officer who was off duty had seen the appellant and another man loading stolen goods into a car. He telephoned the police. The two men ran off, but the appellant was caught running across a field and was arrested. When he was searched, a household knife was found in his pocket. When asked why he had it with him, he replied, 'For self-defence, because some lads from Blyth are after me.'
>
> Since it was a household knife, it was accepted by the prosecution that it was not, to go back to s 10(1) [of the Theft Act 1968], an article made or adapted for use for causing injury to or incapacitating a person. The prosecution accepted that they had to prove that it was intended by the person having it with him (the defendant) for such use . . .
>
> It is agreed by counsel that the prosecution must prove that the appellant knew that he had a knife with him at the relevant time. Clearly that is right, because otherwise he cannot have the relevant intent. As I have said, the prosecution submit that if he knowingly had the knife with him at the time of the burglary with the intention of using it to cause injury to or incapacitate the lads from Blyth if he met them, the offence is proved. It is not necessary to prove the intention to use the knife to cause injury etc during the course of the burglary.
>
> In our view that submission is correct. The mischief at which the section is clearly aimed is that if a burglar has a weapon which he intends to use to injure some person unconnected with the premises burgled, he may nevertheless be tempted to use it if challenged during the course of the burglary and put under sufficient pressure . . .

11.5.2 TIME AT WHICH DEFENDANT MUST HAVE WITH HIM THE FIREARM, ETC

If the allegation of burglary is brought under s 9(1)(a) the prosecution have to prove that *at the time of entering the building* as a trespasser with the intention to commit one of the specified offences (theft, grievous bodily harm, rape, criminal damage) the defendant had with him the firearm or other weapon.

If, on the other hand, the allegation of burglary is brought under s 9(1)(b), the time at which the defendant must be in possession of the firearm or other weapon is *the time at which he commits or attempts to commit one of the specified offences* (theft or grievous bodily harm): see *R v O'Leary* (1986) 82 Cr App R 341 (CA).

Lord Lane CJ:

. . . The facts of the case, which are not in dispute, were these. In the early hours of 31 January 1985 the appellant entered a house in South East London, almost certainly in search of money and valuables, though such an intent, namely the intent at the time of entry to steal, was not alleged against him. At the time of that entry he was unarmed. He looked round the house downstairs. It seems he found nothing there which interested him, except a kitchen knife with which he armed himself.

He then went upstairs. The occupants of the house, husband and wife, were disturbed. A struggle ensued in the course of which all three, husband, wife and the appellant, received injuries. The appellant demanded and was given, he at that point being armed still with the kitchen knife, some cash and a bracelet . . .

. . . Count 2 of the indictment reads as follows:

> Statement of Offence: Aggravated Burglary contrary to s 10(1) of the Theft Act 1968.
>
> Particulars of Offence: Michael O'Leary on 31st day of January 1985 entered as a tres-passer a building known as 104 Lyndhurst Grove, London SE15, and stole therein a sum of money, a bracelet, a number of keys and a cash card belonging to John Marsh, and at the time of committing the said burglary had with him a weapon of offence, namely a knife.

If he had been charged under subsection (1)(a), the offence of burglary would be completed and committed when he entered and it would be at that point that one would have to consider whether or not he was armed. But in the case of subsection (1)(b), which is the one under which he was charged, the offence is complete when, and not until, the stealing is committed, provided again of course that he has trespassed in the first place. The prosecution did not have to prove an intent to steal at the time of entry as the charge is laid here. Indeed such an intent is irrelevant to the charge as laid.

It follows that under this particular charge, the time at which the defendant must be proved to have had with him a weapon of offence to make him guilty of aggravated burglary was the time at which he actually stole. As already indicated, at that moment, when he confronted the house-holders and demanded their cash and jewellery, which was the theft, he still had the kitchen knife in his hand . . .

The judge ruled, as this court has indicated he should have ruled, namely that the material time in this charge for the possession of the weapon was the time when he confronted the householders and stole . . .

R v Kelly (1992) 97 Cr App R 245 (CA)

Potts J:

. . . The prosecution's case was that on 19 June 1991, in the early hours of the morning, the appellant broke into a house in Brixton using a screwdriver to effect entry. He was surprised by the occupants of the house, a young couple, Mr Sheterline and Ms Matthews, while removing a video recorder from the living room . . . The relevant part of [Mr Sheterline's evidence] reads as follows:

> I went back into the living room and looked towards the bar and shouted, 'Oi, what do you want?' On hearing this, a black man sprung up from behind the bar. He looked unshaven

with short black hair and was wearing a black hooded anorak with the hood down. He said to me, 'Where's the remote for the video?' I threw my knife over to the TV and video recorder which are in the far left-hand corner of the room and handed both remote control units to him. Whilst I was there, he said, 'Unplug the TV and video'. He had already turned the light off and he had pulled the hood up over his head and I suddenly felt him push something into the left-hand side of my rib cage. I could see it had a brown handle with a blunt metal end to it. It looked like a chisel.

I said to the man, 'Can I turn the light on because I can't see what I'm doing.' He said, 'No'. I said, 'Don't hurt us, just take the stuff and go, we won't say anything.'

The appellant then attempted to leave the house with the video in one hand and the screwdriver in the other, but he was apprehended by the police who had attended in response to information received from a member of the public. When the appellant emerged from the house, a policeman saw him holding the screwdriver in his hand.

. . . Thus the charge derives from s 9(1)(b) of the Act and the time at which the appellant must be proved to have had with him a weapon of offence to make him guilty of aggravated burglary was the time he actually stole: the screwdriver would become a weapon of offence on proof that the appellant intended to use it for causing injury to, or incapacitating Mr Sheterline or Ms Matthews at the time of the theft, thereby aggravating the burglary: s 10(1)(b). This construction follows from the clear language of s 10 of the Theft Act, and is consistent with its purpose.

11.5.3 '. . . HAS WITH HIM . . .'

This phrase connotes a degree of immediate control over the firearm or weapon.

R v Kelt [1977] 1 WLR 1365 (CA)

The defendant was charged that he 'had with him a firearm . . . with intent to commit an indictable offence' contrary to s 18 of the Firearms Act 1968.

Scarman LJ:

. . . [T]here must be a very close physical link and a degree of immediate control over the weapon by the man alleged to have the firearm with him . . .

. . . [T]he judge [must] make it clear to the jury that possession of the firearm is not enough, that the law requires the evidence to go a stage further and to establish that the accused had the firearm with him. Of course the classic case of having a gun with you is if you are carrying it. But, even if you are not carrying it, you may yet have it with you, if it is immediately available to you. But if all that can be shown is possession in the sense that it is in your house or in a shed or somewhere where you have ultimate control, that is not enough.

R v Pawlicki [1992] 1 WLR 827 (CA)

The defendant was charged that he 'had with him a firearm' contrary to s 18 of the Firearms Act 1968.

Steyn LJ:

... A man who leaves a shotgun at home while he proceeds to the next town to rob a bank is still in possession of the shotgun but he does not 'have it with him' when he commits the robbery at the bank. Under s 18 [of the Firearms Act 1968] the words 'have it' import an element of propinquity which is not required for possession. [Further] 'having with him a firearm' is a wider concept than carrying the firearm.

11.6 GOING EQUIPPED FOR STEALING, ETC

The offence 'going equipped' under s 25 of the Theft Act 1968 (as amended by the Fraud Act 2006), is not related solely to burglary but is clearly of particular relevance as an ancillary offence. The rationale of the offence clearly being that intervention prior to the commission of offences such as burglary and theft (including robbery) is in the public interest. As originally enacted the offence extended to those found in possession of articles for the use in burglary, theft or a 'cheat' – the latter term being used to denote the offence of obtaining property by deception that was created by s 15 of the Theft Act 1968. The Fraud Act 2006 abolished the deception offence under s 15 replacing it with a range of fraud offences under ss 2 to 4 of the 2006 Act. Consequently s 25 of the 1968 Act was amended to remove references to a 'cheat'. Section 6 of the 2006 Act creates a new offence of being in possession of articles for use in committing a fraud; see further Chapter 10.7.

Section 25 of the Theft Act 1968 (as amended by the Fraud Act 2006) provides:

(1) A person shall be guilty of an offence if, when not at his place of abode, he has with him any article for use in the course of or in connection with any burglary or theft.

(2) A person guilty of an offence under this section shall on conviction on indictment be liable to imprisonment for a term not exceeding three years.

(3) Where a person is charged with an offence under this section, proof that he had with him any article made or adapted for use in committing a burglary or theft shall be evidence that he had it with him for such use.

(4) Any person may arrest without warrant anyone who is, or whom he, with reasonable cause, suspects to be, committing an offence under this section.

(5) For the purposes of this section an offence under s 12(1) of this Act of taking a conveyance shall be treated as theft.

The elements of the offence of 'going equipped' are:

(1) that the defendant is not at his 'place of abode'; and

(2) that he 'has with him' (ie has in his possession) certain articles; and

(3) that those articles are for use to commit burglary or theft.

11.6.1 PLACE OF ABODE

R v Bundy [1977] 1 WLR 914 (CA)

Lawton LJ:

. . . The particulars of the offence . . . were as follows: that the defendant and a man called Evans 'on 21 April 1975, when not in their places of abode, had with them a piece of piping, a hammer, a pipe threader and three pieces of stocking for use in the course of or in connection with theft'.

. . . On arresting the defendant and his passenger, the police searched the motor car [which the defendant had been driving]. In it they found the articles referred to in the particulars of offence. It was accepted in this court that there was evidence on which the jury could properly have decided that all the articles were articles for use in the course of or in connection with theft . . .

At the trial, in the witness box, [the defendant's] evidence was that about four or five weeks before his arrest, he had borrowed the motor car in which he was arrested from a friend, and that he had lived in that motor car, travelling around in it . . .

. . . [I]t is manifest that no offence is committed if a burglar keeps the implements of his criminal trade in his place of abode. He only commits an offence when he takes them from his place of abode. The phrase 'place of abode', in our judgment, connotes, first of all, a site. That is the ordinary meaning of the word 'place'. It is a site at which the occupier intends to abide. So, there are two elements in the phrase 'place of abode' – the element of site and the element of intention. When the defendant took the motor car to a site with the intention of abiding there, then his motor car on that site could be said to be his 'place of abode', but when he took it from that site to move it to another site where he intended to abide, the motor car could not be said to be his 'place of abode' during transit.

When he was arrested by the police he was not intending to abide on the site where he was arrested. It follows that he was not then at his place of abode. He may have had a place of abode the previous night, but he was away from it at the time of his arrest when in possession of articles which could be used for the purpose of theft . . .

11.6.2 '. . . HAS WITH HIM . . .'

This phrase, which also appears in s 10 of the Act (aggravated burglary), connotes a 'degree of immediate control': see *R v Kelt* (above); *R v Pawlicki* (above).

11.6.3 '. . . FOR USE FOR BURGLARY OR THEFT . . .'

'Burglary' means burglary for the purposes of s 9 of the Act; 'theft' means theft for the purposes of s 1 of the Act or taking a conveyance contrary to s 12 of the Act.

It can be proved that the defendant had the requisite intention in either of two ways:

(1) if the article in question is 'made or adapted' for use in burglary or theft (e.g. a jemmy or a bunch of skeleton keys), this very fact is evidence that the defendant intended to use the article for such purpose (so, effectively, a burden of proof is placed on the defendant to show that he had the article with him for an innocent purpose); or

(2) if the article is innocuous in itself (e.g. a screwdriver), the prosecution have to prove that

the defendant intended to use it for burglary or theft (much will depend, of course, on the circumstances in which the defendant is found to be in possession of the article).

The defendant must have intended to use the article at some time in the future (in other words for an offence of burglary or theft which has not yet been committed). It is not enough that the article has been used in an offence of burglary, theft or cheat which has already been committed.

R v Ellames [1974] 1 WLR 1391 (CA)

A robbery took place in the course of which certain articles, including a sawn-off shotgun, were used. The appellant was charged with robbery and with going equipped for stealing contrary to s 25(1) of the Theft Act 1968. The case against the appellant was that, although he might not have been present at the robbery, he had helped with the planning of it, and that afterwards he had helped the robbers to escape, and in particular that he had helped in hiding the articles used in the robbery.

Browne J:
. . . [NB references to 'cheat' in this judgment reflect the fact the prosecution occurred prior to the changes introduced by the Fraud Act 2006] In our judgment, the words in s 25(1) of the 1968 Act: 'has with him any article for use' mean 'has with him for the purpose' (or 'with the intention') 'that they will be used'. The effect of s 25(3) is that if the article is one 'made or adapted for use in committing a burglary, theft or cheat', that is evidence of the necessary intention, though not of course conclusive evidence. If the article is not one 'made or adapted' for such use, the intention must be proved on the whole of the evidence – as it must be in the case of an article which is so made or adapted, if the defendant produces some innocent explanation. We agree with the learned authors of Smith and Hogan's *Criminal Law* that s 25 is directed against acts preparatory to burglary, theft or cheat; that:

> Questions as to D's knowledge of the nature of the thing can hardly arise here, since it must be proved that he intended to use it in the course of or in connection with [burglary, theft or cheat]; and that the *mens rea* for this offence includes 'an intention to use the article in the course of or in connection with any of the specified crimes'.

An intention to use must necessarily relate to use in the future. . . . It seems to us impossible to interpret s 25(1) of the 1968 Act as if it read: 'has with him any article for use or which *has been used* in the course of or in connection with any burglary, theft or cheat'. Equally, it is impossible to read s 25(3) as if it said: 'had it with him for or *after* such use'.

In our judgment the words 'for use' govern the whole of the words which follow. The object and effect of the words 'in connection with' is to add something to 'in the course of'. It is easy to think of cases where an article could be intended for use 'in connection with' though not 'in the course of' a burglary etc, e.g. articles intended to be used while doing preparatory acts or while escaping after the crime . . .

In our view, to establish an offence under s 25(1) the prosecution must prove that the defendant was in possession of the article, and intended the article to be used in the course of or in connection with some future burglary, theft or cheat. But it is not necessary to prove that he intended it to be used in the course of or in connection with any *specific* burglary, theft or cheat; it is enough to prove a general intention to use it for *some* burglary, theft or cheat; we think that this view is supported by the use of the word 'any' in s 25(1). Nor, in our view, is it necessary to prove that the defendant intended to use it himself; it will be enough to prove that he had it with him with the intention that it should be used by someone else. For example, if in the present case it had been proved that the defendant was hiding away these articles, which had already been used for one robbery, with the intention that they should later be used by someone for some other robbery, he would be guilty of an offence under s 25(1).

FURTHER READING

Mackenna, Sir Bernard, 'Blackmail: a criticism' [1966] Crim LR 466 'Coercion, threats, and the puzzle of blackmail', in G Lamond, AP Simester and ATH Smith (eds), *Harm and Culpability*, 1996, Oxford: OUP, 215

Pace, PJ, 'Burglarious trespass' [1985] Crim LR 716

Smith, JC, 'Burglary under the Theft Bill' [1968] Crim LR 367

CRIMINAL DAMAGE

12.1 INTRODUCTION

The offence of criminal damage was created by the Criminal Damage Act 1971, replacing the Malicious Damage Act of 1861. As an offence against property, some forms of criminal damage clearly share some of the features of the offence of theft, for example property belonging to another. There may indeed be situations where the prosecution may have a choice of bringing either theft or criminal damage charges. To destroy another's property is undoubtedly an appropriation for the purposes of theft. The determining factor may be that criminal damage does not require proof of dishonesty. For a period of almost 20 years from 1983, a key feature of criminal damage was the fact that *Caldwell* recklessness applied to both the 'simple' and 'aggravated' forms of the offence. As will have been seen from Chapter 3.3, *Caldwell* no longer governs recklessness in this area following the House of Lords' decision in *R v G* [2003] 4 All ER 765.

Section 1 of the Criminal Damage Act 1971 provides:

> (1) A person who without lawful excuse destroys or damages any property belonging to another intending to destroy or damage any such property or being reckless as to whether any such property would be destroyed or damaged shall be guilty of an offence.
>
> . . .

(3) An offence committed under this section by destroying or damaging property by fire shall be charged as arson.

12.2 PROPERTY BELONGING TO ANOTHER

Property, for the purposes of the Criminal Damage Act 1971, is defined by s 10(1), which provides:

(1) In this Act 'property' means property of a tangible nature, whether real or personal, including money and:
   (a) including wild creatures which have been tamed or are ordinarily kept in captivity, and any other wild creatures or their carcasses if, but only if, they have been reduced into possession which has not been lost or abandoned or are in the course of being reduced into possession; but
   (b) not including mushrooms growing wild on any land or flowers, fruit or foliage of a plant growing wild on any land.
   For the purposes of this subsection 'mushroom' includes any fungus and 'plant' includes any shrub or tree.

The term 'belonging to another' is defined by s 10(2), which provides:

(2) Property shall be treated for the purposes of this Act as belonging to any person:
   (a) having the custody or control of it;
   (b) having in it any proprietary right or interest (not being an equitable interest arising only from an agreement to transfer or grant an interest); or
   (c) having a charge on it.
(3) Where property is subject to a trust, the persons to whom it belongs shall be so treated as including any person having a right to enforce the trust.

Although the offence created by s 1(1) of the Criminal Damage Act 1971 requires the destruction or damage of property 'belonging to another', it is possible to be guilty of an offence under s 1(1) even though the property damaged belongs to the defendant, provided that someone else also has a proprietary right in the property. For the offence of aggravated criminal damage under s 1(2) of the Criminal Damage Act 1971 it does not matter to whom the property belongs.

12.3 DAMAGE OR DESTROY

Damage need not be permanent: it is enough if taking remedial steps costs time, labour and expense, or if the value or usefulness of the property has been damaged.

Cox v Riley (1986) 83 Cr App R 54 (DC)

Stephen Brown LJ:

... The justices in the case state that they found the following facts: (1) the defendant was employed by Hi-Tech Profiles Limited to work on a computerised saw owned by that company; (2) that the computerised saw relied for its operation on a printed circuit card being inserted into it, containing programs which enabled the saw to be operated so that it could cut window frame profiles of different designs; (3) that the printed circuit card was of no use to the company unless it contained programs which enabled it to cause the saw to operate as (2) above; (4) that on 30 July 1984 the defendant blanked the computerised saw of all its 16 programs thereby erasing the said programs from the printed circuit card by operating the program cancellation facility, contained within the computerised saw, once for each individual program removed; (5) that the defendant's action rendered the computerised saw inoperable, save for limited manual operation, which would cause production to be slowed dramatically ...

They ask this court the following question: can the erasing of a program from printed circuit card which is used to operate a computerised saw constitute damage within the meaning of the Criminal Damage Act 1971? ...

The question of damage has been considered by the Court of Appeal, Criminal Division, on 29 November 1984 in the unreported case of *Henderson and Battley*. The court was presided over by Lawton LJ and he was sitting with Cantley J and Sir John Thompson. Cantley J gave the judgment of the court.

In that case the facts were different, but it is relevant on the meaning of damage. In that case the charge was one of damaging a development land site, intending to damage that property or being reckless as to whether it would be damaged. The facts concerned a development site in the Isle of Dogs which had been cleared for development. It was flat except for a pile of crushed concrete which was kept there intentionally so that it could be used eventually in the laying of temporary roads whilst the development was carried on.

On the occasion in question 30 lorry loads of soil and rubble and mud were tipped on to the site. The appellants in that case, pretending to act with authority, had been operating the site, as Cantley J said, impudently as a public tip and charging their customers for the rubbish which was tipped. There was a submission before the trial judge which was repeated before the Court of Appeal that what they had done could not be said to have damaged the land, bearing in mind that this was a site cleared for building development. The argument was that the land was not damaged because the land beneath the piles of rubbish which had been tipped upon it was in the same condition as it was before the rubbish was tipped upon it. It was argued that there must be a distinction between the cost of putting something right and actual damage.

Cantley J said in the course of this judgment at 3B of the transcript:

There is of course such a distinction, but if as here there is evidence that the owner of the land reasonably found it necessary to spend about £2,000 to remove the results of the appellants' operations it is not irrelevant to the question of whether this land, as a building site, was damaged. Ultimately whether damage was done to this land was a question of fact and degree for the jury. Damage can be various kinds. In the *Concise Oxford Dictionary* 'damage' is defined as 'injury impairing value or usefulness'. That is a definition which would fit in very well with doing something to a cleared building site which at any rate for the time being impairs its usefulness as such. In addition, as it necessitates work and the expenditure of a large sum of money to restore it to its former state, it reduces its present value as a building site. This land was a perfectly good building site which did not need £2,000 spending on it in order to sell or use it as such until the appellants began their operations.

. . . It seems to me that the principle as explained by Cantley J applies in full measure to the present case. Undoubtedly . . . the defendant in this instance for some reason, perhaps a grudge, wished to put out of action, albeit temporarily, the computerised saw, and he was able to do that by operating the computer blanking mechanism in order to erase from the printed circuit card the relevant programs. That made it necessary for time and labour and money to be expended in order to replace the relevant programs on the printed circuit card . . .

It seems to me to be quite untenable to argue that what this defendant did on this occasion did not amount to causing damage to property, and for this reason I would dismiss the appeal.

I would answer the question posed by the justices . . . with the emphatic answer yes.

R v Whiteley (1991) 93 Cr App R 25 (CA)

The appellant was a 'computer hacker'. He gained unauthorised access to a computer network ('JANET') and altered data contained on disks in the system, thereby causing the computers in question to fail and to be unable to operate properly; the computers had to be shut down for periods of time.

Lord Lane CJ:

. . . The prosecution case was twofold. First, that the appellant caused criminal damage to the computers by bringing about temporary impairment of usefulness of them by causing them to be shut down for periods of time preventing them from operating properly; second, that he caused criminal damage to the disks by way of alteration to the state of the magnetic particles on them so as to delete and add files; the disks and the magnetic particles on them containing the information being one entity and capable of being damaged.

The jury acquitted the appellant on those counts which were based upon the first leg of the prosecution case, namely criminal damage to the computers. The counts on which they convicted were based upon the second leg, namely the allegation of damage to the disks . . .

The evidence before the jury was that the disks are so constructed as to contain upon them thousands, if not millions, of magnetic particles. By issuing commands to the computer, impulses are produced which magnetise or demagnetise those particles in a particular way. By that means it is possible to write data or information on the disks and to program them to fulfil a variety of functions. By the same method it is possible to delete or alter data, information or instructions which have previously been written on to the disk . . .

. . . What the Act requires to be proved is that tangible property has been damaged, not necessarily that the damage itself should be tangible. There can be no doubt that the magnetic particles upon the metal discs were a part of the disks and if the appellant was proved to have intentionally and without lawful excuse altered the particles in such a way as to cause an impairment of the value or usefulness of the disk to the owner, there would be damage within the meaning of s 1. The fact that the alteration could only be perceived by operating the computer did not make the alterations any the less real, or the damage, if the alteration amounted to damage, any the less within the ambit of the Act . . .

. . . Any alteration to the physical nature of the property concerned may amount to damage within the meaning of the section. Whether it does so or not will depend upon the effect that the alteration has had upon the legitimate operator (who for convenience may be referred to as the owner). If the hacker's actions do not go beyond, for example, mere tinkering with an otherwise 'empty' disk, no damage would be established. Where, on the other hand, the interference with the disk amounts to an impairment of the value or usefulness of the disk to the owner, then the necessary damage is established . . .

 COMMENTS AND QUESTIONS

1   Although *Cox v Riley* and *R v Whiteley* remain good law on the interpretation of the Criminal Damage Act 1971, and so the general principles they lay down remain valid, damage to computers is now governed by the Computer Misuse Act 1990.

2   *Roe v Kingerlee* [1986] Crim LR 735 confirms that it is not necessary that the damage caused should be permanent before an act can constitute criminal damage. Whether or not the application of graffiti to a structure will amount to causing criminal damage will be a question of fact and degree for the tribunal of fact. Hence in *Hardman and Others v The Chief Constable of Avon and Somerset Constabulary* [1986] Crim LR 330, HHJ Llewellyn-Jones sitting at Bristol Crown Court determined that human silhouettes painted on an asphalt pavement to represent vaporised human remains could amount to criminal damage notwithstanding that the 'paint' used was a fat-free unstable whitewash, which was soluble in water. There had been damage, which had caused expense and inconvenience to the local authority.

3   Further evidence that damage can be caused even where the interference with property is transient and remediable is provided by *R v Fiak* [2005] All ER (D) 103 – the court holding that wetting a blanket and floor with clean water could amount to damage for the purposes of the 1971 Act.

12.4 WITHOUT LAWFUL EXCUSE

A defendant charged with criminal damage has available to him the normal range of general defences in criminal law, in particular common law defences based on duress, necessity and self-defence (ie reasonable force to protect property). As will be seen below, however, s 5 of the

Criminal Damage Act 1971 makes specific provision for situations where the defendant can claim to have been acting with lawful excuse where he damages or destroys property. As the absence of lawful excuse is one of the elements of the offence, the burden is on the prosecution to establish beyond all reasonable doubt that the defendant did not have any lawful excuse as defined in s 5.

Section 5 provides as follows:

Section 5 of the Criminal Damage Act 1971: 'without lawful excuse'

(1) This section applies to any offence under s 1(1) above and any offence under s 2 or 3 above other than one involving a threat by the person charged to destroy or damage property in a way which he knows is likely to endanger the life of another or involving an intent by the person charged to use or cause or permit the use of something in his custody or under his control so to destroy or damage property.

(2) A person charged with an offence to which this section applies shall, whether or not he would be treated for the purposes of this Act as having a lawful excuse apart from this subsection, be treated for those purposes as having a lawful excuse:

    (a) if at the time of the act or acts alleged to constitute the offence he believed that the person or persons whom he believed to be entitled to consent to the destruction of or damage to the property in question had so consented, or would have so consented to it if he or they had known of the destruction or damage and its circumstances; or

    (b) if he destroyed or damaged or threatened to destroy or damage the property in question or, in the case of a charge of an offence under s 3 above, intended to use or cause or permit the use of something to destroy or damage it, in order to protect property belonging to himself or another or a right or interest in property which was or which he believed to be vested in himself or another, and at the time of the act or acts alleged to constitute the offence he believed:

        (i) that the property, right or interest was in immediate need of protection; and

        (ii) that the means of protection adopted or proposed to be adopted were or would be reasonable having regard to all the circumstances.

        (iii) For the purposes of this section it is immaterial whether a belief is justified or not if it is honestly held.

        (iv) For the purposes of subsection (2) above a right or interest in property includes any right or privilege in or over land, whether created by grant, licence or otherwise.

        (v) This section shall not be construed as casting doubt on any defence recognised by law as a defence to criminal charges.

(3) For the purposes of this section it is immaterial whether a belief is justified or not if it is honestly held.

(4) For the purposes of subsection (2) above a right or interest in property includes any right or privilege in or over land, whether created by grant, licence or otherwise.

(5) This section shall not be construed as casting doubt on any defence recognised by law as a defence to criminal charges.

R v Denton [1981] 1 WLR 1446 (CA)

Lord Lane CJ:

[The defendant was charged with] arson contrary to s 1(1) and (3) of the 1971 Act, the particulars being that the defendant:

> on the 3rd day of January 1980 without lawful excuse damaged by fire a building known as Barnfield Mill belonging to Leslie Fink & Co Ltd and the contents thereof belonging to Albus Products Ltd intending to damage such property or being reckless as to whether such property would be damaged.

The facts of the case are somewhat unusual. There is no dispute that on 3 January 1980 the defendant set light to some machinery in the cotton mill. The machinery was very badly damaged, and as a result of that conflagration damage was also done, to a much lesser degree it is true, to the building itself. The total damage to stock and building was said to be some £40,000.

On Monday 17 March 1980, the defendant presented himself at the police station and told the police that he had in fact started that fire. He described how he had done it, and he then made a statement under caution, in which he gave his reason for having started the fire: that it was for the benefit of the business, because the business was in difficulties, and, although he was going to get no direct benefit from it himself, he thought he would be doing a good turn to the financial status of the company if he were to set light to the premises and goods as he did . . .

When it came to the trial . . . he gave evidence that his employer, whom we will refer to as 'T' for obvious reasons, had asked him to put the machines out of action and he had agreed to set light to them. The reason given to him by the employer for that request was because the company was in difficulties; the way that T put it was: 'There is nothing like a good fire for improving the financial circumstances of a business.'

. . . It was agreed on all hands for the purpose of this case that T was the person who, any evil motives apart, was entitled to consent to the damage. It was likewise conceded that the defendant honestly believed that T occupied that position and was entitled to consent.

. . . It is quite apparent . . . that in so far as the 1971 Act is concerned it is not an offence for a man to damage or injure or destroy to set fire to his own premises.

One therefore turns to see what the situation would have been had T made a confession in the same, or similar, terms as that made by the defendant, and to see what would have happened to the Crown's argument if the two of them, T and the defendant, stood charged under s 1(1) of the 1971 Act in the Crown Court. It is not an offence for a man to set light to his own property. So T would have been acquitted. But if the Crown is correct, the defendant, the man who had been charged with the task of actually putting the match to the polystyrene, and setting the fire alight, would have been convicted.

Quite apart from any other consideration, that is such an anomalous result that it cannot possibly be right. The answer is this: that one has to decide whether or not an offence is committed at the moment that the acts are alleged to be committed. The fact that somebody may have had a dishonest intent which in the end he was going to carry out, namely to claim from the insurance company, cannot turn what was not originally a crime into a crime. There is no unlawfulness under the 1971 Act in burning a house. It does not become unlawful because there may be an inchoate attempt to commit fraud contained in it; that is to say it does not become a crime under the 1971 Act, whatever may be the situation outside of the Act.

... Indeed it seems to us, if it is necessary to go as far as this, that it was probably unnecessary for the defendant to invoke s 5 of the 1971 Act at all, because he probably had a lawful excuse without it, in that T was lawfully entitled to burn the premises down. The defendant believed it. He believed that he was acting under the directions of T and that on its own, it seems to us, may well have provided him with a lawful excuse without having resort to s 5 ...

Note: Strictly speaking, the owner of the property was the limited company, not T. However, the decision of the court is sustainable on the basis that the defendant believed that T was entitled to authorise the destruction of the property. The present case may be contrasted with *R v Appleyard* where the managing director was convicted of destroying property belonging to his company; it was said that the company was a separate legal entity and so the defendant could not consent to the destruction of its property.

R v Hill; *R v Hall* (1989) 89 Cr App R 74

The appellants were convicted of criminal damage, having cut through the perimeter fencing of RAF bases. They appealed on the ground that the issue of lawful excuse had not been dealt with adequately by the trial judge. In particular they sought to rely on their assertion that if they could show that such bases were not secure, they would be closed and the surrounding properties would be at reduced risk of being targeted by hostile states armed with nuclear weapons.

Lord Lane CJ:

The learned judge ... came to the conclusion that the causative relationship between the acts which [the appellants] intended to perform and the alleged protection was so tenuous, so nebulous, that the acts could not be said to be done to protect viewed objectively ... with reference to the provision that the lawful excuse must be based upon an immediate need for protection ... the judge came to the ... conclusion that on the applicant's own evidence the applicant could not be said to have believed under the provisions of section 5(2)(b)(i) that the property was in immediate need of protection ... The judge in each case relied upon a decision of this court in *Hunt* (1978) 66 Cr App R 105. We have the advantage also of having that report in transcript. We also have before us a more recent decision of this court in *Ashford and Smith* [1988] Crim LR 682 ... in which very similar considerations were raised to those which exist in the present case. It also has the advantage of having set out the material findings of the court in *Hunt* which were delivered by Roskill LJ. I am referring to p 4 of the transcript in *Ashford and Smith*, and it will help to set out the basis of the decision not only in *Ashford and Smith* but also in *Hunt* if I read the passage. It runs as follows:

The judge relied very largely upon the decision of this court in *Hunt* (1978) 66 Cr App R 105. That was a case in which the appellant set fire to a guest room in an old people's home. He did so, he said, to draw attention to the defective fire alarm system. He was charged with arson, contrary to section 1(1) of the Criminal Damage Act 1971. He sought to set up the statutory defence under section 5(2) by claiming to have had a lawful excuse in doing what he did and that he was not reckless whether any such property would be destroyed. The trial judge withdrew the defence of lawful excuse from the jury and left the issue of recklessness for them to determine. The jury by a majority verdict convicted the appellant. On appeal [it was held that] applying the objective test, the trial judge had ruled correctly because what the appellant had done was not an act which in itself did protect or was capable of protecting property; but in order to draw attention to what in his view was an immediate need for protection by repairing the alarm system; thus the statutory defence under section 5(2) of the Act was not open to him; accordingly, the appeal would be dismissed.

Giving the judgment of the court Roskill LJ said, at p 108:

Mr Marshall-Andrews' submission can be put thus: if this man honestly believed that that which he did was necessary in order to protect this property from the risk of fire and damage to the old people's home by reason of the absence of a working fire alarm, he was entitled to set fire to that bed and so to claim the statutory defence accorded by section 5(2). I have said we will assume in his favour that he possessed the requisite honest belief. But in our view the question whether he was entitled to the benefit of the defence turns upon the meaning of the words 'in order to protect property belonging to another'. It was argued that those words were subjective in concept, just like the words in the latter part of section 5(2)(b) which are subjective. We do not think that is right. The question whether or not a particular act of destruction or damage or threat of destruction or damage was done or made in order to protect property belonging to another must be, on the true construction of the statute, an objective test. Therefore we have to ask ourselves whether, whatever the state of this man's mind and assuming an honest belief, that which he admittedly did was done in order to protect this particular property, namely the old people's home in Hertfordshire? If one formulates the question in that way, in the view of each member of this court, for the reason Slynn J gave during the argument, it admits of only one answer: this was not done in order to protect property; it was done in order to draw attention to the defective state of the fire alarm. It was not an act which in itself did protect or was capable of protecting property.

Then the judgment in *Ashford and Smith*, delivered by Glidewell LJ continued as follows:

In our view that reasoning applies exactly in the present case. *Hunt* is, of course, binding upon us. But even if it were not, we agree with the reasoning contained in it. Now it is submitted by Mr Bowyer [for the applicants] to us that the decision in *Hunt* and the decision in *Ashford and Smith* were wrong and that the test is a subjective test. In other words the submission is that it was a question of what the applicant believed and accordingly it should have been left to the jury as a matter of fact to decide what it was the applicant did believe.

We are bound by the decision in *Hunt* just as the court in *Ashford and Smith* were bound, unless that case can be demonstrated to have been wrongly decided in the light of previous authority . . . we think that *Hunt* was correctly decided, for this reason. There are two aspects to this type of question. The first aspect is to decide what it was that the applicant, in this case Valerie Hill, in her own mind thought. The learned judge assumed, and so do we, for the purposes of this decision, that everything she said about her reasoning was true. I have already perhaps given a sufficient outline of what it was she believed to demonstrate what is meant by that. Up to that point the test was subjective. In other words one is examining what is going on in the applicant's mind. Having done that, the judges in the present cases . . . turned to the second aspect of the case, and that is this. He had to decide as a matter of law, which means objectively, whether it could be said that on those facts as believed by the applicant, snipping the strand of the wire, which she intended to do, could amount to something done to protect either the applicant's own home or the homes of her adjacent friends in Pembrokeshire. He decided, again quite rightly in our view, that that proposed act on her part was far too remote from the eventual aim at which she was targeting her actions to satisfy the test. It follows therefore, in our view, that the judges in the present two cases were absolutely right to come to the conclusion that they did so far as this aspect of the case is concerned, and to come to that conclusion as a matter of law, having decided the subjective test as the applicants wished them to be decided. The second half of the question was that of the immediacy of the danger. Here the wording of the Act, one reminds oneself, is as follows: She believed that 'the property . . . was in immediate need of protection'. Once again the judge had to determine whether, on the facts as stated by the applicant, there was any evidence on which it could be said that she believed there was a need of protection from immediate danger. In our view that must mean evidence that she believed that immediate action had to be taken to do something which would otherwise be a crime in order to prevent the immediate risk of something worse happening. The answers which I have read in the evidence given by this woman (and the evidence given by the other applicant was very similar) drives this court to the conclusion, as they drove the respective judges to the conclusion, that there was no evidence on which it could be said that there was that belief.

R v Baker and Wilkins [1997] Crim LR 497

The appellants were both convicted of criminal damage to the front door of a house belonging to a Mr Wonnacott. They claimed that they had forced entry to the house to retrieve Stephanie, the infant daughter of the appellant Baker, whom they believed to be in danger because she had been left in the house unattended by Baker's estranged partner, Stephanie's father. One of the issues for the Court of Appeal was whether the appellants could claim that they had acted with a lawful excuse if they believed it was necessary to break in to rescue the child.

Brooke LJ:
. . . In a very brief ruling the [trial] judge said that he intended to direct the jury that the intention to recover the child would not constitute lawful excuse, or a defence, or would make any violence lawful in respect of the affray charge. He later summed-up to the jury on this basis . . .
. . . so far as Count 4 was concerned, there was an argument based on the wording of Section 5(2)(b) of the Criminal Damage Act 1971. This provides that there is lawful excuse for destroying or damaging property where this is done in order to protect property belonging to the defendant which is in immediate need of protection and where the means of protection adopted are reasonable. It was said that if the statute provides this express definition of reasonable excuse, it is possible to infer *a fortiori* that damage to property, when this is reasonably done for the protection of one's child, constitutes reasonable excuse . . .
We turn . . . to the possible defence that the desire to rescue Stephanie provided a lawful excuse for the appellants to batter down the door of the house in which she was detained in order to secure her release. [The relevant provisions of the Criminal Damage Act 1971 were recited.]

> . . . It is quite clear that the circumstances provided for in section 5(2)(b) do not arise in the present case, since Stephanie did not represent property within the meaning of that section.
>
> For the purposes of this appeal we are bound to assume that if a legitimate defence existed, there was an issue fit to be put to a jury on the evidence that the appellants honestly believed that Stephanie was being unlawfully detained, and the question we have to consider is whether and in what circumstances the criminal law permits someone holding such a belief in relation to a child, to take the law into their own hands, to use a colloquialism, and to batter down the door of the house in which she is detained in order to try to effect a rescue.

12.5 AGGRAVATED CRIMINAL DAMAGE

Section 1(2) of the Criminal Damage Act 1971 creates an aggravated (ie more serious) form of the offence, where D intends that the criminal damage will endanger life, or is at least reckless as to whether or not this is the case. Many of the elements of the offence are the same as those for the simple offence under s 1(1), for example the damage to or destruction of property. Note however that the offence can be committed by the defendant damaging or destroying his own property. Section 1(2) provides:

> A person who without lawful excuse destroys or damages any property, whether belonging to himself or another:
>
> (a) intending to destroy or damage any property or being reckless as to whether any property would be destroyed or damaged; and
> (b) intending by the destruction or damage to endanger the life of another or being reckless as to whether the life of another would be thereby endangered,
>
> shall be guilty of an offence.

R v Steer [1988] AC 111 (HL)

The defendant went to the bungalow of his former business partner, David Gregory, against whom he bore a grudge. Armed with an automatic .22 rifle the defendant fired a shot aimed at the bedroom window. He then fired two further shots, one at another window and one at the front door. No one was hurt, and there was no evidence that the first shot had been aimed at Mr Gregory. The defendant was charged, *inter alia*, with criminal damage with intent to endanger the lives of Mr and Mrs Gregory or being reckless whether their lives would be endangered.

> Lord Bridge of Harwich:
> My Lords . . ., it is to be observed that the offence created by subsection (2), save that it may be committed by destroying or damaging one's own property, is simply an aggravated form

of the offence created by subsection (1), in which the prosecution must prove, in addition to the ingredients of the offence under subsection (1), the further mental element specified by subsection (2)(b) . . .

We must, of course, approach the matter on the footing, implicit in the outcome of the trial, that the respondent, in firing at the bedroom window, had no intent to endanger life, but accepts that he was reckless whether life would be endangered.

Under both limbs or s 1 of the Act of 1971 it is the essence of the offence which the section creates that the defendant has destroyed or damaged property. For the purpose of analysis it may be convenient to omit the reference to destruction and to concentrate on the references to damage, which was all that was here involved. To be guilty under subsection (1) the defendant must have intended or been reckless as to the damage to property which he caused. To be guilty under subsection (2) he must additionally have intended to endanger life or been reckless whether life should be endangered 'by damage' to property which he caused. This is the context in which the words must be construed and it seems to me impossible to read the words 'by the damage' as meaning 'by the damage or by the act which caused the damage' . . .

I would accordingly dismiss the appeal. The certified question should be answered as follows:

On the true construction of s 1(2)(b) of the Criminal Damage Act 1971 the prosecution are required to prove that the danger to life resulted from the destruction of or damage to property; it is not sufficient for the prosecution to prove that it resulted from the act of the defendant which caused the destruction or damage.

R v Webster and Others; R v Warwick [1995] 2 All ER 168 (CA)

In *R v Webster* appellants pushed a coping stone weighing 1 to 2 cwt from the parapet of a railway bridge onto a two-carriage passenger train passing below. The stone landed on the first carriage, showering the passengers with glass fibre and polystyrene-type material from the roof. Only a corner of the stone penetrated the roof. Nobody received any physical injury, although passengers were shocked by the event. In *R v Warwick* the appellants were involved in a car chase with the police. On a number of occasions one of the appellants stood up through the sun-roof of the car in which he was being carried as a passenger and hurled bricks through the windows of pursuing police cars. The appellant who was driving the car also rammed a police car. In both cases the issue arose as to the *mens rea* required in respect of the aggravated form of criminal damage under s 1(2), in particular the extent to which the appellants had to be shown to have intended that criminal damage should endanger life, or at least be reckless as to this consequence.

Lord Taylor of Gosforth CJ:

. . . what has to be proved under s 1(2)(b) is not whether and how life was in fact endangered (if it was) but whether and how it was intended to be endangered or there was an obvious risk of it being endangered . . . In our view, the true construction of s 1(2) is that the *actus reus* is defined in the first two lines of the subsection, while paras (a) and (b) deal with *mens rea* and are conjunctive in the way described by Staughton LJ. Otherwise, the gravamen of an offence involving damage by missile would depend not on the defendant's intention but on whether he was a good shot in seeking to carry it out.

Thus, if a defendant throws a brick at the windscreen of a moving vehicle, given that he causes some damage to the vehicle, whether he is guilty under s 1(2) does not depend on whether the brick hits or misses the windscreen, but whether he intended to hit it and intended that the damage therefrom should endanger life or whether he was reckless as to that outcome. As to the dropping of stones from bridges, the effect of the statute may be thought strange. If the defendant's intention is that the stone itself should crash through the roof of a train or motor vehicle and thereby directly injure a passenger, or if he was reckless only as to that outcome, the section would not bite. That would follow from the *ratio* in *R v Steer* and is no doubt why Lord Bridge made the comment he did about missiles from motorway bridges. If, however, the defendant intended or was reckless that the stone would smash the roof of the train or vehicle so that metal or wood struts from the roof would or obviously might descend upon a passenger endangering life, he would surely be guilty. This may seem to many a dismal distinction.

. . .

. . . If the intention [in *R v Webster*] was that the stone itself should endanger the life of the passengers, then the 'pusher' would not be guilty of this offence . . . In our view, by convicting each of the appellants . . . the jury must be taken to have found . . . that each of them intended the stone itself to crash through the roof and endanger life. The conviction on that basis alone cannot be sustained. However, the jury's finding of an intent by each appellant to endanger life by causing the stone itself to penetrate the roof must, in common sense, carry the implication that they were each reckless as to endangering life by whatever damage the stone might do when it fell. If the intention was for the stone to penetrate the roof, there was clearly an obvious risk that it might endanger life by bringing parts of the roof down into the compartment, quite apart from other obvious risks such as derailment if it fell in front of the train or struck the driver's cab, incapacitating him or the controls.

In the circumstances, we consider the proper course is for us to . . . substitute in each case a conviction . . . of 'being reckless as to whether the life of another would thereby be endangered'. This we do.

. . . [In] *R v Warwick* . . . If the intention was to break the windscreen or window by hurling a brick or stone, the jury would be entitled to infer that there was an intention to shower the driver with broken glass. If as a result of being so showered he were to lose control of the vehicle so that his life and that of his passengers or other road users were endangered, a jury could properly find that that danger was caused and intended to be caused by the broken glass, i.e. the damage to the vehicle. Clearly . . . an intention to render the windscreen opaque, or recklessness as to its becoming so, could invoke the section. Likewise, if a defendant deliberately rams a vehicle in moving traffic, it would be open to a jury to infer an intention to disable the vehicle, for example by damaging the suspension, by damaging the steering, by buckling the bodywork onto the tyres and thereby causing a blowout. Any of these forms of damage in moving traffic could well endanger life and in our judgment it would be open to a jury, hearing evidence of deliberate ramming of a police car, to infer that the intention was to endanger life by damaging the vehicle.

The circumstances in this case are clearly distinguishable from those in *R v Steer*. To shower the driver of a moving vehicle with broken glass or ram his vehicle in moving traffic are clearly distinguishable from merely piercing the window or door of a stationary house by discharging an air rifle . . .

12.5.1 THE MENTAL ELEMENT: INTENTION OR RECKLESSNESS

Both forms of criminal damage under s 1(1) and s 1(2) require either intention or recklessness. Regarding recklessness, the objective approach based on the speech of Lord Diplock in *R v Caldwell* [1982] AC 341 no longer applies. To incur liability the defendant must at least be aware of the risk of criminal damage, and for the aggravated offence aware of the risk that life would be endangered by the criminal damage; see *R v G* [2003] 4 All ER 765 extracted at Chapter 3.2.1.

12.5.2 THE MENTAL ELEMENT: MISTAKEN BELIEF

R v Smith (David Raymond) [1974] QB 354 (CA)

The appellant, as a tenant of a ground floor flat, installed some electrical wiring for use with stereo equipment. The appellant also, with the landlord's permission, put up roofing material and asbestos wall panels and laid floorboards. There was no dispute that the roofing, wall panels and floorboards became part of the house and, in law, the property of the landlord. In due course the appellant was given notice to quit. In accessing the wiring to remove his stereo equipment the appellant damaged the roofing, wall panels and floorboards he had installed. When interviewed by the police, the appellant said, 'Look, how can I be done for smashing my own property? I put the flooring and that in, so if I want to pull it down it's a matter for me.' The appellant was charged with criminal damage of the landlord's property, contrary to s 1(1) of the Criminal Damage Act 1971. The appellant's defence was that he honestly believed that the damage he did was to his own property, that he believed that he was entitled to damage his own property and therefore that he had a lawful excuse for his actions causing the damage.

James LJ:

. . . [His Lordship quoted from s 1 of the Criminal Damage Act 1971 and then considered a number of arguments raised by counsel for the appellant. His Lordship concluded]:

Construing the language of s 1(1) we have no doubt that the *actus reus* is 'destroying or damaging any property belonging to another'. It is not possible to exclude the words 'belonging to another' which describe the 'property'. Applying the ordinary principles of *mens rea*, the intention and recklessness, and the absence of lawful excuse required to constitute the offence, have reference to property belonging to another. It follows that in our judgment no offence is committed under this section if a person destroys or causes damage to property belonging to another if he does so in the honest though mistaken belief that the property is his own, and provided that the belief is honestly held it is irrelevant to consider whether or not it is a justifiable belief . . .

12.5.3 THE MENTAL ELEMENT: THE EFFECT OF INTOXICATION UNDER S 5

Jaggard v Dickinson [1981] QB 527 (CA)

The defendant, who had been drinking, entered a house at 35 Carnach Green, occupied by a Mrs Raven, wrongly believing it to be no 67 Carnach Green, a house of identical outward appearance. The house at no 67 was occupied by a friend of the defendant, a Mr Heyfron. The defendant's relationship with Mr Heyfron was such that, in the words of the justices, she had his consent at any time to treat his property as if it were her own. She had an understanding with the owner of no 67 that she could enter the house at any time she pleased. In order to access 35 Carnach Green, the defendant broke the glass in the hallway of the house and then went to the back door, where she broke another window, and gained entry to the house, damaging a net curtain in the process. The defendant denied liability for criminal damage on the basis that, due to her state of self-induced intoxication, she had wrongly but genuinely believed that she was destroying property with the owner's consent.

Mustill J:

. . . It is convenient to refer to the exculpatory provisions of s 5(2) as if they created a defence, whilst recognising that the burden of disproving the facts referred to by the subsection remains on the prosecution.

The justices held that the defendant was not entitled to rely on s 5(2) of the Act of 1971, since the belief relied upon was brought about by a state of self-induced intoxication.

In support of the conviction [counsel for the prosecutor] advanced an argument which may be summarised as follows: (1) Where an offence is one of 'basic intent', in contrast to one of 'specific intent', the fact that the accused was in a state of self-induced intoxication at the time when he did the acts constituting the *actus reus* does not prevent him from possessing the *mens rea* necessary to constitute the offence: see *R v Morgan* [1976] AC 182 and *R v Majewski* [1977] AC 443. (2) Section 1(1) of the Act of 1971 creates an offence of basic intent: *R v Stephenson* [1979] QB 695. (3) Section 5(3) has no bearing on the present issue. It does not create a separate defence, but is no more than a partial definition of the expression 'without lawful excuse' in s 1(1). The absence of lawful excuse forms an element in the *mens rea*: see *R v Smith (David)* . . . Accordingly, since drunkenness does not negative *mens rea* in crimes of basic intent, it cannot be relied on as part of a defence based on s 5(2).

Whilst this is an attractive submission, we consider it to be unsound, for the following reasons. In the first place, the argument transfers the distinction between offences of specific and of basic intent to a context in which it has no place. The distinction is material where the accused relies on his own drunkenness as a ground for denying that he had the degree of intention or recklessness required in order to constitute the offence. Here, by contrast, the defendant does not rely on her drunkenness to displace an inference of intent or recklessness; indeed she does not rely on it at all. Her defence is founded on the state of belief called for by s 5(2). True, the fact of the defendant's intoxication was relevant to the defence under s (2), for it helped to explain what would otherwise have been inexplicable, and hence lent colour to her evidence about the state of her belief. This is not the same as using drunkenness to rebut an inference of intention or

---

recklessness. Belief, like intention or recklessness, is a state of mind: but they are not the same states of mind.

Can it nevertheless be said that, even if the context is different, the principles established by *R v Majewski* [1977] AC 443 ought to be applied to this new situation? If the basis of the decision in *R v Majewski* had been that drunkenness does not prevent a person from having an intent or being reckless, then there would be grounds for saying that it should equally be left out of account when deciding on his state of belief. But this is not our view of what *R v Majewski* decided. The House of Lords did not conclude that intoxication was irrelevant to the fact of the accused's state of mind, but rather that, whatever might have been his actual state of mind, he should for reasons of policy be precluded from relying on any alteration in that state brought about by self-induced intoxication. The same considerations of policy apply to the intent or recklessness which is the *mens rea* of the offence created by s 1(1), and that offence is accordingly regarded as one of basic intent: see *R v Stephenson* [1979] QB 695. It is indeed essential that this should be so, for drink so often plays a part in offences of criminal damage; and to admit drunkenness as a potential means of escaping liability would provide much too ready a means of avoiding conviction. But these considerations do not apply to a case where Parliament has specifically required the court to consider the accused's actual state of belief, not the state of belief which ought to have existed. This seems to us to show that the court is required by s 5(3) to focus on the existence of the belief, not its intellectual soundness; and a belief can be just as much honestly held if it is induced by intoxication, as if it stems from stupidity, forgetfulness or inattention. It was, however, urged that we could not properly read s 5(2) in isolation from s 1(1), which forms the context of the words, 'without lawful excuse', partially defined by s 5(2). Once the words are put in context, so it is maintained, it can be seen that the law must treat drunkenness in the same way in relation to lawful excuse (and hence belief) as it does to intention and recklessness; for they are all part of the *mens rea* of the offence. To fragment the *mens rea*, so as to treat one part of it as affected by drunkenness in one way, and the remainder as affected in a different way, would make the law impossibly complicated to enforce.

If it had been necessary to decide whether, for all purposes, the *mens rea* of an offence under s 1(1) extends as far as an intent (or recklessness) as to the existence of a lawful excuse, I should have wished to consider the observations of James LJ delivering the judgment of the Court of Appeal in *R v Smith (David)* . . . I do not however find it necessary to reach a conclusion on this matter, and will only say that I am not at present convinced that, when these observations are read in the context of the judgment as a whole, they have the meaning which the prosecutor has sought to put upon them. In my view, however, the answer to the argument lies in the fact that any distinction which has to be drawn as to the effect of drunkenness arises from the scheme of the Act of 1971 itself. No doubt the *mens rea* is in general indivisible, with no distinction being possible as regards the effect of drunkenness. But Parliament has specifically isolated one subjective element, in the shape of honest belief, and has given it separate treatment, and its own special gloss in s 5(3). This being so, there is nothing objectionable in giving it special treatment as regards drunkenness, in accordance with the natural meaning of its words.

In these circumstances, I would hold that the justices were in error when they decided that the defence furnished to the defendant by s 5(2) was lost because the defendant was drunk at the time. I would therefore allow the appeal.

12.5.4 THE MENTAL ELEMENT: AGGRAVATED CRIMINAL DAMAGE

Attorney General's Ref (No 3 of 1992) [1994] 1 WLR 409 (CA)

Schiemann J:

. . . The point of law which has been referred to us was formulated as follows:

> Whether on a charge of attempted arson in the aggravated form contemplated by s 1(2) of the Criminal Damage Act 1971, in addition to establishing a specific intent to cause damage by fire, it is sufficient to prove that the defendant was reckless as to whether life would thereby be endangered.

The acquittals which have given rise to this reference had the following background according to the prosecution evidence. Following previous attacks upon their property the complainants maintained a night-time watch over their premises from a motor car (a Ford Granada). In the early hours of the morning the respondents came upon the scene in a vehicle. Inside this car, a Sierra, was a milk crate containing a number of petrol bombs, matches, a petrol can and some rags. As the Sierra approached the complainants, four inside their car and two persons on the pavement talking to them, a lighted petrol bomb was thrown towards them from the Sierra. The prosecution's case was that it was thrown at the Granada and its occupants. The petrol bomb in fact passed over the top of the Granada and smashed against the garden wall of a house a pavement's width away from the car. The Sierra accelerated away but crashed, and the respondents were arrested.

At the trial count 1 of the indictment alleged attempted aggravated arson, specifying in the particulars of offence, *inter alia*, an intent to endanger life. Count 2 alleged attempted aggravated arson, specifying in the particulars of offence, *inter alia*, recklessness as to whether life would be endangered . . .

[The trial judge directed acquittal on both counts; the present appeal is concerned only with the acquittal on count 2] . . .

. . . [A]lthough in the present reference the question is posed in relation to arson, it has not been submitted that the presence or absence of fire makes any difference to the answer to the question posed which applies to any form of attempted criminal damage. So we omit any further reference to the element of fire in this judgment . . .

So far as the completed simple offence is concerned, the prosecution needs to prove (1) property belonging to another was damaged by the defendant; (2) the state of mind of the defendant was one of the following, (a) he intended to damage such property, or (b) he was reckless as to whether any such property would be damaged.

In the case of the completed aggravated offence the prosecution needs to prove (1) the defendant in fact damaged property, whether belonging to himself or another; (2) that the state of mind of the defendant was one of the following, (a) he intended to damage property, and intended by the damage to endanger the life of another, or (b) he intended to damage property and was reckless as to whether the life of another would be thereby endangered, or (c) he was reckless as to whether any property would be damaged and was reckless as to whether the life of another would be thereby endangered.

It is to be noted that the property referred to under (1) (to which we shall hereafter refer as 'the first-named property') is not necessarily the same property as that referred to in (2) (to which we shall refer as 'the second-named property'), although it normally will be.

Thus a man who (1) owns a crane from which is suspended a heavy object and (2) cuts the rope (the first-named property) which holds the object with the result that (3) the object falls and hits the roof of a passing car (the second-named property) which roof (4) collapses killing the driver, would be guilty if it could be shown that he damaged the rope, was reckless as to whether this would damage the car, and was reckless as to whether the life of the driver of the car would be endangered by the damage to the car.

All the foregoing is common ground. The problem which has given rise to this reference relates to an attempt to commit the aggravated offence in circumstances where the first-named property is the same as the second-named property in the instant case a car. It amounts to this: whether, if the state of mind of the defendant was that postulated in (2)(b) above, namely that he intended to damage property and was reckless as to whether the life of another would thereby be endangered, and whilst in that state of mind he did an act which was more than merely preparatory to the offence, he is guilty of attempting to commit that offence . . .

So far as attempting to commit the simple offence is concerned, in order to convict on such a charge it must be proved that the defendant (a) did an act which was more than merely preparatory to the commission of the offence and (b) did an act intending to damage any property belonging to another.

One way of analysing the situation is to say that a defendant, in order to be guilty of an attempt, must be in one of the states of mind required for the commission of the full offence, and did his best, as far as he could, to supply what was missing from the completion of the offence. It is the policy of the law that such people should be punished notwithstanding that in fact the intentions of such a defendant have not been fulfilled.

If the facts are that, although the defendant had one of the appropriate states of mind required for the complete offence, but the physical element required for the commission of the complete offence is missing, the defendant is not to be convicted unless it can be shown that he intended to supply that physical element . . .

We turn finally to the attempt to commit the aggravated offence. In the present case, what was missing to prevent a conviction for the completed offence was damage to the property referred to in the opening lines of s 1(2) of the 1981 Act, what in the example of a crane, which we gave earlier in this judgment, we referred to as 'the first-named property'. Such damage is essential for the completed offence. If a defendant does not intend to cause such damage he cannot intend to commit the completed offence. At worst he is reckless as to whether the offence is committed. The law of attempt is concerned with those who are intending to commit crimes. If that intent cannot be shown, then there can be no conviction.

However, the crime here consisted of doing certain acts in a certain state of mind in circumstances where the first-named property and the second-named property were the same, in short where the danger to life arose from the damage to the property which the defendant intended to damage. The substantive crime is committed if the defendant damaged property in a state of mind where he was reckless as to whether the life of another would thereby be endangered. We see no reason why there should not be a conviction for attempt if the prosecution can show that he, in that state of mind, intended to damage the property by throwing a bomb at it. One analysis of this situation is to say that although the defendant was in an appropriate state of mind to render him guilty of the completed offence the prosecution had not proved the physical element of the completed offence, and therefore he is not guilty of the completed offence. If, on a charge of attempting to commit the offence, the prosecution can show not only the state of mind required for the completed offence but also that the defendant intended to supply the missing physical element of the completed offence, that suffices for a conviction. That cannot be done merely by the prosecution showing him to be reckless. The defendant must intend to damage property, but there is no need for a graver mental state than is required for the full offence . . .

We answer [the referred question] in the affirmative.

We add that, in circumstances where the first-named property is not the same as the second-named property, in addition to establishing a specific intent to cause damage by fire to the first-named property, it is sufficient to prove that the defendant was reckless as to as to whether any second-named property was damaged and reckless as to whether the life of another would be endangered by the damage to the second-named property.

12.6 OTHER OFFENCES UNDER THE CRIMINAL DAMAGE ACT 1971

Section 2 of the Criminal Damage Act 1971: threats to destroy or damage property

A person who without lawful excuse makes to another a threat, intending that that other would fear it would be carried out:

(a) to destroy or damage any property belonging to that other or a third person; or

(b) to destroy or damage his own property in a way which he knows is likely to endanger the life of that other or a third person,

shall be guilty of an offence.

Section 3 of the Criminal Damage Act 1971: possessing anything with intent to destroy or damage property

A person who has anything in his custody or under his control intending without lawful excuse to use it or cause or permit another to use it:

(a) to destroy or damage any property belonging to some other person; or

(b) to destroy or damage his own or the user's property in a way which he knows is likely to endanger the life of some other person,

shall be guilty of an offence.

12.7 RACIALLY MOTIVATED CRIMINAL DAMAGE

Section 30 of the Crime and Disorder Act 1998: racially or religiously aggravated criminal damage

(1) A person is guilty of an offence under this section if he commits an offence under section 1(1) of the Criminal Damage Act 1971 (destroying or damaging property belonging to another) which is racially or religiously aggravated for the purposes of this section.

(2) A person guilty of an offence under this section shall be liable:

    (a) on summary conviction, to imprisonment for a term not exceeding six months or to a fine not exceeding the statutory maximum, or to both;

    (b) on conviction on indictment, to imprisonment for a term not exceeding fourteen years or to a fine, or to both.

(3) For the purposes of this section, section 28(1)(a) above shall have effect as if the person to whom the property belongs or is treated as belonging for the purposes of that Act were the victim of the offence.

Section 28 of the Crime and Disorder Act 1998 (as amended by the Anti-Terrorism, Crime and Security Act 2001) defines 'racially or religiously aggravated' for the purposes of s 30 – it is set out at Chapter 5.7 in the context of racially aggravated assaults.

 ## COMMENTS AND QUESTIONS

1   In *Lloyd v Director of Public Prosecutions* [1992] 1 All ER 982, the Divisional Court rejected the contention that there was a general defence of lawful excuse available to a motorist who damaged a car clamp that had been used to detain his illegally parked car. Nolan LJ observed: '. . . as a general rule, if a motorist parks his car without permission on another person's property knowing that by doing so he runs the risk of it being clamped, he has no right to damage or destroy the clamp. If he does so he will be guilty of a criminal offence'.

2   The offence of arson, and the aggravated forms of criminal damage carry the possibility of life imprisonment. All other offences under the 1971 Act carry the possibility of up to 10 years' imprisonment following conviction on indictment.

3   Would the defendants in *R v Baker and Wilkins* have been able to succeed with a defence of necessity at common law? Consider *R v Jones* [2004] EWCA Crim 1981, where the defend-ants unlawfully gained entry to RAF bases in order to damage military equipment. They were charged with criminal damage and sought to rely, *inter alia*, on lawful excuse under s 5(2) of the 1971 Act – i.e. damaging military equipment to prevent further damage to property by the use of that military equipment. The court expressed the view that lawful excuse was not limited to situations where the defendant, viewed objectively, acted to prevent harm to prop-erty caused by another's unlawful conduct. The court noted that no such restriction on the availability of the defence was provided for under s 5(2), although many would regard such a restriction as desirable. Consequently the court certified the following point of law of general public importance as arising in the appeal: 'Is the defence of lawful excuse under section 5 of the Criminal Damage Act 1971 available to a defendant who acts to protect the property of another abroad from damage that will be caused by the executive's lawful exercise of pre-rogative power to wage war?'

4   It is for the trial judge to determine whether or not s 5(2) lawful excuse issues arise, and therefore whether or not the jury needs to be directed on the issue. For example in *R v Kelleher* [2003] EWCA Crim 2846, where the appellant admitted that he had 'decapitated' a statue of Baroness Thatcher in order to bring attention to his opposition to the policies she

had advocated, the Court of Appeal endorsed the trial judge's view that no issues of lawful excuse under s 5(2) could arise.

FURTHER READING

Elliot, DW, 'Endangering life by destroying or damaging property' [1997] Crim LR 382

CHAPTER 13

DEFENCES WHERE *MENS REA* IS DENIED

13.1 VOLUNTARY INTOXICATION

The rules governing the defence of intoxication are to be found at common law. Where a defendant, through his own volition, becomes intoxicated he may nevertheless have a partial or complete defence to the offence with which he is charged, depending on whether the offence is classified as being one of specific or basic intent. In general terms, where the offence is classified as requiring specific intent the defendant who successfully pleads the defence of intoxication will be acquitted of that specific intent crime, but convicted instead of the lesser included basic intent crime. Hence in a case where the defendant is charged with murder, he might be acquitted on the basis of his voluntary intoxication, but convicted instead of manslaughter. Similarly with an offence such as causing grievous bodily harm with intent contrary to s 18 of the Offences Against the Person Act 1861. The defendant might be acquitted under s 18 because of his intoxication but convicted of the lesser included basic intent crime of malicious wounding contrary to s 20 of the 1861 Act. An intoxicant for these purposes is not limited to class A or class B drugs or alcohol, but can, in theory, extend to any substance which has the effect of altering the defendant's consciousness; see further *R v Hardie* [1985] 1 WLR 64, extracted below.

13.1.1 WHAT AMOUNTS TO A STATE OF INTOXICATION?

DPP v Beard [1920] AC 479

Lord Birkenhead LC (at p 499):
... where a specific intent is an essential element in the offence, evidence of a state of drunkenness rendering the accused incapable of forming such an intent should be taken into consideration in order to determine whether he had in fact formed the intent necessary to constitute the particular crime. If he was so drunk that he was incapable of forming the intent required he could not be convicted of a crime which was committed only if the intent was proved.

13.1.2 THE BASIC INTENT/SPECIFIC INTENT DICHOTOMY

In _DPP v Morgan_ [1976] AC 182, Lord Simon of Glaisdale (at p 216) observed that: 'By crimes of basic intent I mean those crimes whose definition expresses (or, more often, applies) a _mens rea_ which does not go beyond the _actus reus_. The _actus reus_ generally consists of an act and some consequence. The consequence may be closely connected with the act or remotely connected with it: but with a crime of basic intent the _mens rea_ does not extend beyond the act and its consequence, however remote, as defined in the _actus reus_.' The problem with Lord Simon's explanation of the basic/specific intent dichotomy is that it is not borne out by practice. Murder is regarded as a specific intent crime, yet no one would claim that the _mens rea_ – intention to kill – goes beyond the _actus reus_ – killing. A simpler way of approaching the issue is to proceed on the basis that any crime for which recklessness would be sufficient _mens rea_ can be regarded as a crime of basic intent for the purposes of the defence of intoxication.

13.1.3 THE RATIONALE FOR THE OPERATION OF THE DEFENCE OF INTOXICATION

R v Lipman [1970] 1 QB 152 (CA)

Widgery LJ:
... Both the defendant and the victim were addicted to drugs, and on the evening of 16 September 1967, both took a quantity of a drug known as LSD. Early on the morning of 18 September, the defendant, who is a United States citizen, hurriedly booked out of his hotel and left the country. On the following day, 19 September, the victim's landlord found her dead in her room. She had suffered two blows on the head causing haemorrhage of the brain, but she had died of asphyxia as a result of some eight inches of sheet having been crammed into her mouth.

The defendant was returned to this country by extradition proceedings, and at the trial he gave evidence of having gone with the victim to her room and there experienced what he described as an LSD 'trip'. He explained how he had the illusion of descending to the centre of the earth and being attacked by snakes, with which he had fought. It was not seriously disputed that he had killed the victim in the course of this experience, but he said he had no knowledge of what he was doing and no intention to harm her. He was charged with murder, but the jury evidently accepted that he lacked the necessary intention to kill or to do grievous bodily harm . . .

For the purposes of criminal responsibility we see no reason to distinguish between the effect of drugs voluntarily taken and drunkenness voluntarily induced. [His Lordship then quoted from the speech of Lord Birkenhead in *DPP v Beard* [1920] AC 479, 499, 500 and from the speeches of Lord Denning in *Bratty v AG for Northern Ireland* [1963] AC 386, 410 and *AG for Northern Ireland v Gallagher* [1963] AC 349, 381. His Lordship went on to hold:] Those authorities show quite clearly, in our opinion, that it was well established that no specific intent was necessary to support a conviction for manslaughter based upon a killing in the course of an unlawful act and that, accordingly, self-induced drunkenness was no defence to such a charge.

In the case of manslaughter by neglect, however, it has been recognised that some mental element must be established . . . [His Lordship quoted from the speech of Lord Atkin in *Andrews v DPP* [1937] AC 576, 582, 583 and from the judgment of Edmund Davis J in *R v Church* [1966] 1 QB 59, 69. He continued:] All that the judgment in *Church's* case says in terms is that whereas, formerly, a killing by any unlawful act amounted to manslaughter, this consequence does not now inexorably follow unless the unlawful act is one in which ordinary sober and responsible people would recognise the existence of risk.

. . . We can dispose of the present application by reiterating that when the killing results from an unlawful act of the prisoner no specific intent has to be proved to convict of manslaughter, and self-induced intoxication is accordingly no defence. Since in the present case the acts complained of were obviously likely to cause harm to the victim (and did, in fact, kill her) no acquittal was possible and the verdict of manslaughter, at the least, was inevitable . . .

4 November 1969: The Appeal Committee of the House of Lords (Lord Wilberforce, Viscount Dilhorne and Lord Pearson) refused leave to appeal.

DPP v Majewski [1977] AC 443 (HL)

Lord Elwyn-Jones LC:

My Lords, Robert Stefan Majewski appeals against his conviction on 7 November 1973, at Chelmsford Crown Court on three counts of assault occasioning actual bodily harm and three counts of assault on a police constable in the execution of his duty . . .

The appellant's case was that when the assaults were committed he was acting under the influence of a combination of drugs (not medically prescribed) and alcohol, to such an extent that he did not know what he was doing and that he remembered nothing of the incidents that had occurred . . .

The appeal raises issues of considerable public importance. In giving the judgment of the Court of Appeal Lawton LJ rightly observed, at 404, that:

> The facts are commonplace – indeed so commonplace that their very nature reveals how serious from a social and public standpoint the consequences would be if men could behave as the [appellant] did and then claim that they were not guilty of any offence.

Self-induced alcoholic intoxication has been a factor in crimes of violence, like assault, throughout the history of crime in this country. But voluntary drug taking with the potential and actual dangers to others it may cause has added a new dimension to the old problem with which the courts have had to deal in their endeavour to maintain order and to keep public and private violence under control. To achieve this is the prime purpose of the criminal law. I have said 'the courts', for most of the relevant law has been made by the judges. A good deal of the argument in the hearing of this appeal turned on that judicial history, for the crux of the case for the Crown was that, illogical as the outcome may be said to be, the judges have evolved for the purpose of protecting the community a substantive rule of law that, in crimes of basic intent as distinct from crimes of specific intent, self-induced intoxication provides no defence and is irrelevant to offences of basic intent, such as assault . . .

What then is the mental element required in our law to be established in assault? This question has been most helpfully answered in the speech of Lord Simon of Glaisdale in *R v Morgan* [1976] AC 182, 216:

> . . . I take assault as an example of a crime of basic intent where the consequence is very closely connected with the act. The *actus reus* of assault is an act which causes another person to apprehend immediate and unlawful violence. The *mens rea* corresponds exactly. The prosecution must prove that the accused foresaw that his act would probably cause another person to have apprehension of immediate and unlawful violence, or would possibly have that consequence, such being the purpose of the act, or that he was reckless as to whether or not his act caused such apprehension. This foresight (the term of art is 'intention') or recklessness is the *mens rea* in assault. For example of a crime of basic intent where the consequence of the act involved in the *actus reus* as defined in the crime is less immediate, I take the crime of unlawful wounding. The act is, say, the squeezing of a trigger. A number of consequences (mechanical, chemical, ballistic and physiological) intervene before the final consequence involved in the defined *actus reus* – namely, the wounding of another person in circumstances unjustified by law. But again here the *mens rea* corresponds closely to the *actus reus*. The prosecution must prove that the accused foresaw that some physical harm would ensue to another person in circumstances unjustified by law as a probable (or possible and desired) consequence of his act, or that he was reckless as to whether or not such consequence ensued.

How does the fact of self-induced intoxication fit into that analysis? If a man consciously and deliberately takes alcohol and drugs not on medical prescription, but in order to escape from reality, to go 'on a trip', to become hallucinated, whatever the description may be and thereby disables himself from taking the care he might otherwise take and as a result by his subsequent actions causes injury to another – does our criminal law enable him to say that because he did not know what he was doing he lacked both intention and recklessness and accordingly is entitled to an acquittal?

Originally the common law would not and did not recognise self-induced intoxication as an excuse. Lawton LJ spoke of the 'merciful relaxation' to that rule which was introduced by the judges during the 19th century, and he added, at 411:

> Although there was much reforming zeal and activity in the 19th century, Parliament never once considered whether self-induced intoxication should be a defence generally to a criminal charge. It would have been a strange result if the merciful relaxation of a strict rule of law had ended, without any Parliamentary intervention, by whittling it away to such an extent that the more drunk a man became, provided he stopped short of making himself insane, the better chance he had of an acquittal . . . The common law rule still applied but

there were exceptions to it which Lord Birkenhead LC tried to define by reference to specific intent.

There are, however, decisions of eminent judges in a number of Commonwealth cases in Australia and New Zealand, (but generally not in Canada nor in the United States) as well as impressive academic comment in this country, to which we have been referred, supporting the view that it is illogical and inconsistent with legal principle to treat a person who of his own choice and volition has taken drugs and drink, even though he thereby creates a state in which he is not conscious of what he is doing, any differently from a person suffering from various medical conditions like epilepsy or diabetic coma and who is regarded by the law as free from fault. However our courts have for a very long time regarded in quite another light the state of self-induced intoxication. The authority which for the last half century has been relied upon in this context has been the speech of the Earl of Birkenhead LC in *DPP v Beard* [1920] AC 479, who stated at 494:

> Under the law of England as it prevailed until early in the 19th century voluntary drunken-
> ness was never an excuse for criminal misconduct; and indeed the classic authorities
> broadly assert that voluntary drunkenness must be considered rather an aggravation than
> a defence. This view was in terms based upon the principle that a man who by his own
> voluntary act debauches and destroys his will power shall be no better situated in regard to
> criminal acts than a sober man.

Lord Birkenhead LC made a historical survey of the way the common law, from the 16th century on, dealt with the effect of self-induced intoxication upon criminal responsibility. This indicates how, from 1819 on, the judges began to mitigate the severity of the attitude of the common law in such cases as murder and serious violent crime when the penalties of death or transportation applied or where there was likely to be sympathy for the accused, as in attempted suicide. Lord Birkenhead LC concluded at 499, that (except in cases where insanity is pleaded):

> the law is plain beyond all question that in cases falling short of insanity a condition of
> drunkenness at the time of committing an offence causing death can only, when it is
> available at all, have the effect of reducing the crime from murder to manslaughter. From
> this it seemed clear – and this is the interpretation which the judges have placed upon the
> decision during the ensuing half century – that it is only in the limited class of cases
> requiring proof of specific intent that drunkenness can exculpate. Otherwise in no case can
> it exempt completely from criminal liability . . .

I do not for my part regard that general principle as either unethical or contrary to the principles of natural justice. If a man of his own volition takes a substance which causes him to cast off the restraints of reason and conscience, no wrong is done to him by holding him answerable crimin-ally for any injury he may do while in that condition. His course of conduct in reducing himself by drugs and drink to that condition in my view supplies the evidence of *mens rea*, of guilty mind certainly sufficient for crimes of basic intent. It is a reckless course of conduct and recklessness is enough to constitute the necessary *mens rea* in assault cases: see *R v Venna* [1976] QB 421, *per* James LJ at 429. The drunkenness is itself an intrinsic, an integral part of the crime, the other part being the evidence of the unlawful use of force against the victim. Together they add up to criminal recklessness . . .

My noble and learned friends and I think it may be helpful if we give the following indication of the general lines on which in our view the jury should be directed as to the effect upon the criminal responsibility of the accused of drink or drugs or both, whenever death or physical injury to another person results from something done by the accused for which there is no legal justification and the offence with which the accused is charged is manslaughter or assault at common law or the statutory offence of unlawful wounding under s 20, or of assault occasioning actual bodily harm under s 47 of the Offences Against the Person Act 1861.

In the case of these offences it is no excuse in law that, because of drink or drugs which the accused himself had taken knowingly and willingly, he had deprived himself of the ability to exercise self-control, to realise the possible consequences of what he was doing, or even to be conscious that he was doing it. As in the instant case, the jury may be properly instructed that they 'can ignore the subject of drink or drugs as being in any way a defence' to charges of this character . . .

Lord Salmon:

. . . I accept that there is a degree of illogicality in the rule that intoxication may excuse or expunge one type of intention and not another. This illogicality is, however, acceptable to me because the benevolent part of the rule removes undue harshness without imperilling safety and the stricter part of the rule works without imperilling justice. It would be just as ridiculous to remove the benevolent part of the rule (which no one suggests) as it would be to adopt the alternative of removing the stricter part of the rule for the sake of preserving absolute logic. Absolute logic in human affairs is an uncertain guide and a very dangerous master. The law is primarily concerned with human affairs. I believe that the main object of our legal system is to preserve individual liberty. One important aspect of individual liberty is protection against physical violence.

If there were to be no penal sanction for any injury unlawfully inflicted under the complete mastery of drink or drugs, voluntarily taken, the social consequence could be appalling. That is why I do not consider that there is any justification for the criticisms which have been made of the Court of Appeal's decision in *R v Lipman* (extracted above) . . . [offences] like manslaughter, are . . . offences of basic intent and do not require the proof of any specific intent in order to establish guilt. According to our law as it has stood for about 150 years, in such cases evidence that the injuries were inflicted by a man not knowing what he was doing because he was intoxicated by drinks or drugs which he has voluntarily taken is wholly irrelevant. Certainly this rule seems, in practice, to have worked well without causing any injustice. The judge always carefully takes into account all the circumstances (which vary infinitely from case to case) before deciding which of the many courses open should be adopted in dealing with the convicted man.

If, as I think, this long-standing rule was salutary years ago when it related almost exclusively to drunkenness and hallucinatory drugs were comparatively unknown how much more salutary is it today when such drugs are increasingly becoming a public menace? My Lords, I am satisfied that this rule accords with justice, ethics and common sense, and I would leave it alone even if it does not comply with strict logic. It would, in my view, be disastrous if the law were changed to allow men who did what Lipman did to go free. It would shock the public, it would rightly bring the law into contempt and it would certainly increase one of the really serious menaces facing society today. This is too great a price to pay for bringing solace to those who believe that, come what may, strict logic should always prevail . . .

Lord Russell of Killowen:

. . . There are those who consider that the pendulum should swing the whole way from the old attitude of the criminal law that self-induced intoxication was if anything an aggravation of the crime committed while under its influence, to an attitude whereunder if the intoxication deprives a man of the ability to appreciate what he was doing he cannot be held guilty of any crime at all, save one of absolute liability or in which drunkenness is itself a constituent element of the crime. A man who has no knowledge of what he does cannot, it is said, be a guilty man, whatever may have deprived him of that knowledge. There is, at least superficially, logic in that approach: but logic in criminal law must not be allowed to run away with common sense, particularly when the preservation of the Queen's Peace is in question. The ordinary citizen who is badly beaten up would rightly think little of the criminal law as an effective protection if, because his attacker had deprived himself of ability to know what he was doing by getting himself drunk or going on a trip with drugs, the attacker is to be held innocent of any crime in the assault. *Mens rea* has many aspects. If asked to define it in such a case as the present I would say that the element of guilt or moral turpitude is supplied by the act of self-intoxication reckless of possible consequences. (In the early history of the criminal law it was always recognised that intoxication not self-induced – the surreptitiously laced drink – gave rise to quite different considerations: and this was because it was not the man's 'fault'. And so nowadays.) If, however, the crime charged was, as described in *DPP v Beard* [1920] AC 479, one which required a 'specific intent' to constitute the crime, and the self-induced intoxication was such that he had not the required specific intent, the accused is not to be found guilty of that particular crime: though commonly there will be a lesser crime to which the intoxication – however mind-stealing – will be no defence: murder and manslaughter are such: assault causing grievous bodily harm with intent to cause grievous bodily harm, and assault causing grievous bodily harm or actual bodily harm is another example . . .

13.1.4 THE DEFENDANT WHO DELIBERATELY INTOXICATES HIMSELF IN ORDER TO COMMIT A CRIME

Attorney General for Northern Ireland v Gallagher [1963] AC 349 (HL)

Lord Denning:
My Lords, every direction which a judge gives to a jury in point of law must be considered against the background of facts which have been proved or admitted in the case. In this case the accused man did not give evidence himself. And the facts proved against him were:

> He had a grievance against his wife. She had obtained a maintenance order against him and had been instrumental in getting him detained in a mental hospital. He had made up his mind to kill his wife. He bought a knife for the purpose and a bottle of whiskey – either to give himself Dutch courage to do the deed or to drown his conscience after it. He did in fact carry out his intention. He killed his wife with the knife and drank much of the whiskey before or after he killed her.

There were only two defences raised on his behalf: (1) Insanity; (2) Drunkenness.

The Lord Chief Justice directed the jury that the *time* when they had to consider whether he was insane or not (within the *M'Naghten* Rules) was before he started on the bottle of whiskey. 'You should direct your attention,' he said to them, 'to the state of his mind before he opened the bottle of whiskey.' If he was sane at that time, he could not make good the defence of insanity 'with the aid of that bottle of whiskey'. Immediately after the jury retired, Mr Kelly took up this point of *time*. He suggested that it was inaccurate and inconsistent with the *M'Naghten* Rules. But the Lord Chief Justice adhered to his view. He declined to modify his charge to the jury on the matter. 'If I'm wrong,' he said, 'I can be put right.' It was on this very point of *time* that the Court of Criminal Appeal reversed him. His direction was, they said, 'inconsistent with the *M'Naghten* Rules', which fix the crucial time as 'the time of the committing of the act', that is, the time of the killing and not at an earlier time.

The question is whether the direction of the Lord Chief Justice as to the *time* was correct. At least that is how I read the question posed by the Court of Criminal Appeal. It is complicated by the fact that, according to the medical evidence, the accused man was a psychopath. That does not mean that he was insane. But it sharpens the point of the question. He had a disease of the mind. It was quiescent before he started on the whiskey. So he was sane then. But the drink may have brought on an explosive outburst in the course of which he killed her. Can he rely on this self-induced defect of reason and put it forward as a defence of insanity?

My Lords, this case differs from all the others in the books in that the accused man, whilst sane and sober, before he took to the drink, had already made up his mind to kill his wife. This seems to me to be far worse – and far more deserving of condemnation – than the case of a man who, before getting drunk, has no intention to kill, but afterwards in his cups, whilst drunk, kills another by an act which he would not dream of doing when sober. Yet by the law of England in this latter case his drunkenness is no defence even though it has distorted his reason and his will power. So why should it be a defence in the present case? And is it made any better by saying that the man is a psychopath?

The answer to the question is, I think, that the case falls to be decided by the general principle of English law that, subject to very limited exceptions, drunkenness is no defence to a criminal charge, nor is a defect of reason produced by drunkenness. This principle was stated by Sir Matthew Hale in his *Pleas of the Crown*, 1, p 32, in words which I would repeat here: 'This vice' (drunkenness) 'both deprives men of the use of reason, and puts many men into a perfect, but temporary frenzy . . . By the laws of England such a person shall have no privilege by this voluntary contracted madness, but shall have the same judgment as if he were in his right senses.'

This general principle can be illustrated by looking at the various ways in which drunkenness may produce a defect of reason:

a   It may impair a man's powers of perception so that he may not be able to foresee or measure the consequences of his actions as he would if he were sober. Nevertheless he is not allowed to set up his self-induced want of perception as a defence. Even if he did not himself appreciate that what he was doing was dangerous, nevertheless if a reasonable man in his place, who was not befuddled with drink, would have appreciated it, he is guilty: see *R v Meade* [1909] 1 KB 895, as explained in *DPP v Beard* . . .

b   It may impair a man's power to judge between right or wrong, so that he may do a thing when drunk which he would not dream of doing while sober. He does not realise he is doing wrong. Nevertheless he is not allowed to set up his self-induced want of moral sense as a defence. In *Beard's* case Lord Birkenhead LC distinctly ruled that it was not a defence for a drunken man to say he did not know he was doing wrong.

The general principle which I have enunciated is subject to two exceptions:

1   If a man is charged with an offence in which a specific intention is essential (as in murder, though not in manslaughter), then evidence of drunkenness, which renders him incapable of forming that intention, is an answer: see *Beard's* case. This degree of drunkenness is reached when the man is rendered so stupid by drink that he does not know what he is doing (see *R v Moore* (1852) 3 Car & Kir 319), as where, at a christening, a drunken nurse put the

baby behind a large fire, taking it for a log of wood (*Gentleman's Magazine*, 1748, p 570); and where a drunken man thought his friend (lying in his bed) was a theatrical dummy placed there and stabbed him to death (1951) *The Times*, 13 January. In each of those cases it would not be murder. But it would be manslaughter.

2   If a man by drinking brings on a distinct disease of the mind such as *delirium tremens*, so that he is temporarily insane within the *M'Naghten* Rules, that is to say, he does not at the time know what he is doing or that it is wrong, then he has a defence on the ground of insanity: see *R v Davis* (1881) 14 Cox CC 563 and *Beard's* case.

Does the present case come within the general principle or the exceptions to it? It certainly does not come within the first exception. This man was not incapable of forming an intent to kill. Quite the contrary. He knew full well what he was doing. He formed an intent to kill, he carried out his intention and he remembered afterwards what he had done. And the jury, properly directed on the point, have found as much, for they found him guilty of murder. Then does the case come within the second exception? It does not, to my mind, for the simple reason that he was not suffering from a disease of the mind brought on by drink. He was suffering from a different disease altogether. As the Lord Chief Justice observed in his summing up: 'If this man was suffering from a disease of the mind, it wasn't of a kind that is produced by drink.'

So we have here a case of the first impression. The man is a psychopath. That is, he has a disease of the mind which is not produced by drink. But it is quiescent. And whilst it is quiescent he forms an intention to kill his wife. He knows it is wrong but still he means to kill her. Then he gets himself so drunk that he has an explosive outburst and kills his wife. At that moment he knows what he is doing but he does not know it is wrong. So in that respect – in not knowing it is wrong – he has a defect of reason at the moment of killing. If that defect of reason is due to the drink, it is no defence in law. But if it is due to the disease of the mind, it gives rise to a defence of insanity. No one can say, however, whether it is due to the drink or to the disease. It may well be due to both in combination. What guidance does the law give in this difficulty? That is, as I see it, the question of general public importance which is involved in this case.

My Lords, I think the law on this point should take a clear stand. If a man, whilst sane and sober, forms an intention to kill and makes preparation for it, knowing it is a wrong thing to do, and then gets himself drunk so as to give himself Dutch courage to do the killing, and whilst drunk carries out his intention, he cannot rely on this self-induced drunkenness as a defence to a charge of murder, nor even as reducing it to manslaughter. He cannot say that he got himself into such a stupid state that he was incapable of an intent to kill. So also when he is a psychopath, he cannot by drinking rely on his self-induced defect of reason as a defence of insanity. The wicked-ness of his mind before he got drunk is enough to condemn him, coupled with the act which he intended to do and did so. A psychopath who goes out intending to kill, knowing it is wrong, and does kill, cannot escape the consequences by making himself drunk before doing it. That is, I believe, the direction which the Lord Chief Justice gave to the jury and which the Court of Criminal Appeal found to be wrong. I think it was right and for this reason I would allow the appeal.

I would agree, of course, that if before the killing he had discarded his intention to kill or reversed it – and then got drunk – it would be a different matter. But when he forms the intention to kill and without interruption proceeds to get drunk and carry out his intention, then his drunken-ness is no defence and nonetheless so because it is dressed up as a defence of insanity. There was no evidence in this case of any interruption and there was no need for the Lord Chief Justice to mention it to the jury.

I need hardly say, of course, that I have here only considered the law of Northern Ireland. In England a psychopath such as this man might now be in a position to raise a defence of diminished responsibility under s 2 of the Homicide Act 1957 . . .

13.1.5 IS ALL VOLUNTARY CONSUMPTION OF INTOXICANTS TO BE REGARDED AS RECKLESS?

R v Hardie [1985] 1 WLR 64 (CA)

Parker LJ:

. . . Shortly after 9.15 pm on 2 January 1982, fire broke out in a wardrobe in the bedroom of the ground-floor flat at 55 Bassingham Road, London SW10. At that time there were in the flat the appellant, Mrs Jeanette Hardie, with whom the appellant had been living at the premises since May 1974, and who had changed her name to Hardie by deed poll in 1976, and her daughter Tonia. The upstairs flat was occupied by a Mrs Young. Shortly before 2 January, the appellant's relationship with Mrs Hardie had broken down and she had insisted that he must leave. He did not wish to do so, but on the morning of 2 January he packed a suitcase. At about lunchtime the appellant found two bottles of tablets in a cabinet. One contained Valium which Mrs Hardie had had in 1974 and the other tablets to assist urination.

The appellant's evidence in regard to this was that he had never taken Valium before, that he took one about 12 pm to calm him down for he was in a distressed state, that it did not have much effect, that he and Mrs Hardie had then gone shopping, that he had taken two more in front of her and she had said, 'take as many as you like, they are old stock and will do you no harm', that he had taken two more shortly afterwards, that he may have taken two of the other tablets also, and that shortly thereafter on return to the house he had fallen into a deep sleep and could thereafter remember only periods. He was in fact collected from the flat by his mother and remained with her until returning to the flat again at 9.15 pm. It was not disputed that he must have started the fire for he was alone in the bedroom when it started. Having started it, he emerged, returned to the sitting room where were Mrs Hardie and Tonia and stayed there. Shortly afterwards Mrs Hardie heard sounds from the bedroom, went there and found smoke and flames coming from the wardrobe. There was evidence that before, at the time of and after the fire the appellant was exhibiting signs of intoxication and that such signs might have resulted from the taking of Valium some hours earlier.

The defence was that the appellant was so affected by the Valium that he could remember nothing about the fire and had not the necessary *mens rea* to constitute either of the offences charged. On the basis no doubt of *R v Majewski* [1977] AC 443 and *R v Caldwell* [1982] AC 341, the judge directed the jury in effect that, as the Valium was voluntarily self-administered, it was irrelevant as a defence and its effect could not negative *mens rea* . . .

. . . It is clear from *R v Caldwell* [1982] AC 341 that self-induced intoxication can be a defence where the charge is only one specific intention. It is equally clear that it cannot be a defence where, as here, the charge included recklessness. Hence, if there was self-intoxication in this case the judge's direction was correct. The problem is whether, assuming that the effect of the Valium was to deprive the appellant of any appreciation of what he was doing it should properly be regarded as self-induced intoxication and thus no answer . . .

R v Majewski was a case of drunkenness resulting from alcoholic consumption by the accused whilst under the influence of non-medically prescribed drugs. *R v Caldwell* [1982] AC 341 was a case of plain drunkenness. There can be no doubt that the same rule applies both to self-intoxication by alcohol and intoxication by hallucinatory drugs, but this is because the effects of both are well known and there is therefore an element of recklessness in the self-administration of the drug. *R v Lipman* [1970] 1 QB 152 is an example of such a case.

'Intoxication' or similar symptoms may, however, arise in other circumstances. In *R v Bailey (John)* [1983] 1 WLR 760 this court had to consider a case where a diabetic had failed to take sufficient food after taking a normal dose of insulin and struck the victim over the head with an iron bar. The judge directed the jury that the defence of automatism, i.e. that the mind did not go with the act, was not available because the incapacity was self-induced. It was held that this was wrong on two grounds (a) because on the basis of *R v Majewski* [1977] AC 443 it was clearly available to the offence embodying specific intent and (b) because although self-induced by the omission to take food it was also available to negative the other offence which was of basic intent only . . .

In the present instance the defence was that the Valium was taken for the purpose of calming the nerves only, that it was old stock and that the appellant was told it would do him no harm. There was no evidence that it was known to the appellant or even generally known that the taking of Valium in the quantity taken would be liable to render a person aggressive or incapable of appreciating risks to others or have other side effects such that its self-administration would itself have an element of recklessness. It is true that Valium is a drug and it is true that it was taken deliberately and not taken on medical prescription, but the drug is, in our view wholly different in kind from drugs which are liable to cause unpredictability or aggressiveness. It may well be that the taking of a sedative or soporific drug will, in certain circumstances, be no answer, for example, in a case of reckless driving, but if the effect of a drug is merely soporific or sedative the taking of it, even in some excessive quantity, cannot in the ordinary way raise a conclusive presumption against the admission of proof of intoxication for the purpose of disproving *mens rea* in ordinary crimes, such as would be the case with alcoholic intoxication or incapacity or automatism resulting from the self-administration of dangerous drugs.

In the present case the jury should not, in our judgment, have been directed to disregard any incapacity which resulted or might have resulted from the taking of Valium. They should have been directed that if they came to the conclusion that, as a result of the Valium, the appellant was, at the time, unable to appreciate the risks to property and persons from his actions they should then consider whether the taking of the Valium was itself reckless. We are unable to say what would have been the appropriate direction with regard to the elements of recklessness in this case for we have not seen all the relevant evidence, nor are we able to suggest a model direction, for circumstances will vary infinitely and model directions can sometimes lead to more rather than less confusion. It is sufficient to say that the direction that the effects of Valium were necessarily irrelevant was wrong.

In *R v Bailey (John)* [1983] 1 WLR 760 the court upheld the conviction notwithstanding the misdirection, being satisfied that there had been no miscarriage of justice and that the jury properly directed could not have failed to come to the same conclusion. That is not so in the present case. Properly directed the jury might well have come to the same conclusion. There was, for example, evidence that the Valium really did not materially affect the appellant at all at the relevant time, but we are quite unable to say that they must have come to the same conclusion . . .

13.1.6 THE RELATIONSHIP BETWEEN INTOXICATION AND MISTAKE OF FACT

R v Richardson and Irwin [1999] 1 Cr App R 392 (CA)

Clarke J:

On May 29 1998 in the Crown Court at Guildford before Mr C Beaumont, sitting as a Recorder, and a jury, the appellants were convicted by a majority of 11 to one of inflicting grievous bodily harm contrary to section 20 of the Offences Against the Person Act 1861. The Recorder imposed a community service order of 100 hours and each of the defendants was directed to pay compensation of £750 to the victim.

They now appeal against conviction by leave of the trial judge, who granted a certificate pursuant to section 1(2)(b) of the Criminal Appeal Act 1968 that the case was fit for appeal. The judge granted the certificate on the ground that:

> There was a redirection in that the jury were directed that the intention of the defendant should be on the basis of a reasonable (ie not under the influence of drink) man and not (as they were) under the influence of drink.

The Recorder added that he did not agree that there was a redirection but gave leave because he thought that the point was arguable.

The facts of the case can be shortly stated. Both appellants were at the material time students at Surrey University. The complainant, Simon Rose, was also a student at the university. There was evidence that the appellants, the complainant, and the other prosecution witnesses were all friends who regularly drank together at the university. The only possible exception was Nigel Richardson.

On the night in question it was effectively agreed in evidence that the appellants, the complainant and others had been drinking at the student union bar and returned to the appellant Irwin's accommodation. It was said that they had had four to five pints of lager. The accommodation consisted of a duplex flat in which one student occupied the lower floor and Irwin occupied a mezzanine floor up a flight of stairs.

When they arrived there they began joshing Irwin about a girlfriend of his who was also there. They also started what was apparently known as 'bundling', which the Recorder described as 'all jumping about and just regular sort of horseplay'. It was a regular occurrence among the group.

About 2 am the appellants, the complainant and another student, Dean Johnson, went up the stairs into Irwin's part of the accommodation. According to both the complainant and Dean Johnson, Irwin said, 'Let's get Simon over the edge'. There was something of a struggle, apparently all part of the horseplay. However, during the course of this the complainant was lifted over the edge of the balcony and was dropped, as a result of which he fell about 10 to 12 feet and suffered injuries which they must have concluded were really serious and thus grievous bodily harm.

The complainant alleged that that was done by the two appellants. The appellant Irwin agreed that they were the only two involved in it, although the appellant Richardson alleged that the fourth person present, Dean Johnson, was also involved. Irwin gave evidence shortly to this effect. He admitted that he was involved in the tussle which led to the complainant falling over the balcony. However, it was his case that such tussles were a regular occurrence among the group and that the complainant consented to it. It was further his evidence that it was not within any of their contemplations that the complainant should actually fall over the balcony, rather the complainant slipped out of his arms when he was seeking to hold him. Richardson did not give evidence but had admitted in interview that when Irwin had hold of the complainant he, Richardson, held his ankles. Richardson let go of Rose's ankles, and very shortly after that, a period which Richardson put in his interview at some three seconds, Irwin let go of his arms and the complainant fell.

[With regards to the charge under s 20 of the Offences against the Person Act 1861] a key issue before the jury was whether the appellants acted maliciously and the essential question in this appeal is whether the Recorder correctly directed the jury in this regard and, if he did not, whether the convictions are safe.

As we understand it, it was not the prosecution case that the appellants had intended to drop the complainant and cause him harm, but that they acted maliciously in the sense that they each actually foresaw that dropping the complainant would or might cause harm and that they nevertheless took the risk of doing so.

As we understand it, absent the effects of drink, it is common ground that in order to establish the offence under section 20 the prosecution had to prove that in the case of each defendant he either intended the dropping of the complainant to cause him some harm, or that he actually foresaw that it would or might do so: *R v Savage; Director of Public Prosecutions v Parmenter* (1992) 94 Cr App R 193, [1992] 1 AC 699, HL, *per* Lord Ackner at 214, and 751 where he said this:

> Therefore in order to establish an offence under section 20 the prosecution must prove either the defendant intended or that he actually foresaw that his act would cause harm.

As so often, the instant case is complicated by the fact that the appellants had had a good deal to drink. It was therefore possible that the jury might conclude that they did not actually foresee that the dropping of the complainant could cause him injury, if only because they did not foresee the risk of dropping him. The reason that they did not do so was the amount of drink which they had consumed.

It appears to us to be clear on the authorities that in considering what *each* defendant actually foresaw the jury must disregard the fact that the appellants had been drinking.

. . . In *Director of Public Prosecutions v Majewski* . . . the House of Lords did not give guidance as to how juries should be directed in cases such as this. However, . . . [the] matter was expressly considered by the Courts-Martial Appeal Court in *Aitken, Bennet and Barson* (1992) 95 Cr App R 304. In that case the judge advocate had directed the court in this way at p 308:

> . . . you must be satisfied so that you feel sure that each defendant, when he did the act, either foresaw that it might cause some injury, not necessarily serious injury, or wound to some person; in other words, he or she does not have to foresee the particular type of wound or injury which resulted, but foresaw that he might cause some injury, albeit of a minor nature – that is the first – or would have foreseen that the act might cause some injury, had he not been drinking.

It was submitted that the last part of that direction, namely 'would have foreseen that the act might cause some injury, had he not been drinking', was a direction, having regard to the reasoning in *Parmenter*. The court . . . considered the matter in considerable detail. It held that the House of Lords in *Parmenter* did not intend to go behind the clear dicta in *Majewski*, which we have quoted. Its conclusion was that the judge advocate's direction with regard to what it called 'self-induced intoxication' was correct.

It follows that in the instant case, if the matter was to be raised at all, the Recorder should have given a direction to like effect . . .

There were a number of issues which the jury had to consider. As we understand it Mr Dunlop opened the case on the basis that the jury had to be sure that each defendant foresaw the risk that Mr Rose might fall or be dropped and sustain harm. He did not invite the jury to consider the case on the alternative basis that the particular defendant might not have actually foreseen harm, but that he would have done so if he had not been drinking. That would of course have been a less favourable formulation from the defendant's point of view than the one in fact advanced. The prosecution's final speech was also put on the basis of actual foresight and it was that case which the defence speeches were designed to meet. We see no reason why the prosecution should not confine the way in which it put the case in the way described. However the Recorder introduced the alternative into his summing up. In our judgment it would have been better if before doing so he had indicated his intention to counsel before they addressed the jury so that they might take that possibility into account in their addresses to the jury.

It follows from the conclusions which we have stated that, as we see it, the Recorder should have directed the jury along these lines, which seem to us to be consistent with the standard Judicial Studies Board directions:

> The complainant, Rose, suffered bodily harm because he slipped or was dropped from the top of the stairwell. No question of self-defence arises. To convict either defendant you must be sure: (1) that he alone or with the other defendant put Rose into the position from which he slipped or was dropped; (2) that Rose did not consent to being put there; (3) that he realised that Rose did not consent; (4) that his actions in putting Rose there were deliberate, i.e. not accidental; (5) that when doing this either (a) he realised that Rose might slip or be dropped and thus sustain some degree of bodily harm, albeit of a minor character, or (b) would have realised that had he not been drinking. Questions (3) and (5)(a) are about the defendant's state of mind. When considering both you must take account of the evidence that the defendant's mind was affected by alcohol. In relation to question (3) you cannot convict if you find that the defendant did mistakenly believe or might have mistakenly believed that Rose did consent. Take the evidence of his consumption of alcohol into account when considering this. Similarly in relation to question (5)(a) you cannot convict if you find that the defendant did not realise or might not have realised that Rose might slip or be dropped and be injured. Here too you must take account of the evidence of the defendant's consumption of alcohol into account. In the same way the alcohol consumed by Rose bears on question (2).

There was, in our judgment, no need to mention the word recklessness. It is to be noted that if question (5)(b) was to be included it asks not about what the reasonable man would have realised, but what the defendant would have realised. In this case, as Mr Edwards has pointed out, the defendants were not hypothetical reasonable men, but university students.

COMMENTS AND QUESTIONS

1   In *R v Cole and Others* [1993] Crim LR 300, the Court of Appeal held that, whilst the defence of intoxication was made out if the defendant was incapable of forming the necessary intent,

it was also made out where, even though the defendant was so capable, the intent was not actually formed.

2   *R v Bowden* [1993] Crim LR 380 makes clear that the fact that the defendant did something whilst drunk that he would not have done when sober did not, of itself, give rise to the defence of intoxication. A drunken intent was nevertheless an 'intent'; see further *R v Kingston*, considered below.

3   Intoxication is regarded as voluntary if the defendant knowingly took alcohol or other intoxicating drugs. It is irrelevant that he might have misjudged the extent to which he would become intoxicated; see *R v Allen* [1988] Crim LR 698, below.

4   In his speech in *DPP v Majewski* (above) Lord Elwyn-Jones refers to a defendant who voluntarily consumes intoxicants and thereby '. . . disables himself from taking the care he might otherwise take. . .'. Does this mean that a defendant, charged with a basic intent crime, who became intoxicated through his own volition, can still escape liability where there is evidence that, even if he had been sober at the time of the *actus reus*, he would not have been aware of the risk of the prohibited consequence occurring?

5   *R v Cullen* [1993] Crim LR 936, and *R v Richardson and Irwin* (above), suggest that even in respect of basic intent crimes, the jury should be asked to consider whether the defendant would have been aware of the risk in question had he been sober.

6   In *R v O'Grady* [1987] 1 QB 995, the Court of Appeal held that, where a defendant makes a mistake of fact causing him to believe that he is justified in using force to defend himself, and that mistake arises from his voluntary intoxication, he is not entitled to rely on self-defence. In this respect the court further held that no distinction was to be made between offences of basic or specific intent – see further Chapter 14).

13.2 INVOLUNTARY INTOXICATION

Following the 'logic' of *DPP v Majewski* (above) a defendant who commits the *actus reus* of an offence whilst in a state of intoxication brought about by involuntary consumption of intoxicants should escape liability on the basis that he was not at fault in becoming intoxicated. The common law has not, however, adopted an entirely logical response to this problem. Where the effect of the involuntary intoxication is that the defendant was in a state of automatism at the time the *actus reus* was committed, which might be the case, for example, where a third party surreptitiously places LSD in the defendant's food, the defendant should escape liability entirely. The third party could be charged as the principal offender acting through an innocent agent.

Where the defendant is in a state of involuntary intoxication falling short of automatism he can still avail himself of the defence of intoxication in respect of specific intent crimes, following the principles laid down in *DPP v Majewski*, above. If such a defendant is charged with a basic intent crime he would be advised to rely on both *DPP v Majewski* and *R v Hardie* to the effect that he was not 'reckless' in becoming intoxicated, hence there is no prior fault on which to base liability.

13.2.1 MISTAKE AS TO THE NATURE OF THE SUBSTANCE CONSUMED

In *R v Allen* [1988] Crim LR 698, the appellant was convicted of buggery and indecent assault. It was the appellant's alternative line of defence that if, contrary to his basic assertion that he was not the attacker, he was so drunk at the time that he was not responsible for his actions and was in effect acting in a state of automatism; and that that drunken condition was due to his involuntarily having imbibed a quantity of alcohol which he was not responsible for consuming. The appellant gave evidence that he had consumed some drink in a public house and had later been given wine by a friend. He had not realised that the wine had a high alcohol content. The second line of defence was not left to the jury by the judge. The appellant appealed against conviction on the ground that the judge erred in ruling that involuntary drunkenness could not be a defence to a crime of non-specific intent. The court held, dismissing the appeal, the judge was correct in ruling that there was no evidence before him that the drinking was other than voluntary. Further, where an accused knows that he is drinking alcohol, such drinking does not become involuntary for the reason alone that he may not know the precise nature or strength of the alcohol that he is consuming.

13.2.2 INVOLUNTARY CONSUMPTION OF INTOXICANTS FALLING SHORT OF INTOXICATION

R v Kingston [1995] 2 AC 355 (HL)

The respondent was a homosexual with paedophiliac predilections. He became involved in a dispute over business matters with a couple named Foreman. The Foremans employed Penn to obtain damaging information that they could use against the respondent. As part of this plan Penn invited a youth to his room, and supplied the youth with a soporific drug in a drink. The youth gave evidence at the trial that he remembered nothing between a time when he was sitting on the bed in Penn's room and when he woke up, still in Penn's room, the following morning. Whilst the boy was asleep the respondent went to the room and indulged in gross sexual acts with the boy. As part of the plan Penn made a recording of what took place and took some photographs. The respondent maintained that he had only engaged in the sexual acts with the boy because he too had been tricked by Penn into consuming a drug that had lowered his inhibitions. The Court of Appeal allowed the respondent's appeal on the basis that *mens rea* brought about by another's trick or deception could not give rise to criminal liability. The Crown appealed to the House of Lords.

Lord Mustill:

My Lords, this appeal concerns the effect on criminal liability of involuntary intoxication . . . It is clear . . . that [the Court of Appeal's decision] . . . was explicitly founded on general principle. There can be no doubt what principle the court relied upon, for at the outset the court . . . recorded the submission of counsel for the respondent:

The law recognises that, exceptionally, an accused person may be entitled to be acquitted if there is a possibility that although his act was intentional, the intent itself arose out of circumstances for which he bears no blame.

The same proposition is implicit in the assumption by the court that if blame is absent the necessary *mens rea* must also be absent.

My Lords, with every respect I must suggest that no such principle exists or, until the present case, had ever in modern times been thought to exist. Each offence consists of a prohibited act or omission coupled with whatever state of mind is called for by the statute or rule of the common law which create the offence. In those offences which are not absolute the state of mind which the prosecution must prove to have underlain the act or omission – the 'mental element' – will in the majority of cases be such as to attract disapproval. The mental element will then be the mark of what may properly be called a 'guilty mind'. The professional burglar is guilty in a moral as well as a legal sense; he intends to break into the house to steal, and most would confidently assert that this is wrong. But this will not always be so. In respect of some offences the mind of the defendant and still less his moral judgment, may not be engaged at all. In others, although a mental activity must be the motive power for the prohibited act or omission, the activity may be of such a kind or degree that society at large would not criticise the defendant's conduct severely or even criticise it at all. Such cases are not uncommon. Yet to assume that contemporary moral judgments affect the criminality of the act, as distinct from the punishment appropriate to the crime one proved, is to be misled by the expression *mens rea*, the ambiguity of which has been the subject of complaint for more than a century. Certainly, the *mens* of the defendant must usually be involved in the offence; but the epithet *rea* refers to the criminality of the act in which the mind is engaged, not to its moral character . . .

I would therefore reject that part of the respondent's argument which treats the absence of moral fault on the part of the appellants as sufficient in itself to negative the necessary mental element of the offence . . .

. . . His second ground is more narrow, namely that involuntary intoxication is already recognised as a defence by authority which the House ought to follow . . .

[His Lordship discussed the older authorities, and then went on:] There is, however, another line of authority to be considered, for it is impossible to consider the exceptional case of involuntary intoxication without placing it in the context of intoxication as a whole. The area of the law is controversial, as regards the content of the rules, their intellectual foundations, and their capacity to furnish a practical and just solution. Since the law was not explored in depth during the arguments and since it is relevant only as part of the background it is better not to say any more about it than is strictly necessary. Some consideration of the law laid down in *R v Majewski* [1977] AC 443 is however inevitable. As I understand the position it is still the law that in the exceptional case where intoxication causes insanity the *M'Naghten* Rules (*M'Naghten's* case (1843) 10 Cl & F 200) apply: see *DPP v Beard* [1920] AC 479, 501 and *Attorney General for Northern Ireland v Gallagher* [1963] AC 349. Short of this, it is no answer for the defendant to say that he would not have done what he did had he been sober, provided always that whatever element of intent is required by the offence is proved to have been present. As was said in *R v Sheehan* [1975] 1 WLR 739, 744c, 'a drunken intent is nevertheless an intent'. As to proof of intent, it appears that at least in some instances self-induced intoxication can be taken into account as part of the evidence from which the jury draws its conclusions; but that in others it cannot. I express the matter in this guarded way because it has not yet been decisively established whether for this purpose there is a line to be drawn between offences of 'specific' and of 'basic' intent. That in at least some cases a defendant cannot say that he was so drunk that he could not form the required intent is however clear enough. Why is this so? The answer must I believe be the same as that given in other common law jurisdictions: namely that such evidence is excluded as a matter of policy . . .

There remains the question by what reasoning the House put this policy into effect. As I understand it two different rationalisations were adopted. First that the absence of the necessary consent is cured by treating the intentional drunkenness (or more accurately, since it is only in the minority of cases that the drinker sets out to make himself drunk, the intentional taking of drink without regard to its possible effects) as a substitute for the mental element ordinarily required by the offence. The intent is transferred from the taking of drink to the commission of the prohibited act. The second rationalisation is that the defendant cannot be heard to rely on the absence of the mental element when it is absent because of his own voluntary acts. Borrowing an expression from a far distant field it may be said that the defendant is estopped from relying on his self-induced incapacity.

Your Lordships are not required to decide how these two explanations stand up to attack, for they are not attacked here. The task is only to place them in the context of an intoxication which is not voluntary. Taking first the concept of transferred intent, if the intoxication was not the result of an act done with an informed will there is no intent which can be transferred to the prohibited act, so as to fill the gap in the offence. As regards the 'estoppel' there is no reason why the law should preclude the defendant from relying on a mental condition which he had not deliberately brought about. Thus, once the involuntary nature of the intoxication is added the two theories of *Majewski* fall away, and the position reverts to what it would have been if *Majewski* [1977] AC 443 had not been decided, namely that the offence is not made out if the defendant was so intoxicated that he could not form an intent. Thus, where the intoxication is involuntary *Majewski* does not subtract the defence of absence of intent; but there is nothing in *Majewski* to suggest that where intent is proved involuntary intoxication adds a further defence . . .

To recognise a new defence of this type would be a bold step. The common law defences of duress and necessity (if it exists) and the limited common law defence of provocation are all very old. Since counsel for the appellant was not disposed to emphasise this aspect of the appeal the subject was not explored in argument, but I suspect that the recognition of a new general defence at common law has not happened in modern times. Nevertheless, the criminal law must not stand still, and if it is both practical and just to take this step, and if judicial decision rather than legislation is the proper medium, then the courts should not be deterred simply by the novelty of it. So one must turn to consider just what defence is now to be created. The judgment under appeal implies five characteristics:

1   The defence applies to all offences, except perhaps to absolute offences. It therefore differs from defences such as provocation and diminished responsibility.
2   The defence is a complete answer to a criminal charge. If not rebutted it leads to an outright acquittal, and unlike provocation and diminished responsibility leaves no room for conviction and punishment for a lesser offence. The underlying assumption must be that the defendant is entirely free from culpability.
3   It may be that the defence applies only where the intoxication is due to the wrongful act of another and therefore affords no excuse when, in circumstances of no greater culpability, the defendant has intoxicated himself by mistake (such as by shortsightedly taking the wrong drug). I say that this may be so, because it is not clear whether, since the doctrine was founded in part on the dictum of Park J in *Pearson's* case, 2 Lew 144, the 'fraud or stratagem of another' is an essential element, or whether this was taken as an example of a wider principle.

4   The burden of disproving the defence is on the prosecution.

5   The defence is subjective in nature. Whereas provocation and self-defence are judged by the reactions of the reasonable person in the situation of the defendant, here the only question is whether this particular defendant's inhibitions were overcome by the effect of the drug. The more susceptible the defendant to the kind of temptation presented, the easier the defence is to establish.

My Lords, since the existence or otherwise of the defence has been treated in argument at all stages as a matter of existing law the Court of Appeal had no occasion to consider the practical and theoretical implications of recognising this new defence at common law, and we do not have the benefit of its views. In their absence, I can only say that the defence appears to run into difficulties at every turn. In point of theory, it would be necessary to reconcile a defence of irresistible impulse derived from a combination of innate drives and external disinhibition with the rule that irresistible impulse of a solely internal origin (not necessarily any more the fault of the offender) does not in itself excuse although it may be a symptom of a disease of the mind: *AG for South Australia v Brown* [1960] AC 432. Equally, the state of mind which founds the defence superficially resembles a state of diminished responsibility, whereas the effect in law is quite different. It may well be that the resemblance is misleading, but these and similar problems must be solved before the bounds of a new defence can be set.

On the practical side there are serious problems. Before the jury could form an opinion on whether the drug might have turned the scale witnesses would have to give a picture of the defendant's personality and susceptibilities, for without it the crucial effect of the drug could not be assessed; pharmacologists would be required to describe the potentially disinhibiting effect of a range of drugs whose identity would, if the present case is anything to go by, be unknown; psychologists and psychiatrists would express opinions, not on the matters of psychopathology familiar to those working within the framework of the Mental Health Acts but on altogether more elusive concepts. No doubt as time passed those concerned could work out techniques to deal with these questions. Much more significant would be the opportunities for a spurious defence. Even in the field of road traffic the 'spiked' drink as a special reason for not disqualifying from driving is a regular feature. Transferring this to the entire range of criminal offences is a disturbing prospect. The defendant would only have to assert, and support by the evidence of well-wishers, that he was not the sort of person to have done this kind of thing, and to suggest an occasion when by some means a drug might have been administered to him for the jury to be sent straight to the question of a possible disinhibition. The judge would direct the jurors that if they felt any legitimate doubt on the matter – and by its nature the defence would be one which the prosecution would often have no means to rebut – they must acquit outright, all questions of intent, mental capacity and the like being at this stage irrelevant.

My Lords, the fact that a new doctrine may require adjustment of existing principles to accommodate it, and may require those involved in criminal trials to learn new techniques, is not of course a ground for refusing to adopt it, if that is what the interests of justice require. Here, however, justice makes no such demands for the interplay between the wrong done to the victim, the individual characteristics and frailties of the defendant, and the pharmacological effects of whatever drug may be potentially involved can be far better recognised by a tailored choice from the continuum of sentences available to the judge than by the application of a single yea-or-nay jury decision. To this, there is one exception. The mandatory life sentence for murder, at least as present administered, leaves no room for the trial judge to put into practice an informed and sympathetic assessment of the kind just described. It is for this reason alone that I have felt any hesitation about rejecting the argument for the respondent. In the end however I have concluded that this is not a sufficient reason to force on the theory and practice of the criminal law an exception which would otherwise be unjustified. For many years mandatory sentences have impelled juries to return merciful but false verdicts, and have stimulated the creation of partial defences such as provocation and diminished responsibility whose lack of a proper foundation has made them hard to apply in practice. I do not think it right that the law should be further distorted simply because of this anomalous relic of the history of the criminal law.

All this being said, I suggest to your Lordships that the existing work of the Law Commission in the fields of intoxication could usefully be enlarged to comprise questions of the type raised by this appeal, and to see whether by statute a merciful, realistic and intellectually sustainable solution could be newly created. For the present, however, I consider that no such regime now exists, and that the common law is not a suitable vehicle for creating one . . .

13.3 CODIFICATION AND LAW REFORM PROPOSALS

Clause 22 of the draft Criminal Code Bill (DCCB) (see Law Com No 177 Vol I) sought to codify *Majewski* with some minor clarifications. Although the defence of intoxication has been the subject of a much more searching review by the Law Commission since – see its Consult-ation Paper (LCCP 127) and the Report *Legislating the Criminal Code: Intoxication and Criminal Liability* (Law Com 229) – the Home Office Offences Against the Persons Bill (see clause 19) adopts the approach adopted in clause 22 – hence it is reproduced here along with the commentary from Law Com 173 Vol II.

Clause 22 of the DCCB provides:

22(1) Where an offence requires a fault element of recklessness (however described), a person who was voluntarily intoxicated shall be treated –

    (a) as having been aware of any risk of which he would have been aware had he been sober;

    (b) as not having believed in the existence of an exempting circumstance (where the exist-ence of such a belief is in issue) if he would not have so believed had he been sober.

(2) Where an offence requires a fault element of failure to comply with a standard of care, or requires no fault, a person who was voluntarily intoxicated shall be treated as not having believed in the existence of an exempting circumstance (where the existence of such a belief is in issue) if a reasonable sober person would not have so believed.

(3) Where the definition of a fault element or of a defence refers, or requires reference, to the state of mind or conduct to be expected of a reasonable person, such person shall be understood to be one who is not intoxicated.

(4) Subsection (1) does not apply –

    (a) to murder (to which section 55 applies); or

    (b) to the case (to which section 36 applies) where a person's unawareness or belief arises from a combination of mental disorder and voluntary intoxication.

(5)(a) 'Intoxicant' means alcohol or any other thing which, when taken into the body, may impair awareness or control.

   (b) 'Voluntary intoxication' means the intoxication of a person by an intoxicant which he takes, otherwise than properly for a medicinal purpose, knowing that it is or may be an intoxicant.

   (c) For the purposes of this section, a person 'takes' an intoxicant if he permits it to be administered to him.

(6) An intoxicant, although taken for a medicinal purpose, is not properly so taken if –

   (a) (i) it is not taken on medical advice; or

      (ii) it is taken on medical advice but the taker fails then or thereafter to comply with any condition forming part of the advice; and

   (b) the taker is aware that the taking, or the failure, as the case may be, may result in his doing an act capable of constituting an offence of the kind in question;

     and accordingly intoxication resulting from such taking or failure is voluntary intoxication.

(7) Intoxication shall be taken to have been voluntary unless evidence is given, in the sense stated in section 13(2), that it was involuntary.

The commentary in Vol II Law Com 177 states:

Clause 22: Intoxication

8.33 This clause provides for the effect of intoxication upon the liability of a person who causes the external elements of an offence. It aims to reproduce the present law on this topic with modifications recommended by the Criminal Law Revision Committee. It is a somewhat complex clause because it restates relatively complex law. We have kept it as simple as possible by omitting aspects of the corresponding clause in the Code team's Bill that we regarded as strictly speaking redundant (as we explain below). The provision of a simpler clause on intoxication could only result from a major law reform exercise. That was not in question as an aspect of the present project. But, like the majority of the Criminal Law Revision Committee, we are not in any case persuaded that the law as stated in clause 22 would be seriously unsatisfactory.

8.34 *Involuntary intoxication; offences requiring intention, knowledge, etc.* The legal position in relation to situations not referred to by clause 22 is to be deduced from the rest of the Code, read with the enactment creating the offence charged. Thus, the clause has nothing to say about evidence of involuntary intoxication, which is accordingly to be treated like any other evidence tending to show that the defendant lacked the fault required for the offence charged. If the evidence shows no more than that the defendant more readily gave way to passion or temptation than he would have done if he had been sober, it may be a mitigating factor but it will not be a defence. Again, when the offence charged requires proof of intention, knowledge or belief, evidence of voluntary intoxication is to be treated like any other evidence tending to show that the defendant lacked the state of mind in question. This is presently the position in relation to any offence classified as an offence of 'specific intent'. And once again, with such an offence as with any other, intoxication will have no bearing on liability to conviction if it merely affected the defendant's emotional reaction or reduced his inhibitions. There is no need for express provision on these matters.

8.35 *Offences of recklessness.* So far as proof of the fault element of an offence is concerned, the law at present has a special rule for the effect of voluntary intoxication where the offence charged is one of so-called 'basic intent'. We agree with the view of the Criminal Law Revision Committee that this should be replaced by a rule, modelled upon the corresponding provision of the American Law Institute's Model Penal Code, relating to any offence requiring a fault element of recklessness. Subsection (1)(a) provides that a person who was voluntarily intoxicated is to be treated, for the purposes of such an offence, as having been aware of any risk of which he would have been aware had he been sober. Subsection (1) applies to an offence requiring recklessness 'however described'. So, for example, if any offences requiring 'malice' survive the enactment of the Code, they will be governed by the subsection since 'maliciously' is satisfied by proof of recklessness, as defined in clause 18(c); and the same will be true of any offences enacted after the Code which employ the concept of recklessness but use different terminology to describe it.

8.36 Subsection (1) applies to an offence requiring a fault element of recklessness even where it also requires, expressly or by implication, an element of intention or knowledge. So, for example, any charge of rape no doubt implies an allegation of an intention to have sexual intercourse; but paragraph (a) nonetheless applies to an alleged 'fault element of recklessness' constituted by the defendant's having been aware that the woman was not consenting to the intercourse.

8.37 A defendant who was intoxicated may, however, deny that he intended to do any act at all, having no control over, or awareness of, his movements. Charged with recklessly causing serious personal harm by beating a woman, he says that because of his drugged condition he was unconscious. Clause 33 (1)(b) makes it clear that he cannot rely on his condition as a 'state of automatism' if it arose from voluntary intoxication. He is to be treated as having beaten the woman, being aware of any risk of causing harm of which he would have been aware had he been sober.

8.38 *Belief in exempting circumstances*. Just as a person may, because of intoxication, lack the state of mind required for an offence, so he may have the state of mind required for a defence – as when, being drunk, he mistakenly believes that P is making a murderous attack on him and retaliates, as he supposes, in self-defence. As with the fault elements of offences, we believe that it is unnecessary to refer in this clause to the relevant effect of involuntary intoxication. Evidence of involuntary intoxication will, without special provision, be treated like any other evidence tending to show that the defendant held any belief or had any other state of mind which is an element of a defence.

8.39 Where intoxication is voluntary, its effect depends on the fault element of the offence charged. Subsection (1)(b) follows the recommendation of the Criminal Law Revision Committee:

> . . . in offences in which recklessness constitutes an element of the offence, if the defendant because of a mistake due to voluntary intoxication holds a belief which, if held by a sober man, would be a defence to the charge but which the defendant would not have held had he been sober, the mistaken belief should be immaterial.

8.40 A slightly stricter rule must apply to offences not requiring a fault element of recklessness. Subsection (2) therefore provides that, where the offence charged involves a fault element of failure to comply with a standard of care, or requires no fault, the defendant is to be treated as not having believed in the existence of an exempting circumstance if a reasonable sober person would not have so believed.

8.41 In *Jaggard v Dickinson* [1981] QB 527 [see Chapter 12.4.3] the defendant was allowed to rely on a drunken belief that she was damaging property belonging to a person who would consent to her doing so. The effect of subsection (1)(b) is to reverse this decision. This is justified, not only on the ground that it follows from the Committee's recommendations, but also because that decision creates an anomalous distinction (between mistake as to the nonexistence of an element of an offence and mistake as to the existence of a circumstance affording a defence) which it would be wrong to perpetuate in the Code.

8.42 *Mistake and offences requiring intention.* The same anomaly would be introduced if the Code were to adopt a *dictum* of the Court of Appeal in *O'Grady* to the effect that a defendant, on a charge of an offence of 'specific intent' equally with one of 'basic intent', would not be able to rely upon evidence of an intoxicated mistaken belief in an occasion for self-defence. The court was concerned that one who kills because of a drunken mistake should not be 'entitled to leave the court without a stain on his character'. But a conviction of manslaughter will of course be available (and similarly, in a case of serious personal harm, a conviction of an offence of recklessly causing such harm); and it would, we believe, be unthinkable to convict of murder a person who thought, for whatever reason, that he was acting to save his life and who would have been acting reasonably if he had been right. Moreover, the Code should if possible provide consistently for all defences; it would not he appropriate to try to devise a special rule for self-defence alone, or generally for the use of force in public or private defence (clause 44) or in defence of property (clause 185). In all the circumstances we are satisfied that the *dictum* referred to must be ignored in framing the present clause. The result is consistent with the view of the Criminal Law Revision Committee on this topic.

8.43 *Intoxication and reasonableness.* It would seem obvious that, when the law prescribes a standard of reasonable behaviour, this must relate to the standard to be expected of a sober person. But the fact that the point has been argued in the Court of Appeal in two modern cases suggests the desirability of including in the Code the principle that those cases establish, to avoid the matter being reopened. The principle is stated in subsection (3). In *R v Young* [1984] 1 WLR 654 the Court of Appeal thought that, in determining whether a person 'has reason to suspect', it is 'an unnecessary gloss to introduce the concept of the reasonable man'. It is, however, impossible to state a principle concerning intoxication or sobriety without a reference to a person. It does not necessarily follow that the judge need refer to such a person in directing the jury, though it may sometimes be convenient to do so.

8.44 *Exceptions from subsection (1): (a) murder.* Murder has to be excepted (by subsection (4)(a)) from the application of subsection (1) because the fault required by clause 54(b) ('A person who causes the death of another . . . intending to cause serious personal harm and being aware that he may kill') is a variety of recklessness. If murder were not excepted, a person who, because of intoxication, was unaware that he might kill might be treated as being aware of that risk and so liable to conviction of murder. This would be a departure from long established law and from the recommendation of the Criminal Law Revision Committee. The exception reproduces existing law in accordance with that recommendation. It is justified because manslaughter, being punishable with life imprisonment, is sufficient to protect the public interest.

8.45 *(b) Voluntary intoxication and mental disorder in combination.* The courts have accepted that a person's unawareness or mistaken belief may be due to a combination of voluntary intoxication and mental disorder. In *R v Burns* (1973) 58 Cr App R 364 where the defendant's unawareness may have been due partly to brain damage and partly to drink and drugs taken otherwise than on medical advice, the Court of Appeal held that he was entitled to an absolute acquittal. Yet neither of the concurrent causes alone would have entitled him to an absolute acquittal of the offence of 'basic intent' with which he was charged. Some such cases would be better dealt with by a mental disorder verdict under clause 36: the defendant is acquitted but made amenable to the special disposal powers available to the court. A mental disorder verdict will be returned (so long as clause 22 (1) does not apply) where the defendant was suffering at the time of the act from 'mental disorder' as defined in clause 34. The kind of mental disorder relevant in practice would be a state of automatism (not resulting only from the intoxication itself) that is associated with an underlying condition and likely to recur. A mental disorder verdict would be more satisfactory than an 'insanity' verdict under the present law because the court will have wide powers of disposal under the recommendations of the Butler Committee instead of being obliged to order indefinite detention of the offender. Subsection (4)(b) therefore provides that subsection (1) shall not apply in a case of combined intoxication and mental disorder.

8.46 *Definitions: (a) 'Intoxicant'*. It is desirable to define 'intoxicant' (and, by implication,'intoxication') for the purposes of the Code because the meaning it has to bear, like its meaning under the existing law, is probably wider than that attributed to it in ordinary speech. There is only one aspect of intoxication which is relevant for present purposes and that is its effect on a person's awareness of circumstances and of the possible results of his conduct and on his ability to control his movements. Subsection (5)(a) therefore defines an intoxicant as anything which, when taken into the body, may impair awareness or control. The paragraph makes specific reference to alcohol not only because it is the most common intoxicant but also in order to direct the reader's mind more readily to the kind of effect envisaged. The definition is wide enough to include the vapour which is inhaled by a glue-sniffer as well as drugs taken orally or by injection.

(b) 'Voluntary intoxication'. When a person who takes an intoxicant knows that it is or may be an intoxicant his resulting intoxication is in general 'voluntary', as subsection (5)(b) provides. But it seems to be accepted in the present law that intoxication arising from the proper use of drugs for medicinal purposes does not have the consequences in the criminal law of voluntary intoxication; and this is clearly right in principle. A person who becomes voluntarily intoxicated may, without any further fault on his part, become guilty of serious crime. It would be entirely wrong that such a consequence should follow from acting either on medical advice or without medical advice but in all respects properly for a medicinal purpose.

(c) 'Takes' an intoxicant. In the interests of economy of statement, a person's permitting an intoxicant to be administered to himself is said by subsection (5)(c) to be a case of 'taking' it.

8.47 *When an intoxicant is not taken 'properly for a medicinal purpose'*. When drugs are taken on medical advice that advice may include conditions as to the circumstances in which the drug is to be taken. The effect of taking drugs and failing to comply with the conditions may be that the taker becomes intoxicated. If, in consequence of something he then does, he is charged with an offence requiring recklessness or a lower degree of fault, or with an offence of strict liability, the question arises whether the intoxication is 'voluntary' so as to attract the operation of subsection (1) or (2).

8.48 The same question arises where drugs are taken without specific medical advice but for a medicinal purpose and with similar results. As stated in the preceding paragraph, the answer is that it depends, in both types of case, on whether the drugs were taken 'properly' for a medicinal purpose (subsection (5)(b)). Subsection (6) explains that drugs taken on medical advice are properly taken unless (i) the taker fails to comply with the conditions of the advice and (ii) he is aware that he may as a result do an act capable of constituting an offence of the relevant kind. Drugs taken without medical advice but for a medicinal purpose are properly taken unless the taker is aware he may as a result do such an act.

8.49 Subsection (6) is based on the decisions of the Court of Appeal in *Bailey* and *Hardie (Paul Deverall)*. It appears from these decisions that what the taker of the drugs must be aware of in order to incur liability varies according to the nature of the offence charged. If he is charged with an offence of violence he must have been aware that he might behave aggressively. If he is charged with reckless driving it is sufficient that he was aware that his conscious control of what he was doing might be affected. This is expressed as a general principle that the defendant should be regarded as voluntarily intoxicated only if he was aware that his taking of the drugs (if not on medical advice), or his failure to comply with a condition of the advice under which he took them, might result in his doing an act capable of constituting an offence of the kind in question.

8.50 *Evidential burden as to nature of intoxication.* It would, we believe, be arguable, in the absence of special provision, that whenever there is evidence of the defendant's having been so intoxicated that he did not form the intention required for the offence charged, the burden lies on the prosecution to prove that the intoxication was 'voluntary' within the meaning of subsection (5)(b) (see clause 13 (1)(a)). We do not think that such a burden should rest on the prosecution in the absence of any evidence tending to show that the intoxication was involuntary. Subsection (7) therefore puts an evidential burden to that effect upon the defence.

8.51 The subsection does not go so far as to require the defence to prove that the intoxication was involuntary. The Code team included a provision imposing such a requirement in their Bill (in square brackets in view of their doubts about its correctness). They had regard in doing so to a recent provision to the same effect in section 6(5) of the Public Order Act 1986, based on a Law Commission recommendation. The question whether intoxication was involuntary, whenever it is relevant, will in effect be the question whether the defendant acted without the fault required for the offence charged or had a defence based on a belief that an exempting circumstance existed. We do not now think that it would be appropriate to place on the defence a burden of proving absence of fault or to distinguish, in respect of the incidence of the burden of proof, between a defence of mistaken belief that involuntary intoxication may exceptionally provide and other defences of general application. There was some support on consultation for abandonment of the Code team's bracketed provision; and relevant judicial statements appear to assume that the burden is on the prosecution.

13.4 SANE AUTOMATISM

A defendant who raises the defence of sane automatism is claiming that he was unaware of his actions and thus unable to control them. If the defence succeeds it normally amounts to a complete defence. Involuntariness can obviously be seen as a denial of *mens rea*, but if one accepts that voluntariness is an aspect of *actus reus* as well, in the sense that an act is only *reus* if it is voluntary, the defence could also succeed where the offence alleged is one of strict liability.

Hill v Baxter [1958] 1 QB 277 (DC)

Lord Goddard CJ:

This special case stated by justices for the County Borough of Brighton concerns two informations preferred against the respondent, the first for the dangerous driving of a motor vehicle contrary to s 11(1) of the Road Traffic Act, 1930, and the second for failing to conform to a Halt sign contrary to s 49(b) of the Act. The facts found by the justices are that at 10.45pm on the evening of 12 April this year the respondent drove a motor van along Springfield Road, Brighton, in a westerly direction and where that road crosses Beaconsfield Road he ignored an illuminated Halt sign, drove across the road junction at a fast speed and came into collision with a car which was being driven northwards in Beaconsfield Road. The respondent's van then carried on for a short distance and overturned. A police constable arrived and found the respondent in a dazed condition and at the hospital to which he was taken he said:

> I remember being in Preston Circus going to Withdean. I don't remember anything else until I was searching for my glasses. I don't know what happened.

The justices found that to be in Springfield Road on the way to Withdean from Preston Circus involved a substantial and unnecessary detour but that the respondent must have exercised skill in driving in order to reach Springfield Road by whatever route he took. The justices apparently accepted the respondent's evidence and found that he remembered nothing from the time when he was at Preston Circus till the accident had happened. They were of opinion that the respondent was not conscious of what he was doing after leaving Preston Circus and to this finding they add the words 'with the implication that he was not capable of forming any intention as to his manner of driving'. They dismissed the informations, accepting a submission that loss of memory could only be attributed to the respondent being overcome by illness without warning . . .

The first thing to be remembered is that the statute contains an absolute prohibition against driving dangerously or ignoring Halt signs. No question of *mens rea* enters into the offence; it is no answer to a charge under those sections to say 'I did not mean to drive dangerously' or 'I did not notice the Halt sign'. The justices' finding, that the respondent was not capable of forming any intention as to the manner of driving, is really immaterial. What they evidently meant was that the respondent was in a state of automatism . . .

I agree that there may be cases where the circumstances are such that the accused could not really be said to be driving at all. Suppose he had a stroke or an epileptic fit, both instances of what may properly be called acts of God; he might well be in the driver's seat even with his hands on the wheel but in such a state of unconsciousness that he could not be said to be driving. A blow from a stone or a swarm of bees I think introduces some conception akin to *novus actus interveniens*. In this case, however, I am content to say that the evidence falls far short of what would justify a court holding that this man was in some automatous state. There was no evidence that he was suffering from anything to account for what is so often called a 'black-out' and which probably, if genuine, is epileptic in origin . . .

13.4.1 THE DEGREE OF INVOLUNTARINESS REQUIRED FOR AUTOMATISM

Attorney General's Ref (No 2 of 1992) [1994] QB 91 (CA)

The defendant had crashed his lorry into a stationary vehicle on a motorway. The prosecution's case was that the defendant had been overcome by sleep at the wheel. The defendant contended that he should be acquitted on the basis that he was in a state of automatism at the time of the crash as a result of the 'hypnotic' effect of the white lines on the road. The defendant was acquitted and the following point of law was referred to the Court of Appeal:

'Whether the state described as "driving without awareness" should, as a matter of law, be capable of founding a defence of automatism.' This formulation relates to expert evidence given in the particular case. However, we take the point more generally to raise the question: 'What are the requirements and limits of the defence of automatism?'

Lord Taylor of Gosforth CJ:

. . . Both the prosecution and the defence had obtained expert evidence. For the defence, there was a report from Professor Brown, a chartered psychologist and assistant director of the Medical Research Council's Applied Psychology Unit in Cambridge. The Crown had obtained a report from Professor Horne, director of the Sleep Research Laboratory at Loughborough University. It was agreed by counsel that the evidence of each of these experts should be adduced and the judge admitted it. Professor Horne was called as part of the prosecution case. The respondent did not give evidence but relied upon Professor Brown's expert testimony which is central to this reference.

Professor Brown described to the court a condition known as 'driving without awareness' and on the basis of his evidence it was contended for the defence that the respondent was in a state of automatism at the time of the accident and was therefore not to be regarded as driving at all. Professor Horne did not accept Professor Brown's analysis. However, the judge in summing-up to the jury left the defence of automatism based upon Professor Brown's evidence as an issue properly open for the jury's consideration.

It is common ground that, for the purposes of this reference, the court should proceed on the basis of Professor Brown's evidence at its highest. He said that 'driving without awareness' is not a scientific term but a provisional, or interim, descriptive phrase coined at a conference he had attended. He said that there are two essential components to the act of driving: collision avoidance and steering within highway lanes. In a state of 'driving without awareness', the driver's capacity to avoid a collision ceases to exist. This is because repetitive visual stimuli experienced on long journeys on straight, flat, featureless motorways can induce a trance-like state in which the focal point of forward vision gradually comes nearer and nearer until the driver is focusing just ahead of his windscreen. He therefore fails to see further ahead in the central field of vision. However, peripheral vision continues to send signals which are dealt with subconsciously and enable the driver to steer within highway lanes.

Professor Brown said this condition can occur insidiously without the driver being aware it is happening. However, he also said that usually a driver would 'snap out' of the condition in response to major stimuli appearing in front of him. Thus flashing lights would usually cause him to regain full awareness. Professor Brown was unable to explain why that had not happened in the present case. In fact, the respondent told the police when interviewed that he had seen the flashing lights some quarter of a mile before reaching them. Professor Brown was also unable to explain why the respondent should have steered, apparently deliberately, onto the hard shoulder.

Despite his phrase 'driving without awareness', Professor Brown agreed that the driver's body would still be controlling the vehicle, that there would be subconscious motivation to his steering and that although 'largely unaware of what was happening ahead' and 'largely unaware of steering either' the unawareness was not total. Asked if nothing intrudes into the driver's consciousness when he is in this state, the professor said: 'I would not go so far as to say nothing, but very little'. There must, as a matter of common sense, be some awareness if, as Professor Brown accepted, the driver will usually be caused to 'snap out' of the condition by strong stimuli noticed by his eyes . . . The contention on behalf of the Attorney General is that on the evidence given by Professor Brown, even taken at its highest, there was no basis for leaving the defence of automatism to the jury.

. . . The extent of the loss of control is crucial in the present case . . . In our judgment, the 'proper evidential foundation' was not laid in this case by Professor Brown's evidence of 'driving without awareness'. As the authorities cited above show, the defence of automatism requires that there was a total destruction of voluntary control of the defendant's part. Impaired, reduced or partial control is not enough. Professor Brown accepted that someone 'driving without awareness' within his description, retains some control. He should be able to steer the vehicle and usually to react and return to full awareness when confronted by significant stimuli.

Accordingly, in our judgment the recorder ought not to have left the issue of automatism to the jury in this case and the answer to the point of law as formulated is, 'No'.

13.4.2 CONDITIONS GIVING RISE TO AUTOMATISM

Bratty v Attorney General for Northern Ireland [1963] AC 386 (HL)

The defendant strangled a young woman whilst suffering from an attack of psychomotor epilepsy. The House of Lords considered whether this could be regarded as a case of sane automatism, or whether it was more appropriate to regard it as falling within the scope of insanity (i.e. insane automatism).

Lord Denning:
No act is punishable if it is done involuntarily; and an involuntary act in this context – some people nowadays prefer to speak of it as 'automatism' – means an act which is done by the muscles without any control by the mind, such as a spasm, a reflex action or a convulsion; or an act done by a person who is not conscious of what he is doing, such as an act done whilst suffering from concussion or whilst sleep-walking. The point was well put by Stephen J in 1889: 'Can anyone doubt that a man who, though he might be perfectly sane, committed what would otherwise be a crime in a state of somnambulism, would be entitled to be acquitted? And why is this? Simply because he would not know what he was doing'; see R v Tolson (1889) 23 QBD 168, 187. The term 'involuntary act' is, however, capable of wider connotations: and to prevent confusion it is to be observed that in the criminal law an act is not to be regarded as an involuntary act simply because the doer does not remember it. When a man is charged with dangerous driving, it is no

defence for him to say 'I don't know what happened. I cannot remember a thing'; see *Hill v Baxter* [1958] 1 QB 277. Loss of memory afterwards is never a defence in itself, so long as he was conscious at the time; see *Russell v HM Advocate* [1946] SC (J) 37; *R v Podola* [1960] 1 QB 325. Nor is an act to be regarded as an involuntary act simply because the doer could not control his impulse to do it. When a man is charged with murder and it appears that he knew what he was doing, but he could not resist it, then his assertion 'I couldn't help myself' is no defence in itself; see *AG for South Australia v Brown* [1960] AC 432: though it may go towards a defence of diminished responsibility, in places where that defence is available; see *R v Byrne* [1960] 2 QB 396: but it does not render his act involuntary so as to entitle him to an unqualified acquittal. Nor is an act to be regarded as an involuntary act simply because it is unintentional or its consequences are unforeseen. When a man is charged with dangerous driving, it is no defence for him to say, however truly, 'I did not mean to drive dangerously'. There is said to be an absolute prohibition against that offence, whether he had a guilty mind or not; see *Hill v Baxter* [1958] 1 QB 277 at 282 by Lord Goddard CJ. But even though it is absolutely prohibited, nevertheless he has a defence if he can show that it was an involuntary act in the sense that he was unconscious at the time and did not know what he was doing, see *HM Advocate v Ritchie* 1926 SC (J) 45, *R v Minor* (1955) 15 WWR (NS) 433 and *Cooper v McKenna ex p Cooper* [1960] Qd LR 406.

Another thing to be observed is that it is not every involuntary act which leads to a complete acquittal. Take first an involuntary act which proceeds from a state of drunkenness. If the drunken man is so drunk that he does not know what he is doing, he has a defence to any charge, such as murder or wounding with intent, in which a specific intent is essential, but he is still liable to be convicted of manslaughter or unlawful wounding for which no specific intent is necessary, see *Beard's* case [1920] AC 479 at 494, 498, 504 . . .

My Lords, I think that the difficulty is to be resolved by remembering that, whilst the *ultimate* burden rests on the Crown of proving every element essential in the crime, nevertheless in order to prove that the act was a voluntary act, the Crown is entitled to rely on the *presumption* that every man has sufficient mental capacity to be responsible for his crimes: and that if the defence wish to displace that presumption they must give some evidence from which the contrary may reasonably be inferred. Thus a drunken man is presumed to have the capacity to form the specific intent necessary to constitute the crime, unless evidence is given from which it can reasonably be inferred that he was incapable of forming it; see the valuable judgment of the Court of Justiciary in *Kennedy v HM Advocate* 1944 SC (J) 171, 177 which was delivered by Lord Normand. So also it seems to me that a man's act is presumed to be a voluntary act unless there is evidence from which it can reasonably be inferred that it was involuntary. To use the words of Devlin J, the defence of automatism 'ought not to be considered at all until the defence has produced at least *prima facie* evidence'; see *Hill v Baxter* [1958] 1 QB 277, 285; and the words of North J in New Zealand 'unless a proper foundation is laid'; see *R v Cottle* [1958] NZLR 999 at 1025. The necessity of laying the proper foundation is on the defence: and if it is not so laid, the defence of automatism need not be left to the jury, any more than the defence of drunkenness (*Kennedy v HM Advocate* 1944 SC (J) 171), provocation *(R v Gauthier* (1943) 29 Cr App R 113, CCA) or self-defence (*R v Lobell* [1957] 1 QB 547) need be.

What, then, is a proper foundation? The presumption of mental capacity of which I have spoken is a provisional presumption only. It does not put the legal burden on the defence in the same way as the presumption of sanity does. It leaves the legal burden on the prosecution, but nevertheless, until it is displaced, it enables the prosecution to discharge the ultimate burden of proving that the act was voluntary. Not because the presumption is evidence itself, but because it takes the place of evidence. In order to displace the presumption of mental capacity, the defence must give sufficient evidence from which it may reasonably be inferred that the act was involuntary. The evidence of the man himself will rarely be sufficient unless it is supported by medical evidence which points to the cause of the mental incapacity. It is not sufficient for a man to say 'I had a black-out': for 'black-out' as Stable J said in *Cooper v McKenna ex p Cooper* 'is one of the first refuges of a guilty conscience and a popular excuse'. The words of Devlin J in *Hill v Baxter* should be remembered: 'I do not doubt that there are genuine cases of automatism and the like, but I do not see how the layman can safely attempt without the help of some medical or scientific evidence to distinguish the genuine from the fraudulent.' When the only cause that is assigned for an involuntary act is drunkenness, then it is only necessary to leave drunkenness to the jury, with the consequential directions, and not to leave automatism at all. When the only cause that is assigned for it is a disease of the mind, then it is only necessary to leave insanity to the jury and not automatism. When the cause assigned is concussion or sleepwalking, there should be some evidence from which it can reasonably be inferred before it should be left to the jury. If it is said to be due to concussion, there should be evidence of a severe blow shortly beforehand. If it is said to be sleepwalking, there should be some credible support for it. His mere assertion that he was asleep will not suffice.

Once a proper foundation is thus laid for automatism, the matter becomes at large and must be left to the jury. As the case proceeds, the evidence may weigh first to one side and then to the other: and so the burden may appear to shift to and fro. But at the end of the day the legal burden comes into play and requires that the jury should be satisfied beyond reasonable doubt that the act was a voluntary act.

R v Quick and Paddison [1973] 1 QB 910 (CA)

Quick was employed at Farleigh Mental Hospital as a charge nurse. He was convicted of assaulting a patient, Mr Green, who sustained two black eyes, a fractured nose, a split lip which required three stitches and bruising of his arm and shoulders. At his trial Quick sought to rely on the defence of automatism. His evidence was that he had been a diabetic since the age of seven. On the day of the assault Quick had taken insulin, had had a very small breakfast and no lunch, and had then drunk some whisky and a quarter of a bottle of rum. Quick contended that the state of automatism had arisen from hypoglycaemia, a condition brought about when there is more insulin in the bloodstream than the amount of sugar there can cope with. The trial judge ruled that the only defence that could be based on that evidence was one of insanity. Quick changed his plea to guilty and then appealed on the basis that the trial judge had been wrong in law to reject the evidence of automatism.

Lawton LJ:

. . . Our examination of such authorities as there are must start with *Bratty v AG for Northern Ireland* [1963] AC 386, because the judge ruled as he did in reliance on that case. Bratty had been accused of the murder of a young girl. He put forward three defences; first, that at the material time he was in a state of automatism by reason of suffering from an attack of psychomotor epilepsy; second, that he was guilty only of manslaughter since he was incapable of forming an intent on the ground that his mental condition was so impaired and confused and he was so deficient in reason that he was not capable of forming such intent; and third, that he was insane.

The trial judge left the issue of insanity to the jury (which they rejected) but refused to leave the other two issues. The House of Lords adjudged on the evidence in *Bratty's* case that he had been right to rule as he did, but accepted that automatism as distinct from insanity could be a defence if there was a proper foundation in the evidence for it. In this case, if Quick's alleged condition could have been caused by hypoglycaemia and that condition, like psychomotor epilepsy, was a disease of the mind, then Bridge J's ruling was right. The question remains, however, whether a mental condition arising from hypoglycaemia does amount to a disease of the mind. In *Bratty v AG for Northern Ireland* [1963] AC 386, all their Lordships based their speeches on the basis that such medical evidence as there was pointed to Bratty suffering from a 'defect of reason from disease of the mind' and nothing else. Lord Denning discussed in general terms what constituted a disease of the mind. [His Lordship then quoted from the speech of Lord Denning at 412.]

If [Lord Denning's] opinion is right and there are no restricting qualifications which ought to be applied to it, Quick was setting up a defence of insanity. He may have been at the material time in a condition of mental disorder manifesting itself in violence. Such manifestations had occurred before and might recur. The difficulty arises as soon as the question is asked whether he should be detained in a mental hospital. No mental hospital would admit a diabetic merely because he had a low blood sugar reaction; and common sense is affronted by the prospect of a diabetic being sent to such a hospital, when in most cases the disordered mental condition can be rectified quickly by pushing a lump of sugar or a teaspoonful of glucose into the patient's mouth.

The 'affront to common sense' argument, however, has its own inherent weakness, as Sir Joseph Moloney pointed out. If an accused is shown to have done a criminal act while suffering from a 'defect of reason from disease of the mind', it matters not whether the condition of the mind is curable or incurable, transitory or permanent: see *per* Devlin J in *R v Kemp* [1957] 1 QB 399, 407. If the condition is transitory, the Secretary of State may have a difficult problem of disposal; but what happens to those found not guilty by reason of insanity is not a matter for the courts . . .

Applied without qualification of any kind, Devlin J's statement of the law would have some surprising consequences. Take the not uncommon case of the rugby player who gets a kick on the head early in the game and plays on to the end in a state of automatism. If, while he was in that state, he assaulted the referee, it is difficult to envisage any court adjudging that he was not guilty by reason of insanity. Another type of case which could occur is that of the dental patient who kicks out while coming round from an anaesthetic. The law would be in a defective state if a patient accused of assaulting a dental nurse by kicking her while regaining consciousness could only excuse himself by raising the defence of insanity.

. . . In this quagmire of law seldom entered nowadays save by those in desperate need of some kind of a defence, *Bratty v AG for Northern Ireland* [1963] AC 386, 403, 412, 414 provides the only firm ground. Is there any discernible path? We think there is. Judges should follow in a common-sense way their sense of fairness. This seems to have been the approach of the New Zealand Court of Appeal in *R v Cottle* [1958] NZLR 999, 1011 and of Sholl J in *R v Carter* [1959] VR 105, 110. In our judgment no help can be obtained by speculating (because that is what we would have to do) as to what the judges who answered the House of Lords' questions in 1843 meant by disease of the mind, still less what Sir Matthew Hale meant in the second half of the 17th century. A quick backward look at the state of medicine in 1843 will suffice to show how unreal it would be to apply the concepts of that age to the present time. Dr Simpson had not yet started his experiments with chloroform, the future Lord Lister was only 16 and laudanum was used and prescribed like aspirins are today. Our task has been to decide what the law means now by the words 'disease of the mind'. In our judgment the fundamental concept is of a malfunctioning of the mind caused by disease. A malfunctioning of mind of transitory effect caused by the application to the body of some external factor such as violence, drugs, including anaesthetics, alcohol and hypnotic influences cannot fairly be said to be due to disease. Such malfunctioning unlike that caused by a defect of reason from disease of the mind, will not always relieve an accused from criminal responsibility. A self-induced incapacity will not excuse (see *R v Lipman* [1970] 1 QB 152), nor will one which could have been reasonably foreseen as a result of either doing, or omitting to do something, as, for example, taking alcohol against medical advice after using certain prescribed drugs, or failing to have regular meals while taking insulin. From time to time difficult borderline cases are likely to arise. When they do, the test suggested by the New Zealand Court of Appeal in *R v Cottle* is likely to give the correct result, viz, can this mental condition be fairly regarded as amounting to or producing a defect of reason from disease of the mind?

In this case Quick's alleged mental condition, if it ever existed, was not caused by his diabetes but by his use of the insulin prescribed by his doctor. Such malfunctioning of his mind as there was, was caused by an external factor and not by a bodily disorder in the nature of a disease which disturbed the working of his mind. It follows in our judgment that Quick was entitled to have his defence of automatism left to the jury and that Bridge J's ruling as to the effect of the medical evidence called by him was wrong. Had the defence of automatism been left to the jury, a number of questions of fact would have had to be answered. If he was in a confused mental condition, was it due to a hypoglycaemic episode or to too much alcohol? If the former, to what extent had he brought about his condition by not following his doctor's instructions about taking regular meals? Did he know that he was getting into a hypoglycaemic episode? If yes, did he not use the antidote of eating a lump of sugar as he had been advised to do? On the evidence which was before the jury Quick might have had difficulty in answering these questions in a manner which would have relieved him of responsibility for his acts. We cannot say, however, with the requisite degree of confidence, that the jury would have convicted him. It follows that his conviction must be quashed on the ground that the verdict was unsatisfactory.

 COMMENTS AND QUESTIONS

1   In *R v Bingham* [1991] Crim LR 433 (CA), the defendant, a diabetic, was charged with theft of a can of Coke and sandwiches, worth £1.16, at a time when he had £90 in his pocket. He had paid for one can of Coke, and was stopped on leaving the store, following which he replied to questions with 'no comment'. His defence was automatism based on the claim that, at the time, he was suffering from hypoglycaemia and was unaware of his actions. The judge refused to leave that defence to the jury. The Court of Appeal allowed his appeal on the basis that the judge failed to distinguish between hyperglycaemia and hypoglycaemia, the former being too much sugar in the blood, and the latter too little. Hyperglycaemia, being caused by the internal condition of diabetes, could come within the *M'Naghten* Rules and lead to a verdict of not guilty by reason of insanity; see further Chapter 13.5.2. Hypoglycaemia, by contrast, was not caused by the initial disease of diabetes, but by the treatment in the form of too much insulin, or by insufficient quality or quantity of food to counterbalance the insulin. That could give rise to a defence of automatism.

2   In *R v T* [1990] Crim LR 256, the court accepted evidence that post-traumatic stress disorder could give rise to automatism. By contrast, in *R v Sandie Smith* [1982] Crim LR 531, evidence of severe premenstrual tension was not accepted as giving rise to automatism. Aside from the issue of whether there was sufficient evidence of automatism in the latter case, the determining factor was the court's desire to exercise some jurisdiction over the accused. If a plea of automatism is successful the defendant is free to go – the courts cannot compel him or her to receive treatment for the condition giving rise to the automatism.

13.4.3 SELF-INDUCED AUTOMATISM

R v Bailey [1983] 1 WLR 760 (CA)

The defendant was a diabetic. The evidence was that he had attacked a man named Harrison whilst suffering from hypoglycaemia. The Court of Appeal considered the extent to which the defence of automatism ought to be available where there was evidence that the automatism might have occurred due to the actions of the victim himself.

Griffiths LJ:

. . . Automatism resulting from intoxication as a result of a voluntary ingestion of alcohol or dangerous drugs does not negative the *mens rea* necessary for crimes of basic intent, because the conduct of the accused is reckless and recklessness is enough to constitute the necessary *mens rea* in assault cases where no specific intent forms part of the charge: see *R v Majewski* [1977] AC 443, 476 in the speech of Lord Elwyn Jones LC and in the speech of Lord Edmund-Davies where he said, at p 496, quoting from Stroud, *Mens Rea*, 1914, p 115:

> The law therefore establishes a conclusive presumption against the admission of proof of intoxication for the purpose of disproving *mens rea* in ordinary crimes. Where this presumption applies, it does not make 'drunkenness itself' a crime, but the drunkenness is itself an integral part of the crime, as forming together with the other unlawful conduct charged against the defendant, a complex act of criminal recklessness.

The same considerations apply where the state of automatism is induced by the voluntary taking of dangerous drugs: see *R v Lipman* [1970] 1 QB 152 where a conviction for manslaughter was upheld, the appellant having taken LSD and killed his mistress in the course of an hallucinatory trip. It was submitted on behalf of the Crown that a similar rule should be applied as a matter of public policy to all cases of self-induced automatism. But it seems to us that there may be material distinctions between a man who consumes alcohol or takes dangerous drugs and one who fails to take sufficient food after insulin to avert hypoglycaemia.

It is common knowledge that those who take alcohol to excess or certain sorts of drugs may become aggressive or do dangerous or unpredictable things, they may be able to foresee the risks of causing harm to others but nevertheless persist in their conduct. But the same cannot be said without more of a man who fails to take food after an insulin injection. If he does appreciate the risk that such a failure may lead to aggressive, unpredictable and uncontrollable conduct and he nevertheless deliberately runs the risk or otherwise disregards it, this will amount to recklessness. But we certainly do not think that it is common knowledge, even among diabetics, that such is a consequence of a failure to take food and there is no evidence that it was known to this appellant. Doubtless he knew that if he failed to take his insulin or proper food after it, he might lose consciousness, but as such he would only be a danger to himself unless he put himself in charge of some machine such as a motor car, which required his continued conscious control.

In our judgment, self-induced automatism, other than that due to intoxication from alcohol or drugs, may provide a defence to crimes of basic intent. The question in each case will be whether the prosecution have proved the necessary element of recklessness. In cases of assault, if the accused knows that his actions or inaction are likely to make him aggressive, unpredictable or uncontrolled with the result that he may cause some injury to others and he persists in the action or takes no remedial action when he knows it is required, it will be open to the jury to find that he was reckless . . .

In the present case the recorder never invited the jury to consider what the appellant's knowledge or appreciation was of what would happen if he failed to take food after his insulin or whether he realised that he might become aggressive. Nor were they asked to consider why the appellant had omitted to take food in time. They were given no direction on the elements of recklessness. Accordingly, in our judgment there was also a misdirection in relation to the second count in the indictment of unlawful wounding.

But we have to consider whether, notwithstanding these misdirections, there has been any miscarriage of justice and whether the jury properly directed could have failed to come to the same conclusion . . . We think it very doubtful whether the appellant laid a sufficient basis for the defence to be considered by the jury at all. But even if he did we are in no doubt that the jury properly directed must have rejected it. Although an episode of sudden transient loss of consciousness or awareness was theoretically possible it was quite inconsistent with the graphic description that the appellant gave to the police both orally and in his written statement. There was abundant evidence that he had armed himself with the iron bar and gone to Mr Harrison's house for the purpose of attacking him because he wanted to teach him a lesson and because he was in the way . . .

13.4.4 AUTOMATISM – CODIFICATION AND LAW REFORM PROPOSALS

The draft Criminal Code Bill proposes the following as its codification of the defence of sane automatism:

33(1) A person is not guilty of an offence if –
    (a) he acts in a state of automatism, that is, his act –
        (i) is a reflex, spasm or convulsion; or
        (ii) occurs while he is in a condition (whether of sleep, unconsciousness, impaired consciousness or otherwise) depriving him of effective control of the act; and
    (b) the act or condition is the result neither of anything done or omitted with the fault required for the offence nor of voluntary intoxication.
(2) A person is not guilty of an offence by virtue of an omission to act if –
    (a) he is physically incapable of acting in the way required; and
    (b) his being so incapable is the result neither of anything done or omitted with the fault required for the offence nor of voluntary intoxication.

The commentary on this clause in Vol II of Law Com 177 provides as follows:

11.1 'Automatism' has been referred to as 'a modern catch-phrase' to describe 'an involuntary movement of the body or limbs of a person'. In general a person is not criminally liable for such a movement or its consequences. On one analysis an 'involuntary movement' is not an 'act'. In Code terms, however, even an unconscious movement of a person is an 'act', but one done 'in a state of automatism'. This permits flexible use of the word 'act' as a key term in the Code and makes 'a state of automatism' also available as a Code expression. The word 'involuntary' is not needed – happily, in view of the variable use to which it tends to be put.

11.2 Limited function of subsection (1). The main function of clause 33 (1) is to protect a person who acts in a state of automatism from conviction of an offence of strict liability. It is conceded that he does 'the act' specified for the offence; but the clause declares him not guilty. One charged with an offence requiring fault in the form of failure to comply with a standard of conduct may also have to rely on the clause. On the other hand, a state of automatism will negative a fault requirement of intention or knowledge or (normally) recklessness; so a person charged with an offence of violence against another, or of criminal damage, committed when he was in a condition of impaired consciousness, does not rely on this clause for his acquittal but on the absence of the fault element of the offence.

11.3 Conditions within the subsection. Subsection (1)(a) refers to acts of two kinds:

(i) an act over which the person concerned, although conscious, has no control: the 'reflex, spasm or convulsion'. Such an act would rarely, if ever, be the subject of a prosecution;

(ii) an act over which the person concerned does not have effective control because of a 'condition' of 'sleep, unconsciousness, impaired consciousness or otherwise'. We believe that the references to 'impaired consciousness', and to deprivation of 'effective' control are justified both on principle and by some of the leading cases. The governing principle should be that a person is not guilty of an offence if, without relevant fault on his part, he cannot choose to act otherwise than as he does. The acts of the defendants in several cases have been treated as automatons although it is far from clear, and even unlikely, that they were entirely unconscious when they did the acts and although it cannot confidently be said that they exercised no control, in any sense of that phrase, over their relevant movements.

11.4 The case law, however, is not consistent. In *Broome v Perkins*, D drove five miles home, very erratically, in a hypoglycaemic state. The evidence was that he may well not have been conscious of what he was doing. The Divisional Court directed a conviction of driving without due care and attention, on the ground that D's mind must have reacted to stimuli, made decisions (to swerve, brake, restart after stopping) and given directions to his limbs. His actions were regarded as not 'involuntary' or 'automatic'. Yet it seems clear that D's condition was such that he could not choose to behave otherwise than as he did. Cases such as those we have mentioned above appear not to have been referred to. Finding it necessary to choose between the authorities, we propose a formula under which we expect (and indeed hope) that a person in the condition of the defendant in *Broome v Perkins* would be acquitted (subject to the question of prior fault).

11.5 *Prior fault.* Subsection (1)(b) excepts from the protection of the subsection cases in which the state of automatism itself is the result of relevant fault on the part of the person affected or of voluntary intoxication. A person charged with an offence that may be committed by negligence can be convicted if his state of automatism was the result of his own negligent conduct. Under clause 22 (1)(a) a person who was unaware of a risk by reason of voluntary intoxication is credited, when charged with an offence of recklessness, with the awareness that he would have had if sober; and clause 33 (1)(b) ensures that he cannot escape liability for the offence by a plea of automatism. Paragraph (b) is intended to produce the same results as the common law.

11.6 *Physical incapacity*. Subsection (2) provides the necessary corresponding rules for a case in which physical incapacity prevents the doing of that which there is a duty to do. The law does not condemn a person for not doing what cannot possibly be done – unless, once again, it is in a relevant way his fault that he cannot possibly do it.

13.5 INSANE AUTOMATISM

In broad terms, a criminal court may be concerned with the issue of insanity at two stages. First, was the defendant insane at the time of the alleged offence? Second, is the defendant fit to stand trial? Where it is accepted on both sides that D was insane at the time of the offence, or is unfit to stand trial, the court (sitting without a jury) will nevertheless have to investigate whether or not the defendant committed the *actus reus* of the offence charged. The purpose of this exercise is to ensure that the defendant is only detained where there is evidence that he actually committed the *actus reus* alleged; see further the Criminal Procedure (Insanity and Unfitness to Plead) Act 1991, as amended by the Domestic Violence, Crime and Victims Act 2004. Where a special verdict is returned that the accused is not guilty by reason of insanity – or findings have been made that the accused is under a disability and that he did the act or made the omission charged against him – the court has the power to make the defendant the subject of a hospital order (with or without a restriction order); a supervision order; or an order for his absolute discharge.

Insanity is a general defence in criminal law and can be raised, if the defendant so wishes, in relation to minor offences; see *R v Horseferry Road Magistrates' Court ex p K* [1997] QB 23. As the defence involves a denial of *mens rea* it will not avail a defendant charged with a strict liability offence; see *DPP v H* (1997) *The Times,* 2 May.

13.5.1 THE TEST FOR INSANE AUTOMATISM

M'Naghten's case (1843) 10 Cl & F 200

Daniel McNaghten was acquitted of shooting Sir Robert Peel's secretary, in what today would probably be termed a state of paranoia. The question of insanity and criminal responsibility was the subject of debate in the legislative chamber of the House of Lords. The House invited the judges of the courts of common law to answer five abstract questions on the subject of insanity as a defence to criminal charges. The answer to the second and third of these questions combined was given to Tindal CJ on behalf of all the judges, except Maule J, and constituted what have become known as the *M'Naghten* Rules.

Tindal CJ:

... The jurors ought to be told in all cases that every man is to be presumed to be sane, and to possess a sufficient degree of reason to be responsible for his crimes, until the contrary be proved to their satisfaction; and that to establish a defence on the ground of insanity, it must be clearly proved that, at the time of the committing of the act, the party accused was labouring under such a defect of reason, from disease of the mind, as not to know the nature and quality of the act he was doing; or, if he did know it, that he did not know he was doing what was wrong.

It will be noted from the above that the rules envisage the defendant's defect of reason as manifesting itself in one of two ways – automatism, or a failure to appreciate that the actions were 'wrong'. [This latter manifestation of insanity is considered later in this chapter.] The defendant is presumed to be sane unless he proves (and the burden is on him to show), on the balance of probabilities, that he was insane at the time of the alleged offence. It follows that the jury do not have be satisfied beyond reasonable doubt that the defendant was insane; it is sufficient that they are satisfied that it is more likely than not that he was insane at the relevant time: see *Sodeman v The King* [1936] 2 All ER. Note that in *R v Clarke* [1972] 1 All ER 219, Ackner J observed: '... The *M'Naghten* Rules relate to accused persons who by reason of a disease of the mind are deprived of the power of reasoning. They do not apply and never have applied to those who retain the power of reasoning but who in moments of confusion or absent-mindedness fail to use their powers to the full.'

13.5.2 DISEASE OF THE MIND FOR THE PURPOSES OF INSANITY

R v Kemp [1957] 1 QB 399 (Devlin J, Bristol Assizes)

Devlin J:

... The facts of the case in relation to which this point has to be considered are that the accused, who is charged with causing grievous bodily harm to his wife, struck her during the night with a hammer with such violence as to inflict a grievous wound. The accused is an elderly man of excellent character and he and his wife have always been thought to be a devoted couple, and it seems that there is strong evidence to show that the act was entirely motiveless and irrational. I say strong evidence to show, though that is a matter which the jury will have in due course to decide: for the purpose of my ruling I assume that in accordance with the evidence to which I have referred, the act was committed, as the doctors on all sides think it was, while the accused was in a mental condition which made him not responsible for his actions. Their view upon this – and all three are agreed – is that he did the act, as he says he did, not knowing anything about it and that he has not any real memory of it. It is not merely a question of his striking his wife when in some mental derangement, nor appreciating that what he was doing was wrong; it is a case in the view of all three doctors in which he was not conscious at the time that he did the act, that he picked up the hammer or that he was striking his wife with it ...

It is common ground on the evidence that the accused was suffering from a physical disease, namely arteriosclerosis, or hardening of the arteries. It had not reached – and this, I think, is clear from the evidence, at any rate I assume so for this purpose – the stage at which the accused was showing any general sign of mental trouble. Apart from a depression, not an irrational depression, produced by his poor state of health, there were no signs of mental trouble ...

I shall say by way of commencement that there is, according to the evidence, no general medical opinion upon what category of diseases are properly to be called diseases of the mind. Both doctors have expressed their views, but they have expressed their views as personal views and not ones for which they can call in aid any general body of medical opinion. Doctors' personal views, of course, are not binding upon me. I have to interpret the rules according to the ordinary principles of interpretation, but I derive help from their interpretations in as much as they illustrate the nature of the disease and the matters which from the medical point of view have to be considered in determining whether or not it is a disease of the mind.

The broad submission that was made to me on behalf of the accused was that this is a physical disease and not a mental disease; arteriosclerosis is a physical condition primarily and not a mental condition. But that argument does not go so far as to suggest that for the purpose of the law diseases that affect the mind can be divided into those that are physical in origin and those that are mental in origin. There is such a distinction medically. I think it is recognised by medical men that there are mental diseases which have an organic cause, there are disturbances of the mind which can be traced to some hardening of the arteries, to some degeneration of the brain cells or to some physical condition which accounts for mental derangement. It is also recognised that there are diseases functional in origin where it is not possible to point to any physical cause but simply to say that there has been a derangement of the functioning of the mind, such as melancholia, schizophrenia and many other of those diseases which are usually handled by psychiatrists. This medical distinction is not pressed as part of the argument for the accused in this case, and I think rightly. The distinction between the two categories is quite irrelevant for the purposes of the law, which is not concerned with the origin of the disease or the cause of it but simply with the mental condition which has brought about the act. It does not matter, for the purposes of the law, whether the defect of reason is due to a degeneration of the brain or to some other form of mental derangement. That may be a matter of importance medically, but it is of no importance to the law, which merely has to consider the state of mind in which the accused is, not how he got there.

The distinction that emerges from the evidence of Dr Gibson and which has been argued by [counsel for the accused] is a different one. It is that this is something which is capable of becoming a mental disease but has not yet become one. It has not created any degeneration of the brain and the argument is that it is merely interfering temporarily with the working of the brain by cutting off the supply of blood in the same way as concussion might, or something of that sort. I am invited to say that this disease at this stage is purely physical; when it interferes with the brain cells so that they degenerate, it then becomes a disease of the mind. This would be a very difficult test to apply for the purposes of the law. I should think it would be a matter of great difficulty medically to determine precisely at what point degeneration of the brain sets in, and it would mean that the verdict depended upon a doubtful medical borderline.

The law is not concerned with the brain but with the mind, in the sense that 'mind' is ordinarily used, the mental faculties of reason, memory and understanding. If one read for 'disease of the mind' 'disease of the brain', it would follow that in many cases pleas of insanity would not be established because it could not be proved that the brain had been affected in any way, either by degeneration of the cells or in any other way. In my judgment the condition of the brain is irrelevant and so is the question of whether the condition of the mind is curable or incurable, transitory or permanent. There is no warranty for introducing those considerations into the definition in the *M'Naghten* Rules. Temporary insanity is sufficient to satisfy them. It does not matter whether it is incurable and permanent or not.

I think that the approach of [counsel for the Crown] to the definition in the rules is the right one. He points out the order of the words 'a defect of reason, from disease of the mind'. The primary thing that has to be looked for is the defect of reason. 'Disease of the mind' is there for some purpose, obviously, but the prime thing is to determine what is admitted here, namely whether or not there is a defect of reason. In my judgment, the words 'from disease of the mind' are not to be construed as if they were put in for the purpose of distinguishing between diseases which have a mental origin and diseases which have a physical origin, a distinction which in 1843 was probably little considered. They were put in for the purpose of limiting the effect of the words 'defect of reason'. A defect of reason is by itself enough to make the act irrational and therefore normally to exclude responsibility in law. But the rule was not intended to apply to defects of reason caused simply by brutish stupidity without rational power. It was not intended that the defence should plead: 'Although with a healthy mind he nevertheless had been brought up in such a way that he had never learned to exercise his reason, and therefore he is suffering from a defect of reason.' The words ensure that unless the defect is due to a diseased mind and not simply to an untrained one there is insanity within the meaning of the rule.

Hardening of the arteries is a disease which is shown on the evidence to be capable of affecting the mind in such a way as to cause a defect, temporarily or permanently, of its reasoning, understanding and so on, and so is in my judgment a disease of the mind which comes within the meaning of the rules . . .

R v Sullivan [1984] 1 AC 156 (HL)

Lord Diplock:

My Lords, the appellant, Mr Sullivan, a man of blameless reputation, has the misfortune to have been a lifelong sufferer from epilepsy. There was a period when he was subject to major seizures known as grand mal; but, as a result of treatment which he was receiving as an out-patient of the Maudsley Hospital from 1976 onwards, these major seizures had, by the use of drugs, been reduced by 1979 to seizures of less severity known as petit mal; or psychomotor epilepsy, though they continued to occur at a frequency of one or two per week.

One such seizure occurred on 8 May 1981, when Mr Sullivan, then aged 51, was visiting a neighbour, Mrs Killick, an old lady aged 86 for whom he was accustomed to perform regular acts of kindness. He was chatting there to a fellow visitor and friend of his, a Mr Payne aged 80, when the epileptic fit came on. It appears likely from the expert medical evidence about the way in which epileptics behave at the various stages of a petit mal seizure that Mr Payne got up from the chair to help Mr Sullivan. The only evidence of an eyewitness was that of Mrs Killick, who did not see what had happened before she saw Mr Payne lying on the floor and Mr Sullivan kicking him about the head and body, in consequence of which Mr Payne suffered injuries severe enough to require hospital treatment.

As a result of this occurrence Mr Sullivan was indicted upon two counts: the first was of causing grievous bodily harm with intent contrary to s 18 of the Offences Against the Person Act 1861; the second of causing grievous bodily harm contrary to s 20 of that Act. At his trial, which took place at the Central Criminal Court before Judge Lymbery and a jury, Mr Sullivan pleaded not guilty to both counts. Mrs Killick's evidence that he had kicked Mr Payne violently about the head and body was undisputed and Mr Sullivan himself gave evidence of his history of epilepsy and his absence of all recollection of what had occurred at Mrs Killick's flat between the time that he was chatting peacefully to Mr Payne there and his return to the flat somewhere else to find that Mr Payne was injured and that an ambulance had been sent for. The prosecution accepted his evidence as true. There was no cross-examination.

Counsel for Mr Sullivan wanted to rely upon the defence of automatism or, as Viscount Kilmuir LC had put it in *Bratty v AG for Northern Ireland* [1963] AC 386, 405, 'non-insane' automatism; that is to say, that he had acted unconsciously and involuntarily in kicking Mr Payne, but that when doing so he was not 'insane' in the sense in which that expression is used as a term of art in English law, and in particular in s 2 of the Trial of Lunatics Act 1883, as amended by s 1 of the Criminal Procedure (Insanity) Act 1964. As was decided unanimously by this House in *Bratty*, before a defence of non-insane automatism may properly be left to the jury, some evidential foundation for it must be laid.

The evidential foundation that counsel laid before the jury in the instant case consisted of the testimony of two distinguished specialists from the neuro-psychiatry epilepsy unit at the Maudsley Hospital, Dr Fenwick and Dr Taylor, as to the pathology of the various stages of a seizure due to psychomotor epilepsy. Their expert evidence, which was not disputed by the prosecution, was that Mr Sullivan's acts in kicking Mr Payne had all the characteristics of epileptic automatism at the third or post-ictal stage of petit mal; and that in view of his history of psychomotor epilepsy and hospital records of his behaviour during previous seizures, the strong probability was that Mr Sullivan's acts of violence towards Mr Payne took place while he was going through that stage.

The evidence as to the pathology of a seizure due to psychomotor epilepsy can be sufficiently stated for the purposes of this appeal by saying that after the first stage, the prodram, which precedes the fit itself, there is a second stage, the ictus, lasting a few seconds, during which there are electrical discharges into the temporal lobes of the brain of the sufferer. The effect of these discharges is to cause him in the post-ictus stage to make movements which he is not conscious that he is making, including, and this was a characteristic of previous seizures which Mr Sullivan had suffered, automatic movements of resistance to anyone trying to come to his aid. These movements of resistance might, though in practice they very rarely would, involve violence . . .

The *M'Naghten* Rules have been used as a comprehensive definition for this purpose by the courts for the last 140 years. Most importantly, they were so used by this House in *Bratty v AG for Northern Ireland* [1963] AC 386. That case was in some respects the converse of the instant case. Bratty was charged with murdering a girl by strangulation. He claimed to have been unconscious of what he was doing at the time he strangled the girl and he sought to run as alternative defences non-insane automatism and insanity. The only evidential foundation that he laid for either of these pleas was medical evidence that he might have been suffering from psychomotor epilepsy which, if he were, would account for his having been unconscious of what he was doing. No other pathological explanation of his actions having been carried out in a state of automatism was supported by evidence. The trial judge first put the defence of insanity to the jury. The jury rejected it; they declined to bring in the special verdict. Thereupon, the judge refused to put to the jury the alternative defence of automatism. His refusal was upheld by the Court of Criminal Appeal of Northern Ireland and subsequently by this House . . .

In the instant case, as in *Bratty*, the only evidential foundation that was laid for any finding by the jury that Mr Sullivan was acting unconsciously and involuntarily when he was kicking Mr Payne, was that when he did so he was in the post-ictal stage of seizure of psychomotor epilepsy. The evidential foundation in the case of Bratty, that he was suffering from psychomotor epilepsy at the time he did the act with which he was charged, was very weak and was rejected by the jury; the evidence in Mr Sullivan's case, that he was so suffering when he was kicking Mr Payne, was very strong and would almost inevitably be accepted by a properly directed jury. It would be the duty of the judge to direct the jury that if they did accept that evidence the law required them to bring in a special verdict and none other. The governing statutory provision is to be found in s 2 of the Trial of Lunatics Act 1883. This says 'the jury shall return a special verdict . . .'

My Lords, I can deal briefly with the various grounds on which it has been submitted that the instant case can be distinguished from what constituted the *ratio decidendi* in *Bratty v AG for Northern Ireland* [1963] AC 386, and that it falls outside the ambit of the *M'Naghten* Rules.

First, it is submitted that the medical evidence in the instant case shows that psychomotor epilepsy is not a disease of the mind, whereas in *Bratty* it was accepted by all the doctors that it was. The only evidential basis for this submission is that Dr Fenwick said that in medical terms to constitute a 'disease of the mind' or 'mental illness', which he appeared to regard as interchangeable descriptions, a disorder of brain functions (which undoubtedly occurs during a seizure in psychomotor epilepsy) must be prolonged for a period of time usually more than a day; while Dr Taylor would have it that the disorder must continue for a minimum of a month to qualify for the description 'a disease of the mind'.

The nomenclature adopted by the medical profession may change from time to time; *Bratty* was tried in 1961. But the meaning of the expression 'disease of the mind' as the cause of 'a defect of reason' remains unchanged for the purposes of the application of the *M'Naghten* Rules. I agree with what was said by Devlin J in *R v Kemp* [1957] 1 QB 399, 407, that 'mind' in the *M'Naghten* Rules is used in the ordinary sense of the mental faculties of reason, memory and understanding. If the effect of a disease is to impair these faculties so severely as to have either of the consequences referred to in the latter part of the rules, it matters not whether the aetiology of the impairment is organic, as in epilepsy, or functional, or whether the impairment itself is permanent or is transient and intermittent, provided that it subsisted at the time of commission of the act. The purpose of the legislation relating to the defence of insanity, ever since its origin in 1800, has been to protect society against recurrence of the dangerous conduct. The duration of a temporary suspension of the mental faculties of reason, memory and understanding, particularly if, as in Mr Sullivan's case, it is recurrent, cannot on any rational ground be relevant to the application by the courts of the *M'Naghten* Rules, though it may be relevant to the course adopted by the Secretary of State, to whom the responsibility for how the defendant is to be dealt with passes after the return of the special verdict of 'not guilty by reason of insanity'.

To avoid misunderstanding I ought perhaps to add that in expressing my agreement with what was said by Devlin J in *Kemp*, where the disease that caused the temporary and intermittent impairment of the mental faculties was arteriosclerosis, I do not regard that learned judge as excluding the possibility of non-insane automatism (for which the proper verdict would be a verdict of 'not guilty') in cases where temporary impairment (not being self-induced by consuming drink or drugs) resulted from some external physical factor such as a blow on the head causing concussion or the administration of an anaesthetic for therapeutic purposes. I mention this because in *R v Quick* [1973] QB 910, Lawton LJ appears to have regarded the ruling in *Kemp* as going as far as this. If it had done, it would have been inconsistent with the speeches in this House in *Bratty* [1963] AC 386, where *Kemp* was alluded to without disapproval by Viscount Kilmuir LC at 403, and received the express approval of Lord Denning at 411. The instant case, however, does not in my view afford an appropriate occasion for exploring possible causes of non-insane automatism.

The only other submission in support of Mr Sullivan's appeal which I think it necessary to mention is that, because the expert evidence was to the effect that Mr Sullivan's acts in kicking Mr Payne were unconscious and thus 'involuntary' in the legal sense of that term, his state of mind was not dealt with by the *M'Naghten* Rules at all, since it was not covered by the phrase 'as not to know the nature and quality of the act he was doing'. Quite apart from being contrary to all three speeches in this House in *Bratty v AG for Northern Ireland* [1963] AC 386, this submission appears to me, with all respect to counsel, to be quite unarguable. Dr Fenwick himself accepted it as an accurate description of Mr Sullivan's mental state in the post-ictal stage of a seizure. The audience to whom the phrase in the *M'Naghten* Rules was addressed consisted of peers of the realm in the 1840s when a certain orotundity of diction had not yet fallen out of fashion. Addressed to an audience of jurors in the 1980s it might more aptly be expressed as 'He did not know what he was doing'.

My Lords, it is natural to feel reluctant to attach the label of insanity to a sufferer from psycho-motor epilepsy of the kind to which Mr Sullivan was subject, even though the expression in the context of a special verdict of 'not guilty by reason of insanity' is a technical one which includes a purely temporary and intermittent suspension of the mental faculties of reason, memory and understanding resulting from the occurrence of an epileptic fit. But the label is contained in the current statute, it has appeared in this statute's predecessors ever since 1800. It does not lie within the power of the courts to alter it. Only Parliament can do that. It has done so twice; it could do so once again . . .

R v Hennessy [1989] 1 WLR 287 (CA)

Lord Lane:

. . . The facts which gave rise to the charges, so far as material, were these. On Thursday 28 May 1987, two police constables, Barnes and Grace, were on duty in St Leonards-on-Sea on the Sussex coast, among other things looking for a Ford Granada car which had been stolen. They found the car. It was unattended. They kept it under watch. As they watched they saw the appellant get into the car, switch on the headlights and ignition, start the car and drive off. The appellant at the wheel of the car correctly stopped the car at a set of traffic lights which were showing red against him. PC Grace then went over to the car as it was stationary, removed the ignition keys from the ignition lock, but not before the appellant had tried to drive the motor car away and escape from the attention of the policeman. The appellant was put in the police car. On the way to the police station an informal conversation about motor vehicles took place between the appellant and the police officers, in particular about the respective merits of the new Rover motor car and the Ford Sierra. Indeed, the appellant appeared to PC Barnes not only to be fully in possession of his faculties but to be quite cheerful and intelligent. Indeed he went so far as to say to the police officer that if he had only got the car, which he was in the process of removing, into the open road, he would have given the policemen a real run for their money.

However after having been at the police station for a time, the appellant was at a later stage escorted by PC Barnes to hospital. He seemed to be normal when he left the cell block at the police station, but when he arrived at the hospital he appeared to be dazed and confused. He complained to the sister in the casualty ward that he had failed to take his insulin and indeed had had no insulin since the previous Monday when he should have had regular self-injection doses.

He was given insulin, with which he injected himself, and the hospital discharged him and he was taken back to the police station.

The appellant gave evidence to the effect that he had been a diabetic for about 10 years. He needed, in order to stabilise his metabolism, two insulin injections on a daily basis, morning and afternoon. The amount required would depend on factors such as stress and eating habits. He was on a strict carbohydrate diet. At the time of the offence he said he had been having marital and employment problems. His wife had submitted a divorce petition some time shortly before, and he was very upset. He had not been eating and he had not been taking his insulin. He remembered very few details of the day. He could recall being handcuffed and taken to the charge room at the police station. He remembered being given insulin at the hospital and injecting himself and he remembers feeling better when he got back to the police station afterwards. He said he did not recall taking the car . . .

The defence to these charges accordingly was that the appellant had failed to take his proper twice-a-day dose of insulin for two or three days and at the time the events in question took place he was in a state of automatism and did not know what he was doing. Therefore it is submitted that the guilty mind, which is necessary to be proved by the prosecution, was not proved, and accordingly that he was entitled to be acquitted.

The judge took the view, rightly in our view, that the appellant, having put his state of mind in issue, the preliminary question which he had to decide was whether this was truly a case of automatism or whether it was a case of legal 'insanity' within the *M'Naghten* Rules . . . He concluded that it was the latter, and he so ruled, whereupon the appellant changed his plea to guilty and was sentenced to the terms of imprisonment suspended which we have already mentioned. The judge then certified the case fit for appeal in the terms which I have already described.

The *M'Naghten* Rules in the earlier part of the last century have in many ways lost their importance; they certainly have lost the importance they once had, but they are still relevant in so far as they may affect the defence of automatism. Although the rules deal with what they describe as insanity, it is insanity in the legal sense and not in the medical or psychological sense . . .

The importance of the rules in the present context, namely the context of automatism, is this. If the defendant did not know the nature and quality of his act because of something which *did not* amount to defect of reason from disease of the mind then he will probably be entitled to be acquitted on the basis that the necessary criminal intent which the prosecution has to prove is not proved. But, if, on the other hand, his failure to realise the nature and quality of his act was due to a defect of reason from disease of the mind, then in the eyes of the law he is suffering from insanity, albeit *M'Naghten* insanity . . .

The question in many cases, and this is one such case, is whether the function of the mind was disturbed on the one hand by disease or on the other hand by some external factor. The matter was discussed, as counsel for the appellant has helpfully pointed out to us, by the House of Lords in *R v Sullivan* . . . [see above] . . . The point was neatly raised in *R v Quick, R v Paddison* . . .

Thus in *R v Quick* the fact that his condition was, or may have been, due to the injections of insulin meant that the malfunction was due to an external factor and not to the disease. The drug it was that caused the hypoglycaemia, the low blood sugar. As suggested in another passage of the judgment of Lawton LJ, hyperglycaemia, high blood sugar, caused by an inherent defect and not corrected by insulin is a disease, and if, as the defendant was asserting here, it does cause a malfunction of the mind, then the case may fall within the *M'Naghten* Rules.

The burden of the argument of counsel for the appellant to us is this. It is that the appellant's depression and marital troubles were a sufficiently potent external factor in his condition to override, so to speak, the effect of the diabetic shortage of insulin on him. He refers us not only to the passage which I have already cited in *R v Quick*, but also to a further passage in *Hill v Baxter* [1958] 1 QB 277 at 285 which is part of the judgment of Devlin J, sitting with Lord Goddard CJ and Pearson J, in the Divisional Court of Queen's Bench Division. It reads as follows:

> I have drawn attention to the fact that the accused did not set up a defence of insanity. For the purposes of the criminal law there are two categories of mental irresponsibility, one where the disorder is due to disease and the other where it is not. The distinction is not an arbitrary one. If disease is not the cause, if there is some temporary loss of consciousness arising accidentally, it is reasonable to hope that it will not be repeated and that it is safe to let an acquitted man go entirely free. If, however, disease is present, the same thing may happen again and therefore since 1800 the law has provided that persons acquitted on this ground should be subject to restraint.

That is the submission made by counsel as a basis for saying the judge's decision was wrong and that this was a matter which should have been decided by the jury.

In our judgment, stress, anxiety and depression can no doubt be the result of the operation of external factors, but they are not, it seems to us, in themselves separately or together external factors of the kind capable in law of causing or contributing to a state of automatism. They constitute a state of mind which is prone to recur. They lack the feature of novelty or accident, which is the basis of the distinction drawn by Lord Diplock in *R v Sullivan*. It is contrary to the observations of Devlin J, to which we have just referred in *Hill v Baxter*. It does not, in our judgment, come within the scope of the exception 'some external physical factor such as a blow on the head . . . or the administration of an anaesthetic . . .' (see *R v Sullivan* [1984] AC 156 at 172) . . .

R v Burgess [1991] 1 QB 92 (CA)

Lord Lane CJ:

On 20 July 1989 in the Crown Court at Bristol before Judge Sir Ian Lewis and a jury the appellant was found not guilty by reason of insanity on a charge of wounding with intent. He was ordered to be admitted and detained in such hospital as the Secretary of State should direct.

He now appeals against that verdict by certificate of the trial judge under s 12 of the Criminal Appeal Act 1968.

The appellant did not dispute the fact that in the early hours of 2 June 1988 he had attacked Katrina Curtis hitting her on the head first with a bottle when she was asleep, then with a video recorder and finally grasping her round the throat. She suffered a gaping 3 cm laceration to her scalp requiring sutures.

His case was that he lacked the *mens rea* necessary to make him guilty of the offence, because he was 'sleepwalking' when he attacked Miss Curtis. He was, it was alleged, suffering from 'non-insane' automatism and he called medical evidence, in particular from Dr d'Orban and Dr Eames, to support that contention.

The prosecution on the other hand contended that this was not a case of automatism at all, but that the appellant was conscious of what he was doing. If, contrary to that contention, he was not conscious of what he was doing, then the case fell within the *M'Naghten* Rules, and accordingly the verdict should be not guilty by reason of insanity. The prosecution called an equally eminent expert in the shape of Dr Fenwick.

Where the defence of automatism is raised by a defendant two questions fall to be decided by the judge before the defence can be left to the jury. The first is whether a proper evidential foundation for the defence of automatism has been laid. The second is whether the evidence shows the case to be one of insane automatism, that is to say a case which falls within the *M'Naghten* Rules, or one of non-insane automatism.

The judge in the present case undertook that task and on the second question came to the conclusion that (assuming the appellant was not conscious at the time of what he was doing), on any view of the medical evidence so far as automatism was concerned, it amounted to evidence of insanity within the *M'Naghten* Rules and not merely to evidence of non-insane automatism.

The sole ground of appeal is that the ruling was wrong.

The jury then had to decide on the basis of the judge's direction, which of course followed his ruling, whether the appellant was conscious when he struck Miss Curtis, in which case the verdict would be guilty, or whether he was not guilty by reason of insanity. As already indicated, they came to the latter conclusion.

The facts required setting out in a little more detail.

Miss Curtis occupied the flat immediately above that of the appellant. The two were on friendly terms. They were in the habit of watching video tapes together in her flat. She realised that the appellant was probably in love with her. She did not wish to allow their relationship to develop beyond mere friendship. The appellant was then 32 years of age. He was sexually inexperienced and of a somewhat solitary disposition. He had always behaved impeccably towards her and had made no physical advances. He had hopes that her friendship towards him might develop into something deeper.

On the evening in question the appellant came up to her flat with the video tapes. They had one glass of Martini each. There is no suggestion of any intoxication. Having watched one video tape, she fell asleep on the sofa. The next thing she knew was that something hard had hit her on the head. This must have been about one to one and a half hours later, so it seems. She woke up, dazed, to find herself surrounded by broken glass and confronted by the appellant with the video recorder held up high, clearly intending to bring it down on her head, which he did. He was speaking loudly. He seemed vicious and angry – quite out of character. She fell to the floor, whereupon he put a hand round her throat. With great presence of mind, she managed to say, 'I love you Bar', whereupon he appeared to come to his senses and to show great anxiety for what he had done. He later telephoned for an ambulance. It seems that he must have unplugged the video recorder, detaching the various leads, and then carried it round to where Miss Curtis lay . . .

[His Lordship quoted the material part of the *M'Naghten* Rules (set out at the start of this chapter) and went on:]

The reason for the finding of not guilty in these circumstances is of course the absence of the intent which must be proved to accompany the defendant's actions before guilt can be established.

What the law regards as insanity for the purposes of these enactments may be far removed from what would be regarded as insanity by a psychiatrist.

There can be no doubt but that the appellant, on the basis of the jury's verdict, was labouring under such a defect of reason as not to know what he was doing when he wounded Miss Curtis. The question is whether that was from 'disease of the mind'.

The first point that has to be understood is that the phrase is 'disease of the mind' and not 'disease of the brain' . . .

The appellant plainly suffered from a defect of reason from some sort of failure (for lack of a better term) of the mind causing him to act as he did without conscious motivation. His mind was to some extent controlling his actions, which were purposive rather than the result simply of muscular spasm, but without his being consciously aware of what he was doing. Can it be said that that 'failure' was a *disease* of the mind rather than a defect or failure of the mind not due to disease? That is the distinction, by no means always easy to draw, upon which this case depends, as others have depended in the past.

One can perhaps narrow the field of enquiry still further by eliminating what are sometimes called the 'external factors' such as concussion caused by a blow on the head. There were no such factors here. Whatever the cause may have been, it was an 'internal' cause. The possible disappointment or frustration caused by unrequited love is not to be equated with something such as concussion. On this aspect of the case, we respectfully adopt what was said by Martin JA giving the judgment of the court in the Ontario Court of Appeal in *R v Rabey* (1977) 17 OR (2d) 1 at 17, 22, which was approved by a majority in the Supreme Court of Canada (see [1980] 2 SCR 513 at 519 where the facts bore a similarity to those in the instant case although the diagnosis was different):

> Any malfunctioning of the mind, or mental disorder having its source primarily in some subjective condition or weakness internal to the accused (whether fully understood or not), may be a 'disease of the mind' if it prevents the accused from knowing what he is doing, but transient disturbances of consciousness due to certain specific external factors do not fall within the concept of disease of the mind . . . In my view, the ordinary stresses and disappointments of life which are the common lot of mankind do not constitute an external cause constituting an explanation for a malfunctioning of the mind which takes it out of the category of a 'disease of the mind'. To hold otherwise would deprive the concept of an external factor of any real meaning.

This distinction between 'internal' and 'external' factors appears in the speech of Lord Diplock in *R v Sullivan* [1984] AC 156 at 172 [from which his Lordship then quoted].

What help does one derive from the authorities as to the meaning of 'disease' in this context? Lord Denning in *Bratty v AG for Northern Ireland* [1963] AC 386 at 412 said:

> On the other hand discussed by Devlin J, namely what is a 'disease of the mind' within the *M'Naghten* Rules, I would agree with him that this is a question for the judge. The major mental diseases, which the doctors call psychoses, such as schizophrenia, are clearly diseases of the mind. But in *R v Charlson* [1955] 1 WLR 317, Barry J seems to have assumed that the other diseases such as epilepsy or cerebral tumour are not diseases of the mind, even when they are such as to manifest themselves in violence. I do not agree with this. It seems to me that any mental disorder which has manifested itself in violence and is prone to recur is a disease of the mind. At any rate it is the sort of disease for which a person should be detained in hospital rather than be given an unqualified acquittal.

It seems to us that if there is a danger of recurrence that may be an added reason for categorising the condition as a disease of the mind. On the other hand, the absence of the danger of recurrence is not a reason for saying that it cannot be a disease of the mind. Subject to that possible qualification, we respectfully adopt Lord Denning's suggested definition.

There have been several occasions when during the course of judgments in the Court of Appeal and the House of Lords observations have been made, *obiter*, about the criminal responsibility of sleepwalkers, where sleepwalking had been used as a self-evident illustration of non-insane automatism . . .

One turns then to examine the evidence upon which the judge had to base his decision and for this purpose the two medical experts called by the defence are the obvious principal sources. Dr d'Orban in examination-in-chief said:

> On the evidence available to me, and subject to the results of the tests when they became available, I came to the same conclusion as Dr Nicholas and Dr Eames, whose reports I had read, and that was that [the appellant's] actions had occurred during the course of a sleep disorder.

He was asked, 'Assuming this is a sleep-associated automatism, is it an internal or external factor?' He answered: 'In this particular case, I think that one would have to see it as an internal factor.'

Then in cross-examination:

> Q: Would you go so far as to say that it was liable to recur?
> A: It is possible for it to recur, yes.
> Judge Lewis: Is this a case of automatism associated with a pathological condition or not?
> A: I think the answer would have to be yes, because it is an abnormality of the brain function, so it would be regarded as a pathological condition.

Dr Eames in cross-examination agreed with Dr d'Orban as to the internal rather than the external factor. He accepted that there is a liability to recurrence of sleepwalking. He could not go so far as to say that there is no liability of recurrence of serious violence but he agreed with the other medical witnesses that there is no recorded case of violence of this sort recurring.

The prosecution, as already indicated, called Dr Fenwick, whose opinion was that this was not a sleepwalking episode at all. If it was a case where the appellant was unconscious of what he was doing, the most likely explanation was that he was in what is described as a hysterical dissociative state. That is a state in which, for psychological reasons, such as being overwhelmed by his emotions, the person's brain works in a different way. He carries out acts of which he has no knowledge and for which he has no memory. It is quite different from sleepwalking.

He then went on to describe features of sleepwalking. This is what he said:

> First, violent acts in sleepwalking are very common. In just an exposure of one day to a sleepwalking clinic, you will hear of how people are kicked in bed, hit in bed, partially strangled – it is usually just arms round the neck, in bed, which is very common. Serious violence fortunately is rare. Serious violence does recur, or certainly the propensity for it to recur is there, although there are very few cases in the literature – in fact I know of none – in which somebody has come to court twice for a sleepwalking offence. This does not mean that sleepwalking violence does not recur; what it does mean is that those who are associated with the sleeper take the necessary precautions. Finally, should a person be detained in hospital? The answer to that is: Yes, because sleepwalking is treatable. Violent

night terrors are treatable. There is a lot which can be done for the sleepwalker, so sending them to hospital after a violent act to have their sleepwalking sorted out makes good sense.

Dr Fenwick was also of the view that in certain circumstances hysterical dissociative states are also subject to treatment.

It seems to us that on th[e] evidence the judge was right to conclude that this was an abnormality or disorder albeit transitory, due to an internal factor, whether functional or organic, which had manifested itself in violence. It was a disorder or abnormality which might recur, though the possibility of it recurring in the form of serious violence was unlikely. Therefore, since this was a legal problem to be decided on legal principles, it seems to us that on those principles the answer was as the judge found it to be. It does however go further than that. Dr d'Orban, as already described, stated it as his view that the condition would be regarded as pathological. Pathology is the science of diseases. It seems therefore that in this respect at least there is some similarity between the law and medicine . . . This appeal must accordingly be dismissed.

13.5.3 RELATIONSHIP BETWEEN SANE AND INSANE AUTOMATISM

Bratty v Attorney General for Northern Ireland [1963] AC 386 (HL)

Viscount Kilmuir LC:

. . . To establish the defence of insanity within the *M'Naghten* Rules the accused must prove on the preponderance of probabilities, first a defect of reason from a disease of the mind, and, second, as a consequence of such a defect, ignorance of the nature and quality (or the wrongfulness) of the acts. We have to consider a case in which it is sought to do so by medical evidence to the effect that the conduct of the accused might be compatible with psychomotor epilepsy, which is a disease of the mind affecting the reason, and that psychomotor epilepsy could cause ignorance of the nature and quality of the acts done, but in which the medical witness can assign no other cause for that ignorance. Where the possibility of an unconscious act depends on, and only on, the existence of a defect of reason from disease of the mind within the *M'Naghten* Rules, a rejection by the jury of this defence of insanity necessarily implies that they reject the possibility.

The Court of Criminal Appeal also took the view that where the alleged automatism is based solely on a disease of the mind within the *M'Naghten* Rules, the same burden of proof rests on the defence whether the 'plea' is given the name of insanity or automatism. I do not think that statement goes further than saying that when you rely on insanity as defined by the Rules you cannot by a difference of nomenclature avoid the road so often and authoritatively laid down by the courts.

What I have said does not mean that, if a defence of insanity is raised unsuccessfully, there can never, in any conceivable circumstances, be room for an alternative defence based on automatism. For example, it may be alleged that the accused had a blow on the head, after which he acted without being conscious of what he was doing or was a sleepwalker. There might be a divergence of view as to whether there was a defect of reason from disease of the mind (compare the curious position which arose in *R v Kemp* [1957] 1 QB 399). The jury might not accept the evidence of a defect of reason from disease of the mind, but at the same time accept the evidence that the prisoner did not know what he was doing. If the jury should take that view of the facts they would find him not guilty. But it should be noted that the defence would only have succeeded because the necessary foundation had been laid by positive evidence which, properly considered, was evidence of something other than a defect of reason from disease of the mind. In my opinion, this analysis of the two defences (insanity and automatism) shows that where the only cause alleged for the unconsciousness is a defect of reason from disease of the mind, and that cause is rejected by the jury, there can be no room for the alternative defence of automatism. Like the Court of Criminal Appeal, I cannot therefore accept the submission that the whole of the evidence directed to the issue of insanity should have been left to the jury to consider whether there was automatism due to another cause. It was conceded before this House, and this is stated in the judgment of the Court of Criminal Appeal, that there was nothing to show or suggest that there was any other pathological cause for automatism.

Lord Denning:

. . . if the involuntary act proceeds from a disease of the mind, it gives rise to a defence of insanity, but not to a defence of automatism. Suppose a crime is committed by a man in a state of automatism or clouded consciousness due to a recurrent disease of the mind. Such an act is no doubt involuntary, but it does not give rise to an unqualified acquittal, for that would mean that he would be let at large to do it again. The only proper verdict is one which ensures that the person who suffers from the disease is kept secure in a hospital so as not to be a danger to himself or others. That is, a verdict of guilty but insane.

Once you exclude all the cases I have mentioned, it is apparent that the category of involuntary acts is very limited. So limited, indeed, that until recently there was hardly any reference in the English books to this so-called defence of automatism . . . In striking contrast to *Charlson's* case [1955] 1 WLR 317, is *R v Kemp* [1957] 1 QB 399. A devoted husband of excellent character made an entirely motiveless and irrational attack upon his wife. He struck her violently with a hammer. He was charged with causing her grievous bodily harm. It was found that he suffered from hardening of the arteries which might lead to a congestion of blood in the brain. As a result of such congestion, he suffered a temporary lack of consciousness, so that he was not conscious that he picked up the hammer or that he was striking his wife with it. It was therefore an involuntary act. Note again the important point – no plea of insanity was raised but only the defence of automatism. Nevertheless, Devlin J put insanity to the jury. He held that hardening of the arteries was a 'disease of the mind' within the *M'Naghten* Rules and he directed the jury they ought so to find. They accordingly found Kemp guilty but insane.

My Lords, I think that Devlin J was quite right in *Kemp's* case in putting the question of insanity to the jury, even though it had not been raised by the defence. When it is asserted that the accused did an involuntary act in a state of automatism, the defence necessarily puts in issue the state of mind of the accused man: and thereupon it is open to the prosecution to show what his true state of mind was. The old notion that only the defence can raise a defence of insanity is now gone. The prosecution are entitled to raise it and it is their duty to do so rather than allow a dangerous person to be at large . . .

Upon the other point discussed by Devlin J, namely what is a 'disease of the mind' within the *M'Naghten* Rules, I would agree with him that this is a question for the judge. The major mental diseases, which the doctors call psychoses, such as schizophrenia, are clearly diseases of the mind. But in *Charlson's* case, Barry J seems to have assumed that other diseases such as epilepsy or cerebral tumour are not diseases of the mind, even when they are such as to manifest themselves in violence. I do not agree with this. It seems to me that any mental disorder which has manifested itself in violence and is prone to recur is a disease of the mind. At any rate it is the sort of disease for which a person should be detained in hospital rather than be given an unqualified acquittal.

It is to be noticed that in *Charlson's* case and *Kemp's* the defence raised only automatism, not insanity. In the present case the defence raised both automatism and insanity. And herein lies the difficulty because of the burden of proof. If the accused says he did not know what he was doing, then, so far as the defence of automatism is concerned, the Crown must prove that the act was a voluntary act, see *Woolmington's* case. But so far as the defence of insanity is concerned, the defence must prove that the act was an involuntary act due to disease of the mind, see *M'Naghten's* case (1843) 10 Cl and F 200, 210, HL . . .

This brings me to the root question in the present case: Was a proper foundation laid here for the defence of automatism, apart from the plea of insanity? There was the evidence of George Bratty himself that he could not remember anything because 'this blackness was over me'. He said 'I did not realise exactly what I was doing', and added afterwards 'I didn't know what I was doing. I didn't realise anything.' He said he had four or five times previously had 'feelings of blackness' and frequently headaches. There was evidence, too, of his odd behaviour at times, his mental backwardness and his religious leanings. Added to this there was the medical evidence. Dr Sax, who was called on his behalf, said that there was a possibility that he was suffering from psychomotor epilepsy. It was, he said, practically the only possibility that occurred to him. Dr Walker, his general practitioner, said you could not leave the possibility out of account. Dr Robinson, a specialist, who gave evidence on behalf of the Crown, said he thought it was extremely unlikely that it was an epileptic attack, but could not rule it out. All the doctors agreed that psychomotor epilepsy, if it exists, is a defect of reason due to disease of the mind: and the judge accepted this view. No other cause was canvassed.

In those circumstances, I am clearly of opinion that, if the act of George Bratty was an involuntary act, as the defence suggested, the evidence attributed it solely to a disease of the mind and the only defence open was the defence of insanity. There was no evidence of automatism apart from insanity. There was, therefore, no need for the judge to put [non-insane automatism] to the jury. And when the jury rejected the defence of insanity, they rejected the only defence disclosed by the evidence . . .

13.5.4 WHERE THE DEFENDANT DID NOT REALISE HIS ACTIONS WERE WRONG

As indicated above, the defence of insanity may be available to a defendant who was aware of his actions but, because of his defect of reason, did not realise that his actions were wrong. The issue here has been as to the correct interpretation of the word 'wrong'. Does it mean morally wrong, or legally wrong? Earlier cases such as *R v Codere* (1916) 12 Cr App R 21 suggested that a defendant might not be able to avail himself of the defence of insanity, even where he was unaware that his actions were contrary to law, if he nevertheless realised that his conduct was wrong according to the ordinary standards adopted by reasonable persons. As will be seen below, *R v Windle* suggests that it is sufficient that the defendant was unaware that his actions were illegal.

R v Windle [1952] 2 QB 526 (CA)

The appellant was convicted of the murder of his wife. He was a man, 40 years of age, of little resolution and weak character, and was married to a woman 18 years his senior. His married life was very unhappy; his wife was always speaking of committing suicide and the doctors who gave evidence at the trial were of opinion, from the history of the case, that she was certifiably insane. The appellant frequently discussed his home life with his workmates, until, as one of them said, they were sick and tired of hearing about it. Eventually a workmate said to the appellant, 'Give her a dozen aspirins', and on the following day the appellant gave his wife 100 tablets. He sent for a doctor and told him that he had given his wife so many aspirins. She was taken to hospital, where she died. The appellant informed the police that he had given his wife 100 aspirins, and added: 'I suppose they will hang me for this?' At his trial a defence of insanity was put forward. A doctor was called for him who said that the appellant was suffering from a form of communicated insanity known as *folie à deux*. It was said that if a person was in constant attendance on another of unsound mind, in some way the insanity might be communicated to the attendant, so that, for a time at any rate, the attendant might develop a defect of reason or of mind. Rebutting medical evidence was allowed to be called for the prosecution, and the doctors called on either side expressed the opinion that the appellant, when administering the fatal dose of aspirin to his wife, knew that he was doing an act which the law forbade.

The trial judge, Devlin J, having heard the evidence, ruled that there was no evidence of insanity, as defined in the rules in *M'Naghten's* case (1843) 10 Cl & F 200, to be left to the jury. He accordingly withdrew that issue from them, and they found the appellant guilty of murder.

Lord Goddard CJ:

... In this particular case, the only evidence given on the issue of insanity was that of the doctor called by the appellant and of the prison doctor who was allowed to be called by the prosecution to rebut, if indeed it were necessary, any evidence which had been given. It was probably right that the prison doctor should be called as he had had the appellant under constant observation. Both the doctors gave their evidence in a way that commended itself to the judge, and both, without hesitation, expressed the view that the appellant knew, when administering this poison, for such as it was, to his wife, that he was doing an act which the law forbade. I need not put it higher than that.

It may well be that, in the misery in which he had been living, with this nagging and tiresome wife who constantly expressed the desire to commit suicide, he thought that she would be better out of this world than in it. He may have thought that it would be a kindly act to release her from what she was suffering from – or thought she was suffering from – but that the law does not permit. In the present case there was some exceedingly vague evidence that the appellant was suffering from a defect of reason. In the opinion of his own doctor, there was a defect of reason which he attributed to communicated insanity. In my opinion, if the only question in this case has been whether the appellant was suffering from a disease of the mind, I should say that that was a question which must have been left to the jury. That, however, is not the question.

... A man may be suffering from a defect of reason, but if he knows that what he is doing is 'wrong', and by 'wrong' is meant contrary to law, he is responsible. Mr Shawcross, in the course of his very careful argument, suggested that the word 'wrong', as it was used in the *M'Naghten* Rules, did not mean contrary to law but had some kind of qualified meaning, such as morally wrong, and that if a person was in such a state of mind through a defect of reason that, although he knew that what he was doing was wrong in law, he thought that it was beneficial or kind or praiseworthy, that would excuse him . . .

. . . Counsel for the appellant argued that the *M'Naghten* Rules only applied to cases in which delusions were present. The court cannot agree with that. It is true that when the judges who formulated the rules were summoned by the House of Lords the occasion had special reference to *M'Naghten's* case, but ever since that date the rules have been generally applied in all cases of insanity, whatever the nature of the insanity or disease of the mind from which the person accused is suffering.

In the opinion of the court there is no doubt that in the *M'Naghten* Rules 'wrong' means contrary to law and not 'wrong' according to the opinion of one man or of a number of people on the question whether a particular act might or might not be justified. In the present case, it could not be challenged that the appellant knew that what he was doing was contrary to law, and that he realised what punishment the law provided for murder. That was the opinion of both the doctors who gave evidence . . .

 ## COMMENTS AND QUESTIONS

1   To what extent is the distinction between diabetes as a disease of the mind resulting in insanity (see *Hennessy*, above) and lack of insulin as an external factor giving rise to automatism (*Bingham*, above) sustainable and credible?

2   As the above extracts indicate, the issue of insanity often arises not because the defendant has raised the defence, but because the trial judge indicates that it is the only defence, on the facts, that he is willing to leave to the jury.

3   Given that a defendant charged with murder who suffers from a mental illness will now plead diminished responsibility (see further Chapter 4.6.3), why would any defendant charged with a lesser offence actively seek to raise the issue of insanity? Would a defendant not be better advised simply to plead guilty?

4   Does the decision in *Windle* mean that a defendant, who knows his actions are wrong by all reasonable and civilised standards, but who is nevertheless unaware of the fact that they are prohibited by law, will be able to avail himself of the defence of insanity?

5   Suppose D kills P because he wrongly believes P is trying to kill him. Suppose that this belief springs from D's insane delusions. Would D be able to plead insanity? He believes he is acting in self-defence, hence he believes his actions are not unlawful. Is it true to say, therefore, that he is unaware that his actions are wrong?

6   Suppose D claims he was ordered by God to commit an offence of theft or criminal damage – does this amount to a plea of insanity? See further *R v Bell* [1984] Crim LR 685.

7   To what extent does the defence of insanity provide a defence based on ignorance of the criminal law?

13.5.5 CODIFICATION AND LAW REFORM PROPOSALS

Clauses 34–40 of the draft Criminal Code Bill (DCCB) (Vol I of Law Com 177) propose significant reforms in its restatement of the law relating to a general defence of mental illness, as follows:

34 In this Act –

'mental disorder' means –

(a) severe mental illness; or

(b) a state of arrested or incomplete development of mind; or

(c) a state of automatism (not resulting only from intoxication) which is a feature of a disorder, whether organic or functional and whether continuing or recurring, that may cause a similar state on another occasion;

'return a mental disorder verdict' means –

(a) in relation to trial on indictment, return a verdict that the defendant is not guilty on evidence of mental disorder; and

(b) in relation to summary trial, dismiss the information on evidence of mental disorder;

'severe mental illness' means a mental illness which has one or more of the following characteristics –

(a) lasting impairment of intellectual functions shown by failure of memory, orientation, comprehension and learning capacity;

(b) lasting alteration of mood of such degree as to give rise to delusional appraisal of the defendant's situation, his past or his future, or that of others, or lack of any appraisal;

(c) delusional beliefs, persecutory, jealous or grandiose;

(d) abnormal perceptions associated with delusional misinterpretation of events;

(e) thinking so disordered as to prevent reasonable appraisal of the defendant's situation or reasonable communication with others;

'severe mental handicap' means a state of arrested or incomplete development of mind which includes severe impairment of intelligence and social functioning.

35(1) A mental disorder verdict shall be returned if the defendant is proved to have committed an offence but it is proved on the balance of probabilities (whether by the prosecution or by the defendant) that he was at the time suffering from severe mental illness or severe mental handicap.

(2) Subsection (1) does not apply if the court or jury is satisfied beyond reasonable doubt that the offence was not attributable to the severe mental illness or severe mental handicap.

(3) A court or jury shall not, for the purposes of a verdict under subsection (1), find that the defendant was suffering from severe mental illness or severe mental handicap unless two medical practitioners approved for the purposes of section 12 of the Mental Health Act 1983 as having special experience in the diagnosis or treatment of mental disorder have given evidence that he was so suffering.

(4) Subsection (1), so far as it relates to severe mental handicap, does not apply to an offence under section 106(1), 107 or 108 (sexual relations with the mentally handicapped).

36 A mental disorder verdict shall be returned if –

(a) the defendant is acquitted of an offence only because, by reason of evidence of mental disorder or a combination of mental disorder and intoxication, it is found that he acted or may have acted in a state of automatism, or without the fault required for the offence, or believing that an exempting circumstance existed; and

(b) it is proved on the balance of probabilities (whether by the prosecution or by the defendant) that he was suffering from mental disorder at the time of the act.

37 A defendant may plead 'not guilty by reason of mental disorder'; and

(a) if the court directs that the plea be entered the direction shall have the same effect as a mental disorder verdict; and

(b) if the court does not so direct the defendant shall be treated as having pleaded not guilty.

38(1) Whether evidence is evidence of mental disorder or automatism is a question of law.

(2) The prosecution shall not adduce evidence of mental disorder, or contend that a mental disorder verdict should be returned, unless the defendant has given or adduced evidence that he acted without the fault required for the offence, or believing that an exempting circumstance existed, or in a state of automatism, or (on a charge of murder) when suffering from mental abnormality as defined in section 57(2).

(3) The court may give directions as to the stage of the proceedings at which the prosecution may adduce evidence of mental disorder.

39 Schedule 2 has effect with respect to the orders that may be made upon the return of a mental disorder verdict, to the conditions governing the making of those orders, to the effects of those orders and to related matters.

40 A defendant shall not, when a mental disorder verdict is returned in respect of an offence and while that verdict subsists, be found guilty of any other offence of which, but for this section, he might on the same occasion be found guilty –

(a) on the indictment, count or information to which the verdict relates; or

(b) on any other indictment, count or information founded on the same facts.

The commentary explains the thinking behind these proposals:

Disability in relation to trial

11.7 *Reform proposals*. The defendant's mental disorder (or his being a deaf-mute) may operate as a bar to his trial on indictment or to the progress of his trial beyond the end of the prosecution case. If the defendant is found to be 'under disability' the court will order his admission to a hospital to be specified by the Secretary of State. The Committee on Mentally Abnormal Offenders (chairman: Lord Butler; hereafter called 'the Butler Committee') gave elaborate consideration to the law and procedure relating to disability and made important recommendations for reform. The Committee made a cogent case for change on a number of issues, including the extension of a disability procedure to the magistrates' court and the provision of flexible disposal powers in relation to a defendant under disability. But some of the Committee's procedural proposals were controversial. A consultative document issued by the Home Office in April 1978 referred in particular to serious doubts as to the practicability of a recommendation that if the defendant is found to be under disability there should nevertheless be a 'trial of the facts' – at once if there is no prospect of the defendant's recovering, or as soon (during periods of adjournment not exceeding six months in total) as he may prove unresponsive to treatment.

11.8 *Location in the Code*. We hope that the important matter of disability will be further considered as soon as possible with a view to reform. We do not, however, share the Code team's preference for including provisions on disability in Part 1 of the Code. It is true that the Butler Committee proposed that a finding of disability and an acquittal based on a mental disorder verdict should give rise to similar disposal powers. But compatibility between the two disposal regimes can be achieved without enacting the relevant provisions side by side. Those relating to disability are procedural in nature and in due course their proper place will be in the projected Part 111 of the Code.

Code provisions on mental disorder

11.9 *Butler Committee*. The Butler Committee proposed substantial reform of the law and procedure relating to the effect of mental disorder on criminal liability and the disposal of persons acquitted because of mental disorder. The necessity of incorporating in the projected Criminal Code an appropriate provision to replace the outdated 'insanity' defence was one justification given by the Committee for its review of the subject. We ourselves are persuaded that implementation of the Committee's proposals would greatly improve this area of the law. We have, however, found it necessary to suggest some important modifications of those proposals. Clauses 34 to 40 therefore aim to give effect to the policy of the Butler Committee as modified by us in ways that will be explained in the following paragraphs.

11.10 *The present 'insanity defence'*. Before considering the structure of the proposed law, it will be convenient to refer to that of the present law. The *M'Naghten* Rules together with statutory provisions, produce a 'special verdict' ('not guilty by reason of insanity') and the automatic committal of the acquitted person to a hospital to be specified by the Secretary of State, in two kinds of case.

(i)   The first case is that where it is proved (rebutting the so-called 'presumption of sanity') that, because of 'a defect of reason, from disease of the mind,' the defendant did not 'know the nature and quality of the act he was doing'. If the defendant 'did not know what he was doing', he must have lacked any fault required for the offence charged; so, in modern terms at least, this first element in the *M'Naghten* Rules has the appearance of a rule, not about guilt, but about burden of proof and disposal. The defendant should in any case be acquitted, but he must prove that he should be; and his acquittal is to be treated as the occasion for his detention as a matter of social defence.

(ii) The second case is that where, because of 'a defect of reason, from disease of the mind', the defendant 'did not know he was doing what was wrong.' This is a case, then, in which the Rules afford a defence properly so called: a person who would otherwise be guilty is not guilty 'by reason of insanity'. But, once again, social defence requires his detention in hospital.

11.11 *Structure of the proposed provisions*. Clauses 35 and 36, following the structure proposed by the Butler Committee, are similarly concerned with two kinds of case, in each of which there is to be a verdict of acquittal in special form ('not guilty on evidence of mental disorder'). On the return of a mental disorder verdict the court would have flexible disposal powers, the availability of which would undoubtedly give clauses 35 and 36 greater practical importance than the insanity defence now has.

(a) Clause 35(1). In one case all the elements of the offence are proved but severe mental disorder operates as a true defence. This is equivalent to case (ii) above.

(b) Clause 36. In the other case an acquittal is inevitable because the prosecution has failed to prove that the defendant acted with the required fault (or to disprove his defence of automatism or mistake); but the reason for that failure is evidence of mental disorder, and it is proved that the defendant was indeed suffering from mental disorder at the time of the act. This differs from case (i) above in casting no burden on the defendant of proving his innocence.

11.12 *Summary trial*. The Butler Committee recommended that a magistrates' court should acquit on evidence of mental disorder in the same circumstances as a jury. Our clauses so provide. The general principles of the substantive criminal law applicable to offences triable either way must be the same whatever the mode of trial in the particular case. A defendant who lacked the fault required for the offence charged will of course be entitled to an acquittal wherever he is tried. And if severe mental illness or severe mental handicap at the time of the offence entails an acquittal on trial on indictment, it must do so also on summary trial. A defence of severe mental illness may, of course, make summary trial inappropriate. That is a consideration that could be taken care of by procedural provisions. But, assuming that mental disorder is capable of arising as an issue on summary trial, the Code must clearly provide for the same substantive consequences as on trial on indictment.

Clause 34: Mental disorder: definitions

11.13 *'Mental disorder'; 'severe mental illness'; 'severe mental handicap'*. These terms are considered below, in the context of the provisions in which they are crucial. The Butler scheme renounces the outdated terms 'insanity' and 'disease of the mind'.

11.14 *'Return a mental disorder verdict'*. Each of the situations defined in clauses 35(1) and 36 calls for the return of 'a mental disorder verdict'. The word 'verdict' is strictly speaking inapt to refer to the determination of a magistrates' court. But it greatly simplifies drafting to refer to the 'return' of a 'mental disorder verdict' as the relevant outcome of summary trial as of trial on indictment, and to explain that language in the definition section: a jury will declare that the defendant 'is not guilty on evidence of mental disorder'; the magistrates will 'dismiss the information on evidence of mental disorder'.

Clause 35: Case for mental disorder verdict: defence of severe disorder

11.15 Subsection (1) provides that even though he has done the act specified for the offence with the fault required, a defendant is entitled to an acquittal, in the form of a mental disorder verdict, if he was suffering from severe mental illness or severe mental handicap at the time. This implements the Butler Committee's conceptions with some modifications.

11.16 *Attributability of offence to disorder: a rebuttable presumption*. One aspect of the Committee's recommendation has proved controversial. The Committee acknowledged that –

it is theoretically possible for a person to be suffering from a severe mental disorder which has in a causal sense nothing to do with the act or omission for which he is being tried;

but they found it 'very difficult to imagine a case in which one could be sure of the absence of any such connection'. They therefore proposed, in effect, an irrebuttable presumption that there was a sufficient connection between the severe disorder and the offence. This Proposal is understandable in view of the limitation of the defence to a narrow range of very serious disorders; and its adoption would certainly simplify the tasks of psychiatric witnesses and the court. Some people, however, take the view that it would be wrong in principle that a person should escape conviction if, although severely mentally ill, he has committed a rational crime which was uninfluenced by his illness and for which he ought to be liable to be punished. They believe that the prosecution should be allowed to persuade the jury (if it can) that the offence was not attributable to the disorder. We agree. Subsection (2) provides accordingly. We believe that it must improve the acceptability of the Butler Committee's generally admirable scheme as the basis of legislation.

11.17 *'Severe mental illness'* is defined in clause 34 in the terms proposed by the Butler Committee. Severe mental illness, for the purpose of this exemption from criminal liability, ought, in the Committee's view, to be closely defined and restricted to serious cases of psychosis (as that term is currently understood). The Committee recommended, as the preferable mode of definition, the identification of 'the abnormal mental phenomena which occur in the various mental illnesses and which when present would be regarded by common consent as being evidence of severity'. We believe that this symptomatic mode of definition has much to commend it. The psychiatric expert will give evidence in terms of strict 'factual tests', rather than of abstractions (such as 'disease of the mind' or 'severe mental illness' itself) or diagnostic labels. The method allocates appropriate functions to the law itself (in laying down the test of criminal responsibility), to the expert (in advising whether the test is satisfied) and to the tribunal of fact (in judging, by reference to the whole of the case, whether that advice is soundly given).

11.18 *Content of the definition*. We are grateful to the Section for Forensic Psychiatry of the Royal College of Psychiatrists for responding to our request for advice on the content of the definition of 'severe mental illness'. We are told that there was a suggestion, at the time of the Butler Committee's Report, that the list of symptoms in the definition might not be sufficiently comprehensive, but that this suggestion had had little support. Our advisers expressed their own satisfaction with the proposed criteria of severe mental illness and with the way in which they are expressed.

11.19 *'Severe mental handicap'* is defined in clause 34. The expression used by the Butler Committee was 'severe subnormality', which was defined in the Mental Health Act 1959, section 4, in terms apt for the Committee's purpose. But the expression 'severe mental impairment' has since replaced 'severe subnormality' in mental health legislation (the latter term having fallen out of favour). 'Severe mental impairment' has the following meaning:

> a state of arrested or incomplete development of mind which includes severe impairment of intelligence and social functioning and is associated with abnormally aggressive or seriously irresponsible conduct on the part of the person concerned.

This definition is not a happy one for present purposes; exemption from criminal liability on the ground of severe mental handicap ought not to be limited to a case where the handicap is associated with aggressive or irresponsible conduct. We therefore propose that the expression 'severe mental handicap' be used, with the same definition as 'severe mental impairment' down to the word 'functioning'. This will give effect to the Butler Committee's intentions and has the approval of our Royal College advisers.

11.20 *Burden of proof*. Subsection (1) permits proof of severe disorder by either prosecution or defendant. Normally it will be for the defendant to prove it, as his defence to the charge. This is as proposed by the Butler Committee. But there may be a case in which the defendant adduces evidence of mental disorder on an issue of fault or automatism and the prosecution responds with evidence of severe disorder and in such a case it may be the prosecution evidence (or a combination of prosecution and defence evidence) which results in a mental disorder verdict under clause 35(1).

11.21 *Evidence of severe disorder*. Subsection (3) provides that such evidence must be given by two appropriately qualified doctors, as recommended by the Butler Committee.'

11.22 *Exception*. A severely mentally handicapped person cannot commit an offence under clause 106(1), 107 or 108 involving sexual relations with another such person. Subsection (4) ensures that such a person, if charged with one of those offences, receives an unqualified acquittal.

11.23 *Broad effect of the clause*. Evidence of mental disorder may be the reason why the court or jury is at least doubtful whether the defendant acted with the fault required for the offence. The Butler Committee recommended that, although in such a case there must be an acquittal, this acquittal should be in the qualified form 'not guilty on evidence of mental "disorder" ' where it is proved that the defendant was in fact suffering from mental disorder at the time of his act. Clause 36 gives effect to this recommendation, significantly modified by the adoption of a narrower meaning of 'mental disorder' than that proposed by the Committee.

11.24 *Cases covered by the clause*. The clause adapts the Committee's proposal to the conceptual structure of the Code. First, it provides that the mental disorder verdict is not to be returned unless evidence of mental disorder is the only reason for an acquittal. The provision must not affect a case in which the defendant is entitled to an acquittal on some additional ground having nothing to do with mental disorder. Second, it refers not only to absence of fault but also (a) to automatism and (b) to a belief in a circumstance of defence.

(a) Automatism is mentioned because the acquittal of one who acted in a state of automatism is not grounded only in absence of 'fault' (see clause 33).

(b) A person may commit an act of violence because of a deluded belief that he is under attack and must defend himself. Within the scheme of the Code – which draws a distinction between elements of offences (including fault elements) and defences – such a person would not, when relying on his delusion, be denying 'the fault required for the offence'. His mentally disordered belief must therefore be separately mentioned in the paragraph.

11.25 The clause deals also with the case where the defendant lacked the required fault because of the combined effects of mental disorder and intoxication. We have discussed this case in our comments on clause 22 (intoxication).

11.26 *'Mental disorder': the Butler Committee's proposal*. The Butler Committee proposed to adopt in principle the Mental Health Act definition of 'mental disorder' – namely, 'mental illness, arrested or incomplete development of mind, psychopathic disorder and any other disorder or disability of mind' – subject only to the exclusion of 'transient states not related to other forms of mental disorder and arising solely as a consequence of (a) the administration, misadministration or non-administration of alcohol, drugs or other substances or (b) physical injury.'

11.27 We are surprised that such an extremely wide definition, designed for the very different purposes of the Mental Health Act, should have been thought suitable as the basis of a qualified acquittal, subject only to the exclusion of certain 'transient states not related to other forms of mental disorder'. If this proposal were followed, the result might be to subject too many acquitted persons to a possibly stigmatising or distressing verdict and to inappropriate control through the courts' disposal powers. The cases attracting a mental disorder verdict under this clause should, we think, be strictly limited. We therefore exclude 'mental illness' (not being 'severe') and 'any other disorder or disability of mind' from our definition. We also exclude 'psychopathic disorder' as being, we believe, irrelevant to the existence of 'fault' in the technical sense.

11.28 *'Mental disorder': the proposed definition*. We define 'mental disorder' in clause 34 to include (only):

(a) 'severe mental illness' (as defined in the same section): the defendant who lacked fault, or believed in the existence of an exempting circumstance, because of a psychotic distortion of perception or understanding, will receive a mental disorder verdict and be amenable to the court's powers of restraint.

(b) 'arrested or incomplete development of mind': this category from the Mental Health Act definition of 'mental disorder' survives our amendment of the Butler Committee's proposal. We must, however, express a doubt as to whether it should do so. Some persons against whom fault cannot be proved might receive mental disorder verdicts, and become subject to the protective powers of the criminal courts, although under the present law they would receive unqualified acquittals. It may be thought more appropriate to leave any acquitted persons within this category who represent a danger to themselves or others to be dealt with under Part 11 of the Mental Health Act 1983.

(c) (in effect) pathological automatism that is liable to recur: it would not, we think, be acceptable to propose that the courts should lose all control over a person acquitted because of what is now termed 'insane automatism'. Paragraph (c) of our definition requires the 'state of automatism' (see clause 33 (1)) to be 'a feature of a disorder . . . that may cause a similar state on another occasion'. This qualification confines the mental disorder verdict to those possibly warranting some form of control that the court can impose. It may nevertheless be felt by some that the paragraph includes too much. The Butler Committee wished, in particular, to protect from a mental disorder verdict a diabetic who causes a harm in a state of confusion after failing to take his insulin. We do not think, however, that there is a satisfactory way of distinguishing between the different conditions that may cause repeated episodes of disorder; nor do we think it necessary to do so. There is not, so far as we can see, a satisfactory basis for distinguishing between (say) a brain tumour or cerebral arteriosclerosis on the one hand and diabetes or epilepsy on the other. If any of these conditions causes a state of automatism in which the sufferer commits what would otherwise be an offence of violence, his acquittal should be 'on evidence of mental disorder'. Whether a diabetic so affected has failed to seek treatment, or forgotten to take his insulin, or decided not to do so, may affect the court's decision whether to order his discharge or to take some other course. What is objectionable in the present law is the offensive label of 'insanity' and the fact that the court is obliged to order the hospitalisation of the acquitted person, in effect as a restricted patient. With the elimination of these features under the Butler Committee's scheme, the verdict should not seem preposterous in the way that its present counterpart does.

11.29 *Burden of proof*. A mental disorder verdict under clause 36 will not be appropriate unless the court or jury is satisfied that the evidence of mental disorder that has prevented proof of fault – to take the most likely example – in fact establishes that he was suffering from such disorder. If the court or jury is not so satisfied, there will be an ordinary acquittal. As in the case of clause 35(1), proof may derive from prosecution or defence evidence, or indeed from a combination of the two.

Clause 36 follows the Butler Committee in requiring the mental disorder to be proved on the balance of probabilities: but since the defendant is *ex hypothesi* entitled to an acquittal, there is an obvious argument for requiring proof beyond reasonable doubt of the case for exposing him, through a mental disorder verdict, to the disposal powers of the court.

Clause 37: Plea of 'not guilty by reason of mental disorder'

11.30 This clause gives effect (with a verbal amendment) to the Butler Committee's recommendation that a defendant should be allowed to plead 'not guilty on evidence of mental disorder'.

Clause 38: Evidence of mental disorder and automatism

11.31 *Question of law.* Subsection (1) puts it beyond doubt that it is the function of the court (and not, in particular, of medical witnesses) to interpret the definitions of 'automatism' and 'mental disorder' in clauses 33(1) and 34 respectively. The allocation of this function to the court is important for the purposes of clauses 33(1) and 36 as well as of subsection (2) of the present clause.

11.32 *Prosecution evidence.* The Butler Committee proposed that the prosecution should, as at present, be restrained from adducing evidence of mental disorder until the defendant raises an issue that justifies its doing so; but the Committee thought that, '[i]f the defendant admits doing the act and contests the case solely on his state of mind, it is right that all the evidence as to his state of mind can be given, and if the evidence is that he was mentally disordered when he did the act there should be a [mental disorder] verdict rather than an ordinary acquittal'. Subsections (2) and (3) give effect to these views.

11.33 *Notice of defence.* The Butler Committee proposed that the defence should be required to give notice of an intention 'to adduce psychiatric or psychological evidence on the mental element – whether in relation to the [mental disorder] verdict or the defence of automatism'; and the Code team included in their Bill a provision to give effect to this proposal in a modified form. Since then the Crown Court (Advance Notice of Expert Evidence) Rules 1987 have been made. The Code team's provision, in its application to trial on indictment, would substantially duplicate those Rules. In any case, we have elsewhere in our Bill forborne to offer rules requiring advance notice of defences. The subject merits further consideration in the present context, as does the Code team's further suggestions that the prosecution should (subject to judicial direction) be able to give evidence of mental disorder as part of its case in chief if a relevant defence has been notified.

Clause 39: Disposal after mental disorder verdict

11.34 *Proposal for flexible powers.* By far the most important aspect of the Butler Committee's scheme of reform was the proposal as to the consequences of a mental disorder verdict. The Committee recommended that the court be given quite flexible powers, including the power to order inpatient treatment in hospital (with or without a restriction order), outpatient treatment, certain forfeitures, or a driving disqualification, and the power to discharge the acquitted defendant without any order.

11.35 The details of this proposal no doubt still require consideration by the government departments concerned and it would not be realistic for us, without the benefit of necessary consultation, to offer a complete set of relevant provisions. We can only express the hope that this important reform will be undertaken without further delay. It should be clear that enactment of our clauses 35 and 36, providing for mental disorder verdicts, depends upon abolition of the mandatory consequences of the present equivalent verdict.

11.36 Clause 39 provides for a Schedule of provisions concerning the disposal of persons found not guilty on evidence of mental disorder.

Clause 40: Further effect of mental disorder verdict

11.37 This clause gives effect to a subsidiary recommendation of the Butler Committee.

FURTHER READING

Jones, TH, 'Insanity, automatism and the burden of proof on the accused' (1995) 111 LQR 475

Loughman, A, 'Manifest Madness: Towards a New Understanding of the Insanity Defence' (2007) 70 Mod LR 379

Mackay, RD, 'Fact and fiction about the insanity defence' [1990] Crim LR 247

Mackay, RD, 'Intoxication as a factor in automatism' [1982] Crim LR 146

Mackay, RD and G Kearns, 'The continued underuse of unfitness to plead and the insanity defence' [1994] Crim LR 576

Mackay, RD and B J Mitchell, 'Sleepwalking, Automatism and Insanity' [2006] Crim LR 901

Orchard, G, 'Surviving without *Majewski* – a view from down under' [1993] Crim LR 426

Paton, E, 'Reforming the intoxication rules: the Law Commission's Report' [1996] Crim LR 382

Virgo, G, 'Reconciling principle and policy' [1993] Crim LR 415

Ward, AR, 'Making sense of self-induced intoxication' [1986] CLJ 247

CHAPTER 14

DEFENCES OF COMPULSION

14.1 INTRODUCTION

This chapter brings together materials relating to what can be loosely described as the 'compulsion-based' defences. These are:

- Duress *per minas*
- Duress of circumstances
- Necessity
- Self-defence

Duress *per minas* (i.e. duress through threats from a third party) arises where D succumbs to threats from another person (the duressor). Typically these will be threats that unless

D commits a particular crime D, or another person with whom D has a connection, will be killed or will suffer grievous bodily harm.

Duress of circumstances differs only in that the threat of death or grievous bodily harm does not arise from the wrongful actions of a third party but from extraneous circumstances, such as D escaping from prison to escape from a fire, or driving the wrong way down a one-way street to escape from an unruly mob.

Whether or not there is a distinct third category of 'pure' necessity at common law is the subject of some debate, but *Re A (Children) (Conjoined Twins: Surgical Separation)* [2000] 4 All ER 961, suggests that the courts may be willing, on a case-by-case basis, to recognise such a defence where D (although not subject to any threats or compulsion himself) commits a criminal offence to prevent another from having to suffer death or grievous bodily harm.

Self-defence, sometimes referred to as 'private defence', actually encompasses three situations where D may feel compelled to act to prevent harm:

- D using reasonable force to protect himself from unlawful violence
- D using reasonable force to protect others from unlawful violence
- D using reasonable force to protect his property from unlawful harm

The Criminal Law Act 1967 also provides the statutory defence of using reasonable force to prevent the commission of a criminal offence – this is wider than the common law defence in that, for example, D could rely on the statutory defence to use reasonable force to prevent harm to property belonging to other persons.

14.2 DURESS *PER MINAS*

Duress *per minas* – or duress by threats – occurs where D commits an offence and claims that at the time he did so because his will to resist was overborne by threats of death or grievous bodily harm made against him by another person. As Lord Simon observed in *DPP for Northern Ireland v Lynch* [1975] 1 All ER 913, 932: '. . . as a result of experience and human valuation, the law draws [a line] between threats to property and threats to the person . . .'. Although D may himself be the subject of the threats to kill or do grievous bodily harm, the defence is available where the threats are made to third parties, for example D's family; see further *R v Ortiz* (1986) 83 Cr App R 173, and *R v Harley and Murray* [1967] VR 526. In *R v Hasan* [2005] UKHL 22 (considered below), Lord Bingham, by way of *obiter*, commented that:

> In the light of . . . Court of Appeal decisions such as *R v Conway* [1989] QB 290 and *R v Wright* [2000] Crim LR 510, the current (April 2003) specimen direction of the Judicial Studies Board suggests that the threat must be directed, if not to the defendant or a member of his immediate family, to a person for whose safety the defendant would reasonably regard himself as responsible. The correctness of such a direction was not . . . appears to me, if strictly applied, to be consistent with the rationale of the duress exception.

To succeed with the defence D will have to provide evidence that a reasonable person would also have succumbed to the threats, and that the person making the threats specified that a criminal offence would have to be committed by D. See *R v Cole* [1994] Crim LR 582, where D could not rely on duress by threats since the money lenders threatening him regarding unpaid debts had not stipulated that D had to commit robbery to meet their demands.

14.2.1 THE IMMINENCE OF THE THREAT

R v Hudson and Taylor [1971] 2 QB 202 (CA)

The appellants witnessed a fight in a pub that resulted in a man named Wright being put on trial. At that trial the appellants failed to identify Wright as the assailant. Wright was acquitted and, in due course, the appellants were charged with perjury. At their trial they admitted that the evidence which they had given was false but set up the defence of duress. The basis of the defence was that, shortly after the fight involving Wright, Hudson had been approached by a group of men who had a reputation for violence and was warned that if she told the truth in court she would be attacked. The jury were directed that, as a matter of law, the defence of duress was not open to the appellants in these circumstances.

Lord Parker CJ:

. . . Despite the concern expressed in Stephen's *History of the Criminal Law of England*, Vol 2, 1883, p 107 that it would be 'a much greater misfortune for society at large if criminals could confer [immunity] upon their agents by threatening them with death or violence if they refuse to execute their commands' it is clearly established that duress provides a defence in all offences including perjury (except possibly treason or murder as a principal) if the will of the accused had been overborne by threats of death or serious personal injury so that the commission of the alleged offence was no longer the voluntary act of the accused.

This appeal raises two main questions: first, as to the nature of the necessary threat and, in particular, whether it must be 'present and immediate'; second, as to the extent to which a right to plead duress may be lost if the accused has failed to take steps to remove the threat as, for example, by seeking police protection.

It is essential to the defence of duress that the threat shall be effective at the moment when the crime is committed. The threat must be a 'present' threat in the sense that it is effective to neutralise the will of the accused at that time. Hence an accused who joins a rebellion under the compulsion of threats cannot plead duress if he remains with the rebels after the threats have lost their effect and his own will has had a chance to re-assert itself: *R v M'Growther* (1746) Fost 13; *AG v Whelan* [1934] IR 518. Similarly a threat of future violence may be so remote as to be insufficient to overpower the will at that moment when the offence was committed, or the accused may have elected to commit the offence in order to rid himself of a threat hanging over him and not because he was driven to act by immediate and unavoidable pressure. In none of these cases is the defence of duress available because a person cannot justify the commission of a crime merely to secure his own peace of mind.

When, however, there is no opportunity for delaying tactics, and the person threatened must make up his mind whether he is to commit the criminal act or not, the existence at that moment of threats sufficient to destroy his will ought to provide him with a defence even though the threatened injury may not follow instantly, but after an interval. This principle is illustrated by *Subramaniam v Public Prosecutor* [1956] 1 WLR 965, when the appellant was charged in Malaya with unlawful possession of ammunition and was held by the Privy Council to have a defence of duress, fit to go to the jury, on his plea that he had been compelled by terrorists to accept the ammunition and feared for his safety if the terrorists returned.

In the present case the threats . . . were likely to be no less compelling, because their execution could not be effected in the courtroom, if they could be carried out in the streets of Salford the same night. In so far, therefore, as the recorder ruled as a matter of law that the threats were not sufficiently present and immediate to support the defence of duress we think that he was in error. He should have left the jury to decide whether the threats had overborne the will of the appellants at the time when they gave the false evidence.

[Counsel for the Crown], however, contends that the recorder's ruling can be supported on another ground, namely that the appellants should have taken steps to neutralise the threats by seeking police protection either when they came to court to give evidence, or beforehand. He submits on grounds of public policy that an accused should not be able to plead duress if he had the opportunity to ask for protection from the police before committing the offence and failed to do so. The argument does not distinguish cases in which the police would be able to provide effective protection, from those when they would not, and it would, in effect, restrict the defence of duress to cases where the person threatened had been kept in custody by the maker of the threats, or where the time interval between the making of the threats and the commission of the offence had made recourse to the police impossible. We recognise the need to keep the defence of duress within reasonable bounds but cannot accept so severe a restriction upon it. The duty, of the person threatened, to take steps to remove the threat does not seem to have arisen in an English case but, in a full review of the defence of duress in the Supreme Court of Victoria (*R v Harley and Murray* [1967] VR 526), a condition of raising the defence was said to be that the accused 'had no means, with safety to himself, of preventing the execution of the threat'.

In the opinion of this court it is always open to the Crown to prove that the accused failed to avail himself of some opportunity which was reasonably open to him to render the threat ineffective, and that upon this being established the threat in question can no longer be relied upon by the defence. In deciding whether such an opportunity was reasonably open to the accused the jury should have regard to his age and circumstances, and to any risks to him which may be involved in the course of action relied upon.

In our judgment the defence of duress should have been left to the jury in the present case, as should any issue raised by the Crown and arising out of the appellants' failure to seek protection . . .

R v Abdul-Hussain and Others [1999] Crim LR 570 (CA)

The appellants were mostly Shiite Muslims from Southern Iraq. In the summer of 1996, they were living in Sudan and feared return to Iraq at the hands of the Sudanese authorities. On 27 August 1996, at Khartoum Airport, the appellants boarded a Sudanese Airbus bound for Amman in Jordan. Once the flight was in Egyptian airspace the appellants hijacked the plane. At first the flight was diverted to Cyprus, but having stopped there for refuelling, eventually landed in London. The appellants were charged with hijacking, contrary to section 1(1) of the Aviation Security Act 1982, and pleaded the defence of duress based on their fears of torture or death if they were deported from the Sudan to Iraq. The trial judge ruled that duress was not available as a defence as the threats relied upon to substantiate the defence were not sufficiently imminent.

Rose LJ:

In the light of the submissions made to us, we derive the following propositions from the relevant authorities:

1   Unless and until Parliament provides otherwise, the defence of duress, whether by threats or from circumstances, is generally available in relation to all substantive crimes, except murder, attempted murder and some forms of treason (*R v Pommell* [1995] 2 Cr App R 607 at 615C). Accordingly, if raised by appropriate evidence, it is available in relation to hijacking aircraft; although, in such cases, the terror induced in innocent passengers will generally raise issues of proportionality for determination, initially as a matter of law by the judge and, in appropriate cases, by the jury.

2   The courts have developed the defence on a case-by-case basis, notably during the last 30 years. Its scope remains imprecise (*Howe* [1987] AC 417, 453G–54C; *Hurst* [1995] 1 Cr App R 82 at 93D).

3   Imminent peril of death or serious injury to the defendant, or those to whom he has responsibility, is an essential element of both types of duress (see *Southwark LBC v Williams* [1971] 1 Ch 734, *per* Lord Justice Edmund-Davies at 746A; *Loughnan*, by the majority at 448 and the dissentient at 460; and *Cole* at p 10).

4   The peril must operate on the mind of the defendant at the time when he commits the otherwise criminal act, so as to overbear his will, and this is essentially a question for the jury (*Hudson and Taylor* at 4; and *Lynch* at 675F. It is to be noted that in *Hudson and Taylor* Lord Parker CJ presided over the court, whose reserved judgment was given by Widgery LJ (as he then was)).

5   But the execution of the threat need not be immediately in prospect (*Hudson and Taylor* at 425). If in *Cole* the court had had the advantage of argument, as to the distinction between imminence, immediacy and spontaneity which has been addressed to us, it seems unlikely that the second half of the paragraph at p 10 of the judgment which we have cited would have been so expressed. If, and in so far as anything said in *Cole* is inconsistent with *Hudson and Taylor*, we prefer and are, in any event, bound by *Hudson and Taylor*, as, indeed, was the court in *Cole*.

6   The period of time which elapses between the inception of the peril and the defendant's act, and between that act and execution of the threat, are relevant but not determinative factors for a judge and jury in deciding whether duress operates (*Hudson and Taylor; Pommell* at 616A).

7   All the circumstances of the peril, including the number, identity and status of those creating it, and the opportunities (if any) which exist to avoid it are relevant, initially for the judge, and, in appropriate cases, for the jury, when assessing whether the defendant's mind was affected as in 4 above. As Lord Morris of Borth-y-Gest said in *Lynch* at 675F in the passage previously cited, the issue in *Hudson and Taylor* was 'whether the threats were so real and were at the relevant time so operative and their effect so incapable of avoidance that, having regard to all the circumstances, the conduct of the girls could be excused'.

8   As to 6 and 7, if Anne Frank had stolen a car to escape from Amsterdam and been charged with theft, the tenets of English law would not, in our judgment, have denied her a defence of duress of circumstances, on the ground that she should have waited for the Gestapo's knock on the door.

9   We see no reason of principle or authority for distinguishing the two forms of duress in relation to the elements of the defence which we have identified. In particular, we do not read the court's judgment in *Cole* as seeking to draw any such distinction.

10   The judgment of the court, presided over by Lord Lane CJ and delivered by Simon Brown LJ, in *Martin*, at 345 to 346 (already cited) affords, as it seems to us, the clearest and most authoritative guide to the relevant principles and appropriate direction in relation to both forms of duress. Subject to questions of continuance (which did not arise and as to which, see *Pommell* at 615D), it clearly reflects Lord Lane's judgment in *R v Graham* (1981) 74 Cr App R 235 at 241, which was approved by the House of Lords in *Howe* in 458G. It applies a predominantly, but not entirely, objective test, and this court has recently rejected an attempt to introduce a purely subjective element divorced from extraneous influence (see *Roger and Rose*, 9th July 1997).

11   Clauses 25 and 26 of the Law Commission's draft Criminal Law Bill do not represent the present law. Accordingly, reference to those provisions is potentially misleading (see the forceful note by Professor Sir John Smith QC [1998] Crim LR 204, with which we agree). Applying these principles to the present case, we are satisfied that the learned judge was led into error as to the applicable law. We have considerable sympathy with him. No submissions were addressed to him as to the distinction between imminence, immediacy and spontaneity, and he sought to follow the judgment of this court in *Cole*, where, likewise, no such submissions had been advanced. In our judgment, although the judge was right to look for a close nexus between the threat and the criminal act, he interpreted the law too strictly in seeking a virtually spontaneous reaction. He should have asked himself, in accordance with *Martin*, whether there was evidence of such fear operating on the minds of the defendants at the time of the hijacking as to impel them to act as they did and whether, if so, there was evidence that the danger they feared objectively existed and that hijacking was a reasonable and proportionate response to it. Had he done so, it seems to us that he must have concluded that there was evidence for the jury to consider.

We stress that the prosecution did not seek to rely on a want of proportionality or to contend that duress was not capable of applying after the plane had landed at Larnaca. It follows that, in our judgment, in the light of how he was invited to approach the matter, the judge should have left the defence of duress for the jury to consider. Although the position of some of the defendants differed – in particular, Hoshan held documents which permitted him to travel freely and Maged Naji's case raised an additional argument in relation to voluntariness – we see no reason, for present purposes, to draw a distinction between the defendants. In relation to all of them, the jury should have been permitted to consider duress.

We express no view as to proportionality or the continued availability of duress after Larnaca because, as we have said, these matters were not relied on before the judge and because, more significantly, there is no sufficient material before us as to the evidence on these matters. In any event, having concluded, for the reasons given, that the judge was wrong to withdraw the defence from the jury, the convictions of the appellants at the first trial must be regarded as unsafe. Their appeals are therefore allowed and their convictions quashed. For the fourth time in five years this court emphasises the urgent need for legislation to define duress with precision.

R v Hasan [2005] UKHL 22

For the facts, see below.

In relation to the availability of the defence of duress the judge put four questions to the jury, one of which was:

3   Could the defendant have avoided acting as he did without harm coming to his family? If you are sure he could, the defence fails and he is guilty.

In the House of Lords, Lord Bingham was critical of the 'indulgent' approach taken by the Court of Appeal in *R v Hudson and Taylor*, suggesting that it undermined the view that 'execution of a threat must be reasonably believed to be imminent and immediate if it is to support a plea of duress'. He added:

> I cannot, consistently with principle, accept that a witness testifying in the Crown Court at Manchester [as was the case with the defendants in *R v Hudson and Taylor*] has no opportunity to avoid complying with a threat incapable of execution then or there . . . It should . . . be made clear to juries that if the retribution threatened against the defendant or his family or a person for whom he reasonably feels responsible is not such as he reasonably expects to follow immediately or almost immediately on his failure to comply with the threat, there may be little if any room for doubt that he could have taken evasive action, whether by going to the police or in some other way, to avoid committing the crime with which he is charged.

14.2.2 THE DIRECTION TO THE JURY IN CASES OF DURESS *PER MINAS*

> ### *R v Graham* [1982] 1 WLR 294 (CA)
>
> Lord Lane CJ:
> . . . The facts of the case were as follows. The appellant was the victim's husband. He is a practising homosexual. His wife was aware of this and indeed at the material time they were living in a bizarre *ménage à trois* with another homosexual called King. They were living in the flat above two other homosexuals, named Gillis and Minter, with whom the appellant occasionally had sexual relations. The appellant and King were jointly charged with the murder. King pleaded guilty. The appellant admitted playing an active part in the events leading to the killing and admitted seeking to conceal the killing after it had happened.
>   His defence was twofold: first, that he lacked the necessary intent, and he drew attention particularly to the drink and drugs he had taken; and, second, that whatever his intentional actions may have been, they were performed under duress because of his fear of King.
>   We are satisfied that the directions given to the jury by the trial judge, on the issues of murder and manslaughter, on joint enterprise and on the relevance of drink and drugs to those issues, were impeccable. Other minor complaints made in the notice of appeal are also without foundation. The only live issue is, as counsel for the appellant concedes, whether the direction to the jury on the question of duress was correct.

The evidence relevant to this issue was this. The appellant had suffered for some time from an anxiety state. He was taking Valium tablets on prescription. There was medical evidence to the effect that Valium, if taken in excess, would make him more susceptible to bullying, but that by mid-1980 he would have developed some tolerance to the drug. King was said to be a man of violence. There was evidence of altercations. In 1978 King had tipped the appellant and his wife off a settee because they were embracing and he was jealous. The appellant, it seems, knew of another incident in 1978 when some other woman had been assaulted by King and had had her ribs broken. In June 1980, said the appellant, King had 'swiped him over the head'.

On Friday 27 June 1980, the day before the killing, King attacked the wife with a knife. The appellant intervened and, for his trouble, cut his finger when he tried to grab the knife. As a result of this incident, the wife on the following day left and went to the appellant's mother's home. The appellant and King stayed behind and, together with the man Gillis, occupied their time in the flat drinking, talking and indulging in homosexual activities. The appellant said that he had a lot to drink during this time and had taken Valium tablets in excess of the quantity which had been prescribed for him. He also said that during the time that the three were together, he thought that King was going to attack him with a knife, but the incident came to nothing. Gillis left soon after midnight.

King then suggested getting rid of the wife once and for all. The two of them hatched a plan. The appellant telephoned his wife in the small hours, told her falsely that he had cut his wrists and asked her to come home at once. Meanwhile, King bandaged both of the appellant's wrists and he, the appellant, lay face down on the floor pretending to be seriously hurt. When the wife arrived, she knelt down beside the appellant to see how he was. King had the flex from a coffee percolator in his hands. He attempted unsuccessfully to put it round the wife's neck while she was kneeling. The appellant and his wife then both got up and King said: 'What's it feel like to know that you are going to die, Betty?' That remark was repeated. King then put the flex round the wife's neck and pulled it tight, hauling her off her feet onto his back as if she were a sack of coals. She put her hands up to the flex at her neck, whereupon King told the appellant to cut her fingers away. The appellant said in evidence that he picked up a knife but could not bring himself to use it. King thereupon put the wife on the floor, still holding the flex. He told the appellant to take hold of one end of it. The appellant said in evidence that he did so. He added that it was only in fear of King that he complied with the order. He said that, in any event, the plug at the end of the flex which he was holding came off as he exerted pressure on it. If that were the case, it would remain in doubt whether the appellant's act made any contribution to the death. It should, however, be noted that in the voluntary statement, which he made to the police, he had admitted pulling on the flex for about a minute. Whatever the precise sequence of events, it was beyond doubt that the ligature around the wife's neck was responsible for her death.

Thereafter, the appellant helped King to dispose of her body by wrapping it up, carrying her out of the flat and dumping it over an embankment. Each of the two men then took one of her earrings; the appellant rifled her handbag for anything he could find of use, and spread the rest of the contents near her body to make it look as though she had been robbed. He then made telephone calls suggesting that she had gone missing.

The Crown at the trial conceded that, on those facts, it was open to the defence to raise the issue of duress. In other words, they were not prepared to take the point that the defence of duress is not available to a principal in the first degree to murder. Consequently, the interesting question raised by the decisions in *Lynch v DPP for Northern Ireland* [1975] AC 653, and *Abbott v R* [1977] AC 755 was not argued before us. We do not have to decide it. We pause only to observe that the jury would no doubt have been puzzled to learn that whether the appellant was to be convicted of murder or acquitted altogether might depend on whether the plug came off the end of the percolator flex when he began to pull it . . .

The direction which the judge gave to the jury required them to ask themselves two questions. First, a subjective question which the judge formulated thus: 'Was this man at the time of the killing taking part because he feared for his own life or personal safety as a result of the words or the conduct on the part of King, either personally experienced by him, or genuinely believed in by him?' Neither side in the present appeal has taken issue with the judge on this question. We feel, however, that for purposes of completeness, we should say that the direction appropriate in this particular case should have been in these words: 'Was this man at the time of the killing taking part because he held a well-grounded fear of death (or serious physical injury) as a result of the words or conduct on the part of King?' The bracketed words may be too favourable to the defendant. The point was not argued before us.

The judge then went on to direct the jury that if the answer to that first question was 'Yes', or 'He may have been', the jury should then go on to consider a second question importing an objective test of reasonableness. This is the issue which arises in this appeal. Counsel for the appellant contends that no second question arises at all; the test is purely subjective. He argues that if the appellant's will was in fact overborne by threats of the requisite cogency, he is entitled to be acquitted and no question arises as to whether a reasonable man, with or without his characteristics, would have reacted similarly.

Counsel for the Crown, on the other hand, submits that such *dicta* as can be found on the point are in favour of a second test; this time an objective test. He argues that public policy requires this and draws an analogy with provocation. He submits that while the judge was right to pose a second question, he formulated it too favourably to the appellant. The question was put to the jury in the following terms:

> Taking into account all the circumstances of the case, including the age, sex, sexual propensities and other characteristics personal to the defendant, including his state of mind and the amount of drink or drugs he had taken, was it reasonable for the defendant to behave in the way he did, that is to take part in the murder of his wife as a result of the fear present at the time in his mind? The test of reasonableness in this context is: would the defendant's behaviour in all the particular circumstances to which I have just referred reflect the degree of self-control and firmness of purpose which everyone is entitled to expect that his fellow citizens would exercise in society as it is today? . . .

There is no direct binding authority on the questions whether the test is solely subjective or, if objective, how it is to be formulated . . .

As a matter of public policy, it seems to us essential to limit the defence of duress by means of an objective criterion formulated in terms of reasonableness. Consistency of approach in defences to criminal liability is obviously desirable. Provocation and duress are analogous. In provocation the words or actions of one person break the self-control of another. In duress the words or actions of one person break the will of another. The law requires a defendant to have the self-control reasonably to be expected of the ordinary citizen in his situation. It should likewise require him to have the steadfastness reasonably to be expected of the ordinary citizen in his situation. So too with self-defence, in which the law permits the use of no more force than is reasonable in the circumstances. And, in general, if a mistake is to excuse what would otherwise be criminal, the mistake must be a reasonable one.

It follows that we accept counsel for the Crown's submission that the direction in this case was too favourable to the appellant. The Crown having conceded that the issue of duress was open to the appellant and was raised on the evidence, the correct approach on the facts of this case would have been as follows: (1) was the defendant, or may he have been, impelled to act as he did because, as a result of what he reasonably believed King had said or done, he had good cause to fear that if he did not so act King would kill him or (if this is to be added) cause him serious physical injury? (2) if so, have the prosecution made the jury sure that a sober person of reasonable firmness, sharing the characteristics of the defendant, would not have responded to whatever he reasonably believed King said or did by taking part in the killing? The fact that a defendant's will to resist has been eroded by the voluntary consumption of drink or drugs is not relevant to this test.

We doubt whether the Crown was right to concede that the question of duress ever arose on the facts of this case. The words and deeds of King relied on by the defence were far short of those needed to raise a threat of the requisite gravity. However, the Crown having made the concession, the judge was right to pose the second objective question to the jury. His only error lay in putting it too favourably to the appellant.

R v Hasan [2005] UKHL 22

For the facts, see below.

In relation to the availability of the defence of duress the first of four questions put to the jury by the trial judge was:

1: Was the defendant driven or forced to act as he did by threats which, rightly or wrongly, he genuinely believed that if he did not burgle [the] house, his family would be seriously harmed or killed? If you are sure that he was not forced by threats to act as he did, the defence fails and he is guilty. But if you are not sure go on to [the second question];

Lord Bingham concluded that this test for belief was too favourable to the defendant. He observed:

It is evident that the judge, very properly, based himself on the JSB's specimen direction as promulgated in August 2000. That specimen direction included the words, adopted by the judge, 'he genuinely believed'. But the words used in *R v Graham* and approved in *R v Howe* were 'he reasonably believed'. It is of course essential that the defendant should genuinely, i.e. actually, believe in the efficacy of the threat by which he claims to have been compelled. But there is no warrant for relaxing the requirement that the belief must be reasonable as well as genuine. There can of course be no complaint of this departure from authority, which was favourable to the defendant.

14.2.3 RELEVANCE OF THE DEFENDANT'S CHARACTERISTICS

As with the defence of provocation, there has been a continuing debate as to the extent to which the characteristics of the individual defendant ought to be taken into account when applying the objective test of the reasonable person of average fortitude in the defence of duress. In *R v Horne* [1994] Crim LR 584 the Court of Appeal held that a person of reasonable firmness was an average member of the public; not a hero necessarily, and not a coward. If the standard for comparison was a person of reasonable firmness it was irrelevant for the jury to consider any characteristics of the defendant that showed that he was not such a person, but was pliant or vulnerable to pressure. Similarly in *R v Hegarty* [1994] Crim LR 353, the appellant's 'grossly elevated neurotic state' was also ignored, although the Court of Appeal confirmed that the jury had to consider the response of a sober person of reasonable firmness 'sharing the characteristics of the defendant', such as age, sex and physical health. Factors such as drug addiction are seen as being self-induced conditions, not characteristics, and are therefore excluded from the application of the objective test; see *R v Flatt* [1996] Crim LR 576 (CA).

R v Bowen [1997] 1 WLR 372 (CA)

The appellant was convicted on five counts of obtaining services by deception and sentenced to 18 months' imprisonment. He appealed against conviction on the basis that the judge should have included in his direction that the sober person of reasonable firmness was someone who shared the defendant's characteristics.

> Stuart-Smith LJ:
> The classic statement of the law is to be found in the judgment of the Court of Appeal in *Graham* [1982] 1 WLR 294 at 299 . . .
> But the question remains, what are the relevant characteristics of the accused to which the jury should have regard in considering the second objective test? This question had given rise to considerable difficulty in recent cases. It seems clear that age and sex are, and physical health or disability may be, relevant characteristics. But beyond that it is not altogether easy to determine from the authorities what others may be relevant . . .
> What principles are to be derived from [the] authorities? We think they are as follows:
>
> (1) The mere fact that the accused is more pliable, vulnerable, timid or susceptible to threats than a normal person are not characteristics with which it is legitimate to invest the reasonable/ordinary person for the purpose of considering the objective test.
> (2) The defendant may be in a category of persons who the jury may think less able to resist pressure than people not within that category. Obvious examples are age, where a young person may well not be so robust as a mature one; possibly sex, though many women would doubtless consider they had as much moral courage to resist pressure as men; pregnancy, where there is added fear for the unborn child; serious physical disability, which may inhibit self-protection; recognised mental illness or psychiatric condition, such as post-traumatic stress disorder leading to learned helplessness.

(3) Characteristics which may be relevant in considering provocation, because they relate to the nature of the provocation itself, will not necessarily be relevant in cases of duress. Thus homosexuality may be relevant to provocation if the provocative words or conduct are related to this characteristic; it cannot be relevant in duress, since there is no reason to think that homosexuals are less robust in resisting threats of the kind that are relevant in duress cases.

(4) Characteristics due to self-induced abuse, such as alcohol, drugs or glue-sniffing, cannot be relevant.

(5) Psychiatric evidence may be admissible to show that the accused is suffering from mental illness, mental impairment or recognised psychiatric condition provided persons generally suffering from such condition may be more susceptible to pressure and threats and thus to assist the jury in deciding whether a reasonable person suffering from such a condition might have been impelled to act as the defendant did. It is not admissible simply to show that in the doctor's opinion an accused, who is not suffering from such illness or condition, is especially timid, suggestible or vulnerable to pressure and threats. Nor is medical opinion admissible to bolster or support the credibility of the accused.

(6) Where counsel wishes to submit that the accused has some characteristic which falls within (2) above, this must be made plain to the judge. The question may arise in relation to the admissibility of medical evidence of the nature set out in (5). If so, the judge will have to rule at that stage. There may, however, be no medical evidence, or, as in this case, medical evidence may have been introduced for some other purpose, e.g. to challenge the admissibility or weight of a confession. In such a case counsel must raise the question before speeches in the absence of the jury, so that the judge can rule whether the alleged characteristic is capable of being relevant. If he rules that it is, then he must leave it to the jury.

(7) In the absence of some direction from the judge as to what characteristics are capable of being regarded as relevant, we think that the direction approved in *R v Graham* without more will not be as helpful as it might be, since the jury may be tempted, especially if there is evidence, as there was in this case, relating to suggestibility and vulnerability, to think that these are relevant. In most cases it is probably only the age and sex of the accused that is capable of being relevant. If so, the judge should, as he did in this case, confine the characteristics in question to these.

How are these principles to be applied in this case? [Counsel for the appellant] accepts, rightly in our opinion, that the evidence that the appellant was abnormally suggestible and a vulnerable individual is irrelevant. But she submits that the fact that he had, or may have had, a low IQ of 68 is relevant since it might inhibit his ability to seek the protection of the police. We do not agree. We do not see how low IQ, short of mental impairment or mental defectiveness, can be said to be a characteristic that makes those who have it less courageous and less able to withstand threats and pressure. Moreover, we do not think that any such submission as is now made, based solely on the appellant's low IQ, was ever advanced at the trial. Furthermore, it is to be noted that in two places the judge told the jury that if they thought the appellant passed the subjective test they should acquit him. We are quite satisfied that in the circumstances of this case the judge's direction was sufficient. He directed the jury to consider the only two relevant characteristics, namely age and sex. It would not have assisted them, and might well have confused them, if he had added, without qualification, that the person of reasonable firmness was one who shared the characteristics of the appellant. For these reasons, the appeal will be dismissed.

14.3 THE AVAILABILITY OF THE DEFENCE OF DURESS *PER MINAS*: MURDER AND ATTEMPTED MURDER

Duress is not a defence to murder, and this is so whether the accused is a principal offender or an accessory: see *R v Howe* (extracted below). Similarly, duress is not available on a charge of attempted murder: see *R v Gotts* (extracted below).

R v Howe [1987] AC 417 (HL)

The appellants, Howe and Bannister, were charged with involvement in two murders. Count 1 involved the murder of Elgar. The appellants claimed that they had participated in the murder under duress. They feared that if they did not assist with the murder, the person making the threats, Murray, would torture and kill them. Count 2 alleged that the appellants had carried out the killing of a man named Pollitt, again acting under duress from Murray. On appeal the House of Lords had to consider the availability of the defence of duress to a defendant charged with murder as a principal offender and to a defendant charged as an accomplice to murder.

> Lord Griffiths:
>
> ... For centuries it was accepted that English criminal law did not allow duress as a defence to murder. It was so stated in Hale's *Pleas of the Crown* (1736) Vol 1, p 51, repeated by Blackstone in his *Commentaries on the Laws of England*, 1857 edn, Vol 4, p 28, and so taught by all the authoritative writers on criminal law. It was accepted by those responsible for drafting the criminal codes for many parts of the British Empire and they provided, in those codes, that duress should not be a defence to murder. In *R v Tyler and Price* (1838) 8 C & P 616, Denman CJ told the jury in emphatic language that they should not accept a plea of duress that was put up in defence to a charge of murder against those who were not the actual killers. Fifty years later, in *R v Dudley and Stephens* (1884) 14 QBD 273, the defence of necessity was defined to the men who had killed the cabin boy and eaten him in order that they might survive albeit only Stephens was the actual killer. The reasoning that underlies that decision is the same as that which denies duress as a defence to murder. It is based upon the special sanctity that the law attaches to human life and which denies to a man the right to take an innocent life even at the price of his own or another's life.
>
> There are surprisingly few reported decisions on duress but it cannot be gainsaid that the defence has been extended, particularly since the second war, to a number of crimes. I think myself it would have been better had this development not taken place and that duress had been regarded as a factor to be taken into account in mitigation as Stephen suggested in his *History of the Criminal Law of England* (1883) Vol 2, p 108. However, as Lord Morris of Borth-y-Gest said in *DPP for Northern Ireland v Lynch* [1975] AC 653, 670, it is too late to adopt that view. And the question now is whether that development should be carried a step further and applied to a murderer who is the actual killer, and if the answer to this question is no, whether there is any basis upon which it can be right to draw a distinction between a murderer who did the actual killing and a murderer who played a different part in the design to bring about the death of the victim ...
>
> In *Abbot v R* [1977] AC 755, the majority in the Privy Council applied the law of duress in accordance with English authority and denied it as a defence to a murderer who took part in the

actual killing. The minority would have extended the defence even to the actual killer, pointing out the illogicality of allowing it to the principal in the second degree or the aider and abettor and denying it to the principal in the first degree.

Since that time the whole question of duress has been studied by the Law Commission: see Law Commission Report, *Criminal Law, Report on Defences of General Application* (Law Com 83), dated 27 July 1977. The report sets out the arguments for and against the defence and deals in particular with whether it should apply to murder. They balanced the argument based upon the sanctity of human life that denies the defence to a murderer against the argument urged by the majority in *DPP for Northern Ireland v Lynch* [1975] AC 653, that the law should not demand more than human frailty can sustain. They preferred the latter argument and accordingly recommended that a defence of duress should be available to all crimes including murder . . .

Against this background are there any present circumstances that should impel your Lordships to alter the law that has stood for so long and to extend the defence of duress to the actual killer? My Lords, I can think of none. It appears to me that all present indications point in the opposite direction. We face a rising tide of violence and terrorism against which the law must stand firm recognising that its highest duty is to protect the freedom and lives of those that live under it. The sanctity of human life lies at the root of this ideal and I would do nothing to undermine it, be it ever so slight.

On this question your Lordships should, I believe, accord great weight to the opinion of the Lord Chief Justice who by virtue of his office and duties is in far closer touch with the practical application of the criminal law and better able to evaluate the consequence of a change in the law than those of us who sit in this House. This is what Lord Lane CJ had to say in his judgment in this case [1986] QB 626, 641:

> It is true that to allow the defence to the aider and abettor but not to the killer may lead to illogicality, as was pointed out by this court in *R v Graham (Paul)* [1982] 1 WLR 294, where the question in issue in the instant case was not argued, but that is not to say that any illogicality should be cured by making duress available to the actual killer rather by removing it from the aider and abettor. Assuming that a change in the law is desirable or necessary, we may perhaps be permitted to express a view. The whole matter was dealt with *in extenso* by Lord Salmon in his speech in *Abbott v R* [1977] AC 755 to which reference has already been made. He dealt there with the authorities. It is unnecessary for us in the circumstances to repeat the citations which he there makes. It would, moreover, be impertinent for us to try to restate in different terms the contents of that speech with which we respectfully agree. Either the law should be left as it is or the defence of duress should be denied to anyone charged with murder, whether as a principal in the first degree or otherwise. It seems to us that it would be a highly dangerous relaxation in the law to allow a person who has deliberately killed maybe a number of innocent people, to escape conviction and punishment altogether because of a fear that his own life or those of his family might be in danger if he did not; particularly so when the defence of duress is so easy to raise and may be so difficult for the prosecution to disprove beyond reasonable doubt, the facts of necessity being as a rule known only to the defendant himself. That is not to say that duress may not be taken into account in other ways, for example, by the parole board. Even if, contrary to our views, it were otherwise desirable to extend the defence of duress to the actual killer, this is surely not the moment to make any such change, when acts of terrorism are commonplace and opportunities for mass murder have never been more readily to hand.

My Lords, in my view we should accept the advice of Lord Lane CJ and the judges who sat with him, and decline to extend the defence to the actual killer. If the defence is not available to the killer what justification can there be for extending it to others who have played their part in the murder? I can, of course, see that as a matter of common sense one participant in a murder may be considered less morally at fault than another. The youth who hero-worships the gang leader and acts as lookout man whilst the gang enter a jeweller's shop and kill the owner in order to steal is an obvious example. In the eyes of the law they are all guilty of murder, but justice will be served by requiring those who did the killing to serve a longer period in prison before being released on licence than the youth who acted as lookout. However, it is not difficult to give examples where more moral fault may be thought to attach to a participant in murder who was not the actual killer; I have already mentioned the example of a contract killing, when the murder would never have taken place if a contract had not been placed to take the life of the victim. Another example would be an intelligent man goading a weak-minded individual into a killing he would not otherwise commit.

It is therefore neither rational nor fair to make the defence dependent upon whether the accused is the actual killer or took some other part in the murder. I have toyed with the idea that it might be possible to leave it to the discretion of the trial judge to decide whether the defence should be available to one who was not the killer, but I have rejected this as introducing too great a degree of uncertainty into the availability of the defence. I am not troubled by some of the extreme examples cited in favour of allowing the defence to those who are not the killer such as a woman motorist being hijacked and forced to act as getaway driver, or a pedestrian being forced to give misleading information to the police to protect robbery and murder in a shop. The short, practical answer is that it is inconceivable that such persons would be prosecuted; they would be called as the principal witnesses for the prosecution.

As I can find no fair and certain basis upon which to differentiate between participants to a murder and as I am firmly convinced that the law should not be extended to the killer, I would depart from the decision of this House in *DPP for Northern Ireland v Lynch* [1975] AC 653 and declare the law to be that duress is not available as a defence to a charge of murder, or to attempted murder. I add attempted murder because it is to be remembered that the prosecution have to prove an even more evil intent to convict of attempted murder than in actual murder. Attempted murder requires proof of an intent to kill, whereas in murder it is sufficient to prove an intent to cause really serious injury.

It cannot be right to allow the defence to one who may be more intent upon taking a life than the murderer. This leaves, of course, the anomaly that duress is available for the offence of wounding with intent but not to murder if the victim dies subsequently. But this flows from the special regard that the law has for human life; it may not be logical but it is real and has to be accepted.

I do not think that your Lordships should adopt the compromise solution of declaring that duress reduces murder to manslaughter. Where the defence of duress is available it is a complete excuse. This solution would put the law back to lines upon which Stephen suggested it should develop by regarding duress as a form of mitigation. English law has rejected this solution and it would be yet another anomaly to introduce it for the crime of murder alone. I would have been more tempted to go down this road if the death penalty had remained for murder. But the sentence for murder, although mandatory and expressed as imprisonment for life, is in fact an indefinite sentence, which is kept constantly under review by the parole board and the Home Secretary with the assistance of the Lord Chief Justice and the trial judge. I have confidence that through

this machinery the respective culpability of those involved in a murder case can be fairly weighed
and reflected in the time they are required to serve in custody . . .

R v Gotts [1992] 2 AC 412 (HL)

The appellant was convicted of attempted murder, the trial judge having rejected counsel for
the appellant's submissions that duress was available as defence. The House of Lords (Lord
Keith and Lord Lowry dissenting), dismissed the appeal.

Lord Jauncey:

My Lords . . . On appeal (*Director of Public Prosecutions for Northern Ireland v Lynch* [1975] AC
653), it was held by a majority of this House that the defence of duress was available to a person
charged with murder as a principal in the second degree. In a dissenting judgment Lord Simon of
Glaisdale referred, at p 687A, to the need for the law to draw a line somewhere and went on to
pose the question: 'But if an arbitrary line is thus drawn, is not one between murder and traditionally lesser crimes equally justifiable?' It is, in my view, taking too much out of these observations
to treat them as recognising the availability of the defence of duress to a charge of attempted
murder.

In *Abbott v R* [1977] AC 755, the Privy Council by a majority held that on a charge of murder
the defence of duress was not available to a principal in the first degree who took part in the
actual killing. Mr Farrer relied on a passage from the dissenting judgment of Lord Wilberforce
at p 772:

> *Director of Public Prosecutions for Northern Ireland v Lynch* having been decided as it
> was, the most striking feature of the present appeal is the lack of any indication, in the
> judgment of the majority, why a flat declaration that in no circumstances whatsoever may
> the actual killer be absolved by a plea of duress makes for sounder law and better ethics.
> In truth, the contrary is the case. For example D attempts to kill P but, though injuring him,
> fails. When charged with attempted murder he may plead duress (*R v Fagan* (1974)
> unreported, 20 September, and several times referred to in *Lynch*). Later P dies and D is
> charged with his murder; if the majority of their Lordships are right, he now has no such
> plea available.

The observations as to attempted murder were *obiter* and I do not consider that *R v Fagan*, a
Northern Irish case, which proceeded upon a concession by the Crown that the defence was
available to a charge of attempted murder, can be treated as authoritative.

The last and most important of the three cases is *R v Howe* . . . This case '[restored] the law to
the condition in which it was almost universally thought not be prior to *Lynch*': *per* Lord Hailsham
of Marylebone LC at p 430. Accordingly, duress is no defence to murder in whatever capacity the
accused is charged with that crime.

My Lords, I share the view of Lord Griffiths that 'it would have been better had [the development
of the defence of duress] not taken place and that duress had been regarded as a factor to be
taken into account in mitigation as Stephen suggested in his *History of the Criminal Law of
England*, Vol II, p 108': *R v Howe* [1987] AC 417, 439 – a view which was expressed in not
dissimilar terms by Lord Hunter in the Scottish case of *Thomson v HM Advocate* (1983) SCCR

368, 372: 'I doubt whether – at any rate in the case of very serious crimes – it is sound legal policy ever to admit coercion as a full defence leading, if established, to acquittal.' At the time of the earlier writings on duress as a defence, offences against the person were much more likely to have involved only one or two victims. Weapons and substances capable of inflicting mass injury were not readily available to terrorists and other criminals as they are in the reputedly more civilised times in which we now live. While it is not now possible for this House to restrict the availability of defence of duress in those cases where it has been recognised to exist, I feel constrained to express the personal view that given the climate of violence and terrorism which ordinary law-abiding citizens have now to face Parliament might do well to consider whether that defence should continue to be available in the case of all very serious crimes. I am aware that in expressing this personal view I am at odds with the recommendations of the Law Commission Report, *Criminal Law Report on Defences of General Application* (1977) (Law Com 83), but I am also aware that during some 14 years since its publication Parliament has, perhaps advisedly, taken no action thereafter.

However, in this appeal there is no question of your Lordships being asked to deny the defence in circumstances where it has previously been held to be available. I have already expressed the opinion that earlier writings leave the matter at large. I do not consider that the *obiter dictum* of Lord Wilberforce in *Abbott v R* [1977] AC 755 to which I have already referred, supported as it is only by *R v Fagan*, 20 September 1974, which proceeded upon a concession, can be regarded as authoritative and there are no other observations in any of the three recent cases to a similar effect. There are, however, two *obiter dicta* in *R v Howe* [1987] AC 417 to which I must refer. Lord Hailsham, dealing with a defence argument as to the illogicality of allowing the defence of duress to a charge of attempted murder but not to one of murder, said, at p 432:

> More persuasive, perhaps, is the point based on the availability of the defence of duress on a charge of attempted murder, where the actual intent to kill is an essential prerequisite. It may be that we must meet this *casus omissus* in your Lordships' House when we come to it. It may require reconsideration of the availability of the defence in that case too.

I understand Lord Hailsham there to be accepting that the question was still open for decision by his House and that his use of the word 'reconsideration' was not intended to connote a change in established law. Lord Griffiths dealt with the matter more positively, at p 445:

> As I can find no fair and certain basis upon which to differentiate between participants to a murder and as I am firmly convinced that the law should not be extended to the killer, I would depart from the decision of this House in *Director of Public Prosecution for Northern Ireland v Lynch* [1975] AC 653 and declare the law to be that duress is not available as a defence to a charge of murder, or to attempted murder. I add attempted murder because it is to be remembered that the prosecution have to prove an even more evil intent to convict of attempted murder than in actual murder. Attempted murder requires proof of an intent to kill, whereas in murder it is sufficient to prove an intent to cause really serious injury. It cannot be right to allow the defence to one who may be more intent upon taking a life than the murderer.

As the question is still open for decision by your Lordships it becomes a matter of policy how it should be answered. It is interesting to note that there is no uniformity of practice in other common law countries. The industry of Mr Miskin who appeared with Mr Farrer disclosed that in Queensland, Tasmania, Western Australia, New Zealand and Canada duress is not available as a defence to attempted murder but that it is available in almost all of the states of the United States of America. The reason why duress has for so long been stated not to be available as a defence to a murder charge is that the law regards the sanctity of human life and the protection thereof as of paramount importance. Does that reason apply to attempted murder as well as to murder? As Lord Griffiths pointed out in the passage to which I have just referred, an intent to kill must be proved in the case of attempted murder but not necessarily in the case of murder. Is there logic in affording the defence to one who intends to kill but fails and denying it to one who mistakenly kills intending only to injure? If I may give two examples:

(1a) A stabs B in the chest intending to kill him and leaves him for dead. By good luck B is found whilst still alive and rushed to hospital where surgical skill saves his life.

(1b) C stabs D intending only to injure him and inflicts a near identical wound. Unfortunately D is not found until it is too late to save his life.

I see no justification of logic or morality for affording a defence of duress to A who intended to kill when it is denied to C who did not so intend.

(2a) E plants in a passenger aircraft a bomb timed to go off in mid-flight. Owing to bungling it explodes while the aircraft is still on the ground with the result that some 200 passengers suffer physical and mental injuries of which many are permanently disabling, but no one is killed.

(2b) F plants a bomb in a light aircraft intending to injure the pilot before it takes off but in fact it goes off in mid-air killing the pilot who is the sole occupant of the airplane.

It would in my view be both offensive to common sense and decency that E, if he established duress, should be acquitted and walk free without a stain on his character notwithstanding the appalling results which he has achieved, whereas F who never intended to kill should, if convicted in the absence of the defence, be sentenced to life imprisonment as a murderer.

It is, of course, true that withholding the defence in any circumstances will create some anomalies but I would agree with Lord Griffiths (*R v Howe* [1987] AC 417, 444A) that nothing should be done to undermine in any way the highest duty of the law to protect the freedom and lives of those that live under it. I can therefore see no justification in logic, morality or law in affording to an attempted murderer the defence which is withheld from a murderer. The intent required of an attempted murderer is more evil than that required of a murderer and the line which divides the two offences is seldom, if ever, of the deliberate making of the criminal. A man shooting to kill but missing a vital organ by a hair's breadth can justify his action no more than can the man who hits that organ. It is pure chance that the attempted murderer is not a murderer and I entirely agree with what Lord Lane CJ [1991] 1 QB 660, 667 said: that the fact that the attempt failed to kill should not make any difference.

For the foregoing reasons I have no doubt that the Court of Appeal reached the correct conclusion and that the appeal should be dismissed.

14.4 THE AVAILABILITY OF THE DEFENCE OF DURESS *PER MINAS*: WHERE A DEFENDANT VOLUNTARILY EXPOSES HIMSELF TO THE RISK OF THREATS

R v Sharp [1987] 1 QB 853 (CA)

The appellant had been involved in a number of robberies with two other men. He claimed that one of the other men, Hussey, had threatened to blow his head off if he did not carry on with a plan to rob a post office. The Court of Appeal considered the proper direction on duress where a defendant joined a criminal gang and was then forced by gang members to participate in the commission of offences.

> Lord Lane CJ:
>
> . . . No one could question that if a person can avoid the effects of duress by escaping from the threats, without damage to himself, he must do so. In other words if there is a moment at which he is able to escape, so to speak, from the gun being held at his head by Hussey, or the equivalent of Hussey, he must do so. It seems to us to be part of the same argument, or at least to be so close to the same argument as to be practically indistinguishable from it, to say that a man must not voluntarily put himself in a position where he is likely to be subjected to such compulsion.
>
> . . . [W]e are fortified in the view which I indicate, which, to jump ahead, is that this is part of the common law and always has been, by certain matters which appear in the speeches of their Lordships in *DPP for Northern Ireland v Lynch* [1975] AC 653. Although *Lynch's* case has been the subject of certain adverse comment since the date of those speeches, nevertheless the passages to which we wish to refer have not, as far as we know, been the subject of criticism.
>
> First of all in the speech of Lord Morris of Borth-y-Gest appears this passage, at 668:
>
>> Where duress is in issue many questions may arise such as whether threats are serious and compelling or whether (as on the facts of the present case may specially call for consideration) a person the subject of duress could reasonably have extricated himself or could have sought protection or had what has been called a 'safe avenue of escape'. Other questions may arise such as whether a person is only under duress as a result of being in voluntary association with those whom he knew would require some course of action. In the present case, as duress was not left to the jury, we naturally do not know what they thought of it all.
>
> A little later Lord Morris of Borth-y-Gest again said, at p 670:
>
>> In posing the case where someone is 'really' threatened I use the word 'really' in order to emphasise that duress must never be allowed to be the easy answer of those who can devise no other explanation of their conduct nor of those who readily could have avoided the dominance of threats nor of those who allow themselves to be at the disposal and under the sway of some gangster-tyrant. Where duress becomes an issue courts and juries will surely consider the facts with care and discernment.
>
> Here of course, I interpolate, Hussey was the archetypal gangster-tyrant.
>
> I turn from Lord Morris of Borth-y-Gest to the speech of Lord Wilberforce, at 679:

It is clear that a possible case of duress, on the facts, could have been made. I say 'a possible case' because there were a number of matters which the jury would have had to consider if this defence had been left to them. Among these would have been whether Meehan, though uttering no express threats of death or serious injury, impliedly did so in such a way as to put the appellant in fear of death or serious injury; whether, if so, the threats continued to operate throughout the enterprise; whether the appellant had voluntarily exposed himself to a situation in which threats might be used against him if he did not participate in a criminal enterprise (the appellant denied that he had done so); whether the appellant had taken every opportunity open to him to escape from the situation of duress. In order to test the validity of the judge's decision to exclude this defence, we must assume on this appeal that these matters would have been decided in favour of the appellant.

Finally, so far as the passages in favour of the contention which we are supporting are concerned, in the speech of Lord Simon of Glaisdale appears this passage, at p 687:

I spoke of the social evils which might be attendant on the recognition of a general defence of duress. Would it not enable a gang leader of notorious violence to confer on his organisation by terrorism immunity from the criminal law? Every member of his gang might well be able to say with truth, 'It was as much as my life was worth to disobey'. Was this not in essence the plea of the appellant? We do not, in general, allow a superior officer to confer such immunity on his subordinates by any defence of obedience to orders: why should we allow it to terrorists? Nor would it seem to be sufficient to stipulate that no one can plead duress as a defence who has put himself into a position in which duress could be exercised on himself . . .

In other words, in our judgment, where a person has voluntarily, and with knowledge of its nature, joined a criminal organisation or gang which he knew might bring pressure on him to commit an offence and was an active member when he was put under such pressure, he cannot avail himself of the defence of duress . . .

R v Hasan [2005] UKHL 22

Hasan had worked for a period of time as a 'minder' for Claire Taeger, who ran an escort agency and was involved in prostitution. Hasan was subsequently succeeded in this role by a man named Sullivan who had a reputation for violence. Hasan's evidence was that he had been driven to a house by an associate of Sullivan's and told to commit a burglary under threat of serious harm. Having conceded to these threats Hasan was, in due course, charged with aggravated burglary.

In relation to the availability of the defence of duress the judge put four questions to the jury, the last of which was:

Did the defendant voluntarily put himself in the position in which he knew he was likely to be subjected to threats? If you are sure he did, the defence fails and he is guilty. If you are not sure, he is not guilty.

Hasan was convicted, but on appeal, the Court of Appeal allowed his appeal, holding that, the defence of duress would only be excluded where the defendant was aware of the risk that the group he was associating with might try to coerce him into committing criminal offences of the type for which he was being tried. The Crown appealed to the House of Lords, contending that the trial judge's directions on the third and fourth questions involved no misdirection, and that the direction on the first question was favourable to the defendant.

The certified question in relation to the fourth question posed by the trial judge was formulated in these terms:

> Whether the defence of duress is excluded when as a result of the accused's voluntary association with others:
>
> (i)   he foresaw (or possibly should have foreseen) the risk of being subjected to any compulsion by threats of violence, or
>
> (ii) only when he foresaw (or should have foreseen) the risk of being subjected to compulsion to commit criminal offences, and, if the latter,
>
> (iii) only if the offences foreseen (or which should have been foreseen) were of the same type (or possibly of the same type and gravity) as that ultimately committed.

The Crown argued in favour of (i) in its objective form. Hasan argued in favour of the third answer omitting the first parenthesis.

Deciding in favour of the Crown's arguments, and holding that *R v Baker and Ward* [1999] 2 Cr App R 335 mis-stated the law, Lord Bingham observed:

> To resolve that issue one must remind oneself [that the] . . . defendant is seeking to be wholly exonerated from the consequences of a crime deliberately committed. The prosecution must negative his defence of duress, if raised by the evidence, beyond reasonable doubt. The defendant is, *ex hypothesi*, a person who has voluntarily surrendered his will to the domination of another. Nothing should turn on foresight of the manner in which, in the event, the dominant party chooses to exploit the defendant's subservience. There need not be foresight of coercion to commit crimes, although it is not easy to envisage circumstances in which a party might be coerced to act lawfully . . . There remains the question . . . [of] . . . whether the defendant's foresight must be judged by a subjective or an objective test: i.e. does the defendant lose the benefit of a defence based on duress only if he actually foresaw the risk of coercion or does he lose it if he ought reasonably to have foreseen the risk of coercion, whether he actually foresaw the risk or not? I do not think any decided case has addressed this question, and I am conscious that application of an objective reasonableness test to other ingredients of duress has attracted criticism . . . The practical importance of the distinction in this context may not be very great, since if a jury concluded that a person voluntarily associating with known criminals ought reasonably to have foreseen the risk of future coercion they would not, I think, be very likely to accept that he did not in fact do so. But since there is a choice to be made, policy in my view points towards an objective test of what the defendant, placed as he was and knowing what he did, ought reasonably to have foreseen. I am not persuaded otherwise by analogies based on self-defence or provocation for reasons I have already given. The policy of the law must be to discourage association with known criminals, and it should be slow to excuse the criminal conduct of those who do so.

The correct direction on this issue, as restated by Lord Bingham, would now be as follows:

> If a person voluntarily becomes or remains associated with others engaged in criminal activity in a situation where he knows or ought reasonably to know that he may be the subject of compulsion by them or their associates, he cannot rely on the defence of duress to excuse any act which he is thereafter compelled to do by them.

Baroness Hale agreed that the Crown's appeal should be allowed, but dissented from the majority as regards the reformulation of the defence of duress. In particular she expressed concern that the formulation favoured by the majority might work unfairly in the case of a battered wife forced by her abusive partner to commit offences:

> The battered wife knows that she is exposing herself to a risk of unlawful violence if she lives [with an abusive partner] but she may have no reason to believe that her husband will eventually use her broken will to force her to commit crimes. For the same reason, I would say that it must be foreseeable that duress will be used to compel the person to commit crimes of some sort. I have no difficulty envisaging circumstances in which a person may be coerced to act lawfully. The battered wife knows very well that she may be compelled to cook the dinner, wash the dishes, iron the shirts and submit to sexual intercourse. That should not deprive her of the defence of duress if she is obliged by the same threats to herself or her children to commit perjury or shoplift for food . . . It is one thing to deny the defence [of duress] to people who choose to become members of illegal organisations, join criminal gangs, or engage with others in drug-related criminality. It is another thing to deny it to someone who has a quite different reason for becoming associated with the duressor and then finds it difficult to escape. I do not believe that this limitation on the defence is aimed at battered wives at all, or at others in close personal or family relationships with their duressors and their associates, such as their mothers, brothers or children. The Law Commission's Bills [setting out proposed reformulations of the defence of duress] all refer to a person who exposes himself to the risk 'without reasonable excuse'. The words were there to cater for the police infiltrator (see Law Com No 83, para 2.37) but they are also applicable to the sort of association I have in mind. The other elements of the defence, narrowly construed in accordance with existing authority, are more than adequate to keep it within bounds in such cases . . . [in relation to the certified question on this part of the appeal – see questions (i), (ii) and (iii) above] . . . I would have chosen option (ii), together with the further explanation of the concept of 'voluntary association with others'.

In summary, therefore, the ruling changes the defence of duress in three important respects:

(a) the defendant's belief in the duressor's threats of death or serious harm must be genuine and reasonable;

(b) a defendant who has a genuine opportunity to negate the effect of the threats, for example by going to the police, and fails to do so, will not be allowed to rely on the defence;

(c) the defence will no longer be available to a defendant who voluntarily associates with others whom he realised (or ought to have realised) would put him under pressure of any sort to commit a criminal act.

 COMMENTS AND QUESTIONS

1   Lord Lane CJ in *R v Graham* expresses the view that 'Provocation and duress are analogous'. To what extent is this a correct view in the light of *Attorney General for Jersey v Holley (Jersey)* [2005] UKPC 23, considered at Chapter 4.6.4.5?

2   Suppose D, a former member of a violent and ruthless criminal gang who has been 'going straight' for the last few years, is approached by X, a former partner in the criminal gang. X tells D that he must commit a burglary or D's family will be killed. Would D be able to avail himself of the defence of necessity?

3   Given that a defendant may raise the defence of self-defence if he honestly but mistakenly believes he is being attacked (see 14.11 below), why should a defendant who honestly but mistakenly believes that the threats constituting duress are genuine be treated any differently?

14.5 DURESS BY THREATS – CODIFICATION AND LAW REFORM PROPOSALS

The current views of the Law Commission are contained in its Report (Law Com No 304) *Murder, Manslaughter And Infanticide* published in November 2006. Assuming that its proposals for reforming the homicide offences were to be brought into effect – see the outline summary at Chapter 4.1.2 – the Commission supports the proposals that:

> duress should be a full defence to first degree murder, second degree murder and attempted murder.
>
> For duress to be a defence to first degree murder, second degree murder and attempted murder, the threat must be one of death or life-threatening harm.
>
> The defendant should bear the legal burden of proving the qualifying conditions of the defence on a balance of probabilities.

The report continues:

> *A full defence to first degree murder*
> 6.36 We acknowledge that the majority of consultees who favoured duress being a defence to first degree murder agreed with our provisional proposal that it should be a partial rather than a full defence to first degree murder. At the same time, a significant minority thought that it should be a full defence and, on balance, we are now persuaded that it should be.

6.37 Previously, the Commission has recommended that duress should be a full rather than a partial defence to murder:

> ... where the duress is so compelling that the defendant could not reasonably have been expected to resist it, perhaps being a threat not to the defendant himself but to an innocent hostage dear to him, it would be ... unjust that the defendant should suffer the stigma of a conviction even for manslaughter. We do not think that any social purpose is served by requiring the law to prescribe such standards of determination and heroism. [*Report on Defences of General Application* (1977) Law Com No 83, para 2.43 cited with approval by the Commission in *Legislating the Criminal Code: Offences against the Person and General Principles* (1993) Law Com No 218, para 30.17.]

6.38 In the CP, we provisionally proposed a different approach in relation to first degree murder. There were two main reasons:

(1) we thought it important that there should be consistency with the partial defences of provocation and diminished responsibility, both of which we were proposing should reduce first degree murder to second degree murder;

(2) it would not be right for a person who had intentionally killed to be completely exonerated.

Reasons for questioning our provisional proposal that duress should be a partial defence to first degree murder

6.39 We now believe that, in this context, we exaggerated the importance of treating duress in a manner that was consistent with the way provocation and diminished responsibility fitted into our proposed structure. Professor Ormerod commented:

> ... I am not convinced that duress has been shown to be sufficiently similar to provocation and diminished responsibility to warrant like treatment. An argument could be made that it ought to be treated like self-defence, and therefore ought to afford a complete defence. In truth, the defence is distinct from all of the others. It has a strong objective element which allies it with provocation, and it focuses on external pressures triggering a response, but it is a defence in which D has made a more calculated choice. Similarly, with diminished responsibility, the defences might be regarded as excuses (whatever that may mean), but duress is very different from the quasi-medicalised defence (unless we are treating them both as some form of diminished capacity defence).

6.40 We also acknowledge that we exaggerated the strength of the case for duress being a partial defence to first degree murder merely because, under our proposals, there would be more categories of murder. We now accept that, while having more categories of murder may make it easier to effect a compromise between competing views, the mere fact that there are more categories of murder does not assist in deciding whether or not as a matter of principle duress should be a full defence to first degree murder.

6.41 In the CP, we stressed that if D intentionally kills he or she deserves to be stigmatised despite killing under duress. However, we now believe that we paid insufficient attention to the fact that, for the defence to succeed, D must satisfy the very stringent requirements of the defence including satisfying a jury that a reasonable person, sharing his or her characteristics, might have acted in the way that D did.

6.42 Further, during the consultation process it became clear that significant anomalies might arise were duress to be a partial defence to some homicide offences but a full defence (or no defence) to others. It is hard, for example, to see why duress should be a full defence (or no defence) to attempted murder but a partial defence to first degree murder, given that only chance may distinguish whether the one offence or the other has been committed. While it might not be impossible to find a justification in relation to each individual offence, the overall structure threatens to become incoherent.

Reasons for concluding that duress should be a full defence to first degree murder

6.43 The argument that duress should be a full defence to first degree murder has a moral basis. It is that the law should not stigmatise a person who, on the basis of a genuine and reasonably held belief, intentionally killed in fear of death or life-threatening injury in circumstances where a jury is satisfied that an ordinary person of reasonable fortitude might have acted in the same way. If a reasonable person might have acted as D did, then the argument for withholding a complete defence is undermined. In the words of Professor Ormerod, 'if the jury find that the defendant has, within the terms of the defence, acted reasonably, it seems unfair to treat him as a second degree murderer or even a manslaughterer'.

6.44 Further, the option also accords with the way that duress operates as a complete defence in relation to other offences and it is, therefore, conducive to coherence and consistency as we pointed out above.

6.45 One respondent who favoured duress being a partial defence to first degree murder did so because he thought that this was the best way of accommodating each side in the moral debate. We see the force of this argument. However, we believe that if the arguments of principle and morality point decidedly in one direction, our recommendation should reflect what we believe to be a principled approach rather than one based on a desire to accommodate the different viewpoints.

6.46 An important counter-argument is that the law rightly attaches special sanctity to innocent human life and that this should preclude duress ever being a full defence to first degree murder. We now depart from this view, in so far as we believe that the 'sanctity of life' argument was not meant to deal with examples such as ten-year-olds or peripheral secondary parties becoming involved in killing under duress. The 'sanctity of life' argument may be more confusing than illuminating in this context.

6.47 Those who are opposed to duress being a full defence to first degree murder argue that cases of intentional killing under duress can never be completely deserving of excuse, but some are more deserving of excuse than others. For that reason, so the argument runs, duress should result in a conviction of second degree murder where the sentence can reflect the circumstances of each case.

6.48 Of course, views may differ as to what makes a case more or less deserving of excuse. For example, some, but not all, will think that a person is more deserving of excuse if he or she commits first degree murder under duress in order to secure a net gain of life. Alternatively, some will believe that those who commit first degree murder under duress in order to save the life of an innocent third party are more deserving of excuse than those who do so to save themselves, particularly if the killing also secures a net gain of life. Others will point to the case of a secondary party such as a taxi driver who is threatened with death unless he or she drives a gang to a location where he or she knows they are intending to kill a householder.

6.49 By contrast, others will point to the case of a drug addict who, threatened by his or her supplier to whom he or she is in debt, commits a murder to placate his or her supplier to whom he or she owes money.

6.50 Although, amongst those who would prefer duress to be a partial defence to first degree murder, there may not be unanimity as to what makes a case more (or less) deserving, they are as one in stressing the range of circumstances in which duress may be pleaded. In their view, what is required is a flexible sentencing regime which, while recognising that a person who intentionally kills under duress ought always to be stigmatised, allows the trial judge to pass a suitably severe or lenient sentence depending on the circumstances.

6.51 We see the attraction of this view. However, we believe that there is more force in the views expressed by consultees who believe that duress should be a complete defence to first degree murder. For example, the Criminal Bar Association argued that, if duress were not a complete defence to first degree murder, it would give the impression that, in law, 'it is better to prevent the death of a stranger than to prevent the death of one's children'. Similarly, Mr Justice Elias said that withholding duress as a complete defence implies that the criminal law should support the view that 'people ought to act in an exceptionally moral and courageous way. They are being punished for giving way to what will often be enormous fear and wholly understandable human frailty'.

6.52 We also think it important to bear in mind the stringent qualifying conditions that attach to the defence. In particular, the majority of the House of Lords in [R v Hasan] were firmly of the view that the defence ought not to be available to D if he or she saw or ought to have foreseen the risk of being subjected to any compulsion by threats of violence. We believe that this will serve to exclude the most unmeritorious cases where the defence should simply not be available. It is true that it will not in itself exclude all undeserving cases but we believe that juries should be trusted not to accept the defence in undeserving cases.

6.53 Above all, we believe that it is essential to recognise and accord proper weight to the fact that for the defence to succeed, a jury must form a judgment that a reasonable person in D's position might have committed first degree murder. If a jury forms that judgment, we believe that D should be completely exonerated despite having intentionally killed.

Distinguishing cases according to whether or not the defendant acted in response to a threat against his or her own person

6.54 We have considered whether it would be appropriate to distinguish cases of duress according to whether D has intentionally killed in order to save the life of an innocent third party as opposed to his or her own life. Some believe that there is a clear moral difference between acting on a threat directed at another and acting on a threat directed at oneself. However, we believe that it would be unsatisfactory to recommend reform based on such a distinction.

6.55 Consider these examples. A child is threatened with life-threatening harm by his or her psychopathic father unless he or she helps him to perpetrate a murder. A pregnant woman is threatened with death unless she kills V. She yields to the threat in order to safeguard the life of her unborn baby who, while in the womb, has no legal recognition for the purposes of the criminal law, apart from the offences of child destruction, attempting to procure a miscarriage and offences under the Abortion Act 1967. An uncle threatened with death commits murder in order to preserve his own life so that he can donate a kidney to his desperately ill nephew. In our view, it would be wrong to deny such persons a complete defence merely because they acted in order to preserve their own lives.

Distinguishing between principal offenders and secondary parties

6.56 We have also considered whether it would be appropriate to distinguish cases depending on whether D was a principal offender or a secondary party. At one stage, we were inclined to do so. However, for two reasons, we believe that it would be undesirable.

6.57 First, it assumes, wrongly, that a secondary party acting under duress is necessarily less culpable than a principal offender acting under duress. For example, a husband and his wife are told that their child will be killed unless they kill V who is the husband's brother. They agree that the wife will perpetrate the killing and the husband will keep watch. It would be wrong to afford the husband but not the wife a complete defence. Likewise, a psychopathic father threatens his child with serious physical harm unless the child commits a murder while the father keeps watch. We believe that, unhesitatingly, most people would brand the father as the more culpable. The jury should be trusted to employ the objective test to distinguish deserving from undeserving cases, without this added legal complication.

6.58 Further, it would put a premium on determining whether someone was a principal offender or a secondary party. For example, a husband and wife are threatened that their child will be killed unless they kill V. They decide to kill V by poisoning. Before V joins them for lunch, together they measure out a fatal dose of strychnine which the wife sprinkles over V's soup. V drinks the soup and dies. On one view, the wife is the principal offender because she is the most direct and immediate cause of V's death. Her husband is a secondary party. Suppose, however, that, in order to introduce the fatal dose into V's soup, the husband lifts V's soup bowl across the dining table and then, after the wife ladles out the soup, replaces the bowl. Alternatively, the husband's sole contribution is to pass a spoon to V. We believe that to make the liability of the husband and wife dependent on whether or not one was a principal offender and the other a secondary party would result in liability being dependent on fine distinctions that would reflect poorly on the law, particularly where the issue is whether one or other, or both, is guilty of first degree murder.

Consistency with provocation and diminished responsibility

6.59 It might be thought that our recommendation is inconsistent with our recommendations that provocation and diminished responsibility should operate as no more than partial defences to first degree murder.

6.60 On the assumption that provocation, diminished responsibility and duress are all defences that operate by way of excusing D, the way that the current law treats these defences is illogical. Provocation and diminished responsibility each has a weaker moral claim to excusatory status in the law of murder than duress. It is true that provocation is grounded on the view that D has lost his or her self-control whereas in cases of duress D has made a conscious, albeit an unwilling, choice. It is also true that in cases of diminished responsibility, D is partially excused because it is recognised that his or her responsibility for intentionally killing is lessened. However, in cases of provocation and diminished responsibility, D has not killed in order to preserve innocent life and yet he or she has a partial excuse. By contrast, a person who pleads duress is one who has sought to avoid the death of or serious physical harm to an innocent person (not necessarily him or herself) by doing no more than is required to avert that harm. Yet, provocation and diminished responsibility excuse murder while duress does not.

6.61 More importantly, it is inappropriate to characterise duress as an excusatory defence in the same way that provocation and diminished responsibility are excusatory. Although it cannot be said of all cases, some instances of duress come close to being a justification for killing rather than an excuse. To give an example of duress of circumstances, the roped climber who cuts the rope after his or her companion has accidentally slipped and is dragging them both to oblivion is a case in point. The same claim cannot be made in respect of either provocation or diminished responsibility. No act of killing comes close to being justified if committed solely in response to provocation or as a result of diminished responsibility. Viewed in this light, the case for distinguishing duress from provocation and diminished responsibility becomes more compelling.

6.62 The fact that we are recommending a reformulated partial defence of provocation does not detract from the above. It would be wrong to conclude that the reformulation, by removing the loss of self-control requirement and at the same time requiring that D must have a "justifiable sense of having been seriously wronged", places the defence on a justificatory basis. The first limb of the reformulation is seeking to do two things. First, it avoids the well-known problems caused by the loss of self-control requirement. Secondly, it is emphasising that the provocation must be of such gravity that if a person responds to it by intentionally killing, he or she merits being partially excused despite his or her conduct lacking any justification.

6.63 The second limb of the reformulated partial defence of provocation focuses on an intentional killing in response to a fear of serious violence. At first blush, it might be thought that this places the defence on a more justificatory footing. However, it is important to emphasise that the defence comes into play only if the justificatory defence of self-defence is unavailable or unsuccessful. If self-defence is unavailable or unsuccessful it will be because D used an unreasonable amount of force in the circumstances. In such cases D's conduct cannot be characterised as justified.

. . .

A possible refinement of our recommendation

6.66 Under our recommendation, duress would be a full defence to first degree murder if D satisfies the qualifying conditions on a balance of probabilities and the jury concludes that a sober person of reasonable fortitude in the circumstances of D might have committed first degree murder.

6.67 However, we envisage that in some cases, while D may be able to satisfy the qualifying conditions, the jury will conclude that no sober person of reasonable fortitude in the circumstances of D would have committed first degree murder. We believe that such cases are much more likely to arise if D is a principal offender as opposed to a secondary party.

6.68 It would be possible to adopt an 'all or nothing' approach by virtue of which D would either be convicted of first degree murder or completely exonerated depending on whether or not he or she satisfies all the elements of the defence. However, that might be thought to be too severe on those who had proved that they genuinely and reasonably believed that they, or a person for whom they reasonably felt responsible, would be killed or very seriously harmed unless they committed first degree murder.

6.69 In such cases, a conviction for second degree murder would recognise the perilous circumstances in which, without any fault on their part, they had (or reasonably thought they had) been placed while acknowledging that they ought to be convicted of a very serious offence because no reasonable person would have acted as they did.

. . .

Additional recommendations: Fear of death or life-threatening harm

6.73 A large majority of consultees were in favour of the proposal that for duress to be a defence to murder or attempted murder, then the threat must be one of death or life-threatening harm.

6.74 It is true that, under the current law, the defence can succeed if the threat was one of death or serious harm, whether or not life-threatening harm. However, we believe that the special harm involved or intended in cases of first degree murder, second degree murder and attempted murder justifies a higher threshold.

6.75 We are conscious that some consultees have reservations about the threat having to be one of life-threatening harm. Some believe that it would exclude deserving cases such as a parent witnessing his or her child being tortured. Others believe that the concept 'life-threatening' is too vague and ambiguous. However, it is important to recognise that the threat does not have to be objectively life-threatening. It is the reasonableness of D's perception of the threat that is critical. D would have to prove that he or she honestly and reasonably believed that the nature of the threat was such that, if implemented, would involve a risk to life. The jury would be entitled to take into account the age and vulnerability of the person being threatened with harm. Thus, a jury might well conclude that D reasonably believed that a threat of torture to his or her five-year-old child involved a risk of life-threatening harm while taking a different view if the threat of torture was directed at D's spouse.

6.76 We recommend that for duress to be a full defence to first degree murder, second degree murder and attempted murder, the threat must be one of death or life-threatening harm.

Additional recommendations: Reasonably held belief

6.77 We did not pose a direct question to consultees as to whether D's belief that a threat of death or life-threatening harm had been made and would be implemented had to be reasonably held. A few consultees questioned the need for the belief to be reasonably held. It was suggested that the requirement was unnecessary because a jury would be unlikely to conclude that an unreasonable belief was an honestly held belief. One consultee thought that a reasonableness requirement would make it more difficult for children and the mentally vulnerable to make out the defence.

6.78 Previously the Law Commission has expressed support for the proposition that D's belief should only have to be honestly held. Further, neither provocation nor self-defence imports a test of reasonableness. However, in this respect, there are important differences between duress, on the one hand, and provocation and self-defence, on the other hand. The defence of duress revolves around a threat of death or serious-harm that will materialise at some point in the future should D not do what he or she has been told to do. Typically, D will have time to reflect on and assess the nature and strength of the threat. As Professor Ormerod commented, 'D has made a more calculated choice'.

6.79 By contrast, in cases of provocation and self-defence, typically there is a more immediate temporal or physical nexus between the actions of the victim (V) and the action of D that is precipitated by the actions of V. In relation to self-defence, the law recognises this even in relation to that aspect of the defence – the degree of force used by D – where there is a reasonableness requirement . . .

6.80 It is clear that at common law, D's belief in the existence of the threat and that it will be implemented must be reasonably held. It would be anomalous that if D is pleading duress as a defence to theft his or her belief in the existence of the threat must be reasonably held but not if D is pleading duress as a defence to first degree murder, second degree murder or attempted murder.

6.81 At the same time, we see no reason why the particular circumstances of D should not be capable of being taken into account in determining whether or not his or her belief was reasonably held. This would enable account to be taken of the age and vulnerability of D. It would also accord with the decision in *Martin* (David Paul). The Court of Appeal held that expert testimony that D was suffering from a recognised psychiatric condition which made him more likely than others to regard things said or done as threatening and to believe that they would be carried out was admissible evidence. We do not believe that [*R v Hasan*] casts doubt on that decision.

6.82 Contrary to the view that we have previously expressed, we now believe that for duress to be a full defence to first degree murder, second degree murder and attempted murder, the defendant's belief as to the existence of the threat and to its being implemented must be not only honestly held but also reasonably held.

Additional recommendations: The defendant's characteristics for the purpose of the objective limb of the defence

6.83 Two consultees, Professor Ronnie Mackay and Nicola Padfield, disagreed with our proposal that the relevant characteristics should not include those which bear on D's capacity to withstand duress. Professor Mackay argued that to alter the common law rule in *Bowen*, in which it was held that relevant characteristics include psychiatric syndromes and mental illnesses, would be unfair and is driven by a suggested need for consistency with provocation. Professor Mackay argues that the two pleas are very different in nature. Professor Mackay further argues that it is speculative to suggest that the decision in *Attorney General for Jersey v Holley* [2005] UKHL 22, [2005] 2 AC 467 will mean that *Bowen* will no longer be followed.

6.84 Despite Professor Mackay and Nicola Padfield's objections, we believe that in deciding whether a person of reasonable firmness would have acted as D did in a case of first degree murder, second degree murder and attempted murder, the jury should be able to take into account all of the circumstances of D, including his or her age, other than those which bear upon his or her capacity to withstand duress. This recommendation is consistent with our recommended reformulation of the partial defence of provocation. We believe that it would be anomalous if there were to be a significant distinction between the characteristics that are relevant to provocation and duress.

6.85 We appreciate that our recommendation, if implemented, would result in a narrower test for first degree murder, second degree murder and attempted murder than the *Bowen* test which would apply to all other offences. However, we consider that this is justified for two reasons. First, given the seriousness of the harm caused (or intended) in cases of first degree murder, second degree murder and attempted murder, it is important that a strict objective standard is maintained to limit the scope of the defence. Secondly, unlike other offences, the partial defence of diminished responsibility would be available to mentally disordered persons charged with first degree murder. We acknowledge that, under our recommendations, diminished responsibility would not be available to those charged with second degree murder or attempted murder. However, since both these offences attract a discretionary life sentence, any mental disorder can be taken into account in sentencing.

6.86 We believe that, in deciding whether a person of reasonable firmness might have acted as the defendant did, the jury should be able to take into account all the circumstances of the defendant, including his or her age but not any other characteristics which bear upon his or her capacity to withstand duress.

. . .

Burden of proof to be consistent between first degree murder and second degree murder
6.140 As we stated at paragraph 6.90, in the further consultation that we undertook, we asked whether the burden of proof should be the same for first degree murder and second degree murder. All consultees were of the view that the burden of proof should be the same for first degree murder and second degree murder.

6.141 We recommend that on a charge of first degree murder, second degree murder and attempted murder, the defendant should bear the legal burden of proving the qualifying conditions of the defence of duress on a balance of probabilities.

14.6 DURESS OF CIRCUMSTANCES

The defence of duress of circumstance is effectively coterminous with duress *per minas*, both in terms of the direction given to the jury and the offences in respect of which it is available (i.e. duress of circumstances cannot be raised as a defence to murder or attempted murder). What distinguishes the two forms of duress is the nature of the threat. With duress *per minas* X is saying to D 'Rob the bank or I'll kill you!' With duress of circumstances, X need not specify the offence to be committed by D. D fears death or grievous bodily harm will occur simply because of X's words or actions (for example where X is a member of an angry mob gesticulating at D), and commits the offence in question (for example driving away in excess of the speed limit) in order to avoid such harm occurring. It may even be the case that D's compulsion arises from natural causes, where, for example D exceeds the speed limit, or drives with excess alcohol, because he needs to move his car from the vicinity of a blazing building.

R v Willer (1986) 83 Cr App R 225 (CA)

The appellant was convicted of reckless driving. He contended that he had been confronted by a gang of shouting and bawling youths, 20–30 strong, one of whom had shouted: 'I'll kill you, Willer'. The appellant realised that the only conceivable way he could escape from the gang of youths was to mount the pavement and drive through a small gap into the front of a shopping precinct. The Court of Appeal considered the availability of duress of circumstances.

Watkins LJ:
. . . one begins with the reasons advanced by the assistant recorder for declaring that the defence of necessity was not available to the appellant. He seems to have based himself upon the

proposition, though saying that necessity was a defence known to English law, that it was not, albeit available to the appellant in respect of the journey through the gap into the car park in front of the shopping precinct, available to him upon the return journey because he was not at that stage being besieged by the gang of youths. We feel bound to say that it would have been for the jury to decide, if necessity could have been a defence at all in those circumstances, whether the whole incident should be regarded as one, or could properly be regarded as two separate incidents so as to enable them to say that necessity applied in one instance but not in the other. For that reason alone the course adopted by the assistant recorder was we think seriously at fault. Beyond that upon the issue of necessity we see no need to go further, for what we deem to have been appropriate in these circumstances to raise as a defence by the appellant was duress. The appellant in effect said: 'I could do no other in the face of this hostility than to take the right turn as I did, to mount the pavement and to drive through the gap out of further harm's way, harm to person and harm to my property.' Thus the offence of duress, it seems to us, arose but was not pursued. What ought to have happened therefore was that the assistant recorder upon those facts should have directed that he would leave to the jury the question as to whether or not upon the outward or the return journey, or both, the appellant was wholly driven by force of circumstance into doing what he did and did not drive the car otherwise than under that form of compulsion, i.e. under duress . . .

R v Conway [1989] 1 QB 290 (CA)

The appellant was convicted of reckless driving. He had driven off at high speed, ignoring a 'No Entry' sign, when two plain-clothes police officers had approached his car and asked to speak to a man called Tonna who was a passenger in the appellant's car. The appellant contended that he had not known that the two men were police officers and that he feared for Tonna's safety because of attempts on Tonna's life six weeks previous to this incident. The Court of Appeal considered the availability of duress of circumstances.

Woolf LJ:

. . . We conclude that necessity can only be a defence to a charge of reckless driving where the facts establish 'duress of circumstances', as in *R v Willer* 83 Cr App R 225, i.e. where the defendant was constrained by circumstances to drive as he did to avoid death or serious bodily harm to himself or some other person.

As the editors point out in Smith and Hogan, *Criminal Law*, 6th edn, 1988, p 225, to admit a defence of 'duress of circumstances' is a logical consequence of the existence of the defence of duress as that term is ordinarily understood, i.e. 'do this or else'. This approach does no more than recognise that duress is an example of necessity. Whether 'duress of circumstances' is called 'duress' or 'necessity' does not matter. What is important is that, whatever it is called, it is subject to the same limitations as 'do this or else' species of duress. As Lord Hailsham of St Marylebone LC said in his speech in *R v Howe* [1987] AC 417 at 429:

There is, of course, an obvious distinction between duress and necessity as potential defences; duress arises from the wrongful threats or violence of another human being and necessity arises from any other objective dangers threatening the accused. This, however, is . . . a distinction without a relevant difference, since on this view of duress it is only that species of the genus of necessity which is caused by wrongful threats. I cannot see that there is any way in which a person of ordinary fortitude can be excused from the one type of pressure on his will rather than the other . . .

It follows that a defence of 'duress of circumstances' is available only if from an objective standpoint the defendant can be said to be acting in order to avoid a threat of death or serious injury. The approach must be that indicated by Lord Lane CJ in *R v Graham (Paul)* [1982] 1 WLR 294 at 300 . . .

Adopting the approach indicated by Lord Lane CJ, and not that argued by [counsel for the appellant], which involved a subjective element, we ask ourselves whether the judge in the Crown Court should have left the defence of 'duress of circumstances' to the jury, notwithstanding the submission made by his counsel that it was 'impossible to run the defence of necessity . . . or indeed (to) leave it to the jury'.

On the facts alleged by the appellant we are constrained to hold that the judge was obliged to do so, notwithstanding his counsel's submission at the hearing . . . [H]is client's defence was that he drove as he did because he was in fear for his life and that of Tonna. Although it is unlikely that the outcome of the jury's deliberations would have been any different, they should have been directed as to the possibility that they could find the appellant not guilty because of duress of circumstances, although they were otherwise satisfied that he had driven recklessly . . .

R v Martin [1989] 1 All ER 652 (CA)

The appellant was convicted of driving whilst disqualified. His wife has suicidal tendencies. On a number of occasions before the day in question she had attempted to take her own life. On the day in question her son, the appellant's stepson, had overslept. He had done so to the extent that he was bound to be late for work and at risk of losing his job (it was claimed) unless the appellant drove him to work. The appellant's case was that he genuinely believed that his wife would carry out her threat of suicide unless he did as she demanded. Despite his being disqualified from driving, therefore, the appellant drove his stepson to his place of work. En route he was apprehended by the police. The Court of Appeal considered the availability of duress of circumstances as a defence.

Simon Brown J:

. . . Sceptically though one may regard that defence on the facts (and there were, we would observe, striking difficulties about the detailed evidence when it came finally to be given before the judge in mitigation), the sole question before this court is whether those facts, had the jury accepted they were or might be true, amounted in law to a defence. If they did, then the appellant was entitled to a trial of the issue before the jury. The jury would of course have had to be directed properly on the precise scope and nature of the defence, but the decision on the facts would have been for them. As it was, such a defence was pre-empted by the ruling. Should it have been?

In our judgment the answer is plainly not. The authorities are now clear. Their effect is perhaps most conveniently to be found in the judgment of this court in *R v Conway* [1988] 3 WLR 1238. The decision reviews earlier relevant authorities.

The principles may be summarised thus: first, English law does in extreme circumstances recognise a defence of necessity. Most commonly this defence arises as duress, that is pressure on the accused's will from the wrongful threats or violence of another. Equally however it can arise from other objective dangers threatening the accused or others. Arising thus it is conveniently called 'duress of circumstances'.

Second, the defence is available only if, from an objective standpoint, the accused can be said to be acting reasonably and proportionately in order to avoid a threat of death or serious injury.

Third, assuming the defence to be open to the accused on his account of the facts, the issue should be left to the jury, who should be directed to determine these two questions: first, was the accused, or may he have been, impelled to act as he did because as a result of what he reasonably believed to be the situation he had good cause to fear that otherwise death or serious physical injury would result; second, if so, would a sober person of reasonable firmness, sharing the characteristics of the accused, have responded to that situation by acting as the accused acted? If the answer to both those questions was Yes, then the jury would acquit; the defence of necessity would have been established.

That the defence is available in cases of reckless driving is established by *R v Conway* itself and indeed by an earlier decision of the court in *R v Willer* (1986) 83 Cr App R 225. *R v Conway* is authority also for the proposition that the scope of the defence is no wider for reckless driving than for other serious offences. As was pointed out in the judgment, 'reckless driving can kill' (see [1988] 3 WLR 1238 at 1244).

We see no material distinction between offences of reckless driving and driving whilst disqualified so far as the application and scope of this defence is concerned. Equally we can see no distinction in principle between various threats of death; it matters not whether the risk of death is by murder or by suicide or indeed by accident. One can illustrate the latter by considering a disqualified driver being driven by his wife, she suffering a heart attack in remote countryside and he needing instantly to get her to hospital.

It follows from this that the judge quite clearly did come to a wrong decision on the question of law, and the appellant should have been permitted to raise this defence for what it was worth before the jury . . .

R v Pommell [1995] 2 Cr App R 607 (CA)

The appellant's home was searched under warrant and a loaded gun found. When questioned the appellant stated: 'I took it off a geezer who was going to do some people some damage with it . . . Last night someone come round to see me, this guy by the name of Erroll, and he had it with him with the intention to go and shoot some people because they had killed his friend and he wanted to kill their girlfriends and relatives and kids, and I persuade him, I took it off him and told him that it's not right to do that.' The appellant, in due course, advanced the defence of duress of circumstances in respect of the charge of possessing an unlicensed firearm.

Kennedy LJ:

. . . Before us there is substantially one ground of appeal. It is that the judge should not have ruled as he did and when he did in relation to the defence of necessity. [Counsel] for the appellant contends that the defence which he was seeking to advance should not have been so summarily dismissed. Evidence should have been called in the normal way, and then, if the evidence emerged as was anticipated, the judge should have left to the jury the issue of whether or not the defence of necessity was made out . . .

. . . [W]e turn to consider the defence of necessity. There is an obvious attraction in the argument that if A finds B in possession of a gun which he is about to use to commit a crime, and if A is then able to persuade B to hand over the gun so that A may hand it to the police, A should not immediately upon taking possession of the gun become guilty of a criminal offence. However, if that is right, then in 1974, at least in the result, the case of *Woodage v Moss* was wrongly decided.

The strength of the argument that a person ought to be permitted to breach the letter of the criminal law in order to prevent a greater evil befalling himself or others has long been recognised (see, for example, Stephen's *Digest of Criminal Law*), but it has, in English law, not given rise to a recognised general defence of necessity, and in relation to the charge of murder, the defence has been specifically held not to exist (see *Dudley and Stephens* (1884) 14 QBD 273). Even in relation to other offences, there are powerful arguments against recognising the general defence. As Dickson J said in the Supreme Court of Canada in *Perka et al v R* (1985) 13 DLR (4th) 1 at 14:

. . . no system of positive law can recognise any principle which would entitle a person to violate the law because in his view the law conflicted with some higher social value.

The Criminal Code has specified a number of identifiable situations in which an actor is justified in committing what would otherwise be a criminal offence. To go beyond that and hold that ostensibly illegal acts can be validated on the basis of their expediency, would import an undue subjectivity into the criminal law. It would invite the courts to second-guess the legislature and to assess the relative merits of social policies underlying criminal prohibitions.

However, that does not really deal with the situation where someone commendably infringes a regulation in order to prevent another person from committing what everyone would accept as being a greater evil with a gun. In that situation it cannot be satisfactory to leave it to the prosecuting authority not to prosecute, or to individual courts to grant an absolute discharge. The authority may, as in the present case, prosecute because it is not satisfied that the defendant is telling the truth, and then, even if he is vindicated and given an absolute discharge, he is left with a criminal conviction which, for some purposes, would be recognised as such.

It was, as it seems to us, to meet this difficulty that the limited defence of duress of circumstances has been developed in English law in relation to road traffic offences. It was first recognised in *Willer* (1986) 83 Cr App R 225, where the accused drove onto a pavement and in and out of a shopping centre in order to escape a gang of youths seeking to attack him and his passenger. *Willer* was followed and applied in *Conway* (1989) 88 Cr App R 159, in which the Court of Appeal quashed a conviction on a charge of reckless driving. Having considered existing authorities, textbooks and the proposals of the Law Commission, the court in that case said at 164:

. . . it is still not clear whether there is a general defence of necessity or, if there is, what are the circumstances in which it is available.

In our judgment, that is still the position, but the court in *Conway* went on to say that necessity can be a defence to a charge of reckless driving where the facts establish duress of circumstances, that is to say when the defendant is constrained to drive as he did to avoid death or serious bodily harm to himself or some other person.

Then came *Martin*, a decision to which we referred earlier in this judgment, and *DPP v Bell* [1992] RTR 335, where the defendant, whose alcohol level was over the prescribed limit, was pursued to his car and, fearing serious injury, drove some distance down the road. The Crown Court allowed his appeal on the basis of duress of circumstances, and an appeal by way of case stated was dismissed. The Divisional Court particularly noted the finding of fact that the appellant drove only some distance down the road and not, for example, all the way home, so that the defence of duress of circumstances continued to avail him. In *DPP v Jones* [1990] RTR 33, it was held that any defence of necessity available to a driver would cease to be available if he drove for a longer period than necessary. Commenting on the case of *Bell*, Professor Sir John Smith has written:

> All the cases so far have concerned road traffic offences but there are no grounds for supposing that the defence is limited to that kind of case. On the contrary, the defence, being closely related to the defence of duress by threats, appears to be general, applying to all crimes except murder, attempted murder and some forms of treason . . . (See [1992] Crim LR 176.)

We agree.

That leads us to the conclusion that in the present case the defence was open to the appellant in respect of his acquisition of the gun. The jury would have to be directed to determine the two questions identified in the passage which we have cited from the judgment in *Martin*. That leaves the question as to his continued possession of the gun thereafter. In our judgment, the test laid down in *Martin* is not necessarily the appropriate test for determining whether a person continues to have a defence available to him. For example, a person takes a gun off another in the circumstances in which this appellant says he did and then locks it away in a safe with a view to safeguarding it while the police are informed. When the gun is in the safe, the test laid down in *Martin* may not be satisfied: there would then be no immediate fear of death or serious injury. In our judgment, a person who has taken possession of a gun in circumstances where he has the defence of duress by circumstances must 'desist from committing the crime as soon as he reasonably can' (Smith and Hogan, *Criminal Law*, 7th edn, p 239). This test is similar to the test in *Jones*, to which we have already referred. In deciding whether a defendant acted reasonably, regard would be had to the circumstances in which he finds himself. Can it be said, in this case, that there was no evidence upon which a jury could have reached the conclusion that the appellant did desist, or may have desisted, as soon as he reasonably could? In answering this question, the jury would have to have regard to the delay that had occurred between, on the appellant's account, his acquisition of the gun and ammunition at 12.30 to 1 am, and the arrival of the police some hours later. The appellant has offered an explanation for that delay but, as it seems to us, the defence of duress of circumstances could not avail him once a reasonable person in his position would have known that the duress, in this case the need to obtain and retain the firearm, had ceased. In the present case the judge said that the failure of the appellant to go immediately to the police 'robs him of a defence'. We accept that in some cases a delay, especially if unexplained, may be such as to make it clear that any duress must have ceased to operate, in which case the judge would be entitled to conclude that even on the defendant's own account of the facts, the defence was not open to him. There would then be no reason to leave the issue to the jury. However, the situation does not seem to us to have been sufficiently clear cut to make that an appropriate step in the present case. In the first place, the delay of a few hours overnight might not be regarded as being unduly long and, second, the defendant did offer an explanation for it, therefore, in our judgment, the proposed defence should have been left to the jury.

We have considered whether the reloading of the gun and the fact that the appellant had the gun in his bed deprived him of the defence. Must a person who has acquired a gun in circumstances in which he has the defence of duress of circumstances not only desist from committing the offence as soon as he reasonably can but, in the meanwhile, act in a reasonable manner with the gun? The answer is that if he does not do so, it will be difficult for the court to accept that he desisted from committing the offence as soon as he reasonably could. Therefore, in our judgment, the acts of reloading and putting the gun in the bed do not of themselves deprive him of the defence, but are matters which may be taken into account by the jury in deciding the issues to which we have already made reference . . .

14.6.1 POLICY LIMITATIONS ON DURESS OF CIRCUMSTANCE

In *R v Martin* (above) the suicidal tendencies of the appellant's wife were accepted by the court as laying a foundation for the defence of duress of circumstances. Contrast this with *R v Rodger and Another* (1997) *The Times,* 30 July, where the Court of Appeal refused to allow a plea of duress of circumstance in respect of an appellant who had escaped from prison citing his own suicidal tendencies as the basis for the defence. The court held that the defence had to be based on something extraneous to the appellant. The issue has subsequently arisen in a number of cases involving defendants convicted of offences under the Misuse of Drugs Act 1971 in respect of their use of cannabis as an alternative pain killer. The defendant claimed that they had acted under duress of circumstances (i.e. forced by the absence of any other effective remedy) in possessing and cultivating the drug. As will be seen from the extracts below, the court have not been willing to accept these arguments, partly because the circumstances were not extraneous to the appellants, but primarily because to allow the defence would introduce uncertainty into the operation of the 1971 Act, and would also undermine the legislative framework. The contention that not permitting the defence of necessity in these circumstances would amount to inhuman and degrading treatment in breach of Art 3 of the European Convention on Human Rights was rejected by the Court of Appeal in *R v Altham* [2006] EWCA Crim 7.

R v Quale and other appeals; *Attorney General's Reference (No 2 of 2004)* [2005] EWCA Crim 1415.

The Court of Appeal considered a numner of appeals, and a reference from the Attorney-General raising the issue of whether the defence of duress of circumstance could be raised in respect of the medicinal use of cannabis where defendants were charged with offences under the Misuse of Drugs Act 1971.

Mance LJ (having reviewed the authorities):

[53]. In the light of these authorities, we are not persuaded by Mr Fitzgerald's [counsel for one of the defendant] attempts to derive from individual authorities in different areas a coherent overarching principle applicable in all cases of necessity. Such an attempt appears to us to pay too little attention to the particular context of individual decisions, and not to correspond with the

case-by-case approach suggested by the authorities. However, there is a recognised defence of duress by threats, to which it is clear that the defence of necessity by circumstances bears a close affinity. Save that, in the present cases at least, the offences in question are not readily seen as involving any individual victim, the arguments which Lord Bingham mentioned in *Hasan* in favour of a confined definition appear to us applicable to any defence of necessity by circumstances.

. . .

56. The necessitous medical use on an individual basis which is at the root of the defences suggested by all the appellants . . . is in conflict with the purpose and effect of the legislative scheme. First, no such use is permitted under the present legislation, even on doctor's prescription, except in the context of the ongoing trials for medical research purposes. Secondly, the defences involve the proposition that it is lawful for unqualified individuals to prescribe cannabis to themselves as patients or to assume the role of unqualified doctors by obtaining it and prescribing and supplying it to other individual 'patients'. This is contrary not only to the legislative scheme, but also to any recommendation for its change made by the Select Committee and Runciman Reports. Further, it would involve obvious risks for the integrity and the prospects of any coherent enforcement of the legislative scheme. A parallel but lawful market in the importation, cultivation, prescription, supply, possession and use of cannabis would have to come into existence, which would not only be subject to no medical safeguards or constraints, but the scope and legitimacy of which would in all likelihood be extremely difficult to ascertain or control . . . Neither judges nor juries are well equipped to resolve issues as to when and how far the deliberate policy of clear legislation should give way in a particular case to countervailing individual hardship, or as to what the overall effect of such derogations would be on the whole legislative scheme.

57. We are not concerned with the question whether a defence of duress by threats or of necessity by circumstances may ever be available in relation to offences under the drugs legislation, where the general scheme and policy of the legislation would not be in question. We have no doubt it may. To take an obvious example, if A forces B at gun-point to take into his possession cannabis or to smoke a cannabis joint, there would be no offence, and the defence of duress by threats is regularly suggested, though less regularly accepted by juries, in relation to charges of illegal importation of drugs. We will not either encourage or discount the possibility that there may be occasions when a defence of necessity might also run. A contrived but possible example mooted in argument concerned the patient on an island, in need of a further supply from a chemist of a particular drug licensed for prescription by a doctor to ensure his or her continued health, in circumstances where the only doctor capable of prescribing it had died or was stormbound on the mainland. If (improbably) no prescription could be obtained in any way, might the chemist be justified in giving out a further supply without a prescription? But, whatever the answer to such an exceptional case, it has nothing to do with the situation before us. We are concerned with sufferers whose conduct contravenes the legislative policy and scheme on a continuing and regular basis, but who maintain nonetheless that this is excusable. Mr Fitzgerald submitted at one point that, in contrast to the evident ill which would (for example) result if prison-breach were held to be excusable (cf Rodger & Rose), any ill-effects of cannabis itself or of non-compliance with the statutory prohibitions could be seen as relatively minor compared with the risk of serious injury or pain to an individual defendant; and that it should be left to the jury in any particular case to weigh the potential ill-effects which might result (either generally or to the particular defendant) from such non-compliance against the potential benefits to the particular

defendant; and that the jury should, on that basis, determine whether or not to enforce the statutory prohibition taking account of whatever degree of need a defendant might show impelled him or her to act as he or she did. The jury has a well-established power to return a verdict of not guilty, whatever the law and however clear it may be. But to require the judge to direct the jury that they should weigh in the balance the pros and cons of enforcing the clear policy of a statutory scheme in any particular case is, in our view, a different matter. It would involve a positive invitation to the jury to act contrary to the law and to take over the role of the legislative authorities.

14.7 A COMMON LAW DEFENCE OF NECESSITY?

Historically the courts have refused to accept that there could be a distinctive defence of necessity at common law. This reluctance, in part, explains the emergence of the defence of duress of circumstances and, it is submitted, the difficulty in explaining why the cases where duress of circumstance has been recognised might not also be seen as examples of necessity.

It may be possible to draw a distinction between duress of circumstance and necessity on the basis that, with the former, the defendant must show that he was 'constrained by circumstances' to act as he did (see *R v Conway*, above), or that he was 'impelled to act as he did' (see *R v Martin*, above). The latter defence, however, might be available to a defendant who, though not threatened himself, simply takes action, which, although it involves the commission of a criminal offence, is the lesser of two evils in the situation as it presents itself to him. Developed along these lines there would be no need to show that the defendant had no choice but to act, or indeed that the evil he sought to avoid necessarily involved a threat of death or grievous bodily harm. As will have been seen from the extracts considered thus far, however, the courts are some way from identifying or accepting such a distinctive role for the defence of necessity.

R v Dudley and Stephens (1884) 14 QBD 273

Lord Coleridge CJ:

. . . [T]his is clear, that the prisoners put to death a weak and unoffending boy upon the chance of preserving their own lives by feeding upon his flesh and blood after he was killed, and with the certainty of depriving him of any possible chance of survival. The verdict finds in terms that 'if the men had not fed upon the body of the boy they would probably not have survived', and that 'the boy being in a much weaker condition was likely to have died before them'. They might possibly have been picked up next day by a passing ship; they might possibly not have been picked up at all; in either case it is obvious that the killing of the boy would have been an unnecessary and profitless act. It is found by the verdict that the boy was incapable of resistance, and, in fact, made none; and it is not even suggested that his death was due to any violence on his part attempted against, or even so much as feared by, those who killed him . . .

There remains to be considered the real question in the case – whether killing under the circumstances set forth in the verdict be or be not murder. The contention that it could be any-thing else was, to the minds of us all, both new and strange, and we stopped the Attorney General in his negative argument in order that we might hear what could be said in support of a prop-osition which appeared to us to be once dangerous, immoral, and opposed to all legal principle and analogy. All, no doubt, that can be said has been urged before us, and we are now to consider and determine what it amounts to. First it is said that it follows from various definitions of murder in books of authority, which definitions imply, if they do not state, the doctrine, that in order to save your own life you may lawfully take away the life of another, when that other is neither attempting nor threatening yours, nor is guilty of any illegal act whatever towards you or anyone else. But if these definitions be looked at they will not be found to sustain this contention . . .

. . . Now it is admitted that the deliberate killing of this unoffending and unresisting boy was clearly murder, unless the killing can be justified by some well-organised excuse admitted by the law. It is further admitted that there was in this case no such excuse, unless the killing was justified by what has been called 'necessity'. But the temptation to the act which existed here was not what the law has ever called necessity. Nor is this to be regretted. Though law and morality are not the same, and many things may be immoral which are not necessarily illegal, yet the absolute divorce of law from morality would be of fatal consequence; and such divorce would follow if the temptation to murder in this case were to be held by law an absolute defence of it. It is not so. To preserve one's life is generally speaking a duty, but it may be the plainest and the highest duty to sacrifice it. War is full of instances in which it is a man's duty not to live, but to die. The duty, in case of shipwreck, of a captain to his crew, to the crew to the passengers, of soldiers to women and children, as in the noble case of the *Birkenhead*; these duties impose on men the moral necessity, not the preservation, but of the sacrifice of their lives for others, from which in no country, least of all, it is to be hoped, in England, will men ever shrink, as indeed, they have not shrunk. It is not correct, therefore, to say that there is any absolute or unqualified necessity to preserve one's life . . . It is not needful to point out the awful danger of admitting the principle which has been contended for. Who is to be the judge of this sort of necessity? By what measure is the comparative value of lives to be measured? Is it to be strength, or intellect, or what? It is plain that the principle leaves to him who is to profit by it to determine the necessity which will justify him in deliberately taking another's life to save his own. In this case the weakest, the youngest, the most unresisting, was chosen. Was it more necessary to kill him than one of the grown men? The answer must be 'No':

So spake the Fiend, and with necessity,
The tyrant's plea, excused his devilish deeds.

It is not suggested that in this particular case the deeds were 'devilish', but it is quite plain that such a principle once admitted might be made the legal cloak for unbridled passion and atrocious crime. There is no safe path for judges to tread but to ascertain the law to the best of their ability and to declare it according to their judgment; and if in any case the law appears to be too severe on individuals, to leave it to the sovereign to exercise that prerogative of mercy which the constitution has intrusted to the hands fittest to dispense it.

It must not be supposed that in refusing to admit temptation to be an excuse for crime it is forgotten how terrible the temptation was; how awful the suffering; how hard in such trials to keep the judgment straight and the conduct pure. We are often compelled to set up standards we cannot reach ourselves, and to lay down rules which we could not ourselves satisfy. But a man has no right to declare temptation to be an excuse, though he might himself have yielded to it, nor allow compassion for the criminal to change or weaken in any manner the legal definition of the crime. It is therefore our duty to declare that the prisoners' act in this case was wilful murder, that the facts as stated in the verdict are no legal justification of the homicide; and to say that in our unanimous opinion the prisoners are upon this special verdict guilty of murder.

Re A (Children) (Conjoined Twins: Surgical Separation) [2000] 4 All ER 961

Jodie and Mary were conjoined twins. The parents of the twins and the doctors treating them faced a dilemma. If no action was taken both would die, as the weaker twin, Mary, would slowly cause the death of Jodie. If an operation to separate the twins was carried out successfully, Jodie had an excellent chance of survival, whilst Mary's death would be an inevitable consequence of such an operation. The Court of Appeal was asked to rule on the legality of an operation to separate the twins, and looked specifically at the extent to which doctors performing such surgery would be entitled to defences of duress, necessity and self-defence (i.e. reasonable force used in defence of others).

Brooke LJ:

In the present case we are concerned with what is said by some of those who appeared before us to be a case of private necessity in the eyes of the criminal law. Bracton, writing in the thirteenth century *On the Laws and Customs of England* (Selden Society Edition 1968, at Vol 2, 340–41) identified this type of necessity, in the context of the law of homicide, in these terms:

> Of necessity, and here we must distinguish whether the necessity was avoidable or not; if avoidable and he could escape without slaying, he will then be guilty of homicide; if unavoidable, since he kills without premeditated hatred but with sorrow of heart, in order to save himself and his family, since he could not otherwise escape [danger], he is not liable to the penalty for murder.

Five hundred years later the same concept of necessity, which still forms part of our law today, was expressed as follows by Lord Hale in his *Pleas of the Crown*, Vol 1, 51:

> . . . but if he cannot otherwise save his own life, the law permits him in his own defence to kill the assailant; for by the violence of the assault, and the offence committed upon him by the assailant himself, the law of nature and necessity hath made him his own *protector cum debito moderamine inculpatae tutelae* as shall be further shewed, when we come to the chapter of homicide *se defendendo*.

Later in the same volume Hale identifies two kinds of necessity which justify homicide: necessity which is of a private nature, and the necessity which relates to the public justice and safety (with which we are not here concerned). He added (at p 478):

> The former is that necessity which obligeth a man to his own defence and safeguard, and this takes in these enquiries: (1) What may be done for the safeguard of a man's life . . . As touching the first of these, viz homicide in defence of a man's own life, which is usually called *se defendendo* . . . Homicide *se defendendo* is the killing of another person in the necessary defence of himself against him that assaults him.

Blackstone, in Volume IV of his *Commentaries on the Laws of England*, had recourse to the law of nature as the source of a person's authority to use proportionate force in self-defence, saying at p 30: 'In such a case [viz a violent assault] he is permitted to kill the assailant, for there the law of nature, and self-defence its primary canon, have made him his own protector.'

During the seventeenth century there were suggestions that the right of self-preservation extended beyond the right to use appropriate force in self-defence. Thus in his *Elements of the Common Laws of England* (1630) Lord Bacon wrote:

Necessity is of three sorts – necessity of conservation of life, necessity of obedience, and necessity of the act of God or of a stranger. First, of conservation of life; if a man steal viands to satisfy his present hunger this is no felony nor larceny. So if divers be in danger of drowning by the casting away of some boat or barge, and one of them get to some plank, or on the boat's side to keep himself above water, and another to save his life thrust him from it, whereby he is drowned, this is neither *se defendendo* nor by misadventure, but justifiable.

Similar sentiments appear in Thomas Hobbes's *Leviathan* at p 157:

If a man by the terror of present death, be compelled to doe a fact against the Law, he is totally Excused, because no Law can oblige a man to abandon his own preservation. And supposing such a Law were obligatory; yet a man would reason thus, if I do it not, I die presently; if I doe it, I die afterwards; therefore by doing it, there is time of life gained; Nature therefore compels him to the fact. When a man is destitute of food, or other thing necessary for his life, and cannot preserve himselfe any other way, but by some fact against the law; as if in a great famine he take the food by force, or stealth, which he cannot obtaine for mony nor charity; or in defence of his life, snatch away another mans Sword, he is totally Excused, for the reason next before alledged.

Both these extensions of the doctrine of necessity have been authoritatively disapproved as propositions of English law. For the disapproval of the idea that in order to save himself a man is entitled to deprive another of the place of safety he has already secured for himself, see *R v Dudley and Stephens* ... *per* Lord Coleridge CJ ... and *R v Howe* ... For the equally strong disapproval of the idea that if a starving beggar takes the law into his own hands and steals food he is not guilty of theft, see *Southwark LBC v Williams* [1971] 1 Ch 734 *per* Lord Denning MR at pp 743H–D and Edmund-Davies LJ at pp 745E–746C ... *R v Dudley and Stephens* ... has sometimes been taken as authority for the proposition that necessity can never under any circumstances provide a legal justification for murder. While it is true that a passage in the speech of Lord Hailsham in *R v Howe* [1987] 1 AC 417 at p 429C–D might be interpreted to this effect, in my judgment neither that passage nor a similar passage in Lord Mackay of Clashfern's speech at p 453C–D displays any evidence that they had in mind a situation in which a court was invited to sanction a defence (or justification) of necessity on facts comparable to those with which we are confronted in the present case. I accept Miss Davies's submission that *R v Dudley and Stephens*, endorsed though it was by the House of Lords in *R v Howe*, is not conclusive of the matter.

We have also been shown how the Law Commission tackled this troublesome doctrine in the criminal law between 1974 and 1993. In 1974 a very experienced Working Party was brave enough to recommend codified proposals for a general defence of necessity (Law Commission Working Paper No 55, pp 38–39). Three years later the Commission itself retreated so far from this proposition that it recommended that there should be no general defence of necessity in any new Code, and that if any such general defence existed at common law it should be abolished (Law Com No 83 (1977), p 54). It felt that it would be much better if Parliament continued to create special defences of necessity, when appropriate. Because euthanasia was so controversial, and because the Criminal Law Revision Committee was engaged in work on offences against the person, the Commission thought it better to leave to that committee any questions relating to the provision of a defence in that area of the law.

This retreat, influenced by the responses it had received on consultation, particularly from practitioners (see pp 24–25), evoked a storm of protest from academic commentators (see, for instance, the articles entitled 'Necessity' by Glanville Williams [1978] Crim LR 12 and 'Proposals and counter proposals on the defence of necessity' by PHJ Huxley [1978] Crim LR 141, and the powerful criticism (to the effect that the proposals represented 'the apotheosis of absurdity') by Sir Rupert Cross in a Canadian university law journal cited by Professor Glanville Williams in a footnote on p 202 of the 2nd edn of his *Textbook on Criminal Law* (1983)).

Professor Williams returned to the topic of necessity in Chapter 26 of that book. He observed at p 602 that the main difficulty felt by the Law Commission appeared to have been in respect of certain 'human rights', whereas the doctrine of necessity was an expression of the philosophy of utilitarianism. He referred, however, to a suggestion by an American writer, Paul Robinson, to the effect that the recognition of important values did not entirely exclude a defence of necessity. In the determination of cases where those values did not appear, their existence could not affect the outcome, and even where they did appear, they could be given special weight in estimating the balance of interests.

In his powerful Section 26.3 ('Necessity as a reason for killing') Professor Williams addressed the issues with which we are confronted in this case. He began his treatment of the subject by saying that many people believed in the sanctity of life, and consequently believed that killing was absolutely wrong. It was for this reason, he said, that the defence of necessity, if allowed at all, was given very narrow scope in this area. He distinguished private defence from necessity (although the two overlapped) on the grounds that (unlike necessity) private defence involved no balancing of values, while on the other hand private defence operated only against aggressors (who, with rare exceptions, were wrongdoers) whereas the persons against whom action was taken by necessity might not be aggressors or wrongdoers. In this context, he mentioned *R v Bourne* [1939] 1 KB 687 (where Macnaghten J had suggested in his summing-up that there might be a duty in certain circumstances to abort an unborn child to save the life of the mother), as an example of the defence of necessity, even though it was a case not of homicide but of feticide.

Professor Williams came to the heart of the matter at p 604:

Might this defence apply where a parent has killed his grossly malformed infant? Doubtless not. It may of course be argued that the value of such an infant's life, even to himself, is minimal or negative, and that if parents are obliged to rear him they may be disabled from having another and normal child. But it is not a case for applying the doctrine of necessity as usually understood. The child when born, unlike the fetus, is regarded as having absolute rights. Besides, there is no emergency. The usual view is that necessity is no defence to a charge of murder. This, if accepted, is a non-utilitarian doctrine; but in the case of a serious emergency is it wholly acceptable? If you are roped to a climber who has fallen, and neither of you can rectify the situation, it may not be very glorious on your part to cut the rope, but is it wrong? Is it not socially desirable that one life, at least, should be saved? Again, if you are flying an aircraft and the engine dies on you, it would not be wrong, but would be praiseworthy, to choose to come down in a street (where you can see you will kill or injure a few pedestrians), rather than in a crowded sports stadium. But in the case of cutting the rope you are only freeing yourself from someone who is, however involuntarily, dragging you to your death. And in the case of the aircraft you do not want to kill anyone; you simply minimise the slaughter that you are bound to do one way or the other. The question is whether you could deliberately kill someone for calculating reasons. We do regard the right to life as almost a supreme value, and it is very unlikely that anyone would be held to be justified in killing for any purpose except the saving of other life, or perhaps the saving of great pain or distress. Our revulsion against a deliberate killing is so strong that we are loth to consider utilitarian reasons for it. But a compelling case of justification of this kind is the action of a ship's captain in a wreck. He can determine who are to enter the first lifeboat; he can forbid overcrowding; and it makes no difference that those who are not allowed to enter the lifeboat will inevitably perish with the ship. The captain, in choosing who are to live, is not guilty of killing those who remain. He would not be guilty even though he kept some of the passengers back from the boat at revolver-point, and he would not be guilty even though he had to fire the revolver.

His Lordship went on to consider the current recommendations of the Law Commission, contained in the Report *Offences Against the Person and General Principles* (Law Com 218, 1993), extracted below. He then turned to examine the work of academic writers on this topic.

Those who prepared [Law Com 218] would have been familiar with a modern update of the 'two men on a plank' dilemma (which dates back to Cicero, *de Officiis*) and the 'two mountaineers on a rope' dilemma which was mentioned by Professor John Smith in his 1989 Hamlyn Lectures (published under the title *Justification and Excuse in the Criminal Law*). At the coroner's inquest conducted in October 1987 into the Zeebrugge disaster, an army corporal gave evidence that he and dozens of other people were near the foot of a rope ladder. They were all in the water and in danger of drowning. Their route to safety, however, was blocked for at least ten minutes by a young man who was petrified by cold or fear (or both) and was unable to move up or down. Eventually the corporal gave instructions that the man should be pushed off the ladder, and he was never seen again. The corporal and many others were then able to climb up the ladder to safety.

In his third lecture, *Necessity and Duress*, Professor Smith evinced the belief at pp 77–78 that if such a case ever did come to court it would not be too difficult for a judge to distinguish *R v Dudley and Stephens*. He gave two reasons for this belief. The first was that there was no question of choosing who had to die (the problem which Lord Coleridge had found unanswerable in *R v Dudley and Stephens* at p 287) because the unfortunate young man on the ladder had chosen himself by his immobility there. The second was that unlike the ship's boy on the *Mignonette*, the young man, although in no way at fault, was preventing others from going where they had a right, and a most urgent need, to go, and was thereby unwittingly imperilling their lives.

I would add that the same considerations would apply if a pilotless aircraft, out of control and running out of fuel, was heading for a densely populated town. Those inside the aircraft were in any event 'destined to die'. There would be no question of human choice in selecting the candidates for death, and if their inevitable deaths were accelerated by the plane being brought down on waste ground, the lives of countless other innocent people in the town they were approaching would be saved.

It was an argument along these lines that led the rabbinical scholars involved in the 1977 case of conjoined twins to advise the worried parents that the sacrifice of one of their children in order to save the other could be morally justified. George J Annas, *Siamese Twins: Killing One to Save the Other* (Hastings Center Report, April 1987 at p 27), described how they:

> ... reportedly relied primarily on two analogies. In the first, two men jump from a burning aeroplane. The parachute of the second man does not open, and as he falls past the first man, he grabs his legs. If the parachute cannot support them both, is the first man morally justified in kicking the second man away to save himself? Yes, said the rabbis, since the man whose parachute didn't open was 'designated for death'. The second analogy involves a caravan surrounded by bandits. The bandits demand a particular member of the caravan be turned over for execution; the rest will go free. Assuming that the named individual has been 'designated for death', the rabbis concluded it was acceptable to surrender him to save everyone else. Accordingly, they concluded that if a twin A was 'designated for death' and could not survive in any event, but twin B could, surgery that would kill twin A to help improve the chance of twin B was acceptable.

There is, however, no indication in the submission we received from the Archbishop of Westminster that such a solution was acceptable as part of the philosophy he espoused. The judge's dilemma in a case where he or she is confronted by a choice between conflicting philosophies was thoughtfully discussed by Simon Gardner in his article 'Necessity's newest inventions' (Oxford Journal of Legal Studies, Vol II, 125–35). He explored the possibility of rights-based justifications based on a principle that otherwise unlawful actions might be justified where the infraction was calculated to vindicate a right superior to the interest protected by the rule, but he was perplexed by the idea that judges in a democracy could make their own decisions as to what was right and what was wrong in the face of established law prohibiting the conduct in question. The whole article requires careful study, but its author concluded that in jurisdictions where rights were guaranteed, the judicial vindication of a guaranteed right would be seen as protecting democracy rather than contravening it. This consideration does not, however, assist us in a case where there are conflicting rights of apparently equal status and conflicting philosophies as to the priority, if any, to be given to either.

Before I leave the treatment afforded to the topic of necessity by modern academic writers of great distinction (there is a valuable contemporary summary of the issues in the Ninth Edition of Smith and Hogan's *Criminal Law* (1999) at pp 245–52), I must mention the section entitled 'Justifications, necessity and the choice of evils' in the 3rd edn (1999) of *Principles of Criminal Law* by Professor Andrew Ashworth. After referring to the facts of the Zeebrugge incident he said at pp 153–54:

> No English court has had to consider this situation, and it is clear that only the strongest prohibition on the taking of an innocent life would prevent a finding of justification here: in an urgent situation involving a decision between n lives and n + 1 lives, is there not a strong social interest in preserving the greater number of lives? Any residual principle of this kind must be carefully circumscribed; it involves the sanctity of life, and therefore the highest value with which the criminal law is concerned. Although there is a provision in the Model Penal Code allowing for a defence of 'lesser evil', it fails to restrict the application of the defence to cases of imminent threat, opening up the danger of citizens trying to justify all manner of conduct by reference to overall good effects. The moral issues are acute: 'not just anything is permissible on the ground that it would yield a net saving of lives'. Closely connected with this is the moral problem of 'choosing one's victim', a problem which arises when, for example, a lifeboat is in danger of sinking, necessitating the throwing

overboard of some passengers, or when two people have to kill and eat another if any of the three is to survive. To countenance a legal justification in such cases would be to regard the victim's rights as morally and politically less worthy than the rights of those protected by the action taken, which represents a clear violation of the principle of individual auto-nomy. Yet it is surely necessary to make some sacrifice, since the autonomy of everyone simply cannot be protected. A dire choice has to be made, and it must be made on a principle of welfare or community that requires the minimisation of overall harm. A fair procedure for resolving the problem – perhaps the drawing of lots – must be found. But here, as with self-defence and the 'uplifted knife' cases, one should not obscure the clearer cases where there is no need to choose a victim: in the case of the young man on the rope-ladder, blocking the escape of several others, there was no doubt about the person who must be subjected to force, probably with fatal consequences.

I turn now from twentieth century academic writing and the work of the Law Commission and its specialist working parties to consider the way in which Parliament and the courts have addressed these issues.

So far as I am aware, Parliament has never even debated these issues in a general sense, in spite of the recommendations of the Law Commission and the increasingly insistent pleas for Parliamentary assistance which have been made by senior judges in the context of the rapidly developing new defence of 'duress of circumstances'. Parliament has, however, to an increasing extent included 'necessity' defences or justifications in modern offence-creating stat-utes, and where such provisions are present the Parliamentary intention is clear. In 1974 the Law Commission's Working Party identified such provisions in the Infant Life Preservation Act 1929 s 1(1), the Education Act 1944 s 39(2)(a), the Fire Services Act 1947 s 30(1), the Road Traffic (Regulation) Act 1967 s 79, the Abortion Act 1967 s 1(1) and the Road Traffic Act 1972 s 36(3). The Criminal Damage Act 1971 s 5(2)(b) provides another example from that period, and this statutory process has continued up to the present day, although, as is common with piecemeal law reform, the defences are not always framed along the same lines.

The Abortion Act provides a particularly good example of this process at work, expanding and clarifying the law for the benefit of the courts and for everyone else who, for whatever reason, needs to have recourse to the law in this controversial area. Before its enactment Macnaghten J in the case of *R v Bourne* derived a 'necessity' defence out of the word 'unlawfully' in Section 58 of the Offences Against the Person Act 1861 ('Any person who unlawfully uses an instrument with intent to procure a miscarriage shall be guilty of felony'). Macnaghten J said at p 691 that he thought that the word 'unlawfully' imported the meaning expressed by the proviso in s 1(1) of the Infant Life Preservation Act 1929 ('Provided that no person shall be guilty of an offence under this section unless it is proved that the act which caused the death of the child was not done in good faith for the purpose only of preserving the life of the mother'). He went on to direct the jury at p 693:

> In such a case where a doctor anticipates, basing his opinion upon the experience of the profession, that the child cannot be delivered without the death of the mother, it is obvi-ous that the sooner the operation is performed the better. The law does not require the doctor to wait until the unfortunate woman is in peril of immediate death. In such a case he is not only entitled, but it is his duty to perform the operation with a view to saving her life.

That, as I have observed earlier, was the common law defence of necessity at work when a judge was interpreting what he believed Parliament must have meant when it used the word 'unlawfully' in a codifying statute. Parliament's current intentions in this field are now clearly set out in the substituted Section 1(1) of the Abortion Act 1967. It would of course be very helpful, once Parliament has had the opportunity of considering the implications of the judgments in the present case, if it would provide similar assistance to the courts and to all other interested parties (and in particular parents and medical practitioners) as to what is legally permissible and what is not legally permissible in the context of separation surgery on conjoined twins. Parliament would of course now have to take account of the relevant provisions of the European Convention of Human Rights when formulating any new legislation.

In addition to the major work that has been undertaken by Parliament in creating statutory excuses or justifications for what would otherwise be unlawful, the courts have also been busy in this field, at all events in those cases where a defendant maintains that he/she was irresistibly constrained by threats or external circumstances to do what he/she did.

So far as duress by threats is concerned, it was common ground between counsel that the solution to the present case is not to be found in the caselaw on that topic . . . The work of academic writers and of the Law Commission has, however, led to one significant development in the common law. This lies in the newly identified defence of 'duress of circumstances'. The modern development of this defence began in the field of driving offences.

In *R v Kitson* (1955) 39 Cr App R 66 the defendant, who had had a lot to drink, went to sleep in the passenger seat of a car driven by his brother-in-law. When later charged with driving the car under the influence of drink, he said in his defence that when he woke up, he found that the driving seat was empty, and the car was moving down a hill with the handbrake off. He managed to steer the car into a grass verge at the bottom of the hill. He was convicted of driving a car under the influence of drink, and when the Court of Criminal Appeal dismissed his appeal on the basis that the ingredients of the offence were made out, and he had undoubtedly been driving the car within the meaning of the Act, nobody suggested that he was entitled to rely on a defence of necessity or duress of circumstances.

Thirty years later, this potential line of defence first saw the light of day in *R v Willer* . . . A similar issue arose in *R v Conway* [1989] QB 290, another case of reckless driving . . . [Brooke LJ referred to *R v Martin*, *R v Pommell*, and *R v Abdul-Hussain* and continued] . . . I mention these . . . to show that the Court of Appeal is now willing to entertain the possibility of a defence of duress even in a case as extreme as this if it is arguable that 'the will of the accused has been overborne by threats of death or serious personal injury so that the commission of the alleged defence was no longer [his] voluntary act' (see *R v Hudson* [1971] 2 QB 202 *per* Lord Parker CJ at p 206E). The defence is available on the basis that if it is established, the relevant actors have in effect been compelled to act as they did by the pressure of the threats or other circumstances of imminent peril to which they were subject, and it was the impact of that pressure on their freedom to choose their course of action that suffices to excuse them from criminal liability.

I have described how in modern times Parliament has sometimes provided 'necessity' defences in statutes and how the courts in developing the defence of duress of circumstances have sometimes equated it with the defence of necessity. They do not, however, cover exactly the same ground. In cases of pure necessity the actor's mind is not irresistibly overborne by external pressures. The claim is that his or her conduct was not harmful because on a choice of two evils the choice of avoiding the greater harm was justified.

. . . I have considered very carefully the policy reasons for the decision in *R v Dudley and Stephens*, supported as it was by the House of Lords in *R v Howe*. These are, in short, that there were two insuperable objections to the proposition that necessity might be available as a defence for the *Mignonette* sailors. The first objection was evident in the court's questions: Who is to be the judge of this sort of necessity? By what measure is the comparative value of lives to be measured? The second objection was that to permit such a defence would mark an absolute divorce of law from morality.

In my judgment, neither of these objections are dispositive of the present case. Mary is, sadly, self-designated for a very early death. Nobody can extend her life beyond a very short span. Because her heart, brain and lungs are for all practical purposes useless, nobody would have even tried to extend her life artificially if she had not, fortuitously, been deriving oxygenated blood from her sister's bloodstream.

It is true that there are those who believe most sincerely – and the Archbishop of Westminster is among them – that it would be an immoral act to save Jodie, if by saving Jodie one must end Mary's life before its brief allotted span is complete. For those who share this philosophy, the law, recently approved by Parliament, which permits abortion at any time up to the time of birth if the conditions set out in s 1(1)(d) of the Abortion Act 1967 (as substituted) are satisfied, is equally repugnant. But there are also those who believe with equal sincerity that it would be immoral not to assist Jodie if there is a good prospect that she might live a happy and fulfilled life if this operation is performed. The court is not equipped to choose between these competing phil-osophies. All that a court can say is that it is not at all obvious that this is the sort of clear-cut case, marking an absolute divorce from law and morality, which was of such concern to Lord Coleridge and his fellow judges.

There are sound reasons for holding that the existence of an emergency in the normal sense of the word is not an essential prerequisite for the application of the doctrine of necessity. The principle is one of necessity, not emergency: see Lord Goff (in *In Re F* at p 75D), the Law Commis-sion in its recent report (Law Com No 218, paras 35.5–35.6), and Wilson J in *Perka* (at p 33).

There are also sound reasons for holding that the threat which constitutes the harm to be avoided does not have to be equated with 'unjust aggression', as Professor Glanville Williams has made clear in Section 26.3 of the 1983 edition of his book. None of the formulations of the doctrine of necessity which I have noted in this judgment make any such requirement: in this respect it is different from the doctrine of private defence.

If a sacrificial separation operation on conjoined twins were to be permitted in circumstances like these, there need be no room for the concern felt by Sir James Stephen that people would be too ready to avail themselves of exceptions to the law which they might suppose to apply to their cases (at the risk of other people's lives). Such an operation is, and is always likely to be, an exceptionally rare event, and because the medical literature shows that it is an operation to be avoided at all costs in the neonatal stage, there will be in practically every case the opportunity for the doctors to place the relevant facts before a court for approval (or otherwise) before the operation is attempted.

According to Sir James Stephen, there are three necessary requirements for the application of the doctrine of necessity: (i) the act is needed to avoid inevitable and irreparable evil; (ii) no more should be done than is reasonably necessary for the purpose to be achieved; (iii) the evil inflicted must not be disproportionate to the evil avoided.

Given that the principles of modern family law point irresistibly to the conclusion that the interests of Jodie must be preferred to the conflicting interests of Mary, I consider that all three of these requirements are satisfied in this case.

Finally, the doctrine of the sanctity of life respects the integrity of the human body. The pro-posed operation would give these children's bodies the integrity which nature denied them. For these reasons I, too, would dismiss this appeal.

Robert Walker LJ:

The House of Lords has made clear that a doctrine of necessity does form part of the common law: see *Re F (Mental Patient: Sterilisation)* [1990] 2 AC 1 (especially in the speech of Lord Goff at pp 74–78) . . . Duress of circumstances can therefore be seen as a third or residual category of necessity, along with self-defence and duress by threats. I do not think it matters whether these defences are regarded as justifications or excuses. Whatever label is used, the moral merits of the defence will vary with the circumstances. The important issue is whether duress of circumstances can ever be a defence to a charge of murder . . .

The special features of this case are that the doctors do have duties to their two patients, that it is impossible for them to undertake any relevant surgery affecting one twin without also affecting the other, and that the evidence indicates that both twins will die in a matter of months if nothing is done. Whether or not that is aptly described as duress of circumstances, it is a situation in which surgical intervention is a necessity if either life is to be saved.

I do not find any clear principle in *R v Howe, R v Gotts* or *R v Abdul-Hussain* which applies to the clinical dilemma which faces the doctors in this case. Like the other members of the court I have derived assistance from the minority judgment of Wilson J given in the Supreme Court of Canada in the case of *Perka and Other v R* . . .

Wilson J's reference to a conflict of duties in relation to abortion must be treated with caution because of the well-established rule that English law (like Canadian law, but here differing markedly from the teaching of the Roman Catholic church) does not regard even a viable full-term fetus as a human being until fully delivered: see the account in *Rance v Mid-Downs HA* [1991] 1 QB 587, 617–23 to which I have already referred, and also *St George's Healthcare NHS Trust v S* [1999] Fam 26, 45–50. There is in law no real analogy between Mary's dependence on Jodie's body for her continued life, and the dependence of an unborn fetus on its mother.

In truth there is no helpful analogy or parallel to the situation which the court has to consider in this case. It is unprecedented and paradoxical in that in law each twin has the right to life, but Mary's dependence on Jodie is severely detrimental to Jodie, and is expected to lead to the death of both twins within a few months. Each twin's right to life includes the right to physical integrity, that is the right to a whole body over which the individual will, on reaching an age of understanding, have autonomy and the right to self-determination: see the citations from *Bland* collected in the *St George's Healthcare* case at pp 43–45.

In the absence of Parliamentary intervention the law as to the defence of necessity is going to have to develop on a case-by-case basis, as Rose LJ said in *R v Abdul-Hussain*. I would extend it, if it needs to be extended, to cover this case. It is a case of doctors owing conflicting legal (and not merely social or moral) duties. It is a case where the test of proportionality is met, since it is a matter of life and death, and on the evidence Mary is bound to die soon in any event. It is not a case of evaluating the relative worth of two human lives, but of undertaking surgery without which neither life will have the bodily integrity (or wholeness) which is its due. It should not be regarded as a further step down a slippery slope because the case of conjoined twins presents an unique problem.

There is on the facts of this case some element of protecting Jodie against the unnatural invasion of her body through the physical burden imposed by her conjoined twin. That element must not be overstated. It would be absurd to suggest that Mary, a pitiful and innocent baby, is an unjust aggressor. Such language would be even less acceptable than dismissing Mary's death as a 'side effect'. Nevertheless, the doctors' duty to protect and save Jodie's life if they can is of fundamental importance to the resolution of this appeal.

R v Jones [2004] EWCA Crim 1981

The defendants had unlawfully gained entry to RAF bases in order to damage military equipment. They were charged with criminal damage and sought to rely on, *inter alia*, the defence of necessity, i.e. their actions had been necessitated by the need to prevent unlawful aggression against Iraq by the UK and US military forces using the base.

Latham LJ [having referred to *R v Martin* [1989] 1 All ER 652, *R v Abdul-Hussain* [1999] Crim LR 570 and *R v Shayler* [2001] All ER (D) 99]:

The question that we have to determine is whether or not on the basis of these decisions, the court will have to grapple with the question of the legality of the government's decision to declare war on Iraq. The defendants say that it is necessary because that is the 'evil' which they felt impelled to do their best to obviate by their actions. Alternatively, using the terminology of Simon Brown J in *Martin*, it is only available to them if from an objective standpoint, they could be said to be acting reasonably or proportionately; and a determination of the legality of the war would be necessary in order to answer that question.

It seems to us, however, that this approach fails to put the defence in its proper context. Necessity is potentially a domestic defence to a domestic offence. We have already held that no domestic crime is engaged. The executive's action in declaring and waging war is, in itself, a lawful exercise of its powers under the prerogative. The court will accordingly have to consider the extent to which necessity might afford a defence to the defendants in the light of their beliefs on that basis. The extent to which their beliefs as to the facts will enable the defendants to establish any of the elements of the defence, in particular the requirement that they should be so acting in relation to people for whom they could reasonably regard themselves as being responsible is not a question we are called upon to answer.

14.8 SELF-DEFENCE

At common law the scope of the defence of self-defence extends to using such force as is reasonable in the circumstances for the purposes of:

(1) self-defence;
(2) defence of another person;
(3) defence of property.

By virtue of s 3(1) of the Criminal Law Act 1967, reasonable force can also be used in the prevention of crime and in making a lawful arrest (see s 3(1) of the Criminal Law Act 1967).

Where an accused puts forward a defence, he bears what is known as an 'evidential' burden of proof in relation to it. This does *not* mean that he has to prove his defence to the satisfaction of the jury. All it means is that the accused has to adduce sufficient evidence of the defence for the judge or magistrates to decide that it is worthy of consideration. Thus, the 'legal' burden of proof is borne by the prosecution: it is for the prosecution to prove beyond reasonable doubt that the defence is negated. These rules apply whether the case is being tried in a magistrates' court or in the Crown Court. As Lord Slynn explained in *DPP (Jamaica) v Bailey* [1995] 1 Cr App R 257 (PC): '. . . hopeless defences which have no factual basis of support do not have to be left to the jury. But it is no less clear, in their Lordships' view, that if the accused's account of what happened includes matters which, if accepted, could raise a *prima facie* case of self-defence this should be left to the jury even if the accused has not formally relied upon self-defence'.

The concept of 'force' is a broad one that can be left largely to the common sense of the jury – see *R v Renouf* [1986] 1 WLR 522. It can encompass threats as well as direct or indirect contact. As Milmo J observed in *R v Cousins* [1982] 1 QB 526 (CA): '. . . It is, of course, true that the charge against the appellant was not that he used force but that he threatened to use force. However, if force is permissible, something less, for example a threat, must also be permissible if it is reasonable in the circumstances.'

14.8.1 THE CONCEPT OF REASONABLE FORCE

Palmer v R [1971] AC 814 (PC)

Lord Morris of Borth-y-Gest:
. . . The only question that is raised for determination is whether in cases where on a charge of murder an issue of self-defence is left to the jury it will in all cases be obligatory to direct the jury that if they found that the accused while intending to defend himself had used more force than was necessary in the circumstances they should return a verdict of guilty of manslaughter . . .

. . . Their Lordships conclude that there is no room for criticism of the summing-up or of the conduct of the trial unless there is a rule that in every case where the issue of self-defence is left to the jury they must be directed that if they consider that excessive force was used in defence then they should return a verdict of guilty of manslaughter. For the reasons which they will set out, their Lordships consider that there is no such rule . . .

On behalf of the appellant it was contended that if, where self-defence is an issue in a case of homicide, a jury came to the conclusion that an accused person was intending to defend himself, then an intention to kill or to cause grievous bodily harm would be negatived: so it was contended that if in such a case the jury came to the conclusion that excessive force had been used the correct verdict would be one of manslaughter: hence it was argued that in every case where self-defence is left to a jury they must be directed that there are the three possible verdicts, viz guilty of murder, guilty of manslaughter, and not guilty. But in many cases where someone is intending to defend himself he will have had an intention to cause serious bodily injury or even to kill, and if the prosecution satisfy the jury that he had one of these intentions in circumstances in which or at a time when there was no justification or excuse for having it, then the prosecution will have shown that the question of self-defence is eliminated. All other issues which on the facts may arise will be unaffected.

An issue of self-defence may of course arise in a range and variety of cases and circumstances where no death has resulted. The test as to its rejection or its validity will be just the same as in a case where death has resulted. In its simplest form the question that arises is the question: Was the defendant acting in necessary self-defence? If the prosecution satisfy the jury that he was not then all other possible issues remain . . .

In their Lordships' view the defence of self-defence is one which can be and will be readily understood by any jury. It is a straightforward conception. It involves no abstruse legal thought. It required no set words by way of explanation. No formula need be employed in reference to it. Only common sense is needed for its understanding. It is both good law and good sense that a man who is attacked may defend himself. It is both good law and good sense that he may do, but may only do, what is reasonably necessary. But everything will depend upon the particular facts and circumstances. Of these a jury can decide. It may in some cases be only sensible and clearly possible to take some simple avoiding action. Some attacks may be serious and dangerous. Others may not be. If there is some relatively minor attack it would not be common sense to permit some action of retaliation which was wholly out of proportion to the necessities of the situation. If an attack is serious so that it puts someone in immediate peril then immediate defensive action may be necessary. If the moment is one of crisis for someone in imminent danger he may have to avert the danger by some instant reaction. If the attack is all over and no sort of peril remains then the employment of force may be by way of revenge or punishment or by way of paying off an old score or may be pure aggression. There may no longer be any link with a necessity of defence. Of all these matters the good sense of a jury will be the arbiter. There are no prescribed words which must be employed in or adopted in a summing up. All that is needed is a clear exposition, in relation to the particular facts of the case, of the conception of necessary self-defence. If there has been no attack then clearly there will have been no need for defence. If there has been attack so that defence is reasonably necessary it will be recognised that a person defending himself cannot weigh to a nicety the exact measure of his necessary defensive action. If a jury thought that in a moment of unexpected anguish a person attacked had only done what he honestly and instinctively thought was necessary that would be most potent evidence that only reasonable defensive action had been taken. A jury will be told that the defence of self-defence, where the evidence makes its raising possible, will only fail if the prosecution show beyond doubt that what the accused did was not by way of self-defence. But their Lordships consider, in agreement with the approach in the *De Freitas* case (1960) 2 WLR 523, that if the prosecution have shown that what was done was not done in self-defence then that issue is eliminated from the case. If the jury consider that an accused acted in self-defence or if the jury are in doubt as to this then they will acquit. The defence of self-defence either succeeds so as to result in an acquittal or it is disproved, in which case as a defence it is rejected. In a homicide case the circumstances may be such that it will become an issue as to whether there was provocation so that the verdict might be one of manslaughter. Any other possible issues will remain. If in any case the view is possible that the intent necessary to constitute the crime of murder was lacking then that matter would be left to the jury . . .

R v Shannon (1980) 71 Cr App R 192 (CA)

Ormrod LJ:

. . . [Counsel] for the appellant has criticised the learned judge's summing-up on the basis of the well-known passage in the speech of Lord Morris of Borth-y-Gest giving the advice of the Privy Council in *Palmer v R* [1971] AC 814, 831 and 832. He submits that the learned judge overlooked one important sentence in that advice which reads thus: 'If a jury thought that in a moment of unexpected anguish a person attacked had only done what he honestly and instinctively thought was necessary, that would be most potent evidence that only reasonable defensive action had been taken.'

This proposition is, as it were, a bridge between what is sometimes referred to as 'the objective test', that is what is reasonable judged from the viewpoint of an outsider looking at a situation quite dispassionately, and 'the subjective test', that is the viewpoint of the accused himself with the intellectual capabilities of which he may in fact be possessed and with all the emotional strains and stresses to which at the moment he may be subjected.

The learned judge dealt fully with the relevant evidence and the law, and finally left this question to the jury: 'Has the prosecution satisfied you that Mr Shannon used more force than was reasonable in the circumstances; because that goes solely to the question: Did he lawfully kill Mr Meredith?' This summarises the burden of his direction to the jury.

[Counsel for the appellant] argues that the judge ought to have invited the jury to consider whether the appellant, at the moment of stabbing, 'honestly and instinctively thought that this action was necessary' to his defence and to have told them that if they thought that that was right and provided an adequate reason for the stabbing, it would be strong evidence that only reasonable defensive action had been taken.

[Counsel for the appellant] in effect urged that the learned judge had concentrated so much on the state of the appellant's mind in relation to the intent necessary to establish the charge of murder that he had, unwittingly, obscured this subjective element in self-defence.

Taken in isolation it is not an easy concept to explain to a jury, or for a jury to understand and apply, although Lord Morris regarded the defence of self-defence as 'one which can and will be readily understood by any jury'. It is however easier to understand in its context and, if full justice is to be done to [counsel's] submission in this case, it is necessary to read what Lord Morris said *in extenso* at [1971] AC 814, 831, 832.

. . . The whole tenor of this statement of the law [ie what Lord Morris said] is directed to the distinction which has to be drawn between acts which are essentially defensive in character and acts which are essentially offensive, punitive, or retaliatory in character. Attack may be the best form of defence, but not necessarily in law. Counter-attack within limits is permissible; but going over to the offensive when the real danger is over is another thing. This, we think, is the distinction which Lord Morris was endeavouring to explain, and which he thought a jury would readily understand.

Various indicators are used by the judges to enable juries to make this crucial distinction. If the act or acts go beyond what the jury think reasonably necessary for defensive purposes, that points to the offensive rather than the defensive character of the act; if the attack is finished, the subsequent employment of force may be, in Lord Morris's words, 'by way of revenge or punishment or by way of paying off an old score or may be pure aggression'; if other people have come to the assistance of the person attacked before some act of violence is done to the assailant, this too may indicate that the victim has gone over to the offensive. But these are only indicators to be used by the jury in making their commonsense assessment on the facts as they find them; they are not conclusive tests in themselves of self-defence on the one hand or of aggression on the other. This is where Lord Morris's references come in to 'a person defending himself cannot weigh to a nicety the exact measure of his necessary defensive action' and to such a person's 'honest and instinctive' belief that his act was necessary. These considerations, depending on the facts of the particular case, may have to be weighed by the jury before coming to their conclusion 'self-defence' or 'no self-defence'.

The learned judge, in the course of his summing up, used verbatim several extracts from Lord

Morris's statement of the law in *Palmer v R* (above), but throughout the summing up, and at the end he left the jury with the bald question, 'Are you satisfied that the appellant used more force than was necessary in the circumstances?' without Lord Morris's qualification that if they came to the conclusion that the appellant honestly thought, without having to weigh things to a nicety, that what he did was necessary to defend himself, they should regard that as 'most potent evidence' that it was actually reasonably necessary. In other words, if the jury came to the conclusion that the stabbing was the act of a desperate man in extreme difficulties, with his assailant dragging him down by the hair, they should consider very carefully before concluding that the stabbing was an offensive and not a defensive act, albeit it went beyond what an onlooker would regard as reasonably necessary . . .

In the judgment of this court the evidence of the appellant, if accepted by the jury, raised the questions (a) whether the stabbing was in fact the act of a desperate man trying to defend himself and to force his assailant to let go of his hair and (b) whether, although not reasonably necessary by an objective standard, nonetheless, to use Lord Morris's words, the appellant honestly and instinctively thought that it was; in which case his honest belief would be 'most potent evidence' that he had only taken defensive action; in other words, in the circumstances the stabbing was essentially defensive in character. The case for the prosecution, on the other hand, if accepted by the jury, was a perfect illustration of a man going over to the offensive and stabbing by way of revenge, punishment, retaliation or pure aggression.

The learned judge touched on this aspect of the matter when he was directing the jury on the issue of intent in relation to the charge of murder. At the end of the summing-up he said this:

> If you think that he lashed out because he lost his temper, having been treated in this painful, humiliating, frightening way, then you may think – it is a matter for you – that because he lost his temper in those circumstances he gave little or no thought to what might be the consequences of lashing out and in those circumstances he did not form the intent suggested. That is the matter which you must consider, clearly. The more a man loses his temper, the less likely he may be to consider what are likely to be the consequences of his acts even though when he is in a balanced state of mind he realises that if you lash out with scissors and it lands and you do it with force then it is going to do a lot of personal injury.

But on the issue of self-defence he effectively excluded the state of the accused's mind. In other words, by leaving that issue to the jury on the bald basis of 'Did the appellant use more force than was necessary in the circumstances?' the learned judge may have precluded the jury from considering the real issue, which, to paraphrase Lord Morris in *Palmer v R* (above) was: 'Was this stabbing within the conception of necessary self-defence judged by the standards of common sense, bearing in mind the position of the appellant at the moment of the stabbing, or was it a case of angry retaliation or pure aggression on his part?'

It is, we think, significant that in relation to intent, that is applying the test of what was in the accused's mind, the jury concluded that it was not murder but only manslaughter on the basis of no intent to cause really serious bodily harm, but seem to have excluded the appellant's state of mind in considering self-defence . . .

R v Whyte [1987] 3 All ER 416 (CA)

The appellant became involved in an argument with another man named Khan. The appellant stabbed Khan and gave evidence to the effect that he had acted in self-defence.

Lord Lane CJ:

. . . In most cases, where the issue is one of self-defence, it is necessary and desirable that the jury should be reminded that the defendant's state of mind, that is his view of the danger threatening him at the time of the incident, is material. The test of reasonableness is not, to put it at its lowest, a purely objective test. We have been referred to two authorities. The first is an opinion of the Privy Council in *Palmer v R* [1971] AC 814 and the second is *R v Shannon* (1980) 71 Cr App R 192, a decision of this court which of course is binding on us. The effect of those two decisions seems to be this. A man who is attacked may defend himself, but may only do what is reasonably necessary to effect such a defence. Simple avoiding action may be enough if circumstances permit. What is reasonable will depend on the nature of the attack. If there is relatively a minor attack, it is not reasonable to use a degree of force which is wholly out of proportion to the demands of the situation. But if the moment is one of crisis for someone who is in imminent danger, it may be necessary to take instant action to avert that danger.

Although the test is what is sometimes called an objective one, yet nevertheless, to quote the words of Lord Morris in *Palmer v R* [1971] AC 814 at 832:

If a jury thought that in a moment of unexpected anguish a person attacked had only done what he honestly and instinctively thought was necessary, that would be most potent evidence that only reasonable defensive action had been taken.

In *R v Shannon*, to which we have already referred, the trial judge had directed the jury to consider the question, 'Are you satisfied that the defendant used more force than necessary in the circumstances?' without going on to consider the qualification of what the defendant may have done in a 'moment of unexpected anguish'. On the facts of *R v Shannon*, that was clearly a fatal flaw which led to the conviction being quashed.

The judge in the present case likewise omitted to mention the qualification which Lord Morris had suggested should be made and which *R v Shannon* says should be made in appropriate circumstances.

It is a trite observation, but nevertheless true, that the requirements of a summing-up will depend on the particular facts of the case. Whereas on the facts of *R v Shannon* the court correctly held that the qualifying effect mentioned by Lord Morris should have been given, one has to look at this case to see whether it was similarly necessary here. The jury in convicting him of the s 18 offence must have come to the conclusion that he had deliberately stabbed Mr Khan with the knife, despite what he himself said. They were directed correctly on the question of accident. The appeal on that point has been abandoned. So the jury must have decided that the knife was deliberately used by the appellant on Mr Khan. At the very best, from the appellant's point of view, the jury must have come to the conclusion that he stabbed Mr Khan because Mr Khan had hit him in the face with his hand. Now I am assuming in favour of the appellant that the facts were, with that small amendment about accident, as the appellant himself stated them to be. It is highly likely that the jury entirely disbelieved the appellant.

Was it necessary in those circumstances that the judge should mention the qualifying factor as mentioned by Lord Morris? In our judgment it was not. There was no question raised by the appellant that he, acting in the agony of the moment, went too far, that he failed to weigh accurately the precise degree of the attack which he was suffering. It is perfectly plain that on any view the use of an already prepared knife, the blade having been extended, in circumstances such as this, could not possibly be reasonable under any circumstances, whether the direction in *Palmer v R* was given or not.

For those reasons we think that in this particular case it was not necessary for the judge to give the *Palmer* direction, although as a matter of abundance of caution he might perhaps have given it . . .

14.8.2 WHETHER THERE IS A DUTY TO RETREAT FROM THREATENED VIOLENCE

R v Julien [1969] 1 WLR 839 (CA)

Widgery LJ:

. . . The third point taken by counsel for the appellant is that the learned deputy chairman was wrong in directing the jury that before the appellant could use force in self-defence he was required to retreat. The submission here is that the obligation to retreat before using force in self-defence is an obligation which only arises in homicide cases. As the court understands it, it is submitted that if the injury results in death then the accused cannot set up self-defence except on the basis that he had retreated before he resorted to violence. On the other hand, it is said that where the injury does not result in death (as in the present case) the obligation to retreat does not arise. The sturdy submission is made that an Englishman is not bound to run away when threatened, but can stand his ground and defend himself where he is. In support of this submission no authority is quoted, save that counsel for the appellant has been at considerable length and diligence to look at the textbooks on the subject, and has demonstrated to us that the textbooks in the main do not say that a preliminary retreat is a necessary prerequisite to the use of force in self-defence. Equally, it must be said that the textbooks do not state the contrary either; and it is, of course, well-known to us all that for very many years it has been common form for judges directing juries where the issue of self-defence is raised in any case (be it a homicide case or not) that the duty to retreat arises. It is not, as we understand it, the law that a person threatened must take to his heels and run in the dramatic way suggested by counsel for the appellant; but what is necessary is that he should demonstrate by his actions that he does not want to fight. He must demonstrate that he is prepared to temporise and disengage and perhaps to make some physical withdrawal; and to the extent that that is necessary as a feature of the justification of self-defence, it is true, in our opinion, whether the charge is a homicide charge or something less serious. Accordingly, we reject counsel for the appellant's third submission . . .

R v Bird [1985] 1 WLR 816 (CA)

The appellant became involved in an argument with her ex-boyfriend, Darren Mander, and poured a glassful of Pernod over him. He retaliated by slapping the appellant around the face.

During these altercations the appellant lunged at Mander with her hand. She was holding the Pernod glass in her hand at the time. The glass hit Mander causing him to lose one eye. In evidence the appellant insisted that she had been acting in self-defence.

Lord Lane CJ:

... The grounds of appeal are these. First of all, the judge was in error in directing the jury that before the appellant could rely on a plea of self-defence, it was necessary that she should have demonstrated by her action that she did not want to fight. That really is the essence of the appellant's case put forward by her counsel to this court . . .

The court in *R v Julien* was anxious to make it clear that there was no duty, despite earlier authorities to the contrary, actually to turn round or walk away from the scene. But, reading the words which were used in that judgment, it now seems to us that they placed too great an obligation on a defendant in circumstances such as those in the instant case, an obligation which is not reflected in the speeches in *Palmer v R*.

The matter is dealt with accurately and helpfully in Smith and Hogan, *Criminal Law*, 5th edn, 1983, p 327 as follows:

> There were formerly technical rules about the duty to retreat before using force, or at least fatal force. This is now simply a factor to be taken into account in deciding whether it was necessary to use force, and whether the force was reasonable. If the only reasonable course is to retreat, then it would appear that to stand and fight must be to use unreasonable force. There is, however, no rule of law that a person attacked is bound to run away if he can; but it has been said that: '. . . what is necessary is that he should demonstrate by his actions that he does not want to fight. He must demonstrate that he is prepared to temporise and disengage and perhaps to make some physical withdrawal'. It is submitted that it goes too far to say that action of this kind is necessary. It is scarcely consistent with the rule that it is permissible to use force, not merely to counter an actual attack, but to ward off an attack honestly and reasonably believed to be imminent. A demonstration by D [the defendant] at the time that he did not want to fight is, no doubt, the best evidence that he was acting reasonably and in good faith in self-defence; but it is no more than that. A person may in some circumstances so act without temporising, disengaging or withdrawing; and he should have a good defence.

We respectfully agree with that passage. If the defendant is proved to have been attacking or retaliating or revenging himself, then he was not truly acting in self-defence. Evidence that the defendant tried to retreat or tried to call off the fight may be a cast-iron method of casting doubt on the suggestion that he was the attacker or retaliator or the person trying to revenge himself. But it is not by any means the only method of doing that . . .

R v McInnes [1971] 1 WLR 1600 (CA)

Edmund Davies LJ:

... The incident which led to the murder charge was of a kind only too frequently occurring in these days, namely a fracas between two perfect strangers which resulted in the violent death of one of them as the result of a knife wound. The appellant belonged to a group of youths commonly called 'greasers', who adopted a particular form of dress which includes leather jackets.

Hostility generally exists between them and 'skinheads', who are youths differently dressed and having close-cropped heads. The deceased belonged to neither of these groups. The deceased was killed at about 9.30 pm on Saturday 22 August 1970, at a fair being held at Platt Fields in Manchester, and his death was caused by a knife wound in the left side of the body. The knife used had penetrated the heart. The wound was about 2 inches deep and about 3 feet 11 inches from the deceased's left heel . . .

. . . We turn to the two criticisms advanced in relation to the manner in which the learned judge treated the topic of self-defence. Before doing this, however, it should again be observed that, while both prosecuting and defence counsel (very understandably in all the circumstances) dealt at length with this plea, it was one never advanced by the appellant himself in evidence. On the contrary, he insisted throughout that he never thrust the knife forward, and that the wounding and killing of the deceased were due to no aggressive action on his part.

The first criticism of the learned judge's treatment of self-defence is that he misdirected the jury in relation to the question of whether an attacked person must do all he reasonably can to retreat before he turns on his attacker. The direction given was in these terms:

> In our law if two men fight and one of them after a while endeavours to avoid any further struggle and retreats as far as he can, and then when he can go no further turns and kills his assailant to avoid being killed himself, that homicide is excusable, but notice that to show that homicide arising from a fight was committed in self-defence it must be shown that the party killing had retreated as far as he could, or as far as the fierceness of the assault would permit him.

. . . In our judgment, the direction was expressed in too inflexible terms and might, in certain circumstances, be regarded as significantly misleading. We prefer the view expressed by the High Court of Australia (in *R v Howe* (1958) 100 CLR 448 at 462, 464, 469) that a failure to retreat is only an element in the considerations on which the reasonableness of an accused's conduct is to be judged (see *Palmer v R* [1971] 2 WLR 831 at 840), or, as it is put in Smith and Hogan's *Criminal Law*, 1969, 2nd edn, p 231:

> . . . simply a factor to be taken into account in deciding whether it was necessary to use force, and whether the force used was reasonable.

The modern law on the topic was, in our respectful view, accurately set out in *R v Julien* [1969] 1 WLR 839 at 843 by Widgery LJ in the following terms:

> It is not, as we understand it, the law that a person threatened must take to his heels and run in the dramatic way suggested by counsel for the appellant; but what is necessary is that he should demonstrate by his actions that he does not want to fight. He must demonstrate that he is prepared to temporise and disengage and perhaps to make some physical withdrawal; and to the extent that that is necessary as a feature of the justification of self-defence, it is true, in our opinion, whether the charge is a homicide charge or something less serious.

In the light of the foregoing, how stands the direction given in the present case? Viewed in isolation, that is to say, without regard to the evidence adduced, it was expressed in too rigid terms. But the opportunity to retreat remains, as the trial judge said, 'an important consideration', and, when regard is had to the evidence as to the circumstances which prevailed, in our view it emerges with clarity that the appellant could have avoided this fatal incident with ease by simply walking or running away – as, indeed, he promptly did as soon as the deceased had been stabbed . . .

14.8.3 WHERE THE FORCE USED EXCEEDS THAT WHICH IS REASONABLE

R v McInnes [1971] 1 WLR 1600 (CA)

Edmund Davies LJ:

The final criticism levelled against the summing-up is that the learned judge wrongly failed to direct the jury that, if death resulted from the use of excessive force by the appellant in defending himself against the aggressiveness of the deceased, the proper verdict was one of not guilty of murder but guilty of manslaughter. Certainly no such direction was given, and the question that arises is whether its omission constitutes a defect in the summing up.

The Privy Council decision in *Palmer v R* provides high persuasive authority which we, for our part, unhesitatingly accept, that there is certainly no rule that, in every case where self-defence is left to the jury, such a direction is called for. But where self-defence fails on the ground that the force used went clearly beyond that which was reasonable in the light of the circumstances as they reasonably appeared to the accused, is it the law that the inevitable result must be that he can be convicted of manslaughter only, and not of murder? It seems that in Australia that question is answered in the affirmative (see Professor Colin Howard's article, 'Two problems in excessive defence' (1968) 84 LQR 343), but not, we think, in this country. On the contrary, if self-defence fails for the reason stated, it affords the accused no protection at all. But it is important to stress that the facts on which the plea of self-defence is unsuccessfully sought to be based may nevertheless serve the accused in good stead. They may, for example, go to show that he may have acted under provocation or that, although acting unlawfully, he may have lacked the intent to kill or cause serious bodily harm, and in that way render the proper verdict one of manslaughter . . .

Section 3(1) of the Criminal Law Act 1967 provides: 'A person may use such force as is reasonable in the circumstances in the prevention of crime . . .' and in our judgment the degree of force permissible in self-defence is similarly limited. Deliberate stabbing was so totally unreasonable in the circumstances of this case, even on the appellant's version, that self-defence justifying a complete acquittal was not relied on before us, and rightly so. Despite the high esteem in which we hold our Australian brethren, we respectfully reject as far as this country is concerned the refinement sought to be introduced that, if the accused, in defending himself during a fisticuffs encounter, drew out against his opponent (who he had no reason to think was armed) the deadly weapon which he had earlier unsheathed and then 'let him have it', the jury should have been directed that, even on those facts, it was open to them to convict of manslaughter. They are, in our view, the facts of this case. It follows that in our judgment no such direction was called for . . .

R v Clegg [1995] 1 AC 482 (HL)

Lord Lloyd of Berwick:

My Lords, on the night of 30 September 1990 the appellant, Lee William Clegg, a soldier serving with the Parachute Regiment, was on patrol in Glen Road, West Belfast, when the driver of a stolen car and one of his passengers were shot and killed. Private Clegg was charged with murder of the passenger, and attempted murder of the driver. His defence was that he fired in self-defence. He was convicted on 4 June 1993, after a trial before Campbell J without a jury. His appeal to the Court of Appeal was dismissed. The Court of Appeal held that the firing of the shot which killed the passenger was, on the facts found by the judge, a grossly excessive and disproportionate use of force, and that any tribunal of fact properly directed would so have found. The certified question of law for your Lordships is whether a soldier on duty, who kills a person with the requisite intention for murder, but who would be entitled to rely on self-defence but for the use of excessive force, is guilty of murder or manslaughter.

The patrol consisted of 15 men under the command of Lieutenant Oliver. It was accompanied by a police constable from the Royal Ulster Constabulary. The purpose of the patrol was to catch joyriders. But this was not explained to Private Clegg. The patrol was divided into four teams or 'bricks'. Brick 11 formed a vehicle checkpoint at a bridge on the Glen Road about six miles west of Belfast. Brick 10A, consisting of Lieutenant Oliver, Private Clegg, Private Aindow and another, were moving down the road towards Belfast. Private Aindow was on the right-hand side of the road. The others were all on the left-hand side. Bricks 12 and 14 were still further down the road, around a corner. As the stolen car approached the bridge from the west, it was stopped by a member of Brick 11. The car then accelerated away in the centre of the road towards Brick 10A with its headlights full on. Someone in Brick 11 shouted to stop it. All four members of Brick 10A fired at the approaching car. Private Clegg's evidence was that he fired three shots at the windscreen, and a fourth shot into the side of the car as it was passing. He then replaced his safety-catch. According to Private Clegg he fired all four shots because he thought Private Aindow's life was in danger. However, scientific evidence showed, and the trial judge found as a fact, that Private Clegg's fourth shot was fired after the car had passed, and was already over 50 feet along the road to Belfast. It struck a rear-seat passenger, Karen Reilly, in the back. It was later found lodged beneath her liver. The judge found that Private Clegg's fourth shot was an aimed shot fired with the intention of causing death or serious bodily harm. Although another bullet passed through Karen Reilly's body, Private Clegg's fourth shot was a significant cause of the death.

In relation of the first three shots, the judge accepted Private Clegg's defence that he fired in self-defence or in defence of Private Aindow. But with regard to the fourth shot he found that Private Clegg could not have been firing in defence of himself or Private Aindow, since, once the car had passed, they were no longer in any danger.

Having rejected Private Clegg's defence in relation to the fourth shot, the judge went on to consider, as was his duty, whether there was any other defence open on the evidence, even though Private Clegg had not raised the defence himself. One possible defence was that Private Clegg fired the fourth shot in order to arrest the driver. Section 3(1) of the Criminal Law Act (Northern Ireland) 1967 provides:

A person may use such force as is reasonable in the circumstances in the prevention of crime, or in effecting or assisting in the lawful arrest of offenders or suspected offenders or of persons unlawfully at large.

The judge held that there was insufficient evidence to raise such a defence. Accordingly he convicted Private Clegg of murder.

When the case reached the Court of Appeal, the court reviewed the whole of Private Clegg's evidence. In a number of his answers he had said that he fired to stop the driver of the car after it had, as he thought, struck Private Aindow. Accordingly there was, in the court's view, evidence on which the judge should have considered the defence under s 3 of the Act of 1967.

It should be noted in passing that the car did not, in fact, strike Private Aindow. The judge held that bruising found of Private Aindow's left leg was caused, not by the car, but by another soldier stamping on him in order to create the appearance that he had been struck by the car. In those circumstances, Private Aindow was charged with perverting the course of justice as well as attempted murder. He was convicted on the former count and sentenced to two years' imprisonment. His appeal on that count was dismissed.

Having held that there was evidence to raise the defence under s 3, the Court of Appeal went on to consider whether any miscarriage of justice had actually occurred by reason of the failure of the judge to consider that defence. Section 3 of the Act of 1967 allows a person to use 'such force as is reasonable in the circumstances'. So the question for the Court of Appeal was whether Private Clegg, in firing the fourth shot, used only such force as was reasonable in the circumstances, or whether the force which he used was excessive.

In the course of his cross-examination Private Clegg was asked whether he was aware of any circumstances which would have justified him in firing after the car had passed. He replied that he had no reason to fire at that stage.

Q 29: And if you had fired any more you know of no justification for that action?

A 29: That's correct. That's why I applied my safety-catch as the car went past me.

There was no suggestion in Private Clegg's evidence, as the Court of Appeal pointed out, that he thought that the driver was a terrorist, or that if the driver escaped he would carry out terrorist offences in the future. In those circumstances the use of lethal force to arrest the driver of the car was, in the court's view, so 'grossly disproportionate to the mischief to be averted' that any tribunal of fact would have been bound to find that the force used was unreasonable. It follows that if the defence under s 3 had been raised, which it was not, it would have failed. Accordingly, Private Clegg's appeal was dismissed . . .

The point raised in the present case might have arisen for decision by your Lordships in *AG for Northern Ireland's Ref (No 1 of 1975)* [1977] AC 105. That case also concerned a soldier on patrol in Northern Ireland. He shot and killed an unarmed man, who ran away when challenged. The trial judge found that, unlike the present case, the prosecution had failed to prove that the soldier intended to kill or cause serious bodily harm, and further found that the homicide was justifiable under s 3 of the Act of 1967 on the ground that the use of force was reasonable in the circumstances. The questions for the opinion of the House were first whether, on the facts set out in the reference, the soldier had committed a crime at all and second whether, if so, the crime was murder or manslaughter. The House held that the first question was not a question of law at all, but a pure question of fact, which, on the facts proved at the trial, had been answered in favour of the soldier; and that the second question, though a question of law, did not arise on the facts. But it is to be observed that Viscount Dilhorne said in relation to the second question at 148:

> I now turn to the second point of law referred, whether if a crime was committed in the circumstances stated in the reference it was murder or manslaughter. The Attorney General indicated that he would like it to be held that it was manslaughter and, while I appreciated his reasons for doing so, I can find no escape from the conclusion that if a crime was committed, it was murder if the shot was fired with intent to kill or seriously wound. To hold that it could be manslaughter would be to make entirely new law. If a plea

of self-defence is put forward in answer to a charge of murder and fails because excessive force was used though some force was justifiable, as the law now stands the accused cannot be convicted of manslaughter. It may be that a strong case can be made for an alteration of the law to enable a verdict of manslaughter to be returned where the use of some force was justifiable but that is a matter for legislation and not for judicial decision.

. . . I do not find it necessary to go through the earlier English authorities relied on by counsel, since they were all reviewed at length by Lord Morris of Borth-y-Gest in *Palmer v R* [1971] AC 814. I respectfully agree with his analysis. Counsel did not advance any fresh arguments. In my opinion the law of England must now be taken to be settled in accordance with the decision of the Privy Council in that case. Thus, the consequence of the use of excessive force in self-defence will be the same in the law of England, Scotland, Australia, Canada and the West Indies. I consider later whether, despite this uniformity, some change in the law may, nevertheless, be desirable.

The second question is whether there is any distinction to be made between excessive force in self-defence and excessive force in the prevention of crime or in arresting offenders. In *AG for Northern Ireland's Ref (No 1 of 1975)* [1977] AC 105 Lord Diplock said, at 139, that the two cases were quite different. But I do not think it possible to say that a person who uses excessive force in preventing crime is always, or even generally, less culpable than a person who uses excessive force in self-defence; and even if excessive force in preventing crime were in general less culpable, it would not be practicable to draw a distinction between the two defences, since they so often overlap. Take, for example, the facts of the present case. The trial judge held that Private Clegg's first three shots might have been fired in defence of Private Aindow. But he could equally well have held that they were fired in the prevention of crime, namely to prevent Private Aindow's death being caused by dangerous driving. As is pointed out in Smith and Hogan, *Criminal Law*, 6th edn, 1988, p 244; 7th edn, 1992, p 255, the degree of permissible force should be the same in both cases. So also should the consequences of excessive force.

The third question is whether it makes any difference that Private Clegg was a member of the security forces, acting in the course of his duty . . .

. . . In most cases of a person acting in self-defence, or a police officer arresting an offender, there is a choice as to the degree of force to be used, even if it is a choice which has to be exercised on the spur of the moment, without time for measured reflection. But in the case of a soldier in Northern Ireland, in the circumstances in which Private Clegg found himself, there is no scope for graduated force. The only choice lay between firing a high-velocity rifle which, if aimed accurately, was almost certain to kill or injure, and doing nothing at all.

It should be noticed that the point at issue here is not whether Private Clegg was entitled to be acquitted altogether, on the ground that he was acting in obedience to superior orders. There is no such general defence known to English law, nor was any such defence raised at the trial . . . The point is rather whether the offence in such a case should, because of the strong mitigating circumstances, be regarded as manslaughter rather than murder. But so to hold would, as Viscount Dilhorne said in *AG for Northern Ireland's Ref (No 1 of 1975)* [1977] AC 105, 148, be to make entirely new law. I regret that under existing law, on the facts found by the trial judge, he had no alternative but to convict of murder . . .

14.8.4 LAW REFORM PROPOSALS – THE USE OF EXCESSIVE FORCE

The problem of the defendant who is justified in using some force by way of self-defence, but who in fact uses excessive force and thereby kills the victim, was considered in the Law Commission's Report *Partial Defences to Murder* (Law Com 290). Having weighed the arguments for and against introducing a partial defence to murder whereby a defendant's liability could be reduced to manslaughter if it was found that the use of force by way of self-defence had been justified, but that the defendant had gone beyond what was reasonable in the circumstances, the Commission decided not to propose a new partial defence, but to broaden the redrafted defence of provocation to encompass situations where the defendant had responded to the fear of violence. In its subsequent report *Murder, Manslaughter And Infanticide* (Law Com No 304) was published in November 2006, the Commission put forward its proposals for a reformed defence of provocation that would encompass the use of lethal force as a response to a fear of serious violence – see extracts from paras 5.48 to 5.55 of the Report at Chapter 4.6.4.6

14.9 THE STATUTORY DEFENCE OF REASONABLE FORCE – CRIMINAL LAW ACT 1967

Section 3(1) of the Criminal Law Act 1967 provides:

> A person may use such force as is reasonable in the circumstances in the prevention of crime, or in effecting or assisting in the lawful arrest of offenders or suspected offenders or of persons unlawfully at large.

Whereas at common law it has been argued that the use of force to protect others requires proof of some nexus between the defendant and those he seeks to protect, under s 3 a defendant can use force to protect a complete stranger from a criminal attack as he will be using force to prevent the commission of a criminal offence. Similarly, at common law, a defendant can rely on self-defence to protect his property from attack. Under the statute the defendant could use reasonable force to protect anybody's property from criminal damage or theft. The 'crime' that the defendant seeks to prevent for these purposes means a crime in domestic law – it cannot be relied upon to prevent acts regarded as crimes under customary international law; see *R v Jones* [2006] UKHL 16.

14.10 CROWN PROSECUTION GUIDANCE ON SELF-DEFENCE

The Tony Martin case (considered below at 14.11) provoked much discussion in the media regarding the rights of householders confronted by burglars, and the extent to which the law ought to be changed to tip the balance in favour of the householder using force in such situations. The government view was that no change was required and in February 2005 the Crown Prosecution Service, in conjunction with the Association of Chief Police Officers published the following guidance:

Householders and the use of force against intruders – Joint Public Statement from the Crown Prosecution Service and the Association of Chief Police Officers

What is the purpose of this statement?

It is a rare and frightening prospect to be confronted by an intruder in your own home. The Crown Prosecution Service (CPS) and Chief Constables are responding to public concern over the support offered by the law and confusion about householders defending themselves. We want a criminal justice system that reaches fair decisions, has the confidence of law-abiding citizens and encourages them actively to support the police and prosecutors in the fight against crime. Wherever possible you should call the police. The following summarises the position when you are faced with an intruder in your home, and provides a brief overview of how the police and CPS will deal with any such events.

Does the law protect me? What is 'reasonable force'?

Anyone can use reasonable force to protect themselves or others, or to carry out an arrest or to prevent crime. You are not expected to make fine judgements over the level of force you use in the heat of the moment. So long as you only do what you honestly and instinctively believe is necessary in the heat of the moment, that would be the strongest evidence of you acting lawfully and in self-defence. This is still the case if you use something to hand as a weapon.

As a general rule, the more extreme the circumstances and the fear felt, the more force you can lawfully use in self-defence.

Do I have to wait to be attacked?

No, not if you are in your own home and in fear for yourself or others. In those circumstances the law does not require you to wait to be attacked before using defensive force yourself.

What if the intruder dies?

If you have acted in reasonable self-defence, as described above, and the intruder dies you will still have acted lawfully. Indeed, there are several such cases where the householder has not been prosecuted. However, if, for example:

- having knocked someone unconscious, you then decided to further hurt or kill them to punish them; or
- you knew of an intended intruder and set a trap to hurt or to kill them rather than involve the police;
- you would be acting with very excessive and gratuitous force and could be prosecuted.

What if I chase them as they run off?
This situation is different as you are no longer acting in self-defence and so the same degree of force may not be reasonable. However, you are still allowed to use reasonable force to recover your property and make a citizen's arrest. You should consider your own safety and, for example, whether the police have been called. A rugby tackle or a single blow would probably be reasonable. Acting out of malice and revenge with the intent of inflicting punishment through injury or death would not.

Will you believe the intruder rather than me?
The police weigh all the facts when investigating an incident. This includes the fact that the intruder caused the situation to arise in the first place. We hope that everyone understands that the police have a duty to investigate incidents involving a death or injury. Things are not always as they seem. On occasions people pretend a burglary has taken place to cover up other crimes such as a fight between drug dealers.

How would the police and CPS handle the investigation and treat me?
In considering these cases Chief Constables and the Director of Public Prosecutions (Head of the CPS) are determined that they must be investigated and reviewed as swiftly and as sympathetically as possible. In some cases, for instance where the facts are very clear, or where less serious injuries are involved, the investigation will be concluded very quickly, without any need for arrest. In more complicated cases, such as where a death or serious injury occurs, more detailed enquiries will be necessary. The police may need to conduct a forensic examination and/or obtain your account of events.

To ensure such cases are dealt with as swiftly and sympathetically as possible, the police and CPS will take special measures, namely:

- an experienced investigator will oversee the case; and
- if it goes as far as CPS considering the evidence, the case will be prioritised to ensure a senior lawyer makes a quick decision.

It is a fact that very few householders have ever been prosecuted for actions resulting from the use of force against intruders.

Helpful as this guidance is, it still leaves some issues, particularly the rights of the 'criminal' i.e. the burglar or the robber to use force in self-defence. For example, if P, a householder attacks a burglar D, can D use reasonable force to protect himself? *R v Rashford* [2005] All ER (D) 192 suggests that D will be permitted to use reasonable force against P in such a case provided P's violence against D is disproportionate and D is in immediate danger from which there is no other means of escape. By implication this would suggest that if P's violence is proportionate, it is therefore lawful and D is thus not entitled to defend himself against it by using force on P.

14.11 THE RELEVANCE OF THE DEFENDANT'S PERCEPTION OF THE NEED TO ACT IN SELF-DEFENCE AND THE FORCE REQUIRED

Beckford v R [1988] AC 130 (PC)

The defendant was a police officer who attended a domestic dispute armed with a shotgun and ammunition. He had been advised that the deceased, Chester Barnes, was terrorising a woman with a gun. The defendant fired at the deceased killing him and subsequently claimed to have acted in self-defence. The main issue on appeal was whether, for the purposes of assessing the availability of the defence of self-defence, the defendant was entitled to be judged according to the facts as he had honestly believed then to be.

Lord Griffiths:

The common law recognises that there are many circumstances in which one person may inflict violence upon another without committing a crime, as for instance, in sporting contests, surgical operations or, in the most extreme example, judicial execution. The common law has always recognised as one of these circumstances the right of a person to protect himself from attack and to act in the defence of others and if necessary to inflict violence on another in so doing. If no more force is used than is reasonable to repel the attack, such force is not unlawful and no crime is committed. Furthermore a man about to be attacked does not have to wait for his assailant to strike the first blow or fire the first shot; circumstances may justify a pre-emptive strike.

It is because it is an essential element of all crimes of violence that the violence or the threat of violence should be unlawful that self-defence, if raised as an issue in a criminal trial, must be disproved by the prosecution. If the prosecution fail to do so the accused is entitled to be acquitted because the prosecution will have failed to prove an essential element of the crime, namely that the violence used by the accused was unlawful.

... a genuine belief in facts which, if true, would justify self-defence, [must] be a defence to a crime of personal violence because the belief negatives the intent to act unlawfully. Their Lordships therefore approve the following passage from the judgment of Lord Lane CJ in *R v Williams (Gladstone)* 78 Cr App R 276, 281, as correctly stating the law of self-defence:

The reasonableness or unreasonableness of the defendant's belief is material to the question of whether the belief was held by the defendant at all. If the belief was in fact held, its unreasonableness, so far as guilt or innocence is concerned, is neither here nor there. It is irrelevant. Were it otherwise, the defendant would be convicted because he was negligent in failing to recognise that the victim was not consenting or that a crime was not being committed and so on. In other words the jury should be directed first of all that the prosecution have the burden or duty of proving the unlawfulness of the defendant's actions; second, if the defendant may have been labouring under a mistake as to the facts, he must be judged according to his mistaken view of the facts; third, that is so whether the mistake was, on an objective view, a reasonable mistake or not.

In a case of self-defence, where self-defence or the prevention of crime is concerned, if the jury came to the conclusion that the defendant believed, or may have believed, that he was being attacked or that a crime was being committed, and that force was necessary to protect himself or to prevent the crime, then the prosecution have not proved their case. If, however, the defendant's alleged belief was mistaken and if the mistake was an unreasonable one, that may be a powerful reason for coming to the conclusion that the belief was not honestly held and should be rejected. Even if the jury come to the conclusion that the mistake was an unreasonable one, if the defendant may genuinely have been labouring under it, he is entitled to rely upon it.

... There may be a fear that the abandonment of the objective standard demanded by the existence of reasonable grounds for belief will result in the success of too many spurious claims of self-defence. The English experience has not shown this to be the case. The Judicial Studies Board with the approval of the Lord Chief Justice has produced a model direction on self-defence which is now widely used by judges when summing-up to juries. The direction contains the following guidance:

> Whether the plea is self-defence or defence of another, if the defendant may have been labouring under a mistake as to the facts, he must be judged according to his mistaken belief of the facts: that is so whether the mistake was, on an objective view, a reasonable mistake or not.

Their Lordships have heard no suggestion that this form of summing-up has resulted in a disquieting number of acquittals. This is hardly surprising, for no jury is going to accept a man's assertion that he believed that he was about to be attacked without testing it against all the surrounding circumstances. In assisting the jury to determine whether or not the accused had a genuine belief, the judge will of course direct their attention to those features of the evidence that make such a belief more or less probable. Where there are no reasonable grounds to hold a belief it will surely only be in exceptional circumstances that a jury will conclude that such a belief was or might have been held ...

R v Oatridge (1992) 94 Cr App R 367 (CA)

The appellant and the deceased had lived together. The deceased was a diabetic who became abusive and violent when drunk, and there was evidence that he had, on a number of occasions, struck the appellant during arguments. One evening both the appellant and the deceased returned to the flat that they shared after spending the evening apart drinking with friends. The deceased had been drinking much more heavily than the appellant. A quarrel ensued during which the appellant stabbed the deceased once with a knife, just below the sternum, severing a main pulmonary artery. The deceased died shortly afterwards. The appellant remained at the scene and summoned the emergency services. She admitted to the police that she had stabbed the deceased, stating: 'I stabbed him, he was at me, what else could I do ... He came in drunk, we had a fight. What could I do, I had to defend myself.' The appellant was convicted of murder and appealed.

Mustill LJ:
In many cases of self-defence the following questions must be asked: (1) Was the defendant under actual or threatened attack by the victim? (2) If yes, did the defendant act to defend himself

against this attack? (3) If yes, was his response commensurate with the degree of danger created by the attack? In answering this question allowance must of course be made for the fact that the defendant has to act in the heat of the moment and cannot be expected to measure his response exactly to the danger. (These questions are of course a considerable oversimplification, particularly since they omit reference to burden of proof. But they will suffice to illustrate the point at issue in the present appeal.) There are however occasions where a further question must be asked: (1a) Even if the defendant was not in fact under actual or threatened attack, did he nevertheless honestly believe that he was? . . . If this question is answered in the affirmative (or, more correctly, the prosecution does not establish that it should be answered in the negative), then the third question must be modified, so as to read: (3a) Was the response commensurate with the degree of risk which the defendant believed to be created by the attack under which he believed himself to be?

We return to the present case . . . In our opinion two questions arise on the appeal against the verdict of guilty. First, did the judge in fact give direction on mistaken belief? Second, if he did not should he have done so, in the light of the issues arising on the evidence? The first question does not bear elaborate analysis. Although there was a reference to honest belief, this was in the context of the 'agony of the moment' aspect of reasonable response, which is only indirectly linked with mistake as to the nature of the attack. The thrust of the summing-up was . . . to point up the radical issue as to whether the deceased really was setting out to strangle the appellant, and the question whether she might honestly have believed that he was even if in fact he was not, was not explored at all. We are fortified in the view that when [counsel for the defendant] raised the question of subjective belief, [counsel] for the Crown submitted that any direction on the topic would have to include a reference to the effect of drink on the appellant's belief, the judge did not say anything further to the jury. As we understand the matter it was not disputed before us, or at any rate not disputed with any great vigour, that the summing-up did not deal with honest mistake, and as the argument developed it emerged that the real question for decision was whether in the circumstances any such direction was required.

. . . Two points stand out: (1) Although the medical evidence suggests that the attack actually made was in pure physical terms not of great severity, it took place against the background of quite serious violence and threats of worse. (2) In one of the passages quoted the choice was not between a potentially lethal attack and a trifling assault. Even on the prosecution's case the victim tried unsuccessfully to get the appellant out of the front door by force, and then (being unsuccessful) grasped her by the throat.

It seems to us on these facts that the possibility of the appellant honestly believing that on this particular occasion the victim was really going to do what he had previously threatened – even if in fact this was not what he was going to do – was not so fanciful as to require its exclusion from the case as a piece of unnecessary clutter. This being so, although we respectfully endorse the learned judge's desire to keep the case as simple as possible, we consider that on this occasion he went too far. What the jury would have made of it if the point had been developed we cannot tell, but each of us considers that the jury might have felt that the possibility of mistake could not be excluded, in which case the question on proportionate response would have been crucially different . . . the appeal must be allowed.

R v Owino [1996] 2 Cr App R 128 (CA)

The appellant and his wife had a volatile relationship where heated arguments were common-place. The appellant was convicted on several counts of causing harm to his wife during these heated exchanges. He contended that, if he had caused any harm to his wife he had been acting in self-defence and that the trial judge had erred in not directing the jury accordingly.

Collins J:

. . . Unfortunately, the learned judge did not refer to self-defence at all in his summing up, and the jury retired shortly after 1 pm without any such direction being given to them. It was perfectly plain that such a direction ought to have been given . . . With the greatest of respect to the learned judge, if, as indeed was clear, the issue of self-defence had been raised on the evidence, he had a duty to put it to the jury and to direct the jury upon it . . .

Complaint is made by Mr Mendelle [counsel for the appellant] that [the trial judge] did not deal with [self-defence] . . . adequately as he ought to have done. Mr Mendelle essentially submits that he failed to direct the jury . . . that any force used must be unlawful, in the sense that it must have been excessive – more than was reasonable for self-defence; and further, that the test of what was reasonable was subjective, in the sense that the defendant could not be convicted unless he intended to use force which was more than was necessary for lawful self-defence. He relies on the authority of *Scarlett* [1993] 4 All ER 629 to support that proposition.

Before I come to the case of *Scarlett* specifically, it is our view that the law does not go as far as Mr Mendelle submits that it does. The essential elements of self-defence are clear enough. The jury have to decide whether a defendant honestly believed that the circumstances were such as required him to use force to defend himself from an attack or a threatened attack. In this respect a defendant must be judged in accordance with his honest belief, even though that belief may have been mistaken. But the jury must then decide whether the force used was reasonable in the circumstances as he believed them to be.

Scarlett was a case where a landlord of a public house had been ejecting, and perfectly lawfully and properly ejecting, a drunken customer from his public house. The allegation was that he had used excessive force in the course of ejecting him so that the customer fell down the steps of the entrance to the pub and unfortunately hit his head and was killed. What Mr Mendelle relies upon in the case of *Scarlett* is a passage at pp 295, 296 and p 636 of the respective reports, where Beldam LJ, giving the judgment of the court, said this:

> Where, as in the present case, an accused is justified in using some force and can only be guilty of an assault if the force used is excessive, the jury ought to be directed that he cannot be guilty of an assault unless the prosecution prove that he acted with the mental element necessary to constitute his action an assault, that is 'that the defendant intentionally or recklessly applied force to the person of another'. Further, they should be directed that the accused is not to be found guilty merely because he intentionally or recklessly used force which they consider to have been excessive. They ought not to convict him unless they are satisfied that the degree of force used was plainly more than was called for by the circumstances as he believed them to be and, provided he believed the circumstances called for the degree of force used, he is not to be convicted even if his belief was unreasonable.

In this case the learned judge gave no direction to the jury that the prosecution, to establish an assault, had to prove that the appellant intentionally or recklessly applied excessive force in seeking to evict the deceased.

The passage which we have cited could, if taken out of context, give rise to a suggestion that the submission by Mr Mendelle is well-founded. But what, in the context, the learned Lord Justice was really saying was, in our view, this: he was indicating that the elements of an assault involved the unlawful application of force. In the context of an issue of self-defence or reasonable restraint, which was what *Scarlett* was essentially about, then clearly a person would not be guilty of an assault unless the force used was excessive; and in judging whether the force used was excessive, the jury had to take account of the circumstances as he believed them to be. That is what is made clear in the first part of the sentence, which we will isolate and read again:

> They ought not to convict him unless they are satisfied that the degree of force used was plainly more than was called for by the circumstances as he believed them to be and, provided he believed the circumstances called for the degree of force used, he is not to be convicted even if his belief was unreasonable.

So far as the second half of the sentence is concerned, what we understand the learned Lord Justice to have been saying was that, in judging what he believed the circumstances to be, the jury are not to decide on the basis of what was objectively reasonable; and that even if he, the defendant, was unreasonable in his belief, if it was an honest belief and honestly held, that he is not to be judged by reference to the true circumstances. It is in that context that the learned Lord Justice talks about '[belief] that the circumstances called for the degree of force used', because clearly you cannot divorce completely the concept of degree of force and the concept of the circumstances as you believe them to be. In our judgment, that is effectively all that the learned Lord Justice was saying.

What he was not saying, in our view (and indeed if he had said it, it would be contrary to authority) was that the belief, however ill-founded, of the defendant that the degree of force he was using was reasonable, will enable him to do what he did. As Kay J indicated in argument, if that argument was correct, then it would justify, for example, the shooting of someone who was merely threatening to throw a punch, on the basis that the defendant honestly believed, although unreasonably and mistakenly, that it was justifiable for him to use that degree of force. That clearly is not, and cannot be, the law.

In truth, in the view of this court, the law was properly and adequately set out in the case of *Williams* [1984] 3 All ER 411, which was cited and referred to in *Scarlett* and the court in *Scarlett* was not going beyond what is set out in *Williams* . . .

R v Martin [2001] All ER (D) 435 (Oct)

The appellant lived alone in a remote farmhouse. His house was burgled at night by two men, Barras and Fearon. The appellant opened fire on the two intruders with his 12-bore Winchester pump-action shotgun. He did not give any warning. Barras was shot in the back and in his legs and Fearon was also shot in both legs. Barras collapsed and died a short distance from the house. At his trial for the murder of Barras and the attempted murder of Fearon, the appellant unsuccessfully advanced a defence of self-defence and was sentenced to life imprisonment. One of the issues considered on appeal was the extent to which the appellant's mental characteristics should have been taken into account in assessing the reasonableness of the force used by way of self-defence.

Lord Woolf CJ:

5. In judging whether the defendant had only used reasonable force, the jury has to take into account all the circumstances, including the situation as the defendant honestly believes it to be at the time, when he was defending himself. It does not matter if the defendant was mistaken in his belief as long as his belief was genuine.

6. Accordingly, the jury could only convict Mr Martin if either they did not believe his evidence that he was acting in self-defence or they thought that Mr Martin had used an unreasonable amount of force . . .

7. As to the first issue, what Mr Martin believed, the jury heard his evidence and they could only reject that evidence, if they were satisfied it was untrue. As to the second issue, as to what is a reasonable amount of force, obviously opinions can differ. It cannot be left to a defendant to decide what force it is reasonable to use because this would mean that even if a defendant used disproportionate force but he believed he was acting reasonably he would not be guilty of any offence. It is for this reason that it was for the jury, as the representative of the public, to decide the amount of force which it would be reasonable and the amount of force which it would be unreasonable to use in the circumstances in which they found that Mr Martin believed himself to be in. It is only if the jury are sure that the amount of force which was used was unreasonable that they are entitled to find a defendant guilty if he was acting in self-defence.

8. These features of the defence of self-defence are critical to the outcome of this appeal. They are difficult to criticise and mean that Mr Martin is faced with the fact that the jury must have decided that when he shot the two men, he was either not acting in self-defence or, if he was, he used excessive force.

Lord Woolf CJ then referred to expert medical evidence, not available at the time of the trial, suggesting that the appellant suffered from a mental condition that would have caused him to perceive a much greater danger to his physical safety than the average person, and may also have caused him to suffer 'a genuine period of amnesia' when dealing with the intruders. Counsel for the appellant therefore sought to argue that if the jury had considered and accepted the expert evidence as to this, this would have made the jury more willing to accept that the appellant acted reasonably in firing the gun as he did.

65. Mr Wolkind [for the appellant] relied on the recent decision of the House of Lords in *R v Smith* [2001] 1 CAR 31. This was also a provocation case that Mr Wolkind contended could be applied to the similar issues which arise when a defendant relies on self-defence. In that case Smith was relying upon evidence that he suffered from clinical depression. There was no dispute that the evidence was admissible and relevant on the issue as to whether he was provoked, the subjective issue. The problem was as to whether the evidence was admissible as being relevant on the objective issue of loss of self-control. As to this the majority of their Lordships came to the conclusion that the jury were entitled to take into account some characteristic, whether temporary or permanent, which affected the degree of control which society could reasonably expect of a defendant and which it would be unjust not to take into account.

66. Is the same approach appropriate in the case of self-defence? There are policy reasons

for distinguishing provocation from self-defence. Provocation only applies to murder but self-defence applies to all assaults. In addition, provocation does not provide a complete defence; it only reduces the offence from murder to manslaughter. There is also the undoubted fact that self-defence is raised in a great many cases resulting from minor assaults and it would be wholly disproportionate to encourage medical disputes in cases of that sort. Lord Hobhouse in his dissenting speech in *Smith* recognised that in relation to self-defence too generous an approach as to what is reasonable could result in an 'exorbitant defence' (p 93 para 186). Lord Hoffmann also appeared conscious of this. As a matter of principle we would reject the suggestion that the approach of the majority in *Smith* in relation to provocation should be applied directly to the different issue of self-defence.

67. We would accept that the jury are entitled to take into account in relation to self-defence the physical characteristics of the defendant. However, we would not agree that it is appropriate, except in exceptional circumstances which would make the evidence especially probative, in deciding whether excessive force has been used to take into account whether the defendant is suffering from some psychiatric condition.

68. The only other issue, as to which the medical evidence could possibly be relevant, so far as self-defence is concerned, is as to what Mr Martin believed the situation to be when he fired the shots. However he himself gave evidence as to this and it was for the jury to decide the extent to which they could act on his evidence.

. . .

72. While we recognise [that the new expert evidence regarding the appellant's mental state] could be said to [be admissible] . . . on the issue of self-defence in this case we do not consider it would have advanced the defence of self-defence. While it is true that the jury were unaware of Dr Joseph's diagnosis that Mr Martin suffered from a paranoid personality disorder and so consequently might have perceived a greater danger to his physical safety than an average person in his situation, they did have the evidence of Mr Martin himself (on which Dr Joseph based his diagnosis) including that Mr Martin was terrified for his life. They knew that Mr Martin was a very eccentric man indeed and that he was obsessed with the security of his home. A large part of the summing-up was spent dealing with this evidence with the judge making clear the undoubted relevance of what Mr Martin believed the situation to be. The jury could have been in no doubt but that their judgment of Mr Martin's actions had to be made by placing themselves in Mr Martin's shoes. In our judgment had that part of Dr Joseph's opinion on this aspect of the case been before the jury it would not have affected their decision and its omission does not render his conviction unsafe.

14.11.1 WHERE THE DEFENDANT'S MISTAKE REGARDING SELF-DEFENCE ARISES BECAUSE HE IS INTOXICATED

As will have been seen from the case extracts at 14.11 a defendant who mistakenly believes he is entitled to use reasonable force to defend himself is entitled to be judged on the facts as he honestly believes them to be. What if, however, D makes his mistake of fact because of his voluntary intoxication? Logic might suggest that D should be entitled to be judged on the facts as he wrongly believed them to be if there is evidence that he would have made the relevant mistake of fact even if sober. As the following extract indicates, the law adopts a more 'broad brush' approach and simply prohibits D from relying on a drunken mistake of fact as a basis for self-defence.

R v Hatton [2005] All ER (D) 308 (Oct)

D had killed P by beating him to death with a sledgehammer. There was evidence that D had consumed over 20 pints of beer on the evening in question and that he may have believed P to have been an SAS soldier attacking him with a sword. The issue of the relevance of D's intoxication to any mistake he might have made regarding the need to act in self-defence was considered by the trial judge who ruled that it was not open to D to rely on a mistake induced by drunkenness. D was convicted of murder, and appealed against his conviction.

The Court of Appeal, dismissing the appeal, held that the decision in *R v O'Grady* [1987] 3 All ER 420 was to be followed, and rejected the argument that it was *obiter* for the purposes of this case because O'Grady had been convicted only of manslaughter.

Lord Phillips LCJ:

[10]. Mr Newman [counsel for Hatton] accepts [that his] submission is inconsistent with the judgment of this court in *O'Grady*. He submits, however, that the observations in that case were wrong in principle and were *obiter dicta*, so that we need not and should not follow them. We turn at once to that case.

. . .

[13]. . . . Lord Lane then stated the conclusion of the court in the following passage:

How should the jury be invited to approach the problem? One starts with the decision of this Court in *Williams (Gladstone)* (1984) 78 Cr App R 276, namely that where the defendant might have been labouring under a mistake as to the facts he must be judged according to that mistaken view, whether the mistake was reasonable or not. It is then for the jury to decide whether the defendant's reaction to the threat (real or imaginary) was a reasonable one. The Court was not in that case considering what the situation might be where the mistake was due to voluntary intoxication by alcohol or some other drug.

We have come to the conclusion that where the jury are satisfied that the defendant was mistaken in his belief that any force or the force which he in fact used was necessary to defend himself and are further satisfied that the mistake was caused by voluntarily induced intoxication, the defence must fail. We do not consider that any distinction should be drawn on this aspect of the matter between offences involving what is called specific intent, such as murder, and the offences of so-called basic intent, such as manslaughter. Quite apart from the problem of directing a jury in a case such as the present where manslaughter is an alternative verdict to murder, the question of mistake can and ought to be considered separately from the question of intent. A sober man who mistakenly believes he is in danger of immediate death at the hands of an attacker is entitled to be acquitted of both murder and manslaughter if his reaction in killing his supposed assailant was a reasonable one. What his intent may have been seems to us to be irrelevant to the problem of self-defence or no. Secondly, we respectfully adopt the reasoning of McCullough J already set out.

This brings us to the question of public order. There are two competing interests. On the one hand the interest of the defendant who has only acted according to what he believed to be necessary to protect himself, and on the other hand that of the public in general and the victim in particular who, probably through no fault of his own, has been injured or perhaps killed because of the defendant's drunken mistake. Reason recoils from the conclusion that in such circumstances a defendant is entitled to leave the Court without a stain on his character.

. . .

16. In a commentary to *O'Grady*, after the report in the Criminal Law Review, Professor John Smith commented that the decision proceeded on the basis that self-defence was a complete defence to a charge of homicide which was unfounded. A defendant who relied on a reasonable reaction to a drunken mistake to establish a defence to murder could not rely on the drunken mistake as a defence to manslaughter: see the decision of the House of Lords in *Majewski*. Professor Smith commended the recommendation of the Criminal Law Revision Committee (Fourteenth Report, Cmnd 7844 para 2777) that the evidence of voluntary intoxication adduced in relation to a defence should be treated in the same way as evidence of voluntary intoxication adduced to negative the mental element in a crime of specific intent.

17. Professor Smith commented that the decision in *O'Grady* was *obiter* because the appellant had been convicted only of manslaughter. Professor Smith returned to this theme in a commentary in the Criminal Law Review in *O'Connor*. He argued that this court was wrong to regard *O'Grady* as binding authority because *O'Grady* was convicted only of manslaughter, so anything said about the law of murder on appeal must have been unnecessary to the decision and *obiter*. Perhaps nor surprisingly, the same argument was advanced in the tenth edition of *Smith and Hogan's Criminal Law* at page 247, and is repeated in the current edition. Mr Newman adopted that argument. Mr Kelson QC for the Crown contended that this court in *O'Connor* had been right to regard *O'Grady* as binding authority.

18. We have used the term '*obiter dicta*' because it is a recognised legal term of art that is not readily reproduced by an English phrase. The term describes judicial statements which are peripheral to the reason for the decision, the *ratio decidendi*. *Halsbury's Laws*, 4th Ed, dealing at paragraph 1237 with 'Judicial Decisions as Authorities' accurately states 'The enunciation of the reason or principle upon which a question before the court has been decided is alone binding as precedent.' In considering whether the relevant statements of Lord Lane in *O'Grady* were *obiter* it is necessary to consider what was in issue and what was the reason or principle applied by the court in resolving that issue.

. . .

23. With this background we come to *O'Grady*. At issue in that case was whether the trial judge had correctly directed the jury in relation to self-defence on a charge of murder. As Professor Smith has pointed out, that question was approached on the express premise that where self-defence provides a defence to a charge of murder, it will equally provide a defence to an alternative charge of manslaughter. The reasoning of the court drew no distinction between murder and manslaughter. Having given judgment the court certified that its decision raised a point of law of general public importance, namely: 'Is a defendant who raises the issue of self-defence entitled to be judged upon the basis that he mistakenly believed it to be the situation when that mistaken belief was brought about by self-induced intoxication by alcohol or other drugs?' That was the

issue that this court addressed. It was a general issue, not restricted to the offence of man-slaughter. To that issue the court gave the answer 'No'. We do not believe that upon a proper application of the law of precedence we can treat the general principle that was the reason for this court's decision as being mere *obiter dicta* so far as the law murder is concerned. We are obliged to follow *O'Grady* and to reject Mr Newman's contention that the judge should have directed the jury to consider whether the appellant's drunkenness might have led him to make a mistake as to the severity of any attack to which he may have been subjected by [the deceased].

COMMENTS AND QUESTIONS

1   Once the threat has been removed, or subsided, the right to act in self-defence falls away. Hence in *Priestnall v Cornish* [1979] Crim LR 310, where the victim had retreated into his car after an altercation with the defendant following a road rage incident, and had therefore ceased to be a threat, the defendant was held not to have been acting in self-defence in continuing to attack the victim as, by then, the defendant had had every means of retreat open to him.

2   If D uses reasonable force to stop B (who is 9 years old) from attacking C, can D rely on s 3(1)? See the extract from *Re A* (below). If D comes upon A attacking B and he uses reasonable force to restrain A, can he rely on s 3(1) if A is, in reality, defending himself from an attack by B?

3   Where D makes a genuine mistake as to the need to act in self-defence he is judged on the facts as he believed them to be and, provided the force used was reasonable in the circum-stances as he believed them to be, he will be acquitted – see *Beckford*. If D is genuinely in a situation where he is justified in using force by way of self-defence, but makes a mistake as to the extent of the force required and uses more force than is reasonable, does the decision in *Clegg* mean that he has no defence? If so is this fair?

4   Compare *R v Martin* [2001] All ER (D) 435 (Oct), above, with *Shaw (Norman) v R* [2002] Crim LR 140, where the Privy Council held that (for the purposes of the defence of self-defence in Belize) a proper direction to the jury on self-defence would be: (a) did D honestly believe that it was necessary to defend himself? If so, (b) on the basis of the facts and the danger perceived by D, was the force used reasonable? Such an approach would have been more favourable to Tony Martin, given the fresh evidence of mental abnormality – should domestic law adopt this approach?

14.12 SELF-DEFENCE AND NECESSITY

As will have been seen from the above extracts, self-defence (whether at common law or under statute) arises where D claims that he was compelled to act to prevent a greater evil, whether this be harm to himself, others, harm to his property or the prevention of crime. The defence of necessity does not, of course, extend to killing another person in order to save one's own life. How can this be reconciled with the fact that the law allows D to kill another in self-defence?

The answer lies, in part, in the status of the victim. In *R v Dudley and Stephens* (see Chapter 14.8 above) the cabin boy killed by the defendants was an 'innocent' party. Where D kills P in order to prevent a murderous attack by P, P ceases to be an 'innocent' party – in effect he becomes fair game. This can cause difficulties where P is under the age of criminal responsibility – in such cases is it really accurate to say that P is not 'innocent'? The following extract addresses the matter.

Re A (Children) (Conjoined Twins: Surgical Separation) [2000] 4 All ER 961

For the facts see 14.8 (above). Ward LJ considered whether operating to save one conjoined twin in the knowledge that it would cause the certain death of the other would offend the 'sanctity of life' principle.

Ward LJ:

The second reason why the right of choice should be given to the doctors is that the proposed operation would not in any event offend the sanctity of life principle. That principle may be expressed in different ways but they all amount to the same thing. Some might say that it demands that each life is to be protected from unjust attack. Some might say as the joint statement by the Anglican and Roman Catholic bishops did in the aftermath of the *Bland* judgment that because human life is a gift from God to be preserved and cherished, the deliberate taking of human life is prohibited except in self-defence or the legitimate defence of others. The Archbishop defines it in terms that human life is sacred, that it is inviolable, so that one should never aim to cause an innocent person's death by act or omission. The reality here – harsh as it is to state it, and unnatural as it is that it should be happening – is that Mary is killing Jodie. That is the effect of the incontrovertible medical evidence and it is common ground in the case. Mary uses Jodie's heart and lungs to receive and use Jodie's oxygenated blood. This will cause Jodie's heart to fail and cause Jodie's death as surely as a slow drip of poison. How can it be just that Jodie should be required to tolerate that state of affairs? One does not need to label Mary with the American terminology which would paint her to be 'an unjust aggressor', which I feel is wholly inappropriate language for the sad and helpless position in which Mary finds herself. I have no difficulty in agreeing that this unique happening cannot be said to be unlawful. But it does not have to be unlawful. The six-year-old boy indiscriminately shooting all and sundry in the school playground is not acting unlawfully for he is too young for his acts to be so classified. But is he 'innocent' within the moral meaning of that word as used by the Archbishop? I am not qualified to answer that moral question because, despite an assertion – or was it an aspersion? – by a member of the Bar in a letter to *The Times* that we, the judges, are proclaiming some moral superiority in this case, I for my part would defer any opinion as to a child's innocence to the Archbishop for that is his territory. If I had to hazard a guess, I would venture the tentative view that the child is not morally innocent. What I am, however, competent to say is that in law killing that six-year-old boy in self-defence of others would be fully justified and the killing would not be unlawful. I can see no difference in essence between that resort to legitimate self-defence and the doctors coming to Jodie's defence and removing the threat of fatal harm to her presented by Mary's draining her life-blood. The availability of such a plea of quasi self-defence, modified to meet the quite exceptional circumstances nature has inflicted on the twins, makes intervention by the doctors lawful.

14.13 SELF-DEFENCE – CODIFICATION AND LAW REFORM PROPOSALS

The most recent examination of the use of force by way of defence has been in the context of the Law Commission's review of offences against the person, *Legislating the Criminal Code: Offences Against the Person* (Law Com 218). Its proposals as regards the lawful use of force are set out in clauses 27–29 of the Criminal Law Bill attached to the report.

27(1) The use of force by a person for any of the following purposes, if only such as is reasonable in the circumstances as he believes them to be, does not constitute an offence –

    (a) to protect himself or another from injury, assault or detention caused by a criminal act;

    (b) to protect himself or (with the authority of that other) another from trespass to the person;

    (c) to protect his property from appropriation, destruction or damage caused by a criminal act or from trespass or infringement;

    (d) to protect property belonging to another from appropriation, destruction or damage caused by a criminal act or (with the authority of the other) from trespass or infringement; or

    (e) to prevent crime or a breach of the peace.

(2) The expressions 'use of force' and 'property' in subsection (1) are defined and extended by sections 29 and 30 respectively.

(3) For the purposes of this section an act involves a 'crime' or is 'criminal' although the person committing it, if charged with an offence in respect of it, would be acquitted on the ground that –

    (a) he was under ten years of age, or

    (b) he acted under duress, whether by threats or of circumstances, or

    (c) his act was involuntary, or

    (d) he was in a state of intoxication, or

    (e) he was insane, so as not to be responsible, according to law, for the act.

(4) The references in subsection (1) to protecting a person or property from anything include protecting him or it from its continuing; and the reference to preventing crime or a breach of the peace shall be similarly construed.

(5) For the purposes of this section the question whether the act against which force is used is of a kind mentioned in any of paragraphs (a) to (e) of subsection (1) shall be determined according to the circumstances as the person using the force ('D') believes them to be.

    In the following provisions of this section references to unlawful or lawful acts are to acts which are or are not of such a kind.

(6) Where an act is lawful by reason only of a belief or suspicion which is mistaken, the defence provided by this section applies as in the case of an unlawful act, unless –

    (a) D knows or believes that the force is used against a constable or a person assisting a constable, and

    (b) the constable is acting in the execution of his duty,

    in which case the defence applies only if D believes the force to be immediately necessary to prevent injury to himself or another.

(7) The defence provided by this section does not apply to a person who causes conduct or a state of affairs with a view to using force to resist or terminate it.

But the defence may apply although the occasion for the use of force arises only because he does something he may lawfully do, knowing that such an occasion may arise.

28(1) The use of force by a person in effecting or assisting in a lawful arrest, if only such as is reasonable in the circumstances as he believes them to be, does not constitute an offence.

(2) The expression 'use of force' in subsection (1) is defined and extended by section 29.

(3) For the purposes of this section the question whether the arrest is lawful shall be determined according to the circumstances as the person using the force believed them to be.

29(1) For the purposes of sections 27 and 28 –

    (a) a person uses force in relation to another person or property not only where he applies force to, but also where he causes an impact on, the body of that person or that property;

    (b) a person shall be treated as using force in relation to another person if –

        (i) he threatens him with its use, or

        (ii) he detains him without actually using it; and

    (c) a person shall be treated as using force in relation to property if he threatens a person with its use in relation to property.

(2) Those sections apply in relation to acts immediately preparatory to the use of force as they apply in relation to acts in which force is used.

(3) A threat of force may be reasonable although the actual use of force would not be.

(4) The fact that a person had an opportunity to retreat before using force shall be taken into account, in conjunction with other relevant evidence, in determining whether the use of force was reasonable.

The commentary in the report provides the following rationale for these proposals:

Introduction

36.1 The Draft Code brought together for the first time various elements in the existing common law relating to the justifiable use of force, and expressed that part of the law in a rational statutory form. In LCCP 122 we provisionally proposed the statutory adoption of a similar clause, which would in effect codify the existing common law, and some related statutory additions, while at the same time eliminating some of the inconsistencies and uncertainties that have been produced by the unconnected development of different areas of the law.

36.2 It is, however, important to note that even the rationalised version of the common law that we proposed in LCCP 122, and which we recommend in this Report, does not cover all cases in which a person may use force against the person or property of another without incurring criminal liability. The law set out in the Criminal Law Bill covers a wide range of possible events, and seeks to define the circumstances in which the defence of justified use of force will apply with as much clarity as possible, in order to assist courts and other users in those cases where issues of the use of force for self-protection or cognate purposes most often arise . . .

36.3 The most significant element in this part of the law is the present common law of self-defence. The basis of the present law of self-defence is that a person has a defence to a criminal charge if he acts to prevent the commission of an unjustifiable attack on himself or another, and the steps that he takes are reasonable in the circumstances as he believes them to be. The attack will often itself be criminal, but it need not necessarily be so in order to fulfil the requirements of the present law of self-defence. The present common law has a number of important features, which we stress here because they form the basis of the general statutory provision that we put forward in LCCP 122, and which is reproduced in substance in the Criminal Law Bill.

36.4 The essential justification of the defendant's acts is that he has acted for *self-protection*. No act that is done for motives of revenge, or in a spirit of informal punishment, can even potentially qualify for consideration under this defence.

36.5 The question for the jury is whether the defendant's acts of self-protection were reasonable in the circumstances that he believed to exist. That question has two distinct elements.

36.6 First, the defendant is judged according to the facts as he believed them to be. That was clearly established in the present law by the judgment of Lord Lane CJ in *Gladstone Williams* and further confirmed by the Privy Council in *Beckford v R*. This element, as Lord Lane pointed out, is of importance in eliminating the possibility that the accused was acting under a genuine mistake of fact. His Lordship emphasised that the reasonableness or unreasonableness of any belief alleged by the defendant is relevant to the question of whether the defendant held the belief at all: because if an unreasonable belief is alleged the jury are likely to have difficulty in thinking that the accused may be telling the truth. But, again to cite Lord Lane, 'If the belief was in fact held, its unreasonableness, so far as guilt or innocence is concerned, is neither here nor there.'

36.7 In his judgment the Lord Chief Justice referred to the recommendation of the CLRC in its Fourteenth Report that:

> The common law of self-defence should be replaced by a statutory defence providing that a person may use such force as is reasonable in the circumstances as he believes them to be in the defence of himself or any other person.

The court considered that that proposition already represented the common law. The statutory expression of the law of self-defence that we proposed in LCCP 122, and which we repeat in the Criminal Law Bill, therefore gives effect to the CLRC's desire that the defence should be put on a statutory footing, and incorporates the statement of the law that was considered to be correct both by the CLRC and by the court in *Gladstone Williams*.

36.8 In practice, the principle that the accused must be judged on the facts as he believed them to be is unlikely frequently to be decisive of the outcome of a case. It will not often be the case, and the jury are unlikely often to think, that the defendant may have mistakenly believed that, for instance, he or another person was about to be attacked, when a reasonable person in the defendant's position would not have so believed. But, for instance in a confused situation of brawling or disorder in a street or public house, or where there is a heated argument between two individuals, A may genuinely mistake B's raising of his hand as the immediate precursor of an attack on A, rather than as merely his seeking to emphasise a point or to summon help. Somewhat similarly, police officer A may wrongly and indeed unreasonably believe that B whom he is arresting is armed, and use the amount of force against him that would be reasonable if his belief were true; or he may make a mistake of identity, and think that B, an innocuous person, is C, a dangerous armed criminal. In such circumstances it would be unjust, as the Court of Appeal said in *Gladstone Williams*, if A, provided he did no more than would have been reasonably required to avoid an expected attack on himself, and not in a spirit of aggression or revenge, were to be exposed to criminal liability simply because of his mistaken or even negligent belief.

36.9 The second requirement of the present law of self-defence is that while, as emphasised in *Gladstone Williams*, the defendant is judged according to what he believed the circumstances to be, he will only be able to claim the benefit of this defence if he has acted (objectively) reasonably in the light of those circumstances. This requirement is equally as important as that just discussed. It is not for the defendant himself to adjudicate upon the reasonableness of the steps that he takes to prevent the offence, because that would unfairly and dangerously exculpate defendants who had an irresponsible, irrational or anti-social notion of the extent to which it is acceptable to react when threatened with attack. The reasonableness of the defendant's reaction is rather to be adjudicated upon by the jury, as a means of applying an external control to the conduct of persons who think themselves to be under attack.

The approach of the Criminal Law Bill

37.1 In LCCP 122 we proposed the adoption of the principles set out above, and their extension beyond the central case of self-defence to other cases where, in the present law, a defendant may be excused if he acts to protect valid personal and social interests: in particular, if he acts to protect property, or to prevent crime or in the arrest of offenders.

37.2 In these latter cases, the law is already broadly the same as that obtaining in the case of defence of the person. There are, however, some anomalies, and some unjustifiable gaps or uncertainties in the provision that the law currently makes. Clause 28 of the Bill that we submitted for consultation under LCCP 122 aimed to rationalise these problems, in line with the general principles of self-defence set out above. There was no significant dissent on consultation from that approach, which we have therefore felt justified in following through in the Criminal Law Bill. It may however be helpful if we summarise the gaps or illogicalities in the present law that clauses 27–30 of the Criminal Law Bill address.

37.3 The Criminal Damage Act 1971, section 5(2)(b), enables a person to rely on his purpose of protecting property as a 'lawful excuse' for the destruction of, or damage to, property belonging to another. The Criminal Law Act 1967, section 3(1), has been interpreted as providing a defence to a charge of reckless driving where a driver forces another car off the road in order to effect a person's arrest, at least where the 'force' used is 'reasonable in the circumstances'. But no provision at present identifies as a 'lawful excuse', for an act directed against property, the purpose of defending a person against unlawful force or of releasing a person from unlawful detention. Conversely, no provision at present expressly permits, in defence of property against an attack (as opposed to prevention of the crime that that attack may constitute), a use of force other than force directed against other property. The law is thus in need of the rationalisation provided by the Criminal Law Bill, since it ought surely to be made explicit that the purpose of protecting valuable property against vandalism is a defence to a use of modest force against the vandal; as, equally, it ought to be made explicit that force against property may be excusable when used in protection of a person as well as when used in protection of other property.

37.4 The Criminal Law Bill (together with amendments to the Criminal Damage Act) aims to improve further on existing law by providing consistently for the various purposes for which force may be lawfully used. The lawfulness of force used to protect a person against a violent attack ought not to depend upon whether its purpose is described as preventing the aggressor's crime or as the defence of the victim: the same act may have both purposes. But at present the use of force in the prevention of crime, as in effecting an arrest, is governed by section 3 of the Criminal Law Act 1967, and the use of force in self-defence or the defence of another is governed by the common law; and the principles are probably not quite the same.

37.5 A further important anomaly in the present law is that, as stressed in paragraph 36.9 above, the common law only allows such force in defence of the person as is objectively reasonable; whereas section 5(2)(b) of the Criminal Damage Act 1971 permits a person to damage or destroy another's property in order to protect his own property if he believes the means of protection that he employs to be reasonable. That cannot be right. It is anomalous that different, and less stringent, standards should apply when a person is defending his property than when he is defending his person, or defending another person; and it is in any event undesirable in any case, for the reasons suggested in paragraph 36.9 above, that the reasonableness of an accused's conduct should be judged by him rather than by objective external standards supervised by the court.

37.6 The Criminal Law Bill does not propose the complete repeal of section 5 of the Criminal Damage Act, and its replacement by the general provisions of the proposed new clauses. We think that it will be easier for those who have to deal with this chapter of the law if section 5, which has stood for twenty years, is retained as a special defence in cases of damage to property, even though it will substantially overlap with the new clause. That however is subject to the important qualification that the defence provided by the Criminal Damage Act should be amended to bring it into line, in respect of the requirement that the defendant's conduct should be objectively reasonable, and not merely reasonable in his own estimation, with the common law of self-defence that is described above. That step, which was proposed in LCCP 122, 117 and not dissented from on consultation, is therefore provided for in the Criminal Law Bill.

37.7 On consultation on LCCP 122 there was no substantial disagreement with the approach contained in that Consultation Paper and outlined above. In particular, no respondent disagreed with the principle established in *Gladstone Williams* that the accused should be judged according to the circumstances that he believed to exist. We are therefore able with some confidence to put forward in the Criminal Law Bill a scheme that is in substance the scheme contained in LCCP 122 and, indeed, in the Draft Code.

37.8 Respondents to consultation did, however, make some valuable comments on the detailed drafting of the Bill annexed to LCCP 122, and our own further consideration has also caused us to review that draft in some respects. That has been done principally in order to clarify the application of the law in cases where people act under a mistake as to the other party's intentions, for instance where D mistakenly thinks that P is about to attack him or steal his property, and takes what would, if he were right, be reasonable pre-emptive action. Such cases may not arise, or be prosecuted, very frequently, but prosecutors and courts require guidance when they do.

37.9 Clauses 27–30 of the Criminal Law Bill set out a statement of the law in a form that is intended to give as complete guidance as is possible to police, prosecutors and the citizen in considering this part of the law, and to the courts in applying it . . . these clauses bring what is in effect the present common law immediately and clearly to the attention of all those concerned with cases where self-defence or related matters are in issue. These basic provisions are grouped in clause 27. Provisions addressing special cases, and more detailed and explanatory matter, are placed in clauses 28–30.

37.10 The rest of this part of the Report comments on the provisions of those clauses. It will be convenient in that discussion to refer to the person using the force as 'D', and to the person against whom the force is used as 'P'.

PURPOSES FOR WHICH THE USE OF FORCE CAN BE JUSTIFIED

The concept of use of force

38.1 Clauses 27–30 of the Criminal Law Bill set out the circumstances in which the use of 'force' against the person or property of another will not constitute a criminal offence. The clauses apply generally, to all offences, though in practice they are most likely to come into play where self-defence is relied on as a defence to charges of assault or of the more serious offences against the person that are contained in clauses 2–4 of the Criminal Law Bill; and in cases of homicide.

38.2 The basic meaning of 'force' is not likely to cause difficulty, and the Criminal Law Bill contains no definition of this simple everyday concept. Some particular cases, including threats to use force, and the detention of a person without actually using force, are, however, dealt with in clause 29 of the Criminal Law Bill.

Types of conduct that may justify the use of force

38.3 The purposes for which the use of force may be justified, if the force is reasonable in the circumstances that D believes to exist, are listed in clause 27(1). A further purpose, the use of force in effecting or assisting in a lawful arrest, is, for the reasons explained in paragraph 38.31 below, separately set out in clause 28 of the Criminal Law Bill. It is important to note that all these categories are not mutually exclusive: for instance, where D acts to prevent P from assault-ing him he will be simultaneously protecting himself from a criminal assault; and protecting him-self from a tortious trespass; and seeking to prevent the commission of a crime by P. The question in any case will, therefore, be whether D's acts fall within any one of the categories listed in clauses 27 and 28.

38.4 In accordance with the basic requirement of the defence of self-defence, that was men-tioned in paragraph 36.4 above, the essence of all these cases is that they should have as their motive the *protection* of persons or property, or the *prevention* of crime or breach of the peace.

38.5 We have endeavoured in the Criminal Law Bill to set out the various cases in a way that identifies for users the nature of, and justification for, the particular categories. For that reason, we have abandoned the use of the generalised concept of protection against 'unlawful' force or injury, in favour of separately identifying protection against criminal and against tortious acts . . .

. . .

38.7 We now comment briefly on the cases listed in clause 27(1). In accordance with the current law as explained in paragraphs 36.6–36.8 above, whether a situation falls within one of the categories in which the use of force may be justified is to be determined according to the circum-stances as the defendant, D, believed them to be. That rule is stated explicitly in clause 27(5) of the Criminal Law Bill. If D knows or believes that the circumstances are such that P's acts do not fall into any of the categories of conduct against which force may *prima facie* be legitimately used, then he cannot claim the protection of this defence. But if he, even wrongly, believes that P's conduct is such that it would amount to a crime, or to a trespass against D, then it would seem wrong that he should be burdened with criminal liability if he reacts reasonably to protect person or property from a feared attack.

38.8 '*Self-defence*'. Paragraphs (a) and (b) reproduce the present law of self-defence, that was described in paragraphs 36.4–36.8 above. For reasons that are explained in paragraph 38.19 ff below, it is convenient to deal separately with protection against criminal and against tortious interference with the person, though in all but the most unusual cases the two categories will overlap. The Bill's extended definition of 'force', as including force in relation to property, cures what might otherwise be a lacuna in the present law, where there is no explicit provision justifying acts directed at property for the purpose of defending a person from unlawful injury or detention.

38.9 Paragraphs (a) and (b) apply, as does the present law, to the reasonable defence of others, as well as to the defence of the person actually using the force; so for that reason it is not strictly accurate to describe the paragraphs as dealing with self-defence. One particular aspect of the use of force by D to protect a third party should however be noted.

38.10 Paragraph (b) addresses acts by P that are trespasses to the person but which are not or may not be a *criminal* act: principally where there is or may be doubt as to whether P's attack takes place with the mental element necessary for criminal liability. In respect of the protection of others from trespass, the Criminal Law Bill confirms the proposal of LCCP 122 that where an act of P directed against a third party is merely trespassory and not criminal, D should only be able to use force to prevent it with the agreement of that third party. This limitation on officious intermeddling in the affairs of others is perhaps of more practical importance in relation to acts done to protect the property of others, which we discuss in paragraph 38.15 below.

38.11 *Protection of property.* Where D is charged with criminal damage and his defence is that he was acting in defence of his own property, for instance where D kills P's dog that he claims was attacking his sheep, his liability will continue to be adjudicated on by the rules laid down under the Criminal Damage Act 1971. The provisions of paragraphs (c) and (d) of clause 27(1) of the Criminal Law Bill are however required to confirm, what is not expressly provided in the current law, that the same principles as apply in cases of self-defence extend also to the use of force against a person to protect property. What would be reasonable in such circumstances would, of course, be adjudicated upon in the light of the force having been used to protect property rather than a person: it being generally more reasonable to use serious force to protect a person than when merely property interests are at stake.

38.12 In respect of the non-criminal acts on the part of P to which the defence *prima facie* applies, we consider that 'trespass' as used in paragraphs (c) and (d) will better focus attention on the type of case in which this defence might properly arise than did the more general formula of 'unlawful appropriation, destruction or damage' that we proposed in LCCP 122.

38.13 Paragraphs (c) and (d) of clause 27(1) of the Criminal Law Bill do, however, refer, as did the LCCP 122 Bill, to 'infringement' of property. That, together with the definition of 'property' in clause 30(1) of the Criminal Law Bill as including any right, interest or privilege over property, keeps this defence in line with the Criminal Damage Act, where the defence provided by section 5(2)(b) extends to the protection of an interest in property including, by section 5(4), any right or privilege in or over land. Under the Criminal Law Bill, therefore, reasonable force may be permissibly used to prevent unlawful interference with the exercise of such a right (for instance, an easement or a right to fish) rather than merely to protect the property itself.

38.14 The interest or right protected must, however, be in or over tangible property. We had originally, in LCCP 122, thought that the defence of reasonable use of force could appropriately, if in practice not very frequently, be applied in relation also to interferences with intangible property. However, it has been brought to our attention that the Copyright, Design and Patents Act 1988, while providing for certain acts of self-help on the part of a copyright owner, places strict limits on such acts. The decision to place limitations on the protection of intangible property even in the case of perhaps the paradigmatic example of such property, copyright, is, we think, an indication that Parliament sees legal action rather than the direct protection of rights as the appropriate course in such cases. We do not think it appropriate that we should potentially undermine that policy by extending the present defence to cases of protection of intangible property.

38.15 Clause 27(1)(d) of the Criminal Law Bill envisages the use of force by D to protect the property of a third party. Where that protection is against trespass or infringement of a non-criminal nature, D does not have the benefit of this defence unless he acts with the authority of the third party. That distinction seems to us to be a sensible one. Where D is intervening to prevent a criminal act, he should not have to seek the permission of another party; and in any event will have the protection of the defence of prevention of crime under clause 27(1)(e) of the Criminal Law Bill. Where, however, P's interference is objectionable only because it is tortious against a third party, and not against D, D should not be encouraged to intervene in that dispute unless he does so on behalf of the third party. At the same time, however, in cases of emergency, where D judges that he has to act without the authority of the third party, and without the opportunity to warn or question P about his activities, then D will be able to rely on the defence of necessity. Cases of such a sort, where P's activities do not constitute or threaten the commission of a crime, are likely to be rare. We think it right that, before D intervenes in such non-criminal activity directed at a third party, the element of urgent need that characterises the defence of necessity should be present.

38.16 *Prevention of crime.* Clause 27(1)(e) of the Criminal Law Bill, in respect of the prevention of crime, covers the same ground as section 3 of the Criminal Law Act 1967. It will replace that section in relation to criminal liability for the use of force for that purpose. Section 3 will continue in operation in respect of civil liability for the use of force.

38.17 This category of excuse will often overlap with those already discussed; since, as pointed out above, one who protects himself, or his or another's property, from criminal interference will almost necessarily also be preventing or terminating the commission of a crime. However, conversely, clause 27(1)(e) is not otiose, since D may act to prevent crime in circumstances where he is not protecting the person or property of himself or another: for instance, where D restrains P, who is clearly dangerously intoxicated, from driving P's motor vehicle.

38.18 *Breach of the peace.* Specific reference to prevention or termination of a breach of the peace is required because breach of the peace is a wider concept than 'crime', and prevention of such a breach of the peace is, particularly in public order situations, a common occasion for the legitimate use of force. Paragraph (e) makes it clear that it is not an offence to use reasonable force either to prevent a person's being put in fear of the kind that constitutes a breach of the peace, or to remove the cause of such fear where it already exists.

Defence against non-culpable acts: particular cases

38.19 There will occasionally arise cases where a person should have a defence of reasonable protection against the acts of another, although those acts are not in fact 'criminal' because of some particular circumstance, or some characteristic of his, that exculpates him from criminal liability. That lack of criminal liability on the part of the actor does not, however, reduce the threat that his acts pose to others. For instance a person may be attacked with a dagger by a nine-year-old child, or by a person suffering from severe mental illness; or P may be forced by threats made by X that afford him a defence of duress to make a murderous attack on D.

38.20 Often such acts will or may be tortious, even if not criminal, and therefore fall under clause 27(1)(b) of the Criminal Law Bill. However, there may be difficulties of fact in establishing the state of mind necessary for tortious liability in the case of infants or persons with mental disability; and the effect on tortious liability of duress operating on the defendant is far from clear. It is not acceptable that the determination of the criminal liability of persons who protect themselves from such attacks should, even in the rare cases where that question may arise, depend on complicated enquiries into the law of tort, and the possible failure of the defence of reasonable use of force because, for reasons that are perfectly valid within the law of tort, the attacker is not subject to civil liability.

38.21 To avoid these difficulties, the Criminal Law Bill provides that the defence will be available in a number of cases where the fact of what would otherwise be a criminal act occurs, but for particular reasons the actor would not be subject to criminal liability. [See clause 27(3)] . . .

38.22 Paragraph [27(3)](c) is required to cover those cases where P, if charged, would be acquitted on grounds of 'automatism' or involuntary act. For instance, in the perhaps not very likely case of P attacking D while in a hypoglycaemic episode, or suffering from concussion, D should not incur criminal liability if he takes reasonable steps to defend himself. The reference to possible exculpation of P from criminal liability because of his intoxication is necessary principally to account for the special case, identified by the Court of Appeal in *Kingston*, where although P has the intent to commit the forbidden act, his conduct is not criminal because his ability to resist the desire to do that act was reduced or excluded by involuntary intoxication.

38.23 It should be emphasised that, in practice, it is not often likely to be necessary for D to have recourse to the special provisions of clause 27(3) in order to establish that the case falls within one of the categories listed in clause 27(1). That is because, as we explained in paragraph 38.7 above, those categories are assessed on the facts as D believes them to be. In most cases where D is attacked by a person who is under age, insane, acting in a state of automatism, or in the very limited circumstances where intoxication makes his act non-criminal, D will not have directed his mind to those special facts. He will know no more than the facts that, if they stood alone, would make the attack on him criminal in nature. Those facts justify him in morality and common sense and, by the operation of clause 27(1) of the Criminal Law Bill, in terms of criminal liability, in defending himself against an apparently criminal act. But D may in some cases know or believe the further facts that do or may render P's conduct non-criminal: perhaps the clearest example is likely to be where D knows that P is under ten years of age. It is only in such cases that clause 27(3) is necessary, to ensure that D can defend himself against acts that are 'criminal' in all respects except that, for a particular reason that happens to be known to D, P would not be convicted if charged in respect of them.

Defence against non-culpable acts: mistaken belief or suspicion
38.24 The cases dealt with above involve specific circumstances that exempt P from criminal liability for what may, nonetheless, be an attack against which D is entitled to defend himself or another. A problem of a more general nature arises where P would, if prosecuted, escape liability because he believed in circumstances that gave him a defence: often, the defence of reasonable use of force. We may give some examples of cases that could arise, in all of which D might legitimately wish or see the need to use force against P.

(i)   P, a store-detective, wrongly thinks that D has not paid for goods that D is in the course of removing from the store. He attempts to arrest D. P has reasonable grounds for suspecting D to be committing theft, and therefore his arrest is lawful. D uses force to resist the arrest.

(ii)   P comes upon a fight in the street between D and X. D is in fact lawfully attempting to make a 'citizen's arrest'. P, not realising that, and thinking that D is gratuitously attacking X, intervenes to restrain D. D in turn uses force to resist.

(iii) P, a plain clothes police officer, is ordered to arrest X, a dangerous criminal. He mistakenly thinks that D is in fact X, and attempts to arrest him, using force that would be reasonable if he were arresting X. D resists, using force.

(iv)   P knows that D is a supplier of controlled drugs. He wrongly thinks that D has a load of such drugs in his car, and is about to drive the car to hand the drugs over to a customer. P is in the process of disabling D's car, to prevent the supply of the drugs, when D comes on the scene, and uses force to prevent P from completing his work on the car.

(v)   P is employed by X to demolish the garden shed at X's country cottage. P by mistake goes to the wrong house, X not being present, and starts to demolish the shed of D, X's next door neighbour. D intervenes to restrain P.

(vi)   P takes the wrong overcoat from the cloakroom at a hotel. D, the cloakroom attendant, thinking that P is stealing the coat, attempts to take the coat from him by force.

38.25 As in the cases discussed in paragraph 38.23 above, it will normally not be necessary to have recourse to a special rule in order to deal justly with D's case. In most cases of the type exemplified above, D will not know the special facts that render P's acts non-criminal. For example, in case (ii) D is most likely to think, in the confusion of the melee in the street, that P is intervening unlawfully to assist X; or in case (iii) that P, who he does not know to be a police officer, is a thug making a criminal attack upon him. In these circumstances D will, under the general rule laid down by clause 27(1) of the Criminal Law Bill, be judged according to the reasonableness of his reaction in those believed circumstances.

38.26 What, however, if D knows of P's mistake? Then, in the circumstances as D believes them to be, P's actions are lawful. Nevertheless, it can hardly be right that the present defence should be withheld from D if he acts reasonably to protect himself or his property. In all the cases stated P's act is lawful only because of a mistake or suspicion on the part of P that is in fact incorrect. D is nonetheless put in a position of potential peril, that is not in any way lessened by P's error, and the fact D knows of the error should not shut him out from the defence.

38.27 This case is dealt with by clause 27(6) of the Criminal Law Bill, which provides that where an act potentially falling into one of the categories set out in clause 27(1) is lawful (according, as provided by clause 27(5), to the circumstances as D believes them to be) by reason only of a mistaken belief or suspicion on the part of the actor, then the defence of reasonable use of force will continue to be available in respect of steps taken in response to that act.

38.28 It should again be emphasised, however, that in none of these cases is D given carte blanche to use whatever force he pleases, just because the situation that he is facing comes potentially within the reach of the present defence. He must act reasonably in the circumstances as he believes them to be. If he knows that P is only acting as he does because of a mistake on P's part, it may often be reasonable initially not to use force at all to rectify the situation, but rather to explain to P the nature of his mistake. That would very likely be the case where P's error has caused him to interfere only with property, as in paragraph 38.24(vi) above. Where, however, P's mistake leads him to use force against D, there may not be time for, and it would not be reasonable to expect D to delay so that he can make, explanations. D should not in such circumstances find himself suffering criminal liability if all that he does is to act reasonably to secure his immediate protection.

38.29 The approach that we now recommend to these difficulties, as explained in paragraphs 38.22–38.28 above, relies on a narrower and more specific statutory formula than did the Bill presented for consultation under LCCP 122, which envisaged the acts of P being deemed to be 'unlawful' for the purpose of this defence if P 'lacked the fault required for the offence or believed that an exempting circumstance existed'. That formula would undoubtedly cover all the cases discussed above, but it would go much wider than them: because very many perfectly innocuous acts are criminal but for the fact that the actor lacks the fault required for criminal liability. Let us cite a simple case. D may hire his motor car to P. P, in driving another person's car away, would be committing a crime were it not for the fact that by reason of D's permission he lacks the fault (dishonesty; and an intention permanently to deprive the owner) that is required for him to be guilty of theft. To include a case where D, wanting to break his contract, uses force to reverse his previous decision to lend the car to P within even the potential ambit of the present defence would be to deprive those having to make decisions about the application of the law of much of the guidance that it is the aim of the Criminal Law Bill to provide. It is true that in practice D would be unlikely to benefit from the defence, because where D knows that P's acts are innocent it can hardly ever be reasonable for him to use any force to interfere with those acts. We think, however, that the Criminal Law Bill should do as much as it can to state expressly the cases where the availability of the defence can even potentially arise, and not put all the burden on the ultimate test of whether D's action was reasonable.

Use of force in effecting or assisting in a lawful arrest

38.30 Section 3 of the Criminal Law Act 1967, referred to in paragraph 38.16 above, permits the use of reasonable force in effecting lawful arrest, as well as in the prevention of crime. That objective is, and has long been regarded as being, as much a proper occasion for the use of reasonable force as are the cases listed in clause 27(1) of the Criminal Law Bill that are discussed above.

38.31 It is, however, convenient to deal separately with this case, as is done in clause 28 of the Criminal Law Bill, because where D uses force to make a lawful arrest, the simple and single test of whether his conduct potentially falls within the present defence should be whether the arrest would have been lawful in the circumstances as he believed them to be. The somewhat elaborate provisions that are required in other cases, to elucidate those cases where D is reasonably protecting himself against acts that in fact are or may not be objectively criminal, do not arise in this case.

38.32 It will therefore make for clarity if the simple rule in the arrest case is stated separately. This will be of particular importance in cases involving police officers. Clause 28 emphasises that the general rule that the criminality of a defendant's conduct is to be judged according to the circumstances as he believed them to be extends to protecting from criminal punishment conduct that is reasonable in effecting an arrest where the officer, or citizen, believes, even if mistakenly, that circumstances exist that would make the arrest lawful.

38.33 It may also be worth repeating that the only effect of this clause is to assist in determining whether the arrester commits a criminal offence by his use of force. Other provisions deal with, for instance, civil liability for that use of force [see Clause 28 of the Criminal Law Bill] . . .

Other features of this defence

Force against a constable in the execution of his duty . . .

39.2 [Clause 27(6)] . . . is a special public policy exception to the general rule, described in paragraphs 38.26–38.27 above, that, where D knows of P's mistake, D may still take reasonable steps to resist P's attack on him. The exception applies where P, although mistaken, is a police constable acting in the execution of his duty. It can be illustrated from the most usual type of case in which the exception might arise.

39.3 Various provisions, notably in the Police and Criminal Evidence Act 1984, permit citizens, and in a wider range of circumstances constables, to make arrests on grounds of suspicion of commission of an offence, provided that the arrester has reasonable grounds for that suspicion. If such an arrest is attempted on D, who in fact knows that the suspicion is incorrect, he will, save where the special exception in respect of constables applies, have the defence provided by clause 27(5) and the first part of clause 27(6) of the Criminal Law Bill if he merely uses defensive force that is reasonable in the circumstances. Here again, as we suggested in paragraph 38.28 above, in many cases the reasonable reaction may be the giving of an explanation rather than the use of force: but if force is reasonably used to resist, D should not be criminally liable for so acting.

39.4 There are, however, special considerations where the arrester is a constable. If a constable making the arrest has reasonable grounds for his suspicion, even if that suspicion is mistaken, he is acting in accordance with his duty, and not unlawfully: see the provisions of the Police and Criminal Evidence Act 1984 referred to in paragraph 39.3 above. If D knows that the arrester is a constable, and for the reasons mentioned above the constable is in fact acting in the execution of his duty, the arrest may not be resisted even though the constable's suspicion is known by the person arrested to be mistaken. This special exception, in the case of force used against a person known to be a constable, who is in fact acting in the execution of his duty, accords with existing authority. It is usually thought to be justified or required by the need to encourage obedience to constables who are in fact (as the statement of the exception requires) acting in the execution of their duty. There was no substantial disagreement on consultation that that exception should be maintained.

39.5 Clause 27(6) further provides, however, that this principle does not hold where the person using force 'believes the force to be immediately necessary to prevent injury to himself or another'. For example, a constable, mistaking an innocent person for a dangerous armed criminal, may be about to use disabling or even lethal force to neutralise the imminent threat to himself or others that he believes the 'criminal' to represent. In these circumstances the innocent person may use reasonable force to save himself from injury if he believes that it is immediately necessary to do so. This rule probably coincides with existing law, and, again, it was not the subject of substantial challenge on consultation.

Must the use of force be, or be thought to be, immediately necessary?

39.6 In LCCP 122 we discussed at some length whether there should be a requirement that the defence is only available where the defendant fears or is subject to an immediate attack upon him. Such a requirement is in any event only appropriate for the particular case of self-defence; and even there it adds an unnecessary element of complication and formality, since in every case where there has been an element of 'pre-emptive' action by the defendant the court and jury will have to decide whether that action was reasonable in the circumstances.

39.7 We therefore provisionally proposed that no such express requirement should be contained in the Criminal Law Bill. Of those who addressed this matter on consultation the majority, including the General Council of the Bar and the Society of Public Teachers of Law, agreed with our provisional conclusion. We have therefore adopted that approach in the Bill, which includes no additional rule that the use of force by the defendant must, as a separate requirement, be shown to have been immediately necessary.

Preparatory acts

39.8 Clause 29(2) ensures that criminal liability (most obviously, under legislation prohibiting the possession of firearms and offensive weapons) will not attach to an act immediately preparatory to a use of force permitted by the clause.

'Self-induced' occasions for the use of force

39.9 The effect of the first part of clause 27(7) is that clause 27 provides no defence to a person who deliberately provokes the very attack against which he then defends himself. On the other hand, the second part of the subsection preserves the liberty of the citizen to go about his lawful business even if he knows that he is likely to be met by unlawful violence from others. If he does so and is attacked, he may defend himself.

Opportunity to retreat

39.10 Clause 29(4) restates the law on the significance of a defendant's having had an opportunity to retreat before using force. Although the fact that he had such opportunity is relevant to the court's or jury's consideration of whether his use of force was reasonable, it is not conclusive of the question and is simply to be taken into account together with other relevant evidence.

Circumstances unknown to and unsuspected by the actor

39.11 It follows from the requirement that the defendant be judged according to the circumstances as he believes them to be that he cannot rely on circumstances unknown to him that would in fact have justified acts on his part that were unreasonable on the facts as he perceived them. Although opinion was not unanimous on consultation, we think it right to maintain this long-standing common law rule. Citizens who react unreasonably to circumstances should not be exculpated by the accident of facts of which they were unaware.

Relation to other defences

Necessity and duress of circumstances

40.1 Cases may arise where it is felt unreasonable for a person to be put in peril of a criminal charge by doing acts to protect the person or property of himself or others, but where the circumstances do not fall even under the comparatively broadly expressed terms of the present defence. The present defence largely follows the present law by envisaging the use of force to avoid the consequences of a direct attack by another upon person or property. Cases will arise, however, where D needs to, and should properly, react to other types of danger. For instance, D may beat off, and thereby injure, a dog that is attacking him, or is attacking his or another's small child; or he may pull down another person's wall or fence in order to provide a fire-break against a fire that is threatening a residential area. Alternatively, the danger may accrue from another human being, but not take the form of any sort of direct or deliberate interference with D: for instance, P's entirely lawful driving of his motor-car may threaten a child that has carelessly run into the road.

40.2 Other instances of legitimate action by D which however fall outside the limits of the defence of justified use of force as defined in the Criminal Law Bill can easily be imagined. We have already mentioned, in paragraph 38.15 above, intervention in an emergency to protect another person's property, from non-criminal interference, but without the authority of that person. More generally,

D may in some circumstances legitimately act to save P from himself, for instance if D restrains a small child to prevent him from wandering over a cliff or going too close to a fire. Few if any such cases would be seriously considered for prosecution. But if they were, in such cases, and in the examples suggested in paragraph 40.1 above, there remains available, as a safeguard, either the defence of duress of circumstances, under clause 26(1) of the Criminal Law Bill; or the developing defence of necessity, discussed in paragraphs 35.5–35.6 above. As we have already emphasised, the Criminal Law Bill's rationalisation of the defence of justifiable use of force does not in any way affect the common law on those defences, just as they already cohabit with the existing common law defence of self-defence on which the defence of justifiable use of force is based.

40.3 It would not be possible to adapt the defence of justified use of force to cover all such possible cases without producing a defence expressed in unduly wide terms, which would be in danger of taking the concept and defence of necessity further than the courts have yet seen fit to do. Extension of the defence of necessity is only appropriate on a case-by-case basis, in the context of such cases as are actually sought to be made the subject of criminal liability. The defence in the Criminal Law Bill, rather, provides for the application of clear and consistent principles in cases of the type that experience suggests are in practice most likely to be addressed by the criminal law, and in which guidance is required as to the appropriateness of the application of criminal sanctions.

'NECESSARY ACTION: A NEW DEFENCE', CMV CLARKSON [2004] CRIM LR 81
JUSTIFICATION AND EXCUSE

[A] . . . critical question is whether the excuse/justification distinction does indeed provide the key to distinguishing the defences so as to help shape the contours of the specific rules for each defence.

In essence, the distinction between justification and excuse is as follows: actors are excused; acts are justified. Excused conduct is wrong but because of the excusing condition we can understand the predicament of the person who commits a wrongful act and can conclude that a judgment of blameworthiness is inappropriate. Justification on the other hand involves an assessment of the value of the conduct. Such conduct can be beneficial in the sense of promot-ing a greater good . . . there remains the argument that such a distinction is still necessary because certain consequences flow from it. While there are several (perhaps speculative) reasons for distinguishing justification from excuse generally, the most commonly cited ones and certainly the ones most relevant to the defences under discussion are as follows. A victim is permitted to defend herself against an excused attack but not a justified attack. For example, if a defendant is threatened with death unless she steals my book, I am permitted to use reasonable force to protect my property. On the other hand, it is claimed that I may not resist or defend my interests against a justified attack. For example, 'the owner of a field should not be allowed to resist one who would burn it to stop a spreading fire'. Further, it is claimed that one may assist a person's justified conduct (e.g. others may help the defendant in burning my field) but one may not assist excused conduct (others may not help the defendant to steal my book).

This analysis, which presupposes a clear distinction between justified and excused conduct, is, however, problematic. Take, for example, the much-discussed situation that arose during the sinking of the *Herald of Free Enterprise*. Passengers were climbing a ladder to safety. One of them was so petrified that he 'froze' on the ladder blocking the exit-route of the others. He could not be persuaded to move so he was pushed from the ladder and died. When the other passengers were trying to throw the man from the ladder, would he be permitted to defend himself? The above orthodoxy would result in the following conclusion. If the actions of the other passengers were regarded as excused (duress of circumstances) he could defend himself. If their actions were regarded as justified (necessity or self-defence) he could not. Such a conclusion is patently unacceptable. Whether the actions of the passengers can be categorised as being understandable/ forgivable (excuse) or as a net benefit/tolerated/done for good reasons (justification) should not affect the moral status of the man on the ladder. By not being culpable in any way, he is an innocent and like the innocent victim who is attacked by a defendant acting under duress he may protect his own autonomy interests by defending himself. One needs to separate the two perspectives. From the passengers' perspective, his presence on the ladder poses an unjust threat – like an attack by an innocent – and so from their perspective necessary force may be used. However, from the man on the ladder's perspective, he is faced with what he regards as an unjust threat and may defend himself. A possible objection to this approach is that if A has a right to kill B, B cannot have a right to kill A as this would amount to anarchy. For this reason, notions of 'rights' here are inappropriate. The law is permitting – in the sense of forgiving or regarding as having acceptable reasons – the passengers to eject him from the ladder. The judgment is about *their* normative position and the moral quality of *their* actions. Assuming their beliefs and actions were reasonable (of which more later), the judgment with regard to them should not be affected by the normative position or moral status of the man on the ladder. Equally, from his perspective, judgments about his ability to defend himself should not be determined by the normative position of the passengers.

Let us assume, alternatively, that the man on the ladder was not petrified and unaware of the implications of his actions, but was deliberately blocking the passengers' exit-route because, say, he was the moral equivalent of a 'suicide-bomber' and wanted to kill all the passengers and was prepared to die himself to achieve that objective. In this latter scenario, nothing has actually changed from the passengers' perspective; the man on the ladder is posing the same unjust threat and necessary action is permitted. However, from the ladder-man's perspective much has changed. His normative position is radically different. He is effectively attacking the passengers. He is now not permitted to defend himself: not because their actions are 'justified' but because any defensive action on his part would simply be regarded as further action in pursuance of his original 'attack'. Moving to a more mundane example of street fighting, this explains why the aggressor who attacks a person who then responds with reasonable self-defensive force will not be legally permitted to defend himself. It has nothing to do with whether the response is justified or excused. It is simply that any defensive action by the initial aggressor will be regarded as part and parcel of the initial attack.

'ABOLISHING PROVOCATION AND REFRAMING SELF-DEFENCE – THE LAW COMMISSION'S OPTIONS FOR REFORM' – SUSAN SM EDWARDS [2004] CRIM LR 181

Self-defence and men's 'equality of arms'

The construction of self-defence, whilst a restrictive defence for both genders, has nevertheless been skewed to the detriment of women since a defendant's action is only considered 'reasonable' when the killing is a proportionate response to an immediate threat of deadly force. This requires the person to show that the force used to repel an immediate attack is based on honest belief and is of reasonable amount. The law has been interpreted strictly. With regard to the battered woman who kills she frequently expresses her predicament in everyday language as one of the necessity to take self-defensive action. The effect of repeat violence on her perception and anticipation of further violence is relevant to her reasonableness and justification in mounting a defence of self-defence. Efforts to assimilate the 'effect' of violence on her knowledge of his behaviour and her perception of likely harm or death and hence legal argument that self-defence is 'reasonable in the circumstances' (Criminal Law Act 1967) have been thus far unsuccessful. The question of whether the force used is reasonable in the circumstances is a question for the jury. The harshness of the rule has been somewhat mitigated by the guidance given to juries following *Palmer*. Nevertheless, the defence remains exorbitantly gendered largely situated in the particular ontology of the proportionality requirements.

Proportionality – an incommensurability crisis

Under the common law the 'mode of resentment' was a rule of law. For provocation the retaliation had to be proportionate as it did in self-defence . . . Whilst proportionate force is no longer a legal rule in provocation, it remains pivotal in self-defence. The rule developed at a time when the archetypal killing involved two adult men, not a child killing an adult, nor a woman killing her male partner. Men killing men and men killing women continues to present as the more typical relationship of victim to suspect, but children do on occasion kill adults and women on occasion do kill men. However, the law continues to treat women homicide defendants as if they were indeed men in respect of size, strength, ability to box, spar, and land a punch. So when women defend themselves against male violence with an instrument as they are inclined to do . . . and as a result kill, their 'mode of resentment' is treated for all legal purposes as 'excessive' . . . The terminology 'excessive' is misplaced . . . it is this cognitive intransigence that I refer to as the 'incommensurability' crisis in legal method and reasoning. The 'proportionate' requirement embodies a mathematical and physical abstraction, which disavows the qualitative and quantitative difference of gender, *inter alia*, physical attributes, and unequal access to inherent body force. Women who use weapons in self-defence, do so in order to arm themselves against the *a priori* disproportionate force of men in order to achieve a notional equality between unequals. Women use such force as they consider necessary to repel the real possibility of a disproportionate and life-threatening male force, which in their mind is in the continuous present.

. . .

The other side of the same coin is that the law has ignored the physical disparity between the sexes so that when men kill women, using body force such as strangulation, instead of this force being regarded as excessive when used against a person of smaller frame and when that person is also disabled from using physical force through social conditioning, the law construes body force as a mitigating factor. Again the law reifies context such that body force *per se* is rendered less serious and sometimes even rendered benign. Weapons and body force have different consequences for the construction of intention . . . when men kill spouses they are less likely to be convicted of murder if they use body force than if they use weapons 47 per cent to 56 per cent . . . when women kill, they almost exclusively use weapons. Of course, that is not to say that weapons are the only determining factor in homicide outcomes, the use of a weapon or body force is part of the circumstances to which the court must have regard in assessing murder, manslaughter/provocation and self-defence. Before anyone is misled by the statistical fallacy . . . that really there is nothing biased about provocation since women are more likely to receive a conviction for manslaughter than murder as compared to men, it is always to be remembered that women kill almost always in an effort to survive the beatings and threats of beating from violent men. Men kill in anger because they can: the reasons [men] have for acting in [this] particular way implies the applicability of a law-like proposition to this particular action. And further, when women are the victims whether men use body force or weapons, both methods are disproportionate and excessive.

FURTHER READING

Brudner, A, 'A theory of necessity' (1987) 7 OJLS 338

Buchanan and Virgo, 'Duress and mental abnormality' [1999] Crim LR 517

Gardner, J, 'Justifications and reasons', in AP Simester and ATH Smith (eds), *Harm and Culpability*, 1996, Oxford: OUP

Giles, M, 'Self-defence and mistake: a way forward' (1990) 53 MLR 187

Harlow, C, 'Self-defence: public right or private privilege' [1974] Crim LR 528

Horder, J, 'Occupying the moral high ground? The Law Commission on duress' [1994] Crim LR 334

Simpson, AWB, *Cannibalism and the Common Law*, 1984, Chicago: University of Chicago Press

Smith, JC, 'The right to life and the right to kill in law enforcement' (1994) 144 NLJ 354

Smith, KJM, 'Duress and steadfastness: in pursuit of the unintelligible' [1999] Crim LR 363

INDEX